The American South

A HISTORY

❖

WILLIAM J. COOPER, JR.

and

THOMAS E. TERRILL

Alfred A. Knopf   New York   1990

THIS IS A BORZOI BOOK
PUBLISHED BY ALFRED A. KNOPF, INC.

Text edition published in the United States by McGraw-Hill, Inc.,
New York. Trade edition published in the United States by Alfred
A. Knopf, Inc., New York. Trade edition distributed by Random
House, Inc., New York.

Library of Congress Cataloging-in-Publication Data
Cooper, William J. (William James)
The American South
Includes bibliographical references.
1. Southern States—History.   I. Terrill, Thomas E.
II. Title.
F209.C64   1990   975   90–4671
ISBN 0-394-58948-3

This book was set in Palatino by the College Composition Unit
in cooperation with Waldman Graphics, Inc.
The editors were Christopher Rogers, David Follmer, and Fred H. Burns;
the designer was Wanda Siedlecka;
the production supervisor was Richard Ausburn.
Arcata Graphics/Halliday was printer and binder.

Jacket Art: Detail from "New and Correct Map of the United States of America," 1783, Abel Buell, New Haven. By permission of the Trustees of the
British Library.

FIRST TRADE EDITION

For
William Cooper and Holmes Cooper
and
Andrea Terrill and Mitchell Terrill

About the Authors

❖

William J. Cooper, Jr. is a Boyd Professor at Louisiana State University. He received his A.B. degree from Princeton University and his Ph.D. from The Johns Hopkins University. Professor Cooper has spent his entire professional career on the faculty at Louisiana State University, where he also served as dean of the Graduate School from 1982 to 1989. He has held fellowships from the Institute of Southern History at Johns Hopkins, from the Charles Warren Center at Harvard, from the Guggenheim Foundation, and from the National Endowment for the Humanities.

He is the author of *The Conservative Regime: South Carolina, 1877–1890* (1968); *The South and the Politics of Slavery, 1828–1856* (1978); and *Liberty and Slavery: Southern Politics to 1860* (1983). He has also edited two books and written numerous articles. In addition, since 1979, he has been editor of the *Southern Biography Series* published by the Louisiana State University Press.

Thomas E. Terrill is Professor of History at the University of South Carolina. He received his Ph.D. from the University of Wisconsin and has been the recepient of fellowships from the National Endowment for the Humanities and from the Rockefeller Foundation. Most recently, he has been Fulbright Lecturer, University of Genoa Italy.

In addition to publishing several books as well as publications in periodicals and proceedings, he has helped produce a feature film for national television, a documentary, and a television course for undergraduate and graduate students. His most recent book is his co-edited *The American South Comes of Age.*

Contents

———— ❖ ————

Preface

————— ❖ —————

Our ambition has been to write a comprehensive history of the South from colonial times to the present. *The American South: A History* underscores our belief that it is impossible to divorce the history of the South from the history of the United States. Much of *The American South* therefore emphasizes the complex interaction between the South as a distinct section and the South as an inescapable part of the United States. The resulting tension has often propelled section and nation toward collision.

We develop major themes that give coherence and meaning to southern history from the seventeenth century to the twentieth, with attention to crucial changes over time. We stress the dynamics of the relationship between black and white southerners that have shaped the southern experience for more than three centuries. While for much of its history the South was overwhelmingly rural and agricultural, it is now increasingly urban and industrial. We describe each of these worlds and trace the connections among them. We also treat thoroughly the issue of social class, which, along with race, has been central in southern history, and we discuss the great wars—especially the Revolutionary War, the Civil War, and World War II—that have so powerfully influenced the history of the section and the nation. At least from the time of the Revolution southerners have felt a strong urge to explain and defend themselves and their section. We investigate that urge and chart its results.

In order to write a full history of the South, we start with the colonial era. We focus on the British colonies because those who settled here—both black and white, with their institutions, values, and experiences—fundamentally formed what would come to be called the South. The first half of the book covers the more than two and a half centuries between the first permanent settlement in Virginia in 1607 and the Civil War, in which the South, as the Confederate States of America, attempted to establish its independence. The second half of the book concentrates on the momentous decades from the defeat of the southern Confederacy in 1865 to our own time.

In recent years scholarship in southern history has grown tremendously and been profoundly reshaped. Significantly revised interpretations based on wide-ranging research and altered perspectives have transformed how historians understand traditional subjects, such as political leadership and plantation economics. At the same time, historians have come to give previously neglected topics such as the slave family, blacks since slavery, southern industrial workers, and women a great deal more attention. We have strived to incorporate this outpouring of scholarship to present a fresh look at the whole of southern history. We conclude the book with a substantial bibliographical essay that provides a guide to the major literature on the history of the South.

While working on this book we received the generous assistance of students, colleagues, and friends. Several former graduate students at Louisiana State University and one still enrolled helped enormously: Bradley Bond, Ralph Eckert, Kenneth Startup, and especially Eric Walther. At the University of South Carolina, James A. Dunlap, III did likewise. Colleagues and friends who were willing to listen, to suggest, and to read include Robert Becker, Keen Butterworth, David L. Carlton, Lacy K. Ford, Jr., Gaines M. Foster, Michael F. Holt, David Katzman, Daniel Littlefield, David W. Murphy, Sydney Nathans, Paul Paskoff, George Rable, Charles Royster, Allen H. Stokes, Jr., Robert M. Weir, R. Jackson Wilson, and Bertram Wyatt-Brown. Without their counsel and expertise this would surely be a lesser book. Marlene LeBlanc handled arduous typing duties with good cheer. Polly Brown, Philip C. Cockrell, and Joanne McMullen also helped in numerous ways with the preparation of the manuscript, as did W. Lynn Shirley, who designed some of the maps.

Since the start of work on this book we have been associated with three superb editors. Jane Garrett deserves our thanks. David Follmer initiated this project; he, along with Jack Wilson, brought us together and started us down the road that led to this book. From David, Christopher Rogers inherited us and the history of the South. Chris has been unswerving in his support of our effort, and extraordinarily patient. He coped magnificently with postponements and missed deadlines. He kept faith with us.

Patricia and Sarah also kept the faith and, for a far longer time than any wives should have to, they heard about southern history in general and this discussion of it in particular.

All those people and scores more unnamed scholars of the southern past whose research and writing illuminated our path have assisted us immensely. This book is ours, however, and we accept full responsibility for it.

William J. Cooper, Jr.
Thomas E. Terrill

Prologue

The Enduring South

—————— ❖ ——————

*T*he South, Wilbur Cash wrote in his celebrated book *The Mind of the South* (1941), is "not quite a nation within a nation but the next thing to it." The sources of that enduring distinctiveness are many and complex. As early as 1750, a generation before Americans went to war against Great Britain to secure their political independence, clear differences distinguished the southern colonies from the northeastern and middle Atlantic colonies. Those differences persisted after the American Revolution and intensified during the first half of the nineteenth century. By 1860, though the similarities among the states remained powerful, the gap between the South and the rest of the country had grown into a chasm that seemingly could not be bridged by any compromise. The American South had become synonymous, though not entirely identical, with plantations, cotton, and black slavery—with places such as Davis Bend, Mississippi.

Thirty-odd miles south of Vicksburg, Mississippi, Davis Bend was a fertile peninsula formed by a large horseshoe curve of the Mississippi River. Today, more than four generations since the flood tides of war swept over it, Davis Bend and the people who lived there in 1860 provide a useful focus for examining southern identity before that time and since. The bend got its name from Joseph Davis, a large landholder in the area and the elder brother of Jefferson Davis, president of the Confederacy. He had prospered as a lawyer in Natchez, Mississippi, a booming cotton and commercial center that served as the capital of Mississippi until 1817, when the territory became a state. He was intensely interested in politics, and when his youngest brother, Jefferson, developed an interest in a political career, he frequently turned to Joseph for advice.

Joseph Davis bought most of the 11,000 acres of Davis Bend from the federal government in 1818 and obtained the rest from several frontier farmers who had been the first whites to settle and clear the area. Davis sold off 6,000 acres of the bend to friends. Then in 1827, when he was forty-two, he left his law practice and with his sixteen-year-old bride, three daughters from his earlier marriage, and a few slaves he had inherited from his father established a plan-

tation at the bend. Eight years later, Jefferson Davis started a plantation of his
own on 800 acres that Joseph had given him.

　During the next three decades, Joseph Davis became a very wealthy man. In
1860 he was one of only nine planters in Mississippi with more than 300 slaves.
He had a spacious mansion and almost a village of outbuildings, which included a cluster of slave cottages. To protect his holdings from flooding by the
great river that almost encircled it, Davis and the other leading planters at Davis
Bend built a mile-and-a-half-long levee that was six to eighteen feet high.
Davis's twenty-five-acre flower garden was so spectacular that passengers disembarked from river steamboats to tour it. No doubt the tourists knew they
were in the American South and that their host was a southerner. Neither Davis
nor his plantation was typical of the South, though both were typical of what
many southerners aspired to.

　Davis's background did resemble that of a majority of antebellum southerners. His grandfather, son of a Welsh immigrant, was born in Philadelphia
around 1730 and moved as a young man to the colonial South, first to South

DAVIS BEND, MISSISSIPPI　(New York Public Library, Schaumberg Collection)

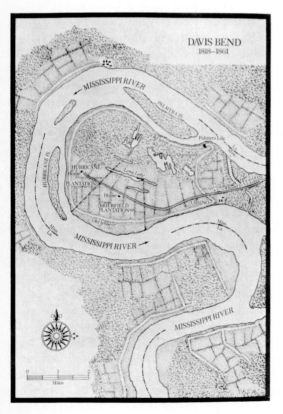

Carolina, then to Georgia. Joseph's father, Samuel, fought in the American Revolution, married a South Carolina woman he met while serving in the military, and took up farming near Augusta, Georgia, on land the state had given him for his military service. The family moved to Kentucky in 1793, a year after the territory had become a state, and there they produced two of that region's principal products: tobacco and horses. In 1810 the Davis family moved again, still pursuing the frontier; eventually they settled in southwestern Mississippi, an area that only nine years earlier had been ceded by the Choctaws. Settlers such as the Davises kept continual pressure on Indians to vacate western land so that whites could safely settle there. In the 1830s the Choctaws and Chickasaws gave up the last of their holdings in Mississippi and moved west beyond Arkansas to what was called Indian Territory. Whites later followed the Indians, took over most of their land, and created the state of Oklahoma; the name means "home of the Indian."

On their newly acquired land in Mississippi the Davises cultivated cotton as their major cash crop. To clear the land and plant, cultivate, and harvest the cotton, they relied on their own labor and the handful of slaves Samuel had bought. Improving fortunes allowed them to build a substantial home graced by a veranda—a large step up from the four-room log cabin the family had occupied in Kentucky. The family of Samuel Davis strongly resembled the great majority of whites who populated the South from its earliest years to the Civil War: yeoman farmers who pushed south and west for more than a century and a half in search of cheap, fertile soil, frequently acquiring a few slaves, always bending their backs as they tried to improve their lot and station.

Their pursuit of the southern version of the American dream propelled such families from Virginia into the Carolinas and Georgia, southward into Florida, and westward as far as Texas before 1860. These pioneering farmers often settled in areas very different from the great plantation regions of which Davis Bend was a part. They made up the great majority of farmers in the mountains of Appalachia and the Ozarks and were predominant in the valleys and rolling hills of the piedmont and along the vast coastal plain that ran from the Chesapeake through Florida and on to the Texas gulf coast. Other southerners made their places in the cities and towns of the overwhelmingly agricultural South. Such places were sites for commercial enterprise and some manufacturing. Urban areas also afforded desired refinements for their residents and for the surrounding countryside.

Joseph Davis, for instance, found Natchez a good place for an ambitious attorney, and Jefferson Davis attended a private academy near there as well as one in Kentucky. Like many ambitious Americans at the time, the youngest Davis seems to have believed that advanced education could improve his prospects. Thus, Jefferson graduated from academies to Transylvania University in Lexington, Kentucky, where he spent a year. Founded in 1780, Transylvania developed into the first center of learning west of the Appalachians and south of the Ohio River. Jefferson Davis completed his formal education at West Point. After an unexceptional academic career, he spent most of his seven-year army career at frontier posts in Wisconsin, Illinois, and Oklahoma.

Jefferson Davis briefly returned to the military in the 1840s, when he fought with distinction in the Mexican War. After 1835, however, he devoted most of his energies to his plantation and to his highly successful political career. Despite ill health, Davis drove himself to build first an impressive plantation estate and then an impressive political career. The latter pursuit required innumerable stump speeches, interminable rounds of political meetings, and mountains of correspondence with constituents and fellow politicians. Several heated disputes stopped just short of duels. Davis survived dirt roads, mud roads, carts, wagons, carriages, lurching spark-spewing trains, sailing ships, steamboats, inns, hotels, good food, bad food, and tobacco-spitting, importuning, and sometimes sweaty constituents from Mississippi to Washington and back. Davis represented his state in the United States House of Representatives and the Senate and served as a highly competent, dedicated secretary of war in the administration of President Franklin Pierce. Like other southerners in his day and later, Jefferson Davis was an American in his efforts to succeed and in his national loyalties. Indeed, Davis was convinced that as a leader first of the South in Congress and later of the Confederate States of America, he was risking civil war and his life and fortune to preserve the Constitution, which he saw as the bulwark of liberty.

To Davis, the election of Abraham Lincoln posed a revolutionary threat; Lincoln's election meant the triumph of the antislavery movement—a movement dedicated to destroying southern rights. Announcing his resignation from the Senate in January 1861, Davis told his fellow senators and the nation that

JOSEPH DAVIS (Eleanor S. Brock-
enbrough (Library, Museum of the
Confederacy, Richmond, Virginia)

the southern states had been forced to secede from the Union because the Republicans who were coming to power "denie[d] us equality...refuse[d] to recognize our domestic institutions which preexisted the formation of the Union, our property which was guarded by the Constitution." He accused Lincoln of making "a distinct declaration of war upon our institutions." Davis asked that the states which chose to secede be allowed to do so peacefully, but if the North insisted that the South "remain as subjects to you, then, gentlemen of the North, a war is to be inaugurated the like of which men have not seen."

In 1860 and 1861 the southern states seceded from the Union to prevent the federal government from intruding on their rights and abolishing slavery, the cornerstone of white southern society. To preserve that society the South took up arms against the Union. As a consequence, the Union intruded massively in the South—and with devastating impact—from 1861 until the end of Reconstruction in 1877. After the Civil War, the South erected a defense to ward off unwelcome outside intrusions in its race relations and other aspects of its life. The most concrete form of that defense was the "Solid South," or the thorough dominance of the South by the Democratic party. Fashioning itself as "the party of white supremacy," the Democratic party grounded its appeal on maintaining white unity in the South, keeping southern blacks subordinate ("in their place"), and preventing interference with that arrangement.

Erected during the 1870s and 1880s, the Solid South remained in place until after World War II. Breaches in the one-party politics of the Democratic South appeared earlier, however, under the federal government's efforts to combat the depression of the 1930s. The Solid South cracked during the 1948 presidential election, then shattered during the civil rights revolution of the 1950s and 1960s. Propelled by America's post-1940 economic boom and by massive federal spending in the region, a more prosperous, two-party South found a comfortable place in the Sunbelt and in national politics and became a much greater force in the nation than it had been at any previous time since the 1860s.

The South's failed attempt to reshape America by leaving the Union in 1860 defined the region and its people for all the generations that have followed. Thus the South and southerners can be defined as the states that seceded and the people who supported secession and identified themselves then and later with what they believed was its noble cause. But identifying the South and southerners in terms of the Civil War yields too narrow a definition. Though that definition has the advantage of clarity, it seriously distorts the realities of the past and even the present. So, in this book, the southern states are defined as the eleven Confederate states plus Kentucky, Maryland, and, after the Civil War, Oklahoma, the creation of latter-day pioneers who erected a Dixie on the plains. Kentucky and Maryland nearly seceded. Both provided troops for the Confederacy, as did Missouri, a state deeply divided by the Civil War. This state-based definition of the South is hardly free of ambiguities. Parts of West Virginia, for instance, are more southern than west Texas, southern Florida, and parts of Kentucky and Oklahoma ever were, and substantial numbers of West Virginians served in the Confederate armed forces.

Using the Civil War as a reference point to define southerners is even more misleading. Not all southerners in the 1860s supported secession or identified with its cause, though they often suffered from the defeat of the Confederacy. Unionist sentiment was strongest in the South among mountain whites. Depredations during the war reinforced the Unionist feelings of many people, particularly in Appalachia. Black southerners celebrated the defeat of the Confederacy for obvious reasons. African-Americans lived all over the South in 1860, but usually on plantations such as those at Davis Bend, and they had interacted with whites since the seventeenth century to create much of what made the South. Without that interaction there would have been no South as the term and the region are commonly understood. Moreover, southern blacks and whites had and have striking cultural similarities and strikingly similar historical experiences. Both have experienced economic inferiority, and both have been disdained as cultural and moral inferiors. The labor, skills, and ideas of blacks have been critical to the development and evolution of the South. For the sake of convenience and clarity, however, southerners are white in this book unless we explicitly state otherwise or unless the context implies a different interpretation.

The Davises, especially Joseph Davis, certainly knew how important blacks were to them. They acknowledged the importance of blacks to their lives, in part by being lenient masters. Some local whites disparaged Joseph Davis's slaves as "Mr. Davis's free negroes." The neighbors may have had Benjamin Thornton Montgomery in mind when they said such things. Born into slavery in northern Virginia in 1819, Montgomery grew up as the companion of his young master. He moved westward involuntarily to Natchez in 1836 when, without notice or explanation, he was sold to a slave trader. The trader took Montgomery with a gang of other recently purchased slaves to the booming slave markets of Mississippi's black belt. There Joseph Davis bought Montgomery, but the young slave soon ran away. Unfamiliar with his new surroundings, Montgomery was caught almost immediately. When Davis questioned Montgomery about his attempted escape, he quickly realized Montgomery's considerable capacities and encouraged them. Montgomery, who had learned to read and write from his young master in Virginia, eventually became a mechanic, inventor, surveyor, builder, and merchant. He and his wife, Mary Lewis Montgomery, who was also literate, arranged, with Davis's approval, for the schooling of their children. Montgomery played a major role in the life of Davis Bend before and after the war reached the peninsula.

In January 1861, Jefferson Davis left Washington and returned home. In February he left Davis Bend to be inaugurated as president of the Confederacy. In April 1862, Joseph Davis took his family and about a hundred slaves and fled his river home to escape the advance of Union forces. Most of their slaves deserted them during their hasty retreat, and some of them later descended upon the mansion to pillage clothing and furniture. Union troops did even more damage when they arrived. Not long afterward, Benjamin Montgomery reasserted his leadership. Eventually, after the war, he bought the plantation from

Joseph Davis, with whom he had maintained regular communication. For several years Montgomery succeeded, but forces beyond his control doomed his efforts. Eventually the community at Davis Bend dissolved. Even the river took its toll: the main channel of the Mississippi swept across the neck of the peninsula and turned Davis Bend into Davis Island.

The war destroyed the slave-based plantation society of the antebellum South: the South of planters, slaves, and highly profitable cash crops, which once was so easily identifiable, faded. Within a generation another, also easily identifiable South emerged: a region of chronic underdevelopment, poverty, one-party politics, and Jim Crow, a rigid racial caste system. Once again, to the rest of Americans the South was the deviant region. And it seemed not to change at all until World War II. That perception was wrong, however, just as was the perception that the antebellum South had been unchanging.

The South did not stand still from 1865 to 1940. The New South, a more urban, industrial South, began to appear soon after the Civil War, but it did not emerge fully until the 1920s. Still, low incomes persisted, race relations remained frozen, and one-party politics and impotence on the national scene seemed permanent conditions. But before World War II, each of these fundamental characteristics of the South after the Civil War began to change. The depression of the 1930s and the New Deal of President Franklin Roosevelt hastened change, and World War II accelerated the process by which the Sunbelt South emerged.

BENJAMIN THORNTON MONT-
GOMERY (Library of Congress)

In the years since 1945, the economics, politics, and race relations of the South have changed so much that the South of the 1990s, the Sunbelt South, seems to have almost no connection with the South of Jefferson Davis or the South after the Civil War, even with the South of the 1930s. The South is now more prosperous than it has been at any previous time since the 1850s. Unlike the antebellum South, however, the Sunbelt South resembles the rest of the country in its politics and its race relations. Though vestiges of poverty, one-party politics, and Jim Crow remain, the picture of the poor, backward South has dissolved into an image of prosperity.

Defining southern identity is not so easy as it once was. One of the region's loyal sons and keen observers declared in 1973 that "the South is just about over as a separate...place." But another perceptive student of the South said in 1983 that he "knows when he is in the South." The South may have lost some of its distinctiveness, but much remains. The South remains the United States' most obviously distinctive region in ways that are still very important: in culture and religion, in ethnic composition, in its sense of having a unique past, and in its sense of place. Southerners have deep attachments to their region. Those attachments have been expressed, among other ways, in the determination of southerners to remain Americans with a special regional identity even in the homogenized culture of the late twentieth century. That determination helps explain why the South has endured as the United States' most distinctive region for more than two hundred years and why the history of the South continues to fascinate so many people.

This book tries to answer two questions: What was and is the American South? What was and is a southerner? The answers to these questions depend largely on where and when they are asked. The answers are easier and clearer at some times than at others. The answer to the question about southern identity is harder and less clear now than at any previous time since the mid-eighteenth century. Still, the South endures. It endures in part because not even a flood of changes has washed away critical connections between the past and the present in the South.

The American South

A HISTORY

The Geography
of the South

———— ❖ ————

These maps delineate the major physical, geographical, and political features of the southern part of the United States. The physical characteristics of the land and the chief rivers did not change fundamentally between the seventeenth and the nineteenth centuries, though, of course, the rivers were named at different times. The political landscape of the South did change dramatically over time, however. The map on page 4 depicts the southern colonies in the middle of the eighteenth century. The following map shows the South at the end of the antebellum era. It locates the slave states in relationship to the rest of the country, marks their boundaries, and notes their dates of admission to the Union. The last map focuses on a key aspect of the colonial period by identifying the most important Indian tribes in the Southeast and specifying their locations.

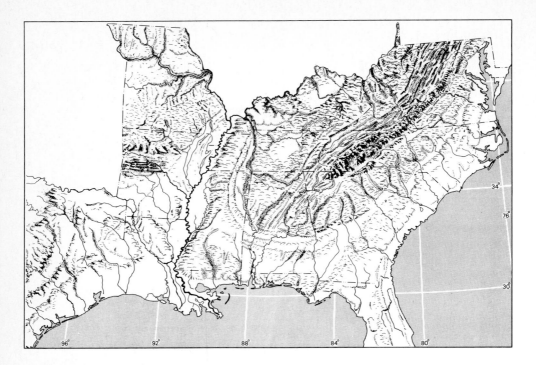

PHYSIOGRAPHIC FEATURES OF THE SOUTH (Reprinted by permission of Louisiana State University Press from *Atlas of Antebellum Southern Agriculture* by Sam Bowers Hilliard. Copyright © 1984 by Louisiana State University Press, 1984.)

GEOGRAPHIC FEATURES OF THE SOUTH

SOUTHERN RIVERS

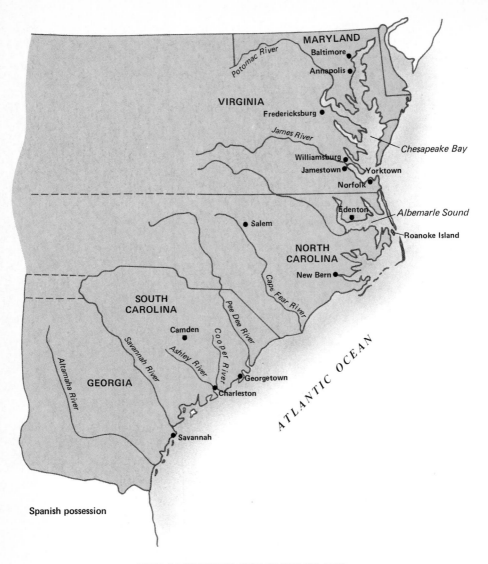

MARYLAND
Potomac River
Baltimore
Annapolis

VIRGINIA
Fredericksburg
James River
Williamsburg
Jamestown
Yorktown
Norfolk

Chesapeake Bay

Salem
Edenton
Albemarle Sound
Roanoke Island

NORTH
CAROLINA
New Bern

SOUTH
CAROLINA
Camden
Pee Dee River
Cape Fear River
Cooper River
Ashley River
Savannah River

GEORGIA
Altamaha River
Georgetown
Charleston
Savannah

ATLANTIC OCEAN

Spanish possession

THE SOUTHERN COLONIES IN 1750

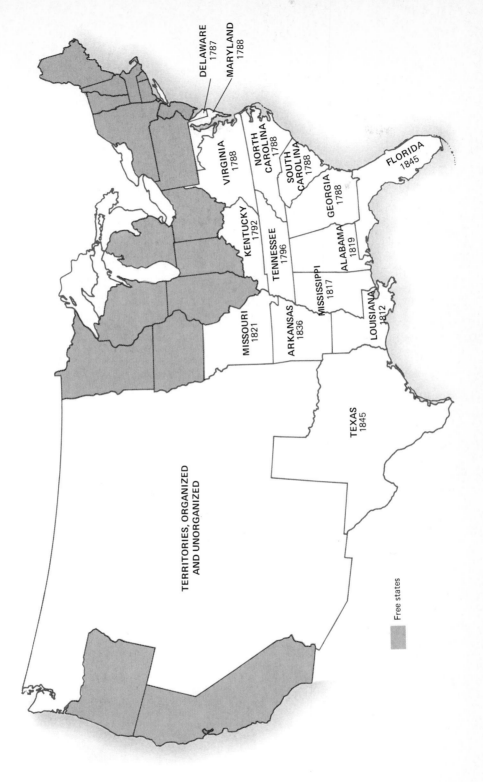

DELAWARE
1787

MARYLAND
1788

VIRGINIA
1788

NORTH
CAROLINA
1788

SOUTH
CAROLINA
1788

GEORGIA
1788

FLORIDA
1845

KENTUCKY
1792

TENNESSEE
1796

ALABAMA
1819

MISSISSIPPI
1817

LOUISIANA
1812

MISSOURI
1821

ARKANSAS
1836

TEXAS
1845

TERRITORIES, ORGANIZED
AND UNORGANIZED

Free states

THE SLAVE STATES IN 1860

MAJOR INDIAN TRIBES ENCOUNTERED BY THE COLONISTS

1

The Beginnings

❖

Young George Percy landed in Virginia in May 1607. He arrived as one of 105 settlers who had sailed across the Atlantic from England in three small ships. In honor of their king, James I, they named their settlement Jamestown. A former soldier and the eighth son of an English nobleman, the twenty-six-year-old Percy and his compatriots were imbued with the notion that they were engaged in a great enterprise to benefit both England and the English.

Percy left an eyewitness account of the early months at Jamestown. His "first sight" of "faire meddowes and goodly Tall trees and such Fresh-waters running through the woods" entranced him. Abundance matched beauty. "Mussels and Oysters...lay upon the ground as thicke as stones." This new land also offered "fine and beautifull Strawberries, foure times bigger and better than ours in England." Exploring, Percy discovered the "most pleasant Springs" and "the goodliest Corne fields that ever was seene in any Countrey." "The soile," he reported, was "good and fruitfull, with excellent good Timber." "The ground all flowing over with faire flowers of sundry colours and kindes" reminded Percy of a "Garden or Orchard in England."

Percy found that the natives could be as inviting as the land. They "entertained" the English "very kindly." "After they had feasted us," Percy wrote, "they shewed us, in welcome their manner of dancing." To Percy it seemed that he and the other settlers had landed in "Paradise."

But thorns infested Percy's garden. Relations with the natives were not always friendly. Percy recorded that one night, "when wee were going abord [our ship]," the natives appeared "creeping upon all foure...like Beares, with their Bowes in their mouthes." They "charged us very desperately in the faces" and wounded two Englishmen. The English fired, according to Percy, and "the sharpnesse of our shot" helped drive the natives "into the Woods." Armed conflict, in which both natives and settlers died, alternated with amity, but it never disappeared.

Other thorns tore at the English. Noting that "our men were destroyed with cruell diseases," Percy cataloged the horrors of "Swellings, Flixes, Burning Fevers." Death visited regularly, "many times three or foure in a night; in the

morning, their bodies trailed out of their Cabines like Dogges to be buried."
Percy's melancholy list of the dead reads like a daily obituary, complete with
cause of death. In September he cried out, "There were never Englishmen left
in a foreigne Countrey in such miserie as we were in this new discovered Virginia."

Rapid, unexpected death remained a constant for many decades, but the
English did not give up their colony. Percy himself rose to the governorship
before he returned to England in 1612. His "Paradise" kept drawing replace-
ments for the settlers who succumbed to the "miserie." They enabled
Jamestown to survive to become the first permanent English settlement in
North America. As Percy indicated, the English gazeteer of the New World lo-
cated Jamestown in Virginia. Named in the 1580s in honor of Queen Elizabeth
I, the Virgin Queen, Virginia was the most significant English claim in North
America. Virginia became the first and thus the oldest English colony in what
was to become the United States. It was obviously the oldest in that part of the
United States that came to be called the South.

ENGLISH BACKGROUND

The English began seriously to discuss the possibilities of colonization during the reign of Elizabeth I, queen of England from 1558 to 1603. During
Elizabeth's time the English were emerging from a period of turmoil and
tribulation, both political and religious. Under her the English rejoiced over
a newly discovered unity and sense of common purpose. Elizabeth and her
advisers recognized that England lived in a precarious political world, in
which powers jockeyed for position while keeping an eye on the greatest
among them, Spain. Elizabeth wanted to establish England's sovereignty beyond any question; she also wanted to secure her country's place among the
great powers of Europe.

England's turn toward colonization of the New World naturally followed.
Among the Englishmen who determined that England's flag must be planted in
the New World, Sir Walter Raleigh stood out. A favorite of Elizabeth's, Raleigh
received her blessings on his attempt to colonize the land the queen authorized
him to call Virginia. Raleigh took action upon the precepts laid down by the
leading English thinker on colonization, Richard Hakluyt the younger. In 1584,
in *A Discourse Concerning Westerne Planting*, Hakluyt eloquently pleaded for colonization. England, he piously asserted, had a duty to extend Protestantism,
but his emphasis was on economics and politics: England needed to build up its
trade and to supply domestic requirements from English colonies, not from foreign nations. In Hakluyt's scheme, prosperous colonies would enrich the
mother country. He also saw colonies as a means to build up the royal navy and
as providing critical military bases. After all, Hakluyt reminded his readers, England was involved in a great economic and political contest with Spain. Accordingly, England must act or risk disaster. Thus, for Hakluyt, colonization
held out the combined promise of financial gain and political security.

While Hakluyt talked of national goals, such men as Raleigh mingled these noble ends with personal ambition. Gain and glory for England could also mean gain and glory for the Englishmen who carried out the great mission set forth by Hakluyt. Raleigh's first colonizing expedition left England in April 1585 for the outer banks of North Carolina, the finger islands that stretch along the Atlantic coast. The previous year a reconnaissance party had decided upon this location as the best place for Raleigh to begin his colonial enterprise. In the summer of 1585 the colonists, all of whom were male, went ashore on Roanoke Island, almost at the center of the outer banks. The colony did not last; after only one checkered year all the survivors returned to England. Undaunted, Raleigh prepared for another try. This time he made more complete preparations, and by including whole families he signaled to his country and his queen that he meant to succeed. Although Raleigh intended this second group of colonists to settle in the Chesapeake, they ended up in July 1587 on Roanoke Island, the site of the failed first attempt. No matter; the colonists set about the work of constructing shelter, providing food, and establishing relations with the Indians.

Raleigh intended to support and resupply his colony, but war with Spain delayed him. To confront the great Spanish Armada of 1588 all ships and sailors were needed at home. By the time a relief party reached Roanoke Island, in the summer of 1590, three years after the establishment of the second colony, it came upon one of the great mysteries of American history. No English man, woman, or child could be found, only the word *Croatoan*, the name of a nearby island, carved on a tree. A search of Croatoan turned up no trace of the colony. Precisely what became of the second Roanoke colony remains unknown. Most probably the settlers were either killed or absorbed by the local Indians. Most authorities believe that both killing and absorption took place.

OTHERS, EUROPEAN AND NATIVE

The English were not the first Europeans to set foot on the territory later known as the southern colonies. Spain, the greatest power in Europe in the sixteenth century, had led the European movement into the New World. The Spanish advance began in 1492, when Christopher Columbus, searching for a western route to the Orient, discovered America. The Spanish colonial empire, which extended from Mexico through Central America into South America and was a powerful presence in the Caribbean, had outposts in southeastern North America as well. The first Spaniard—indeed, the first European—to set foot in the region was Juan Ponce de León, who in 1513 claimed Florida for Spain. In 1539 Hernando de Soto landed on the western coast of Florida and headed inland. Over the next four years de Soto's expedition traversed an immense territory, from North Carolina to the Mississippi River. Although de Soto's journey resulted in no consequential Spanish influence, the Spanish did establish in 1565 the first permanent European settlement in North America, at St. Augustine, Florida. Some forty years earlier, Spanish explorers and colonists had attempted a colony along the central coast of South Carolina. Just after they established St. Augustine they tried again along the southern part of that coastline, but after twenty years their effort failed. Despite the exploration and the attempted settlements, little of the Spanish presence survived outside of Florida. Spain controlled Louisiana and the lower Mississippi Valley in the late eighteenth century, but it governed too short a time to make an indelible imprint there.

Still another great European colonizing power touched the shores of the South. Exploring for France, the Italian Giovanni Verrazzano made landfall on the North Carolina coast in 1524. Afterward he sailed along the eastern sea-

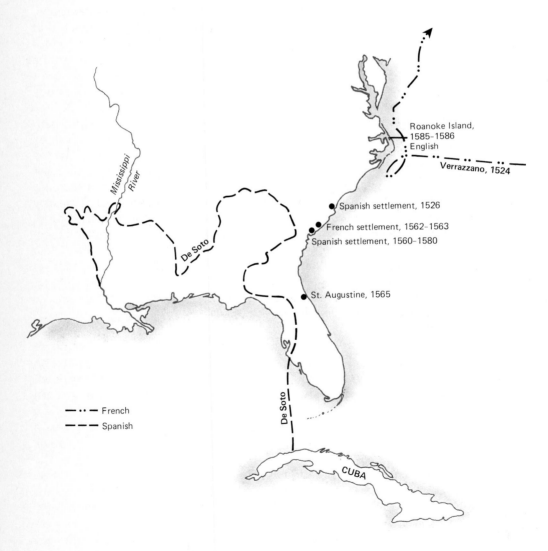

EARLY EXPLORATION IN THE SOUTH

board, though he did not establish a settlement. In the 1560s France did attempt settlements in southern South Carolina and in northern Florida, but the French had even less success and impact than did the Spanish, who promptly drove them out of Florida. The French, however, made their chief effort not in the southeast but along the coast of the Gulf of Mexico. In 1682 the Sieur de la Salle, starting from French Canada, eventually paddled down the Mississippi River all the way to the gulf. The Mississippi Valley he claimed for his king, Louis XIV, and in his honor named it Louisiana. A few years later La Salle returned by sea with the goal of setting up a French colony. His expedition ended in his death at the hands of his own men. Not until the new century and the founding of New Orleans in 1718 by the Sieur de Bienville did the French seriously colonize Louisiana. Although the French in the Mississippi Valley had practically no affect on the development of the British colonies in the Southeast, they had a permanent influence on Louisiana.

The Europeans who explored and colonized the Southeast did not enter an unpopulated land. A substantial native or "Indian" population lived through-out the region, and in the Northeast as well. The name originated with Colum-bus, who gave it to the natives he encountered because he thought he had reached the Indies, off the coast of Asia. An attempt to determine the number of Indians in the Southeast raises a vexing question. Various answers have been suggested, the figures ranging up to 1.5 million. This total seems excessive, but clearly a considerable Indian population greeted the English, French, and Span-ish who came ashore between the Chesapeake and Florida. Although the expe-riences of the Indian groups with the Europeans varied, a common thread did form a pervasive pattern. Contact with Europeans resulted in demographic di-saster for the Indians. Warfare certainly contributed to their downfall, but dis-ease wreaked even more widespread destruction. Biologically unprepared for the diseases the Europeans brought with them, the Indians were devastated. Again, accurate figures are impossible to ascertain, but without doubt entire tribes disappeared within a single generation.

The English did not find a unified Indian people. Three major tribes inter-acted with the English—the Powhatan Confederacy in Virginia, the Cherokee in the western Carolinas, and the Creek in Georgia. None of these tribes was pre-pared culturally to deal with the English. Neither they nor any of the smaller tribes had any conception of an economic and social culture that prized unlim-ited acquisition of land and resources. They also could not cope with a people who had a written language, which permitted coordination and planning over time.

JAMESTOWN

In the beginning Jamestown provided no clue that it would be merely the first step in a process that in the next century and a half would colonize the South-east. On the contrary, Jamestown often seemed headed toward the fate of its predecessor, Roanoke Island. Settlement at Jamestown was the project of the

London Company of Virginia, also known simply as the Virginia Company, a joint-stock company authorized in 1606 by James I. Designed to permit the cost of colonization to be spread among several or several hundred investors, the joint-stock company offered a means to avoid the need for a single investor, such as Sir Walter Raleigh, to finance an expensive colonial venture without help. To attract settlers the Virginia Company offered shares to people who would invest their labor in Virginia as well as to those who would invest their money in England. The charter of the company also permitted a measure of self-government through a council that the colonists in Virginia would set up. Thus from the outset the profit motive was fundamental to the people who founded and settled Virginia.

For at least the first two decades a secure future for Jamestown was far from certain. For the voyage out 105 settlers signed on to plant the British flag in Virginia. As George Percy's narrative makes clear, these colonists soon found themselves in a precarious position. During the first winter the population dwindled to thirty-eight. Poor planning and a lack of leadership resulted in near starvation, which invited disease and brought the colony to the brink of extinction. In fact, Jamestown hung on only because of the assistance, especially the food, given by the Powhatans.

The colonists also found a leader who had the ability and conviction to drive them to save themselves. The first in a long line of Virginia notables, Captain John Smith took over leadership of the colony in 1608. Around forty years of age when he assumed responsibility for the precarious settlement on the banks of the James, Smith brought a military background to his task. He had been a soldier of fortune who had fought on the continent. A member of the Virginia Company, he arrived at Jamestown with the first party of settlers. Once there, he concentrated on exploration and securing food from the Indians. On an exploring venture during the first summer, Smith participated in one of the most famous episodes of early American history. By his own account—and there is no solid reason to disbelieve him—he was captured by Chief Powhatan and scheduled for execution. The chief's daughter Pocahontas, then twelve or thirteen years old, rushed forward and took Smith's head in her arms, thus preventing his executioners from clubbing him to death. After this dramatic incident, Pocahontas spent much time in Jamestown. She converted to Christianity and in 1614 married one of the settlers, John Rolfe. Two years later she and their young son accompanied him to England, where she "carried her selfe as the Daughter of a King, and was accordingly respected." Pocahontas never saw her homeland again; in 1617, just as the Rolfes were starting back to Virginia, she fell ill and died.

During Smith's year as president of the council he organized the colonists for work. He also focused their attention on developing an agriculture that would provide a consistent supply of food. When Smith left the colony, he had not guaranteed success but he had staved off disaster. In 1624 Smith published his *Generall Historie of Virginia*, in which he presented Virginia as a natural paradise that offered a bountiful future for the English. Never underestimating his

CAPTAIN JOHN SMITH,
LEADER OF EARLY JAMES-
TOWN (Library of Congress)

own role in the brief history of the colony, John Smith believed that Virginia was destined for greatness.

Despite Smith's enormous contributions to the security of Jamestown, the settlement remained in jeopardy. Jamestown, along with the farms and homes that grew up around it, confronted three serious challenges. First, the Virginia Company never provided properly for the sustenance of the colony. For almost twenty years ruin seemed imminent. Financial problems plagued the company back in London, and the ensuing loss of interest in the enterprise afflicted the colonists in Virginia. Finally in 1624 King James I revoked the company's charter and Virginia became a royal colony. Second, the colonists had to contend with their more powerful Indian neighbors. During the initial decade, relations between colonists and Indians were reasonably good, but they deteriorated after the death of Powhatan. Then in 1622 came an attack—the colonists called it a massacre—in which at least one-fifth of the population was killed. Desultory fighting went on until the mid-1640s, when the colonists finally overpowered the Powhatan Confederacy. Their triumph was almost total. One hundred years after settlement the 200 Powhatan villages had been reduced to 12.

JOHN SMITH'S MAP OF VIRGINIA, 1612 (John Smith's *Generall Historie*, 1624. New York Public Library)

GROWTH AND CONFLICT IN VIRGINIA

Even more deadly than either the negligence of the company or the danger from the Indians was disease. Between 1607 and 1622 more than 4,000 men, women, and children had come to the colony. After the Indian assault only around 1,240 people remained. The Indians had killed 347 colonists; some 3,000 others had lost their lives to disease. The mortality rate that had frightened George Percy was staggering. Between 1625 and 1640 new colonists arrived at the rate of 1,000 annually, but by 1640 the population had reached only 8,000. Because there were just over 1,000 people in the colony in 1625, the total went up by some 7,000, less than half the number of new arrivals. A new disease environment multiplied by the typhus that resulted from contaminated water ravaged the immigrants. John Smith's description of Virginia as a natural paradise notwithstanding, what nature provided most colonists in Virginia was an early grave.

The easy availability of land and the hope of financial reward kept hopeful people coming to the pestilential place. Those who succeeded in this rough, dangerous world were not noted for honesty and kindness. William Tucker came to Virginia before 1620 to sell goods entrusted to him by a group back in

JAMESTOWN: THE EARLY YEARS, A MODERN MURAL (Thomas L. Williams)

England. Although he evidently sold what he brought, he delivered neither cash nor accounts to the people in England he represented. While he cheated his backers, he was dealing with his fellow colonists in similar fashion. Settlers objected to merchants "who have by needlesse and unprofitable Commodities ...ingaged the inhabitants of debts of Tobacco, to the value almost of theire ensuinge croppe...amonge whom we have good cause to complayne of Captayne Tucker, who hath farr exceeded all other marchaunts in the [prices] of their goodes." Tucker did not outperform Abraham Peirsey, who arrived in Virginia in 1616 as manager of the company's storehouse. Though Peirsey sold his goods for two or three times more than the intended price, the business always showed a loss. Even after a decade he had never paid the company for its goods. That practice helped him leave upon his death in 1628 "the best Estate that was ever yett knowen in Virginia." Edward Blancy rose in part by marrying a widow and grabbing the estate of a man who happened to have a surname identical with that of his wife's first husband. Even a treasurer of the colony who desired more servants simply assigned sixteen tenants of the company as his own servants.

Tobacco held the key to potential wealth. Unlike the Spanish colonies in Mexico and South America, Virginia yielded no gold and no silver, but it had the golden weed, tobacco. The success of tobacco in Virginia resulted in large part from the efforts of John Rolfe. Although Rolfe is known primarily for his marriage to Pocahontas, he made a far more lasting impact on the colony, and ultimately on American history, by developing tobacco marketable in Europe.

The plant was not native to Virginia. Englishmen had learned to like it from the Spanish, who had brought it to Europe from the West Indies at an early date. The Indians of Virginia did grow and smoke a kind of tobacco, but the English found it bitter. Obtaining some seed from the West Indies, Rolfe managed to produce a milder and more palatable product. Others rushed to follow his lead; tobacco grew even in the streets of Jamestown. The first shipments left for England in 1617.

Although tobacco brought wealth to colonial Virginia, even in the seventeenth century the English disagreed sharply about its use. Those who championed it described the plant as a gift from a bountiful nature. The "esteemed weed" moved one of its partisans to write:

> Earth ne're did breed
> Such a joviall weed,
> Whereof to boast so proudly.

Its enemies, however, denounced tobacco as the "chopping herbe of hell." And the opponents counted among their number King James himself. The king had no use for the chief commodity of his first North American colony. Three years before Jamestown, in a condemnation quite modern in its particulars, he castigated smoking as "a custome lothsome to the eye, hateful to the nose, harmfull to the braine, dangerous to the lungs, and in the blacke stinking fume thereof, neerest resembling the horrible Stigian smoke of the pit that is bottomelesse." James was on the losing side, however, for his own subjects as well as the continental Europeans eagerly took up the tobacco habit.

If Virginia was to realize fully the economic promise tobacco offered, changes had to be made. The introduction of fruit trees added to the vitamin supply. After midcentury the colony required ship captains to disembark new arrivals in either fall or winter so that they might become somewhat acclimatized before the rigors of summer. Although these measures did not make Virginia a healthy place, they probably helped somewhat to curb the spread of disease. Still, an increase in population depended chiefly on migration from England, which after 1640 included more women than had previously entered the colony. The additional women improved the male-female balance and contributed to the rise in the colonial birthrate. The population rose from 8,000 in 1644 to more than 14,000 in 1653, then to almost 32,000 in 1662, and to just under 45,000 in 1680. By 1700 it topped 58,000.

These years also witnessed the rise of many of the families that were to dominate the colony in the eighteenth century. Among the men who came in the 1650s and 1660s, many were younger sons of the English landed gentry; some were even members of the aristocracy. Though not of the nobility, these individuals were neither the common folk nor the riffraff. They were gentlefolk who wanted to replicate the society they had left behind. They left because their England afforded them no opportunity to rise to the wealth and influence they believed they deserved. In Virginia these gentry strove to give substance to title.

William Byrd I, progenitor of one of the most notable families in colonial Virginia, reached the colony about 1670. He came to live with an uncle, Thomas Stegg, Jr., whose father had migrated a generation earlier. Upon Stegg's death, Byrd inherited his estate, and with determination and ruthlessness he transformed his inheritance into one of the greatest of colonial fortunes. He raised tobacco, and he also moved forcefully into other endeavors. Setting up a trading station at the falls of the James River—the future site of Richmond—on the outer edge of English settlement, Byrd traded over hundreds of miles with various Indian tribes. He also dealt extensively in indentured servants and slaves. Passing up no opportunities, Byrd became an accomplished looter when times became unsettled.

Hardship, competition, the risk of failure—nothing daunted Byrd or the other immigrants. Virginia remained in large part a rude frontier where ordinary planters lived chiefly on Indian corn and water. Beef in summer, pork in fall, and game supplemented the monotonous regular diet. This open, mostly unregulated environment gave hard-driving men the chance to make their mark. And they were not always scrupulous about how they did it. Colonel Philip Ludwell, for example, used the stroke of a pen to give himself a comparative advantage. Every man who came to the colony received fifty acres of land for every person he brought with him. Ludwell had forty people, so he was entitled to 2,000 acres. But he wanted more, and with his own hand he added a zero to each number. He did not bring 400 immigrants, but he did get 20,000 acres of land. In this hurly-burly world, the likes of the first William Byrd and Philip Ludwell laid the foundations for the life of cultivation and graciousness later enjoyed by their families and by such others as the Carters, the Lees, the Randolphs—the first families of Virginia.

Social conflict pervaded this process. The conflicting interests among the older colonial elite, the hard-driving newcomers, and newly freed indentured servants—the unfree whites who formed the bulk of the labor force before 1675—made for tense, even violent times. By 1660 the peopling of the older sections of the tidewater counties made readily available acres scarce indeed. Newly freed servants and new immigrants found it more and more difficult to obtain decent land in settled areas. Their alternatives were to rent from established landowners—not their choice—or to take up land farther inland, a move that often meant trouble with the Indians. The land hungry saw the Indians as their enemies, as possessing the land they desired. Yet the royal governor and others among the elite did not want a renewed struggle with the Indians. After the triumph of the mid-1640s the colonial government designated its near neighbors, who now lived peaceably beside the whites and paid tribute in kind, as "tributary" Indians.

Governor William Berkeley in 1667 captured precisely the background of the strife rankling Virginia society: "Consider us as a people press'd at our backes with Indians, in our Bowills with our servants." This tension exploded in

Bacon's Rebellion, which shook the colony between the spring and fall of 1676. At that time eager, ambitious young men, such as William Byrd I, rallied behind the leadership of thirty-year-old Nathaniel Bacon, who had been in Virginia only a year. Bacon arrived with close ties to the elite; Governor Berkeley had even placed his future foe on his council. Disagreement over Indian policy eventually led Berkeley and Bacon to armed combat. Bacon demanded a commission from the governor to attack the Indians, but Berkeley, fearful of the repercussions, refused. Despite the governor's refusal, Bacon and his followers set out.

In the ensuing conflict the upper hand seemed to belong first to one side, then to the other. In May, Berkeley branded Bacon a rebel and proceeded to capture his former associate. But once he had Bacon in his grasp, the governor imposed no punishment. Instead, hoping to end the trouble and reunite his colony, he pardoned the rebel. Bacon was not to be deterred, however. In June he brought a strong force to Jamestown and at gunpoint forced the governor to give him the commission he sought, authorizing a move against the Indians. With Bacon on the march, the governor declared the commission fraudulent and called on the people to help him stop Bacon. But it was Berkeley who was stopped. Defeated, the governor retreated to the eastern shore of the Chesapeake Bay while the victorious Bacon entered Jamestown with 400 men on foot and 120 horsemen. On September 19 he and his men torched the town—the church, public buildings, private homes, even the tavern. Outside of Jamestown homes and plantations were looted, including the governor's. William Byrd got his share.

Yet in the end Bacon's Rebellion failed. In late October Bacon died, probably of dysentery. No one else rose to replace him as leader. When Governor Berkeley returned and regained control, he had at least twenty of Bacon's lieutenants executed. The governor retained his authority, but the brutality of both sides underscored the severity of the crisis.

Bacon's Rebellion was the most violent episode in the social melee that was seventeenth-century Virginia. The future, however, was not on the side of continued turmoil. Colonists' willingness to move to new land along with the firm adoption of a new labor system worked for a more settled social order. The new century would usher in social peace and a more ordered society, though the new order commanded a heavy price.

MARYLAND

While the story in Virginia unfolded, just to the north and on the Chesapeake another colony was being established. The origins of Maryland differed from those of its older neighbor. Maryland grew out of a land grant and charter King Charles I gave in 1632 to George Calvert, Lord Baltimore, though technically they went to George's son Cecilius, the second Lord Baltimore because George died before completion of the transaction. The charter gave Calvert proprietorship of Maryland, which meant that initially he had title to all the land and that he could establish the rules for colonization. A Roman Catholic, Calvert wanted a colony in which no discrimination would be practiced against his fellow Catholics, though he never saw Maryland simply as a haven for his coreligionists. At the same time Calvert wanted to profit from his landholdings like any other English lord. To that end he envisioned a land system dominated by lords of manors who controlled immense acreages.

The first group of 200 settlers, including a cadre of Roman Catholic priests, landed in southern Maryland in 1634 and established St. Mary's City as the first colonial capital. By summer their numbers had grown to 350. Like the settlers who journeyed to Virginia, the original Marylanders all hailed from England. And in fact the social and economic course of Maryland followed a pattern quite similar to that of Virginia.

The structured, almost medieval social organization that Calvert planned for Maryland never came to pass. His system of literal lords of the manor never became important; after a decade only sixteen were in place. Instead, the almost wide-open practices common in Virginia prevailed. Without question large landowners stood at the top of Maryland's social order, but, as in Virginia, many had made their way up through ambition, drive, and good fortune. By the end of the century, again as in Virginia, the great families that would dominate affairs in the eighteenth century had emerged from the grasping pack.

On the religious front Roman Catholics retained their security throughout the century. Almost from the beginning Protestants outnumbered them, but the Catholics' association with the proprietor helped their cause. Then the Maryland Toleration Act of 1649 gave legislative sanction to nondiscriminatory practices. Although the law did not declare religious diversity a public good, it did require toleration. And toleration became the hallmark of the colony until 1691, when Protestants succeeded in obtaining a royal charter, which turned Maryland into a royal colony and ended the proprietorship of the Calvert family. Substantial changes occurred: the capital was moved from St. Mary's City, in the center of the Catholic population, to Annapolis, a Protestant stronghold; the Church of England became the established church; Roman Catholics were denied the right to vote, to hold office, and to hold religious services outside their homes.

Maryland was the only southern colony in which the royal period did not last until the Revolution. In 1715, after only a quarter century, the crown restored the proprietorship of Maryland to the fourth Lord Baltimore, who had converted to Protestantism. With the restoration the original charter of 1632 again became valid. Though the anti-Catholic statutes remained on the books, the political proscriptions were lifted from Catholics who professed allegiance to the king, and the colonial government did not rigorously enforce the prohibition against public religious services.

For the growth of Maryland it really did not matter who had basic authority. By 1650, 4,500 settlers were in colony. In 1690, on the eve of the royalist takeover, their numbers had increased more than fivefold, to 24,000. In 1720, after the reinstatement of the proprietor, the population stood at just about 66,000. And by the eve of the Revolution it had edged above 200,000.

THE CAROLINAS

After the founding of Maryland, colonization in the South subsided for almost forty years. Internal problems in the mother country, which eventually led to civil war and the execution of King Charles I in 1649, and so to the temporary end of the monarchy, accounted for this considerable loss of momentum. But just as the fall of the monarchy halted colonization, its restoration under Charles II in 1660 signaled a resurgence. To reward eight of his major supporters, Charles gave them a substantial land grant in the New World. This land, which stretched southward from Virginia, was called Carolina—from Carolus, the Latin form of Charles—and its owners were known as the Lords Proprietors of Carolina.

In planning a colony for Carolina the proprietors certainly wanted to profit, and like Cecilius Calvert, they envisioned an almost medieval social organization. A document known as the Fundamental Constitutions formed their blueprint. Prepared chiefly by John Locke, the great English philosopher and political theorist, the Fundamental Constitutions blended notions advanced for the seventeenth century with an archaic social structure. The plan guaranteed religious freedom, but it authorized the establishment of the Church of England. It also provided for a stratified, hereditary nobility with such exotic titles as landgrave and cacique. Although the Fundamental Constitutions provided a master plan for the Lords Proprietors' new colony, converting theory into practice proved to be impossible.

In 1680, ten years after the proprietors established their colony, they relocated their settlement a short distance, to the present site of Charleston. The proprietors hoped to promote Carolina not only among their English compatriots but in New England and Barbados, an English-owned colony in the West Indies, which they believed overpopulated. New Englanders had no impact on South Carolina, but Barbadians had an enormous influence. During the initial decades the Barbadian immigrants became the driving force in the colony. They were willing to relocate in the new colony because Barbados's land area was not large enough to permit all of its ambitious families to establish rich plantations. The Barbadians arrived in South Carolina with the goal of creating in their new home the plantation economy they had envied back in Barbados. Despite their commitment to plantation life, the colony remained basically a wilderness until the turn of the century.

French Huguenots soon joined the Barbadians in Carolina. Driven out of France by the Catholic majority, the French Protestants had no difficulty accepting the Barbadians' vision for the colony. The career of one Huguenot immigrant testifies both to the harsh conditions in South Carolina and to the determination of its settlers. Judith Manigault and her husband left France in the mid-1680s and, after a stop in England, traveled on to South Carolina. Arriving in 1689, the Manigaults settled in the swampy country along the Santee River, approximately forty miles north of Charleston. Judith and her husband worked side by side felling trees, sawing wood, and raising crops. Their life was difficult. "I have been for six months together without tasting bread, working the ground like a slave; and I have even passed three or four years without always having it when I wanted it," she wrote a brother back in Europe. Even so, she thanked God for the good things in her life, especially the strength to bear the rigors of South Carolina. By the time of Judith's death in 1711 at age forty-two, some seventy families lived in this Santee region, where they farmed and traded with Indians.

The early settlers struggled until the success of rice. In the beginning the South Carolina economy was based on livestock and skins, chiefly deerskins, which they traded with the Indians. A staple crop to support a growing, prosperous economy remained elusive. Although attempts to grow rice were made in the 1670s and 1680s, these efforts did not produce enough for home consumption, and certainly not enough for export. Even by 1690, when growers managed to increase their yields, they still had severe problems with the task of removing the husks from the grains of rice. But over the next twenty years Carolinians did learn to produce an economically viable crop. This success came in conjunction with the importation of slaves into the colony. Some of the slaves entering South Carolina came from areas of western Africa where rice had long been a mainstay of the diet. It seems likely that the newly arrived Africans were the key to the development of South Carolina's rice culture. They knew how to plant, cultivate, harvest, and thresh rice. The slaves surely supplied the labor in the rice fields, and it is probable that they also helped provide the knowledge critical to the successful cultivation of what became the great Carolina staple. A report to London in 1700 made the point that South Carolinians had "now found out the true way of raising and husking Rice."

The favorable outcome of the venture with rice significantly affected the growth of the colony's population. In 1680 no more than 1,000 people lived around Charleston, and by 1700 their numbers had reached only 2,260, of whom 900 were women. Then with the success of rice cultivation prosperity and confidence began to take hold. Many of the planters who prospered with rice and rose to eminent positions in the colony had Barbadian and Huguenot roots. By 1710 the population moved beyond 10,000; by 1730 it had shot up to 30,000; and by 1770 it stood at 125,000.

Although Charles II's grant to the Lords Proprietors included North Carolina, that colony had a different settlement pattern from South Carolina's. The initial settlements in the seventeenth century occurred before 1650, in the same outer banks area where the Roanoke Island colonies had foundered back in the 1580s. The colony was originally known as Albemarle, the name of one of the sounds separating the outer banks from the mainland. In 1691, North Carolina replaced Albemarle as the name of the colony. This second and permanent colonization originated in Virginia, when some settlers made the short journey

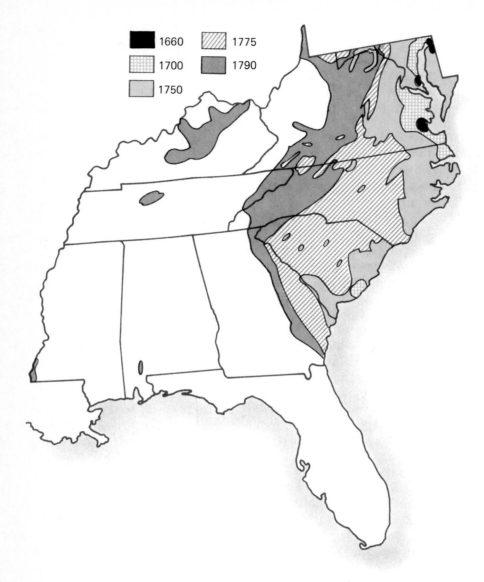

■ 1660	▨ 1775
▦ 1700	▨ 1790
▨ 1750	

GROWTH OF SETTLEMENT IN THE SOUTHERN COLONIES, 1660–1775

from the James River region to the outer banks, and the colony of Albemarle became the colony of North Carolina. By midcentury a few hundred people were raising livestock and attempting to grow tobacco there.

When the Lords Proprietors assumed control of North Carolina, they experienced some of the same problems they confronted in South Carolina. Despite the proprietors' intentions, the Fundamental Constitutions were never enforced. They were just as impractical in North Carolina as they were in South Carolina. The interests of the settlers in North Carolina often differed from those of the Lords Proprietors, and tension governed the relationship between the two factions. Finally in 1719 the Lords Proprietors formally surrendered their charter and North Carolina became a royal colony.

During the last twenty years of the seventeenth century settlement expanded inland. In that period and in the early years of the eighteenth century the colony greeted a variety of groups that broadened its ethnic base. French Huguenots and German and Swiss Protestants joined the colony. In the colonial era North Carolina never became so prosperous as Virginia or South Carolina, but its population steadily increased. Between 1680 and 1700 the number of North Carolinians doubled, from about 5,000 to 10,000. During the next three decades the population rose to 30,000. As in the other southern colonies, growth was enormous after 1730. By 1750 almost 73,000 people lived in the colony, and by 1770 their numbers exceeded 197,000. Some North Carolinians emulated their prosperous neighbors, growing tobacco in the Virginia border areas and rice in the southeastern corner, close to South Carolina. But most North Carolina farmers concentrated on animals, corn, and other foodstuffs. Naval stores—turpentine, pitch, rosin—obtained from the abundant pine forests formed a critical part of the colonial economy.

GEORGIA

The boundaries of Georgia, the last English colony established in the South, were initially within the area granted to the Lords Proprietors of Carolina. The first plans to settle Georgia were devised in South Carolina in an effort to create a buffer between that colony and Spanish Florida, but none of these early attempts succeeded. After both Carolinas became royal colonies, the English government took a different tack. In 1732 the crown approved a charter setting up a Board of Trustees and granting to the trustees a twenty-one-year lease on Georgia.

In colonizing Georgia the trustees had two major goals. The first was the traditional strategic aim of establishing a barrier between increasingly prosperous South Carolina and the Spanish in Florida. Then the trustees had the notion that Georgia would serve as a haven for certain social unfortunates, such as debtors, who in eighteenth-century England faced imprisonment. This philanthropic vision extended beyond the creation of a new home for people trapped by unfortunate circumstances; the trustees envisioned a new society unlike any that existed in the older colonies. They would restrict landholding to a maximum of 500 acres per person, and they banned slavery. The trustees wanted Georgians to benefit the mother country by developing crops and products not available elsewhere in the empire: instead of the veterans of colonial southern agriculture like tobacco and rice, they would cultivate mulberry trees to feed silkworms, grapes for wine, and spices.

The first settlers landed in 1733 at a place they called Savannah. Leading the

115 original settlers was James Oglethorpe, the only trustee to come to Georgia. The thirty-seven-year-old Oglethorpe became the dominant figure in early Georgia. Born in London into a prominent family, Oglethorpe served in Parliament, where his chairmanship of a committee on the condition of English jails stirred his interest in America. He made the journey to Georgia to see that the colony started off in the right direction. This original contingent included few of the social unfortunates the trustees wanted to aid. Neither did it have many who knew anything about agriculture. These new Georgians were chiefly artisans and tradespeople from small English towns. Led by Oglethorpe, who proved himself an able colonizer and leader, they set about clearing land for homes and crops, erecting a fort for defensive purposes, and laying out the town of Savannah. In the initial years the trustees sent over assistance and some 1,800 charity colonists, whose passage the trustees paid. Scottish soldiers and German Protestants supplemented the English majority. From Savannah the colony expanded inland and down the coast to the Altamaha River.

Michael Burkholder was the kind of settler the trustees hoped would immigrate to their colony. A German who still spoke his native tongue, Burkholder in the early 1740s owned about 500 acres outside Savannah. The Burkholder family farmed the land, and in addition they worked as skilled artisans. Michael Burkholder had mastered several crafts, including carpentry, millwrighting, and wheelwrighting. His oldest son and his son-in-law were shoemakers and carpenters, and his eldest daughter was a seamstress. Burkholder made sure that his five younger children learned the trades that their father and older siblings practiced.

Despite the great hopes of the trustees and the immigration of such colonists as the Burkholders, Georgia did not prosper, and many of the colonists blamed the trustees' cherished goals: restrictions on landowning, exotic crops, and the absence of slaves. After 1745 the interest of the trustees waned. Simultaneously the colonists grew more independent, and some of the inland settlements became practically autonomous. Finally in 1752, at the end of the trustees' lease, the crown assumed control of the colony. Even before Georgia became a royal colony, however, the trustees had begun to relax some of the old restrictions; the authorized size of landholdings was increased and slaveholding was permitted. The kind of determination and drive that produced the economic elite in the Chesapeake and in Carolina became evident in Georgia. These people constantly pressed for the changes that they believed would permit them to match the prosperity of the planters in South Carolina. In the two decades remaining before the Revolution, the economic fortunes of Georgia improved so strikingly that the population grew from just over 5,000 in 1750 to more than 23,000 in 1770.

*U*NFREE LABOR, WHITE AND RED

All of the colonies had one overpowering need: able-bodied men and women to work. The colonists faced the enormous task of converting the forests of their new domain into cultivated fields that would produce the tobacco, the rice, and the other crops necessary not merely for their survival but for the generation of the wealth they dreamed about. In the pre-machinery days of the seventeenth and eighteenth centuries, that feat required the strong backs, arms, and legs of many human beings. Those who could pay their way across the Atlantic could never achieve that goal. First, and fundamentally, this group never had the numbers to get the work done. Second, many of these people had been lured to the New World by the hope of making a fortune, and to succeed they had to have others working for them. And the pestilent environment of the seventeenth century provided few incentives to free persons of limited means. People who could exercise some choice over their destination in the New World tended to choose healthier areas, such as New England.

To fill this critical need the southern colonists looked to unfree labor. That was a familiar concept to the colonists, for English law provided for the hiring out of servants to masters, usually for a fixed term. In the seventeenth century the powerful magnet of land drew to the Chesapeake colonies a substantial number of indentured servants, English men and women who paid for their transatlantic voyage by selling their labor for a specified period, usually five to seven years. These landless, unfree laborers, chiefly young, unmarried, and unskilled men but also young, unmarried women, expected their labor to enable them in time to become landowners. Of course they expected that as landowners they would acquire servants to work for them.

In seventeenth-century Virginia and Maryland indentured servants were the mainstays of the labor force. Probably from one-half to three-fourths of all new arrivals in the Chesapeake between 1630 and 1680 came as indentured servants. Until the end of the terms specified in their contracts, these laborers were considered the chattel property of the masters who had purchased their indentures. According to the usual contract, masters had to provide clothing, food, and shelter; in return the indentured servants contributed their labor. The servants did have the basic civil rights shared by all of the king's subjects, regardless of circumstances. In the colonies a body of statute law developed to govern the master–servant relationship.

At times the system seemed to work as intended. Servants performed their required labor and subsequently became landowners themselves. John Cage was an illiterate indentured servant in Maryland in the 1640s. The owner of Cage's service evidently tried to keep him in servitude past his legal term, but Cage won a court judgment against his master. The records indicate that in 1650 Cage held title to 150 acres of land. He also served for a time as a county juror and later on apparently possessed a few servants of his own. In Virginia during the same period the Seager family made even greater strides. Oliver Seager, most likely a former servant, in 1652 had 200 acres of land in Middlesex County. After Oliver's death his son Randolph took charge of the property. Randolph Seager, too, became a county official, but a more successful one than John Cage, for in the next few years he held a variety of offices—juror, estate appraiser, constable. At his death in his early thirties he was a respected property owner.

Indentured servitude did not always lead to such careers, however. The fate that befell Elizabeth Abbott and Elias Hinton in Virginia in the 1620s indicates the horror that could await an indentured servant. Abbott and Hinton labored for the Proctors, husband and wife, who had at least four other servants. Hinton toiled chiefly in the tobacco fields; Abbott apparently worked mostly in or around the Proctor home. Both Proctors inflicted corporal punishment on their servants, and they certainly did not discriminate between the sexes. Both of them beat Abbott and Hinton unmercifully. Abbott claimed that on one occasion she was beaten with fishhooks. Hinton's final beating seems to have been with a rake. Neither Abbott nor Hinton survived their common ordeal. In October 1624 the Proctors were arrested and charged with beating both servants to death.

Most indentured servants probably did not fare so well as Cage and Seager or suffer so incredibly as Abbott and Hinton. Regardless of individual experiences, indentured servants dominated the labor force in the seventeenth century, but they practically disappeared after 1700. They never were so important in the Carolinas and Georgia as in Virginia and Maryland. This different experience of the older and younger colonies testifies to an especially momentous shift in the source and the identity of unfree laborers. Between 1650 and 1700 indentured servitude gave way to another form of unfree labor, slavery.

From an early date the colonists enslaved Indians, though the extent of Indian slavery varied widely. Indian slavery never became fundamental to the labor system of the Chesapeake. Over the course of much of the seventeenth century some Virginians tried to make slaves of Indians. Although the historical record is not absolutely clear on this issue, it is probable that few Indians in Virginia or Maryland ended up as slaves. Indian slavery was much more widespread in South Carolina between 1670 and 1700. More Indians lived in and near the colony, and the various tribes traded their captives from tribal wars to the whites for enslavement. Shortly after the beginning of the eighteenth century frontier conflicts boosted Indian slaves to their largest total, around 1,400, but by then the days of Indian slavery were almost over. The Indian population, even in South Carolina, never was large enough to provide a sufficient labor force for the whites. Moreover, the susceptibility of Indians to the whites' diseases made them unsatisfactory as slaves. Besides, the possibility always existed that Indian slaves could escape and melt back into the Indian population of the interior.

UNFREE LABOR, BLACK

By 1700 colonists from the Chesapeake to South Carolina had fixed on a much more plentiful group to furnish their slaves. Like the Indians, these people were not white, but unlike the Indians, they were not native to the New World. Neither were the whites' diseases so lethal to them, nor did they have a nearby hinterland. Black Africans became the great slave force of the colonial South. The enslavement of blacks did not begin in one location at one point in time. It developed in the Chesapeake, particularly in Virginia, over several decades. The first blacks, some possibly slaves, appeared in Jamestown in 1619; by 1660 a system of black slavery was clearly in place. Black slaves had not yet generally replaced white indentured servants as the major source of unfree labor, but their introduction signaled the beginning of significant change. Intimate ties bound together those two complementary developments—the rise of black slavery and the decline of white indentured servitude.

Until 1650 the black population of Virginia grew very little. The first blacks who arrived in 1619 numbered around twenty; a half-dozen years later the total remained basically unchanged at twenty-three, compared to more than 1,200 whites. During the next quarter century the whites far outdistanced the blacks. In 1649 the white population stood at approximately 15,000, while the black had reached only 300.

The historical record does not make precisely clear the status of the blacks in Virginia between 1619 and 1649. The evidence does permit two generalizations, however. First, not all of these blacks were slaves; in fact, most probably were not. Some were free people; others, probably the majority, were indentured servants. Second, at times they were treated quite differently from whites. The first census, in 1629, distinguished white people from black people and often provided no personal names for blacks. In 1640 blacks were denied the right to bear arms, and they received harsher penalties than whites who had committed the same offenses. On occasion punishment for blacks was a lifetime in servitude. In 1640 three runaway servants, two white and one black, were captured. Each of the white servants was sentenced to four additional years of servitude; the black found himself bound for life. That some blacks were also being sold for life, a condition never applied to whites, also indicates that white society viewed the servant status of at least some blacks differently. Executors settling an estate in 1647 gave eight blacks to a master "to have hold occupy posesse and injoy and every one of the afforementioned Negroes forever." In addition, black servants commanded a higher price than white servants, which certainly indicates a different kind of servitude.

Although in 1650 white indentured servants still overwhelmingly supplied the unfree labor, changes taking place in the colony were setting the circumstances that would foster the massive growth of black slavery. The disparity between the costs of white and black servants dramatized that shift. In the 1640s and early 1650s a white servant with an indenture of five years or more cost around 1,000 pounds of tobacco, but a black commanded approximately 2,000 pounds of tobacco. A seasoned male or female black could bring between 2,000 and 3,000 pounds. Late in the 1650s prices rose for both blacks and whites, but a substantial differential still held. While white servants brought as much as 3,000 pounds, blacks sold for 4,000 pounds. That white masters would pay 50 percent and even 100 percent more for blacks than for whites underscores the fundamental transformation that was taking place.

Worsening relations between white servants and their masters significantly influenced the new direction. The increasing number of young men completing their servitude and clamoring for their own land led to social and political strain. This increasing tension among the whites finally erupted in 1676 in Bacon's Rebellion. The white elite had to decide whether it wanted to sustain a system that seemingly guaranteed social turmoil and strife.

To the Virginia elite, blacks offered two powerful advantages over whites as the major source of unfree labor. A black could be held in bondage for life, a condition that could never apply to an English person. A black man could also be permanently barred from the company of landowners and placed outside of political life, as no Englishman could be.

The embrace of Africans as the servant class had a further important ramification for the leaders of colonial Virginia, and for the subsequent history of the South. Whites of every social class could join together as whites vis-à-vis the black slaves. Thus racial identity became a powerful force for white unity. The growth of black slavery did help the cause of social peace among whites. The turmoil that sparked Bacon's Rebellion and racked Virginia in much of the seventeenth century did not carry over into the eighteenth.

The enslavement of blacks satisfied many needs for the white colonists. Certainly the English in Britain and in Virginia had knowledge of both blacks and slavery before the introduction of blacks into the colony. White Virginians were aware that for the bulk of the sixteenth century, blacks had been transported from Africa to work as slaves in Spanish colonies in the New World. They also knew that the English colony of Barbados had instituted slavery in the 1630s.

Critical was the black color of the Africans. To the English of the Elizabethan age, that blackness separated Africans from themselves. And just as important, it signified inferiority. In the eyes of the English the black Africans were not only different from but inferior to themselves. The reasons for that attitude were complex. In the sixteenth century no two words in the English language carried more psychological power than *black* and *white*. *White* stood for goodness and purity, *black* for sinfulness and evil. Color symbolism alone, however, did not construct racism. What the English learned about the living conditions and social activities of equatorial Africa reinforced the sharp contrast conveyed by *white* and *black*. Of course, few English people had visited tropical Africa; they formed their impressions by reading the accounts of travelers. Those reports described men and women wearing loincloths and living in straw huts. Moreover, those Africans did not worship the Christian God. To the English convinced of the superiority of their own civilization and cultural attainments the Africans appeared uncivilized, heathen, even savage. In their minds a people who wore practically no clothes, who had no grand buildings, and who were not Christian could in no way be equal to the English or to any other Europeans. That these uncivilized Africans had black skins only underscored the fundamental distinction the English perceived between themselves and the Africans. Then the actual enslavement of Africans in the New World confirmed for many English people their perception of the basic inferiority of blacks. A calculus of racial debasement and prejudice took hold.

THE SUCCESS OF SLAVERY

Thus both economics and race made essential contributions to the enslavement of blacks. Although scholars disagree as to which of the two factors had primary importance as a motivating force, all students of colonial slavery concur that both were critical ingredients in the origins of slavery. Each reinforced the other.

Between 1650 and 1700 black slavery went into the bedrock of Chesapeake society. By 1670, Virginia counted some 2,000 blacks, considerably more than the 300 of twenty years earlier. The number grew steadily through the remainder of the century until by 1700 at least 10,000 blacks lived in the colony. Maryland went from just over 1,000 blacks in 1670 to more than 3,000 in 1700. The increasing statutory recognition of slavery matched the growing numbers. As early as 1661 Virginia law recognized that some blacks served for life. During the next three decades a succession of statutes dealt in increasing detail with various aspects of slavery. Finally in 1705 the first codification of slave law took place in Virginia. In the new century the number of slaves increased massively.

South of the Chesapeake no such lengthy incubation period occurred. The Fundamental Constitutions of Carolina made provision for slavery. And coming from a society where slavery was firmly implanted, the Barbadian immigrants to South Carolina thought in terms of slavery from the beginning. Although indentured servants did come into Carolina, they never occupied a central place there. By 1700 approximately a third of South Carolina's population was black, and only ten years later blacks outnumbered whites. Even Georgia turned to black slaves as the chief source of unfree labor within twenty years of its settlement. The southern colonies made no more momentous decision in all of the seventeenth century than the establishment of black slavery.

2

The Economic and Social World

---------- ❖ ----------

The availability of land had an enormous impact on the social, economic, and political structure of the colonial South. As a South Carolinian wrote in the aftermath of the Revolution, "From the first settlement in this country...the facility of procuring landed property gave every citizen an opportunity of becoming an independent freeholder." Land was the greatest economic asset of the colonies, in the North as in the South. Not only was land plentiful throughout the colonial period; its price remained generally reasonable. Over time land in the older, coastal regions did increase substantially in cost, but prices in newer areas remained within the financial reach of multitudes of colonists. In addition to general availability and reasonable cost, land was owned in fee simple; in other words, the overwhelming majority of landowners possessed their acres with none of the encumbrances associated with feudal land tenure.

Landownership was important for a great deal more than economic advancement. In the seventeenth and eighteenth centuries landownership provided the necessary key to respected social position and to participation in politics. Although laws generally excluded the landless from political participation, the proscription had a much broader base than statutes. A general societal attitude placed the landless outside social respectability. As a result, ownership of land became a basic requirement for both social mobility and broad political activity.

The male heads of southern colonial families surely owned land. Heading the list of landowners in the colonial South, and certainly impressing most historians, were the plantation magnates, planters who possessed enormous acreages. William Byrd I, who at one time counted 179,000 acres as his own, and Robert "King" Carter with 300,000 acres exemplify the grandees. Often these men did not simply appear and disappear within a generation, though dissipation of fortunes did occur. Many of the great families of the Revolutionary era— the Carrolls, the Lees, the Masons—benefited from the economic success of their forebears.

*T*HE BREADTH OF LANDOWNING

Despite the grandeur of great names and plantations, the most striking feature of landownership in the colonial South was its breadth. Although social conflict over landowning had plagued Virginia for a time in the mid-seventeenth century, by the eighteenth century the great majority of white male southerners owned their own land. At the end of the colonial period no more than 30 percent of the white population in Virginia made up the landless group. In North Carolina the figure dropped to 25 percent, and in South Carolina scarcely 14 percent of the white population occupied the landless category. These figures on landownership compare favorably with those of the northern colonies, where the landless totaled approximately 25 percent of the population.

Within the landowning class a middle group occupied a prominent place. In South Carolina, 30 percent owned more than 500 acres, but fully 60 percent held between 100 and 500 acres, while 30 percent had title to between 100 and 300 acres. The landed aristocracy was less important in North Carolina, where middle-class farmers or yeomen formed a clear majority of the population.

By the middle of the eighteenth century many of these farmers were prospering, and the ongoing westward expansion that characterized the century made it entire'y possible for a yeoman to become rich and even for a poor person to achieve economic independence. The geographic mobility across the broad expanse of the Southeast helped maintain a significantly high rate of social mobility. Westward expansion permitted the continuing creation of new elites—people who garnered the power and prestige accorded to the large planters. Even before 1750 this expansion spilled into the piedmont of Virginia and the Carolinas; by the close of the Revolution it crossed the Appalachians, and in the nineteenth century it reached to the Mississippi and beyond.

The creation of new elites meant a constant renewal of the upper classes. In fact, the upper class of the colonial South never became a fixed, static order. Although many of the great Virginia families, such as the Byrds, Lees, and Randolphs, could date their status back to the seventeenth century, new families constantly moved into the upper orders. Recent studies have demonstrated that families who made their mark as late as 1720 contributed to the leadership of the colony. In the younger colonies to the south the social order was even more fluid. Individuals moved into the upper class on past mid-century.

The pervasive ownership of land, along with social mobility, had enormous political and social consequences. Together they muted the potential for class conflict, though class differences and economic disparities clearly existed. But because landownership allowed participation in politics and prevented any upper class from formally stigmatizing those below as perpetually inferior or worthless, the possession of land guaranteed social and political status to most whites in the eighteenth century.

THE PLANTATION SYSTEM

The chief economic importance of land lay in the production of crops for the market. Fewer than twenty years after the settlement of Virginia commercial agriculture had become the engine driving the economy of the colony. The first tobacco shipments left Jamestown for England in 1617. During the following decade a burst of tobacco-backed prosperity created the first colonial fortunes. Those fortunes were inextricably tied to the land and to the production of a staple crop for an overseas market. Plantations and planters got an early start in the South.

The term *plantation system* aptly describes this economic activity, even though agriculturalists of all sorts engaged in it. Almost from the beginning the plantation, or large commercial farm, provided the main impetus to the southern agricultural machine. Smaller farmers often raised the same money crops, and they usually hoped to expand their farms into plantations.

The economic pattern established in Virginia formed the model for subsequent colonies. Settled in 1634, Maryland early committed itself to tobacco, just as its older neighbor had done. Although tobacco did not become the economic mainspring of the younger colonies south of the Chesapeake, staple crop agriculture surely became their central economic activity. By the beginning of the eighteenth century, only thirty years after the settlement of South Carolina, its colonists were turning to the cultivation of rice, which in the new century generated an astonishing prosperity. Even in North Carolina, where the plantation system did not attain the importance it did elsewhere, the richest areas embraced the system. The youngest colony, Georgia, tried desperately to emulate its nearest neighbor, South Carolina. By mid-century, after a brief, unsuccessful effort with exotic crops and an equally unsuccessful attempt to do without the plantation system, Georgians had embraced both rice and slaves.

The system of plantation agriculture grew and flourished despite massive social and economic changes. The initial crops of tobacco and rice remained important throughout the eighteenth century and even into the nineteenth, but others appeared early, and over time an increasingly smaller proportion of southern farmers cultivated the two crops that first brought wealth to southern planters. By the middle of the eighteenth century indigo had become a major supplement to rice in South Carolina, and before the Revolution wheat had become a major money crop of the tidewater in Virginia and Maryland. Cotton, which became the monarch of nineteenth-century southern agriculture, had no economic importance during the colonial period. Afterward, however, it fit perfectly into a time-tested economic machine.

Tobacco governed the colonial Chesapeake. In 1697 the Maryland assembly recognized that "the trade of this province ebbs and flows according to the rise

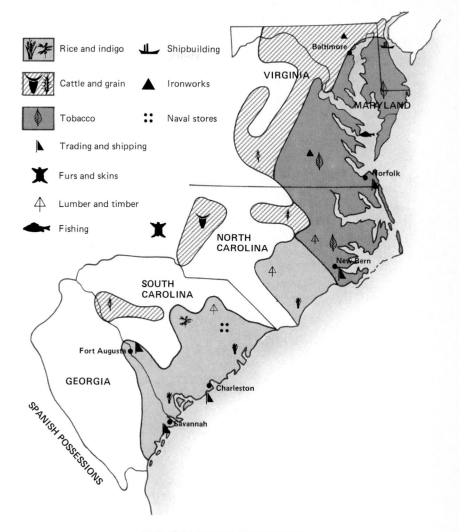

Rice and indigo — Shipbuilding

Cattle and grain — Ironworks

Tobacco — Naval stores

Trading and shipping

Furs and skins

Lumber and timber

Fishing

VIRGINIA

Baltimore

MARYLAND

Norfolk

NORTH CAROLINA

New Bern

SOUTH CAROLINA

Fort Augusta

GEORGIA

Charleston

Savannah

SPANISH POSSESSIONS

THE COLONIAL ECONOMY

or fall of tobacco in the market of England." That observation held for Virginia as well as Maryland throughout the colonial era. Although little evidence is available on the size of the crop, figures on British imports provide a good sense of tobacco production because most tobacco was exported, and the bulk of it made at least its first stop in England. In Virginia the production of tobacco underwent three basic phases. From the beginning of tobacco cultivation in the first decade after Jamestown until the 1680s production soared. During the next thirty years the output leveled off at around 28 million pounds annually. Then in 1715 began another round of growth, which lasted until the Revolution. By

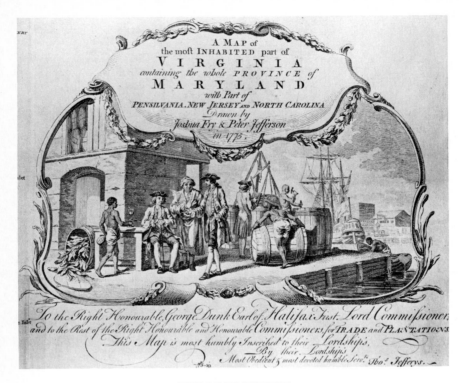

TOBACCO WHARF

1740 some 50 million pounds were being produced each year; on the eve of the Revolution the poundage reached 100 million. Over the course of the colonial period tobacco prices experienced substantial movement. They fell consistently during the seventeenth-century growth, but gains in productivity maintained income for growers. Prices remained stable from the 1680s until the middle of the eighteenth century, with a slight increase early in the period. As demand increased from mid-century to the Revolution, prices moved upward.

Although tobacco dominated the Chesapeake, other crops and products contributed to the agricultural economy. Grains, chiefly wheat, became more and more important through the eighteenth century. Even in the tidewater, the birthplace of tobacco cultivation, some planters and farmers began to shift from the weed to wheat. In the Shenandoah Valley, settled in the middle of the century, grain assumed prime importance from the beginning. The production of beef and pork assisted in the diversification of Chesapeake agriculture.

Farther south rice predominated. Between 1700 and 1750 rice generated enormous wealth in South Carolina. Production expanded rapidly, from 1.5 million pounds in 1710 to 20 million pounds in 1730. The increase never ceased; by 1750 rice production rose more than two and a half times, to 50 million pounds, and during the next twenty-five years it doubled again. During this mighty surge in production the price fluctuated, but from mid-century stability prevailed, so that rice planters could count on a rise in income as production increased. After 1750 rice cultivation expanded into lower North Carolina and southward into Georgia. Still, South Carolina remained indisputably the center of rice production; in 1770, for example, South Carolina exported four and a half times more rice than did Georgia.

Rice clearly led in the southernmost colonies, but by mid-century a second crop became a notable supplement. Indigo was an important source of dye for the British textile industry. It had been grown earlier in South Carolina, but not successfully until Eliza Lucas tried her hand at it. A remarkable individual, Eliza Lucas—she later became Eliza Pinckney—at age twenty was managing her father's plantation. With indigo seed sent by her father from the West Indies and with technical help from an experienced West Indian, she made a rousing success of indigo farming. Scores of planters rushed to emulate her. With encouragement from both the colonial and British governments, production boomed. In 1748 exports from Charleston totaled just under 140,000 pounds; by 1775 more than a million pounds left the port. Indigo was also grown on a smaller scale in Georgia.

Of course not every farmer in the southern colonies raised staple crops for export. Especially in the back country, numerous farmers cared not at all about tobacco, rice, or indigo; their concern was to provide food for themselves. The chief thrust of southern agriculture, however, was indisputably commercial, and increasing numbers of back-country farmers ambitious for economic and social advancement moved toward the goal by selling grain and meat both within their colony and to other colonies. In addition, they hunted and trapped to take advantage of the vigorous market for skins, particularly deerskins. During the second quarter of the eighteenth century, when tobacco cultivation moved into the Virginia piedmont, farmers already there greeted it warmly. In sum, there was no substantial brake on the commercial engine propelling colonial southern agriculture.

OTHER ECONOMIC ACTIVITIES

Although agriculture clearly dominated the colonial economies, it did not stand alone. Probably the two most important nonagricultural economic activities were the mining and processing of iron and the extraction of pitch, tar, and other naval stores from the southern forests. Virginia, Maryland, and Pennsylvania were the major iron producers among the colonies. Mining began in Virginia as early as 1716. Furnaces, forges, and rolling mills followed, especially in the Shenandoah Valley and in western Maryland. The Virginians and Marylanders produced chiefly bar iron and pig iron, which they marketed primarily in the colonies, though exports did take place. Forest products also contributed substantially to the South's economy. Although the production of pitch, tar, and other naval stores occurred almost everywhere, the Carolinas led the way by a wide margin, with North Carolina at the top. By the eve of the Revolution the Carolinas accounted annually for around 200,000 barrels of pitch, tar, and turpentine. Another, but sharply different kind of forest product also contributed to the economic health of the more southerly colonies: deerskins. Trade in deerskins thrived mostly in South Carolina until the middle of the eighteenth century. This trade often orginated with Indian hunters who dealt with white traders. Early in the century some 53,000 skins left Charleston each year for England. By the 1740s annual exports totaled between 600 and 700 hogsheads of skins.

With iron, forest products, deerskins, and a host of lesser activities all supplementing agriculture, the southern colonies enjoyed a generally prosperous economy. Comparative studies of colonial wealth underscore that conclusion; the most thorough study used data from the year 1774. The sum of private physical wealth, including land and slaves, placed the southern colonies substantially ahead of both the middle colonies and New England: southern colonies, £60.5 million; the middle colonies, £26.8 million; New England, £22.2 million. The per capita values formed a similar pattern, with the southern colonies again clearly in front. Slaves accounted for one-third of the total physical wealth of the southern colonies. When slaves are removed from consideration, however, the southern colonies were still in first place, though with a reduced margin. In nonfarm business equipment and inventory, however, New England and the middle colonies far outdistanced the South. That fact underscores the overwhelming importance of agriculture to the colonial southern economy. When all factors are considered, the evidence points clearly to a strong, productive economy.

The activities of town merchants, often also planters or at least future planters, facilitated the smooth operation of the economic system. Such towns as Annapolis and Charleston supported an enterprising, energetic merchant class. In Virginia the most important merchants were often agents of British firms; in South Carolina the merchants tended to be independent, though they worked closely with British firms. One of South Carolina's leading merchants was Henry Laurens. In 1744, at age twenty, the short, swarthy Laurens was sent to London for commercial training and to establish business contacts. Upon returning to Charleston in 1747, he received a considerable inheritance from his father, who had built up the largest saddlery business in the city. Young Henry went into the mercantile business and prospered. The export of rice and the import of African slaves dominated his affairs. In time Laurens extended the range of his activities by buying land and slaves and growing rice. By the eve of the Revolution he was primarily a planter.

In the overwhelmingly rural world of the colonial South, villages and towns were widely scattered; there were no cities in any modern sense. Yet to the colonists their towns performed vital functions as the seats of colonial government, the loci of trade, and the centers of cultural activities.

By the time of the Revolution the total population of the southern colonies numbered more than one million people, but no more than 25,000, or only 2.5

percent, lived in towns of over 1,000 inhabitants. Although population statistics for the colonial period do not permit a detailed analysis, information does exist that provides a good sense of the sizes of southern towns. In the seventeenth century no single place had enough inhabitants to be called even a good-sized town. Throughout the eighteenth century the largest town by far was Charleston. From a population of just over 2,000 in 1700, Charleston advanced to 6,800 in 1740, to 8,000 in 1760, and to 12,000 in 1770. The fastest growing town in the late colonial era, however, was Baltimore, Maryland, which leaped from a village of about 200 in 1750 to a bustling port of 6,000 in 1775. In 1720 Williamsburg could count only 500 residents, and in 1780 just under 1,500. On the eve of the Revolution, Savannah had only 750 inhabitants; Wilmington, North Carolina at the same time was home to only 500.

THE PLANTERS

Great planters, located chiefly in the Chesapeake and the low country of the Carolinas and Georgia, dominated the economy and the society of the colonial South. In the eighteenth century these grandees were usually sons and grandsons of men who had made their mark or at least made a substantial beginning on the family position and fortune in the second half of the seventeenth century or very early in the eighteenth. These men ruled over thousands of acres and hundreds of slaves. Quite often they constructed impressive mansions on their plantations, and some of them also owned elegant town houses, especially in Charleston or Annapolis. Their children either went to school in England or studied at home under private tutors.

Landon Carter of Virginia, born in 1710, was one of the men at the very top of the southern social order. The fourth son of Robert "King" Carter, whose regal nickname signals his standing, Landon did his father proud. After an educational sojourn in England, Landon returned to Virginia at seventeen and entered his father's planting-trading business. His determination to succeed and his careful attention to his agricultural pursuits underlay Landon's enormous success as a planter. Starting with some 15,000 acres, he accumulated 50,000 acres and owned some 500 slaves by the time of his death in 1778. From his plantation headquarters, Sabine Hall in Richmond County, he maintained and managed his agricultural empire. He focused his efforts on tobacco and cereals, though he also raised flax and hemp. An avid reader as well as a committed agriculturalist, Carter read books on history, medicine, and religion, in addition to agricultural literature. In the manner of his class, Carter provided a governess and tutors for his children. He had clothing and wine shipped from England. A glimpse at his wealth comes from his gift of £800 sterling to each of his four daughters upon their marriages—at a time when an annual living wage for a laborer was around £20 sterling.

Nothing set such grandees as Landon Carter so visibly apart from the mass of whites or so impressed later generations as the plantation mansions they constructed. These palaces in the wilderness represented to their builders—and still do to many people today—the ideal of a landed gentry. Mansions such as Carter's Sabine Hall, William Byrd II's Westover, and Thomas Lee's Stratford Hall, all in Virginia, and John Drayton's Drayton Hall in South Carolina are more famous than the names of the great planters who lived in them. Most of these country seats are of Georgian architecture, the classically influenced style that predominated in English public and private buildings during the eighteenth century. And without question the great planters attempted to replicate the English manor house. The first of this type erected in the colonies was the Governor's Palace in Williamsburg, completed about 1720, which set the tone for plantation mansions until the Revolution. The most impressive town houses, such as the Hammond House in Annapolis and the Miles Brewton House in Charleston, also followed the Georgian pattern. Architectural handbooks available from Britain after 1720 provided invaluable assistance to every family determined to build a palace of its own.

Plantation magnates often set their homes in rural, parklike surroundings, preferably fronting on a river. To travelers along the streams of the Virginia tidewater and the South Carolina low country, the numerous structures stretching away from an impressive mansion gave the appearance of a country village. An Englishman who traveled on the Virginia rivers in the 1730s observed "pleasant Seats on the Bank which Shew like little villages, for having Kitchins, Dayry houses, Barns, Stables, Store houses, and some of them 2 or 3 Negro Quarters all Separate from Each other but near the mansion houses.... Most of these have pleasant Gardens and the Prospect of the River render them very pleasant." The centrally located mansion of two or even three stories, most often of brick, conveyed opulence and grandeur. The exterior image was matched by an interior that featured paneled and pilastered walls, parquet floors, molded ceilings, marble fireplaces, and a magnificent staircase.

WESTOVER, THE PLANTATION SEAT OF THE BYRD FAMILY (Thomas J. Waterman, photographer HAS, Library of Congress)

HENRY LAURENS,
MERCHANT AND PLANTER
(Library of Congress)

At times wealthy planter-merchants constructed their showplaces in towns, especially in Annapolis and Charleston. One of the most impressive homes in Charleston belonged to Miles Brewton. Like Henry Laurens, Brewton started as a merchant, prospered in the slave trade, and invested his profits in rice acreage and slaves. Around 1765 he built an exquisite town house separated from the street by a magnificent iron fence with a double gateway. Marble steps led up to a marble platform before the front door. Inside, a mahogany staircase with triple-arched window ascended to the second floor. A visitor in 1773 commented on the blue satin curtains, the blue wallpaper emblazoned with gilt, the elegant glassware, and the finely crafted goblets. Landscaped gardens and extensive servant or slave quarters dominated the grounds. Whether in countryside or town, these grand houses stood as monuments to the determined, hard-driving, wealthy individuals and families who rose to the top of the southern colonial world.

THE FARMERS OR YEOMEN AND SOCIAL MOBILITY

Of course the vast majority of southern whites possessed neither wealth, plantation manor houses, nor elegant town houses. They lived in far simpler dwellings, though the construction of their homes changed over time. In seventeenth-century Virginia the cottage predominated. Built of plaster and laths, often with a thatched roof, these cottages frequently lacked finished floors,

DRAYTON HALL, HOME OF THE DRAYTON FAMILY NEAR CHARLESTON
(South Caroliniana Library, University of South Carolina)

even windows and doors. Sometimes they had a chimney of logs chinked with clay, but just as commonly the family's meals were cooked in a fire pit in the middle of a room; a hole through the roof permitted the smoke to escape. After the cottage came the simple rectangular frame house of one story; a half story could be added later as the family grew and its fortunes improved. The log cabin did not appear until after 1720, and throughout the colonial period it was found chiefly in the piedmont, where the Scotch-Irish replicated the cabins they had known in Pennsylvania.

Farmers who prospered in the back country and the piedmont built their own plantation houses. Although considerably more substantial than the commonplace small frame houses and log cabins, they did not begin to match in sophistication and scale the manor houses of the tidewater and low-country magnates. Like many of the smaller houses, they were of frame construction. Private homes of brick rarely appeared in the pre-Revolutionary back country. Tall and thin, normally of two stories, these frame houses usually had roofed porches with simple wooden columns over the ground floor. A massive chimney at either end spoke of stability and substance.

Without question economic and social mobility marked the back country. The abundance of land and the relative ease of obtaining it ensured the upward movement of numerous folk. In the middle decades of the eighteenth century, Lunenburg County, Virginia, south of the James River in the area known as the Southside, offered substantial opportunity to new settlers, even to those who had been landless. Lydell Bacon, who bought 197 acres of land there in 1747, had increased his holdings to 1,060 acres by 1769. In 1748 John Hix worked for a small planter, but by 1769 he had acquired 395 acres and two slaves. Not quite so successful was George McLaughlin, who started as a laborer in 1748 and by

1769 owned 250 acres; still, those acres gave him the status of independent landowner.

The rolling, heavily forested piedmont was Scotch-Irish country. Most of these people moved south from Pennsylvania in the middle third of the eighteenth century, though a smaller number arrived in southern ports directly from Ireland. In the piedmont they cleared land, built cabins, and raised crops and children. Within a generation they turned a wild, rude country into

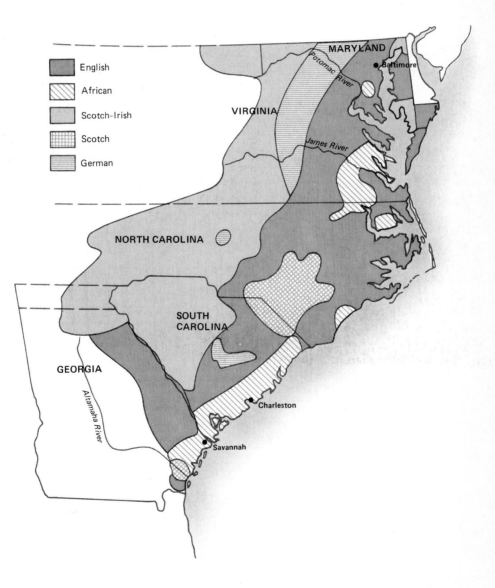

English

African

Scotch-Irish

Scotch

German

CONCENTRATION OF KEY IMMIGRANT GROUPS AT THE END
OF THE COLONIAL PERIOD

farms and plantations. At the outset the new Scotch-Irish differed from the established English. Socially and economically the Scotch-Irish ranked below the English colonists, whose wealth and social position they could not yet match.

Many of the settlers who opened the piedmont prospered with the development of their new homeland. In the early 1730s the Calhoun family joined hundreds of their fellow Scotch-Irish in emigrating from Northern Ireland to the New World. In 1733 they settled in western Pennsylvania, but a few years later they headed southward through the Shenandoah Valley to Augusta County, on the southwestern Virginia frontier. There they set about accumulating a considerable acreage. Within a decade these frontier settlers had become prosperous independent farmers. But in the mid-1750s they again looked south, this time toward piedmont South Carolina, where land had been opened by agreement between colonial officials and the Cherokees. The Calhouns became the first white family to settle in northwestern South Carolina. One of the Calhouns, Patrick, received an initial land patent of 200 acres, and through hard work and enterprise he added significantly to that total. In 1770 Patrick was elected to the colonial assembly. Twenty years later he was one of the largest slaveholders in his section of the state, with thirty-one slaves. Patrick Calhoun had traveled not only from Pennsylvania through Virginia to South Carolina but also from frontier settlement to farm to plantation. His son spent his life defending his vision of the land Patrick had pioneered; his name was John C. Calhoun.

Not everyone in the piedmont experienced the success of the Calhouns. In 1747 James Carter made his way down from Virginia to the Yadkin River country in North Carolina. One of the first settlers in the area, he seemed to prosper with it. Six years after arriving he bought 350 acres and became a deputy surveyor in charge of purchasing and surveying the town lands of Salisbury, soon to become the major town in Carter's county. He became a major in the militia and in 1754 went to the colonial assembly or legislature. But then Carter's creditors pressed for payment of money he had borrowed, evidently to help him get started. In 1756 he raised money by selling two slaves, but not enough to keep his creditors from taking legal action against him. The next year the sheriff sold Carter's land to pay his debts. Carter also faced charges of embezzlement, extortion, and misappropriation of state funds. The unpaid debts and the accusations cost him his reputation as well as his land. He had recovered neither when he died in 1765. Carter's sad career demonstrates that times and places of opportunity do not automatically guarantee success for everyone.

WOMEN

In the seventeenth century two critical conditions governed the lives and roles of female colonists. The first was a highly unbalanced sex ratio. Early in the century men outnumbered women by 3 or 4 to 1 in the Chesapeake. In colonies settled toward the end of the century a similar pattern prevailed. Of almost 700 settlers in South Carolina during the 1670s, only around 200 were women.

Though the imbalance in the Chesapeake lessened through the century, there were always so many more men than women that every woman who wanted a husband could easily find one, whatever her financial or social position. The second critical factor was the initial status of many of the women who immigrated to the southern colonies. More than half of them arrived as indentured servants; as indentured servants women came under the same legal restraints and were subjected to same compulsion as men. The owners of their indentures controlled their work.

Women performed a wide variety of tasks. The indentured servants, of course, had little say about what they did. Many of them worked in fields alongside men. Although promotional literature designed to attract women in Britain to sign on as indentured servants promised no fieldwork, such promises often turned out to be no more than propaganda. But many wives and daughters not bound by indentures also knew the rigors of fieldwork. In addition the chores of milking cows, making butter and bread, raising chickens, butchering and preserving meat, growing vegetables, brewing cider and beer, sewing and washing and mending clothes, and of course child care all fell to women.

Free women tended to marry between the ages of twenty and twenty-three, earlier by three years than their counterparts in England and servants in the colonies. Servants usually married quite soon after the removal of their indentures, and many of them made a significant leap upward socially by becoming the wives of substantial farmers or planters. Colonial women tended to have more children than women in England. Most families needed the labor of many children, and infant mortality was high. Mothers had responsibility for the control and rearing of children, both boys and girls. The terrible mortality rates of the seventeenth century, which affected adults as well as infants, often made for nontraditional families of complex composition. A family might include a widow, a widower, adults who had not yet married, stepchildren, and orphans along with servants.

The legal status of women in England carried over to the colonies. Women could not vote or hold public office or serve in the militia or on juries. Despite this political proscription, they did have the right to own land and to engage in business. In fact, during the seventeenth century women not uncommonly became executors of their husbands' estates. When a woman married, however, she legally surrendered all of her possessions to her husband. Any money she might earn was legally his, and he had the right to beat her so long as he used a stick no wider than his thumb. To this day we speak of a general principle based on observation rather than precise measurement as a "rule of thumb."

The increasing stability of the colonies in the eighteenth century affected women's lives in ways that were not always favorable. As the imbalance in the sex ratio declined, women had fewer opportunities to move rapidly upward through marriage. Now a woman was more likely to marry a man of her own social class, and her social mobility depended on his fortunes. With the turn to slavery and the resulting decline of indentured servants, fewer women and men entered the colonies as servants. This drop in the number of female indentured servants helped to lower the age of women at marriage. The growing distinction among classes also had an effect on women; the line separating the plantation mistress from the laborer's wife was sharper than it had been in the 1600s. In the eighteenth century labor was divided more clearly along gender lines. A far smaller proportion of women engaged in fieldwork, certainly not the plantation ladies and often not the wives and daughters of independent farmers.

With the decline in fieldwork most women spent their time in housework. The specific nature of that work varied considerably according to class. On plantations women were occupied chiefly in the supervision of the slaves who actually performed the various tasks—preserving and cooking food, cleaning the house, caring for the children, making and mending clothes for the slaves as well as for the family of the master. White women, a step down the social ladder, actually performed all the duties only supervised by the plantation mistress. Of course the arduousness of those labors depended on the family's wealth, on the geographical location of the home, and on the family's individual circumstances.

Quite a few women, however, found pursuits outside the home, out of either necessity or choice. From the Chesapeake to Georgia, all midwives were women. One of the most active and successful midwives, Catherine Blaikly of Williamsburg, had delivered some 3,000 babies by the time of her death in 1771 at seventy-six years of age. A talented woman who moved with striking success into an area usually reserved for men was Clementina Rind, whose husband owned the *Virginia Gazette* of Williamsburg. When he died in 1773, she took over the paper, and she did so well with it that she was named state printer by the Virginia assembly. In midcentury, Eliza Lucas Pinckney, by successfully cultivating indigo, made a major contribution to southern agriculture.

In the eighteenth century the legal status of women changed little, but in practice notable differences appeared. Fathers less frequently gave daughters land; ownership was concentrated more and more in male hands. More husbands wrote wills directing that their widows' inheritances were to be reduced if they remarried. And fewer and fewer wives served as executors of their husbands' estates. These shifts did not necessarily signify a substantial reduction either in the place of women in the society or in their treatment. Their primary significance lies in the evidence they provide of increasing social stability in the southern colonies and simultaneously a growing concern for the family continuity represented by the male line.

THE BREADTH OF SLAVE OWNING

Land provided the foundation for economic advancement, social status, and political activity in the colonial South, and black slavery reinforced that foundation. From the seventeenth century ownership of black slaves in addition to land identified the economically privileged. The possession of slaves became a badge of upper-class status; practically every family of the colonial aristocracy counted black bondsmen and bondswomen among its most prized possessions.

From the very beginning slave owning was associated with planting, and the large planters came to own hundreds of slaves. After all, the chief purpose of slaves was agricultural labor, and the more acres a family cultivated, the more slaves it was likely to own. Large holdings appeared early and grew over time. Robert "King" Carter owned more than 700 slaves before 1730. George Mason of Virginia, Gabriel Manigault of South Carolina, and the Marylander Charles Carroll of Carrollton also numbered their human property in the hundreds.

The breadth of slave owning was even more impressive than the size of some holdings, and this breadth equaled in importance the extent of land-owning, though the number of whites who owned slaves was always smaller than the number who owned land. Slaves did not belong to wealthy planters alone. Evidence abounds that in the eighteenth century the middle levels of white society also participated directly in slave ownership. By the 1770s nearly half of the families in the Chesapeake counties of Maryland owned slaves. Charleston's merchants and mechanics bought slaves just as eagerly and readily as did planters. Almost half of the city's mechanics who left wills between 1760 and 1785 were slave owners. Of the 190 artisans of colonial Charleston who could be identified in the 1790 census, 159 were specified as slave owners. An account of a Charleston slave sale in 1756 lists merchants, a mariner, and a widow along with planters as purchasers. Most bought fewer than five slaves.

The westward movement spurred the growth of slavery, for slavery gener-ally accompanied colonial expansion. As white settlers pushed toward the pied-mont from the older tidewater section, they carried slaves and slavery as part of their economic and cultural baggage. Most white southerners on the frontier envisioned a prosperous future for themselves, and they saw slavery as a nec-essary function in the equation that yielded prosperity. Exceptions did exist, however. The Germans who settled in the Shenandoah Valley of Virginia and around Salem, North Carolina, generally eschewed slaveholding.

Such deviations did not stem the westward march of slavery. When the cen-ter of tobacco cultivation in Virginia moved away from the tidal rivers to the shadow of the Appalachian Mountains, slaves still toiled in the fields. The great Charleston merchant and slave trader Henry Laurens attested to the intimate connection between geographical expansion and the growth of slavery. To as-sociates in England, Laurens wrote in 1763, "We have now a large field for Trade opening in these colonies & a vast number of people seting [sic] down upon our frontier Lands...will take...a Cargo by one or two [slaves] in a Lot and it has been from such folks that we have always obtain'd the highest prices."

THE CASE OF GEORGIA

The best testimony to the intermixing of slavery with expansion and prosperity comes from Georgia. Georgia did not welcome its first British settlers until 1733, some 126 years after Jamestown. More to the point, the first Englishmen arrived in Georgia long after slavery had become an integral part of the society of both the Chesapeake colonies and the Carolinas. Yet the philanthropic founders of the new colony wanted to dispense with such institutions as slavery and large plantations, and the laws set up by the governing trustees outlawed both. These restrictions, however, did not last long.

Early on Georgia coveted slaves. Mired in what they viewed as poverty and backwardness, Georgians by the 1740s demanded new materials with which to build prosperity. Slaves stood high on their list. As in political matters Georgia looked for guidance to its older neighbor, South Carolina. By the 1740s slaves and rice had made South Carolina prosperous indeed. White Georgians saw the introduction of slavery as the solution to their economic problems. The agitation of the colonists prevailed, and in 1750 the trustees repealed their prohibition of slavery. Five years later the Georgia assembly enacted its first slave code, modeled on the South Carolina code of 1740.

The drive for slavery in Georgia derived from both individual and community interests. Individual Georgians believed slavery the surest means to guarantee their personal advancement. Even before the 1750 repeal, settlers had circumvented the slavery prohibition by leasing slaves from South Carolina for ninety-nine years, with the full purchase price paid as advance rent. Collectively, Georgians wanted their colony to develop and to prosper, and almost everyone saw slavery as an essential part of that development. When Georgia did in fact begin to prosper after 1750, many people pointed to slavery as the primary cause. Increasing real estate values, burgeoning production of rice, and growing personal fortunes all stemmed, in the minds of many planters and merchants, from Georgia's commitment to the peculiar institution.

THE SLAVE TRADE AND THE GROWTH OF SLAVERY

By the middle of the eighteenth century each of the southern colonies from the Chesapeake to the Savannah had firmly committed itself to black slavery. Of course slavery was legal in all colonies because it was legal in the British Empire, though it never became so important north of the famous Mason-Dixon line—the name given to the boundary between Maryland and Pennsylvania— as it did south of the line. By 1770 the colonies below the line had nearly nine times more slaves than the colonies above it. Across the southern colonies the percentage of slaves in the population grew substantially, but only in South Carolina did the number of blacks exceed the number of whites. That situation dated from at least 1710. By 1740 slaves numbered fully one-fourth of the southern colonial population. During the next three decades the proportion of slaves increased by more than half until on the eve of the Revolution they accounted for almost 40 percent of the population of the southern colonies.

In the seventeenth century most slaves who arrived in both the Chesapeake and Carolina came from the West Indies, but in the next century slave traders brought them directly from Africa. The slave trade was part of a larger pattern,

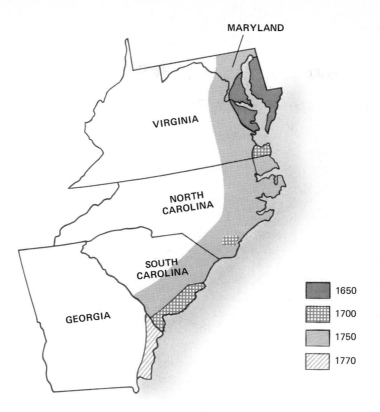

THE SPREAD OF SLAVERY, 1650–1770

a three-cornered trade. From Europe to Africa went such items as liquor, tobacco products, jewelry, firearms; to pay for these things, Africa sold slaves to
the New World; and finally the products of slave plantations in the New
World—chiefly sugar, tobacco, and rice—were shipped to Europe. The Europeans converted the sugar into rum, which they shipped to Africa, and the trade
went on.

That the beginning of colonial empires in the New World occasioned a
transatlantic slave trade surprised no one. For centuries black slaves had been
brought out of central Africa, first across the northern desert, then after the
middle of the fifteenth century by ship to the Iberian Peninsula. When the European empire builders thought about filling the demand for labor in their new
colonies, Africa came readily to mind. The Portuguese became the first great
transporters of African slaves, but soon other competitors shouldered them
aside. The Dutch and the French participated vigorously. The greatest slave
traders, however, were the English, who dominated the trade at its peak in the
eighteenth century.

The European traders operated along the African coast. The massive European takeover of central Africa did not commence until the mid-nineteenth century, in the waning decades of the transatlantic slave trade and after England had relinquished its place as the number one slave trader to become the staunchest opponent of the trade. On the coast the Europeans set up what they termed castles or factories—in reality trading posts. Agents of the European powers lived in them and managed the transfer of goods for human beings. The slave-trading vessels, known as slavers, anchored offshore until a full cargo of slaves was available. Once loaded, the ships headed west for the plantations of South America, the West Indies, and North America.

The Europeans could not have functioned so effectively as they did without the assistance of Africans. The arrival of seaborne European slave traders did not introduce slavery to Africans. The overland slave trade with the Mediterranean world was long established. Moreover, slavery was practiced in equatorial Africa. Africans became slaves of other Africans usually because of defeat in battle or for the payment of debt. Although this kind of slavery had become a part of the African world, it had neither the motive nor the outcome of the commercially driven slavery that characterized the institution in the New World. The voracious demand created by the colonial empires had a thunderous impact on African society. Now Africans mounted expeditions designed to capture other Africans to sell to the Europeans. Sometimes the captors marched the captives over hundreds of miles to reach the coast and the slavers. The cooperation of Africans made it unnecessary for the Europeans to attempt to conquer the African interior.

The numbers of people forcibly transported across the Atlantic stagger the imagination. Although precision is impossible, the best estimates place the total number of Africans removed to the New World at around 10 million. This massive, enforced population movement occurred over more than three and a half centuries. The transatlantic slave trade began in the very early sixteenth century, grew through the seventeenth century, flourished in the eighteenth, and tapered off and finally died in the nineteenth.

The great bulk of these Africans did not, however, end up in what became the United States. Imports into British North America up to 1790 totaled around 275,000. From 1790 until the outlawing of the trade in 1808, another 70,000 came in. Then after 1808 the illegal trade probably smuggled in another 50,000 before the Civil War. Those figures add up to 395,000 slaves the trade landed in British North America. To this total, however, must be added the 28,000 brought into Louisiana during the French and Spanish periods, which ended in 1803. The sum approaches 425,000 human beings, surely a significant figure, but one that represents only 4.5 percent of all Africans brought to the New World. More than twice that many Africans—860,000—were transported to the great French sugar island of Saint-Domingue between 1681 and 1791. Yet in 1791, at the end of the slave trade to Saint-Domingue, only 480,000 slaves survived there. In contrast, despite the tiny percentage of Africans who were brought to the

United States, the United States became the only major slave country in which slaves sustained and even increased their population. By 1800 the number of slaves in this country reached almost 1 million. In the next six decades the American slave population more than quadrupled, to over 4 million. During those sixty years no more than around 70,000 slaves entered the country, either legally or illegally—a number too small to effect this impressive growth.

Why the slave population reproduced itself with such success in the United States but nowhere else has no simple explanation. Several circumstances, however, undoubtedly influenced this outcome. The milder climate in the American South generally subjected the slaves to a less frightful disease environment. The more evenly balanced sex ratios that obtained in the South were more conducive to a family structure and natural reproduction. Perhaps most important, southern planters never adopted the basic philosophy prevalent in some other slave societies, especially some of the sugar islands: that of working slaves to death and then replacing them. It seems that on the whole, slaves in the southern colonies and states received better physical care than those in bondage in the Caribbean and South America.

For the slaves bound for the New World the oceanic passage was an unspeakable horror. Men, women, and even children were crammed into narrow spaces averaging no more than four feet high. Rarely did they receive proper food and water, and the ship captains had little concern about sanitation in the slave areas. Almost unbelievable discomfort pervaded the densely packed slave deck. Seasickness and dysentery—both almost inevitable in the circumstances—resulted in frightful conditions.

Many accounts of slavers overwhelm our sensibilities. An observer described "400 wretched beings...crammed into a hold 12 yards in length...and only 3½ feet in height." According to this eyewitness, "the suffocating heat of the hold" created a panic among the Africans desperate for air. Stark terror resulted. "The smoke of torment and the 54 mangled crushed bodies lifted up from the slave deck" testified to the horror.

For the captains of the slavers and for their employees, of course, slaving was an economic enterprise designed to make money. Thus they had a vested interest in landing as many Africans alive and reasonably healthy as possible. Available evidence indicates that they learned how to make the trip safer. Over the course of the eighteenth and nineteenth centuries the rate of loss among the slaves declined. Statistics from the slavers of the Royal African Company, which dominated the English trade in the eighteenth century, reveal distinct improvement in mortality rates. In the 1680s the mean loss stood at 23.4 percent; by 1791 it had dropped to 8.8 percent. Although substantial annual variations occurred over time, they did so in a lower range. The death rate among the crews of slavers, by contrast, remained around 20 percent throughout the period. The white crewmen were devastated by tropical diseases, mainly malaria and yellow fever, for which no successful treatment existed during the life of the trade.

SLAVES IN A NEW WORLD

After the wrenching experiences of capture, sale, and ocean crossing, Africans arriving in the Chesapeake or Carolina faced adjustment to a new and different world. Much that they knew and cherished—family, tribe, religion—they had left behind in Africa. In the colonies they confronted fundamental problems. For most of them the tribe had provided a basic identity; now they had somehow to forge a new one, for any African could end up on a farm or plantation with no one from his or her own tribe. Language could pose severe difficulties. As the Africans spoke a wide variety of languages, they had to overcome substantial barriers to establish basic communication with fellow slaves as well as with the master. Many found themselves isolated in the matter of religion as well. Because the trade demanded young people, few older people such as religious leaders crossed the Atlantic. Moreover, the plants and other materials used in their native religions were seldom available in the colonies. As far as religion was concerned, then, the new slaves had been cast adrift.

In this cultural vacuum the Africans had to find their way. They did have one immediate bond: their color. Their blackness separated them from their white masters and helped them overcome lost tribal identities. The slaves also developed a pidgin language combining various African tongues with English, which permitted them to communicate among themselves. In areas of extremely heavy slave population slaves retained their own language. Probably the most famous of these pidgin languages, Gullah, the language of the sea islands of South Carolina and Georgia, survived well into the twentieth century. The old religious ways also tended to disappear, but in the colonial period no central religious experience pervaded the slave world.

During most of the seventeenth century very few slaves lived in either the Chesapeake or the Carolinas. As late as 1670 Virginia could claim no more than 2,000 slaves; that number increased to 10,000 by 1700. Considerably fewer had been brought into South Carolina before the eighteenth century. These small numbers meant that most slaves were scattered over a broad geographic area; additionally most slaveholders owned very few slaves. In Virginia the average number of slaves per holding between 1650 and 1700 was eight.

This kind of spatial pattern made it extraordinarily difficult for the newly arrived Africans to create families or even to look to each other for emotional and psychological support in the face of the incredible experience of their ocean passage and the unknown future of servitude to white masters. The sharp imbalance in the sex ratio made the establishment of any kind of family structure even more unlikely. With slaves so spread out geographically and with comparatively few women, complete slave families were not common. On a single farm or plantation they were rare indeed. Although slaves surely did establish families in the seventeenth century, especially after 1650, quite often they did not live together under a single master. Most owners, however, permitted visiting privileges so that husbands could see wives and children, and many owners tried to keep mothers and small children together. The seven children born in the 1670s and 1680s to Ann Joice, a slave of the Darnall family of Prince George's County, Maryland, either remained on the Darnall plantation or ended up with nearby planters. Life for the slave family never became easy, but never again was it so fractured as in the seventeenth century.

In the early days most black slaves worked alongside their owners to create farms out of a wilderness. Clearing forests, breaking land, erecting structures essential for living, and, of course, cultivating crops were the work and life of seventeenth-century slaves. In the Chesapeake they entered an economy already committed to tobacco, which had become the key to prosperity before slavery assumed any importance. White masters put African slaves to work on a crop unfamiliar to them. In South Carolina, however, the presence of a dominant staple did not precede the arrival of slaves. In fact, the evidence indicates that masters and slaves struggled together to find the Carolina version of tobacco. When in the 1690s the Carolina planters settled upon rice as their ticket to economic success, slaves contributed significantly to that decision. The colony would become at the same time enormously wealthy and the home of the largest percentage of slaves in the colonies.

SLAVE FAMILIES AND RELIGION

With the massive increase of the slave population during the eighteenth century, conditions for the slaves changed markedly. While the numbers of imported Africans shot up, the numbers of blacks born in the colonies also increased substantially as well. The presence of a significant native-born slave force provided for the transmission of tradition and culture. Slaves fresh from Africa often found themselves living among others born on this side of the ocean. This reality eased somewhat the arduous task of acculturation faced by the Africans. They were not flung utterly alone into a totally white world. Moreover, this constant mixture gave rise to a culture both African and colonial.

The expansion of the slave population did not, however, erase the sexual imbalance. Always more men than women arrived from Africa. Still, in large part because of the native-born, the ratio became less one-sided. Because men continued to outnumber women, women tended to marry young. The younger a woman marries, the greater the number of her child-bearing years and the more children she bears. The development of large plantations and the stability of independent farmers contributed to the presence of family units among the slaves belonging to one master, though the practice of marrying "away" did not end.

The evidence is clear on the existence of slave families. The Carters of Virginia, who owned hundreds of slaves and thousands of acres, certainly knew about slave families. John Carter bought a woman and her children who had been separated from their husband and father by the terms of their owner's will. A runaway carpenter, Sam, came back to his Carter master after only a week because Sam thought "it a hard case to be separated from his wife." Still another Carter wanted a seventy-one-year-old slave grandfather to live with his grandchildren. A 1761 list of fifty-five slaves belonging to a Mrs. Allen of North Carolina details family ties across generations. The list specifies that the slaves lived in six families, except for the eight who were single. It also indicates that most of the fifty-five were the children of three sets of parents. Names surely crossed generational boundaries. Some slaves were named for their fathers, and a child born in 1759 was named for her maternal grandmother. As slave families proliferated in the colonial South, a common African practice, polygamy, became a casualty. The colonies simply had too few women to permit polygamy to succeed. By 1733 only one of the 249 male slaves on Robert "King" Carter's plantation had more than one wife.

Of course the religion of the masters did not encourage polygamy. Yet in the colonial era Christianity did not penetrate the slave world as it would in the nineteenth century. Before the Great Awakening, which shook the southern colonies in the 1740s, religion did not occupy a central place in the lives of most whites, either. Even after the Great Awakening many Anglicans did not share in the fervor it aroused, and most substantial slave owners belonged to the Church of England. In any case, some slave owners feared that converting the slaves to Christianity might ultimately lead to emancipation. A major argument for slavery turned on the heathenism of the enslaved. Removal of that condition, in the minds of some masters, might lead to questions, even within the Anglican establishment, about the legitimacy of an institution that kept Christians in bondage for life.

Because Christianity did not generally become the religion of slaves, no single religious experience predominated among them. Some slaves did profess Christianity; their conversion had been prompted by individual owners or by zealous preachers. Discovering how many were actually believing Christians is impossible, though during the colonial era the number probably remained small. Other slaves, particularly newcomers from Africa, clung to their native religion as long as they could, but maintaining the African practices in the colonies proved difficult. For the great majority of slaves religion most likely meant a combination of their African heritage, including charms and folk beliefs, and a smattering of Christian practices and teachings. But in all probability religion did not assume the importance for colonial slaves that it would for their descendants in the nineteenth century.

THE WORK AND CONTROL OF SLAVES

Whatever their religious preferences, slaves had one chief purpose: work. And work they did. Overwhelmingly slaves toiled in the fields to grow tobacco, rice, indigo, and grain. The hard physical labor essential for agricultural production before the age of mechanization was the lot of the slave. On farms and plantations slaves also engaged in a variety of other jobs, such as caring for animals,

repairing buildings, and clearing new land. The routinized labor that characterized so many agricultural tasks did not confront most slaves with unfamiliar
work patterns.

Many slaves had been exposed to similar activities in Africa. Consider the
work of slaves in growing rice. Slaves who dropped grains of rice into a hole
they had created by pressing a heel into the soft dirt and who then brushed
earth over the seeds with a foot were following a pattern familiar in West Africa. Later in the season, when slaves walked in line through rice fields with
hoes in hand, another African practice appeared in the colonial South. To win-
now or "fan" the harvested rice the slaves made broad, flat baskets based on
African designs.

Although the majority of slaves, male and female, were field hands, most
engaged in several activities and some of them became skilled artisans. Especially on large plantations masters prided themselves on the abilities of the carpenters, wheelwrights, blacksmiths, brick masons, and masters of other crafts
within their slave force. Some plantations boasted spinners, weavers, tanners,
and even distillers. Other slaves on large estates devoted their time to caring for
the manor house and for their owner's family. The tasks given Ben, a slave belonging to Landon Carter, illustrate the variety of jobs assigned even to individual slaves. Ben waited upon his master, served as a coachman, tended
horses, and occasionally labored in the tobacco house. Carter, who thought that
Ben "work[ed] very well," also designated him to pick up and bring to the plantation such items as oysters, salt, and wool.

But no matter their specific job assignment, from common field hand to liv-
eried coachman, all were slaves. They or their fathers or occasionally their
grandfathers had been involuntarily sold into slavery in a strange land. They
had been bought and paid for along the African coast. Once they were landed
in a port such as Charleston, they ended up in the hands of a slave trader who
sold them for any service the new owner decreed, wherever the owner desired.
Others, particularly in the Chesapeake, were hauled along the tidal rivers by
the ship captain who displayed his human wares at docks and landings.

Slave life could be brutal. As in eighteenth-century England, where the theft
of a loaf of bread could lead to the gallows, punishment could be harsh. A visitor to South Carolina reported seeing a suspended cage containing a bound
slave. Birds had already attacked. Blood and wounds covered his body, and his
eyes had been plucked out of their sockets. A planter explained that the offending
slave had killed a plantation official, and that "the laws of self-preservation rendered such execution necessary." Some planters critized their peers' treatment of
slaves. The great Virginia planter William Byrd II complained that his neighbor's
"poor Negroes are a kind of Adamites, very scantily supply'd with cloaths and
other necessaries." Byrd considered such lack of care a "Scandal."

Most planters, however, provided their slaves with adequate food, clothing,
and shelter. To the planters, their own self-interest required no less. After all,
slaves were valuable property; they represented a good portion of the wealth of
the master class. While masters generally attempted to provide for the physical

well-being of their bondsmen and bondswomen, they were conscious of the raw power fundamental to the master–slave relationship. And most did not hesitate to exercise their authority. Again William Byrd offers pertinent testimony. He recognized that force was an integral part of the system. "Numbers make them insolent," he observed, "& then foul means must do what fair will not...these base Tempers require to be rid with a tort [sic] rein, or they will be apt to throw their Rider."

3

The Intellectual, Political, and Religious World

❖

Although the political development of the southern colonies shared much with that of the other mainland colonies, particular aspects of the southern experience had a profound impact on the subsequent history of the region's political culture. Specific ideas, institutions, and practices shaped the form of southern politics even before the Revolution.

Liberty was the central political idea of the colonial South. Although before the 1760s southerners spent little time writing about the theoretical and philosophical dimensions of liberty, they had no doubt as to its fundamental meaning: according to the *Oxford English Dictionary*, "freedom from arbitrary, despotic rule or control." In the immediate political context of seventeenth- and eighteenth-century England, liberty meant some kind of representative government that would ensure such freedom. In England the Parliament represented the interests and protected the liberty of the king's subjects.

The distance that separated the New World from the mother country prevented any agency of the British government from performing this critical task in the colonies. An ocean voyage of 3,000 miles, requiring at least three months for the round trip, made the possibility of immediate guardianship precarious indeed. Living in a relatively small country, politically active Englishmen, both rural and urban, felt something akin to political control. Thus political liberty included connotations of geographic propinquity between the government and the governed. The colonists' intellectual defense of their assemblies clearly revealed this conjunction between liberty and local governmental control.

THE ASSEMBLIES

Colonial assemblies appeared early. The House of Burgesses was founded in 1619, only a dozen years after the first settlement at Jamestown. The establishment of assemblies in the other colonies, northern as well as southern, followed the example set by Virginia, usually in even less time. These transplanted Englishmen were determined to replicate one of their most treasured institutions.

These assemblies did not come into existence simply to protect the perceived interests of a colony. Perhaps even more important, assemblies provided a vehicle for the protection of local and private rights, economic as well as political. Through the assembly, planters in various parts of a colony had a say in the governing both of the entire colony and of their own bailiwicks. To southerners liberty was never just an abstract concept. It always involved their perceptions of their self-interest. Most of them were concerned chiefly about their own liberty. Control of one's own affairs lay at the heart of liberty, of freedom from outside interference. By this definition, an individual—a tobacco planter, for example—must have his interests represented in the colonial government or risk losing his liberty. Pertinent here is the experience of the House of Burgesses. Originally the burgesses met with the Governor's Council, but by the 1650s the council was coming to be associated with the office of the governor and with executive or royal power. As a result, the burgesses felt that they must give a clear identity to their house in order to protect the interests of the local planters they represented. Thus liberty demanded a distinct house of Burgesses.

The assemblies rapidly assumed considerable authority. Even before the seventeenth century had run its course, they had successfully asserted their power and prerogative. As early as the end of the 1650s the House of Burgesses, composed of local magnates, possessed real power in Virginia. By then London could no longer effectively control affairs in the colony without the concurrence of the burgesses. When the Maryland assembly considered it appropriate to do so, it rejected legislation proposed by the proprietor, and the proprietor had to acquiesce in the assembly's decision. In South Carolina during the 1680s the Lords Proprietors sent in new people to wrest control of the colony from a group that treated proprietary instructions and directions in cavalier fashion. The colonists had disregarded directives on debts, Indian trade, and land distribution. The resulting conflict between old and new colonists only fueled the efforts of the antiproprietary faction and did nothing to undermine the growing authority of the assembly. The Glorious Revolution of 1688 in England, which rejected the doctrine and practice of supreme royal power, confirmed for the colonists the special place of their assemblies. Just as the Parliament stood in England as the protector of liberty, the colonial assemblies assumed the role of guardian against tyranny. Of course, in the eyes of the colonials that role had been the purpose of the assemblies from the beginning, but after 1688 that purpose, from the colonial perspective, fit neatly into the larger scheme of British affairs. Translated into practical terms, this theoretical role meant that the colonists were even more determined to protect their perception of their own interests by defending and by pressing the authority of their assemblies. The historian of the southern assemblies termed this great theme "the quest for power." Surely it was a quest for power—power to guarantee the liberty of the colonists by protecting their self-interest.

ASSERTION OF POWER BY THE ASSEMBLIES

Southern colonists did not wait for the Revolutionary crisis to make fundamental claims for their right to an assembly. The crown always maintained that assemblies existed only through a royal grant of privilege. Southerners rejected that position; they had more in mind than simply the political reality and the political power of their assemblies. In 1739 the South Carolina Commons House of Assembly adopted a resolution justifying its right to exist on the grounds of the basic right of Englishmen to legislative representation. "No Usage or Royal Instruction," the assembly asserted, "can take away the force of it in America." This resolution explicitly claimed for the South Carolina assembly, and by extension for all assemblies, the privileges of the House of Commons in London.

Two episodes that antedate the Revolutionary crisis reveal the determination of the assemblies and the political distance they willingly traveled to guard their sense of their liberty. The Pistole Fee Controversy in Virginia in the mid-1750s involved the power of the purse, the power to tax; the Gadsden Election Controversy, which rocked South Carolina in the early 1760s, turned on the authority of the assembly to determine its own membership.

These conflicts arose because royal governors attempted to impose their policies or their will in areas the assemblies considered their exclusive domain. In Virginia, Governor Robert Dinwiddie, who arrived in 1752, proclaimed a fee or tax of one pistole, a small Spanish coin, for use of his seal on a land patent. The House of Burgesses declared that it alone had the right to tax the people of Virginia. Addressing the governor, the burgesses asserted, "The Rights of the Subject [any of the king's subjects, even those in Virginia] are so secured by Law, that they cannot be deprived of the least part of their Property, but by their own Consent." Both sides stood their ground, the lawmakers echoing the cry made in a public toast: "Liberty and property and no pistole!" The dispute was finally settled in 1754 when the royal government in London technically upheld the governor but so restricted the imposition of the fee that the burgesses could feel vindicated.

Claiming a violation of South Carolina's election law, Governor Thomas Boone refused in 1762 to administer the oath of office to Christopher Gadsden, a recently elected member of the assembly. The assembly had perceived no problem and had seated Gadsden. The governor also maintained that the assembly existed solely at the pleasure of the crown, not by any basic right the colonists enjoyed as English subjects. Outraged by the governor's action, which it denounced as "a most precipitate, unadvised, unprecedented Procedure of the most dangerous Consequence," the assembly declared that no one else could decide its membership, and it refused to conduct any further business with the governor "until his Excellency shall have done justice to this House." This conflict also went to London for resolution. Though the decision in 1764 did criticize the assembly, it did not uphold Boone, who left the colony. With Boone gone and London making no move to challenge its claim to legitimacy, the assembly clearly had won.

Both the Pistole Fee Controversy and the Gadsden Election Controversy reveal just how tenaciously the colonists clung to their vision of their liberty. Despite the position of the governors as agents of royal power, the assemblies refused to bow or to bend. As they defined the issue, none could be more fundamental. The essence of liberty—protection against outside control, against despotic power—was at stake. The legislators saw themselves as manning the battlements at the most crucial points. They acted on the premise that "liberty and property once lost, a people have nothing left worth contending for."

REGULATION

The duty to safeguard liberty did not stop at a colony's boundaries. The colonists themselves expected their assemblies to guard them no less zealously on the issues that affected all the colonies. This function of the assembly never seriously clashed with the interests of the dominant elite, as they dominated the assemblies. For others, however, the action or the inaction of the assemblies as the guarantors of liberty could generate considerable distress.

This relationship between the colonies and their assemblies provides the most fruitful approach to an understanding of the Regulator movement, which sprang up in the back country of both North and South Carolina during the 1760s. Although the movement varied slightly in the two colonies, it had the same thrust in both. The Regulator movement did not represent a revolt of the oppressed against the privileged. In South Carolina substantial backcountry men led voting, independent farmers in an attempt to gain effective expansion of the colonial legal system into their home area. They wanted courts and sheriffs close at hand to protect liberty and property from lawless bands. Small to middling planters in North Carolina led approximately 75 percent of the backcountry population in an attempt to protect their local rights. The North Carolina Regulators detested the pervasive corruption in their local political and judicial institutions, a corruption at least countenanced by the assembly. The Regulators feared that sheriffs' abuse of their tax-collecting authority, with neither oversight nor correction coming from the assembly, endangered both their prosperity and their freedom. They adopted the name Regulator because "their primary goal was to gain the right to regulate their own local government."

Neither group of Regulators gained an immediate victory, but their efforts did not go for naught. In South Carolina the legal system did finally make its way into the backcountry, though not before the Regulation had degenerated into a vigilante movement trying to impose morality. In North Carolina, Regulation had a more fractious, even belligerent career that ended in fighting and bloodshed. Even there, however, the Articles of Settlement of 1768 left most Regulator partisans with the belief that the movement had benefited them. In neither colony did the Regulation herald any long-term divisiveness, for during the ensuing war with England the great majority of the Regulators fought for the colonial cause against the mother country.

THE ELITE AND DEFERENCE

The assemblies existed to protect and benefit their creators and constituents. In each colony the economic and social elite made up the political elite. This elite was the dominant force in the assemblies, and its members clearly envisioned the assemblies as their assemblies, organized not only to defend their interests but to advance them.

Throughout the colonial South, both in space and in time, great planters formed the keystone of the elite. From the seventeenth-century Chesapeake to eighteenth-century Georgia the men who managed the slave plantations also directed political affairs in their colonies. Although the planters surely dominated, they shared political power with two complementary groups. Everywhere the leading lawyers and the large merchants participated directly in legislative activity. Especially in South Carolina with its port of Charleston, the largest city in the colonial South, nonplanters enjoyed particular influence; in fact, the lawyers and merchants of the city usually led the assembly. The division of the southern elite into planters, lawyers, and merchants can easily be exaggerated, however, for often one man engaged in two of the three occupations. In Maryland most of the great planters were also intimately involved in commercial affairs. Many of the leading planters in Virginia were also lawyers—Thomas Jefferson, for example. The wealthy Charleston merchant Henry Laurens became a major rice planter after making his fortune in trade. Men of other influential South Carolina political families, such as the Rutledges and the Pinckneys, were lawyers first and planters second. In sum, it is unhistorical to divide the colonial southern elite into agricultural, commercial, and professional interests, as though those interests were mutually exclusive.

The elite thought of themselves and comported themselves accordingly. They treated the people they considered their social inferiors differently from the way they treated their peers, and they expected the inferiors to accept the differentiation. In the middle of the eighteenth century William Bull, Sr., lieutenant governor of South Carolina, acted on such premises. After Sunday services Bull often invited the congregation of Prince William's Parish to his plantation. Bull personally received his peers of the gentry inside his home while the other parishoners, a majority, remained outside with Bull's overseer as their immediate host. This overtly discriminatory behavior occasioned neither surprise nor antagonism. Both groups, the upper and the lower, expected the treatment they received.

The religious structure buttressed this ranking of society. In each southern colony the Anglican or Episcopal church was the established church: only the Anglican church had official government sanction, and public funds paid its clergy. Everywhere the Anglicans counted among their communicants the major portion of the economic, social, and political elite. Dissenting Protestant churches appealed chiefly to the lower order of society. The Roman Catholic church mattered only in Maryland, where its membership did include some of the wealthiest families, such as the Carrolls. But Catholic influence and relative strength declined in Maryland throughout the colonial era.

The vestry of the established church exercised considerable influence in the parishes, which became important units of local government. A body of prominent laymen, the vestry had responsibility for such diverse matters as relief for the poor, church construction, public education, and the hiring of ministers. The vestry was so important locally that notable non-Anglicans who wanted to influence local affairs sometimes got themselves elected vestrymen, even though the law specified that only Anglicans could serve. Just as the elite of a parish made up the vestry, the same elite furnished the assembly delegates. Assemblymen and vestrymen were often identical. Vestrymen and assemblymen controlled the church, local affairs, and the assemblies, and they expected their social inferiors to support their efforts.

No evidence indicates substantial chafing at this system, either at Bull's Sunday soirees or anywhere else. In the eighteenth century few of the independent or yeoman farmers, who constituted the great bulk of the southern white population, disputed this social system. Although the majority could vote and many did, practically nobody challenged the assumption of the upper class that it alone could provide proper political leadership. In the Carolina backcountry the yeomen normally looked to men of the higher economic and social ranks for political leadership. Even the politically active skilled artisans in Charleston and Savannah never questioned the political role of those they thought of as their betters. Many of these artisans were legally qualified to sit in the assembly, but custom awarded such seats to the elite, and before the Revolution artisans never challenged the custom. Instead they supported the individuals they perceived as helping them. The son of a Virginia farmer and carpenter spoke for his class across the South when he remembered: "We were accustomed to look upon what were called *gentle folks*, as beings of a superior order."

This political behavior is indisputably deferential politics. Not only did the gentry rule; the farmers and artisans expected them to do so and supported their exercise of authority. Important as it was, though, the politics of deference did not alone shape southern political life.

THE DEMOCRATIC CHARACTER OF POLITICS

Colonial southern politics also had a democratic configuration. The great majority of white southerners, who at any one time were of course not of the upper class, also had the right to be active politically through voting. Throughout the period each colony determined its own franchise requirements, and each restricted the franchise. Everywhere by the eighteenth century ownership of property was a prerequisite for voting, though occasionally, as in the South Carolina Electoral Act of 1721, payment of a stipulated tax sufficed. No matter the specific statutory provision at any given time, the southern colonials shared the view that only those with a tangible stake in society should have the right to vote. Although the precise number of people franchised and disfranchised is impossible to ascertain, it is clear that in the eighteenth century a majority of the white males could vote in each colony. This politically relevant group probably included from 60 percent to 90 percent of the adult white males. The percentage varied over time as well as by colony. Of course, the legal right to vote does not automatically ensure the exercise of that right.

For the broad franchise to influence the political process significantly, the enfranchised must vote. Before the 1760s interest in voting and electoral activity varied. In some places and at some times interest and activity quickened; in other places and at other times they flagged. Elections in Virginia for the House of Burgesses usually stimulated electoral activity, though not every contest brought an outpouring of voters. The first election for the Georgia assembly, in 1754, was fiercely contested both in the countryside and in Savannah, but in other years elections were quiet. Except in Charleston and its vicinity, South Carolinians generally showed little interest in voting before the 1760s. In the city and its environs, however, elections occasioned a flurry of activity.

The interest in elections came in no small part from the efforts of men who hungered for office. As early as 1699 the House of Burgesses lamented the excesses of office seekers and sought to restrict them, but with little success. Electioneering techniques used by successful candidates for the burgesses included meeting and speaking with prospective voters. Candidates met with church congregations; they visited in private homes and stayed overnight when campaign exertions carried them substantial distances from home. And all tried to bring joy to the voters in the way George Washington did in Frederick County in 1758. On that occasion Washington's agent supplied 160 gallons of spirits to 391 voters. Barrels of whiskey open on the courthouse green were not an unusual sight in the hurly-burly of a hot contest. Virginia probably led the way in electioneering, but such practices were certainly not unknown elsewhere. Even in young Georgia, electoral excitement in 1768 inspired two women to sally forth in a carriage to win votes for their political hero.

THE POLITICIANS

In this active electoral process the mere possession of money, social rank, and even a famous name did not guarantee political success. Conscious of their power to approve and to reject bids for office, colonial voters demanded that candidates treat them with respect. Though the candidates were not of the same class as the bulk of the voters, they had to possess characteristics that the voters approved and supported. The essential ingredient in political success, then, was not name or wealth, for many men who had both failed to achieve notable political careers. Before anything else, the aspiring political leader had to be ambitious for political place. Ambition was essential because victory usually required effort. A veteran Virginia politician who had known both victory and defeat perfectly understood the requirement, and obviously himself as well. Writing to a friend, he announced that he was "once again in a state to venture on the stormy sea of politics and public business." The requisite ambition mustered, the candidate had "to practice the arts by which [the voters'] approval could be won." Political leadership required the savvy and acumen that could transform economic and social privilege into victory at the polls.

John Robinson and Willie Jones mastered the complexities. As longtime speaker of the House of Burgesses and treasurer of the colony in the mid-eighteenth century, John Robinson gained wide popularity in Virginia. But equally important for Robinson's favorable public image was his personality. "A jewel of a man," according to one associate, Robinson possessed "a benevolence which created friends and sincerity which never lost one." Widely admired, Robinson, in the minds of politically conscious Virginians, was a man whose "opinions must be regarded."

JOHN ROBINSON, LEADER
OF COLONIAL VIRGINIA
POLITICS (Colonial Williamsburg
Collection)

In neighboring North Carolina just a bit later, Willie Jones proved himself an equally adept practitioner of the political art. Even those who disagreed with him marveled at his political astuteness. As one of them observed, Jones "stimulated the passions, aroused the suspicions, [and] moderated the ardor of his followers." He managed to do so because he "stole his way into [their] hearts" by "smoking his pipe, and chatting of crops, ploughs, stock, dogs, and c." Many citizens believed Jones, the sophisticated planter, the most influential public man in his state.

The qualities that blended to create the master politicians of the colonial South differed little from those that characterized leaders of subsequent generations. Most politicians, understanding that their success depended on the political culture that nourished them, vociferously defended its goodness and doggedly guarded its institutions and privileges against outside encroachment. Attacks on their own class or the deference it received were rare. Products of a system few questioned seriously, they adopted defense of it as a cardinal principle.

PARTICIPATORY POLITICS

Colonial southern politics, then, was both deferential and democratic. Without question the upper class dominated the political system, but that system was fluid and marked by constant interaction between elector and elected. Historians who emphasize either deference or democracy to the exclusion of the other oversimplify, because any valid general characterization of the system must account for both. This political process can perhaps best be described as "participatory politics."

All involved in the process, whether vote seekers or voters, recognized that popular rule underlay the liberty of their political system. Political institutions existed to guard the rights of the people, and the people's representatives worked to protect their constituents and to carry out their wishes. A former royal governor of North Carolina thoroughly understood this truth. In 1733 he described the colonials as a people "who are subtle and crafty to admiration, who could neither be outwitted nor cajoled, who always behave insolently to their governors." And ready to protect these difficult folk stood assemblymen bound to them by culture and votes. The voters of Orange County, North Carolina, instructed their assembly delegates: "Gentlemen, we have chosen you our Representatives at the next General Assembly and when we did so we expected and still do expect that you will speak our Sense in every case when we shall expressly declare it, or when you by any other means discover it." That sentiment ranged far beyond North Carolina. Failure to attempt to discern the sense of electors returned assemblymen to the ranks of electors. Without question representatives were aware that they spoke for a larger body than themselves. From at least the early 1720s the South Carolina assembly clearly responded to public opinion; thoughts of the electorate were never out of assemblymen's minds. In 1767 the Georgia assembly refused to grant a gubernatorial request because, the assemblymen explained, to grant it would violate the trust the people had placed in them.

One of the most famous political scandals in the colonial South underscored this relationship between the gentry who dominated the assemblies and the voters. Upon the death in 1766 of John Robinson, for twenty-eight years the treasurer of Virginia as well as the speaker of the House of Burgesses, the discovery was made that he had embezzled more than £100,000 of public money, which he lent to himself and close associates. Although particulars of the scandal did not become public knowledge, its general outlines appeared in the press, and rumors about its details permeated the colony. Aware that their continued power depended on the reputation they enjoyed among the electorate, the burgesses instituted legal procedures against Robinson's estate to recover the money. They also separated the offices of speaker and treasurer; never again would the same man hold both offices simultaneously. In addition they created a committee to conduct semiannual audits of the public accounts—audits that would be published.

In this instance the political elite surely acted to preserve and protect their power, but by their actions they acknowledged that such prerogatives depended on the support of social and economic inferiors who participated in the political process. In fact, the post-Robinson reforms probably strengthened the position of the elite in Virginia because the reforms demonstrated responsible leadership. They were in the best interest of all Virginians, not just of the burgesses.

CONFLICT WITH INDIANS

Through most of the colonial era the public issues with which southern politicians dealt tended to concern finance, land, and place. Often routine, they occasionally sparked heated controversy, which enlivened the political arena. Colonial assemblies and politicians also had to confront questions of defense, which usually meant relations with neighboring Indian tribes. From the moment of contact until the Revolution the Indian question remained unresolved.

The militia assumed central importance in the colonists' stance toward the Indians. Based on the principle that free men had the duty to guard and to protect their society, by fighting if necessary, the militia had a long history in England. Drawing on their English heritage, the colonists early on created militias, chiefly to contend with the presence and potential threat of the Indians. Laws made clear that white males from their late teens to middle age had a responsibility to contribute to the safety of their colony by serving in the militia. A militiaman usually had to supply his own weapon, ammunition, clothing, and provisions. Training was generally haphazard, a matter of drills and reviews on muster days scattered throughout the year. On those occasions military training tended to take second place to social festivities. The laws normally authorized the governor to name the militia officers, and he appointmented them with an eye more to the prominence of their families than to their military expertise. Yet the militia understood its purpose and recognized that it could be called up in time of danger.

Though the Powhatan tribes had almost wiped out the Jamestown settlers in 1622, their strength declined rapidly in the face of white Virginians determined to beat them down. The tribes rose up one last time in 1644 and killed some 500 colonists. The Virginians retaliated to good effect, but the Indian problem did not totally disappear, for the Indians remained intimately involved with the extension of white settlements. This fact was an essential ingredient in Bacon's Rebellion. Still, after 1650 the Indians of Virginia were almost as powerless as those in Maryland, who never did have sufficient numbers to pose a serious obstacle to the settlers' advance.

No other significant difficulties with the Indians arose in Virginia before the settlement of the Shenandoah Valley in the mid-eighteenth century. At that time the Virginia frontier became embroiled in the larger Anglo-French contest for North America. Virginians in the western reaches of the colony confronted Indians backed by the French. These tribes were not descendants of the tidewater people put down a century earlier; they hailed rather from western Pennsylvania and the Ohio Valley. When the British finally defeated the French in 1763, the Virginia frontier quieted down, though the danger to exposed settlements never entirely disappeared.

The story of North Carolina reads much the same, though the events took place somewhat later. The sparseness of settlers and the small size of their scattered settlements worked against serious problems between colonists and Indians before 1700. But after 1700 a growing population resulted in a more determined expansion into the interior of the colony, which in turn led to troubles with the major local tribe, the Tuscarora. The fifteen Tuscarora villages, with a total of some 2,000 men of fighting age, were located along the chief rivers in eastern North Carolina. These people were understandably outraged when colonists captured Tuscarora women and children and sold them into slavery, and they had no higher opinion of the colonists' relentless advance to the west. Finally in 1711 hostilities erupted into a war that lasted two years. In that contest the combined militias of North and South Carolina and Virginia decisively defeated the Tuscarora forces. The Tuscarora War ended any real danger to the colonists in eastern North Carolina; nor could the Indians any longer delay the settlers' push into the central part of the colony.

South Carolina and Georgia had a different experience because they had to contend with larger numbers of Indians and also because of the Spanish presence in Florida. The Spanish were as wary of British encroachment as the Indians. From their citadel of St. Augustine, little more than 250 miles from Charleston, they recruited Indian allies to confront the British. The Creeks, who lived mostly in western Georgia and what became Alabama, provided important assistance to the Spaniards.

In South Carolina the first generation of settlers engaged in an ongoing contest with various tribes, often aided by the Spanish. The critical contest came against the Yamassee, a tribe located initially in eastern Georgia. Before 1700, however, the Yamassee began to move across the Savannah River and establish towns in lower South Carolina. Relations worsened until in 1715 the Yamassee, supported by the Creeks and the Spanish, assaulted the British settlements. The colonists fought back and overwhelmed their Indian opponents. The Indians' defeat in the Yamassee War ended their threat to the settlers in the low country.

Georgia was a battleground almost from the beginning. Settled in part to provide a buffer between an increasingly wealthy South Carolina and Spanish Florida, Georgia fulfilled its mission. Possible Spanish moves against either or both colonies constantly concerned officials of both, and with good reason. The Spanish viewed with dismay the British settlement of coastal Georgia, which placed British settlers no more than 100 miles from St. Augustine. But neither the Spanish nor their Indian allies could drive the British out of Georgia. The military fate of the youngest British colony was sealed in 1742 when Georgians under James Oglethorpe soundly defeated a Spanish force that had landed on the Georgia coast. This victory over the Spanish at Bloody Marsh secured South Carolina as well as Georgia. And after 1763, when Spain lost Florida to Great Britain as a consequence of the French and Indian War, Spain could no longer threaten the security of the southernmost British colonies.

The success of Carolinians and Georgians along the seacoast did not guarantee a similar result in their conflict with the Cherokees in the western reaches of their colonies. From the beginning the colonists in both Carolinas and later in Georgia had traded profitably with the Cherokees, but disagreements had always arisen over proper boundaries. As settlements pushed farther and farther inland during the middle third of the eighteenth century, boundary disputes became increasingly rancorous, and almost inevitably sporadic violence broke out.

Toward the end of the 1750s the Cherokees numbering some 3,000 men were becoming increasingly unhappy with the colonial authorities. The issue of colonial intrusion into Cherokee lands could not be settled; all efforts to resolve the issue failed. Finally, fearing seemingly unending encroachments on their land, the Cherokees in 1759 attacked outlying western settlements in both Carolinas. Stung, the colonists retaliated. Led by the South Carolina militia, around 1,300 men marched against the Cherokees. By 1761 a series of hard blows by the colonials had so weakened the Cherokees that they could no longer effectively resist the white onslaught. They gave up more and more of the land the colonists coveted until, by an agreement reached in 1765, they turned over most of northwestern South Carolina and retreated into the mountains. This outcome settled the Cherokee question until the Revolution.

RELIGION

Although the issue of physical security engaged the southern colonists just as it did their counterparts elsewhere, religious concerns did not assume the importance in the South that they did in New England, at least not until the mid-eighteenth century. Throughout the colonial period, for the majority of white southern colonials religion meant the Church of England, also known more popularly as the Anglican or the Episcopal church—the established church in all the southern colonies.

In establishing the Church of England, the assembly in every colony placed its authority behind the institution's financial and political support. Yet the established church was operating without a spiritual leader in North America. The church hierarchy in England never appointed a bishop to head the colonial church. From New England to Georgia the church had to look to London for guidance and authorization for its activities. The absence of a bishop caused serious difficulties for the colonial church. Among the most pressing problems was a shortage of clergy. With no bishop on the scene, men who felt called to the Anglican ministry had to journey to England for instruction and ordination. A paucity of Anglican ministers in the colonies was guaranteed.

During the colonial era the church did not occupy a central place in the lives or thoughts of most of its communicants. With no resident spiritual leader, with far too few clergy, with an absence of theological rigor, and with a frown on emotion, the Anglican church did not generate either fervor or excitement among its members. Its decorous formalities only rarely stirred hearts and minds. The church did, however, provide a mainstay for the social order and for the elite who dominated it. The elite were overwhelmingly of the Episcopal persuasion. Their dominance of the vestry, as we have seen, complemented their dominance of the assemblies. For the elite, church and state were almost one.

All colonists not loyal to the Church of England were labeled dissenters. Dissent existed in the southern colonies from the beginning. Roman Catholics had a critical role in the founding and settling of Maryland, but the history of dissent in the southern colonies does not focus on Roman Catholics. In Maryland they quickly became a minority, though a generally tolerated one. Elsewhere they could not be found. In the colonial South, dissenters were non-Anglican Protestants.

Protestant dissent ranged across a wide spectrum. At one end stood the Huguenots, the French Calvinists who came mostly into South Carolina in the late seventeenth and early eighteenth centuries. In a relatively short time the Huguenots so thoroughly assimilated with the Anglicans that many became Anglicans themselves. By midcentury some of the leading South Carolina families, such as the Manigaults, boasted Huguenot names and Anglican loyalties. At the other end of the spectrum stood the Quakers, who had no interest in assimilation; no one else wanted to mix with them, either. In the eyes of the ascendant groups, the Quakers' pacifism, their refusal to take oaths, and later their antislavery stance made them social misfits and religious radicals. Quakers did not have an easy time, though no southern colony emulated New England and prescribed the death penalty for holding to Quaker beliefs. The Quakers never became a major social force, and their main settlement in central North Carolina remained largely isolated.

THE GREAT AWAKENING

The significant impact of dissent came from the evangelicals, chiefly the Baptists, Methodists, and Presbyterians. Their influence at once generated and stemmed from a general religious movement that spanned the colonies. The Great Awakening, a series of religious revivals that swept through the colonies in the mid-eighteenth century, originated in New England. The Great Awakening first visited the South around 1740 in the Chesapeake and then spread southward. In the southern colonies the Awakening represented in part a reaction against the formalism and lethargy of the Anglican church. Many southern colonials, eager for a more emotional and more vigorously active religious experience, looked for it beyond the established church. Widespread sentiment against public support for the church so closely tied to the colonial elite helped to propel the Great Awakening.

Revival meetings were the key features of the Great Awakening. Preachers spoke to eager crowds in buildings of every kind and in open fields. Many of these evangelists were itinerants, preachers who traveled from place to place; at each stop they called on their listeners to join the march toward salvation. The revivalists' message emphasized the necessity of an individual religious experience. Stressing the sinfulness of all, the revivalists called out that all must become aware of their sorry spiritual state. Awareness would then lead to conversion; at that point God's grace would save the believer. This was, of course, a far cry from the formalities of the established church.

Among the legion of preachers calling for repentance and renewal certain men had a tremendous influence over their audiences. Many people thought George Whitefield was the greatest orator and preacher of his day. After coming to Georgia in 1737 as an Anglican minister, Whitefield went back to England, then returned to this side of the Atlantic two years later to launch a speaking tour that took him to every southern colony. Whitefield preached the new Methodist faith, which grew out of Anglicanism, though a separate church did not appear until after the Revolution. Methodism appealed to Anglicans who believed that their church had become staid and static. It spread rapidly among the unchurched as well, especially in the poorer classes. No one was more zealous in the cause of Methodism than Whitefield. His powerful, eloquent sermons, in which he often trounced the Anglican clergy as unregenerates, attracted hearers and made converts from the Potomac to Georgia.

Samuel Davies, born in Delaware in 1723, labored with equal intensity to propagate the Presbyterian faith in the Virginia piedmont and backcountry. A magnificent preacher, a prolific hymnist, and a gifted organizer, he put together in 1755 the first presbytery, the governing structure of this Calvinist church, in the southern colonies. Hanover Presbytery became the mother presbytery for the Presbyterian church in the South.

The Methodists, the Presbyterians, the Baptists—all profited from the Great Awakening. In the three decades before the Revolution each of these denominations built a substantial presence in every colony. The Baptists spread into the southern colonies from New England and the middle colonies. With their emphasis on the autonomy of each congregation and their willingness, even eagerness, to accept untrained clergy, the Baptists matched the Methodists in rapid growth. During the first half of the century small groups of Presbyterians moved through such ports as Charleston into the backcountry. But the great Presbyterian migration came in midcentury. Moving southward from Pennsylvania into the Valley of Virginia and on down into the piedmont of both Carolinas and Georgia, Scotch-Irish Presbyterians grew into a powerful force on the frontier. Although their organizational structure and their insistence on an educated clergy helped keep their numbers below those of the Baptists and Methodists, their cohesiveness and energy made their presence felt.

The Church of England simply could not match the dynamics of the evangelicals, and it watched with dismay as increasing numbers of its more enthusiastic members broke away to join the Methodists. Undoubtedly many Anglicans had no interest in competing with dissenters. Others did, but they found the going tough. One of the most dedicated was the Reverend Charles Woodmason, a native Englishman who put on the clerical collar after some ten years of various activities in South Carolina. Woodmason took as his mission the carrying of the Church of England into the backcountry of his own colony. Away from the low-country parishes he found considerable hostility, especially among the Presbyterians, who made every effort to undermine his missionary endeavor. Woodmason reported that to thwart his crusade the Presbyterians on one occasion provided two barrels of whiskey for the crowd gathered for his services. This tactic worked, for "the Company got drunk by 10 o'th clock and we could hear them firing, hooping, and hallowing like Indians." According to the outraged Woodmason, the nefarious Presbyterians never let up. To the mind of this harassed evangel of Anglicanism, one of their schemes was particularly diabolical: they "[took] down Advertisements for calling our People together." The offending Calvinists often altered the date and place of Woodmason's services. "When I came," a frustrated Woodmason complained, "there were no People—and on other days the People would meet and no Minister." Woodmason's tribulations underscored the extreme difficulty the established church confronted with the surge of the evangelical faiths.

The Great Awakening did not change the fact of establishment, though it did have a significant impact on the Anglican church. The Awakening provoked discussion on the issue of establishment itself; many of the evangelicals asked why their taxes should support the Church of England alone or at all. In addition the substantial anticlerical sentiment voiced by so many spokesmen of the Awakening injured the reputation and the position of the Anglican clergy. In Virginia even within the established church conflict erupted between clergy and laity over control of the ministers' salaries. This infighting hurt the ministers, who appeared overly concerned about worldly matters, and it also struck at the moral authority of the Anglican church, which could ill afford such blows. Moreover, an assault against the established church could easily become a strike at the social order in which it occupied such a conspicuous place. Without question the Great Awakening contributed to tensions in colonial society, but the social fabric remained fundamentally intact at the onset of the Revolution.

CULTURE AND EDUCATION

The southern colonies were on a cultural as well as a geographical frontier. From Jamestown to the Revolution, neither concern for education nor the life of the mind assumed major importance for most colonists. The overwhelming majority of whites spent their lives in hard physical labor to wrest a living from soil and forest. The gentry who lived in the manor houses of the Chesapeake and the Carolina low country attempted to replicate the culture of the mother country in the New World. In the colonial South, as in most of the Western world during the seventeenth and eighteenth centuries, only the upper classes had an opportunity to cultivate artistic and intellectual pursuits, even one as fundamental as reading. Those who did were so few and in general so widely separated from one another that they could not institutionalize education or the arts beyond the local level.

The educational enterprise, as understood today, simply did not exist in the southern colonies. No colony supported a public school system. In the eighteenth century the larger towns, such as Annapolis and Charleston, did have free common schools, but they reached very few young people. The upper classes tended to hire tutors to educate their children. The tutors, many of them recent graduates of northern colleges and often aspiring clergymen, introduced the scions of the gentry to the mysteries of Greek, Latin, mathematics, some history, and occasionally modern foreign languages. Some plantation families hired a tutor solely for their own children; others joined together to employ a tutor to instruct all of their children jointly. The wealthiest tobacco and rice families not uncommonly sent their sons to England for the best education the mother country offered. In this endeavor prosperous southern colonials acted differently from their counterparts in the middle colonies and New England, who rarely turned to England for the schooling of their young. Two reasons probably account for this difference: first, the richest planters had more money; second, the southern gentry were trying to emulate the English country squires in every way they could.

In the almost 170 years that elapsed between the settling of Jamestown and the outbreak of the Revolution, only one college opened its doors in the southern colonies. Chartered in 1693, the College of William and Mary at Williamsburg, Virginia, is the second oldest institution of higher learning in the United States. Only Harvard, with a 1636 birth date, has a more ancient lineage. The primary force behind the founding of William and Mary was the Reverend John Blair, a native Englishman and Anglican minister, who came to Virginia as the commissary or agent of the bishop of London. Conscious of the woeful shortage of pastors in the colony, Blair wanted a college to help provide an educated clergy for the Anglican church. The colonial William and Mary was an all-purpose institution. It had an Indian school and a grammar school as well as a collegiate course. Beset by difficulties in the beginning and quite weak early in the eighteenth century—a report in 1712, for example, indicated a total enrollment of twenty-two students—the college had become stronger by mid-century. Although William and Mary never met Commissary Blair's goal of providing the requisite number of trained ministers for the established church, it did educate many of the elite of the colony, several of whom became prominent during the Revolutionary crisis; two of its most illustrious alumni were Thomas Jefferson and James Monroe. To foster scholarship and debate, the college established the first chapter of the Phi Beta Kappa Society in 1776.

The gentry attempted to provide for themselves the cultural attractions favored by the British upper classes, and in the major towns, especially in Charleston, Annapolis, and Williamsburg, they made considerable headway. In the 1710s Williamsburg had an operating playhouse and acting company. By mid-century two professional touring troupes entertained Virginians in Williamsburg and also in smaller towns such as Fredericksburg. Beginning in those same years, acting companies performed in Annapolis. As early as 1703 visiting players entertained Charleston audiences; professional companies appeared thereafter, and before 1740 a theater had been built. The colonials preferred and attended the plays most popular in England at the time; Shakespeare was always the favorite.

Even before 1750 concerts had become as commonplace as dramatic productions. Musical groups were active throughout Maryland. Williamsburg featured chamber music concerts and by 1766 could boast of an orchestra. Charleston was the home of the most distinctive musical program in the southern colonies. Professionals from both England and the continent performed there. Concerts were presented on a subscription basis as early as 1733; the first performance of an opera in the American colonies took place in Charleston in 1735. Musical societies abounded. The most notable and the oldest in America, the St. Cecilia Society, established in 1762, sponsored an orchestra with paid musicians. Though surely not London, the largest colonial towns provided remarkable cultural offerings for their time and their location.

THE WRITTEN WORD

Southern colonials did not gain fame for their authorship. Traditionally the colonial South has been judged a literary desert in comparison with New England. More recent investigations, however, have led to the discovery that southern colonials produced writing of considerable quality and quantity. From poetry to plays to histories to sermons, the output of southerners equaled in distinction that of writers to the north. That fact has generally been established, though studies of the southern literary effort do not yet match in thoroughness and sophistication the scholarship applied to the writings of New Englanders.

Certainly histories rank among the most important of colonial southern writings, and they have received the most attention. In the southern colonies this genre originated with Captain John Smith, who brought out his *Generall Historie of Virginia* in 1624. The writing of history remained largely a Virginia enterprise. Two particularly notable eighteenth-century successors to Smith were Robert Beverley and Hugh Jones, both of whom published histories of the oldest colony. All three of these early historians had a dual purpose: not only to describe and explain events but to make Virginia attractive to new settlers. All published their works in London.

Beverley, a native Virginian, member of a notable family, and public man who served in the House of Burgesses, wrote more as a Virginian than as an Englishman. He used a wide range of sources for *The History and Present State of Virginia* (1705; a second edition appeared in 1722), which he wrote while in England. Beverley's thorough account of seventeenth-century Virginia criticized some officials and official policies (the criticism was muted in the second edition), and he argued that the "slothful Indolence" of Virginians kept them from making the most of the colony's abundant resources. At the same time, he declared Virginia "the best poor Man's country in the World" and predicted a bright future for it.

Unlike Beverley, Hugh Jones was born in England; he first arrived in Virginia as an Anglican minister, with an appointment to the faculty of William and Mary. Jones's *Present State of Virginia* (1724) focused more on the contemporary world than on the past. The laziness that worried Beverley did not bother Jones. On the contrary, Jones spoke almost admiringly of the outlook and characteristics of Virginians. Celebrating the environment, he predicted a bountiful future for the colony. Even so, he advocated a more diversified economy, but admitted that the understandable commitment of Virginians to agriculture made diversification unlikely.

Undoubtedly the most noteworthy literary figure was another Virginian, William Byrd II. Born in 1674 into one of the leading families in the colony, Byrd engaged in an impressive variety of activities. With an English education and numerous long visits to the mother country—he spent half his life there—as well as experiences on the continent, Byrd was a cosmopolitan person. He wanted to recreate in Virginia the life of an English country gentleman, and with his plantation mansion, Westover, as his seat he largely succeeded. A man of business, he managed his land and his slaves so well that he not only maintained his substantial inheritance but added to it. At his death in 1744 he owned 174,000 acres. A man of public affairs, he was active in politics, both in Virginia and as a representative of various Virginia interests in London. But for William Byrd II, the life of the mind was also essential. He rose every morning at five to begin his daily reading in Greek, Hebrew, or Latin. Byrd's literary efforts ranged widely, from essays to diaries to public papers to history, though much that he wrote remained unpublished during his lifetime. His diaries, the source of much of our knowledge of his life and world, were discovered only in this century. Byrd's best-known works, *The Secret History of the Dividing Line* (around

WILLIAM BYRD II, GREAT
PLANTER AND NOTABLE
AUTHOR (Colonial Williamsburg
Collection)

1730) and *The History of the Dividing Line* (probably late 1730s), tell about the survey of the North Carolina–Virginia boundary conducted in 1728; Byrd had headed the Virginia party. These two books—satirical, witty, trenchantly observant of people and customs and places, marvelously written—represent a considerable literary achievement.

In a quite different area southern colonials did work of substantial intellectual merit. Colonial Americans, including southerners, moved rapidly and with respect into the best scientific circles in Europe. After all, they lived in virtually a virgin laboratory for the observation and collection of flora and fauna. The garden of William Byrd II won fame for the variety of its rare species. Dr. John Mitchell, also a Virginian, became a fellow of the British Royal Society as a result of his writings on plants and animals in his colony. Another fellow of the Royal Society, Dr. Alexander Garden of South Carolina, won fame for his work on botanical and zoological topics. In addition, the first museum in the colonies was founded in Charleston in 1773.

The southern colonies also vigorously participated in the establishment of a critical vehicle for the expression of ideas as well as for the improvement of communications. The first newspaper in the colonial South appeared in Annapolis in 1727; under several proprietors the *Maryland Gazette* carried on until the Revolution. Charleston in 1732 and Williamsburg in 1736 joined Annapolis as homes of newspapers, or gazettes, as they were invariably called. The *North Carolina Gazette* started publication in New Bern in 1751. Finally the youngest colony got its own gazette with the appearance in 1763 of the Savannah *Georgia Gazette*. In each of the other colonies, as in Maryland, these newspapers became practically permanent fixtures from their initial publication on to the Revolution. Only in North Carolina did a significant interruption occur.

The southern colonists did not live in a cultural wasteland any more than they operated in a political wilderness. Located on the western boundary of the British Empire, they, along with their fellow colonists to the north, took part in the English cultural world. Just as integrally they participated in British imperial politics. As the last third of the eighteenth century began, the attention of the colonists turned inevitably toward the increasing tension between their own view of their place in the empire and the colonial role envisioned for them by the government in London.

4

The Revolution

❖

*I*n 1763 Great Britain finally defeated France in the long struggle for domination of eastern North America. In the aftermath of this great victory, which significantly increased the size of the British Empire, the British government adopted policies that caused a profound shift in the posture of the mother country toward her North American colonies. Before 1763, London had basically followed a laissez faire policy that had given the colonies wide latitude to devise their own political institutions and develop their own ideas about their relationship with the mother country, about who had what rights and powers.

But beginning in 1763, Britain intervened more directly in colonial affairs. The Proclamation of 1763 barred settlers from crossing the Appalachians into the Ohio Valley, a major prize of the war. Never before had the British attempted to exercise such control over westward expansion. The royal government also planned to station an unprecedented 6,000 additional troops in the colonies. The administration of a large dominion, including the maintenance of a substantial army in North America, made government more expensive. That increased cost, added to the massive debt incurred during the war with France, placed an enormous burden on the British government and on British taxpayers. The government decided that the colonists should help carry the burden by contributing directly to the royal treasury.

QUESTIONS OF AUTHORITY

In every colony objections were raised. The blocking of expansion pleased few. Nobody wanted the army. The prospect of taxes imposed by Britain was anathema. Quickly the colonists' antagonism to the new empire focused on taxes, which became a reality in 1765 when Parliament passed the Stamp Act. Calling for taxes similar to those already collected in England, the Stamp Act placed a tax on all kinds of printed matter, from legal documents to newspapers.

Immediately the colonists resisted. They insisted that Parliament could not tax them, could not take their property, because they had no representatives sitting in Parliament. Nurtured on the practice of actual representation, which

required assemblymen to act as the advocates and protectors of their home areas and of the constituents who elected them, the colonials rejected the contention that they were represented by every member of Parliament, who virtually
represented every subject of the Crown in every corner of the British Empire.
From New England to Georgia colonials took up their pens to contest this new
and, to them, threatening turn in British policy.

The colonials did more than write and speak—a great deal more. Direct action revealed the depth of the colonists' distress. Massachusetts called for a
Stamp Act Congress, which met in New York in October 1765 with delegates
from nine colonies, including three from the South. The Congress passed a series of resolutions. Protest went far beyond resolutions when mobs took to the
streets. They intimidated officials, burned stamps in fact and stamp-tax collectors in effigy, looted homes, and occasionally vented their anger on anyone
they happened to encounter. Finally colonists began to defy the law by using
unstamped materials. In the face of such massive opposition, British officials
could not carry out the provisions of the law. The Stamp Act became a dead
letter.

Although Parliament attempted to defuse this explosive situation by repealing the Stamp Act in 1766, at the same time it passed the Declaratory Act, which
declared that the colonies were subordinate to Parliament and that laws enacted
by Parliament were binding on America. Promptly Parliament moved to translate the Declaratory Act into concrete policy. The next year it authorized the
Townshend Acts, which imposed taxes on such items as glass, paper, and tea.
The colonies, southern as well as northern, responded in 1769 by beginning a
movement to refuse to import goods from Great Britain, and informed colonials
everywhere vowed not to buy British goods. Over the next few years the situation continued to deteriorate. Several laws passed by Parliament in 1774
heightened fears and tension. Among these so-called Intolerable Acts was one
that empowered the royal governor of Massachusetts to fill by appointment
many offices that had been elective. Britain's determination to bring the colonists to heel was met by an equal implacability in the colonies. The Intolerable
Acts, aimed chiefly at dissidents in Massachusetts, alarmed people everywhere.
Legislative committees of correspondence, extralegal bodies set up first in 1773
in Virginia and then in almost every other colony to promote intercolony cooperation and solidarity, alerted all to the danger perceived in British actions.
From the Virginia committee the call went out for all colonies to send delegates
to a meeting in Philadelphia. The First Continental Congress, held in September and October 1774, was attended by delegates from every colony except
Rhode Island. A Second Continental Congress followed in 1775; in April of that
year shots were fired at Lexington and Concord. Then in 1776, with the pro-
mulgation of the Declaration of Independence, the colonies proclaimed themselves to be the United States of America, an independent nation. Through all
of these cataclysmic events the southern colonies acted in concert with the
northern colonies.

THE SOUTH IN 1775

Mason-Dixon Line

MD.

VA.

N.C.

S.C.

GA.

*L*IBERTY *ENDANGERED*

Liberty—on this concept turned the ideological conflict between England and its colonies. The idea of liberty came to the fore in the works of certain political writers in seventeenth- and eighteenth-century England. These works were widely read on this side of the ocean long before 1763, and Americans took to heart their basic precept that liberty required freedom from outside control. In this view, control, beginning with interference in such areas as taxation, was a prelude to tyranny.

Taxation assumed critical importance because taxes involved property. To tax meant taking from citizens a portion of their property. And property was inextricably tied to liberty. The colonial writers clearly made the connection, and no one did so more graphically than the Virginian who declared: "Liberty and property are like those precious vessels whose soundness is destroyed by the least flaw." Thus, when Parliament taxed, it took away liberty as well as property.

In the political lexicon of the eighteenth century, the opposite of liberty was slavery. Slavery had a particular political meaning: the absence of liberty. In its political definition slavery characterized a society or a people that had lost its power to resist oppression, and that loss led inevitably to tyranny. Tyranny was seen as inevitable in such circumstances because the English writers and the colonists shared the conviction that an endemic political corruption, a greedy grasping for place and reward, hovered over every society, ready to swoop up liberty in the claws of slavery.

When colonists spoke about slavery, they were not merely employing a rhetorical device. Although the political meaning and the political use of the term were just as familiar to New Englanders as to southerners, the idea of political slavery had special force among southerners. They lived with the institution of slavery and among tens of thousands of slaves. Although not every white person owned slaves, the institution of slavery was so widespread that almost all whites, those who did not own slaves as well as those who did, the lower classes as well as the upper, knew at firsthand what slavery entailed. All the characteristics associated with political slavery—dependence, tyranny, oppression, defenselessness—glowed especially brightly among people in the South, for those words described their own human institution.

Conscious of this association, southerners directly connected their political contest against England with their domestic institution. When southerners cried out, as they so often did, "Slavery or independence!" there could be no mistaking their meaning. This conclusion is all the more inescapable because almost every prominent crier owned slaves. Their vigorous language created a powerful rhetorical weapon, a weapon grasped by conservatives as well as radicals. It mattered little where a southerner appeared along the spectrum of opposition to England, from firebrands demanding independence to moderates urging caution to conservatives anxious about the tumult. All saw and pictured the plight of the colonies and themselves in terms of the institution they knew so well. Lacerating "the oppressive and unconstitutional measures of the British government," the radical Charleston merchant Christopher Gadsden posed the alternatives for his fellow citizens. Firm resistance to British oppression, he wrote in 1769, would guarantee "the honorable rank of Freemen," but acquiescence in evil and unconstitutional taxes meant inevitable degradation. "Whatever we may think of ourselves," Gadsden warned, "we are as real slaves as those we are permitted to command, and differ only in degree. For what is a slave, but one that is at the will of his master and has no property of his own."

Gadsden did not speak in a strange dialect. A conservative lawyer from Edenton, North Carolina, James Iredell, declared that if Americans submitted to the absolute claims of Parliament, then Americans became dependent, a condition not "of free men, but of slaves." To Iredell, submission and dependence were "the very definition of slavery." Before the outbreak of hostilities George Washington had not been a major spokesman for independence, but he had no doubt that England aimed "by every piece of art and despotism to fix the shackles of slavery upon us." Washington believed that failure to establish a clear-cut

American position would force all Americans to "submit to every imposition, that can be heaped upon us, until custom and use shall make us as tame and abject slaves, as the blacks we rule over with such arbitrary sway." Others echoed these sentiments: America had to stand against England or became "a sink for slaves." The connection southerners made between their own institution of slavery and their view of their conflict with England was never more sharply drawn as by a writer in the Charleston *South Carolina Gazette*: "not to be, *is better than* to be a slave."

VIEWS ON SLAVERY

This conscious and explicit juxtaposition of their political position with their institution of slavery forced white southerners to look closely at their institution for the first time. They were risking their lives and property for liberty while holding slaves. Although by 1770 slaves constituted 40 percent of the population with a value counted in the hundreds of thousands of pounds sterling, the vast majority of the white South had given neither the institution nor its growth much serious thought before the Revolutionary crisis. Now, however, thoughts about slavery flooded the consciousness of the South. Some southerners did recognize the contradiction in their position, in calling for liberty in a land of slavery. The tension created by this paradoxical stance brought forth tormented cries from some slaveholders. Yet the only concerted effort to resolve this tension by actively working for emancipation was made by the Quakers, and they were so few and occupied such a marginal position in southern society that they had little impact either on the behavior of slave owners or on the course of slavery.

The most visible antislavery spokesmen in the Revolutionary South appeared in Virginia. Many Virginia public men who called the colonies to arms against England also denounced the morality of owning slaves. To name them is to call the roll of Revolutionary heroes: Thomas Jefferson, George Mason, Richard Henry Lee—the list goes on. Some brilliant, all articulate, these men agonized over the fundamental contradiction between their deep belief in liberty and their possession of human slaves. As they saw it, their personal dilemma mirrored the quandary of their society. Despite their conviction that slavery was an unmitigated evil—a conviction one cannot doubt after absorbing the anguish that pervades their writings about slavery—they led no crusade against that special horror. Very few of them even emancipated their own slaves. Patrick Henry in 1773 spoke for this class of Virginia slaveholders when he wrote:

> Would any one believe that I am Master of Slaves of my own purchase! I am drawn along by ye general inconvenience of living without them; I will not, I cannot justify it. However culpable my conduct, I will so far pay my devoir to virtue as to own the excellence and rectitude of her precepts and to lament my want of conformity to them.

Having indicted himself, Henry mourned that "we cannot reduce this wished for Reformation to practice."

Thus the intense intellectual and spiritual antislaveryism of the great Virginians had no comparable practical dimension. During the entire span of the Revolutionary era Virginia adopted only two measures that can be counted as antislave, and neither was a direct attack on the institution. Moreover, the men with the great names can claim complete credit for neither. Opposing the international slave trade throughout the period, Virginia's public men spoke for the planters who, unlike their counterparts farther south, needed and wanted no additional slaves. Thus a substantial economic motive reinforced the ideological preference of the Jeffersons and the Henrys. They also warmly supported legislation pushed by the Quakers and passed in 1782 which permitted private manumission by individual masters. Because of this feeble antislavery record, many recent historians have challenged the depth of the antislavery sentiments voiced by Virginia's heroes. Without getting tangled in that interpretive thicket, one can draw two conclusions from the evidence. No doubt can exist about the genuineness of the intellectual and spiritual turmoil caused by the clash between slavery and liberty; and that turmoil engendered no significant alteration in slavery in Virginia.

South of Virginia antislavery sentiments were rare indeed. Those that did occur, however, were both more public and more forceful than the largely private trauma of the Virginians. The most powerful public indictment of slavery during the Revolutionary period came from the southernmost limit of British settlement. At Darien, on the southern border of settled Georgia, citizens met in January 1775 to align themselves with the rebellion against Great Britain. These Georgians, some of them slave owners, promulgated a set of resolutions specifying both British evils and American goals. The fifth resolution thundered:

> To show the world that we are not influenced by any contracted or interested motives, but a general philanthropy for all mankind of whatever climate, language, or complexion, we hereby declare our disapprobation and abhorrence of the unnatural practice of slavery in America (however, the uncultivated state of our country, or other specious argument may plead for it), a practice founded in injustice and cruelty and highly dangerous to our liberties (as well as lives), debasing part of our fellow creatures below men, and corrupting the virtues and morals of the rest, and is laying the basis for the liberty we contend for (and which we pray the Almighty to continue to the latest posterity) upon a very wrong foundation.

The Darien resolution had no repercussions, absolutely none.

The Henry Laurens family carried the antislavery banner in South Carolina. Henry acted much like the Virginians he matched in wealth and social position. As early as 1763 he condemned slavery, and he often spoke about his deep wish to emancipate his slaves. But when he contemplated manumission, his self-assurance seemed to leave him. He never found the proper opportunity. Henry's son John shared his father's detestation of slavery. To a friend in 1776 he confessed, "I think we Americans at least in the Southern Colonies, cannot contend with good grace for liberty, until we have enfranchised our slaves." As well as anyone ever did, the twenty-two-year-old John Laurens illuminated the irony of the Revolutionary South: "How can we whose jealously [sic] has been claimed more at the name of oppression sometimes than at the reality, reconcile to our spirited assertions of the rights of mankind, the...abject slavery of our Negroes...?"

Nothing had an effect. The Virginians, like Hamlet, found it easier to lament their quandary than to act to end it; the Darien resolution never had an echo; the Laurenses failed to move their state. The utter ineffectiveness of all efforts to pierce the armor of slavery testifies to the strength of the institution in the South. The reasons were many.

THE STRENGTH OF SLAVERY

The massive financial investment in slavery made successful moves against it most unlikely. Slaves were property, and the right to hold property was an integral part of liberty. No white southerner thought seriously about general emancipation without compensation because property owners had an inherent right to their property, including human property. And for Americans the Revolutionary struggle turned in part on their charge that England was endangering their liberty by unconstitutionally depriving them of their property. Unless the owners of slave property decided upon voluntary manumission, the states would have to provide owners with huge sums in compensation. Sums of such magnitude were simply unavailable.

The war with England revealed the close tie southerners saw between slavery and land as congenial, even intimate, forms of property. To encourage enlistment, several states offered a bounty of land to each man who signed up for military service upon his honorable discharge. Georgia, South Carolina, North Carolina, and Virginia increased that offer: every veteran who received a land bounty would receive also at least one slave. As property, black slaves could be given by the state to individuals, and the state recognized slaves as desirable gifts that perfectly complemented the reward of land. After all, the overwhelming majority of the greatest fortunes in the South rested on those twin pillars, land and slaves.

Although no full-blown proslavery argument emphasizing the racial inferiority of the South's slaves appeared during the Revolutionary era, the absence of such an argument did not indicate that white southerners took no notice of the difference in color between themselves and their black slaves. To them that difference was a clear sign of inferiority. That belief antedated the introduction of slavery into British North America. Even that most enlightened of southerners, Thomas Jefferson, shared the conviction that blacks stood several cultural levels below whites. Like most of his fellow southerners, Jefferson considered that inferiority insurmountable; blacks could not be raised to equality with whites, at least not for a long time.

This certainty about the inequality of blacks and whites added significantly to the difficulties of emancipation. Even those white southerners who most wished slavery gone—and Jefferson surely belonged to this group—were convinced that emancipated slaves could not remain near their former masters. In the minds of even sincere antislavery southerners an inundation of their society by substantial numbers of freed black slaves meant cataclysm. To them such an eventuality would lead to the inevitable degradation of their society and would end in the two things they dreaded most: miscegenation and race war. This conviction that whites and free blacks could not live together meant that emancipation would match slavery as an evil, unless another home could be found for the newly freed blacks. Thus, even for antislavery southerners the race problem equaled the slave problem in horror and potential danger. The solution to the latter led to the former, for which they had no solution.

The reaction to efforts to put slaves in uniform when war came reveals how deeply white southerners dreaded the consequences of emancipation. In 1775 the royal governor of Virginia, Lord Dunmore, called for slaves to rally to the king's banner in return for ultimate emancipation. Enraged, Virginia and Maryland planters denounced Dunmore for his "diabolical schemes against good people," which threatened lives and property with "the *very scum* of the country." Planters feared not only the loss of slaves who might run away to join Dunmore; more to be feared were blacks with guns in their hands, aiming at them.

Similar proposals to make slaves soldiers of the Revolution generally failed. Some 5,000 blacks did take up arms against the king, but the vast majority came from the northern states. The southern states considered the employment of black slaves to fight for the freedom of whites, but as all recognized, such a step would have to result in freedom for blacks as well, at least for those who had borne arms. Besides, if the southern states placed weapons in the hands of slaves, would the British fail to follow suit, and would racial war not then compound the horrors that the conflict had already brought? The South could accept neither possibility. Only Maryland ever authorized the enlistment of slaves. Even in the face of military disaster, which surely loomed over the South in 1780, all other states remained adamantly opposed.

*T*HE DECISION TO REVOLT

While white southerners decided their future with slavery, they carried on their great conflict with England within the framework of southern politics. The men who led the southern colonies against Great Britain after 1763 were, for the most part, men of place and position. Although the crisis did provide an opportunity for the rise of new leaders, such as Patrick Henry, many of those who stood firm for the colonial position had been serving in assemblies or in other prominent posts. Such men as Henry Laurens had won the plaudits and respect of their fellow citizens from the Potomac to the Savannah.

These leaders of the southern colonies in revolt often did not agree on political timing and occasionally seemed to disagree even on the ultimate political goal. The particular stance taken did not depend on old or new prominence, though most recently prominent men advocated advanced positions. As firebrands of rebellion Patrick Henry and Christopher Gadsden early accepted the possibility that the colonials could secure their liberty only outside the British Empire. The cautious, careful Henry Laurens, by contrast, came slowly to a belief in political separation; he took that decisive step only after his experiences with the imperial customs system convinced him that a general corruption would indeed clamp slavery on him and his fellow colonials. In Georgia, Lachlan McIntosh, a planter and later wartime general, worried more about his financial prospects than about the question of empire until finally, in the winter of 1774–1775, British actions and the warnings of his friend Henry Laurens persuaded him that his continued liberty required participation in the rebellion. Though zealous in denouncing British threats to American liberty, Rawlins Lowndes, longtime leader in South Carolina politics, hoped against hope that the two sides could avoid a total break. In fact, not until 1776 did Lowndes back complete political independence.

Clearly, then, differences of opinion on a critical question existed among leading southerners. Emphasis on that difference and a focus on such terms as *radical* and *conservative*, however, can obscure a profound similarity among those southerners, from Henry to Lowndes. All of them spoke the same language, even with the same inflection. Each of them riveted his argument on the primary issue: liberty versus slavery. All of them agreed that the colonials must resist the Stamp Act, the Townshend duties, the Intolerable Acts; all of them insisted that the British must recognize the rights of the colonies. In sum, all concurred that the colonies and the colonists must protect themselves against what they described as the shackles of British slavery.

Southern leaders knew that no matter how mighty their effort against England, it would never succeed without widespread public support. To preserve the liberty they worshiped, they would have to arouse the public so that leaders and led shared the perception of a common danger to the freedom of all. Many of the southern elite wrote pamphlets spelling out the colonial position and castigating British machinations. Pamphlets were surely important, especially in expanding the colonial definition of liberty. Perhaps even more noteworthy in galvanizing the white masses of the South were oral appeals for the defense of precious liberty. Although this conclusion does not lend itself to ready proof, the nature of southern politics and the character of southern society strongly suggest its accuracy. The general sharing among white southerners of the liberty-slavery rhetoric bugled by speakers to their listeners certainly made simpler the task of leadership. All white southerners understood the vast chasm between freedom and slavery.

Revolutionary activity was emotional as well as practical, and the emotion injected into southern politics by spokesmen for independence had an enormous influence on those politics. It made careers. At the very beginning of his public career Patrick Henry made the elders of Virginia politics nervous. As a young member of the House of Burgesses in 1765 he startled them and aroused Virginia with a bold speech and forceful resolutions condemning the Stamp Act. Most senior burgesses agreed with Henry's position but not with his tactics. They feared that the excitement aroused by his eloquent tongue could jeopardize their control of the House as well as stimulate popular opposition to England. No matter the opinion of his elders, Henry stayed on his rhetorical course. Throughout the crisis he constantly rallied Virginians with his mighty outcries against British tyranny. And even if the story is apocryphal, his trumpet blast "Give me liberty or give me death!" dramatizes the passion of Henry's appeal. Unfortunately, only fragments of his powerful speeches have survived; most of what is known about them comes from people who heard them. Still, no doubt can exist about the power of his oratory. He stood as indisputably the greatest orator of the Revolution, and he still ranks as one of the greatest orators in all American history. Attempting to describe the magnificence of Henry's oratory, Thomas Jefferson called Henry the Homer of the spoken word. Soon the most popular political figure in Virginia, Henry was elected governor six times and enjoyed public adulation as well as public office until his death in 1799.

In Maryland the Revolutionary turmoil provided a similar political opportunity to Samuel Chase. An ambitious young lawyer, Chase had just begun his climb up the political ladder when news of the Stamp Act broke upon the colonies. Sensing the visceral opposition to the act, Chase seized the opening it provided him to win recognition as a champion of the people. Little by little he inched to the forefront of the colonial cause in Maryland. He excelled in the tumult and excitement of emotional politics. When the stamp-tax distributor for the colony arrived in Annapolis, a group of Chase's followers prevented his landing. Then Chase himself directed a mock burning and burial of the unfortunate official, who was ultimately hounded out of the colony by such tactics. From the Stamp Act forward into the Revolution, Chase solidified his position as a popular leader. He emerged not only as a chieftain of the Revolutionary cause but also as a powerful force in Maryland politics, a position he retained into the 1790s.

WAR BEGINS

When the war of words and of committees turned into a shooting war, the southern colonies joined the fight. The military conflict began in New England with a small engagement, hardly more than a skirmish. In April 1775 a British column with orders to capture or destroy munitions headed west out of Boston toward Concord, less than twenty miles away. Along the way at Lexington some seventy militiamen stood in opposition. Shots rang out; to this day who fired first is unknown. The British continued on to Concord, where they met another militia detachment, and again a brief fire-fight took place. The alarm was sounded and militiamen from the surrounding countryside gathered to strike the British. As the British returned to Boston, the militiamen harassed them all the way. War had begun—a great war that would last eight years and alter the course of history.

The next month the Second Continental Congress convened in Philadelphia. Accepting the fighting around Boston as the beginning of war, the Congress acted to protect American interests. The Congress moved in two directions. First, it created the Continental Army by authorizing the raising of troops to be sent to Boston. The Continental Army would become the mainstay of American military efforts in the long struggle against the British. Second, the Congress named a commanding general for the force it had created. It unanimously chose George Washington of Virginia, a forty-three-year-old slave owner and planter who had fought with the British in the French and Indian War. Washington promptly traveled northward to Cambridge, Massachusetts, where on July 3 he took command of American forces.

General Washington and the Continental Army, or the Continental Line, composed the national force in the Revolution. During the course of the Revolution more than 232,000 men eventually enlisted in the Continental Army, some 59,000 of them from the southern states. Of course General Washington never commanded this many men at any one time; during the last two years of the war, for example, the Continentals in service totaled just over 33,000. These units could be sent wherever the commanding general ordered and under the direction of any officer he named, subject to the agreement of Congress. Washington reported directly to the Congress. Ever conscious of the authority possessed by the Congress, Washington never attempted to substitute himself for it, though the action or inaction of the Congress often frustrated him. With Washington in command of the army there was never a hint that the military would usurp political power; he never challenged the ultimate authority of the Congress.

The Continental Line, however, could not alone stop the British. The Line could never man the far-flung battlefields of the Revolution against the much larger British force. Augmenting the Continentals and performing an essential service for the American cause were the state militias. Enlistments in the various militias numbered 145,000 throughout the eight years between 1775 and 1783; the southern states accounted for around 80,000 of that total. But far fewer were available at any one time. Each state had a militia that had been created during the colonial period. Its units owed and paid allegiance not to the Second Continental Congress but to the governor and legislature of their state. Although the militias provided essential manpower in numerous critical situations, they generally retained the right to conduct their own affairs. Usually they operated within state borders and crossed those lines only when state authorities permitted such movements. With George Washington, the Continental Army, and the several militias, the Americans prepared to face regulars of the British army supplemented by German mercenaries hired by the royal government to help put down the rebellion.

The war did not spread rapidly throughout the colonies. New England, chiefly the immediate Boston area, was the first battlefield. The major campaigns of 1776 and 1777 took place in New Jersey, New York, and Pennsylvania. The first substantial action in the South occurred in June 1776 when the British failed in an assault on Charleston Harbor. Two and a half years later, however, in December 1778, the British claimed their first significant southern triumph when they captured Savannah. Still, for the first five years of the Revolutionary War the South remained a distinctly secondary theater.

THE SOUTHERN WAR

The situation changed dramatically in 1780; now the South became the chief battleground. As early as 1778 the British began planning for a substantial southern thrust. The precise aims of their strategy remained unclear. Their initial goal, the capture of a significant seaport to serve as a supply base, made absolute sense, but after that task was accomplished the British strategists never had a clear sense of either the appropriate next step or their ultimate military aim, other than the general goal of ending the rebellion.

The British southern strategy began gloriously. In March 1780 a force of some 12,000 men commanded by Major General Sir Henry Clinton moved against Charleston, the largest city and port in the South. With the assistance of the royal navy Clinton laid siege to Charleston, defended by more than 6,500 troops under Major General Benjamin Lincoln. After two months, on May 12, 1780, Lincoln surrendered his entire command. Charleston was to remain in British hands for the duration of the war.

The fall of Charleston resulted in the greatest British victory of the war, yet the British failed to follow up their magnificent triumph. Clinton decided to divide his force and his effort. With one-third of his army, Clinton returned to New York. Behind in Charleston he left Major General Charles Lord Cornwallis with 8,000 soldiers; Cornwallis had instructions to defend Charleston and to disrupt all American activities in South Carolina. He was also to render every assistance to the British loyalists in the state.

Distressed by the turn of events in the South, the Continental Congress acted to shore up the American position. To restore American fortunes the Congress chose Major General Horatio Gates, a hero of the 1777 victory at Saratoga. In North Carolina in July Gates assumed command of a reconstituted Army of the Southern Department. Immediately he headed his army into South Carolina and toward Charleston. Alerted that a new enemy was in the field, Cornwallis marched westward from Charleston to confront Gates. On August 16 just north of the village of Camden the two armies met. Although he outnumbered Cornwallis almost 2 to 1, Gates's hastily organized force, heavily dependent upon militiamen, was no match for Cornwallis's troops. When the British advanced with fixed bayonets, the militiamen panicked and fled from the field, with Gates alongside. Gates's Continentals fought well but were overwhelmed; American casualties were twice those of the British. Following so quickly upon the loss of Charleston, the disaster at Camden seemed to give the South to the

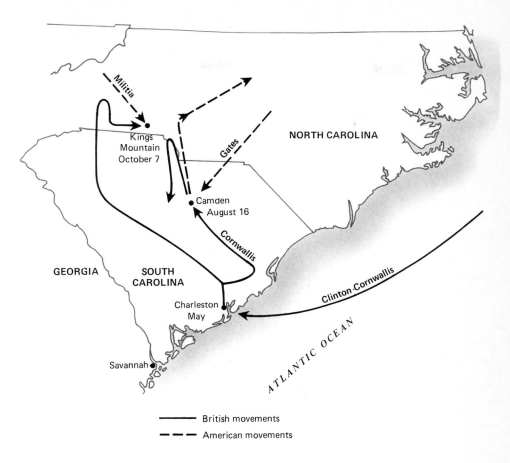

Kings
Mountain
October 7

Militia

Gates

NORTH CAROLINA

Camden
August 16

Cornwallis

GEORGIA

SOUTH
CAROLINA

Charleston
May

Clinton-Cornwallis

Savannah

ATLANTIC OCEAN

——————— British movements

– – – – American movements

SOUTHERN CAMPAIGNS, 1780

British. The American side, however, did not cave in. After Camden, Cornwallis sent a detachment of almost 1,000 men to sweep the western Carolinas. Responding, around 1,000 militiamen from both Carolinas, Virginia, and Georgia met the British on October 7 at Kings Mountain, in northwestern South Carolina, and smashed them. Cornwallis's work was not yet done.

The war in the South was not restricted to organized field armies. In fact, often the most vicious and bloody contests took place between detachments of loyalists, or tories, who fought for the British, and bands of Americans, who called themselves patriots. In the Carolinas and Georgia bitter civil strife sparked a nasty guerrilla war. Tories were found in every colony, in the North as well as the South, but they were especially strong in the Carolinas and Georgia. Toryism cut across social lines. Wealthy seacoast planters and merchants in both Carolinas stood by their king. Many backcounty farmers also supported the royalist cause. The reasons were undoubtedly complex; among the most vigorous tories were Scots Highlanders who had migrated to the Carolinas in the mid-eighteenth century.

Tories did more than profess loyalty to the crown; they took up arms against the rebellion. In almost every major contest in the Carolinas and Georgia, tory units accounted for a significant portion of the British army. Without them the British would have had a much more difficult task. At the same time, the tories' willingness to fight for the British pitted neighbors and friends against each other in what was almost fratricidal conflict.

At times the patriot-tory contest almost became a war of extermination. In February 1781 a group of patriots in North Carolina practically massacred some four hundred tories moving to reinforce Cornwallis. The patriots, wearing uniforms similar to those of British solders, mounted a saber attack on the unsuspecting loyalists as they waited along a road for what they thought was the passage of a British unit. The butchery resulted in 90 dead and 150 wounded. Even prisoners were not safe; some were hacked to pieces with broadswords. The tories responded in kind. One of the most successful and brutal tory leaders, William "Bloody Bill" Cunningham, operated in mid-South Carolina. Bloody Bill supposedly developed his mighty hatred for all patriots after a band of them murdered his brother. His thirst for retaliation knew no limits. In November 1781 he and a raiding party attacked about fifteen patriots barricaded in a fortified house. After several hours of hard fighting, Cunningham set the house on fire, forcing the little garrison to surrender. Cunningham promptly hanged the leader, but the improvised gallows broke, leaving its intended victim dazed but alive. Bloody Bill reacted swiftly: he ran the fellow through with his sword. Following his lead, Bloody Bill's men killed all the other prisoners.

The viciousness of the tory-patriot war could have become even more terrible had the Indians living on the Carolina-Georgia frontier become combatants for either the British or the Americans. Certainly in 1775 neither side could predict the path the Indians might follow. After years of intrusion by whites into Indian territory, Indians had reason to distrust them all. The British were eager for the Indians' involvement, but only under their guidance and direction. They had no interest in any independent action the Indians might undertake. The Americans wanted the Indians to stay out of the conflict because they feared the physical and psychological impact of Indian war parties ranging across the backcountry of Georgia and the Carolinas. To keep the Indians at bay they played on tribal factionalism and distributed copious supplies of "rum and good words."

The nature of the Indian front was settled early on. In 1776 the British persuaded the Cherokees, the dominant tribe in the region, to attack the Carolina frontier. In June the Indians hit; they destroyed property, took prisoners, and killed several dozen whites. The Americans called up some 6,000 men to punish the Indians. The chief contingent, more than 1,000 men under South Carolina leadership, marched into Cherokee country and by late summer had destroyed all the Cherokee towns in their path. This offensive broke the power and the will of the Cherokees. Other tribes, aware of what had happened to the Cherokees, never became major participants. White frontier families remained alert, however; raids were always possible, and sometimes they materialized. This reality kept some of the frontier militiamen in their home district. Still, after the Cherokee incident of 1776 the southern Indian front remained basically quiet.

THE ADVENT OF NATHANAEL GREENE

In the aftermath of Gates's disaster at Camden, Congress acted to strengthen the American cause in the South. The Congress recognized that something had to be done to revive the military effort there. In part because its past choices of commanders, including Generals Lincoln and Gates, had been so spectacularly unsuccessful, Congress asked General Washington to choose a new commander for the southern army. In October Washington picked Nathanael Greene, a Rhode Island native, then quartermaster general of his army. The thirty-eight-year-old Greene, standing just under six feet, with broad shoulders and a florid complexion, headed south. In early December, at Charlotte, North Carolina, he took over the remnant of Gates's force, no more than 1,500 men. Greene confronted a military situation that would have tested the ablest commander. His army was a wreck and supplies and morale were low. The very desperation of the situation in the Charlotte camp necessitated action. Greene divided his small army and sent one portion to eastern South Carolina, the other under Daniel Morgan to the western part of the state. Although dividing his army violated the maxims of military textbooks, Greene believed the action essential for the sustenance of his men. Moreover, the division might cause Cornwallis to split his own forces, thus making Charleston vulnerable to a quick strike.

Cornwallis had become increasingly unhappy with the restrictions placed on him by Clinton. Clinton had ordered him to disrupt American activities in South Carolina, even to pacify the state, but also to hold to his base at Charleston and guarantee its security. Cornwallis, however, came to believe that he could not quiet South Carolina until all possibility of aid from neighboring North Carolina and even Virginia had been eliminated. He proposed to eliminate it by breaking away from his base at Charleston and driving against Greene and anyone else who was out there.

Cornwallis confronted two basic problems. First, he had to decide how to contend with Greene's force, the major field army against him. Greene complicated matters when he divided his troops. Second, his forces had to march and camp in country that was home to numerous patriot bands, some of them led by superb guerrilla fighters. Such commanders as Francis Marion (the famous Swamp Fox), Thomas Sumter, and Andrew Pickens made life utterly miserable for Cornwallis and his soldiers. Dispatch riders disappeared; patrols and scouting parties were ambushed; supply trains ended up in patriot hands; cavalry detachments were routinely cut up, even slaughtered. And after rapid, brutal strikes the patriots melted away into the forests and swamps. The British could not bring these guerrillas out into the open for a conventional fight, in which their own superior numbers and weaponry could give them the advantage.

Deciding that Greene was his chief enemy, Cornwallis focused on him. He followed his opponent's lead by sending a detachment to defeat the portion of Greene's army in western South Carolina. In mid-January the Americans and British met at Cowpens, where, in a minor tactical masterpiece, combined Continental-militia units under Daniel Morgan defeated the British-tory force. At the news from Cowpens, both commanders rushed to unify their forces. Greene saw an opportunity to strike Cornwallis's main army, and Cornwallis was determined to catch and punish Morgan. Learning that a reunited British force had advanced into North Carolina, Greene retreated. Although he would have preferred to stand and fight, Greene listened to his subordinates, including Morgan, who warned him that their tired, poorly supplied troops were in no condition to face the united British army.

Across the North Carolina piedmont the two armies moved until Greene crossed into Virginia. There Greene heard that Cornwallis had rallied to his colors a large number of loyalists. With these reinforcements he might be able to bring both Carolinas under tight British control. These reports were exaggerated, but Greene believed he had no choice but to head back into North Carolina. He and Cornwallis met in battle for the first time on March 15, 1781, at Guilford Courthouse, North Carolina, just north of Greensboro. The Americans had superiority in numbers but the British had the more professional and dis-

GENERAL NATHANAEL GREENE, COMMANDER IN THE SOUTH, 1781 (Independence National Historical Park Collection)

ciplined troops. After a hard, at times savage fight, Greene gave way and ordered a retreat. But Cornwallis was too bloodied to take advantage of his battlefield success. After Guilford Courthouse the two armies that had been
fighting or chasing each other for four months marched away from each other.

This turnabout resulted chiefly from Cornwallis's needs and his ambitions.
Even though he commanded the field after Guilford Courthouse, he was in no
position to follow up his tactical victory. After weeks of marching and fighting,
his army required refurbishing and resupply. In order to get that essential task
done, Cornwallis had to return to the coast and a British base. Thus he headed
for the nearest port: Wilmington, North Carolina. From there Cornwallis in-

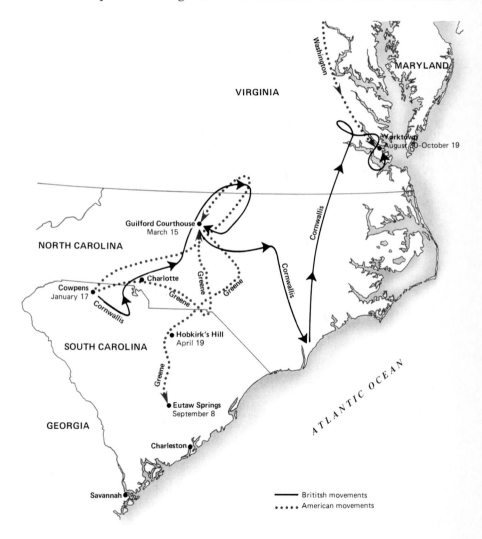

SOUTHERN CAMPAIGNS, 1781

formed Clinton in New York that his campaign had been a raging success. This wildly inflated claim did not deceive Clinton. Determined to recoup his military fortunes and enhance his own fame, Cornwallis decided to take his army up into Virginia. Greene was looking in the opposite direction. With Cornwallis in Wilmington, he saw the way open to Charleston and started his troops southward. Even though Cornwallis was under orders to protect Charleston and had been informed of Greene's movements, he headed for Virginia and hoped-for glory.

Cornwallis's shift to Virginia did not leave Greene a completely open road to Charleston, for various British and loyalist units still remained in South Carolina. In April a British detachment stopped Greene at Hobkirk's Hill, just north of Camden, almost at the site of Gates's debacle. But Greene was only momentarily halted; he kept his army together and on the scene. Moreover, an aroused countryside increased problems for the British. In the summer Greene continued on and in September he struck the British again at Eutaw Springs, no more than fifty miles from Charleston. Although Eutaw Springs ended as basically a tactical draw, Greene pushed onward. By the end of 1781 the British in South Carolina found themselves confined largely to Charleston. Except for Savannah and Charleston, both Carolinas and Georgia were securely in American hands. Nathanael Greene had performed masterfully. By keeping his army together, by using the partisans, by hard fighting, and with a clear sense of his purpose, he turned disaster into triumph.

YORKTOWN

While Greene crept closer to Charleston, Cornwallis assumed command of all British forces in southern Virginia. Cornwallis finally posted his 7,000 troops at Yorktown, on the York River just up from the Chesapeake Bay. There he thought the royal navy could easily reinforce and resupply him, or if need be evacuate him to New York. Cornwallis's chief goal, however, had nothing to do with evacuation. He wanted to mount a campaign in the interior of Virginia, the state he now designated as the main theater of the war.

But George Washington, sitting in New York state, had other plans. For six years the Virginian had been fighting in the North; now he saw an opportunity to hit the British hard in his native state. The key to his hopes was the expected arrival of the French fleet in American waters. When the French had learned of the American victory at Saratoga in 1777, they had seen in an alliance with the victors a splendid opportunity to strike at their old enemy, England. They had been helping the struggling Americans since 1778. In August 1781, Washington learned that the French fleet would appear in the Chesapeake. The possibility of a Franco-American combined land-sea attack on Cornwallis excited him. Immediately he set his plans in motion. With most of his troops he headed for Virginia, though he left a small force to demonstrate against New York City and mask his primary movement.

By late September, Washington had arrived in front of Yorktown. His army, strengthened by 3,000 French soldiers who had accompanied the fleet, totaled some 9,000 troops, the largest he had ever led. An attempt by the royal navy to relieve Cornwallis was stopped by the French fleet. With superior numbers and artillery, Washington decided on a siege to take Yorktown. Finally on October 19, 1781, Cornwallis surrendered. Clad in new uniforms, the British troops marched to the surrender ceremony with their bands playing melancholy tunes, including one aptly titled "The World Turned Upside Down." Yorktown was the greatest American military victory of the Revolution.

Today we consider the triumph at Yorktown to mark the end of the Revolutionary War, but at the time that eventuality was not so clear. In fact, the war continued until the peace treaty was finally completed and adopted more than a year later. The great significance of Yorktown lay in its power to persuade the British government to abandon its effort to end the Revolution by force and to begin negotiations. Those negotiations took place in Europe and did not produce a final treaty until September 1783. Meanwhile, skirmishes continued in the South throughout 1782. The British presence did not end until December 1782, when the British garrison finally sailed out of Charleston Harbor.

THE IMPACT OF THE WAR

The Treaty of Paris, ratified by Congress in April 1783, formalized the independence the United States had won on the battlefield. A new nation joined the ranks of independent states. The future development of the southern states could never be totally separated from the country they had helped create. In 1783 southerners, like all other Americans, rejoiced that they had successfully turned back Britain's effort to keep them politically dependent. After eight long years of warfare the Americans had prevailed, but the Revolution surely left its imprint on them.

The human cost cannot be tallied with any real precision. Thousands of soldiers from the southern states in both the Continental Line and militia units were killed or wounded on various battlefields. Their families had to learn to cope with their loss and make their way in the world without their dead sons, brothers, husbands, fathers. Although eighteenth-century campaigns largely spared civilians, the fury of the partisan war surely reached to noncombatants. The impossibility of obtaining precise numbers makes it extremely difficult to assess the effect of war-related casualties on the South. Certainly the human damage of the Revolution, though powerful to those directly involved, did not even begin to approach the trauma suffered by the South in 1865. The evidence does not indicate that the human price of the Revolution seriously hindered the course of the South.

The southern countryside largely escaped any substantial or long-lasting physical damage. The British army never adopted a systematic policy of destroying homes, fields, villages, or towns. Eighteenth-century armies generally did not engage in widespread destruction. The leading southern cities also emerged relatively unscathed. In Charleston, for example, some homes and buildings were destroyed during the siege, but the city remained largely intact at the end of the war. An overwhelmingly rural and agricultural area, the South did not present numerous obvious targets. Without a vigorous scorched-earth policy, which the British never adopted, little chance existed for massive destruction in the South. And it did not occur.

Even the often brutal tory-patriot conflict did not massively scar the landscape, but it did lead to harsh action against the tories. Most states banished those who had been especially active on the side of the Crown. When the last British troops pulled out of the various states, many loyalists went with them. Although practices varied among the states, all of them confiscated tory property. In Maryland alone the value of confiscated tory lands amounted to more than £500,000. Without question tories lost millions of pounds, chiefly in land, to the victors.

The British did not raze the southern countryside, but they did affect slavery. Recognizing slaves as valuable assets to their enemies, the British acted wherever they could to deprive the Americans of their slaves. Occasionally, as in the Lord Dunmore episode, the British promised freedom for slaves who left their American owners. More often the British impressed slaves to perform various tasks for the British army in areas they swept or controlled. The British were not seriously promoting emancipation; they perceived their actions as injuring their foes. Certainly thousands of slaves ended up under British control, and many never returned to their owners. When the British evacuated Charleston, they took more than 5,000 slaves with them; another 4,000 left Savannah with British troops. Many of those unfortunates ended up in slavery in the Caribbean or East Florida, though some found freedom in Canada. But for their former American owners the result was loss.

In the South, however, slavery survived. And survival, after the ideological turmoil and the military operations, underscored the importance of slavery to the South and, even more important, the widespread conviction among southerners that slavery was permanent. In the year of the Declaration of Independence, 1776, Henry Laurens declared that he could not liberate his slaves because his neighbors would identify him as "a promoter not only of strange, but of dangerous doctrines." A decade later Thomas Jefferson agreed only with great reluctance to the publication of his *Notes on Virginia*, which contained Virginia-style antislavery sentiments. Originally he had intended only a small, anonymous edition for private circulation; Jefferson feared that wider distribution of the work under his name would produce an adverse reaction that might fasten slavery even more tightly to Virginia and the South. Laurens's concerned inaction and Jefferson's troubled hesitation make it abundantly clear that the force of Revolutionary rhetoric, ideology, and even war had moved the South no closer to the abandonment of slavery. In fact, the opposite occurred. In 1784 and 1785 more than 1,200 Virginians signed petitions to the assembly protesting the private manumission act of 1782. Thus Jefferson worried needlessly; slavery was already powerfully attached to his Virginia. With slavery having withstood the cumulative force of the Revolution, the white South emerged from the experience more consciously committed to slavery than it had ever been before.

SLAVERY AND LIBERTY

This vigorous commitment to black slavery did not diminish the South's fervor for white liberty. White southerners had made a revolution in the name of liberty. Victorious, they had a voracious appetite for the precious commodity they had preserved. Thus southerners simultaneously loved liberty and maintained slavery. To explain this irony some historians have argued that slavery paved the way for southern faith in republicanism by eliminating the lowest class of whites, who otherwise could have threatened the stability and unity of the social order. The whites, all of whom stood above the slaves economically and socially, joined together to give thanks for the enslaved blacks, who made harmony and republicanism, and thus liberty, possible for whites. Other scholars have pointed out that the love of liberty also flourished in such places as Massachusetts, where slavery was inconsequential. They have also emphasized that numerous southerners saw slavery as a blight on the republicanism of the South even as they could envision no way to be rid of it. The critical fact, however, lies in the powerful influence slavery had on the southern attitude toward liberty. It mattered not at all whether white southerners viewed slavery as the foundation of their liberty or as a moral curse. All of them, both those who bemoaned slavery and those who supported it, saw slavery as a condition to be avoided at all hazards, no matter the cost.

Thus their acute awareness of slavery led white southerners to a highly developed sense of liberty. Noting the universality of a "high sense of personal independence" among white Virginians, Edmund Randolph, one of them, thought it derived from the "system of slavery," which nurtured a "quick and acute sense of personal liberty, a disdain for every abridgement of personal independence." White southerners embraced liberty with an all-consuming passion, a passion that had powerful political manifestations. The first great manifestation came when slave owners led the South into the Revolution. Political revolutions against legitimate authority are not normally led by the dominant economic and social class of a society. Yet in the colonial South men of great wealth were revolutionaries. The names of such men as Charles Carroll of Carrollton, George Washington, James Iredell, Henry Laurens, and Lachlan McIntosh head a long list of the elite in every colony. No, these individuals and their peers did not advocate a social revolution that would destroy their privilege or their future. Still, they strode with open eyes into war against the greatest military power of their time, a war all recognized as a war of revolution. When they accepted war, they risked not only their personal safety but also their position and property in possible social unheaval and economic catastrophe. These wealthy slave owners made a revolution because they believed it essential to protect themselves from the despicable yoke of slavery. But their war for their own liberty never meant liberty for their slaves. Quite the contrary—the triumph that secured their liberty tightened the bonds on their slaves. From 1776 to 1860 the liberty white southerners celebrated always included the freedom to preserve the slavery of blacks.

THE FORM AND SUBSTANCE OF POLITICS

Just as the Revolution had a profound impact on slavery, it significantly influenced the course of southern politics. The rampant emotionalism of Revolutionary politics fundamentally affected political affairs. Throughout the years between the Revolution and the Civil War, southern politics was an emotional business. At every critical instant politicians stepped forward with historical choruses to the performances of the Patrick Henrys and the Samuel Chases. Repeatedly the appeal to emotion made careers and shaped momentous decisions.

The rhetoric of the Revolution imparted to southern politics more than emotion. Its substance also enjoyed a long, prosperous political life. Appeals to the people accenting the fragility of their liberty and emphasizing the threat of various demons to obliterate it filled southern editorials, platforms, pamphlets, and podiums right down to 1860. No political cause could hope to succeed unless it gave a clear signal that its primary goal was to guarantee the liberty of the people, a liberty that for white southerners was always entwined with slavery.

While the Revolution influenced the character of southern politics, it also modified its structure. The participatory politics that had characterized the colonial South weathered the storm of the Revolution, but not without significant alterations. A decade and more of emphasis on the rights of all citizens modified the equation of democracy and deference that equaled participatory politics. The experience of war added to the democratic side of the equation. This additional weight was evident in the changing attitude of the lower classes toward the upper, in the kinds of men who assumed political responsibility, and in the very basis of government.

Because of the Revolution, white southerners of the lower social orders began to question the deference they had previously shown to their social betters. When dealing with such broad societal attitudes the focus has to be on trends, not absolutes. In the colonial period some lower-class southerners had surely refused to fit neatly into their expected role; just as surely after the Revolution many others continued to feel comfortable with the old deferential ways. But the Revolution did spawn a general shift away from deference, a shift illustrated by an episode in South Carolina in 1784.

In that year the South Carolina assembly threatened to banish from the state one William Thompson, a tavernkeeper, for insulting John Rutledge, a former governor and a prominent figure in the ruling group. In a public address defending himself Thompson stood deference on its head. Acknowledging that Rutledge "conceived me his inferior," Thompson announced that he could not understand Rutledge's attitude. As a former officer in the Revolutionary army, Thompson said, he was asking for no more than the respect he deserved. Calling himself "a *wretch* of no higher rank in the Commonwealth than that of Common-Citizen" and identifying himself with "those who...go at this day, under the opprobrious appelation of, the *Lower Orders of Men*," Thompson pitched into "*John Rutledge*, or any of the NABOB *tribe*," who claim "to compose the grand hierachy of the State." Thompson argued that an independent people required leaders who were "*good, able, useful* and *friends to social equality*," and nothing more. Not only did Thompson fail to act deferentially, he assaulted the citadel of deferential government.

More and more men who shared William Thompson's views began to populate the assemblies, or legislatures, as they came to be called. In Virginia the number of wealthy men in the legislature declined by half after the war. In Maryland and South Carolina, too, more ordinary citizens sought and won election to the legislature. Military leadership brought to prominence such rough-hewn, untutored men as Elijah Clarke of Georgia. A backcountry guerrilla leader, Clarke used his wartime reputation to embark on a notable postwar career in his state. Individuals such as Clarke would probably not have become important figures before 1775. The war breached forever the old walls of political leadership as the sanctuary of the privileged.

The disestablishment of the Anglican church also contributed to the weakening of deference. Everywhere in the 1780s legislatures dismantled the legal framework that had given Anglicanism a special place in southern life. When the church lost its privileges, the gentry lost one of the props that elevated it above the common people. While the Anglican church lost its status as the established church, the evangelical denominations surged across the South. Led by the Baptists and the Methodists, these churches brought increasingly large numbers of southerners into their folds. Emphasizing individualism and shunning any trappings of rank or privilege, the evangelicals offered only meager assistance to a concept of deference already beleaguered by secular forces. Although most of the political leaders in the late eighteenth century still retained their Anglican ties, the increasing political influence of the evangelicals testified to the rapid growth of their congregations.

The arrival of this new kind of public man did not escape the notice of the traditional ruling class. Many of them echoed the dismay expressed by a Virginian when he saw "men not quite so well dressed, nor so politely educated, nor so highly born" take their legislative seats. Henry Laurens complained that the new legislators, knowing nothing of parliamentary procedure, thought government required "no more words than are necessary in the bargain and sale of a cow." The Henry Laurenses also feared that their new associates might not be amenable to control by the gentry.

That fear was justified, to a point. Although no social revolution took place in any southern state, the new men in the legislatures certainly made their presence felt. Largely at their behest, legislatures in every southern state but Georgia reformed regressive tax structures. The chief reform, repealing a land tax based on acreage and substituting an ad valorem land tax, headlined a generally successful effort to base taxes more on wealth than on individuals or acreage alone.

The Revolution also modified the basis of government. A common theme ran through the state making and constitutional writing that pervaded the entire country during the war years. Southerners as well as other Americans gave all but complete power to their assemblies or legislatures. Each state had an executive that all eventually called the governor, but he had practically no authority. Basically a figurehead, the governor, though often a man of prominence and popularity, was deprived even of the veto. This political emasculation of the executive was a reaction to royal governors and to the king, executives both and, of course, integral parts of the British imperial system. Neither had absolute power, and in the colonies the royal governor shared power with the colonial assembly, which had increased its prerogatives considerably by the time of the Revolution. Still, the royal governor had power; he could terminate a legislative session and could veto legislation. In theory even more than practice, the assemblies were only a part of a large governmental machine. But during the Revolutionary crisis the cries of liberty for the people and the shouts that the people must rule merged to underwrite full authority for the legislature, the hall of the people. In the legislature sat southerners of all kinds, who as voices of the people and guardians of their liberty controlled public affairs in their states.

This democratic turn did not signify the death of deference, not at all. A great name, family, and wealth remained important. These attributes still commanded respect from multitudes of southerners, and they continued to provide the surest ticket to political advancement. The great debate in the late 1770s and 1780s over the proper relationship between the southern states and the central government of the infant United States conclusively confirmed the ongoing authority of the traditional southern ruling class.

A NATIONAL SETTING

Just as the rhetoric and ideology of the Revolution forced the South to ponder slavery, political organization for the Revolution obliged the South for the first time to consider itself as part of a larger political whole. Before the First Continental Congress in 1774, no single political group or institution devoted to making policy for all the colonies had existed in British North America. The convening of the Second Continental Congress in 1775 reinforced the new departure in colonial politics. Then with the Declaration of Independence promulgated by the Congress in 1776, the Congress asserted itself as the political voice of the new United States of America. Thus in only two years a marked transformation in governance had taken place.

Until 1774 each colony was a single polity loyal to London, whence came general political direction. Although all the colonies had shared certain patterns of development and although groupings of colonies—the southern, New England—had common institutions, each acted as an individual political entity. The colonies saw no need to adjust competing goals or to reconcile differences with one another because no common political center existed to direct the course of thirteen colonies as one political unit. But the union of all the colonies in the rebellion against England changed that long-standing political situation.

The Second Continental Congress, which assumed direction of the war effort—at first by common agreement, then under the Articles of Confederation—had to make decisions and formulate policies for a union of all the states, not for a single state or a group of states. In this new environment delegates from the thirteen states sitting in Congress had to face the political reality that the interests of the states they represented often diverged. The southern delegates certainly discovered this fact of political life, and the discovery necessarily led to the adoption of identifiable political positions.

The Second Continental Congress, which first convened in 1775, served as the government of the United States until the implementation of the Constitution almost a decade and a half later. This Congress had to wage war and simultaneously devise a plan of government that would give the country more than an ad hoc regime. To wage war it had to collect money and decide on war aims; to plan a government it had to sanction a method of taxation and fix the location of sovereignty, or ultimate authority. Although Congress began to debate the form of a permanent government in 1776, not until late in 1777 did it agree on the Articles of Confederation and transmit the document to the states for consideration. With attention fixed on the war, four years passed before all thirteen states approved the Articles. During those years, the southern delegates in Congress identified the interests of their states and acted to safeguard them. As the Marylander Samuel Chase informed the Congress as early as 1776, "We [the South] shall be governed by our interests, and ought to be."

Slavery dominated those interests. To southerners, whether or not slavery continued to exist was not a fit subject for congressional debate. In July 1776—the very month independence was declared—a South Carolinian put it boldly to Congress: "If it is debated whether slaves are their property, there is an end of the confederation." While among themselves white southerners discussed their future with black slaves, albeit in generally muted fashion, they had no intention of allowing any nonsoutherners to enter their conversation. The southerners got what they demanded: the Congress never directly threatened the sanctity of slavery.

Southerners' concern with slavery, however, extended beyond the security of the institution itself. Because the Articles did not give it the power to tax, Congress had to rely on funds supplied by the states or requisitioned from them. In debating how much money should come from each state, Congress considered basing the amount on the populations of the states. The southern delegates immediately raised objections to any formula that counted slaves on an equal basis with whites. Expressing the views of his fellow southern delegates, Samuel Chase minced neither words nor sentiment. Chase told Congress that slaves were property just like any other property; as such, they should not be considered members of political society any more than livestock, because "they have no more interest in it." No matter the importance of slavery to the South, southerners had no intention of permitting their slaves to become a national asset, available to pay the costs of Congress and country. Congress finally had to abandon the attempt to include slaves in any requisition plan. Just as adamantly the southern delegates refused to consider slaves as part of their population for purposes of troop assessments.

This congressional discussion about the position of slavery dramatized the new world that the southern states and southerners had entered. With the Revolution won and the United States established, the shaping of the new nation assumed paramount importance.

5

The South in the New Nation

❖

Many historians of the South have argued over the beginnings of southern distinctiveness, over when the South began to exhibit the unique features and common attitudes that by the mid-nineteenth century set it apart from the rest of the country. Various scholars have located this allegedly momentous occurrence at various points in time. This issue, however, is misleading. Distinct characteristics of the South, such as plantation agriculture and black slavery, began in the seventeenth century. The conscious commitment to slavery made by the South during the Revolutionary crisis simply confirmed the powerful place slavery had come to occupy in the preceding century. The suggestion that in one year or at one time a particular southern distinctiveness appeared is misguided. Yet in the 1770s and the 1780s southerners did begin to speak of themselves as southerners.

No one articulated this view of southernness more clearly than the Virginian Thomas Jefferson. For the benefit of a French writer, Jefferson in 1785 spelled out what he called "my idea of the character of the several states." He sharply separated northern and southern characteristics. Northerners he described as "cool, sober, laborious, . . . jealous of their own liberties, and just to others." Southerners, by contrast, were "fiery, Voluptuary, indolent, . . . zealous for their own liberties, but trampling on those of others." Whether or not Jefferson's assessment was correct is less important than his conviction that he could identify distinctions between North and South.

Southerners also began to think in terms of specific southern interests. This development was part of a general process that was unfolding everywhere under the influence of the Continental Congress and the war. During this period observers elsewhere began to speak of the South as a distinctive region. Even so, nothing fundamental had changed in the southern states; southern economic and social institutions remained basically what they had been. Change had taken place, but beyond the borders of the southern states. With the Con-

101

tinental Congress and the Articles of Confederation representing a union of American states, southerners found themselves in a new arena that demanded a new assessment of themselves and their interests.

SELF-INTEREST

In the immediate postwar period southerners identified interests other than slavery and taxation. Tobacco, rice, and other commodities found their greatest market beyond the South. With the British Empire no longer governing trade, new patterns had to appear. Southerners knew they would not be transporting their own goods, for shipping was not one of the South's strengths. The mercantile community in the North, with its vigorous shipping industry, wanted Congress empowered to regulate external and internal commerce, the latter known as the coasting trade—the movement of goods between American ports. Many southerners objected because they feared Congress might exclude foreign ships from the coasting trade, leaving southern trade and prosperity at the mercy of northern merchants. Southerners pressed for competition among shippers, whom they expected to be eager for their business. Western trade issues also concerned southerners. The ongoing drive to the West made the South acutely aware of the Mississippi River, which was absolutely critical to the prosperity of Kentucky and Tennessee. People on both sides of the Appalachians recognized that central truth. Almost all southerners considered access to the Mississippi essential.

This belief in the intimate relationship between southern destiny and the Mississippi explains southerners' fierce opposition to the proposed Jay-Gardoqui Treaty of 1786. The treaty grew out of discussions between John Jay of New York, the American foreign secretary, and Diego de Gardoqui, the Spanish minister to the United States. Jay wanted to boost American commerce while Gardoqui wanted to arrest American expansion. In possession of Florida and Louisiana, Spain feared encroachment on its empire by the vigorous young nation to the north. The two diplomats reached an agreement that had the Mississippi as its fulcrum. In return for the United States' renunciation of claims to navigate the Mississippi for twenty-five years, Spain would open its markets to American commerce. The South was stunned. The government seemed to have no regard for southern interests. United southern opposition guaranteed that Jay and the proponents of the treaty could never muster the nine votes they needed for congressional ratification. To southerners the episode said that the North was ready to sacrifice southern concerns on the altar of its commercial desires.

Perceiving clearly their common interests, southerners also understood that they often clashed with those of the North. A southerner in Congress in 1782 referred to "these great struggles between Northern and Southern interests." In the same year the nationally minded Virginian James Madison noted that southern congressmen exhibited "an habitual jealously [*sic*] of a predominance of Eastern interests."

The recognition of particular southern concerns extended beyond the political leadership to southern voters, who expected their leaders to protect their interests. Although under the Articles the actual voters for congressional delegates were legislators, they spoke for the citizens who had placed them in the legislatures. Challengers for public office were quick to charge incumbents with negligence in safeguarding the South. No politician, no matter his name, experience, or reputation, could exempt himself from the requirement that he stand as a sentinel for the South. The enemies of Richard Henry Lee, who in 1776 had introduced in Congress the resolution for independence, charged in the Virginia legislature that he "favored New England to the injury of Virginia." Lee thought this accusation "so contemptibly wicked" that he did not want to take the time to refute it. But he did, and his defense was offense. To his political enemies he cried, "I defy the poisonous tongue of slander to produce a single instance in which I have preferred the interest of N.E. to that of Virg." Despite this challenge, the charge that Lee was less than zealous in safeguarding southern interests almost cost him his seat in Congress. If the southern issue could threaten a leader as notable as Lee, it could surely have an enormous impact on men with lesser reputations.

A distinct sectional consciousness can be seen in the voting patterns of southern congressmen. Students of the Continental Congress have identified a southern voting alignment that became increasingly evident as the 1770s gave way to the 1780s. By the mid-1780s southern congressmen had achieved such cohesion in their voting that the South was able to dominate the Congress. New England and the middle states also tended to vote in concert, but they did not match the South in solidarity. In sum, southerners identified their special interests in a larger arena and acted vigorously to uphold their position.

UNITY AND DISUNITY

The congressional consensus on areas of critical concern to the South did not mean that southerners knew no political disunity. Southerners, like all other Americans, disagreed over a variety of issues in the 1780s, and they split most markedly over financial matters. Such disputes pervaded the country. Although the disputes focused on state finances, the financial question ultimately had national implications.

Though the particulars of financial politics varied from state to state, an underlying cause provided thematic unity to the arguments over money. Rampant inflation fueled by the issuing of paper money during the Revolution had been replaced by vigorous deflation after the war. As the amount of paper currency in circulation declined, the importance of specie, or "hard money," increased. Specie was scarce in the South. The shortage of money led to hard times and anger and tough legislative fights. Almost everywhere the general financial issue assumed a political shape of two dimensions: taxes and debts.

The debate over taxation focused on two issues: the tax structure—on what basis should taxes be assessed?—and whether or not taxes should be high enough to meet the levies requested by Congress. Though southern legislatures engaged in some restructuring of state taxes, they generally refused to meet requests from Congress. State officials knew that their economies would suffer under the pressure of additional taxes. These officials also knew that they would personally suffer the wrath of hard-pressed constituents if voters were saddled with higher taxes to pay for a central government that was enthusiastically supported by very few.

In their financial distress many southerners clamored for legislative relief from debt payment as well as from tax increases. They demanded "stay laws" that would postpone the collection of legally contracted debts; and planters who still owed prewar debts to British merchants wanted those merchants barred from initiating action in state courts, despite the provision of the peace treaty upholding the right of creditors to collect such debts. Legislators heard these cries and acted in response to them, but not without opposition, for any proposal to delay or obstruct payment of legitimate debts outraged domestic creditors and others who believed that the integrity of an individual and of a society depended on the honoring of all obligations.

The clash did not simply line up poor debtors against rich creditors. The opposing sides had a more complex membership, in part because some southerners, especially planters, fell into both camps. They were lenders, but they also borrowed—from fellow planters, from American merchants, and before the Revolution from British merchants. To complicate matters further, those who believed that the treaty with England took precedence over the policy of individual states argued that one state could not undercut the treaty rights of British merchants. Despite these complications, legislators responded to the shouts for relief. The elected representatives of an aroused people who expected action could hardly do otherwise. After hard legislative fights the efforts to shackle local lenders and to thwart British creditors largely succeeded.

Recent students of this period have found the beginnings of political parties in the division over financial issues. State financial politics became connected with large national concerns because the partisan lineup in the southern states brought the local conflict into national focus. The political sides on the financial issues did not form solely or chiefly along economic lines. Partisanship depended more on general outlook or world view than on financial status or occupation. On one side, the men who opposed meeting the needs of Congress, who supported stay laws and restrictions on British merchants, insisted that the state and the desires of its citizens must come first. On the other side of the financial issues were men whose education, business and social activities, and wartime experiences had given them a broader, more nationalist outlook. They denounced their states' unwillingness to support the Congress. They foresaw a drifting, ineffective Congress that would make for a feckless nation.

NATIONALISM

These more nationalist-oriented southerners believed that the Congress and the Articles of Confederation needed an injection of strength and purpose. If these essentials were to be found, the central government had to have the power to raise its own revenue. But, in the view of these nationalists, money alone would not suffice to give pride and momentum to the nation. They were convinced that some way had to be found to make the relationship between the central government and the citizens more intimate. To these men the nation created by the Revolution was not yet secure in the dangerous world of nations. Like-minded men sounded the same warnings north of the Mason-Dixon line. Nationalists everywhere worried that national goals and the common good would be overpowered by the localist orientation of the state legislatures. They feared that the division over financial issues might undermine social and political stability. And they dreaded even more the possibility that the United States would disintegrate into several parts, most likely into the sections so clearly revealed in congressional voting. This political subdivision would create a series of little Americas that could never fend off the preying empires of Great Britain and Spain. Such a horrendous outcome would inevitably conclude with the destruction of republicanism. In short, the Revolution would fail.

Southerners were surely not the only Americans thinking this way. The stronger national government the nationalists wanted was a government republican in both form and substance. A popular base and elected representatives were essential. Men in the rest of the country shared this opinion, but the nationalist viewpoint had especially prominent advocates in the South. No American was a more forceful advocate of radical change than James Madison, who fought the political and ideological battles of the 1780s in both the Congress and the Virginia legislature.

James Madison was a bright star in the galaxy of political leaders who directed American affairs in the first generation of national life. Born in Virginia in 1751, Madison graduated from Princeton in 1771 and with the onset of the Revolution began a political career that would span forty years. His physical presence contrasted sharply with his political eminence. A short, frail man—he was only five feet four inches tall and weighed but a hundred pounds—he occasionally had difficulty making himself seen. But he never had any trouble getting his contemporaries to pay attention to what he wrote or said. Madison displayed a remarkable combination of political abilities. A close student of politics, he was thoroughly grounded in the thought of the classical and continental political theorists, and no American of his time surpassed him in ability to wrestle with the most fundamental questions of government. And Madison was as successful a politician as he was a theorist. He was an effective legislator; in Philadelphia he was a major force in shaping the Constitution. With good reason historians have called him the father of the Constitution. In the ratification debate he assumed a critical role both in Virginia and in the nation. During the early 1790s, in conjunction with his personal and political confidant Thomas Jefferson, he founded a major political party. In 1801 he became secretary of state and in 1809 the fourth president of the United States. Whether Americans agreed with him or not, most of them respected his learning, his determination, and his political skills.

Many southerners shared Madison's conviction that the Articles of the Confederation had to be fundamentally altered, but many others predicted that any central government with power to raise its own revenue would run roughshod over both the states and liberty. When the Articles had been drafted in the 1770s, southerners had been among the most insistent that the states must keep more power than they gave to the central government. As Madison noted, "a jealousy of congressional usurpations" preoccupied many southerners. A surrender of power by the states, they argued, could turn liberty into despotism. The nationalist thrust of Madison and his allies seemed to be opening up the same kind of outside threat to local control that had sparked the Revolution. From this political vantage point, the specter of a powerful American central government appeared to be as great a menace as the government of George III.

DRAFTING THE CONSTITUTION

Under the Articles of Confederation disputes between and among states were not easily solved. In an attempt to deal with commercial problems that had arisen, Virginia in 1786 called for a conference to meet in Annapolis, Maryland. Attendance was poor and little could be accomplished. The delegates, under James Madison's urging, pressed the Congress to call a convention with power broad enough to consider changes in the Articles. Congress issued such a call, and delegates from twelve states (Rhode Island sent none) convened in Philadelphia in May 1787.

The delegates went far beyond their mandate. Rather than alter or amend the Articles, they fashioned a totally new governmental plan, the Constitution. They were generally convinced that radical action was essential. The delegations, including those from the southern states, consisted overwhelmingly of men who shared James Madison's commitment to the necessity of a stronger central government. Although each member of this extraordinarily able group had his eyes fixed on a secure future for the United States of America, not all agreed on the means to ensure that security. Those from large states clashed with those from small states on apportionment of power; delegates who pushed for an especially strong executive debated with colleagues who feared what they called undue concentration of power. Through all the debates, votes, and compromises, the southern delegates never forgot the special interests of the

South. Madison was on target when he declared that the differences among states derived "principally from the effects of their having or not having slaves"; the fundamental division of interests "lay between the Northern and Southern."

The deliberations of the Constitutional Convention underscored the direct connection between the South's perception of southern interests and slavery. Southerners made clear their refusal to tolerate any discussion of the future of slavery, and they insisted that their slaves must be no liability to them; indeed, they expected their slaves to benefit them politically. Southern delegates urged that slaves be counted for representation when the convention decided to base representation in the lower house of Congress on population, but not when the convention opted for a direct tax based on population. After much discussion, delegates agreed that the solution to this problem required the use of fractional counting. The black slaves would count for representation and taxation, but less than white people. Finally the conflict ended with the famous three-fifths compromise—a slave would count for three-fifths of a white citizen for the purposes of both representation and taxation. Southerners spoke forcefully. Observing that some delegates intended "to deprive the Southern States of any show of Representation for their blacks," a North Carolina delegate pronounced the verdict of the South. The South, he declared, "would never confederate on any terms that did not rate [slaves] at least as ⅗. If the Eastern States meant therefore to exclude them altogether the business was at an end."

From 1775 to 1787 the South repeatedly insisted that the national government keep its hands off slavery. Southerners also demanded that any national government must agree that slavery could benefit the South in any new political arena. The obverse also held: slavery must never penalize the South. As the Constitution took shape, the South won all of its fundamental demands on slavery.

Though southerners stood united on the institution of slavery as in their interest, they strongly disagreed on the international slave trade. Opposition to the continuation of the trade centered in the upper South, especially in Virginia. Although the Virginians who worried about the morality of slavery were either unwilling or unable—and usually both—to do anything about the institution itself, they could assault the slave trade. An attack on the trade neither damaged slavery in Virginia nor threatened slaveholders. By the 1770s many white Virginians believed their black population large enough; moreover, any restriction on the importation of slaves could only increase the value of those already in Virginia. Thus opposition to the slave trade posed no economic menace to Virginia or to Virginia slaveholders. In this instance ideological inclination and economic self-interest meshed perfectly.

South of Virginia planters wanted more slaves. In the Carolinas and Georgia the plantation system was spreading. Seacoast and backcountry alike were undergoing considerable economic growth, and planters believed they needed more slaves to fuel that growth. Politicians in the lower South never joined the Virginia-led chorus against the slave trade. The disunity on this issue broke wide open when the Constitutional Convention considered halting the trade. Prodded by the Virginia delegation, the convention seemed prepared to outlaw the trade in the Constitution. Reacting vigorously, delegates from the three southernmost states based their agreement to the Constitution squarely on their right to import slaves. Without that right, as a South Carolinian put it, "the expectation is in vain." In the face of such adamant opposition, the convention compromised: the Constitution would not outlaw the trade, but it would empower the new federal Congress to decide the matter twenty years after ratification. Although neither the Virginians nor the Carolinians rejoiced over this solution, both accepted it as a reasonable way out of a vexing situation.

THE RATIFICATION CONTEST

Because the Philadelphia convention, which met from May to September, conducted its affairs in secret, no debate on the Constitution took place in the South until the contest over ratification. The debate raged for a year, until the autumn of 1788. During that year the opponents of the Constitution challenged the proposed form of government vigorously. The structure and substance of this discussion illuminate just what the South saw as its basic political values and goals. The major battle in the South was fought in conventions called by each state to approve or reject the Constitution. The division over ratification basically continued the localist-nationalist contest that had marked southern politics in the 1780s.

As advocates of both sides articulated their perceptions of the critical issues, the constitutional fight underscored the South's participatory politics. Throughout the months of decision the Federalists (who advocated ratification of the Constitution) and the Anti-Federalists (who opposed it) constantly appealed to the people for support. Both sides insisted that the course they advocated would benefit "the people." Such rhetoric had a long history in the region between the Potomac and the Savannah. These polemics cannot be dismissed as cynical and meaningless rhetoric. During and after the Revolutionary crisis, southerners, along with most other Americans, had given extraordinary power to the concept of the sovereignty of the people. Committees, conventions, elections, instructions to delegates and representatives, unending appeals to the people—all gave significant weight to what may seem an empty phrase: sovereignty of the people. All the contestants in the South took seriously the voice and role of the people.

At the same time that the people received plaudits aplenty, the men with the great names massively influenced the fate of the Constitution. They propelled the Constitution forward, and often men who had served in Philadelphia stood in the front rank of the Federalist charge. James Madison, Charles Pinckney of South Carolina, James Iredell of North Carolina—such men led the forces that pushed for the Constitution. Those forces represented the planter-lawyer-merchant upper class that had directed the course of southern politics

from the colonial era through the Revolution. The great majority of this traditional leadership class championed ratification, but just enough of them
called for rejection to limit the inclusiveness of the upper-class constitutional
club.

The Constitution did not get the same reception from all the southern ratifying conventions. It found its warmest welcome in Georgia, where it won
quick and almost unanimous approval, probably because of the desire for military assistance to protect a frontier exposed to both Spanish and Indians. Its
coldest response came in North Carolina, which initially rejected it. Maryland
and South Carolina approved of the new plan by substantial margins, though
not without strenuous objections. The deepest division, the hardest fight, and
the closest margin of victory came in Virginia.

OPPOSITION

Enemies of the Constitution charged that it would weaken liberty in the South
and in the United States at large by establishing "most clearly a consolidated
government." For Anti-Federalists this consolidated government was "extremely pernicious, impolitic, and dangerous" because it resulted from what
they termed an enormous transfer of power from the states to the central government. As they saw it, states would lose control over such critically important
areas as governmental expenditures because the power to tax provided the central government with its own source of revenue. In addition, the revised basis
for apportionment and the new voting procedure in a radically different Congress reduced both the image and the reality of state power. Whereas the Articles based both apportionment and voting on the states alone, each state having
one vote, the Constitution added a second chamber to Congress, brought population into the apportionment formula, and required each member of Congress
to vote as an individual. The size of a delegation in the House of Representatives would depend solely on the population of its state; and though each state
would send two people to the Senate, the senators, just like the members of the
House, would cast their ballots as individuals. Southern Anti-Federalists never
used "consolidation" as a synonym for "union." They carefully separated the
two; they wanted the latter but not the former. These southerners followed the
traditional political dictum that liberty depended on the power to control one's
own affairs, one's own destiny. One of them shouted, "Liberty! What is liberty?
The power of governing yourselves. If you adopt this Constitution, have you
this power? No!"

This was not the only argument advanced by the southern Anti-Federalists
against the Constitution. A friend of George Washington voiced an anxiety
shared by many southerners when he wrote, "If the Constitution is carried into
effect, the States south of the potowmac [sic], will be little more than appendages to those to the northward of it." No other single question preoccupied the
southern Anti-Federalists so much as the security of slavery. To the Virginia

convention Patrick Henry repeated his lament about the evil of slavery and the impossibility of doing anything about it, but he went on to declare that "in clear, unequivocal terms" the Constitution gave the North the power to abolish slavery. Farther south no qualms about slavery accompanied fear for its health under the proposed Constitution. Rawlins Lowndes painted a melancholy scene in somber colors: "When this new Constitution should be adopted, the sun of the Southern States would set, never to rise."

SUPPORT

The Federalists met their opponents directly on every point. Emphasizing that the Constitution "takes its rise, where it ought, from the people," the old South Carolina Revolutionary Christopher Gadsden pronounced in a public letter that "all essentials to a republican government, are, in my opinion, well secured." The individual most responsible for the Constitution found perplexing as well as wrongheaded the argument that it organized a consolidated government. Before the Virginia convention James Madison countered such assertions by dwelling on the continuing importance of states in the new nation, which to his mind proved the error of all talk about consolidation. Madison maintained that a consolidated government would eliminate the power of the states, but that the Constitution did no such thing.

On one vitally important interest, slavery, southern Federalists never squirmed. Madison expressed amazement that any southerner could think that ratification of the Constitution signaled abolition. Madison, who certainly should have known, assured Virginians that "there is no power to warrant it in the [Constitution]." A South Carolinian proclaimed, "We have a security that the general government can never emancipate [slaves], for no such authority is granted." In an attempt to end all talk about the insecurity of slavery under the Constitution, a delegate to the Virginia convention who had also served in Philadelphia spoke authoritatively: *"The Southern States, even South Carolina herself, conceived this property to be secure by* [the Constitution]." No one *"had the smallest suspicion of the abolition of slavery."*

The most striking feature of the rhetoric employed in the ratification struggle was the common theme articulated by Federalists and Anti-Federalists alike. Both sides underscored liberty—specifically, whether or not the Constitution protected it. Everyone agreed on its absolute primacy. Moreover, all concurred that preservation of liberty required protection of the South's special interests, paramount among them slavery. At the close of the Revolutionary and Constitution-making epoch all white southerners conceded that slavery was embedded in their society. They did not believe that their society could withstand any fundamental alteration of the system because such a transformation meant inevitable disorder, even upheaval. The white South did not agree on the virtue or vice of its marriage to black slavery, but it cried in unison that slavery must remain its partner, and that it was strictly a southern concern. Without control of slavery, white southerners agreed, they could not possess their own liberty. Thus on the morning of the ratification of the Constitution, just as during the Revolution, slavery and liberty were inextricably intertwined in the southern mind.

UNDER THE CONSTITUTION

The ratification of the Constitution and the creation of a different national political arena did not bury local interests under an avalanche of nationalist fervor. Although all Americans desired success for the fledgling nation, they also anticipated success for themselves and for their particular interests. From the outset southerners in Congress recognized that their northern colleagues did not take a disinterested view of public affairs. Commenting on the first session of the First Congress, a South Carolina senator observed, "Here I find men scrambling for partial advantage, State interests, and in short, a train of these narrow, impolitic measures that must, after a while shake the Union to its very foundation." Even James Madison, the ardent evangelist of the new government, admitted that congressional votes during the initial session indicated that northerners were looking out for themselves. And all the while they criticized the self-interest of the northerners, southerners maneuvered to advance their own interests.

An attempt in the First Congress to give Congress power over slavery clearly demonstrated the determination of the southerners. In February 1790 various antislavery groups petitioned Congress to assert itself on the slavery issue. In response the House of Representatives set up a special committee to specify the power of Congress over slavery. The committee, with only one southern member, reported that before 1808 Congress could interfere with neither the international slave trade nor slavery; the clear implication was that Congress could interfere at will after 1808. Southerners on both sides of the slave-trade question joined to emasculate the report. They united behind an amendment proposed by Madison: "That Congress have no authority to interfere in the emancipation of slaves, or in the treatment of them within any of the States; it remaining with the several states alone to provide any regulation therein." The passage of Madison's amendment meant congressional adoption of the southern view that the Constitution did not permit Congress to act against slavery. This policy settled upon during the second session of the First Congress, remained intact for seventy years, until the Union itself broke apart.

The debate on Congress's jurisdiction over slavery did nothing to alter the South's perception that an assault on slavery was the primary threat to its liberty. For most southerners that threat materialized in the first great struggle over the basic course the new nation would follow.

HAMILTON'S VISION

At the center of the great contest stood Alexander Hamilton of New York, secretary of the treasury in President George Washington's cabinet. Hamilton envisioned a country growing powerful and wealthy through the active agency of the central government, which would promote economic and political measures to support American commercial and financial endeavors. Hamilton had no intention of guarding local interests; in his mind they all paled beside the overriding necessity of giving life to the United States of America—one nation, not its constituent parts.

Hamilton wanted to bind the self-interest of American citizens to the nation so that the prosperity of the citizenry would be dependent on the success of the nation. The means would come through public credit: the federal government would assume all the remaining Revolutionary debts of the states, combine them with the federal debt, and fund the total as a new public debt. To facilitate this citizen-nation financial relationship he advocated a national bank chartered by Congress and capitalized with both public and private funds. Believing that the growth of manufacturing was essential for the nation's strength, he also proposed direct government subsidies to manufacturers and a tariff that would keep out cheaper foreign goods and at the same time provide revenue to operate the federal government. This grand design had a foreign policy component—good relations with Great Britain, our chief trading partner, even if to secure them the United States had to acquiesce in Britain's control of the seas. Anglo-American trade provided the tariff revenue to run the government, and Hamilton saw Britain as a source of capital for American economic growth. The South did not occupy a large place in Hamilton's national vision. Merchants, shippers, financiers, and manufacturers were much more numerous and important in the North. Thus his program had sectional favoritism built into it, though Hamilton did not think in such terms.

THE SOUTH OPPOSES

Not surprisingly, the South led the opposition to Hamilton's plans. Directed chiefly by the indefatigable James Madison, the opposition spanned the South. Of the southern states only South Carolina, with the largest city and major commercial center in the South, Charleston, offered Hamilton much support, and that support was to diminish significantly through the 1790s. Southern self-interest was surely involved. All southern states except South Carolina had already paid a substantial portion of their Revolutionary debts; thus in their eyes, Hamilton's funding scheme would require them to help others when no one had helped them. Concluding that Hamilton's program would favor commercial and financial interests in the North, southerners could see no good reason to back it.

But more than self-interest was involved. Southerners argued that Hamilton exhibited entirely too little concern for the words and intentions of the Constitution. As Madison pointed out, the Constitution made no provision for a national bank. He and his colleagues feared that such a broad interpretation would undermine the Constitution, to the public's jeopardy. And when Congress passed the bank bill in February 1791, southerners cast almost all the nay votes.

Most southerners saw no reason to interfere in an economy that permitted their agrarian society to flourish. Although many northerners agreed on the virtues of an agrarian society, its advocates and defenders were concentrated in the South. All were appalled by Hamilton's desire for structural changes in the American economy. The idea of turning the United States into a manufacturing country with a monetary system based on a funded debt and a national bank clashed with their fundamental view of society. To most southerners the agrarian society of large and small freeholders which had produced them was the best of all possible worlds. They wanted the nation to grow and prosper, but not to change in any significant sense. That this growth necessitated territorial expansion southerners recognized and approved, but this kind of expansion did not necessitate structural change. In a basic sense, Hamilton wanted to make a social and economic revolution, and the southerners did not. To be sure, their vision of society meshed with their self-interest in the 1790s, but it was not simply a function of self-interest. The public and private utterances of southerners during these years leave no doubt that their fervent commitment to their world was grounded in idealism. At the same time, the reality of their world did not always coincide with their vision of it.

This world view explains why Madison and his supporters opposed Hamilton's foreign policy. Their image of Great Britain in the 1790s remained what it had been two decades earlier—a corrupt society in which public debt and manufacturing had led to extremes of wealth and poverty, which had destroyed liberty. Believing, basically correctly, that Hamilton wanted to refashion the United States after the British pattern and that such a transformation would mortally wound the Revolution by destroying the republic, they wanted no friendship with Great Britain. Madison countered Hamilton's program by proposing a policy of commercial discrimination that would force Britain, in dire need of American products, to end restrictions on American trade.

To his opposition Alexander Hamilton seemed bent on tearing apart what the Revolution had won. Aware that they were setting the foundation stones of a new nation, all the builders understood that the emplacement would have a profound influence on the completed structure. Only this understanding explains the bitterness and viciousness of politics in the 1790s. The Virginia legislature pointed directly to the terrible danger southerners saw when it warned in 1790 that Hamilton's program entailed "a change in the present form of federal government fatal to the existence of American liberty."

When Congress enacted most of Hamilton's proposals, partisanship sharpened and led to the formation of competing parties. In the South national issues generated the private and public activity that resulted in political parties. The administration party, with President Washington as its chief luminary and Hamilton's program as its platform, called itself the Federalist party.

FEDERALISTS AND THE SOUTH

The Federalists appeared to have distinct advantages in their efforts to cultivate the South. George Washington headed the list. The first great national hero, Washington occupied a special place in the South. A son of Virginia, Washington proudly identified himself with his native state. As a slave-owning planter he was a member of the group that had long dominated southern politics. When Washington traveled through the South in 1791, celebration marked his tour—for himself, for the young nation, and for the local leaders who made his cause their own. And because the Federalists controlled the national administration, they could employ patronage in their own interest. Although patronage in the 1790s did not begin to match that of later years, it still provided an opportunity to reward friends and win political loyalty. Washington placed prominent southerners in the cabinet and in responsible diplomatic and judicial posts. At the local level, the Treasury Department and the Post Office provided numerous jobs that the administration used to build political loyalty in the states.

With the great hero at their head, local luminaries in strategic posts, and patronage to dispense, the Federalists seemed prepared to dominate southern politics; they needed only an issue or program to promote in the South. But, aside from calling for allegiance to Washington, they had none. This liability was quickly apparent when Hamilton's policies became the cornerstone of the Federalist program. Few southern Federalists publicly supported Hamiltonianism, and practically none was enthusiastic about it. The proposal to cultivate Great Britain was particularly difficult to accept. In 1795 President Washington set off a political conflagration when he submitted to the Senate a treaty that had been negotiated by John Jay. Republicans denounced the Jay Treaty for prohibiting any American commercial discrimination against Great Britain for ten years, and southerners especially condemned the provisions that aided British merchants in recovering sums they had advanced to Americans before the Revolution. From the Potomac to the Savannah public meetings railed against Jay's handiwork; in the Federalist stronghold of Charleston a mob burned the diplomat in effigy. The treaty was ratified by the Senate with no votes to spare, and in the House the motion to appropriate funds to finance the treaty's provisions was carried by only three votes.

Southern Federalists had still another massive problem. Washington excepted, no southerner who publicly identified himself with the administration's policies enjoyed broad appeal and respect in the South. Of course given the onerous problems that the major issues posed for southern Federalism, the emergence of such a man would have required the possession of almost magical political talents. The lack of a southern junior partner for Washington was of special concern in view of the dominance of the national leadership by northerners, particularly Alexander Hamilton of New York and Vice President John Adams of Massachusetts.

Without easily salable issues to take before southern voters and with no prominent national leaders rising from their ranks, southern Federalists had to rely on the prestige of George Washington. Reliance on Washington, however, was at best a short-term strategy. He would not tower over the political scene forever. Southern Federalists would find themselves in a desperate political situation if they should have to face a determined, organized opposition with both southern leaders and southern-oriented issues.

THE REPUBLICAN PARTY

Even after Congress approved Hamilton's program, its opponents kept working to build a political party that would have a chance to take power by winning elections. Although scholars do not agree on the precise date of the party's formation, a great majority of them agree that by 1793 a political party did exist—a party in the sense that a group of men armed with policy goals and a commitment to use the political process had come together to win control of the national government. These men began to call themselves Republicans.

James Madison and Thomas Jefferson were the two most important leaders of this new body, and the designation Republican fit precisely their conception of the party. To them the Revolution had secured American liberty by overthrowing a monarchy and instituting a republic. What they interpreted as Hamilton's attempt to impose the British system on the United States placed republicanism and liberty in mortal danger. When Madison and Jefferson constantly attacked the "monarchists" who wanted to destroy liberty, they were aiming at the Federalists. The question was not whether an American king would actually be placed on an American throne but whether a republican America would survive.

Denouncing the British system, Madison and Jefferson insisted that America must retain its agrarian character. To the Virginians an agrarian society needed no national bank, no subsidies, no funded debt; in their view, these were plagues that destroyed liberty. Moreover, an agrarian country did not require a powerful central government, because such a country did not need the fearful economic functions envisioned by Hamilton. The Republicans preached states' rights to emphasize that only local control guaranteed liberty.

For Madison this attitude marked a turnabout since the 1780s, when he had called for a stronger central government. Then Madison had believed that the Revolution and Americans' liberty were threatened by the weakness of the central government. Now, facing Hamilton's program, he saw the greatest danger

THOMAS   JEFFERSON   (The White House Collection)

to liberty in the consolidation of the national government. "Let it be the patriotic study of all," Madison wrote, "to maintain the various authorities established by our complicated system, each in its respective sphere." Strict construction and states' rights became the rallying cry of Republicanism.

This rhetoric fit easily with the South's long-standing concern about outside authority. Articulated Republican fears in the 1790s harked back to worry about British oppression, to concern about the North's domination of the government under the Articles of Confederation, to the misgivings expressed by the Anti-Federalists in 1787 and 1788. Although Madison had changed, many southerners could adopt his new stance without changing at all. The fact that outside or northern forces were engineering this new consolidation compounded the distress of Madison and his followers. Not only were the consolidationists outsiders; they wanted to implement policies disadvantageous to the South, at least as most southerners perceived them. In sum, political heritage, local prejudice, and self-interest coalesced to give the Republicans a powerful hold on the South.

To eliminate the Federalist threat, Madison, Jefferson, and other Republican leaders chose the electoral process as the highway for their political offensive. Two basic facts dictated that choice. First, the Republicans vigorously proclaimed their devotion to the Constitution; their mission was to rescue it from the Federalists. Second, because they believed in the right thinking of the people, the electoral process had to give them power. The Republicans worked to

JAMES MADISON (Courtesy of
The New-York Historical Society,
New York City)

ensure that their message reached voters. Republican leaders established newspapers that gave a Republican hue to their political coverage. These newspapers
also served as an outlet for public letters and essays, which gave the leadership
an opportunity to reach a wide audience and to set the tone of public debate.
Complementing the public press, the leaders' private correspondence pressed
their views and urged active participation. They set up committees, selected
and put before voters faithful Republican candidates, and worked for their election. By mid-decade the caucus of loyal Republicans at both national and local
levels had become a key feature of party organization and discipline.

Republicans hoped to transform the nation. Jefferson and Madison did not
think of their political handiwork as designed only for the South. Any attempt
to label the Republican party only a southern movement is simply unhistorical,
but the special relationship between the Republican party and the South cannot
be denied. The South and southerners played a critical role in the creation of the
party, in the formulation of its ideology, and in its electoral success.

THE SOUTH AS REPUBLICAN

Southerners certainly heeded the Republicans' call. In both the First Congress
(January 1790–March 1791) and the Second Congress (March 1791–March 1793)
southerners made up the bulk of the opposition to Hamilton's program. The

admission to the Union of Kentucky in 1792 and Tennessee in 1796 added to
Republican ranks, for Federalism never prospered west of the Appalachians.
Only Maryland and tiny Delaware seemed to be Federalist havens among the
slave states, but even in Maryland the Republicans challenged the Federalists
vigorously. The presidential election of 1796 clearly indicates the dominance of
Republicanism in the South. For southerners the presidential candidates—
Jefferson of Virginia and John Adams of Massachusetts—personified the rela-

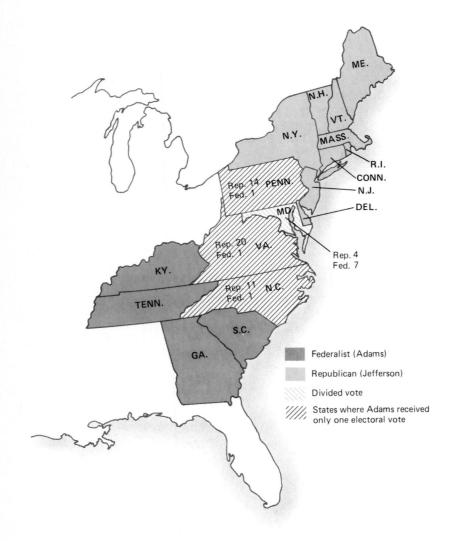

THE ELECTION OF 1796

tive orientations of the two parties. Some Federalist leaders hoped to confuse the southern scene by manipulating the electoral process mandated by the Constitution, which specified that each presidential elector would vote for two candidates regardless of party. (This process was changed to the present system, in which electors vote for the presidential and vice presidential candidates nominated by a single party, by the Twelfth Amendment, adopted in 1804.) In this scheme the name of Thomas Pinckney of South Carolina was injected on the Federalist side as either vice president or possibly even president. Despite this strategem, the Republicans scored a lopsided victory. From Maryland southward Jefferson won 54 electoral votes, whereas Adams garnered but 9, 7 in Maryland. Despite Adams's miserable showing in the South, he won the election by three electoral votes, 71 to Jefferson's 68. Adams won because he trounced Jefferson in the free states, where Jefferson could claim only Pennsylvania.

Without question the South was the most strongly Republican part of the nation. For southerners the great political contest was fought over national issues; from the birth of the nation southerners had taken a special interest in national politics. Their determination to maintain absolute control over their peculiar institution of slavery gave southerners good reason to be acutely aware of national events. And the debate in 1790 over congressional power and slavery did nothing to diminish that interest. When Alexander Hamilton proceeded to move the nation down a path most southerners believed inimical to their interests and dangerous to their liberty, national affairs became even more salient. To guard their interests, their institutions, themselves—their liberty—southerners banded together in a party they perceived as carrying their flag, with a southerner as commander in chief and southerners as important subordinates. To most southerners the Republican party manned the political frontier as the great army protecting southern interests and southern liberty.

THE FEDERALIST SURGE

After John Adams took the oath of office as the second president on March 4, 1797, the Federalist party had little reason to expect its status in the South to improve noticeably. Adams's inauguration signaled the retirement of George Washington, and there was no one to replace him.

Yet the relationship between the Adams administration and the South did not follow the expected path. Deterioration in the nation's relations with France unexpectedly revived southern Federalists' fortunes. Facing the possibility of war, the administration began to build up the army. George Washington was named commanding general; the great leader returned to face a new crisis. All this rejuvenated the southern Federalists. In 1798 and 1799 southerners elected more Federalists to Congress than they ever had done before or would do in the future. They even breached the Republican citadel of Virginia, which in 1799 sent eight Federalists along with eleven Republicans to Congress.

For southern Federalists it was a heady time; they seemed on the verge of breaking out of their minority mold. But their success in 1798 and 1799 lacked a secure foundation. War and Washington had served as a crutch for a lame party. Without that crutch the southern Federalists would once again stumble.

While President Adams worked to avoid war with France, he also moved to secure the position of his administration by stifling dissent. In 1798 Congress passed a series of acts designed to achieve that goal. The Naturalization Act extended the time required for immigrants—who the Federalists believed filled Republican ranks—to become citizens from five to fourteen years, and the Alien Act empowered the president to deport aliens regarded as dangerous. The Sedition Act, which made it a federal crime to attack government officials, struck directly at Republican critics of the Adams administration. The Sedition Act was no empty gesture; it was enforced. Government lawyers prosecuted Republicans, especially editors, and Federalist judges sent them to jail.

To protect their party and their understanding of American liberty, the Republican chieftains counterattacked. The tactics they employed fastened the Republican party ever more tightly to the South. When Jefferson confided to an associate, "It is true that we are completely under the saddle of Massachusetts and Connecticut, and that they ride us very hard, cruelly insulting our fellings as well as exhausting our strength and subsistence," he entwined sectionalism with politics. Still, for Jefferson ideological commitment to liberty outweighed sectional loyalty. Even so, the sectional dimension clearly in his mind reinforced the intimate bond between the Republican party and the South.

*T*HE REPUBLICAN RESPONSE

Underscoring the traditional southern and Republican emphasis on the rights of the states and on local control, Jefferson and Madison used state legislatures as their forums. Each man wrote a set of resolutions proclaiming the unconstitutionality of the Alien and Sedition acts and denouncing the federal government's violation of the rights of the states. Madison's resolution went to the legislature of Virginia, Jefferson's across the mountains to Kentucky. Both men stressed that the central government possessed only those powers strictly delegated to it by the Constitution. All other powers remained with the states, the contracting parties that had created the Constitution.

Although both men had the same intention, they differed in one important respect. Madison contented himself with denouncing the administration's behavior in formal fashion and urged other states to follow Virginia's lead; he provided no precise remedy for the evil he defined. Jefferson, in contrast, boldly advanced the idea that because the Constitution did not specify an ultimate arbiter of disputes, each state had "an equal right to judge for itself, as well of the infractions as the mode and measure of redress." This extreme conclusion—the seed of nullification and secession—was further than Madison and the Kentucky Republicans were willing to go. That Jefferson had broached the idea of secession remained secret for decades. Though Kentucky's resolution was milder than Virginia's, both were strong documents. In asserting the legitimacy of states' rights and condemning the broad use of federal power, they expressed attitudes that would enjoy a long, prosperous life in the South.

A head-on collision between Federalists and Republicans—between the central government and the states—was averted when John Adams secured a diplomatic settlement with France. With the relaxation of tension between France and the United States, the parties turned to the voters to settle their differences.

THE ELECTION OF 1800

Primed for political combat, Federalists and Republicans prepared to battle for southern votes under their tested commanders, Adams and Jefferson. Partisan feelings were even stronger in 1800 than they had been in 1796 because of the passion and anger generated by the war scare. Federalists castigated Republicans as anarchists, atheists, and regicides; Republicans condemned Federalists for "delug[ing] the world with crimes and blood." The immense organizational and publicity effort mounted by both sides only intensified the partisanship. Newspapers, committees, electoral tickets, pamphlets, broadsides—all combined to make the presidential election of 1800 a foretaste of those that would come a generation later.

The outlook for southern Federalists appeared simultaneously bright and somber. In view of their performance in 1798 and 1799, many Federalist leaders hoped that 1800 would reveal a solid Federalist base in the South, at least from Maryland to South Carolina. In Georgia and the trans-Appalachian states of Tennessee and Kentucky the Federalists made little effort and expected little return. At the same time there were problems. The passing of the war scare not only eliminated their most emotional issue; it also left them as authors of an unpopular tax measure. To finance the military buildup Congress in 1798 had passed a direct tax on land, slaves, and houses. Southerners bore a heavy portion of this tax load, and by 1800 they had grown weary of the burden. In addition, the death of George Washington in December 1799 deprived southern Federalists of the one man who had given many southerners cause for loyalty to the Federalist party. Sectional strife also plagued the party. In the month of Washington's death, southern and northern Federalists fought over the speakership of the House of Representatives; the northern majority refused to accept a southern speaker. Once again a scheme was hatched to defeat Adams in the electoral college by making the South Carolinian Charles Cotesworth Pinckney a contender for president or vice president.

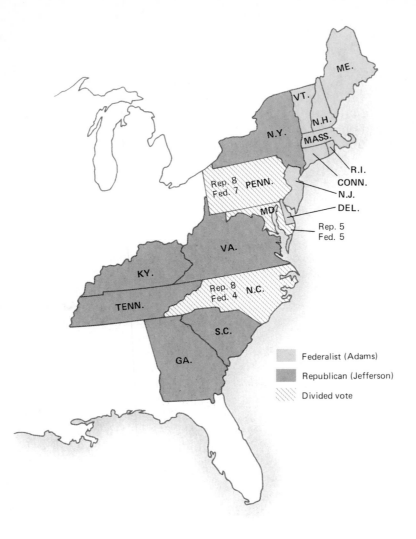

Rep. 8
Fed. 7

Rep. 5
Fed. 5

Rep. 8
Fed. 4

Federalist (Adams)

Republican (Jefferson)

Divided vote

THE ELECTION OF 1800

The Republicans, in contrast, were united, and they enjoyed a strong southern base. Their leaders believed a strong showing in the South was essential for
national victory because of Federalist strength in the North, especially in New
England. With their candidate a southerner and their party attuned to southern
issues, the Republicans bugled their call to southern voters: they protected
southern interests, whereas the Federalists endangered them.

The election confirmed the overwhelming dominance of the Republicans in
the South and left the Federalists once again with no more than political

crumbs. Among the slave states only in tiny Delaware, which Adams carried, and in Maryland, which he divided evenly with Jefferson, did the Federalists do well. Overall Jefferson won 53 of the 65 southern electoral votes. In the country as a whole Jefferson defeated Adams by only 8 electoral votes, a narrow turnabout from 1796, when Adams had won by 3. But in the South neither election had been at all close; each had produced a Republican landslide. In 1800 Republicans had more to cheer about than their huge victory in the presidential race. State and local elections generally followed a similar pattern, so that the Republicans erased the gains the Federalists had made during the war scare.

Although the Republican party was indisputably dominant in the South, it was not simply a southern party. Through the 1790s Jefferson and Madison wooed northerners; the results of 1800 could only have pleased them. The party won all 12 electoral votes in New York and 8 of 15 in Pennsylvania, and without them Jefferson would have lost. The Virginia–New York connection was to remain crucial to the success of the Jeffersonian Republican party. The appearance of Aaron Burr of New York on the ballot demonstrated the Republicans' determination to bridge the sectional gap. To cement a North-South alliance the Republicans nominated Burr, Hamilton's political archenemy, with the expectation that he would run second to Jefferson and so would become Jefferson's vice president. In 1800 presidential electors still did not cast votes for a vice president; each elector voted for two candidates. But the Burr candidacy proved almost too successful. As all Republican electors named both Jefferson and Burr, each man received the same number of electoral votes, though Jefferson was the undoubted Republican choice for president. Because of the tie, under the Constitution the House of Representatives had to choose a winner, and it did so on February 17, 1801, when it selected Jefferson as president. The Jefferson-Burr deadlock led directly to the Twelfth Amendment, which specifies that electoral votes for president and vice president be cast separately.

Tangled electoral voting notwithstanding, the Republican party controlled the southern political world. The Federalists could not match them. The Republicans possessed the leadership and the issues that best fit southern interests.

THE MARCH WESTWARD

While the political wars raged, the South was in motion. Since colonists first moved up the tidal rivers away from the seacoast in the late seventeenth century, the West, the land beyond settlement, had attracted southerners like a bright rainbow. Surely riches awaited the hardy folk who ventured there. The prosperity that followed each successive advance stirred dreams of bountiful streams, rich valleys, fertile bottomlands.

In the 1780s and 1790s the march westward led chiefly to Tennessee and Kentucky. Before the Revolution these areas—claimed by North Carolina and Virginia, respectively—had known only explorers and hunters. The most famous of them was Daniel Boone, who first explored Kentucky in 1769 and in

1775 established Boonesboro on the Kentucky River. By 1780 fewer than 10,000 whites had settled in either territory, but by 1790 their numbers reached almost 32,000 in Tennessee and beyond 61,000 in Kentucky. Kentucky became the fifteenth state in 1792; Tennessee became the sixteenth in 1796. Mississippi Territory, formerly controlled by Spain but organized by Congress in 1798, also witnessed settlement around its capital, Natchez. This horizontal expansion of the South occasioned no basic change in southern institutions, which traveled west with settlers.

The conviction that opportunity abounded was the chief motive for migration. Seeing Kentucky for the first time, a new settler could not contain himself. He had never before seen "So Rich a Soil, Covered in Clover in full Bloom, the Woods alive in wild game." To his dazzled eyes "it appeared that nature in the profusion of her Bounties had spread a feast for all that lives." The "Sight so delightful to our View and grateful to our feelings almost Induced us...to Kiss the Soil of Kentucky." All classes joined the westward trek, though the majority were probably yeomen. The land bounties offered by North Carolina and Virginia to veterans of the Revolution provided considerable incentive. All ranks were eligible for these free allotments of western land. North Carolina's bounties were based on rank, from 600 acres for a private to more than 7,000 acres for a colonel.

The family of Mary Dewees joined the migration. After starting from Philadelphia, Mary, her husband, her children, and her brother found themselves in western Virginia in late 1788. From there they pushed on to Kentucky, where, to Mary's dismay, her brother left the Dewees and headed away alone. For Mary the trek was at the same time wondrous and dangerous. She recorded that the early winter chill and the howls of wolves made the evening fires especially inviting. Much of the food came from the abundance of game—deer, turkeys, ducks, and geese. Finally in early 1789 the Dewees decided where they would plant their roots in the new land. Mary described a spot with plentiful trees, near a spring and a beautiful pond. Once her home was established, Mary wrote that she had not been happier in years. Though not all shared Mary's final enthusiasm, thousands of individuals and families duplicated the Dewees' journey from east to west.

Land speculators also played a role in the opening of the trans-Appalachian South. The buying up of vast western tracts in the hope of reaping financial rewards was an honorable tradition in the South. Some of the most respected southerners, George Washington and James Madison among them, invested eagerly in the proposition that western land would bring them wealth. Many speculators in the 1780s and 1790s bought up cheaply the land claims of veterans who had no intention of moving west. One of the most successful was William Blount of North Carolina, who parlayed western land grants into a fortune. By 1791 Blount and his associates had acquired almost 165,000 acres of land in Tennessee. Probably the most infamous of the speculators were the four companies engaged in what became known as the Yazoo land frauds. In 1795 they bribed the Georgia legislature to grant them 35 million acres of Georgia's southwestern land claims for only $500,000. This blatantly corrupt action caused such a public uproar in Georgia that the next legislature repealed the act authorizing the grants. Ultimately the legal wrangle over the Yazoo speculation led to a major decision by the United States Supreme Court. Its ruling in *Fletcher* v. *Peck* in 1807 extended the obligation of contracts from private persons to states and defined Georgia's 1795 statute as a contract protected by the Constitution. Therefore, the Court ruled, the repeal of the statute was unconstitutional. For the first time the United States Supreme Court invalidated a state law.

*T*HE WEST AND SLAVERY

The mountains formed no barrier to slavery. Although early figures are unreliable, slaves surely accompanied whites in their westward trek. The initial federal census in 1790 placed 3,417 slaves in Tennessee and 12,430 in Kentucky. The constitutions written by both in preparation for statehood protected the institution of slavery. When Kentucky revised its constitution in 1799, an effort was made to plan for gradual emancipation. The move failed, however. The first census taken after both states entered the Union, in 1800, clearly demonstrated that slavery had become woven into the social fabric. In ten years the number of slaves in Kentucky had more than tripled, to over 40,000 (18 percent of the population), while in Tennessee the count had increased more than fourfold, to 13,584 (13 percent of all Tennesseans). Throughout the slave era the two states stood as staunch slave states.

The question of slavery in the West led to one of the most notable legislative acts in American history, the Northwest Ordinance of 1787—almost the only act passed by the Articles government that is remembered. The Northwest Ordinance forbade slavery in the Northwest Territory, the area north of the Ohio River and east of the Mississippi. This massive domain had been claimed by Virginia, but in 1781 Virginia ceded it to the nation. Supported by southern votes in Congress, the ordinance is often pointed to as an enlightened action against slavery by southerners of the Revolutionary generation. That stance is then favorably contrasted with the stern advocacy of slavery in the territories by a later generation of southerners. The southern position, however, was not so clear-cut. Few southerners questioned the legitimacy of slavery in Tennessee and Kentucky, which were slave areas before they became states. In fact, white southerners were taking black slaves across the Appalachians at the very time Congress enacted the ordinance. Moreover, when the Mississippi Territory was organized in 1798, Congress did not prohibit slavery within its boundaries.

Southern congressmen supported the Northwest Ordinance for several reasons. Possibly most important was that in the 1780s southerners did not think of themselves as representing a minority position. On the contrary, many were convinced that the South would become dominant over the North. When the Northwest was populated by southerners, as they were convinced it would be, their orientation would prevail. At the same time, it is probable that others

THE NORTHWEST ORDINANCE, 1787

viewed the Ohio River as the western extension of the Mason-Dixon line, the border between Maryland and Pennsylvania, which separated slavery from freedom. Evidence suggests, too, that some southerners supported the exclusion of slavery from the Northwest to preclude possible competition for southern tobacco interests.

In 1800 a vibrant, confident South looked toward the new century. Southern citizens and southern culture had passed beyond the old colonial borders. A political organization embraced enthusiastically by the South prepared to take control of the national administration. From the southern perspective, all was secure.

6

Republican Ascendancy

❖

The victory of Thomas Jefferson in 1800 delighted most southerners. In the eyes of the overwhelming majority, the bitter battles of the 1790s had been struggles over the fundamental definition of the national identity and the basic orientation of the new nation. Most southerners, then, felt vindicated by the triumph of the leader and party they identified as their own. The South had surely been essential to Jefferson's triumph; without the electoral votes he won in the slave states, he would have been thrashed by his Federalist opponent, John Adams. Particularly important, southerners could interpret the results as proof positive that the nation and the South were aimed in the same direction, that they shared the same values and goals. The South and the nation were one.

When the fifty-eight-year-old Thomas Jefferson entered the White House in 1801, he had been a famous public man for twenty-five years; and through all that time he remained a Virginia planter and slave owner with an abiding commitment to his state and to his occupation. Jefferson combined intellectual and political talents in a manner matched by no other president. Truly a Renaissance man, an eighteenth-century intellectual equally at home in political philosophy and in science, an architect who created monuments to the art, Jefferson was also a skilled politician. He was a major builder of the Republican party, and in little more than half a decade he led the party to national victory. Neither his intellectual achievement nor his political success diminished his conviction that the agrarian world that produced him was the best of all possible worlds. All his life he had owned slaves, eventually more than two hundred of them; they worked his lands and built his cherished home, Monticello. And he could never reconcile the institution of slavery with his devotion to freedom. Yet it was his dedication to liberty—a liberty that required local control by local citizens and local government—that, in combination with his belief in the racial inferiority of blacks, kept him from any move against slavery. Not only was Jefferson united with the chief southern economic and social institutions; his view of politics meshed nicely with the general southern view. And nothing Jefferson did in the 1790s threatened anything white southerners held dear. On the contrary, he advocated principles and practices that would secure those values and interests. Although Jefferson could never be called a sectional provincial, southerners identified overwhelmingly with him and his political cause.

Jefferson did not stand alone as a victor. In the Congress and across the South, Republicans assumed office. Jefferson would have a Republican Congress to help him redirect the future of the country, and southerners made possible that executive-legislative unity. To the Seventh Congress, which first convened in December 1801, the states below the Potomac sent eight Federalists and fifty-nine Republicans. By the time the Tenth Congress met, even that paltry Federalist contingent had been halved. Federalists began to disappear from the slave states. The Republican surge signaled to southerners that the nation had become reoriented in the direction toward which the South had pointed: agrarianism, not commercialism; local control, not central control. Thus, for southerners, sectional concerns were national concerns.

*T*HE LOUISIANA PURCHASE

The two major initiatives of Jefferson's presidency took the Republicans down a different road, one that forced the South to consider quite carefully the fit between power and ideology. The Louisiana Purchase was the crucial event of Jefferson's first administration. In the president's mind the acquisition of Louisiana would give an enormous boost to his fledgling nation. The addition of the 828,000 square miles of Louisiana enabled Jefferson and his supporters to dream of a boundless agrarian empire. The idea of boundlessness was compelling because Americans had taken 150 years to cross the Appalachians, only a few hundred miles from the Atlantic Ocean. Based on that experience, settlers would not reach the western edge of Louisiana or the Rocky Mountains, two thousand miles from the Appalachians, for centuries. The acquisition of Louisiana enabled southerners to envision their domain as expanding indefinitely. Their society had unlimited space for growth, for white farmers and black slaves. Kentucky and Tennessee, the extension of the seaboard South which joined the Union in the 1790s, came in as slave states. The treaty that transferred Louisiana from France to the United States specifically protected property rights in slaves. And the congressional legislation that organized the territory under American jurisdiction did not prohibit the introduction of additional slaves.

The Louisiana Purchase represented the first acquisition of territory that had not been part of or claimed by the United States in 1787, when the Constitution was written. And nowhere did the Constitution specifically authorize additions to the national domain. For a president who had boasted about allegiance to the letter of the Constitution, this lack of authorization was troublesome. Jefferson wanted Louisiana desperately, but he considered a constitutional amendment necessary. It would not have to precede the transfer of money for land, but Jefferson believed that constitutional sanction should be given after the fact.

THE SOUTH IN 1800

Not all of the president's advisers shared his concern. Most congressional and administrative leaders, southerners included, had no doubts about the constitutionality of the purchase. Furthermore, they argued that raising the constitutional question would provide an additional weapon to the Federalists, who opposed adding Louisiana. Jefferson disagreed on the basic issue, but he did agree not to publicize his reservations. He stated clearly the reason for his doubt: "Our peculiar security is in the possession of a written Constitution. Let us not make it a blank paper by construction." But he would not risk giving up his great prize, political as well as ideological. He ultimately satisfied himself with the observation that "the good sense of the country will correct the evil of construction when it shall produce ill effects." When Jefferson forwarded the treaty to the Senate, he did not mention his uncertainty about its constitutionality. With opposition localized among the Federalists, the Senate accepted the Louisiana Purchase on October 20, 1803, by a vote of 26 to 6. Southerners and most other Americans applauded.

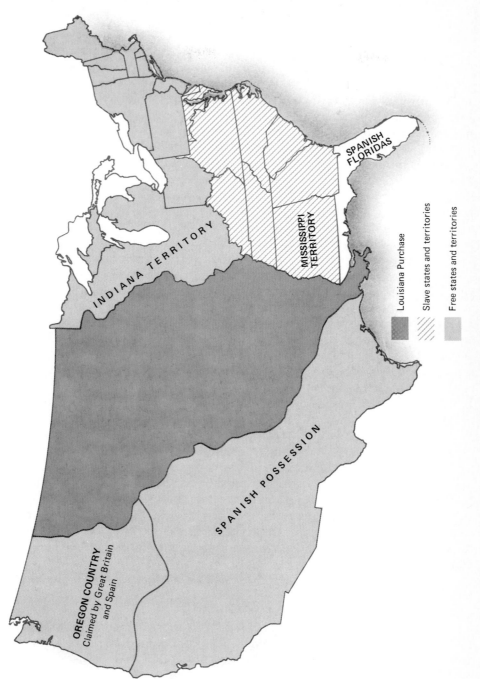

INDIANA TERRITORY

MISSISSIPPI TERRITORY

SPANISH FLORIDAS

SPANISH POSSESSION

OREGON COUNTRY
Claimed by Great Britain and Spain

Louisiana Purchase

Slave states and territories

Free states and territories

THE LOUISIANA PURCHASE

THE EMBARGO

In contrast to Jefferson's effort to buy Louisiana, the most important event of his second administration turned into dismal failure. From its beginning the Jefferson presidency had been caught up in the great Anglo-French conflict raging in Europe. Claiming neutrality and the right to trade with belligerents, Jefferson and his secretary of state, James Madison, had pressed both Britain and France to recognize and accept the American position. Because the powerful royal navy gave Britain control of the sea, conflict occurred most often with the former mother country. America demanded unfettered trade; Britain exercised the prerogative of power and refused to permit any commerce that would aid France, its great enemy.

Perceiving no alternative except war and rejecting that possibility, Jefferson decided to shut down American trade completely. In 1807 he submitted to Congress a bill that banned from American ports any ship seeking to enter from a foreign port or to depart for one. It authorized collectors of customs to search and detain vessels, even those in the coasting trade. Never before had a president embarked on such an ambitious program to compel obedience to national legislation. Despite this about-face from Republican teaching about the proper character of the central government, Republicans did not hold up the bill's passage. It raced through Congress—one day in the Senate, three in the House—and won the overwhelming majority of Republican votes, including those of southerners. On the state level Republicans also indicated that they stood squarely behind their president.

The embargo brought American commerce to a standstill. The economic impact on the country was devastating. The embargo strangled mercantile and shipping interests in every seaport, but especially in New England, the center of American shipping. Neither did the embargo exempt southern agriculturalists. After all, southern planters raised staple crops for an export market, a market now closed. Palpable distress gripped South and North. Republicans had inflicted a severe economic blow on the heartland of the party. The value of rice exports fell from $2.4 million in 1807 to a paltry $221,000 in 1808, a decline of 90 percent in one year. During the same year Virginia's exports dropped from $4.8 million to just over $0.5 million. Exports from Georgia in 1808 reached less than 1 percent of the 1807 total.

No matter the depths of their distress, most southern Republicans did not take to open opposition. The South Carolina House of Representatives vowed complete support for the embargo; the governor of Georgia proposed strong laws to relieve debtors unable to pay creditors because of the halt in trade. By 64 to 1 the Kentucky legislature announced its continuing adherence to the embargo. Attempts both by dissident Republicans and by Federalists to turn economic disadvantage into political advantage failed miserably.

The South's steadfastness illuminates the southern view of politics, ideology, and power. Had the Adams administration or even the second Washington administration done what Jefferson did, the Republican party, with its southern contingent in the vanguard, would have cried out against executive usurpation, tyranny, and oppression. This kind of attack on Jefferson and his policies rarely occurred. Although a coterie of southern Republicans did launch such an assault, they persuaded few of their fellows. For most southerners the identity of the men holding power was far more important than the niceties of constitutional theory or political philosophy. Southerners trusted themselves and their own leadership not to endanger fundamentally either southern interests or southern liberty. After all, most southerners perceived the Republican party as the guardian of liberty and of the South in the nation.

This view does not relegate ideology to the scrap heap. Ideology remained crucial because the South and its chosen political emissary would not always control the national government. They had not done so in the 1790s, and the time would come again when southerners would doubt that they had an emissary. Then the distinct southern ideological bent would guide the reaction to political reality as the South perceived it.

THE TERTIUM QUIDS

Not every southerner supported Jefferson's major policies, but the character of dissent emphasized the South's general allegiance to the party. Although individuals both in and out of Congress opposed specific measures for various reasons, the only serious continuous opposition appeared in 1805. Led by Virginia Congressman John Randolph of Roanoke and his North Carolina colleague Nathaniel Macon, these southern Republicans attacked Jefferson and the Republican majority for undermining "republican principles." Calling themselves Tertium Quids (a third way) to emphasize their separateness both from the administration and from the Federalist party, these southerners demanded strict adherence to the pristine Republican doctrine of the 1790s. They considered themselves guardians of the sacred text of the Virginia and Kentucky resolutions, which, to their way of thinking, Jefferson had violated. On the national level Quids were strongest in the House of Representatives, where they numbered approximately a dozen.

John Randolph, the most vigorous Quid and the most fiercely individualistic politician of his time, refused to be bound by party loyalty or commonly accepted behavior. He sometimes appeared in the House, booted, spurred, and flicking his riding crop, with a slave boy trailing behind. Then in his high-pitched voice, with a flagon of porter occasionally providing sustenance, he lacerated opponents. "Meddling fools and designing knaves are governing the country," slashed Randolph. National affairs had been "committed to Tom, Dick, and Harry, the refuse of the retail trade of politics." The Quids called on the Republicans never to desert principles that had given birth to the party: local power, small government, and a just fear of the executive. A small band, the Quids were never able to control the legislative process, but their abilities and efforts served to remind all Republicans of their political birthright.

The Quids spoke the language of the Republican tradition and made every effort to alert their fellow southerners to the administration's apostasy, but they enjoyed few legislative triumphs and persuaded few southerners to rally round their flag. Possibly Randolph was right when he claimed that many congressional Republicans expressed Quid principles in private but voted the administration line. But purists such as Randolph and his associates could never attract much support in the South so long as governmental power was being exercised by a party that southerners identified as their own. John Randolph would not be the last notable southern political ideologue to discover that fact about his fellow southerners. Mainstream southern Republicans attacked the Quids for endangering the party and for "tend[ing] to invigorate the declining spirit of federalism." Even the economic pain inflicted on the South by the Embargo Act failed to strengthen the Quid force.

THE FEDERALISTS

No one turned to the Federalist party. The care the Quids took to distance themselves from it revealed the sorry political reputation of southern Federalists. To the Quids the Federalists stood for everything that was wrong and dangerous about the American government. And the Quids were not the only southerners who had no use for the Federalist party. After the defeat of John Adams in 1800, southern Federalists rushed toward political extinction. A brief look at election figures underscores the serious political disease debilitating southern Federalism. Charles Cotesworth Pinckney of South Carolina headed the Federalist ticket in the elections of 1804 and 1808, but he had little success in the slave states: he won only two electoral votes the first time and five the second. After the congressional elections of 1807 and 1808 the Federalists held but seven seats south of the Potomac, whereas in 1800 they had had twice that many. In 1800 the South Carolina legislature had been almost half Federalist; by 1808 the Federalists held only one-seventh of the seats. That same precipitous decline halved Federalist legislators in both North Carolina and Virginia.

A tale told by a Republican editor in North Carolina was clearly on the mark. It seems two Federalists were passing the time of day. One exclaimed, "Federalism begins to look up!" His more realistic comrade replied, "Very true, being on its back now, it can look no other way." Not only did Federalists lose most of the races they ran, they ran fewer and fewer. By 1806 and 1807 Federalist candidates appeared in only 8 percent of congressional races in the southeastern states. When the party held a nominating caucus in New York in the summer of 1808 to choose a presidential ticket, only one southerner attended. The exuberant, energetic young leaders who guided the Federalist party to resurgence in the North had no counterparts in the South. Despite the two presidential candidacies of Charles Cotesworth Pinckney, southern Federalists never matched the influence of southern Republicans at the national level. Southern Federalism did hold the loyalty of a few substantial men, at least along the Atlantic seaboard north of Georgia, but in time their numbers declined, and they never invigorated their party.

Several reasons underlay the Federalist debacle. Southerners supported the Republicans in the 1790s because Republicans dealt with the issues in ways that most southerners approved, and in power the Republicans moved on those fronts. They let the Alien and Sedition acts languish and finally die. They repealed the direct tax and cut the federal budget. Then the entire South cheered the Louisiana Purchase. Division on state issues remained unimportant; Federalists rarely tried to use them to advance the Federalist cause. The hardship caused by the embargo seemingly should have given Federalists an entrée to southern voters, yet it did not.

A more fundamental disability plagued southern Federalists: the Federalist party never succeeded in identifying itself with the hopes and fears of most southerners. In the 1790s Republicans had tarred Federalists with the brush of antisouthernism. The stain remained, and after 1800 it seemed ineradicable. In 1812 Charles Cotesworth Pinckney urged the Federalist caucus not to run a southerner for president because he did not believe the party could win a single electoral vote in the South.

In direct contrast, a common identity bound together the South and the Republican party. The South accepted the party as its representative and protector. Not even the Quids, good southerners all and with a striking southern political accent, could loosen the bonds between southerners and the party they cherished as their own. Before any serious political restiveness could threaten the Republicans' authority in the South, the general perception of the party as advocate and guardian of the South would have to change. As Jefferson's presidency demonstrated, such a momentous shift would require a thunderous shock.

THE COMING OF WAR

Although the Republican party in the South turned back the Quids with ease and faced but feeble opposition from Federalists, the administration of James Madison, who succeeded Jefferson in the White House in 1809, found itself in a difficult situation. The predicament of the administration was caused chiefly by the failure of its economic diplomacy. The embargo had caused economic devastation at home and had had absolutely no impact on British policy. Despite the embargo and other measures passed by Congress to take its place, the British government would not agree that as a neutral nation the United States could trade with any nation it pleased, and certainly not with Britain's great foe, France. Through Madison's first term the British maintained in force the orders-in-council that forbade all ships to enter continental ports unless they had first passed through a British port and secured new clearances. In addition, the British navy continued the practice of impressment—British naval officers forcibly removed American citizens from American ships and pressed them into service

POWERFUL FORCES IN
SOUTHERN AND NATIONAL
POLITICS FROM THE WAR
OF 1812 TO 1850

John C. Calhoun (Brady Collection, National Archives)

in the royal navy. Between 1803 and 1812 more than 5,000 American sailors
were thus forced into the king's uniform. Just as Jefferson had done, Madison
found himself in a diplomatic box. And by 1812, after five years in this untenable position, Madison and many of his countrymen had had enough.

Southerners joined in the demand that the administration and country
stand up to what they termed British intimidation. Sure about their own power
in the nation and about the course of the nation, southerners entered the second decade of the nineteenth century with a viewpoint that contrasted sharply
with the attitude they had brought into the new century. The maturing of a second generation of Republican politicians reinforced their altered outlook. When
the first session of the Twelfth Congress convened in November 1811, new
names populated the roster of southern Republican congressmen. Half were in
their first or second term, and many of them had only faint memories of the
1790s. They had reached political maturity after the great victory of 1800.

Moving quickly to the prominence and influence that were to characterize
them during the next four decades, Henry Clay of Kentucky and John C.
Calhoun of South Carolina heralded the arrival of this new generation. These
two dynamic young congressmen—Clay was thirty-four, Calhoun only twenty-
nine—embodied the basic forces shaping southern society and politics. They
spoke for those who saw no threat from national power. Calhoun was a prod-

Henry Clay (Brady Collection, National Archives)

uct of the great Scotch-Irish tide that had flowed into the Carolina piedmont before the Revolution. After Calhoun graduated from Yale in 1804, he returned to his native state, where he practiced law, planted, and politicked. In 1811 he married Floride Bonneau Colhoun, a tidewater heiress who was also a distant cousin. His marriage intimately involved him in the great confluence of two major groups in the white South, the upland Scotch-Irish and the tidewater plantation magnates. And southern unity would become the watchword of his politics.

Henry Clay of Kentucky was the first man from west of the Appalachians to become a major force in American politics. Born in Virginia in 1777, he emigrated to Kentucky as a lad. At twenty he was admitted to the bar. He married into a prominent family and accumulated land and black slaves while he acquired an enviable reputation for charm and eloquence. A tall, lanky fellow with a captivating personality, Clay quickly became a political leader. His presence and vitality helped him achieve what today would be impossible—he was elected Speaker of the House of Representatives in his first term.

With no break in the diplomatic impasse in sight, the United States drifted toward war with Great Britain. Southern politicians stood among those most eager for war. Sounding the war tocsin loudest were young southerners who had come to Congress after Madison's election to the presidency. Youthful Republican stalwarts such as Calhoun and Clay had seen at firsthand the failure of the embargo. They were supremely conscious of what seemed like the impotence of their country. Through these southern eyes the nation seemed dangerously close to losing independence and sliding back into slavery under Great Britain. To these southerners the fruits of the Revolution were at stake.

Most historians today believe that the United States went to war in 1812 to salvage national honor and to preserve the liberty of the country. This conclusion meshes perfectly both with the major ideological tenets of Republicanism and with the attitude of southerners. To be sure, some southerners, chiefly westerners, did worry about Indian depredations on the frontier, and some also coveted Spanish Florida. Most, however, shared a grave concern about what they saw as the growing weakness of the country. In the eyes of many southerners, their country seemed cowed, appeared unwilling or unable to defend its most precious possession, liberty. Far from enjoying the independence it had fought for, it was once again dependent on the arbitrary whim of Great Britain. Independence required determination to preserve liberty, even if violence were required. A generally united South urged military action on the Madison administration.

PARTY AND SECTION AND WAR

Many other Republicans opposed war just as vigorously as the War Hawks—the name given to the major congressional spokesmen for conflict—advocated it. Antiwar forces were centered in the Northeast, especially in New England. Many of the opponents argued that the United States had no just cause to oppose Great Britain on the battlefield. Moreover, they thought war would be ruinous, for the country was not prepared to fight a great power.

Faced with a diplomatic policy that was not working and a divided party, the most prominent southern Republicans saw no easy solutions. President Madison had been a key architect of the commercial diplomacy that had characterized Republican policy since the 1790s. In a 1792 pamphlet he had even denounced war while urging and pointing the way toward universal peace. But Madison was a dedicated nationalist, and by 1812 he had concluded that the United States could not protect its sovereignty and its independence without standing firm against the British. Moreover, many of his strongest political supporters were clamoring for war. Thus recognition that his commercial diplomacy was not working, political pressure, and fear that the country could again become subservient to Great Britain all pushed the president on June 1, 1812, to ask that Congress declare war.

By June 18 Congress had acceded to the president's request and declared war on Great Britain. Although the United States never went to war more divided than in 1812, the South stood united behind the president. The Senate voted for war by the narrow margin of 19 to 13; no southern senator joined the minority. In the House the final tally gave a 79–49 margin for a declaration of war; only three southern Republicans cast negative ballots. The war vote was partisan—Republicans voted for war, Federalists against. But the overwhelming dominance of Republicans in the South gave to a partisan vote a distinctly sectional dimension. The defection of almost twenty northern Republicans on the war question emphasized the South's commitment both to the party and to its decision for war.

The government conducted the War of 1812 according to traditional Republican dogma. The Republican party had long denounced both standing (or professional) armies and taxes; in the Republican lexicon both were mortal threats to liberty. Volunteers, Republicans believed, would always rush forth and turn back any enemies the nation might face. This war would surely provide the ultimate test for these theories. The opponent was a great power and it had the most powerful navy in the world.

The Republican leadership did not envision major fighting anywhere within the national borders. The great goal of the war effort was to capture Canada and so to drive Great Britain off the North American mainland. Though Canada was far from the South, southern War Hawks eagerly joined the clamor to bring Canada under the American flag. In the House, John C. Calhoun cried, "In four weeks from the time that a declaration of war is heard on our frontier the whole Upper and a part of Lower Canada will be in our possession." Henry Clay bragged that "the militia of Kentucky are alone competent to place Montreal and Upper Canada at [our] feet." But rhetoric far outdistanced action; when Congress authorized building up the army by 25,000 men, only 400 enlistments came from Clay's hotbed of martial ardor.

THE RISE OF ANDREW JACKSON

While southerners were chorusing their eagerness to annex Canada, some attention was being given also to the southwest frontier, particularly by those who lived near it. Their concern focused on Spanish Florida; they worried that the Spanish, with British support, would urge the Creeks, known as Red Sticks, to attack whites in southwestern Georgia and in what would become Alabama. That fear became reality in the summer of 1813, when the Creeks attacked Fort Mims, just above Mobile, and killed some 60 percent of its 550 defenders and occupants.

Alarmed, the governor of Tennessee called out his militia to put down the uprising. In charge of the troops ordered to deal with the Creeks was Andrew Jackson, major general of the Tennessee militia. A man of ferocious energy, almost demonic determination, and incredible toughness, Jackson was a superb warrior.

In late 1813 he led his force across the Tennessee River into the heart of Alabama. He promptly engaged the Creeks and won a victory at Talladega, but then in winter combat his troops suffered repulses and heavy casualties. A budding mutiny among some of the volunteers endangered Jackson's authority and the campaign. Facing the challenge directly and with loyal soldiers prepared to do his bidding, Jackson threatened to shoot any man who left the army for Tennessee. The belief that the fearsome Jackson would carry out his threat kept the army in the field. With the approach of spring, Jackson once again advanced toward his enemy. On March 27, 1814, Jackson with 3,000 men attacked a main Creek camp on the Tallapoosa River. The resulting Battle of Horseshoe Bend was a disaster for the Creeks. The Tennesseans killed all but about 500 of an estimated 9,000 Creek fighting men and took prisoner 500 women and children. In August the Creeks finally signed the Treaty of Fort Jackson, dictated by General Jackson, by which they turned over to the United States some 20 million acres of land in southern Georgia and Alabama. The man the Indians called Sharp Knife had broken the power of the Creeks forever. Now the way was open for white settlement of the Southwest.

At the other end of the South, the Chesapeake, southerners experienced at firsthand the military woes that were the American norm during the war. Just as Jackson was wrenching the Southwest away from the Creeks, a major British expedition of 4,000 veterans and a supporting fleet entered Chesapeake Bay. In August the British landed in Maryland and marched toward Washington. At Bladensburg, on the outskirts of the capital, they encountered a militia force that outnumbered them. But no Andrew Jackson commanded these Americans; facing British veterans, and with President Madison watching, they turned and ran almost without firing a shot. The British overran Washington and burned most public buildings, including the Capitol and the White House. They found Baltimore more difficult. There both land and naval attacks failed. From a British ship where he had been detained, an American civilian watched the naval bombardment of Fort McHenry. When at dawn he detected the American flag still flying over the fort, Francis Scott Key wrote on an old letter a poem that later was set to music and widely admired. He called it "The Star-Spangled Banner."

NEW ORLEANS AND THE END OF THE WAR

After Baltimore and Fort McHenry the southern theater of war shifted back to the Southwest. Upon leaving Baltimore, the British went to Jamaica, where they joined a major British force aimed at New Orleans. Preparing to face the expected British onslaught was Andrew Jackson, who had been promoted to major general in the regular United States Army and put in command of all troops in the Southwest. Although the Americans anticipated a British strike, they did not know precisely where the enemy would land. Initially Jackson considered Mobile the most likely spot, but by December 1814 he had arrived in the city the British had chosen as their target, New Orleans.

Once in New Orleans, Jackson prepared energetically to meet the British threat. He threw his forceful personality directly into the fray. Determined that he alone, not city officials, would make all the crucial decisions concerning the

Washington D.C.
burned August 24, 1814

MISSOURI
TERRITORY

—— U.S. movements
•••• British movements

MISSISSIPPI RIVER

MISSISSIPPI
TERRITORY

Horseshoe Bend
March 27, 1814

Jackson 1814

LOUISIANA

SPANISH
TERRITORY

Jackson
1814–1815

Ft. Mims

Pensacola

New Orleans
January 8, 1815

SPANISH TERRITORY
(FLORIDA)

Pakenham
1814–1815

GULF OF MEXICO

THE WAR OF 1812 IN THE SOUTH

civilian population as well as the army, he declared martial law in the city. The American troops required someone with a hand as strong as Jackson's. His force consisted of almost 900 U.S. Army regulars, 6,000 to 7,000 militiamen from Kentucky, Louisiana, and Tennessee, and a few hundred free blacks organized in a separate battalion; he even had a band of pirates. Immediately Jackson began work on the neglected defenses of the city. When he learned that the British had disembarked and moved units to within seven miles of New Orleans, he reacted swiftly. With 5,000 men he made a night attack, which checked the British advance.

After that engagement Jackson worked strenuously to build a defensive line at Chalmette's plantation, some five miles east of the city. While Jackson's men threw up breastworks, the British commander, Sir Edward Pakenham, a veteran of the Napoleonic campaigns, waited for reinforcements. Finally in early January Pakenham was ready. His tactics were unimaginative. Con

ANDREW JACKSON, THE GREAT HERO (Metropolitan Museum of Art, Harris Brisbane Dick Fund, 1964)

vinced that British soldiers who had faced the mighty French armies could easily overpower Jackson's unprofessional Americans, Pakenham decided to send his troops straight at the Americans. This decision forced the British troops to march across a narrow front, with the Mississippi on their left and a cypress swamp on their right, directly toward the American cannon and rifles.

In the foggy dawn of January 8, 1815, the Redcoats advanced with bayonets fixed. Under orders to hold their fire until the British came within easy range, the Americans watched their foe moving toward them. Finally the command rang out. American artillery raked the British lines as Jackson's infantrymen flung a sheet of lead at the Redcoats. The British made two direct assaults in the face of this withering fire before their line splintered. No soldiers could forever withstand the deadly fusillade, and they had nowhere to turn. General Pakenham, urging his men forward, was hit twice. As he was calling up his reserves, he was killed by a shell fragment.

Jackson won a great victory. Failing to break Jackson's line, the British retreated to their transports. They paid a fearful price on that January morning. Of some 5,300 men in the attacking force, almost 2,100 were killed and wounded, including three generals. The Americans, in stark contrast, suffered fewer than 20 killed, around 60 wounded and missing. General Pakenham had expected to return to England a great hero; instead his body went home in a cask of rum. The hero was Jackson, who directed the greatest American victory of the war.

Jackson's triumph had far-reaching consequences. Back in the summer of 1814 peace negotiations between American and British commissioners had begun in Ghent, Belgium. By late fall the two sides had settled on an agreement that stipulated the *status quo ante bellum*. In other words, the United States would come out of the war with its territory intact while the British made no concessions on neutral rights or impressment. On Christmas Eve, 1814, the Treaty of Ghent was signed. Thus the Battle of New Orleans was fought after a peace treaty had been completed. But New Orleans represented considerably more than an empty victory. A victorious British army sitting in New Orleans would have mocked American claims to the republic's 1812 boundaries. At New Orleans, no matter what took place in Ghent, the future of the Southwest was at stake. Jackson's battlefield victory guaranteed American control of both the Mississippi Valley and the Southwest.

Jackson's defeat of the British coupled with his destruction of the Creeks as a fighting force pointed up the vulnerability of Spanish Florida. With the Indians crushed and the British turned back, Spain could not hope to hold Florida very long against an expanding United States. The weakness, even the impossibility, of Spain's position was dramatized in 1818, when General Jackson marched into Florida in pursuit of marauding Seminoles and runaway slaves. He drove the Indians southward and seized the Spanish garrisons at St. Marks and Pensacola. Although Jackson did not remain in Florida, the administration of James Monroe used Jackson's foray to press Spain. Secretary of State John Quincy Adams told the Spanish that if the United States had to send another expedition against Indians into Florida, American troops would remain. Accepting the inevitable, Spain in 1819 agreed to a treaty that transferred Florida to the United States.

All of these notable events between 1814 and 1819—the destruction of the Creeks, the defeat of the British, the acquisition of Florida—came about in no small part because of one man, Andrew Jackson. Jackson became something Americans had not seen since George Washington: a genuine national hero. Though indisputably a national hero, Jackson had a special identity in the South. His great exploits had come in the South, and most of the officers and men who fought with him were southern. He had been born in South Carolina and as a young man had moved to Tennessee, where he began to accumulate the two possessions most prized by white southerners, land and black slaves. Southerners would not soon forget Andrew Jackson.

A NATIONALIST COURSE

Though the war had ended triumphantly at New Orleans and with the United States intact, leaders in the administration and in the Congress knew that the country had had quite a close call. Huzzahs aroused by the news from New Orleans swelled to grandiloquent expressions of national pride, but the men who made policy realized that United States was utterly unprepared for a war with a major power. Britain's preoccupation with Europe had been as instrumental as Jackson's victory in preserving the United States. Next time the country might not be so fortunate. That knowledge had a powerful effect on the Republican party and on the South. The party, with its southern cohort in agreement, decided that the power and authority of the central government would have to be strengthened.

Even before the war was over, President Madison acted to increase the federal government's power. In his annual message to Congress in December 1814, presented as Jackson prepared to meet the British attack on New Orleans, the Madison administration called for a protective tariff, a national bank, and a system of internal improvements. Southerners not only supported this new direction, they led the way. After all, Madison was a Virginian. In the Congress every southern state provided votes for the bills pushed by the administration and directed through the legislative process by such southern Republicans as John C. Calhoun and Henry Clay.

As these measures made their way through Congress in 1816 and 1817, not every southern Republican supported every one of them. Southerners in the House voted more than 2 to 1 in favor of a national bank but by a small majority opposed the tariff of 1816. More voted against than for internal improvements, but a substantial number did support such expenditures. A Quid-like opposition that based its objections solely on doctrinal purity had little importance. The irrelevance of traditional Republican doctrine was eloquently expressed by Nathaniel Macon, the old Quid from North Carolina. Lamenting the passage of the bank bill, Macon seemingly eulogized the Republicanism he cherished when he said, "I am at a loss to account for the fact that I seem to be the only person of those who were formerly in Congress, that still cannot find the authority for a bank in the constitution of the U.S."

For southern Republicans the voting pattern in Congress was instructive. The pattern had a double weave. One thread indicated that for many southerners the old ideology, which focused on a small government with limited powers and honored agrarianism as the essence of republican society, had been suppressed or had disappeared. A second thread carried the legacy of tradition. By voting chiefly for measures that would help their localities, southerners could salve their political consciences. Unlike Calhoun and Clay, most had not become dedicated nationalists. President Madison provides a superb illustration of this divided mind. He accepted a bank and the tariff, but in the end he vetoed the internal improvements bill because the Constitution did not specifically authorize the central government to build roads and canals. Neither, of course, did it specifically authorize a national bank or a protective tariff.

SOUTHERNERS AND THE NEW NATIONALISM

Madison along with others of his generation had moved a considerable distance from their position of the 1790s. Of that generation only John Randolph,

Nathaniel Macon, and their small congregation held fast to the gospel preached by Republicans in an earlier time. Adjusters such as Madison believed that the responsibilities of power at times overrode ideology. Jefferson himself had demonstrated that conviction with both Louisiana and the embargo. Then the war seared the president and the colleagues who shared his responsibility and witnessed the same unnerving events. Frightened by the weakness of the government which the war had exposed, they believed that an increase in strength was essential. Thus they consciously traveled down a new political road.

This assessment, however, does not account for the behavior of Calhoun, Clay, and others of the younger generation in every southern state. Generally these men had not participated directly in the politics of the 1790s. They had come of political age when their party was in the ascendancy. To them the exercise of power meant the Republicans' exercise of power. And because of the South's position in the party, it necessarily meant the South's exercise of power. These young southerners did not distrust either their party or themselves. They demanded war in 1812 to prevent Great Britain from crippling their country. The war persuaded them that the energetic spirit they had fostered required additional bone and muscle. Without hesitation they moved to add substance to spirit. National power had never endangered them. Always they had seen it exercised by their own elders, even by themselves. They had never seen it turned against the South or against southern interests as they perceived them.

Peace and the spectacular triumph at New Orleans confirmed the exuberant southerners in their nationalism. Building a nation, they were caught up in swirling events. They had met Great Britain a second time and survived, even prevailed. They had also finally done away with their old political enemies. The Virginian James Monroe swept the nation in 1816 to become the third successive southern Republican president. The Federalist candidate, Rufus King of New York, carried only Delaware, Connecticut, and Massachusetts. In the South the Federalist party became politically extinct. It was a heady time.

THE MARCH WESTWARD CONTINUES

The South did not expend its energy solely on legislation and elections. Southerners participated vigorously in the westward drive that between 1815 and 1820 significantly expanded the nation's settled borders. In those five years organized states for the first time reached the Mississippi. In the old Northwest Territory, beyond the Ohio River, both Indiana and Illinois joined the Union. In the Southwest settlers also pushed toward the great river. Mississippi became a state in 1817, followed by Alabama in 1819. Those two, along with Louisiana, which had entered the Union in 1812, expanded the South considerably.

This expansion contributed to the political strength of the South. From the time of the Constitutional Convention southerners had expected expansion to help them dominate the new nation. The ascendancy of the Republican party indicated that they indeed dominated it, and expansion had surely helped. The

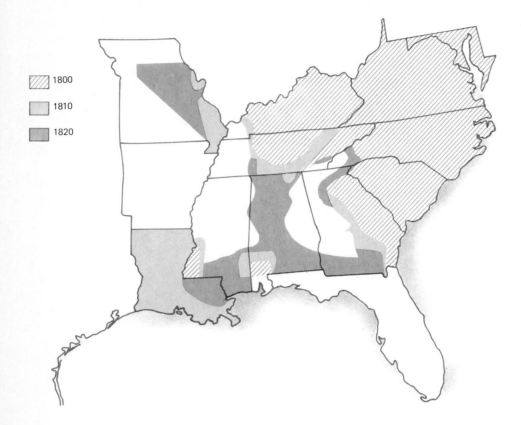

1800

1810

1820

POPULATION MOVEMENT IN THE SOUTH, 1800–1820

first fruits, Tennessee and Kentucky, had lengthened the Republican column. Then Jefferson purchased Louisiana, which seemed to give permanence to southern political as well as economic and ideological aspirations. Alabama and Mississippi buttressed the South's political power. As southern states were added to the Union, the three-fifths clause of the Constitution, which permitted 60 percent of the slave population to be counted for the purposes of apportioning congressmen in a state, continuously added to the number of presidential electors claimed by the South and increased the region's national political strength. After the admission of Alabama in 1819 the Union had eleven slave and eleven free states.

The South had long cast covetous eyes on Spanish Florida. Andrew Jackson's exploits there in 1818 captured the South's attention and won the plaudits of western southerners, though some seaboard southerners were alarmed by Jackson's direct action. When the United States acquired Florida in

1819, southerners certainly expected it to end up under their influence. And when President Monroe named General Jackson as the first governor of the Florida Territory, southerners were sure that it had done so.

In 1819 the South had no reason to change its mind about the ultimate result of expansion. New southern states reinforced the political legions of the Republican party, the party southerners viewed as their own. With the remainder of vast Louisiana and nearby Florida on the horizon, the future of expansion seemed equally hospitable to southern interests.

THE DISSENTERS

Although nationalist fervor did dominate the South, a minority of southerners stood in opposition to the new faith. This opposition centered on Virginia, but not all Virginia Republicans belonged to it. The dissenters held fast to the doctrines of the 1790s and repeated Quid rhetoric against what had become mainstream Republicanism. Old Quids such as John Randolph of Roanoke continued to emphasize pure Republicanism as they had done before the War of 1812, but they were seldom called Quids now and they were not among the chief spokesmen for this new opposition; that honor went to powerful Virginia Republicans who had opposed the Quids a decade earlier. The most important opponents were leaders of the Richmond Junto, a loosely knit organization that dominated Republican (and later Democratic) politics in Virginia for a generation. Thomas Ritchie, editor of the Richmond *Enquirer*, the best-known Republican newspaper in the South—according to the aged Jefferson, it was the only paper in the nation worth reading—warned his readers that the nationalist course undermined the hallowed truths of the 1790s.

Not only did the policies of the Madison and Monroe administrations concern the Richmond Junto and its followers; decisions of the United States Supreme Court distressed them mightily. Ironically, the author of many of the opinions that so rankled the Virginians was one of their own, with a difference. John Marshall was just as Virginian as Ritchie or anyone else, but he was a Federalist. Appointed chief justice by President Adams in 1801, Marshall remained loyal to Federalist concepts of power and authority throughout the Republican ascendancy. In the postwar years two major Court decisions gave legal sanction to the nationalist course. In 1816 in *Martin* v. *Hunter's Lessee* the Supreme Court affirmed on broad grounds that it could review and reverse, if it thought proper, all cases under the laws, treaties, or Constitution of the United States, whether they originated in federal or state courts. In effect this decision reduced state courts to inferior tribunals. Then in *McCulloch* v. *Maryland* in 1819 the Supreme Court gave powerful sanction to the broad, or classically Federalist, interpretation of the Constitution. Affirming the constitutionality of the Bank of the United States, Chief Justice Marshall announced that the Congress could pass any law that was necessary and proper to conduct national business, the only exceptions being measures expressly prohibited by the Constitution. The

old strict-construction argument that the Constitution had to authorize specifically any particular measure before it could be considered constitutional made
no headway before Marshall's court.

The southerners troubled by congressional laws and Supreme Court decisions wrote, spoke, and voted in a distinct minority until 1819. In that year two
cataclysmic events rocked the South and the Republican party: the onset of the
Missouri crisis and a financial panic. The shock waves from these massive up-
heavals caused fundamental shifts that altered the southern landscape and
turned a minority into a majority.

THE ONSET OF THE MISSOURI CRISIS

The Missouri crisis struck at the vitals of the South. No one was surprised when
Congress in 1819 considered a bill to admit Missouri as a slave state. Slavery
had been legal in Missouri under both the French and the Spanish, and because
the treaty by which the United States acquired Louisiana guaranteed the preservation of slavery, it had been a legitimate part of an American Missouri since
1803. And Congress had certainly admitted new slave states. Between 1792 and
1817 Kentucky, Tennessee, Louisiana, and Mississippi had all come in with little fanfare. Nor did Alabama experience any difficulty in that same year, 1819.

Missouri, however, became a great battleground when Congressman James
Tallmadge of New York offered a two-part amendment to the statehood bill.
First, no more slaves would be allowed to enter Missouri; second, all slave children born after statehood would become free at age twenty-five. Tallmadge
proposed a gradual emancipation plan, for he advocated no change in the status of the 10,000 slaves already in Missouri. Thus Missouri would remain a
slave state for decades, though not forever.

The origins of the Tallmadge Amendment remain unclear. In the years preceding 1819 antislavery activity had not been significant in either Congress or
the country at large. The evidence suggests that both moral and political motives prompted Tallmadge's proposal. Many northerners were unhappy with
the Constitution's three-fifths clause, which added notably to southern strength
in the House of Representatives and in the electoral college. To these
northerners the three-fifths clause underlay the South's domination of the national government, and they wanted that domination ended. Refusal to permit
the three-fifths advantage to cross the Mississippi seemed to be a way to keep
the South's power from expanding. Too, many northerners were morally of-
fended by slavery; they believed it mocked the Declaration of Independence
and blemished American liberty. Moreover, much of Missouri lay directly west
of Illinois, a free state. To some northerners the admission of a slave Missouri
would take slavery beyond its traditional bounds, north even more than west.

The Tallmadge Amendment ignited a political firestorm. Southerners united
in denouncing it. As a result, sectional lines drew taut and Republican unity
broke down. With free-state congressmen considerably outnumbering those

from the slave states, a sectional vote would mean passage for the amendment. On February 17, 1819, that is exactly what happened. But later in the month the Senate rejected the amendment. When the Fifteenth Congress adjourned on March 3, the issue of Missouri's statehood had not been decided. The convening of the new Sixteenth Congress in December 1819 brought no agreement; the same split between the two chambers blocked any action.

THE SOUTH'S REACTION

The South's unity rested on three pillars. First, southerners refused to permit what they called outside interference with slavery. Since the Constitutional Convention southerners had declared that slavery was their institution and that only they could decide its future. Now the Tallmadge Amendment sought to restrict southern expansion into the Louisiana Purchase. But southerners wanted no barriers to expansion, which had always been central to their economic and political strength. Finally, the thrust of the Tallmadge Amendment undermined the South's conception of the country. The supporters of the amendment denounced slavery as an aberration in the United States, a nation dedicated to freedom and liberty. The time had come, they insisted, for Congress to put on the road to extinction the nefarious, un-American institution of slavery. The argument that liberty and slavery could not coexist fundamentally challenged the southern view of liberty and slavery. At least since the Revolution most white southerners had equated their own liberty with their right to decide the fate of their black slaves. In southern eyes a threat to their control of their slaves automatically jeopardized their liberty.

In the congressional debates that stretched through the winter of 1819–1820 southerners emphasized themes that would dominate southern political rhetoric and thinking for the remainder of the antebellum era. They emphatically reaffirmed that they would tolerate no outside interference with slavery. Southern speakers took two different tacks to make this fundamental point. The Virginians especially repeated their time-honored laments about the evil of slavery, but as always, they simultaneously insisted that slavery was solely a southern concern. At the same time a bold new southern voice staunchly defended slavery. For the first time in the national legislature southerners defended slavery as a positive good. Some southerners proclaimed that "Christ himself gave a sanction to slavery." Others painted warm, bucolic pictures of plantation life and the human affection that bound masters and slaves in friendship and harmony. Of course these apostles of bondage joined their less committed southern brothers in refusing totally to permit any outside involvement with slavery.

Although such an audacious defense had never before been heard in Congress, this language did not mean that the white South had reached some kind of historic crossroads in its attitude toward slavery. The defense clearly spelled out the South's contention that slavery was a permanent institution, but no evidence exists to indicate that the Missouri crisis prompted a hardening of attitudes on the subject. During both the Revolutionary era and the ratification of the Constitution, the South had made clear its commitment to slavery. Changes had occurred by 1819, but outside, not inside, the South. A new antislavery mood had surfaced in the North, and for the first time the South faced a sustained public attack on slavery; it responded with a public defense. Missouri did demonstrate that the South was willing to take such a stance, but the basic commitment had been consciously powerful since the Revolution.

In attacking the Tallmadge Amendment southerners for the first time made an extended connection between states' rights and slavery. Previously they had often appealed to states' rights to justify a broad definition of their interests; now they fused states' rights with slavery. Southerners argued that the Constitution made no provision for placing conditions or restrictions on a new state such as those proposed by the Tallmadge Amendment. When advocates of restriction countered calls for states' rights with assertions that the Tallmadge Amendment was needed to guarantee republican government, southerners recoiled in horror. Carried to its logical extreme, that doctrine could impose conditions not just on new states but on old ones. In the southern interpretation of the northern argument, slavery could be endangered everywhere. Constitutionally speaking, the Missouri crisis propelled the South's reaction against postwar nationalism into a headlong rush back to the 1790s, to the Virginia and Kentucky resolutions. As in that earlier time, self-interest and ideology meshed perfectly. During the lengthy debates southerners talked about more than slavery and states' rights; they raised the ominous specter of disunion. One senator cried that the North's determination to interfere with slavery could end only in "a brother's sword crimsoned with brother's blood."

THE MISSOURI COMPROMISE

The Missouri crisis never became a secession crisis because Congress found a solution. The Missouri Compromise of 1820 had three elements: (1) the admission of Missouri as a slave state, (2) the admission of Maine as a free state, and (3) a slavery/freedom boundary line drawn through the Louisiana Purchase along 36°30' westward from the Mississippi River; it marked the southern border of Missouri.

Not all senators and representatives were happy about the compromise. When the three parts were presented to the Senate as a package, the vote revealed deep sectional differences. Slave-state senators supported it 20 to 2; free-state senators voted against it 18 to 4. It seems obvious that southerners saw the package as their victory. A 10-to-1 margin could not be interpreted as anything less than a perceived triumph. In the House the three parts of the compromise were presented separately, and southerners voted overwhelmingly for two parts and rejected one—the 36°30' line.

Thirty-seven southern congressmen voted against the territorial line, considering it too great a concession. They agreed with Nathaniel Macon that "to

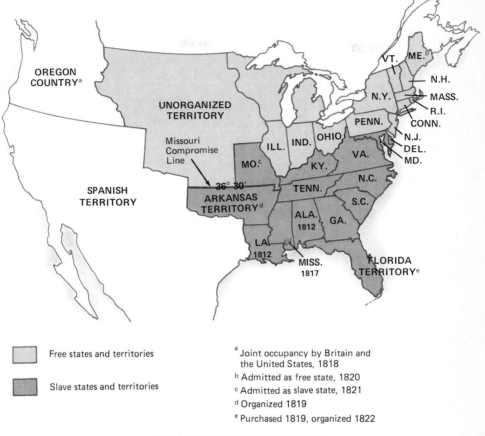

Free states and territories

Slave states and territories

[a] Joint occupancy by Britain and the United States, 1818
[b] Admitted as free state, 1820
[c] Admitted as slave state, 1821
[d] Organized 1819
[e] Purchased 1819, organized 1822

THE MISSOURI COMPROMISE

compromise is to acknowledge the right of Congress to interfere and to legislate on the subject. This would be acknowledging too much." The major Republican editor, Thomas Ritchie, warned that acceptance of the territorial division would set a dangerous precedent by inviting the North to disregard southern interests. "If we yield now, beware," he cried, "[the North] will ride us forever." But despite their pleadings and warnings, Macon, Ritchie, and their colleagues failed to undo the compromise, which finally passed the Congress in March 1820. The crisis had passed.

The vantage point of hindsight causes wonder why the South gave in on the territorial point, which would later become the critical issue. In 1820 the southerners obviously considered paramount the admission of Missouri as a slave state. They wanted a slave state west of the Mississippi, in the Louisiana Purchase, and to get what they wanted many of them willingly gave up their right to take slaves into much of the rest of the Purchase. That the proposal for the 36°30′ line originated within the proslavery camp demonstrates conclusively that in 1820 they viewed the slave state they could get now as considerably more important than other slave states they might get later. To southerners the admission of Missouri proved that the expansion of their peculiar institution, which had been so important in the first generation of the new nation, had a beachhead on the far shore of the future.

Although a few southerners objected to the territorial restriction on constitutional grounds, most did not. The virtual absence of such opposition from a major discussion of constitutional powers and slavery clearly indicates that in 1820 most southerners who thought about the subject believed that Congress had the power to act on slavery in the territories. After all, precedent had been set with the Northwest Ordinance of 1787, which prohibited slavery north of the Ohio River. Likewise, Congress legislated on slavery in the Mississippi Territory in 1798, and again in 1804 in the Louisiana Purchase, and once more in 1819 in the Arkansas Territory. Congress's refusal to prohibit slavery in each of those cases certainly did not imply limits on congressional power or opposition to the exercise of that power by southerners as well as northerners.

THE PANIC OF 1819

At the same time the Missouri crisis wracked the Congress, the Panic of 1819, the first great economic depression in American history, assaulted the American economy. The South was not spared. The panic brought an abrupt halt to the postwar prosperity that had helped create a widespread economic nationalism. That prosperity had been based in large part on agricultural exports, and cotton was the most important item on the list. The explosion in the price of cotton led to a sharp demand for the two commodities essential for its production, land and slaves. The cotton boom focused on the Southwest—the new states of Alabama and Mississippi, and to a lesser extent Louisiana, Georgia, and Tennessee. The purchase of land and slaves required more capital than most families had. Thus credit became absolutely essential to fuel the boiler that generated prosperity.

To thousands of southerners—on plantations, on farms, in the stores that supplied them and the banks that lent them money and the trading offices that speculated on them—the financial feast came to an abrupt end long before all the anticipated courses had been served. At the beginning of 1819 cotton sold for 33 cents a pound; by fall it brought less than half that amount. The utter collapse of cotton prices, caused in large part by overproduction, signaled a precipitous decline of the entire economy. The prices of other agricultural products followed cotton downward. Slave prices also tumbled. Early in 1819 the cost of a prime field hand reached $800 in Richmond and $1,100 in New Orleans; the dollar value had doubled since the war. But by 1821 the price in Richmond fell to less than $600 and in New Orleans it plummeted to $800. Bank shares, rents, real estate all collapsed after the wreck of agriculture. Bankruptcy seemed at worst imminent, at best only inevitable. Sudden, totally unexpected, the panic had a massive impact on the South, political as well as economic.

Its fury certainly jolted William T. Palfrey, a planter in St. Mary Parish, Louisiana. Noting that land prices were rising and that his slave force was increasing, Palfrey greeted the spring of 1819 with optimism, but by autumn his outlook had changed. Though his cotton had "never looked as well as it does now," the price was "so unfavorable" that even the value of slaves was collapsing. Palfrey described a "depression in price that will make a melancholy elimination in the amount of Dollars." By the spring of 1820 his situation had worsened. Despite an abundant crop, he had to keep borrowing. The notes piled up, and William Palfrey feared for his financial survival. Though he managed to hold on, many others who faced similar difficulties went under.

POLITICAL REPERCUSSIONS

On the state level the panic led to a return of financial politics, especially in the Southwest, where the aftermath of the panic seemed to replay the 1780s. Talk of stay laws, debates about circulating currency, disputes between creditors and debtors, and arguments about the proper role of banks pervaded the political arena. Both Tennessee and Kentucky enacted stay laws. Tennessee also created the Bank of Tennessee, with the power to issue $1 million in paper money and to make loans not exceeding $1,000 to a single borrower. Georgia and Alabama organized comparable institutions with similar stipulations on loan ceilings and distribution. Factions within the dominant Republican party coalesced on opposite sides of these financial issues.

This political warring brought to state politics a bitterness not seen since the 1780s. In the furor of depression politics, financial issues such as the role of banks and the rights of creditors and debtors became entangled with the most precious of all southern commodities, liberty. Creditors and opponents of banks charged that the power of banks gave them an unnatural privilege that imperiled both the independence of the community and the control individuals had over their own affairs. Many southerners viewed the banks and the paper money they issued as qualitatively different from the traditional land and slaves. The cries against this kind of privilege echoed the Republican assault on Hamilton's financial policy. In turn, politicians who considered banks and creditors as performing valuable services denounced their opponents as demagogues who denied property rights and strained the social fabric, thus endangering liberty.

The panic also had major repercussions on the relationship between the South and the rest of the nation. Facing financial ruin, many southerners searched for villains, and banks served as easily identifiable ones. Banks had provided much of the credit that underwrote the cost of land and slaves, and many banks had seriously overextended themselves. When the financial crunch came, banks retrenched and called in loans. And the financial pincers were being applied not only by local banks. The second Bank of the United States, with headquarters in Philadelphia and branches throughout the country, including ten in the slave states, had opened its doors in 1817. Both individuals and local banks did business with the national bank, which exercised no more fiscal judgment than most southern banks did. Like them, it became overextended and found itself in a precarious financial position. By the summer of 1818 the bank had almost a 10-to-1 imbalance between its specie reserve (gold and silver coins on deposit) and its immediate liabilities. And without the government-backed insurance guarantees that protect bank depositors today, a prudent balance between specie reserves and liabilities offered the only protection to depositors. To save itself, the bank retrenched with ferocity, and its southern branches were forced to do so as well.

The Bank of the United States survived, but at the partial expense of hard-pressed southerners, who cried that "the Bank was saved and the people were ruined." Though devastated southerners condemned their own banks as "horse-leeches [that] drained every drop of blood they could from a suffering community," they identified the Bank of the United States as playing an especially evil role. In the graphic image of one antibank enthusiast, southerners discovered themselves "in the jaws of the monster! a lump of butter in the mouth of a dog! one gulp, one swallow, and all is gone."

With the bank indicted as the chief villain, it took but a step to include in the indictment as accessories the nationalism and broad construction of the Constitution which had spawned the bank. Because energetic government sanctioned by an elastic view of the Constitution had permitted the creation of the bank, they became the real menaces. Most southerners found such an interpretation particularly compelling because it enabled them to speak in the congenial language they had spoken so powerfully during the Revolution and on through the 1790s. Fear of an oppressive central authority and the necessity for local control to protect liberty—once again this twin message became the cry of the South.

Antipathy toward the Bank of the United States not only brought back the old fears of national power; it also rekindled sectional animosity. Although the bank was certainly active in the South, its main office was in Philadelphia, after all. Its southern enemies had no difficulty in branding it a northern institution that benefited mainly northern financial interests.

The rejuvenated antagonism to a broad view of the Constitution and an active federal government also revealed itself when Congress considered another tariff bill in 1820. Southerners led the opposition to this measure, which called for an increase in the duties imposed by the 1816 law. They argued that an increased tariff would give a favored status to manufacturers, and that Congress should not provide an artificial stimulus to manufacturing. Southerners also asserted that a protective tariff would benefit a special interest against the people, or a nonsouthern interest against the South. The vote was more sectional than it had been in 1816. Only a tiny southern group, mostly from Kentucky and

Maryland, voted aye. The votes of southern senators were crucial when by one vote the Senate indefinitely postponed the bill.

In response to the panic and to the Missouri Compromise, southerners united in rejecting nationalism, but this unity disintegrated as financial politics splintered the states. Yet the unity as well as the divisiveness rested on a widely shared perception that liberty was threatened. That perception would have enormous import in southern politics in general and in the relationship between the South and the Republican party in particular.

7

A New Political Structure

❖

The pressures generated by the Missouri crisis and the Panic of 1819 broke the Jeffersonian Republican party apart. The tension between the advocates of national power and the guardians of local authority proved greater than the old party's ability to contain them. For southerners the struggle was especially momentous because of the intimate ties between the party and the South. For southerners the events of 1819 revived and reinforced the lesson of the 1790s—power exercised by the national government could menace the vital interests of the South

During the Missouri controversy, the panic, and the debate over an increased protective tariff in 1820 and in 1824, southern leaders once again warned of the dangers of a strong national government buttressed by a broad interpretation of the Constitution. For the first time in Congress southerners in 1823 declared the protective tariff unconstitutional. Asserting correctly that the Constitution nowhere explicitly endorsed protection, they concluded that Congress had no authority to protect domestic manufacturing. The passage of the new tariff in 1824, despite overwhelming southern opposition, confirmed the lessons of Missouri. The South could no longer count on the Republican party to do its bidding.

The constitutional retrenchment so evident in debates over protection reached into the most sensitive areas. Southerners began to see broad construction as a potential threat to more than their economic interests and the unrestricted expansion of slavery. Nathaniel Macon confided to a friend, "If Congress can make banks, roads, and canals under the Constitution they can free any slave in the United States." John Randolph of Roanoke expanded on Macon's fearful theme in a speech to the House in 1824; in opposition to a bill that merely authorized widespread federal surveys for roads and canals, Randolph exposed the core of the South's apprehension about national power.

> If congress possess the power to do what is proposed by this bill, they may emancipate every slave in the United States. . . . And where will they find the power? They

156

may . . . hook the power upon the first loop they find in the Constitution; they might take the preamble—perhaps the war making power—or they might take a greater sweep, and say, with some gentlemen, that it is not to be found in this or that of the granted powers, but results from all of them—which is not only a dangerous but the *most dangerous* doctrine.

BACKGROUND TO 1824

The debate over the future orientation of the Republican party focused on the contest to choose a successor to James Monroe in the White House. The third member of the Virginia dynasty, Monroe was reelected in 1820 without opposition. For Monroe reelection brought the best of all possible political worlds—the disappearance of the Federalist party as a national entity. No Federalist opposed Monroe in 1820. To Monroe that signified the victorious conclusion of the great political war begun in the 1790s. The serious issues facing his party and the internal conflicts raging within it held little interest for him. With his powdered wig and buckled breeches, Monroe was an artifact in fashion as well as in politics. Although Monroe seemed oblivious of the swirl around him, forceful men in his cabinet and in the Congress figured prominently in it. That southerners dominated this group pointed up the special relationship between the South and the party.

Only Monroe's secretary of state, John Quincy Adams of Massachusetts, carried northern colors in the great political parade of 1824. Both Secretary of the Treasury William H. Crawford of Georgia and Secretary of War John C. Calhoun of South Carolina ardently desired the presidency. The Kentuckian Henry Clay, as Speaker, the most influential man in the House of Representatives and the most popular as well, eagerly hoped for the top prize. Each of these four brought impressive legislative or administrative credentials to the presidential race. The fifth candidate also had a notable public record, but one of a different sort. Although he had served in both House and Senate, in fact was a sitting United States senator in 1824, Andrew Jackson had never been a major figure in the national legislature. None of his competitors, however, could match his public visibility and fame. His military exploits had made him the most widely known American of his time, save possibly for the Revolutionary patriarchs Jefferson and John Adams. Never in American history has a stronger group vied for the presidency.

Although four southerners dominated the field, they neither stood together ideologically nor agreed on the future direction of the party. Calhoun, Clay, and Crawford had all been part of the new nationalism after the War of 1812. Calhoun and Clay had been especially energetic in advancing the postwar Republican doctrine of vigorous government. Crawford was not quite so outspokenly in favor of the new orthodoxy, though he never took serious issue with it. Despite his vote for the Tariff of 1824, Jackson escaped identification with any particular ideology. His heroic public image was grounded in his military exploits, not in his stand on public policy or in his political philosophy.

The traditional Republican leaders in the seaboard states adopted Crawford as the man who could ensure the demise of the unholy "Federalism" that in their view had seeped into the party. Why these men settled upon Crawford is unclear; perhaps because he was less tainted with the new nationalism than any other major figure. Although William H. Crawford is a forgotten man today, his contemporaries considered him a political leader of the first rank. The Crawford backers had no intention of remaining a local interest group. In a conscious effort to replicate the old Virginia–New York alliance, they joined with Martin Van Buren, the politically astute manager of the dominant faction in the New York Republican party. Called Radicals because in their mind they advocated a radical return to the old ways and thoughts, these men believed they would purify the party.

Though clearly distinguishable from Crawford, Calhoun and Clay did not stand together. At this time Calhoun was in transit between an ardent nationalism that could not imagine the interest of the South "to be opposed to the rest of the Union" and a zealous sectionalism that saw a growing Union threatening the security of the South. In making this momentous shift Calhoun was following his state, which was rapidly deserting postwar nationalism, and also his own conviction that increasing federal power could endanger the South. Even though he was actively participating in the southern shift, Calhoun failed to generate significant support outside South Carolina. For many southern Republicans he had been too able on the other side for too long. Clay, on the other hand, remained a stalwart behind the nationalist program he had helped to shape. He even talked about an American System in which the national bank, the protective tariff, and internal improvements would all work together for the benefit of the nation. Although enormously popular with his fellow politicians, he could not translate that goodwill into general southern support. In the South he was on the wrong side of the crucial issue.

A NEW POLITICS

With Calhoun and Clay severely circumscribed and Adams shackled by his New England identity, Crawford appeared well on his way to securing the leadership of a new generation of southern Republicans. But just as triumph seemed within his grasp, he collided with the formidable presence of Andrew Jackson. They never met in a face-to-face debate. Their direct competition occurred within the structure of southern politics, and the collision permanently altered the structure. Crawford's managers wanted to win in the old-fashioned Republican way, with the caucus of congressional Republicans awarding Crawford its presidential nomination. The caucus held an honored place in Republican tradition; Jefferson, Madison, and Monroe had all received its blessings and its nomination. In 1824 Crawford's managers saw their man as next in line.

But in the states and the nation a new politics overpowered Crawford. Though ideologically the southern Republicans were reverting to a familiar, secure position, in practice they were rushing toward the future. Denouncing Crawford's campaign as "the few political managers against the body of the people," his opponents called on the voters to defend their right of choice by crushing Crawford and the caucus. In North Carolina, Crawford's opponents organized a People's party to discredit his campaign. The Tennessee legislature announced that the election should be left "to the *people themselves*." Of course, the anti-Crawfordites expected to win practical political gains by freeing the selection process from the caucus.

They did succeed in destroying the caucus by defining its destruction as a practical manifestation of democracy and the preservation of liberty. The caucus became a dead letter. When it met in February 1824, duly called by Crawford leaders, only 66 Republicans attended while almost 200 stayed away. Although Crawford won the caucus's endorsement, the victory was hollow. To the multitude of southern Republicans the caucus meant nothing.

With the caucus slain and a rowdier, more popular politics victorious, appeals to the mass of voters became essential for political triumph. Managers could certainly still plot and plan; after all, such planning had brought down the caucus. Still, the result meant more direct contact with voters. In this kind of context no one in the race could match Jackson. As one of his opponents put it, "It is very difficult to electioneer successfully against General Jackson—his character and services are of the kind which *alone* the people can appreciate and feel." In fact, Jackson's strength caused Calhoun to reassess his position. Finding his candidacy overwhelmed by Jackson's surge, Calhoun opted for the vice presidency, a post for which he was unopposed.

The election demonstrated Jackson's power. He won all the electoral votes in five states along with a majority in Maryland and Louisiana. His total was 55, only one less than that of all of his opponents combined. In 1824, for the first time in a presidential election, a notable popular vote was cast. Here Jackson's dominance was unmistakably clear. Winning more than 78,000 popular votes, Jackson outdistanced his nearest rival, Crawford, by more than 2½ to 1. Moreover, his vote exceeded the combined votes of all other candidates. Even the sainted Jefferson might not have been Jackson's match among southern voters.

Although Jackson trounced his opponents in the South, the national outcome was not so clear-cut. As none of the candidates won a majority of electoral votes, the job of electing the president fell to the House of Representatives, where the Constitution accorded each state one vote. In the House the southern vote did not follow precisely the pattern of the general election. Emphasizing his close ties to the leadership of the seaboard states, Crawford not only held Virginia and Georgia but also gained North Carolina, which had gone for Jackson. The border South went solidly for John Quincy Adams, largely because

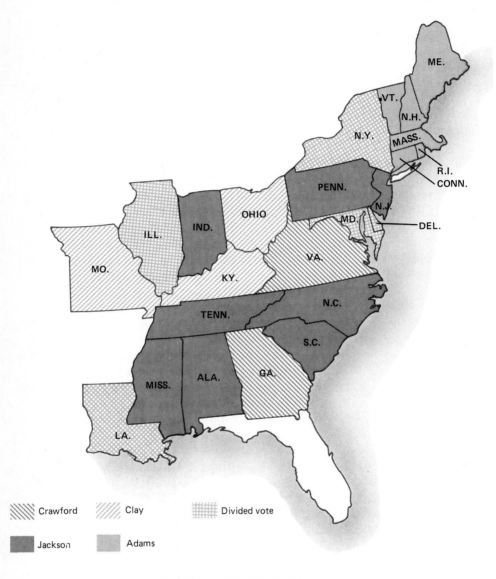

THE ELECTION OF 1824

Clay brought his two states of Kentucky and Missouri into the Adams camp. Clay's influence in the House also helped Adams get Louisiana and Maryland, where Jackson had won a majority of the electoral votes. Although these four slave states provided votes essential for Adams's victory in the House, they were congressional votes only, based on little or no popular support.

A NEW ALIGNMENT

For the South the most important result of Adams's election came in the almost immediate coalescence of the several Republican factions into two, pro- and anti-administration. President John Quincy Adams and Henry Clay, who became his secretary of state, led the pro-administration forces. Alignment with Adams was the logical move for Clay, ideologically as well as politically. Both Adams and Clay were confirmed nationalists; moreover, Clay saw Jackson as his great rival in the West. Andrew Jackson took command of the forces against the administration. In Jackson's view, the people's choice had been subverted because Adams and Clay had made a corrupt bargain—the presidency for Adams and the secretaryship of state for Clay. The State Department was looked upon as a special prize because Madison, Monroe, and Adams had stepped directly from there to the White House. In the Jacksonian interpretation, the House would surely have ratified the popular choice and selected Jackson but for the intrigue masterminded by Clay. No reliable evidence supports the case for an unsavory deal between Adams and Clay, but the Jackson men made effective use of the charge. Standing with the Jacksonians was Vice President Calhoun, who recognized Clay as Adams's political heir. Besides, Calhoun's move away from his strong nationalist orientation was rapidly gaining momentum.

The events of 1824 provided the springboard for a new political force that to southerners descended directly from the original Republican party. This new force had a visible, heroic leader, Andrew Jackson. It also had numerous southerners in significant positions. Calhoun was perhaps the most notable, but he had colleagues in every state. The party also laid claim to ideological purity with the accession of Thomas Ritchie and his old Republican confederates in Virginia, who joined only after overcoming their anxiety about Jackson's military background. Despite that reservation, they saw no other way to defeat the revived Federalism of another Adams. Quite aside from leaders and ideology, powerful ties formed between southern voters and Jackson, a kinship clearly shown in 1824. The Jackson party also replicated Jefferson's tie with the North. With Ritchie and Van Buren making the connection, even the same states led the way. A final similarity with the early Republicans made clear the southern idiom of the Jackson party. John Quincy Adams was the first northern president in two and a half decades, since the administration of his father, John Adams. That coincidence underscored the South's perception of a reprise of the Republican-Federalist rivalry.

As president, John Quincy Adams fueled the fires of southern opposition. The most nationally minded of any president up to his time, Adams envisioned an active central government energetically carrying out a vigorous nationalist program. In pushing for specific measures, Adams antagonized southerners in particular. No issue proved more divisive than the effort to drive Indians from their lands. When Georgia, in violation of a treaty between the United States and the Cherokees, acted to survey the Indian lands in preparation for forcing the Cherokees to relinquish them to white settlers, President Adams opposed the state's action. But to no avail—he could find little support in Congress for a firm policy in the face of an intransigent Georgia. Georgia won; the Cherokees and Adams lost; the white South cheered. For southerners, who eagerly desired Indian lands in Alabama and Mississippi as well as in Georgia, self-interest and ideology meshed. States' rights protected their interests. Southerners were also appalled when Adams wanted to send an American delegation to a conference of Latin American and Caribbean nations in Panama. Because American diplomats would mingle there with black delegates from Haiti, a country founded by a slave rebellion, southerners greeted Adams's announcement with a barrage of criticism. In Congress southerners delayed passage of the appropriations bill so long that the conference adjourned before the American delegation arrived.

President Adams also fought the southerners on what was rapidly becoming the most pressing economic issue. Long a protectionist, he supported an increase in duties proposed in 1828. Although the Tariff of 1828 was in no way the complete responsibility of John Quincy Adams, it did go through Congress during his administration, and he did sign into law the highest tariff enacted before the Civil War. Its enemies, chiefly southerners, called the Tariff of 1828 an "abomination" both because of its record rates and because of the labyrinthine politics of its passage. In their efforts to stop it, southerners tried to drive a wedge between northern and western farmers, who wanted higher duties on such products as raw wool, and manufacturers, who advocated protection of finished goods, not raw materials. The southern effort failed under the combined weight of the protectionists. Although some Jackson supporters from the North and West voted aye to solidify support for their candidate in such states as Pennsylvania, where protection was a major concern, southerners identified the measure with the Adams camp. Jackson himself had not publicly supported it, and most southerners believed he would work to lower the tariff if he could be installed in the White House.

In the presidential election of 1828 the South made its preference absolutely clear. Adams and his supporters, known as National Republicans, were literally buried under a Jackson avalanche. Below the border Jackson took every electoral vote; along the border only Maryland, which split its vote, provided Adams with any electoral votes. More southerners voted than in any previous presidential election, and in many states the popular margins for Jackson were astounding. He won in Alabama by more than 8 to 1, in Tennessee by 20 to 1; and in Georgia he garnered 100 percent of the popular votes.

With the election of 1828 a new political age dawned. In the South the political sun shone with special brightness. Southerners overwhelmingly perceived Andrew Jackson as their political savior, who would deliver them from the threat of a powerful central government with all its evils. The overwhelming belief in Jackson is a telling commentary on the South's perceptions of policy and power. Most southerners never doubted that Jackson was with them on the great question of national versus local power. Yet Jackson had never taken a

strong public stand on the most salient question. Because of his southern identity and his heroic image, southerners simply assumed that he stood where
they did. He was the new Jefferson. When Jefferson was in power he had
moved in unexpected directions, but southerners had generally remained
steadfast behind him and his party. If Jackson followed that pattern, would he,
like Jefferson, still hold the loyalty of most southerners?

Swept into power on a flood tide of southern support, Andrew Jackson in
his first administration confronted three issues critical to the South—the tariff,
the second Bank of the United States, and Indians. His actions brought forth
both praise and blame from a South that had backed him solidly.

NULLIFICATION

In the late 1820s nothing so distressed the majority of southerners as did the
tariff. And most expected Jackson to get the high rates of 1828 lowered. The
most vigorous antitariff sentiment was found in Virginia and South Carolina,
where ideological sensitivity matched financial concern. To the purists a protective tariff violated the Constitution. They insisted that Jackson remove this
blotch from the holy constitutional writ. Jackson, however, did not move so directly as the southern antitariff zealots demanded. He had never adopted a doc-
trinaire antitariff position. Besides, Jackson recognized that a protective tariff
helped his party in critical northern states.

Jackson's dilatoriness in moving against the Tariff of 1828 led to a major national and constitutional crisis. This crisis was precipitated by South Carolina,
which by 1830 had replaced Virginia as the self-proclaimed guardian of the
southern ideological birthright. Living as they did in the only state with a population more than half slave, many white South Carolinians had become hyper-
sensitive about the potential danger posed by national power to the institution
of slavery. South Carolina proclaimed the faith of the newly baptized, for the
state had undergone a conversion. No other southern state had been more enthusiastic about the postwar nationalism of the Republican party. But during
the 1820s South Carolina began a political and ideological trek that would place
the state in the vanguard of states'-rights extremists.

As South Carolina moved toward intransigence, its most notable political
son, John C. Calhoun, took his post as captain of the guard that watched over
southern interests. Calhoun provided the theoretical framework as well as the
political leadership for the unhappy South Carolinians. In 1828 the South Carolina legislature published Calhoun's *South Carolina Exposition and Protest*, but his
authorship was kept secret until 1831. In this work, after describing in detail
what he saw as the unfairness of the tariff, Calhoun spelled out his theory of
constitution making and the Union. Claiming with justification that he drew
upon the Virginia and Kentucky resolutions, Calhoun insisted that the Union
was a compact of states. In Calhoun's view, the individual states had created
the Union, and as creators they were sovereign.

Moreover, he argued, the states gave the federal government only the particular powers enumerated in the Constitution, and no more. Thus a measure such as the protective tariff, which did not have specific constitutional sanction, was patently unconstitutional and a clear usurpation of power. As a remedy for such an abuse Calhoun spoke of a state veto. Because the individual states retained their sovereignty, Calhoun maintained, a state could interpose its will between its citizens and the federal government. Thus an individual state could veto or nullify any federal law it defined as unconstitutional. This veto could be exercised by the people of a state acting through a state constitutional convention, in Calhoun's theory the ultimate constitutional power. In Calhoun's scheme, this state veto also protected a minority from the unconstitutional acts of a majority. But Calhoun's minority rights were those of interest groups, such as southern planters and states, not of individuals. In fact, in 1832, when South Carolina nullified the tariff, the opponents of nullification were forced to conform or face the loss of their political rights. Calhoun did provide a legal way to overturn nullification: an amendment to the Constitution approved by the required three-fourths of the states would make any policy legitimate.

While Calhoun penned probing essays on the nature of the Constitution and American federalism, others in his state acted—and without Calhoun's public support. As early as the fall of 1830 they attempted to call a convention so that South Carolina could nullify the Tariff of 1828. Facing stiff opposition from Jackson supporters who claimed that the president should be given more time and from others who considered that the basic idea behind nullification was preposterous, they failed.

Undaunted, the nullifiers mounted a forceful, energetic effort to awaken the state to the dangers they saw. Even the lowered tariff enacted in 1832 failed to satisfy them, for it retained the hated principle of protection. After its passage the nullifiers again tried for a state constitutional convention in a campaign that forced Calhoun to take sides publicly. This time the nullifiers persuaded a sufficient number of their fellow South Carolinians that the action of the national government threatened their well-being as well as the sovereignty of their state. In November 1832 the convention met and solemnly nullified the tariffs of 1828 and 1832. After March 1, 1833, the convention declared, both tariffs would be null and void in South Carolina. It also stipulated that any attempt by the national government to use force would bring disunion. Later, the effective date of nullification was postponed until after Congress adjourned in order to allow national lawmakers a final chance to give up protection.

The reaction was instantaneous, and not to the nullifiers' liking. Andrew Jackson denounced nullification as treason. In a public proclamation, known as the Nullification Proclamation, he announced that any attempt to enforce nullification would by definition be an attack on the Union. Deeds accompanied words when the president poured troops into the Charleston forts and asked Congress to go on record in support of any action that might be required to suppress nullification.

The other southern states offered South Carolina no tangible assistance. Although most of them continuously railed against the tariff, none joined South Carolina in nullification. Nullification was both too radical and too arcane. Though southerners almost universally agreed that the tariff was hurtful, few believed that it mortally endangered vital interests. The theory itself perplexed many. In Calhoun's construct a state could be simultaneously inside and outside the Union. To many southerners South Carolina was behaving rashly.

With the nullifiers and President Jackson seemingly headed for collision, the president maneuvered to avoid a head-on crash. In his annual message in December 1832 he advocated that Congress lower the tariff rates even further. That month Calhoun, who had resigned the vice presidency, returned to Washington as a United States senator. Even as Calhoun vigorously defended his state before the Senate, he sought some way to avert a confrontation between state and nation. He pressed forward on two fronts: he urged caution and delay upon his hotheaded comrades back home, and he cooperated even with his ideological enemy Clay to get a compromise tariff.

Finally in March 1833, with Calhoun and Clay in league, Congress passed a compromise tariff that lowered rates in slow stages to the 20-percent level by 1842. At the same time Congress overwhelmingly approved Jackson's Force Bill, which reaffirmed the president's right to use force if South Carolina in any way interfered with the enforcement of federal laws. President Jackson signed both bills. Reconvening, the nullifiers claimed victory. The convention rescinded its nullification of the tariff laws, and in a final meaningless act nullified the Force Bill.

The legacy of the nullification crisis was not at all clear-cut. At first glance Jackson's firmness seemed to leave no doubt that the federal government would be supreme over state governments. But among the nullifiers the conviction prevailed that they had stood up to the central government and it had come to terms with them. Thus confrontation could lead to success. At the same time, Jackson's ringing pronouncements about the authority of the federal government frightened some of his southern partisans, people who gave no support to nullification. To these stalwart states'-righters, Jackson's view of federal prerogatives was every bit as disturbing as nullification. They began to wonder whether they had misplaced their political faith.

THE BANK

Even while the stormclouds of nullification gathered, still another whirlwind swirled around the president. The second Bank of the United States had not played a significant part in Andrew Jackson's first campaign for the White House, but as president he quickly thrust the bank to the center of the political arena. Almost from the beginning the president questioned the bank's value to the country as well as its constitutionality. But he did not put the bank at the top of his agenda; after all, its charter ran until 1836. Believing—in a massive political miscalculation—that the bank could overpower all opposition, the congressional faction headed by Henry Clay obtained a recharter in 1832, four years in advance. If Jackson vetoed the recharter, they thought, he would be driven out of office in 1832. So whether he signed it or not, they would win. They were wrong. In a ringing veto message, Jackson denounced the bank as unconstitutional and castigated it as a parasite feeding off the people. Southerners generally supported the president's stand. Most southern congressmen did not vote for recharter, and few supported the unsuccessful effort to override the veto. The mass of states'-rights, strict-construction southerners viewed the bank as a "reptile," a "sin against the Constitution." To most southerners the very purpose of the Jackson movement was to halt and, if possible, to do away with everything connected with the abhorrent postwar nationalism. They cheered the veto.

Jackson, however, did not want the bank to have even the four years of life left to it. After his reelection he moved in the autumn of 1833 to withdraw all federal deposits from the bank. The law permitted withdrawal only if dereliction or mismanagement could be demonstrated. There was no such demonstration, but Jackson ordered the federal funds removed anyway. To southerners, ever alert for unwarranted assumptions of power, Jackson's course seemed just as dangerous as the bank had been. "It is certainly," wrote one in language as vigorous as the president's, "the most atrocious, high handed despotick measure that ever was before assumed by the most absolute monarch." That was surely an exaggeration, but just as surely Jackson had moved beyond a strict reading of the law. And coming just after his claims for federal and executive authority in the nullification crisis, his removal of the deposits reinforced those earlier concerns that Andrew Jackson had become a power-mad president who could not be trusted to protect the sacred truths of strict construction and limited federal power.

INDIAN POLICY

Although Andrew Jackson claimed and exercised considerable federal power, his Indian policy closely followed states'-rights precepts and delighted most southern Jacksonians. Jackson, of course, had gained much of his fame as an Indian fighter, and he surely believed that whites were destined to own and farm the land possessed by Indians all the way from Georgia to the Mississippi River.

Like most other southern whites, Jackson took a paternalistic view of the Indians. Though he did not agree that the only good Indian was a dead Indian, he believed that whites were better guardians of the Indians' welfare than the Indians themselves. He did think that the Indians could survive either with their traditional customs or by adopting the civilized ways of the whites, but he was convinced that they must do so beyond the Mississippi, beyond both the mercenary influence of the whites and the competing authority of the states.

Andrew Jackson knew firsthand the southern whites' lust for the Indians' land. When Jackson announced his position in his first annual message to Congress in December 1829, he did not equivocate: the federal government must stand by Georgia in its contest with the Cherokees. Otherwise, "the objects of this Government are reversed, and...it has become a part of its duty to aid in destroying the States which it was established to protect." No states'-rights zealot could have put the case more forcefully.

Jackson's actions matched his words. Not only the Cherokees but the Choctaws and Chickasaws felt the full force of Jackson's determination. Jackson saw only one possibility: the Cherokees must move west, and he pressed that course upon them. Finally in 1835 the Cherokees yielded. By the Treaty of New Echota they agreed to accept $5 million and land in the Indian Territory (Oklahoma) in exchange for their land in Georgia. The majority of Cherokees did go west—most of them removed by force—but a thousand or so fled into the mountains of North Carolina, where eventually they were provided a reservation.

Even before the Cherokee treaty, Jackson had secured for white settlement the lands of the Choctaws and Chickasaws in Alabama and Mississippi. Those tribes were given stark alternatives: move or be exterminated. By 1832 they bowed to the inevitable and agreed to cross the Mississippi. They, too, received land in the Indian Territory.

In pushing the Indians out of the old Southwest, Andrew Jackson had wielded the power of the federal government to do just what those states wanted. Now millions of acres of land in Georgia, Alabama, and Mississippi were opened to white settlers, and they poured in. No white person in the South forgot who had made those lands available to whites. Thus the distress occasioned among many southerners by Jackson's stance on nullification and withdrawal was tempered by his acquisition of Indian land.

JACKSON AND ABOLITION

President Andrew Jackson had to contend with a new, and to southerners frightening, development concerning slavery. When William Lloyd Garrison began publication of his *Liberator* in Boston in 1831, the antislavery movement took on a new, uncompromising tone. Concern about the morality of slavery had been around a long time; some southerners had even shared it. But before 1830 the overwhelming majority of antislavery Americans, northerners as well as southerners, saw slavery as a vexing dilemma, one that history had presented to the country. They certainly did not include slaveholders as an essential part of the problem. And they believed that slavery could be eliminated only gradually and over a long period. Garrison and his abolitionist colleagues hurtled into gradualism and bowled it over. They demanded immediate and uncompensated emancipation of all slaves. Moreover, they condemned slave owners as corrupt, both as a group and as individuals. To them a slavemaster was by definition immoral. Though these abolitionists were not numerous, they had a substantial political impact. To southerners it seemed that a herd of wild bulls was preparing to trample over them.

Abolitionists moved on two major political fronts. First, they mailed pamphlets and other publications into the South as well as across the North. Southerners were outraged to find these "incendiary publications," as southerners termed them, on their doorsteps. In Charleston in July 1835, citizens removed the materials from the post office and burned them in a public bonfire. The president, a slave owner himself, shared their anger, and in his forthright manner he moved against the abolitionists. His postmaster general directed that no abolitionist tract could be delivered unless the addressee had requested it. That order eliminated the incendiary publications in slave country, because few southerners wanted to receive them and those who did certainly did not want to be publicly identified as being on the mailing list of Garrison and his friends.

On another front, the abolitionists focused directly on the people who were expected to respond to the pleas of citizens—United States congressmen. To the House of Representatives came a multitude of petitions requesting the abolition of slavery in the District of Columbia, over which Congress had complete authority. The reception of these petitions and their presentation to the House enraged southern congressmen. To solve this problem, the Democratic party, with Jackson's agreement, supported a proposition known as the gag rule, which declared that all petitions would be immediately put on the table without formal presentation to the House.

THE RISE OF THE WHIGS

In the contest to succeed Jackson, victory went to a northerner, Martin Van Buren of New York. Even before the nullification crisis he had bested Calhoun, the early contender for Jackson's favor. When Jackson installed Van Buren as vice president in 1832, Van Buren clearly became the heir apparent. Even though Jackson had blessed him, most southern Jacksonians had serious reservations about a northern president. After all, the only previous two northern presidents—the Adamses, John and John Quincy—had been largely responsible for the success of new, southern-dominated parties. Adding the highly flammable issue of abolition to that natural liability could surely alienate southerners, no matter how devoted they might be to Andrew Jackson. As most southerners saw it, Jackson could be trusted, but they were not at all sure about Van Buren. By the time the Democratic party gave Van Buren its presidential nomination in May 1835, a surging opposition challenged the Democrats' supremacy in the South.

The Democrats had good reason to worry. The halcyon days of 1828 and 1832, when Andrew Jackson had run roughshod over the token opposition put up by the National Republicans were long gone; the presidential election of 1836 promised to be a donnybrook. The National Republican party, burdened by the Adams administration and a platform urging a vigorous national government, never made any headway in the South.

Andrew Jackson's overwhelming strength had more than a little to do with the growth of an effective opposition to his party. So many people expected so much that some were sure to be disappointed. The first were the antitariff zealots, who were dismayed when Jackson did not obliterate the principle of protection. Then many people who distrusted a powerful executive were frightened by Jackson's Nullification Proclamation and his actions in the withdrawal affair. Joining these more ideologically inclined southerners were those politicians who lost out in the race for place and reward within the Democratic party. By 1834 these dissidents, added to the National Republicans, formed a sizable group. But they certainly were a variegated crew, ranging from nullifiers to American System men, from ideologues to opportunists. The politically astute, however, recognized that only one formula afforded any chance for political health and victory in the South. Success could be attained, as a former Jacksonian editor noted, only "by the Nationals coming down to our standard of strict Construction of the Constitution and by no other means." This new party bore no ideological resemblance to the defunct National Republican party.

These southerners, along with other Americans opposed to Jackson, created the Whig party. The term *Whig*, borrowed from the British tradition, denoted someone opposed to executive authority, and Andrew Jackson certainly represented such authority. Only opposition to Jackson glued the Whigs together. Between 1834 and 1836 the national Whig party did not present anything resembling a united political front. Nothing so dramatized early Whig disunity as the election of 1836, in which the party presented three sectional candidates for the presidency: Daniel Webster of Massachusetts, William Henry Harrison of Ohio, and Hugh L. White of Tennessee. The choice of White is instructive about early southern Whiggery. A former Jacksonian—in fact, a close friend of Jackson—White stood for those who believed that Jackson had deserted time-honored principles and had turned over the party to time-serving politicians.

Although southern Whiggery between 1834 and 1836 was in a large sense a part of the states'-rights renewal that had been building for more than a decade, the excitement it helped to create derived from something at once more fundamental and more emotional. The abolitionists' all-out assault on slavery and slave owners frightened and angered the South. Their tactics demanded constant vigilance and unyielding defense. In such a time, southern Whigs argued, only tried native sons could be trusted with leadership.

"The cause of Judge White is the cause of the South," shouted the enthusiastic Whigs. The Democrats, Whigs charged, had tainted credentials: Martin Van Buren was a political chameleon, and he even had abolitionist friends. In the face of this onslaught, the Democrats found it impossible to make 1836 a referendum on the old National Republican–Jacksonian economic issues. The universal complaint of southern Democrats, "Judge White is cutting into our ranks," forced a direct response to the Whigs. Southern Democrats defended Van Buren while they paraded the prosouthern actions of the Jackson administration—the ouster of the Indians, the destruction of the Bank of the United States, the hampering of the abolitionists. White could never win, they insisted, because the race was not just between White and Van Buren. Pointing out that three Whig candidates were running, the southern Democrats claimed that a large vote for White could send the election to the House of Representatives, where chicanery and dealmaking would prevail. With 1824 and Adams's triumph over Jackson fresh in memory, the Democrats had a responsive audience.

The southern Jacksonians stemmed the Whig surge, but the challenging party made a good showing. Although Van Buren won, the Whigs below the border took two states and won 49 percent of the popular vote. Such a showing by a second party was unprecedented in the South. Neither the Federalists nor the National Republicans had ever come close to this kind of performance. Along the border the Whigs also did well, carrying Kentucky and Maryland, but even the National Republicans had never been feeble there. The result on the border was another sign of the difference between those states and the slave states farther south, for the successful Whig candidate in the border states was William Henry Harrison, not Hugh White.

THE POLITICAL ARENA

The presidential election of 1836 took place in a political arena with wide-open doors. Although those doors had never been fully closed, after 1830 the democratization of southern politics intensified, in law as well as in practice. By the mid-1830s white male suffrage prevailed everywhere except in Louisiana, which embraced it in 1845, and Virginia, which did so in 1851. By 1830 the voters, not the legislature, chose presidential electors in every state but South Carolina, where legislators retained that prerogative through the Confederacy. After Maryland went to a popularly elected governor in 1837, every state did so but Virginia, where the voters took on that responsibility in 1851, and South Carolina, where they never did. After 1835 only four states maintained property qualifications for the holding of some offices, and only the two Carolinas retained them in the 1850s. In every state except South Carolina, most local offices were thrown open to popular elections.

Political campaigns after 1830 expanded upon the lively, even boisterous practices that had marked southern politics since the colonial era. The young John A. Quitman expended every effort to attain a seat in Mississippi's legislature. At a large gathering just before the election, Quitman astonished and wooed the crowd with his feats of running, jumping, boxing, and wrestling. He capped an impressive performance by outshooting the area's leading marksman. Then with a sure political touch he offered his prize, a fat ox, to the dejected loser and won the cheers and political support of the onlookers.

One of the greatest extravaganzas took place in Georgia during the heated presidential contest in 1848. In late August the Democrats staged a massive two-day rally just outside Atlanta. The trains as well as the roads were jammed with political pilgrims. Thousands crowded the grounds, and "as the shades of night set in, the whole surrounding county was illuminated by fires enkindled at the numerous encampments, and every house, out-house, barn and shed in the vicinity, which could afford a shelter, was filled to overflowing." Speakers, bands, barbecues, and more speakers entertained the throng. The speeches went on almost nonstop; beginning on Monday afternoon, they continued into

(a)

(b)

THESE PAINTINGS BY GEORGE C. BINGHAM CONVEY A SENSE OF THE
POLITICAL CULTURE IN THE JACKSONIAN ERA.
(a) Stump speaking (Collection of Boatmen's National Bank of St. Louis)
(b) Election day (St. Louis Art Museum Purchase)

the night, started up again Tuesday morning, and stopped only at midnight. Special cheers went to the group that brought "a six pounder [cannon], and to the whole-souled Democrats, who took charge of it, the loud thunder of whose artillery was in unison with the enthusiasm that pervaded the whole mass." The faithful enjoyed themselves immensely while party orators urged them on to even greater exertions for the Democratic party.

In this intensified campaign activity the canvass assumed a pivotal role. Canvassing—or making a political speaking tour through a congressional district or a state—began in the 1830s and soon became commonplace. Often the canvass originated with one candidate, but two or more competing contestants quickly joined to make it a procession. The arduousness of some of these tours staggers the modern imagination. Possibly the most Herculean canvasses marked the tight gubernatorial battles fought in Tennessee between James K. Polk and his Whig opponents. During his first and only successful race, in 1839, Polk rode more than 1,300 miles in a little more than two months to make forty-three scheduled speeches and numerous impromptu ones in thirty-seven of his state's sixty-four counties. In 1843, he and his Whig opponent crisscrossed Tennessee for some 2,300 miles and spoke for five or six hours each day. It took these knights of the hustings four months to complete their strenuous crusade.

Southern voters certainly responded to these massive efforts. One-half of those eligible voted in 1836; that percentage reached beyond 75 in 1840 and 1844. In 1860 some 70 percent of southern voters cast ballots. Hotly contested state and congressional races brought out voters in equal and even greater numbers. These turnouts clearly prove that southern politicians did not have passive constituents. Keen observers of southern politics noted that southern voters were particularly well informed about political issues. It seemed that in the South "everybody talked politics everywhere," even the "illiterate and shoeless." This political sophistication impressed Daniel R. Hundley, an Alabamian with a Harvard law degree who lived in Chicago. Hundley thought the average southerner "on the whole much better versed in the lore of politics and the provisions of our Federal and State Constitutions" than his northern counterpart. Hundley attributed this awareness, which extended all the way to the "poor men in the South," to the political discussions that pervaded the "public barbecues, court-house-day gatherings, and other holiday occasions."

ANOTHER PANIC

Martin Van Buren hardly had time to move into the White House before the Panic of 1837 struck. For the second time in less than twenty years massive tremors shook the economy. Falling prices and wages, increasing unemployment, business failures, and foreclosures wracked the entire nation. The South was hit just as hard as it had been in 1819. In one sense, 1837 replicated 1819: the collapse of cotton prices heralded general depression. The weighted annual price in New Orleans tumbled from just over 15 cents a pound in 1835 to just over 13 cents in 1836, then plunged all the way to 9 cents in 1837—a drop of 40 percent in only two years. Slave prices followed the downward movement of cotton. In major markets they declined by as much as one-third in three years. This plunge in the prices of cotton and slaves wreaked havoc throughout the southern economy. The booming Southwest was especially hard hit. Planters and farmers retrenched and struggled to survive; some pulled through, others did not. Merchants, factors, and bankers found themselves playing the same desperate game.

The troubles that befell the Georgia planter John A. Cobb underscore the personal devastation caused by the panic. Owner of 150 slaves on his Jefferson County plantation and of an imposing mansion in Athens, John Cobb also invested in Georgia gold mines, banks, and railroads. During the panic his bank and railroad stock depreciated rapidly and his gold mine produced virtually nothing. By 1840 Cobb's debts totaled almost $75,000 and his creditors were demanding payment. Unable to meet his obligations, Cobb suffered a mental collapse. His son Howell tried to help and most of his slaves were sold, but the hard times made it impossible to find a buyer for the plantation. Bright hopes had been dashed and a proud man defeated. This sad story was repeated countless times across the South.

The panic also had profound political repercussions for parties in the South. Simply put, economic depression helped the southern Whigs. Voters blamed the party in power for hard times, just as they do now, and the Whigs benefited. After 1837 the Whigs generally gained in state elections, and they looked forward optimistically to 1840.

President Van Buren's response to the panic also had a significant political impact. To remedy the economic ills besetting his country the president proposed the Independent Treasury, or the Subtreasury, which would divorce the government and banks. Instead of making use of various state banks to hold government deposits—Jackson's alternative to the Bank of the United States—Van Buren proposed that the federal government be its own banker. This approach appealed to John C. Calhoun, who had never been altogether comfortable with the Whigs, though he had been loosely associated with them since 1834. Moreover, Calhoun was especially pleased by Van Buren's ringing affirmation of states' rights and his forthright stand against abolition. As a result, Calhoun announced his return to the Democratic party. His shift had immediate political fallout because the partisan allegiance of his followers could influence the orientation of state politics. In Mississippi, for example, the shift of the Calhounites gave the Democrats the upper hand.

THE ELECTION OF 1840

The Democrats were hard-pressed as the presidential election approached. Van Buren had numerous southern friends along with the loyal support of the party, but he generated no enthusiasm among southern voters, even among Democrats. No matter how vehement his declaration of friendship for the

South or how vigorous his denunciation of abolition, most southerners could not overlook Van Buren's origins or his unsavory political reputation.

The Whigs were united behind one candidate: Henry Clay. No, the southern Whigs had not turned into National Republicans; rather Henry Clay presented a new political face. Jettisoning his American System, his economic nationalism, he wooed the South with advocacy of states' rights and condemnation of abolitionists. As they embraced Clay, most southern Whigs also prepared to become part of a truly national party. The Whigs scheduled their first national convention for December 1839 in Harrisburg, Pennsylvania. Organizationally the southern Whigs were moving forward while ideologically they remained firmly in place.

Although most slave states sent delegates to Harrisburg and to a man voted for Clay on the first ballot, the convention turned elsewhere for its candidate. To southerners, however, the nomination of William Henry Harrison of Ohio posed no problem: Harrison was a native Virginian and a member of a prominent family. As a congressman he had voted with the South in the Missouri crisis, and in the 1830s he denounced abolition. The convention also helped the southerners in two other ways. John Tyler, a stalwart states'-rights Whig from Virginia, was named vice president. And when the delegates, unable to agree on a platform, decided not to adopt one, the southerners were left free to run their campaign as they saw fit.

In the South the campaign of 1840 replayed that of 1836. Economic issues did not dominate the campaign. Even though the hard times surely made Whigs more attractive and Democrats less so, the parties did not emphasize specific economic programs, except for the Independent Treasury. Each party stressed its claim to be the protector of southern interests and accused the other of infidelity to those interests. The Whigs condemned Van Buren as unsavory and untrustworthy, and promoted Harrison as a true son and friend of the South. The Democrats, in turn, praised Van Buren's firm stance against abolition and his unswerving friendship for the South. Harrison they pictured as unprincipled and tainted with abolitionism.

The campaign of 1840 had a momentous impact on the South. Harrison carried seven slave states; even more impressive, he won more than half the popular vote below the border. Two-party politics had definitely arrived in the South. Although the South's allegiance had shifted since the 1790s, it had shifted en bloc. First the Jeffersonian Republicans and then the Jacksonian Democrats dominated southern politics. The Federalist party in the South had controlled only local pockets; the National Republicans were even weaker. But after 1840 two vigorous parties, each claiming to be the champion of the South, competed on an almost equal footing across the slave states.

THE POLITICS OF SLAVERY

The political war that began between Democrats and Whigs in the mid-1830s brought a special character to southern politics. This uniqueness is best described as the politics of slavery. The politics of slavery encompasses the inter-change among the major forces that influenced antebellum southern politics: the institution of slavery, parties and politicians, the political structure, and the fundamental values of southern white society.

These basic forces did not suddenly spring up full-blown in the 1830s, yet before the competition between Democrats and Whigs, southern politics could not properly be called a politics of slavery. The existence of two competing par-ties, the increased democratization of politics, the volatility of the antislavery issue—together they simultaneously caused and demanded a more intense ef-fort by politicians to reach a larger number of voters. To succeed in a two-party world, southern politicians had to beat not only opponents in their own orga-nization but those in another as well. That competition increased the intensity of electoral politics.

The existence of a second competitive party was crucial. For the first time in the South, parties seriously competed with each other to defend southern in-terests. From the beginning of parties in the 1790s southerners had looked upon the political party as an advocate for the South in the nation. Because southern-ers understood that they had a special stake in the direction of national policy, no party could flourish in the South unless it had an identity as such an advo-cate. A party's prosperity in the South depended on the conviction of southern voters that it gave first place to its duty to protect southern liberty in the nation. The rise of abolitionism compounded that political truth.

If a party was to prosper in the politics of slavery, it had to have a northern connection that, at the least, accepted the southern interpretation and use of slavery-related issues. Because in the southern view the chief purpose of a po-litical party was to protect southern interests in the nation, a national party was essential. But southern partisans had to have the support or at least the acqui-escence of their northern comrades on slavery-related issues. If the northerners opposed the position of their southern brethren, then the basis for a national party in the South was undermined. Besides, southern politicians in that party would become vulnerable to the charge that they held to party alliance only for place and reward, not to guard the South. Unchecked, that onslaught could en-danger the attacked with political extinction.

The faithfulness of northern associates was a requirement not only for suc-cess at the polls but for the personal honor of the individual southern politician. His party's defense of southern liberty allowed a southern politician to blend his ambition for power and place with the holy mission of defending the South. His lust for the perquisites of office could be ennobled by his stated desire to protect southern liberty. But if his party refused to stand with the southerners on slavery-related questions, then his opponents in the South could castigate him as a grabber for place and, even worse, as uncaring about special southern concerns. Such a charge carried with it the stain of dishonor, and no southern politician could afford such a stigma. Unless he could demonstrate the lie of such stigmatizing, then he stood dishonored as an individual and before his community. Both this vilifying and the essential defenses against it remained unceasing.

Southern politicians, both Democratic and Whig, shared the belief that a national party provided the best protection for southern interests. Representing a minority section, the southern party men grounded their strategy for guarding special southern concerns on cooperating with northerners to gain national power. Such a national party precluded a sectional assault on the South because the North was politically tied to the South. To northerners, southerners offered the prize of national political power and the rewards stemming from it. To southerners, an alliance with the North offered the surest means of protecting their liberty.

THE SPECIAL PLACE OF CALHOUN

This party solution to the problem of protecting the South in the nation dominated the South to 1860. Before the 1850s only one major political force rejected the party solution. John C. Calhoun pronounced the fundamental premise of the party men fraught with peril. To his mind they wrote a fatal prescription for the South because they failed to appreciate both the numerical superiority of the North and the potential political power of antislavery ideology. In view of the minority position of the South in the nation, Calhoun feared the time would come when the more powerful North would feel "an obligation of conscience to abolish [slavery]." Thus he viewed as a slow-acting poison the political strategy so vigorously touted by the party men.

Calhoun's political force had an unsettling effect on southern politics because he rejected the rules followed by the party men. He and they approached the politics of southern safety from opposite directions. The politics of slavery that captured Democrats and Whigs came out of southern culture and produced a rhetoric designed for the South and southern voters. Most southern politicians were concerned about the success of their party, both in their home states and in the nation. Rhetoric spotlighting slavery was a political weapon designed to best the opposing party in the southern political arena. Accordingly, the politicians aimed it at southern, not northern, audiences. Calhoun, on the other hand, cared most about maintaining the parity of the South as a section in the nation. Although Calhoun surely wanted support from southern voters, his major goal was to confront the North with demands.

Distrusting the unwritten party compact, Calhoun wanted an open, public declaration from the North that southern liberty would never be endangered. He envisioned a declaration coming from Congress which would abide by his and the South's theory of the Constitution, the protection it gave to slavery and to southern liberty. Although Calhoun believed that the Constitution protected the South in 1840 just as it had done in 1789, he believed also that the rise of abolition necessitated a reaffirmation of that protection.

While the party men were preaching the politics of accommodation, Calhoun was crying out for a politics of confrontation. To ensure southern success when the confrontation occurred, he worked to unify the South. Urging southerners to turn away from partisan loyalties, Calhoun insisted that "the South should overlook all minor differences and unite as one man in defense of liberty."

Despite his attacks on parties, Calhoun did act with them at times, always on his own terms. After rapprochement with the Democrats in 1837, much of his political influence grew out of the close association of many of his followers with that party. Calhoun made a mighty effort to win the Democratic presidential nomination for 1844. When he lost, he did not accept defeat as a good party loyalist. Though Calhoun could look with disdain upon parties and keep his distance from them when it suited him to do so, he could neither convert nor defeat them.

Calhoun never attained the southern unity he so desperately wanted. Wherever he turned, from the 1830s to his death in 1850, he met the implacable force of party. Despite his dire warnings, he was never able to baptize the mass of southerners in his antiparty church. The major southern party leaders condemned Calhoun as a man consumed by ambition and as a fomentor of political difficulties. They called him "John Crisis Calhoun."

*P*ARTISANSHIP AND ECONOMICS

The politics of slavery formed the fundamental boundary lines within which parties in the South had to function. A party that crossed those lines risked political extinction, but within them parties could differ sharply on substantive questions. And parties surely did. Within the states and at the national level Democrats and Whigs fought bitterly over concrete issues. Democrats praised their party for resting on "the sovereignty of the people" and condemned the Whigs as aristocrats wedded to "odious distinction"—in southern politics a death sentence if allowed to stand. A newly elected governor of Tennessee compared the Democratic party with "the Church Militant: both fight against error—one in the moral, the other in the political field." Turning aside Democratic accusations, Whigs cried that they guarded "popular liberty" from the Democratic "political wireworkers" who threatened "the subversion of civil liberty." Whigs proclaimed that only their party guaranteed "the Liberties of the People."

The first Democratic–Whig division over economic questions took place after the Panic of 1837. Just as in the 1780s and after 1819, the aftermath of the panic saw deep division within the South over economic and financial policy. Politicians took divergent approaches to the problems of the times, and the like-minded coalesced under party banners. Such differences had not been instrumental in the formation of the southern Whig party or in the origins of two-party politics in the South; in the late 1830s, however, partisan loyalties sharpened responses to the depression.

Banking became the focal point of concern. The panic that devastated planters and farmers also hammered banks. Banks had become an important part of the growing southern economy, and they enjoyed bipartisan support. In discussing the formation of banks, a Democratic editor in Arkansas observed, "No party question was raised; it was deemed indispensable that we should have institutions of the kind." Banks furnished much of the credit that financed economic expansion, chiefly the purchase of land and slaves. When the panic struck, it not only delivered banks a heavy blow, it also obliterated the general public support that banks had enjoyed.

From the panic on into the 1840s, attitudes toward banks and banking separated Democrats from Whigs. Although events and issues were not identical in every state, a general political pattern did emerge. Whigs generally favored banks and Democrats usually opposed them. The use of banknotes (or paper money) in addition to coins (hard money or specie); the suspension by banks of specie payments—that is, the refusal of banks to redeem paper money for coins; even the need for banks at all—these issues dominated public debate. Taking an almost classic Jeffersonian stance, Democrats attacked banks with their paper money and credit as harmful to the economic health and independence of southern agriculturalists. Whigs, on the other hand, pictured banks in partnership with agriculture in a common quest for prosperity. Whigs argued that states ought to encourage banking because it was essential for economic development. Democrats countered that states should not become involved in such matters; in their view, the economic future depended on individual initiative and effort. Across the slave states newspapers and election platforms were filled with discussion about banks and banking policy. In state after state bitter legislative battles over financial questions sharply divided Democrats and Whigs.

ECONOMICS AND NATIONAL POLITICS

The division over financial policy in the states received powerful reinforcement at the national level. President Van Buren's proposal of the Independent or Subtreasury, which would divorce government revenue and banks, divided Whigs and Democrats from its introduction in 1837 until its passage in 1840. Whigs insisted that banks and the government should cooperate while Democrats argued for separation. The division over the Independent Treasury did not, however, indicate any basic shift in partisan approaches to national economic policy. Southern Whigs and southern Democrats alike remained faithful to their common credo of limited government. Economic nationalism captured neither party. The strict constructionism of Henry Clay in the late 1830s and the campaign of 1840 testified to the hold that the traditional southern approach to national power had on the Whigs as well as the Democrats.

But in the early 1840s southern Whigs broke from the southern consensus and adopted economic nationalism. This sudden transformation grew out of the political turmoil following the death of President William Henry Harrison after only one month in office. Henry Clay in the United States Senate was determined to dominate the party through his influence in Congress. And a Clay Whig party would be dedicated to Clay's traditional program—economic nationalism or the American System, including a national bank and a protective tariff. After his short, unhappy fling with strict construction in the late 1830s, which had failed to gain him the presidency, Clay returned to his long-held views on energetic government and national economic policy. In a special session of Congress beginning in May 1841, Clay moved to repeal the Independent Treasury and create a new national bank.

Opposing him stood President John Tyler. The first vice president to assume the highest office upon the death of a sitting president, Tyler was a states'-rights Virginian who had broken with the Democrats over nullification. Just because he had moved into the White House, Tyler had no intention of giving up his political heritage. The creation of a national bank struck at the core of his constitutionalism. Twice in the summer of 1841 Tyler vetoed Clay-sponsored bank bills. Those vetoes broke the unity of the newly victorious Whig party.

Southern Whigs could not hope to remain neutral in this controversy. They clung to Clay. This marked transformation, which placed southern Whiggery foursquare behind Clay's American System, had both political and economic roots. Clay had become the voice of the party; Tyler was branded as an apostate. Loyalty to the party, built up in two presidential elections and countless state contests, dictated that southern Whigs remain with an organization that promised opportunities and rewards. Besides, with the South still mired in depression, they thought a new economic approach just might turn into a political tonic. When a Tennessee Whig editor in 1843 called his state "A WHIG STATE—A NATIONAL BANK STATE—A TARIFF STATE—A CLAY STATE," he defined the southern Whig party.

The political distance traveled by United States Senator Willie P. Mangum of North Carolina illustrates the dramatic shift in southern Whiggery. Mangum had been a Jacksonian who had supported Jackson's veto of the bill rechartering the second Bank of the United States. After Jackson's withdrawal of deposits, however, he turned toward the Whigs and campaigned vigorously for Hugh L. White. Then he backed the states'-rights version of Henry Clay for the Whig presidential nomination in 1839. But in 1841 Mangum became the ally of the real Henry Clay. When the congressional Whigs read President John Tyler out of the Whig party, Mangum chaired the party meeting. In his journey Mangum was joined by tens of thousands of Whigs below the Potomac.

OTHER PARTISAN ISSUES

Financial politics did not furnish the only evidence of partisanship in the states. Consider the dispute in Alabama over state support for public education. Alabama was so overwhelmingly Democratic that it never voted for a Whig presidential candidate, nor did the Whigs ever control the legislature. Thus the Democratic position that the state should basically stay out of education was never really threatened during the Democratic-Whig years. Yet Alabama Whigs never gave up trying to change state policy. They maintained that a strong educational system was necessary to improve the people and the state. To increase the visibility and political liability of the Whigs' position on this question, the Democrats who dominated the legislature often put Whigs in charge of the education committee. Invariably the committee brought in reform bills, which the Democrats proceeded to kill on the floor. Then they gleefully took to the public the message that the Whigs accused Alabama farmers and voters of "ignorance, poverty, filthiness, vulgarity and indecency." An exaggeration, to be sure, but the Democrats were convinced that such charges helped keep the Whigs in a minority position.

Not all local issues revolved around the proper activities of a state government. In the North Carolina gubernatorial election of 1848 the Democratic candidate, David Reid, proposed the elimination of the provision that only propertyholders were eligible to vote for state senators. White manhood suffrage obtained in elections for president, for governor, for congressmen, and for the state House of Representatives, but the state constitution limited the right to vote for state senators to white men who owned at least fifty acres. The Democrats, who had been generally whipped by the Whigs throughout the 1840s, hoped they had found an issue that would turn North Carolina politics around. Applying to their proposal the magnetic term "equal suffrage," the Democrats proclaimed, "Equality in the exercise of suffrage among free white men who are citizens of our State, is one of the first principles of Democracy." This assault put the confident Whigs on the defensive, but they quickly rallied. Reverting to the rhetoric of an earlier time, they took the Democrats to task for trying to "humbug" the people with "newfangled clap-trap." Whigs mocked the Democrats' discovery that the voters had been "laboring under a tyranny and oppression" that they had not known they were experiencing. In the end Reid lost, but by fewer than 1,000 votes; the Democrats had never done so well in a North Carolina gubernatorial contest. "Equal suffrage" remained a partisan issue until the 1850s, when the fifty-acre requirement was finally removed from the North Carolina constitution.

Possibly the clearest illustration of bitter partisan division can be seen in Tennessee, a state almost evenly divided between Democrats and Whigs. In 1841 both of Tennessee's seats in the United States Senate had to be filled. Of course, the United States Constitution directed that state legislatures select United States senators. (The Seventeenth Amendment, which transferred that right to the people, was not adopted until 1913.) Traditionally in Tennessee a joint session of House and Senate had chosen senators. If that practice were to be followed in 1841, the Whigs would win, because more Whigs than Democrats sat in the House, though the Democrats did control the Senate. But it was not to be. In the Senate a group of thirteen ferociously committed Democrats refused to go into a joint session to elect senators. Their absence prevented a quorum, so that no election could take place. For two years, between 1841 and

1843, Tennessee had no representation in the United States Senate. These principled or stubborn Democrats became known as the "Immortal Thirteen," who saved Tennessee from the evil policies of "this motley crew" of Whigs. A leader of the Immortal Thirteen, the future president Andrew Johnson, defended his and his colleagues' actions as protecting the fundamental interests of Tennesseans from the "vile wretch[es]" and the "heterogeneous mass" that composed the Whig party. The Whigs, appalled, spoke of democracy ruined and tyranny triumphant. This fight was surely a struggle over place and power, but it also occurred over the meaning of place and power, not only for political advantage but also for public policy.

Other local issues transcended party lines. The most fundamental of these issues rested on geography or state sectionalism, and they often caused internal divisions within the parties. Western Virginia and western North Carolina chafed over apportionment plans that gave more power in the state legislature to the older, eastern areas. Stretching back to the colonial era, these provisions clearly discriminated against the westerners, and the fights over them pitted west against east more than Whig against Democrat. Yet more Whigs than Democrats supported western aims because the east in both states tended to be Democratic. In eastern Tennessee, however, Democrats and Whigs usually joined to advocate state aid for projects that would improve transportation in their rugged land. Another source of friction lay in the three-fifths clause of the United States Constitution. Several states, among them Alabama and North Carolina, followed that example in apportioning legislative seats. Opponents, most of whom represented areas with few slaves, demanded what they called the white-basis plan of apportionment, which would completely exclude slaves from consideration. In North Carolina the white-basis plan tended to be associated with Whigs, in Alabama with Democrats, but before 1860 neither state adopted it. These sectional differences strained party lines because a party that forcefully adopted one position on a geographical issue alienated its own loyalists on the other side. Statewide parties found no easy solution to this problem.

Local political differences, those strictly partisan as well as those enmeshed with state sectionalism, existed for the life of the Democratic–Whig competition in the South. Some of the arguments antedated those parties; some outlasted them. The disagreements could be identified with the Democrats and Whigs only so long as those parties retained their political vitality, and that life span depended on their allegiance to the politics of slavery.

DEMOCRATS AND WHIGS

Divided over economic and other issues, the two parties carried their message to southern voters, most of whom were allied with one or the other. Pinpointing the distinctions between Democratic and Whig constituencies is a vexing task. Detailed investigations have generally failed to reveal dramatic differences between Democrats and Whigs on the basis of wealth, social class, or slave ownership. The best evidence suggests that Whigs, whatever their class or occupation, were more commercially oriented and lived in more commercially oriented towns and counties. This conclusion certainly fits with the divergent positions on financial issues taken by the two parties in the 1840s. Because of the overwhelming homogeneity of the southern white population, such ethnocultural forces as antagonism between Roman Catholics and Protestants, between native-born Americans and immigrants, were not at all central in southern party differences. Those forces did have a substantial impact in the North, but not in the South. Whatever the motivation for party affiliation, the identifications became intense and were reinforced by partisan rivalry in constant electoral battles.

Though the party preferences of various political subdivisions within states may be identified, patterns of partisan loyalty are difficult to establish with any certainty. Motivation in the political population depended in large part on family, neighborhood, friendship, local magnates, and similar forces—forces basically immeasurable and extraordinarily difficult for the historian to uncover, except in individual cases. Both parties, however, drew the bulk of their voting strength from planters and farmers. That was guaranteed by the dominance of agriculture in the South.

8

Plantations and Farms

❖

During the first six decades of the nineteenth century, just as in the years before 1800, the South was overwhelmingly agricultural. And the major thrust of this agricultural economy remained unchanged—the production of staple crops for market, often an export market. The plantation, the large agricultural enterprise, continued to occupy a central position in southern agriculture. In the antebellum era four crops, two traditional and two new, dominated commercial agriculture, but these crops were not grown across the entire region. Significant regional differences underscored the variety in southern agriculture.

Tobacco

The oldest major crop in the South, tobacco, which first brought wealth to Virginia in the 1620s, was still a major money crop two centuries later. Although tobacco retained its importance for many farmers and planters, its chief growing areas shifted. Tobacco culture spread from the Virginia and Maryland tidewater to the Virginia piedmont by the second half of the eighteenth century. In the nineteenth century tobacco largely disappeared from the tidewater. By mid-century the center of tobacco farming in the eastern South had moved below the James River to south-central Virginia, the area known as the Southside, and to the adjacent counties of north-central North Carolina. In Maryland the counties along the western shore of the Chesapeake continued to raise the ancient crop, but it was all but absent from the eastern shore. Tobacco had also assumed importance across the mountains in Kentucky and Tennessee, which by 1860 produced more tobacco than any other state except Virginia.

Tobacco country was not necessarily prosperous country. Prices were fairly good until 1807, but the Embargo Act hurt tobacco producers, and so did the War of 1812. When agricultural prices rose after the war, prosperous seasons returned for tobacco growers. But the Panic of 1819 put an end to the first good times in a decade. Favorable prices returned briefly in the 1830s, only to be swallowed up in the Panic of 1837. Finally the general prosperity of the 1850s

brought a decade of strong prices. The table below shows what happened. In
the five major tobacco states production fell by over 34 million pounds between
1839 and 1849. But between 1849 and 1859 poundage shot up nearly 181 million
pounds, a 109 percent increase during the decade and a 73 percent increase
over the 1839 total.

Tobacco Production (millions of pounds)

	1839	1849	1859
Virginia	75.3	56.9	124.0
North Carolina	16.9	12.0	32.9
Maryland	24.9	21.4	38.4
Kentucky	53.4	55.5	108.1
Tennessee	29.6	20.1	43.4
Total	200.1	165.9	346.8

The rejuvenation of tobacco in the 1850s was based on more than a general
upturn in agricultural prices. Around 1850 the Slade brothers, Eli and Elisha, of
Caswell County, North Carolina, developed a new variety of tobacco that had a
brighter color. A new curing process preserved the yellow color. Termed Bright
Yellow, this variety of tobacco brought considerably more per pound than did
the traditional dark variety. During the 1850s techniques for cultivating Bright
Yellow were publicized. Initially Bright Yellow served as the wrapper for plug
tobacco, but after the Civil War it became the basic ingredient in cigarettes.
Bright Yellow clearly helped the price, but even more important for tobacco
growers, the price held firm during the explosion in production.

Although Bright Yellow transformed price and use, cultivation practices
changed little from those of the colonial era. Early in the spring workers burned
the vegetation on small, carefully selected parcels of land to sterilize the soil and
destroy weeds. Then on these seedbeds the tiny tobacco seeds were sown. In
late spring the young tobacco plants were transplanted to the fields where they
would grow to maturity. But transplanting did not signal the end of careful attention. Plowing and hoeing were necessary to control grass and weeds, and
the growing tobacco plant required suckering and topping. Suckering—the
pulling off of subordinate leaves—encouraged the growth of the large leaves
that brought good prices. In addition the main stem of the plant had to be broken
off, or topped, to prevent the plant from going to seed. Both of these time-consuming tasks had to be performed by hand, as did the onerous and continuous job
of picking green tobacco worms off the leaves. At maturity the plants were cut and
hung in log tobacco houses or barns, where slow fires and smoke cured the leaves.
The cured tobacco was packed in hogsheads, large barrels that in the antebellum
years contained almost 1,500 pounds of the weed, and transported to market.

Because of the intensive hand labor involved in growing tobacco, a single
worker, free or slave, could care for only two or three acres. Tobacco did not
require expensive equipment. Careful attention to the many details of planting,

MAJOR HEMP, TOBACCO, RICE, AND SUGAR CANE REGIONS, 1860

cultivation, and harvesting held the key to a successful crop. Tobacco could provide quite a decent return per acre. In 1850 the gross value of the average yield
was about five times that of wheat.

Tobacco was a suitable crop for both large planters and small farmers, and
both grew it. Fully 90 percent of the farmers in the Roanoke River valley, the
center of Virginia's tobacco culture, raised the weed. The average tobacco acreage per farm in these seven counties was between eight and nine, far from massive. The larger growers cultivated the bulk of the crop. In Charlotte County,
for example, 17 percent of the growers produced 57 percent of the crop. One of
the greatest tobacco planters was Samuel Hairston of Pittsylvania County, who
owned more than 1,500 slaves. In 1855 his plantations were worth $600,000 and
his total wealth was placed at more than $3 million.

The potentially high rate of return for tobacco did cause one serious problem: it often caused farmers and planters to forget that the crop severely de-

pleted the resources in the soil. Three or four years of tobacco could destroy the fertility of any piece of land. Agricultural reformers urged the rotation of crops and some growers managed to maintain the fertility of their acres by this means, but many more simply shifted tobacco to another portion of their holdings. Because most growers, even substantial ones, raised relatively few acres of tobacco, they found it simpler and more profitable to abandon a depleted parcel and plant their seedlings somewhere else.

In the colonial period most tobacco was exported, but in the nineteenth century an increasingly large share of the crop went to American manufacturers, who processed it for a domestic market. Although the amount of unprocessed tobacco exported grew to an all-time high of 198,846 hogsheads in 1859, by that time almost half of the crop remained in the United States. Much of it went to the nearby Virginia towns of Danville, Lynchburg, Petersburg, and especially Richmond, where in 1860 more than 10,000 workers labored to manufacture snuff, cigars, and the massively popular plug (or chewing) tobacco. The tobacco enterprise epitomizes the old ways and the new directions that marked the South of the mid-nineteenth century. The oldest staple, which had been critical in Virginia for more than two centuries, provided the raw material for an increasingly important industry, the manufacture of tobacco products. And in the last decade before the Civil War both were prospering. In 1860 tobacco occupied a central place in a thriving agricultural and industrial economy.

RICE

Rice, the crop that had first brought wealth to South Carolina, continued to be a major staple in the nineteenth century. In the 1800s rice had not moved far from its domain centered in South Carolina—along the coast between Georgetown and the Savannah River, with a slight northern extension along the Cape Fear River in North Carolina and a more substantial thrust along the Georgia coast down to the Altamaha River. The rice area expanded so little because cultivation depended on the tidal flow of rivers, and even on restricted portions of the rivers. The acres devoted to rice had to be above the level where salt water intruded but still within the powerful influence of tides.

Along the tidal rivers of lower South Carolina and Georgia—the Waccamaw, the Pee Dee, the Santee, the Cooper, the Ashley, the Combahee, the Savannah, the Altamaha—stood the heaviest concentration of great slave plantations in the South. Slaves accounted for 90 percent of the total population, and their owners were among the wealthiest and most baronial of all the slave masters. On James H. Couper's Hopeton Plantation, on the Altamaha, some 500 blacks toiled in the rice fields. Robert F. W. Allston, of Georgetown District, possessed 590 slaves, who worked his seven rice plantations totaling 4,000 acres. The prince of the rice planters was Nathaniel Heyward, whose plantations on the Combahee River he called "gold mines." When Heyward died in 1851, his estate included more than 2,000 slaves, 5,000 acres of riceland,

and a larger acreage of timber. The value of the estate exceeded $2 million—in an age with no income taxes.

These enormously wealthy planters presided over an enterprise that combined a paradoxical mix of modern technology and primitive cultivation practices. Considerable engineering sense and skill were essential to a successful rice operation. To protect the crop from overflowing rivers and simultaneously to permit the regulated use of the tidal flow required an elaborate system of dikes, levees, canals, and sluice gates. All that building and maintenance necessitated an immense amount of labor; hence the huge slave gangs. Unlike tobacco, rice could not be produced by small operators. The massive investment required for slaves, construction, and milling shut out all but the wealthy.

The actual preparation of the land and the cultivation and harvesting of the crop differed little from practices of ancient times. The key implement was the hoe. Slaves with hoes in hand broke the land and prepared it for planting. Slaves, again with hoes, worked through the young rice several times to keep out grasses and weeds. Then when harvest time came, hoes were replaced by sickles, which the slaves used to cut the rice. Experiments were made with reapers, but they simply did not work well in the boggy ground.

The milling of rice—the removal of the kernel from the husk with as little breakage of the grain as possible—took place at three locations. Initially most large plantations had their own mills, but advancing technology so increased the size and sophistication of the machinery that plantation mills gave way to commercial mills. By midcentury commercial mills in Georgetown, Charleston, and Savannah handled the bulk of the crop milled in this country. But by 1850 most of the rice was shipped to Europe for milling as well as for sale.

Rice production did not match the sharp advances posted by the other major staples in the nineteenth century. In the decade before the Civil War it declined by some 13 percent. Exports showed no appreciable increase between the 1790s and 1860. Though South Carolina's share of the crop shrank from 74 percent to 63 percent between 1849 and 1859, the state retained its traditional position as the first state of rice. In the same period, Georgia's share of the total rice crop more than doubled, to 28 percent. North Carolina, which had a small gain in production, remained a distant third. Even when production declined, the price, which had reached its antebellum high in 1816 at 6.1 cents a pound, failed to remain strong. Between 1840 and 1860 it generally hovered around 3 cents a pound. Because rice planters were large operators, they could make money despite low prices. But in contrast to the rest of southern agriculture, rice was static. Rice certainly did not hold the key to either the prosperity or the economic future of the South.

SUGAR CANE

Like rice, sugar cane faced geographical constraints. Because it needed a growing season of at least eight months and plentiful rainfall, successful commercial

cultivation was impossible above 31° latitude. In antebellum America this cli-
matic requirement restricted sugar cane to southern Louisiana and sparsely settled Texas and Florida. As late as 1860, Louisiana produced 96 percent of the
American crop.

Sugar cane came relatively late to Louisiana. It had no significance during
French domination, which ended in 1763. Not until the Spanish period was
nearing its close, in the mid-1790s, did commercial production of sugar cane
take hold. The efforts of one man had a great effect on the development of the
crop in Louisiana. In the 1770s Etienne de Boré emigrated from France to Louisiana, to a plantation some six miles above New Orleans, currently the site of
Audubon Park. In the early 1790s Boré, desperately searching for a profitable
crop, turned to sugar cane. Success, however, required more than the harvesting of a crop; it also necessitated transformation of the juice of the cane into
sugar—the process of granulation. With determination and the assistance of an
experienced sugar maker who had emigrated from Saint-Domingue after the
great slave rebellion, Boré prevailed. In 1795 he made a profit of $5,000 on a
crop that he sold for $12,000. Boré's pathbreaking effort led other planters to see
sugar cane as their economic future.

In the nineteenth century sugar cane became the leading crop of southern
Louisiana. As early as 1802 some seventy-five plantations produced around 6
million pounds of sugar. By the mid-1820s production had climbed to 30 million
pounds annually. Substantial growth continued through the antebellum years.
In 1860 the total was 221,840 hogsheads, each containing about 1,100 pounds of
sugar.

Making a profitable cane crop was complicated and difficult. The anticipated arrival of the first killing frost, which would ruin the cane, controlled the
growing season. Unlike the West Indies, Louisiana did have frosts, and the first
usually arrived in early November. The cane had to come out of the fields before then even if it were not fully ripe. Some cane was cut before it was completely mature, but the fertility of the rich delta soil compensated for the lack of
maturity. Frost also influenced planting practices. In the frostfree West Indies,
the cane was replanted only once in every ten or twelve years, because new
cane sprouted from the roots of the previous crop. Louisiana's frost shrank the
twelve years to three; thus one-third of the crop had to be replanted each year.
Stalks were placed in a furrow and covered with earth by a field hand wielding
a plow or a hoe.

The low, fertile land of the cane region made for special requirements. Because most cane was planted along the lower Mississippi or its appendages on
land basically at sea level, levees became absolutely essential to prevent flooding. The low elevation in conjunction with the high rainfall—almost 60 inches
annually—required an extensive network of ditches to facilitate draining and
bridges to make possible movement on and across plantations. A visitor to one
plantation of 1,360 acres estimated that it contained 100 miles of ditches and 200
bridges within its boundaries. In the days before the internal combustion engine, building and maintaining these structures entailed an immense amount of

labor. A planter had to have lots of people around. Obviously sugar cane did not attract many small operators. In the major sugar parish of Ascension in 1859, only six cane farmers had fewer than 900 improved acres.

The milling process further stacked the odds against all but substantial planters. The mill turned cane juice into sugar; molasses was the chief by-product. Initially, crude mills were driven by oxen or horses, but the introduction of steam power in 1822 transformed their operations. By 1854 over 75 percent of the mills in Louisiana were operated by steam. Throughout the antebellum era various technical improvements, such as vacuum pans for more efficient granulation, made sugar mills even more complex and required considerable technical knowledge and ability to run. To construct an up-to-date mill or to revamp an old one a planter could expect to spend a minimum of $12,000.

Not surprisingly, wealthy planters dominated sugar production. In 1860 John Burnside of New Orleans owned five cane plantations totaling 7,600 acres of improved land valued at more than $1.5 million. His sugar mills and other equipment were worth $250,000, and his slaves more than $500,000. His 1859 crop amounted to 3,060 hogsheads, which had a value of at least $250,000. Magnolia Plantation in Plaquemines Parish had over 2,200 acres, with 950 in cultivation; it fronted the Mississippi for more than two miles and had a massive levee system to prevent flooding. In 1861 Magnolia produced a gross income of $148,000 from the sale of sugar and molasses. William J. Minor, of Natchez, Mississippi, owned three cane plantations and 400 slaves, together worth approximately $1 million. As a group the sugar barons of the 1850s outdid in opulence their fellow slave owners across the South.

The marketing of sugar differed from that of the other major staples. The domestic market absorbed nearly all the sugar produced. Before the Louisiana Purchase, in fact, the United States had imported sugar from Louisiana. Now that Louisiana was a state and the American population was growing, markets never became a major preoccupation for cane planters. They spent their time striving to maintain a tariff that would give them an advantage over lower-priced West Indian sugar. And they succeeded for the entire period, but after the Tariff of 1846 at a considerably lower rate.

Sugar cane growers faced the same fluctuations in prices and weather that plagued all farmers and planters. Still, sugar was a vigorous and prosperous part of the economy. From 1840 to 1860 the price remained generally good, and in the 1850s it was excellent. The general sugar economy certainly shared in the prosperity of the last antebellum decade. No decline or fall was in sight.

Cotton

Although tobacco, rice, and sugar cane were important staples, none matched the undisputed monarch of nineteenth-century agriculture. Cotton was king. A visitor who journeyed through the region in 1827 noted that he never lost sight of cotton in one form or another. In Charleston he found the wharves "piled up with mountains of Cotton, and all your stores, ships, steam and canal boats crammed with and groaning under the weight of Cotton." On the main streets of the city pedestrians had to "dodg[e] from side to side to steer clear of the cotton waggons." When he moved inland to Augusta, he found cotton boats crowding the Savannah River and cotton warehouses covering entire blocks. As he traveled westward toward Montgomery, cotton fields, cotton bales, and cotton gins seemed omnipresent. Montgomery, he discovered, was "overstocked with cotton, and no boats to take it away." Finally the visitor reached New Orleans, where on his first night he attended a play put on in "a steam cotton-press house." A fitting end to this cotton pilgrimage came when he asked for directions to a gambling emporium. He would find it "at the Louisiana Coffee-house, just below the cotton-press, opposite to a cotton ware-house." This thousand-mile journey from the Atlantic to the Gulf of Mexico had been one long odyssey of "Cotton! Cotton!! Cotton!!!"

This trip from South Carolina to Louisiana did not encompass the whole of the area that was to become the antebellum cotton kingdom. By 1860 cotton fields stretched from North Carolina in the east to Texas in the west and from Tennessee down to Florida. Before the Civil War the cotton kingdom was never static. It was established in the late 1790s and early 1800s in South Carolina and Georgia, where its center remained until the 1820s. After the War of 1812 and the opening of the Southwest, cotton moved west rapidly until by midcentury the gulf states dominated production.

The alluvial lands along the lower Mississippi River, including portions of Arkansas, Louisiana, and Mississippi, were the richest cotton country in the South. Enriched by the periodic flooding of the Mississippi and its tributaries, this soil provided a magnificent home for cotton. Not far behind was the Alabama black belt, which stretched across the center of the state and angled toward the northwest as it approached the Mississippi line, where it spilled over into a few counties. The black belt was named not for the thousands of slaves who toiled on its farms and plantations but for the heavy black clay that produced the bountiful crops of white gold. Other notable cotton areas were the Tennessee River Valley in northern Alabama and southern Tennessee and the river valleys of eastern Texas.

This massive geographical expansion required fertile land and a labor supply, which the Southwest and slaves provided, but it rested in large part on a major technological advance, the invention of the cotton gin. In the early years the future of cotton was clouded by the difficulty of separating the cotton fiber, or lint, from the cotton seed. Cotton cloth came from the lint, not the seed, and until the two were separated, the process of making cotton cloth could not begin. Accomplishing this separation by hand was slow and tedious work, and basically uneconomical. Improvement was essential before the growing of cotton could become a major enterprise.

The key step was taken by a Yankee inventor during a sojourn on a Georgia plantation. Upon graduation from Yale in 1792, the New Englander Eli Whitney

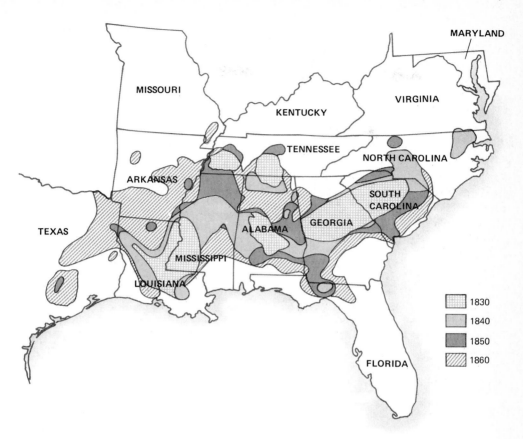

THE SPREAD OF COTTON, 1830–1860

headed south to be a tutor and ended up on a plantation owned by the widow of General Nathanael Greene. Here he began to work on a mechanical cotton gin, a machine that would pull the lint from the seed. In 1793 he built a machine that had a cylinder with wire teeth which rotated against a hopper filled with cotton and tore the lint from the seed. He added another cylinder with brushes revolving in the opposite direction to remove the lint from the wire teeth. The cotton gin was born. Improvements would be made—circular saws eventually replaced the wire teeth, for example—but the basic idea was in place, and it worked. Before the end of the decade cotton gins dotted the southern countryside. The birth of the cotton gin heralded the coming of the cotton revolution.

The revolution involved short-staple (or upland) cotton, not long-staple (or sea island) cotton. Long-staple cotton—the designation came from the length of the lint after it was separated from the seed—came into Georgia from the Bahama Islands in the mid-1780s. The name sea island became common because this variety of cotton was grown only on the sea islands of South Carolina and Georgia, where it was a near neighbor of rice. And like rice, sea island cotton supported a few extremely wealthy planters. Production, like the growing area, remained largely stable: 11.6 million pounds were exported in 1820, 15.6 million pounds in 1860. The longer staple gave this cotton a silky texture, and the cloth made from it commanded a high price. Sea island cotton cost several times more than its upland cousin (so named because it was grown away from the coast). Between 1820 and 1860 the annual average price in Charleston, the central market, never dropped below 16.6 cents a pound and often reached 30 cents and more, all the way to a high of 47 cents in 1860. The corresponding prices for upland cotton in New Orleans ranged between 5.5 and 17.9 cents and rarely exceeded 11 cents.

The rapid geographical expansion of upland cotton was matched by an explosion in production. At the beginning of the century just over 73,000 bales were produced; by 1820 that number had almost quintupled, to just over 335,000 bales. The same kind of jump occurred during the next two decades: the number of bales topped 1.0 million in 1835 and reached 1.35 million in 1840; by 1860 the cotton states raised and ginned 4.5 million bales of cotton. The price farmers and planters received for their cotton was never fixed or certain. It boomed early, but collapsed after the Panic of 1819; in New Orleans the average annual price fell from 21.5 cents in 1818 to 11.5 cents in 1822. Through the remainder of the 1820s and on into the 1830s the price fluctuated, but by the mid-1830s it seemed to stabilize at a reasonable level. The Panic of 1837 ravaged the price, which plummeted from 13.3 cents in 1836 to 7.9 cents in 1839 and kept on falling to a low of 5.5 cents in 1844. Throughout the 1840s, difficult years for most cotton planters, cotton prices remained generally depressed. But the 1850s were quite another story. Expanding production, which more than doubled in the decade, did not undermine prices. Cotton brought a profitable 11.1 cents in 1860, only 0.6 cents less than in 1850. The Panic of 1857, unlike its predecessors of 1819 and 1837, had no adverse effect on cotton prices. This was a farmer's dream: price stability at a profitable level and production rising sharply. In the final antebellum decade cotton led the way to a general agricultural prosperity. Southerners could reasonably believe that cotton was indeed king.

The particulars of cotton cultivation enabled both large planters and small farmers to grow it successfully. The seed was planted in the spring, then hoed and cultivated until the cotton plants were large enough to be out of danger from grass and weeds. To make a crop one needed only one's labor, a plow, and a draft animal to pull it. Of course, the greater the acreage planted, the more labor, plows, and animals that were needed. Normally horses or mules were used on cotton farms—mostly mules in the chief cotton regions. The amount of cotton planted depended on the size of the labor force available to pick the crop. When cotton bolls ripened and opened in the fall, people had to go into the fields and pick them, and picking a given acreage required more people than cultivating did. Depending on acreage and weather, the picking season could extend over several months, even into winter. Unpicked cotton had no value, so growers had no incentive to raise more than they could harvest. A reasonable estimate is that for each laborer, free or slave, six to nine acres would be planted.

Once picked, the cotton had to be ginned and packed into bales before shipment to market. Although by mid-century considerable improvements had been made on Whitney's gin, the antebellum gins never became the technological equals of rice or sugar mills. Most substantial plantations had their own gins to process their cotton and that of neighbors as well. Few small operators ran their own gins; they generally used the facilities on nearby plantations. In areas of few plantations, a farmer or group of farmers would operate a gin that serviced numerous small farmers.

Although small farmers did raise cotton, economies of scale favored the large planters. Most recent studies make clear that larger growers made more use of fertilizer, improved varieties of seed, and progressive cultivation practices than did small operators. Moreover, the substantial planters usually possessed the best land, produced the bulk of the crop, and made the greatest profit. In 1860, for example, in the richest cotton area, the alluvial river bottoms of the lower Mississippi Valley, the top 10 percent of the planters controlled 50 percent of the improved acreage and produced just over 50 percent of the cotton. This group of large planters also possessed 55 percent of the total agricultural wealth—the sum of real and personal property owned by all farmers and planters.

Cotton certainly formed the foundation for some of the greatest plantation fortunes. From 1801, when Wade Hampton I of Columbia, South Carolina, received $90,000 for a 600-bale crop, cotton provided wealth and power. Hampton went on to amass an agricultural empire with massive cotton estates in South Carolina and Mississippi along with a huge sugar cane plantation in Louisiana. At his death in 1859, Frederick Stanton of Natchez, Mississippi, owned plantations in Louisiana and Mississippi totaling over 15,000 acres. In that same year his three major plantations turned out 3,054 bales of cotton valued at $122,000. In the mid-1840s the former slave trader Isaac Franklin owned almost 11,000 acres in Tennessee and Louisiana. Between 1847 and 1849 his plantations produced on the average more than 1,100 bales annually. Farther to the east the fields of Joseph Bond of Macon, Georgia, yielded 2,100 bales of cotton in 1858.

General prosperity and expansion in the cotton economy depended on markets. And the textile mills of the Industrial Revolution had a voracious appetite for southern cotton. The Industrial Revolution came first to Great Britain, which remained the largest buyer of southern cotton all the way down to 1860. But the spread of the textile industry to the continent and its rapid growth in the United States created new consumers avid for the fleecy staple. In fact, as the table below shows, during the final two antebellum decades the continental and American markets for cotton were growing at a more rapid rate than the British, though it, too, expanded sharply.

	1839–1840 (bales)	1859–1860 (bales)	Percent increase
Great Britain	1,022,000	2,344,000	130
Continental Europe	453,000	1,069,000	136
United States	336,000	953,000	184

Those numbers make it easy to understand why most cotton growers in the 1850s thought their market inexhaustible and their crop indispensable.

OTHER CROPS AND LIVESTOCK

Although southern agriculture came to seem synonymous with its major money crops—tobacco, rice, sugar cane, cotton—they were not grown on every farm or plantation. In some areas, mostly in the upper and border South, other crops predominated. In the bluegrass region of Kentucky and in the counties along the Missouri River in Missouri, farmers and planters depended on hemp, used chiefly as bagging and rope for cotton bales. Hemp first gained importance in Kentucky in 1790, and Kentucky remained its major producer. In the 1850s hemp production declined there, though it increased in Missouri. By the 1860s those two states raised 75 percent of the American crop. American hemp, however, never captured what seemed to be its most likely market, the United States Navy. The navy preferred the water-rotted hemp imported from Russia rather than the dew-rotted native variety. And down to 1860, despite political pressure, the navy and the growers never got together.

By 1860 wheat was grown in every slave state except Louisiana and Florida, but production centered in the upper South and in the border states. In the South per capita production of wheat increased in the last antebellum decade, though the South's share of the national crop declined because of the surge of Middle Western wheat. In the tidewater and the Shenandoah Valley of Virginia, in eastern Tennessee, and in Kentucky and Maryland wheat was a significant crop. Much of the wheat grown in these areas remained in the South, where it supplemented the food supply.

Of all the crops in the antebellum South, corn was the most widely grown. Every slave state raised corn. The leaders were Missouri, Kentucky, and Tennessee. Southern production went up continually, to more than 436 million bushels in 1859. At the same time the South's share of the national crop declined from almost two-thirds in 1839 to just over one-half twenty years later. As with wheat, the burgeoning Middle West outpaced the South in production of corn. Although as a commercial source of corn the South did not compete with the Middle West, southern corn production was essential to meet food and forage requirements throughout the plantation South.

The South also had a sizable livestock population. Cattle were found in every state. As early as the eighteenth century, the people who lived in the forests and backcountry of the Southeast kept herds of cattle. In the nineteenth century, herders joined the westward trek, but the continued growth of farms and plantations reduced their numbers and importance. Although cattle pervaded the South, by 1860 the westernmost southern state, Texas, was already emerging as dominant in cattle, and that dominance was to become pronounced in the postwar decades.

Hogs provided the basic meat in the southern diet. Pork was a dietary mainstay for blacks and most whites. Few people of either race passed many days without pork in some form—fried, roasted, or boiled, alone or mixed with vegetables. Almost every family with any land at all kept some hogs, but even so, a commercial market for hogs did exist, chiefly to feed the cities and the larger plantations. So pork became a cash crop for some southerners, especially in Tennessee and Kentucky, which between 1840 and 1860 had the greatest concentration of hogs. Much of this pork went southward to sugar cane and cotton plantations.

Not surprisingly, the South had a huge number of work animals. In a largely nonmechanized agricultural economy, draft animals were essential. Least numerous were oxen, though they were evenly distributed through the region. Horses abounded. From the sturdiest workers to the sleekest racers, horses formed a natural part of the southern world. Most southerners, whether they favored carriages, wagons, or saddles, could not contemplate transport for business or pleasure apart from horses.

The animal most closely identified with southern agriculture enjoyed little of the favored image often bestowed upon horses. The mule was singularly a southern animal; in 1860 southerners owned almost 90 percent of the nation's mule supply. Mules had infrequent encounters with carriages and races; they spent their lives in plow harnesses. Though horses outnumbered them, mules spanned the southern region. The major plantation areas, such as the Alabama black belt and the alluvial lands along the lower Mississippi, had a substantial mule population that worked in the cotton and cane fields. The large number of mules in Kentucky, Tennessee, and Missouri was accounted for by the raising of stock for sale to the plantations and farms of the deep South.

ECONOMIC TRENDS

Across the southern countryside and in the towns and cities as well, prosperity depended on the health of agriculture. In view of the diversity of crops planted in the region, one economic condition did not always prevail throughout the slave states. With the rise of cotton, however, its fate had an enormous impact on the economic well-being of the South.

Although the volumes and prices of crops fluctuated from year to year and localities experienced their economic ups and downs, it is possible to generalize about sectionwide trends. At the same time, the existence of local variations must never be forgotten. Between the last years of the eighteenth century and the end of the antebellum era, the southern agricultural economy underwent five general periods:

1. Before the War of 1812: The introduction of cotton into South Carolina and Georgia along with reasonable prices for rice made for prosperity. Though not so dynamic as the rice country, the Chesapeake area knew generally good prices for tobacco. But the Embargo Act of 1807 caused abrupt change; trade stopped and economic stagnation pervaded the region.

2. The War of 1812 to the Panic of 1819: The war years were difficult but peace brought a return of good times, even a boom in cotton country. The boom was brief, however.

3. The Panic of 1819 to the Panic of 1837: Although the Panic of 1819 delivered a crushing blow, a slow comeback took place in the 1820s. Rice remained stable and sugar cane did well. By the 1830s a new enthusiasm stirred the South; once again times were flush in the Southwest. Many people became excited at the prospect of railroads that would connect the South with the Midwest.

4. The Panic of 1837 to the late 1840s: The panic struck ferociously; this period represented the deepest and most prolonged depression in the antebellum period. In some places cotton prices plunged to less than 5 cents a pound. Tobacco and rice also suffered, though sugar cane held on. As hard times wore on, optimism all but disappeared in bitter political fights over financial policy.

5. The late 1840s to 1861: Prosperity returned; the depression was a rapidly fading memory. Across the South the 1850s was the most prosperous single decade thus far in the nineteenth century—and it would not be matched until the twentieth. Everything went the southern way. Substantial increases in the production of most staples did not depress prices, which either rose or at least remained stable. The Panic of 1857, unlike its two predecessors, had little affect on the boisterous southern economy.

These five periods describe the general direction of the southern economy at specific times. That framework does not at all mean that within a particular period everyone prospered or suffered. At all times some individuals were making fortunes while others were going broke, and some managed to do both. Nor were economic conditions identical across the section in every year or in every decade. The Panic of 1837, for example, did not hammer sugar cane so hard as cotton. Other factors entered into the equation as well. The western cotton belt, especially the alluvial land along the lower Mississippi, was more fertile and productive than the eastern. Thus when prices were good, western planters tended to be more prosperous than their eastern counterparts; and when prices dropped, the easterners usually experienced greater hardships.

*F*INANCE AND A MARKET ECONOMY

In the South the size of farms exceeded the national average, and economies of scale did exist. Larger farms and plantations were generally more efficient and more prosperous than smaller ones. Of course there were exceptions, but large operators had a clear advantage, especially in the major staple regions. That southern farms and plantations averaged more acres than those elsewhere in the country was not accidental. In a time before much mechanization, the most serious drawback to expansion in agriculture was the need for large numbers of hands to do the work. Most American farm families had to depend solely on their own efforts because hired help was scarce. Throughout the antebellum years land remained available and cheap in the newer states and the less settled regions. Families that wanted to make their own way, and most did, could relatively easily buy farms of their own. Thus a substantial population of permanent agricultural laborers never developed. In the South, however, slaves provided the labor needed to build huge agricultural operations. Thus slavery gave to southern agriculturalists with ambition, determination, and good fortune the opportunity to move far beyond the limits imposed by a restricted labor supply in other regions.

Like most other businesses, southern agriculture required capital. Some agriculturalists—small farmers bent on self-sufficiency and the very wealthiest—might rarely need credit, but for most of them credit was just as essential as sunshine and rain. The cost of planting a crop, marketing it, and supplying the physical needs of a slave force, to say nothing of acquiring more acres or slaves, required larger expenditures of money at one time than most agriculturalists had readily available. Thus, like most other business operators, southern farmers borrowed. They borrowed from family members and friends but chiefly from banks and factors. From 1820 onward banks operated in most slave states, though their character, number, and wealth varied enormously. By 1860 Virginia counted sixty-five banks and neighboring North Carolina had fifty; Arkansas and Florida, by contrast, had fewer than five. As far as banking was concerned, the South was in general a poor relation to the rest of the country. In 1860 the bank capital in New York City exceeded $100 million, a figure greater than any southern state could claim and more than the combined total of all the banks in Baltimore, Louisville, St. Louis, New Orleans, Mobile, Charleston, and Richmond.

Most planters, however, did not deal directly with banks to finance their crops. Instead they worked with factors, middlemen who performed an indispensable economic function in the antebellum South. Factors operated between the grower and purchaser of staple crops. But a factor was more than a broker— a person who merely brings together seller and buyer. Factors conducted business in their own names, and they often made advance payments to planters against the money they expected to receive when their crops were sold. Quite often the factor became a planter's major source of credit. And if the factor did not provide credit himself, he arranged a line of credit for the planter. Factors supplied planters with a variety of critical information and services. To provide market information in both the United States and Europe was an essential duty of a factor. With that information and their factors' advice, planters decided when to sell their crops and in what market. Many factors served as purchasing agents for their planter clients. In this role factors bought goods and supplies ranging from slave provisions to clothes and furniture for the planter family. Thus the factor was at the same time a supply merchant, a crop broker, a fount of financial information, and a source of financing. For these services planters paid factors a commission, usually 2.5 percent of the gross proceeds from the sale of a crop.

Every major market center, especially the seaports, had numerous factors. In New Orleans, Maunsel White's career spanned the first half of the nineteenth century. White arrived in Spanish Louisiana from Ireland in 1801. Early on he became active in the factoring business, and for decades he was one of the leading factors in the greatest southern seaport. White of course arranged for the sale of crops, chiefly cotton and sugar cane, and advanced money to planters. In the supply part of his business White purchased and sent to his planter clients an enormous variety of goods, including skins, lace caps, bonnets, cordage, meat, and lard. White did business with an impressive list of planters, including Zachary Taylor and Andrew Jackson, whose affairs White handled from 1826 until Jackson's death in 1845.

White's successful career as a factor led him to other activities. He became a large property owner in New Orleans and a substantial sugar cane planter. His major plantation, Deer Range, downriver from New Orleans, was valued at $200,000. Committed to his city and state, he contributed generously to the infant University of Louisiana (renamed Tulane University in 1884). When White died at Deer Range in 1863, he had been witness to massive transformations in the economics and politics of Louisiana and the South. Such men as White were integral parts in the antebellum agricultural system.

Most farmers and small planters, however, did not deal with factors. They sold their crops to local merchants or to neighboring larger planters, often for cash. Credit could be involved; merchants or planters might provide various supplies, which would be paid for from the proceeds of the crop sale. For the smaller operators, then, the market tended to be local. They had only an indirect connection with the larger financial world of New Orleans, New York, and England, though that world had considerable influence on local prices. Farmers across the South had to make a decision about the market, about whether or not to participate in it. As landowners—and the overwhelming majority of all southern agriculturalists owned their land—they could determine their own course. In the eighteenth century many farm families shunned the market in favor of self-sufficiency; they focused on providing the food and clothing they needed. But in the nineteenth century, especially with the spread of cotton, more and more families became involved in growing crops for the market. The decision to participate in the market economy did not necessarily mean a shift to slave labor. Half of the farms in the cotton states had no slaves, but only one-quarter grew no cotton.

This movement from self-sufficiency to participation in the market was an ongoing process. Not all farm families made the shift at the same time; some made it, then changed their minds; others never made it. Despite the diversity, the trend was unmistakable. More and more southern farm families joined the ranks of those enmeshed in the market; they produced a crop to sell. For most farmers going with the market was a major decision. A way of life was at stake. To say yes meant that providing food and clothing for the family took second place to the production of a money crop, usually cotton. But to say no could mean being left behind. When new areas came into the market, everyone tended to push for railroads and other improvements in transportation. A family with a crop to sell had to be concerned about marketing, about the availability of an efficient, inexpensive means to transport that crop to market. And wagons crammed with a few bales of cotton and pulled by a team of mules over miserable roads for considerable distances simply were not good enough.

*T*HE FOOD SUPPLY

With so many southerners committed to growing crops for the market, the question of feeding family and slaves had to be faced. Concentration on a staple crop and the market could lead to bare cupboards and an empty pantry. Even so, individual insufficiency did not necessarily mean any widespread shortage of food. The South produced ample food to feed its population, white and black.

Regional differences and variations did exist, however. Major plantation regions with large slave populations and a massive commitment to staple crops tended to import foodstuffs from other areas. Cities, too, had to obtain food supplies elsewhere. Generally speaking, these needs were supplied within the region. The commodity most in demand was meat, chiefly pork. From commercial hog farms in the upper and border South, especially in Tennessee and Kentucky, drovers brought hogs down into the great cotton belt and the cane country. Cattle often followed the same routes. Coastal areas were serviced from New Orleans with animals first brought downriver to the Crescent City. Seaports along the Gulf of Mexico and the South Atlantic not only received cargos from New Orleans for distribution in their hinterlands, they also sent seafood inland.

The internal southern grain trade differed from the pattern established for meat. The major grain in the southern diet, corn, was so abundant that it never had to be transported over any great distance. Most cities' shipments came from nearby growers. Wheat was less plentiful and often had to be brought from other states. Charleston, for example, in 1850 brought wheat in by rail from northern Georgia, North Carolina, and even Tennessee. In the same year Mississippi and Louisiana received shipments that originated in the upper and border slave states and even in the Midwest.

THE FORMATION OF PLANTATION DISTRICTS

In some parts of the South, such as the rice districts, plantations were dominant and farms were few. Other areas, such as northeastern Alabama, had many farms but few plantations and slaves. But in most of the South plantations and farms coexisted. In the major staple regions plantations were surely more important economically but they did not drive out farms. Away from those counties farms often had more significance, yet plantations could be found in substantial numbers.

Plantations had been a part of the Chesapeake and the South Carolina coast since the eighteenth and in some cases even the seventeenth centuries. By the mid-nineteenth century plantations were still characteristic of those two colonial bastions. In most of the South, however, plantations appeared only after 1800, and in the burgeoning Southwest usually not until after the War of 1812, when settlement began in earnest.

In the Southwest much of the best land that eventually supported plantation agriculture had initially been public land. In the 1820s numerous speculators and even squatters led in the creation of rich plantation districts. In 1818 John Brahan, the receiver of the public land office in Huntsville, Alabama, bought for $317,622 more than 44,000 acres in the rich Tennessee River Valley. Much of that land, sold and resold, became prime cotton plantations. John Coffee of Tennessee, a friend as well as a military and business colleague of Andrew Jackson, used his position as government surveyor to purchase for himself and some friends almost 23,000 acres, many of which became the cores of thriving plantations.

In the 1820s and 1830s the Alabama black belt became a magnet both for men looking to make their first mark and for established families in the seaboard states seeking to renew or increase their wealth. All saw the magnificent black soil as the fount of riches. The purchase in Perry County alone of more than 90,000 acres in only five years, between 1830 and 1835, underscores the furious pace of settlement. Elisha King came to the black belt in 1819 as an obscure settler from Georgia. In 1820 he acquired 1,028 acres in Perry County and planted cotton. By his death in 1852 he was master of almost 8,000 acres and 186 slaves. In 1835 sixty-five-year-old James Lide, a substantial planter, left his home in Darlington District, South Carolina, for Dallas County in search of a secure source of wealth. With him came his wife, six children, one daughter-in-law, and six grandchildren.

But the Southwest had no monopoly on the creation of plantation districts, even after the War of 1812. In the older states plantations found their way into areas that had not previously known them. In upcountry South Carolina the development of plantation agriculture went on continuously between 1820 and 1860, albeit at an uneven pace. In some counties plantations took hold early; in others it never did; and in most there was a lengthy transition period. Thus throughout the antebellum era the upcountry knew change. By 1850 the upcountry produced over half of the cotton grown in South Carolina but it had

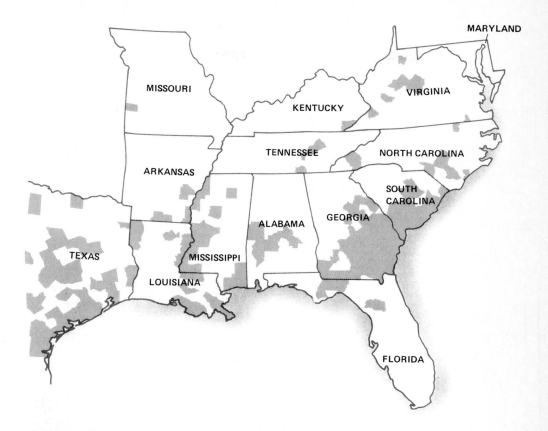

THE PLANTATION BELT, 1860 (Areas Where Farms Averaged 600 Acres or More)

only 36 percent of the slave population, which totaled over 50 percent for the state as a whole.

Hancock County, Georgia, in the lower piedmont between Augusta and Milledgeville, made its transformation only in the 1850s. During the decade the more affluent planters bought up land that previously had belonged to small farmers. That process diminished the number of landowners in Hancock by 16 percent. As a result, the white population declined from 4,201 in 1850 to 3,871 in 1860. At the same time the slave population rose from 7,306 to 8,137. With the multiplication of plantations, land values in the county shot up by 47 percent. The number of holdings valued at $10,000 or more quadrupled. Such property accounted for only 4 percent of all holdings in 1850 but in 1860 represented fully 15 percent.

Families pushed out by the growth of plantations usually followed one of two possible courses. Many of them joined the never-ending westward migration. This move might be to the adjoining county, to the next state, or to a location hundreds of miles away. In fact, many of these migrants left voluntarily; they were not really forced away. Responding to the call of newer lands and greater wealth in the West, tens of thousands of Virginians, Carolinians, and even Georgians traveled west during the last antebellum generation. These people happily sold out and headed toward the sunset in the hope of becoming rich or richer. When the Lide family left South Carolina for the Alabama black belt, several other families from the neighborhood moved with them. Practically an entire community went west at one time.

Others moved only because they had no choice. In the race for wealth they finished out of the running, their poor showing caused by bad luck, lack of ambition, or simply no interest in becoming enmeshed in the burgeoning market economy. These families generally tried to find a spot in advance of the plantation frontier where they could farm and live in their traditional manner. It was a hard living, though, and when the spread of plantations gave them an opportunity to sell their land and pay their debts, they sold out and moved on. Many moved often.

Although many families left the newly created plantation districts, either voluntarily or involuntarily, others remained and slid down into landlessness. White tenant farmers and farm laborers did exist in the South before 1860, though their numbers did not begin to match the post–Civil War figures. In Hancock County, Georgia, for example, the census of 1860 listed 198 farm laborers. Among them was David Ware, who migrated there from North Carolina around 1840. Toward the end of the decade he became a tenant on a plantation owned by Andrew J. Lane. Ware worked hard and prospered. By 1850 he owned five horses, 100 hogs, and two dozen cows; he also produced 650 bushels of corn, 100 bushels of peas and beans, 400 bushels of sweet potatoes, three tons of hay, and three bales of cotton. Ware seemed on his way up the social and economic ladder, but disaster struck. In 1852 his home burned, and he was forced, apparently evicted, from Lane's plantation. The record is unclear as to whether Lane wanted Ware gone, but that is a distinct probability. The result for Ware is clear, though we do not know the reason: his fortunes hurried downward. According to his former landlord, Ware's holdings "dwindled down to nothing." The census of 1860 carried David Ware as a farm laborer.

In 1860, as during the previous two centuries, the prosperity of the South and of southerners depended on the land. And as southerners contemplated the last four decades of the nineteenth century, they had every reason for confidence and optimism.

9

The Institution of Slavery

❖

When people talk about slavery, they are usually talking about the slavery of the 1840s and 1850s. They seem to assume that the institution always had the form it did then. But slavery changed over time. Though the institution of 1850 inherited many features of the slavery of a hundred years earlier, it was not an exact replica. Slavery responded to and shared in the continuities and changes that marked all other facets of southern life between the colonial era and the Civil War.

CHANGE AND CONTINUITY

Major similarities spanned the decades. None was more important or more obvious than the place of work. In 1860 just as in the seventeenth century, the overwhelming majority of slaves worked as agricultural laborers. For two centuries they had provided the muscle power of southern agriculture. Two aspects of ownership also followed the colonial pattern—concentration and distribution. Although precise figures for the colonial period are not available, in all probability the planters owned most of the slaves. Certainly they did in 1860. But many other people owned slaves too, among them artisans and small farmers. Even before the Revolution slaveholding had been broadly democratic, and it still was in the 1840s and 1850s.

In still another important way the late antebellum institution resembled its youthful predecessor. As white settlers pushed inland to the piedmont and toward the mountains, black slaves moved along with them. This westward advance did not slow in the nineteenth century. When white southerners reached the Mississippi, when they arrived in Texas, their black slaves stood beside them.

Although similarities were powerful, sharp differences separated colonial slavery from its nineteenth-century descendant. Perhaps the most obvious distinction was the absence of slaves freshly arrived from Africa. Under the authority of the Constitution, Congress prohibited the international slave trade as of January 1, 1808. Despite the legal ban on importation, slaves were smuggled into the South down to 1860, but the numbers were not large. The best modern studies put the figure at around 50,000 over more than fifty years. This small group had no significant impact on the culture or demography of a slave population that increased from just under 1 million in 1800 to 4 million in 1860.

Though an outlawed international trade largely disappeared, a thriving internal slave trade assumed major importance. During the colonial period slaves were certainly sold in colonial seaports for employment in the backcountry. These slaves, however, moved relatively short distances, and the continued importation of Africans precluded the growth of an intercolonial slave trade. But the rush west after 1815 necessitated the movement of slaves from the eastern South to the western South. When it was no longer possible to bring in substantial numbers of slaves from Africa or elsewhere in the New World, the interstate slave trade burgeoned. It played an instrumental role in the westward movement of the slave population.

In a quite different sphere, and paradoxically, momentous change took place in the slaves' religion and probably in their family life. Before the Revolution, Christianity had made little headway among slaves, as whites showed little interest in intruding into their slaves' religious life. That situation changed with the massive growth of the evangelical denominations in the nineteenth century. Christianity became a major influence in the slave world. Whites pushed it and slaves willingly accepted it, though not without placing their own distinctive imprint on their masters' religion. At the same time, family life became more important in the slave community. Studies of the colonial period are few and evidence is scarce, but recent scholarship has underscored the primary role of the slave family in the last antebellum generation.

The increasing importance of Christianity and family point not only to change in the life of the slaves but also to a change in whites' perception of their bondsmen and bondswomen. In the nineteenth century whites began to speak of their slaves as part of their own family, a practice not common before the Revolution. This shift, so critical for whites as well as blacks, has been aptly characterized as "the domestication of African slavery."

THE DISTRIBUTION AND CONCENTRATION OF SLAVES

During the 1840s slavery spread across the South, all the way to the Rio Grande. After Texas and Florida became states in 1845, slavery was legally protected and constitutionally sanctioned in fifteen states plus the District of Columbia. The institution, however, was not evenly distributed throughout the thousands of square miles covered by those states. By 1860 the proportion of the population accounted for by slaves ranged from almost zero in some areas to 90 percent in others.

Slavery did not flourish in regions where the topography and the soil failed to support plantation agriculture. The great Appalachian heartland, reaching from western Virginia down to northeastern Alabama and encompassing western North Carolina, eastern Tennessee, and northern Georgia, provided a home for few slaves. This part of the South was generally inhospitable to plantations and plantation culture. When the Civil War came, much of western Virginia broke away and in 1863 joined the Union as West Virginia. Simultaneously eastern Tennessee furnished military units to the United States Army and was arguably home to more Union sympathizers than any other part of the Confederacy. Slaves were also exceedingly scarce in the piney woods of southeastern Mississippi, the mountains of northwestern Arkansas, and the vast barrenness of western Texas.

At the other end of the distribution scale came the sea islands that stretched along the South Carolina–Georgia coast from north of Charleston to the Florida line. There rice and sea island cotton plantations teemed with slaves; this is one of the regions where slaves constituted 90 percent of the population. Whites were equally outnumbered along both banks of the Mississippi River above and below Vicksburg, where rich alluvial soil supported enormous cotton plantations.

Most of the South fell between these two extremes. Over the South the slave population totaled 33 percent of the entire population. In every state slaves congregated in the sections of richest soil and most prosperous agriculture—Alabama's black belt, the cotton belt of central Georgia, the sugar parishes in southern Louisiana, the tobacco counties of Southside Virginia. The institution pervaded the whole of only one state, South Carolina. In 1860 South Carolina retained the position it had held since the early eighteenth century as the blackest of southern colonies or states, with a slave population of 55 percent. Elsewhere, only in Mississippi did the percentage of slaves reach 50 percent.

From the oldest settled area along the Chesapeake Bay to the newest in Texas, slavery was firmly implanted and growing. In the last antebellum decades all signs pointed to the continued growth of the institution that in the South was already two centuries old. The number of slaves in every state except Maryland and Delaware grew between 1840 and 1860, though the impact of the interstate slave trade moderated the increase in the older eastern states. With a slave population in 1860 of only 1.4 percent, Delaware was a slave state in name only. State law still protected the institution, but economically, ideologically, and politically its influence was rapidly declining. Maryland remained a slave state but it was unmistakably following Delaware's lead. The sharp decline in the percentages of both slaves and slave owners distinguished Maryland from the states below the Potomac. Far to the west in Missouri, where a battle over slavery had sparked a national crisis in 1820, a similar pattern prevailed. Only Kentucky retained a percentage of slaves and owners that still marked it as a thriving slave state. The border states, then, marked more than a geographic border; by 1860 they also marked a social, economic, ideological, and political border.

Just as slaves were not distributed evenly across the South, their concentration varied. In 1860, 393,967 southerners owned slaves, an increase of 13.8 per-

cent over the number of owners in 1850. Still, only 4.9 percent of the white population in the slave states owned even one slave. But the owners of record were
certainly not the only white southerners directly involved with slavery. According to census figures, a family in 1860 averaged five members. Thus, to obtain a
more accurate count of the southerners intimately involved with slavery requires multiplying the number of titular owners by the average family size. The
result, almost 2 million people, represented fully one-quarter of the white population, and in the eleven states that made up the Confederacy the number
equaled 30 percent. With such a substantial proportion of white southerners
having a direct stake in slavery, the powerful influence of the institution is easily understandable.

Just as the ownership of slaves plunged deep into southern white society, it
also spread across a broad economic spectrum. Slave ownership in the mid-
nineteenth century followed the pattern established during the colonial period.
It was a democratic enterprise. In 1860, 72 percent of the owners possessed
fewer than ten slaves and more than half owned fewer than five. In 1850 those
percentages had been 73 and 50. In both years the largest category of owners
barely made it into the slave-owning class with only one slave. In 1850 owners
of one slave totaled 68,820; a decade later that number reached 77,324. These
masters were obviously not great planters living in manor houses or riverfront
palaces. Most were small farmers or artisans who worked alongside the slave
who made them legally part of the master class.

Historians usually consider that planter status required the possession of at
least twenty slaves. Though the categories often employed are somewhat arbitrary, they are helpful: small planters were those who owned between 20 and
50 slaves; large planters, from 50 to 100; great planters, more than 100. Though
the owners in none of these three categories were very numerous, they were
still consequential. The substantial planters accounted for only 11 percent of all
slaveholders in 1850 and 12 percent in 1860, but they and their plantations gave
a special identity to the antebellum South.

The slave owners who dominated the southern economy and stood at the
social summit of southern society could not match in splendor some of their
labor-owning colleagues elsewhere in the world. Until 1861, Russia also had a
social and economic system based on human bondage. The institution of serfdom was fully established in the seventeenth century. By the nineteenth century the great nobles of Russia had accumulated massive numbers of serfs.
Prince Iusupov counted 54,703; Count Vorontsov had 54,703; Count N. P.
Sheremetev's serfs reached the staggering total of 185,610. In 1858 more than
2,400 landlords owned between 500 and 1,000 serfs and 1,382 had more than
1,000. No slave owner could match those serf owners. According to the 1860
census, only fourteen southerners owned more than 500 slaves and of them only
one possessed more than 1,000. Thus, while wealthy and powerful in their own
domain, southern slaveowners were neither the greatest nor the richest masters.

From the slaves' perspective, the pattern of ownership was the exact oppo-

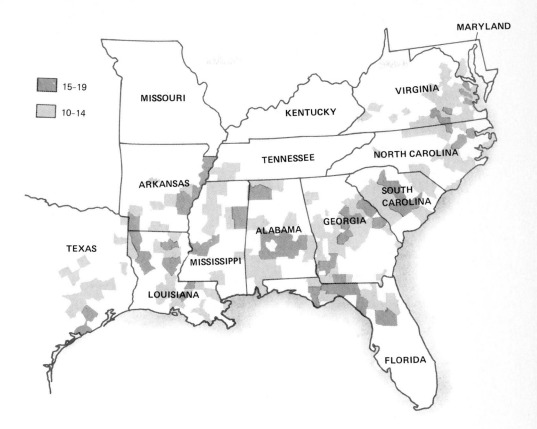

15–19

10–14

AREAS WHERE NUMBER OF SLAVES AVERAGED 10–19 PER HOLDING, 1860

site of the one the masters saw. Most whites who possessed slaves had very few, but most slaves were members of considerably larger holdings. In 1860 planters with more than twenty slaves accounted for only 12 percent of all slave owners, but they owned 48 percent of all the slaves. In contrast, 71 percent of the masters with fewer than ten slaves held only 32 percent of the slaves. These numbers show clearly that almost half of the slave population labored for the planter class.

Like so much else in southern history, slave ownership did not make up a neat, tidy package. Slave owning was certainly not uncommon in the South. Without a doubt the wide extent of ownership over more than a century was of critical importance in securely fastening slavery on the society. Simultaneously, the skewed ownership pattern underscored the special position of the landed planter class.

AREAS WHERE NUMBER OF SLAVES AVERAGED 20 OR MORE PER HOLDING, 1860

SLAVE CODES

All southern states grouped laws governing slaves in "slave codes." The first codification of statutes pertaining to slaves occurred in Virginia in 1705; in the nineteenth century such codes governed the master-slave relationship across the South. In describing the condition of servitude the codes were invariably harsh. The codes had a simple basic thrust—the total submission of all slaves to their masters, and by extension to all whites. The Louisiana Code of 1806 did not mince words:

> The condition of the slave being merely a passive one, his subordination to his master and to all who represent him is not susceptible of modification or restriction... he owes to his master, and to all his [master's] family, a respect without bounds, and an absolute obedience, and he is consequently to execute all orders which he receives from him, his said master or from them.

The codes specified restrictions on slaves' activities. Slaves were forbidden to play drums or horns. They had no legal standing in court; no court accepted their testimony. Laws directed slaves to step aside when whites passed. Other statutes forbade the teaching of reading or writing to slaves, even by their masters. Slave marriages were not recognized by the law. Slaves were forbidden to gamble or trade with whites, free blacks, or other slaves. They were not permitted to possess guns. Limitations on the sale of slaves, even the taking away of children from mothers, barely existed. The slave was property, or chattel, and so could be freely bought or sold. In 1861 the Alabama Supreme Court cogently described the inevitable effect of slavery as "a complete annihilation of the will." The slave "ha[d] no legal mind, no will which the law [could] recognize."

The codes sharply circumscribed the lives of slaves. The Alabama Code of 1852 was forceful and direct: "No slave must go beyond the limits of the plantation on which he resides, without a pass, or some letter or token from his master or overseer, giving him authority to go and return from a certain place." Slaves who violated this law were to be "apprehended and punished."

The racial character of slavery underlay the enforcement of restrictions on slaves' movements. Any white could halt and demand identification from any black. Blacks out on the road had to be prepared to prove either that they were free persons or that they had permission to be away from their home plantation. From the Red River Valley of central Louisiana, Solomon Northup reported that fear of the omnipresent whites served as a massive deterrent to unauthorized movement. Northop, a free black from New York who had been kidnapped and sold into slavery, confessed that apprehension about scrutiny by whites along the roads helped keep in check his great desire to escape his bonds. Although the entire white community acted as a brake on the free movement of slaves, one group had the specific responsibility of enforcing the laws governing their movements—the slave patrol.

Across the rural South the slave patrol provided a visible sign of white authority. Officially sanctioned by law, the patrol had enormous powers vested in it by the state or the white community. In view of the Anglo-American judicial tradition, the legal conception of the patrol and the functions assigned to it were extraordinary. The patrols possessed both judicial and executive power. The Alabama slave code of 1852 charged patrols "to enter in a peaceable manner, upon any plantation; to enter by force, if necessary, all negro cabins or quarters, kitchens and outhouses, and to apprehend all slaves who may there be found, not belonging to the plantation or household, without a pass from their owner or overseer; or strolling from place to place without authority." The patrols in Avoyelles Parish, Louisiana, were authorized to "take up and punish slaves that they [found] away from their Masters' premises without a permit." Thus patrols acted as sheriff, judge, and jury. And without any question slaves feared the patrols. Reminiscences of former slaves are filled with that fear.

Although the slave patrol was a formidable force for the preservation of white authority, it must not be equated with a totalitarian police force. Patrols were not the enforcement arm of an omnipotent state. Despite statutes calling for service by the great majority of the white male population and specifying a regular schedule of patrolling, men shunned such duty and the patrols operated sporadically, unless rumors circulated that a slave had killed a white person or that the slaves in the region were fomenting rebellion; then patrol activity increased sharply. A patrol was like a group of deputy sheriffs on call. When the white community felt the need for its services, the patrol could respond quickly.

PATTERNS OF MANAGEMENT

Slave owners had to manage their slaves. Because 95 percent of all slaves worked on farms or plantations, the overwhelming majority of owners were engaged in agricultural management. Because of the great variety both in the classes of owners and among individuals within those classes, however, it is not possible to describe precisely the practices followed by all owners. Still, a general pattern can be discerned.

Small farm families who owned few slaves usually combined their managerial responsibilities with their own physical labor. These families, the largest group of slaveholders, normally worked in the fields beside their slaves. Together they prepared the ground, planted seeds, cultivated the growing crop, and harvested it at maturity. In the off-season they joined in such tasks as repairing fences, refurbishing buildings, and clearing land. Though the master might assign his slaves a specific duty, such as caring for livestock, in which his own family did not participate, the white farm family and their black slaves labored together in a common enterprise.

The large farmers and the small planters were really interchangeable; the distinction between them is largely semantic. Although in our time the word *planter* connotes a wealthy operator of a large agricultural enterprise, in the antebellum South *planter* and *farmer* were synonymous. This person owned from ten to twenty or more slaves. These slaves were usually managed in one of two ways, but in neither instance did the master or his family engage in physical labor with their chattels. Instead, the master devoted his time to giving orders and managing the agricultural enterprise.

The first type of organization was quite simple. The planter or farmer personally directed the activities of the slaves. No other white person came between master and slaves. The master usually chose one slave to act as foreman of the group, or, in antebellum terms, the driver—the slave who drove the other slaves to work. With the help of the driver the master directly oversaw the labor of the slave force.

The second type of organization introduced another white person, a second figure of white authority over black slaves: the overseer. On farms and plantations of this sort the overseer occupied a central place, and on larger estates he was absolutely critical. The master issued orders to the overseer, who transmitted them to the slaves. At times the overseer would also work with drivers, who were responsible to the overseer just as the overseer was to the master. But with or without drivers, the overseer had responsibility for the daily labor performed by the slaves. Master and slaves might still have direct and frequent contact, but the presence of an overseer altered the relationship between owner and owned. To the slaves the overseer became the most visible, almost omnipresent symbol of white authority.

Large estates—the sort of plantations most people have in mind when they think of the antebellum South—had complex hierarchical organizations. No master of such an enterprise could possibly manage alone all of the wide variety of day-to-day activities of the many slaves the plantation needed—at least 50, often more than 100. The successful owner of a large plantation had to be an able manager of financial operations and of personnel. Market conditions, crop prices, interest rates, shipping costs all had to be carefully considered and weighed when critical decisions were to be made—how many acres to plant, when to sell the crop, whether to borrow money for expansion. The planter had to be able to cope with poor harvests as well as good ones, with low prices as well as high. Unless he managed his finances well, he had little chance to succeed at anything else. Of course, reasonably content, hard-working, productive slaves were indispensable to the financial success and stability of the plantation.

Overseers

To ensure that he had just such a slave force on his estate, the large planter needed assistance. The large plantation could not function without an overseer; he was the key subaltern. The overseer carried out the general policy set by the master. He translated the wishes, goals, and orders of the master to the slaves. *They* may be a more accurate term than *he*, for a large plantation where more than 100 slaves labored over thousands of acres often employed more than one overseer. With no automobiles, radios, or telephones, one person could effectively oversee only a limited area of activity. Whether he worked alone or as one of several, the overseer regularly made decisions in regard to the planting, cultivating, and harvesting of the crops as well as the disciplining of the slaves.

Overseers were generally assisted by slave drivers. White assistant overseers were rare. If more than one overseer was employed, each usually had assigned tasks and a corps of slaves to supervise. The slave drivers performed the same essential functions on the large estates as on the small ones. The larger the plantation, the more drivers.

Without overseers the slave plantation could not have functioned as it did. In the antebellum South *overseer* had a very specific meaning: a white man who managed slave labor on a plantation. The overseer was the man in the middle; he stood between the owner and the slave. To the former he was the employee who made sure that the slaves worked to make crops and produce wealth. To the slaves he was the embodiment of white authority, of the power vested by the state in the owner.

Overseeing was at best a difficult job. It required a technical knowledge of agriculture—about preparing the land, about planting, about cultivation, about harvesting. An overseer had to be well versed in the particularities of the major money crop grown in his region—cotton, tobacco, rice, or sugar cane—and of the crops produced for food and forage, especially corn. In a time before government-supported agricultural colleges and agricultural extension services, the overseer's expertise was essential for a productive and profitable plantation. Many owners were also agricultural experts, but some of them spent little time on their plantations. The overseer was always on the scene.

Overseers also had to be expert at what today would be called labor relations. Sometimes the tasks assigned the overseer seemed impossible. His fundamental mission had twin goals that often conflicted. On the one hand, owners demanded the largest possible crop; on the other, they usually directed their overseers not to work the slaves too hard, not to overtax them, and certainly not to impose such harsh working conditions as to cause unrest. Plowden Weston, a large rice planter in Georgetown District, South Carolina, told his overseers that he would judge their performance by "the general well being of the negroes; their cleanly appearance, respectful manners, active and vigorous obedience; their completion of their tasks well and early; the small amount of punishment; the excess of births over deaths; the small number of people in hospital, and the health of the children." Failure in either respect—a poor crop or dissatisfied slaves—often led to dismissal. Thus overseers had to find and then hold to a middle way, but that way proved to be elusive. The overseer had to concern himself with more than his employer's guidelines. The slaves under his charge were not simply passive pawns who blindly followed his commands. Slaves often complained directly to their owners about mistreatment by the overseers. Whether or not an overseer had actually mistreated the slaves, such charges could never be cavalierly dismissed. Slaves were valuable. And most owners viewed job security for overseers as considerably less important than a seemingly satisfied slave force. As a result, the successful overseer had to strike a balance between the concerns of the master and those of the slaves.

The difficulty of the overseer's position is seen in the turnover of overseers on most plantations. Many planters hired a new overseer every year. Trouble with overseers occupies a large place in the letters of planters. Time and time again planters complained to friends and relatives that their overseers were unsatisfactory. Dismissals of overseers and searches for new ones were constant topics. And always the complaint was either that the overseer failed to make a crop or that he mishandled the slaves. In the minds of most planters, mismanagement of slaves could fall into any of three categories. Most often it meant harsh treatment, but at times it signified just the opposite, loss of control. Occasionally owners intervened because of what they termed familiarity—the sexual involvement of male overseers with female slaves.

The problems faced in 1856 by Martin Phillips, a planter in Hinds County, Mississippi, illustrate the tension between owners and overseers. Less than one month after hiring an overseer named Champion, Phillips became dissatisfied. He let Champion go for laxness in enforcing plantation rules, but the two reconciled their differences and Phillips gave Champion a reprieve. More problems quickly arose, however, and in the middle of the growing season Phillips fired Champion again, this time permanently. Before 1856 was over, the harried Phillips tried two more overseers, with equally unsatisfactory results.

Most overseers worked for resident planters, but absentee ownership was not uncommon. James K. Polk, the eleventh president of the United States, lived in central Tennessee, south of Nashville; he also owned a cotton plantation in Yalobusha County, in the northern part of Mississippi. Living on and running Polk's plantation was a series of overseers, none of whom seemed to stay there very long. Polk tried to visit this plantation at least once a year, but he really managed it through correspondence with his various overseers and with a neighboring planter, who kept him posted on activities at his Mississippi property. The friend assured Polk that despite many difficulties, the plantation was not facing ruin. In an era when transportation and communications were slow, Polk's overseers seemingly had far greater freedom of action than many others. Yet Polk's experience mirrored that of most planters who resided on their plantations with their overseers. Neither distance nor the lack of it made simple the owner-overseer relationship.

This vexing part in the slave regime carried few social pluses. An overseer stood much lower on the social ladder than a planter, and it mattered not at all if the plantation was less than prosperous. An occasional overseer was a younger son of a small planter, but most overseers were young men who had grown up on farms, with and without slaves. Some of these people hoped to use overseeing as a stepping-stone to landownership and even slaveholding. In short, they wanted to become planters. Some did make the transition, and in that sense the role of overseer assisted social mobility in white society. One who did was Jordan Myrick. A native of Brunswick County, Virginia, he moved in 1803 at age seventeen to the South Carolina rice country, where he went to work as an overseer on a Cooper River plantation. After twenty-five years of employment with the same planter, Myrick was able to buy a small rice estate and thirty-three slaves. There is no way of knowing how many men repeated Myrick's experience, but the record clearly indicates that the number was not large.

An overseer's salary varied with crop and region. On average, wages were higher on sugar cane and rice plantations than in cotton and tobacco country. Three reasons account for this disparity. First, cane and rice plantations tended to be larger operations and to have more slaves in residence. Second, cane and rice were more complicated crops to raise and so required more technical expertise. Third, the sugar and rice mills of the antebellum era were considerably more advanced technologically than the cotton gins. Overseers generally had to be knowledgeable about the critical first step that turned raw agricultural pro-

duce into a marketable commodity. Overseers' salaries ranged from $700 to
$2,000 a year on cane and rice plantations, from $200 to $1,000 on cotton and
tobacco plantations. In an emergency a cotton planter could hire an overseer
for $20 to $25 a month. An overseer was also provided with a house and
usually with land and labor for a vegetable garden. Inflation over the years
makes the purchasing power of antebellum wages very difficult to estimate,
but the vast majority of overseers did not find the job a springboard to
wealth.

The difficulty of succeeding in every aspect of the job underlay both the
widespread dissatisfaction expressed by planters and the high turnover among
overseers. A few planters dispensed with overseers and took on the work themselves, with the aid of slave drivers. Bennett Barrow, a large cotton planter in
West Feliciana Parish, Louisiana, denounced overseers as "good for nothing"
and "a perfect nuisance." They made no positive contribution to southern society, Barrow complained; "I hope the time will come when every overseer in
the country will be compelled to adopt some other mode of making a living."
With the assistance of slave drivers, he kept a tight grip on the more than 200
slaves who tilled his acres. But Barrow was an exception. The overseer occupied
such a central place in the plantation South that the structure of the plantation
and even of the regime could not survive without him.

SLAVE DRIVERS

Overseers could not function effectively without slave drivers. Except for the
handful of slave overseers, drivers were the slaves most important for the
smooth operation of a plantation. Drivers held positions of responsibility. For
this post, owners and overseers chose the men they considered the most loyal
and dependable of their slaves. On some plantations the position became associated with a particular family and was passed on from father to son.

Drivers were usually placed in charge of a gang of fellow slaves. The number of slaves in a gang varied, but it usually was about ten. An overseer charged
a driver to see that his gang effectively carried out its assigned task of the moment—planting, plowing, harvesting, repairing fences, clearing land, or any of
the countless other jobs necessary to make a crop and keep a plantation going.
The driver, in turn, was responsible to the overseer for the work of his gang.

Although he had genuine responsibility, the driver was still a slave. Though
the members of his gang recognized the driver as a subordinate of overseer and
master, and thus an extension of white authority, they also saw him as one of
themselves. And just as the driver made sure that the slaves worked, he also
represented them to the overseer. He attempted to protect his gang from impossible work assignments, from infringements on what slaves saw as their rights—
the length of the noon break, for example, or the number of rest periods.

Planters acknowledged the special position of the driver. The driver often
lived in a more spacious cabin than the field hands and other slaves. He might
also enjoy a larger vegetable garden, better clothes, a more varied diet, extra

privileges, such as more time off or special niches for his wife and children. Planters wanted all slaves to understand clearly that drivers were distinctive.

Drivers had an exceedingly difficult role to play, if they played it well. They were direct extensions of white authority into the slave community; at the same time, they spoke for that community to white authority. Like his overseer, the driver found himself in the middle—between black and white, slave and free— but he viewed the middle position from a different perspective. He faced a conflict that the overseer escaped because he was white. Some drivers tried to resolve the conflict by identifying their interests with those of the whites. The most responsible drivers acted to maintain harmony and order on the plantation. Though they never forgot the interests of the white people for whom they worked, they also worked for their fellow blacks by articulating their interests and desires to their masters.

WESTWARD MOVEMENT AND THE INTERSTATE SLAVE TRADE

When southern whites moved westward, so did black slaves. White southerners had become so dependent on slave labor that they considered it essential for their prosperity. Many slaves accompanied masters who migrated from the Southeast to the Southwest. Others went with kinsmen or agents of planters who invested in southwestern lands but sent others to manage the new plantations. In both instances slaves remained with their old owners or at least with people closely associated with them. Although the slaves did experience a sharp and usually permanent separation from their original homes, they were not wrenched totally away from familiar whites or even from their own kin and friends, unless the master had left older slaves with his relatives or friends, or had sold some slaves to finance his own move. The slaves who journeyed with relatives or agents of their master experienced a more pronounced separation from the old familiar ways. On the journey and in the West their ultimate authority would be not the old master but someone else in his family or his employ. That change might be for better or for worse. They also left behind friends and kin whom the master retained on the home plantation.

There is no way to know precisely how many slaves went west along either of those two roads. Travelers reported numerous caravans of masters and slaves traveling west together, especially in the 1820s and 1830s. Not all of the whites they saw accompanied by slaves were planning to settle in the West, however; some were slave traders.

The interstate slave trade was a thriving business that grew with westward expansion. It commenced in serious fashion in the 1820s and became a major operation between 1830 and 1860. The traders, who moved scores of thousands of slaves between 1,000 and 2,000 miles, were the latter-day counterparts of the great merchants of colonial seaports who funneled slaves to tidewater plantations and backcountry farms. But the colonial merchants, no matter their wealth, never operated on the geographical scale of the nineteenth-century traders.

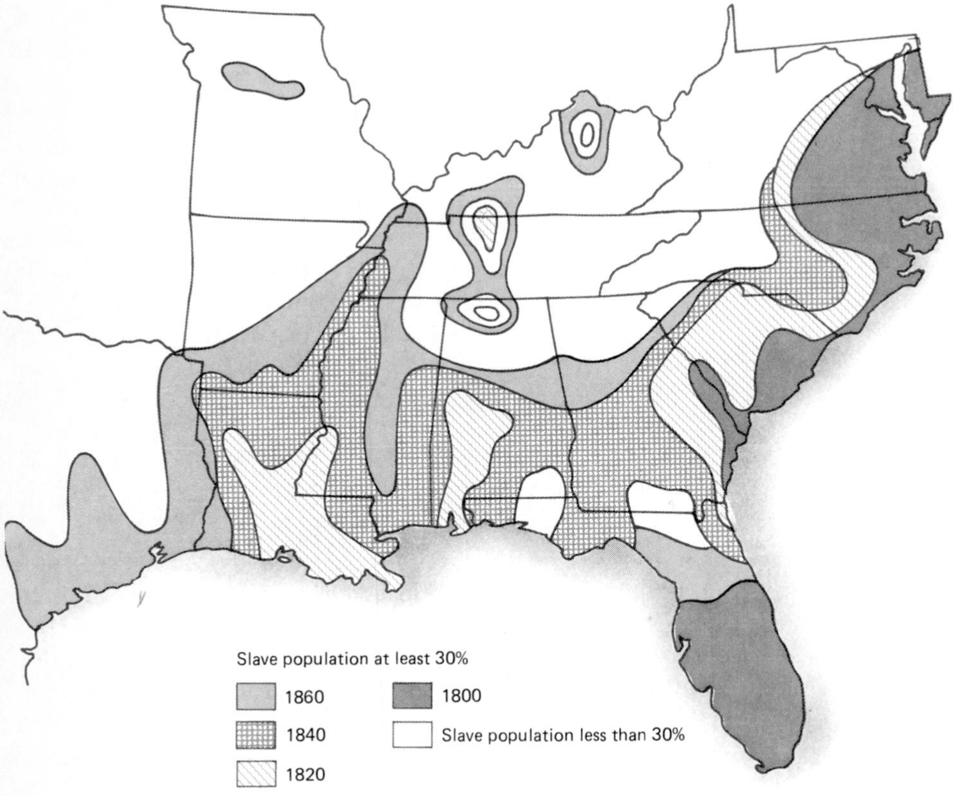
Slave population at least 30%
1860
1840
1820
1800
Slave population less than 30%

THE EXPANSION OF SLAVERY, 1800–1860

These traders bought slaves in the eastern states, initially Virginia and Maryland, later the Carolinas and Kentucky as well. The newly purchased slaves were then shipped west (or south in the case of Kentucky) either by the purchasing company or by other traders. Although nearly every town of any size had a slave market, two in the West became the key distribution points at the western end of the slave trade: New Orleans and Natchez.

Those cities represented the ends of the two great trade routes, by sea and by land. Slaves shipped from the Chesapeake and from ports to the south and west—Wilmington, Charleston, Louisville—were destined for New Orleans. The ships that carried them were specially fitted for the trade. Slaves bound for the West went overland in what were called slave coffles—groups of slaves, sometimes 100 or more, moving under the watchful eyes of professional traders. It is impossible to ascertain precisely the number of slaves going west by ship or on foot. Each method was important, and each was widely used.

SLAVES MOVING WEST

Perhaps the largest and best-known slave-trading firm was Franklin & Armfield. From 1828 until 1841, Franklin & Armfield was a major force in the interstate slave trade. The senior partner, Isaac Franklin, a Tennessean born in 1784, began to trade in slaves as early as 1819. In 1828 he formed a partnership with a nephew, John Armfield, to purchase slaves and transport them from Virginia to the Southwest. The two partners handled separate ends of the business. Headquartered in Alexandria, just across the Potomac from Washington, Armfield was the buyer; his assignment was to obtain slaves to meet the demands of planters and farmers in the Southwest. To accomplish his mission Armfield certainly did not operate in secret. Washington newspapers carried notices under the Franklin & Armfield banner: "Cash for any number of likely Negroes, of both sexes, from 12 to 25 years of age." The company advertised for "field hands" and "mechanics of every description." And for them, Armfield told prospective sellers, "we will give higher prices, in cash, than any other purchaser who is now, or may hereafter come into the market."

Armfield bought slaves either through his own agents or from local traders and held them temporarily at the company's headquarters in Alexandria, to which he welcomed visitors, even abolitionists. By all accounts, Armfield presided over a well-run establishment. One abolitionist visitor reported surprise at finding the slave quarters clean and the slaves well cared for. He made the establishment sound almost like a hotel. But of course the guests could not check out. Eventually they would be transferred to the Southwest.

Franklin waited in the West, where he supervised the selling end of the business. Armfield sent slaves west both by water and by land. Most left Alexandria in ships, either owned or leased by the firm, headed for New Orleans. Many of the slaves were sold there, but some were transshipped to points farther up the Mississippi or even up the Red River. A substantially smaller segment of this human traffic marched overland to Natchez. An observer reported in 1833 that Franklin & Armfield's annual shipments numbered between 1,000 and 1,200 men, women, and children.

THE DIMENSIONS OF THE SLAVE TRADE

The slave trade, so well represented by Franklin & Armfield, was critical to the economic health of the South. After the international slave trade closed in 1808, southerners had no other way to populate the growing West with slaves. Some traders smuggled slaves into the country, but the best evidence indicates that the number of slaves smuggled between 1808 and 1860 totaled only around 50,000, far fewer than were needed to meet the demand generated by the expanding southwestern frontier. It has been estimated that between 1800 and 1860 more than 800,000 slaves moved by all routes from east to west. By the 1850s the annual total reached 25,000. At this level the traffic had a value of some $20 million a year.

The slaves shipped west were chiefly under thirty years of age and came from the natural population growth of the eastern slave states. As Franklin & Armfield's advertisements indicate, traders preferred young slaves, both male and female. Young, vigorous slaves could better withstand the rigors of the journey to the lower Mississippi Valley. Besides, they brought the highest prices from planters, who wanted strong bodies to labor on cotton and sugar cane plantations. The impressive ability of southern slaves to reproduce themselves accounts for almost all the human cargo of the interstate slave trade. In the older eastern states, slave populations in general did not decline between 1820 and 1860, but their rate of increase was not comparable to the rate for the entire South. Too many of their sons and daughters took the involuntary westward trip.

The enormous size of the interstate trade often prompts questions about slave breeding. From the days of the abolitionists to our own time some people have talked of slave-breeding farms and plantations, presumably conducted just like an animal-breeding operation. Whether commercial slave breeding was practiced is a vexing problem. Massive literary evidence lends no credence to any argument for sizable breeding establishments. Recently more quantitative-oriented historians, known as cliometricians or econometricians, have attempted to throw light on this issue. After studying a computer sample of cotton plantations and incorporating statistics on the ages and sexes of slaves, they conclude that less that 1 percent of the more than 5,200 farms and plantations in the sample could have been slave-breeding centers—that is, farms or plantations with three times as many women as men between the ages of fifteen and forty-four plus an unusually large percentage of children under age fourteen. The tiny percentage in this instance along with the absence of literary evidence leads to only one logical conclusion. Although it is reasonable to assume that in a society as large and diverse as the antebellum South some entrepreneurs may have bred slaves in the expectation of making a profit by selling their offspring at some time in the indefinite future, such operations were rare. Slave breeding never assumed any commercial importance in the South.

Southerners clearly recognized the centrality of the trade. They knew that their economic health and political power depended on the movement of slaves from east to west. And they acted on that knowledge. As early as 1807, when Congress outlawed the international trade, southerners made sure that no prohibitory laws touched any other aspect of slavery, including the interstate trade. Southerners in Congress continued to fend off all attempts to tamper with their slave trade. An important weapon in the southern arsenal against the Republican party in the late 1850s was the charge that Republicans intended to interfere with the trade through the interstate commerce clause of the Constitution. The potential of such interference southerners depicted as dangerous.

Most southerners were not hypocrites about the trade—almost every community of any size had its slave market—though some were clearly troubled by it. Perhaps the most vigorous denunciation of the men who traded in human beings came from the pen of Daniel R. Hundley, an Alabama native and ardent defender of the South. In 1860 Hundley described the typical trader as "a coarse, ill-bred person, provincial in speech and manners, with a cross-looking phiz, a whiskey-tinctured nose, cold, hard-looking eyes, a dirty tobacco-stained mouth, and shabby dress."

Yet traders were by no means social pariahs. The trade made Isaac Franklin a wealthy, respected planter. At his death his estate was valued at $750,000. It included Angola, a large plantation fronting the Mississippi River in Louisiana; Angola is now the name and site of the Louisiana State Penitentiary. In Charleston, Louis de Saussure and Thomas Gadsden, holders of aristocratic names and prominent social positions, were major slave traders. These men followed in the path of the great eighteenth-century merchant Henry Laurens, whose dealing in slaves helped make him rich and powerful. In neither the eighteenth nor the nineteenth century did the occupation of buying and selling slaves do anything to lower one's social standing, if one had such standing to begin with, or to prevent one from acquiring high status, if one were successful.

THE PROFITABILITY OF SLAVEHOLDING

Slave owning was itself a commercial enterprise. Although at times masters and slaves developed a deep, caring reciprocal relationship, the slave plantation or farm had to return a profit on the capital invested in it. Unless he made some money, the master would not forever remain an owner of slaves and acres. The profitability of slaveholding had two separate but related dimensions: the individual slave owner and the South as a whole.

Slavery as a labor system was financially rewarding for masters. Of course, over the years individual slave owners prospered and went bankrupt, just as businessmen of all sorts have always done, but masters could expect to make money. This conclusion is generally accepted by historians. Current scholarly investigations of profitability differ considerably in methodology from earlier approaches. Historians used to look only at account books and ledgers of individual planters, then use accounting procedures to decide whether or not that individual planter made or lost money. That approach remains useful for study of people who left full financial records. But in the late 1950s scholars began to employ economic theory and economic models in an effort to generalize about profitability. Using this new methodology, the cliometricians or econometricians have made a powerful case for the profitability of slavery. They are convinced that slavery returned a profit for masters across the South. This view has swept the field; now most historians of slavery and the South accept the proposition that in general masters who invested in a slave plantation could anticipate a return that matched investments in business enterprises in the North.

This generalization about profit is subject to two qualifications. First, there were economies of scale; larger plantations tended to generate a better return than smaller plantations and farms. Second, sectional variations within the South determined the formula by which profit was calculated. In the Southwest, enormously fertile land produced tremendous crops and profits. But back in the older, eastern states, the income from slave sales made up a critical component of the equation that yielded return on investment. In these areas agriculture alone could not normally guarantee a rate of return that meant prosperity. Thus the interstate slave trade was essential for the maintenance of prosperity in the Southeast as well as for the source of labor in the Southwest.

The economic prosperity of the South matched the financial success of slave owners. Slave labor underlay an economy that performed impressively during the last antebellum generation. Although the Panic of 1837 struck the South and the nation a severe blow, the slave states began to recover in the mid-1840s and went on to sustained growth and prosperity. Between 1840 and 1860 the value of slaves increased from just under $3 billion to more than $6 billion. Cotton gave the South a comparative advantage that supported an explosion in production which did not splinter prices. The number of bales produced from 1840 to 1860 shot up from 1.35 million to 4.5 million while the price moved upward from around 9 cents to about 11 cents a pound. Although historians do not

agree about either the short-term or the long-term effects of slavery on industrial growth, capital invested in manufacturing in the South leaped from just
over $53.0 million in 1840 to $163.7 million in 1860. In the two decades between
1840 and 1860, per capita income in the South advanced by 39 percent, above
the national average. In the middle of the nineteenth century a growing economy and general prosperity gave the slave South every reason for optimism.

10

The World of the Slaves

❖

In 1860 some four million black slaves lived in the South, a fourfold increase since the beginning of the nineteenth century. The influence of slavery was felt in every aspect of the white South. External events had a tremendous impact on the course of slave society. The technological developments that modernized the textile industry, first in Britain and later in the United States, stimulated a seemingly insatiable demand for cotton. The invention of the cotton gin made it economically feasible to grow enough cotton to meet a good part of that demand. And the opening of the old Southwest following the War of 1812 ensured the massive horizontal expansion of cotton agriculture.

Two other events affected the cultural values that shaped the slave world. The rise of evangelical Christianity in the late eighteenth and early nineteenth centuries paved the way for the Christianization of the slaves. The almost simultaneous closing of the international slave trade precluded any substantial infusion of newly enslaved Africans into the American slave population. And in the absence of large numbers of imported slaves, no major challenge was offered to the direction taken by an increasingly American slave community.

WORK

The agricultural work performed by most slaves had a seasonal and rhythmic pace that depended on the crop. Slaves were involved in every phase of agricultural production—preparing the ground, cultivating the crop, harvesting it, and doing the curing, ginning, or milling necessary to prepare it for market.

Few slaves were exempt. Masters generally permitted only the very young, the very old, and the infirm to escape work. On plantations children generally started out as one-quarter hands, progressed as young teenagers to one-half hands, and finally became full or prime hands. Where age at last slowed their work, they moved back down the slope from full to one-quarter hands. This rating system was applied to both men and women. Many women worked in the fields beside the men, though on large plantations some served as household workers and nurses.

On plantations two basic schemes of work prevailed, the task system and the gang system. As the gang system pervaded the cotton kingdom, it became the dominant mode in the slave South. This was the system of slave gangs supervised by drivers, and ultimately by overseers. A traveler in Mississippi in the 1850s saw the gang system in action. He "found in the field thirty ploughs, moving together, turning the earth from the cotton plants, and from thirty to forty hoers, the latter mainly women, with a black driver walking among them with a whip, which he often cracked at them.... All worked very steadily." The gangs usually worked from sun to sun. An overseer reported that he rarely started his gangs "fore daylight." A field hand in South Carolina spoke of long hours. "I was always obliged to be in the field by sunrise," he remembered, "and I labored till dark." From sunrise to sunset—that was the norm.

The task system was prevalent in the rice country and was widely used in the cultivation of hemp, but it found few adherents elsewhere. This system, too, organized slaves in small work groups under drivers and overseers, but the

COTTON PICKING UNDER A WATCHFUL OVERSEER (State Historical Society of Wisconsin)

basic work assignment differed. Instead of keeping at a job every working hour, each slave had a specific task or tasks to accomplish. On his rice plantations in Georgetown District, South Carolina, Robert F. W. Allston expected an able-bodied man with a spade to break 1,500 square feet (one-thirtieth of an acre) of riceland in a day, after it had been turned by a plow. On Allston's plantations the overseers set the daily tasks and the drivers saw to their completion. On Oxmoor, the plantation seat of the Bullitt family near Louisville, Kentucky, a slave was required to break 100 pounds of hemp a day. Slaves had to finish the task or tasks assigned to them, which might or might not take up all the day-light hours.

The work of slaves was not always directly connected with crops. Some jobs, such as feeding and caring for livestock, had to be done every day; other duties occupied slaves during the slack times in the cycle of crop production. Slaves did the work essential to keep the plantation or farm in good running order. They built new fences and buildings, maintained and repaired old ones, cleaned ditches, cleared new ground, and engaged in a multitude of other ac-tivities so that the chief enterprise, the production of a staple crop, could suc-ceed.

On large estates some slaves became specialists, the skilled artisans of the plantation world. Though they were never so numerous as the field hands, these experts were a critical part of the work force. Neither the farming nor the household operations of a plantation could function smoothly without their skills. The northern traveler Frederick Law Olmsted found a variety of special-ized jobs on a cotton plantation outside Natchez. Here the work of 135 slaves was dedicated to raising cotton. The sixty-seven field hands and their drivers were supported by a specialist group that included a blacksmith, a carpenter, a wheelwright, a teamster, a keeper of the stable, a hog tender, a cattle tender, two seamstresses, a midwife, a nurse, and a cook for the overseer. The manor house on the typical plantation required at least cooks, butlers, maids, nurses for the children, and gardeners. Obviously not every plantation slave was a common field laborer. Slaves filled numerous skilled and even managerial po-sitions.

WORK STRATEGIES

To motivate their slaves to work, most masters employed two basic strategies—incentive and force, the proverbial carrot and stick. Incentive had two dimen-sions. The first was a general demonstration that the master cared about the slaves. He demonstrated his concern by treating them fairly, providing decent housing and ample food, and keeping families together. An owner who made clear to the slaves that their welfare was important to him won their loyalty, occasionally even praise. Solomon Northup described his master, William Ford, as a "kind, noble, candid, Christian man." As long as he belonged to Ford,

Northup did his very best. Northup acted upon his conviction that "fortunate was the slave who came to [Ford's] possession."

Masters also developed a variety of incentives designed to cultivate loyalty and reward specific acts. Permitting slaves, at least favored slaves, to have their own gardens was not uncommon. The Florida planter George Jones allowed the head of each slave cabin a quarter-acre allotment or "garden patch" behind the cabin. That patch enriched the slaves' diet with a variety of vegetables, such as tomatoes, corn, yams, okra, and collards. Others went even further and permitted slaves to sell surplus vegetables, even cotton. On his Hill of Howth plantation in Greene County, Alabama, William Gould permitted his slaves to grow their own cotton. In 1840 his cotton book recorded the pounds of cotton produced by his slaves: "David 1140, Jordan 730, Phil 850, Bill 1000, Bob 947, Peter 1050, Augustus 500 and Squire 475."

Many provided rewards for faithful and superior service. A Tennessee planter noted in his diary that he had "given the servants a Dinner on Saturday in commemoration of their faithful working." Thomas Dabney of Hinds County, Mississippi, provided small cash prizes—just a few cents—for his best cotton pickers. Hugh Davis of Alabama was one of many planters who divided slaves into rival teams that competed for prizes, which ranged from cash to food supplements to extra time off.

This incentive system was not a one-way street. Evidence abounds that slaves influenced their own situations. By custom and often by law, Sunday was the slaves' day. Except for punishment and essential duties, masters left the slaves to their own activities. When slaves did labor for their masters on Sunday, payment of a wage underscored the unusual circumstances. Payment for work on Sunday was so widespread that the practice was seemingly institutionalized. In 1836 the Supreme Court of Louisiana declared that "slaves are entitled to the produce of their labor of Sunday; even the master is bound to remunerate them, if he employs them." In the face of such a deep-seated tradition—which the slaves, of course, considered a right—only a reckless master would fail to honor it.

Direct communication with owners provided an opportunity for slaves to protect their interests, especially against overseers. A planter wrote to his overseer in 1858 that the slaves were to be permitted "to come to [him] with their complaints and grievances and in no instance shall they be punished for so doing." The slaves of such masters had a direct influence on their treatment, for those masters responded to their slaves' opinions. "I found so much dissatisfaction among the negroes that I placed under [my overseer's] charge," wrote an Alabama planter, "that I could not feel satisfied to continue him in my employment." Slaves' reports of an overseer's abuse of pregnant women relayed by the plantation physician brought a prompt and firm response from the Georgia planter-politician Howell Cobb. Although the slaves' situation was certainly not enviable, they were not totally helpless. They could act, and they did act to defend their interests.

At the same time, the use of force was an omnipresent reality in the slave South. Almost all well-run plantations had rules that stipulated specific punishments for violations: extra work, cancellation of a scheduled Saturday-night dance, solitary confinement or the stocks, and a multiplicity of other deprivations and restrictions. But eventually all had to rely on force, especially the whip, which became the symbol of white authority. The use and abuse of the whip varied widely. While the whip cracked rarely on some plantations and on others often, it was never absent. Bennett Barrow of Louisiana, a hard master, did not hesitate to use his; some of his slaves averaged a whipping a month. On some Sea Island plantations every slave's back was scarred. Whipping offenses included running away (the most serious), stealing, and poor work. Every slave realized that he or she might feel the sting of the lash. And the accounts of former slaves indicate their acknowledgment of its power. The universal application of physical force by white upon black had a profound impact on both. Its meaning has never been more acutely discerned than by a conscientious North Carolina slaveholder: "It is a pity that agreeable to the nature of things Slavery and Tyranny must go together and that there is no such thing as having an obedient and useful Slave, without the painful exercise of undue and tyrannical authority."

INDUSTRIAL SLAVES AND SLAVE HIRING

Some 5 percent of slaves worked in industrial enterprises, ranging from lumbering operations to city factories. The number of such slaves increased over time as the southern industrial economy expanded, though the figures remained small throughout the slave era. Almost every kind of industrial endeavor relied on the labor of slaves.

Three of the most important southern industries made widespread use of slaves. Efforts to bring cotton mills to the cotton fields took slaves from the fields to the factories. By 1860 more than 5,000 slaves labored in textile mills. Edward McGehee's mill in Mississippi and the Saluda factory in South Carolina each employed more than 100 slaves in their operations. The southern iron industry depended on slave labor. Slaves made up the bulk of the labor force at most upper-South ironworks. These works ranged from small companies with only a few slaves to large, sophisticated establishments that owned hundreds of them. The ironworks controlled by Senator John Bell in the Cumberland River region of Tennessee owned 365 slaves. The most famous of all southern iron manufacturers, the Tredegar Iron Company of Richmond, Virginia, used more than 100 slaves during the 1850s. Southern tobacco factories used slave labor almost exclusively. Centered in Virginia, this industry provided the workplaces for thousands of slaves. In the 1850s fifty-two tobacco plants employed 3,400 slaves in Richmond alone.

A slave named Tooler operated the chafery and refining forges at Buffalo Forge, an ironworks in the Shenandoah Valley near Lexington, Virginia. The position demanded considerable skill. Tooler worked iron before it was wrought into bars. The master assigned work quotas to his slaves, and encouraged additional effort by setting up a credit system that rewarded slaves who exceeded their quotas. When slaves had amassed credit they could draw on their accounts for such goods as sugar, tobacco, coffee, clothes, and even cash. Because of the responsibility of his position, Tooler could earn between $3 and $5 a ton for extra work. Occasionally he withdrew cash from his account for trips to Lynchburg, Virginia, possibly to see his wife. Tooler remained a slave at Buffalo Forge until 1865.

Other industries also used slaves extensively. The transportation industry, chiefly railroads and steamboats, was completely dependent on slaves. Almost all southern railroads were constructed with slave labor, and slaves performed myriad tasks on steamboats. Skilled slave machinists worked in Daniel Pratt's famous cotton gin factory in Alabama. The 153 slaves who worked at a brick plant in Biloxi Bay, Mississippi, produced 10 million bricks annually. Slaves drove the printing press of the Charleston *Courier*. They mined coal in Virginia and Kentucky and gold in North Carolina. They staffed saltworks and operated tanneries. In short, slaves could be found in almost every industry in the South.

Although most slaves worked directly for their owners, whether in field or factory, some owners hired out their slaves to other whites. A widespread practice in both agricultural and nonagricultural areas, slave hiring increased the flexibility of the system and occasionally of the slaves' lives. Many planters hired slaves from each other at harvest time. Some manufacturing enterprises, especially in the upper South, routinely hired surplus slaves from the countryside. Railroads often hired slaves for construction crews from slave owners along the routes. Many city families hired rather than bought domestic servants.

The contracts that governed such arrangements specified the fee to be paid to the slave's owner, the term of the hire (usually from January to Christmas), and the kind of work to be performed. The hirer agreed to provide proper clothing, food, and general care. On January 1, 1832, C. W. Thurston of Louisville "promised to pay James Brown Ninety dollars for the hire of Negro Phill until 25 Dec. next. And we agree to pay taxes and doctor bills. Clothe him during said time and return him...with good substantial cloth or...shoes and socks and a blanket."

A small number of slaves was permitted to hire their own time, though the practice was illegal nearly everywhere. This system was generally restricted to cities, and chiefly to those in the upper South. These people, usually artisans, had considerably more freedom of movement than other slaves. This device permitted masters to escape the cost of feeding, clothing, and housing the artisan while reaping financial rewards from the slave's skill. Allowed to find work for themselves, these slaves had only two obligations: to stay out of trouble and to make payments to their masters at regular intervals. In describing the terms by which he hired his time to work in the Baltimore shipyards, Frederick Douglass spelled out the guidelines that governed such arrangements: "I was to

be allowed all my time; to make all bargains for work; to find my own employment, and to collect my own wages; and, in return for this liberty, I was required, or obliged, to pay...three dollars at the end of each week, and to board
and clothe myself." Masters expected prompt and regular payment. The account books of James Rudd of Louisville show the system at work. Rudd permitted his slave Yellow Jim to hire out his own time for $5 a week. In eight
years Rudd collected nearly $1,900 from him. Of course, this flexibility could
have drawbacks for a master. Rudd noted the most serious in his ledger: "December 11, 1853, Ranaway."

DIET AND DRESS

Work requires energy, and for human beings food provides the energy. Thus if
slaves were to work at all productively, they had to have sufficient food. The
evidence indicates that the vast majority of slaves had ample food. In a system
as large and diverse as southern slavery, surely some slaves did not have
enough to eat, but they were few and not characteristic of the system. Although
most historians agree on the quantity of food provided to slaves, they tend to
differ on its quality. The question of quality can never be answered authoritatively because the enormous variety of individual circumstances makes it impossible to establish precise diets for the bulk of the slave population.

The foundation of the slave diet consisted of pork and corn. At times sweet
potatoes and, in the coastal region, rice were substituted for corn. Molasses was
also quite commonly part of the basic menu. The standard plantation ration was
a peck of cornmeal and three to four pounds of pork for every slave, distributed
weekly. The pork ration usually consisted of bacon and fatback, not hams and
chops. An unrelenting diet of pork and corn was surely monotonous, but fresh
vegetables and fruits in season, grown either in the slaves' plots or in the owner's gardens and orchards, provided variety and essential minerals as well.
Slaves and masters raised chickens, too, and some slaves supplemented their
provisions by trapping and fishing. It is impossible to know the complete range
of these supplemental foods or the frequency with which slaves enjoyed them.
Some slaves always had many of them available; others rarely saw anything but
corn and pork.

Though slaves' diets varied widely, some generalizations can be made. Despite the variations, the quantity and quality of the slave diet enabled the vast
majority of slaves to live productive lives. Malnutrition was not common. The
diets of slaves and of most whites were quite similar. The average white family
in the countryside ate almost exactly what the slaves ate. Wealthy families on
plantations and in the cities surely ate better than slaves, but they also ate better
than most other whites. Corn, pork, and molasses were the staple foods of the
rural South, for both black slave and free white.

Slaves probably enjoyed more variety in their diets than they did in their
clothing. Most masters were not generous with their allotments of clothes. Mas-

ters typically made two allotments a year: a set of lightweight clothes for each slave at the beginning of summer, a heavier outfit for winter. Both were coarse and plain. The issue often included a hat or cap for the man and a kerchief for the women. A slave usually had only one pair of shoes, brogans, for in warm weather no one wore shoes, and young children usually went naked. The paucity of clothes along with the absence of socks could bring suffering in cold weather.

Hand-me-downs from whites, chiefly to house servants and other favorites, enabled those so favored to add individuality to their clothing. Others might spruce up their drab attire by boiling it with dye extracted from local plants. Some augmented their meager allotments with items purchased in rural stores with money they received as rewards or from the sale of produce.

Most slaves displayed considerable ingenuity in their dress. They used strips of discarded material and clothing and anything else available to turn their slave garb into distinctive outfits. In a real sense they created their own wardrobe, limited though it surely was. Travelers constantly commented on the incredible variety in slaves' clothing. Masters also testified to their slaves' determination to individualize their dress. Notices of runaway slaves printed in newspapers often carried careful descriptions of the clothing the runaways were wearing when they were last seen.

*H*OUSING

The term *slave quarters* has a double meaning. It can refer to an individual structure or dwelling in which slaves lived, or to a group of slave dwellings. And on plantations most masters preferred that the dwelling places of their slaves be grouped together.

In both meanings slave quarters had tremendous variety. A family that owned only one or two slaves, or perhaps a single slave family, might provide quarters for them in their own house, or in a shed attached to the house or to a barn, or in a small cabin close to the house. Such a cabin was usually a clapboard structure, small and rectangular, commonly twelve feet by ten. The floor was usually of trampled earth. If the cabin had a window, it was provided with wooden shutters but not with windowpanes. If it had a chimney, it was commonly made of sticks and clay.

Masters on large farms and plantations employed a greater variety of building materials, though the simple wooden shack or cabin was pervasive. Some masters embellished them, though. Whitewash improved the appearance of crude cabins. Wooden floors, glass windowpanes, and brick hearths made for warmer, more comfortable living. Brick chimneys increased safety. Some prosperous masters, chiefly in the upper South, even built their whole quarters of brick. Sturdy brick quarters remain today on the grounds of Boone Hall Plantation, near Charleston. Along the Atlantic coast from Carolina to Florida, tabby was widely used for slave cabins. Made from sand, oyster shells, and water, tabby made for solid, secure structures. At Kingsley Plantation, in northeast Florida, a row of tabby cabins still stands. They testify to the strength of tabby and to the organization of the quarters.

Whatever the basic construction material they favored, masters grouped their cabins together. Most plantations had a single grouping, but some had several quarters of a few cabins each. James Couper, for example, at his Cannon's Point Plantation on St. Simon's Island, Georgia, constructed his slave cab-

(a)

(b)

VARIOUS TYPES OF SLAVE CABINS
(a) Ruins of tabby cabins, Kingsley Plantation, Florida (Courtesy of Kingsley Plantation State Historical Site, Fla.)
(b) Brick cabins, Boone Hall Plantation, South Carolina (Courtesy of Bradley Bond)

ins in groups of four. Most cabins in a plantation's slave quarters were identical or very similar. Sometimes larger cabins were provided for drivers and other outstanding slaves. Some cabins at Kingsley Plantation have two rooms, the larger with a tabby floor. With around 455 square feet of living space, they were intended for slave notables.

Masters with a mind to both their own profits and the welfare of their slave force planned thoughtfully for their slave quarters. The description provided by a planter along the Big Black River in Mississippi indicates the care taken by concerned masters.

> There being upward of 150 negroes on the plantation, I provide for them 24 houses made of hewn post oak, covered with cypress, 16 by 18, with close plank floors and good chimneys, and elevated two feet from the ground. The ground *under* and around the houses is swept every month, and the houses, both inside and out, white-washed twice a year. The houses are situated in a double row from north to south, about 200 feet apart, the doors facing inwards, and the houses being in line, about 50 feet apart. At one end of the street stands the overseer's house, workshops, tool house, and wagon sheds; at the other, the grist and saw-mill, with good cisterns at each end, providing an ample supply of pure water.

Toward the end of the antebellum era many major planters had slave quarters on their minds. They were planning for the future. A glimpse into the future they envisioned can still be had at Horton Grove, in Durham County, North Carolina. In the late 1850s this area belonged to Paul Cameron. Among the largest and wealthiest planters in the South, Cameron owned almost 800 slaves and 30,000 acres in North Carolina, Alabama, and Mississippi. In 1851

(c) Wooden slave "apartments," Horton Grove, North Carolina (Courtesy of Kenneth M. McFarland and the Stagville Center, Durham, N.C.)

Paul's father, Duncan Cameron, designed and built at Horton Grove what to-day would be called fourplexes. Each building had two stories and contained four wood-floored rooms, two on the first floor and two on the second, each almost seventeen feet square. A hallway four feet wide separated the rooms, providing space for a stairway leading from the first floor to the second. The houses sat well above the ground on high pilings. The brick walls were faced with board-and-batten siding; the inside walls were whitewashed. A brick chimney at either end of the building provided a fireplace for each of the rooms. A tin roof reduced the possibility of fire.

DISEASE

Shelter, food, and clothing all had an influence on the health of slaves. Their health depended basically on genetics, the practices of their owners, and the state of medical knowledge before 1860.

A genetic trait limited mainly to black people has to do with blood cells— misshapen blood cells known as the sickling trait. This trait had both a positive and a negative impact on the health of slaves. It helped make them highly im-mune to the more virulent forms of malaria, a fact noticed both by planters and by medical authorities in the antebellum South. To them it meant that blacks were naturally suited to labor in hot climates where malaria and other fevers were common. This relative genetic immunity had evolved in Africa, where ma-laria was a constant threat. While it was helpful in warding off malaria, hemo-globin abnormalities may very well have made slaves susceptible to miscar-riage, aching joints, and leg ulcers, all often noted as health problems among slaves. Slaves were also particularly susceptible to respiratory diseases. Al-though the specifics of their blood-cell makeup affected their susceptibility, their historical experience also contributed to it. Africans had little experience with pulmonary infection before they were brought to the cooler climate of North America, and it wreaked havoc on them. Epidemiological research has proved that even mild "domesticated" diseases can devastate previously unex-posed populations. Thus Europeans coped more successfully with respiratory illnesses than with fevers while Africans had the opposite experience.

The attitude of masters was also a force in the health of slaves. Most slave owners showed real concern for their slaves, for two reasons. The first was self-interest. Slaves were valuable, and it made enormous sense to maintain their health. A sick and physically incapacitated slave could not work so productively as an able-bodied one, and a dead slave represented a total financial loss. Thus the economics of slave owning instructed masters to do everything possible to keep their slave force healthy. Self-interest had still another dimension. With whites and blacks living and working in close contact, disease within the slave population could quickly spread to the families of the master and the overseer. No one understood the dynamics of contagion but everyone knew it occurred. The second reason was humanitarian. Most slave owners professed a sincere interest in the well-being of their slaves. The same Christian culture and morality that underlay masters' respect for slaves' marriages and their families prompted a deep concern for their physical health. This motive did not, of course, influence every master, but it was generally pervasive throughout the South.

The records testify to the planters' provision of medical care. Many masters and mistresses acted as doctors and nurses on their plantations. A former slave remembered his mistress: "She was with all the slave women every time a baby was born. Or, when a plague of misery hit the folks she knew what to do and what kind of medicine to ease off the aches and pains." Between 1842 and 1847 the Alabama planter James Tait paid a yearly average of $160 for doctors' services. In 1847 the overseer on John A. Quitman's plantation in Terrebonne Parish, Louisiana, arranged for a physician to visit the place twice a week through the year. Between 1850 and 1856 William P. Gould paid one doctor $2,667.49 for visits to his fifty slaves.

Although most masters tried to aid their sick slaves, the slaves often spurned that assistance and turned to their own folk remedies. In every locale, if not on every plantation, an herb doctor or conjurer practiced a folk medicine that relied on herbs and roots. This was one means by which slaves retained strong ties with their African past. A former slave from South Carolina recalled, "Oh, de people never didn' put much faith to de doctors in dem days. Mostly, dey would use de herbs in de fields for dey medicine." These remedies may or may not have relieved physical distress, but they certainly helped give the slaves a sense of self-worth. They had a medicine just as the masters did, and both were ineffective. The pervasive bleeding practiced by white doctors for almost every possible ailment had no more restorative power than the green figs and salt that the herb doctors prescribed for cholera.

Neither white nor slave medicine helped very much because no one really understood the germ theory of disease. In the eighteenth century and the first half of the nineteenth, medical knowledge was still quite primitive. Cholera, which felled white and black alike, is caused by bacteria and is contracted chiefly through contaminated water. No one understood the connection, and no one developed any effective counter to it. Four times between 1830 and 1860 cholera epidemics ravaged parts of the South. Whites and blacks suffered together, but because of their almost universal poverty and poor living conditions, blacks were hit harder.

Despite less than ideal living conditions, the slave population multiplied. Between 1800 and 1860 the number of slaves more than quadrupled, from just under 1 million to 4 million. As only around 70,000 new slaves entered the country during the period, this impressive growth cannot be attributed to the international slave trade.

MASTERS AND SLAVE FAMILIES

The natural increase in the slave population raises the question of slave families. Did slaves form families? The answer is both yes and no. The negative comes directly from the law; no slave code gave legal sanction to a slave's marriage or to the resulting family. The much more important response, however, is positive. In practice slave families flourished, with the strong support of masters. Although slave families had no legal standing, they rested on the firm foundation of custom, morality, and self-interest.

Morality and self-interest motivated the commitment of slave owners to their slave families. In a Christian culture the family is sacred, and even if not every master was a practicing Christian, the South was surely a Christian culture. Masters continually spoke of their slaves as part of their extended family. The privileged position held by the concept of family easily encompassed the slaves. Most masters encouraged their slaves to live in families. They not only permitted slave marriages, they often performed them. And slave cabins were usually allocated to families. As the Virginian William Massie explained, keeping his family, free and slave, together "would be as near that thing happiness as I ever expect to get."

Self-interest also formed a part of the master's profamily stance. Slaves committed to each other formed a mighty force for obedience and work. With a family structure the slave cabin became a place of solace, warmth, and love. Slaves' attachment to their spouses, their children, and their parents provided a source of comfort that owners believed, justifiably, would enhance their slaves' overt loyalty to the person who permitted their unions—the master. Masters understood this reality; there can be no other explanation for their willingness to permit their slaves to marry other masters' slaves. A male slave whose wife lived on another plantation customarily was permitted time off each week to spend with her, and their children added to the wealth of the neighbor, not to the husband's master.

Whites and blacks testified to the importance of slave marriages. Masters involved themselves in the slaves' ceremonies, from the simplest to the most lavish. The customary slave wedding was simple: the couple jumped over a broomstick, to the applause of their families and friends. One marriage took place in a field, bride and groom standing between the handles of a plow. Masters occasionally hosted the broomstick ceremony in their homes. Mistresses often provided wedding finery for favored slaves (especially house servants), filled the house with flowers, and invited their neighbors to witness the ceremony and toast the newlyweds at a sumptuous feast. Of course there was an element of sham in these costume affairs, and some slaves surely chafed at the role written for them by master and mistress. Still, for most of the participants, white and black, those festivities symbolized the commitment of free and slave to family. Just as the kind of ceremony varied, so did the person who performed it. Masters often officiated; so did ministers, both white and black. All recognized the seriousness of what was happening.

For the slaves the wedding, extralegal though it was, was a time for joy, but joy tempered by the realization that the master who permitted the marriage could also control its duration. A former slave from Virginia commented: "We slaves knowed that them words wasn't bindin'. Din't mean nothin' lessen you say, 'What God has joined, caint no man pull asunder.' But dey never would say dat. Jus' say, 'Now you married.' " No slave wedding included the words "till death do you part." A black preacher pronounced his own version of the familiar pledge: "Till death or buckra [whites] part you."

For masters the breakup of slave families by sale drove a wedge between the mutually supporting motives of morality and self-interest underlying support of those families. Most slave owners anguished over the choice between financial loss and the separation of family members. Although most planters chose business over sentiment, even a cursory glance at the manuscript record makes clear the intensity of the ordeal. Facing massive debts, Thomas B. Chapin, who grew sea island cotton on St. Helena Island, South Carolina, had to make this choice. "Nothing can be more mortifying and grieving to man," he recorded in his journal, "than to select out some of his Negroes to be sold. You know not to whom, or how they will be treated by their new owners. And Negroes you find no fault with—to separate families, mothers & daughters, brothers & sisters. ..." Most masters who confronted Chapin's dilemma acted as he did, though many suffered considerable losses to keep families together or at least to sell members within visiting distance. Nothing else about slavery so troubled southern whites as the separation of families, and reformers called for legal restrictions against it. In his 1860 book *Social Relations in Our Southern States*, Daniel R. Hundley, a stalwart defender of the institution, advocated that it be placed "upon a more humane basis than it rests upon at present" by legislation disallowing "families to be broken up and sold to separate masters." Hundley's appeal, like others before it, went unheeded. In 1860 slave codes had not been changed. Slaves' marriages and the security of their families were in the hands of their masters.

SLAVES AND THEIR FAMILIES

Recent scholarship has demonstrated conclusively that slaves lived in families and took their family life seriously. Slaves were generally monogamous after marriage, though their mores attached no stigma to premarital sex. The reality of slave life, however, caused quite a few men and women to have more than one spouse before they finally were widowed. The sale of either husband or wife often led both to form a new union.

Slaves' commitment to the concept of family was not destroyed by separation. In 1828 the Pettigrews of North Carolina acquired a four-year-old girl named Patience. Separated from her family of origin Patience grew up in the community of Pettigrew slaves. At seventeen she had a daughter by Dick Buck. The couple married two years later. Dick's father, William, died the following year, and they named their first son for him. Living a conventional family life, Patience and Dick became the parents of seven children in all.

The behavior of emancipated slaves during and immediately after the Civil War makes clear the meaning of family in the slave community. Across the

South roads were filled with slaves traveling toward hoped-for reunions with loved ones from whom they had become separated. Ben and Betty Dodson had been apart for twenty years. When they met in a refugee camp, Ben was overcome with joy. "Glory, glory, hallelujah!" he shouted. Embrace alternated with disbelief, then finally reassurance: "Dis is my Betty, shuah. I foun' you at las'. I's hunted an' hunted till I track you up here. I's boun' to hunt till I fin' you if you's alive." It is impossible to know how many former slaves shared the good fortune of Ben and Betty Dodson, but surely William Carter of Georgia, whose father had been purchased by a Virginia planter, spoke for many when he said that the best thing about being free was that "he could come back to us."

Slaves' names also indicated the strength of their families. Masters knew slaves only by their first names; a master's recognition of a slave's surname was rare indeed. Yet slave families often adopted surnames, which other slaves knew and respected. When the daughter of a Mississippi planter asked her nurse, "Mammy, what makes you call Henry Mr. Ferguson?" the nurse's response spoke volumes about the slaves' sense of family and self-worth. "Do you think 'cause we are black that we cayn't have no names?" The prevalence of family surnames became quickly apparent upon emancipation, when slaves used them openly.

Not all families had surnames, but those that did not promptly adopted one when they became free. The new surnames came from a variety of sources. Some adopted the name of their most recent master; some opted for that of an earlier, more fondly remembered owner. Other families chose to identify with their emancipator; Lincolns and Abrahams were not uncommon. Still others selected the names of people they admired or simply chose a name they liked. Whatever the source, the publicly announced surname helped give concreteness to a sense of family that had survived the rigors of servitude.

The slave family had great strength, and both black and white knew its power. This truth was never more dramatically described than by the great political orator John Randolph of Roanoke, who was also a large slaveholder. Randolph was asked to identify the person whom he ranked as the very best speaker. "The greatest orator I ever heard," he responded, "was a woman. She was a slave and a mother and her rostrum was an auction block."

SLAVES AS CHRISTIANS

Only religion matched family in importance to most slaves. Family and religion reinforced each other. The Christian religion emphasized the value of the family and the family embodied the earthly representation of God's love. Both provided a powerful moral sensibility to the life of the slaves.

White southerners showed little interest in Christianizing their slaves before the rise of evangelical Christianity in the last quarter of the eighteenth century. The Great Revival, however, made religion a much more vital part of the white community than it had been earlier, and the newly converted lost no time in seeking to convert other people, both white and black. The uses of Christianity in the ongoing effort to control a large and growing slave population soon became apparent to them. To most white southerners, a Christian slave was somehow less threatening to them and their society than a heathen.

Whites certainly tried to evangelize the slaves. Individual planters urged Christianity on their own slave family. The major denominations mounted substantial home mission campaigns aimed at slaves. White ministers, in sermons delivered to both whites and blacks, preached the efficacy of the Gospel for slaves. Ministers especially dedicated to slave conversion wrote pamphlets and books advising their ministerial brethren on the proper approach to win the souls of slaves. A number of white churches even welcomed blacks as members, though most provided a separate seating area for the slave congregation. Many masters also encouraged slaves to have separate services on plantations. These sponsored events, however, usually had white preachers, or at least a white presence if a black were preaching. In many urban areas blacks—both slave and free—had their own churches, presided over by a black minister, almost always a free man.

The message that whites preached to blacks focused exclusively on individual salvation. The white clerics and lay people did preach that one God watched over and loved all, that Jesus Christ died for all and was lord of all; on those fundamental questions blacks and whites received identical messages. But one theme dominated the sermons delivered to the slaves by the whites: servants, obey your masters. Just as all must obey their heavenly master, so slaves must obey their earthly master. The reward for faithful service to both masters was heaven.

Slaves responded enthusiastically to Christianity, but not precisely as whites either wanted or believed. Slaves accepted Christianity for several reasons. Many were committed Christians; for them the Christian message was the key to life. But more mundane considerations also made Christianity attractive. Particular events, such as funerals, provided opportunities for legitimate emotional release that might otherwise make whites uneasy. Finally, the role permitted and assumed by black preachers gave both them and their congregations a sense of pride.

The substance of slave Christianity did not coincide precisely with the message preached by whites. Slaves took the Christian message and molded it into a living, vital religion that spoke meaningfully to them as individuals and to their condition. The theology of the slaves affirmed life and love, certainly central themes in their spirituals. Rejecting the notion that their bondage stemmed from some fault in themselves, slaves rejected also the doctrine of original sin. The theology of the slaves emphasized deliverance, and that message dominated their spirituals. In one of them slaves sang:

> But some ob dese days my time will come,
> I'll year dat bugle, I'll year dat drum,
> I'll see dem armies, marchin' along,
> I'll lif' my head an jine der song.

Moses, who led God's chosen people out of bondage, was a hero almost equal to Jesus. In fact, Jesus and Moses often seemed forged into one deliverer.

Slaves grasped at one major tenet of their masters' theology—the concept of heaven. The slaves accepted St. Paul's message that equality would reign in heaven (so did many whites, for that matter). In God's kingdom there would be neither bond nor free, for all would be one in Jesus Christ. To slaves this vision of heaven diminished the whites' claim of superiority on earth. The prospect of equality in heaven undermined the pretensions of the earthly powerful.

To slaves no one expounded their Christianity so forcefully as the black preacher. And it is almost impossible to overestimate his importance in the slave community. Many slave preachers could read the Bible, despite laws forbidding the teaching of reading to slaves. Many more had memorized huge sections of Scripture. To most slaves and not a few whites, black preachers were more powerful proclaimers of the Gospel than whites. The evidence is indisputable that even in the mid-nineteenth century, blacks ministered to whites as well as to their own. Slave preachers helped lead the slave community in extraordinarily difficult circumstances to forge an identity founded on self-worth.

Though slave Christianity had immense emotional and psychological value for the slaves, it had no political strength. Slave Christianity sounded no call to revolution and inspired no armed prophets. Without a belief in original sin and bearing no responsibility for their enslavement, slaves felt no compulsion to prove or to improve themselves. There was no millennialism, no specified time when all wrongs would be righted. Slaves took this world as it was and struggled in it. The widespread adoption of Christianity by the slaves also precluded any religiously charged cultural clash between blacks and whites. Though they prayed for different things, both worshiped the same God.

REJECTION OF BONDAGE

The absence of a revolutionary thrust in the slaves' religion did not at all mean that slaves accepted enslavement as their proper station in life. It is impossible to know precisely what every slave thought, and undoubtedly there were some who internalized the white view of them as slaves. The evidence is overwhelming, however, that the vast majority of slaves rejected the whites' perception of them. Though by the mid-nineteenth century practically no slave had ever known any other condition, slaves were well aware of the sharp difference between slavery and freedom. And they opted for freedom. When Frederick Law Olmsted asked a Louisiana slave what he would do if he were free, the answer made clear that freedom meant options.

If I was free, massa; if I was free (with great animation), I would—well sar, de fus thing I would do, if I was free, I would go to work for a year, and get some money for myself,—den—den—den, massa, dis is what I do—I buy me, fus place, a little house, and little lot land, and den—no; den—den—I would go to old Virginny, and see my mudder. Yes, sar, I would like to do dat fus thing; den, when I com back, de fus thing I'd do, I'd get me a wife; den, I'd take her to my house, and I would live with her dar; and I would raise things in my garden, and take 'em to New Orleans, and see 'em dar, in de market. Dat's de way I would live, if I was free.

During the war years, the approach of Union armies signaled the dawning of a new day. Across the South slaves left farms, plantations, and their masters to become refugees. A few remained on the home place with their owners and became the source of the postwar scenario that depicted loyal servants standing firmly with their white people in the face of Yankee invasion. Although those few provided a factual basis for a story enmeshed in white tradition, they were a small minority. Time and again whites were astonished to see the slaves they accounted as faithful, loyal, and contented march off to the armies in blue.

Before that day came, many bondsmen and bondswomen made known their unhappiness. Overt rejection of bondage took many forms. Minor acts of sabotage occurred regularly. A slave with a hoe could chop young cotton plants as well as grass. Buildings burned, equipment ruined, food stolen—all could indicate the slaves' rejection of their oppression. These acts, however, could become a double-edged sword. Masters could and did retaliate with repressive measures that affected all the slaves on a plantation or farm, not just those who had acted. Thus pressure from within the slave community could curtail such activities.

Possibly the most common expression of dissatisfaction was running away. Slaves ran away from their owners for many reasons, but principally to escape anticipated punishment or to see family members on other farms and plantations. Some also slipped away simply because they could not take their bondage any longer. Most runaways either returned of their own accord or were soon caught, usually within a week. It was extremely difficult for slaves to lose themselves in the population. Whites could identify neighborhood blacks, and if they saw one they did not recognize, they could demand to see a travel permit. Some runaways managed to stay away as long as they did only because other slaves provided them with food and occasionally even shelter at night.

While hunting in Louisiana in the 1820s, the famous artist John James Audubon encountered a runaway. This fugitive (he is not named) had found a precarious sanctuary for himself and his family in one of the swamps in the southern portion of the state. The slave told Audubon that he had run away because he and his family had been split up on the auction block. Escaping from his new home on a stormy night, he had made his way into the swamp. Then he spirited his wife away from her plantation and even managed to secure some of their children. In these circumstances survival was doubtful, and even a runaway as enterprising as this one needed assistance. Only supplies provided by house servants at their original plantation had enabled this daring family to survive as long as they had. Audubon returned with the slave family to their original master and persuaded him to reunite them by buying them back. Unfortunately, the stories of most runaways did not have such a happy, if bittersweet, ending.

The historical record indicates that the overwhelming majority of slaves formed their identity in psychological and emotional terms that generated a positive view of their worth within the boundaries of enslavement. Slaves could and did stand for their perception of their worth. As best they could, slave husbands and fathers provided for and protected wives and children. Slave wives and mothers loved, served, and comforted husbands and children. All the while these bondsmen and bondswomen were convinced both that God had not created them to be slaves and that someday they would be delivered from slavery. They awaited their day of jubilee.

Some slaves, however, simply could not remain in the pattern, even a pattern broad enough to encompass minor sabotage. Chronic troublemakers, the whites called them. They were constantly disrespectful of whites; they continually disregarded plantation rules; they ran away time and time again; some even dared to raise a hand against overseer or master. When a slave was seen to fit this category, whites moved promptly. When punishment failed, the usual reaction was to sell the troublemaking slave—and the sale normally meant the transfer of the slave a substantial distance away.

REBELLION

These individual acts, however, only rarely coalesced into a direct challenge to the slave system, and the few slave revolts that did occur paled in comparison with the cataclysms that rocked the Caribbean and South America. In 1823, for example, thousands of slaves rose in Demerara, British Guiana, and 2,000 took part in a major battle. The South experienced nothing remotely like the massive rebellion on Saint-Domingue led by Toussaint L'Ouverture, which began in 1794 and resulted a decade later in the overthrow of French authority and the creation of a black state, Haiti.

Tangible reasons account for this difference between the South and most other New World slave societies. In the South whites were numerically dominant. Although by 1860 the slave population totaled over 4 million, 8 million whites were living in the slave states. Slaves did have a substantial majority in a few areas, such as the sea islands of South Carolina and Georgia, but they were too isolated to have any hope of success in a land where the whites controlled both weapons and police power. The whites could confront any rebellion with militia units and even elements of the regular United States Army in addition to hastily organized but well-armed planters and farmers.

Neither sanctuaries nor friendly groups that could harbor or aid slave rebels existed. The only sparsely settled areas—such as the mountains of western North Carolina and the swamps of southern Louisiana—were remote, and to reach them rebellious slaves would have to travel significant distances through thickly settled countryside. And almost every southern white agreed that slave rebellion was the greatest disaster that could strike their society. Mutinous slaves would have to confront this phalanx of whites without any hope of allies.

No group in the South would aid them. By 1860 the Indians had been subjugated, but even earlier, when numerous independent Indian tribes lived in the South, they failed to provide either sympathizers or a haven for slaves seeking escape from the system. From colonial times most Indian tribes owned slaves themselves and were on the lookout for runaways. The Seminoles of Florida would harbor runaways, but they lived on the periphery of the slave South. No tribe constituted even a minor threat to the social stability of slavery.

In addition to the adverse calculus of power, emotional and psychological forces in the southern slave community worked against revolt. Religion and family gave a meaning to life, even within a harsh and cruel system. As a result, most slaves developed neither the ideology nor the desperation that open rebellion required.

Throughout the centuries of slavery in the American South, only five major conspiracies or revolts can be documented. Two occurred before statehood, one in colonial South Carolina in 1739, the other in territorial Louisiana in 1811. The only revolt in the colonial South, the Stono Rebellion, took place near Charleston, South Carolina, in September 1739. Of central importance in this uprising were the differences between England and Spain. Spanish authorities in St. Augustine, Florida, promised freedom to any slave who escaped to Spanish territory, and over time some South Carolina slaves had managed to get there. When war was declared between England and Spain, some twenty slaves, led by a man named Jemmy, seized the opportunity to make a break for Florida. As a first step they broke into a store, decapitated the two owners, and made off with small arms and powder. As they headed southward they acquired reinforcements until they numbered between sixty and one hundred. Almost as soon as the uprising began, the alarm was sounded. Late that same day between twenty and one hundred local planters and farmers banded together and attacked the rebels. With this attack the rebellion disintegrated, though it took the whites the better part of a month to track down all the participants. Casualties included about twenty-five whites and thirty-five slaves killed.

In January 1811 slaves in St. John the Baptist and St. Charles parishes, up the Mississippi River from New Orleans, assaulted the system. Evidently without any planning, the slaves on one plantation attacked the planter and killed his son. Armed with cane knives, axes, and clubs, they started downriver toward New Orleans, killed another white, and steadily gained recruits until their force included at least 200 men and perhaps as many as 500. Armed planters in the area immediately sounded the alarm and took to the field. When word reached Brigadier General Wade Hampton, in command of the United States Army forces in New Orleans, he rushed upriver with both regular troops and militiamen. Within two days the combination of local and official forces crushed the rebellion, which left more than sixty slaves killed or executed. To demonstrate to the slave population the fate that awaited rebels, the victors displayed the heads of decapitated rebels on poles along the Mississippi from the plantation of origin all the way to New Orleans.

The two most elaborately planned rebellions never went beyond the conspiracy stage. Discovery of the plots by whites prevented either from developing into an open revolt. During the summer of 1800 a group of slave artisans
planned an attack on Richmond, Virginia. The genesis of this uprising is
murky, but in all likelihood these bondsmen were inspired by widespread talk
of the French Revolution and the overthrow of tyranny, following hard on the
American Revolution, with its rhetoric of liberty and freedom. The leading conspirators were people whose owners permitted them considerable latitude to
travel about the countryside and talk with other slaves. Several, including
Gabriel Prosser, a blacksmith, could read. Prosser and his associates recruited
around Richmond for months, with the intention of capturing the arsenal to
arm themselves and then kidnapping the governor. Their success was to signal
a general rising in the countryside; the ultimate goal of the rebellion remains
unclear. Approximately two hundred men were scheduled to enter Richmond
on the night of August 30, 1800. Prosser's hopes were undone by his widespread recruiting efforts. Slaves aware of the plot informed their masters, who
took their warnings seriously. The governor, the future president James Monroe, called out the militia to patrol suspected rendezvous areas. Almost simultaneously a violent thunderstorm disrupted the conspirators' attempts to unite.
Although no attack ever occurred and no whites died, white authorities investigated, held trials, and executed about twenty of the plotters, including Gabriel
Prosser.

The uncovering of a plot by slaves and free blacks to take over their city
terrified white Charlestonians in the summer of 1822. This plan was conceived
by a remarkable man, Denmark Vesey, a literate carpenter who had purchased
his own freedom. Chafing at the continuing enslavement of others in his family, Vesey sought to strike at the system. As associates Vesey enlisted other
skilled artisans, both slave and free. In his preparations he was influenced by
the Bible, by antislavery speeches made in Congress during the Missouri Compromise debates, and, through his most important lieutenant, Gullah Jack, by
African religion. Vesey's scheme involved at least eighty conspirators organized
into teams with specific targets. Vesey assigned the key points of the municipal
guardhouse and the arsenal to his own team. With those posts captured and
weapons secured, the rebels hoped to command the city. What they planned to
do then is uncertain, but Vesey seems to have contemplated sailing to Haiti. But
it was not to be. When several slaves privy to the plot became frightened and
informed their masters, whites at first listened in disbelief, then became convinced and moved swiftly into action. On June 16 the militia squelched the conspiracy before it became a revolt and before any white person could be killed.
Immediately investigations were mounted and trials held. In the next two
months thirty-five rebels, including Vesey, were executed, and thirty-seven
more were banished from the state.

The bloodiest and most famous of all southern slave revolts took place in
Southampton County, Virginia, in 1831. Between August 21 and 23 of that year
the slave Nat Turner led between sixty and seventy slaves in a rebellion that

cost more than sixty white and numerous black lives. In critical ways this revolt differed from the conspiracies formulated by Prosser and Vesey. Its setting was a rural county, not a city. Although its chieftain could read and write, he was a field hand, not an artisan. Also no evidence indicates that Turner planned his assault over as long a period as Prosser and Vesey had done or with the care that marked their efforts. That was probably a major reason Turner actually attacked the white community. Turner acted so precipitously that no one had time to inform on him.

Turner was a formidable figure. In his call to rebellion he relied chiefly on the Bible. Something of a mystic, Turner exhorted his listeners to follow him as an instrument of the Lord. Convinced that God had chosen him to lead, Turner emerged as a Christian prophet who inspired others to follow.

Turner made final plans on Sunday afternoon, August 21; that night, armed with axes, he and his band struck. Although Turner's revolt began in his own neighborhood, his immediate goal lay some ten miles distant: the county seat and the arms stored there. The name of the village was, ironically, Jerusalem. Beyond that initial goal it is not at all clear precisely what Turner intended to do. Turner never reached Jerusalem. Late in the afternoon of August 22, whites engaged Turner's forces in a pitched battle and dispersed them. The next morning another group of whites, aided by slaves, broke up the remnants of Turner's party. Most of the rebels were killed or captured, but Turner escaped and remained at large for nine weeks. While the search for him continued, his followers were tried and twenty were executed; ten others were transported out of the state. Finally, on October 30, Turner was captured. He was tried at the Southampton County Court on November 5 and hanged six days later.

These five incidents left a powerful legacy. The possibility of a slave revolt was seldom far from whites' minds. In the aftermath of each revolt some slaves met violent deaths at the hands of whites uncertain about the extent of the conspiracy and determined to demonstrate their control. A white Virginian drove home the point in the wake of Nat Turner's revolt. Whites reacted so vigorously, he explained, because of "the suspicion eternally attached to the slave himself—the suspicion that a Nat Turner might be in every family; that the same bloody deed might be acted over at any time and in any place; that the materials for it were spread through the land, and were always ready for a like explosion." Whites had always to be prepared for it.

11

Learning, Letters, and Religion

---- ❖ ----

The life of the mind occupied an important place in southern history from the Revolution to the Civil War. At the same time, the South could not be called an intellectual society, nor did it offer great rewards for intellectual endeavors. In those respects, however, the South differed little from the rest of the country. In a fundamental sense, an intellectual act created the United States. Much of the modern thought of Europe in the eighteenth century surrounded and permeated the coming, the conduct, and the outcome of the American Revolution. The conviction that through our reason we can determine our fate underlay this intellectual ferment. The southern Revolutionaries were in the mainstream of this movement, even at the forefront; emphatically they were not outsiders. The basic documents of the Revolution, chiefly the Declaration of Independence and the Constitution, embody this faith in human reason, and Southerners heavily influenced both documents. Thomas Jefferson of Virginia wrote the Declaration; although the Constitution did not have a single author, several southerners, led by the Virginian James Madison, greatly influenced its final form. Thus just as the South was instrumental in building the nation, southern intellectuals were among the leaders who charted its direction.

INTELLECTUALS AND THE SOUTH

These men did not fit the common view of alienated intellectuals; they were men of action. Although such men did not disappear after the Revolution, their influence in politics declined during the nineteenth century. Only John C. Calhoun matched the Founding Fathers in power of intellect and public influence, and the role he played differed from theirs. That difference is instructive about antebellum southern history. Jefferson and Madison devoted their efforts to building a nation of which the South was a part. Calhoun began in the same

244

vein, but became famous for his attempt to protect the South against the nation. Whereas initially the South was part of a whole, by the 1820s many southerners began to view nation and section as divisible. After Calhoun, southern intellectuals concerned about politics—such men as Nathaniel Beverly Tucker of Virginia and William Gilmore Simms of South Carolina—found their political homes within southern sectional radicalism, a movement to destroy the nation.

Southern public men were not uniquely intellectual, but intellectuals did play active and important roles in southern politics. A certain irony was at work here. Between 1775 and 1860 intellectuals as public men were intimately a part of southern political life, yet politics had no appeal for them; public life in its broadest sense can be said to have co-opted them. In the modern world intellectuals are known as critics of their society, as outsiders; in the antebellum South intellectuals were concerned with the support and defense of the South and its institutions, not the criticism of it.

Many southern intellectuals, like their counterparts elsewhere, identified themselves as members of a particular group and gave themselves a special mission. "Sacred circle," the term Simms used to describe himself and the other men who shared his work and goals, tells much about the perspective of southern intellectuals. They had a sacred duty to the South—to understand it, to explain it, even to defend it, but not to criticize it or question its fundamental organization.

In the Revolutionary generation southern intellectuals found their chief occupation in defending the colonies against a perceived British tyranny and in creating a new polity. The next great intellectual movement, which came a half century later, emphasized defense of the South against a perceived northern tyranny. These later intellectuals did not advocate change, however. On the contrary, they warned of the danger of change. Rather than work to create something new, they stressed the need to protect what had been built. This fervent activity focused on and revolved around the institution of slavery.

Southern intellectuals never got away from slavery. In the Revolutionary era they struggled to reconcile the institution with their ideology. Although they did not put forth an overt defense of slavery, neither did they mount a direct assault on it. To emphasize the joy of liberty and the horror of bondage while holding tens of thousands of human beings in slavery troubled many intellectuals. In private, most of them wished slavery gone. Wishing was their major activity, for they simply could not devise any practical plan that they believed could work. They recognized that persuading the white South to give up slavery now would be incredibly difficult, probably impossible, no matter what plan they might propose. When the time was right, slavery would fall of its own weight. Thus they satisfied themselves that somehow progress would eventually destroy slavery. As late as 1814 the most eloquent of the Revolutionaries, Thomas Jefferson, left the end of slavery to "the younger generation."

That generation, however, moved in exactly the opposite direction. It created an intellectual defense of slavery unprecedented in the South and unique in the New World. Slavery had of course had its defenders before the second quarter of the nineteenth century. As early as the 1780s the Reverend William Graham, rector and principal instructor at Liberty Hall Academy (now Washington and Lee University), defended slavery in a lecture that he gave annually to the senior class. Drawing on both the Bible and the ideology of race, Graham anticipated the proslavery ministers of a later time. Christianity, he maintained, sanctioned slavery, and to his mind slavery was the proper status for inferior blacks. During congressional debates on Missouri in 1820 and 1821 several southerners found no difficulty in reconciling slavery with the Bible. Some of them described slavery as a patriarchal system based on reciprocal loyalty between kind masters and faithful slaves. Later in the 1820s similar arguments flowed from the pens of other southern stalwarts. Still, before 1830 no full-blown systematic defense of slavery had appeared.

*T*HOMAS R. DEW AND THE CLERGY

The first major text in the proslavery canon came from the pen of Thomas R. Dew, a professor at the College of William and Mary. In 1832, when Dew was thirty years old, he published his *Review of the Debates in the Virginia Legislature of 1831 and 1832*, a commentary on wide-ranging debates in the legislature on the future of slavery in Virginia. In rejecting the arguments of Virginia antislavery spokesmen and making the case for slavery, Dew laid the foundation that would hold up the mature proslavery argument over the next three decades. Professor Dew discussed slavery in practical, historical, and philosophical terms. He stressed the nature of slaves as property and underscored the massive financial investment—tens of millions of dollars—that Virginians had in their slaves. In a society that honored and protected private property, Dew insisted, the rights of propertyholders had to be guarded. It had been proposed that the state purchase slaves from their owners and set them free; Dew considered that suggestion impractical. The financial burden would be unbearable; moreover, finding a home outside Virginia for the emancipated slaves would be impossible. With that point Dew underscored the powerful issue of race. No whites in Virginia, even the most vigorous opponents of slavery, envisioned free blacks remaining in the state. Thus by showing the impossibility of removing the freed slaves, Dew undermined the argument for emancipation.

But Dew did not rest his case solely on practical grounds. He went on to place southern slavery in the mainstream of Western history. Pointing to the great civilizations of the past—the Greek, the Hebrew, the Roman—Dew stressed that the institution of slavery flourished in each. He drew upon both secular and religious texts to demonstrate the legitimacy of slavery. On the basis of his study of Aristotle, who had considered Greek slavery justified by the manifest inequality among peoples, Dew found slavery perfectly suited for blacks and for the South. In the history of the children of Israel, as recorded in the Old Testament, Dew found divine sanction for slavery—a sanction upheld by the New Testament, for Jesus Christ made no attack on slavery. Thus, according to Dew, the slaveholding South was the legitimate descendant of both classical civilization and the Judeo-Christian tradition. Slavery, in sum, was a worthy part of the good society. After Dew, the intellectual defenders of slavery focused on three major areas: religion, history and social organization, and science.

Protestant Christianity, with its reliance on the unerring accuracy of Holy Scripture, was the bedrock of southern society. In this society a Bible-centered argument for slavery assumed central importance. If white slave owners could not believe that the Bible sanctioned slavery, they would face a terrible moral and psychological dilemma.

The southern clergy took the lead in defending slavery as divinely inspired and biblically sanctioned. That had not always been the case. In the late eighteenth and early nineteenth centuries many southern ministers questioned the morality of slavery, but those doubts faded as the white South began to articulate its commitment to the institution. Standing foursquare behind slavery, the preachers pointed to the Old Testament patriarchs, instruments of God and slave owners to a man. Never, they correctly maintained, did the laws of Israel condemn slavery; on the contrary, those laws protected servitude. Turning to the New Testament, they depicted both Jesus and Paul as supporters, if not champions, of slavery. They emphasized that the Son of God had lived in a slave society and had never attacked the institution of slavery. If he did not attack it, he must have supported it. Southern clerics took as their chief text Paul's letter to Philemon, by which he returned the runaway slave Onesimus to his lawful owner. In the southern view, if the great apostle acted in such fashion, how could anyone in the nineteenth century dare to question the legitimacy or morality of slavery?

The blackness of southern slaves buttressed the clerical position. Believing totally, as did almost every other white American, that blacks were an inferior race, the proslavery clergy searched for the scriptural origins of that inferiority. They found it in Genesis, where Noah cursed his grandson Canaan. According to the King James version—the Bible of the pre-Civil War South—Canaan would be "a servant of servants"; God would bless and "enlarge" Noah's favored sons, and Canaan would be their servant. For southerners, who regularly used *servant* to stand for *slave*, the meaning could not be doubted. And in fact they interpreted the language correctly; both the Revised Standard Version and the New English Bible use the word *slave*. To the southern clergy the issue could not have been clearer. Were not their own people blessed and enlarged? In their minds, God himself had favored them and chosen the descendants of Canaan for bondage; since the time of Genesis blacks had been fulfilling the role specially assigned to them. Thus for the religious defenders of slavery, the blackness of southern slaves only confirmed their scriptural argument.

The ministerial guardians of slavery stood at the front rank of their profession. It was not only the less educated, the less able, the less recognized who took up the cause. Eminent Episcopalians, Presbyterians, Baptists, and Methodists across the South proclaimed that the "master who rules his slaves and provides for them, according to Christian principles, [can] rest satisfied, that he is not in holding them, chargeable with moral evil, nor with acting in this respect, contrary to the genius of Christianity." In fact, the ministers saw the evangelization of the slaves as one of their great callings. The Reverend James H. Thornwell of South Carolina explained, "We feel that the souls of our slaves are a solemn trust and we shall strive to present them faultless and complete before the presence of God." To that end each of the major Protestant denominations launched a mission campaign to the slaves during the final antebellum generation. Conferences were held, instructional pamphlets and books were published, and missionaries were sent to preach to the slaves, all carrying the message that Christianity could save their souls, but on earth their Christian duty required loyalty and obedience to their masters.

HISTORY AND SOCIETY

Appeals to the authority of history and emphasis on the proper social organization matched the religious defense in importance. On these points southerners extended and developed themes that Dew had touched upon. Southern intellectuals who participated in this endeavor covered a wide range—such public men as John C. Calhoun and James H. Hammond; literary figures such as the leading writer of the region, William Gilmore Simms; academics such as Nathaniel Beverly Tucker of the College of William and Mary and George Frederick Holmes, who settled in 1857 at the University of Virginia; publicists and journalists such as James D. B. De Bow, editor of *De Bow's Review*. These men and their colleagues built their case for slavery with four major building blocks: history, the racial inferiority of blacks, the equality of whites, and the physical well-being of slaves in comparison with that of free laborers.

The proslavery spokesmen emphasized that slavery was an integral and a legitimate part of Western history. Constantly they pointed out that the cherished and admired products of Greece and Rome—the poetry, the philosophy, the art, the political theory—all sprang from a slave-based society. The conclusion seemed inescapable: slavery represented not barbarism but high culture and virtue.

Although they placed their institution in a broad historical context, the southern apologists also focused on its particular identity. Slavery was especially appropriate to the South, they held, because of its racial character. Southerners argued that slavery provided the best—indeed, the only—way for two such dissimilar races to live in the same place. To southerners the racial inferiority of blacks—on which most northern and European contemporaries agreed—made any other social arrangement impossible. Advocates of slavery asserted that the inferior blacks were especially well-suited to be slaves. As slaves, they had their physical needs met by their owners; an all-encompassing social welfare system protected them from the vagaries of a world they were not equipped to face unaided. To the southerners, moreover, the inferiority of blacks provided a great opportunity for the superior whites. According to this script, southern whites were engaged in a massive civilizing effort, which in time could lift up the slaves from ignorance and social savagery. This secular civilizing mission would match in value and efficacy the conversion efforts of the churches. In this scheme slavery became a highway to Christian civilization for blacks. Its end, of course, was not in sight.

To the defenders of slavery no benefit surpassed in importance the aristocracy of color made possible by the institution. In their view slavery underlay a real equality among whites. Southerners insisted that every society had its degraded class, its poverty-stricken menials, or, in the arresting phrase of the South Carolina planter intellectual James H. Hammond, its "mudsills." That reality, in the southern argument, necessitated a harsh division among whites based on economics. In the South, however, race, not economics, marked the fundamental dividing line in society. "The poor white laborer at the North is at the bottom of the social ladder," read the southern brief, "whilst his brother here has ascended several steps and can look down upon those who are beneath him, at an infinite remove." In the proslavery text, the presence of black slaves rather than white workers in the mudsill class guaranteed equality among southern whites and thus a political democracy unmatched elsewhere in the civilized world.

And under slavery even the black mudsills in the South fared better than their white counterparts elsewhere. Southern defenders maintained that the Industrial Revolution was responsible for terrible human carnage. Pointing to the desperate condition of many factory workers in the North and in England, southerners described those laborers as far worse off than slaves. Those "wage slaves," they charged, were "free but in name." The South Carolinian William J. Grayson published in 1856 a long poem in heroic couplets, *The Hireling and the Slave*. To Grayson and his compatriots the caring master provided for the physical wants of the slave while industrial employers left their workers to fend for themselves. As Grayson put it, "The slave escapes the perils of the poor." The moral dimension of free versus slave the southerners rejected as distorting the true situation of the slave and the laborer.

A NEW THRUST

In the mid-1850s the defenders of slavery advanced in a new direction that took them from the particular to the general. This thrust drew upon the mainstream arguments about the care of the master and wage slavery, but it moved beyond the peculiar institution of black slavery to a more theoretical advocacy of slavery as a superior social system regardless of racial characteristics. In an attempt to underscore its objectivity, this argument clothed itself in the garments of the new science of society that was beginning to capture the interest of Western intellectuals. In 1854 Henry Hughes of Mississippi published his *Treatise on Sociology: Theoretical and Practical*. In the same year the Virginian George Fitzhugh wrote *Sociology for the South; or the Failure of Free Society*, and three years later he followed it with *Cannibals All! or Slaves without Masters*.

Hughes and Fitzhugh argued that slavery served both masters and slaves so well that it should govern social relations in all societies, not just in the South. In their view, slavery should not be restricted to biracial situations; the value of slavery was so enormous that white laborers would fare much better as true slaves than they did as wage slaves. Though Hughes shunned the word *slavery* in favor of the more scientific-sounding *warranteeism*, his argument was clearly based on southern slavery. Fitzhugh pictured the social reality of the industrial world as a vicious system in which capital cruelly exploited labor. To his mind, only slavery, by combining capital and labor, could inject humane values into industrial society. Then justice and decency would prevail. Without the introduction of slavery, Fitzhugh predicted class warfare, even revolution.

Among scholars Hughes and especially Fitzhugh have known a popularity they never knew in their own time. Scholars have found them fascinating chiefly for two reasons: first, they attacked perceptively and forcefully the evils of the Industrial Revolution; second, they took the proslavery argument to its logical conclusion. In the South of the 1850s, however, talk of enslaving white workers, or even of making them warrantees, did not get far at all. By that time all adult white males had the right to vote in an essentially democratic political process. Neither white voters nor the politicians who courted their votes had any interest in pushing slavery across the racial boundary. Quite to the contrary, they stressed black slavery as the cornerstone of white equality. When ardent southerners compiled proslavery writings with a view to spreading their message, they omitted Hughes and Fitzhugh. The first of these compendiums, *The Pro-Slavery Argument as Maintained by the Most Distinguished Writers of the Southern States*, came out in Charleston in 1852, before the major work of either Hughes or Fitzhugh. But the considerably heftier *Cotton Is King and Pro-Slavery Arguments*, published in Augusta, Georgia, in 1860, also excluded the self-proclaimed sociologists of slavery.

A SECOND NEW DIRECTION

Southerners turned to still another of the new sciences to bolster their institution of slavery. This one focused exclusively on race. Numerous men of science on both sides of the Atlantic embraced ethnology, the science of racial differences, during the mid-nineteenth century. Racial origins and types were the consuming interest of ethnologists, who then believed that human beings had multiple origins. According to the early ethnologists, different human races originated at different times. This position was anathema to the clerics, who insisted that all human beings were literally descended from Adam and Eve. The foremost southern proponent of ethnology was Dr. Josiah Nott of Mobile, Alabama. A native of South Carolina and graduate of South Carolina College, Nott had studied medicine at the College of Physicians and Surgeons in New York

City and received his medical degree from the University of Pennsylvania before settling in Mobile in the 1830s. A widely respected clinician and surgeon, Nott also worked hard to improve medical education and to professionalize the practice of medicine.

Nott was also a scholar who became an active and respected member of the transatlantic community of ethnologists. Totally committed to his society and believing that the truths of science should govern social and moral relationships, Nott worked to put science behind slavery. To his mind, ethnology provided indisputable evidence in support of slavery. He and his fellow ethnologists believed that different races had not only different origins but different capabilities. In an attempt to demonstrate that blacks were inferior to whites and that they constituted a separate and distinct species, Nott took cranial measurements, compiled statistical data, and investigated the position of black people in ancient civilizations, such as the Egyptian. In 1854 he published with George Gliddon of Philadelphia, another leading American ethnologist, his major work, *Types of Mankind: or Ethnological Researches, Based upon the Ancient Monuments, Paintings, Sculptures, and Crania of Races, and upon Their Natural, Geographical, Philological and Biblical History.*

Nott realized that the religious orthodoxy of the South would cause problems for him and his argument. Most southerners, after all, accepted the biblical account of creation. To blunt the criticism he anticipated, Nott tried to present his scientific investigation as a Christian duty, but his effort availed him little. Though he thought of himself as fighting the battle of scientific truth against ignorance, his "science" was seriously flawed, and the biology of Charles Darwin soon replaced the ethnological explanation for the origin of species. In the South ethnology was never widely accepted. Because Nott and his doctrine were so vigorously assailed, most proslavery theorists tried to avoid both Nott and the question of racial origins. Yet Nott's work is one more demonstration that thoughts of slavery preoccupied southern intellectuals.

The reason for the burgeoning and ramification of the proslavery argument lends itself to no single, final answer. At the same time the historical record does permit reasonable certainty about the primary motives that prompted southerners to take up the proslavery cudgels. One possibility can be quickly eliminated; the defenders of slavery never really believed that their efforts could change prevailing opinion in the North. In their view, most of the North had already made up its mind, and any positive impact proslavery writings might have would be incidental.

The evidence points to three basic causes underlying the birth and maturation of the proslavery argument. Self-defense was significant. It is not accidental that the growth of the proslavery argument paralleled the growth of an articulate antislavery and antisouthern opinion in the North. In the face of what they saw as unfair and unwarranted condemnation of themselves and their institutions, southerners felt compelled to strike back. To them silence would signal either acquiesence or agreement. Rejecting both, southerners turned to a positive defense of slavery. In doing so they provided a buttress for the white

South. Any wavering or defensive or doubting southerners could turn to the proslavery canon and find extensive arguments for the worth and rightness of slavery. That the proslavery argument helped weld a basic southern unity on the issue of slavery cannot be doubted. Finally, the southern intellectuals who built the defense of slavery also had a part in its development. Searching for a way to be of use to the society that needed them, these men committed a substantial portion of their intellectual talent to erecting an edifice designed to emphasize the legitimacy and value of their society. By that act these southern intellectuals joined their counterparts in the North and Europe.

SCIENCE

Intellectual activity in the antebellum South was not confined to the formal defense of slavery. The contributions to science made by colonial southerners were exceeded by those of southern scientists in the nineteenth century. No true scientific community existed in the South before 1860, but notable southerners did participate in the larger American and even European worlds of science. The most famous and popular southern scientist of his time was Matthew Fontaine Maury. Born in Virginia in 1806, Maury spent most of his life in the United States Navy. After a stagecoach accident in 1842, he found himself at a desk job in Washington. There he pursued his wide-ranging studies of winds and currents, which generally aided navigation and specifically enabled him to chart the course of the Gulf Stream.

Southerners did especially significant research in geology. Arguably the ablest scientist active in the South was William Barton Rogers, a native Pennsylvanian who as a teenager came to Virginia with his father, a science professor at William and Mary. In 1828, at twenty-four, William Rogers took over his deceased father's position at William and Mary; seven years later he moved to the University of Virginia. Rogers's work on the structure of the Appalachian Mountains gained him a national and an international reputation. Unhappy with the intellectual atmosphere at the university and with the state's support of his efforts, Rogers left Virginia in 1853 for his wife's New England, with the hope of establishing a polytechnic school. In 1862 he became the first president of the Massachusetts Institute of Technology.

Younger than Rogers and also exceptionally talented, Joseph LeConte taught in the 1850s first at the University of Georgia, his alma mater, and then at South Carolina College. Before entering upon his academic career in the South, LeConte studied at Harvard with the foremost American scientist of his day, Louis Agassiz. LeConte's first major publication, based on work begun on a research trip with Agassiz, discussed the formation of the keys and peninsula of Florida. LeConte was building his scientific reputation when the Union divided. He served the Confederacy as a scientist, but after 1865 he went west to the University of California at Berkeley, where he had a distinguished career.

Between 1820 and 1860 every southern state except Florida and Louisiana funded a geological survey. To conduct these surveys the legislators employed capable scientists, including William Rogers in Virginia. Legislators voted to spend money on such surveys because they anticipated economic advantages to result from them. They expected that agriculture would benefit from a better understanding of soils, and the identification of mineral deposits would benefit mining and industry. Surely economic development would follow. Although the Panic of 1837 for a time curtailed financial support for these projects, they continued to the end of the antebellum era.

Edmund Ruffin, a Virginia planter who became a political radical during the sectional crisis, was one of the foremost agricultural reformers in America. Distressed about the declining fertility of his own and other tidewater plantations, Ruffin as early as 1818 began a series of experiments in an attempt to halt the debilitation of the land. From study of the chemistry of soils he concluded that the acidic conditions in Virginia required neutralization before productivity could return. His own trials proved that marl, a fine shell deposit, would lower the acid content of the soil and make it productive once again. In his *Essay on Calcareous Manures*, published in 1833, and in an agricultural journal he founded, Ruffin pushed for agricultural reform. Although not all Virginia farmers and planters promptly followed his lead, he had a positive influence that extended beyond his state. North Carolina, South Carolina, and Georgia invited him to conduct agricultural surveys and advise on the renovation of worn-out lands.

Southerners made valuable contributions to other areas of science as well. When Dr. Josiah Nott was not writing his ethnological defenses of slavery, he was making detailed observations that increased the medical profession's knowledge about yellow fever and publishing widely on surgical techniques. Joseph Jones, a young Georgia physician with a bent for research, used his experiences as a Confederate surgeon to comment extensively on gangrene, the deadly scourge of the wounded, civilian as well as military. Dr. Jones also showed the potential of public health studies with his analyses of the sick and wounded in Confederate armies and of illness and mortality among Union prisoners of war. In Charleston, which had the finest museum of natural history in the South, the Lutheran clergyman John Bachman wrote substantively on the state's flora and fauna. Though no major centers of science appeared anywhere in the antebellum South, the men discussed here and their colleagues took part in investigations that added to the scientific knowledge of their day.

HISTORY AND BELLES LETTRES

The South also had an honorable tradition of history and belles lettres stretching from the Revolution to the Civil War. Early on southern writers became caught up in explaining their section and its mores. The first such work after the Revolution was Thomas Jefferson's *Notes on Virginia*, written in 1781–1782, then revised and published privately in France in 1785, and finally published two years later in England in what Jefferson regarded as the definitive version. The *Notes* are at the same time a history, a geography, and a meditation. Originally intended to answer inquiries from France, the Revolutionary ally, *Notes* gave Jefferson the opportunity to comment on several topics of importance to him. Jefferson's concern about slavery and race—he considered the two to be inextricable—and his championship of the agrarian life pointed to the major themes of much of his later writing. The *Notes* presented both agriculture and slavery as essential to the identity of Virginia and of the South.

In the half century following the *Notes*, southerners made their most important literary efforts in history and biography. The first historian of the post-Revolutionary South was a transplanted Pennsylvanian. David Ramsay, a medical doctor, married a daughter of Henry Laurens, who gave him entrée to the elite of South Carolina. Ramsay believed that literature and the arts were "fixing their long and favorite abode in this new western world." Ramsay made his own contribution to literature with *A History of the Revolution in South Carolina* (1785), followed by a longer *History of the American Revolution* (1789). In the new century he published his *History of South Carolina* (1809). Although none of Ramsay's books broke a new literary path, his work does demonstrate the early determination of southerners to tell their story and to take literature seriously.

Southern writers who followed Ramsay continued to focus on the region's past. Probably the most notable was the Virginian William Wirt. A native of Maryland, Wirt at twenty headed for Virginia, and he did well there. Wirt served in both the legislative and judicial arms of the state government; he was attorney general in James Monroe's cabinet; and in 1832 he made an unsuccessful try for the presidency. All the while he thought of himself as a man of letters. Beginning with the anonymous publication of a series of essays in 1803, Wirt wrote chiefly about the society of his Virginia. He spent a dozen years on his major work, *Sketches of the Life and Character of Patrick Henry*, which appeared in 1817. His *Patrick Henry* reached far fewer readers than another biographical study that came out a few years earlier. Like Wirt, Mason Locke Weems was a Marylander who ended up in Virginia. A man of many occupations—he was at various times an itinerant bookseller and an Anglican clergyman—Weems published in 1805 his *Life of Washington*, probably the most popular biography in early nineteenth-century America. Embellished by tales of his own invention— we owe to Weems the legend that young Washington fessed up to cutting down his father's cherry tree—Weems's book went through forty editions before his death in 1825 and a multitude of others thereafter.

The writing of fiction in the South emerged in earnest with the work of John Pendleton Kennedy of Baltimore, who had an enormous influence on plantation fiction. Kennedy's first novel, *Swallow Barn*, published in 1832, described in charming and romantic terms a Virginia plantation of 1800 vintage. The plantation depicted by Kennedy could not be surpassed as a scene of warmth and high human values—hospitality, devotion to family, a sense of honor among the gentry, kindly relations between masters and slaves. Although he found slavery morally indefensible, as a true son of the upper South he took the position that only southerners could deal with slavery; any interference by the North was absolutely unacceptable.

Kennedy spent much of his life in the larger world of business, and he also devoted time to the Whig party, which rewarded him with the post of secretary of the navy in President Millard Fillmore's cabinet. His literary focus, however, remained on the southern past. His *Horse-Shoe Robinson* (1835) and *Rob of the Bowl* (1838) deal with the pre-1800 South. Set in Virginia and South Carolina during the Revolution, *Horse-Shoe Robinson* focuses on the conflicts that raged between patriots and tories. *Rob of the Bowl* moves even further back in time, to seventeenth-century Maryland.

Two other writers who worked with southern themes approached their subject from quite opposite political directions, though both were Virginians. Nathaniel Beverly Tucker, a patrician and half brother of John Randolph of Roanoke, wandered a bit before settling in the Old Dominion. A lawyer, he served as a federal judge in Missouri before returning to Virginia and a faculty appointment at the College of William and Mary. Deeply involved in sectional politics, Tucker in 1836 published his best-known novel, *The Partisan Leader: A Tale of the Future*. Purporting to describe events in 1849, Tucker discusses the evils of the tariff and the North and the joys of the master-slave relationship and the South. He even depicts the formation of a successful southern confederacy. William Alexander Caruthers, by contrast, disliked slavery and attempted to foster sectional goodwill. Hailing from the Virginia uplands, not the tidewater, Caruthers devoted much of his work to more western regions. *The Kentuckians in New York* (1834) weaves a story out of the journeys of southerners and northerners to each other's homes; the plot of *Knights of the Horseshoe* (1845) hinges on a colonial expedition into the Shenandoah Valley. In *The Cavaliers of Virginia* (1834–1835), Caruthers tells a Gothic tale of Bacon's Rebellion.

None of those writers matched in importance the two men who stood far ahead of all their literary colleagues—Edgar Allan Poe and William Gilmore Simms. Poe, a significant figure in the history of American writing, occupies a unique position in southern letters. Though born in Boston, he was reared in Virginia and identified himself with the South, whose institutions, including slavery, he defended. Although he did contribute substantial critical pieces to the *Southern Literary Messenger*, the section's leading magazine, in neither his poetry nor his fiction did Poe make significant use of southern subjects or materials. His characters and plots were not tightly connected to time or place. From a purely artistic viewpoint he surpassed all his southern contemporaries, but his work falls outside the southern experience.

*W*ILLIAM *GILMORE SIMMS*

William Gilmore Simms, though no match for Poe as a literary artist, stood as the preeminent man of letters in the antebellum South. Born in Charleston in

1806, Simms remained a partisan of South Carolina, and though he traveled beyond its borders, he never lived anywhere else. His loyalty to his native state
was the cornerstone of his powerful commitment to the South. Yet Simms was
no provincial; as a young man he traveled to the North, and he was well known
in the literary and publishing circles of New York City, where he found both
lifelong friends and publishers for his books.

Simms began his literary career as a poet but gained his greatest renown as
a novelist. During his lifetime he published more than thirty novels—far too
many, for the mediocrity of some of them still haunts his reputation; but in
quality his best work approaches that of James Fenimore Cooper and Simms's
great model, Sir Walter Scott. Simms wrote chiefly about the South, both the
southwestern frontier and his own South Carolina. His interest in the Southwest stemmed from a youthful journey to Mississippi, where his father had
moved. Simms rejected his father's advice to make his fortune in the West, but
he did use the region as a setting for four border romances, most notable among
them *Guy Rivers* (1834) and *Richard Hurdis* (1838).

After Simms's second marriage in 1836, to a plantation heiress, he settled at
Woodlands Plantation, some seventy-five miles west of Charleston. Without
question his best fiction dealt with his state. The Indian conflicts of the 1710s

WILLIAM GILMORE SIMMS,
THE LEADING MAN OF LET-
TERS IN THE ANTEBELLUM
SOUTH (Courtesy South Carolini-
ana Library, University of South
Carolina)

provided the background for *The Yemassee* (1835). His finest novels, such as *The Partisan* (1835) and *Woodcraft* (1852), treated the bitter strife between South Carolina's patriots and tories. Although Simms's work tended to be melodramatic, it had distinct strengths: superb descriptions of the landscape, development of memorable characters, an honest depiction of the Revolutionary conflict, careful attention to social class. In none of Simms's fiction, however, did he question the fundamental social institutions of his society.

Simms's devotion to the South prompted him to take up other literary tasks. Believing an appreciation of their past essential for South Carolinians—and by extension for all southerners—he published in 1840 a *History of South Carolina* and followed it three years later with a geography of his state. Simms also devoted considerable effort to biographical studies and published works on a founding colonist, John Smith (1840) and two Revolutionary heroes, Francis Marion (1844) and Nathanael Greene (1849). Although Simms's own writing consumed most of his time, he also strove to create a southern literary community by assisting and encouraging young writers and by working on literary journals, which he envisioned as highways connecting all southern literary endeavors with each other. From 1840 to 1860 he was either editing such journals or contributing to them, often both. Such periodicals tended to have short lives in the antebellum South. Only the *Southern Literary Messenger*, published in Richmond from 1834 to 1864, enjoyed a reasonably lengthy life span.

Although at one level Simms never achieved his goal, at another he knew hard-won success. The magazines never flourished as he hoped and southerners never became the serious literary consumers he wished, but Simms kept alive the ideal of a literary community in the South. And by 1860, thanks in large part to his efforts, Charleston was developing into the kind of literary center that he envisioned.

THE HUMORISTS

Although Simms's novels often had a strong comic dimension, he is not included among the writers known as humorists. In the antebellum era humor became a distinct genre, though it had origins in the colonial period. Humorous writing was not peculiar to the South; New England had its Down East comedy and other areas also had their humorists. The first major southern humorist set a high standard. Born in Augusta, Georgia, in 1790, Augustus Baldwin Longstreet had a varied career. A graduate of Yale and of Tapping Reeve's Law School in Litchfield, Connecticut—to both of which he followed his friend John C. Calhoun—Longstreet began as a lawyer, then became a newspaper editor. Later he was ordained as a Methodist minister, and that work led him into education. He served as president of four colleges—two small denominational institutions, the University of Mississippi, and South Carolina College. Even with this active life Longstreet became the Adam of antebellum humorists. His *Georgia Scenes*, published in 1835, was a collection of stories that had appeared earlier in two Georgia newspapers. This was a publishing route that would become familiar to other southern humorists. Longstreet's stories revolved around the everyday life of the common white people of Georgia—horse trading, market day, social occasions and festivities, fights. With dialect a prominent feature, these tales provide a marvelous sense of who these Georgians were and how they lived. In a real sense *Georgia Scenes* is a historical source as well as a collection of comic stories.

Among the best of Longstreet's numerous literary descendants were Johnson J. Hooper and Joseph G. Baldwin. Hooper was a North Carolinian who emigrated to Alabama, where he moved about to pursue several occupations in addition to writing stories. Collected as *The Adventures of Captain Simon Suggs...*, Hooper's work came out in 1845. Unlike Longstreet, who invented a variety of leading characters, Hooper focused on only one. Through Simon Suggs, a wily trickster, Hooper satirized such serious subjects as political campaigns and camp meetings. Hooper found the comedy in everybody, the clever along with the gullible. Adopting a different approach, Joseph G. Baldwin used humor to describe a specific time and place. A Virginian who moved to the southwestern frontier in the hectic years just before the Panic of 1837, Baldwin wanted to convey the wide-open, turbulent society he entered. *The Flush Times of Alabama and Mississippi* (1853) recounts the essentially frontier character of a new area before settled ways and institutions took over. In humorous fashion Baldwin contrasts the Southwest, where nothing was nailed down, with his native Virginia, where everything was in place. Though *Flush Times* is fiction, it conveys a superb sense of those times.

The most original of all the southern humorists was George Washington Harris, a Pennsylvanian who migrated to eastern Tennessee. At various times he captained a steamboat, farmed, and engaged in other endeavors. In the 1850s he wrote stories about the most powerful comic figure created in the antebellum South, Sut Lovingood. Harris's *Sut Lovingood: Yarns Spun by a "Nat'ral Born Durn'd Fool,"* published in book form in 1867, describes the common whites of antebellum eastern Tennessee. Harris treats basically the same topics that most of his fellow humorists addressed, though he makes more pronounced use of the violence and crudity of primitive life. Social and religious occasions, superstitions, love and marriage, and sharp traders make up the bulk of Harris's plots. The heavy dialect in these stories discourages readers today, but the tales have a vitality and exuberance unmatched in antebellum southern fiction.

These four men and their numerous colleagues made two major contributions to southern history and letters. First, their works provide a description of the everyday life of the common white folk that is almost unique in its detail. They remained largely silent on the blacks. It is almost as if they lived and wrote in a slaveless world. For them and their society, slavery was a serious business; no one poked fun at it. A second and equally important contribution lies in the powerful legacy of their humor. In the late nineteenth and the twentieth centuries the great southern writers who made humor a central part of their works, most notably Mark Twain and William Faulkner, drew directly on the techniques and subjects of Longstreet, Harris, and their fellows.

For all its indisputable merits, the literary corpus of the antebellum South does not approach in distinction the literature produced in the North, chiefly in New England. These years have been said to represent the flowering of New England, and a galaxy of brilliant writers give substance to that claim. Herman Melville, Nathaniel Hawthorne, Ralph Waldo Emerson, Emily Dickinson— these writers had no equals in the slave states. Like their southern contemporaries, they were products of their region, but they brought to their art an intellectual detachment and a sense of irony about their own world which we do not find in the southerners. Those qualities are essential for literary achievement of the highest order. Caught up in defending their society, southern writers were unable to perceive the massive intellectual distance between irony and ridicule. They were too committed to their society, with its peculiar institution, to produce great literature. They could not distinguish detachment and criticism from hatred. The South would have to wait until another century for its literary flowering.

SCHOOLING

The story of education in the antebellum South reads very much like that of literature. Some of its parts had true merit, but the whole was not distinguished. Southern education moved into the nineteenth century without a secure foundation, for education was never a central concern in the colonial South.

During the antebellum era no statewide public school system existed. Southerners never heeded Thomas Jefferson's cry that the state ought to assume the responsibility of educating its young people. Even Jefferson's own Virginia rejected his proposals. By 1860 some states had made a respectable beginning while others were performing abysmally. In some cities, however, public schools made substantial headway. Charleston, Louisville, Mobile, and others had excellent schools, and without question the schools were better in the cities than in rural areas.

All too frequently a state made elaborate plans and then did nothing. A few states, however, went beyond planning to action. Kentucky and North Carolina made the best effort. In the 1830s the Kentucky legislature supported public schools by appropriating over half of the surplus revenue received from the federal government before the Panic of 1837 and by adopting a tax of 2 cents on all property in the state. In 1839 North Carolina permitted counties to levy taxes for schools, but the system remained decentralized until 1853, when the office of state superintendent of schools was created. Its first incumbent, Calvin H. Wiley, who for a score of years had been urging popular education, guided

North Carolina to undisputed leadership in public education. By 1860 some 150,000 of the state's 220,000 white children were enrolled in more than 3,000 schools. No other state could match that record.

The southern states also had charity schools, a particular form of public school. In order to qualify their children for enrollment in these free schools, families had to declare themselves unable to pay for their children's education. Proud people—and southerners were surely proud —usually refused to make the necessary declarations of indigency. As a result, these schools were undersubscribed. In Alabama six years after the establishment of a charity system the state superintendent of education reported that nearly one-half of the eligible children did not attend.

Private academies, often called field schools, filled a crucial place in secondary education. In a basic sense they replaced the colonial system of educating children either with private tutors or by sending them to England. In the nineteenth century the South had more private secondary schools than any other section of the country. According to the 1850 census, the South had 2,700 academies to New England's 2,100 and the Middle West's 1,000. Many of these academies offered a vigorous and rigorous education that emphasized the classics and the Bible. Possibly the best known was headed by Moses Waddel, who held forth in Willington, South Carolina. A minister as well as teacher and headmaster, Waddel taught for six days and preached on Sundays. His curriculum focused on Greek, Latin, mathematics, religion, and public speaking. He counted among his alumni many notable southern leaders, but undoubtedly the most famous was John C. Calhoun.

The general failure of secondary education in the South is readily apparent in the figures on illiteracy. According to the 1850 census, 20.3 percent of southern whites were illiterate—a damning indictment of the educational system, or more precisely a dramatic indication of the lack of one. In the Middle States only 3 percent of the white population were illiterate, and in New England the comparable figure was less than 0.5 percent. Comparing the number of schools and teachers in South and North, the wide disparity in illiteracy is not surprising. The 1850 census indicates that the white population of the North was two and a half times larger than that of the South, but the number of both schools and teachers was three times greater in the North. Although the South added substantial numbers of schools and teachers in the final antebellum decade, the wide sectional gap remained.

The reasons for the lag in southern educational were many. First, the population density in the southern states, even among the most populous, worked against a vigorous public school system. Virginia had only 14 white inhabitants per square mile and North Carolina but 12. Massachusetts, in contrast, had 127 inhabitants for each square mile. This density pattern underscores the overwhelming rural character of the South. And in view of the state of communications, roads, and modes of travel in the first half of the nineteenth century, an effort to bring children together regularly over considerable distances would have faced formidable difficulties. In addition, neither wealthy planters nor middling farmers pressed southern legislatures to spend money on education. Neither group as a whole saw much benefit in public education for them or their children. Feeling no pressure, legislators did not rush into an area that many believed was a private matter, not a state function. Thus by the outbreak of the Civil War most public school systems in the South were rudimentary at best.

COLLEGES

The South had a much stronger record in higher education. Unlike the North, the post-Revolutionary South did not have a strong colonial base on which to build colleges. The College of William and Mary was really the only institution of higher learning in the southern colonies. The South witnessed no flurry of new private colleges after the Revolution, but a movement for public ones spread through the seaboard states. Pushed by the upper social order, public higher education became such a popular cause that the first state-supported colleges were established in the South. The debate still rages on which such school is the oldest. The University of Georgia (then known as Franklin College) received the first charter, in 1785, but it did not open until 1801. Although the University of North Carolina was not chartered until 1789, it welcomed students in 1795. South Carolina College was founded in 1801. Not until 1816, however, did the Virginia legislature give its blessing to the University of Virginia, and then only after the insistent advocacy of Thomas Jefferson. Undoubtedly the existence of William and Mary influenced the delayed entry of Virginia.

The desire for public institutions of higher learning did not remain restricted to the older states. The establishment of colleges became an integral part of the western march. The University of Tennessee, which was established in 1794 as East Tennessee College, received state assistance in 1807. Alabama founded its university in the very year it became a state, 1819. Mississippi and Louisiana waited for a time; the University of Mississippi dates from 1844; the University of Louisiana (which after the Civil War became Tulane University) came into being four years later. Before 1860 most southern states could boast of a state-supported college.

Some of these schools were quite good; the best were probably the University of Virginia and South Carolina College. Without question the University of Virginia was the most influential. Jefferson, its founder, was both the political and intellectual father of the university. He not only urged the legislature to establish it but designed the campus and the buildings, planned the curriculum, and brought in the first faculty members, many from Europe. Jefferson's university had the first elective curriculum in the country and introduced the teaching of modern foreign languages. Its antebellum faculty included such academic stalwarts as the scientist William B. Rogers and the literary critic George Frederick Holmes. The University of Virginia was the only southern school that attracted many out-of-state students. South Carolina College became a strong institution under the presidency of Thomas Cooper, a Scottish chemist. Committed to a particular political philosophy as well as to academics, Cooper preached an extreme states'-rights doctrine to a generation of Carolina leaders. Among its faculty South Carolina College could boast the most outstanding political scientist in the country, the German-born Francis Lieber. Lieber left for Columbia University in 1857, however, after questions were raised about his fervor for slavery. The college also had the services of the youthful geologist Joseph LeConte.

Three states also supported military colleges. State leaders expected these institutions to train officers for state militias, but the academies had another purpose as well: their military discipline provided an acceptable means for governing and educating proud, unruly planters' sons who rejected all other efforts to regulate their behavior. The Virginia Military Institute (VMI), founded in 1839, is the oldest southern military school. Its most famous citizen was a professor who taught physics and artillery tactics to cadets and then later commanded many of them in battle, Thomas J. "Stonewall" Jackson. The Citadel, South Carolina's version of VMI, accepted its first students in 1842. The Citadel certainly succeeded with its military education, for during the Civil War some 90 percent of its living alumni became officers in the Confederate States Army. The last of the military schools to be established, Louisiana State Seminary of Learning and Military Academy (now Louisiana State University), opened its doors in 1860, with a former United States Army officer as superintendent. Although it had little time to educate students before the war broke out, it certainly had an impact on the conflict. With the onset of hostilities, all students and faculty joined the Confederate forces. The superintendent, however, went with the Union, where he served with considerable distinction; his name was William Tecumseh Sherman.

Public colleges did not, however, occupy the entire stage of higher education. Nonpublic institutions did exist, though prior to 1830 they were neither notable nor numerous; the one significant exception was Transylvania University, opened in Lexington, Kentucky, in 1789. By 1820 Transylvania was flourishing, with offerings in law and medicine as well as an undergraduate curriculum. When religious problems plagued the school in the mid-1820s, however, its light dimmed.

In the years between 1830 and 1860 religion became a major force in southern higher education. Spurred by the evangelical movement that surged throughout the South, the major denominations established colleges in almost every state. Many disappeared almost as quickly as they were founded; others were little more than high schools. Some not only survived but became well-known institutions. The Baptists started Wake Forest in North Carolina, Furman in South Carolina, and Baylor in Texas. The Methodists were responsible for Randolph-Macon in Virginia, Trinity (now Duke University) in North Carolina, and Emory in Georgia. The Presbyterians founded Hampden-Sydney in Virginia, Davidson in North Carolina, and Austin in Texas.

The church leaders whose efforts and determination ensured the success of this collegiate movement had two basic motives. One was clearly religious, or more precisely sectarian; the other had secular overtones. First, the churchmen became concerned that the public institutions either suffered from a lack of orthodoxy or failed to stress religion at all. These clerics and laymen wanted their young people educated in an environment where the doctrinal teachings of their particular denomination were emphasized. Second, a substantial portion of the religious educators believed that the public colleges had become too aristocratic as well as too worldly. As they saw it, their schools would not nurture displays of wealth and social position. To curtail snobbishness and preoccupation with wealth, some of them—Wake Forest was one—decreed that all students must engage in manual labor.

The last sectarian college established before the Civil War differed from the others in one important respect. When the Episcopalians founded the University of the South in Sewanee, Tennessee, in 1860, they certainly expected their school to inculcate Episcopalian values and doctrine; but they also wanted to educate young men as true southerners. Created as the sectional crisis deepened and southern self-consciousness heightened, Sewanee had a mission both sectarian and secular.

THE GROWTH OF EVANGELICAL RELIGION

The best estimates indicate that in 1800 only about 10 percent of white southerners belonged to a church. Some others attended a church occasionally. In the decade and a half before 1800 a network of evangelical churches had been created on both sides of the Appalachians, in the new western states as well as the old seaboard states, but they were the outposts of a faithful few. A New Englander who worked as a tutor in Richmond in the mid-1790s pictured the South as a religious wasteland. "Christianity is here breathing its last," he wrote home. "I cannot find a friend with whom I can even converse on religious subjects."

Yet only a few years later the South got religion. The spiritual fires that swept over that wasteland in the nineteenth century were sparked by a camp meeting in south-central Kentucky in the summer of 1800. A camp meeting was exactly what it sounds like. People from the surrounding area came together for a meeting. Expecting to stay a few days, they set up tents and lean-tos. In this environment, where people congregated to share a religious experience, the emotion that was generated among the faithful was contagious. The spiritual energy released during the Great Revival spread east, south, and west. A great interdenominational appeal, though clearly Protestant, swept across the South.

Properly understood, the Great Revival was the southern Great Awakening. In a fundamental sense, the revival never ended: religion assumed a permanently conspicuous place in the society. By 1860 the proportion of church members had more than doubled, and twice that many more—fully 40 percent of southern whites—actively participated in organized churches. The evangelical denominations both led and pushed this religious turnabout. Spearheaded by the Baptists and Methodists, who by 1860 claimed 80 percent of all southern church members, evangelical Protestantism captured the South.

Between the Great Revival and 1860 revivals became fixtures of southern life. The Methodists institutionalized the camp meeting, which became a key feature of the denomination. Essential to the success of Methodism were the circuit riders, the tireless ministers who served the isolated churches of the southern countryside. Each circuit rider served a number of churches spread over a considerable distance. On the frontier a circuit could encompass a hundred miles and twenty or more churches. The men who rode the circuits combined religious conviction with the courage of pioneers.

The experience of one William Redman, responsible for the White River Circuit in Arkansas, underscores the resoluteness of these mobile messengers. Because of the distance between his congregations, the Reverend Redman often slept alone on the ground with a saddlebag for a pillow. During one night he had just begun to drift off to sleep "when the sudden, terrific scream of a panther brought him to his feet." As he clung to his horse, which threatened to bolt, he feared "the blood-thirsty animal would rend him to pieces." But to Redman's great relief, the panther decided to look elsewhere for his nighttime meal. On the following morning Redman "paid his devotions to the God of Daniel, who had delivered him from so great a danger," then resumed his journey with "rejoicing." Only the dedication and zeal of itinerant preachers such as the Reverend Redman made possible the phenomenal growth of Methodism.

The other two evangelical denominations took a somewhat different tack. Both the Baptists and, to a lesser extent, the Presbyterians embraced the revival as central to their mission, but neither warmed to the camp meeting. The Baptists were particularly suited to capitalize on the changing role of religion in southern society. Because Baptists believed in the absolute independence of individual churches, no ecclesiastical hurdles hindered the organization of a Baptist church anywhere a group wanted one. And because Baptists were not concerned about the educational attainments of their clergymen, anyone who desired to do so and who could find a congregation could become a minister. Instant churches and preachers were commonplace.

The Presbyterians did not match their evangelical brethren in growth. Their governance precluded the instantaneous church, but an even greater impediment was their insistence on an educated clergy. Those two considerations, added to a theology more intellectual than emotional in character, ensured that the Presbyterians would never match the Baptists and Methodists in growth rate or numbers. The Presbyterians attracted a larger portion of the social and economic elite than their evangelical competitors, but here again they were overshadowed, for the spiritual home of the upper orders was the Episcopal or Anglican church, the smallest of the major denominations and the one least affected by evangelicalism.

SALEM BLACK RIVER PRESBYTERIAN CHURCH (1846)
Sumter District, South Carolina. This structure emphasizes the influence of
religion in the countryside. (Courtesy of Patricia H. Cooper)

Neither the Roman Catholics nor the Jews challenged the overwhelming
cultural as well as religious domination of the Protestants. Jews, who constituted less than 1 percent of the southern population in the first half of the nineteenth century, had arrived in the South before 1750. Locating mostly in cities—
Charleston, for example, had a significant Jewish community—Jews as a group
exercised little influence. They generally adopted the mores and the outlook of
the larger society. Roman Catholics were more numerous than Jews but were
no more influential, except in Louisiana. With its Franco-Spanish heritage, Louisiana accounted for more than half of the Catholics in the antebellum South.
Outside Louisiana most Catholics, like most Jews, lived in cities along the seaboard and on the border with the free states. They, too, became part of the social, political, and cultural world fashioned by the dominant Protestants.

In the nineteenth century the evangelicals stood at the center of southern
society. Whereas evangelicals had been outsiders in the eighteenth century,
they made up the southern establishment in the nineteenth. Their prominent
laymen occupied central posts in the society and their leading ministers, a number of them originally from the North, became molders of opinion and influential public spokesmen. The churches exercised considerable moral authority in
the South. When such men as the South Carolina Baptist Richard Furman, the
Mississippi Methodist William Winans, the Presbyterians Benjamin Palmer of
Louisiana and James H. Thornwell of South Carolina, and James Otey, Episco-

pal bishop of Tennessee, chose to speak, they had an audience. In towns, in villages, and in individual congregations, local clergymen enjoyed similar status and influence.

THE MESSAGE

On major issues the clergy's blessing, or at least its support, was critical. The churches and their teachings permeated southern society. The churches did not attack slavery or any other institution central to the society. In the late eighteenth century some clerics, especially among the Methodists of the upper South, questioned the morality of slavery, but the extent of such opposition can be exaggerated, and even those limited reservations disappeared in the nineteenth century. Ministers placed their influence and the authority of God behind the organization of southern society in general and behind slavery in particular. Religious southerners did not have to choose between the promptings of their political chieftains and the exhortations of their spiritual guardians; they were not at odds. According to the gospel pronounced from numerous pulpits, even secession was ordained by the Almighty.

The attention of southern Protestants focused chiefly on personal conversion and the spiritual health of the individual soul. The southern clergy were not out to remake the world. A pervasive Calvinism underscored the widespread belief that imperfect people lived in an imperfect world. The concept of perfectionism, which stimulated and fueled reform movements in the North, was largely absent from the southern religious vocabulary. Southern clergy surely strove to uplift their congregations, but they had no vision of a perfect society. Ministers inveighed against immoral behavior, and local churches, acting as keepers of morality, enforced a moral code that defined as sins such acts as adultery, fornication, intoxication, and in the most solemn congregations even dancing. But always the focus was on the individual.

The influential Presbyterian minister and theologian James H. Thornwell, who also served as president of South Carolina College, captured the essence of southern Protestantism when he wrote that too many people regarded the church as "a moral institute of universal good, whose business it is to wage war upon every form of human ill, whether social, civil, political or moral, and to patronize every expedient which a romantic benevolence may suggest as likely to contribute to human comfort, or to mitigate the inconveniences of life." Nonsense! proclaimed Thornwell. In his view, God did not intend that "all ill shall be banished from this sublunary state, and earth be converted into a paradise, or that the proper end of the Church is the direct promotion of universal good." God was sovereign, and "the power of the church...is only ministerial and declarative." Cementing himself and his religion to a literal reading of God's word, Thornwell asserted, "The Bible, and the Bible alone, is [the church's] rule of faith and practice. Beyond the Bible she can never go and apart from the Bible she can never speak."

JAMES H. THORNWELL,
PRESBYTERIAN MINISTER
AND EDUCATOR (Courtesy of
South Caroliniana Library, Univer-
sity of South Carolina)

Yet southern Protestantism did have a distinct reform dimension. Ministers were especially concerned about greed, or what one of them termed "a lust for mammon"—in our language, the almighty dollar. Ministers saw greed as a vicious cancer eating away at the vitals of southern society. Unchecked, the preachers predicted, it would destroy any hope for a godly South. From their pulpits ministers thundered against putting money and the desire for it ahead of the Bible and God. Christian citizens, they asserted, must be educated in Christian principles. This Christian education would take place in schools and colleges as well as churches. The perceived need for a Christian education to counter the tendency to greed became a primary motive in the founding of denominational colleges, and it spurred the extraordinary efforts made by ministers to keep academies going.

The sin of greed was a constant theme during the antebellum period, and it probably received special attention in the 1850s, a decade of general prosperity. In the ministers' view, southern society never purged itself of this transgression; spiritual transformation never occurred. From this vantage point the preachers launched their one major criticism of slavery. They urged slave owners to follow the biblical precepts defining a truly patriarchal system. According to the clergymen, decisions by masters to work slaves unduly hard and to break up families signaled greed, not Christian stewardship. Sermon after sermon urged slave owners to focus on becoming Christian stewards of what God had placed in their trust.

In an effort to foster and encourage slavery according to biblical precepts, the major denominations engaged in a mission to the slaves. While seemingly directed solely at converting and ministering to slaves, this crusade also encouraged Christian slaveholding. This combination produced for the ministers the twin blessings of slavery. Carrying the Gospel to slaves could result in the salvation of souls otherwise lost and also could offer masters the opportunity to demonstrate their allegiance to Christian principles. The major purpose of the mission to the slaves was to bring the institution more in line with the Bible's teachings as the ministers saw them. Never did they set out to destroy slavery, and it is impossible to overestimate the importance of the clergy's support of slavery.

SECTIONAL STRIFE

The commitment of southern churches and their ministers to southern institutions was underscored in the sectional divisions of the largest denominations. In the mid-1840s both the Baptists and the Methodists in the South broke with their northern brethren in disputes directly connected with slavery. In 1844 the general conference of the Methodist church asked the Methodist bishop of Georgia to take a leave from his episcopal office until he had disposed of the slaves he had acquired along with his second wife. Incensed by this action, which in their minds was tantamount to declaring slaveholding unchristian, southern Methodists moved to set up their own church. The next year in Louisville, the Methodist Episcopal Church, South, came into being. In that same year Baptists in the South, meeting in Augusta, organized the Southern Baptist Convention and withdrew from the national organization because its foreign mission board refused to appoint slaveholding missionaries.

The remaining two major Protestant denominations escaped sectional division before 1861. In 1837, before the Baptists and Methodists split, the Presbyterians had been divided by questions that were chiefly theological, though they did have implications for the church's involvement in social reform. The conservative Old School predominated in the South; these southerners had no difficulty getting along with their fellow traditionalists in the North. The liberal New School, which was more strongly oriented toward social action, counted few adherents below the Mason-Dixon line. As a result, an organized southern Presbyterian church did not come into existence until 1861. It lasted as a separate entity until 1983, however. Episcopalians never really divided; in fact, the church remained remarkably free of sectional disputes. An Episcopal Church in the Confederate States was formed in 1861, but when the war ended, the Episcopalians quickly reunited.

The bulwark provided by the churches and the clergy enabled antebellum southerners to live secure in the conviction that their society and its major social institution had God's approval.

12

The Free Social Order

❖

Rich planters, poor whites, black slaves—the stereotype of an antebellum social order comprised of these three groups alone has survived more than a century. In the generation before 1860 it was adopted and preached by the abolitionists; the Republicans also made it a staple of their propaganda. In our own time popular novelists and moviemakers have conveyed it to millions in bold portraits with no blurred images. This distorted picture has little connection with historical reality.

The reality was considerably more complex. That conclusion is not simply the assessment of modern scholars who have carefully studied antebellum society. In 1860 Daniel R. Hundley, a native Alabamian, divided white southerners into seven classes. It is certainly possible to quarrel with Hundley's categories and it would surely be unprofitable to classify every individual in the antebellum South, but recognition of the region's social diversity and complexity is essential to an understanding of the social order.

PLANTERS

The vast majority of southern white males fell into one of two broad categories: planters and yeomen. To be sure, substantial differences were to be found among planters. The planter class ranged from grand seigneurs reigning over acres and slaves accumulated across several generations to hard-charging buccaneers driving newly acquired slaves to carve plantations out of the virgin land west of the Mississippi to plain, hard-working folk tilling a modest acreage with a modest slave force. And over time thousands of planters moved from one group to another.

The homes of the planters were as various as the lives they led. In the years after 1815 the stately Georgian mansion that housed the tidewater aristocracy of the colonial era still adorned the old seaboard states. The 1820s, however, witnessed the advent of the architectural style that would prevail in the antebellum South and eventually become both symbol and stereotype of the antebellum regime. Based on the design of the classical Greek temple, the Greek Revival style, with its imposing columns, originated in the upper South and spread quickly throughout the region. Some houses—Andrew Jackson's Hermitage outside Nashville, for instance—were quite simple behind their great columns. Others, such as Gaineswood in Demopolis, Alabama, were complex and lavish structures. In the Mississippi Valley the Greek Revival meshed with the Creole tradition in such magnificent structures as Houmas House in Ascension Parish, Louisiana.

Although the Greek Revival mansions denoted success and status in every slave state, by the 1850s new styles and new wealth led in new directions. The Italianate style, borrowed from Italian villas, added semicircular arches and towers. It was popular for a time but never drove the Greek Revival from its pinnacle. The enormous riches that sugar brought to some planters in the decade before 1860 resulted in houses of unprecedented size and opulence. Possibly the largest residence constructed in the antebellum South still stands today beside the Mississippi in Iberville Parish, Louisiana. Built for John Hampden Randolph in 1859, Nottoway, or the White Castle, a Greek Revival–Italianate mansion, contains 64 rooms, 200 windows, and 165 doors. Randolph wanted Nottoway to outshine a wealthy neighbor's home, Belle Grove, a house of comparable magnificence which no longer stands. The desire for conspicuous display which motivated the construction of these two enormous houses did not die in 1861. Belle Grove and Nottoway clearly point the way to the "cottages" of Newport.

Most planters did not live in splendid columned mansions, though few were so unpretentious as the Mississippi slave owner who named his home Log Hall. The most common plantation residence was a simple rectangular frame

GAINESWOOD, DEMOPOLIS, ALABAMA, 1843–1859, PROBABLY DESIGNED BY THE OWNER, NATHAN B. WHITFIELD (Courtesy of Patricia H. Cooper)

HOUMAS, ASCENSION PARISH, LOUISIANA, 1840s, CENTER OF THE
HAMPTON FAMILY SUGAR PLANTATION (Courtesy of Patricia H. Cooper)

house of two stories with a chimney at either end. Such homes usually had either two or four rooms on each floor, divided by a central hall. They might or
might not be painted. A number of these plain farmhouses still stand in the
southern countryside. Over time some of these houses were enlarged by rooms
extended rearward or by the addition of a wing or wings; these additions rarely
provided any architectural distinction. A family that really prospered or that
had social ambitions might place a portico or columns, most often two, at the
front of their house in an effort to mimic the Greek Revival mansion.

A glimpse at the lives and activities of some of these planters affords insight
into the planter class. At the ancestral home called Shirley, on the James River
in tidewater Virginia, Hill Carter, scion of one of the most notable families in
the state, lived in a manner his grandfather would have recognized and applauded. A guest provided an eyewitness account of a dinner at Shirley in 1833.
The event began at 3 P.M., when the host led the family and their guests, in
pairs, to the dining room. At one end of the table he carved a saddle of mutton
while at the other his wife ladled soup. Two young slave boys served from plat-
ters brimming with ham, beef, turkey, duck, eggs, greens, sweet potatoes, and
hominy. After champagne was served, the upper tablecloth was removed and
desserts were brought in: plum pudding, tarts, ice cream, and brandied

NOTTOWAY, IBERVILLE PARISH, LOUISIANA, 1859, BUILT FOR JOHN HAMPDEN RANDOLPH (Courtesy Louisiana Office of Tourism)

peaches. After desert the second tablecloth was removed and on the mahogany table were placed figs, raisins, almonds, and, in front of Hill Carter, "2 or 3 bottles of wine—Madeira, Port, and a sweet wine for the ladies. After the glasses are filled, the gentlemen pledge their services to the ladies, and down goes the wine." After the second glass the ladies retired, but "the gentlemen...circulate[d] the bottle pretty briskly." Any man who wished to follow the women from the table, however, could do so at his leisure without insulting his host. After music and conversation, the guests headed for home.

John Palfrey never knew such ease or such bounty. Immigrating to Louisiana from Massachusetts shortly after the Purchase, he went bankrupt both as a ship's chandler and as a plantation manager. Finally he managed to obtain land west of New Orleans, where in 1811 he began to clear land and put up crude buildings with the help of twenty-three slaves. Surveying his past as a bankrupt and a widower, he named his new plantation Forlorn Hope. For a decade and a half floods and disease kept prosperity at a distance. After 1830, when he turned to sugar cane, Palfrey's situation brightened, and he knew some good fortune until his death in 1843. But for thirty years Palfrey's life had been one of uncertainty and struggle.

The experience of the Wade Hampton family of South Carolina bore little relation to Palfrey's. Wade I came to prominence out of the South Carolina piedmont after notable military service during the Revolution. He established himself near Columbia and became one of the first successful planters of short-staple cotton in the state. Commissioned as a brigadier general in the United States Army, Hampton found himself in American Louisiana, where he put his business acumen to work. Purchasing substantial acreage in sugar country,

Wade I added a sugar barony to his established cotton estate. With drive and entrepreneurial skill, Wade I built up an agricultural empire. After his death his son Wade II and his grandson Wade III ruled their imperial domain from their plantation palace outside Columbia. At its height the Hampton holdings included vast cotton plantations in Mississippi as well as in South Carolina and a major sugar plantation in Louisiana. Precisely how many slaves the family owned is uncertain, but in all probability the number exceeded 1,000 in the three states.

Richard Eppes never knew the grandeur of the Hamptons. Born into a good but not first-rank family in Virginia, Richard attended the University of Virginia and graduated in 1842. He had intended a medical career, but he abandoned that plan when he inherited the family plantation. Although Eppes built up his slave force and his landholdings, he remained basically a farmer. He often rose at 4:30 in the morning to supervise the work on the plantation. A scientific farmer, he eagerly read the works of the agricultural reformers, bought machinery, used fertilizers, and was active in the local agricultural society. With little time for or interest in cultural matters, Eppes enjoyed smoking "segars," entertaining visitors, and attending the local Episcopal church, where he served on the vestry. He believed strongly in the immortality of the soul and confided to his diary that he hoped to be reunited in heaven with his first wife.

Obviously, the individuals who made up the planter class varied enormously; at the same time, important similarities bound them together. Almost all were engaged in commercial agriculture, though the crops and the scale of production varied. Thus the economic course of agriculture, especially of cotton, was fundamental to their financial well-being. All of these planters owned slaves. Whether they owned twenty or two hundred slaves, a considerable portion of their wealth was tied up in human property. The issue of slavery and its future was central to their lives. Not surprisingly, agriculture and slavery formed the heart of public discussion in the South. The special concerns of the planters became central for the entire region.

Southern slave owners in the nineteenth century lived in a world dominated by the expansion of capitalism made possible by the Industrial Revolution. Slave owners had a unique relationship with this new, powerful economic order. They shared basic characteristics with capitalists: the profit motive, the view of land and slaves as investments, a willingness to relocate to take advantage of an opportunity, an interest in investing in such enterprises as banks, railroads, and manufacturing. At the same time, planters possessed slaves; in economic terms, they owned their labor. By the nineteenth century their system was economically anachronistic and at odds with a concept central to capitalism: free labor. In the capitalist system workers were free to offer their labor to the highest bidder. If the highest bid was less than they needed to stay above poverty or if the working conditions were brutal, they were theoretically free to take a better offer if they could find one. The concept of free labor, with its actual or implied contract, was the bedrock of the emerging capitalism. To the new capitalists, slavery was an outmoded and immoral economic arrangement;

to most southerners it was economically viable and humane. These conflicting perspectives on slavery contributed significantly to the growing tension between the free and slave societies.

In sum, most slave owners were enmeshed in the capitalist world at the same time that they stood somewhat apart from it. They did not perceive an inevitable conflict between slavery and sustained economic growth.

YEOMEN AND POOR WHITES

Although the planters receive the most attention, it was the yeoman farmers who occupied the central place in southern society. Neither rich nor poor, the yeomen were property-owning farmers who might or might not own slaves. Between 80 and 90 percent of all small farmers in the antebellum South owned

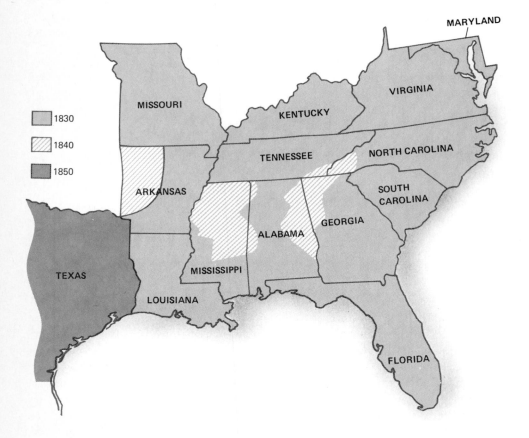

POPULATION MOVEMENT IN THE SOUTH, 1830–1850

their own land. These people were surely not a peasantry. Most yeomen did not own slaves. No great social distance separated a farmer who owned three or four slaves from one who had none, though a person with a dozen or fifteen slaves stood considerably higher on the social scale than either. Just as the planter class covered a broad social and economic spectrum, so did the yeomanry.

Self-sufficiency and commitment to the market economy varied among them. As growers of tobacco, grain, livestock, and particularly cotton for money, most yeomen had at least some involvement in the market. They were neither pariahs nor ciphers in antebellum society. Property owners, they were also political citizens who could and did vote. Some families remained in a particular area over generations while others became part of the great westward movement. In addition, the economic and geographical expansion of the South permitted movement up the social ladder.

A glimpse at two very different families lends insight into the yeoman class. Jacob Eaton and his family lived on a 160-acre farm in the North Carolina piedmont. Jacob with his wife and their eight children lived in a three-room log house with a loft where the boys slept. In 1860 they owned seven slaves, in all probability one family. With their help the family raised their crops and tended their animals. Mrs. Eaton and her daughters spun their cotton into thread on spinning wheels, wove the thread into cloth, and made their own clothing. The strong feeling of place and kinship within the family found expression in the family cemetery, where generations were buried.

The family of Samuel Davis, in contrast, followed the moving frontier. As a child Samuel moved with his parents from Philadelphia to colonial Georgia. There he grew up and fought in the Revolution. As a reward for his military service, the state gave him land near Augusta, and he farmed it until 1793, when he moved to Kentucky. There in Christian County he raised tobacco, corn, and wheat. Early in the new century Samuel once again headed west; after a brief stop in southern Louisiana he settled in Wilkinson County, Mississippi, where he commenced farming once again, this time with cotton as a market crop. Although he had a few slaves, at various times ranging from two up to a dozen, he always worked in his fields beside them. Throughout his peregrinations Samuel Davis strove to better his circumstances, but upon his death in 1824 he was still the yeoman farmer he had always been. Although Samuel himself never moved up into the planter class, his son Jefferson surely did.

Below the yeomen on the social scale were the people designated as poor whites, both in the nineteenth century and by modern scholars. This group has also been called white trash, rednecks, crackers, and other names equally demeaning. Even the slaves joined in with their derisive "po' buckra." These poor whites lived largely on the margin of southern society. In the rural South they included owners of small plots of unproductive soil as well as tenants and agricultural laborers; the last two were not nearly so numerous as they were to become in the years after the Civil War and especially in the twentieth century. In some parts of the South, chiefly away from the main agricultural areas, trap-

EPPS HOUSE, AVOYELLES PARISH, LOUISIANA, 1852, HOME OF A
YEOMAN WHO OWNED A FEW SLAVES (Courtesy of Patricia H. Cooper)

pers, hunters, and herders fit into this category. Unsuccessful artisans and laborers in towns and cities added to their number. In the antebellum years this
lower class had little impact on the course of southern development. Impressive
economic growth and massive geographical expansion offered sufficient opportunities for escape and mobility, both economic and social, to keep this lowest
segment of the white social order small.

HARMONY OR DISHARMONY

Many scholars have pondered whether planters exploited such men as Jacob
Eaton and Samuel Davis or whether class conflict between the upper and lower
orders characterized the antebellum South. This question is not at all new. Two
southerners who wrote toward the end of the antebellum regime came down
vigorously on opposite sides of the issue. Daniel Hundley, in his *Social Relations
in Our Southern States* (1860), found unity and harmony in southern society, and
he thought the yeomen central to the society. The North Carolinian Hinton
Helper, by contrast, argued in *The Impending Crisis of the South* (1857) that slave
owners and the very system of slavery exploited the nonslaveholders by severely restricting the possibilities for economic advancement. Helper, however,
did not at all challenge white supremacy. In fact, a virulent racism informs *The
Impending Crisis*; Helper believed that blacks must leave the South. Although

both industry and the general economy in the South were growing, the South certainly did not match the North. Just how severely slavery circumscribed southern economic growth and opportunity for southern farmers is difficult to say at this remove, but most scholars believe that Helper's basic point is correct. Few southerners of the 1850s shared that view, however. They believed, with good reason, that slavery powered an economic engine of considerable force. Suffice it to say here that the expansion of the southern economy provided sufficient wealth and opportunity to preclude any significant attacks on the regime for holding down the mass of its white citizens. Class antagonism and tension surely existed, and given the appropriate conditions, they could become powerful forces in southern society. The strains of wartime would bring some into the open, but before 1860 class conflict did not threaten the social order.

Of the many reasons for this basic social harmony, five stand out:

1. Race: An omnipotent racism convinced all whites that only bondage enabled black and white to coexist without massive social trauma. This racism also made believable an ideology that placed all whites on an equal social and political level, despite sharp economic and social distinctions. John C. Calhoun articulated this view forcefully: "With us the two great divisions of society are not the rich and poor, but white and black; and all the former, the poor as well as the rich, belong to the upper class, and are respected and treated as equals, if honest and industrious."

2. Politics: By the Jacksonian era all white male adults had the right to vote, and they exercised it. Specific policies underscored the strength of the average white southerner. Tax policy in the lower South, for example, provides concrete evidence of their political standing. In those states the principal source of tax revenue was the tax on slaves—paid, of course, by slave owners. The land tax remained quite low; even when it rose somewhat in the 1850s, it generally stayed below two mills on the dollar. In addition, planters had to pay a luxury tax on race horses, pleasure carriages, private libraries, pianos, and similar property. This system was not at all like the ancien régime in prerevolutionary France, where the lower classes paid to support the upper classes.

3. Economic relations: Planters and yeomen, slaveholders and nonslaveholders quite often shared the same economic world. In only a very few areas, such as the sea islands, did planters operate in isolation from yeomen. Elsewhere the two groups provided essential services and materials to each other. Planters with cotton gins ginned the cotton raised by yeomen. Yeomen sold livestock and grain to planters. Planters who needed additional labor at critical times often hired the slaves of yeomen, and even the yeomen themselves, whether or not they owned slaves.

4. Social mobility: Social mobility had always been a hallmark of southern society. Never, even in the colonial era, had the path to the top been

blocked. The prosperity of the 1850s certainly did not encourage the belief that stagnation would ever completely close the path leading upward.
It is true that the substantial increase in slave prices during that decade,
which made it more difficult to become a first-time slave owner, worried
some southerners; they feared increasing class conflict if prices should
rise high enough to close off that option for good. That was indeed a legitimate concern, but such a situation did not arise before 1860. No one
can be sure what would have happened if the war had not come.

5. Kinship: The incredible geographic and economic growth of the South,
    along with the fluidity of social lines, guaranteed that members of indi-
    vidual families would range across the economic and social spectrum. Fa-
    thers, sons, brothers, mothers, daughters, sisters, not to mention collat-
    eral relatives, could find themselves significantly differentiated by wealth
    and social position. At times people who were successful turned their
    backs on kin who were less fortunate. It has always been so. But many
    others proudly recognized family ties that spanned wide economic and
    social chasms.

THE PLACE OF WOMEN IN SOCIETY

Literary and historical mythology has tended to picture southern white women
as spoiled belles idling away their time in languid conversation on their veran-
das, but few antebellum women would recognize themselves in that portrait.
Of course, the advice literature of the time, widely read in the South as well as
the North, portrayed the ideal woman as submissive, pure, and pious; domestic
ideology thrived in countryside and city alike. In many ways southern families
embodied the more general ideals and practices of Victorian America rather
than those of a distinctively southern society. Some historians have argued that
the subordination of women was critical to the security and ideology of a slave
society, but in fact few southern intellectuals paid much attention to the place of
women in their society.

Whether patriarchy was the official southern ideology is by no means clear.
Some southern men often behaved like imperious lords of the manor, but so
did many northern husbands. To be sure, southern writers urged women to
cultivate a "quiet submission to the state of subordination ordained by heavenly
wisdom." Louisa Cheves McCord, a remarkable South Carolinian who wrote
forcefully and prolifically on political and economic questions, argued that
women were "made for duty, not for fame." Yet in the South women were also
expected to exert moral authority in the home; what has been called "domestic
feminism" appeared as women assumed increasing control over the rearing,
education, and religious instruction of their children. Southerners tended to
place more emphasis on female virtue than northerners because any question
raised about a woman's respectability would besmirch a family's honor—a most

sensitive point in the South and an issue of such explosiveness that it sometimes led to duels.

The myth of the lazy belle notwithstanding, most southern women were too busy to worry about their place in southern ideology. Regardless of class, they worked at a wide variety of household and agricultural tasks. The advice literature and family documents alike portray women as scurrying about their kitchens and gardens, cooking for their families, sewing, and managing slaves. In their domestic routines their lives differed little from those of their northern counterparts, though there appears to have been somewhat less domestic discontent in the South and certainly less overt feminism than in the Northeast.

In many ways southern families were in transition between traditional and modern attitudes toward family life. "Companionate" marriage became increasingly the pattern in the South in the decades immediately preceding the Civil War: young people chose their own mates. Even parental influence on the selection of a spouse steadily declined. Both young people and their advisers placed more and more emphasis on romance and less and less on finance. Planters who still tried to arrange "good matches" for their daughters could not always get their way.

This greater freedom was also reflected in the decision of many women either to delay marriage or to stay single. Some young women expressed reluctance to give up their independence; because marriage greatly limited their property rights and means of escape were few, they feared making a bad choice. As one put it, "Liberty is sweeter to me than matrimony." The census data suggest that the rate of marriage in the southern states was about the same as that for the rest of the country.

THE PLACE OF WOMEN IN MARRIAGE

Once married, the southern woman lost most of her legal rights. Some states had laws permitting husbands to punish their wives physically, and even after these abuses were outlawed in the 1840s and 1850s, juries seldom convicted wife-beaters and judges handed down absurdly light sentences. Women trapped in bad marriages had few means of escape. If a woman left her husband, she also abandoned any property she had brought into the marriage and entered a world with few opportunities for single women, especially for those who had fallen into disgrace. And to leave one's husband was disgraceful.

Divorces were rare. Early in the nineteenth century divorce required the passage of a private bill in a state legislature, and most politicians set a high standard for acceptance of such a petition. Both men and women had difficulty obtaining divorces. As several states converted divorce into a judicial proceeding, the law shifted in favor of women. Every southern state except South Carolina, which had no divorce law, added adultery, cruelty, and desertion to the usual bigamy, impotence, and consanguinity as grounds for divorce. Lawmakers also gave courts wide discretion in defining "cruelty," and a number of judges would grant divorce on the grounds of mental cruelty. Of course some patriarchal elements survived. The woman had to prove her virtue beyond question and usually had to show that she had been a duly submissive wife. Yet southern judges, who tended to see themselves as paternalistic defenders of the weak, became increasingly generous in awarding property and child custody to women. Despite legal reforms and the growing number of divorces, the social stigma against divorce remained, and the antebellum divorce rate was minuscule.

Marriage and motherhood were still the destiny of most southern women. Women well understood that some men measured a woman's value by her fertility. Marriage began a lengthy round of pregnancies. The manuscript census for any southern county shows children spaced at intervals of two years or less; births only thirteen months apart were commonplace. After ten years of marriage, Elizabeth Perry of South Carolina had been pregnant ten times; these pregnancies had ended in four live births, two stillbirths, and four miscarriages. In St. Francisville, Louisiana, one thirty-seven-year-old woman had already borne sixteen children, and a neighbor ruefully remarked, "Her family may yet be much larger." Most women welcomed children, but the excitement soon wore off. "Babies to you are no novelty," one mother informed a friend, "and even to me the novelty is fast wearing away for I'm sometimes completely worn out in mind and body. Poor little girls I pity them all no matter whose they are."

Birth control techniques commonly used by educated northern women were only slowly adopted in the South. A mother of thirteen could only comment wearily: "I have so many little children and no prospect of ever stopping." Delayed weaning, abstinence, and coitus interruptus were evidently the only birth control techniques widely known and practiced in the South. Most southern states outlawed abortions performed after the quickening of the fetus, but no evidence suggests that abortions at any stage of pregnancy had ever been common in the South.

In addition to the burdens of child rearing, women faced seemingly endless rounds of household chores. Class differences appeared in the type and amount of housework done by women. On a typical day Jane Beale, a poor widow with nine children living in Fredericksburg, Virginia, put up pickles, cut out cloth, washed lamp chimneys, listened to her children recite their lessons, cleaned up the yard, whitewashed part of the house, cut up peaches, mended clothes, rid the beds of insects, and fed and milked the cow. After getting her youngsters to bed, she at last sat down to chat with her brother Sam—with, of course, knitting in her lap. For more comfortably situated women, the tasks were different but only slightly less demanding. Along with her mother and half sister in Marietta, Georgia, Mary Roberts worked hard to maintain a neat and respectable home. Rising early in the morning, she prepared breakfast and then hustled her nieces and nephews off to school. Then it was out to the yard to look after the ducks, turkeys, and chickens. She reserved the afternoon for reading, writing, sewing, and a walk outside. Visits from neighbors and friends might disrupt this routine. In the evening she read aloud to the family. Planters' wives, too, had their daily chores, and most ran their households carefully, but they had much more leisure than the typical farm woman. Ella Thomas sewed, cared for her children, worked in the garden, but still had time to read popular novels and the four magazines to which she subscribed.

THE LIFE OF THE FEMALE SPIRIT AND MIND

Although class differences certainly existed in southern society, evangelical religion sometimes helped women bridge these social distances. Like their menfolk, southern women tended to be Methodists or Baptists. Perhaps because church membership was one of the few public activities open to them, women flocked to the churches. Religion linked women to the world even as it led them to shun worldliness and materialism, but this connection did not threaten domestic ideology. Ministers argued that wives found it easier than their husbands to obey Christ because they had already learned the lessons of submission at home. Membership statistics are notoriously unreliable, but at least twice as many women as men joined southern churches, and the ratio may have been as high as 4 to 1. The reasons for this disparity are unclear, but contemporaries argued that women were more devout because they had more sorrows than men, a greater sense of dependence, and even a nervous system better suited to spiritual commitment. Perhaps women responded to the promise of a status in God's kingdom denied to them on earth.

Perhaps, too, they understood that religion increased women's influence in the home. The image of the pious mother and wife trying to convert her heathenish menfolk was not simply a product of the evangelical imagination. Accepting the ministers at their word, many southern women asserted their spiritual superiority by begging, prodding, and cajoling men into joining the church. And this proselytizing could easily move from the private to the public sphere. During the revivals that swept through the antebellum South, converts were far more numerous among women than among men. Bolder women gave their testimonies at prayer meetings, led prayers, and spoke in tongues, despite occasional criticism from nervous preachers anxious about preserving their spiritual authority.

A short road led from churchwork to more secular forms of benevolence. The South lagged behind the rest of the country in benevolent organizations, but southern women held fairs, directed poor relief, and participated in many other activities that raised implicit questions about domestic ideology. As one wife told her husband in describing plans for a hospital benefit concert, it was silly for women to withdraw from community life simply because they married. Yet whatever the potential of such efforts, they hardly threatened male authority. "Ladies' societies" remained dependent on the support of ministers and church elders, and for the most part confined their efforts to safely conservative channels. In Charleston, for example, aristocratic women worked with poor women and orphans, not only to ease suffering but to convince the downtrodden that the local elite had their best interests at heart. The reformers' fondest hope was to turn these impoverished females into models of Victorian respectability. In a region that had few cities, women moved slowly and cautiously toward establishing reform societies outside the church. Some women engaged in poor relief, temperance work, and some agitation for educational reform, but most had more than enough to do with their own domestic duties. Numerous men praised southern women for staying at home with their families and cultivating genteel manners rather than following the busybody examples of their northern sisters.

Some southern intellectuals worried about the possible effects of northern feminism on southern women, but they need not have been concerned. Few southern women were either familiar with or sympathetic to the cause. Louisa McCord agreed with male conservatives that enfranchising women would "unsex" them. Even women who felt initially attracted to such radical ideas usually drew back from following their own reasoning to any logical conclusion. After thumbing through a French feminist novel, a young woman regretted doing so. "I do not like that kind of reading," she wrote, "it scares me of myself and makes me rebel against my lot." Therefore women as well as men kept the South "safe" from the women's rights movement.

Within the limits of social conservatism the intellectual horizons of elite women expanded during the antebellum decades. Novels enjoyed great popularity, but well-to-do parents encouraged their daughters to read histories and classical literary works along with some Greek and Roman mythology. The great majority of southern women, though, probably read little or nothing during their lifetimes beyond a few schoolbooks, the Bible, and some devotional works, if they could read at all. In 1850 the adult female literacy rate ranged from a high of 86 percent in Mississippi to a low of 64 percent in North Carolina. Overall the literacy rate was 4 to 16 percentage points lower for southern women than for southern men. New England and the Middle Atlantic states, by contrast, generally had female literacy rates above 90 percent. Functional illiteracy was undoubtedly a greater problem than the available statistics suggest because many antebellum women read nothing. Nowhere were southern class differences more apparent than in the social distance between a planter's daughter thumbing through Shakespeare and a poor white woman who could not decipher a sales receipt or sign her name.

Many upper-class fathers took a keen interest in their daughters' education and worried about everything from their study habits to their social activities. These men hoped to encourage spirited and undisciplined adolescents to grow into intelligent and respectable young ladies. In other words, they stressed the type of education that would make their daughters into successful wives and mothers. The history of women's education in the nineteenth-century South therefore became a story of brave beginnings and limited achievements. Ideological barriers did as much as tight finances to slow improvements.

Advocates of improved education for women had to be cautious in making their case. Better schooling, they argued, would improve women without changing them; the educated woman would still be the "heart" of the home, whose "head" would still be the husband. Learning science, mathematics, or Latin would not exempt women from domestic chores.

For more ambitious parents and their daughters the multiplication of female academies during the antebellum decades seemed promising. But most of these schools enrolled fewer than a hundred students and experienced serious financial troubles. Yeoman families could not afford institutions where tuition alone ran to more than $100 a year. Only the elite enjoyed the luxury of sending their children to good boarding schools.

At least the new academies and female colleges did expand educational opportunities for the daughters of the planters. Southerners still doubted that girls needed to study advanced mathematics, Latin, or Greek, but reformers called for more history, philosophy, science, and mathematics in the curriculum. During the 1850s several schools added geometry and trigonometry to their course offerings. Such ornamental subjects as painting, drawing, needlework, and music declined in importance. Surprisingly few institutions emphasized the "domestic arts." By 1850 a southern girl of means could follow a curriculum in many ways comparable to that of her brothers. Yet for the most part, women's education remained conservative, haphazard, and woefully inadequate. Most so-called colleges were nothing more than glorified academies. Despite curricular reform, tight budgets and reactionary attitudes hemmed in women on every side. The women of yeoman and poor white families had even fewer opportunities and faced the full force of social as well as sexual prejudice.

WOMEN IN THE ECONOMIC AND POLITICAL SYSTEMS

The subordination of women rested on a firm legal foundation. Despite some use of prenuptial agreements, most women gave up their property rights when they married. State legislatures slowly expanded women's property rights, but the purpose was more to protect estates from fortune hunters, and thus to safeguard the interests of women's male relatives, than to improve women's status.

Such legal disabilities made widows reluctant to remarry and even gave single women pause. Yet the road to financial independence was all but closed to unmarried women. The typical female head of household in the antebellum South owned little or no property, and for those who chose to remain unmarried, economic mobility remained a most elusive goal.

Avenues of opportunity were few. The 1860 census listed housekeeper, seamstress, and farmer as the most common female occupations, though census takers classified many women who managed farms or plantations as "housekeepers." Women who worked in their husbands' businesses were also often overlooked. But even when the undercounting is taken into account, it remains true that most women who worked outside the home labored at menial jobs. Women might supplement other family income by doing laundry or making clothes, but they could hardly make enough to support themselves or their children.

In the course of the Industrial Revolution many of the traditional female crafts, such as spinning and weaving, were transferred from the home to the factory. More and more women worked in the textile mills; by 1860 white women made up more than 10 percent of the labor force in five of the future Confederate states. On the eve of the Civil War, several thousand southern women worked in factories, but the general employment picture was hardly bright.

Educated women might teach school, if for no other reason than the respectability of the profession. But even when women overcame the expected objections of their male relatives, the classroom did not represent a golden opportunity. Some women offered private lessons in their homes, a practice that clearly tied their income to the number of pupils they could accommodate and hold. Teachers earned as little as $200 a year and seldom found the profession altogether satisfying. A handful of women wrote for a living, but with indifferent results, from both literary and financial standpoints.

Despite limited opportunities, women played an important role in the southern economy. In addition to their domestic activities, they ran farms and plantations. Although some women deplored slavery and a few even condemned the institution, historians have too often permitted this unrepresentative group to speak for a largely silent or proslavery majority. And even the appearance of antislavery sentiments could be deceiving. The famous diarist Mary Boykin Chesnut lived comfortably with both her antislavery sentiments and her slaves; she enjoyed the luxury of clean white sheets, fresh cream in her coffee, breakfast in bed, and more than enough leisure to denounce slavery in her diary. It would also be a mistake to confuse exasperation with slaves, often expressed in diaries and letters at the end of a long day, with abolitionism. Most women simply accepted slavery without thinking much about it.

A few women dealt with slaves in the most basic manner on plantations they operated. When Rachel O'Connor's husband died, probably between 1815 and 1820, she took over the management of the family plantation in West Feliciana Parish, Louisiana. Over the next quarter century Rachel O'Connor made a success of it by determination and hard work. Starting out with a single overseer for assistance, she produced as many as 150 bales of cotton annually along with corn, potatoes, and other essentials for the provisioning of her slaves and livestock. She took great pride in the care she gave her slaves, and evidently was both an effective and humane mistress. The record indicates neither runaways nor serious resistance to her authority.

Life as a slave-owning planter was never simple for Rachel O'Connor. At times she struggled to obtain vital credit, and at others she battled disease. At one point seventeen of her slaves and her overseer were down with cholera. During the 1830s she bought more land and increased the size of her operation. A confident and competent planter, by the end of that decade, upon the retirement of her white overseer, she turned his job over to a young male slave.

When age and illness slowed her down, a neighbor hired another white over-seer to give overall direction. By Rachel O'Connor's death at age seventy-two in 1846, she had built up an estate of 1,000 acres of land and eighty-one slaves. Despite the resentment of some nearby male slave owners that a female planter lived amongst them, Rachel O'Connor made her way successfully in a tough, male-dominated world.

Widows and single women made up about 10 percent of the slaveholding class. The education of these mistresses began in early childhood, when they observed how slavery worked and, if the family was wealthy, were given personal servants. And though the vast majority of white women were not ultimately responsible for the work and welfare of a slave force, work with and on behalf of slaves made enormous demands on their time and energy.

In this complicated world of black and white families, white women became active and for the most part willing participants in the slave system. Although the prevalence of the "good mistress" has been greatly exaggerated, such persons did exist. A marvelously complex paternalism, in which most white women played their expected roles, developed out of an oppressive system. Devoted mistresses paid attention to the health and general well-being of each slave. They nursed the sick and held religious services in the quarters.

But an inevitable concomitant of paternalism is condescension. The house-wife who slipped a slave child corn bread and sausage under the table was treating the child as one would a pet dog. Such "privileges" as riding in a car-riage at the foot of the mistress and sleeping under her bed bespoke more deg-radation than status. Some mistresses relied on their slaves to do the smallest tasks. The thoughtless exploitation of black labor occurred daily in southern homes, but even white women with antislavery convictions seldom recognized its significance. In hot weather slaves fanned their mistresses to keep them cool. White women pleasantly remembered such scenes; slaves remembered falling asleep and getting whipped.

Despite the close bonds that occasionally developed between mistresses and their female slaves, race and class tended to overcome sexual solidarity. Hu-mane mistresses saw their duty as attempting to civilize the blacks on their place. Such considerations led to the famous scenes of tearful women protect-ing slaves from the lash or preventing sales that would break up slave families. Yet for every woman who tried to soften the harsher aspects of the institution, there were others who did not hesitate to order whippings and could them-selves apply the lash with a will. Brutality and sadism were by no means a male monopoly. One angry mistress brutally pressed a recalcitrant slave girl's head under a rocking chair; another, in a fit of exasperation brought on by a poorly cooked potato, put out a slave's eye with a fork.

If women willingly participated in some of the most brutal acts, they were themselves victims of the system. Miscegenation, one of the great chinks in the slaveholders' moral armor, greatly troubled many white women. Yet rather than condemn slavery, most condemned black women for luring white men into sin. Rather than call into question their husbands' behavior, these women

conveniently blamed the slaves. Even Mary Chesnut concluded her famous lament on miscegenation by denouncing the promiscuity of blacks. Whatever
their doubts or possible feelings of guilt, busy women suppressed them and became absorbed by their many household duties. Most mistresses did far more to
sustain slavery than to subvert it.

The mounting abolitionist crusade elicited a defensive response from
southern women, much as it did from southern men. Women seldom discussed a defense of slavery in their diaries and letters, but many implicitly
accepted the major tenets of the proslavery argument. Southern women novelists obliquely supported slavery; only Louisa McCord made any substantial
contribution to proslavery literature. McCord's essays on political economy
in general and slavery in particular demonstrated that women could be effective polemicists.

Women of course occupied a marginal position in southern political culture.
As one writer put it, "one of [women's] highest privileges is to be politically
merged in the existence of their husband[s]." But even in public life the fiction
of marital unity sometimes broke down. Many women commented on public
issues only in their private writings or in family discussions, but yeoman and
upper-class women could be fierce partisans. The wives of politicians not only
closely followed their husbands' careers but offered astute advice on politics.
Ambitious and sophisticated women might display more drive than their husbands.

Of course women had few opportunities to express their opinions on a
more public stage, but subtle changes took place in their relations with the masculine world of politics. Beginning with the 1840 presidential campaign, women
marched in parades, attended rallies, and listened to speeches. A few even
wrote to public officials to express their opinions on controversial issues.

As sectional tensions mounted during the 1850s, women became increasingly likely to comment on political questions. A spattering of comments on the
issue of slavery in the territories became a flood after John Brown's raid, an
event that became a powerful symbol of the threat posed by antislavery agitation to southern domestic life. The election of 1860 did not arouse much female
interest, but the secession debates did. The dissolution of the Union and the
firing on Fort Sumter made many women pay attention to public events for the
first time in their lives. Perhaps even more than men, women weighed the
question of secession to see how this step would affect family and local interests. And more than many men, they worried about the bloody consequences
of disunion. Women took a more active part in family political discussions, and
a few even broke with fathers and husbands during the crisis.

Secession also gave women expanded public roles. From sporting secession
cockades to attending rallies for southern rights to sewing flags and uniforms,
women became increasingly active. To be sure, conservative social values inhibited them. Women usually refused to speak at flag-presentation ceremonies; no
one suggested they enter public life or fight for their country. The model for
female courage remained largely passive—the Spartan mother sending her men-

folk off to battle. During the secession crisis, women mouthed men's words: liberty, honor, southern rights, abolition fanatics. But they also glimpsed the human faces and future sufferings beneath the abstractions.

FREE BLACKS

Between the dominant white community and the slaves lived the free blacks. Before the Revolution they formed quite a tiny group. Statistics for the colonial era are largely unavailable and certainly imprecise, but they send a clear signal about the size of this group. Maryland in 1755 had 1,817 free blacks; as late as 1780 Virginia could count even fewer. Centered in the Chesapeake, these people had probably always been free. They or their forebears had come to the colonies as indentured servants or as laborers in some other capacity.

The Revolution had a major impact on the free black population in the Chesapeake. Without question their numbers shot up; by 1790 Maryland had 8,043 and Virginia 12,766. This substantial increase came from two sources. The lesser of the two was the freedom given slaves for military service by Maryland and Delaware. Although the number involved was small, it did add to the total, and this practice, though restricted, helped absorb runaway slaves into the growing free population. The major impetus to the growth of free blacks came from manumission. In 1782 Virginia passed a law enabling masters to free slaves by deed or by will; within a decade Maryland, Delaware, and Kentucky followed suit. Influenced by the Revolutionary ideology of freedom and inalienable rights, hundreds of masters in these states of the upper South broke the chains of their slaves. These newly emancipated blacks generally remained in the countryside to work as agricultural laborers. This was certainly an auspicious beginning, though emancipation never moved into the lower South, and even in the upper South free blacks remained a small percentage of the black population.

In the portions of the old Southwest which had been under French and Spanish control a different pattern prevailed. Louisiana and such towns as Mobile and Pensacola had free black communities that originated in liaisons between white masters and their black slaves. With the support of the central governments back in Europe, white fathers often emancipated their illegitimate mulatto offspring. The number leaped from under 200 in 1769 to 2,000 in 1800. Unlike their counterparts in the American upper South, these free blacks congregated in urban areas. They also strove to make themselves indispensable to the whites. During the Revolution the free blacks fought in Louisiana and Florida with the Spanish against the British, and in 1815 they again did battle with the invading British, this time under American authority.

After 1800, however, the growth of the free black population slowed. The enormous geographic and economic expansion heralded by the purchase of Louisiana in 1803 and by the rise of cotton changed the economic calculus of slavery. Also as time passed the ideological influence of the Revolution, never deep or pervasive where slavery was concerned, waned. Virginia in 1806 drastically tightened the 1782 emancipation law by requiring that a manumitted slave leave the state within one year or face reenslavement. Tougher laws spanned the region. They became almost totally restrictive in Kentucky, where emancipation had no legal effect until the freed slave left the state, and in Mississippi, where each individual manumission required a special act of the legislature. The size of the free black population in 1860 shows clearly just how effective nineteenth-century legislation and practice had been. Only 261,918 free blacks lived in the slave states, 86 percent of them in their traditional home, the upper South. Since 1800 the number of slaves had more than quadrupled while the free blacks increased at a considerably lesser rate, some two and a half times. The free blacks were surely not holding their own against the surge of slavery.

Free blacks found their legal situation tenuous at best. Whites systematically barred them from the rights and symbols associated with freedom, especially American freedom. Because the law presumed that all blacks were slaves, free blacks had to have documents proving their freedom. Several states restricted their movements, and all banned free blacks from certain occupations; blacks could not, for instance, enter the printing trade. They could not participate in politics or testify in court against whites. Owning guns was prohibited, and stiff criminal penalties were standard. In the public arena—in theaters, railroads, and steamboats, for example—segregation along with inferior facilities and accommodations prevailed.

In the nineteenth century free blacks remained on the economic margin. In the upper South most still lived in the countryside. Although a few became landowners—1,200 black Virginians enjoyed that status in 1860—the great majority (75 percent in North Carolina) found employment as rural laborers. Across the South free blacks generally fared much better in the urban areas, where most in the lower South lived. There the men worked at such skilled trades as carpentry, masonry, and tailoring. In the upper South quite a few were employed as factory hands. Some jobs seemed universal: men worked as waiters and women as domestics.

Free blacks did not form a phalanx; class differences surely existed among them, at times notably so. In the cities, especially in the lower South, a three-caste system grew up. A largely mulatto upper class that monopolized the best jobs available to free blacks made every effort to separate itself from the mass of poorer free blacks, few of whom had any white blood. This system was prevalent in the Caribbean but never became that strong in the South outside of older cities such as New Orleans and Charleston. Although this division was clear within the black community and to some whites, the powerful racism pervading the South ensured that the basic social lines were drawn along racial, not economic, lines. To the overwhelming majority of whites a black was a black, whether free or slave, whether mulatto or not. As a result, all free blacks teetered precariously on a precipice.

BLACK MASTERS

Despite the sharp and deep racial divide that characterized the antebellum South, a few free blacks became masters of black slaves. This group, never large, numbered some 3,600 in 1850. The great majority were artisans in such cities as Charleston, where in 1860 more than 70 percent of South Carolina's black masters resided. The slaves of most of these men were their own wives and children. A free person could purchase a spouse from a willing owner. If a free black husband owned his wife, their children were slaves, because status was inherited from the mother. When manumission statutes tightened, husbands and fathers could not easily free wives and children.

A handful of free blacks operated slave plantations just as their white counterparts did. The Metoyer family of Natchitoches Parish, Louisiana, in 1850 possessed thousands of acres and more than 400 slaves. The Metoyer clan, which traced its roots to a slave who was emancipated by her French master in the late eighteenth century, built a slave empire that rivaled all but the very largest. Most of the Metoyers married the mulatto sons and daughters of neighboring white planters, who accepted the Metoyers as fellow slaveholders, if not as equals. In their enclave, centered on the still-standing Melrose Plantation, the Metoyers constructed a Roman Catholic church, operated schools, and ran several businesses.

The South Carolinian William Ellison in 1816, at age twenty-six, gained his freedom from his owner, who was probably his father. As a slave Ellison

MELROSE, NATCHITOCHES PARISH, LOUISIANA, 1833, BUILT FOR LOUIS METOYER (Courtesy Louisiana Office of Tourism)

learned several trades, including work on cotton gins, and cotton gins became his road to wealth. Upon being freed Ellison migrated to Sumter District, where he manufactured and sold his own gins. Prospering, Ellison began to buy land and slaves. By 1860 he owned fifty-nine slaves, who worked on his plantation and in his gin shop. The local planter elite permitted Ellison to join their Anglican church, though the pew he was given was set apart from the others at the rear. Just like the children of successful whites, who tended to marry the sons and daughters of the tidewater aristocracy, Ellison's children married into the free black elite of Charleston. His commitment to the slave regime was seemingly total. He sold slaves, mostly children, and bought slaves, mostly adult males. William Ellison died in 1861, but during the war the Ellison plantation, run now by his sons, produced foodstuffs for the Confederate army.

The Metoyers and the Ellisons were exceptions to the rule. Toward the end of the 1850s the free blacks' position was shifting from perilous to critical. Free blacks just did not fit into the white South. And many whites, including those in the legislatures, began to ask questions that posed great danger to all free blacks. If, as the proslavery argument maintained and most whites believed, blacks were specially suited for slavery, then why were not all blacks enslaved? If blacks possessed uniquely slavelike characteristics, why were any blacks at all not only free but masters of slaves? Legislatures began to provide ominous answers. In 1859 the Arkansas legislature passed a law ordering all free blacks out of the state by January 1, 1860. Any who remained after that date would have a choice: either choose a master and voluntarily submit to servitude or be sold into slavery. Arkansas was not an isolated case. In their final sessions before the war both Missouri and Florida lawmakers passed similar legislation. Mississippi was on the verge of doing so. Debate in other states made it clear that the elimination of free blacks from the slave states had become a possibility. Even the Ellisons and their peers in South Carolina were not immune to the threat; they, too, feared what the white majority might do. Without question the legal status of free blacks was eroding rapidly and dangerously. The evidence strongly indicates that freedom for any blacks was about to disappear in several states. But the onset of war riveted white attention on a different danger.

LIBERTY AND HONOR

The dominant whites who threatened the free blacks were surely a diverse lot. Vast differences in wealth, education, manners, diet, and outlook on life separated the squires of tidewater plantations from the hardscrabble farmers of the mountain ridges and piney woods. At the same time, southern whites shared certain fundamental values.

As the increasing difficulties faced by the free blacks underscored, all white southerners believed in the superiority of the white race, or in white supremacy. It is impossible to exaggerate the power of race. Without question it occupied a central position in the southern view of slavery; to southern whites it made both necessary and possible the solidarity of whites vis-à-vis the black slaves. Historians have shown, however, that similar views about white supremacy held in the North, and in western Europe as well. Thus while a general conviction about white superiority defined an essential portion of southern values, it surely did not make up the whole.

Critical to understanding the southern mentality is comprehending its passionate commitment to liberty. Liberty meant the opposite of slavery, and like their Revolutionary forefathers, southerners of the nineteenth century knew precisely what slavery entailed: loss of control over one's family, loss of control over one's future, loss of control over one's very person. To white southerners confronting this stark truth, their liberty was utterly crucial. They did not separate their devotion to liberty from their knowledge of slavery. Maintaining their liberty necessitated retaining dominion over their institution of slavery. From the southern perspective, failure on that front would result in their own enslavement.

To white southerners loss of control over slavery threatened not only their liberty but their honor. In the white southern mind liberty and honor could not be pried apart. Welded together, they became the core of the southern psychology. A man who possessed liberty could call himself honorable; no free man would allow his reputation to be besmirched by dishonor. With honor gone, liberty became problematical. The absence of liberty and honor carried the awful connotation of the degraded slave. Thus for white southerners, escape from the dreaded status of slave required the maintenance of their liberty and honor, no matter the cost.

The great novelist William Faulkner dramatized the pervasiveness and power of southern honor in his story "An Odor of Verbena." Though the story takes place during the Reconstruction years, the values that influence the characters and actions are clearly antebellum. Young Bayard Sartoris, faced with avenging the killing of his father, feels the pressure of a solid wall of community conviction. Honor demands that he act. If he fails to act, Bayard's personal honor will be tarnished and he will be shamed before the community. Whites of both the upper and lower social orders, men and women, a former slave, even the killer of Bayard's father—all expect Bayard to observe the code that requires a man to preserve his honor through action identifiable by the community as well as by himself. Bayard ultimately decides against killing, but still he must confront his father's killer in order to retain both his personal honor and his honor in the community. The two cannot be separated. The values of the individual and the community reinforce each other.

It is difficult to comprehend this southern sense of honor today, for in our time honor has little meaning, even as a civic virtue. But for antebellum southerners life itself was less precious than honor. Most agreed with Andrew Jackson, who condemned the slanderer as far worse than the murderer because the murderer took only life whereas the slanderer took honor. A man who permitted slander to go unchallenged was a man shamed and degraded before his community and in his own eyes. Community opinion and personal opinion merged. Just as the collective South had to protect its honor, individual southerners had to prove that no slavelike characteristics tarnished their honor. Duels still were fought in the South long after they had disappeared from the rest of the nation. That politicians and newspaper editors made up a disproportionate share of the duelers underscores the intimate connection between the determination to protect one's private honor and the public requirement that it be guarded. With public attention riveted on them, neither politicians nor editors could ever turn aside from a challenge. The duel both permitted and demanded protection of honor.

The duel came to America with class-conscious European officers who crossed the ocean to fight in the Revolution. British, French, and German officers brought the tradition of private warfare to vindicate the honor of gentlemen. The practice impressed Americans, and not just those who lived below the Mason-Dixon line, at least not in the aftermath of the Revolution. Undoubtedly the most famous duel in American history took place in 1804 in New Jersey when Aaron Burr killed Alexander Hamilton.

The duel, however, became increasingly associated with the South. Northerners condemned dueling and it all but disappeared in the North, especially after the Burr-Hamilton contest. Officially the South took an identical stand. As early as 1802 North Carolina set the death penalty for dueling; ten years later South Carolina mandated a prison term and a substantial fine for everyone involved in a duel. All the other southern states passed similar legislation.

But the idea of the duel had penetrated to the essence of white southern society. Laws could not eradicate it. The roster of southern politicians who fought on the field of honor includes such notables as Andrew Jackson, Henry Clay, and John Randolph of Roanoke, as well as scores of individuals not so well known. These duels rarely replicated the romanticized contest of two swordsmen. Almost without exception the weapon of choice was a gun; the firearms used ranged from pistols to rifles, even shotguns. To escape legal prohibitions, duelists often slipped across state lines for their combat or met on islands in rivers separating states. Legislatures also exempted individual duelists from the penalties of antidueling laws just as readily as they passed such laws. The leading handbook on dueling illustrates the paradox of the attempt to outlaw an institution that embodied the fundamental values of southern society. Written in 1838 by John L. Wilson, a former governor of South Carolina, *The Code of Honor; or Rules for the Government of Principals and Seconds in Duelling* provided directions on such mechanics as the issuing of challenges and the duties of seconds; and it also had much to say about the high moral principles and social value of dueling.

One man's response to a duel in 1809 helps us to understand the powerful social force behind the practice. Upon hearing that Henry Clay had survived a duel, a close friend expressed delight. "Your firmness and courage is admited [sic] now by all parties," he wrote. Then Clay's companion came to the heart of the southern view of the duel. "I had rather heard of your Death," he informed

Clay, "than to have heard of your backing in the smallest degree." But this was no apostle of dueling. On the contrary, he "disapprove[d] [*sic*] Dueling in general, but it seems absolutely necessary sometimes for a mans dignity." General disapprobation salved by the unquestioning acceptance of particular necessity seems to have been the guiding principle of most white southerners.

Although the duel affected chiefly the upper orders of society, worship of the two-headed god Liberty-Honor permeated the white social order. A Scottish traveler who gave special attention to working people was convinced that southern "men of business and mechanics" tended more than their northern counterparts to "consider themselves men of honor" and "more frequently resent any indignity shown them even at the expense of their life, or that of those who venture to insult them." Daniel R. Hundley, the Alabamian who lived in the North and an acute observer of southern mores, concluded that the men in the middle order of southern society possessed "the stoutest independence" and would never allow themselves to be humiliated by anyone. In his story "The Fight," Augustus Baldwin Longstreet captured precisely the place occupied by liberty and honor among them. After Billy Stallings insulted Bob Durham's wife, Bob felt his honor tarnished and in a ritual akin to the duel he demanded satisfaction from Billy. Admitting "I've said enough for a fight," Billy accepted the challenge. Thereupon with fists and teeth the two Georgians proceeded to defend their honor.

Though men took the action, the rest of the family formed important parts of the concept of southern honor. Women seldom wielded enough power to bring honor to a family, but they could certainly bring it dishonor, especially through sexual immorality. Yet women were responsible for upholding not only the morality but the piety of the home.

Upper-class women displayed intense pride in their families, chiefly in the accomplishments of their male relatives. But at the same time, women well understood the gap between the ideals of honor and daily behavior. In casual conversations, usually with other women, they often commented on the general helplessness of menfolk, especially around the house. They often seemed skeptical of male bravado and even joked about having to obey their "lord and master." They certainly knew about breaches of honor, if not in their own households, in those of their relatives and neighbors.

If southern women differed at all from southern men on the question of honor, they possibly took it somewhat less seriously; they particularly deplored the use of violence to avenge perceived insults. One would be hard-pressed to find a southern woman defending dueling or fighting. But their relative isolation from the rough-and-tumble masculine world prevented them from confronting the complexities in the notion of southern honor. Indeed, property and divorce laws were in large part designed to insulate women from the world of competition, the better to uphold patriarchal authority.

Therefore in most senses female honor remained a negative concept, defined by the absence of scandal rather than positive achievement. A man's honor did not exactly depend on his wife's fulfillment of her traditional role, but her failure to fulfill it would at least set tongues wagging and could raise more serious questions.

By the same token, the sexual double standard helped maintain the virtue of the white woman while reinforcing the macho image of the independent-minded southern man. Although miscegenation cast dishonor on the family as well as on the guilty man, such offenses were more often than not passed over in silence or dismissed as the more or less natural behavior of highly sexed men. Despite a few notable complaints about such polite hypocrisies, these questions hardly threatened either the stability of the social order or the conventional beliefs of antebellum southerners.

Slavery as a Subject of Discussion

Slavery's position as the bedrock of the southern god Liberty-Honor meant that the South neither could nor would permit anyone else, any outsider, to control it, or even to discuss its future. Not that all white southerners agreed on every aspect of slavery. It is impossible to know precisely how many southerners at any one time or over time thought slavery a good, a necessity, or an evil. Even so, the evidence will not support the case that very many whites ever opposed the institution or felt guilty about it. Whatever the opinion of individual southerners, the collective South stood as one with the thoughtful commentator who wrote in 1833: "So interwoven is [slavery] with our interest, our manners, our climate and our very being, that no change can ever possibly be effected without a civil commotion from which the heart of a patriot must turn with horror."

Because the white South was in such complete agreement with that view, substantial public discussions about the value of slavery were quite rare. Such conversations surely occurred during the Revolutionary period, but in the debates over whether or not to ratify the Constitution, both supporters and opponents focused on the need to protect slavery. Certainly the last major discussion—and it was the first in a half century—took place in the Virginia legislature during the winter of 1831–1832. The argument against slavery had added force at that time because of Nat Turner's revolt, which had occurred in August 1831 and terrified white Virginians. Some legislators called boldly for preparations for the end of the long association between Virginia and slavery. These men—most of them from the transmontane region of the state, where few slaves lived—argued that slavery was injurious to the economy of the state and to the mores of its white citizens. These enemies of slavery also believed that the end of slavery must be accompanied by the emigration of blacks. They saw no way for free whites and large numbers of free blacks to live side by side. Other legislators emphasized the immense investment in slaves and praised the morality of the institution. They maintained that the vast sum needed to effect even gradual emancipation could not be raised. In 1830 Virginia had more than

470,000 slaves valued at around $100 million, at a time when the annual state budget totaled less than $500,000. Moreover, the supporters of slavery thought large-scale emigration utterly impractical. When the vote took place, slavery won comfortably. The questions raised about slavery had no more practical impact than they had had fifty years earlier.

The state and the legislature permitted this open questioning of slavery for two major reasons. First, at this moment Virginia and the South had not yet felt the full fury of the abolitionists' assault. Second, the questioners were not outsiders but Virginians who were upholding a Virginia tradition, though a distinctly minority one.

After the onslaught of abolition the debate was not repeated. From the southern viewpoint, any questioners aligned themselves with either abolitionists or free-soilers, both of whom southerners identified as groups who wanted to enslave the South. No white southerners who cherished liberty and honor wanted to be associated with such people; neither would the larger society permit any of its own to associate publicly with those it defined as endangering the South.

13

Political Parties and the Territorial Issue

———— ❖ ————

W hite southerners participated in a political world dominated by the two great parties, the Democratic and the Whig. Across the South in the early 1840s, Democrats and Whigs battled over economic and financial policies. The bitter scrapping over these issues at both the national and state levels seemed to herald a return to old political ways. Earlier the Jeffersonian Republicans and the Federalists as well as the Democrats and the National Republicans had divided over questions of national economic power, including a national bank and the tariff. After 1840, Whigs and Democrats took opposite sides on that same basic issue. Partisan squabbling in the states over banking and related financial matters reinforced the division in national politics. The political parties appeared to have shoved aside slavery-related topics to concentrate on economics and finance.

As the presidential election of 1844 approached, Democrats and Whigs prepared to carry on the fight over finance which had characterized state contests and congressional debates. To lead them in their newfound cause southern Whigs joined their northern comrades in uniting behind Henry Clay. Support for Clay quickly turned into adulation. As new converts to the doctrine of national economic power—Clay's American System—southern Whigs were in an extravagant mood. One of them caught it perfectly: "Clay the high comb cock. The election begins and ends. Clay is the president and the nation redeemed." The Democrats, by contrast, were defensive and somewhat lethargic. Martin Van Buren apparently would win their presidential nomination for a third time. By the end of 1843 he had vanquished all competitors, including Calhoun, who had made his strongest bid for the presidency. Most southern leaders supported Van Buren, but he had never generated much excitement among southern voters. They simply did not respond to him, even though on the slavery issue he had always done what southern Democrats had asked. Without much thought the Democrats prepared to combat Clay's nationalism with their time-honored theme of states' rights.

*T*HE POWER OF TEXAS

But it was not to be. President John Tyler enjoyed being president and wanted to remain in the White House. At the least he wanted to leave his mark. To achieve either goal he needed an issue, a dramatic one. Usually dismissed as an unimportant president, John Tyler was in fact of enormous importance. Between 1815 and 1860 only Andrew Jackson and John C. Calhoun had more influence on southern politics, and a legitimate argument can be made that Tyler ranked with the other two. A Virginian immersed in the political and plantation world of his native state, Tyler naturally thought about the South. As a veteran of Hugh White's campaign for the presidency in 1836, Tyler knew that no other issue so aroused southerners as a perceived outside threat to slavery, which, of course, jeopardized their conception of their liberty. If Tyler could succeed in stirring up the South, he might sweep past Van Buren to become the Democratic choice; if the Democrats rejected him, he might even initiate a third party based in the South.

The political hopes of John Tyler formed the background for the drive to annex Texas. After revolting from Mexico in 1836, Texas proclaimed itself an independent republic. Because American immigrants led the revolt and the new country, many people in Texas and in the United States wanted Texas to join the Union. But the existence of slavery in Texas made annexation a delicate issue. Such political considerations checked both Andrew Jackson and Martin Van Buren, because they worried about the possible effect of annexation on northern Democratic unity, but not John Tyler. Texas became his issue for arousing the South. Tyler and his advisers also convinced themselves that annexation was in the national interest. By the summer of 1843 they believed that Great Britain had designs on Texas, which included abolishing slavery and challenging the dominance of American cotton in the British market. The Tyler men, joined by Calhoun, who became secretary of state in February 1844, were confident that with Texas they could gain the attention and support of the South. They anticipated southern public opinion "boil[ing] and effervesc[ing] ...more like a volcano than a cider Barrel."

Texas could cause such a thunderous reaction because it touched the raw nerve of southern politics. The threat of abolition on their border—Texas physically touched Arkansas and Louisiana—would arouse southerners. When somebody other than themselves talked about tampering with slavery on their own ground—and Texas was practically so—southerners heard only one sound, the clanking of the shackles that would end their freedom to control their own affairs.

The force of Texas first hit the southern Democrats. The Tyler men, including Calhoun, had close ties to the Democratic party, and they still hoped to thwart Van Buren. The Tyler-Calhoun combine could hope that Texas would "unsettle all calculations as to the future course of men and parties." And it surely did; the reaction among southern Democrats was volcanic. They reached for Texas as the drowning reach for lifelines. The southern Democrats thought they had an issue that could give even Van Buren popularity. They were savoring the possibility of victory when Van Buren let loose a bombshell: he announced his opposition to the immediate annexation of Texas. Dumbfounded, southerners searched for an explanation. They never imagined that he would stand against them; always before he had done what they asked on slavery-related matters. Van Buren's opposition to Texas meant his political death in the South. Most important, he broke the party compact as southerners interpreted it. By refusing to follow the South's lead on a critical slavery-related issue, Van Buren, as one southern political observer understood, had violated "the *sanctum sanctorum*."

In the Democratic national convention of 1844 the southerners led the successful fight to deny Van Buren the nomination. In his stead the convention chose James K. Polk, a Tennessee Jacksonian who planted cotton and owned slaves. The convention also adopted a pro-Texas platform. Southern Democrats were thrilled; even Calhoun cheered. In the South the party had not known such exuberance and unity since 1828.

While the southern Democrats were overjoyed, nervousness gripped the southern Whigs, who feared the impact of Texas on their party because northern Whigs were adamantly opposed to annexation. All worried that it might lead to war, because Mexico still claimed Texas. Southern Whig senators joined with their northern colleagues to kill Tyler's treaty of annexation, but still Texas would not go away; it knocked the southern Whigs off balance. For the first time in presidential politics they felt the initiative slipping away. The Texas blitz exploded Whig unity. Southern Whigs wanted to win with Clay and their economic program, but Texas struck too deep. With *slavery* and *liberty* on everyone's lips, southerners of all persuasions responded to the issue of Texas. Whigs began to talk more and more about Texas and less and less about banks and tariffs. Not that they accepted the Democrats' call for immediate annexation, but they tried to blur partisan lines. The state convention of Georgia Whigs caught the party in motion: "We are in favor of the annexation of Texas to the United States, at the earliest practicable period consistent with the honor and good faith of the nation." Whigs ranged across the Texas landscape. Defection did occur, but it never became widespread. Many Whigs argued for annexation, with various conditions. Some remained firmly opposed. Others stayed with their leaders, who tried to straddle Texas. Pressed by northern Whigs not to deviate from his initial stand against Texas, Clay was buffeted by powerful southern winds. Hard-pressed southern Whigs implored Clay to open the Texas door, at least a bit. Trapped in these political crosswinds, Clay tried to make all happy. He published three public statements supposedly clarifying his position on Texas, but none of them satisfied anyone. By no means did Clay go all the way to the Democratic position, but he bent to the necessity of southern politics.

Texas obliterated economics. The Texas issue proved again that in the South nothing could withstand the force of a political issue closely connected with slavery and liberty. The politics of slavery made it impossible for economic nationalism to prevail over Texas as an issue. Although southern Whigs were never of one mind on Texas, it shattered their unity. And the constant Democratic pressure made its restoration impossible.

The election results confirmed the triumph of Texas. Clay carried only four states; below the border he polled fewer votes than Harrison had won in 1840. The almost 60,000 new voters cast Democratic ballots. Despite their backing away from outright opposition to annexation, the southern Whigs managed to hold only their committed vote. Because of the Whigs's variety of stances on Texas, from ardent championship to outright opposition, Clay and Polk did not offer the South a clear choice. A vote for Polk was surely an aye vote, but a vote for Clay could have been an aye, a nay, or a maybe.

Before Polk's inauguaration in March 1845, Tyler achieved his goal of bringing Texas into the Union. A joint resolution of Congress, not a treaty, authorized his action, which he took literally in the last hours of his presidency. Texas as a political issue was over, but the force it unleashed became even more potent.

POLK AND THE MEXICAN WAR

When James K. Polk became president, he approved Tyler's last-minute action. With Texas in the Union, Polk could turn his full attention to his own presidential agenda, which contained two main objectives. He wanted economic reform that would bring down the Whig Tariff of 1842 and revive the Independent Treasury of Van Buren's time; and he wanted to ensure the continued westward expansion of the United States. In Polk's mind Texas was not the end but the beginning. He especially coveted California, which still belonged to Mexico.

Polk accomplished his economic goals. Congress, voting along partisan lines, recreated the Independent Treasury and passed the Tariff of 1846, which significantly decreased duties. This triumph of Democratic economic measures really ended the Democratic-Whig rivalry on that front, a rivalry that in the South had begun with the Panic of 1837 and increased with the rise of the Clay Whig party. In the South a national bank and the tariff largely disappeared as political issues.

With them went state financial issues. After 1845 the political rhetoric in the South no longer contained copious references to banks, specie payments, and allied subjects. In the mid-1840s the general upturn in the southern economy, led by rapidly increasing prices for cotton and slaves, dulled the cutting edge of financial weapons. Political resolution of such divisive topics as the chartering of new banks also helped alter the language of southern politics. By 1847 banking was no longer a rousing issue in any of the southern states.

As financial concerns receded, Polk's determination to expand the nation's borders created an issue of great power. His decision to send units of the United States Army under Major General Zachary Taylor to establish the Mexican-Texan, or Mexican-American, border on the Rio Grande and to reach out for California led to war between Mexico and the United States.

When Polk's drive westward brought on armed conflict with Mexico, Democrats, south and north, supported their president. The Democratic party had adopted western expansion as its own natural child. Democrats saw in the westward movement a magnificent opportunity to strengthen the nation and their party. They certainly envisioned no internal party problems from expansion. The declaration of war by Congress in May 1846 occasioned little disaffection. The one notable defector from the party was conspicuous by his loneliness. John C. Calhoun had been an enthusiastic supporter of Polk during the campaign and during the first year of his presidency. He was prepared to back Polk on a defensive posture toward Mexico, but he would not countenance what he called offensive moves. But Calhoun rallied almost no one to his standard. Southern Democratic politicians to a man, including most Calhounites, stood behind the war.

While the southern Democrats sang the praises of expansion and beat the drums of war, the southern Whigs knew little joy. For them Texas had been the worst kind of political medicine. Instead of invigorating the Whigs, it sickened them and their party. For southern Whigs, Texas represented more than the loss of a presidential election they had expected to win; it wounded the party by sundering northerners and southerners. While southern Whigs had divided minds about Texas, northern Whigs vehemently opposed it. While the politics of slavery forced southern Whigs to bend toward Texas, northern Whigs proudly proclaimed their adamant opposition. With Texas finally behind them, southern Whigs wanted no more divisive issues, and they rightly feared that an attempt to add more land to the Union would lead to nothing but disaster. They knew it would strain their party, perhaps this time to the breaking point. Besides, they feared that the South and the nation might also suffer, if expansion led to general sectional antagonism.

The outbreak of war between the United States and Mexico in May 1846 stirred great excitement. The general response across the South approached jubilation. The many newspapers that had clamored for war, especially those in the Mississippi Valley from St. Louis to New Orleans, were overjoyed. The government's call for volunteers to serve in Mexico resulted in an overwhelming turnout. Tennessee was asked to provide 3,000 troops, but nearly 30,000 came forward to join up. Kentucky filled its quota within two weeks after Congress declared war. In Baltimore it took only thirty-six hours to raise the allotted number of citizen soldiers. Many Mississippians complained bitterly that so few of them were called to put on the uniform and follow the flag. These were not isolated instances. In the first year of the war almost twice as many officers and enlisted men went into the ranks of the United States Army from the slave states as from the free states, roughly 45,000 to 24,000. Such prominent southern politicians as Gideon Pillow, a Tennessee associate of President Polk's, and John A. Quitman, an important Mississippi planter and politician, became well-known political generals.

The war proceeded just as most Americans, northerners and southerners, assumed it would. After his initial victorious engagements in the Rio Grande Valley, General Taylor plunged into northern Mexico where he defeated the Mexican army in major battles at Monterrey in September 1846 and again at Buena Vista in February 1847. After those triumphs, which made the Louisiana resident a national hero, the war in the north subsided while the main action shifted southward. In the spring of 1847 an expeditionary force under Major General Winfield Scott captured Vera Cruz, on the eastern coast. After the fall of Vera Cruz, Scott, in a brilliant action, drove inland toward Mexico City, which fell to the Americans in September. The capture of Mexico City basically ended the fighting. The United States had won a great military victory, and the South had surely had a part in it. Of the combat casualties, which totaled some 1,800 killed and wounded, over half came from the slave states.

During the course of the war the South's fervor for it declined somewhat. Among the Democrats, Calhoun never reconciled himself to what was happening. Most Whigs were never happy with either the expansionist policy that brought on the confrontation with Mexico or the declaration of war itself. As the war wore on, they increased their criticism of Polk and his handling of the conflict, but they were careful never to criticize the army. The southern Whigs in Congress believed it their patriotic duty to support the military effort as long as Americans were in combat. The Whigs also remembered what happened to the last party to oppose a war; after the War of 1812 the Federalist party disappeared. At the same time they worried about the political and national difficulties that would result from the expected American victory. In view of their uneasiness about the war, the southern Whigs found themselves in a somewhat uncomfortable position as they celebrated American victories and cheered the winning generals, Scott and especially Taylor.

THE RISE AND FORCE OF THE TERRITORIAL ISSUE

The major postwar problem crystallized before the end of hostilities. If the American victory that all assumed would take place did in fact occur and brought with it the additional territory that Polk went to war to obtain, then the political battle lines were clearly drawn. In fact, they had been staked out early on. When Zachary Taylor first sent his soldiers splashing across the Rio Grande into Mexico, an obscure Democratic congressman from Pennsylvania introduced a measure that would put his name in the history books. On August 8, 1846, as Congress considered an appropriations bill to provide money for negotiations on territorial adjustments with Mexico, David Wilmot proposed an amendment that would forever prohibit slavery in any territory won from Mexico. The immediate response was not partisan but sectional—the South no, the North yes. Still in the summer of 1846 no one was quite sure what the Wilmot Proviso meant. Some thought it simply a sniping attack on President Polk from disaffected Democrats who would soon quiet down. Others feared that the proviso could be a harbinger of a vicious fight over the handling of all future territories. Some thought it terrible and some considered it wonderful. Some wished the proviso would just fade away, but it was not about to do so. The Wilmot Proviso embodied too much that was fundamental about the United States.

The locking of the door to expansion by an antislave or free-soil majority had massive implications. For southerners the Wilmot Proviso carried one ominous message: the South could no longer control its own affairs; the South had lost the power to direct its own destiny. The North would have the South bound by the same shackles that the white South clamped on its black slaves.

For white southerners territorial expansion was not just another political issue that they might win or lose. Expansion had had a central place in southern history since the colonial era. For two centuries new land had offered southerners the traditional avenue to wealth and position, whether in the piedmont, across the Appalachians, in the Southwest, or beyond the Mississippi. Southerners of every economic and social position had taken advantage of the opportunity provided by plentiful, cheap land. Those who aspired to yeoman and planter status as well as those who had already made it saw the West as the place to make it even bigger. For the last antebellum generation neither this attitude toward new land nor the reality of its rewards had diminished. The West was still a magic kingdom drawing southerners with its promises.

The issue of territorial expansion involved more than social mobility and economic opportunity. In an expanding nation the South had always recognized that the extension of southern boundaries was vital for the maintenance of the political power the South must have if it was to protect its interests and guarantee its liberty. In the morning of the Constitution southern leaders believed that the chief benefits of territorial expansion would accrue to their section and permit it to dominate the new nation. Long before the 1840s, however, the southern leadership recognized that continued expansion would not bring domination but still was necessary to keep the South abreast of a North booming in population and wealth. Through the Missouri crisis and into the 1840s the South managed to maintain its political leverage, though it was falling behind in population and total wealth. When both Texas and Florida were admitted to the Union as slave states in 1845, the slave South demonstrated that it had not fallen off the pace. At the end of the decade there were fifteen free and fifteen slave states.

In the southern view, that parity was critical, for political power formed a basic prerequisite for the liberty of a free people. As the South viewed political reality, the closing of the territories to slavery foretold a dismal political fate. New states carved from the territories closed to slavery could only augment the political might of the anti-South forces that had imposed the proviso. Then a people who had not been able to prevent the proviso might become powerless over their own slaves. An increasingly mighty anti-South majority could decree the destruction of slavery itself. Such a catastrophe, if it was to come at all, probably lay far in the future, but temporal distance made the possibility no less real to white southerners. In the late 1840s the South faced the distinct possibility of its first defeat ever on a major slavery question. Never since the Constitutional Convention of 1787, when the South clearly drew the line, had it been vanquished on a momentous slavery issue.

The proviso touched even more than the political power that the South had grown accustomed to and expected. A formal ban on slavery in the territories insulted southerners as individuals and as a community. The proviso's adoption by the rest of the nation, acting through the Congress, stigmatized the South as unclean, as dishonorable. With the proviso as the law of the land, the South would become the American Ishmael, denied full participation in a great national undertaking because it had an un-American social system and held un-American values. White southerners prided themselves on their patriotism and cherished their honor, and the thought of such banishment outraged them. Just as individual southerners unhesitatingly protected their own honor, the collective South struck back at the proviso and all that it implied. The southerners exclaimed that they would never allow anyone to pin a badge of degradation on them. In the southern mind, free-soilers or provisoists became as vile as abolitionists. Most southerners never separated the two groups, because both desecrated the South's image of itself, challenged the right of the South to govern its own destiny, and ultimately threatened the South with destruction of its liberty. Talk of severing the Union should the proviso pass became commonplace.

Whether the insistence of the southerners on their right to take their slaves into the territories meant that they wanted or expected to do so remains a vexing question. Throughout the history of expansion white southerners who responded to the attraction of the West had been accompanied by black slaves. Never had white southerners thought of expansion apart from their institution of slavery. In the southern experience, the two had always converged. In the late 1840s southerners spoke both negatively and positively about carrying slaves beyond Texas, and it is impossible to enumerate precisely the numbers in each camp. The possibility of actually taking slaves into the territories, however, was not the crucial issue in the national debate—at least, not between the introduction of the Wilmot Proviso in 1846 and the passage of the Kansas-Nebraska Act in 1854. During those eight years southerners fought to establish the right to take slaves into the new territories, or at least to prevent the denial of that right. Honor demanded and liberty required not only the struggle but victory. Calhoun expressed the mind and heart of every southerner in 1849:

> What then do we insist on is, not to extend slavery, but that we shall not be prohibited from immigrating with our property, into the Territories of the United States, because we are slaveholders; or, in other words, we shall not on that account be

disenfranchised of a privilege possessed by all others, citizens and foreigners, without discrimination as to character, profession, or color. All, whether savage, barbarian, or civilized, may freely enter and remain, we only being excluded.

Eventually, of course, the political motive so much a part of the southern battle against the proviso would necessitate new slave states. Even if the South secured affirmation of its rights in the territories, the South could not sit quietly by and watch all the common territory turned into free states. When the opportunity arose in the late 1850s to create a slave state in Kansas, the South employed all its political power in an attempt to do so.

THE PARTISAN RESPONSE

By 1847 the Wilmot Proviso held indisputable title as the chief public topic in the South. It occupied first place on the list of concerns for both Democrats and Whigs, neither of whom lost any time in attacking the proviso. A Democratic governor proclaimed "our unalterable purpose of maintaining our rights, at all hazards and to the last extremity." Not to be outdone, a leading Whig newspaper editorialized: "We shall indulge in no bluster or bravado on the [proviso]. Of this, however, the North may be assured, that, whenever the South shall be called upon to *act*, it will present an undivided, stern, inflexible front to its fanatical assailants."

At the same time that the two sides denounced the proviso, each sought some way to keep the national party intact. Party integrity could be maintained if southerners could get their northern colleagues to bypass the proviso or at least meet it obliquely. If not, then the party would cease to serve its major function, guarding southern liberty. Such an outcome guaranteed a political death certificate for the afflicted party.

Along with that danger, the proviso crisis offered a genuine opportunity to southern partisans. If either the Democrats or the Whigs could resolve their intraparty difficulties in a manner clearly advantageous to the South, then they could place their southern opponents in an extremely perilous political position. From the 1790s the first commandment of a successful party in the South had been to protect southern liberty. The politics of slavery only intensified that fundamental law of southern politics. Southern Democrats and southern Whigs strove to place each other on the political chopping block.

The proviso posed immediate problems for southern Democrats. Because it came from certified Democrats, southern Whigs had a ready-made weapon, which they promptly used. Charging that the Democratic party harbored the originators of the proviso, southern Whigs attacked southern Democrats for coddling enemies of the South and for caring less about the safety of the South than about winning place and reward. The hard-pressed Democrats knew exactly the response required by the politics of slavery. Not only did they have to assert unequivocally their loyalty to the South, they also had to prove they were not in the clutches of the provisoists. As they searched for a solution to the pro-viso problem, the southern Democrats met head-on the influence of Calhoun, whose followers, with close ties to Democrats in several states, worked to get the southern Democrats to give their northern brethren an ultimatum.

The final Calhounite–southern Democratic position rested on two pillars. First, they publicly pledged "determined resistance" against the proviso "at all hazards and to the last extremity." Next, they announced that southern Dem-ocrats would support no presidential candidate "who does not unconditionally, clearly, and unequivocally declare his opposition to the principles and provi-sions of the Wilmot Proviso." These two pledges merged to become the dogma of southern Democrats down to the upheaval of 1860.

The southern Democrats hoped for an accommodation with their northern colleagues both because tangible political rewards were associated with national political power and because they still believed that the party provided the surest vehicle for southern safety. Most major northern leaders desired a settlement on the proviso just as fervently as the southerners. As a result, they kept the provisoist minority huddled against the shore, away from the full current. The northerners recognized the potential political dynamite of the proviso, but they also believed that their constituents would stay with them if an acceptable al-ternative to the proviso could be devised.

Searching for a way around the proviso, the Democrats came up with pop-ular sovereignty. Presented by northerners eager to retain their southern con-nection, popular sovereignty became the formula that won the allegiance of Democrats in both sections. Based on the supreme Democratic principle that the people were sovereign, popular sovereignty first declared the Wilmot Pro-viso unconstitutional and then insisted that the settlers in a territory, not the Congress or anyone else, should make the decision on slavery in their territory.

Popular sovereignty added to its political allure by leaving the time frame for the crucial decision on slavery conveniently vague. Although popular sov-ereignty implied that settlers could accept or reject slavery during the territorial stage, its advocates did not talk about territorial legislatures. The doctrine also asserted that all settlers had to abide by the basic principles of the Constitution. Northerners who took the implication as the chief thrust could argue that pop-ular sovereignty allowed the first territorial legislature to ban slavery if it chose to do so. But southerners who stressed the constitutional-principles theme as-serted that a decision on slavery had to await statehood, for territories lacked the authority to decide so fundamental a question as slavery. Only a state had that authority. For southern Democrats, popular sovereignty thus became an extension of their traditional doctrine of states' rights. The obvious inconsis-tency and vagueness inherent in popular sovereignty provided much of its po-litical beauty. Professing loyalty to popular sovereignty, albeit in different ver-sions, both northern and southern Democrats could banish the Wilmot Proviso from their political vocabulary.

Popular sovereignty clearly delighted the vast majority of southern Demo-crats. Only the Calhounites dissented. Calhoun correctly defined popular sovereignty as an ingenious political construct designed to avoid the sectional confrontation he lusted for and believed the proviso would provide. But few southerners shared his desire for confrontation. To them popular sovereignty seemed a perfect doctrine—liberty without confrontation. Southern Democrats believed they could defend it as a guarantee for the South; it also enabled them to represent their northern comrades as denouncing the hated proviso. When the national party, in convention in 1848, placed its imprimatur on popular sovereignty, the southerners cheered. As they saw it, the Democratic party had shunted aside the threat to southern liberty posed by the Wilmot Proviso. To the South, southern Democrats shouted that only they had a foolproof way to guarantee southern liberty, the doctrine of popular sovereignty.

Southern Whigs found themselves perched on the same political precipice occupied by their Democratic opponents. Although they could and did blame the Democrats for giving birth to the proviso, they also had to contend with political reality—every northern Whig in Congress had voted for it. The Wilmot Proviso hit the Whig party even harder than Texas. Northern Whigs supported the proviso just as vigorously as southern Whigs opposed it. Despite this clear sectional division, the national Whig party had not taken an official stand on the proviso. Until it did, southern Whigs had no reason to give up their party. If, like southern Democrats, they could neutralize the proviso, then the Whig party would remain the source of political reward and the guardian of the South it had been since birth. But with the northern leadership more eager to make the proviso its issue than to placate the South, it was most unlikely that the party could reach agreement on a stated formula such as popular sovereignty.

The gods of politics favored the southern Whigs, or so it seemed. The war in Mexico that the party had opposed created several heroes, one of them very special. Major General Zachary Taylor, who had commanded the successful American forces in the early engagements along the Rio Grande and during the invasion of northern Mexico, vaulted from obscurity to instant fame. Though a legitimate military hero, Taylor possessed other characteristics immensely attractive to southern Whigs. A professional soldier, he called Baton Rouge, Louisiana, home; moreover, he owned a cotton plantation in Mississippi and more than a hundred slaves. The likes of Taylor had not been seen in the South since Andrew Jackson—an authentic military hero who was a slaveholding cotton planter. Southern Whigs had never before come close to possessing such a political property. For them Taylor was a godsend, and they quickly made him their champion. That Taylor had no political experience, really no political past of any kind, bothered the southern Whigs not at all. They looked to the future and saw it dominated by the slave-owning hero Zachary Taylor, resplendent in his new Whig uniform.

Zachary Taylor caught on like wildfire. With Taylor as the party nominee, southern Whigs would not need a public party pronouncement against the proviso. They could bring their cause to southern voters in the form of Zachary Taylor, whose name, home, occupation, and possessions were all identified with the South. All by himself Taylor would prove conclusively where the Whig party stood on the proviso; neither he nor the Whig party had to say a thing.

If this political magic was to work, the northern Whigs would also have to accept Taylor. Although the extreme antislavery men refused to back a slaveholder, many northern Whigs, remembering the voters' liking for victorious generals, found Taylor attractive. Besides, they were fumbling for issues; the economic catastrophe they had predicted under Polk had not occurred. Placing the party on record against the proviso and pushing full steam against it would win votes in the North but fracture the party. Moreover, attractive candidates were scarce. If they ran Taylor as a national hero and as a good Whig who as president would surely not veto a congressionally approved proviso, the northern Whigs thought they could win.

The Whig factions made their peace by uniting behind a warrior. The convention that nominated Taylor adopted no platform and thus kept its silence on the proviso. The Southerners were thrilled. To persuade southern voters of their party's ability to defend the South in this moment of crisis they could offer no doctrine, but to their minds they had something vastly superior—a southern hero.

CRISIS AND COMPROMISE

In 1848 the parties in the South asked for votes in return for trust and protection; the Democrats offered a platform, the Whigs a man. The man triumphed. Although each party held its loyalists, Taylor attracted some Democrats and a large share of new voters. He won more than 51 percent of the popular vote and carried states all the way from the Mason-Dixon line to Louisiana. With an energetic dedication to the politics of slavery, the southern Whigs saw themselves standing where the Democrats had stood twenty years earlier—in a position to dominate the South.

They were confident that their southern chieftain would guide them into the political promised land. Under Taylor's leadership they expected to solve the territorial problem that consumed the South, and in a way that would benefit the South and the Whig party. If this vision was to become reality, Zachary Taylor had to act like a good southerner and pull the northern Whigs along with him. The southern Whigs had no doubts.

The Mexican War ended in the spring of 1848, when Mexico ceded to the United States more than 500,000 square miles of its territory, including California and the bulk of the modern Southwest. This outcome translated the Wilmot Proviso from theoretical possibility into hard reality. Events gave neither the nation nor its political leaders time to absorb the implications of the cession before they had to make critical decisions regarding its governance and the status of slavery in it. The gold rush to California in 1849, which excited everyone, mandated prompt governmental action.

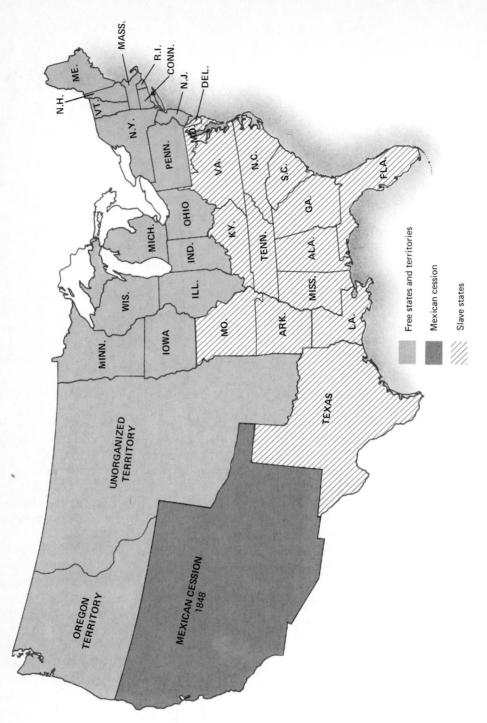

MEXICAN CESSION, 1848

The question of California brought about the crisis of Zachary Taylor's presidency. Taylor wanted to bring in California as a state immediately, to be followed promptly by the rest of the Mexican Cession as a second state, New Mexico. Everyone realized that immediate statehood meant free states, because not enough time had elapsed since the end of the war for more than a handful of slaves to be carried into the area. As a result, the South would be completely shut out of the cession. Southern Whigs cried out in anguish. Although before Taylor's inauguration a number of them had pushed for statehood as a way to solve the terrible problem of the territories, they had backed away. Southern Democrats' definition of Taylor's proposal as an executive proviso and a strong shift in southern public opinion made it impossible for southern Whigs to defend their president's policy. Shocked and bewildered, they implored Taylor to recognize their political plight. But the old general was steadfast; he refused. With leading southern Whigs and Taylor at loggerheads, shouts about impeachment and military force reverberated as far as the White House. Taylor told the beleaguered southerners that his policy would not change, and if they did not like it, he did not care. Southerners, the president made clear, could march with him or he would surely march without them.

Precisely why Zachary Taylor took such an uncompromising position on the territories is exceedingly difficult to understand. Early in his administration, northern Whigs, including proviso stalwarts, became dominant; Whigs below the border had no strong voice among Taylor's advisers. The reasons for that situation are not at all clear. What is clear, however, is that the southerners assumed too much, and while they assumed, others acted. Some historians have argued that Taylor set out to build a new party. More likely his stance was heavily influenced by his view of the West and by his own army career of some forty years. Taylor did not believe that slavery could prosper in the West, and he saw the territorial issue as nationally divisive. When he decided on his policy, he viewed it as in the national interest, and with the habit of command cultivated by four decades as an army officer he announced that his way was the only way, no matter the pleas and needs of southern Whigs. Thus Taylor was an unusual southerner—a large slaveholder who staunchly defended slavery in the states but just as adamantly opposed giving southerners even the right to carry their slaves into the territories.

Taylor's statehood policy and his absolute refusal to consider any alternatives led to a national crisis. To many southerners the president's program eliminated them from national territory paid for in no small part by their blood and treasure. And in fact soldiers from the slave states suffered more battle-related casualties in Mexico than their comrades from the free states. Prodded by Calhoun, who seized what he perceived as an opportunity for his sought-after confrontation, bipartisan groups of southerners called for a meeting in Nashville in the spring of 1850 to consider ultimatums to be presented to the North. Talk of disunion moved out into the open. Out of the crisis came the first serious emergence of fire-eaters, as secessionists were sometimes called. For the fire-eaters the Union could never furnish safety for the South, because to them

TYLER, POLK, AND TAYLOR: THREE
SOUTHERN PRESIDENTS WHO POWER-
FULLY INFLUENCED THE COURSE OF
SOUTHERN POLITICS

John Tyler (Virginia State Library)

the Union aimed to destroy southern liberty. Rejecting Calhoun's desire to ensure southern safety in the Union, they strove to break up the Union, the ultimate act of independence.

Into this political whirlwind stepped Henry Clay. Back in the Senate for the
first time since his defeat for the presidency, Clay reported that "the feeling of
disunion" and sectional animosity "is stronger than I had hoped or supposed it
could be." Convinced that Taylor's insistence on a free California and a free
New Mexico might tear the country apart if nothing were done to mollify angry
southerners, Clay proposed a broad-based compromise. For the North he
would admit California as a free state and halt the slave trade in the District of
Columbia. For the South he would organize the remainder of the Mexican Cession into two territories, New Mexico and Utah, with no mention of slavery,
and enact a tough fugitive slave law that would give the federal government
responsibility for apprehending and returning slaves who had escaped to the
free states. Clay completed his compromise proposals by providing for a settlement of the troublesome Texas–New Mexico boundary dispute.

Clay's compromise deranged parties in the South. Believing that the proposed compromise offered them a haven from the storm caused by Taylor's policy—after all, the fugitive slave bill would affirm the legitimacy of slavery and
the territorial measures would shunt aside the hated proviso—the southern

James K. Polk (Brady Collection, National Archives)

Zachary Taylor (National Portrait Gallery, Smithsonian Institution, Washington, D.C., Gift of Barry Bingham, Sr.)

Whigs leaped to support it. That leap did not restore party unity, however, for most northern Whigs remained with President Taylor, who opposed the compromise. Great irony resulted—antislavery northern Whigs were supporting a southern slaveholding president while southern Whigs fought him desperately. The Democratic response was exactly the opposite. Searching for a way out of the crisis, the northern Democrats considered Clay's package reasonable and backed it. Southern Democrats, heavily influenced by the Calhounites, charged that Clay's compromise sold out the South. The key was California, and to a prompt admission of a free California they cried never.

The strain showed within the South as well as in the national party alliances. Although the great majority of southern Whigs stood behind Clay, a number of leading Democrats who felt that Calhoun had led their comrades astray made common cause with their former Whig opponents. In the three Deep South states of Alabama, Georgia, and Mississippi, party lines broke down completely. There a Democratic minority joined a Whig majority to form Union parties, while a few Whigs combined with most Democrats to form Southern Rights parties. These new combinations had two basic results. In the

short term both traditional parties disappeared; in the long term the Whig party
never reappeared.

From the winter all the way into the summer of 1850 the public mood was
tense. The compromise seemed stalled in Congress. President Taylor remained
unswerving in his determination to bring California in as a free state without
concession to the South. When his opponents accused him of endangering the
Union, he talked of using military force. Then, in July, the sudden death of
Zachary Taylor eliminated an immense obstacle to compromise. A new parliamentary strategy in Congress enabled the compromise to pass: each of its parts
was made into a separate bill. When each bill reached the desk of the new president, Millard Fillmore of New York—never a Taylor confidant—he signed every one into law. The Compromise of 1850 was a fact. Across the country the
decreasing tension was audible; most Americans, North and South, rejoiced.

Without question an immense crisis had passed. With Congress stalemated
and President Taylor unbending, the foundation for a ferocious confrontation
was in place, but a legitimate secession crisis could have occurred only without

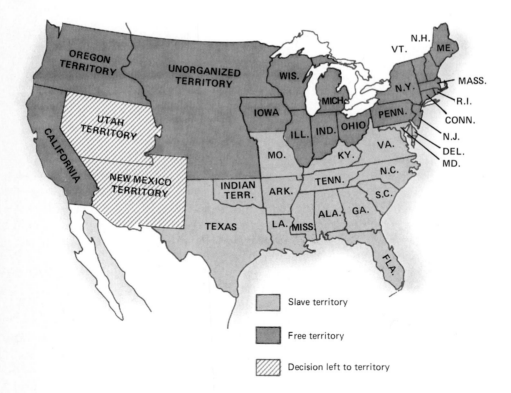

THE COMPROMISE OF 1850

the compromise and with Taylor. Without Taylor and with the compromise, the nation could relax. The overwhelming majority of southerners considered themselves good Americans. They had no desire to leave the Union provided their prized liberty remained secure. The organization of New Mexico and Utah did not overtly deny southern rights in the common territory. And extremely important, the Fugitive Slave Act affirmed the Americanism of the South's peculiar institution. No wedge had been driven between southern and American.

THE ILLNESS AND DEATH OF THE WHIGS

Southerners fell in line behind the compromise, though some did so reluctantly. At every turn southern voters overwhelmingly cast their ballots for candidates and parties that endorsed the compromise. Politicians who had spoken vigorously against it banked their rhetorical fires. The success of the compromise doomed the Southern Rights parties in the Deep South, which had staked their political careers on their opposition to it. The fire-eaters wandered into the wilderness, where they would languish until the end of the decade. Still, southerners were emphatic that their acceptance of the compromise did not at all mean that they valued the Union above all else. The famous Georgia Platform, written by adherents of the compromise in Georgia, affirmed the strong southern accent with which support for the settlement was expressed. The platform proclaimed that Georgia—read the South—would resist even unto secession, if necessary, should Congress prohibit slavery in either New Mexico or Utah, or weaken or repeal the Fugitive Slave Law, or refuse to admit a new slave state, or act against slavery on federal property in a manner "incompatible with the safety, and domestic tranquility, the rights and the honor of the slaveholding states." For southern Americans the Union provided no safe harbor unless it explicitly protected southern interests and honor.

The presidential contest of 1852 underscored the triumph of the compromise. In the South both parties announced their support for it. Southern Democrats who had fought the compromise made peace with those who had supported it, and the reunited party presented a solid front to southern voters. Nationally all Democrats rallied around Franklin Pierce of New Hampshire, who made clear his respect and support for southern institutions as well as his backing of the compromise. Southern Whigs had more problems because many of their northern counterparts still refused to fall in line behind the compromise. In an attempt to mask this serious internal division, the Whig party once again turned to an old general, Winfield Scott, like Taylor a hero of the Mexican War. But the recent experience with Taylor muted many southern Whigs' enthusiasm for Scott. The turmoil in Whig ranks pointed to the possibility of an electoral disaster, which is precisely what occurred. In both popular and electoral votes Pierce crushed Scott, who could not even hold the border. Scott carried only Tennessee and Kentucky; Pierce took everything else, with a larger percentage of the popular vote than any other Democrat had won since Andrew Jackson. No other Whig presidential nominee had ever done so poorly in the slave states as Scott.

This disaster compounded the immense political difficulties the southern Whigs faced. Since the late 1840s they had found it more and more difficult to maintain their political position in the states, even those that had been party strongholds. In state elections in 1852 and 1853 the Democrats devastated the Whigs. Below the border southern politicians vied for eleven governorships, eleven senates, and eleven houses; after 1853 the Whigs controlled only two, the houses in North Carolina and Tennessee. Congressional elections for the Thirty-third Congress, which convened in December 1853, only added to the Whigs' misery. The states below the border elected sixty-five representatives, but no more than fourteen were Whig. In state after state Whig leaders lamented the "decisive breaking up of our party," and almost all of them blamed the ascendency of antislavery northern Whigs for the calamity.

With the Whigs reeling, the Democrats seemed to be moving again toward dominance of southern politics when yet another mighty shock struck the South and the nation. The compromise had barely become national policy when the territorial issue flared up again. This time it had to do with part of the Louisiana Purchase, the Nebraska Territory (basically the present states of Nebraska and Kansas). The trouble began innocently enough. The march westward brought the need for governmental organization in Nebraska, and such expansionist politicians as Senator Stephen A. Douglas of Illinois, Democratic chairman of the Senate Committee on Territories, pushed for congressional action. That should have posed no problem, certainly no sectional problem, for Nebraska was clearly above the Missouri Compromise line that supposedly settled the slavery question in the Louisiana Purchase. Certainly Douglas started out with that view in 1853. But a number of southerners believed that if popular sovereignty had been good enough for New Mexico and Utah and had become the stated policy of the Democratic party, it should also govern the organization of Nebraska. Then southern Whigs, in almost their last thrust with the politics of slavery, proposed the specific repeal of the Missouri restriction against slavery. After much discussion, including a talk with President Pierce at the White House, Senator Douglas agreed to modify his bill by declaring the Missouri Compromise prohibition null and void and by creating a second territory, Kansas as well as Nebraska. The Kansas-Nebraska Act easily got through the Senate in March 1854, but the House took another ten weeks while a bitter struggle took its toll on both parties. The northern Democrats divided; many went with Pierce and Douglas, but an equally substantial number refused to sanction what they perceived as a breach of the Missouri Compromise. Party unity took a substantial blow, and the repercussions were still evident in 1860. The northern Whigs in Congress to a man voted against Kansas-Nebraska, and to make matters even worse for the southerners, the northerners clamored to make their opposition to repeal of the Missouri Compromise line a partisan issue against the Democrats.

For the South, Kansas-Nebraska was a Pyrrhic victory. The passage of the Kansas-Nebraska Act contributed enormously to the growing anti-South feeling in the North and to a political realignment already under way. In the North, free-soil forces, nativism, and anti-Catholicism were pushing toward party reorganization. Kansas-Nebraska propelled that shift. It led directly to the death of the Whig party, which opened the political doors for a new anti-Democratic party. In the North two major contenders, the Know-Nothings (or the Americans) and the Republicans, competed to succeed the Whigs. Nativism in all its manifestations was the prime concern of the Know-Nothings, while the Republicans emphasized free soil and its corollary, antisouthern attitudes.

By the end of 1854 the proud, once powerful Whig party had disappeared as an effective political force in the South. Continued defeats in state elections underscored the party's pathetic condition—"floored, routed, battered, bruised, and whipped," as one loyalist described it with dismal accuracy. And the key reason for that plight was the stiffening antisouthern stance of northern Whiggery. Through its activities between 1849 and 1854 northern Whiggery had demonstrated that it had little sense of southern rights and honor as the South understood them. The impossibility of representing the party as a guardian of the South weakened the commitment of the party faithful and resulted in an avalanche of defeats at the ballot box. Southern Whigs who had always demanded that northern Whigs follow their direction on slavery-related issues had no intention of reversing roles. A prominent spokesman captured the essence of the southern Whigs' predicament: "The Southern Whig cannot stand on a northern platform."

Just as national issues had given birth to the Whig party, so they presided over its death. Local financial issues and intrastate sectionalism could not provide the keystone for the Democratic-Whig system. At both birth and death national issues with particular southern meanings and manifestations were in the ascendancy. The southern Whigs drew the flaming sword of sectional politics to gain their political identity, and they died by that same sword. Party legitimacy in the South derived solely from the ability to protect southern liberty, a power southern Whigs could no longer claim for their party. A party stalwart spoke truthfully when he lamented that the Kansas-Nebraska Act "put an extinguisher upon the Whig party."

THE KNOW-NOTHING EPISODE

The disintegration of the Whig party did not return the South to 1800 or to 1828, when one dominant party claimed the allegiance of almost every politically active southerner. The intense partisanship stemming from two decades of Democratic-Whig rivalry could not and did not disappear. After all, southern Whigs believed that they had left their party because it first left them. There was no mad rush to join the Democrats, though some Whigs did make the shift.

Most, however, yearned for a new political home in a new party that would offer them political sustenance while it honored southern rights.

Almost immediately this hope was fulfilled. As the Whig party disintegrated, the Know-Nothing party spread across the South. It spread so rapidly that it almost seemed fully grown at birth. The adherence of numerous Whigs and major Whig newspapers made it possible for the Know-Nothings to mount campaigns against the Democrats in every slave state in 1855.

The Know-Nothing party arose in the Northeast out of nativist sentiments. It articulated the powerful antagonism many native-born Americans felt toward the immigrants, chiefly Irish, who poured into the seaboard cities in the late 1840s and early 1850s. The Roman Catholicism of most of the newcomers added a religious bias to nativist thinking. The name Know-Nothing signified the successful nativist appeal to working-class men who perceived their jobs and status endangered by the new immigrants. Many of these people believed the Irish were engaged in a conspiracy engineered by the Roman Catholic church to undermine the American republic. They responded in like fashion; clandestine meetings, esoteric rituals, and pervasive secrecy heightened the party's appeal and gave meaning to its name: when questioned about its activities, its members to a man claimed to know nothing about it. Know-Nothings claimed that only they cared seriously about the plight and future of the average working American.

In the South party ideology was not so crucial. With neither large-scale immigration nor a substantial Roman Catholic population, except in Louisiana and the border state of Maryland, southerners cared much less about the ideological tenets of the new party. Even in Louisiana political reality tempered its impact, for the heavily Roman Catholic sugar-planting area, which had been a Whig bastion, became a center of Know-Nothing activity. Southern Know-Nothings wanted most of all a national party with which they could confront the Democrats. The party's northern wing would have to be controlled by conservatives who would make it a citadel against free-soil sentiment. The entire party, then, would have to stand for popular sovereignty in all territories and for the Fugitive Slave Act. Otherwise, the Democrats would destroy the Know-Nothings in the South. Southern Know-Nothings strove to get the national party to meet its needs. The contest over a slavery plank wracked the party's national conventions in 1855 and 1856. In 1855 the southerners got a declaration they approved, but in so doing antagonized many northerners. Then in 1856 the northerners won out. Northern and southern Know-Nothings could not unite on a slavery position that could survive in the politics of slavery.

The southern Democrats constantly slammed them as being unreliable friends of the South. Know-Nothings had no doubt about the political effectiveness of the "battering ram" of slavery used against them. The Know-Nothing party had a short, unhappy life in southern politics. In the state elections of 1855 its candidates were soundly whipped, except along the border. When the presidential election of 1856 came along, they fared no better. The Democrats, with James Buchanan of Pennsylvania, the last in a long line of northern Democrats with southern ties and proclivities, smashed the Know-Nothings, even though they had as a candidate the former president Millard Fillmore, once championed by southern Whigs. Carrying every state but Maryland and winning almost 60 percent of the popular vote, the Democrats sent the Know-Nothings reeling. After the debacle of 1856 the Know-Nothing party was finished as a major contender. It could not survive exposure to the politics of slavery.

After the rapid demise of the Know-Nothings, no new party arose in the South to take its place. The fleeting career of the Know-Nothings indicated that the northern connection so critical for southerners in a national party no longer existed, at least not outside the Democratic party. Aside from northern Democrats, no substantial number of northerners seemed available to participate in a national party dedicated to preserving the southern view of parties. Even so, not all southerners identified themselves as Democrats, though more and more former Whigs and Know-Nothings moved into the party. Those who refused to shift expressed their opposition in a variety of local parties, often called simply the Opposition party. Although they did use local as well as national issues to plague the Democrats occasionally, they never made a national connection. They were not even unified in the South. Certainly they posed no major threat to the dominant Democrats. The Democrats, however, had trouble enough outside the South. The emerging Republican party, a northern phenomenon, which in 1856 had bested the Know-Nothings in the free states, challenged the orientation and power of the Democrats. Within the Democracy itself the smoldering discontent over sectional policy threatened to become a conflagration. The flash point was Kansas.

14

The Crisis of the Union

❖

*I*n the South the disintegration of Whiggery heralded a return to an older version of southern politics, one-party domination. In the North, however, the demise of the Whig party resulted in a new kind of politics—a completely new party that exploded the traditional politics of national parties. The Republican party was strictly a northern party that made no effort to hide its regional identity. Never before had a major party been so thoroughly northern in its orientation and approach to politics. Starting out in opposition to the Kansas-Nebraska Act, the Republican party called on the North to assert its strength or forever be ground down by what it called "the slave power." By late 1856, when it ran its first presidential race, the Republican party had become the chief competition for the Democrats in the free states. Though it lost the election, the Republican party showed impressive strength across the North. Almost overnight it had become a potent political force.

SOUTHERN REACTION TO THE REPUBLICAN PARTY

Southerners of all persuasions were horrified by the emergence of the Republican party. The party platform of 1856, which emphasized the virtues of the Wilmot Proviso while condemning slavery as a "relic of barbarism," reinforced the southern perception that the new party made its stand on an "avowed and unrelenting hostility to the domestic institutions and the equal constitutional rights of the Southern States." Republican orators "poured forth a foul stream of vituperation upon the southern people," and "left no means, however wicked, untried to excite irreconcilable hatred of them in the minds of the people of the North." Even the possibility of a Republican president terrified most southerners.

The rise of the Republican party so traumatized southerners because its electoral success destroyed the traditional arrangements that to southerners had secured their liberty. No southerners, except for a few in the border states, either ran for office as Republicans or helped formulate party policy. Moreover, with their appeal aimed solely at the North, the Republicans' strategy for political victory needed the South not at all, even to win the presidency. No major party had ever so completely repudiated the South. Although neither the Federalists nor the National Republicans enjoyed a strong southern base, each counted prominent southerners among its adherents and each tried to win southern votes. From the southern perspective, the Republican party loomed like a giant tidal wave ready to obliterate the political world finely crafted by three generations of southern politicians. A Republican victory in a national election would mock the essence of liberty, local control. Accordingly, southern eyes saw in a potential Republican triumph a mortal threat.

For southerners the Republicans compounded their sins by not only threatening their liberty but insulting them in the process. When Republicans claimed that slavery violated the American creed, they made white southerners pariahs in their own land. But southerners proudly identified themselves as Americans; they wore their American heritage as a badge of honor. This casting of doubt on their tribal credentials southerners viewed as an unforgivable slander. With their good name slandered, southerners believed their liberty already jeopardized, for in the South good name and integrity of reputation were the personal hallmarks of free and honorable men. Facing what they could characterize only as an outrageous and unprincipled assault on their institutions, their values, their patriotism, and their liberty, the collective South denounced the Republican party.

The existence of the Republican party stiffened commitment to the basic mission that had always given legitimacy and nobility of purpose to political parties in the South—protection of southern interests and liberty in the nation. Now southern politicians confronted a major political foe with the publicly avowed mission of shackling southern power. Proclaiming that it intended to force the South to conform to its vision of the nation, the Republican party announced that its primary aim was to curb the illegitimate power of the South. Never before had southern politicians faced such an ominous challenge.

That challenge reinforced the general mission of defense and protection. Opposition parties immediately began to question Democratic stewardship of southern interests. The politics of slavery had not died with the organized Whig party; the forces it expressed were too fundamental. Every opposing political group slashed at the Democrats for losing sight of their sacred duty—to protect the South. As they had been doing for decades, the Democrats countered vigorously. Even though their opponents were but pale shadows of the once formidable Whigs, the Democrats went after them for their betrayal of the South— betrayal because they preferred to win office and snipe at the Democrats rather than join forces to present a united front to the new determined enemy. According to the Democratic script, the Opposition parties really aided the Republicans. But the Democrats could not simply attack; they also had to defend their unwavering commitment to southern liberty. Kansas provided the opportunity and the requirement.

THE TRAUMA OF KANSAS

After the passage of the Kansas-Nebraska Act, the Territory of Kansas opened for settlement. As in most other such areas, the majority of settlers who poured into Kansas was not interested in the sectional conflict. They wanted land of their own and a better living. But ardent partisans, northerners and southerners, saw Kansas as critical for the future. Each group wanted Kansas to end up on its side, either free or slave. As a result, zeal squeezed out moderation; moderates were unable to manage events or politics in Kansas. Groups of marauders burned, pillaged, and murdered in the name of a larger good. They turned the territory into what many called Bleeding Kansas, a violent microcosm of the sectional crisis. A free Kansas formed a major rallying cry of the Republican party. For many southerners, especially southern Democrats, Kansas became a contest with the hated Republicans.

Confrontations occurred in Washington as well as in Kansas. In May 1856, Senator Charles Sumner, Republican of Massachusetts, delivered in the Senate a long, angry speech titled "The Crime against Kansas." The crime, according to Sumner, was the South's effort to bring slavery to Kansas—in his terms, the "rape" of Kansas. As he lashed out at the South, Sumner also made abusive references to the senior senator from South Carolina, Andrew P. Butler. Butler's cousin, Representative Preston Brooks, took offense at Sumner's remarks and determined that Butler's honor had to be protected. And because Butler was in South Carolina, Brooks decided that he would stand for his kinsman. Two days after the speech Brooks entered the Senate chamber, walked up to Sumner at his desk, and announced that he would punish Sumner for insulting his cousin. Thereupon he proceeded to beat Sumner over the head with his gutta-percha cane. With blows raining upon him and blood spilling about his face, Sumner bolted up, wrenching the desk from the floor, stumbled about, and collapsed. Brooks continued to pound him until others pulled him away. Immediately Sumner became a Republican martyr to the barbaric slave power while the delighted Brooks won the plaudits of southern zealots and his constituents, who reelected him unanimously and gave him a new cane with the inscription "Use Knock-Down Arguments."

In Kansas territorial politics became so inflamed that proslavery and free-soil camps refused to participate in the same political process. From this bitterness emerged the Lecompton Constitution. In 1857, when proslavery forces decided to hold a constitutional convention in preparation for statehood, free-soilers boycotted it. Meeting in Lecompton, this convention adopted a proslavery constitution. Aware that antislavery men significantly outnumbered them, the proslavery men did not submit the issue of slavery to a general referendum, in which it would surely have been defeated. They allowed only a partial referendum; Kansans could vote on the future admission of slaves into the territory, but they could not express an opinion on the slaves already there.

Holding true to Kansas form, the free-soilers did not vote. These facts were as well known in Washington as in Kansas.

For southern Democrats the Lecompton Constitution required a major decision. As Democrats they recognized it as the alleged fruit of popular sovereignty, the gospel of their party. But popular sovereignty meant the wishes of the majority, and the southern Democratic leadership knew full well that no majority in Kansas desired the Lecompton Constitution. They also knew that in a fair vote Kansans would repudiate it. These tainted credentials made acceptance of the Lecompton Constitution extremely difficult for many northern Democrats. Having staked their political future on popular sovereignty, most northern Democrats were prepared to persevere with it despite Republican cries for free soil. But the political potency of those cries made it impossible for the bulk of the northern Democrats to accept the handiwork of Lecompton, a mockery of popular sovereignty. If the southern Democrats made an all-out effort for Lecompton, the ensuing struggle would threaten party unity.

On the other hand, southern Democrats realized that the Lecompton Constitution provided an opportunity to add a slave state to the Union without further ado. The South had not had such an opportunity since 1845. Many southerners felt that if they lost on Kansas, they might never have so good a chance again. Kansas did border on slave territory; it abutted Missouri and was just northwest of Arkansas.

Southerners also believed that if a slave Kansas were refused admission, the great battles over constitutional rights would have been fought in vain. This was especially true because of the southern victory in the Dred Scott case. Handed down by the United States Supreme Court in March 1857, the Dred Scott decision gave constitutional sanction to the southern position on slavery and the territories. The majority decision was written by Chief Justice Roger B. Taney, a Marylander placed on the Court by Andrew Jackson. Although Taney prepared the decision for the seven-man majority, the other six wrote concurring opinions. The two dissenters also filed opinions. Thus all nine members of the Court went on record, confusing the issue more than they clarified it. Still the basic conclusions reached by Chief Justice Taney were clear enough, though scholars have questioned his arguments. Two of them were most crucial: (1) blacks, even free blacks in free states, were not and could not be citizens because the Constitution did not consider them so; (2) the Missouri Compromise was unconstitutional because Congress had no power to exclude slavery from any territory.

Partisan politics also influenced southern Democrats' stance on the issue of Kansas. Their opponents had been attacking them for not caring enough about the South. The interests of the South, according to the Opposition script, aroused little concern among southern Democrats angling for reward and place in the corrupt administration of James Buchanan. If the southern Democrats allowed a new slave state to slip through their grasp, they would hand their opponents a golden political issue. In this atmosphere, party stalwarts in the states pressed the leaders in Washington to act.

Thus both ideology and politics propelled the southern Democrats to demand acceptance of Lecompton and the admission of Kansas as a slave state. When they moved to make these demands party policy, President Buchanan and his administration wheeled into line, but the southerners could not nudge their northern comrades into a united stand. The ablest and most popular northern Democrat, Senator Stephen A. Douglas of Illinois, had made popular sovereignty his political creed ever since Kansas-Nebraska; he had stumped the North for it. And he could not accept the mockery Lecompton made of his doctrine, certainly not with the Republicans mounting a major campaign for his Senate seat. In his march away from Lecompton and the southerners, Douglas led a sizable number of northern Democrats.

Douglas's defection was a grave matter for southern Democrats. His opposition not only decreased the chance that Congress would admit Kansas under the Lecompton Constitution; it also represented the disloyalty of a man southerners had thought a staunch friend. Moreover, Douglas's action challenged the southern conception of the party and its rules. For the first time since Van Buren's rejection of Texas in 1844, a major northern Democratic leader had refused to accept the South's demands on a key slavery issue. But whereas the southerners had overpowered Van Buren, they could not move Douglas.

Despite vigorous efforts, the southerners failed to obtain congressional approval for Lecompton. In control of the Senate, they and the administration stalwarts did win on Lecompton there, even though Douglas opposed it; but they were unable to gain passage in the House, in no small part because of the Douglas Democrats. To camouflage their embarrassing defeat, they managed to have the Lecompton Constitution returned to Kansas for a popular referendum. Although Lecompton was dead, the southerners were able to claim that Congress had not summarily dismissed their policy.

The southern Democrats needed that face-saving device. The Oppositionists savaged them over Douglas's apostasy, over party defections in the House, over the defeat of Lecompton. They kept asking what had happened to the vaunted prosouthern Democratic party. Even the compromise provided ammunition to be used against them. Now they were blasted for betraying principle for lucre: "How harshly does the word [compromise] grate upon the Southern ear. With what unctuous sweetness does it roll from the lips of aspirants for federal position."

The experience of Lecompton devastated the southern Democrats. Although they claimed the party still belonged to them and it did have control of the Senate as well as the administration, the party had been tattered. With Douglas as outcast, a glaring gap cut through the party's northern front. And southern rage only widened the gap. Furious with Douglas and eager to make an example of him, the southerners set out to destroy him. The party was more fractured than it had been since Jackson's second term, when massive defections helped create the Whig party. Battered and fragmented, the Democratic party limped toward 1860.

Economic and Industrial Growth

While the southern Democrats were suffering political setbacks, the economy of the South was growing and prospering, even booming. The dominant agricultural sector knew real prosperity. Production of cotton, sugar cane, and tobacco increased significantly and prices either stayed firm or advanced. By 1860 the value of southern agricultural products reached beyond $525 million. In the 1850s southern farmers and planters experienced the best of all possible agricultural worlds—increasing production with stable or increasing prices.

Not surprisingly, a general optimism governed the mood of the agricultural South. A significant reason for this positive outlook was the widespread conviction that ample, productive land lay yet uncultivated within the borders of the 1850 South. Most southerners believed that they already had within reach the additional land necessary to sustain growth in the agricultural economy and to ensure continuity in the broad landholding pattern, which guaranteed opportunity both for an increasing population and for those squeezed out in other areas. Not only politicians trumpeted the good times; sober-minded agricultural journals also expressed general optimism about the South's economy. Most writers for the journals predicted an exceedingly bright future for southern agriculture.

Without question agriculture dominated the southern economy, but in the last two antebellum decades significant industrial growth occurred. This growth was initially spurred by the Panic of 1837, which severely depressed cotton prices until the mid-1840s. From just over $53 million in 1840, capital invested in manufacturing jumped to $93.6 million in 1850 and then leaped to $163.7 million in 1860. During the 1850s the value of manufacturing output shot up 79 percent, to $186.9 million. This development, however, was not evenly distributed. Industry had become an important part of the economy in Virginia and Kentucky but it was barely visible in Arkansas and Florida. On the whole, the border states and the upper South had a more substantial industrial plant than the lower South. Even so, the cotton South registered impressive relative gains, though the absolute numbers remained small.

In comparison with the rest of the country, however, the South lagged far behind in industrial growth. In 1860 the slave states accounted for 15 percent of the value of manufactured goods produced in the United States; the eleven states that were to form the Confederacy contributed but 10 percent. In that same year the per capita value of New England's manufacturing output was $149.47, in the middle states $96.28, in the Northwest $37.33, and in the South only $17.09.

The South's relative underdevelopment does not negate its significant and increasingly visible gains. Industrialization had made a strong beginning and a variety of industries were prospering in the South. The bellwether of nineteenth-century industrialization, the railroads, had certainly advanced into the South. In the early days of railroading the South could boast the longest road in the world—the South Carolina Railroad, which in 1833 covered the 136 miles between Charleston and Hamburg, a village on the Savannah River opposite Augusta, Georgia. In the 1830s attempts were also made to connect Charleston with the Ohio Valley by crossing the Appalachians. Conflicting political pressures hindered that effort, and the Panic of 1837 struck its death blow. In fact, the panic hampered all railroad construction.

By the 1850s, however, railroads were beginning to cover much of the South, especially east of the Mississippi. Alabama provides a superb example of what was happening in the South. In 1850 the state had only 100 miles of railroad, costing around $2 million. Between 1850 and 1860 the mileage leaped to 610 at a cost of $15 million, raised chiefly from public and private sources within the state. Alabama was a microcosm of the railroad boom sweeping the South. In 1860 more than 10,000 miles of railroad, five times more than in 1850, tracked across the future Confederacy. These railroads were no match for the trunk lines between the Atlantic seaboard and the Northwest, which were reshaping national transportation patterns, but one of these lines, the Baltimore and Ohio, had its eastern terminus in the border-state city of Baltimore. Most of the southern routes went from port cities back into farming country. On the eve of secession a major intersectional artery was being completed, the Illinois Central, which linked New Orleans with Chicago and the Northwest. By the end of the antebellum era few east-west roads existed. Charleston and Savannah were connected with Memphis via Chattanooga and Atlanta, and from Memphis a road ran through Chattanooga and Knoxville on to Richmond. But in both instances several lines, not a single trunk line, made these connections possible.

The massive growth of railroads demonstrates not only southern economic development but also the South's commitment to the industrial component of its economy. Without substantial assistance from state and local governments, this burst of railroad building would not have occurred. Legislatures and localities provided enormous sums for railroad projects. To 1860, the state of Virginia had put up $24 million and Tennessee $17 million. The westernmost southern state, Texas, was also deeply involved in helping railroads; by 1861 the legislature had contributed 5 million acres of land and authorized $1.8 million in state bonds. In one notable instance a state actually went into the railroad business. Although Georgia was surely friendly to private railroads, it built and operated the Western and Atlantic, which connected Atlanta and Chattanooga. Completed in 1851, the Western and Atlantic earned between $800,000 and $900,000 annually during the next decade, and more than half of the money was profit. Across the South (exclusive of Maryland and Missouri) the states invested over $81 million in railroad construction and support while counties and municipalities invested a total of approximately $55 million. These numbers leave no doubt that southerners believed iron rails essential for their economic future.

Other prominent southern industries included ironworks, tobacco processing, and textiles. The iron industry in the South dated back to the eighteenth century. Its colonial capital was Virginia, which retained that title throughout

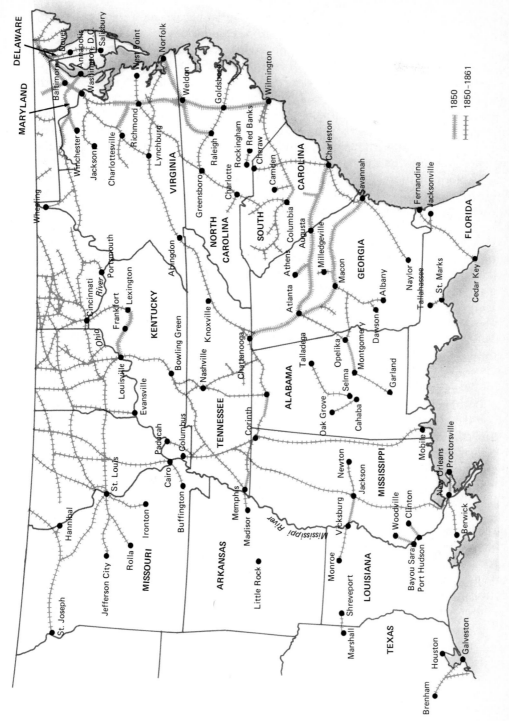

RAILROADS IN THE SOUTH, 1850–1860

Legend:
- 1850
- 1850–1861

DELAWARE

MARYLAND

Baltimore
Dover
Annapolis
Washington, D.C.
Salisbury
West Point
Norfolk

Wheeling

Winchester
Jackson
Charlottesville
Richmond
Lynchburg

VIRGINIA

Weldon
Goldsboro
Wilmington

Raleigh
Greensboro
Rockingham
Red Banks
Cheraw
Charleston

NORTH CAROLINA

Charlotte
Camden

SOUTH CAROLINA

Columbia
Augusta

Savannah

Fernandina
Jacksonville

FLORIDA

Portsmouth
Cincinnati
Ohio River
Frankfort
Lexington

KENTUCKY

Abingdon

Athens
Milledgeville
Macon
Albany

GEORGIA

Naylor
Tallahassee
St. Marks
Cedar Key

Louisville
Evansville
Bowling Green
Nashville
Knoxville
Chattanooga

TENNESSEE

Atlanta
Talladega
Opelika
Montgomery
Dawson
Garland

ALABAMA

Oak Grove
Selma
Cahaba

Mobile
Proctorsville

Paducah
Columbus
Corinth
Memphis
Madison

Cairo
Buffington

St. Louis

Hannibal
Ironton

MISSOURI

Jefferson City
Rolla

Little Rock

ARKANSAS

Mississippi River

Newton
Jackson
Vicksburg
Woodville
Clinton

MISSISSIPPI

Monroe
Shreveport
Marshall

LOUISIANA

Bayou Sara
Port Hudson
New Orleans
Berwick

St. Joseph

TEXAS

Brenham
Houston
Galveston

Frankfort

the antebellum decades. As the industry grew larger and more sophisticated, Richmond became the most important iron-manufacturing center in the slave states. Although Virginia's production soared by almost 200 percent in the 1850s, it remained far behind that of Pennsylvania, the national leader.

Virginia and North Carolina dominated the tobacco industry. In 1860 their factories turned out more than $14.5 million worth of processed tobacco. Fully 60 percent of all plug and smoking tobacco produced in the United States came from these factories. Cigars were made chiefly in the North, and cigarettes did not appear until after the Civil War. Plug or chewing tobacco stood first among tobacco products. Its use was so ubiquitous that spittoons were provided even on the floor of the United States Senate. Favorite brands had hordes of loyal chewers; one of them, Wedding Cake, was shipped from Virginia to England and Germany as well as to American distribution centers such as Baltimore and New York.

The southern textile industry originated early in the nineteenth century, but substantial development did not take place until the 1840s. When cotton prices collapsed following the Panic of 1837, investors turned from cotton fields to cotton mills. In North Carolina alone thirty-two mills were founded during that decade. By 1860 textile mills dotted the fall line from Virginia through the Carolinas and Georgia down to Alabama. The fall line provided most advantageous locations for textile mills, as it provided the water power that ran them. Although southern textile mills did not begin to outproduce the New England mills until late in the century, by 1860 between one-fifth and one-fourth of the national output was accounted for by the slave states.

The South also provided a home to numerous other industrial enterprises. Several involved the processing of southern agricultural products. Rice mills and sugar mills were found mostly in South Carolina, Georgia, and Louisiana, the center of rice and sugar cane farming. The milling of wheat and corn ranked among the leading southern industries. While small mills spanned the region, Baltimore and Richmond were the leaders; Richmond claimed one of the largest grain mills in the world. At rope walks in Kentucky and Missouri the hemp crop was transformed into rope. Sawmilling and the naval stores industry exploited one of the region's most widespread and valuable resources, its forests. The mining of gold in Georgia, of coal in Virginia, and of salt chiefly in Virginia and Kentucky added another dimension to the southern industrial scene. In one area of manufacturing the South had a national monopoly: the building of cotton gins. Remarkable individuals led the southern industrial effort; among the most notable were William Gregg, Joseph Reid Anderson, and Daniel Pratt.

INDUSTRIAL LEADERS AND SUPPORT FOR INDUSTRY

William Gregg was a vigorous apostle of southern industrialism. Born in Virginia in 1800, Gregg moved around until 1824, when he settled in South Carolina. He became a highly successful jeweler in Charleston and Columbia. After a tour of New England in 1844, he returned to South Carolina convinced of the virtues of industry and determined to build up the textile industry. In a pamphlet called *Essays on Domestic Industry*, published in 1845, he advocated the development of manufacturing in the South by the employment of the poor whites in the countryside. Gregg argued that in their current occupations, mostly marginal farming, these people were not making a positive contribution to the economy, but as factory workers they could have a significant effect on the growth of southern industry. He also believed that industrial employment would improve their moral and social condition. Factory work, Gregg thought, should be for whites only; in his judgment, slaves should remain in the fields.

Gregg did more than advocate; he also acted. In order to demonstrate the validity of his ideas he opened a mill in Graniteville, South Carolina, just east of Augusta, in 1846. At Graniteville he replicated the New England mill village. He constructed eighty-five cottages to house his workers. He built a school and instituted a compulsory attendance policy; Gregg himself occasionally acted as truant officer. He promulgated rules for the morality of the village and what he saw as the uplift of the inhabitants. Dancing and drinking were prohibited; churchgoing was encouraged; picnics and lectures on personal improvement

WILLIAM GREGG, TEXTILE ENTREPRENEUR (Courtesy South Caroliniana Library, University of South Carolina)

were featured. The village at Graniteville provided homes for some 300 local employees, who worked under a superintendent and foremen brought down from the North. These workers produced chiefly cheaper grades of cloth, which had a substantial southern market, and some finer goods, which were sold in both the South and the North. Gregg's Graniteville turned out to be a profitable cotton mill; it paid dividends ranging from 7 to 18 percent every year until the Civil War.

Just as Gregg was the most prominent individual in textiles, Joseph Reid Anderson dominated the iron industry. A Virginian educated at West Point, Anderson went to work for Tredegar Iron Works in Richmond in 1841, at age twenty-eight. Seven years later Anderson became the president of Tredegar. Under Anderson's leadership Tredegar grew from a small foundry into one of the largest and best-equipped ironworks in the nation. The company manufactured steam engines for sugar mills and for numerous other enterprises. Securing federal contracts to provide cannon for the United States Navy, Tredegar by 1860 had produced and sold 1,300 of them. Railroads were large customers; Tredegar supplied them with spikes, rails, and even locomotives.

In the 1850s Tredegar employed 800 workers, a figure topped by only three other ironworks in the country. Anderson's decisions about his labor force were important not only for his company but for the whole of southern industry. Unlike Gregg, he had no reservations about using slaves. He made extensive use of them, buying some and hiring others. When white workers went on strike, Anderson fired them and brought in more slaves, who were trained by white foremen. A number of white southerners had claimed that slaves could never be trained to work in an iron mill or any other sophisticated industrial plant. Anderson proved those naysayers wrong. By 1848 slaves held most of the jobs,

GREGG'S TEXTILE MILL, GRANITEVILLE, SOUTH CAROLINA (Courtesy of South Caroliniana Library, University of South Carolina)

JOSEPH R. ANDERSON OF
TREDEGAR IRON WORKS
(Library of Congress)

both skilled and unskilled, in the rolling mills. Twelve years later one-third of the slaves were paddlers, heaters, and rollers; others worked as blacksmiths, strikers, teamsters, and common laborers. Performing effectively, slaves at Tredegar held back neither technological improvements nor profits.

Daniel Pratt, unlike Anderson and Gregg, was not a native southerner. Born in 1799 into a New Hampshire farm family, Pratt learned the carpentry trade as a youth. At twenty he journeyed to Georgia, where he worked first as a carpenter and then for a company that made cotton gins. After a dozen years he moved to Alabama, where in 1838 he founded Prattville, just north of Montgomery. At Prattville, Daniel Pratt presided over an industrial village very much like those he had left behind in New England. In his new village Pratt established several enterprises, including a gristmill, a lumber mill, a textile mill, and a carriage factory, but it was for the manufacture of cotton gins that the village and its founder became famous. As early as 1851 the 200 laborers Pratt employed to make cotton gins produced some 600 gins annually. Pratt accounted for fully 25 percent of the total production of cotton gins. On the eve of the Civil War his property at Prattville was capitalized at more than $500,000.

Gregg, Anderson, and Pratt did not preach the gospel of industrialism to an empty church. As the investment in railroads makes clear, most southerners were eager to back industrial development. An enthusiasm quite like the boosterism usually associated with later years pervaded the South. The principled apprehension that had led the Jeffersonians to oppose the growth of industry and cities was relegated to a minority of ideologues. Even the Democratic party generally adopted the industrial course, though that decision did prompt grumbling and occasionally outright opposition from some of the party faithful. Neither the anti-industry ideologues nor the unhappy Democratic partisans could blunt the thrust of industrial development. The southerners who cheered the railroads and the factories had not turned their backs on agriculture. Most of them repeatedly acknowledged the supremacy of agriculture in the South. A substantial portion of the capital invested in industry came from planters, who had no intention of leaving their plantations or of becoming economic and social vassals to anyone. Spokesmen for industrial growth asserted that industry would buttress agriculture and would increase prosperity. Noting the political contest with the North, proindustry southerners insisted that industrialization also promoted the interests of the South.

No one boosted southern industrial growth more vigorously or more effectively than James D. B. De Bow. Born in Charleston in 1820, De Bow graduated from the College of Charleston and practiced law for a few years before he found his real calling. After attending a commercial convention De Bow decided he wanted to publish a commercial journal in a place with a more vigorous economy and enterprising spirit than his home city. He chose New Orleans, and in January 1846 he brought out the first issue of *De Bow's Review*. Although in the beginning De Bow and his *Review* struggled, by the end of the decade both had become rousing successes. By 1850 *De Bow's Review*, with almost 5,000 subscribers, had one of the largest circulations of the magazines published in the South. The *Review* concentrated on improving and developing the southern economy. De Bow insisted that industry and agriculture complemented each other. To his mind, the South needed vigor and growth in both sectors if it were to reach its economic potential. An energetic champion of slavery and southern rights, De Bow did not believe that industry threatened either. On the contrary, he argued that only significant industrial development would guarantee the preservation of southern rights and institutions. As a promoter of southern industrialism De Bow had no peers in his time.

COMMERCIAL AND URBAN DEVELOPMENT

Banks have an important role in any expanding economy. According to the conventional wisdom, the few banks in the South were poor and dominated by planters hostile to industrial growth. Current scholarship, however, casts considerable doubt on that traditional interpretation. Southern banks grew at healthy and respectable rates. Between 1840 and 1860 the South matched the rest of the country in growth rates of the number of new banks and in increases in deposits and circulating notes, though it lagged somewhat behind the other sections in the values of its loans. These banks supplied an adequate medium of exchange and financed a wide range of projects, chiefly agricultural but industrial as well.

Southern banks were not monoliths. The South had branches of the Bank of the United States during its lifetime, state banks, and private banks, both chartered and unchartered. The banks' chief problem in assisting economic development came in such states as Alabama and Tennessee, where politics heavily influenced their operations. Certainly no sectionwide planter elite worked to prevent banks from participating in commercial and industrial activities. And southern banks surely participated in them.

Thoughts of industry and banks usually bring cities to mind. The South before 1860 has not generally been considered fertile ground for cities. Without question the South was overwhelmingly rural, but so was the North, though it had a larger urban population than the South. Although the South could not match the North in large urban areas, still southern cities occupied an important position in the region. The most notable cities included older ones, such as Charleston and New Orleans, as well as St. Louis, which seemed to spring up almost instantaneously in the 1840s. Between 1800 and 1850 the South outpaced the North in the growth rate of the urban population as compared with the growth rate of the entire population. In 1850 the slave states claimed six of the fifteen largest cities in the country; in 1860, five.

These urban areas were not distributed evenly across the region. The border states claimed the largest, Baltimore, along with three others in the top half-dozen. New Orleans provided the single member of that group located in the lower South, but half of those in the first ten were in states that seceded. At the same time five states lacked a town with more than 10,000 people—North Carolina, Florida, Mississippi, Arkansas, and Texas. Of the ten largest cities, all but two—Richmond and Washington—were either seaports or river ports. So were most of the major northern cities. Until mid-century water afforded the chief mode of transportation, but when railroads began to challenge steamboats, the inland towns and cities began to assume more importance.

In the 1850s a second tier of towns and cities rose toward prominence. Several served as seats of state government. Just as important, they became crossroads of the rails spreading across the region. Among these cities were Columbia, Montgomery, Jackson, Chattanooga, and Atlanta.

The economic base of southern cities was commerce; banking and trade were significant activities. Originally water-borne commerce, both river traffic and ocean shipping, formed the heart of the trade that gave vibrancy to the cities. The arrival of the railroads had no adverse affect on the coastal and river ports; in most instances, railroads either complemented or supplemented shipments that had previously moved by water. Railroads did, however, influence the types of goods the cities handled. The opening of trunk lines between the Atlantic seaboard and the Northwest, for example, greatly reduced the grain

MAJOR SOUTHERN CITIES, 1860

traffic on the Mississippi, and that change had a considerable impact on New Orleans. Still the massive increase of the cotton crop kept both the quantity and the value of trade in New Orleans on the rise.

The activities and problems of southern cities were similar to those in the North. Southern city dwellers organized professional associations and benevolent societies. They joined literary societies and fraternal organizations. Theater, which in the older cities dated back to the colonial era, flourished. Civic pride often helped build and always gloried in first-class hotels, such as the St. Charles in New Orleans. Issues of public safety, fire protection, sanitation, and disease concerned city folk everywhere in the country. Because of the South's warm, humid climate, the link between poor sanitation and the spread of disease posed a particular threat to southern cities, especially those in the lower South. Yellow fever and cholera epidemics terrified all residents of coastal cities; 10 percent of the population of New Orleans died when yellow fever struck in

1853. Ignorance about the close tie between the lack of sanitation and the prevalence of disease ensured serious problems, which would remain until the germ theory of disease triumphed after the Civil War.

One notable factor differentiated southern cities from those in the North: the presence of slaves. Some historians have argued that urban anonymity and the inability of masters to exercise tight control over their bondspeople in heavily populated areas undermined the institution. Little evidence supports such a conclusion, however. It is true that on the whole, urban slaves enjoyed more freedom from their masters' authority than their country counterparts did, mainly because the work of artisans and domestics often took them away from their masters' premises. But the fact of the slaves' blackness and the presumption that all blacks were slaves sharply restricted their activities. Urban slavery in the 1850s was certainly not dying. Though the slave population declined in some Atlantic seaboard cities, it increased in many interior ones. The best explanation seems to be the level of the need for slaves in the countryside. Good times in agriculture increased the demand for slaves, and owners either transferred them from urban occupations to agricultural operations or sold them.

One of the most important functions of towns and cities has gone largely unnoticed by historians. It was there that the planters conferred with bankers, industrialists, lawyers, merchants, and factors who made up the rest of the southern elite. Nowhere else could these seemingly diverse groups come together to discuss the business, financial, and political matters that concerned them all. Thus in a real sense towns and cities helped unify the diverse elements of the antebellum South.

CONFIDENCE AND ANXIETY

No matter where observers of the southern economy looked in the late 1850s, they viewed a scene painted in bold, bright colors: profitable agriculture and prosperous industry, banking, and cities sharing in the prosperity. It was a heady time for southerners. Their slave-based economy appeared strong and solid.

Most scholars claim that the southern economy would have faltered eventually because of an inherent incompatibility between industry and slavery. Some contemporaries had the same thought. These people argued that slavery should remain confined to farms and plantations, for only there could it flourish. To their way of thinking, slaves in factories would erode the southern system they cherished. Not surprisingly, this bleak forecast usually came from the same men who were filled with foreboding about industrial growth. Theirs was a small group, largely unheard and unheeded.

Most southerners of the 1850s envisioned no inevitable conflict between slavery and industry, and there was no good reason for them to foresee such a clash. Until the end of the antebellum period slavery and industry cooperated fully. Most industrialists certainly did not oppose slave labor in their factories. The closest student of industry and slavery concluded that probably 5 percent of the slave population toiled in southern industrial plants. These people worked in every kind of enterprise, from small lumber mills to such large factories as the ironworks in Tennessee controlled by the Whig leader John Bell, in which 365 slaves labored. The books and ledgers of industrial enterprises that employed slaves reveal a widespread prosperity that demonstrates the effectiveness of that labor. The use of slaves in industry also led to innovative business practices. Industrial accidents could be very costly to the factory and mill owners who bought or hired slaves, so some businessmen began to insure the lives of their slaves.

By every economic measure southerners of 1860 were confident, even over-confident. The Panic of 1857, which hit the northern economy hard, struck only a glancing blow at the South; agriculture barely felt it. That experience, after the devastation wreaked by the panics in 1819 and 1837, provided what southerners considered a clear measure of their economic strength. When James H. Hammond, United States senator from South Carolina, proclaimed in 1858, "Cotton is king," most southerners chorused agreement: their cotton ruled the economic world. Grandiose rhetoric aside, a keen student of the antebellum southern economy has concluded that southerners had concrete reasons for their optimism: "Before the war, the South was wealthy, prosperous, expanding geographically, and growing economically at rates that compared favorably to the rest of the country."

This booming economy contributed to a swelling pride, but simultaneously southerners worried about the erosion of their power in the nation. In a fundamental way, the two apparently separate phenomena were closely connected. The same boom that underlay prosperity in the South generated a powerful economic surge in the free states. During the 1850s the North began to stride firmly toward the industrial and financial might that would characterize its economy in the last quarter of the nineteenth century. This expanding economy had a political counterpart, the Republican party. And the Republicans challenged the traditional political role of the South in the nation at the very moment when prosperity and growth marked the southern economy.

THE ELECTION OF 1860

Thus a proud but anxious South both anticipated and dreaded the presidential election of 1860. The once vigorous political champion of southern liberty, now tattered, would either mend or tear itself further in Charleston, the site of the eighth Democratic national convention, which began on April 23, 1860. A love feast it was not. Vindictive southerners were determined to deny Stephen Douglas the party nomination, though he was clearly the most popular Democrat in the North, and some of those states the party had to carry to win the election. In addition the southerners demanded a platform containing a provision for federal protection of slavery in the territories, which they claimed the Dred Scott decision mandated. They knew that Douglas could never accept such a plank; he knew that if the party accepted it, Republicans would destroy Democrats in the North. Neither the southerners nor Douglas would back down. When the convention rejected the southerners' demands, delegates from the lower South walked out. Efforts to reunify the convention failed. Adjournment and a call for reconvening was the best the party could do. The debacle at Charleston provided indisputable proof of the party's disunity.

The public spectacle of a feuding Democratic party was repeated in Baltimore in late June. Baltimore had been the site of every Democratic convention between 1832 and 1852. Many party loyalists hoped that in Baltimore some of the unity of an earlier time would somehow reappear in 1860. But it was not to be; the wrangling was as bitter as ever. Once again the Democratic convention failed to mend itself. In Baltimore party disarray became public dismemberment when each of the two dominant groups called itself the Democratic party and nominated a presidential candidate. The Douglas loyalists gave their nomination to their hero; the breakaway southerners placed their imprimatur on John C. Breckinridge of Kentucky, vice president of the United States. For the first time since its creation, the Democratic party could settle on neither a standard-bearer nor a platform.

Failure to maintain party unity fractured the Democratic effort in the South. A divided Democracy made it extremely difficult for southern loyalists to claim convincingly that their party remained the impenetrable shield of the South. Despite the difficulties, they made their traditional case for their party, but the Democratic troubles brought another force into the southern presidential field. It was composed of Opposition men, former Whigs, and former Know-Nothings. Although this new group called its new political home the Constitutional Union party, it was not a party at all, but an ad hoc reaction to special circumstances. The almost simultaneous occurrence of the disruption of the Democratic party, the threat of the Republicans, and the presidential election caused all anti-Democrats to coalesce into a unit. That only powerful national issues in conjunction with an approaching presidential election could effect this unification, even if temporary, reconfirmed the primacy of national issues in southern politics. Between the collapse of the Know-Nothings and 1860, the numerous anti-Democrats across the South had not been able to arrange themselves into a single force to confront the Democrats. Such unity was impossible because no overriding national issue appeared and because no northern connection existed for a second national party in the South.

But the immediate demands of 1860 led some conservative northerners, opposed to the Republican and Democratic parties alike, to look to Constitutional Unionism as a solution to their problem. Coming together in Baltimore in May, these men called for allegiance to the Constitution and for patriotism and forbearance as the watchwords of all Americans. By awarding their nominations to old-line, conservative Whigs—John Bell of Tennessee for president and Edward Everett of Massachusetts for vice president—the Constitutional Unionists emphasized both their political ancestry and their hopes for the political future. The crisis of 1860 led southern Constitutional Unionists to hope that their temporary northern friends would become permanent allies.

During the election campaign, however, the Constitutional Unionists did not stake out a new direction for southern politics. Leaping to the attack, they condemned the Democrats for failing to secure the South. According to the Constitutional Unionists, the southern Democrats had neglected their sacred mission—to protect southern liberty. Instead the southern Democrats grasped for place and reward while the Republican horde prepared to attack southern liberty. In such dire times, the Constitutional Unionists asserted, southern voters could not put their trust in the faithless Democratic party. The Constitutional Unionist script ended with the obvious conclusion: southerners could count only on the new party.

With the politics of slavery in full bloom, the South voted. No sure champion had arisen to turn back the Republican challenge. With no hero to rally round, southerners divided their votes. Although the southern Democratic candidate, John C. Breckinridge, carried eleven of fifteen slave states, he won a popular majority in only seven. Despite an attempt to persuade southerners that Douglas would protect their interests, the northern Democratic candidate generally received less than 15 percent of the popular vote, and in several states less than 10 percent. He fared little better along the border, except in Missouri, which he carried with just over one-third of the vote. The Constitutional Union party was much stronger. It won the electoral vote of one border state and two in the upper South, and also took 40 percent of the popular vote in the states that would soon form the Confederacy. By every usual measurement the southern Democrats retained their supremacy. Still, Lecompton and the party breakup hurt. More than four of every ten voting southerners cast their ballots for a temporary party—a party that had no history, only claims, and thin ones, that it could guarantee southern liberty, and only the barest hope that it could win the presidential election or even become a force in Congress.

The campaign and election of 1860 dramatized the disintegration of the traditional order in southern politics. For more than three decades the Democratic party had claimed a unique role in protecting southern interests and liberty; on that very issue it had eliminated the Whigs and wrecked the Know-Nothings. Now it was in disarray. The Constitutional Union party was little more than an improvised response to a special political situation. Even though it had no record and campaigned chiefly on hope, it did win the votes of tens of thousands of southerners. That performance signaled the rampant disorder in southern politics. Though these facts were unsettling, southerners were much more distressed by yet another. The hated and feared Republican party won the presidential election. Though the Republican candidate, Abraham Lincoln of Illinois, garnered only a minority of the national popular vote, just 40 percent, he carried every free state save New Jersey, which he divided with Douglas, and won a clear majority in the electoral college, 180 to 123. Now the Republican party, with its antisouthern platform and with no southerners in its inner councils, would control the national administration. In the history of the nation this situation was absolutely unprecedented.

THE FIRE-EATERS

What this Republican triumph heralded many southerners feared they had glimpsed back in October 1859. Then the avenging angel of abolition, John Brown, a bloody veteran of bleeding Kansas, had aimed his fury against slavery at Harpers Ferry, Virginia. An apostle of violence, Brown acted out his favorite biblical passage, "Without the shedding of blood there is no remission of sins." Claiming the role of a prophet charged by God Almighty to root out the evil of slavery, Brown led his band in an assault on the federal arsenal at Harpers Ferry. His professed goal was to foment and lead a slave uprising that would spread southward and sound the death knell of the bondage he hated. Brown's raid failed utterly. Federal troops smashed his attack and captured or killed most of his followers. Brown himself was captured, tried by the state of Virginia for treason, and on December 2 hanged. Although major Republican leaders repudiated Brown's violent tactics, he became almost a saint in northern antislavery circles. Southerners were appalled; countless thousands saw Brown and his crusade as a direct manifestation of Republicanism.

When the despised Lincoln won the election of 1860, southerners saw the slave collar about to be clamped on their own necks. Major Republican leaders had made clear their intention "to take the Government out of unjust and unfaithful hands, and commit it to those which will be just and faithful." This kind of declaration southerners read as the proclamation of conquerors. From their own viewpoint, southerners had been faithful stewards of the Constitution; now their enemies seemed ready to treat them as a vanquished people who had no claim on liberty. By definition absence of liberty meant the presence of slavery. And slavery southerners equated with degradation. In this gloomy vision the white South would become enslaved to tyrannical Republicanism.

This outlook explains why so many southerners framed the overriding issue of 1860 and 1861 as a matter of submission. Slaves submitted; no honorable white person would do so. Although few southerners saw civil war as inevitable, many believed "even that, *if it must come*, would be preferable to submission to Black Republicans, involving as it would all that is horrible, degrading, and ruinous." Many southerners preferred death "to liv[ing] a slave to Black Republicanism." In the words of one, "I would be an equal, or a corpse." Millions shared that sentiment.

With traditional political patterns unraveled and southern liberty facing an epic crisis, the fire-eaters surged into significance. A new and potent force in southern politics, the fire-eaters had sprouted in the crisis of 1850, then with widespread acceptance of the great compromise became dormant during most of the decade, only to blossom at its end. While Democrats and Constitutional Unionists struggled over who could better protect the South in the Union, the fire-eaters aimed to destroy the Union, which they pictured as a dagger poised to plunge into the heart of the South.

The fire-eaters were a small band. The three states where they were most prominent were South Carolina, which had the largest concentration of slaves, 57 percent of the population; Mississippi, second only to South Carolina with 55 percent; and Alabama, with 45 percent of its population slave. Fire-eaters operated on a smaller scale but with impact in Florida, Georgia, Texas, and Virginia. They were scarce elsewhere.

Fire-eaters were not simply large slaveholders. Much of their local leadership seems to have come from relatively young town dwellers in plantation counties. Undoubtedly the intimate relationship between the possession of slaves and the passion for liberty helps explain the citadels of fire-eating. When whites in the centers of black slavery perceived the destruction of slavery at hand, the possibilities assumed terrifying proportions because that destruction would necessarily include, according to the southern calculus, the extermination of their liberty. In 1860 the fire-eaters had no doubt that the future of slavery was at stake. To them Republican domination of the national government meant at once the extinction of black slavery and the imposition of white slavery.

The leading fire-eaters were a diverse lot. The dean of the group was Robert Barnwell Rhett of South Carolina. Sixty years old in 1860, Rhett claimed long adherence to the cause of disunion; he had been a secessionist since the early 1830s. Active in the public world, he served in the Congress from the late 1830s to the early 1850s. In 1852 he resigned his seat as a United States senator in disgust after his state formally refused to oppose the Compromise of 1850. But public office did not provide Rhett's chief platform. He and his son controlled the Charleston *Mercury*, the most prominent fire-eating newspaper in the South. Under the guidance of the Rhetts, it broadcast the message of southern radicalism across the South. Fourteen years younger than Rhett, William Lowndes Yancey of Alabama was the orator of secession. Born in South Carolina, reared in the North in the household of an abolitionist foster father, Yancey came back to the South as a young man and finally settled in Alabama, where he became a major figure among the more radical Democrats. In a time and place where political speaking was a cultivated art, none ranked higher than Yancey. Thousands thronged to hear him cry out, "It is the right to save ourselves from depotism and destruction."

Rhett and Yancey had less politically visible but no less dedicated comrades. None was more interesting than the venerable Edmund Ruffin. Born into a notable Virginia family in 1794, Ruffin was one of the nation's foremost proponents of scientific agriculture. After an unhappy term in the Virginia legislature, he shunned direct involvement in politics, but he wrote numerous secessionist essays. As he was convinced that only blows from the outside could invigorate the "sluggish blood" of his fellow southerners, he cheered John Brown's raid. During the campaign of 1860 he sent to the governor of each slave state a pike he had obtained from Brown's cache of weapons; on each pike Ruffin had af-

(a) (b)

TWO FIRE-EATERS
(a) Robert Barnwell Rhett (Courtesy of South Caroliniana Library, University of South Carolina)
(b) Edmund Ruffin (Brady Collection, National Archives)

fixed a label: "SAMPLE OF THE FAVORS DESIGNED FOR US BY OUR NORTHERN BRETH-REN." Lincoln's election seemed to be God's answer to his prayers.

THE LOWER SOUTH SECEDES

Because the fire-eaters' demand for secession was drastic and unprecedented, their success depended in no small part on outside events. Most southerners considered themselves patriotic Americans; they were far from eager to destroy what their grandfathers had helped create, their fathers had helped nurture, and they helped guide. Secession required a great leap into the political unknown, and most southerners were unlikely to heed the fire-eaters' call unless outside events made it especially attractive. Thus John Brown's raid, the breakup of the Democratic party, and particularly Lincoln's election were bountiful gifts to the fire-eaters from the gods of politics.

The election of Abraham Lincoln was the essential catalyst that enabled the fire-eaters to precipate the revolution they craved. The Republican victory undermined the major pledge of the southern Democrats that they and their party guaranteed the liberty and safety of the South in the Union. Southerners generally viewed the Republican triumph not as a one-time happening but as the culmination of a decade and more of anti-South politics. Southerners of almost every political persuasion agreed when a sober-minded editor depicted Lincoln's triumph as "incontrovertible proof of a diseased and dangerous public opinion all over the North, and a certain forerunner of further and a more atrocious aggression." In short, practically every white southerner looked upon a future Republican administration with combined apprehension and anger. Now one political unknown, the fire-eaters' secession, was matched by another, Republicans in power.

In the lower South the reaction to Lincoln's election was immediate. Governors called legislatures into session, and legislatures called for prompt elections of delegates to convene in December 1860 and January 1861 to consider appropriate actions. Nothing predestined the decision of these conventions. Ultimately the decision for secession was massively influenced by the tactics of the fire-eaters, who understood the opportunity Lincoln's victory provided and with boldness and shrewdness hurried to apply the pressure that would explode the Union.

For the fire-eaters timing was crucial. If they could accomplish secession in any one state, then the basic question would be changed: the other states would then be deciding not simply whether to secede or not, but whether to join or oppose a sister slave state. Recognizing the importance of immediate action, the fire-eaters moved smartly in the state where they had the greatest influence. On December 20, 1860, the South Carolina convention voted unanimously to secede, to break all ties to the old Union. Fire-eaters everywhere rejoiced. An Alabamian was thrilled: "At this point the accumulated aggression of a third of a century fell like shackles at her feet, and free, disenthralled, regenerated, she stood before her devoted people like the genius of liberty, beckoning them on to the performance of their duty."

The relationship between the fire-eaters and the process of secession raises the question of popular support for secession and the unity behind it. Secession was a public issue; no closed-door conspiracy broke up the Union. In every state speeches, editorials, and campaigns engaged the voting South. Initially the fire-eaters led the crusade, with Lincoln's election giving them multitudes of followers; then the traditional political leadership, especially the Democrats, took charge. People who questioned the wisdom of a pell-mell rush to immediate secession, most of whom called themselves cooperationists, lived chiefly in areas and counties with few slaves. In South Carolina, Florida, Mississippi, and Texas a substantial to overwhelming majority of the white population favored immediate secession, and the outcome was never in serious doubt, though only Texas held a popular referendum on the convention's decision.

In the other three states of the lower South—Georgia, Alabama, and Louisiana—the contest was seemingly considerably closer because of the strength of the cooperationists. The popular vote for delegates to the conventions and the early convention votes themselves revealed substantial public backing for the cooperationist position. But too great a distinction can be drawn between immediatists and cooperationists. The cooperationists opposed immediate secession, not secession at any time. Thus the debate in campaigns and conventions focused on tactics rather than on the fundamental issue. Not even all cooperationists belonged to the same camp: for some, cooperation meant a southern convention; for others, a joint statement by two or more states; for still others, simply the secession of another state. In the end, almost every cooperationist in every state quickly and wholeheartedly signed the ordinance of secession. One of their major newspapers warned, "It may prove a fatal, an unretrievably fatal error," if their stance should "be misconstrued into *submission*, or a delay designed eventually to lead to submission."

In the furor of the winter of 1860–1861 the cooperationists could have said nothing else. They agreed that the South had to guard the liberty now jeopardized by Lincoln's victory. Thus to mount an effective opposition to the immediatists they would have had to offer a credible alternative to secession. They had none, at least none that more than a few could agree on. The most striking characteristic of the cooperationists in the crisis was confusion. They could not decide whether to campaign and could not agree on a political goal to articulate if they did. Perhaps in the depths of their being they thought the immediatists were right.

By the first of February 1861 all the states of the lower South had left the Union—South Carolina, December 20, 1860; Mississippi, January 9; Florida, January 10; Alabama, January 11; Georgia, January 19; Louisiana, January 26; Texas, February 1.

THE UPPER SOUTH AND THE BORDER STATES

With eight states in the upper South and on the border still in the Union, the hopes of the fire-eaters still had not been realized. The upper South, which stretched more than a thousand miles from Virginia to Arkansas, did not secede upon Lincoln's election, not even upon his inauguration as president on March 4. The paucity of fire-eaters everywhere and their absence in many places relaxed the political pressure for secession. In the one state where the fire-eaters did have a noticeable voice, Virginia, their influence was offset by the vigorously antisecessionist transmontane region, most of which became West Virginia during the war. That the upper South did not secede along with the lower South did not signify that it looked upon the rise of the Republican party and Lincoln's election as normal occurrences. The rhetoric in these states matched that in their more southerly neighbors. This rhetoric, however, did not propel the upper South into rapid secession because the political equation lacked the crucial multiplier, the fire-eaters. Leaders in the upper South asserted that

Lincoln's triumph had surely challenged southern liberty, but it remained unvanquished in the absence of some overt act such as adoption of the Wilmot Proviso or interference with the interstate slave trade.

At the same time, the upper South did not have a free political hand; it could not escape the politics of slavery. The fact of seven secessions and the formation in February of the Confederate States of America had a massive impact on the upper South. At this juncture states and a combination of states replaced political parties and groups as the motivating force behind the politics of slavery. That politics fundamentally influenced the decision of the upper

MERCURY

SECESSION ANNOUNCE-
MENT BY THE CHARLESTON
MERCURY (New York Public Library)

EXTRA:

Passed unanimously at 1.15 o'clock, P. M., December 20th, 1860.

AN ORDINANCE

To dissolve the Union between the State of South Carolina and other States united with her under the compact entitled "The Constitution of the United States of America."

We, the People of the State of South Carolina, in Convention assembled, do declare and ordain, and it is hereby declared and ordained,

That the Ordinance adopted by us in Convention, on the twenty-third day of May, in the year of our Lord one thousand seven hundred and eighty-eight, whereby the Constitution of the United States of America was ratified, and also, all Acts and parts of Acts of the General Assembly of this State, ratifying amendments of the said Constitution, are hereby repealed; and that the union now subsisting between South Carolina and other States, under the name of "The United States of America," is hereby dissolved.

THE

UNION

IS

DISSOLVED!

South, even though in those four states a majority of voters joined in a new Union party to oppose secession.

With the lower South out of the Union, the question facing people in the upper South was not simply whether to secede but whether to aid their brothers farther south. If in any way the new Confederacy and the old Union came into confrontation, then the upper South would come face to face with its ultimate decision. Its hand would be forced, and the antisecessionists did not at all relish the thought that their future might be controlled by the states that had broken up the Union. Perched perilously between the Union and the Confederacy, the upper South no longer had complete freedom of decision. Confrontation between the Union and the Confederacy, or even a single seceded state, meant for the upper South the choice between freedom and slavery. In the vocabulary of southern politics, coercion by the federal government entailed enslavement of the coerced states and destruction of their citizens' liberty. An antisecessionist Virginia editor spoke bluntly:

> An issue has been made. The subjection of South Carolina or any seceding state, in consequence of their determination not to submit to the policy of the Republicans, is a blow at the entire South—subjection to all. We are, thenceforth, humiliated. We are conquered. We could not hold up our heads in that Union any more.

Thus when the guns roared at Fort Sumter and President Lincoln called for troops to put down the rebellion, the upper South said no. Virginia (April 7), North Carolina (May 20), Tennessee (May 7), and Arkansas (May 6) all seceded.

A distinctly different situation prevailed in the four border states. A small slave population made three of these states "slave" chiefly in a technical and legal sense. Only Kentucky, where slaves accounted for 20 percent of the population, can realistically be said to be a slave state in the social, economic, and political senses. Slaves accounted for only 13 percent of the population in Maryland, 10 percent in Missouri, and less than 2 percent in Delaware. The number of slave owners was correspondingly small—just a fraction over 2 percent of the population in both Maryland and Missouri and no more than one-half of 1 percent in Delaware. Moreover, the percentages of both slaves and slave owners had declined markedly during the 1850s. In them unconditional Unionist sentiment flourished and fire-eaters were rare. This political reality, coupled with an antisecessionist governor in Maryland and the political and military moves of the federal government, made secession impossible.

The percentage of slaves in Kentucky approached that of Arkansas and Tennessee, yet they seceded and Kentucky did not. Geography and political tradition help to explain the behavior of Kentucky. Its northern frontier marked the boundary between freedom and slavery. This proximity to the free states had two important consequences. First, as in the other border states, a powerful, unconditional Unionist sentiment flourished in Kentucky. Second, many Kentuckians wanted to avoid taking sides because they could envision their homeland becoming a major battleground.

The political heritage of Kentucky buttressed this desire to steer clear of overt partisanship. Even after Fort Sumter, Kentucky declared neutrality in any conflict between the United States and the Confederate States. Well aware that their great statesman, Henry Clay, had gained fame as the compromiser in earlier sectional crises, Kentuckians strove to follow his example. In a conscious attempt to emulate Clay, United States Senator John J. Crittenden led the major effort to avert secession and conflict. The compromise he proposed to the Senate was to solve the territorial problem by resurrecting the Missouri Compromise line and extending it all the way to the Pacific Ocean. To legitimize this extension, Crittenden advocated a constitutional amendment that would overcome the Dred Scott ruling against congressional prohibition of slavery in any territory. But neither Republicans nor southern Democrats gave Crittenden much encouragement or support. His failure presaged the failure of his state's hopes for neutrality. Within months both Confederate and Union armies entered the state, and the Union's military superiority settled Kentucky's fate.

THE FORMATION OF THE CONFEDERACY

The Confederate States of America was taking shape even before secession had run its course. On February 4, 1861, delegates from six states of the lower South met in Montgomery, Alabama, to create a new government; later they were joined by a delegation from Texas. Thus seven states initially made up the Confederate States of America. The men in Montgomery acted in more diverse capacities than any other such group in American history.

In their capacity as delegates to a constitutional convention, they went about their deliberations with great unity of purpose. For the mass of southerners in 1861, the Confederate States of America replicated the United States of America, the country they had loved before it had, in their minds, been distorted beyond recognition by the Republicans. The builders of the Confederate States set out to construct a government that would protect the liberty they held so dear. Like their ancestors, they felt compelled to have a written constitution, and they borrowed heavily from the one they knew and admired. The Constitution of the Confederate States adopted the separation of powers, created a federal system, and in general provided the same structure of government that guided the United States.

There were differences, however. Some were mechanical, such as one six-year term for the president and the possibility that in certain circumstances cabinet officers could join debate on the floor of Congress. But the major changes underscored the great themes that had dominated southern politics since the Revolution. In Article I black slavery was specifically recognized and given explicit constitutional sanction and protection: "No bill of attainder, *ex post facto* law, or law denying or impairing the right of property in negro slaves shall be passed." Likewise the Constitution affirmed the legitimacy of slavery in any territory the new nation might come to acquire. One section of the document prohibited a protective tariff. And the concept of states' rights was elevated to a first principle: the preamble declared that the Confederacy derived from "each State acting in its sovereign and independent character."

With the drafting of a constitution completed, the delegates transformed themselves into an electoral college. Again they decided to follow the practice of the United States and elect the president and vice president by state. This first time each state would have one vote. After discussing various possibilities, the delegates unanimously chose Jefferson Davis of Mississippi as president of the Confederate States of America and Alexander Stephens of Georgia as vice president. Both had been notable figures in southern politics. A Mississippi planter and a Democrat, the fifty-three-year-old Davis had been educated at West Point and had served with distinction in the Mexican War and as Franklin Pierce's secretary of war. Before and after his stints in Pierce's cabinet, Davis had been a major figure in the United States Senate. Though a stalwart southern-rights man, Davis was not a fire-eater. The choice of Alexander Stephens, formerly a leading Whig and in 1860–1861 a cooperationist, was dictated in part by the drive for unity: it would underscore the single-mindedness of the new Confederates. Stephens was a graduate of the University of Georgia and a lawyer who for a decade and half had been a major Whig spokesman in the United States House of Representatives. The delegates correctly believed they had selected two eminently qualified, reasonable men to lead their new nation. Of course they had no intention of denying the people of the Confederacy the ultimate right to choose their own leaders. The crisis required immediate action, but the designation of Davis and Stephens was declared to be provisional until a general election could be held. The election was scheduled for November; the permanent president and vice president would be inaugurated in February 1862.

After Davis and Stephens took office, they worked with the delegations, now acting as Congress, to create an administrative structure and a body of laws that would breathe life into the Confederate States of America. In doing so they were mindful that eight slave states remained in the Union. Every effort would be made to secure their partnership in the new country. The infant Confederate government also had to devote attention to its immediate neighbor, the United States. Such matters as the proper political relationship and trading policy had to be settled, but an even more pressing issue was the military posts within the Confederacy still occupied by the United States Army. As states had left the Union, most federal military installations in them either had been captured or had surrendered. In neither instance had any blood been shed. Two major posts, Fort Pickens at Pensacola, Florida, and Fort Sumter in Charleston Harbor, still remained in Union hands. As the Confederate government saw it, a foreign power stood uninvited on its soil. Many Confederates believed that theirs could not be a truly independent country until the Confederate flag flew over every military post within the Confederate States of America.

The Geography
of the Civil War

❖

These maps emphasize critical events leading up to the Civil War and outline the most important military engagements of the conflict. The first two focus on the two crucial political events of 1860 and 1861: the presidential election and secession. The former delineates the sectionalism that dominated the presidential contest while the latter illustrates the range of reactions in the slave states to the outcome of that election. The third map depicts the harbor of Charleston, South Carolina, where the first shots of the war were fired. The final five maps are designed to help clarify the campaigns of the war. They identify the key army movements and specify the locations of the major battles in both the eastern and western theaters.

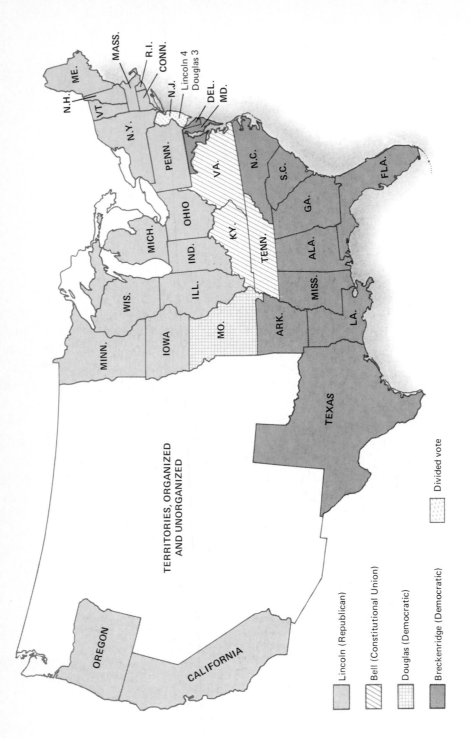

THE ELECTION OF 1860

TERRITORIES, ORGANIZED
AND UNORGANIZED

Lincoln (Republican)

Bell (Constitutional Union)

Douglas (Democratic)

Breckenridge (Democratic)

Divided vote

Lincoln 4
Douglas 3

348

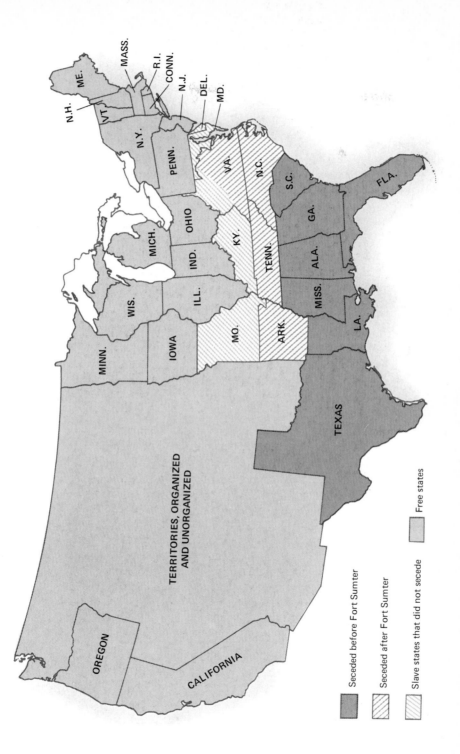

THE PATTERN OF SECESSION

Seceded before Fort Sumter

Seceded after Fort Sumter

Slave states that did not secede

Free states

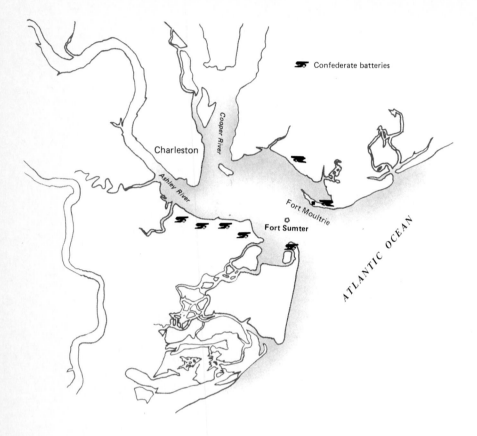

Confederate batteries

Cooper River

Charleston

Ashley River

Fort Moultrie

Fort Sumter

ATLANTIC OCEAN

CHARLESTON HARBOR, 1861

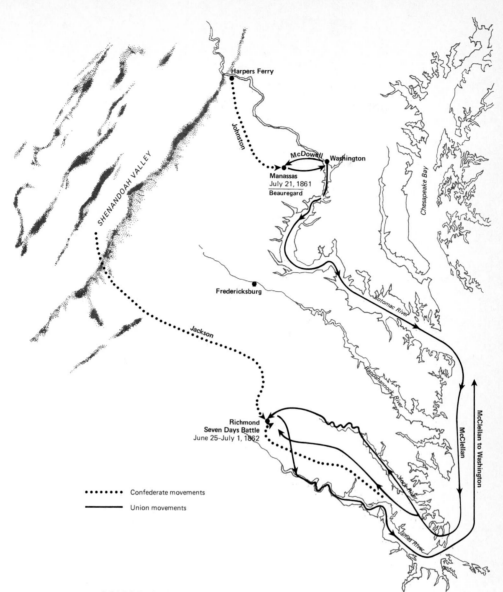

Harpers Ferry

Johnston

SHENANDOAH VALLEY

McDowell   Washington

Manassas
July 21, 1861
Beauregard

Fredericksburg

Chesapeake Bay

Potomac River

Rappahannock River

Jackson

McClellan to Washington

McClellan

Richmond
Seven Days Battle
June 25–July 1, 1862

York River

James River

••••••• Confederate movements

———— Union movements

MAJOR CAMPAIGNS IN THE EAST, 1861–JULY 1862

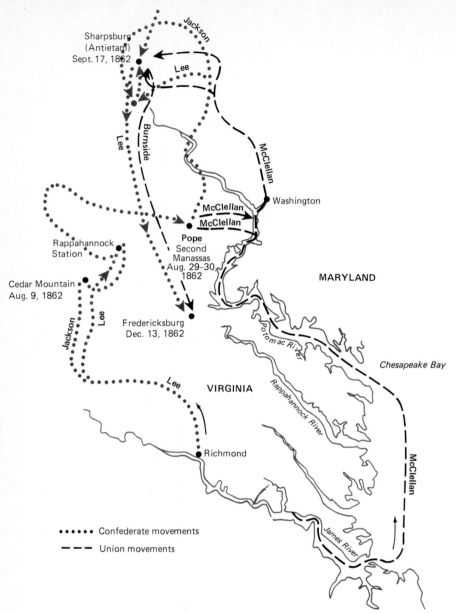

Sharpsburg
(Antietam)
Sept. 17, 1862

Jackson

Lee

Lee

Burnside

McClellan

McClellan

McClellan

Washington

Rappahannock
Station

Pope
Second
Manassas
Aug. 29–30,
1862

MARYLAND

Cedar Mountain
Aug. 9, 1862

Jackson

Lee

Fredericksburg
Dec. 13, 1862

Potomac River

Chesapeake Bay

Rappahannock River

Lee

VIRGINIA

Richmond

James River

McClellan

•••••• Confederate movements

– – – Union movements

MAJOR CAMPAIGNS IN THE EAST, JULY–DECEMBER 1862

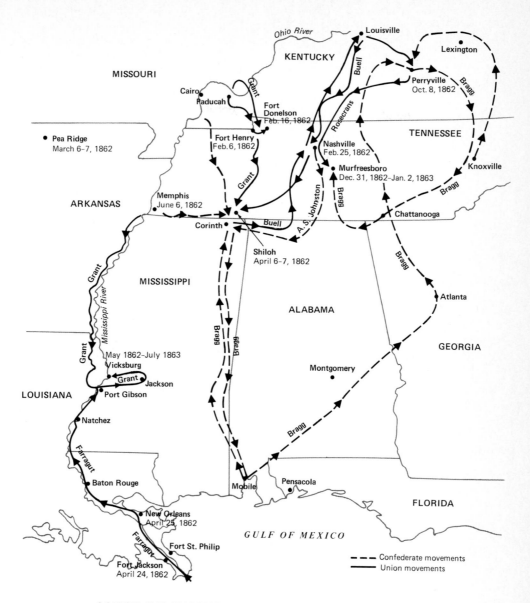

Ohio River

Louisville

Lexington

MISSOURI

KENTUCKY

Buell

Perryville
Oct. 8, 1862

Bragg

Cairo

Paducah

Fort
Donelson
Feb. 16, 1862

Rosecrans

TENNESSEE

Pea Ridge
March 6–7, 1862

Fort Henry
Feb. 6, 1862

Nashville
Feb. 25, 1862

Knoxville

Grant

Murfreesboro
Dec. 31, 1862–Jan. 2, 1863

Bragg

ARKANSAS

Memphis
June 6, 1862

A. S. Johnston

Bragg

Chattanooga

Corinth

Buell

Shiloh
April 6–7, 1862

Bragg

MISSISSIPPI

Grant

Mississippi River

ALABAMA

Atlanta

Bragg

GEORGIA

May 1862–July 1863
Vicksburg

Grant

Jackson

Montgomery

LOUISIANA

Port Gibson

Natchez

Bragg

Farragut

Baton Rouge

Mobile

Pensacola

New Orleans
April 25, 1862

FLORIDA

Farragut

Fort St. Philip

GULF OF MEXICO

Fort Jackson
April 24, 1862

– – – Confederate movements
——— Union movements

MAJOR CAMPAIGNS IN THE WEST, 1861–SUMMER 1863

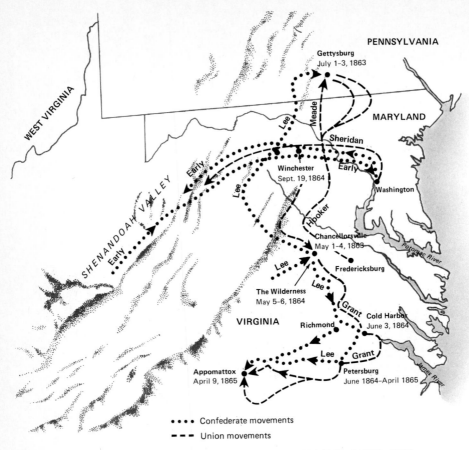

MAJOR CAMPAIGNS IN THE EAST, MAY 1863–APRIL 1865

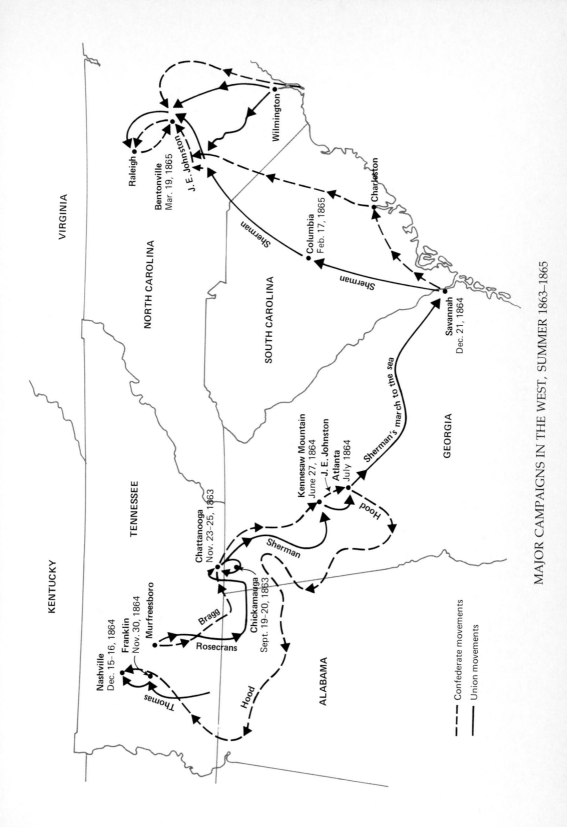

MAJOR CAMPAIGNS IN THE WEST, SUMMER 1863–1865

Nashville
Dec. 15–16, 1864

Franklin
Nov. 30, 1864
Murfreesboro

Thomas

Hood

Bragg

Rosecrans

Chattanooga
Nov. 23–25, 1863

Chickamauga
Sept. 19–20, 1863

Sherman

Kennesaw Mountain
June 27, 1864
J. E. Johnston
Atlanta
July 1864

Hood

Sherman's march to the sea

Savannah
Dec. 21, 1864

Sherman

Columbia
Feb. 17, 1865

Sherman

Charleston

Wilmington

Raleigh

Bentonville
Mar. 19, 1865

J. E. Johnston

KENTUCKY

TENNESSEE

VIRGINIA

NORTH CAROLINA

SOUTH CAROLINA

GEORGIA

ALABAMA

– – – Confederate movements

——— Union movements

15

The Confederate
Experience

❖

Fort Sumter stands three miles from Charleston, at the point where the harbor meets the Atlantic Ocean. Construction on it had begun in the late 1820s, as part of a plan devised after the War of 1812 by Secretary of War John C. Calhoun to defend the nation's seacoast from attack. Still unfinished in the spring of 1861, Fort Sumter had become the most visible symbol of the divided nation. Even though the fort lay entirely within the borders of South Carolina, and thus of the Confederate States of America, the Stars and Stripes still flew over the masonry structure. Manned by a force of eighty-five under the command of Major Robert Anderson, Fort Sumter gave force to President Abraham Lincoln's cry that the Union remained inviolable and challenged the Confederacy's claim to independence.

Fort Sumter became the prize in the first great contest between the Union and Abraham Lincoln and the Confederacy and Jefferson Davis. The stakes were more political than military, for the Sumter garrison, massively outnumbered and outgunned by Confederate troops and artillery, could not hope to win a fight. On the political front, however, the potential rewards and dangers were much greater. Some of Lincoln's advisers, including military leaders, recommended withdrawal from Fort Sumter, but the President rejected their advice. To his mind, to pull out was to concede the Confederacy's independence and possibly to end his cherished dream of keeping the Union whole. Even so, Lincoln realized that a straightforward military reinforcement not only would require a Confederate counteraction but might push both the upper South and the border states into the Confederacy, which would then have fifteen states instead of the seven Deep South states it now had. To double the Confederacy's base was to court disaster for the Union. Rejecting reinforcement as well as withdrawal, Lincoln decided on a master stroke. He announced that he would resupply Fort Sumter. He would send in no new soldiers or guns, only food and medicine for the troops already there. This action, Lincoln proclaimed, would leave unchanged the calculus of power in Charleston Harbor. This masterful maneuver provided a clear sign of the political genius that would make Lincoln such a great president and war leader.

While Lincoln made his momentous decision, President Jefferson Davis and his advisers also pondered the problem of Fort Sumter. Powerful arguments supported the contention that the Confederates should take the fort. The first was that the Union's occupation of Fort Sumter mocked the Confederacy's independence. According to this thinking, the Confederate States of America could not stand as an independent nation so long as another power maintained an uninvited military force within the Confederacy's borders. Second, some Confederates feared, with justification, that hotheads in South Carolina might strike against the fort on their own initiative. Any such action would undermine the authority of the Confederate government and commit it to a course it had not decided upon. Some Confederate leaders also maintained that a Confederate move against Fort Sumter would mobilize the citizenry behind the government and, equally important, bring the upper South within the Confederate fold. Those who opposed direct action stressed the harm that could come from a first strike. Such an attack, they argued, would lose the Confederacy numerous friends in the North and at the same time strengthen Lincoln's hand. But these arguments did not prevail. President Davis decided to demand the surrender of Sumter, and if it were not forthcoming, he would attack.

CONFEDERATE PRESIDENT JEFFERSON DAVIS (Mississippi Department of Archives and History)

From Montgomery orders went to General Pierre G. T. Beauregard of Louisiana, in command of all Confederate forces at Charleston, to demand the surrender of Fort Sumter. If Major Anderson refused, Beauregard was to take the fort. Presented with this alternative, Anderson told the Confederates that he would have to evacuate the fort unless new supplies reached him. Beauregard, aware of the criticalness of the situation in Charleston Harbor, informed his government in Montgomery of Anderson's response. The new directive issued to Beauregard gave him some latitude. If Anderson would provide a specific date for his evacuation, Beauregard was not to open fire. Once again Beauregard contacted Anderson, who did specify a date for withdrawal but added a qualification: he would evacuate Fort Sumter unless controlling instructions from his government directed a different course of action. Beauregard now knew he had no choice; his orders had been explicit. At 4:30 A.M. on Sunday, April 12, the Confederate batteries aimed at Fort Sumter opened fire. After thirty-three hours of bombardment Anderson surrendered. War had begun.

PLANS AND POLICY FOR WAR

With the onset of hostilities, the Confederate government suddenly found itself a war government. Thus almost from its birth the chief mission of the Confederate government became the fighting of a great war.

Jefferson Davis and his advisers faced a formidable task. They led a country that had just been created. This new country had no armed forces, no treasury, no economic or fiscal policy, no foreign policy, or diplomatic missions. It did not even have that most popular scourge of all governments, a bureaucracy. The Confederate leaders had to confront problems in all of these areas simultaneously. They could not address one, solve it, then move to the next. All had to be coped with at once, for all were crucial; none could be postponed. Moreover, all interacted with one another.

The Confederate government began its operations in Montgomery, Alabama. In the center of the Deep South, Montgomery was a logical place for the convening of the delegates from the states that created the Confederate States of America, wrote the Constitution, and selected the first president and vice president. But after Fort Sumter and the secession of Virginia, a movement commenced to move the capital from Montgomery to Richmond. Numerous reasons prompted this pressure. A small town, Montgomery had neither the facilities nor the services to house conveniently either the apparatus or the personnel of the government. Richmond, though no metropolis, offered considerably more. In addition, Richmond was the most important industrial center in the Confederacy. To guarantee its protection, some Confederates argued, it should be made the capital.

Motives other than size and industry also worked in favor of Richmond. Confederates were thrilled when Virginia, the ancient mother and leader of the

South, finally sided with them. Many of them believed it only appropriate that their capital be located in the native state of George Washington and other founders who had led the colonies to victory in the American Revolution. In his inaugural address in Montgomery, President Jefferson Davis proudly equated the Confederates of 1860–1861 with their Revolutionary War ancestors. Southerners, in Davis's mind, "labored to preserve the government of our fathers in its spirit." Accordingly, in May 1861 the entire Confederate government was transferred to Richmond, which remained the capital of the Confederate States of America for the new nation's lifetime.

After April 12 all of the tasks confronting the Confederate leadership coalesced into one immense untaking—the conduct of war. An army had to be raised. Even before Fort Sumter the Confederate Congress had authorized the recruitment of 100,000 volunteers for the Confederate States Army. In May the Congress provided for 400,000 more; by July 1861 the Confederacy, with a white population only one-quarter the size of the Union's, had nearly two-thirds as many men under arms. Although southerners did respond enthusiastically to the colors, the Confederate War Department had difficulty arming them. Some 150,000 muskets were available from captured United States arsenals in the seceded states, but most were obsolete. The first Confederates who joined up brought their own firearms—hunting rifles, shotguns, even ancient flintlock muskets. In 1861 each regiment in the Confederate Army wore its own uniform. Although the government designated the famous cadet gray as the official color, in fact an enormous variety of outfits colored Confederate units. Never did all Confederate soldiers wear a regulation uniform.

At the same time that Confederate authorities strove to find ways to equip their fighting men with the tools of war, they had to make critical decisions about the methods of financing the war. With an overwhelmingly agricultural economy and a tradition of low taxes, the South was not financially ready for a major modern war. Southern leaders believed that the economic power of their cotton would force France and especially Great Britain to intervene on their behalf. No one was quite sure what form such intervention would take, but most envisioned a variety of measures, including financial assistance. With that utterly erroneous faith in European aid and with a massive hostility to taxation, the Confederate Congress at the outset rebuffed the argument of Secretary of the Treasury Christopher Memminger that secure financial support for the war required a levy of taxes.

Denied tax revenue, the Confederate government turned to borrowing. Early in 1861 the government issued $15 million in bonds, which took up most of the available specie in the Confederate states. Then in May a produce loan authorized farmers and planters to pledge a portion of their crop income in return for bonds equal in value to the market price of their pledge. This tactic produced little revenue, as the income from the pledged crops never kept up with the depreciation of Confederate currency. Efforts to raise money in Europe met with no more success, though in late 1862 a loan was negotiated with a French banking house. The Erlanger loan, so called after the banking house, eventually provided between $6 million and $8.5 million to the Confederacy for the purchase of war goods and the repayment of old debts. It was far from enough.

The chief source of revenue was the treasury notes issued by the Confederate government. The introduction into the Confederate economy of large amounts of paper money backed by nothing but hope set off an inflationary spark that soon became a conflagration. In 1864, after three years of this avalanche of paper money, it took $46 to buy what $1 had bought in 1861. From a base of 100 at the beginning of 1861 the price index shot upward to 762 by 1865. This inflationary surge, the result of a reckless fiscal policy, wrecked the economy. Inflation grew so intolerable that popular pressure pushed Congress to enact taxes in an effort to curb it. In 1863 Congress responded by instituting a variety of taxes—excise taxes, license taxes, a 5 percent tax on land and slaves, even an income tax. But the package was too little too late. Lax enforcement and active evasion combined to make the new laws largely ineffective.

Misplaced faith in the omnipotence of cotton governed Confederate diplomatic strategy as well. The Davis administration set one overriding diplomatic goal: to win recognition from the European powers, chiefly France and Great Britain. In cotton the Confederate government thought it had the lever that would force Great Britain to recognize the Confederacy as an independent nation and possibly even intervene in the war on the Confederate side. And when Great Britain adopted a pro-Confederate stance, France would not be far behind.

Confederate authorities might have built up credits in Europe by exporting as much cotton as possible. Instead, to make sure that Great Britain would follow the path they intended, they embargoed all the cotton remaining within their borders. In their view, the British economy could not withstand the absence of Confederate cotton. They made a grave miscalculation. In the first place, cotton was not so central to the British economy as they assumed. Then, to undermine their plans even further, the great crop of 1859 had enabled British merchants and manufacturers to stockpile huge quantities of cotton. Finally, Great Britain had two other sources of cotton within its own empire: Egypt and India. Cotton never forced Great Britain or anyone else to recognize the Confederacy. In short, the cotton the Confederates considered their ace turned out to be a joker.

Even so, the act of a zealous Union naval officer made it appear, at least momentarily, that the Confederacy might get its wish. In November 1861 a Union warship stopped and boarded a British mail packet, the *Trent*, which carried two Confederate diplomats: the Virginian James Mason, traveling to London, and John Slidell of Louisiana, bound for Paris. Mason and Slidell were removed from the *Trent* and taken to a prison in Boston. Huzzahs greeted the news in the North, but London was enraged by the lack of respect shown to the British flag. Tension grew between the two governments, but cool heads and moderation prevailed. The British demanded an apology and the release of the diplomats, and the French sent a supporting note. The Lincoln administration replied that the action had occurred without authorization and ordered the diplomats released. Britain accepted that explanation. Mason and Slidell went on to their posts in Europe; neither succeeded in gaining recognition for the Confederacy.

At home the Confederate leaders had to wrestle with the problems of fighting a war. The Davis administration never developed any written war plans. In a fundamental sense, Davis and his advisers settled on a basic strategy that under the circumstances appeared both logical and reasonable. They had one chief goal, to be let alone. Thus they decided not to go on the strategic offensive; they would not try to secure their independence by attacking the North. This decision resulted in large part from a realistic appraisal of the Confederacy's resources. President Davis wanted to strike at the North, but he realized that he just did not have the means to do so. To a friend he wrote in 1862, "My early...hope was to feed upon the enemy and teach them the blessings of peace by making them feel in its most tangible form the evils of war. The time and place for invasion has been a question not of will but of power." And though in three instances Davis was able to carry the war into enemy territory, he never commanded the sustained power for an offensive strategy.

Instead his troops would stand on the defensive and guard their own territory. From Virginia in the east to the Mississippi River and beyond, the Confederate frontier covered more than 1,000 miles. And the coastline stretching from Virginia on the Atlantic around Florida and across the Gulf of Mexico all the way to the Rio Grande was much longer. If the Union was to subdue the Confederacy, it would have to attack this immense domain. When the Union forces moved into various portions of their territory, the Confederates would strike them at points of opportunity. Thus the Confederates would combine selected offensives with their basic defensive posture. This strategy also included an unstated or undeveloped intention—to wear down the enemy. By luring the Union armies to invade their land—an operation that would require huge numbers of troops and enormous sums to maintain them, and one that was bound to result in substantial casualties—the Confederates hoped to make the North pay a higher price in men, money, and matériel than it could afford. In this view, the Union had neither the will nor the substance to pay the terrible cost necessary to subjugate the Confederacy.

To manage the war the Confederacy had no general staff in the modern sense, with overall command responsibility. Early on the Confederates implemented a departmental command structure: the country was divided into various departments, the commander of each department reporting to the War Department in Richmond. This structure, which seemed rational but worked against cooperation and concentration, remained in place until almost the end of the war. President Davis had a military adviser, but the adviser had no command responsibility. The president acted not only as the constitutional commander in chief but also often as a general in chief, transmitting his orders through the secretary of war. If the numerous departments were to be coordinated in any way, he would have to do the coordinating. To command the major departments Davis assigned the senior generals of the Confederate States

Army, most of whom had been professionals in the prewar United States Army. When their states had seceded and formed the Confederacy, they had resigned their commissions in one army to become officers in another.

THE NAVAL WAR

On the water the Confederates found a different problem. The Confederacy had an immense seacoast and a vast river system, but no navy at all. President Davis gave the task of creating one to former United States Senator Stephen Mallory of Florida. Mallory's job as secretary of the navy was complicated by the Union's decision to impose a blockade on the entire coast for the purpose of impeding both exports such as cotton and imports of war matériel. While Mallory pondered how best to deal with the blockade, he also had to think about protecting the rivers that provided avenues of invasion into the Confederate interior.

Mallory and other officials knew that they could never match the United States Navy ship for ship. To counter the Union's overwhelming numerical superiority, the Confederates turned to technology. As early as May 1861 Secretary Mallory began talking about building a navy of ironclads that could destroy the blockade. Upon investigation, however, Mallory found that because of technological deficiencies and the production of other war matériel, Confederate ironworks could not provide the necessary iron sheeting. To obtain the desired vessels the Confederates entered into contracts with European companies, but Union diplomacy and financial difficulties impeded deliveries. Though the Confederates managed to get some ironclads in the water, their fleet of oceangoing ironclads never materialized.

Their first serious effort resulted in naval history. In 1861 and early 1862 Confederates at Norfolk, Virginia, overhauled the captured Union ship *Merrimac*, clad it in iron, and renamed it the *Virginia*. With this armored vessel, equipped with guns mounted on all sides, the Confederates aimed to smash the blockade. On March 2, 1862, the *Virginia* steamed to the mouth of the Chesapeake Bay to challenge blockading Union ships. The first day was a rousing success. As the *Virginia* sank two ships and forced three others aground, the shots from the Union navy just bounced off its iron coat. On the second day, however, the *Virginia* was met not by wooden ships but by another ironclad. The Union's *Monitor* did not look at all like its southern opponent. A revolving turret with two guns sat on a hull low in the water; observers called the ship "a tin can on a shingle." On March 9 the first battle in history between two ironclads took place. After three hours of hard fighting, neither had substantially damaged the other. But that draw ended the Confederates' dream that ironclads could end the blockade. As for the *Virginia*, when Union forces captured Norfolk in May 1862, the Confederates scuttled the ship. The North went on to build dozens of ironclads based on the design of the *Monitor*.

Because the *Virginia* could not overcome the *Monitor*, the Confederate navy never seriously challenged the Union navy on the high seas. Instead the Confederates sent raiders or cruisers to disrupt Union commerce, a strategy that proved quite successful. Confederate raiders or cruisers captured or destroyed more than 250 merchant ships flying the Stars and Stripes. The most famous of all the raiders, the *Alabama*, built in England and commanded by Captain Raphael Semmes, sank sixty-two merchant vessels and one warship between its commissioning in 1862 and its destruction by the United States Navy in 1864, off the coast of France.

Although Mallory never realized his dream of defeating the blockade with ironclads, the Confederates did construct other ironclads. Generally smaller than the *Virginia*, they were designed to stop Union gunboats on southern rivers. Despite enormous technical and manufacturing difficulties, the Confederate navy managed to place ironclads on the Mississippi and at other strategic spots, such as Mobile Bay. Yet technological shortcomings hampered the effective use of these vessels. Maneuverability on the narrow waterways was always a problem. Most of these ships had short careers. Mechanical shortcomings, chiefly engine failure, caused as many casualties among the ironclads as enemy shot. Many ended up scuttled by their own crews.

*T*HE EASTERN THEATER, 1861–1862

On the ground serious military conflict began in the summer of 1861. The first major battle took place in Virginia, between Richmond and Washington, the corridor that would provide more battlefields than anywhere else during the war. When the Confederate capital was moved to Richmond, a clamor arose in Washington for Union troops to march on the city. Many Washingtonians seemed to regard the coming confrontation as an opportunity for a holiday outing. Confederates, for their part, were confident that they could block any Union advance. Many Confederates, in fact, believed that the South's manliness and fighting skills were so superior that any Confederate force could whip a considerably larger Yankee force.

Americans commenced killing and maiming each other in significant numbers on July 21, 1861, no more than twenty-five miles south of Washington, along a small stream called Bull Run. The First Battle of Manassas, the name given the carnage by the Confederates, provided a foretaste of what this war would be like. First Manassas was no holiday. The congressmen and other picnickers who followed the Union army to watch the gala affair were to have no counterparts at later contests. At First Manassas the roughly 70,000 men in the two armies, fairly evenly divided, demonstrated that both sides could fight and that each would demand a heavy price in suffering and blood from the other. More than 2,700 Union troops were killed, wounded, or missing; the Confederates lost almost 2,000.

First Manassas introduced commanders to real battle. General Pierre G. T. Beauregard, the conqueror of Fort Sumter, found the direction of thousands of soldiers in the turmoil of battle considerably more complicated than aiming artillery at a fixed position. His colleague General Joseph E. Johnston, whose army from the Shenandoah Valley joined Beauregard's on the battlefield, proved that the new mobility provided by the railroad would enable commanders to concentrate troops rapidly at critical points. But for the movement of Johnston's 12,000 men from fifty miles away to reinforce Beauregard, the Union army under Briga1dier General Irvin McDowell would probably have claimed the first victory. But the combination of Beauregard and Johnston overwhelmed the Federals. On the field many Confederate officers who later had important roles in the war gained their first experience commanding soldiers in battle. They included Jubal A. Early, Edmund Kirby-Smith, and Thomas J. Jackson, who received his famous nickname, Stonewall, for a stalwart stand against charging Union units.

The Confederate victory at Manassas taught a hard lesson. Though the Confederates won on that hot July day, their army was too bloodied and too exhausted to take full advantage of its tactical triumph. Those who called for the victorious Confederates to hurry to Washington and end the war had little understanding of the hard blow the battle had dealt the Confederate army. Beauregard and Johnston had blunted the Union advance, but they could neither destroy their enemy nor promptly take the offensive. A similar pattern would appear often over the next four years, on both sides.

After First Manassas the two armies, almost as if suffering from shock, went into practically permanent quarters facing each other. Not until the beginning of 1862 did they begin to stir. A new commander of the Union army fresh from early victories in western Virginia, Major General George B. McClellan, took charge. McClellan planned to use the Union's superiority on the water to move his army from the environs of Washington around the Confederate army to a point below Richmond, on the peninsula between the York and James rivers, where Virginia had first been settled and where George Washington had defeated the British at Yorktown. With the advent of McClellan the main Union army in the East, which became known as the Army of the Potomac, swelled massively, to some 100,000 men.

In the face of this threat, the Confederates struck back with the audacity and imagination that were to be their trademarks in the Virginia theater. Both of these characteristics were intimately associated with two men who became captains of the first rank. General Robert E. Lee, fifty-five years old and serving that spring as military adviser to President Davis, had been born into one of the great Virginia families. But the Lees had lost their economic and political leadership by the time Robert came to maturity. Now that the Lees were no longer great planters, Robert took another road. After graduating from West Point in 1829, he served as a professional soldier. During his more than thirty years as an army officer Lee distinguished himself in the Mexican War and enjoyed a sterling reputation among senior officers. A colonel in 1861, he refused the offer to command the Union field army and, upon the secession of Virginia, resigned his commission. When Virginia joined the Confederacy, he became a full general in its army. In the spring of 1862 Lee was still an unproven general; in fact, in his first combat assignment, in western Virginia, he had lost to George McClellan. Major General Thomas J. "Stonewall" Jackson, only thirty-eight years old, was also a Virginian, but from the transmontane region of the state, not the tidewater. Although he lacked Lee's pedigree, Jackson, too, had graduated from West Point, had been in the regular army, and had participated in the Mexican War. But he had given up his army career, and the 1850s found him on the faculty of the Virginia Military Institute in Lexington.

Together Lee and Jackson derailed McClellan's plan. In order to make Lincoln and his advisers divert units intended for McClellan, Lee urged Jackson

ROBERT E. LEE, THE GREAT
CONFEDERATE WARRIOR
(Cook Collection, Valentine Museum, Richmond, Va.)

stationed in the Shenandoah Valley to advance down the valley toward the Potomac River. In a series of dazzling marches and attacks, the stern, taciturn Jackson confused and defeated several Union generals in the Shenandoah. Jackson's victories worked precisely as Lee had hoped. Because of Jackson's success, the Federals were not able to concentrate as many troops below Richmond as McClellan had hoped.

Because Joseph Johnston had been wounded, Lee now commanded the major Confederate field army, the Army of Northern Virginia. He ordered Jackson to move rapidly and secretly from the Shenandoah Valley to Richmond. When Jackson joined him, Lee intended to take the offensive and destroy McClellan. During the last week in June, in a series of bitter fights known as the Seven Days Battle, Lee did stop McClellan's advance on Richmond, but at a terrible price. During the week's fighting the Federals suffered almost 16,000 casualties out of 100,000 in their army. The Confederates, usually on the attack, took even heavier casualties—more than 20,000, practically one-fourth of their army. These casualty figures meant that with Lee in command ferocity would have to be added to audacity and imagination.

Lee and other Confederate leaders had little time to savor the turning back of McClellan. When information arrived that a new force had started south from Washington, Lee dispatched Stonewall Jackson to counter it. Then, convinced that Jackson was facing a major threat, Lee hurried north from Richmond to join forces with his subordinate. In a daring move that sent Jackson around and deep in the rear of the Federal army, commanded by Major General John Pope, Lee struck and punished the Federals on the same ground where the first great battle had been fought. With the success of the Second Battle of Manassas, Lee and the Confederates had the initiative and the power of decision.

Lee and President Davis decided to go north, to carry the war out of the Confederacy into the Union. Various motives prompted this decision. Without question the general and the president wanted to relieve the pressure on Virginia. They thought of the food available in Maryland and anticipated new recruits for the Army of Northern Virginia. And they hoped that the presence of a major Confederate army in the eastern states, especially a victorious one, would convince the North that the South could not be defeated. When Lee crossed the Potomac, the Confederates had one eye cocked toward England. A triumph on enemy soil might just persuade the British to intervene on behalf of the Confederacy.

But events turned out otherwise. Marylanders did not flock to the Confederate colors. Even more important, a set of Lee's confidential orders fell into the hands of McClellan, once again leading the Army of the Potomac against the Confederates. With that information McClellan moved more rapidly than Lee expected. Confronting this new development, Lee altered his plan of rapid movement through Maryland toward Pennsylvania in favor of regrouping to face McClellan. The two old foes joined battle again along Antietam Creek at Sharpsburg, Maryland. By attacking the Confederates piecemeal instead of in sustained fashion, McClellan frittered away his substantial numerical advantage of 35,000 men. Even though Lee's thin lines held and the Confederates could claim that the Federals had not driven them from the field, Sharpsburg smashed the Confederates' great expectations for this advance into enemy country. McClellan suffered more than 11,000 casualties, but Lee sustained almost 12,000. The combined casualties—about four times as many as the Americans suffered on D-Day in World War II—made this the single bloodiest day of the war. Lee had no choice but to retreat into Virginia. Strategically the Union won a decisive victory at Sharpsburg.

THE WAR IN THE WEST, 1861–1862

While cries of "On to Richmond!" reverberated in the East, critical developments took place in the West. The initial crucial question involved the fate of Kentucky. Of the border states it had the greatest percentage of slaves and the largest number of Confederate sympathizers. The Confederacy hoped that Kentucky would secede and join the new nation, but many Kentuckians remained

THE PRICE OF BATTLE: CONFEDERATE DEAD AT SHARPSBURG (Library of Congress)

loyal to the Union. For Kentucky any North-South conflict would literally become a war of brother against brother. That deep division can be seen in the family of Senator John J. Crittenden, whose attempt at compromise failed in the winter of 1860–1861. One of his sons became a general in the Confederate army, the other a general in the Union army. To escape that horror, Kentucky attempted to remain neutral. Despite an official state proclamation of neutrality, both sides pressed Kentucky, and both took recruits and supplies. For several months, however, neither sent organized forces across the Kentucky border. But in September 1861, to thwart an expected Federal advance, Confederate soldiers entered the state. Technically the Confederacy was the first to violate neutral borders, but Union troops crossed the Ohio River promptly thereafter. Thus the Confederates, commanded by General Albert Sidney Johnston, a stalwart of the prewar United States Army who had a glowing though unproven reputation as a great soldier, occupied a line stretching from east to west through the center of the state. With both sides there in force, the state threatened to become the first great western battleground.

Confederates and Yankees did not, however, fight a major battle for Kentucky. Because of the insight and determination of an unimpressive-looking Union general who chewed on cigars, the Confederates had to pull out of Kentucky without much fighting at all. At the beginning of 1862, Ulysses S. Grant was still a relatively obscure officer, but he would not remain unknown much longer. Grant recognized that two rivers that flowed northward through Tennessee and Kentucky into the Ohio offered an opportunity both to flush Johnston out of Kentucky and to invade the Confederate heartland. The Cumberland River went to Nashville; the Tennessee River cut through the entire state whose name it bore. Grant planned to send a combined navy-army force up the rivers to blast the Confederates by sea and land.

The Confederates were also aware that the Cumberland and Tennessee provided a watery highway into their interior. To block any Union advance, the Confederates constructed two forts on the Kentucky-Tennessee border where only fifteen miles separated the two rivers. Fort Henry, on the eastern bank of the Tennessee, and Fort Donelson, on the western bank of the Cumberland, guarded the water routes. They proved no match, however, for Grant's land-sea attack. Poorly situated, Fort Henry had to contend with the rising waters of the Tennessee as well as the advancing Federals. It did neither successfully and fell on February 6. Ten days later Fort Donelson, plagued by command problems, capitulated to Grant's infantry.

Grant's victory meant disaster for the Confederacy. With his Kentucky line fatally breached and a Federal army in his rear, Johnston pulled out of Kentucky. With Grant astride the two rivers, Tennessee offered no haven, so Johnston retreated southwestward across the state. Not only Kentucky came under Union control; so did central Tennessee, with its important supply point at Nashville and the ironworks of the Cumberland River Valley.

Grant did not rest on his laurels. He pushed on up the Tennessee with the goal of inflicting a crippling blow on the Confederate war effort in the West. Flung back across hundreds of miles and two states, Johnston stopped to regroup in northeastern Mississippi. At some point he had to stand and fight, and Albert Johnston decided the time was now. He had strengthened his army by bringing in every available soldier; he even got General Beauregard as second in command. Moreover, his opponents had temporarily divided their forces. Grant was coming up the Tennessee with the main body, but Federal units sent to Nashville had not yet rejoined him. Grant's army of around 40,000 was encamped on the western bank of the Tennessee just inside the state at Pittsburg Landing, near a small country place of worship called Shiloh Church.

Johnston and Beauregard planned to drive Grant into the Tennessee River before any reinforcements could reach him. At daylight on April 6 the Confederates, 40,000 strong, stormed out of the woods into a generally surprised Union army. Neither Grant nor his generals had expected an attack. During the day the soldiers in gray and blue fought with a ferociousness never before seen on the continent. The bloodletting was appalling. Among the casualties was General Johnston, mortally wounded while urging his men forward. For a time a Confederate victory seemed inevitable, but vigorous stands by individual Federal units kept Grant's line intact. Nightfall found the Confederates short of their goal, and Grant prepared to take the offensive the next day with the reinforcements that arrived during the night. When Beauregard was unable to hold Grant back, he withdrew into Mississippi. The casualties shocked everyone; each side suffered more than 1,700 killed and 8,000 wounded. Though at terrible cost, the Confederates served notice at Shiloh that the western war had not yet ended.

The frightful carnage on Civil War battlefields resulted in large part from technological improvements in weaponry. Chief among these advances was the rifling—the cutting of spiral grooves within barrels—of both infantry and artillery weapons. Rifling imparted a spin to a bullet which greatly increased the range and accuracy of a weapon. The effective range of the basic infantry musket went from 100 yards to 300 or 400 yards. In the face of this enhanced firepower, the traditional infantry charge, widely relied on by most commanders, usually led to disaster. A participant in a Confederate charge described the attack as the "work of death." "Volley after volley of musket balls sweep through the line and mow us down like wheat before the scythe." Witnessing such devastation, a junior officer wailed, "Down! down! go the boys."

After the shooting stopped, grisly sights surrounded the survivors. A Confederate veteran of Chancellorsville described the dead everywhere,

> some with their heads shot off, some with their brains oozing out, some pierced through the head with musket balls, some with their noses shot away, some with their mouths smashed, some wounded in the neck, some with broken arms or legs, some shot through the breast and some cut in two with shells.

Being killed outright, however, was often preferable to being wounded. Because both medical knowledge and sanitary conditions were primitive, many of the wounded died eventually, or survived severely maimed. Military hospitals were appalling places. A Confederate soldier observed:

The sorriest sights...are in those dreadful field-hospitals, established in barns, under large tents, and in houses. The screams and groans of the poor fellows undergoing amputation are sometimes dreadful—and then the sight of arms and legs surrounding those places, as they are thrown into great piles is something one that has seen the results of battle can never forget.

Farther west, beyond the Mississippi, the conflict also raged. In 1861 both sides struggled over control of Missouri, like Kentucky a slave state that had not seceded. For a time in midyear the Confederates controlled most of the southern half of the state, but by early 1862 Confederate forces had been pushed back into Arkansas. In March 1862 a key battle took place in northwestern Arkansas, at Pea Ridge, where a decisive Union victory ended any serious Confederate threat to Missouri. The remainder of the war in this vast area, including Arkansas, northern Louisiana, and Texas—the Confederacy's Trans-Mississippi Department—was not of primary importance. Few troops, long distances, and poor transportation made military operations difficult. Trans-Mississippi's chief contribution to the war effort was as a supplier of such critical items as horses. When Union victories in 1863 closed the Mississippi, eastward traffic slowed and the entire Trans-Mississippi came under military command. With the closure of the great river, President Davis gave the departmental commander, General Edmund Kirby-Smith, the right to exercise civil as well as military authority. Kirby-Smith remained in charge of the Trans-Mississippi for the duration of the war.

The bloodbath at Shiloh had not paralyzed the Confederate leadership. On the contrary, standing and fighting seemed to rejuvenate the Confederates. The shocking loss of New Orleans, the major port of the Confederacy and the guardian of the lower Mississippi, had somehow to be overcome. Only three weeks after Shiloh, New Orleans had fallen to a Union naval task force under David G. Farragut, which had run past the downriver forts defending the city. Determined to turn events around, President Davis replaced Beauregard, who had fallen back deeper into Mississippi, with General Braxton Bragg, an organizer and a disciplinarian. Initially this seemed a wise move, for Bragg determined to take the offensive. By a roundabout rail route he took the bulk of his army to Chattanooga to assist the Confederates defending eastern Tennessee. But once he arrived there, Davis ordered Bragg to invade Kentucky with the combined force of around 50,000 troops.

Such an advance offered enormous potential for the Confederates. With their major western field army in Kentucky, much of the territory lost since Forts Henry and Donelson would seem once again to be within their grasp. Nashville and central Tennessee were still in Federal hands, but the Union forces would evacuate them if the Confederates prevailed in Kentucky. The Confederates hoped not only to recruit Kentucky volunteers and replenish their supplies but to add Kentucky to the roster of Confederate states—a major political triumph. Then the front line would be the Ohio River, not the Tennessee. Strategically, politically, and psychologically the Confederates could gain enormously. But of course this outcome depended on the Confederates' success on the battlefield.

Bragg, who took his army from Mississippi to Kentucky with confidence and decisiveness, lost those characteristics in Kentucky. Once in the state, he did not promptly effect the concentration of all Confederate troops in order to fight the Union forces on ground favorable to him. Nor could he decide on priorities between an aggressive political policy aimed at inaugurating a Confederate governor and a military plan designed to end in Confederate triumph. The campaign that began with such anticipation ended in a muddle. The political goals went nowhere, and the major fight on October 8, at Perryville in the central part of the state, found Bragg outnumbered by Federal forces commanded by Major General Don Carlos Buell. With less than half of his army on the field, he pulled away after a day of fighting. His hopes shattered, Bragg retreated to Tennessee.

A CHANGING WAR

Decisive military victories in Maryland and Kentucky could have put the Confederate States of America in an almost unassailable position. Such triumphs would have put immense pressure on Lincoln to work out some plan for peace. But Lincoln never felt that pressure; it was Jefferson Davis who had to contend with fundamentally altered circumstances.

The strategic reverses suffered by the Confederates in the autumn of 1862 settled the basic international question. Defeat in Kentucky and especially in Maryland exploded the Confederates' dream that Great Britain and perhaps other European powers would intervene on their behalf. Because of Britain's naval power, no one else in Europe would act unless Great Britain led the way. And serious discussions had occurred in England about the proper policy toward the United States and the Confederate States. A weakened United States would certainly be in Britain's interest. And though cotton from Egypt and India had made the loss of the South's cotton less serious than it would have been otherwise, a guaranteed supply from the South would boost Britain's textile industry and general economy. But the foreign policy of the Lincoln administration made clear to the British government that any action to benefit the Confederacy would probably mean war with the United States. Thus England was not going to get involved unless the evidence clearly pointed toward a Confederate victory. And after Sharpsburg and Perryville, the signs indicated confusion at best and the South's defeat at worst. So if the Confederacy were to prevail, it would have to do so without help from England.

The Confederate retreat from Maryland also provided an opportunity for Lincoln to claim the moral high ground. At the outset the Confederacy established independence as its chief war aim, while Lincoln claimed he fought to preserve the Union. As for slavery, Lincoln stated, he would take any stand that would aid preservation of the Union. But after Sharpsburg, Lincoln issued his Emancipation Proclamation, and the elimination of slavery became a second major goal of the war. The proclamation made a decision to help the South even more difficult for England and France because both opposed slavery. Even though the Emancipation Proclamation could not and did not even attempt to free all slaves, it was a significant document. Claiming that his war powers gave him the required authority, Lincoln announced that all slaves held in states still in rebellion on January 1, 1863, would become free. The proclamation did not free slaves in the states of the Union or in those areas of the Confederacy occupied by Union forces. Despite its limitations, it did alter in a basic way the moral calculus of the war.

The Confederates reacted angrily. In a message to the Confederate Congress, President Davis denounced the proclamation as "the most execrable measure in the history of guilty man." He even threatened to treat captured Federal officers as "criminals engaged in inciting servile insurrection." The Union's warning that it would hold Confederate officers for similar treatment guaranteed that Davis's threat would never be carried out. Despite the outcries of the Confederate leaders, many of them recognized that the Emancipation Proclamation put them on the moral as well as the military defensive.

Although disappointed by the refusal of the European powers to intervene and outraged by the Emancipation Proclamation, the Confederate government moved forthrightly to strengthen its ability to carry on the war. The first necessity was manpower. Even before Shiloh and the Seven Days, Confederate authorities recognized that volunteers alone could never meet the requirements for soldiers. On April 1, 1862, the Confederate Congress enacted the first conscription law in American history; it made all white men between the ages of eighteen and thirty-five eligible for military service, though it permitted substitutes and exempted the clergy and men in critical occupations, such as ironworkers, teachers, and state employees. In the fall Congress extended the upper age limit to forty-five and established an exemption for owners and overseers of twenty or more slaves. As troop requirements grew more desperate, Congress continued to respond. In February 1864 it broadened the age brackets to include ages seventeen to fifty and curtailed exemptions.

Though conscription was not popular, it helped to fill Confederate ranks. Some state officials opposed conscription as an invasion of local and states' rights by the central government. The provision permitting owners and overseers of more than twenty slaves to escape the draft brought forth cries that this was a rich man's war and a poor man's fight. Despite the problems, the statistics demonstrate the overall effectiveness of the various conscription bills. The Confederate population included approximately one million white males between seventeen and forty-five; some 750,000 served in the Confederate military. When the men who worked in vital civilian positions are taken into account, it becomes clear that most of those million men directly aided the Confederate war effort. With the help of conscription the Confederate government kept sizable armies in the field until the final months of the war.

Fighting men could accomplish nothing, however, without the materials of war. At the commencement of hostilities the Confederate government had no ready supply of arms; its inventory consisted solely of armaments captured from federal arsenals. But because of the efforts of one of the true geniuses of the Confederacy, Confederate soldiers usually had weapons and ammunition. In April 1861 an obscure captain in the old United States Army accepted a commission as major and assignment as chief of the Confederate Ordnance Department. A native Pennsylvanian, a graduate of West Point, and the son-in-law of a former governor of Alabama, Josiah Gorgas set about arming the defenders of the Confederacy. With immense organizational gifts and astonishing enterprise, Gorgas set to work to turn plowshares into swords. At the outset he sent an agent to Europe to buy arms and ammunition, which entered the Confederacy through the blockade. Then Gorgas set out to create a munitions industry. He built powder mills; the largest, at Augusta, produced one million pounds of gunpowder in 1863 alone. To obtain the essential ingredient, potassium nitrate, or niter, Gorgas mined saltpeter in caves, created niter beds from carcasses of dead animals, and collected the contents of chamberpots. The Tredegar ironworks in Richmond made a wide variety of essential items, such as propeller shafts and plate for ironclads. New foundries to cast cannon were established at Augusta, Columbus, and Macon, in Georgia; a naval gunworks was built at Selma, Alabama. Looking back from the spring of 1864, Gorgas accurately observed in his diary: "Where three years ago we were not making a gun, a pistol nor a sabre, no shot nor shell (except at the Tredegar Works)—a pound of powder—we now make all these in quantities to meet the demands of our large armies." While many men were promoted to high rank because of their performance on the battlefield, Gorgas advanced only to brigadier general, but without him the combat generals would never have been able to lead armies in battle for four years.

The government agencies in charge of procuring and supplying food and clothing had no Josiah Gorgas. Armies often drew from the areas in which they operated for clothing and especially for food. Most soldiers provided most of what they wore, and it was never abundant. Footwear was particularly shoddy and in short supply, though by 1864 shoe factories in Richmond were turning out 800 pairs a day. To feed its troops the government called on planters and farmers to shift from cotton to foodstuffs. The production of cotton declined dramatically, from just under 4 million bales in 1860 to around 300,000 in 1864. The spread of the territory occupied by Union troops surely accounted for some of this decrease, as did the difficulty of marketing the crop; but just as certainly support for the government's efforts contributed significantly. Corn and wheat shipments from farms and plantations to armies crisscrossed the South. Most field armies used nearby food sources as much as possible; the Shenandoah Valley, for example, served as the granary for Lee's Army of Northern Virginia.

HOPE BECOMES DESPAIR

After the Confederate setbacks in Maryland and Kentucky, the war returned southward for the winter. But in neither East nor West did hibernation set in. In

Tennessee, at Murfreesboro or Stones River, and in Virginia, at Fredericksburg, armies fought bloody December battles, neither of which had any significant strategic importance. In mid-December at Fredericksburg, Lee pummeled a new opponent, Major General Ambrose Burnside, from a strong defensive position. At the end of the month, in an uncoordinated attack, Bragg failed in an effort to defeat the Federal army commanded by Major General William S. Rosecrans and to open the road to Nashville, only thirty miles beyond Murfreesboro. After these two inconclusive fights the armies waited for spring.

The spring and summer of 1863 brought two great offensives. In the East Robert E. Lee mounted his second campaign north of the Potomac, while in the West Ulysses Grant struck vigorously at the great Confederate stronghold on the Mississippi, Vicksburg. In May at Chancellorsville, just west of Fredericksburg, Lee in a brilliant battle whipped Major General Joseph Hooker and turned back another Union drive for Richmond. Although Chancellorsville stood as a notable Confederate victory, it demanded a high price. Wounded by fire from his own men, Stonewall Jackson contracted pneumonia and died on May 10. Despite that blow, Lee retained enormous confidence in his officers and men. Having reorganized the Army of Northern Virginia, he once again aimed it at the North. Although Confederate officials no longer seriously contemplated European intervention, President Davis and Lee wanted the war in enemy country. The food, fodder, and other supplies available in Maryland and Pennsylvania would lessen the demand on Virginia. But also the Confederate leadership wanted northerners to experience the presence of armies, troops, and battle. A resounding victory on Union territory could put enormous pressure on Lincoln to recognize the Confederacy and negotiate with the Davis administration. It was not to be, however. Lee's offensive ended in early July in a small Pennsylvania town, Gettysburg. There, after three days of desperate fighting, Lee failed to overcome a Union army commanded by Major General George G. Meade. Having lost more than 25,000 men—over one-third of his troops—Lee once again led his bleeding army back into Virginia.

While Lee was marching northward toward his fateful rendezvous at Gettysburg, Grant was menacing Vicksburg. Vicksburg was of critical importance to the Confederates because along with Port Hudson, just over one-hundred miles to the south in Louisiana, it kept the Mississippi open for communication with the Trans-Mississippi area, which provided horses and other critical items. Jefferson Davis ordered the commander at Vicksburg, Lieutenant General John C. Pemberton, a northerner who had sided with the Confederacy, to hold at all costs. After failing to capture Vicksburg from the north, Grant conducted one of the most brilliant campaigns of the war. On the western bank of the Mississippi he moved his army overland; south of Vicksburg he transported his troops to the eastern bank. Then he moved rapidly northeastward toward Jackson before turning back to the west and driving toward Vicksburg. Knocked off balance by Grant's daring and his rapid movements, the Confederates responded ineffectively. By late May, Grant had Pemberton cooped up in Vicksburg; the siege lasted some six weeks. On July 4, 1863, one day after Lee's defeat at Gettysburg, Vicksburg capitulated. With Port Hudson falling to the Union on July 8, the entire length of the Mississippi came under Federal control.

The losses at Gettysburg and Vicksburg were major blows. In the East the Union forces inflicted heavy casualties on the main Confederate field army and forced it to retreat into Virginia. In the West President Lincoln finally realized a major strategic goal, command of the Mississippi. The bagging of the 30,000 troops in the Vicksburg garrison did nothing to help the Confederate war effort, either. In the Washington-Richmond corridor as well as the Mississippi Valley the Federals had the upper hand and the initiative.

Despite the Confederate disaster at Vicksburg, Bragg's Army of Tennessee remained whole and in the field, though after Murfreesboro he had eventually retreated all the way to Georgia. In September, however, Bragg struck the Union army under Rosecrans in a bitter contest known as the Battle of Chickamauga. Reinforced by 12,000 men from Lee's army, transported by rail to northern Georgia, Bragg overwhelmed his foes and drove them back into Chattanooga. Bragg occupied the heights surrounding the city and attempted to force a surrender, but Chattanooga was still holding out in October, when Grant arrived to take command of the besieged Union forces. Immediately he reopened the Union supply line as a prelude to breaking Bragg's hold on the city. In late November he launched attacks that broke through Bragg's lines; once again the Confederates withdrew into Georgia.

The year 1864 opened with the Confederates on the defensive across the South. In Virginia, on ground just west of his triumphs at Fredericksburg and Chancellorsville, Lee awaited still another march on Richmond. This time his antagonist would be Grant, the conqueror of Vicksburg and Chattanooga, now a lieutenant general in command of all Union armies. While Grant prepared to hurl his troops against Lee, his chief subordinate in the West, Major General William T. Sherman, moved out of Chattanooga and pointed his divisions toward Atlanta and the Army of Tennessee, now under Joseph Johnston, who had replaced the oft-defeated and oft-criticized Bragg.

Grant and Sherman gave Lee and Johnston more than they could handle. The two Confederate generals waged quite different campaigns. From the moment Grant crossed his front in early May, Lee assaulted him on every possible occasion. In a series of bloody engagements—the Wilderness, Spotsylvania Courthouse, the North Anna—Lee delivered fierce blows that would have stopped and probably turned back his previous foes, but Grant kept driving ahead, despite horrendous losses. Finally on June 3 at Cold Harbor, only ten miles from Richmond, Grant launched a frontal assault that resulted in 7,000 Union soldiers killed or wounded, most in the first few minutes. In a month of bitter fighting Lee had inflicted on the Union army casualties about equal to the 60,000 men with whom he started the campaign. And still Grant remained in his front. Lee despaired of what would happen if Grant pinned him in a static position where he could not maneuver. To one of his commanders he predicted with terrible accuracy that if the contest between him and Grant ever "bec[a]me a siege, ... then it [would] be a mere question of time."

Joe Johnston in Georgia never attacked Sherman. By superb handling of his troops in a succession of flanking moves, Sherman thoroughly confused Johnston, who did not seem to understand what his canny opponent was about. After six weeks Sherman had maneuvered Johnston out of mountainous north Georgia to the banks of the Chattahoochee River, with Atlanta in sight and the plains of central and south Georgia beyond. An understandably upset Jefferson Davis could get no plan from Johnston, who informed the president that Sherman's actions would determine his own. Believing he had no choice, Davis relieved Johnston and replaced him with General John B. Hood, a ferocious combat leader who had had an arm maimed at Gettysburg and a leg amputated at Chickamauga but was untested as an army commander. Hood did his president's bidding and fought vigorously, albeit unsuccessfully, for Atlanta. After six weeks and several hard fights, Atlanta fell to Sherman on September 1.

In the fall of 1864 the Confederates faced a bleak military situation. Lee found himself in trenches at Petersburg with overextended lines and his maneuverability gone. Even so, he tried to recreate the circumstances of 1862 by using the Shenandoah Valley to alarm Washington and lessen the pressure on his beleaguered army. Back in the summer he had dispatched Lieutenant General Jubal A. Early with 10,000 troops he could not really spare to stop a Federal incursion in the Shenandoah. After doing so, Early headed down the valley toward the Potomac. He crossed the Potomac and in mid-July came up to the fortifications guarding the northwestern approach to Washington. Lee's hopes were realized when Grant sent an entire corps, more than 15,000 men, up from Petersburg to counter Early. But 1864 was not 1862; the numerical disparity was too great. Even without that corps, Grant maintained inexorable pressure on Lee. At the same time superior Federal numbers forced Early back into Virginia. There he could not contend with the Federal force under Major General Philip Sheridan. By October Sheridan had both decimated Early's little army and laid waste to the Shenandoah. In the trenches at Petersburg, as Grant kept moving southward, Lee could only watch the thin gray line of defenders becoming thinner.

In the West, General Hood received permission from President Davis to strike at Sherman's rear and his supply lines. As a result, the two major armies marched away from each other. While Hood headed for Tennessee with visions of a dazzling victory, Sherman started for Savannah and the sea with his veteran army and without substantive opposition. Christmas brought vastly different tidings to the two sides. Hood made it to Tennessee, but his gross tactical errors and the Union's numerical superiority wrecked the Army of Tennessee. Battles at Franklin and Nashville claimed more than half of his infantry. After a superior Union army under Major General George H. Thomas smashed the Confederates at Nashville, a battered Army of Tennessee limped back into Mississippi, where for all practical purposes it ceased to exist. Simultaneously Sherman was cutting a wide swath through central and south Georgia on his march to the sea. He gave President Lincoln a special Christmas present, the city of Savannah.

THE IMPACT OF THE WAR

The Confederate military effort did not take place in a vacuum. As the battle-field contests began consistently to go against the gray armies, other areas also experienced severe dislocations and setbacks. The economy went out of control. Inflation, inevitable in the absence of a realistic fiscal policy, seemed propelled by gunpowder. Between midsummer and the early fall of 1863 prices rose by 58 percent. Between October 1863 and February 1864 the cost of a barrel of flour in Richmond leaped from $70 to $250. The tightening blockade made any item from abroad difficult to obtain and therefore precious. As advancing Union armies overran more and more Confederate territory, less and less was available to produce foodstuffs for fighting men and civilians alike.

The fate of coffee, a favorite drink of southerners regardless of social standing, indicates the deprivations caused by the war and how southerners attempted to cope with them. Few southerners could contemplate a world without coffee. But by 1862 real coffee practically disappeared for all but the wealthiest, and even they could not count on obtaining it. Southerners never quit struggling to concoct a replacement. Almost every imaginable item was substituted for the unavailable coffee bean. Parched corn, rye, wheat, okra seed, sweet potatoes, and blends of them all ended up in Confederates' coffee ups. No one mistook any of these concoctions for real coffee, however.

onfederate reverses also affected politics. Confederate politics became
politics of personality. In the spring of 1861 southerners had united
nd a president to lead them. Past political loyalties and divi-
dissolved in the cheering moment of the birth of the Con-
a. Old parties did not survive as identifiable entities,
d. Involvement with parties would somehow have
overnment was not identified with a party, its
a party of loyal opposition. When natural
policies arose, it had no institutional
he Davis administration, as well as
n.

eracy and determined to take any
pendence, Jefferson Davis neither en-
nension of his presidency. He did, after
rge Washington, he had to create a nation
e Washington, he did not have the shared
ion as a foundation for his building. Davis's
at events. When Davis supported conscription and
sed the power of the central government, he knew
t the South's tradition of limited government and local
ate victory, in his mind the only legitimate goal, re-
d anyone who opposed one of his policies, including
Stephens and strong-minded governors, became not
ponent on that issue but an enemy of the cause. In a similar

manner Confederates who honestly feared a powerful central government condemned the president as a power-mad despot who did not care about the principles on which the Confederacy was founded. As personal attacks, even ven-
dettas, became commonplace, the Confederate Congress often resembled little
more than a shouting hall.

Davis as war leader was unquestionably committed to securing independence for the Confederate States of America. He tried valiantly to rouse the
people to carry on the fight. In both 1863 and 1864 he traveled into the Deep
South to call on citizens for sacrifice, courage, and determination. His overall
view of the Confederate war effort was certainly reasonable, but he permitted
personal squabbles to influence command and professional decisions. His bitter
conflict with both Joe Johnston and Beauregard made him unwilling to make
the best and fullest use of either general. Although both of them must share the
blame for their bad relations with the president, he did not rise above their pet-
tiness. His commitment to Braxton Bragg, by contrast, lasted long after Bragg,
who had lost the confidence of senior commanders, could function effectively
as commanding general of the Army of Tennessee. As president, Davis permitted his personal likes and dislikes to keep him from making the best use of civilian and military officials. It is easy to criticize Davis's management of the
war, but he confronted an increasingly horrendous situation.

Southern society also felt the impact of war. At the outset whites expressed
great enthusiasm for the Confederate enterprise. They saw themselves as the
true sons and daughters of the American Revolution and as the only faithful
constitutionalists. Moreover, their ministers proclaimed the Confederate enterprise as blessed by God and under His care. From pulpits across the Confederacy the message boomed loud and clear: God was on the side of the South; the
Confederates were His chosen people. Cheers supported the political leadership; volunteers populated the military. But the seemingly unstoppable Union
advances and the hardships of total war eroded both unity and enthusiasm.
Class antagonism surfaced when rich men were permitted to hire substitutes to
do their duty for them, and the exemption from conscription for owners and
overseers of twenty or more slaves especially rankled. Increasing numbers of
men began to avoid military service; desertion came to occupy the attention of
almost every Confederate commander. Most deserters did not come from the
upper orders of society. Some scholars have argued that desertion did at least
as much as battle casualties to undermine the strength of Confederate armies.
That claim is extreme, though undoubtedly desertion hurt and hurt severely.

Avoidance of service and desertion had concrete causes. Most Confederate
men had gone into the military to defend their homes and their families from
invasion. They wanted to protect their liberty. But the tide of the war, particularly after 1863, raised questions of how best to carry out what most Confederate soldiers considered their most sacred mission. By 1864 Union armies were
pouring into almost every state. The invading bluecoats were threatening the
social organization the Confederacy was formed to preserve. To some men, defense of home and family required them to return to protect their loved ones

and property. Confederate defeats spurred desertion. As the situation on the battle lines and the home front became increasingly desperate, the cries of home became louder and louder.

The cries underscored the plight of people on the home front. Trying to obtain his son's release from the army, a father informed the War Department, "If you dount send him home I am bound to louse my crop and cum to suffer. I am eiaghty one years of adge." In her effort to bring her husband back a desperate wife made a forceful case. "Thare is no use," she declared, "in keeping a man thare to kill him and leave widows and poore little orphen children to suffer.... My poor children have no home nor no Father." Many soldiers could have but one response to such pleas. One Confederate civilian went straight to the heart of the issue: "What man is there that would stay in the armey and no that his family is sufring at home?" By the last winter of the war thousands of soldiers disappeared from the ranks. To their minds their fundamental duty lay at home, not in the army.

Four years of war did affect the status of southern women. When so many men from every social and economic class went off to fight, women had to assume many of their duties. In far greater numbers than before 1861 women began to manage farms, plantations, and slaves. The wounding and killing of fathers, husbands, brothers, and sons often turned temporary management into what seemed like a permanent condition. Women worked in factories, engaged in charitable activities, and even commented on political matters. Those endeavors surely differed sharply from the experience of the vast majority of women during the prewar years. Even so, very few tried to make any fundamental alterations in their position in southern society. Most were too busy trying to survive to view their activities as somehow threatening conventional definitions of female propriety. As a result, what appeared to be a striking transformation in the economic and social roles of southern women had mostly short-term effects. When the war ended, most women resumed their traditional roles, and old definitions of the proper relations between the sexes prevailed once more. The war did not create a new southern woman.

THE WAR AND SLAVERY

Although the war did not transform the place of women, it had a momentous impact on black southerners. The South's black slaves contributed immensely to the Confederate war effort. On farms and plantations they produced the food that fed the soldiers. Their labor enabled tens of thousands of whites to enter the ranks. An Alabama newspaper underscored this relationship when it observed that slavery permitted the South "to place in the field a force so much larger in proportion to her white population than the North."

Slaves did a lot more, however, than toil in fields. They made up a substantial percentage of the industrial labor force in mines, ironworks, ordnance plants, and other enterprises. Blacks also helped on specific military projects, such as fortifications—work that their owners did not always volunteer. From the beginning the Confederate government recognized the enormous value of slaves. Accordingly, Congress passed legislation permitting the impressment of slaves for military necessity.

Though most slaves remained faithful to their masters through most of the war, new circumstances strained the old relationship and eventually broke it down. When masters marched off to war they left ultimate control of slaves with others, usually overseers or other family members. Then impressment carried slaves off farms and plantations and put them under the control of government officials. Though disruptive, neither of these situations endangered the system. The advance of Union armies, however, did pose a mortal threat to it. Many slaves took the first opportunity that presented itself to escape to Union lines. To prevent such occurrences, numerous owners transferred their slaves to remote locations in the hope of evading Union forces. Even slaves who had been loyal to masters or the surrogates of masters moved at the approach of blue-clad soldiers, for loyalty to a master stopped when a realistic chance for freedom presented itself.

Developments at Brokenburn Plantation in northeastern Louisiana illustrate just what the war did to slaves and slaveholders. In the spring of 1861 the men went to war with body servants and the public blessings of the house servants and the field hands. In that initial summer Kate Stone, twenty-year-old daughter of the plantation mistress, confided to her diary that "the house servants have been giving a lot of trouble lately—lazy and disobedient....I suppose the excitement in the air has infected them." When the Yankees moved against Vicksburg, just to the east of Brokenburn, during the summer of 1862, Kate worried that they would come and take the family's slaves. Her mother told all the male slaves to hide from the Yankee soldiers. "We think they will," she consoled herself. But in early July, Kate admitted, "Generally when told to run away from the soldiers, they go right to them." In the spring of 1863: "All the Negroes are running away now." By this time many of the Brokenburn slaves had been moved to rented property in the western part of the state. During the summer the remaining whites and blacks headed west. Brokenburn had become a casualty of the war.

By the spring of 1865 the Confederate States of America itself was succumbing. The hungry, ragged veterans in Lee's army and the broken corporal's guard that remained from the Army of Tennessee could no longer hold against the powerful armies of Grant and Sherman. From the trenches at Petersburg, Lee told Davis that he would soon be forced to give up Petersburg, and that move would require the evacuation of Richmond. Called back to command the skeleton of the Army of Tennessee in North Carolina, Joe Johnston could hardly even slow down Sherman, who in the winter had laid waste to South Carolina on his way from Savannah to link up with Grant in Virginia.

Jefferson Davis did not want to contemplate surrender. In a last desperate effort to gain Confederate independence he severed the powerful cultural forces that had given the antebellum South its basic identity and had brought about the creation of the Confederate States of America. At least since the Revolution white southerners had been unable to separate their liberty from their institution of black slavery. Slavery governed the definition of liberty. But in that final, anguished winter Davis split what previously had been unsplittable; he separated liberty from slavery. He reluctantly concluded that to secure liberty the Confederacy must jettison slavery. In this last lunge Davis reached in two directions at once. He dispatched a confidential agent to Europe with instructions to offer Britain and France emancipation in turn for their recognition of the Confederacy. England said never. It was too late. To arrest the disintegration of his armies, Davis simultaneously advocated the enlistment of slaves as soldiers. When one of his generals had broached the idea a year earlier, he had rebuffed it. But in March, with Lee's support, Davis prevailed on a reluctant Congress to enact a law that would permit black slaves to don gray uniforms. The bill did not, however, offer emancipation in exchange for military service. Whether or not slaves would have fought for their masters will never be known. The war ended before the formation of any black regiments.

THE END

The end came in April and May. On April 9, 1865, Palm Sunday, at Appomattox Courthouse, eighty-five miles southwest of Richmond, Lee surrendered the Army of Northern Virginia to Grant. Some two weeks later, just outside Durham, North Carolina, Joe Johnston capitulated to Sherman. By May 4 all Confederate forces east of the Mississippi had surrendered. Still President Davis refused to give up. Calling for continued resistance, he retreated through the Carolinas in the hope of getting to the Trans-Mississippi and carrying on the war from there. But in south Georgia on May 10 a Union calvary detachment captured Davis and his party. Finally on May 26 General Edmund Kirby-Smith surrendered his Trans-Mississippi army. The Confederate States of America ceased to exist.

Although arguments about whether or not the Confederacy could win abound, its defeat was not foreordained. At least three possibilities offered a chance for a different result. The first two would have involved European intervention. Help could have come at the very beginning of the war if Great Britain had refused to permit the Union to blockade Confederate ports. More likely, Great Britain would have acted in the autumn of 1862 had the Confederates won on the battlefield in Kentucky and especially in Maryland. Had Lee triumphed at Antietam, Great Britain might have moved in such a way as to impel Lincoln to make peace with an independent Confederacy. The third chance occurred in the hot, bloody summer of 1864. If Grant had concluded that enough Union blood had soaked the Virginia ground and had followed his predecessors in retreat, or if Sherman had been stopped before Atlanta, then a political shift could easily have occurred in the North which would have forced Lincoln out of office in favor of a peace government. That none of those possibilities turned out to favor the Confederacy does not mean they did not exist. The proper conclusion to draw is that the results on specific battlefields and the character and ability of particular generals and leaders had an enormous impact on the outcome.

Many reasons explain the Union victory and the Confederate defeat. The North enjoyed a substantial advantage in two critical areas—a significantly larger population and a vastly more powerful industrial machine. Neither of them, not even both together, guarantees military success or failure. During both the American Revolution and the Vietnam war the greater power lost. In the 1770s and 1780s America prevailed over Great Britain, then the leading military and industrial power in the world. Almost two hundred years later in the 1960s and 1970s the United States, with almost unlimited military and industrial strength, failed to subdue North Vietnam. The critical difference in war is not material superiority alone but the will to use that superiority. In neither the American Revolution nor the Vietnam war did the stronger side throw all of its might against the weaker with absolute determination to win. But that is precisely what Abraham Lincoln did. He never wavered; he would never relent or hold back. He was willing to use his advantage to the fullest. And he stayed in the fight until he found commanders who had a resoluteness that matched his own. With that kind of leadership the side with the stronger battalions and the larger factories prevailed.

Defeated in open battle, the Confederates did not try to keep their cause alive through guerrilla warfare. Having experienced the brute force of the

COLUMBIA DESTROYED (Kean Archives, Philadelphia)

RICHMOND IN RUINS (Library of Congress)

Union military juggernaut, which had blasted their armies and destroyed their land, they believed they had made their stand and had nothing left to prove. Moreover, they thought that guerrilla activities might very well lead to anarchy and the social disintegration of their homeland. Without question racial considerations were critical in this assessment. Although no one knew where the elimination of slavery might lead race relations, anxiety about the racial situation worked mightily against any cause that could end in lawless marauding in the South.

The South in the spring of 1865 was a broken land. The Confederate experience had cost the South dearly. Slavery and the hundreds of millions of dollars invested in it disappeared with the Confederacy. Physical destruction marred the southern landscape like an ugly scar. Two-thirds of the railroads, the bulk of the industrial plant, countless bridges and buildings, thousands of homes, a huge quantity of livestock—all were destroyed during the war. The human price staggers the imagination. With 260,000 men killed and at least that many more wounded, few white families did not know the grief of a dead or maimed father, husband, brother, or son. Confederate casualties accounted for almost 9 percent of the southern white population. Though the Union suffered 360,000 dead, its casualties did not quite reach 3 percent of the population. In World War II American casualties amounted to only a fraction over one-half of 1 percent of the population. Trying to cope with an uncharted racial course and with massive physical and human devastation, southerners, black and white, faced an uncertain future.

16

After the War

———— ❖ ————

The Civil War reached its climax in April 1865, at Appomattox Court-house. The Confederacy sputtered on until the end of May, but the surrender at the Virginia courthouse was the end of the Confederate States of America, and of much else.

Ham Chamberlayne, a Virginia officer, did not wait for the formal surrender. He wrote his family:

> I am by no means conquered yet....We refused to take part in the funeral at Appomattox C.H. & cut or crept our way out....I am off for Miss. No notion of laying down my arms—Probably make Texas during the Summer....I cant stay here. Twould kill me by inches. I am going off with what I have on. I shall make it, never fear.

Ben Davis, a former slave, remembered another battle and another surrender.

> I saw a big white flag going up toward the skies, like a big white-robed angel, going to heaven. I was too startled at first to grasp what it meant or what it was but, as I got my senses back, I saw it was surrender, surrender, surrender...."We is free, we is free...." We stood there looking up to heaven, thanking God....I stood there after I come to myself and shouted, clapped my hands for joy and shouted and shouted, as if the Holy Spirit was coming down. White folks set their guns down and shouted, "I'm glad of it, I'm glad of it!" And right there midst all that joy and shouting, men were digging graves and others were putting in the bodies, just piling three or four in one grave, like dogs, one on top of the other....It was sad, sad!

Those bodies were among the 260,000 Confederates and 364,000 Federals, including 38,000 blacks, who died along the dreadful, bloody way to Appomattox. One-tenth of all southern white adult males died during the war. Another 282,000 Union troops sustained wounds; Confederate wounded numbered at least half as many. No one counted the permanently disabled or other human costs that are difficult to calculate but no less real. Those costs included mental disability, for combatants and noncombatants alike; reduced opportunities for women to marry and have a family; and increased chances for poverty. How many disillusioned men moved west, as Ham Chamberlayne did, and unlike him, never returned? Other Americans did, of course, migrate to the South after the war, but for years their numbers were exceeded by those moving out of the South. Only after World War II did in-migration begin consistently to exceed out-migration.

The grisly total of the Civil War dead was greater than the sum of all the Americans killed in every war from the American War for Independence up to World War II. Bill Holmes, sometime preacher, sometime farmer from Tennessee, recalled the madness of the bloody battle of Shiloh and his dead friend. "The firing got hot, so I fell down...flat on my belly. I looked and see Burl coming, falling as he come....his heart was shot all to pieces."

Survivors in the South confronted devastation on a scale unprecedented in American history. Major cities and important towns—Atlanta, Charleston, Richmond, Columbia, Selma—lay in ruins. So did two-thirds of southern shipping and most of the 9,000 miles of the southern rail system. Rolling stock, roadbeds, and rails were in shambles, as were warehouses, depots, bridges, shops, water tanks, trestles, and switches. The small but important industrial sector of the South suffered from wear and tear, neglect, and destruction by the military. Worthless Confederate currency and bonds were bitter reminders of past hopes and present despair. Almost all other paper forms of exchange—banknotes, personal notes, state and local bonds—had little value. Not much more could be expected from rail and industrial stocks and bonds. The intricate credit system erected during the antebellum years had collapsed. Personal belongings and real property had in many cases been destroyed. The average value of all real property declined 50 percent, farm property 70 percent. One-third of all livestock was gone, and $3 billion invested in slaves had been transferred from slaveholders to the former slaves, the largest single confiscation and transfer of private property in American history. Production of the principal southern crop, cotton, did not return to prewar levels until 1879. The South's share of the nation's wealth fell from 30 to 12 percent in the 1860s.

> A set of forks with whole tines...is a curiosity. Clocks and watches have nearly all stopped. Hair brushes and tooth brushes have all worn out, combs are broken....Pins, needles and thread, and a thousand such articles, which seem indispensable to housekeeping, are very hard to find.

After the war the South pursued economic recovery and growth vigorously, envisioning a New South, a South with more industry and cities and fewer farms. The pursuit lasted a long time, is continuing, and has been largely successful, yet even today the South trails the rest of the nation in per capita income and in other important measures of economic welfare.

Estimates of the *direct* costs of the war run as high as $6.6 billion, or about $206 for every person living in the North and South in 1861. Those costs, which include expenditures by the Union, the Confederacy, and the states, the costs of running conscription systems, losses in human capital resulting from the deaths and wounds to the soldiers, and the price of wartime destruction, virtually equaled the gross national product of the United States in 1869 ($7.4 bil-

REMAINS OF PLANTATION HOUSE, FREDERICKSBURGH, VIRGINIA
(Library of Congress)

lion). The $206-per-person cost is nearly twice what Americans averaged in individual consumption in 1860. The $6.6 billion expended could have been used to buy the slaves from their owners, pay the freed slaves 100 years of back wages ($3.5 billion), and give each freed family forty acres and a mule. But hindsight cannot undo the tragedy of the Civil War, and figures cannot measure all the costs. Nor does there exist a humane calculus to measure the toll that slavery had taken or that its continuation could have taken on blacks, or on whites. Would slavery have died without the massive defeat of the South? Was the road to emancipation unavoidably strewn with rotting bodies, severed limbs, and destruction? Ben Davis sensed this terrible irony when he shouted that he was free, free at last, and then gasped at the crude burial of the fallen.

The Civil War took an enormous toll in blood and treasure. The conflict also sharpened and magnified sectionalism in the United States even as it abetted the forces of nationalism. The war rendered secession a dead option and greatly enhanced the powers of the federal government even as it underscored the divisions of the country into oversimplified terms, "the North" and "the South." The North became the equivalent of the non-South, or anything that was not the South. The Civil War also made the prewar South the Old South, because the war destroyed the main engine of the prewar South, slave-based plantation agriculture. The war effectively ended the dominance the plantation world had had over almost all of the South before 1865, even in areas remote from plantation agriculture.

The war did not, however, settle the terms on which the former Confederate states would be restored to the Union. Nor did the results of the war clearly determine the place of blacks in American society. Those matters reached some resolution only during Reconstruction and thereafter.

The war left an even more immediate, pressing issue in its wake—survival. The economy of the South had to be made to function again; people had to make a living. Probably neither Ham Chamberlayne nor Ben Davis nor Parson Bill Holmes gave much thought to anything else in 1865. Chamberlayne never made it to Texas, though he did get as far as his uncle's plantation in Mississippi before he returned to Virginia in November. The 1858 graduate of the University of Virginia nearly ruined his health trying to run his family's farm. Then he clerked for a railroad and later edited newspapers. Chamberlayne came to terms with Appomattox. As founder and editor of *The State* in Richmond, he became a leading spokesman for reconciliation between the once warring sections and for the economic diversification of the South.

Ben Davis walked seventy-five miles to Atlanta, joining the people who more than doubled the city's population between 1865 and 1870. But he enjoyed little of the prosperity of the city that showed such remarkable powers of recovery. At first a generous white family gave him food and shelter. Then he scrambled for a living the rest of his life—as a day laborer, factory worker, and preacher. At one point he left his wife and children behind while he worked in Indiana and mailed home his meager savings. In 1938 Davis rocked on his daughter's porch in Athens, Georgia, dispensed potions, advice, and folk medicine, told his life story to an interviewer from a federally funded history project, and awaited his end.

Parson Bill Holmes did likewise. Weary and a bit befuddled, Holmes wandered from past to present and back as he talked about himself to a government interviewer in 1938. At eighteen years of age, Holmes went to war. "We was fighting to keep the slaves. But it's a good thing they's freed. Still, they sure would have hit the nail square on the head if they'd colonized them niggers. It ain't best to have two races of God's children mixed. One is going to boss the other every time that happens." After the war he proposed to Emma. "I told her I wanted to make one crop before we was married. And she says, 'And I want to make some quilts and things.'" Holmes farmed some and then preached as a Primitive Baptist after he "felt a call." He survived three wives and one son lost to drink, gambling, and a barroom brawl, left a "large Holmes family in its several branches," and looked forward to "Heaven, sweet heaven."

In 1938, time and the tumultuous events of World War II had not yet pushed the Civil War from the center of memory in the South. Reconstruction also remained a vivid memory. Debates about why the South lost the Civil War raged in 1938. Only a few historians debated Reconstruction. Everyone else *knew* Reconstruction was bad, that it was an era of unprecedented corruption presided over by vengeful, self-serving, often incompetent politicians. In collective memory Reconstruction had become a morality play between good and evil. But Reconstruction was not that simple or clear-cut.

RECONSTRUCTION

Reconstruction actually began before the defeat of the Confederacy and at a relatively obscure place in the South Carolina tidelands in the fall of 1861. On November 7, Admiral Francis Du Pont led his forces into Port Royal and began to bombard the Confederate defenses there. Sam Mitchell fled what he thought was a violent storm and ran to the safety of his mother, Tyra. "That ain't no thunder," she told him, "that Yankee come to give you Freedom." The next day, Federal troops occupied the area, including Beaufort, the only town of any size on the sound. Overnight the Federals became an army of occupation with responsibilities for defending Port Royal and the one white man—too drunk to flee—and the 10,000 slaves they found there.

Provisions had to be made for these people immediately. Only slightly less pressing was the need to determine the legal status of the slaves. Obviously, what had begun as only a military mission became more than that. The Lincoln administration, especially because it still shied away from any suggestion that the abolition of slavery was one of its war aims, was poorly prepared to deal with the questions raised by the victory at Port Royal.

The story that unfolded at Port Royal in the succeeding months was a re-

EX-SLAVES NEAR HOME OF SAM MITCHELL (Library of Congress)

hearsal for Reconstruction. Thus events at Beaufort revealed something of the way blacks and whites would deal with one another after the war. Moreover, as the diverse groups clustered around Port Royal discovered, distant events and people had enormous impact on their lives. Policies formulated in Washington shaped life and labor on the sound. Equally important was the return of the local whites and the struggles to determine who would have dominance in South Carolina after the war ended.

A critically important fact became very obvious in Port Royal soon after Du Pont's victory: the blacks were not passive lumps of dark clay waiting to be molded by others. The Port Royal blacks, or "contrabands of war" (a politically expedient term employed by the Union government to describe slaves who came within Union lines before emancipation was proclaimed in 1862), mystified, exasperated, and pleased the newly arrived northern whites. They had done the same to their departed owners. The contrabands demonstrated abject dependency, some of which was calculated and some of which was real—a product of their slave experience and their present condition. This dependency confused observers, then and since, and tended to disguise how assertive the former slaves could be. Most had spent their entire lives as slaves. Few had skills as leaders. Even fewer could read and write. Most had worked only as farm hands.

Yet the blacks at Port Royal asserted themselves in ways that belied the guise of dependency. Many, in fact, had acted to secure their own liberty. When Tyra Mitchell's husband told her that their master had ordered him to take him to Charleston to avoid capture by the Federals, she exploded. "You ain't gonna row no boat to Charleston, you go out that back door and keep a-going." Mitchell fled. He returned when Du Pont's victory was certain, worked as a carpenter for the Union army, and eventually bought himself a ten-acre farm nearby. Other blacks along the coast took the first opportunity to join the Port Royal blacks, though the Federals' intentions toward slaves were often unknown and despite warnings from southern whites that the Union forces sold runaways to Cuba.

Blacks were determined to escape slavery and to control their own lives. The contrabands at Port Royal, like the millions of other slaves freed during and after the Civil War, had been hurt but not crushed by the terrible burden of bondage. In fact, they acted a lot like other Americans. They moved quickly to formalize their marriages and to collect their scattered families. They eagerly sought work, education for themselves and especially for their children, and land of their own. The number of blacks who sought schooling overwhelmed the teachers and facilities at Port Royal after Du Pont's victory. The blacks grasped at the American dream of self-improvement, self-employment, and upward mobility. Accordingly, they often resisted working for wages and planting cotton, a crop that had not benefited slaves directly in the past. They preferred to plant food crops and to raise livestock. A number of adult male contrabands fought with distinction in the Union army. Above all, the blacks at Port Royal wanted land.

The prospects for land remained unclear for long, anxiety-filled months, as did the legal status of slaves and the prospects for Union victory. The outcome of these issues depended very largely on events, forces, and decisions beyond Port Royal. In September 1862 President Lincoln committed the Union to emancipation, which was later made effective by the Union's victory in the war. But ownership of the land at Port Royal remained unresolved at the end of the war. That became a critical issue as local whites began to return. And their return raised another pressing question: How would former masters and slaves deal with one another?

By 1865, ownership of the land around Beaufort had become a complex matter. Federal authorities had seized some land for unpaid taxes and sold it at auction. Buyers included whites recently arrived from the North and a few former slaves, who bought small parcels. The great majority of the blacks, however, simply occupied deserted plantations. The ranks of the squatters swelled as the war went on, especially after General Sherman's march to the sea and his Field Order 15, which set aside coastal lands between Charleston and Savannah for use by the refugees. But ownership of these squatter lands was unclear, and that became a critical matter in mid-1865, when the former planters returned.

Most returning planters were welcomed. Some received gifts, loans, and help from their former slaves. But there was a coolness to the welcome. One graciously received planter was "firmly and respectfully informed...: 'We own this land now. Put it out of your head that it will ever be yours again.' " Another planter had his land but found that not one of his old hands would work for him, not even "Old Gib," his former trusted driver.

Land and labor were *the* issues, as they had been before the war. They were necessary for survival, for social position, and for self-respect. In an agrarian world where most people earned their living from the land and nonfarm work was scarce, landlessness and dependency on wages meant uncertain todays and blank tomorrows.

Whatever Old Gib and other freedmen thought and wanted, most of the prewar white landowners soon regained their land, and most of the freedmen remained landless and had no choice but to work the land for others. Less than a year after the planters came back to Port Royal, they received full pardons from President Andrew Johnson, and they were allowed to reclaim most of their land when Federal troops drove the squatters off. Blacks protested to no avail. "Why do you take away our lands? You take them from us who have always been true, always true to the Government! You give them to our all-time enemies! That is not right!" Landless blacks then reluctantly signed work contracts with the planters because when spring came "nature called men, white or black, to plant or starve." As before, decisions made elsewhere—in this case, in Washington—shaped life in Port Royal and throughout the South.

*P*RESIDENTIAL RECONSTRUCTION

President Andrew Johnson, whose Reconstruction policies profoundly affected Port Royal in particular and the South in general, began to outline and implement those policies in May 1865. Like his predecessor, Lincoln, Johnson stressed reconciliation between the Union and the defeated Confederacy and restoration of civil government in the South. In December 1863 Lincoln had issued a "Proclamation for Amnesty and Reconstruction." He had promised a "full pardon" and restitution of all property, save for slaves, to those who had rebelled against the Union and who would take an oath of allegiance to the Union. Some were excluded: officials of the Confederacy, ranking military officers, and some other prominent Confederates. When the numbers of people who took the oath reached at least 10 percent of those who had voted in 1860, they could form a state government, which Lincoln promised to recognize. Lincoln applied his Reconstruction formula in Arkansas and Louisiana in 1864. Both established governments, he recognized them, and they then conducted elections for state and national offices. Both of these new governments, of course, accepted abolition. Neither, however, gave the vote to any blacks, though Lincoln had especially urged Louisiana to do so because of the substantial number of propertied, well-educated blacks in New Orleans. Congress refused to admit the newly elected congressional delegations from Arkansas and Louisiana. Nor would congress count the electoral votes of either state or those of Tennessee, which had a federally sanctioned provisional government, in the 1864 presidential election.

Clearly the Republican Congress had balked at Lincoln's Reconstruction plan. Most congressional Republicans believed that more than the restoration of political control of the South to loyal citizens was required. They believed Reconstruction had to include a clear renunciation of secession, assurances to southern Unionists of personal safety and a political voice, guarantees that slavery had been abolished forever and that blacks had secured civil rights, and, at least for a while, restrictions on the rights of former Confederate leaders to vote and to hold public office. Many congressional Republicans favored some form of suffrage for blacks. In July 1864 Congress passed its own Reconstruction plan: the Wade-Davis Bill (named after its sponsors, Congressman Henry Winter Davis of Maryland and Senator Benjamin Wade of Ohio). Congress gave greater stress to the creation of southern state governments that were loyal to the Union than to sectional reconciliation and the rapid restoration of civil government in the South. The Wade-Davis Bill required that a majority of the voters in each of the former Confederate states take a loyalty oath; it stipulated that only those who could swear they had not willingly supported the Confederacy could vote for delegates to the state constitutional conventions that were charged with establishing new governments; and it created some legal protection, which the federal courts would enforce, for blacks. The Wade-Davis Bill did not, however, enfranchise any blacks, something some Republicans felt should have been done.

Although Congress passed the bill by nearly a unanimous vote, Lincoln vetoed it. Congress could not act further on the measure until it returned for a new session. Wade and Davis reacted promptly, however, with a bitter public attack on Lincoln's veto. It was extraordinary for an incumbent president to be so severely criticized during a presidential campaign by leaders of his own party. Clearly the issues dividing the president and Congress were quite serious, and congressional Republicans reemphasized their position when Congress reconvened in December 1864.

The Republicans had not resolved their differences over Reconstruction policy when Lincoln was assassinated and Andrew Johnson succeeded him in April 1865. Johnson chose to ignore these wide differences and moved quickly on Reconstruction. On May 29, 1865, President Johnson granted a broad amnesty and pardon to southerners who had rebelled and a "restoration of all rights of property, except as to slaves," provided those who had been in rebellion take an oath of future allegiance. Some would require special pardons from the president. These included all the categories of exceptions Lincoln had established earlier plus all those with taxable property worth $20,000 or more. Johnson's addition suggested that he intended to humble the planter elite, a group he had often attacked. If it encouraged the Republicans to believe that the new president was going to be firmer toward the South than Lincoln had been, they soon learned better.

The same day that he issued his proclamation of amnesty and pardon, Johnson appointed William W. Holden as provisional governor of North Carolina and charged him to arrange a convention to draft a new state constitution, abolish slavery, and repudiate secession and the state's war debt. Those who voted for delegates to the convention and the delegates themselves had to be white adult males who had sworn their allegiance to the United States and who had received amnesty or pardons. Shortly thereafter, Johnson made similar arrangements for South Carolina, Florida, Georgia, Alabama, Mississippi, and Texas. Six of these seven states (distance caused delays until April 1866 in Texas) held elections and conventions that met Johnson's stipulations before December 1865. He also accepted Francis H. Pierpoint's government in exile, which the Union had previously supported as the provisional government of Virginia, and he accepted the governments in Tennessee, Louisiana, and Arkansas, which Lincoln had recognized. The president then declared the Union restored in his first State of the Union message, which he sent to Congress as it was opening a new congressional session and as representatives of the former Confederate states waited to be seated in Congress.

Thus, by the time the Senate and the House of Representatives reconvened in December 1865, Johnson had officially welcomed all the former Confederate states except Texas back into the Union. They had met his terms. They had elected new state governments, had repudiated or annulled secession and the Confederate debts, and had abolished slavery, and the required proportion of their voters had sworn allegiance to the Union. Johnson's lenient pardon policy amounted in practice virtually to a general amnesty. About 15,000 applied for special pardons; Johnson granted 13,500 in 1865 alone. Johnson's policies allowed for the restoration to southerners of property that had not already been sold or lost or destroyed—except, of course, slaves. As southerners celebrated the restoration of statehood and civilian government in late 1865, few had any sense that their new state governments might be rejected in the North.

SOUTHERN DEFIANCE: UNCONQUERED REBELS?

Southerners praised President Johnson, for obvious reasons. They had received far better terms that they had expected, including the assurance that they had not lost their lands. They had gotten back some of their lost dignity and had received succor for their war-caused trauma. Their shock was compounded of many elements: exhaustion, great losses of blood and treasure, four years of wartime sacrifices and disruptions—destroyed, damaged, or neglected plantations, farms, railroads, industries, towns, and cities—genuine suffering and deprivation that continued long months after surrender, and the abolition of slavery, the cornerstone of the southern world. Southerners experienced a shattering decline of position, status, and prospects. Save for American Indians and possibly the Revolutionary War loyalists, no group in American history has experienced a decline so severe as that suffered by the planter elite.

Southern honor had been massively assaulted. The deeply religious South confronted a terrifying question: Had the God they believed had ordained and sanctioned their society and its slave foundation found them wanting? Was not the defeat of the South its day of judgment? William Henry Ravenel, South Carolina planter and scientist, felt he could not "avoid the conviction that a righteous God had designed this punishment for our sins." "This is the bitter end of four years of toil and sacrifices," General Josiah Gorgas, chief of ordnance for the Confederacy, confided to his diary in August 1865.

> What an end to our great hopes. Is it possible that we were wrong? Is it right after all that one set of men can force their opinion on another set? It seems so, and that self government is a mocking before the Almighty. He permits it or refuses it as seems good to him. Let us bow in submission and learn to curb our bitter thoughts.

Leaving what had been an enormously profitable rice plantation, William H. Heyward sought refuge in a Charleston hotel, where for a time he lived in virtual solitary confinement in his room. "I am sometimes on the verge of self-destruction. . . . When I go to rest at night, my wish and great desire is that I may never open my eyes another day." Some southerners fled the country, many never to return. Many southerners believed themselves to have been massively wronged, that secession was legal, that the South had followed the revolutionary tradition of 1776, and that the Confederacy had defended republicanism, the American sine qua non, against a power-mad Union. Atrocity stories—real or imagined and heavily embellished—about the conduct of Union armed forces during combat and occupation were widespread and widely believed.

Perhaps worst of all, blacks were out of control. Thousands had fled during the war, more afterward. Former masters worried about how former slaves would react to them, about who would provide critically needed farm labor if blacks did not, whether blacks would seek revenge. Rumors of planned Christmastime rebellions and massacres by blacks swirled. Visions of postemancipation Haiti and Jamaica rose as nightfall came to the thinly populated stretches of the rural South. Actually, physical attacks on the persons of former masters were remarkably rare. Assaults on the property of former slaveholders were more common, though perhaps as often former slaves defended the property of their former masters.

Much more usual was the widespread tendency of blacks to distance themselves from southern whites. Blacks usually greeted former masters warmly, even gave them aid, but refused to work for them. Many former slaves agreed to live in what had been slave quarters only if they could drag the houses to new, dispersed locations away from the old slave compounds. Finally, blacks rejected second-class status in white-dominated churches. They formed black-only congregations within white-majority denominations, usually Baptist or Methodist, or they joined black denominations, such as the African Methodist Episcopal church, which had been founded before 1860.

This distancing of themselves from southern whites puzzled and angered former masters who had treated their slaves paternalistically. Despite its limitations and its frequent violations, paternalism had permeated black-white relations before the defeat of the Confederacy. Paternalism rested on a bond of affection and mutual obligation. Former masters seemed to need an acknowledgment from blacks that that bond had been genuine and that it had not entirely disappeared. Former slaveholders thus complained bitterly about "ungrateful" former slaves and gloated over signs of affection and dependence. Mary Boykin Chesnut seemed genuinely pleased when an elderly nurse came back from a brief flight away with Union troops. She "knew well on which side her bread was buttered; and she knew too, or found out, where her real friends were."

Whites genuinely feared anarchy and bloodshed. They desperately wanted order restored to what seemed like chaos. Whites also anguished about how they would obtain critically needed labor. Convinced that blacks would not work without coercion, whites sought ways to force blacks to labor for them. Strengthened by President Johnson's policies and once again in control of the state and local governments, southern leaders moved quickly in 1865 to assert control over the life and labor of southern blacks. None of the restored southern legislatures gave the vote to any blacks. Most of the new state governments and many local governments revised their vagrancy laws to address the largely illusory problem of idleness among blacks. The result was a legal net to snare the presumably idle and dump them back into the fields. Several states made these changes part of more comprehensive statutes, the infamous Black Codes. Mississippi's Black Code defined a vagrant as anyone who was guilty of theft, had run away, was drunk, was wanton in conduct or speech, had neglected job or family, handled money carelessly, and, lest anyone escape, "all other idle and disorderly persons."

The Mississippi code defined a Negro as anyone who was one-eighth or more Negro (anyone who had at least one black great-grandparent). The code recognized slave marriages as permanent, and allowed blacks to make contracts, hold property, sue and be sued, and be witnesses in cases to which blacks were parties. Interracial cohabitation and marriage were forbidden, and blacks were not permitted to vote, hold public office, serve on juries, or bear arms. Other measures of control included exclusion from many occupations, restrictions on conducting certain businesses, limitations on where blacks could own land, and apprenticeship laws. The last allowed indigent young blacks to be apprenticed involuntarily to whites, with former slave masters receiving preference when apprentices were assigned. The codes also attempted to prevent "enticement" of labor from one employer to another and circumscribed the right of blacks to assemble.

> Any freedman, free negro or mulatto, committing riots, routs, affrays, trespasses, malicious mischief, cruel treatment to animals, seditious speeches, insulting gestures, language or acts, assaults on any person, disturbance of the peace, exercising the function of a minister of the Gospel, without a license from some regularly organized church, vending spirituous or intoxicating liquors, or committing any other misdemeanor, the punishment of which is not specifically provided for by law, shall, upon conviction thereof...be fined not less than ten dollars, and not more than one hundred dollars, and may be imprisoned...[up to] thirty days.

The code also required blacks to be courteous, dutiful, and diligent employees. Unlike white lawbreakers, convicted blacks could be whipped and pilloried. Local ordinances, such as curfew laws, added to the burdens of blacks. South Carolina and Louisiana adopted comparable Black Codes, others had less harsh laws, and several states did not pass such comprehensive measures.

Most states started leasing convicts to planters, coal-mine operators, railroad construction companies, and others. Often brutal in practice, the system passed a substantial portion of the costs of the states' penal systems to the private contractors, and states even made profits from the leases. In turn, the contractors got cheap (and primarily black) workers to whose welfare they could be indifferent. The resulting punishment was often worse than blacks had experienced during slavery. Moreover, Johnson's suggestion, echoing Lincoln's, that a stringently qualified franchise for blacks might have a desirable effect on the North fell on deaf ears. The adoption of the Black Codes proved to be a serious political mistake.

Racial fear and prejudice and a crisis mentality fueled these actions. So did a distorted paternalism and legal precedent. Blacks, it was assumed, were permanently children. Thus blacks needed permanent protection. Conversely, white southerners also insisted that these supposedly perpetual children posed a massive threat. Whether or not such assumptions were genuinely believed, and they probably were in many cases, they contained blatantly logical flaws. Finally, white paternalism squared too neatly with white self-interest. Not too surprisingly, many northern Republicans believed that blacks needed protection from, not by, southern whites.

Southern legislatures did not act in a legal vacuum. They found precedents in the slave codes, which had been voided by emancipation; in vagrancy statutes, north and south; in the northern and southern laws that applied to antebellum free blacks; in the legal codes that had been enacted in the British West Indies after the abolition of slavery there; and even in some of the regulations of the Freedmen's Bureau, the agency created by the federal government to aid blacks in their transition from bondage. Panic reinforced harshness. The most severe legislation was passed before the end of 1865, when anxieties about securing a work force for the next farm season and fears about a black rebellion reached fever pitch. Visions of ruin, starvation, and massacre haunted white lawmakers.

The hopes of the newly freed slaves complicated matters. They did not immediately return to the fields when the war ended, and they did leave plantations in large numbers and move about a great deal. Blacks wanted to explore the boundaries of their new status—to escape reminders of their past, to search for members of their families who had been dispersed by the vagaries of slavery or the war, or merely to see places that had been denied them during their bondage. Cities had a particular attraction. Blacks also waited to see if the federal government would give them the homesteads they believed they had earned by their labor as slaves and thought they had been promised by the Union, especially those who had served in the Union army. Unfortunately and tragically, those promises never had a real chance of becoming reality for the great majority. Finally, former slaves hardly looked forward to returning to someone else's land. By 1866, most did. Necessity prevailed. Southern legislatures had not, however, waited for the invisible hand of economic forces to ease the farm-labor crisis.

These efforts of southern whites to develop a new system of race relations to replace the one that had prevailed during slavery, to establish their superior position in a slaveless South, and to assure themselves of a steady supply of docile black labor bore strong resemblances to slavery itself. The Black Codes in particular were strongly criticized in the North and were prime catalysts for the undoing of the restored state governments that Lincoln and Johnson had created. Northern critics saw these laws as blatant attempts to reestablish slavery. Southern defenders of the vagrancy laws and Black Codes were puzzled, then outraged by what they saw as a double standard. They believed that they had followed precedents in dealing with pressing problems. Their attitude and behavior toward blacks did not differ markedly from what they had heard and seen in their encounters with northern white troops and agents of the Freedmen's Bureau, and they certainly knew that blacks faced serious legal disabilities, flagrant discrimination, and even physical abuse in the North.

Southerners, however, did not realize that in their drive to secure a stable agricultural work force and white dominance they had overreached themselves and now ran the risk of offending northern opinion, which had become closely attuned to southern behavior and attitudes. Northern Republicans began to have grave doubts about the willingness of the southern states to do what the northern Republicans thought was absolutely necessary before the South could rejoin the Union. Northern Republicans began to come to the unsettling conclusion that southerners had not accepted the verdict of the battlefield, that secession and slavery were not dead, that the South was not going to be loyal to the federal government, and that blacks, southern Unionists, and northern immigrants would not be secure and fairly treated in the South. In sum, the South appeared to be a land of defiant, unconquered rebels.

Efforts to determine the mood of the former Confederate states and the conditions there turned pulse-taking into an industry. Journalists sent daily dispatches northward from all over the South, reporting interviews and overheard conversations, pleasant encounters and hostile receptions. Letters and reports flowed northward from travelers and from southerners themselves. These writings reflected the expectations of the writers and their intended readers. President Johnson, for instance, was told that southerners had embraced his restoration program and were loyal to the Union. Congressional Republicans heard otherwise, especially from southern Unionists.

Carl Schurz perhaps penned the most accurate report on conditions and feelings in the South. Schurz was a German-American leader, a Union general, and later an excellent secretary of the interior who was noted for his fairness. Schurz debunked several unsettling rumors. The South was defeated, knew it, and was not planning more armed resistance against the Union. As Schurz pointed out, most southerners were working to reestablish state governments according to Johnson's policies. But Schurz found too little Unionist feeling in the South and too much firm belief that the South had done no wrong. Southerners despised northerners recently arrived in the South, southern Unionists, and, most of all, black troops. Southerners longed for the good old days of slavery and expected blacks to accept something that approximated it, for their own good. Schurz was convinced that southern blacks and southern Unionists urgently needed protection.

What southern political leaders were doing substantiated Schurz's conclusions. First, there were the new laws that applied to freed slaves. Then, not all of the southern states repudiated secession and slavery; they just declared them null and void. Some accepted emancipation only reluctantly. Mississippi and Texas refused to ratify the Thirteenth Amendment (making slavery unconstitutional), and Mississippi and South Carolina declined to repudiate state debts incurred during the war. Mississippi even revived its state militia and manned it with Confederate veterans. Several state constitutional conventions would not fly the Union flag. Confederates dominated the restored state governments, although many of these leaders were old Whigs and reluctant Unionists. The newly elected southern congressional delegations included Confederate cabinet officers, congressmen, generals, and colonels. Georgia even sent the former vice president of the Confederacy to Congress. The fact that Alexander H. Stephens had voted against secession in Georgia's secession convention in 1861 was not enough to offset the stigma he bore in the North as the second-highest official of the Confederacy. Loyalty to proven, beloved leaders was understandable, but sending Stephens to the Senate was worse than foolish.

Several factors may account for these miscalculations. Southern leaders mistakenly believed President Johnson accurately reflected the views of the North and the federal government. Johnson should have been more firm when he advised southern leaders about what was expected of the South. Perhaps Johnson missed the opportunity to demand more of the South in 1865 while the South was still in shock and might have been more accommodating. Yet he and most southern leaders no doubt felt the South was not being defiant and had already paid a high price. The South generally repudiated secession and its Confederate debts, had accepted emancipation and granted some civil rights to the blacks, and had sworn allegiance to the Union and formed new state governments. They had, in fact, met the president's terms. But they had not met those of the Republicans, who, after all, controlled Congress. It became clear in late 1865 that neither Johnson nor most southern leaders paid sufficient attention to what had occurred between Lincoln and Congress over the Wade-Davis Bill or to other issues the Republicans had been raising about Reconstruction.

THE REPUBLICANS AND JOHNSON'S RECONSTRUCTION POLICIES

When Congress reconvened in December 1865, the Republican majority immediately registered its reaction to Johnson's policies, the politics and legislation of restoration in the South, and reports of southern sentiments and behavior it had received. The majority first refused to seat any newly elected southerners in the Senate or the House. (Congress has the constitutional authority to "be the Judge of the Elections, Returns and Qualifications of its own Members.") In taking this action, Congress also raised serious doubts about the future of the new state governments, putting them in a political and constitutional limbo.

Congress subsequently extended the life of the Freedmen's Bureau, which was near expiration, and expanded its duties to include oversight of labor relations between blacks and white employers, provision of impartial courts for blacks in the defeated Confederacy, and supervision of abandoned and confiscated lands in the South. (Johnson's quick restoration of property in the South negated most of the last responsibility.) Congress passed the Civil Rights Bill of 1866 to counter the Black Codes and to negate the Dred Scott decision (1857), which held that blacks could never become citizens. The bill represented a constitutional shift of immense importance in American history. It was the first attempt ever by the federal government to define American citizenship. Also for the first time in federal law, the civil rights of citizens were defined and attempts were made to protect those rights. Congress stated that

> all persons born in the United States and not subject to any foreign power, excluding Indians not taxed, are hereby declared to be citizens, of every race and color, without regard to any previous condition of slavery or involuntary servitude...shall have the right in every State and territory in the United States, to make and enforce

contracts, to sue, be parties, and give evidence, to inherit, purchase, lease, sell, hold and convey real and personal property, and to full and equal benefit of all laws and proceedings for the security of person and property, as is enjoyed by white citizens, and shall be subject to like punishment, pains and penalties, and to none other, any law, statute, ordinance, regulation, or custom, to the contrary notwithstanding.

Federal courts had exclusive jurisdiction over the law. The president was explicitly authorized to act to get speedy trials, and could use army, navy, or militia to enforce the law. President Johnson vetoed both the Freedmen's Bureau Bill and the Civil Rights Bill, and Congress overrode both vetoes to make them law. The gap between the president and the Republican Congress over Reconstruction had become all but unbridgeable.

Congress soon took another major step in keeping with the Republican approach to Reconstruction. It wrote and passed the Fourteenth Amendment to ensure the constitutionality and permanence of the Civil Rights Act of 1866. The first section of the amendment has had lasting, critical importance in American history. Its derivation from the Civil Rights Act is obvious.

All persons born or naturalized in the United States, and subject to the jurisdiction thereof, are citizens of the United States and of the State wherein they reside. No State shall make or enforce any law which shall abridge the privileges or immunities of citizens of the United States; nor shall any State deprive any person of life, liberty, or property, without due process of law; nor deny any person within its jurisdiction the equal protection of the law.

The amendment also provided for a reduction in congressional representation if any state prevented adult male citizens from voting. Despite later massive and blatant violations of this provision, it has never been enforced. Other parts of the amendment declared Federal Civil War debts valid, voided all Confederate debts, and disqualified all former state or federal officials who served the Confederacy during the Civil War from holding office again unless Congress pardoned them. The Republicans made ratification of the amendment a prerequisite for readmission of any Confederate state to the Union. The amendment constituted Congress's plan for Reconstruction. When the South continued to resist that plan, Congress imposed it by passing Reconstructions acts in 1867 and 1868.

A complex set of motives prompted these actions. Congress wanted to assert itself against the executive branch, which during the the Civil War had greatly enhanced its powers at the expense of Congress and the courts. Northern Republicans feared a revived Democratic party in the South and the North. Only part of this fear sprang from purely selfish partisanship. Republicans also genuinely believed that the Democrats had led the nation into a disastrous civil war and that the views of most Democrats on such major issues as the tariff, banking, excise taxes, and internal improvements were wrongheaded and could hurt the nation. Another major factor in the northern Republicans' determination to create and implement their Reconstruction plan was their conviction that they had to protect what the Union had won in battle from a seemingly unbowed South. Republicans also felt compelled to do something to protect Unionists and blacks in the South.

Events in Memphis in the spring of 1866 indicated that these concerns were well founded. When two carriages, one driven by a white and the other by a black, collided on a Memphis street, the collision ignited the powder keg that the city had become. The city's population had doubled in only two years. Irish immigrants and former slaves had poured in. A wave of crime beset the Irish-run city government and police. Former Confederates in Memphis, newly bereft of political power and of much of their wealth, were full of contempt for "damn yankees," whose presence at nearby Fort Pickering was all too apparent. Matters became acute when four regiments of the 4,000 black troops at Pickering were released without pay by the army. Some of them clashed with the Memphis police on April 30. The minor incident involving the carriage drivers grew into three days of riot, arson, rape, and looting, which left forty-six blacks and two whites dead.

Such violent outbursts fed the antisouthern feeling already strong in the North. Angry memories of the war, of great sacrifices, required more than a "make up and forget" policy. The reaction of the Chicago *Tribune* to the Mississippi Black Code reflected those feelings. "We tell the white men of Mississippi that the men of the North will convert the state of Mississippi into a frog pond before they will allow such laws to disgrace one foot of soil in which the bones of our soldiers sleep and over which the flag of freedom waves." The charge of being "too soft" on the South was a political liability for Republican politicians, whose constituents had lost family and friends in combat, had their lives disrupted for four years, and had watched prices, taxes, and the federal debt soar.

Republicans' fears that the Democrats would regain their antebellum political dominance were not fantasies. The dominance of the Republican party was not assured in 1865 and would not be until the 1890s. Only then were the Republicans able to control the White House and both houses of Congress consistently. Divisions among Democrats in 1860 and the secessions that followed had given the Republicans an unusual political opportunity but not a secure upper hand during the Civil War. When the South rejoined the Union, it would be more politically powerful than it had been before the war because emancipation voided the three-fifths rule (by which each slave was counted as three-fifths of a person for apportionment of members of the House of Representatives and of the electoral college). Thus one ironic result of abolition was an increase in the South's strength in Congress and in the electoral college. Moreover, Republicans correctly suspected that President Johnson, a Tennessee Democrat, was attempting to build a new coalition, perhaps a new political party, whose future was tied to the quick restoration of the South. Not incidentally, he hoped that this coalition might get him reelected in 1868. In fact, during the 1866 congressional election, Johnson worked toward those goals by participating in the National Union political movement, a coalition of Democrats and a few prominent Republicans who generally agreed with Johnson on Reconstruction.

THE 1866 ELECTION AND THE FOURTEENTH AMENDMENT

Relations between Johnson and Congress reached an impasse before the 1866 congressional election. In less than twelve months, the good feeling that prevailed when Johnson succeeded Lincoln ended. Johnson failed a basic test of political leadership—he was unwilling and unable to compromise. He did succeed at something else: he forced the Republicans to settle the differences among themselves. Thus the Freedmen's Bureau Act, the Civil Rights Act, and the Fourteenth Amendment were compromise measures for which moderate Republicans were primarily responsible. Contrary to what is often believed, the Radical Republicans, such as Thaddeus Stevens of Pennsylvania and Charles Sumner of Massachusetts, who wanted more sweeping measures, did not control Congress and did not dictate the writing of Reconstruction legislation. Johnson, often portrayed as the victim of a vengeful Congress, thwarted compromise by his political and constitutional rigidity and compounded the difficulty by his fiery rhetoric. In February 1866, for instance, speaking to a group celebrating the birthday of George Washington, Johnson likened opponents of his Reconstruction policy to Judas and himself to Christ: he was willing, he said, for his "blood...to be shed...on an altar to the Union."

The conflict between Johnson and Congress spilled over to the 1866 congressional election, in which the Fourteenth Amendment was the focal issue. Then came a riot in New Orleans which took thirty-eight lives—thirty-four blacks, three white Republicans, and one white rioter. The New Orleans clash was more explicitly political than the riot in Memphis, and it had a major impact on the election. It grew out of attempts by Republicans in Louisiana to protect themselves against a state government controlled by former Confederates whose intentions were all too clear. The Louisiana state Democratic party declared in its 1865 platform:

> Resolved, That we hold this to be a Government of white people, made and to be perpetuated for the exclusive benefit of the white race...that the people of African descent cannot be considered as citizens of the United States, and that there can, in no event, nor under any circumstances, be any equality between the white and other races.

Republican proposals in 1866 to reopen the Louisiana state constitutional convention in order to enfranchise blacks and disfranchise former Confederates alarmed local whites. Democratic politicians harangued. Newspapers circulated rumors of the worst. Local whites, led by the police, refused to wait for the courts to rule on the doubtful legality of reopening the constitutional convention, which had been officially closed. They confronted blacks who were joyously marching to the proposed convention site. The confrontation turned into riot, murderous pursuit, and gunning down. Whites besieged the convention hall, assaulting and killing defenseless blacks and their white allies while ignoring three separate attempts by the assailed to surrender. The New Orleans *Daily Picayune* regretted "the bloody details of yesterday....It was horrifying; but there seemed to be no alternative." President Johnson neither decried the massacre nor expressed sympathy for its victims. Instead, he accused Louisiana Republicans of provoking the rioters.

The New Orleans riot, along with that in Memphis and similar incidents at Chattanooga, Louisville, and Vicksburg, had an electric effect on the northern public and northern Republicans. Given a choice between Johnson's Reconstruction program, which suggested that the South ought to be allowed to reconstruct itself, whatever the consequences, and the Republican program, which was expressed in the Fourteenth Amendment, northern voters overwhelmingly endorsed the Republicans. The Republican party gained the upper hand in every northern state and in West Virginia, Tennessee, and Missouri, and the party held on to its 3-to-1 margin in Congress. But only one former Confederate state, Tennessee, ratified the Fourteenth Amendment. Ten southern legislatures, many unanimously and with Johnson's encouragement, refused to adopt the amendment. "If we are to be degraded," the governors of North and South Carolina declared, "we will retain some self-esteem by not making it self-abasement." Southern honor, the elemental glue of southern society, had to be defended. In this case, the South may have defended its honor, but it squandered an opportunity to be restored to the Union on the mildest terms the Republicans could or would offer. The spurned opportunity set the stage first for Military Reconstruction and then for Radical Reconstruction.

The predominantly Republican Congress reconvened in December 1866, and the Republicans—still divided into conservative, moderate, and radical wings—hammered out a compromise program designed to create a different system of politics in the postwar South. Johnson's ineptitude, the South's intransigence, and the results of the 1866 election caused moderate and even some conservative Republicans to embrace a fundamental position of the Radical Republicans: the South could not be reconstructed unless blacks were given the vote. Congress passed legislation that effectively unhorsed the Johnson state governments, created a series of interim military governors (Military Reconstruction), and laid the basis for Republican control of the former Confederacy (Radical Reconstruction, or the so-called Black Reconstruction).

Southern whites were confused, embittered, and outraged. They felt they had met Johnson's requirements for the restoration of self-government. Now they confronted different terms. They were bitter because the new policy rested on the wholly unacceptable assumption that secession was treasonous, that the South had to bear the burden of war guilt. The North had claimed that the Union was indissoluble and had gone to war in support of that claim. Now Congress was telling the South it had to seek readmission to the Union that the North had claimed was indissoluble. It was monstrously hypocritical, maddening.

Southerners were outraged because Congress was using suffrage requirements and disqualifications for public office to cause a political revolution in the South. Congress stepped into areas traditionally reserved for state action. Congress committed the greatest villainy of all when it gave black adult males the vote.

RECONSTRUCTION: MYTH AND REALITY

Southerners came to view Reconstruction as the Tragic Era. Radical or Black Reconstruction became one of the enduring myths of the South. It was canonized in hundreds of speeches, writings, and even sermons; it was written into textbooks, north and south; and today it is still widely accepted as dreadful fact. Myths combine and blur fact and fiction. They become "truth" and last because they bear some resemblance to reality and have meaning and utility. The myth of a horrific Radical Reconstruction does violence to historical fact. Contrary to the myth, Radical Reconstruction was not interminable, was not uniquely corrupt, was not black—if that means that blacks dominated the South during Reconstruction—and was not imposed at the point of a bayonet by a large army of occupation. Moreover, Radical Reconstruction left some notable achievements.

Virginia experienced Military Reconstruction but never had an elected Republican government. Tennessee was specifically excluded from the Reconstruction acts and was readmitted to the Union in 1866 after it ratified the Fourteenth Amendment. By 1869, Conservatives (coalitions of local white Democrats and former Whigs, common southern phenomena in those years) took control of Tennessee. The state did, however, have to endure the excesses of its Republican governor, William G. "Parson" Brownlow, whose contempt for blacks and former Confederates came in equal parts. North Carolina Conservatives overwhelmed William W. Holden, the Republican governor and a North Carolina native. Then they expelled him on specious grounds, making him the first governor in American history to be thrown out of office. Republican power waxed and waned elsewhere. Only Louisiana, Florida, and South Carolina had Reconstruction governments as late as 1877, and moderate Republicans held sway throughout the period in Florida. Political strife was so intense in Louisiana that the state virtually had no government when Reconstruction ended. And by the last months of 1876, white resistance had reduced Daniel H. Chamberlain, a Republican, to governor of South Carolina in name only.

Corruption in South Carolina reached heights that were not achieved elsewhere, save possibly in Louisiana. Henry Clay Warmoth, onetime Republican governor of Louisiana, declared that members of the state legislature were "as good as the people they represent. Why, damn it, everybody down here is demoralized. Corruption is the fashion." Mississippi Republicans, by contrast, had a remarkably honest record. In some places native whites, both Democrats

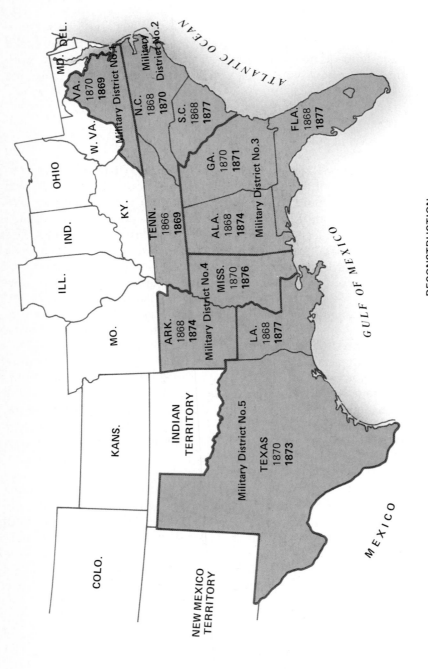

RECONSTRUCTION

1868   Date of readmission to the Union

1870   Date of reestablishment of conservative rule

——   Boundaries of the five military districts

RECONSTRUCTION

and Conservatives, showed a talent for theft from public treasuries which supposedly was unique to southern Republicans. In Alabama and North Carolina, for instance, native Democrats joined forces with home-grown and immigrant Republicans in scandalous transactions involving state bonds issued for urgently needed but financially questionable railroad schemes. The wretchedly corrupt Louisiana Lottery benefited Republicans and Democrats alike. Finally, corruption, to whatever degree it occurred in the South, was not introduced to the South during Reconstruction. Antebellum southern leaders had not always been above helping themselves to public funds.

Southern states during the era of Reconstruction did incur large debts, which became a serious burden. When some states later repudiated them, they were left with tainted credit records. Critics have too readily assumed that those debts were a clear index of public thievery by Republican officials. Some debts were—those of North Carolina, South Carolina, and Georgia in particular. The Republican government in North Carolina in 1868–1869, for instance, committed that state to spend $27.8 million to support railroad construction. More than $17.6 million of that sum was actually spent, but a large portion of it went into politicians' pockets rather than railroads.

Other debts reflected poor financial judgment—which is lamentable but not illegal or immoral. Moreover, the increase of government debt began before Radical Reconstruction and continued afterward in some cases. Throughout the period, Conservatives and Democrats lent a hand in deficit spending. Almost all of the state governments created under Johnson's plan subsidized efforts to rebuild and expand railroads, and several created immigration agencies to attract white workers to replace blacks. Legislatures assisted railroads with corporate charters, land grants, and endorsements of bonds. Repairs and construction of other internal improvements—levees, roads, ports, and harbors—received some help also. In these actions southern legislators were following antebellum precedents. Most of the governments created under the Johnson plan also attempted to deal with the pressing problem of private indebtedness. Banks, whose restoration was crucial to economic recovery, received legal authority to scale down war-inflated debts. Individual debtors also got some relief.

Republican state governments often followed the lead of their predecessors. When Republicans in Alabama implemented their very generous program of aid to railroads, for instance, they did so under legislation passed by Alabama's provisional legislatures in 1866 and 1867. Finally, most of the growth of these debts resulted from needed expenditures for postwar recovery and from the states' assumption of responsibility for new services, such as provision of public schools, which had been almost nonexistent before the war. Aid to railroad construction absorbed by far the greatest portion of the increased expenditures of the southern state governments. This spending pattern continued into the 1870s before necessary budget reductions ended almost all state efforts to assist railroads.

Southern state governments had to increase taxes to get the money they were spending, and those taxes were extracted from a badly weakened economy. The increased tax burden fell especially hard on small landowners. In the past, their tax load had been light because government provided few services and because taxes on slaves had been a major source of state revenue. Emancipation, of course, ended the latter tax. Now almost all public revenue came from taxes on real property, and, coincidentally, the rate of taxation had increased. Thus, ironically, small landowners, who elsewhere in the United States were staunch Republicans, were the most adversely affected by the tax policies of the Republican state governments in the South.

Also contrary to another widely held notion, blacks did not dominate the South during Radical Reconstruction, even numerically. While black voters outnumbered white voters (735,000 registrants to 635,000 in 1867 in the ten unreconstructed states) and had majorities in Louisiana, Mississippi, Alabama, Florida, and South Carolina, only sixteen blacks served in Congress, fourteen in the House and two in the Senate. Several won election as lieutenant governors, and a few others held high state offices. Blacks had a majority in only one southern state legislative body, the lower house in South Carolina.

Black politicians varied in competence and quality of service, just as American politicians have always done. The image of ignorant, arrogant blacks suddenly come to power is grossly unfair. John R. Lynch, a largely self-taught former slave in Mississippi, rose to be Speaker of his state's House of Representatives and won the praises even of southern whites. He later served as an officer in the United States Army and then spent the remainder of his life in Chicago, where he practiced law and tried his hand in real estate. After helping rewrite the constitution of his native state, Francis L. Cardozo was elected secretary of the treasury in South Carolina, a position in which he showed considerable ability and a strong distaste for dishonesty in government. When he died, he was a school administrator in the District of Columbia.

Factors other than their native abilities prevented blacks from achieving political power commensurate with their numbers. Poverty left blacks vulnerable and with more urgent concerns than public office, political organizing, and elections. Slavery had left them with limited experience as organizers and with a tendency to defer to whites. Blacks and their presumed supporters often differed. White Republicans in Georgia even joined with Conservatives in 1870 to deprive black legislators of their seats. Blacks sometimes broke with their white allies, feeling, for instance, that they were not receiving the leadership roles due them. Blacks also divided among themselves. South Carolina black leaders divided along color lines, black versus mulatto, and along antebellum lines, former slaves versus blacks who had not been slaves before the Civil War. Divisions among black Republicans, between black and white Republicans, and between southern- and northern-born Republicans hindered the party and hastened its demise in the South. Those divisions also make a mockery of one of the persistent images of the "tragic era" legend—that Republicans marched like Roman phalanxes across a helpless South. The South was not that helpless, and the Republicans were not that unified in the South or in Washington.

Those who wished to build and maintain a strong Republican party in the South faced enormous odds. To most southern whites, the Republicans symbolized war, invasion, defeat, and abolition. Thus the most economically and politically powerful elements in the South were the most hostile to the party. On the other hand, southern blacks flocked to the Republicans, and understandably so. About 80 percent of the party's supporters were blacks, the least powerful elements in the region. Also, the Republican party had no historical roots in the South; it was an import, not a product of evolutionary growth, as successful political parties have been in the United States. Moreover, northern Republicans favored economic policies—high tariffs, restricted banks, and excise taxes on tobacco and alcohol—which most southerners believed hurt their interests. Finally, sharp factional divisions plagued the Republicans in the South throughout Reconstruction. The seriousness of the difficulties the Republican party encountered in the South is indicated by the failure of the Republicans to sink firm roots in southern soil until after World War II.

White Republicans tried to attract southern whites by various means. One of the most important of these tactics was their championing of the New South, or the idea that the South had to distance itself from its antebellum past, industrialize and urbanize, and diversify and modernize its agriculture, and that to achieve these things government had to aid private enterprise. State aid to railroads was the most obvious and substantial expression of that policy and was based on the belief that recovery and expansion of the South's rail system was necessary for economic development. The cause of the New South appealed particularly to southern Whigs and similar elements among the southern Democrats. Business and political leaders in Atlanta, in northern Alabama, and in Charleston and Richmond joined the New South crusade. White Republicans in the South also tried to appeal to native white leaders through political patronage and by sometimes tempering their commitment to public education. The latter policies, however, risked alienating blacks, who were the principal source of Republican support in the South.

Southern Republicans might have enjoyed greater power after 1865 had they put greater restrictions on voting or officeholding by southern whites. They chose not to do so in part because southern blacks who served as representatives in the conventions that drafted new constitutions for the southern states and who served in southern state legislatures usually opposed such steps. Such actions indicated that Reconstruction often lacked the vindictiveness ascribed to it, even on the part of most blacks, who had the greatest justification for vindictiveness. The reluctance to proscribe southern whites also reflected good sense. Preventing large numbers of southern whites from voting or holding office would very likely have worsened the political turmoil that already existed. Moreover, black leaders understood that blacks were going to live in the South after Reconstruction and were going to have to coexist with southern whites, whose economic power alone gave them enormous leverage over blacks.

Nor was Reconstruction enforced by a massive army of occupation. When the Civil War ended, the United States Army rapidly reduced its forces, and much of what remained was stationed on the western frontier and on the Mexican border. Fewer than 18,000 troops remained in the South in 1866, and only some 6,000 were there in 1876. Immediately after the war, the army helped maintain order in the South and distributed relief. During Military Reconstruction, the army supervised the establishment of Reconstruction governments, but southern whites often found the army was a valuable ally, as in Florida, where the military governor threw his weight behind moderate Republicans and against the more radical Republicans. The army could only occasionally exert force to deter southern whites from excesses. It did so when it was ordered to suppress the Ku Klux Klan. Blacks continued to have mixed feelings about the men in blue, who were too often hostile and sometimes used force to make blacks sign contracts and work as wage laborers and sharecroppers. Southern whites resented the army most when black troops were stationed nearby.

Reconstruction can also be credited with important positive achievements. Southern Republicans drafted state constitutions that recognized blacks' political and civil rights, though they generally left social segregation intact. The Reconstruction constitutions also granted women greater control over their property. Constitutional conventions apportioned legislatures more equitably, expanded the number of elective offices, eliminated property qualifications for officeholding, and checked the power of county political machines. The South eventually accepted many of these constitutional changes. Their permanence despite the numerous revisions of state constitutions since Reconstruction testifies to the merits of the work of the southern Republicans. The South became permanently committed to public education, probably the greatest accomplishment of Reconstruction policy in the South. Other expanded public services included institutions for the poor, the mentally ill, and the physically handicapped. During Reconstruction, Auburn University and the University of Arkansas were created, the University of Alabama and Louisiana State University were reopened, and South Carolina College became the University of South Carolina, with a highly innovative curriculum.

The South began its economic recovery during Reconstruction. The region's rail system was largely restored and was expanded by nearly 7,300 miles. That expansion greatly increased penetration of southern Appalachia. The Freedmen's Bureau spent $1 million on relief for southern blacks and whites and $5 million for education. Working with or alongside teachers from such groups as the American Missionary Association, the New England Freedmen's Aid Society, and the Freedmen's Relief Association, the bureau made significant though modest beginnings toward schooling for blacks. Literacy rose impressively among blacks. Other reminders of these educational efforts remain: Fisk, Hampton, Howard, Atlanta, Talladega, Dillard universities, and others. By 1876 more than half of the white children and two-fifths of the black children in the South were enrolled in school.

The myth of Reconstruction also obscures what did not happen—mass arrests and executions or long imprisonment or deportation of Confederate leaders. Very few southern whites suffered prolonged disfranchisement or disqualification for public office, and the southern states did not suffer extended terms as territories which ended only after a stringent list of requirements were met. One Confederate officer was tried and hanged for war crimes. Captain Henry Wirtz, who had been commander of Andersonville prison, was undoubtedly the victim of a political trial. Jefferson Davis, the former president of the Confederacy, did suffer cruel and humiliating treatment, though briefly. After 1872, when Congress passed the Amnesty Act, only a handful of former Confederate leaders still had to apply for special pardons before they could hold public office. Such pardons were routinely granted.

Southerners did, of course, suffer after the war, but far more as a result of the war itself than as a result of Reconstruction, and blacks suffered far more than whites. Blacks experienced more stark poverty and genuine hunger, and far more of them were the targets of murder, assault, and intimidation. They were deserted by a federal government that was unwilling and unable to secure their political and civil rights and give them a reasonable chance to escape peonage.

The myth that Reconstruction was the Tragic Era persisted because it met an urgent need. Southern whites salved wounds of defeat and feelings of massive wrong with this and other legends: the Lost Cause (the war for southern independence was a noble cause—ignore slavery as the root cause), the Great Alibi (the war made the South economically backward), and the Old South (the antebellum South was an idyllic world peopled by genteel masters, gracious ladies, and happy slaves). A thicket of fact and fiction grew up and thrived with nurturing into a mass that still defies comprehension.

The myth that Reconstruction was the Tragic Era also served to justify efforts of Southern whites to regain and maintain political and economic control. Political "outs"—southern Democrats and Conservatives—found the legends useful for attacking the political "ins." Like northern politicians who waved the Bloody Shirt and shouted "Johnny Reb" and "traitor," southern politicians fulminated about "scalawags" and "carpetbaggers" and Radical and Black Reconstruction. As is often the case, historical reality and political rhetoric parted company. Reconstruction was neither black nor radical. It was not dominated by blacks, and except for the proposal to give blacks full and equal citizenship, it was not a program of revolutionary change. Nor were southern whites a monolithic mass. While they had much in common, they were divided by politics, interests, and geography. The secessionist versus Unionist divisions of the antebellum and war years persisted and were exacerbated by the crushing defeat in the Civil War and the turmoil that followed. Whigs and Democrats continued their long-standing feud. Small farmers often differed with planters, and both usually felt uneasy with the urban South, with manufacturers, merchants, and railroad leaders. Old geographically based differences persisted: upcountry versus low country, mountain versus piedmont, western versus middle versus mountain in Tennessee, hill country versus delta in Mississippi.

The negative image associated with carpetbaggers and scalawags also persists in spite of historical fact. Some carpetbaggers did fit the stereotype: they did throw a goodly portion of their worldly belongings into their carpetbags and head south in pursuit of what they could get. Most, however, were former Union officers and were at least as honest and able as their southern Democratic opponents, and many were more idealistic. Most carpetbaggers had some capital to invest in the South, which they believed had great economic potential, and had a good deal of training and education. Carpetbaggers taught in or administered schools for freedmen, worked for the Freedmen's Bureau, and served as lawyers, physicians, and engineers. Those carpetbaggers who entered politics, one scholar has concluded, "may have been the best educated group of Americans in politics, North or South.... They also invested human capital—themselves—in a drive to modernize the region's social structure, revive its crippled economy, and democratize its politics."

Southern Democrats labeled the Republicans' southern white allies "scalawags," a term for scrub horses or cattle. Drawn from the ranks of former Whigs in the urban South and the black belt and of Unionists in the upland South (western Virginia and North Carolina, eastern Tennessee, and northern Georgia, Alabama, and Arkansas), scalawags joined the Republicans, at least temporarily. They had mixed motives. Some scalawags were simply political opportunists. Some carried over hostility toward the Democrats from antebellum years. Others loathed the planters and the old planter regimes, and some of them had fought against the Confederacy. Scalawags often embraced the Republican party as the party of "progress, of education, of development"; "good roads...free bridges"; "free schools and the advantages of education for your children." The scalawags found that the Republican party—the party that promised a modern South—provided them with the means to pursue concerns that they had had before the Civil War.

Even as southern Democrats decried carpetbaggers, scalawags, and Black Reconstruction, they whitewashed the Ku Klux Klan, the Knights of the White Camellia, and other vigilante groups. Terrorists murdered, maimed, intimidated, whipped, and burned. The toll in lives reached the hundreds. Restoration of the Democrats' political dominance was their prime aim. First, blacks, then white teachers and Republican leaders were their prime targets. The vigilantes left a wide trail that began in Tennessee in 1866, nearly brought civil war to North Carolina in 1869, and reached a climax in South Carolina in 1871, when President Ulysses S. Grant had to declare virtual martial law in nine South Carolina counties. Yet no southern jury ever convicted one vigilante during the Reconstruction era. And prominent southerners acquiesced in, supported, and even led the terrorists. Only in the early 1870s, when this means to achieve control became too risky—when vigilantism triggered federal intervention or threatened to devolve into widespread turmoil—did southern leaders cease secret organized Klan terror. Later in the 1870s, more open and somewhat less violent means were employed by organized local rifle clubs and "Red Shirts," groups that were important in the overthrow of the last of the Reconstruction governments. Thus the myth of Reconstruction as the Tragic Era salved wounds and consciences, excused the fraud and violence that attended the fall of Reconstruction, and justified the subordination of blacks. Eventually the myth of Reconstruction came to be accepted as fact.

THE EMERGENCE OF THE ONE-PARTY SOUTH

The high tide of northern support for Reconstruction passed in 1867, receding almost as quickly as it had risen. Increasingly the South was left to its own devices, and increasingly southern opposition to Reconstruction asserted itself in various ways. The Republicans in Washington lacked public support to do more than they had done. They went as far as circumstances and their ideology would allow when they passed the Fourteenth Amendment, the Reconstruction acts, and the Fifteenth Amendment. The last, which was proposed by Congress in 1869 and ratified in 1870, forbade any state to deny or abridge the right to vote "on account of race, color, or previous condition of servitude." (Ominously for the future, Congress failed to take a more positive position and specifically give blacks the vote. Thus legislatures could, and later did, disfranchise people on nonracial grounds: literacy, poll taxes, "understanding" the Constitution, and so forth.) Having passed this last amendment and no longer needing the unity they had developed to oppose the now departed President Johnson, the Republicans fell back into their conservative, moderate, and radical divisions.

That Republican Reconstruction had passed its climax became very clear during the Grant administration (1869–1877), when the federal government adopted a generally passive attitude toward the South. Neither Congress nor the administration acted to stop the depredations of the Ku Klux Klan, for instance, until they reached epidemic proportions in the 1870s. Finally Congress held extensive hearings and left a voluminous record of murderous outrages and willful disregard of the law which showed that the Klansmen were not noble defenders of virtue and honor, though many Klansmen were of the "better" sort. Congress then passed the Ku Klux Klan Act of 1871, which allowed the federal government to act to prevent interference with voting rights. To enforce the law, the president could suspend the writ of habeas corpus and order the army in, and federal courts had the power to expel Klansmen from juries and inflict heavy penalties for perjury. The Grant administration hesitated, then acted with vigor to enforce the law. Federal agents infiltrated the Klan, the administration suspended habeas corpus in nine South Carolina counties, and thousands of suspected Klansmen were arrested. Some sixty eventually received federal sentences of up to five years, more exchanged guilty pleas for reduced charges, and charges were dropped against perhaps 2,000 who had been indicted for lesser offenses. The worst excesses of the Klan stopped, and the organization became moribund. The strong actions of Congress and the Grant administration and the persistence of Republican strength in the early

1870s helped make the 1872 election the freest and the most democratic presidential election in the South until 1968.

The federal government had to intervene with force in Louisiana in 1873 after elections there produced two legislatures and two governors, products of regular Republicans on the one hand and of an alliance of Democrats and dissident Republicans on the other. President Grant finally had to send troops to enforce a federal court order that supported the regular Republicans. Factional and partisan battles continued, however. So did violence, and it got worse. Black militiamen and local whites fought at Colfax, Louisiana, in April 1873. Two whites and seventy blacks died; about half of the dead militiamen were slaughtered after they had surrendered. The White League, a vigilante group, killed six Republican public officials near Shreveport in August. The following month, White Leaguers routed police and state militiamen in New Orleans: the clash left thirty killed and a hundred wounded. Grant sent troops, again. Their presence calmed matters, but the Democrats continued their ascendancy. And the "bayonet rule" issue surfaced again. In Arkansas, Republican factional strife deteriorated into the Brooks-Baxter "war," while in South Carolina and Florida, Republicans were bitterly divided. By 1874 southern whites controlled the gov-

" Hang, curs, hang! * * * * *   *Their* complexion is perfect gallows. Stand fast, good
fate, to *their* hanging! * * * * * If they be not born to be hanged, our case is miserable."

The above cut represents the fate in store for those great pests of Southern society—the carpet-bagger and scallawag—if found in Dixie's Land after the break of day on the 4th of March next.

KKK WARNING (Collection of the Alabama State Department of Archives and History)

NORTHERN DISILLUSION (American Antiquarian Society)

ernments of Virginia, North Carolina, Georgia, Tennessee, Alabama, and Texas, and they presented growing challenges in South Carolina, Florida, Mississippi, Arkansas, and Louisiana.

That year the Republicans faced severe challenges nationally. Grant and the Republicans were increasingly unpopular. Scandals in the administration, Grant's poor political judgment, weariness after so many years of Republican control of the White House and Congress and the turmoil associated with Reconstruction, and most important, the long depression that began in 1873 took a heavy toll. The Democrats got control of the House of Representatives after gaining seventy-seven seats in the congressional election of 1874, one of the most sweeping victories in American electoral history. For the first time since 1860, the Democrats had a majority in one chamber of Congress, and they had solid grounds for their hope that they could take the Senate and the White House in 1876.

Even as Democrats were savoring their 1874 victories, Mississippi Democrats launched their Mississippi Plan for the 1875 Mississippi state elections. They routed Republicans with appeals to white unity and racial fears, with economic force to intimidate poor dependent black workers and sharecroppers, with rifle clubs and "riots" that they themselves provoked. Dozens died. Voters seemed to vanish. The Republicans got a *total* of 25 votes in 1875 in five counties that previously had had large black voting majorities. The Democrats swept the election and began a long era of white-supremacy politics and one-party rule in Mississippi.

Similar political developments occurred elsewhere in the South. White-supremacy politics and one-party rule became the norm, a norm that persisted until after World War II. The Republican party was driven to the margins of political life while the Democrats achieved overwhelming dominance by making white supremacy the cornerstone of their party. White-supremacy politics had internal and external dimensions. Internally, or within the South, the Democrats argued that whites must unite to exclude blacks from the political process and ensure their own dominance. Any split among whites—if whites divided between the Republican party and the Democratic party, for instance—would allow blacks to play whites against each other and thus escape their subordinate place. Thus white supremacy required the success of the Democratic party. At the same time, the Democrats trumpeted themselves as the party best suited to prevent interference from external or nonsouthern forces in southern race relations, interference that might disrupt what was becoming a rigid racial caste system.

During the early days of Reconstruction, southern Democrats had not adopted such a consistently white-supremacist position. When Republicans first took office in the former Confederate states, some Democrats acquiesced in the new Reconstruction policies, cooperated more or less openly with southern Republican leaders, and even accepted the proposal to give blacks the vote and some civil rights. Concern for political survival and for recognition of their legitimacy by the North figured heavily in their political calculations. Most of these "New Departure" Democrats were in the urban South, in banking, manufacturing, railroading, and commercial enterprises. Some had once been Whigs or had been allied with the Whigs. Almost all of the New Departure Democrats embraced the idea of the New South. Benjamin H. Hill, for instance, began his political career in Georgia as a Whig. A persistent Unionist through the 1850s, Hill left the crumbling ranks of the Whigs and then joined the secessionists. After the Civil War, during which he was a Confederate senator, he denounced Reconstruction and the enfranchisement of blacks. By 1869 he had reversed himself on black suffrage, joined the Democrats, and participated in their revival. He urged his fellow southerners to imitate the North and "go to work to build our own fortunes, get possession of our own affairs": "our material prosperity must now begin."

Practitioners of the politics of moderation, New Departure Democrats frequently worked with Republicans, especially in efforts to obtain state aid for railroads, and they sometimes made serious efforts to attract black voters to the Democratic party, though they assumed that black Democrats would have only a subordinate place in the party. Democrats in Virginia joined a bipartisan coalition to elect a moderate Republican governor in 1870. By electing northern-born Gilbert C. Walker, banker, manufacturer, and railroad man, Virginia managed to be the only former Confederate state not to have a Radical Republican government. A similar coalition in Tennessee elected De Witt Senter governor and opened the way to a constitutional convention that adopted universal manhood suffrage. This broad franchise speeded the return of the Tennessee Democrats to dominance in the state.

"Straight-out" or "straight" Democrats spurned cooperation with Republicans or efforts to appeal to blacks. Instead, following a policy of racial exclusion, or "the white line," they rallied southern whites, many of whom had been politically apathetic, with mass-oriented political tactics. They created grass-roots organizations and mobilized voters with parades, barbecues, and paramilitary organizations or rifle clubs, which, unlike the KKK and the White League, operated openly and publicized their activities.

Angered by rising taxes and growing state debts and wrenched by the depression of the 1870s, the straight Democrats demanded lower taxes and severe budget cuts. To reach these goals they created highly effective nonpartisan pressure groups called taxpayer unions. These organizations usually evolved into more openly partisan political groups. The straight Democrats drew upon their Jacksonian roots in their efforts to reject most forms of state aid to private enterprise. Believing that public schooling had little value and, worse, benefited blacks more than whites, they sought to end or drastically reduce public spending for education.

Led by the straight Democrats, most southern states in the 1870s stopped or revoked land grants to railroads, state purchases or endorsements of railroad bonds, and tax exemptions for corporations. Thus they largely gave up any attempt to use their taxing and spending powers to expand and diversify the economy of the South. Several southern states passed measures to regulate railroad rates. Moreover, the Democrats cut expenditures and taxes by shrinking the size and role of government through very direct means. The Alabama constitution of 1875 limited the legislature to biennial sessions, curtailed its members' pay to $4 a day, and reduced its powers. The executive branch did not escape the attention of the frugal: the number of officials in that branch was reduced, and those that remained took a 25 percent pay cut.

The straight Democrats did not completely reverse the policy of state aid to private enterprise, however. Consisting as they did almost entirely of planters and farmers, they gave their blessings to publicly funded agricultural experiment stations, geological surveys, and even, in Virginia, the Carolinas, and Mississippi, agricultural and mechanical colleges. The straight Democrats also favored measures to ease farm debt and crop-lien laws designed to secure landowners' control of farm labor. The latter became crucially important in the economy of the South.

The triumph of the straight Democrats in the 1870s represented a climax in southern history. Their policies became the accepted policies of the Democratic party, and that party became the only one that had a realistic chance of winning the great majority of offices in the South. Southern whites had clearly reestablished their supremacy over blacks—though they continued to believe that maintaining their position required constant vigilance. Landowners had obtained much stronger legal means of controlling their labor. The crop-lien system, which applied to whites as well as blacks, was not the same as slavery, though it seemed to be, since it kept landless farmers in endless debt. Finally, the Democrats had secured self-perpetuity: they had created the one-party Democratic South. Grounded on white unity, the Democratic party stood ready (and sometimes armed) to protect the racial hierarchy of the South against internal enemies and external threats. About the same time, developments in the border states added to the power of the Democrats in the region and the nation. Relying heavily on appeals to white racism, Democrats enjoyed a resurgence of power in Missouri, West Virginia, Delaware, and Maryland.

The federal government did little after 1872 to oppose these developments. Probably it could have done little that would have had lasting effect. The Grant administration did consider intervening in the 1874 election in Mississippi, but did not do so. Ohio Republicans convinced President Grant that if he sent troops to Mississippi, the Republicans might lose the approaching state elections in Ohio to the Democrats, who would make political capital of the issue of "government by bayonet" in Mississippi. "The whole public are tired out with these annual autumnal outbreaks in the South," the president told the besieged Republican governor of Mississippi, "and the great majority are now ready to condemn any interference on the part of the government." Political considerations and realities outside the South had again shaped the political options available to those developing and implementing policies with respect to the region.

Congress tacitly acknowledged as much when it passed the Civil Rights Act of 1875, the last major Reconstruction law enacted by Congress. Senator Charles Sumner proposed a law to prohibit racial segregation in public schools, in selection of juries, on all forms of public transportation, and in public accommodations. Southern Republicans, especially the factions in which blacks were prominent, gave the bill strong support. But many members of Congress had reservations as to the proposed measure's constitutionality, doubts about its enforceability, and fears of the voters' reaction to it. The death in 1874 of Sumner, one of the keepers of the Republican conscience, may have provided the necessary impetus to secure the act's passage, after removal of the provision applying to public schools. Congress may have believed that the law would have little impact and even less of a future when it was reviewed by the courts. In 1883 the Supreme Court ruled the act unconstitutional. The Court held that though governmental bodies could not legally discriminate by race, individuals could not be prevented by law from doing so.

THE COMPROMISE OF 1877

A year after the Civil Rights Act became law, the 1876 presidential election took place. It ended without a clear victor in the electoral college. The deadlock centered on South Carolina, Louisiana, Florida, and Oregon, where the presidential election results were hotly disputed. Congress took up the dispute in early 1877, exercising its constitutional duty to resolve the undecided election. But the Constitution contained no provision as to how Congress should resolve an inconclusive presidential election. The impasse evolved into a lengthy acrimonious dispute, which was resolved only hours before the Grant administration ended.

Congress created an electoral commission to investigate the disputed state results and to recommend a resolution to Congress. The commission soon found itself in a hopeless thicket when it tried to sort out the election mess in South Carolina, Louisiana, and Florida. So bad was the situation that the governor of Louisiana reportedly offered that state's electoral votes for $200,000. The commission heard testimony that revealed that fraud, violence, and intimidation were common. It was obvious that the Democrats had cast the most ballots in each of the states. Equally obviously, they had also prevented large numbers of blacks from voting. In South Carolina, for instance, the campaign organization put together by Wade Hampton, Confederate hero and future governor, included rifle clubs and Red Shirts. One of his supporters later recalled that some whites voted ten times each at three polling places, that whites paid blacks for their votes, that dead people voted, and that election officials cleverly arranged the tally sheets. Her brother, a bank official and manufacturer, "was an expert at all such manipulations, and I am sure God has forgiven him for all such chicanery with the purpose we all had in view." She did not, however, recall any violence during the election. Others did, and even celebrated it. South Carolina erected a monument to commemorate the Hamburg riot. Two hundred local whites battled a black militia unit at Hamburg, South Carolina, in July 1876; then they killed five militiamen they had captured. After Hamburg and at the request of the Republican governor, Daniel H. Chamberlain, Grant increased the number of troops stationed in South Carolina. Their presence reduced the instances of violence during the election, but only somewhat. Intimidation, violence, and outright fraud played lesser roles in the results in Florida in 1876 than they had done earlier or would do later. In 1876 other factors had greater impact on the election in Florida. White voters slightly outnumbered black voters, the Republicans suffered from bitter factional fights, and the Democrats' campaign was much better organized.

Historians have attempted to determine whether Samuel Tilden, the Democrat, or Rutherford B. Hayes, the Republican, won in the three southern states whose elections were disputed. The generally accepted conclusion, based on careful examination of historical records and elaborate calculations, is that if the elections held in South Carolina, Louisiana, and Florida had been fair, Hayes would have gotten majorities in the first two but Tilden would have taken Florida, and thus the election. The electoral commission did not, however, attempt such a thorough process of sifting and winnowing. The commission had a Republican bias and was operating under severe time constraints. The commission decided by 8 (Republican) to 7 (Democratic) votes to accept the election results as reported by the Republican officials in South Carolina, Louisiana, and Florida. The commission also declared the Republicans the winners in Oregon. The action of the commission made Hayes the victor: he had 185 electoral votes, Tilden 184.

The Democrats countered by threatening to prolong the impasse, perhaps by a filibuster, and maybe get Tilden elected. But the Democrats had serious handicaps. The Republicans had the presidency (at least until March 4), the Senate, the armed forces, and the enormous advantage of being the party of national patriotism, the party that had defended the Union. The commission's action could not realistically be set aside, because Congress had stipulated that the commission's rulings could be vetoed only by both houses of Congress. The Republican Senate was hardly going to reject the commission's decision. Filibustering to delay action beyond March 4, the date for a new administration to begin, required more unity than the Democrats probably had, in light of their own sectional divisions and mounting pressure from the public and from important business interests to settle the election. Democrats, especially in the North, could not risk being again labeled the party of disunion. Northern Democrats showed far less tenacity on Tilden's behalf than did their southern counterparts. These circumstances cast considerable doubt on the assertion that Hayes struck a clear bargain with southern Democrats in order to ensure his election. If Hayes and the southern Democrats had had a firm, explicit bargain, they should not have been the most persistent opponents to the electoral commission's report.

Hayes's representatives did engage in negotiations with the southern Democrats, which laid the groundwork for the Compromise of 1877. They concluded a series of "understandings," which were not entirely clear at the time and still are not. Hayes indicated that he would remove federal troops from the South and that he would not attempt to prop up feeble Republican governments in South Carolina and Louisiana, where both Democrats and Republicans claimed that they had captured the governorships and the legislatures in 1876. In this instance, Hayes was not making big concessions. The Democrats had so much power in both states that the great majority of whites paid taxes to the Democratic governments, not to the Republican governments that still claimed to exist officially. In Louisiana, the Democrats controlled the state courts and the New Orleans police. Hayes could have done little to alter the situation in either state, even from the White House. The Democratic-controlled House of Representatives simply could have refused, as it said it would do, to appropriate funds for the armed forces that would have been required to keep the Republicans in office in South Carolina and Louisiana. Moreover, it is highly doubtful that Hayes could have gotten enough public support to use the army in the South.

Hayes also agreed to appoint a southerner to the cabinet and to give some patronage to moderate southern Democrats. And he did so. Hayes also indicated that he favored the use of more federal funds for internal improvements in the South, such as levees for the Mississippi River and a rail link to connect the South directly with the Pacific Coast, something southerners had long wished for. If, as some historians believe, he committed himself to supporting government subsidies for Tom Scott's Texas and Pacific Railroad, he later changed his mind. Subsequently, as president, Hayes gave government encouragement, but not funds, to Collis P. Huntington's Southern Pacific Railroad to complete a southern transcontinental road. (Completion came in 1882.) Hayes's support for internal improvements struck strong responsive chords in the South, and the South did receive more federal money for internal improvements during the Hayes administration than it had received earlier.

In seeking these understandings, Hayes may have been as concerned about running the country after the election was settled as he was about getting elected. How could any president function effectively and how could there be domestic peace if he had to keep sending troops to one region of the country? Hayes believed that moderation and conciliation might be more productive than a more aggressive approach and would have broad support in the North. Hayes and his advisers also hoped that a conciliatory strategy might help the Republican party to gain strength in the South. They thought that many white southerners, such as former Whigs, shared the Republicans' commitment to economic development and public education. Many did, but few were inclined to seek those goals from within the Republican party in the 1870s or for many years thereafter. Also the vast majority of southern whites believed that white supremacy must be the cornerstone of postbellum southern life. Southern white leaders may have led Hayes to think that blacks and Republicans would receive fair treatment in the South, but they were quite prepared to disappoint him on both points. As Hayes quickly discovered after he was in the White House, southern whites would go to great lengths to secure the supremacy of themselves and the Democratic party. A disillusioned Hayes also found that he could do little to stop them.

Though the Republicans got the main prize, the presidency, they did not do as well as they had thought they would in the House. Hayes Republicans thought they had assurances from southern Democrats that a few of them would break ranks with their party and help the Republicans organize the

House. No such break occurred. The Democrats thus kept control of the House. They also triumphed in South Carolina and Louisiana, ending the last Republican governments in the South. Thus the Democracy now had control of the governments of all the states of the former Confederacy and the border South.

Reconstruction had ended.

Five times during the nineteenth century sectional divisions took the United States to the brink of a bloody conflict. Four times, as C. Vann Woodward, distinguished historian of the American South, has noted, compromise prevailed—in the Missouri Compromise of 1820, at the end of the nullification crisis in the 1830s, in the Compromise of 1850, and in the Compromise of 1877. Compromise failed once, and civil war resulted. "The Compromise of 1877," Woodward writes,

> marked the abandonment of principles and of force and a return to the traditional ways of expediency and concession. The compromise laid the political foundation for reunion. It established a new sectional truce that proved more enduring than any previous one and provided a settlement for an issue that had troubled American politics for more than a generation. It wrote an end to Reconstruction and recognized a new regime in the South. More profoundly than Constitutional amendments and wordy statutes it shaped the future of four million freedmen and their progeny for generations to come. It preserved one part of the fruits of the "Second American Revolution"—the pragmatic and economic part—at the expense of the other part— the idealistic and humanitarian part. The settlement was not ideal from any point of view, nor was it very logical either. But that is the way of compromises.

The blacks at Port Royal certainly understood such matters. Tyra and Moses Mitchell, their son Sam, and other blacks discovered the limits of the freedom the Yankee had come to give them. Southern whites kept or regained ownership of most of the land and, sooner or later, political dominance. Blacks had to accept peonage—sometimes worse—and second-class citizenship. The federal government deserted the blacks when they evicted the squatters at Port Royal. Then the federal government deserted blacks elsewhere in the South and in other ways. If it was ever intended to do so, Reconstruction fell dismally short of bringing sweeping change to the South. That result can be traced largely to the constraints imposed on the federal government by elemental American institutions, beliefs, and traditions.

Redistribution of land from former slaveholders to former slaves fell afoul of the cardinal American principle of the sanctity of private property. Any comprehensive, long-term aid program for blacks or the South conflicted with the nineteenth-century belief that government's responsibilities for the economic welfare of its citizens were severely limited. Congress revered the Constitution and felt the limitations it set acutely. The war may have made the Union supreme, but it was still a union of states to which certain powers were reserved. Blacks were given the vote and then left to work out their future in a hostile South—to, in the words of one contemporary, "root, hog, or die." And the South was left to elevate itself by its own bootstraps.

The United States also lacked the institutional means to carry out broad domestic changes.

> Without the tradition, the means of communication, the legal framework, or the administrative apparatus—in effect, without anything beyond an army and the tenuous cooperation of some local citizens to implement a detailed public policy—reconstruction had guaranteed confusion, disappointment, and recrimination.

The Freedmen's Bureau, for instance, had a budget too niggardly ($5 million), a staff too small (900 people at its peak), and tenure too short (five years) to do much. Even the number of federal troops was reduced to 17,700 by 1868 and to 6,000 by 1876, and one-third to one-half of them served in Texas, where the army patrolled the Mexican border.

Racism, which abounded in the halls of Congress as it did among most white Americans, north and south, severely limited northern whites' willingness to exert themselves on behalf of the former slaves. After all, the North only reluctantly embraced emancipation, then tardily enlisted blacks in the armed forces, and finally, swayed by the valor of blacks in the field and by the excesses of southern whites after the war, gave blacks the vote. The concern and sympathy of northern whites reached their limits there. Other things mattered more: a deep, understandable yearning for peace, for reconciliation with the white South and reunification of the nation, and for steps to bolster the faltering national economy.

Reconstruction left a flawed record, a record that belies both its professed ideals and the myth of the Tragic Era. That record included the happenings at Washington, Atlanta, Montgomery, and other political centers and wherever blacks seized their chance—"You ain't gonna row no boat to Charleston, you go out that back door and keep a-going"—to build new lives in the New South.

17

Economic Reconstruction, 1865–1880

❖

They were driving stakes into the ground when Bryant Watkins found them on his plantation near Greensboro, Alabama. They said that "Yankees" told them half the land belonged to them. "Listen, niggers," replied the planter, according to one of his former slaves,

> "what's mine is mine, and what's yours is yours. You are just as free as I and the missus, but don't go foolin' around my land. I've tried to be a good master to you. I have never been unfair. Now if you wants to stay, you are welcome to work for me. I'll pay you one third the crops you raise. But if you wants to go, you sees the gate."

Thus economic reconstruction began on Bryant Watkins's plantation, as it did on thousands of plantations and farms and in cities and towns in the South as soon as the fighting ended. Economic reconstruction began before Republican Reconstruction, lasted longer, and had a far more lasting impact on the South. Southern whites and blacks had to replace the social and economic organization that slavery had provided. The critically important southern railway network had to be rehabilitated. So did commerce, industry, and cities and towns. Growth came later, occasionally faster than was anticipated. The contours that emerged during economic reconstruction were determined by a blend of past and present. The South's antebellum heritage, the circumstances of the South in 1865 and the several decades thereafter, the limits of human imagination in nineteenth-century America, and national and international forces and events set the patterns for economic reconstruction. Those contours lasted a long time and became the basic elements of the postbellum South.

Economic reconstruction left King Cotton on his throne. The fortunes of cotton and of the South were virtually identical for a long time, though cotton did not grow everywhere in the South and not everyone was part of the vast network associated with it. But growing and marketing cotton were the principal activities and sources of income for southerners as late as 1930. Thus cotton lay at the nucleus of southern social, political, and economic life: the ownership and use of land, obtaining and controlling labor, the rise and fall of individual fortunes as measured by pocketbooks and places in society, and how far the South would distance itself from its antebellum roots and the destruction of war and defeat.

LANDLORDS, SHARECROPPERS, AND TENANTS

Bryant Watkins probably was not thinking so abstractly about the role of cotton in the South's economy that morning. He still had land despite the Civil War, but he no longer controlled his work force as he had·done during slavery. His former slaves owned their labor but no land. The requirements of survival compelled them (and Watkins) to strike a bargain. Watkins's former slaves could use some of his plantation for a portion of the crop they produced. Or they could leave. Watkins and his former slaves made an "arrangement," in this case what came to be called sharecropping. Along with tenancy (land renting), it became a fixture of postbellum southern agriculture. Sharecroppers and tenants were the products of an antebellum culture shaped by wartime destruction and upheaval. Their situations were also defined by the policies of the federal and state governments and by the growing commitment of southern farmers to cash crops, cotton in particular.

Most of the land remained in white hands, often in large parcels. Many whites lost their landholdings, but apparently not nearly so many as family legends suggest. Recent studies indicate that most landowners survived the Civil War in better shape than was once believed. Blacks, of course, had owned little real estate before the war, and most remained landless afterward. Slavery had provided the means for obtaining and organizing black labor in exchange for food, clothing, shelter, other assorted necessities, and an occasional "luxury." Emancipation destroyed that means, and sharecropping and tenancy evolved as the principal ways to obtain farm labor.

The story about the Watkins plantation, as told years later by Simon Phillips, an elderly former slave, suggests a speedy transition from slavery to these new means. Whatever the experience of Watkins and his former slaves was, most southern landlords learned that necessity (hunger), the realities of the marketplace, the power of contracts enforced by laws and the courts, and occasional violence and intimidation could restore much of the control they had previously enjoyed as slaveholders.

Immediately after the war, most former slaveholders despaired of finding adequate labor. Sidney Andrews, a northern reporter, concluded after a trip to Georgia and the Carolinas in 1865 that three-fourths of the whites "assume that the negro will not labor except on compulsion." Only the heartiest of dreamers believed that slavery would be reestablished. Many more thought blacks could not survive as free people, that they would "perish by hunger and disease and melt away as snow before the rising sun," that "being in contact and competition with a superior race," they were "destined to die out" as the Indians had done. Others saw visions of boatloads of immigrants coming to the now slaveless Dixie. Almost all the southern states created commissions and appropriated funds to attract immigrants to the South. These efforts achieved little. In fact, the South had fewer foreign-born residents in 1880 than it did in 1860. Nor did the blacks vanish. If they had done so, the economy of the South would have collapsed completely. Blacks were absolutely essential to the South.

New ways of obtaining labor in the slaveless South actually began to develop before the Civil War ended. The transition began wherever the Union Army captured southern farmlands and where there were blacks. That conjunction occurred before 1864 at Port Royal in South Carolina, along the Mississippi, and in southern Louisiana. The methods employed by the army sometimes violated the concept of free labor. In the occupied parts of Louisiana, for instance, Union soldiers began in 1863 to seize and transport unemployed former slaves to plantations where their labor was needed. The army arranged labor contracts that stipulated terms of employment and obligations between employer and employee. Louisiana planters were delighted and called for more troops. Eventually the Freedmen's Bureau took over this responsibility in Louisiana and then everywhere in the defeated South. The army and bureau also gave the former slaves and many whites emergency relief, and they made some effort to ensure that laborers got fair treatment. The extent of these efforts may be measured by the frequency and intensity of planters' complaints of interference with their labor. Planters wanted help in obtaining workers but not questions about how workers were treated.

The concept of annual contracts for the labor of former slaves soon caught on. By 1867, the role of the bureau as negotiator of labor contracts had shrunk; landowners and tenants preferred to make their own arrangements. Marked improvement in southern farm output by 1868 suggests that the southern farm labor market had overcome the disorganization of the immediate postwar period and that whites had learned at last that blacks would work in the absence of slavery.

Government policies usually strengthened the hands of the landholders and creditors and did little to help blacks become farm owners. Shortly after the Civil War, as you may recall, southern legislatures passed stringent vagrancy laws, some of which were part of the more comprehensive Black Codes. Republican Reconstruction policies did not include provision of land for former slaves; the "forty acres and a mule" so many blacks thought they had been promised did not materialize. Some blacks did manage to purchase land around Beaufort, South Carolina, and other blacks in that state bought land in small parcels and on favorable terms from the South Carolina Land Commission. But this state agency was the only one of its kind during Reconstruction. Elsewhere, a few blacks took advantage of the Southern Homestead Act of 1866. But the slow implementation of the act and the inability of most blacks to meet even the rather small costs of starting a homestead seriously limited the impact of the law. Poverty was and remained the greatest obstacle to blacks in their efforts to join the ranks of the landed, even on a modest scale. Most blacks became tenants or sharecroppers, like those on the Watkins plantation.

Cropping and tenancy evolved into a pattern that unfolded in the course of a year. Landlords and tenants made oral or written contracts or "arrangements" in January or February. Planting began in April, then came cultivation in the summer months, and harvest and "settling up" in the fall. The types of arrangements and the amounts paid depended on the bargaining power of the landlord and that of the prospective tenants or workers. Labor-short landlords offered better terms. Less advantaged tenants—those with few able-bodied workers in their families, with little or no equipment and few or no work animals—had to accept less favorable arrangements. Equal or one-half shares became most common in sharecropping. Farm employers also paid wages in cash.

Landlords disliked cash wages and renting because most had little cash for wages and because rental agreements lessened their control over the crops. Landless farmers, though, preferred to rent. Rental had a higher social status than other arrangements—renters were known to have at least some means, perhaps farm equipment, tools, even a mule. Tenants, moreover, worked without the unwelcome supervision that sharecroppers and laborers experienced, which must have brought unpleasant reminders of slavery for many. Finally, unlike sharecroppers and farm laborers, tenants owned and controlled their crops until they were sold.

BLACKS AND THE LIMITS TO FREEDOM

Although the poverty of the former slaves left them few options, they actively probed the limits of their new freedom. They successfully resisted landowners' attempts to work them in gangs, another reminder of slavery. Blacks, most of whom lacked the means to become renters, preferred sharecropping to working for wages. Their persistence on this point helped make sharecropping a basic institution in the agricultural South. Blacks turned to sharecropping because they believed it allowed them a place in the decision making on the farm, and hence greater personal freedom. But southern courts in the 1870s ruled that croppers were simply laborers and had no control over the crops they grew.

Whether they rented, sharecropped, or worked as wage laborers, blacks—especially women and children—worked less than they used to do as slaves. According to careful estimates, blacks reduced the amount of work they had done as slaves by more than a third. Landlords complained bitterly. A cotton merchandising company surveyed a number of southern planters and concluded that one of the "chief needs" of the planters was "Laborers, laborers, reliable laborers." The planters raised "an almost universal cry for emigrants! emigrants!!" A Georgia planter reported that it was "harder, much harder to get laborers," that many had gone to work on railroad construction or had taken

> to little rude cabins and patches in poor lands, where they set up for themselves.... White labor was diminished by the war, and fifty per cent, more than fifty per cent, of black labor had disappeared from the *fields*. The negroes are not dead, nor gone, as elections show; but they very much quit the fields.... Give us cash capital and labor; *certainty* of labor, and its *control*."

Blacks also objected to living in what had been slave quarters. They often moved old slave houses out of the quarters area, creating a new geography of housing on plantations. In this and in other ways, such as their determination to create and operate their own religious institutions, blacks attempted to distance themselves from whites, to limit the intervention of whites in their lives. Thus blacks initiated some of the forms of postwar racial segregation in order to assert at least a portion of the freedom that emancipation afforded them.

Blacks also distanced themselves from whites and their former slave lives by leaving their masters. Initially, as we have seen, blacks left to follow the Union Army, for a while their preferred protector and provider. Or they went in search of dispersed families, to see places heard of but never before seen, and to seek nonfarm employment. Simon Phillips remembered being "treated good" as a slave, but he left the plantation in 1866 to work in Tuscaloosa (for 17 cents a day). Planters in the less settled areas of the South—Arkansas, Louisiana, Mississippi, and Texas—urgently needed labor, and they offered better terms than those available in the more settled areas. According to an 1866 report to Washington, "every railroad train during this winter has been loaded with negroes going to the west under the promise of increased wages."

Southern legislatures attempted to restrict this movement, to lessen if not destroy the freedom of the labor market. Immediately after the Civil War, for example, they enacted anti-enticement laws that made it a criminal offense to hire or entice away any laborer under contract. Though most of these laws were set aside during Reconstruction, they reappeared in other forms and remained part of the statutes of most southern states well into the twentieth century. It is uncertain whether such laws prevented laborers from seeking and finding the best pay available to them. The limited economic opportunities for former slaves anywhere in the United States long after Appomattox probably had far greater effect than the actions of state legislatures. In any event, by 1919 most blacks lived about where they had when the Civil War ended, in the black belt. This immobility was a physical expression of the limits to the freedom blacks had secured at emancipation. Too few escaped the seemingly endless cycle of poverty that ensnarled too many southern farmers after the Civil War in the "vast pawnshop" that postbellum southern agriculture became.

"FURNISH," CROP LIENS, AND COUNTRY MERCHANTS

Simon Phillips's narrative slighted some important details about the transaction on the Watkins plantation. The land rental undoubtedly included housing, but Phillips did not explain how the former slaves obtained "furnish," or provisions (food, clothing, and medicine), and supplies, equipment, and work animals to begin farming and to carry them through the year until they could harvest and sell their crops. Eventually southerners devised a means to meet those needs, and to finance the production and marketing of their crops. Local merchants and the better-off landowners advanced "furnish" against future crops, secured by crop liens. The holder of a crop lien had a legal claim, second only to that of the landholder against his rented land, to the proceeds of the crop of the indebted farmer. In other words, tenants and croppers were legally bound to settle their debts for land rentals and then for "furnish" before they paid other debts or bought anything for themselves.

Tenants, sharecroppers, and landlords, "furnish" and crop liens, country stores and country merchants evolved into staples of the rural South and in time involved small landholders as well as tenants, whites as well as blacks. When railroads penetrated previously isolated areas and brought greater access to distant markets for sales and purchases, farmers with small landholdings increased their cash-crop farming and became a larger part of the cotton South. Country merchants proliferated, another product of the growth of the southern railway network and cash-crop farming and crop liens. The roles of the landlords and merchants intermingled. Landlords sometimes opened their own stores, and certainly many supplied their own sharecroppers directly. Many merchants acquired substantial landholdings as a result of land foreclosures when debts went unpaid too long.

Merchants became community and political leaders who challenged the power of the planters. They became pillars of the churches, stalwarts of local school boards, community boosters, investors in railroads and industry, and bosses of rural politics. Linked by railroads to such trade centers as Louisville, Nashville, Atlanta, Memphis, and New Orleans, country stores spread the values associated with modern urbanization and industrialization into the rural South.

Country merchants and their stores brought consumerism and the physical artifacts of modern life: ready-made clothes and shoes, kerosene (for everything from illumination to cleaning privies), prepared foods, Pear's and Fels Naphtha soaps, Hoyt's cologne, tobacco (including the most modern form of the noxious weed, cigarettes), *McGuffey's Readers* and other school supplies, corsets and petticoats when they became fashionable, contraceptives, ready-made caskets (for as little as $5), furniture, tableware, eyeglasses, toothbrushes, sporting goods, musical instruments, playing cards, patent medicines. The Chattanooga Medicine Company used mass marketing techniques, such as almanacs and calendars, to sell Wine of Cardui, a mixture of alcohol and herbs that supposedly relieved "female troubles," and Black Draught, a blend of plant extracts and herbs for constipation, which may have been common given the diet of the day. Country stores offered other forms of relief—liquor and, before federal laws restricted their trade, laudanum, opium, calomel, morphine, and paregoric. Some stores had lunch counters that offered sardines, sausages, crackers, oysters, salmon, and other favorites. Most stores had some fancy merchandise. Apparently all sold pistols, a requirement for the suitably attired male. At Christmas they offered oranges and coconut for coconut cake, once-a-year delicacies. Country stores provided postal services, news, and gossip, courting places for persons so inclined, sites for magistrates' courts, and focal points for local politics. The Red Shirts of South Carolina, for example, used country stores as

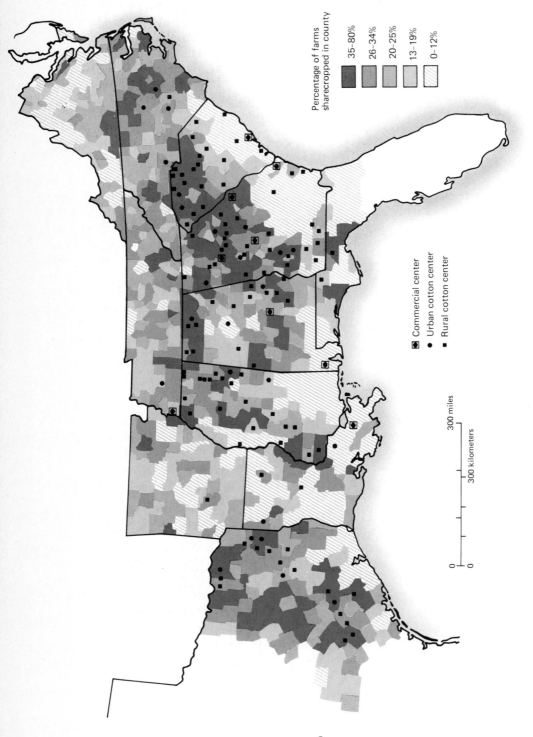

Percentage of farms
sharecropped in county

35–80%
26–34%
20–25%
13–19%
0–12%

■ Commercial center
● Urban cotton center
■ Rural cotton center

THE CROP-LIEN SYSTEM, 1880

300 miles

300 kilometers

0

0

meeting places during their campaign to overthrow the Republican government of the state in 1876.

Many merchants also had cotton gins and grinding mills for grains, services that were vital to southern farmers. They functioned as middlemen in the produce and egg trade, provided informal legal and small banking services, and tendered advice. But, above all, they controlled local credit. Sometimes known simply as "the Man," they dispensed monthly "draws" or "rations" (food, clothing, fertilizer, and so forth) and "toted up" what by the end of the year was a farmer's "run." Successful merchants and landlords supervised their debtors closely. What and when to plant? When to cultivate or harvest, repair fences, dig ditches, cut wood? How to manage animals? What and how much to buy at the store? There were lots of questions about purchases of tobacco, liquor, or other "luxuries," about whether children went to school or to the fields. These questions reminded black and white renters and croppers repeatedly what their station was, that they were not far from slavery. In sickness and death, the Man was there, arranging for the physician or undertaker. The Man was, of course, not invincible. Even Will Varner lost first place in the county to Flem Snopes, his son-in-law.

William Faulkner described Varner in *The Hamlet* as the

> owner of the Old Frenchman place...chief man of the country. He was the largest landholder and beat supervisor in one county and Justice of the Peace in the next and election commissioner in both, and hence the fountainhead if not of law at least of advice and suggestion to a countryside which would have repudiated the term constituency if they had ever heard it. He was a farmer, a usurer, a veterinarian; Judge Benbow of Jefferson once said of him that a milder-mannered man never bled a mule or stuffed a ballot box. He owned most of the good land in the country and held mortgages on most of the rest. He owned the store and the cotton gin and the combined grist mill and blacksmith shop in the village proper and it was considered, to put it mildly, bad luck for a man of the neighborhood to do his trading or gin his cotton or grind his meal or shoe his stock anywhere else.

Will Varner was the looming presence of Frenchman's Bend, Faulkner's fictional hamlet. Country merchants were not creatures of the imagination. They occupied the crossroads of the rural South, literally and figuratively. They were envied for their real and imagined wealth, feared for their power to reduce landowner to tenant, tenant to sharecropper, and suspected and despised for seemingly hard-fisted ways. Critics denounced them for what were perceived to be extortionate interest rates and prices. Merchants, commentators charged, forced farmers to give first place to cash crops and were responsible for the calamitous consequences. Thus southern farmers failed to diversify, bought food that they could have produced themselves, and grew more cotton than they could sell at a reasonable profit. "The merchants...," lamented one critic, "have replaced the former masters and have made peons of them and their former slaves."

Such strong feelings are understandable in light of the erratic fortunes of southern farmers from 1865 to World War II and the enormous human toll that resulted. Southern agriculture did have good years, and some farmers did do well, but most did not. Over the years, tenancy spread and the ranks of landowners shrank. In 1880, somewhat more than one-third of southern farmers were tenants or sharecroppers. Twenty years later one-half were, and more than half of those were white.

Merchants often stood out as the prosperous amid the deprived, as parasites living off a dead or chronically ill body, like Will Varners waiting to foreclose and take the farm and home place away. Merchants held potentially profitable though precarious positions. They supplied farmers whose few assets made them poor credit risks, whose crops had not yet been planted and might never be harvested, and if harvested might not sell for as much as the debt owed. Merchants had legal protection through the crop-lien laws, the first of which was passed in 1866 in Georgia, and more generally through the power they held in relation to borrowers in negotiating contracts. A merchant sometimes "furnished" a sharecropper, for instance, only after the landowner agreed to waive his prior claim to what the sharecropper produced. But collecting debts could be very difficult and, given the resources of many debtors, often not worth the costs involved. Moreover, croppers and renters tended to move on after a year or two, frequently leaving with debts unpaid. Merchants who pressed defaulters could alienate other customers. Still, foreclosed mortgage notices littered courthouse squares.

Merchants reduced their risks by careful supervision of borrowers and their accounts and by charging high interest rates and high prices. They used a two-price system, one price for cash purchases and a considerably higher price for credit purchases. Merchants charged as much as 50 percent interest and even more. In part, they were passing on the costs they incurred by making loans that were not repaid and the costs for their own borrowing, which could be quite high. They bought on credit from manufacturers and wholesalers and borrowed from what local banks there were. These banks borrowed in turn from banks in larger cities.

Country merchants had risks and costs that justified substantial interest rates, but probably not so high as those they charged. Clearly the business was profitable and very attractive. Though no one knows just how country merchants fared, studies suggest that they had satisfactory rates of success and that their numbers grew significantly. Country stores offered solid opportunities. "Clerking" in them became an important avenue for advancement for ambitious young men in the postbellum South. Merchants could go far, apparently without tampering with farmers' accounts. Still, the suspicion lingered that merchants and clerks cheated their customers. The inability of too many farmers to read or to do simple arithmetic complicated matters and fed their bitterness.

MONEY AND INTEREST

The interest rates charged by country merchants reflected the acute shortage of capital in the South after 1865. Neither was a new economic factor. The antebellum South had lacked adequate banking facilities and depended heavily on

STORE LEDGER (South Caroliniana Library)

the factorage system and other outside sources for capital. In 1860 the future Confederate states—exclusive of Texas and Arkansas, for which we have no reports—had 104 banks, including branch banks, with capital of $92 million. That same year, New York, Massachusetts, and Pennsylvania had 567 banks, including branch banks, with $301.5 million in capital.

The Civil War, federal legislation and policy, and general economic trends made matters worse. When the shooting stopped in 1865, southern banking was in shambles, Confederate bonds and money were worthless, and United States greenbacks were almost impossible to find. The elaborate structure for the financing and marketing of southern farm products lay in ruins. The value of southern assets that could be used to secure loans had declined so drastically that loans were hard to obtain and very costly. The value of southern farms and farm implements, for instance, dropped almost 50 percent, that of livestock 25 percent. The average value of southern farms remained about one-half of the national average as late as 1900, and the southern average did not improve much in the next twenty-five years. When emancipation took effect, it liberated what had been one of the principal forms of collateral that slaveholders had.

Federal banking laws affected southern banking adversely. In an effort to increase federal revenues during the Civil War and to make the banking system more stable and less subject to panics, Congress passed the Banking Act of 1863. Banks in towns with fewer than 3,000 people were required to have $50,000 capital to get a national charter, $100,000 in towns with 6,000 to 50,000 people, and $200,000 in larger cities—requirements that were difficult to meet in the postbellum South. Congress also put a 10 percent tax on banknotes issued by state-chartered banks in an effort to force them to join the national bank system. National banks could not make mortgage loans; therefore they could not meet an especially important need of farmers. Other parts of the banking laws and a sectional bias in the granting of national bank charters also inhibited the growth of national banks in the South. In 1900, when the United States had 1,737 national banks with $417.6 million in capital—252 of them, with capital of $75.9 million, were in New York—the eleven former Confederate states had a total of 125 banks with $26 million. Not too surprisingly, southern congressmen and senators figured prominently in the successful efforts to change federal banking laws and create the Federal Reserve System in 1913. Other, now conventional means for raising capital for investment and lending—such as insurance companies and mutual savings banks—were extremely limited in the postbellum South. In 1900 there were only six class A life insurance companies (companies that had at least $10 million in assets) in the entire South. And only after 1890 did the United States have the truly national financial institutions necessary to move capital easily from one region to another, say from the Northeast to the South or the West. The shortage of banks and the lack of development of other financial institutions increased the costs of borrowing in the South.

Moreover, the money supply (the sum total of all forms of money) grew at an unusually slow pace from 1865 to 1879, and in fact contracted severely in the 1870s. That contraction of the money supply is still noted for its severity; only one other such occurrence compares with it, the Great Depression of the 1930s. The reduction of the money supply pushed interest rates up. The depression of the 1870s compounded the difficulties. (Those who recall more recent American experiences with increases in the money supply and interest rates must bear in mind that the circumstances that prevailed in the late nineteenth century differed radically from those of more recent times.) Though not the most severe economic crisis in American history, it was the longest and was quite serious.

The government generally practiced deflationary policies in the late nineteenth century—passing the Resumption Act of 1875; fending off efforts of greenbackers and silverites, who favored a looser monetary policy; passing the

Gold Standard Act of 1898; and, of course, spending little, balancing the federal budget, and even paying off the debt the federal government incurred during the Civil War. This policy may have been virtuous, and certainly it was what most "right-thinking people" believed must be done, but it favored lenders and hurt borrowers.

Banking, money, and monetary policy were part of a larger whole, the longest deflationary trend in American history. Prices fell by one-half between 1865 and 1898. Unfortunately for cotton farmers, the price of cotton fell faster than other prices while credit costs rose, and the Republican policy of protectionism increased the costs of the manufactured goods that southern farmers purchased. Save among the Louisiana sugar growers, a small but politically powerful group, protectionism found little favor with southern farmers. They added high tariffs to their list of grievances, which by the late 1880s had become as long as their patience was short. By then southern farmers were finding common cause with western wheat farmers, who had similar experiences, and they were laying the base for a major political upheaval. But that is a story for a later chapter.

The interest rates southern farmers paid were obviously not simply the product of willful, greedy merchants or other local creditors. Merchants hardly had a free hand with respect to interest rates. "Merchants...were only functional parts of the whole ineffective scheme of production and credit." Nor did they have the power over time to force farmers to produce certain crops, such as cotton, or to buy their food from country stores instead of producing it. But they were widely criticized for supposedly doing these things.

This criticism, though motivated by genuine and understandable alarm about the state of farming and the plight of farmers in the South, rested on dubious assumptions and ignored certain factors. The interests of merchants and their farmer customers were not always in conflict; often they were in harmony. Merchants had reason to want their borrowers and customers to succeed. For one thing, farmers who prospered bought more than farmers who did not. Land acquisitions by the merchants could reach the point of diminishing returns, where the value of land had fallen so far as to make further acquisitions pointless or even costly. Falling land values could also have an adverse effect on land the merchant already owned. Finally, in small communities, merchants and farmers might be friends or relatives, even across color lines.

It is doubtful that merchants had the monopolistic control that critics and some scholars have inferred. They could not prevent others from entering the mercantile business or effectively stem the constant movement of tenants and sharecroppers from one farm to another, from one community to the next. Itinerant peddlers, drummers, fertilizer salesmen, and buyers of cotton and tobacco also traded directly with farmers. Last, the patterns of commodity prices and the response of farmers to those prices did not conform to the notion of a merchant monopoly. Commodity prices were determined by international markets, far beyond the will or the whim of a Will Varner. Southern farmers watched prices carefully and shifted their crop selections accordingly.

Farmers were not mindlessly attached to cotton. In comparison with other production choices open to farmers at any given time, cotton had an advantage and kept it well into the twentieth century. Demand for raw cotton was strong throughout most of the late nineteenth century, though it increased more slowly than it had done before 1860. Start-up costs were low: to begin cotton farming, a family needed little equipment and few work animals. Southerners knew how to grow cotton. Land was readily available through purchase, rent, or working on shares, and the climate of the South and much of its soil were suitable for cotton.

Farmers had few realistic alternatives to cotton as a cash crop in the postbellum South. Diversification may have sounded good, especially when cotton prices fell, but it was not possible for many farmers. Most of them lacked the required capital. The dearth of cities and the slowness of railroad development made for constricted markets and inadequate transportation for would-be truck farmers. Climate, soil types, pests such as the cattle tick, and the undeveloped state of agricultural science precluded the evolution of a more complex farm mix of staple crops, forage, and quality livestock in the cotton South. Farmers there may have wanted to imitate the diversified agriculture of farmers in the North and in the upper South, but even if they had had the money to invest in such pursuits, it would not have been possible to do so until at least 1920. Farmers in the South did practice mixed agriculture when and where they could, especially in the Shenandoah Valley in Virginia.

Almost all farmers grew food for their own tables. Corn was grown virtually everywhere in the South, primarily for food for the family and for livestock. Pigs, usually of poor quality, provided the staple meat. Farmers (outside of Texas) raised little beef cattle and even less poultry. Home-grown potatoes, sweet potatoes, beans, peas, and other vegetables lent some diversity to diets, as did a variety of fruits and berries. Many berries grew wild. Farms in the South produced small amounts of hay, oats, wheat, and nuts. Peanut growing was centered in Alabama, Georgia, and Virginia.

Two important antebellum cash crops—sugar and tobacco—revived after the Civil War. Sugar cane remained in the limited areas of the South where it could be grown and recovered only slowly from the extensive damage it suffered during the Civil War. Cane farming evolved into three basic patterns. Plantations employing large numbers of wage laborers and having large milling facilities produced most of the sugar. Many planters and large farmers also used black and white sharecroppers. Finally, some farmers owned or rented small farms where they grew sugar cane along with other crops.

Kentucky remained the leading tobacco state in the South, followed by Virginia and Tennessee. That situation changed after 1890, when demand for bright-leaf flue-cured tobacco soared to meet the demand of the cigarette manufacturers. Paddy-grown rice, which had long been concentrated along the coasts of South Carolina and Georgia, enjoyed only a modest restoration after 1865. It never again attained its previous prosperity and would eventually lose out to field-grown rice in Texas, Louisiana, and Arkansas. Cattle ranching flourished in Texas. The cattle kingdom, the long drive, and open ranges had a brief legendary reign after 1865. By 1880 it was giving way to barbed-wire fences, systematic beef production, and a more subdued ethos.

At the same time, in large areas of the South—Appalachia, the Ozarks, and the piney woods of Georgia, Alabama, and Mississippi—thousands farmed and lived in a world with little or no cash and few cash crops. They met their needs by scrambling to raise some corn and a few vegetables on parcels of begrudging land, letting their livestock run the woods, and supplying large portions of their diets by hunting, fishing, and picking berries. These small farmers and others like them elsewhere in the South got a good deal of public notice in the late nineteenth century because of their opposition to fencing laws. Designed to fence in livestock in order to protect crops, these laws met stiff opposition from many small farmers who believed these laws would harm them and their way of life. Disputes over these laws revealed class conflicts between the traditional small farmers and the newer, larger commercial farmers and their allies in the banks and mercantile establishments in the towns. Well into the twentieth century, large areas of the South had no effective fence laws.

For too many southern farmers, black and white, the result of hard effort was poverty compounded by isolation. Trips to town, church, revival meetings, and political and agricultural gatherings helped. So did fairs and holiday celebrations. Still, the feeling of isolation remained. Years after he went to Congress and rose to become Speaker of the House of Representatives, Sam Rayburn recalled the loneliness of life on his father's Texas farm. As a boy, Rayburn used to go down and sit by the road that passed the farm and wait to see if someone, anyone, would come by.

Women had it even worse. They bore the greatest burden of responsibilities inside and outside the house. They gave birth to and raised large families at a time when maternal and infant deaths were common. Unless a woman was married to one of the relatively few well-fixed planters or farmers, she did a lot of fieldwork. She also gardened, and she cooked, washed, sewed, ironed, and cleaned long hours without electricity, running water, or indoor plumbing. She had fewer social and recreational opportunities than her husband had. Many women, usually widows, ran farms on their own. Most, widowed or not, aged quickly.

Understandably, many southerners tried to find a living and a life away from the farm. Unfortunately, nonfarm options in the South were not plentiful and seldom attractive. Some urban areas expanded rapidly after 1865, and many people hastened to take advantage of the opportunities of Richmond, Charlotte, Atlanta, Nashville, Louisville, Memphis, and New Orleans. But southern cities were too few, too small, and too poor to act as truly effective safety valves. As late as 1910, only about one in five southerners lived in an urban area, as compared with a national rate of nearly one in two. The same, of course, was true of southern industry. Southern manufacturers employed less than 10 percent of the working people of the South in 1910. Nor did northern cities and industries provide effective avenues of escape for most southerners.

Rapidly expanding northern industries and cities received ample supplies of cheap, unskilled labor from the tide of European immigration that surged, fell back, and surged to new heights between the Civil War and World War I. Lack of skills also circumscribed the choices open to most southern blacks and whites, and the former faced racial discrimination in various forms everywhere in America. Finally, southerners, black and white, demonstrated a strong attachment to the land and to the South. The modest but significant gains blacks made in landholding from 1865 to 1900 may have encouraged them to remain in Dixie.

Puppet Monarch

The burden of southern welfare thus fell on cotton. It could not bear the burden. Cotton culture spread anyway, throughout the lower South and into the lower reaches of the upper South, following the expanding railroad network and its companion system of dirt roads into the Mississippi delta after the restoration and expansion of the levee system in the late 1880s, and increasingly beyond the Mississippi. "Cotton was king, but he was a puppet monarch."

The boom the cotton South experienced in the 1850s did not recur. The demand for cotton rose faster in the antebellum era and particularly in the 1850s than it ever would do again. Also during the 1850s some of the richest cotton-growing soil in the South had come into production. This cotton bonanza was

PERSONAL INCOME PER CAPITA AS A PERCENTAGE OF THE U.S. AVERAGE, 1840–1950, BY REGION

Region	1840	1860	1880	1900	1920	1930	1940	1950
United States	100%	100%	100%	100%	100%	100%	100%	100%
Northeast	135	139	141	137	132	138	124	115
New England	132	143	141	134	124	129	121	109
Middle Atlantic	136	137	141	139	134	140	124	116
North-central	68	68	98	103	100	101	103	106
East	67	69	102	106	108	111	112	112
West	75	66	90	97	87	82	84	94
South	76	72	51	51	62	55	65	73
South Atlantic	70	65	45	45	59	56	69	74
East south-central	73	68	51	49	52	48	55	62
West south-central	144	115	60	61	72	61	70	80
West	—	—	190	163	122	115	125	114
Mountain	—	—	168	139	100	83	92	96
Pacific	—	—	204	163	135	130	138	121

SOURCE: Richard A. Easterlin, "Regional Income Trends, 1840–1950," in Seymour E. Harris, ed., *American Economic History* (New York: McGraw-Hill, 1961), p. 28. Reprinted by permission of McGraw-Hill, Inc.

MORGAN SQUARE, SPARTANBURG, SOUTH CAROLINA, 1884 (Courtesy of the Spartanburg Chamber of Commerce)

not repeated. As figures for per capita income indicate, King Cotton was not able to bring prosperity to his subjects.

For twenty years after the South recovered from the Civil War, when personal incomes declined sharply, the economy kept pace with the rest of the nation, which was enjoying strong growth. After 1910, incomes rose significantly in Texas, Louisiana, and Oklahoma, probably because of oil, and in the Southeast, probably because of industrial growth. Then military spending during World War I gave a strong stimulus to the Southeast. Unlike most Americans, however, southerners saw their incomes drop during the 1920s, before the Great Depression engulfed the country. The failures of King Cotton were widely acknowledged even before 1938, when President Franklin Roosevelt declared that the South was "the nation's No. 1 economic problem."

The cotton South had structural flaws that made it peculiarily vulnerable and that helped to explain much of what lay behind those figures on per capita income. Year after year, farmers in the cotton South acted on virtually the only option they had. They gambled each year that this year they would "pay out"— have enough money from the sale of their crop to pay their debts—and perhaps have some money left over. They went to their creditors again and again. They planted cotton in soil that was too thin for repeated cotton plantings, too sub-

COTTON PRODUCTION IN THE SOUTH, 1850–1987 (THOUSANDS OF BALES)

State	1850[a]	1860[a]	1870[b]	1880[b]	1890[b]	1900[c]	1910
Ala.	564	990	429	670	915	1,094	1,130
Ark.	65	367	248	608	617	706	777
Fla.	45	65	39	55	58	54	65
Ga.	499	702	474	814	1,192	1,233	1,992
Ky.	1		1	1	1	1	3
La.	179	778	351	509	659	700	269
Miss.	484	1,203	565	963	1,155	1,287	1,127
Mo.		41	1	20	16	26	54
N.C.	74	146	145	390	336	433	665
Okla.							923
S.C.	301	353	225	523	747	844	1,280
Tenn.	195	296	182	331	191	235	265
Tex.	58	431	351	805	1,471	2,584	2,455
Va. & W.Va.	4	13		20	5	10	10
Totals for South	2,469	5,385	3,011	5,709	7,363	9,207	11,015

[a]av. 400 lbs.
[b]av. 450 lbs.
[c]av. 500 lbs.
[d]av. 480 lbs.

SOURCE: James C. Bonner, "Cotton," *The Encyclopedia of Southern History*, David C. Roller and Robert W. Twyman, eds. (Baton Rouge, La., 1979), p. 301; U.S. Bureau of the Census, *Agricultural Statistics, 1981* (Washington, D.C., 1982), p. 63; U.S. Bureau of the Census, *1987 Census of Agriculture* (Washington, D.C., 1987), Vol. I, Table 25.

ject to erosion and requiring large amounts of fertilizer, specifically the guano and phosphates that became commercially available after 1865. The toll of erosion mounted to crisis levels and undermined the land, the single most important farm asset. Fertilizers helped raise yield per acre, but productivity in cotton grew less than productivity in any other major American farm commodity. Mechanization came more slowly to cotton farming than to wheat and corn farming. Without greater increases in productivity, too many cotton farmers played a losing game against cotton prices. Too many cotton farmers experienced the "annual defeat of the crop market..., the weekly defeat of the town market and mounting debt, and the small gnawing daily defeats of crumbling barn and fence, encroaching sagebrush and erosion, and one's children growing up in illiteracy."

The cotton South was a land of landlords, tenants, sharecroppers, and country merchants for nearly fourscore years. They seemed fixed, permanent. They stood as specters that could be little softened by nostalgia or ties of kin and friendship and remembered kindnesses. Then, sometime around 1940, no one can say just when, these fixtures of the South began almost magically to vanish. An age had ended and now seems so distant as to be foreign.

COTTON PRODUCTION IN THE SOUTH, 1850–1987 (THOUSANDS OF BALES) (*Cont.*)

1920	1930	1940	1950	1959	1969	1980[d]	1987
718	1,313	773	824	683	498	275	382
869	1,398	1,351	1,584	1,484	1,150	444	817
20	34	11	18	14	10	7.5	33
1,682	1,344	905	610	521	311	86	286
3	9	16	13	11	5		
307	799	718	607	479	516	460	922
958	1,875	1,533	1,497	1,561	1,383	1,143	1,655
64	225	433	472	482	332	177	306
858	764	458	472	319	115	52	94
1,336	854	802	242	458	193	205	306
1,477	836	850	544	411	236	77	102
307	504	436	617	620	428	200	567
2,972	3,793	2,724	5,550	4,156	3,041	3,320	4,072
25	52	13	19	12	3	.2	15
11,596	13,800	11,023	13,069	11,211	8,221	6,447	9,557

SOUTHERN RAILWAYS

Even as the postbellum agricultural system was evolving, southerners were rebuilding and expanding their railways. The Confederacy and the border states of Kentucky and Maryland had more than 9,000 miles of track in 1860. That figure compared well with those of the Northeast (10,000) and the Middle West (11,000), but comparisons with respect to quality of roadbed and facilities (such as stations) and quantity of rolling stock (engines and cars) were not so favorable. The South's dispersed population and limited industrialization made railways less profitable there than in more populous, more industrialized areas.

The Civil War sharpened these contrasts. Four years of combat destroyed or crippled more than half of the South's railroads at a cost of at least $28 million. A South Carolinian observed that "one week we had passably good roads, ...the next week they were all gone." "Sherman hairpins"—rails that Union troops had ripped up, fired, and bent double—indicated what the massive conflict had done to most of the southern rail system. The only major railway in the South to escape serious damage was the Louisville and Nashville. It had thrived. The L&N moved quickly after 1865 to build one of the largest rail empires in the nation, anchoring itself in the booming commerce of its urban namesakes and the coal and iron of northern Alabama.

Coincidentally, the badly damaged railways of the South recovered with remarkable speed to approximate the status quo ante bellum by 1870. Southern railroads obviously had considerable resilience, vigorous leadership, and more. For its military purposes, the Union Army had rebuilt some of the southern railways—one of the few benefits the South received from the war. The L&N was a major beneficiary, having been captured early in the war, then operated and maintained by Union forces. The L&N also enjoyed the continuing leadership of one its developers, James Guthrie. Southern rail companies still owned their rights of way and their roadbeds. Many of the roadbeds, of course, needed repairs. Some railways had the foresight to bank in London during the war or to have stockpiled cotton, which they sold for substantial profits. Even Sherman hairpins were not complete losses: they could be straightened and reused or, if beyond reclamation, sold for scrap.

Most important, southern railroads enjoyed a very strong demand for their services. Government officials and business leaders alike saw the close connection between the railroads and the South's recovery and growth, and they supported efforts to restore and expand the southern rail system. Private creditors and investors postponed settlement of debts. The United States Military Railway Department quickly restored to their former owners the railroads it had seized, and subsequently declined to collect more than half the money owed it for the postwar sales of government-owned rolling stock to southern railways.

Southern state governments, like their antebellum predecessors, lent their support to the restoration of the railways as early as 1866 and before any Radical Reconstruction government was in power. Before the war, southern states had joined the nationwide trend of subsidizing railroads. They had employed a variety of the usual means for doing so: land grants, state guarantees for bonds issued to raise money for railroads, purchases of railroad stock, and even state ownership of railways. Virginia, for instance, had substantial holdings in stock, including three-fourths of the important Richmond and Danville. North Carolina had a similar amount of North Carolina Railroad stock. Prewar Tennessee made direct loans of state bonds to railroads and incurred a debt of $14 million to do so. Georgia owned the Western and Atlantic, which connected Atlanta and Chattanooga. Many smaller communities, too, had subsidized railroads. Continuing the subsidies made sense, given the need to rehabilitate and expand the southern rail system in 1865. Major trade routes that lacked railroads included the intercoastal regions of the South, northern connections for the piedmont through Appalachia, and north-south routes in Mississippi. The more postwar state and local governments subsidized railroads to meet these needs, the more they increased the amount of track they got—and increased the opportunities for political and financial fraud. As we mentioned earlier, paper railroads and theft from the public treasury became synonymous with Reconstruction. The machinations of General Milton S. Littlefield of New York and of George W. Swepson, Tarheel native, nearly doubled the state debt of North Carolina, to over $28 million—an outrageous cost to incur in order to obtain the 136 miles of track laid from 1868 through 1870. South Carolina had a comparable experience. Its debt rose to $25 million, much of it the result of fraudulent railroad schemes involving three Republican governors, at least two black political leaders, and perhaps James L. Orr, provisional governor under President Andrew Johnson and reluctant secessionist Democrat. Under Republican Governor Rufus B. Bullock, new railroad schemes proliferated in Georgia. Political cronies became managers of companies whose workings mystified them. A special relationship with the governor and a satchel of money with which to ply the legislature proved useful in efforts to secure state aid for proposed railroads.

Railroad swindles added significantly to Alabama's horrendous $30 million state debt—swindles perpetrated by Democrats and Republicans alike. Railroads, as we noted earlier, were decisive political forces in Alabama during Reconstruction and remained so afterward. There Reconstruction was closely related to and shaped by the struggle between the Louisville and Nashville and the Alabama and Chattanooga for access to the coal and iron regions of Alabama. The Reconstruction government in Mississippi made state aid for such internal improvements as railways unconstitutional. Thus Mississippi escaped the railroad swindles that were all too common elsewhere; it also had few miles of track laid from 1865 to 1880.

Usually the states that aided railroads the most got the most track laid and were the most swindled. Alabama, Georgia, Arkansas, and Texas led the South in state aid and in new railroad construction from 1865 to 1875. Texas used its vast public land holdings for large grants to the Texas and Pacific and the Southern Pacific, which laid major lines across Texas and finally achieved the antebellum dream of a southern rail connection to the Pacific. The president of the important Little Rock and Fort Smith Railroad recognized that "without...state aid the road could not have been accomplished by our company."

By 1880, railroad mileage in the South (including, in this instance, Maryland, Kentucky, West Virginia, and the District of Columbia, because their figures were included in census reports) reached 19,430 miles, more than double the 1860 total. Nationally, railroad mileage almost tripled between 1860 and 1880, to 87,800. (These figures include the South. They are somewhat misleading because figures for the nonsouthern states include the recently built transcontinental lines.) These disparities reflected the South's need to spend much of its money and energy on postwar rehabilitation of its railroads and the general disruption of the region that southern railroads had to serve. Construction and maintenance costs were lower in the South than elsewhere, but not enough lower to offset these disadvantages. The doubling of the rail system in the South increased access from farm to market, provided urgently needed transportation for industry, and laid or reinforced the foundations for cities, towns, and villages. Railroads also speeded the nationalization of the southern market. Southern consumers could find Standard Oil kerosene, Iowa corn, and New England woolens on the shelves of even small merchants by 1880.

*T*HE GREAT STRIKE OF 1877

Labor troubles also rode the rails. In July 1877 the bloodiest strike in American history began after the Baltimore and Ohio Railroad announced wage cuts for its already underpaid and overworked trainmen. The strike swept across the country, the first nationwide strike in American history. At least forty persons were killed and perhaps $10 million in property was destroyed. The strike largely by-passed the South. Little Rock and New Orleans had minor disturbances. Workers withdrew a strike threat against the Georgia Central after the railroad made some concessions. Black male workers in Galveston, Texas, marched, organized, and successfully allied themselves with white male workers to get a minimum wage of $2 a day. Black laundrywomen in Galveston then demanded and got $1.50 a day. Louisville fared worst. During a one-day riot a black and white mob stoned street lights, stores, houses, the Louisville and Nashville's depot, and the home of its president. Working people in Louisville subsequently elected Workingmen's party candidates to five of the seven seats on the city council. The Little Rock *Arkansas Gazette* congratulated the South "that nearly all of the mob violence...occurred north of the Ohio River." The *Raleigh Observer* chimed in: "Southern people are not as...Northern people, ...person and property, life and liberty are alike safe where Southern men hold sway." This was a curious observation in light of the only recently ended Reconstruction, and it was not the first time or the last that the South would claim too much for its supposedly harmonious employer-employee relations.

More important were the actions of the federal government. President Rutherford B. Hayes took the unprecedented step of sending federal troops to quell domestic disturbances during peacetime. The federal courts acted with dispatch against strikers and real or alleged rioters. The lesson was clear: the federal government would more readily defend the interests of capital than those of labor, *or* those of blacks and Republicans in the South.

BANKRUPTCY, CONSOLIDATION, AND REGULATION

The depression of the 1870s brought more than labor problems to southern railroads. It interrupted expansion and caused about one-half of the southern railroads either to default on their debt payments or to go bankrupt. The failure rate of southern companies was twice the national rate. Obviously, railways in the South were more financially vulnerable than those in other regions.

The defaults and bankruptcies opened many southern railways to takeovers and consolidations. The new owners and managers were more likely to be from outside the South, and, much more significant, they differed in type and orientation from their predecessors. They speculated in railroads more than they ran them, because they made more money by constructing railways, manipulating stocks, and investing in land, timber, and mineral schemes than by actually operating railroads. Railways in the postwar South, as elsewhere in the United States, began to be dominated by large companies that had large assets and potentially great economic and political power. Because railroads needed so much capital to operate, control of them generally shifted to such financial centers as New York. The president of the Louisville and Nashville, for instance, was called a "railway emperor," but by 1880 the company's finances were increasingly controlled from New York.

Faced with hard times and railroad wars, southern railway leaders developed the first successful railroad pool (a form of business merger) in the country. Under the leadership of Albert Fink, an L&N executive, the Southern Railway and Steamboat Association was formed in 1875 to represent the interests of railroads east of the Mississippi River and south of the Ohio and Potomac. It lasted until 1887, when the federal Interstate Commerce Act made railroad pools illegal. The association's twenty-seven member corporations divided markets, settled disputes among members, and tried to make rates stable and uniform. The organization may have been a factor in the steady decline of freight rates in the South.

But the association reinforced the fears of monopoly that railroads aroused. As economic conditions worsened in the 1870s, these fears became important politically. Several southern states created railroad commissions, most of which had only advisory powers. Presumably encouraged by the Supreme Court's decision in *Munn* v. *Illinois* (1877) and prompted by continuing protests, the legislature of Georgia gave its commission power to set rates, and the Georgia commission became a model for others. The presence of the Grange—a farm movement that began in the Middle West and engaged in education and lobbying—and the rumblings of such independent political movements as the Greenbackers may have unsettled the Redeemer governments of the South. Most southern states in 1880 also placed severe constitutional limits on the ways states could subsidize private enterprise. Overindulgence in state-aided railway projects and mounting state debts made sobriety attractive, indeed necessary.

CITIES, TOWNS, AND INDUSTRY

Railroads and their leaders had played and would continue to play a critical and ever larger role in the South. Atlanta, the creature of railroads, formed the political and economic nucleus of postbellum Georgia and eventually became the leading metropolis of the Southeast. As early as November 1865, an observer reported, out of

> ruin and devastation a new city is springing up with marvelous rapidity. The narrow and irregular and numerous streets are alive from morning till night...with a never-ending throng of pushing and crowding and scrambling and eager and excited and enterprising men, all bent on building and trading and swift fortune-making....The four railroads centering here groan with the freight and passenger traffic ...Where all this eagerness and excitement will end no one seems to care to inquire. The one sole idea in every man's mind is to make money.

Atlanta was just one of the interior cities of the South to prosper at the hand of the railroads after 1865. So did Richmond, Nashville, Louisville, and Memphis, and such smaller ones as Augusta, Macon, Little Rock, Chattanooga, Montgomery, Greensboro, Charlotte, and Columbia. Far to the west, Dallas, Houston, Fort Worth, and Shreveport were becoming more than small towns. New Orleans was still the largest city in the South, but it grew little. Charleston, Savannah, Mobile, and Alexandria, all seaport cities, declined relatively. This pattern of growth reflected old and continuing migratory habits, a general movement to urban areas and westward.

But the depression, then disease, slowed urbanization in the 1870s. Hard times slowed urban growth to a crawl and created fiscal crises in many cities and towns. To make matters worse, yellow fever struck Montgomery and New Orleans in 1873. New Orleans lost nearly 4,000 of its 191,000 residents. Cholera afflicted Nashville the same year. Then, five years later, a yellow fever epidemic killed 5,800 of perhaps 45,000 people in Memphis; about half the victims were Irish. The scourge drove Memphis Germans to St. Louis, where they stayed. The killing fever left Memphis temporarily demoralized and permanently changed its ethnic makeup.

Southern cities remained primarily centers for railways, for financial, governmental, and legal services, for merchandising, and for the marketing of farm products. Industrial Birmingham and nearby Bessemer and Sheffield grew little in the 1870s. Anniston was only starting up. The Alabama iron industry had not yet lived up to the expectations of its boosters. The cotton textiles industry, which had entered the first stage of its postbellum growth, built its own villages in rural areas and on the edges of small cities and towns, such as Danville in Virginia, Greensboro, Winston-Salem, and Charlotte in North Carolina, Spartanburg and Greenville in South Carolina, and Columbus and Macon in Georgia. Urbanization in the South increased less than a tenth of a percent in the 1870s, well below the approximately 2 percent increase of the 1860s. In 1880, the percentage of urbanized southerners (8.7) was far short of the national rate of 28.2 percent.

Industry in general developed slowly in the decade and a half after Appomattox. Although the former Confederate states and Kentucky had nearly 30 percent of the nation's people, they produced only about 6 percent of the nation's industrial output in 1879. That output did not, however, include domestic manufactures. Southerners still did a lot of processing of cotton, corn (into meal and, illicitly, liquor), meats, and leathers at home. Virginians still made linen from locally grown flax. Southern manufacturing usually involved first-stage processing of raw materials and agricultural products—ginning, turpentining, lumbering, making of pig iron, spinning and weaving of cotton, pressing of cottonseed oil, making of cigars and plug tobacco, distilling, sugar refining, and flour milling. These industries added little value to their raw materials, required many unskilled workers and few highly skilled ones, paid low wages, and did not generate extensive or related industries in the South.

Cotton textiles are a case in point. Textiles were the only southern industry to grow significantly in the 1870s, and that growth was modest. Investment by southern cotton manufacturers was about 10 percent of that by companies in New England and about half that by those in the middle Atlantic states. Still, southern boosters were cheered by reports of the opening of the Eagle and Phoenix factory at Columbus, Georgia, in 1868, only three years after Union troops burned the Eagle Manufacturing Company to the ground. Columbus, looking northward to Massachusetts' most famous mill towns, claimed to be the "Lowell of the South"; Augusta and other towns disputed Columbus's claim to the title. Local capital, much of it earned during the Civil War and Reconstruction, built these southern Lowells. But they failed to generate related industries, such as machine tool manufacturing. For years southern textile companies bought their machinery from New England manufacturers. Southern textile companies usually produced coarse "gray" goods, which were shipped elsewhere for dyeing and other final processing steps. Only after 1900 did southern textiles begin to compete effectively in the market for fine cottons. In the textile industry's early stages, north and south, women and children made up over half of the modestly skilled, low-wage work force. Southern companies excluded blacks from all but the most menial jobs. Since most of the textile companies were located on the edges of cities and towns or in rural areas, southern textile workers lived in a racially segregated and hierarchically ordered world that was unusual even for its day.

This isolation did not, however, assure companies of the control over workers that nineteenth-century manufacturers thought was essential. Across the Savannah River from Augusta and twelve miles away, in the Horse Creek Valley in South Carolina, workers struck in late 1875 after the Graniteville Manufacturing Company announced a wage cut. The strike was the first of its kind, and it occurred even as South Carolina whites were uniting in a mass movement to expel the Republicans from state office in 1876. The strike lasted a month and before it was over the superintendent of the company had been shot and the factory sabotaged. The company did not rescind the wage cut, but neither did it discipline the strike leaders. The strike clearly indicated that southern white elites were not immune to challenge by other whites, and that divisions among whites were serious and could not be erased by simplistic appeals to white solidarity against blacks and other presumed threats. If the economy faltered, divisions among whites could become sharp and even threatening to those who had assumed leadership in the South after Reconstruction.

When the long depression of the 1870s ended in 1879, southerners celebrated its passing. The editor of the New Orleans *Times-Democrat* rejoiced: "The stagnation of despair has given...place to...hope,...courage,...resolve." Then, in his understandable excitement, he claimed too much: "We are a new people. Our land has had a new birth."

Southern railroads had recovered from the Civil War, had expanded, and were ready to expand even faster. The South's cities and industries remained small but portended better times. But the reign of King Cotton was as powerful in 1880 as it had been in 1865, and it was spreading. So were sharecropping, tenancy, crop liens, and country merchants. The evolution of a South in which cotton was no longer monarch would be slow and painful. Change and changelessness seemed to coexist in the South of the 1870s.

18

The Redeemers and the New South, 1865–1890

❖

The funeral train left Miami, moved up the east coast of Florida, angled northwest through the pines and sand of southeastern Georgia, and finally climbed through rolling hills into Atlanta. Mourners and the curious gathered all along the way. At one place where the train stopped, an old man took his jacket off, laid it on the coffin, and then took it back. "Now thousands couldn't buy...the jacket from me." President Theodore Roosevelt telegraphed his respects. Legislatures, city councils, and dozens of organizations memorialized the deceased. Flags hung at half-staff. Businesses closed. Governors, senators, congressmen, and former soldiers of all ranks, the United Confederate Veterans, the Sons of the Confederate Veterans, and the United Daughters of the Confederacy were in attendance. Railroads charged reduced rates to people who wanted to go the final services and burial.

On January 15, 1904, they laid to rest the mortal remains of Lieutenant General John Brown Gordon, the "very embodiment of the Lost Cause." Gordon had been with General Robert E. Lee at the surrender at Appomattox and was one of the last surviving Confederate generals and the first commander of the United Confederate Veterans. The *Atlanta Constitution* eulogized the general: "Gordon, who found his Calvary at Appomattox, his Gethsemane in the days of reconstruction, has gone beyond to reap the harvest he has so richly earned—on to his immortal Lee, his beloved Jackson and so many of his old command."

In its magnitude and its display of emotion and sentiment, the commemoration of Gordon's death compares with the outpourings of grief at the deaths of Abraham Lincoln, Franklin D. Roosevelt, John F. Kennedy, and Martin Luther King, Jr. The vast display of feeling in 1904 suggested that the South remained fixated on the War for Southern Independence, the Lost Cause. Had the South changed so little since 1865? People who observed Gordon's funeral from a distance must have wondered.

446

The more reflective, more informed smiled. They knew better. They probably savored the irony of having Gordon's last rites in Atlanta, the very embodiment of the New South. Nor, as many were aware, had Gordon himself spent the years since Appomattox merely telling war stories. He had been very busy and sometimes successful in politics and business. Gordon, in fact, had taken an active part as a Redeemer in shaping the New South. The Redeemers were the southern Democrats who presided over the end of Reconstruction, the restoration of native white supremacy and black subordination, the evolution of the one-party South, and the emergence of the New South. The Redeemers did not, however, necessarily encourage or even endorse the New South. Indeed, they were divided among themselves about it, though they did little to oppose it.

Opponents of the Redeemers often called them Bourbon Democrats. The label was borrowed from Napoleonic France. The French Bourbons supposedly represented those who wanted to restore prerevolutionary France, reactionaries who their opponents said could forget nothing old and learn nothing new.

JOHN BROWN GORDON (Hargrett Rare Book and Manuscript Library, University of Georgia Libraries)

Given the Redeemers' habit of referring to one another in public by military titles—general, brigadier, colonel—their frequent appearances in their old gray
uniforms, and their endless talk of "the War," the label seemed appropriate.

Opponents of the Redeemers used the Bourbon label effectively, especially
in the 1880s and the 1890s, but the name distorted reality. The Redeemers were
not an easily definable group with a fixed set of positions on public issues. Historians still debate about the origins of the Redeemers. Were they antebellum
planters who lived into the postbellum South with most of their property and
their agrarian ideas intact and a determination to retain as much of the Old
South as possible? Or were they urban businessmen and landed farmers who
wanted a modernized South, one that differed greatly from the antebellum
South? Or were they something between these two extremes, people who
wanted a more industrialized, urbanized South but one that retained the hierarchical social and economic structures of the Old South?

Rhetoric contributed to the confusion. Postbellum boosters who urged the
South to make a strong commitment to industrialization, urbanization, and diversified agriculture drew sharp contrasts between the South they envisioned—
the New South, as they called it—and the South before the Civil War, the Old
South. The South before 1865 and the one that came after clearly differed in at
least two ways. First, any attempt to create a separate nation or federation of
southern states was dead as a viable political option. The South after 1865 had
to resolve its problems within the framework of the Union. Reconciliation of
North and South thus became a primary concern. Second, slavery was also
dead. As bad as conditions were for blacks after the war and for many years
thereafter, blacks were not chattel anymore. That was an enormous difference,
for blacks especially but also for whites.

New South boosters in their enthusiasm wrongly pictured the Old South as
too little concerned with economic growth and personal profit, disinclined to
work hard, and indifferent and even hostile to industrialization and urbanization. Large-scale planters, the dominant personages of the Old South, supposedly had a leisurely lifestyle, a satisfied indifference to their personal incomes,
and a distaste for cities and factories. Such portrayals of the Old South and the
planters made for effective public imagery but they were woefully inaccurate.
Most of the antebellum planters worked hard, energetically pursued profits and
assets, and made investment decisions in accordance with anticipated returns
and risks. Though they invested most of their money in slaves and land, which
were good investments at the time, they also invested in other things, including
manufacturing plants. Jefferson Davis, for one, hardly fitted into the picture of
the Old South drawn by New South boosters. Nor did such influential cities as
New Orleans, Memphis, Nashville, Louisville, Savannah, Charleston, and
Richmond, to name only the most obvious urban centers of the antebellum
South. Nor did the railroads and the hardly insignificant, though small, iron,
textile, forest products, and tobacco industries of the South before 1865, industries that were generally hailed by southern leaders.

The Redeemers in South Carolina, for instance, defied easy labeling or description. Like their leader, Wade Hampton, most came from planter back-

grounds. They preferred to retain as much of the past as possible, yet they welcomed industry to their desperately poor state. They were eager to expand the textile industry, which had enjoyed modest but significant growth in their state before the Civil War. In this instance, the Redeemers imitated the antebellum South Carolina leaders who had supported the development of railroads and of cotton manufacturing in their state and who had felt comfortable in Charleston. Unlike some Redeemers in other states, South Carolina Redeemers did not become agents for outside investors at the expense of their state and its citizens. Once in office, they avoided some of the more reprehensible policies that Redeemer Democrats in other states followed. The South Carolina Redeemers did not, for instance, desert the public schools. Moreover, they supported black schools and white schools about equally. They also avoided the worst abuses of the convict lease system, which became a scandal in Georgia and Tennessee.

Though the Redeemers everywhere in the South, including South Carolina, revered the Old South that existed as much in their minds as in reality, they did not seek to restore it: they did not oppose change, want to keep sectional hostilities alive, or believe that they could revive slavery. Many Redeemers in fact championed the New South; others spurned it or approached it warily. Very probably all defended the Lost Cause, but it was subject to various interpretations. Some saw a conflict between the Lost Cause and the New South, but not General Gordon. Indeed, he embraced the New South creed.

The commemoration of Gordon's death could also mislead observers in another way. It suggested that southern whites had a cohesive bond forged in combat, a bond that superseded all divisions among whites. In reality, southern whites were divided during the Civil War and during Reconstruction. They continued to disagree after they returned to power. Gordon's political career, in fact, ended amid the massive political turmoil that swept the South as well as the rest of the nation in the 1890s. In the South, that turmoil reflected deep divisions over the direction economic and political change had taken. Disappointment festered to become deep bitterness. The New South promised more than it produced, and the New South creed seemed hollow indeed in the midst of the depression of 1890s, America's worst economic crisis before 1929.

THE NEW SOUTH CREED

The assumptions and ideas that underlay the New South—the modernizing of the postbellum South—evolved by the 1880s, if not earlier, into what has been called the New South creed. The creed became so much a part of the South after 1865 that it seemed inborn. The creed was a simple set of beliefs with a powerful shaping force. It can be stated appropriately in the form of a catechism.

QUESTION: Why did the North defeat the South?
ANSWER: The South could not compete with the North because the South relied too much on cotton and slave-based agriculture. The South failed to de-

velop industries and cities and towns. Southern leaders were too interested in politics and too uninterested in work and making money.

QUESTION: What should the South do?

ANSWER: The South must change its attitudes toward work and what is worthwhile. Work is good and is necessary for success. Financial success is more important than success in politics.

QUESTION: Then what must the South do?

ANSWER: The South must build factories and cities. Its farmers must grow a wider range of crops and use the best methods and tools for farming.

QUESTION: What kind of relationship should the South have with the rest of the nation?

ANSWER: Harmonious. Disharmony wastes energy and, more important, discourages people who might invest in the New South.

QUESTION: What about relations between blacks and whites?

ANSWER: Those must also be harmonious.

QUESTION: Does that mean racial equality?

ANSWER: No! Southern whites must dominate the South. Whites are naturally superior and more civilized, and they know what is best for the blacks. Blacks may have certain civil and political rights, but they cannot have power in proportion to their numbers. Social equality is unacceptable. Miscegenation and interracial marriage are abhorrent.

The New South creed had its apostles. Many of them had newspapers for pulpits. In fact, several of the most prominent were distinguished journalists who improved southern newspapers significantly even as they preached salvation through economic uplift. Francis Warrington Dawson, who immigrated from England in 1861 to join the Confederate Army, founded the Charleston *News and Courier*. Henry Watterson made the Louisville *Courier-Journal* his personal vehicle and it became second only to the Atlanta *Constitution* as a voice for the New South. Richard H. Edmunds's *Manufacturer's Record* was a business journal that reported economic and financial news and beat the drum for the New South. Daniel Augustus Tompkins published the Charlotte *Observer* and the Greenville (S.C.) *News*. A trained engineer and an ambitious entrepreneur, Tompkins also owned several cotton textile mills in the South. Walter Hines Page spread the New South gospel in the pages of the *Atlantic Monthly*, then in his own magazine, *World's Work*.

Among New South evangels the first rank belonged to Henry Grady, editor of the Atlanta *Constitution*. A Georgian whose father was a successful businessman in antebellum Athens, Grady got an undergraduate degree from the University of Georgia and then did graduate work at the University of Virginia. He began his career in journalism in the 1870s. He started work for the *Constitution* in 1880, and when he was just thirty years of age he became part owner and editor of the paper. Grady used the *Constitution* to pronounce and propagate the New South creed, which Atlanta seemed to embody.

Recognition of Grady's stature and abilities brought him an invitation to

HENRY GRADY (Hargrett Rare Book and Manuscript Library, University of Georgia Libraries)

speak at the annual banquet of the New England Club of New York in 1886. Grady needed his skill and his considerable boldness. The New England Club had never before issued such an invitation to a southerner. Before Grady spoke, other speakers rhapsodized about New England and the Puritan heritage and told again the Union version of the Civil War. General William Tecumseh Sherman, an old favorite in Atlanta and several other places in the South, spoke just before Grady did. The general told a war story. He expressed regret that wars necessitated bloodshed and destruction, blamed the war on the "bad ambitions" of antebellum politicians, and asked that bygones be bygones. Then Sherman returned to his seat at the head table to listen to the young Georgian.

Grady opened by declaring a truce and disarming his listeners. "There was a South of slavery and secession—that South, thank God, is dead. There is a South of union and freedom—that South, thank God, is living, breathing, growing every hour." He lauded Abraham Lincoln as the symbol of national unity, "the first typical American" who had "within himself all the strength and gentleness of this republic...the sum of Puritan and Cavalier." Even Sherman got some praise, lightened with humor. "[He] is considered an able man in our parts, though some think he is...careless...about fire."

Having pacified the gathering, Grady went on to other essentials. Southerners had not given in to "sullenness and despair" after their defeat. They had gone to work and rebuilt the South. Atlantans, for instance, had taken the "ashes" Sherman "left...in 1864...and raised a brave and beautiful city....We have fallen in love with work" and "have challenged your spinners in Massachusetts and your iron-makers in Pennsylvania." The South, he claimed, now knew that slavery was wrong. It accepted and even welcomed emancipation. The South had committed itself to public education for black and white alike. "The relations of the Southern people are close and cordial." He anticipated that blacks would continue to improve their lot, but they must do so under the tutelage of "those among whom [their] lot is cast." He did not specify when or whether that tutelage would end. Grady departed momentarily from his roseate tones and put a hard edge on his words when he warned against intervention in southern race relations from outside the region.

The South, Grady concluded, had kept its "faith with" the North by accepting defeat and pledging allegiance to the Union. The war had freed blacks and the whole South.

> The old South rested everything on slavery and agriculture, unconscious that these could neither give nor maintain healthy growth. The new South presents a perfect democracy, the oligarchs leading in the popular movement...a hundred farms for every plantation, fifty homes for every palace—and a diversified industry that meets the complex needs of this complex age. The new South...is stirred with the breath of a new life...she understands that her emancipation came because through the inscrutable wisdom of God her honest purpose was crossed, and her brave armies beaten.

But the "South had nothing for which to apologize." In keeping with the doctrines of the Lost Cause, he declared that the South "believes that the late struggle between the States was war and not rebellion; revolution and not conspiracy, and that her convictions were as honest as yours." Grady recalled his father, who was killed during the Civil War.

> But...the cause in which he suffered and for which he gave his life was adjudged by higher and fuller wisdom than his or mine, and I am glad that the omniscient God held the balance of battle in His Almighty hand and that human slavery was swept forever from American soil—the American Union was saved from the wreck of war....
>
> Now what answer has New England to this message?...Will she make Lincoln's vision of a restored and happy people...a cheat and delusion?

The audience jumped to its feet and cheered. A band played "Dixie." The speech made Grady famous; it was printed over and over again. Grady's favorable reception resulted from more than momentary things—toasts, fine foods, displays of fellowship, and his artful presentation. Grady succeeded in large part because his speech, like the New South creed he was expounding, fitted the national mood and trends and seemed to suit the needs of the South. Americans wanted reconciliation. They wanted to put the Civil War and Reconstruction behind them. Grady spoke to these desires. He also carefully avoided divisive sectional issues, except for race relations. Even there he was on rather safe ground. Few whites in America in 1886 questioned white supremacy. Most believed race relations in the South were strictly a southern affair, beyond either the duty or the capacity of the federal government to alter or influence.

Grady virtually celebrated the victory of the Union, and he glowed with pleasure at the South's embrace of the supposedly northern virtues of hard work and money-getting. Yet southern sensibilities were not neglected as he recited basic tenets of the Lost Cause. Thus Grady defended the Confederate version of the causes of the Civil War and declared that Confederate efforts and sacrifices had been noble. He reassured the South about its past, and his bubbling optimism gave assurance about the present and the future of the region.

Most important, the New South creed and Grady's remarks fitted the predominant American mentality of the day. People nearly everywhere in the United States saw and most experienced the economic boom of the late nineteenth century. The surge of growth was so strong in the 1880s that even the sober-minded got giddy. The economist David Ames Wells wrote in 1889 that the "economic changes that have occurred during the last quarter of the century...have unquestionably been more important and varied than during any former corresponding period in the world's history." Americans read one Horatio Alger rags-to-riches story after another, no matter how prosaically written or how familiar the plots. Americans vulgarized Darwinian theory into a cliché: "survival of the fittest." They apparently never tired of hearing the Reverend Russell Conswell declare that making money was a Christian duty. At least 6,000 audiences heard him deliver his famous sermon, "Acres of Diamonds." The Southern Methodists were not to be outdone by a Baptist. In 1885 they published William S. Speer's *Law of Success*, "a summary of business methods deduced from the crystallized experiences of twelve hundred successful men on public station and private life." In fact, just before Grady spoke to the New England Society, General Sherman expressed the popular ideology of the day when he told the audience that after the Civil War and emancipation, "all men in America, north and south and east and west, stand free before the tribunal of the Almighty, each to work out his own destiny according to his ability, and according to his virtue, and according to his manhood."

Grady was a political kingmaker as well as the principal apostle of the New South. He enjoyed his greatest success with General Gordon and the Georgia gubernatorial election of 1886. When the campaign began, Augustus Bacon seemed assured of the Democratic nomination. In the solid South, nomination was tantamount to election. Bacon, however, had not anticipated Grady's capacity for selling a candidate. Modern image-makers would have been impressed by what the editor of the *Constitution* accomplished.

Grady got the aged Jefferson Davis to come to Georgia to unveil a monument to Benjamin H. Hill, former Confederate and U.S. senator from Georgia. General Gordon escorted Davis from Montgomery, Alabama, to Atlanta. Everywhere large crowds cheered the former president of the Confederacy, and the praise spilled over and onto Gordon, the alleged hero of Appomattox. Skillfully molded by Grady, the praise became a gubernatorial nomination forced upon a supposedly reluctant Gordon.

Gordon's campaign and election were highly appropriate expressions of the ambiguities of the Redeemer South. Gordon may have embodied the Lost Cause; he certainly embodied the New South. Shortly after the Civil War, he took steps then common to the ambitious in the Southeast: he ended a short career in farming and moved to Atlanta. In 1867 he ran unsuccessfully on the Democratic ticket for governor. Coincidentally, he joined the Ku Klux Klan and apparently served for a short time as the Grand Dragon of Georgia. By the early 1870s, the Democrats had defeated the Republicans and ended Reconstruction in Georgia. In the process, Georgia became a one-party state with whites in control. Gordon, Alfred H. Colquitt, and Joseph E. Brown rotated so smoothly between the U.S. Senate and the governor's mansion that they were called "the Georgia triumvirate."

Gordon sought his personal fortune in insurance, book publishing, law, and land speculation. Only the last endeavor proved very profitable. He served as the broker for an English company that purchased 1.3 million acres of Yazoo delta land in Mississippi. He kept company with the likes of Collis P. Huntington and Henry W. Flagler, railroad magnates. Flagler, once a partner of John D. Rockefeller, provided special cars for Gordon's funeral train.

Both Gordon and the Redeemer South depended heavily on imagery, and both differed significantly from the images they projected. The Redeemers did not create "a perfect democracy" or even a rough approximation of one. Nor had southern manufacturers or the southern economy developed sufficiently to challenge those of the Northeast or the Midwest. Nor had family farmers replaced planters. Nor had race relations in any broad sense become (or ever been) "close and cordial." Still, the Redeemers had presided over the early years of the New South. That was the greatest legacy of the Redeemer years. Ironically, another major legacy of those years was the Lost Cause.

*T*HE LOST CAUSE

Even as southerners moved, sometimes ambivalently, toward the New South, they kept memories of the Confederacy alive as the Lost Cause. The term may be derived from the *The Lost Cause*, an 1866 book by Edward S. Pollard which defended the constitutionality of secession. The Lost Cause evolved into a set of commonly held ideas that were ritualized, institutionalized, and often expressed in religious terms. The Lost Cause was the way in which southerners of the Civil War generation and their children understood the war and coped with crushing defeat, and it was the means they chose to convey that understanding to succeeding generations. Variants of the Lost Cause developed, reflecting changes over time. Individuals and groups often gave the Lost Cause their own particular meaning. Clergymen, for instance, often gave the Lost Cause an intensely religious interpretation.

Monuments—most memorably Monument Avenue in Richmond and Stone Mountain, Georgia—and Confederate cemeteries virtually everywhere lent permanence to the Lost Cause. Local memorial associations sprang up soon after the war. Their activities included annual observances of Confederate Memorial Day. Southern state governments declared Robert E. Lee's birthday a holiday. Regional organizations—most important among them the Southern Historical Society (founded in 1869), the United Confederate Veterans (1889), the United Daughters of the Confederacy (1895), and the Sons of the Confederacy (1896)— spread the word of the Lost Cause. So did magazines and periodicals: *The Land We Love, The Southern Review, The Southern Bivouac, The Southern Historical Papers, Confederate Veteran*; so did books: Jefferson Davis's *Rise and Fall of the Confederate Government* and the less measured *U.S. "History" as the Yankee Makes It and Takes It*, by John Coussens, a Confederate veteran. Episcopal High School at Alexandria, Virginia, the University of the South at Sewanee, Tennessee, and Washington and Lee University at Lexington, Virginia, became citadels of the Lost Cause. The name of Washington and Lee contained an irony. Lee, who served Washington College from 1865 until his death in 1870 and probably saved it from collapse, forcefully modernized the school's curriculum during his brief presidency. In renaming the college to honor him, the trustees looked as much to the future as to the past. Groups, in particular the United Daughters of the Confederacy, also watched to see that textbooks were not "Yankeeized," that the right or southern version of history was told. Katherine Du Pré Lumpkin, Georgia-born sociologist and educator, recalled that her father and his friends repeatedly said, "We were never conquered," and sneered at Reconstruction by proclaiming that they were "unreconstructed rebels." In lighter moments they sang:

> I've not been reconstructed,
> Nor took the oath of allegiance,
> I'm the same old red-hot rebel,
> And that's good enough for me!

Her father carefully instructed his children in the Lost Cause. Institutionalized and ritualized into a civil religion, the Lost Cause also had a political impact by reinforcing the solid South.

The Lost Cause rested on several tenaciously defended beliefs. First, the Confederacy had been founded on the fundamental, correct constitutional prin-

J. E. B. STUART MONUMENT UNVEILING, 1907 (Cook Collection, Valentine Museum)

ciple that sovereign states may make and unmake associations, that secession was constitutional, and that the Confederacy had fought nobly for that principle. Second, the South had not been defeated. It had been exhausted by overwhelming numbers and greater resources, not by superior armed forces and military leaders. Third, the Confederacy was a Christian society and better than its adversary, which was too given to money-making and was disorderly, insufficiently Protestant, and a jumble of ethnic groups. The Old South, by contrast, according to Lost Cause doctrine, had been an orderly, hierarchical, moral society based on evangelical Protestantism, less concerned with financial success than with honor and duty. Slavery was part of this good orderly society and had elevated blacks by Christianizing and civilizing them.

Though slavery as an institution fitted neatly into the Lost Cause, the end of the Confederacy did not. Had not southerners believed and received assurances from men of the cloth that God was on their side? The result of the Civil War defied easy explanation. Some lost their faith. Most found other solutions. In some way the South had sinned or erred grievously, and God had punished it to prepare it for another mission, perhaps to provide moral leadership for a reunited America. Those who stressed the religious aspects of the Lost Cause warned against the materialism of the New South, decrying Yankee "mammonism."

The Lost Cause had its martyrs, among whom Robert E. Lee, "Stonewall" Jackson, and Jefferson Davis were the most important. Lee the man was lost in

FLOAT FOR CONFEDERATE VETERANS (Confederate Veteran)

the portrait of a noble aristocrat of the kind many southerners wanted to believe peopled the antebellum South and a faultless Christian knight. Jackson was the common man who rose to high station to serve a great cause. Davis represented abiding uncompromising commitment to correct constitutional principles and a willingness to suffer for them. Blacks also had their place in the Lost Cause—as faithful slaves. Women received their due, too. Women were praised for their heroism and sacrifice during the Civil War and lauded as symbols of home and family, preservers of moral purity and virtue. Such attitudes may help account for, among other things, the great stress put on the Southern Lady and the South's resistance to coeducation after the Civil War. Subtle but important differences in the role of women and in attitudes among and toward women found expression among the preservers of the Lost Cause. Thus, when the Confederate Veterans, the Daughters of the Confederate Veterans, and the Sons of the Confederacy decided in 1906 to erect a monument to Confederate women, their ideas of an appropriate memorial differed significantly. The men favored a monument that celebrated the Confederate woman as subordinate helpmate, while the women wanted a monument that stressed the dignity and strong spirit of the women of the war.

A WOMAN OF THE NEW SOUTH

The debate over how to memorialize Confederate women suggested that the place of women in the postbellum South was changing, or at least that women's attitudes toward themselves and their roles in society were changing, though the changes were gradual and were less obvious than similar developments in the North.

The Civil War had obvious consequences for southern women. During the war itself, many women assumed new responsibilities. Whether those new responsibilities had a long-range effect on women, or on men, is not known. Nor do scholars know much about the effects of the deaths or disabling of so many men during the war. Presumably young women had fewer opportunities to marry and to have families. Some things are clear, however. The defeat of the South greatly improved the lives of women who had been slaves. The experience of most white women was the reverse. Incomes and living standards among whites suffered a general decline and recovered only slowly. Families in reduced circumstances had less to spend on education, for example. If families had the money to educate only one child, a son would be favored over a daughter. The economic circumstances of the postbellum South put great pressures on poorer whites. Many poorer white women—particularly those who were widowed or single—had to seek employment outside of their homes or off the farm. Domestic work offered them little opportunity: that was considered to be black work and was very poorly paid. Industrial work—in cotton mills and tobacco manufacturing particularly—afforded limited but growing opportunities. When cotton manufacturing began its rapid expansion after the 1870s, more than half of its work force was composed of native-born white women.

The changing place of women in the postbellum South was reflected in the life of Rebecca Latimer Felton. Born in 1835 into the family of a Georgia planter and slave owner, she graduated from Madison (Georgia) Female College at eighteen and married Dr. William H. Felton, a thirty-year-old widower, in 1853. A physician and then a minister, Felton was active in politics and reform. The Feltons soon established a school in which both taught on the site of their modest northern Georgia plantation. It was the first of many joint activities.

The Civil War years left deep scars. One of the Feltons' small sons died of measles during the war, another of malaria immediately after the war. Another son, born in 1869, lived until 1926. Their last child, born in 1871, lived only two years. Before the war, in 1857, their only daughter had died. Rebecca Felton's deeply felt evangelical Protestant faith must have been severely tested by these personal tragedies. The Feltons saw the war at firsthand. They cared for wounded and dying soldiers, fled their home to escape Sherman's march to the sea, and returned to their plantation after the war without slaves or much else. Soon they reopened their school, whose operations they had suspended during the conflict.

Rebecca Felton subsequently went from being wife, mother, and educator to political campaign manager, author, newspaper editor and columnist, businesswoman, and suffragist. She was an advocate of women's rights, of temperance, and of education and penal reform. She became the first woman member of the U.S. Senate, having received a token appointment in 1922. She was also a firm religious fundamentalist and a rabid racial segregationist.

Felton was a self-conscious pioneer. Never shy, Felton became openly and heavily involved in politics, a most unusual occurrence in her day. She took advanced positions on many issues: woman's suffrage, equal rights for women in churches, public funding for maternal and child care and sex education, compulsory school attendance; she opposed convict leasing. She believed that secession had been wrong and that the South had fought the war in order to preserve slavery. She defended white women workers in cotton mills and their employers, asserting that the women, some of whom were Civil War widows, had to work, and that the mills were among the few places where they could find employment. She tended to ignore the callous exploitation and the poor working and living conditions in many mills and mill villages. A member of the Women's Christian Temperance Union, she used her fiery pen to preach against drinking, smoking, and gambling. Rebecca Felton—a Georgian—denounced Coca-Cola as habit-forming and the first step toward more serious addictions. An active participant in the United Daughters of the Confederacy, she joined other Daughters in their efforts to obtain pensions and retirement homes for Confederate veterans and their widows.

Women, Felton argued, should be admitted to the University of Georgia on an equal basis with men, and the university should be better supported by the legislature because it offered people of modest means an opportunity for a college education. The Georgia legislature approved coeducation at the university in 1889, but the trustees of the university did not admit women students until 1919. Rebecca Felton was also a major supporter of the Georgia Normal and Industrial College (now Georgia State College for Women), which opened in 1889, and the Georgia Training School for Girls, which opened in 1913. Speaking of the former, Felton took a clearly feminist position: "Don't make it a man's college, patterned after man's ideas and based upon what man had done or can do." In a similar vein, she declared that men should help women with work around the house.

Felton passionately defended the racial caste system of the South. She had a pathological mind-set about race and the purity of white women. The defense of white women against "raving beasts" required drastic measures, even lynchings "a thousand times a week if necessary." Apparently Felton never probed the possible inner sources of her rage, nor did she show comparable concern for black women.

Church leaders, bankers, railroad presidents, and political opponents were targets for a pen that was still active in 1929. Disinclined to forget or forgive, she relished fights and could sling mud with the best. Felton particularly disliked John Brown Gordon, whom she accused of flipflopping on so many political issues that he was a "political gymnast."

As the 1920s drew to a close, Rebecca Felton, unwilling to trust to others or to fate, supervised construction of her own mausoleum and arranged to have her papers, with newly added marginal notes, deposited where scholars and others could use them. She could not stop the highway department from building a sidewalk and paving the road in front of her house, and she could not avoid the higher taxes that resulted. She lived to see the stock market crash in 1929 and the Depression begin. Momentarily forgetting her Protestant piety, she allowed that "things are in a hell of a shape." Yet at her death in January 1930 she left an estate of $250,000. A person of "well defined and firmly fixed opinions upon social, moral and political questions," one observer declared, she "was always ready to defend them."

POLITICAL INDEPENDENTS CHALLENGE THE REDEEMERS

The Redeemers faced more immediate threats from political independents than they did from southern women, even Rebecca Felton. Of these threats, one of the most formidable was her husband, William H. Felton. He led the Independent Democrats in Georgia and was a force to be reckoned with until the 1890s. Running against the Georgia triumvirate, Felton enjoyed his greatest electoral successes in the 1870s, when he won a seat in Congress three times beginning in 1874. Other independents won congressional elections in Georgia, Alabama, and Texas in 1878. In 1880 Tennessee Republicans regained the governorship of the state when the Democrats divided over whether and how to reduce the state debt. Two years later the national Republican party threw its support behind the successful effort of a Mississippi Independent Democrat to win a seat in Congress. Alarmed, the Redeemers talked about the dangers the independents represented because they split white voters and thus risked "Africanizing" the politics of the South. They claimed that "Mahoneism" was on the loose and was a great peril. "Mahoneism" referred to political developments in Virginia. It was there, in the most tradition-bound state in the South, that the most serious challenge to Redeemer policies came in the late 1870s.

After Reconstruction and before the Populist upheaval of the 1890s, Virginia was the scene of the most divisive political conflict in the South. The dispute focused on whether the state should repay (or fund) its debt in full or at a reduced (or readjusted) level. The Readjusters challenged the Funders in the

REBECCA LATIMER FELTON (UPI/Bettmann Newsphotos)

1870s, overwhelmed them for a time, and appeared to be developing a permanent political party. Then, like similar efforts in the South after 1865, this attempt to develop a political movement or party independent of the Democratic party failed. The conflict between the Readjusters and the Funders had elements that were peculiar to Virginia and others that revealed much about the South as a whole after Reconstruction.

The Readjusters and the Funders were offspring of the Virginia Conservatives who came to power after Union occupation forces left in 1870. The origins of the Conservatives lay in a coalition of moderate Republicans, Democrats, and Whigs. This three-part coalition outflanked radical Republicans and kept Radical Reconstruction out of the Old Dominion. Then the Democrats and the Whigs, who called themselves Conservatives in order to bridge the pre-1865 divisions among them, outmaneuvered the moderate Republicans and became preeminent in Virginia politics. The Conservatives strongly resembled the Redeemers of other southern states, though Virginia had no Radical Republican government from which to be "redeemed."

The Virginia Conservatives generally were members of the white elite and served the interests of that elite, often at the expense of other groups. The state debt crisis demonstrated how narrow their vision could be. Virginia had entered the Civil War with a $33 million debt, the result of state subsidies for the construction of railroads, canals, and turnpikes. (State assets in these internal improvements totaled $43 million in 1860.) After four years of war, the debt (the amount of outstanding bonds) had increased to $45 million. None of this sum, it should be noted, was the result of Reconstruction. In 1871 the Conservative-controlled state government passed the Funding Act and committed the state to pay the debt in full. No other southern postwar government funded its debt at such a high rate. The honor of Virginia, said the Conservatives, was at stake. They probably believed what they said, but what they said was at least partially self-serving. Some Conservatives may have owned state bonds, and some served as legal and business representatives of bondholders. Most of the bondholders were from the Northeast and Europe, and many bought the bonds at considerably less than half their face value. The Conservatives also sold the state's holdings in valuable railroad stocks at suspiciously low prices. Apparently some prominent Conservatives profited from these transactions, among them William Mahone, future leader of the Readjusters.

Payment of the debt hobbled the state. Interest payments alone exhausted state revenues. Virginia was chronically in debt in the 1870s, had to borrow just to keep the government operating at all, and virtually eliminated expenditures for social services. Ignoring constitutional requirements that the legislature bear much of the cost of the newly established public school system, Conservative leaders simply stood by while half of the public schools closed and 100,000 students were turned away. Some Conservatives thought this was a regrettable but necessary consequence of preserving the honor of the state. Rather than readjust the debt, close the schools. The governor thought public schools were "a luxury...to be paid for...by the people who wish their benefits." As they would soon discover, the Funders were out of touch with public sentiment.

"Kill the public schools, will you?" a Virginia farmer reportedly warned his representative in the legislature. "Do it and this will be your last winter in Richmond." The warning reflected a widespread sentiment. By the 1870s most Virginians and most other southerners had rejected the long-held idea that public education was for paupers only. But the Conservatives in Virginia persisted. They also acquired a new name, Funders. The Funders put themselves in the politically absurd position of defending the interests of the bondholders, most of whom were not Virginians and who were making very substantial profits on their bonds, against the interests of Virginians. Reports of bribery, theft, and forgery clouded the Conservatives' claim to be defenders of Virginia's honor. Cash payments to high officials apparently had speeded passage of the Funding Act. Consequently, the Readjusters became a major force in Virginia politics by the late 1870s.

William Mahone, the principal leader of the Readjusters, puzzled his contemporaries then and historians since. How much did he mix self-interest with his politics? Was he prompted by conscience or by opportunism? Was he the leader of what might have been a significantly different politics in Virginia and in the South? How responsible was he for the successes of the Readjusters? Their failures? The grandson of an eighteenth-century Irish immigrant to Virginia, son of a moderately prosperous innkeeper, graduate of Virginia Military Institute, railroad engineer and then president of his own line, slaveholder, Democrat, secessionist, member of the state legislature of Confederate Virginia, major general in the Confederate Army, hero of the Battle of the Crater, and highly influential Conservative leader, he hardly seemed the type to break ranks with his fellow Conservatives.

But by 1877 the general sought another battle. The depression of the 1870s had cost him his nascent railroad empire (suggestively named the Atlantic, Mississippi, and Ohio Railroad Company). He may have wanted to revive his railroad through what was then the accepted means, the state legislature. If Mahone could lead the Readjusters to a successful conquest of the legislature, the legislature might look favorably on the state railroad charter he had to have. Whatever his motives, Mahone sided with efforts to reduce the state debt and declared himself "the friend of the public school system of Virginia." He quickly took command of the Readjusters.

Led by Mahone and using the debt issue as an entering wedge, the Readjusters won control of the legislature in 1879 and the governor's office in 1881. They reduced the debt by a third and the interest rate on it from 6 to 3 percent. Virginia's creditors, they argued, should bear some of the costs of Virginia's war-reduced economy and of the revenue losses associated with the secession of West Virginia. The Readjusters' rhetoric had a distinctly modern ring. They decried the flow of capital to the state's creditors rather than to industry and agriculture. Harrison H. Riddleberger, Readjuster chieftain and future U.S. senator, wanted to "combine manufactures with agriculture." The *Staunton Valley Virginian* hailed Virginians as "a new people, living under new conditions, looking to new pursuits, new methods, and new results." In other words, slavery and secession were dead, and Virginia wanted to end its dependence on agriculture.

The Readjusters reformed the tax system by reducing taxes on farmland and small businesses, by ending the policy of self-assessment by the railroads for tax purposes, and by collecting delinquent taxes. At the same time, the Readjusters spent more on social services—on hospitals, asylums, the penitentiary, higher education, and the public schools. The number of schools, teachers, and students more than doubled. Yet Virginia had a budget surplus of $1.5 million in 1883. The Readjusters embraced other activist ideas about the role of government. Some wanted to enact maximum hours laws, restrict child labor, and give aid to the needy. In another break with southern tradition, the Readjusters formally declared their support for protective tariffs. The Readjuster legislature enacted laws to ensure the quality of agricultural fertilizers and to regulate the activities of life insurance companies—but only those based outside of the state. Influenced perhaps by Mahone, the Readjusters did not respond positively to pressures to regulate railroads more vigorously.

The humanitarian reform and public school movements and the activist notions of the proper role of government, found elsewhere in nineteenth-century America, had reached the Old Dominion. As elsewhere, self-interest and the urge to impose social control were factors. The Readjusters defended public schools as an asset for economic growth and as a stimulant to "a general ambition" for "prosperity." Keenly aware of their dependence on black voters, the Readjusters made voting easier for blacks and passed other measures designed to appeal to them. Thus they repealed the Conservative law that made the poll tax a requirement for voting and the law that disfranchised men convicted of petty larceny. These measures also broadened the franchise for low-income whites. Ironically, those whites might then vote against their benefactors if they believed the Readjusters had failed to defend white supremacy adequately. The Readjusters abolished the whipping post (hated vestige of slave times), increased patronage for blacks, created a college (now Virginia State University), and supported the state mental hospital for blacks. Black legislators, whose numbers grew during the Readjuster years, figured prominently in these efforts.

REPUBLICANS AND DEMOCRATS IN VIRGINIA

Mahone attempted to transform the Readjusters into a permanent political party by joining forces with the Republicans. The general cast his lot with the Republicans in 1881, when he went to the U.S. Senate. His vote allowed the Republicans to organize the Senate and thus to elect its officers and control its committees. In return, the general got command of federal patronage in Virginia, essential for political party building. But the Readjusters and Republicans could not overcome the problems that for nearly a century after 1865 plagued challengers of southern Democrats. Circumstances and Mahone's own failings undermined the efforts to make a strong Republican party out of the Readjusters.

The Funders, who formally declared themselves to be Democrats in 1883, had enormous political assets. Self-proclaimed defenders of the South, they stood opposed to the party of Lincoln, which symbolized the Civil War, emancipation, and Reconstruction. Cloaked in Confederate gray and surrounded by the Stars and Bars, they recalled past glories and bitter memories. They promised to maintain a South rooted in tradition, white supremacy, and black subordination. Democrats also drew their leaders from those who were politically active and able to assure the Democrats of ample funds.

The Virginia Democrats also made some timely changes in their course. They distanced themselves momentarily from their Funder past. They adopted the programs of the opposition and imitated Mahone's statewide organization. They declared the debt issue settled, and they committed themselves to keeping the public school system and most other Readjuster reforms. Ironically, the Readjusters' victory on the debt deprived the insurgents of the issue that had been the glue of the Readjuster coalition of blacks and nonelite whites.

Mahone himself weakened the coalition. His imperial style bred harmful divisions among Readjuster and Republican leaders. He perceived other Readjuster and Republican leaders as rivals, so he demanded oaths of loyalty—to himself. He used patronage like a bludgeon. Opponents effectively equated Mahoneism with bossism. Mahone's decision to join forces with the Republicans was a calculated risk in the South, where the party was abhorrent to most voters. That bold step, however, offered the Readjusters the only realistic chance to develop a permanent political party that could challenge the Democrats.

More than anything else, however, the race issue doomed the Readjusters, even though they approached the color line discreetly. The white Readjuster leaders, including Mahone, were white supremacists. They supported racial segregation in schools, handled race and access to public facilities gingerly, and flatly rejected miscegenation and racial intermarriage. "Our party...encourages each race to develop its own sociology separately and apart from unlawful contamination with each other, but under a government which recognizes and protects the civil rights of all." Still, their constituency left them exposed to racist attacks.

The Democrats could win elections without black votes. Their opponents could not—unless an unusual circumstance should arise, such as the crisis over the state debt. Anyone who wished to build a permanent political party that could present a continuous challenge to the Democrats in Virginia had to have strong support from blacks. As the Readjusters metamorphosed into Republicans, they were gored on the horns of a dilemma not of their making. They had to court black leaders and black voters, who understandably and often rightly suspected that white politicians only wanted to use them. But every concession to blacks, born of self-interest or of good conscience, and every black candidate, elected official, or appointee darkened the Readjusters and Republicans in white Virginia.

Conversely, the Democrats claimed to be "the white man's party." The Richmond *Daily Dispatch* put it simply in 1883: "Shall the whites rule...or shall the negroes...?" "I am a Democrat," explained John W. Daniel, Democratic senator, "because I am a white man and a Virginian." These leaders were disposed to exploit race for political advantage. They might even get involved in staging a serious disturbance on the eve of an important election, or they might take advantage of opportunities such a disturbance might offer. Danville seemed a likely place.

Danville was located in Southside Virginia, an area where blacks made up about half of the populace. Danville itself had a black majority, a white carpetbagger mayor, several blacks on the town council, a black judge, and several black policemen. The white minority in the town, according to the "merchants and manufacturers and mechanics" who signed the "Danville Circular" on the eve of the 1883 state election, deeply resented "the injustice and humiliation to which our white people have been subjected and are daily undergoing by the domination and misrule of the Radical or negro party." Danville supposedly hovered on the brink of economic collapse. Actually, it had a booming trade in tobacco, three railroads, and the recently started Riverside Cotton Mills. Also Negro maids allegedly were uppity. How much of the circular was contrived, how much was factual, and how much was believed are impossible to discern. It probably did reflect the feelings of most local whites and the determination of the Democrats in Danville to win the state election and regain control of their town. The authors and signers of the circular warned that if the Democrats lost, *"we are doomed."* Whites also threatened to boycott businessmen who did not support the Democrats and suggested that property owners not rent to blacks or Republicans. Three days before the polls opened, an argument of uncertain origin led to a shooting that left four blacks and one white dead. Inflated into a "riot" and broadcast by poster, telegraph, and mounted courier, the incident became the focal point of what was already a racially oriented campaign.

The resultant emotional upsurge helped the Democrats to a decisive electoral victory in the 1883 state election. They then quickly consolidated their gains. Using their newly won control of the legislature, the Democrats took over the election machinery of the state. That control was critical to their ability to carry the state for Grover Cleveland in the 1884 presidential election and to recapture the governorship and Virginia's congressional delegation. Stuffed ballot boxes, falsified election returns, and intimidated opposition supporters became commonplace. The Democratic leader Hal Flood explained that once the polls closed, election judges, all of whom were Democrats, "changed the ballots to suit themselves." Gerrymandering also helped. The Democrats drew electoral lines for Danville so artfully that its black majority became a minority. So effective were these political practices that sweeping disfranchisement laws (Jim Crow election laws) were not enacted in Virginia until 1902. The Democrats did not need Jim Crow laws to stay in power, at least not for some years.

A historian recalled that during his boyhood in eastern Virginia around World War I, people who remembered Mahone

> spoke of him with horror.... He had threatened Virginia with Negro-Republican rule. His career had been an offense to Virginia's dignity and decency. In campaign after campaign such views were reiterated by the leaders of the ruling Democratic party. The worst charge that could be brought against an opposition candidate was that he had been associated in any way with Mahone and the Readjusters.... The prevailing opinion was that only the Democrats had served the state with honesty, dignity, and integrity.

Mahone had obvious shortcomings, but he deserved better. So did the Readjusters. At the very least, they offered black and nonelite white Virginians a better present and future and all Virginians a wider range of political options and a less racially skewed politics.

The attempt to build a viable opposition to the Redeemers-turned-Democrats failed even in Virginia, where it had considerable advantages, certainly greater advantages than those of similar efforts in other southern states. The debt crisis had been a catalyst for political dissent. In Virginia, unlike several Deep South states, blacks were numerically a minority and could not realistically threaten "black domination." Virginia had not experienced Radical Reconstruction. The Readjusters had able leaders who were natives of the state and relatively immune to the charges of outside intervention that were common during Reconstruction. Still they could not prevail against the postbellum Democrats in Virginia.

THE SOLID SOUTH

As events in Virginia revealed, any opposition to the Democrats faced almost insurmountable odds. Southern Democrats based their defense on the solid South: the South had to remain solidly Democratic because the Democratic party offered the best means of preventing the federal government from intervening in race relations in the South and the best means of keeping blacks in their place within the South. To maintain their two-front strategy of defense of white supremacy (and their own political fortunes and sometimes their own economic positions), southern Democrats were willing to go to great lengths, often well beyond the bounds of the truth and the law. Southern Democrats conjured up visions of past horrors—real, imagined, and embellished. Versions of the past served aims of the present. Particular interpretations of the past and events selectively remembered became fact. Thus the story of Mahone and the Readjusters went through the process that had turned Reconstruction into the Tragic Era. More critically, southern Democrats bludgeoned their opponents with Negrophobia. They exploited rumors, such as the supposed collapse of Danville, for their own gain. The Democrats succeeded in making the South a one-party region and in making that party a white man's party, although they often neglected the interests of many whites. The concern of the Virginia Democrats for the bondholders and their indifference to public education were all too typical of the Redeemers or the postbellum southern Democrats. On whom should the burden of taxes fall? What kind of services—schools, asylums, and so forth—should state and local governments provide? Should railroads and industrial corporations be regulated? Essential questions such as these tended to get obscured in a politics laden with race and memories of the Civil War and Reconstruction. Who was going to challenge heroes of the Lost Cause, General This, Colonel That, Captain Something Else?

The Democrats who triumphed in Virginia and in the rest of the South after Reconstruction dominated the politics of the region throughout the remainder of the century. They left a heritage that lingers even to the present. Their legacy included a one-party politics that became so fixed and persisted so long that the "solid South" or the "Democratic South" seemed to be divinely ordained. And the Democrats assisted Providence. They thwarted whatever possibilities existed for the development of a strong two-party politics. To gain and keep power, the Democrats were willing to risk the "honesty, dignity, and integrity" for which they were noted in some quarters. Fraud and violence at elections did not cease when Reconstruction ended.

Southern Democrats also found bribery effective, as were calculated manipulations of state constitutions and laws. The Democratic legislature in North Carolina removed the threat of black power in areas of the state where blacks were the majority by simply vesting control of county and local governments in itself. The Redeemer constitution in Louisiana achieved a similar effect by expanding the governor's already considerable powers over the legislature and over county and local officials. South Carolina passed its notorious eight-box voting law in 1882. Voters then had to match ballots with boxes, with candidates in proper order, or have their ballots invalidated. Democratic election officials counseled bewildered voters selectively. Southern legislatures gerrymandered without pretense of subtlety. They did not blush to create pretzel-shaped congressional districts that diluted the power of black votes.

The southern Democrats succeeded politically to a remarkable degree. Blessed by the circumstances of the Civil War and Reconstruction and by whites' fear of blacks, the Democrats gave the South unprecedented one-party dominance. In time it became difficult to remember that the South had a two-party tradition, to remember when the South was not solid.

SOUTHERN DEMOCRATS AND BLACKS

Once the Democrats regained office they did not immediately disfranchise black voters. It was not in their interest to do so. Suitably contained and manipulated black voters served the needs of Democratic leaders within the South and without. By various means, fair or foul, the Democrats used ballots cast by blacks to frustrate their challengers. White minorities in black belt counties in Georgia, Alabama, and Mississippi used the ballots of black majorities to offset those cast by whites in white-majority counties. A Mississippi judge told that state's 1890 constitutional convention that

> it is no secret that there has not been a full vote and a fair count in Mississippi since 1875—that we have been preserving the ascendancy of the white people by revolutionary methods. In plain words, we have been stuffing ballot boxes, committing perjury, and here and there in the State carrying the elections by *fraud* and violence until the whole machinery for elections was about to rot down.

Outside the South, the Democrats found the presence of black voters useful for political and economic reasons. That presence was interpreted by the North and by potential investors as an indication that the slavocracy was dead and that the Democrats had rejected their grievous errors of the past and were enlightened. The light of the new day in the South shone so brightly in the eyes of some people that they invented the term "New Departure" Democrats for the Democratic leaders who preached and sometimes practiced accommodation in race relations. The New Departure strategy also diminished the possibility that the federal government might intervene again, politically or militarily.

It is important, however, to remember the limits of the New Departure strategy. Its cornerstone was white supremacy and black subordination. As long as the cornerstone remained securely in place, blacks could continue to have certain political and civil rights: vote, hold office, serve on juries, testify in cases involving whites, and bear arms. They also had access to many public places and to public transit, and not always on a segregated basis.

Blacks voted in large numbers in the South until the late 1890s. But blacks hardly made their electoral decisions freely in many places. Though blacks often constituted a majority of potential voters, southern whites would not let that fact be translated into black majorities in state and local governments. Blacks served in Congress, in state legislatures, and on city councils and local boards of education in such places as Richmond, Jackson, and St. Augustine until the early twentieth century. Four blacks even served as delegates to the 1895 constitutional convention in South Carolina, which was called to disfranchise blacks. The black delegates dissented without effect. (Their remarks, which included a more accurate analysis of Reconstruction than the one that appeared in history textbooks for years, were excluded from the official minutes of the convention.)

Whatever the limits of the race relations policies of the postbellum Democrats, they were more favorable to blacks than the rigid segregationist policies that came during the 1890s. Tragically, however, the policies and actions of the Democrats in pursuit of their own survival nurtured the racism and bloody violence that racked the South in the 1890s.

THE SOLID SOUTH AND NATIONAL POLITICS

The solid South equaled the Democratic South, of course, and that equation had political meaning beyond Dixie and long after the Civil War. The South ensured the Democrats of a substantial portion of any Congress and of electoral votes in a presidential election. The Republicans had similar bastions in many nonsouthern states. The solid South helped to create a nearly even balance of power between the two major parties in the late nineteenth century. The equipoise began as the 1870s started and it lasted until the mid-1890s. Then the Republicans became the dominant party, a position they held until 1930.

Between 1874 and 1894, the Democrats usually controlled the House of Representatives and the Republicans usually controlled the Senate and the White House. Democrats ran well enough in parts of the North to elect a number of congressmen, who joined forces with southern Democrats to control the House. Democrats outside the South had less success in winning statewide elections, and hence less success in capturing seats in the Senate or winning electoral votes in presidential elections. Making the White House Democratic depended on a simple, though not easily applied, formula. To the South add a reasonably attractive Democrat from a large eastern state in which the Democrats are strong, and hope for favorable circumstances. Governor Grover Cleveland of New York fitted this description, and circumstances obliged during the 1884 and 1892 presidential elections when economic difficulties and serious intraparty dissension damaged the Republicans.

Southern Democrats enjoyed considerable success in Congress, even when the Republicans controlled the White House and the Senate. Democrats from the South provided leadership and a substantial vote for the passage of the Interstate Commerce Act in 1887. That law initiated federal regulation of railroads and created the first federal regulatory agency, the Interstate Commerce Commission. Before that, southern congressmen displayed their skills at securing federal funds for river and harbor improvements in the South by making timely bargains with Democrats from the West and Midwest and with Republicans. In 1879 they persuaded Congress to create the Mississippi River Commission. That move put federal money and organization into efforts to solve one of the chronic problems of the southern Mississippi region. The river prevented cultivation of much of the lowlands in the area, and periodic flooding often brought damage or destruction to the lands that were cultivated. Much of the area called the Yazoo delta, for instance, could not be farmed until the Mississippi was better controlled. Convinced that the costs of levee construction and flood control exceeded the capacity of private investors and the states along the lower Mississippi, leaders in the region had sought federal aid. In their successful quest for the Mississippi commission, these leaders cleverly broadened their appeal by claiming that the commission and its funding would ensure improved navigation along the river. Thus they obtained strong support among congressmen, senators, and others throughout the Mississippi Valley.

The attitudes of the eastern Democrats often galled southern Democrats. As they learned in the disputed Hayes-Tilden election and the struggle over the Compromise of 1877, eastern Democrats had little sympathy for efforts to spend federal funds for internal improvements. Eastern Democrats denounced such appropriations as "raids on the Treasury" and worse. Though those views had merit, most southern Democrats believed the easterners wished to stop these appropriations only after they had secured the funds the East had wanted. Southern Democrats also felt that the easterners were insensitive to the acutely needy South.

*T*HE BLAIR BILL

The congressional fight over the Blair Education Bill in the 1880s demonstrated the sharpness of these sectional conflicts within the Democracy. Republican Senator Henry F. Blair of New Hampshire proposed in 1881 that Congress disperse surplus federal funds to the states for educational purposes.

By 1881 the government had retired much of its Civil War debt and was collecting more revenue than it was spending. The obvious remedy—cutting taxes—was not easily applied. There was no income tax to cut. Federal taxes on tobacco and liquor had already been cut, to the delight of the defenders of bourbon and tobacco, who were concentrated in Kentucky, Tennessee, Virginia, and the Carolinas. Tariffs—taxes on imports—produced most of the revenue the federal government collected. Logic pointed to tariff reduction as the best solution, but tariff reduction was a political porcupine best avoided. The Republicans, powerful economic interests, and a small, politically potent group of Democrats made tariff reduction almost impossible at that time. Therefore, the politically embarrassing budget surplus remained and grew. So did the popularity of the Blair Bill.

Blair wanted to apportion funds according to the number of illiterates in each state. Since the South had a higher rate of illiteracy than the rest of the country, it would be the major beneficiary of the Blair Bill. Southern and eastern Democrats generally split over the bill, even though the opponents used arguments that normally had strong appeal to southerners. The bill was denounced as a device to avoid tariff reduction and a dangerous precedent for federal intervention in affairs rightly belonging to the states. Alabama's Senator John Tyler Morgan worried that the Blair Bill would set a precedent for "national prohibition, pure food and drug laws, abolition of penitentiaries, requirements of higher wages for workers, and socialized medicine."

Most southerners in Congress had few such qualms and were little impressed even with arguments based on states' rights. Southern Democrats supported the Blair Bill more consistently than any other group in Congress. Their allies on the issue were Republicans and western Democrats. Eastern Democrats provided the most consistent opposition of all groups. The Senate passed the bill twice, but it never came to a vote in the House because it was tied up in committee. Southern Democrats in the House backed unsuccessful efforts to vote the bill out of committee, but they could not overcome the power of the Speaker of the House, who opposed the measure. John G. Carlisle, a Kentuckian, believed deeply that tariff reduction was critical and that the Blair Bill would hurt attempts to lower import duties. He was also intensely committed to the idea that good government is little government. Finally, when Grover Cleveland, who had similar ideas, was elected president in 1884, all hope for the Blair Bill died.

The debate over and the votes on the education bill suggested that the ideal of limited government was still strong among the Democrats but that it was fading, especially in the South. In any event, southern supporters of the Blair Bill saw an acute need that the federal government might relieve. The South's ability to provide public education, even of dubious quality, faced serious difficulties. The South had less income and wealth to tax than the rest of the country and a greater proportion of school-aged people. Moreover, the South bore the costs of a self-imposed dual school system.

THE LEGACY OF THE REDEEMERS

The fortunes of the southern Democrats became linked in the late nineteenth century with those of Grover Cleveland. It was a mixed blessing. Cleveland's success in the presidential elections of 1884 and 1892 meant more federal patronage for all Democrats. Cleveland appointed Senator L. Q. C. Lamar of Mississippi secretary of the interior and Senator A. H. Garland of Arkansas attorney general in 1885, and in 1893 he selected John G. Carlisle of Kentucky to be secretary of the treasury, Congressman Hilary A. Herbert of Alabama as secretary of the navy, and Hoke Smith of Georgia as secretary of the interior. A year later, Cleveland nominated Senator Edwin D. White of Louisiana for a seat on the Supreme Court, replacing Lamar, whom Cleveland had appointed in 1888 and whose place on the Court became vacant at his death.

Equally important to the white South and the southern Democrats, Cleveland's victories lessened the possibility of federal intervention in the South's peculiar race relations. Cleveland, like most Democrats outside the South, acquiesced in the southern view of race relations. Even as southern race relations entered their most bloody and violent era, Cleveland showed little concern about beleaguered and murdered blacks and no inclination to dispatch troops to the South to defend them. Yet Cleveland took a lively interest in "law and order" in Chicago after the Haymarket Riot (1886), and he used federal troops during the Pullman strike in 1894.

Cleveland joined southern Democrats in calling for tariff reduction, and he even went along with southern Democrats when they insisted that the legislation lowering the tariff had to include an income tax. They saw the income tax as a way to make the wealthier eastern states pay a greater share of federal taxes. Cleveland accepted tariff reduction and the income tax even though many eastern Democrats resented them both.

Unfortunately for southern Democrats, Cleveland did not differ from his fellow eastern Democrats on banking or federal subsidies for internal improvements. Most important, Cleveland stood firmly with the East on monetary policy. Southern Democrats wanted to alter banking laws in order to increase the number of banks and to disperse them more widely. At the very least, they wanted to repeal the 10 percent tax on state-chartered banks. Cleveland and other eastern Democrats opposed any changes in the national banking acts.

The markedly deflationary monetary policy that the federal government followed after 1865 favored the East and hurt the South. Debtors were affected adversely because the costs of borrowing rose steadily. Most southerners were farmers and thus were borrowers, and the South as a section borrowed heavily because it was short of capital. Southern congressmen and senators, therefore, generally supported efforts to stem deflation, and they voted for mildly inflationary measures whenever possible. Cleveland and most of the eastern Democrats held to deflationary policies through the savage depression of the 1890s. For the Democrats, it was a disaster. They became the minority party in national politics in the 1890s, a position to which they were relegated until the 1930s. Consequently, after 1894 the solid South found itself excluded from national power for what seemed like all time.

Yet politically the Redeemers had accomplished much in the quarter-century after 1865. They helped restore whites to political dominance in the South. They managed to handle race relations cleverly enough to ensure white supremacy and to avoid (with very few exceptions) federal intervention in black-white affairs. The Redeemers stood their ground but did not ignore northern sentiments, and so they eased sectional reconciliation. When Senator Charles Sumner died in 1874, for instance, Senator L. Q. C. Lamar of Mississippi eulogized his late Massachusetts colleague who had long been the scourge of the white South. Four years later, General Gordon told a Boston audience: "The causes that divided us are gone, and gone forever. The interests which now unite us will unite us forever."

The Redeemers were also largely responsible for the postbellum Democratic party and its overwhelming dominance in the South. Moreover, southern Democrats in Congress made astute alliances with people outside their section and even outside their party. In doing so, they revived the art of political compromise, which somehow southern leaders had lost during the 1850s. Part of the success of the southern Democrats rested on irony. Emancipation gave the South more seats in the House of Representatives and more votes in the electoral college. Slaves had been counted as three-fifths of a person in apportioning seats in the House and the electoral college. Emancipation converted the fractions to whole numbers, if not whole persons.

The Redeemers also presided over the emergence of the New South, something about which they had mixed feelings. Clearly they were not sure that the New South creed should be the creed of their South. Conversely, they were sure about the Lost Cause. One of their legacies to succeeding generations was a deep reverence for the Confederacy. The Lost Cause, like other Redeemer legacies, was based on and reinforced the bond among whites. That bond was severely tested in the 1890s.

Early death spared Henry Grady the experience of the depression of the 1890s, the accompanying Populist upheaval, and the near-destruction of the political structure the Redeemers had erected. Gordon was not so fortunate. And when he died in 1904, it was probably too early to realize that the handiwork of the Redeemers remained largely intact.

Much of it still does.

19

A Different South Emerges

Rails, Mills, and Towns

———— ❖ ————

The disputants paced off the required distance, turned, fired their pistols, missed, shook hands, and departed. For 1889, it was a peculiar way to conduct business, even in the South. The incident involved more than a momentary revival of the antebellum practice of dueling. The principals were J. D. Williamson, president of the Chattanooga, Rome, and Columbus Railroad, and Patrick Calhoun, senior legal counsel for the Richmond and West Point Terminal Railroad and grandson of John C. Calhoun. Calhoun wanted Williamson to sell his railroad to the Richmond Terminal. Williamson refused.

The issues involved more than the fate of two railway companies. They were part of a much larger story: railroads in the New South. And railroads are related to industrialization and urbanization. But railroads come first because they formed the superstructure of the economy of the New South. They were the elemental precondition to better times.

Railroad mileage in the South doubled between 1865 and 1880. Then it more than tripled between 1880 and 1900. The latter rate of expansion far exceeded that in the rest of the country. Obviously the New South had contracted the railroad mania of the nineteenth century, and for good reasons.

Railroads offered solutions to the geographical barriers that segmented the South and made economic development there difficult in many areas.

Mountain ranges. The Blue Ridge and the Cumberland mountains impose themselves between the Southeast and the Ohio Valley and fragment large areas of Kentucky, Tennessee, Virginia, North Carolina, and Georgia. The Ozarks separate much of Arkansas and Missouri.

Pine and sand barrens. The piedmont is separated from the coastal plains and seaports by stretches of land so sandy that it will support little but scrub pines.

The fall line. Along a line stretching across the piedmont from Virginia to Mississippi, rivers fall to coastal plains. Above the fall line, few rivers are navigable.

The semiarid grasslands. The most prominent geographical features of northwestern Louisiana, Texas, and Oklahoma are semiarid grasslands. Beyond lies the desert of the Southwest, which southern commerce must traverse if it is to reach the west coast and the Pacific.

The Florida peninsula. The Florida land mass runs for more than 400 miles from north to south, reaches 150 miles at its widest point, and has few navigable waterways.

Railroads also supplemented navigable rivers and river systems. The most important of these rivers are those of the Chesapeake region; those of the southeastern coastal plain from Wilmington, North Carolina, to Savannah; the Ohio and Cumberland rivers; and, of course, the Mississippi. Eventually railroads reduced most of these and other navigable waterways to secondary, though still significant, roles in transportation.

Furthermore, railroads helped to translate economic potential into economic reality. They hastened the spread of cotton culture into areas where cotton would not otherwise have been grown profitably because of inadequate transportation. Without railways, the development of most of the interior cities and towns of the South, the southern textile and lumber industries, the cattle industry, and the coal and iron regions of Kentucky, Tennessee, Georgia, and Alabama would have been much delayed. And this list could be much longer.

Railroads also expanded rapidly because they had clear advantages over the alternate means of transportation then available for great areas of the South that lacked ready access to usable waterways. Trains offered speed, flexibility as to location, and less vulnerability to droughts, floods, and other "acts of God." Over time, railroad freight rates declined markedly. Though freight rates on waterways were lower still, rail transportation often cost less in the long run because trains offered better services for most shippers. Advances in the design and construction of rails, engines, cars, and terminal facilities increased railroad productivity. So did improvements in managerial and accounting techniques, air brakes, refrigerated cars, and the adoption of the standard gauge (the distance between rails). Fully implemented in the United States in the 1880s, the standard gauge made a national, interconnected rail system possible and facilitated the integration of the South into the then developing national market.

Given the advantages railroads offered, railroad mania was understandable. No one should be without a railroad—so thought legions of city fathers, town elders, county notables, farmers, manufacturers, and virtually everyone else. Communities lived in dread of being bypassed by the railroad, of being excluded from the Iron Age. Narrower interests, as usual, played their part, too. Hope of handsome profits from land sales to railroads quickened the pulse of landowners. Visions of fortunes to be made from developing land, timber, minerals, factories, and new markets had a similar effect. Other people could and often did make substantial sums by building railroads and by manipulating railway stocks and bonds.

The result was too much of a good thing. Railroads seemed to be everywhere in the South. By 1890 more than three hundred companies operated in the South, though only about sixty of them owned as much as one hundred miles of track. Steady profits or an acceptable return on invested capital proved elusive. Characteristically, railways had high fixed costs. Moreover, the South presented some peculiar vexations. It had fewer capital resources and a weaker economy than did other regions. The South also had a low population density. In 1900 Massachusetts had seven times, New York three times, and Ohio two times more people per square mile than Tennessee, the most densely populated southern state. The dominance of agriculture in the South hurt southern railroads. Farm products created highly seasonal demands on transportation that peaked at harvesttime and fell sharply thereafter. Farm products could not bear such heavy transportation charges as highly processed products, such as machine tools. Neither could first-stage processed raw materials, such as timber, pig iron, and coarse textiles, which were the principal manufactured products of the New South. In comparison with other American railroads, those in the South had some cost advantages, such as lower prices for land and labor, but not enough to offset the regional disadvantages. Thus railways in the South experienced more financial crises than those elsewhere. Railways made critical contributions to the evolution of the New South, but they also increased its vulnerability to economic fluctuations. That weakness became especially apparent in the 1890s.

Railroad Empires

No one should have been surprised when the financially fragile, overbuilt southern rail network nearly collapsed during the economically turbulent 1890s. Companies that controlled 13,000 miles of track (about half of the total mileage in the South) went bankrupt. Hard times hastened the already ongoing process of consolidation of southern lines. By 1902, rail systems that owned more than three-fifths of the lines in the South were established: the Baltimore and Ohio; the Norfolk and Western; the Atlantic Coastline; the Seaboard Airline; the Southern Railway; the Louisville and Nashville; the Illinois Central; the Missouri Pacific; the Missouri, Kansas, and Texas; the Santa Fe; the Texas and Pacific; and the Southern Pacific. Still, rail mileage increased very substantially after 1900 in several southern states: Florida, Louisiana, Arkansas, Texas, and Oklahoma.

The emergence of extensive railroad empires introduced southerners, like other Americans, to the mixed blessings of the Gilded Age and its most important offspring, the corporation. Railroads "were the first American business to

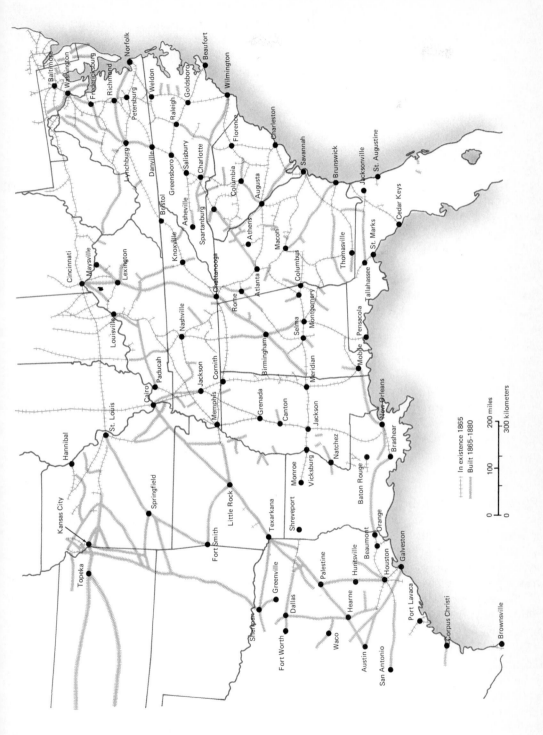

RAILROADS OF THE SOUTH, 1865–1880

Baltimore
Washington
Fredericksburg
Richmond
Petersburg
Norfolk
Weldon
Goldsboro
Beaufort
Raleigh
Wilmington
Lynchburg
Danville
Greensboro
Salisbury
Charlotte
Florence
Charleston
Bristol
Asheville
Spartanburg
Columbia
Augusta
Savannah
Brunswick
Jacksonville
St. Augustine
Cincinnati
Maysville
Lexington
Knoxville
Athens
Macon
Columbus
Thomasville
St. Marks
Cedar Keys
Louisville
Nashville
Chattanooga
Rome
Atlanta
Selma
Montgomery
Pensacola
Tallahassee
Paducah
Cairo
Jackson
Corinth
Birmingham
Meridian
Mobile
St. Louis
Memphis
Grenada
Canton
Jackson
New Orleans
Hannibal
Natchez
Brashear
Springfield
Monroe
Vicksburg
Baton Rouge
Little Rock
Kansas City
Texarkana
Shreveport
Orange
Galveston
Topeka
Fort Smith
Beaumont
Houston
Sherman
Greenville
Dallas
Palestine
Huntsville
Port Lavaca
Fort Worth
Waco
Hearne
Corpus Christi
Austin
San Antonio
Brownsville

┼┼┼┼ In existence 1865
▬▬▬▬ Built 1865–1880

0   100   200 miles
0   300 kilometers

work out the modern ways of finance, management, labor relations, competition, and government regulation."

Their size alone troubled Americans. Big business, it ought to be remembered, was just making its appearance in the United States. Standard Oil and Carnegie Steel, for example, were young concerns. Railroad officials took on the appearance and some of the reality of emperors. They had command over critically needed services and enormous assets. They became heavily involved in politics, not always willingly. Given the nature of the business, they could hardly have done otherwise. The Illinois Central, for instance, became one of the major issues in Mississippi politics. So did the Louisville and Nashville in Kentucky and Alabama. Some saw the hand of the L&N in the notorious Goebel affair in Kentucky, where state elections resulted in two state governments, mountaineer vigilantes roamed the state capital, and the newly elected governor, William Goebel, was assassinated in 1899. In Alabama, regulation of railroads in general and of the L&N in particular dominated the political scene for years.

Railroad leaders were semipublic figures if not quite household names. Among the most notable and notorious were John Inman of the L&N and the Richmond Terminal, Henry W. Flagler of the Florida East Coast Line and pioneer of Florida's tourist industry, Jay Gould of the Missouri Pacific and the Texas and Pacific, Milton Hannibal Smith of the L&N, Collis P. Huntington of the Southern Pacific, and last but certainly not least, J. P. Morgan, who orchestrated the creation of the Southern Railway.

The name of Morgan suggests one of the profound changes that occurred in American railroading in the last years of the nineteenth century. Control passed to the men who were able to supply the capital needed by the increasingly large rail companies—northern, mainly New York, capitalists. The railroads' enormous need for capital helped to centralize and institutionalize the nation's investment markets in New York.

Thus most southern railroads fell under the control of absentee capitalists. Their interests and those of the railroads and of the users of rail services were not necessarily the same. Jay Gould, to cite an extreme example, reputedly built a fortune of at least $75 million by manipulating railway stocks and bonds and by being indifferent to the sound construction, regular maintenance, and good service of the companies he controlled. A recent biography, however, paints a more positive picture of Gould as a businessman and entrepreneur.

More important because of the company's size were the games of high finance played by the Richmond Terminal. Richmond Terminal was a holding company—that is, a company that has a controlling interest in other companies but does not own their physical assets. Byzantine in its organization, Richmond Terminal involved plots within plots. Composed of 105 train lines, it had 8,500 miles of track in 1891, 27 executive committees, a $9 million debt, inadequate revenues, and such a tangle of accounting systems that statements of profit and loss had a fictional quality. The early shock waves of the depression of the 1890s knocked the tottering structure over.

The Southern Railway replaced the Richmond Terminal in 1894, embracing most of the components of the old Terminal company. The Southern launched itself by adopting the $375 million financing plan developed by J. P. Morgan and Company, the nation's premier financial banking firm. Perhaps only Morgan's name and financial genius could have built what became a strong, stable company out of the chaos of the Richmond Terminal. The house of Morgan clearly thought highly of its services. It received $750,000 in stock for its work and $100,000 for expenses. Morgan also got effective control for some years over a railroad that extended from New York to New Orleans, from Jacksonville to Memphis and Cincinnati. Before 1900 the Southern began its very profitable career.

But size and the existence of powerful, often distant, sometimes irresponsible owners were not enough to explain the fear and anger railroads often aroused in the South. Railroads provided an essential service. Their customers were uncomfortably dependent on them, and many railroads had a monopolistic relationship with their customers. The opportunity to charge excessive rates was there. Undoubtedly that opportunity was seized. Shippers often asserted that they were defenseless victims of metallic monsters. Of the aggrieved parties, farmers had the best case. Studies suggest that farmers benefited the least from the lower transportation costs railways brought. Farmers operated very close to the margin during those years, so they were extremely sensitive to real and imagined grievances. Farmers repeatedly vented their anger at railroads and railroad officials, especially during hard times. When farm prices fell in the late 1880s, the Southern Farmers Alliance demanded "the most rigid, honest, and just state and national control and supervision of public...transportation." If that did not work, then the Alliance called for public ownership of railroads. In 1892 the political legatees of the Alliance, the Populists, declared cogently: "We believe that the time has come when the railroad corporations will either own the people or the people must own the railroads." Farmers' discontent with railroads during the late nineteenth century helped make railroad rates one of the major political issues of the day. Whether and how to regulate railroads, monetary policy, banking, and the tariff were the most persistent political concerns of the time. The South had a vital stake in each.

Starting in the 1870s, every southern state passed legislation to create a railroad commission. And, as we noted earlier, southerners played leading roles in writing and passing the Interstate Commerce Act of 1887. The act created the first federal regulatory agency, a landmark on the road America took in response to the modern corporate economy.

By 1900 the southern rail system was largely in place. Imposing physical expressions of the desire to transform the southern economy, railroads carried southerners into a world of corporations, captains of finance, and new forms of government support for and regulation of private enterprise. Rail systems allowed or encouraged the development of new areas, wove the South more tightly into national markets, and made the region and its inhabitants more susceptible to the good and bad fortunes of distant, faceless men and economic forces. J. D. Williamson resisted the persuasion and even the pistols of Patrick Calhoun that day in 1889. But bankruptcy got him and his company.

The Richmond Terminal bought out Williamson's Chattanooga, Rome, and Columbus Railroad in 1890. Four years later, the company regained its independence, but then sold out to the Central of Georgia in 1901. The railroads were full of the promise (and some of the reality) of better days and full of dangers (real and imagined) that seemed beyond the ability of individuals to understand or control. The railroad carried southerners into the Gilded Age, if belatedly. Most wanted to go even if they were not sure where the trip would end.

INDUSTRY IN THE NEW SOUTH

"The time was when the South was exclusively agricultural in its pursuits, but the past few years have seen factories spring up all over the section." It was not quite that way. It seldom is. But the editor of the Americus (Georgia) *Recorder* ought to be forgiven his hyperbole. He had succumbed to the exhilaration many southerners understandably felt as the South recovered first from the Civil War and its aftermath and then from the depression of the 1870s and began a period of substantial growth in the 1880s. Moreover, the editor had correctly sensed the emergence of a South very different from its antebellum predecessor. The South had adopted a new course since 1865; it no longer was willing to stake virtually everything on agriculture.

Just as important was the shape that industrial expansion took in the New South. If the basic contours of the New South are to be understood, the fundamental characteristics of its industrialization must be noted and remembered. First, its industry was based primarily on the processing, often through only the first stages, of the raw materials of the region, materials from forests, mines, and farms. Second, such industries typically rely on low-skill, low-wage labor. The work is usually repetitive, exhausting, and sometimes unhealthy and dangerous. Third, resource-processing industries also are usually dispersed geographically. Consequently, while southern industrial development after 1880 did stimulate urbanization, that urbanization usually took the form of small towns and small cities. Last, southern manufacturing firms, especially those that needed large injections of capital, characteristically looked to sources outside the region. There were exceptions, of course. William Gregg, Edwin M. Holt, and Daniel Pratt, for instance, used their large profits from the Civil War to expand their cotton mills in South Carolina, North Carolina, and Alabama, respectively. In fact, much of the postbellum expansion of southern cotton manufacturing was financed within the region. More usual was the experience of Henry Fairchild de Bardeleben. He was an Alabamian and a stereotypical Gilded Age American businessman, given to uttering maxims about "the survival of the fittest." The son-in-law of Daniel Pratt and heir to his fortune, de Bardeleben envisioned an empire of coal and iron in northern Alabama. He, James W. Sloss, and Truman H. Aldrich—known later as the "captains of the Old Guard of Birmingham"—founded the Pratt Coal and Coke Company in

1878. Three years later they sold it, and in 1886 de Bardeleben built the de Bardeleben Coal and Iron Company with the assistance of capital from London and Baltimore. Within five years the Tennessee Coal, Iron, and Railroad Company (TCI) beat de Bardeleben in a financial war and took over his company. In 1907 United States Steel bought out TCI. Such chains of events illustrate the dependent nature of the industry and the economy of the South. Thus some people contend that the South was an economic colony of the North. That contention will be analyzed later.

FOREST PRODUCTS

As they had done since earliest colonial settlement, southern forests provided materials for a variety of products. Pine trees were tapped for resin and burned for a residue of tar. Resin was distilled into turpentine and rosin. Forest products were used in paints, varnishes, medicines, chemicals, industrial processing, and soap- and papermaking. For many years farmers made tar from pine and "turpentined" as subsidiary activities. This form of domestic manufacturing gave way well before 1900 to larger, company-run operations. After that, turpentiners were usually black males whose existence often resembled serfdom or peonage. Also before 1900, North Carolina lost its leadership in the industry, first to South Carolina, then to Florida, which still retains it. The naval stores industry was small in money terms. The value of its products was only $5.9 million in 1880 and $12.3 million in 1900.

Lumbering gained importance after 1800 and overshadowed the naval stores industry. The demand for southern yellow pine exploded when northern white pine became scarce toward the end of the nineteenth century. Chauncey W. Depew, for one, saw the South as "the Bonanza of the future," with "vast forests untouched" and "enormous veins of coal and iron." The prominent New York Republican, chieftain in the Vanderbilt railway system, and favorite on the banquet circuit, declaimed: "Go south, young man."

Many went, especially after Congress opened federally owned lands in the South without restriction and on a cash basis. The Illinois Central ran special trains to Louisiana and Mississippi to accommodate the rush. When a decade of land speculation ended in 1888, almost 5.7 million acres of federal land in southern states had been sold. By then it must have been almost impossible to remember that Congress had originally intended that much of this land should go to former slaves. At the same time, Florida sold Hamilton Disston of Philadelphia 4 million acres for 25 cents an acre. The Florida legislature endorsed railroad grants with such enthusiasm and personal greed that its arithmetic did not add up. Out of a public domain of 15 million acres, the legislature made grants of 22 million acres. Texas was not to be outdone. It granted railroads 32.4 million acres of state lands, along the way squandering that part of the public domain which had been set aside for the benefit of public education. Groups of capitalists, especially from northern states and England, consumed enormous portions—196,000 acres went to some Chicagoans, 2 million acres to one English syndicate, 1.3 million acres of Mississippi's enormously fertile delta land to Phillips, Marshall, and Company of London. "The living embodiment of the Lost Cause," General John B. Gordon, served as broker for this last transaction. Warnings about environmental consequences were dismissed as "immeasurably stupid" while, in the opinion of one expert forester, "probably the most rapid and reckless destruction of forest known to history" took place. Southern forests provided approximately 1.5 billion board feet of yellow pine in 1869, 2.7 billion in 1879, and 9.7 billion in 1899. By 1910 Louisiana, Mississippi, Arkansas, Texas, and North Carolina joined Washington and Oregon as the nation's leading lumber-producing states.

Lumber companies in the South followed the mobile, dispersed, and highly wasteful patterns so long practiced by the industry in the United States. Companies hacked their way through forests in a great arc from the Southeast to the Southwest. By 1916, production in the South rose to 20.5 billion board feet. Lumbering left vast stretches of cut-over land throughout much of the South. Yet by 1892 Gifford Pinchot, later a major figure in the American conservation movement, had begun the first application of scientific forestry in the United States. Working at Biltmore, the estate of George W. Vanderbilt near Asheville, North Carolina, Pinchot set out to demonstrate "the ability to produce favorable money results, while improving the forest. . . . In other words, forester and lumberman must be combined." Pinchot exhibited his North Carolina work at the Columbian Exposition in Chicago in 1894. Four years later the Biltmore Forest School opened, the first of its kind in the South and one of the earliest in the nation. Although the natives called it Vanderbilt's Folly, Biltmore "became a mecca for advocates of scientific forestry and forest preservation."

Timber companies and sawmills offered backbreaking, dangerous, unhealthy, seasonal, low-wage work that usually involved a minimum of skill. Pinchot's crews earned the lordly sum of 90 cents to $1 a day. (Mules earned 75 cents.) Logging and lumber companies usually hired young men, poor white and black, who lived in the available housing—often company-owned, isolated, and crude. Companies also generally owned the stores, virtually the sole source of supply for food and other necessities. Such circumstances invited abuse. So did the fact that half of the highly dependent labor force was black.

Demand for and exploitation of southern hardwoods followed a course comparable to that of southern pines. Much of the hardwood became furniture. Southern furniture manufacturing reached a landmark in 1884 when it established itself at High Point, North Carolina, the future center of southern furniture making. The proximity of raw materials and low-cost labor played a familiar causal role in this development. Another forest-product industry, pulp and paper, did not become significant in the South until after 1920.

METALS AND MINERALS

The southern states possessed a number of important metals, but their utility depended on their profitability. That was determined by the quantity and quality of the minerals, accessibility to adequate, affordable transportation and technology, and market demands. Iron and coal contributed the most by far to southern incomes before 1900. After that, petroleum began to challenge their leadership. Other minerals—phosphates, clays, and salt, for example—played lesser roles.

Almost all the southern states had iron ore, and by 1860 most had small blast furnaces, bloomeries, and forges to convert the ore into pit, cast, and wrought iron. The last could be shaped into a wide range of useful items. In addition, there were rolling mills, rail mills, and naileries. On the eve of the Civil War, southern iron production accounted for 15 percent (125,000 tons) of the nation's total production. The war stimulated rapid expansion of the industry, in particular at the Tredegar Iron Works in Richmond and at ironworks in Selma and Shelby, Alabama. Those operations also attracted Union troops, who made a shambles of the southern iron industry. Tredegar made the most rapid recovery, but the future lay elsewhere.

The southern iron industry shifted to larger, more efficient operations and to western Virginia, eastern Tennessee, and, especially, central Alabama after 1865. The Elyton (Alabama) Land Company declared itself to be in the business of city building in January 1871: "The city to be built...shall be called Birmingham," after Birmingham, England, center of the English iron industry. Other land developers joined in. They, too, knew about the rich iron ore, coal, and limestone deposits in central Alabama, which provided the material basis for "Magic City." An Alabamian remembered that when she first saw the site of Birmingham "there were only two...houses...nothing else. But my husband pointed up the long valley. 'There lies Birmingham,' he said; 'all that is going to be Birmingham some day.' And he spread his arms out to take in the whole country." "Colonel" James R. Powell, president of the Elyton company and first mayor of Birmingham, got the county seat relocated to Birmingham and reportedly got the New York Press Association to meet there before Birmingham was even listed on any map. A surprise awaited the New Yorkers: "Marshes and mud roads everywhere and yellow pine shacks and a box car for a depot, and gamblers and traders all over the globe. A man had to drink a full quart of whiskey before he could see what Powell said was there."

So valuable was the iron and coal region of northern Alabama that it ignited railroad and industrial wars. Struggles to gain rail access to the region shaped Alabama politics from the end of the Civil War throughout much of Reconstruction. The Louisville and Nashville Railroad beat back the Alabama and Chattanooga and emerged as the principal railroad in the region. Then, guided by Albert Fink, one of the masterminds of American railroading, the L&N bought 500,000 acres of central Alabama to become the "great empire builder of the Alabama mineral region."

In 1881 John H. Inman, "a Southern carpetbagger in Wall Street" who was closely associated with the L&N, formed a group that bought the Tennessee Coal and Railroad Company, reorganized it, and renamed it the Tennessee Coal, Iron, and Railroad Company. TCI entered Alabama in 1886 and began buying up deposits of coal and iron, coking facilities, and blast furnaces. By 1891 it had captured first place in the region. Other companies pursued a similar course. By 1900, mergers created four large corporations—Sloss-Sheffield Iron and Steel Company, the Republic Iron and Steel Company, the Woodward Iron Company, and TCI—which dominated ironmaking in central Alabama. Absentee ownership was another sign of the times. More than 95 percent of TCI shares were owned by New Yorkers or New Englanders. Then in 1907 J. P. Morgan arranged for the purchase of TCI by U.S. Steel.

From 1880 to 1900, southern iron production grew from 397,000 tons to nearly 2 million tons, about 20 percent of total national production. Alabama accounted for more than 60 percent of southern production. By 1900 Birmingham was the largest exporter of pig iron in the United States and the third largest in the world. Southern ironmakers enjoyed lower costs, especially for iron ore and coke and labor. In some years TCI had a peculiar advantage in labor costs. Well connected with such leading Tennessee Redeemers as Governor John C. Brown and Arthur S. Colyar, editor of the Nashville *American*, the company got to lease the entire population of the state penitentiary for use in its coal mines. After visiting the mines in 1886, the United States Commissioner of Labor reported: "Wretched surroundings, bad management, appalling death rate. The prison system in all ways atrocious....But the state makes a large profit from its convict labor."

Transportation costs were higher for southern ironmakers than for their northern competitors. Other problems were more serious. Ironmakers in the South confronted weak demand for their products in their region. They also lacked the capital necessary to adopt the latest technology or to expand enough to enjoy fully the economies of scale then achievable. Although TCI began to make steel in 1899, for instance, it did not have the resources to build the facilities that would have allowed it to make steady profits from steelmaking. Only after U.S. Steel took over TCI and made its capital resources available did steelmaking become a major industry in the South.

Before 1860, coal was mined on a considerable scale in the border states of Maryland and Missouri and on a much smaller scale in several southern states. Post–Civil War industrial and urban growth in the United States stimulated demand for bituminous coal, of which southern Appalachia had a vast supply. That demand and the development of adequate transportation made mining in the region economically feasible. The New River coalfield in West Virginia opened when the Chesapeake and Ohio Railroad reached there in 1872. Some ten years later, the rich Pocahontas field along the Virginia–West Virginia border came into production after the Norfolk and Western Railroad penetrated the area. Only after 1900 was intensive coal mining introduced in eastern Tennessee and eastern Kentucky. Coal production in the southern states rose from about 7 million tons in 1880 to 52.8 million tons in 1900, or about one-fifth of the coal produced in the United States. Coal mining companies threw up company towns and hired blacks and whites. Most came from nearby, but some whites were immigrants from Europe. A crazy quilt of racial and ethnic patterns evolved, from segregation to a rough-hewn integration. Generally, though, blacks got the worst jobs and the least pay.

South Carolina enjoyed a short, small boom in minerals. Phosphate mining grew rapidly in that state after 1880, reached its peak in 1890, and began to fade by 1900. By the last year Florida led the nation. It still does. Phosphate mining, however, never was a large industry. South Carolina, for example, earned only $2.9 million from phosphates in 1890; ten years later, those earnings had declined to a little more than $1 million. Thus, while phosphate was important to the economy of part of the South and was critical for agriculture, phosphate did not have the impact that iron ore had on Alabama or that oil was to have on Texas.

Work in phosphate was hazardous, though not so dangerous as coal mining. Workers, most of whom were black, had to clear the land, cut through to the phosphate, dig out the phosphate rock, convert the rock to liquid with water under high pressure, and then dry and process the mineral. Phosphate workers endured the rigors of heat, cold, and humidity and the dangers of chemical dust and emissions of toxic, potentially explosive gases.

Other mineral resources of the southern states became much more significant in the twentieth century. When cheap hydroelectric power became available and reduced the costs of making aluminum, the amount of bauxite being processed increased dramatically. The importance of oil deposits in the southern states was not clear at the turn of the century. Some Texans had drilled for water at Corsicana in 1894 and gotten oil instead. People suspected there was a good deal more oil beneath the surface in Texas, but even oilmen had not imagined the likes of the Spindletop well near Beaumont. As the drill came closer and closer to the black underground lake in January 1901, the driller upped his production estimates. It might do better than the 50 barrels per day he originally predicted. It might reach 75 barrels. Then they struck oil. As a huge geyser sprayed them black, they celebrated a well that would produce 75,000 barrels a day. The year Spindletop came in, Ohio, Pennsylvania, West Virginia, California, and Indiana were the leading oil-producing states, and total oil production in the United States was 69.4 million barrels. By 1910, production in the United States reached 209.6 million barrels, and by 1920, 442.9 million. By that time Texas, California, and Oklahoma led the nation in petroleum output by a wide margin.

Generally, the chemical industry grew little in the South before the middle of the twentieth century. One facet of the industry, however, developed early— patent medicine. Several factors encouraged the growth of the industry: poverty, the state of medical knowledge and practice, and a wide range of life-threatening and debilitating diseases for which there seemed to be no remedies. The all too common poverty of the South increased the hazards of birth, maternity, and childhood and forced people to have poor diets, to work and live in unhealthy and sometimes hazardous places, and to seek medical aid at the lowest cost. Given the state of medical knowledge and practice before 1900, people were probably wise to avoid most doctors and most hospitals. Yet where could they turn for relief from the ravages of tuberculosis, syphilis, typhoid, malaria, scarlet fever, diphtheria, whooping cough, hookworm, influenza and pneumonia, and cardiovascular diseases? In 1900, life expectancy at birth in the United States was 48.7 for white females, 46.6 for white males, 33.5 for nonwhite females, and 32.5 for nonwhite males. Presumably it was lower for all these groups in the South.

Under such circumstances, the promises of miracles from the makers of nostrums found a ready audience, and drug manufacturers spent large sums for advertising to reach that audience. Makers of patent medicines refined the art of consumer persuasion in the process. Newspaper readers could read almost daily about Berry's Creole Tea (naturally, a New Orleans product), "a perfect tonic" that "makes good blood and a beautiful complexion"; Duffy's Pure Malt Whiskey, which "cured" consumption (tuberculosis), depression, bronchitis, general debility, "La Grippe," malaria, colds, and exhaustion and weakness "from whatever causes"; and Dr. Williams's Pink Pills for Pale People. In addition to newspaper advertising, patent medicine companies churned out a flood of calendars and almanacs, sponsored traveling medicine shows, and papered and painted so many buildings, barns, fences, trees, and hillsides with posters and signs that they triggered a movement to save the landscape. No doubt the substantial quantities of alcohol, cocaine, and opium in these compounds helped sales. Many of the same newspapers that ran advertisements for nostrums also ran notices of private sanitariums that claimed they could cure addiction to alcohol, cocaine, and opium.

Such prominent Americans as Robert E. Lee, Ulysses S. Grant, and Mrs. Grover Cleveland endorsed products. A Mrs. L. L. Lindsay testified at length that Wine of Cardui, at $1 a bottle, had rid her of problems associated with menstruation. She also endorsed Thedford's Black Draught. The remedies so helpful to Mrs. Lindsay were the most profitable products of the most successful patent medicine company in the South, the Chattanooga Medicine Company, founded by two Union army veterans after the Civil War.

Farther to the south, Asa Griggs Candler joined the exodus from the farm to Atlanta, where in the 1880s he opened a wholesale and retail drug business and began some drug manufacturing. In 1891 he curtailed his drug business in order to concentrate on a new product: he had just purchased the rights to a newly formulated headache remedy for $2,000. He soon transformed Coca-Cola, a carbonated beverage, into a drink that promised refreshment, not therapy, and laid down an advertising barrage behind the theme "Refreshingly delicious." Candler sold more than 35,000 gallons of Coca-Cola in 1892, a considerable improvement over the 25 gallons his predecessors had sold in 1886. By 1900, more than 370,000 gallons were sold, some as far away as the Pacific states. Forays into the European market had already begun. Such aggressiveness helps explain why the company sold more than 6.5 million gallons of the liquid refresher in 1912.

PROCESSED FARM PRODUCTS

From 1880 to 1900, manufacturing of materials from southern forests and mines grew in output, but it was dwarfed by the output from processing of farm products. Cotton, of course, led the way, followed by tobacco, then rice and sugar.

The location and methods of rice cultivation and processing in the South changed dramatically after 1880. In that year South Carolina and Georgia led Louisiana in the production and processing of rice. Ten years later the situation was almost reversed. Seaman A. Knapp brought his pioneering ideas about agriculture to the South in the late 1880s. The Iowan, best known for the battle he led against the cotton boll weevil, persuaded farmers in southwestern Louisiana to plant field rice, which they irrigated with water from wells and nearby bayous. Field rice had greater resistance to insects and disease than paddy-grown rice. The soil in the Mississippi delta was better for rice than that of the coastal Southeast, and it also allowed the introduction of heavier machinery than could be used in the coastal rice-growing areas. The use of heavy machinery was the most important of several factors in farmers' ability to increase production while reducing costs. This fortuitous combination helps explain the rapidity with which rice production shifted to Louisiana and then to adjacent areas in Texas and Arkansas. By 1900, Louisiana companies cleaned and polished about two-thirds, or $5.7 million of $8.7 million, of the rice grown in the United States.

Louisiana continued its long-held leadership in domestic sugar production, and by 1900 was second only to New York in sugar refining. Demand outstripped supply, however, even though southern sugar output increased from about 130,000 short tons in the 1880s to about 350,000 in 1900. Americans ate about 73 pounds of sugar per person per year. Because more than 80 percent of that sugar came from abroad, where costs were very low, Louisiana sugar growers operated with narrow profit margins. Low sugar prices and rising labor costs forced the growers to invest heavily in machinery, to rely increasingly on the railroads that penetrated the sugar regions after 1880, to search for and practice the best farming methods, and to form a tightly knit growers' association.

Among its several activities, the Louisiana Sugar Planters' Association effectively encouraged agricultural experiment stations and better refining and marketing techniques. Large-scale engine-powered, centrally located sugar milling and refining replaced the older pattern of widely dispersed, horse-powered operations. Around the turn of the century the association lost ground in its efforts to maintain protective tariffs against imported sugar. The annexation of Hawaii and Puerto Rico in 1898 and a 1903 trade treaty with newly independent Cuba meant that Louisiana sugar would face even stiffer competition.

Meat packing, leather making, flour milling, and distilling in the South remained small and localized. But here, as in the processing of several other major farm products, such as dairy products, the output of the Midwest far exceeded that of the South. Georgia and Virginia manufactured a modest number of agricultural implements. Kentucky, however, established itself as the nation's leading producer of bourbon.

TOBACCO MANUFACTURING

The manufacture of tobacco and cotton products had a much greater impact on the South than the processing of any other agricultural product. Americans in

TOBACCO PRODUCTION IN THE SOUTH, 1850–1987 (IN THOUSANDS OF POUNDS)

State	1850	1860	1870	1880	1890	1900	1910
Ala.	165	233	153	452	162	312	91
Ark.	219	990	595	970	955	832	316
Fla.	999	829	157	21	470	1,126	3,506
Ga.	424	919	289	229	264	1,106	1,486
Ky.	55,501	108,127	105,306	171,121	221,880	314,288	398,482
La.	27	40	16	56	47	102	172
Md.	21,407	38,411	15,785	26,082	12,357	24,589	17,845
Miss.	50	159	61	415	62	63	19
Mo.	17,114	25,086	12,320	12,016	9,425	3,042	5,373
N.C.	11,985	32,853	11,150	26,986	36,375	127,503	138,813
S.C.	74	104	35	46	223	19,896	25,583
Tenn.	20,149	43,448	21,465	29,365	36,368	49,158	68,757
Tex.	67	98	60	221	176	550	162
Va.	56,803	123,968	37,086	79,989	48,523	122,885	132,979
W. Va.	Incl. in Va.	Incl. in Va.	2,046	2,296	2,602	3,087	14,356
Totals	184,984	375,265	206,522	350,265	369,889	668,539	807,940

SOURCE: C. L. Gupton, "Tobacco," *The Encyclopedia of Southern History*, David C. Roller and Robert W. Twyman eds. (Baton Rouge, La., 1979), p. 1237; U.S. Bureau of the Census, *Agricultural Statistics, 1981* (Washington, D.C., 1982), p. 99; U.S. Bureau of the Census, *1987 Census of Agriculture* (Washington, D.C., 1987), Vol. I, Table 25, *passim*.

1860 dipped, smoked, and mostly chewed tobacco. Smokers preferred cigars and pipes, in that order. Cigarettes had only recently begun to gain popularity. Southern farmers produced nearly one-half of the more than 434 million pounds of tobacco grown in the country; much of it was exported. Three border states (Kentucky, which alone provided one-fourth of the nation's output, Maryland, and Missouri) and the southern states accounted for 86 percent of the tobacco grown in the United States when Abraham Lincoln went to the White House. National output grew slightly in the next twenty years, but not in the South. There output declined appreciably, as it did in Maryland and Missouri. Kentucky, however, increased its production by 60 percent, a clear indication that burley, a darker, stronger-tasting tobacco that grew well there, still dominated the market.

But a highly significant shift in the kinds of tobacco grown and consumed was occurring. That shift had a major impact on several areas in the South and in the border states and was a critical factor in the development of two major corporations with southern origins, American Tobacco and R. J. Reynolds. The shift had its beginnings in a Dixie version of a true-to-life Horatio Alger story. Reportedly, Union and Confederate troops, quartered in and around the railroad hamlet of Durham, North Carolina, when General Joseph E. Johnston surrendered to General William T. Sherman in 1865, "borrowed" some tobacco from local tobacco farmers and processors. They liked it. When they got home,

TOBACCO PRODUCTION IN THE SOUTH, 1850–1980 (IN THOUSANDS OF POUNDS) (*Cont.*)

1920	1930	1940	1950	1959	1969	1980	1987
2,031	357	296	356	492	815	826	665
267	95	82	34	23	2		
4,474	9,248	20,322	22,536	23,413	24,142	20,343	12,615
10,585	82,364	94,409	102,505	98,308	94,625	110,550	65,722
504,662	376,649	324,518	404,881	335,099	375,549	416,962	336,364
221	81	374	257	74	91	56	15
17,337	21,624	28,209	35,533	32,568	24,771	22,035	13,752
726	5	17		3	1		
4,075	4,549	5,470	5,237	4,295	4,963	5,263	3,654
280,163	454,223	715,616	661,982	654,439	674,932	761,705	478,051
71,193	83,303	118,963	61,263	81,255	129,169	125,450	87,431
112,368	112,237	109,423	127,324	120,653	111,492	111,981	85,716
27	8	3					
102,391	115,826	136,754	124,904	127,706	117,548	106,791	80,583
7,587	5,362	2,166	3,756	2,976	3,109	2,250	2,159
1,118,107	1,265,931	1,556,622	1,550,568	1,481,304	1,561,209	1,684,212	1,166,727

they wanted more, and they wrote back to Durham for the bright leaf tobacco they savored. This inadvertent advertising made tobacco and Durham synonymous.

The William T. Blackwell Company of Durham seized the initiative, especially after Julian Shakespeare Carr joined the firm. Blackwell and Carr produced a quality product with a memorable trademark, Bull Durham (for the Durham bull, a breeding animal noted for its quality in what was then a predominantly rural America). Mechanizing whenever possible, defending its trademark whenever necessary, and pursuing customers whenever and wherever possible, the Blackwell company enjoyed great success. Like other tobacco manufacturers, it had to confront an oversupply of competitors and a lack of built-in demand. (Unlike food or petroleum, as John D. Rockefeller understood, tobacco is not a necessity, though it may seem that way.) Tobacco manufacturers had to persuade people to use tobacco and their particular products. To do so, Blackwell and Carr spent as much as $150,000 annually for advertising in newspapers. They gave clocks to customers, got testimonials from notables, and plastered pictures of the Durham bull throughout the United States and in parts of Europe and Asia. The Blackwell company built "the largest smoking-tobacco factory in the world," a physical expression of the dominance of the company.

Nearby, Washington Duke and his sons, Benjamin and James Buchanan ("Buck") Duke, watched with fascination, envy, and mounting despair. Though their company, W. Duke and Sons, had done well, Buck Duke concluded that the Dukes "faced a stone wall," that they were overmatched by Bull

Durham, and that they had to find a new product. In 1881 they recruited about a hundred cigarette makers from New York, most of whom were European immigrants. Then, three years later, Duke became the first company to use the Bonsack cigarette machine, the first practical machine for manufacturing cigarettes. The Bonsack immediately reduced the cost of production from 80 cents per thousand cigarettes to 30 cents. Within a year, most of the cigarette makers returned to New York. Within two years, Duke's cigarette production jumped 600 percent. Possessed of intense drive, a competitive urge that strained the bonds of civility, and, most important, nearly exclusive control of the Bonsack machine, Buck Duke, along with Ben Duke and J. W. Watts, built an empire. William T. O'Brien, a machinist and mechanical genius in Duke's employ, contributed greatly to the firm's success by perfecting the Bonsack. Duke marketed with fury and flourish. In the late 1880s he spent as much as $800,000 a year on advertising, including packages embellished by pictures of lovely ladies and sponsorship of touring hockey teams that competed on roller skates. Duke's success, however, may have been attributable primarily to the fact that he was the first tobacco manufacturer to adopt the centralized, departmentalized structure of the modern corporation. In 1890 Duke joined its four other major competitors to form the American Tobacco Company, the "cigarette trust." Under the assumption that competition was bad for profits, the American Tobacco Company used the ample capital it amassed by the sale of cigarettes to make itself dominant in the manufacture of all tobacco products except cigars. American Tobacco also benefited from the fact that tobacco was virtually depression-proof. The company thrived during the 1890s despite the severe economic slump of 1893–1897.

Thorough mechanization of cigarmaking did not become possible until after 1920. Accordingly, cigarmaking remained decentralized, carried on by a large number of small companies spread throughout the country. Several cigar factories opened in Tampa in the 1880s, when Spaniards who made cigars in Cuba moved their operations to Florida in order to escape the political and economic unrest that resulted from Cuba's attempts to end Spanish colonial rule. Eager officials in Tampa subsidized these moves. Tampa had a favorable coastal location, recently acquired rail connections, and an expansive vision. But the heralded growth of the town's economy did not occur as rapidly as the heralds claimed it would. Tampa continued to look like the semitropical outpost it was. It had few houses and even fewer businesses, dirt streets, and alligators in the vicinity, some of whom were inclined to take nocturnal strolls through town. Understandably, the town fathers welcomed the cigar companies, even their Cuban workers. In time, Italian workers came, too. Tampa acquired an ethnic and religious diversity that was unusual in the South. That diversity found disharmonious expression on occasion, as when the Spanish-American War started, when labor and management had a series of bitter conflicts, and when native white Protestants tried to impose prohibition on the town. These disturbances did not, however, seriously hinder the rapid rise of Tampa as a cigarmaking center. By 1900 Florida led the South in this industry and ranked

JAMES B. DUKE (Courtesy Duke University Library)

among the top ten states in the country in the production of America's favorite form of tobacco.

Before the 1880s, work in tobacco factories was seasonal; manufacturers usually suspended operations during the winter months. Most of the workers were black males. Before 1865, slaves made up the majority of the work force. White men managed and supervised. Most of the tasks involved hand labor and a good deal of heavy lifting in hot, dirty, dusty workrooms. Sanitary facilities were crude, if they existed. Workers drank out of common ladles from open buckets and barrels. In *The Romance of a Plain Man* the novelist Ellen Glasgow caught the mood and atmosphere of the tobacco factory before it became heavily mechanized. Ben Starr, who worked as a messenger in a factory—doing, his boss said, "what a nigger can't do"—found the factory workroom intimidating.

At first the stagnant fumes of the dry leaf mingling with the odours of so many tightly packed bodies caused me to turn suddenly dizzy, and the rows of shining black faces swam before my eyes in a blur with the brilliantly dyed turbans of the women. Then I gritted my teeth fiercely, the mist cleared, and I listened undisturbed to the melancholy chant which accompanied the rhythmic movements of the lithe brown fingers.

At either end of the room, which covered the entire length and breadth of the building, the windows were shut fast, and on the outside, close against the greenish panes, innumerable flies swarmed like a black curtain. Before the long troughs stretching waist high from wall to wall, hundreds of negroes stood ceaselessly stripping the dry leaves from the stems; and above the soft golden brown piles of tobacco, the blur of color separated into distinct and vivid splashes of red, blue, and orange. Back and forth in the obscurity these brilliantly colored turbans nodded like savage flowers amid a crowd of black faces, in which the eyes alone, very large, wide open, and with gleaming white circles around the pupils, appeared to me to be really alive and human. They were singing as we entered.... And it seemed to me as I stood there, half terrified by the close, hot smells and the savage colors, that something within me stirred and awakened like a secret that I had carried shut up in myself since birth. The music grew louder in my ears, as if I, too, were a part of it, and for the first time I heard clearly the words:—

> "Christ totes de young lambs in his bosom, bosom,
> Christ totes de young lambs in his bosom, bosom,
> Christ totes de young lambs in his bosom, bosom.
> Fa-ther, de ye-ar-ur Jubi-le-e!...
>
> "Christ leads de ole sheep by still watah, watah,
> Christ leads de ole sheep by still watah, watah,
> Christ leads de ole sheep by still watah, watah,
> Fa-ther, de ye-ar-ur Ju-bi-le-e!"

After the Civil War, tobacco manufacturers moved gradually to year-round operations as the industry grew, mechanized, and shifted its emphasis to smoking tobacco and cigarettes. Whites began to seek employment in the formerly black-dominated factories, and serious racial conflicts among workers followed. One such episode may have been the catalyst for the Danville "riot" of 1883. Blacks, however, continued to make up most of the workers in the older portions of the industry, and they filled the heaviest, dirtiest, and lowest-paying positions in the newer portions of the industry.

Clear race and gender patterns marked the cigarette plants as they became highly mechanized. White men supervised, and white men operated most of the newer, more complex machines. White women, most of them single, performed lighter, cleaner tasks. These jobs were highly repetitive, however, and the women were under a lot of pressure because their pay depended on meeting production quotas. Black women, most of whom were also single, had much less desirable tasks, such as stemming tobacco. Management went to considerable lengths to ensure that white female workers conducted themselves "properly" and were protected from sexual harassment. Employers did not show a comparable concern about black female workers. Black men performed menial and often very heavy work around the factories. Blacks and whites, particularly black men and white women, usually worked in different rooms.

Pay rates reflected these race and gender patterns. Wages for all were modest. Workers in North Carolina in 1879 averaged $101.25 for the year. Workers complained, individually and in groups. A skilled white male worker in Durham declared that his wages in 1887 were so small that he and his wife had trouble meeting their expenses. "We are not in as bad circumstances as some others in the locality," one of them said. "We do not expect to look for any heaven to lay up, but we want, when the time comes when one of our family is called away, to be able to go to the furniture store and purchase what we need to bury the dead."

Groups of workers registered protests in Richmond, Petersburg, and Durham in the 1880s and 1890s. The Knights of Labor attracted a following in these areas in the 1880s, and at the end of the 1890s the National Tobacco Workers Union had some success in the same areas. But racial divisions and economic vulnerability undermined unionization efforts and aborted most of the walkouts that occurred. Perhaps, as one longtime black worker believed, scores would be evened by other means. Elviry Magee stemmed and graded tobacco for sixty years in Danville.

> I tell you one thing, I knows tobacco. I knows all de grades an' blends. I knows bright tobacco an' burley tobacco an' Kaintucky tobacco an' all de rest. You 'members Old Man Hughes what built all dese here schools an' horspitals in town? Well, I learnt Mister John how to grade tobacco when he first come in de factory. Yes, Jesus, I give Mister John his start. I'm po' now an' I was po' den but he come to be a rich man. But it didn't do him no good. De Lawd called him away wi' Bright's misery. I believes one reason was cause he didn't pay niggers nothin'. I was his best hand—he say so hisse'f—an' he didn't never pay me no mo'n fifty to sebenty-five cents a day.

Only cigarmaking had escaped the powerful hold of the American Tobacco Company when the Supreme Court dissolved the company in 1911. The attack on the American Tobacco Company was part of the larger war on "trusts" during the Progressive era. "Trusts" was a term loosely applied to various business structures devised to reduce or eliminate competition—pools, trusts, corporations. American Tobacco produced 85 percent of the plug tobacco, 76 percent of the pipe tobacco, and 86 percent of the cigarettes made in the United States. Moreover, it had cartel agreements with major foreign tobacco manufacturers. The nature of tobacco manufacturing lent itself to such a high degree of concentration. The Dukes, then the American Tobacco Company built their power on the control of essential equipment. Virtually exclusive control of the Bonsack cigarette-making machine made a series of connections possible: from high profits to ample company-controlled capital to monopoly to even higher profits. The monopoly came first in cigarette manufacturing, then in most other areas of tobacco manufacture. Great fortunes followed. From 1878 to 1908 the value of the Duke tobacco interests rose from $78,000 to $39 million.

Such success attracted a good deal of attention and vociferous criticism. More than envy accounted for the criticism. The American Tobacco Company attained its heights by means fair and foul. Competing manufacturing firms, wholesalers, and retailers had good reason to complain about the tactics of the American Tobacco Company. Tobacco farmers joined in, blaming the "tobacco trust" for what they believed were low prices for raw tobacco. Scholarship indicates, however, that the farmers may have been the only people in the tobacco business who had no real basis for their complaints against the Dukes and their associates.

Nor was the company helped by its attachment to the noxious weed. Opposition to tobacco had a long history. James I of England issued his *Counterblaste to Tobacco* in 1604, denouncing the "precious stink" as "loathsome to the eye, hatefull to the Nose, harmfull to the braine, dangerous to the Lungs," and a sin. In the 1890s the antitobacco movement revived itself and took particular aim at the cigarette. Centered in areas where bright leaf did not grow, the movement enlisted adults and children in singing, parading, sermonizing, and pamphleteering. City councils passed laws against selling cigarettes to minors and sometimes even to adults. A subsequent momentary decline in cigarette sales worried Buck Duke. But the antitobacco movement found the public no easier to persuade than had James I. Nor until possibly very recently has any antitobacco campaign enjoyed much success.

The attack on the tobacco trust was successful, however, or so it seemed. In 1911 the Supreme Court ordered the dissolution of the American Tobacco Company (and the Standard Oil Company of New Jersey) for being in violation of the Sherman Antitrust Act (1890). When the American Tobacco Company was dissolved by the Court, it was replaced by an oligopoly of companies that continued to dominate the industry. One of those firms, R. J. Reynolds, had an especially prosperous career after 1911.

The Dukes, who remained in control of the now smaller American Tobacco Company, had other interests by this time. They had started to invest in the development of hydroelectric power and in higher education in the South. They also put capital in banking, insurance, railroads, and textiles. Assured that money invested in cotton mills would earn "at the rate of 40% *net profits*," the Dukes built the first of several large cotton mills in North Carolina in 1892.

COTTON MANUFACTURING

The tobacco barons, led in this case by Ben Duke, again demonstrated their sense for finding lucrative opportunities. In doing so, they joined in a cotton-mill boom that had its origins in the late 1860s and reached fever pitch between 1880 and 1905. The number of active spindles rose from 11,898 to 32,266 to 110,000. (The spindle count is the most common, though admittedly crude, way of measuring the size of a textile industry. It is wise to note whether or not spindles are active in order to differentiate between active and idle industrial plants.) Between 1880 and 1900, consumption of raw cotton expanded seven-fold. The value of the southern cotton mills multiplied almost nine times, to a little more than $95 million; the amount of capital invested increased from $11.1 million to $124.6 million; and the number of workers rose from 16,714 to 97,494. These figures actually underestimate the growth in investment and output because they are expressed in current, not constant, dollars. Prices declined steadily and sometimes markedly in these years; consequently, the value of the dollar went up.

Cotton textiles dwarfed other major manufacturing industries in the South. Even when Maryland, West Virginia, and Missouri are included, the iron and steel industry of the South employed only 22,423 people and represented an investment of $44.7 million in 1900. At the same time, the tobacco industry employed a similar number of people and had an investment of $19.3 million.

The United States Census Bureau noted in 1900 that the "growth of the [cotton textile] industry has been remarkably steady..., attended with not a little public excitement,...failures have been a few, and upon the whole the return upon the investment in Southern cotton mills greatly exceeded that upon factories in the North."

Obviously, such growth reflected a substantial and growing demand for the coarse cottons the South manufactured. (Fabrics are calibrated, coarse to fine, according to the number of threads in a given unit of measure. Fine goods require more complex machinery and more skilled labor.) Southern mills made handsome profits while underselling domestic competitors. (High tariffs imposed by Congress prevented the import of fabrics except for very fine goods used only in luxury items.) Southern textile factories even did rather well during the severe depression of the 1890s, when northern textiles and most other industries faltered or collapsed. Southern mills sold most of their product domestically, but some had substantial foreign sales. Sixty percent of the cotton goods exported from the United States in 1900 came from southern factories. That year South Carolina exported over 45 percent of the production of its cotton mills. Government policies designed to expand foreign commerce received vigorous support from southern cotton manufacturers.

While strong, sustained demand was a great stimulant, advantages in critical items kept costs to southern cotton mills markedly lower than those of their older competitors to the north. Southern firms enjoyed a 7 to 8 percent differential in costs of materials and a 25 percent differential in labor costs. Using newer machinery and concentrating on coarse goods, southern mills employed less skilled labor, an especially important consideration in a labor-intensive industry such as textiles. Southern state and local governments also gave new cotton mills tax breaks. But since tax favors represented such a small portion of the costs of starting and running a cotton mill in those days, they were not very important.

Women and children under sixteen years of age made up a greater part of the industry's work force in the South than elsewhere in the country. Factory hands in 1890 worked sixty hours a week for wages that varied from 15 cents to

COTTON TEXTILE INDUSTRY BY REGION, 1880–1900

	Capital invested and value of product			Number of spindles and looms		
	1880	1890	1900	1880	1890	1900
U.S.[a]	$208,280,346	$354,020,843	$467,240,157	10,653,435	14,188,103	19,050,952
	192,090,110	267,981,724	339,200,320	225,759	324,866	455,752
New England	156,754,690	243,153,249	276,089,821	8,632,087	10,836,155	12,891,787
	143,353,030	181,112,453	191,690,913	184,701	250,166	302,018
Middle[b] Atlantic	31,014,759	51,676,249	61,985,519	1,391,164	1,633,722	1,647,251
	29,389,286	40,664,476	48,961,806	27,318	35,074	38,060
Southern	17,375,897	53,827,303	124,596,874	542,048	1,554,000	4,299,988
	16,356,598	41,513,711	95,002,059	11,898	36,266	110,015

Number of wage earners

	1880	1890	1900
U.S.[a] Total	172,544	218,876	274,929
Men, 16+	59,685	88,837	134,354
Women 16+	84,539	106,607	123,709
Under 16	23,320	23,432	39,866
New England, Total	125,779	147,359	162,294
Men, 16+	45,521	63,749	78,217
Women, 16+	62,554	73,445	73,258
Under 16	17,704	10,165	10,819
Middle Atl.,[b] Total	28,118	31,841	34,843
Men, 16+	8,919	11,580	14,473
Women, 16+	13,185	16,240	16,056
Under 16	6,014	4,021	4,314
Southern, Total	16,317	36,415	97,494
Men, 16+	4,633	12,517	40,528
Women, 16+	7,587	15,083	32,528
Under 16	4,097	8,815	24,438

[a]Includes states not in the three regions here.
[b]Includes Maryland.

SOURCE: U.S. Bureau of the Census, 1900, *Manufactures*, Part III (Washington, D.C., 1902), pp. 19–72.

$1.25 a day and averaged 85 cents. The almost all-white work force came from areas close to the mills. Mills limited blacks to the most menial, dirtiest, least desirable jobs. The Graniteville Manufacturing Company of South Carolina, for instance, drew nearly all of its workers from that state, although the company was located only twelve miles from Augusta, Georgia. As Ben Duke explained to a Massachusetts textile executive and as most southern cotton manufacturers knew, there was an "abundance of cheap white labor." More than other factors, cheap labor accounted for the success of the textile industry in the South.

Southern textile companies also took advantage of current technological advances. The ring spindle, the power loom, and the humidifier allowed for greater speed, and the new spindles and looms required less skill on the part of the operators. Northern companies, by contrast, tended to continue to use the older machinery they had already paid for. The savings that southern cotton mills realized from material and labor costs and from advanced technology more than offset disadvantages in transportation and insurance costs, managerial inexperience, and start-up expenses. By 1900 southern textile manufacturers surpassed northern factories in the production of the coarsest fabrics; then they got the upper hand in fine goods after 1920. Northern textiles never recovered.

The size, extent, and rapid growth of the southern textile industry explain why the industry made such a deep imprint on the South and why it shaped the way the South was perceived from within and without. Thus, if we are to understand the South since 1865, we have to understand the southern textile industry and its characteristics. Unlike iron- and steelmaking and most of tobacco manufacturing, textiles were not concentrated organizationally or geographically. Textiles lent themselves not to monopoly or oligopoly but to a scattering of small to medium-sized firms that usually engaged in only one or two stages of manufacture and that were highly competitive. This competitiveness had enormous influence on the way textile companies dealt with financial adversity and with organized labor.

CARRYING LOOM TO MILLS BY CART (Courtesy of Mildred Gevin Andrews, Mercer University Press)

Most southern companies produced yarn and "gray goods," or coarse fabrics. These goods were then shipped elsewhere, usually to the North, for weaving, bleaching, dyeing, printing, and other final processing. Only years later were extensive facilities for these processes developed in the South. The manufacture of textile machinery followed a similar history, and arrived in the South even later. As a result, the textile industry did not have the same "multiplier effect" on the South as it did in the North, where the industry established itself earlier. Southern textiles therefore did not generate a large pool of skilled machinists and mechanics, a basic necessity for more sophisticated industrial growth.

Southern cotton mills generally grew up along the fall line in the piedmont, where the water power the industry initially depended on could be found. Mills sprang up along an arc more than 700 miles long from Danville, Virginia, to eastern Alabama and away from that arc in eastern North Carolina, the midlands of South Carolina, middle and southern Georgia, eastern and middle Tennessee, and Mississippi. The Carolinas, Georgia, and Alabama were the leading textile states in the South; eventually they came to be leaders for the nation. Most of the plants' sites did not afford enough power to support textile factories on the scale of Lowell or Fall River, Massachusetts, or Manchester, New Hampshire. Thus southern cotton mills contributed to the fundamental demographic patterns of the New South—a profusion of villages and small towns, some medium-sized cities, and several large cities. The textile industry also lent a powerful hand to the shift of economic activity and population growth in the South from the coast to the interior.

Unlike other major businesses in the South, such as railroads and iron and steel, southern cotton manufacturing relied heavily on local sources for capital—merchants, bankers, professionals, successful farmers. The relatively small size of textile firms facilitated this strategy. Efforts to raise capital for cotton mills often were cloaked in civic piety. An evangelist reportedly claimed that "the great morality in Salisbury [North Carolina] was to go to work," and that the "establishment of a cotton mill would be the most Christian act his hearers could perform." Chastened business leaders, so the story went, then built a cotton mill. The "cotton mill campaign," as such efforts have been called, took its basic themes from the ideology of the New South: the belief that "industrialization could cure the region's economic ills...that economic development was...a public service to help the region in general and poor whites in particular."

Southern cotton mills did, of course, provide jobs for families that desperately needed them. Children and women filled many of these jobs. As one textile executive said, "There was no thought...in those times [1880 to 1910] with regard to who should work or how many hours they should work." (His "who" did not include blacks.) The cotton mill provided the "instrumentalities" for "men, women, and children...[to] earn a livelihood,...[to obtain] the bare necessities of life, which could be gotten in the cotton mills of that period only by the combined toil of the whole family....Literally, it was a question of 'bread and meat.' " One scholar and New South enthusiast went too far in 1920 when he asserted that "even machinery was wrapped with idealism and devotion." The Wilmington, North Carolina, *Daily Review* came closer to reality in 1881 when it reported that cotton mills in the South averaged profits of 22 percent and then asked, "Where will philanthropy pay better?"

Undoubtedly cotton mill owners and managers felt some personal ties with their workers. The mills may have been closer to the communities where they were located than were other industries. Face-to-face dealings between labor and management were not uncommon. Nor should claims of concern about factory hands be dismissed out of hand. Caution, however, is urged. Provisions for such amenities as schools, health care, and better housing were closely tied to concerns about profits. Mill managers may have felt some sense of *noblesse oblige*, but that did not preclude their adamant opposition to even the least militant labor unions or their willingness to put black labor in positions normally reserved for whites if their white workers overstepped themselves.

Finally, the southern textile industry became noted for the characteristics of its work force, characteristics that reflected the nature of the industry and its particular chronological and geographical contexts. Most work in textiles was machine-tending, which generally required few and readily learned skills. And this was especially the case in southern cotton mills in the late nineteenth century. Textile factories had very few highly skilled positions, such as mechanic, and they offered little prospect for promotion or for significant improvements in income and status. Cotton mills in the postbellum South relied heavily on women and children. Only about 1900 did male workers begin to outnumber female workers. At the same time, one-fourth of the factory hands were less than sixteen years old. Most employees worked in accordance with the family wage system. Working as families, they earned more than they could on farms, virtually the only other significant occupational alternative open to whites in the Southeast for many years after the Civil War. Landless farmers faced especially poor prospects in agriculture. If people had not made better money in cotton mills than on farms, they would not have gone to the mills. They went, and in large numbers, for many years. For a family with a minuscule income and a preponderance of females, cotton mills had a particular attraction. The harsh physical requirements of agricultural work limited the value of females as farm labor. Nor could low-income white women turn easily to domestic work, which was thought to be appropriate for black women only. It also paid wretchedly. Only after the South became increasingly urbanized was there much demand for white women to work in offices and in retail stores.

Southern textile workers lived in a remarkably segregated world. They usually lived in company houses, often shopped in company stores, and frequently worshiped in churches built and maintained by the mills. Far more than most southerners at the time, mill workers worked and lived in a white world. Blacks were scarcer in a cotton mill than in any other industrial workplace in the South, and when they were allowed to live in a mill village, they were restricted to the most meager dwellings at the edge of the settlement. The textile industry

CHILD LABOR IN A COTTON MILL (Photo by Lewis Hine. George Eastman House Collection.)

in the South had even fewer immigrants among its workers than other southern industries had, and the others had very few. Thus the cotton mills reinforced a long-standing pattern: southern whites were native-born Anglo-Saxons.

But cotton mill hands were not safe from vicious pejoratives in their white sanctuaries. Their contemporaries labeled them "lintheads" and "mill hands." More polite circles preferred "mill people." These terms were fraught with meaning and innuendo. "Linthead" was an Industrial Age colloquialism for "poor white," that elusive label which meant anything from "that alleged Caucasian degenerate no-good who hasn't got any gumption" to "good folks who fell on hard times through no fault of their own." "Linthead" also suggested the existence of an industrial underclass. The term promised hoped-for social distance. "Lintheads" were what many people thought of when they thought of industrial workers in the South. Finally, the label stigmatized a large number of human beings who deserved much better.

Mill workers were not lumps of clay waiting passively to be molded by mill owners. Workers had a substantial role in shaping their work lives and even greater roles in creating and shaping the mill villages in which they lived. Workers restrained management prerogatives by demanding racial segregation in the mill and the village, by slowing the pace of work in the mill, by absenting themselves from work for limited periods of time, and by leaving work altogether. Mills had high absentee and turnover rates, especially when the industry was shorthanded. Workers also registered their dissent by walkouts, strikes, and occasional efforts at unionization. Despite intrusions by management, workers generally controlled their own churches and created their own forms of recreation. Some workers showed their independence by joining holiness and Pentecostal churches. Connected by kinship, workers often policed the life of the village according to their own standards. Older workers set and enforced the rules of dating and courtship. Women practiced folk medicine, meeting medical needs. Some men became noted as musicians, others as athletes on mill baseball and basketball teams. Women carried particularly heavy burdens: they worked outside the home even while they functioned as wife, mother, and homemaker. By 1900 the southern cotton textile industry had grown so large that one long mill village ran along the southern piedmont from southern Virginia to northern Alabama. It was a world that was more firmly shaped by its inhabitants than the epithet "linthead" suggested.

"Linthead" did, however, suggest fierce hate and its opposite, elemental fear. The great dread of several generations of southern whites was that, like others before them, they might have to go to the mills, that their relatives and friends might quit speaking to them, that their children might be physically and verbally abused in school and on the streets, that they might become objects of derision and condescension in local stores and at church. Not much stood between many people and the mills. Failure in farming, a clear and seemingly always present danger for too many people in the New South, often meant going to the cotton mills.

Southerners developed a second, smaller but important industry based on the processing of cotton. Cottonseed mills ground the once neglected seed into cottonseed oil, which was used for salad oils, lard, margarine, and soap, and into meal, which made an excellent fertilizer and feed for cattle. Paper companies used the husks from the seed in fine grades of paper. Between 1880 and 1900 the number of cottonseed mills more than doubled, to about 300 companies with an output worth $30 million. Thus cotton provided the raw material for the New South's largest and most important manufacturing industry, textiles, and for an important smaller industry, cottonseed milling.

URBANIZATION IN THE NEW SOUTH

Cotton also powerfully influenced the contours of urbanization in the New South. Short-staple cotton could be and was grown over an enormous area that ran from Virginia to Oklahoma and covered more than 400,000 square miles. The more than 10 million bales of cotton harvested in 1900, for instance, had to be ginned to separate the seed from the fiber; then the seed was crushed at mills while the fiber was compressed into bales of 500 pounds each, weighed, tested for quality, stored, sold, and shipped and perhaps sold, shipped, and stored several more times. Banks, brokerage houses, and merchants provided the financing required for these processes; others sold insurance to buffer the risks involved in these complex, often lengthy transactions.

The people who provided these services clustered first at sea and river ports, then more and more along the network of rails that covered the cotton belt as the southern rail system expanded rapidly in the late nineteenth century. These clusters followed a stair-step pattern of small towns to large towns to small cities to large cities. Logically, metropolises came next. But in 1900 the South had only one urban center of those dimensions, New Orleans. These clusters grew rapidly after 1880. The number of urban places in the South went from 119 in 1880 to 320 in 1900, four-fifths of which had fewer than 10,000 people. Thus urbanization patterns in the South reflected changes in agriculture and the growth of rail systems more than industrialization. Again cotton demonstrated its power to mold the South.

Urban growth occurred more in the interior than at the once more populous seaports, at Richmond, Danville, Greensboro, Charlotte, Columbia, Atlanta, Nashville, Dallas, and Houston rather than at Wilmington, Charleston, Savannah, Mobile, or New Orleans. Norfolk was the most important exception. Most southern cities and towns continued their primary functions of serving commercial, legal, and governmental needs. Few relied heavily on manufacturing for jobs and incomes. Birmingham provided the most notable exception here. Manufacturing did dominate some smaller cities: tobacco in Durham and Winston after the center of tobacco manufacturing shifted from Richmond; cotton mills in Gastonia, Greenville, Spartanburg, Macon, Columbus; furniture in High Point; cigars in Tampa; and iron in Chattanooga and Birmingham's sister towns of Anniston, Bessemer, Gadsden, and Sheffield.

Urbanization provides a convenient device to measure the degree to which the South, a generation after its massive defeat and the demise of slavery, had begun to resemble the rest of the United States and yet remained distinctive. Urban areas in the South differed from those in the rest of the country in that they were fewer and smaller and had fewer assets. Southern urban areas, even the larger ones, had lower tax rates, lower public debts, and hence fewer services than those elsewhere in the nation. No southern city over 25,000, a Bureau of the Census study found, had a per capita tax levy in 1902 above the national average of $12.89; most were well below the average. Only a few southern cities exceeded the national average for debt per capita. Relatively lower per capita incomes explained most of these differentials. Tightfistedness and the dominance of businessmen may have been factors, too.

Southern towns and cities had made some effort to provide most, if not all, services expected or required of cities at that time: water, sanitation, street improvements, sewer systems, transportation, police and fire protection, schools, some health services, and, in times of economic stress, a modicum of public assistance for the most needy. In the South, as elsewhere in the country, urban communities learned some critical lessons between 1880 and 1900. Firemen and policemen, for example, had to be paid and trained if they were to provide adequate protection, and that protection would be better if they were depoliticized. Unregulated, privately owned utility companies often delivered water, gas (made from coal), electricity, and transportation erratically and expensively. Epidemics threatened the lives of all citizens, not just the less fortunate, and cast shadows over the reputations of communities as places to live or invest. Some learned slowly. Only after yellow fever took 400 lives in New Orleans in the late 1890s did the city take over the defunct sewerage company and start laying sewer pipe. By 1900, southern urban leaders lent strong support to improvement of a wide range of services either through direct government action, such as municipal ownership of services and utilities, or through government regulation of privately owned agencies. Their concern also took the form of greater attention to public schools; they helped establish the first publicly financed high schools in the south. They also encouraged the development of urban parks. Thus these leaders formed the vanguard of Progressivism and its kin, professionalism and bureaucracy, in the South.

Much remained to be done, however. In 1902 a federal census of American cities revealed that Memphis had 17 miles of paved roads and 140 unpaved miles; Atlanta, 63 and 137, respectively. New Orleans had paved only 200 of its 700 miles of roads. Business districts and the better residential areas received the great majority of these improvements. Atlanta called itself "the Chicago of the South" but in 1903 it had only 96,550 people in 11 square miles whereas Chicago had nearly 2 million in 180 square miles. Chicago's financial institutions cleared nearly $7 billion in 1900 while Atlanta's cleared only $96.4 million.

Streetcars, most of which were electrically powered by 1900, did reach the majority of the citizenry. Richmond was the first American city to adopt the electric streetcar, a device that facilitated the evolution of central business districts and the commercial wonder of the age, the department store. Streetcars also hastened the emergence of a residential pattern deeply etched by class and race, and they hurried the growth of suburbs and the extension of the distance between work and residence.

Southern towns and cities had more blacks and fewer foreign-born residents than others in the United States. The Irish had an important political role in such places as Savannah, Charleston, and Memphis. Jewish merchants figured prominently in a number of southern communities. Small enclaves of recently arrived Greeks and Lebanese could be found in many cities and towns. Immigrants from Italy and Cuba left their mark on New Orleans and Tampa, as Mexican-Americans were beginning to do in the Southwest. But no southern city had the variety or numbers of immigrants to be found in most northern cities in those years. The so-called new immigration—the large wave of immigrants from eastern and southern Europe which came between 1880 and World War I—largely by-passed the South. Thus the South remained less ethnically and religiously diverse than the rest of the country.

The proportion of blacks in southern towns and cities varied from less than 10 percent in Houston to more than 50 percent in Charleston and Savannah, averaging about 25 percent. The proportion of blacks did not exceed 5 percent in any city outside the South or in the southern border states, save for Washington (31.1) and Indianapolis (9.4). Southern white urbanites believed that it was of critical importance to control the black populace, more critical than ever now that slavery was ended. Southern towns and cities led the way in the evolution of black-white relations in the South. Racial segregation, with its elaborate edifice of laws, customs, and taboos, had its origins in the urban South. Ironically, racial segregation often represented an advance for blacks. In numerous instances they were admitted on a segregated basis to places where previously they had been excluded altogether.

Southern cities thus formed the vanguard for the development of the South's rigid caste system and the Progressive movement in the region. Southern cities also provided a number of major political figures during the era. Perhaps the most noteworthy were Hoke Smith of Atlanta, governor, senator, and secretary of the interior; Colonel Edward M. House of Houston, a close adviser to Woodrow Wilson; and Josephus Daniels of Raleigh, North Carolina, prominent newspaper editor and secretary of the navy. City-based editors—Francis W. Dawson, Henry Grady, Richard H. Edmonds, and Henry Watterson—played prominent roles in the formation of public opinion. Urbanization went arm in arm with the New South creed. Thus southern urbanites still had more influence on the South than their numbers warranted. Though only a small percentage of southerners lived in urban areas, city-based leaders had and would continue to have a disproportionate voice in the shaping of the South.

A DIFFERENT SOUTH:
AT THE TURN OF THE CENTURY

Thirty-five years after the guns of the Civil War fell silent and twenty years after the longest depression in American history, that of the 1870s, distinctive outlines of a different South had appeared. It was not the New South envisioned by the New South evangels—not yet, anyway—and it was not the antebellum plantation- and slave-based South, obviously, or simply an agrarian, racially divided society with a commercial fringe and a scattering of towns and villages suspended in rustic equilibrium. Though much of the plantation world of the antebellum South remained, it was receding. In its place was a town world or sometimes a city world that was closely tied to a farm world, but that increasingly distanced itself from the farm world.

Some figures do, however, suggest that the changes that had taken place were minimal. Six in ten gainfully employed southerners earned their living from farming, about one in ten from manufacturing. These figures differ significantly from those elsewhere in the country. In 1900, according to the federal census, about 40 percent of Americans lived in urban areas. In the north Atlantic division of the census (Maine, Vermont, Massachusetts, Connecticut, Rhode Island, New York, New Jersey, and Pennsylvania) 68.2 percent of the population lived in urban areas, 35.8 percent in cities of more than 100,000. In the north-central division (Ohio, Indiana, Illinois, Michigan, Wisconsin, Minnesota, Iowa, Missouri, North Dakota, South Dakota, Nebraska, and Kansas) 38.5 percent lived in urban areas, and in the western division (Montana, Idaho, Wyoming, Colorado, New Mexico, Arizona, Utah, Nevada, Washington, Oregon, and California), 40.6 percent. In the south-central division (Kentucky, Tennessee, Alabama, Mississippi, Arkansas, Louisiana, Texas, Oklahoma, and the Indian Territory), by contrast, only 15.5 percent lived in urban areas, and in the south Atlantic division (West Virginia, Virginia, North Carolina, South Carolina, Georgia, Florida, but not Maryland, Delaware, or the District of Columbia), 21.4 percent. These census divisions differed markedly in the proportions of their populations in agriculture and manufacturing.

Cotton was still king; it still had a pervasive, elemental impact on the lives of southerners from Virginia to Texas. Despite considerable effort, the proportion of capital invested in manufacturing still hovered around 11 percent, where it had been for four decades. Southerners also remained overwhelmingly rural. Only Louisiana had as much as 25 percent of its population in urban areas. (Urban, according to the federal census, was any political subdivision of a county with as many as 2,500 souls.) Mississippi, Arkansas, and even North Carolina, one of the South's proudest examples of industrial growth, had less than 10 percent. Finally, in per capita income the South still trailed the nation by about 50 percent, a margin that had not changed in twenty years.

But the South was hardly standing still. From 1880 to 1900 the American economy grew at an extraordinary rate, and the South kept pace with that growth even though it remained behind. The South held its own, for instance, in the growth of per capita income, in investment in industry, and in urban growth. The extension and consolidation of the southern rail system and the emergence of the cotton textile, iron and steel, tobacco, forest products, and coal industries clearly were benchmarks of a different South. Petroleum was only beginning to make its impact. Southern urbanites were forces for change far beyond their numbers and the attainments of their cities. Increasing numbers of southerners, like other Americans, were becoming part of an industrial work force. By 1900 more than 343,000 southerners, many of whom had not yet seen their sixteenth birthday, tended machines in factories or worked in mines and forests. They entered a world where machines increasingly dictated the pace and location of work, where time was measured in minutes and hours rather than from sunup to sundown, where places of work and residence were increasingly distant, and where, most important, they had less individual autonomy on the job than they had had on the farm.

Finally, the South of 1900 was distinguished by more than rails, factories, mines, and growing cities. It was distinguished also by Jim Crow, and by the scars of the Populist upheaval and challenge to the New South. The South that evolved by 1900 had to pass through the cauldron of the 1890s.

20

Shaking the Foundations

The 1890s

❖

The crowd and the dignitaries gathered and waited. Promptly at 10 A.M. on September 18, 1895, President Grover Cleveland pushed an electric signal at Buzzard's Bay, Massachusetts, and the Cotton States and International Exposition opened at Atlanta. Then the president turned to more pressing business, a national financial and economic crisis.

The crowd in Atlanta settled back for a reading of "The Exposition Ode" and the main event of the day, the inaugural address by Judge Emory Speer, who had been an Independent Democrat in the 1870s but had since become a regular Democrat with ties to leaders in Atlanta. Speer's oration was appropriately roseate, reflecting the perspective of the Gilded Age urban boosters who sponsored such expositions. Predictably, Speer looked out and saw progress at every hand, and he poured syrupy praise over all the exhibitors.

But Speer's speech deserves serious attention if for no other reason than that it reflected the times and setting, and consequently provides some significant insights into the American South at the turn of the century. Memories of the Civil War and its aftermath lingered. Sectionalism was very much alive. Accordingly, Speer paid particular attention to sectional reconciliation. He touched lightly on Reconstruction, praised the generosity of the North to the defeated South, applauded the demise of slavery (a "hindrance" to progress in the South), and proclaimed that Confederate veterans would unite with Union veterans to fight if the nation went to war. He declared that "the so-called 'negro question' does not exist," that without resorting to force, whites, secure in this Anglo-Saxon stronghold, were firmly in control of the South. In fact, he gave special stress to Anglo-Saxonism, a form of nativism that flourished at the time almost everywhere in the United States. The desire for sectional harmony, however, did not prevent Speer from pointedly asserting that blacks had better job opportunities in the South than in the North. The judge advocated industrial education for blacks, a theme that Booker T. Washington, president of the Tuskegee Institute in Alabama, expounded earlier in the day. Washington's speech later became famous as "The Atlanta Compromise."

The judge claimed to see things that the New South evangels had preached: thriving commerce in cities and towns, new factories, and a diversified agriculture with burgeoning ranks of farmers who tilled their own land. With respect to commerce and industry, his vision was accurate if somewhat rose-tinted. With respect to agriculture, his vision was seriously blurred. Even the enormous cotton production he proudly advertised was not necessarily a cause for celebration. The vast sea of white fiber that covered much of the South suggested a dangerous overdependence on cotton. And the dangers of that dependency were painfully obvious in much of the South even as Speer spoke.

For the moment, however, the crowd had other things on its mind. It dispersed after the judge ended his oration on what by 1895 had become a standard note in the South: he thanked God for preventing the permanent division of the United States into North and South. The crowd was the first of the more than 1.3 million people to visit the displays sent by cities, states, nations, and associations and to amuse themselves on the midway. Visitors to the exposition could even examine a model jail, which had a gallows that could be "ready at the touch of a button" and a mobproof room. The model jail, unfortunately, was all too relevant for its day.

At the presidential retreat on the coast of Massachusetts, there would have been little tolerance for gallows humor or humor of any kind. The president and his closest advisers faced a grim prospect. In the midst of what was then the worst depression in American history, the federal government appeared to be running out of gold reserves. Since it was widely believed that the government had to have at least a $100 million in gold in reserve if the nation's commercial system was to function, the depletion of the reserve represented a crisis. Working closely and quickly with major bankers, the Cleveland administration eventually resolved the crisis over gold. It could not, however, end the depression. Before the economy recovered, the very foundations of the postbellum South shook. More than a few of the people who reflected on the Cotton States Exposition may have wondered if it symbolized dreams more than realities.

Judge Speer had in fact hinted that his generally happy portrait of the South was distorted. Only the least informed would not have understood what he meant when he acknowledged that "of course there have been seasons of great political excitement when even good men lose the tolerance and mental equipoise which characterizes the majority." Great political excitement indeed swept the South in the 1890s, and economic distress lay at the root of the turmoil. Odes to the New South certainly seemed misguided.

THE DEPRESSION OF THE 1890S

The depression of the 1890s was the worst economic crisis in American history, save for the Great Depression. The economy faltered in early 1893, then began a sharp twelve-month decline in June of that year. Conditions improved mark-edly from June 1894 to December 1895, when a second sharp decline of about twelve months began. Although general prosperity returned by 1898, full re-covery did not come until 1901–1902. The double-cycle depression of the 1890s took a heavy toll. Gross national product fell as much as 10 percent. More than 550 financial institutions closed their doors in 1893 alone; of the 158 national banks that failed, 153 were in the South and West. The rate of business failures in the South exceeded the national average by a wide margin. With the collapse of the byzantine Richmond Terminal, no trunk line in the southern states re-mained solvent. Among manufacturing industries in the South, cotton textiles alone prospered, and even textiles faltered during the economic crisis. The famed "mill boom" made its mark: between 1890 and 1900, the capital invested in southern cotton mills increased 131 percent, the number of plants 67 percent, and the number of spindles more than 100 percent. Most of that vigorous growth, however, occurred at the beginning and the end of the decade. In the middle of the decade, wages declined and cotton mill workers were not fully employed.

Still, cotton mill workers in the South were more fortunate than most work-ers during the depression. Nationwide, unemployment reached 20 percent of the work force, or 3 million people. Distress spilled over into labor disputes, which were not limited to the more industrialized North. The Pullman strike of 1894, which began in Chicago and had its greatest effect in the North and West, riveted public attention at the time and has sustained historians' interest since. Richard H. Edmonds gloated in his *Manufacturer's Record*, "The South has for-tunately demonstrated its freedom from labor riots and from anarchistic teach-ings." Actually, several months before Pullman, Alabama coal miners joined a national soft coal strike. They formed the nucleus of the more than 7,500 Ala-bamians who walked off their jobs that year. Black and white miners jointly confronted hostile mine owners, local law officers, troops sent in by the gover-nor of Alabama, Pinkerton detectives, labor spies, and blacks who were sent in as strikebreakers. Some of these groups, however, may have been sympathetic to the strikers. The strike of the Alabama coal miners became entangled with a bitter state election and with the Pullman strike when Birmingham railroaders joined forces with Eugene V. Debs's American Railway Union. In late August 1894 the Alabama strikers acknowledged defeat and returned to work. At the same time, labor unrest broke out among miners in Virginia. Then, in October, conflicts that began on the wharves of New Orleans led to riots, several deaths, and considerable property damage. Contrary to the biracial character of the New Orleans general strike of 1892, probably the first general strike in Ameri-can history, blacks opposed whites in New Orleans in 1894. Considerable num-bers of workers walked out that year in Georgia, Florida, and Texas; in Ken-tucky, part of the border South, 27,000 workers struck.

But the depression of the 1890s had its greatest impact in the South on farm-ers and their families. Two in three southerners earned their living in agricul-ture, and the majority of those farmers relied on cotton for a cash crop. Declining cotton prices thus had an especially devastating effect. Average at-the-farm prices for cotton fell from 8.4 cents per pound in 1892 to as low as 4.6 cents in 1894—well below what most farmers calculated was the break-even price of 10 cents a pound. At the New Orleans Cotton Exchange, one of the nation's largest, reported prices fell to fifty-year lows. A Louisianan worried that "if there is nothing done to alleviate the suffering among the people, . . . we will have a revolution." A Kentuckian claimed, "We have reached the stage where slow, reasoned arguments cannot any longer affect us. . . . It is a question of bread and meat, and we are ready to fight."

Nature compounded the difficulties. Floods in Mississippi in the early 1890s drove thousands of people from their homes and left many with virtually nothing to eat, destroyed livestock, and left hundreds of acres unusable for years. Then there was too little water. In 1895 and 1896, drought withered crops in Louisiana, Texas, Arkansas, and Mississippi. The winter of 1894–1895 brought the great freeze, which devastated Florida orange growers and caused many to suffer.

Southern farmers created their own storms in the 1890s. More than 3 million of them joined either the Southern Farmers' Alliance or the Colored Farmers' Alliance.* Many of them later swelled the ranks of the Populists, to make the People's party the second most powerful third party in American history. The Populists contributed to and reflected the political upheaval of the decade,

---

*The official name of the Southern Farmers' Alliance was the National Farmers' Alliance and Industrial Union. But the more conventional name, Southern Farmers' Alliance, better reflects the origins and membership of the organization.

BLACK SHARECROPPER HOUSE, 1890s (Courtesy, Georgia Department of Archives and History)

which included two major Republican defeats, victories and then massive defeats for the Democrats, and finally, sweeping Republican triumphs that made the Republicans the dominant party in America for more than three decades. Beaten back in national politics, the Democrats retreated to several strongholds, chief of which was the South. Within the South, the Democrats, "the party of the white man," became even more secure than they had been in 1890. The party, however, underwent major internal changes during the decade. Amid the upheaval of the 1890s, the place of blacks in the South had become at least temporarily less certain than before. But by 1900 Jim Crow was in place, well defined, strongly supported by whites, and, from all appearances, permanent. Thus, though the upheaval of the 1890s ended even before the decade did, the damage done by that upheaval still affected life in the South long afterward.

That there was political turmoil in the South in the 1890s and that it had its origins and base in the rural areas of the region was hardly surprising. That was where most southerners lived and worked, and southern agriculture was in trouble. Too many farmers found that agriculture provided them only a sparse living. Then the depression came. That cotton farmers faced especially desperate times had particular significance, politically and otherwise. They numbered in the thousands and dwelled in all the states of the South, though in small numbers in Virginia and Florida. When their desperation became intense anger and was channeled into agitation and politics, they became a major force in southern and national politics.

Cotton farm families had much to be distressed about. They worked hard and often earned little more than subsistence. Effort did not lead to success. Instead, cotton prices fell, debts mounted, and tenancy grew. By contrast, the railroads, banks, and the army of middlemen who serviced agriculture seemed to thrive. Even the weather appeared to conspire against men and women of the soil. And the boll weevil was coming. It crossed from Mexico to Texas in the early 1890s. Like many other farmers, thousands of cotton growers felt victimized.

By 1890 American agriculture had become a highly complex, commercialized business in which distant forces and persons seemed to control the destinies of thousands. Cotton farmers sold their product for cash at prices determined by the world market. They purchased much, sometimes all, that they ate, as well as manufactured goods, including much of their limited wardrobe; they bought seed, fertilizer, implements, workstock, and livestock; and they made payments on their debts. In sum, like the vast majority of American farmers, they were not self-sufficient. Indeed, farmers in the United States and in much of the rest of the world shared the experience of moving from self-sufficiency (or at least minimal dependence on a cash crop) to commercialized agriculture.

"What a growing part of agriculture all over the world had in common," the English historian E. J. Hobsbawm has written,

> was subjection to the industrial world economy. Its demands multiplied the commercial market for agricultural products—mostly foodstuffs and the raw materials of

the textile industry, as well as some industrial crops of lesser importance—both domestically, through the rapid growth of cities, and internationally. Its technology made it possible to bring hitherto unexploitable regions effectively within the range of the world market by means of the railway and the steamer. The social convulsions which followed the transfer of agriculture to a capitalist, or at least a large-scale commercialized pattern, loosened the traditional ties of men to the land of their forefathers, especially when they found they owned none of it, or too little to maintain their families. At the same time the insatiable demand of new industries and urban occupations for labor, the growing gap between the backward and "dark" country and the advancing city and industrial settlement, attracted them away.

Luke Wadkins experienced these macrocosmic changes on a microcosmic level, at the farm he owned in Georgia's upper piedmont. Wadkins moved from near self-sufficiency to commercialized agriculture between 1860 and 1880. The Wadkins family (the sole source of labor on the farm) grew enough grain, tobacco, vegetables, and cotton (one bale) in 1860 to supply their needs and have something left over for barter or cash exchange. Twenty years later, Wadkins had a farm of ninety acres (worth about $400), of which twenty were in cotton, which produced nine bales. The money value of the cotton and other products of the farm—its *annual* product—was $369. Cash earnings, primarily from cotton, were now important, since the Wadkinses no longer produced adequate provisions for themselves. Also Wadkins had to pay his $131 fertilizer bill and make payments on the credit he had received from merchants.

Wadkins was not unusual. Rupert Vance, a pioneer student of the rural South, concluded that the *average annual gross income* from twenty acres of cotton was (in constant dollars) $472 in 1880, $304 in 1890, and $332 in 1900. Vance and others also found that at the same time the proportion of farms in the cotton states owned by the people who farmed them shrank from 61 percent to 48 percent. "The mortgage," a Georgia farmer wrote, "stayed forever." Or until the bank foreclosed it.

Naturally, understandably, cotton farmers sought relief and redress, and they found many allies within and without the South. Like Americans before them, these dissidents resorted to voluntary associations and pressure groups, then to politics. They had substantial precedent when they did so. In fact, even before the depression of the 1890s had started, more than a million southern farmers had joined the Alliance movement, one of the largest grass-roots movements in American history.

PRELUDE TO THE ALLIANCE MOVEMENT

The 1870s provided the lineal antecedents for the Alliance movement and then the Populist party: the Grange and the Greenbackers. The Grange, or the Order of the Patrons of Husbandry, was the largest and best known of these organizations, and is the only one that still exists. Founded in 1867 by Oliver H. Kelley, an agent of the U.S. Department of Agriculture, the Grange reached its greatest strength in the mid-1870s, then faded. In 1875 it claimed 850,000 members, 350,000 of them in the South.

Convinced that improvement of farm life required better knowledge and more training, the Grange gave particular stress to informal and formal education. These efforts led to lasting institutions in the South: the Agricultural and Mechanical College of Louisiana, now part of Louisiana State University; Mississippi State University; and Texas Agricultural and Mechanical University.

The Grangers addressed themselves to other needs. Local Granges provided social opportunities for farm families—meetings, picnics, barbecues, and the like. Deliberately copying the Masons, the Grange had a secret, elaborate ritual. Unlike the Masons, they welcomed women as members (though not as officers), and some played important parts in the Grange. Some Granges organized buying and selling cooperatives or hired agents to run them. Among the southern states, Arkansas, Tennessee, Louisiana, and Mississippi had the strongest cooperatives.

Regional concerns and preoccupations shaped the Grange in the South. Only whites could join. Councils of Laborers were created for blacks. The separation and names of the councils spoke for themselves and pointed to two of the persistent problems faced by farm groups in the South. First, could the all-important color line be maintained without fatal divisions in the ranks of farmers? Second, did farm groups include landed and landless farmers, farmers with ample means and those without? Which farmers should or could organizations represent? Grangers in the South had a very particular form of uplift in mind when they founded Councils of Laborers. A leading student of farm movements in the South concluded that the Grangers intended "to make the Negro a reliable farm hand, trusty, stable, and industrious." Coincidentally, the Grangers in the South also wanted publicly funded efforts to attract European immigrants in order to lessen their dependence on black labor and to reduce the potential political power of blacks. The Grange avoided one problem that later unsettled farm organizations in the South: it did not engage in partisan politics and thus did not challenge the primacy of the Democrats.

The Patrons of Husbandry in the South took up other regional causes. They lent support to efforts to obtain a southern transcontinental railway. They pleaded for greater diversity in farming and less dependence on cotton, and got involved in abortive attempts to limit cotton production. They lobbied for refunds of the federal tax imposed on cotton immediately after the Civil War, and they pressed for the repeal of the 10 percent federal levy on banknotes issued by state-chartered banks. The state banks, it was hoped, would lower interest rates and make loans more readily available.

Unlike Grangers elsewhere, those in the South did not become heavily involved in efforts to pass railroad regulatory legislation. That issue may have been preempted by the regulatory legislation passed by the Redeemer governments in the 1870s. Thus the legacy of the Grange in the South did not include anything comparable to the widely known, landmark Granger regulatory laws that were enacted in the Midwest in the 1870s. The Grange in the South did, however, provide a legacy on which other farm groups would build. The Grange might have been stronger and accomplished more in the South if Reconstruction and the depression of the 1870s had not imposed themselves. Restoring and maintaining native white political dominance took precedence in most of the southern states in the 1870s. The depression hurt Grange cooperatives and left farmers with even less money to pay the Grange's modest dues. Then currency contraction and deflation—monetary issues that the Grange had largely avoided—became major concerns in the late 1870s and would remain powerful forces in American politics for years to come.

These two monetary issues became ensnarled with partisan politics and sectionalism and with conflicts between interest groups. The Alliance movement, the Populists, the Democrats, and the Republicans became entangled in that snarl. The principal unknotting finally came in two major steps: the Gold Standard Act of 1898 and the Owen-Glass Act, which created the Federal Reserve System, in 1913.

The monetary issues had their roots in the Civil War. In order to ease an acute currency shortage in 1862, the federal government created treasury notes (known popularly as "greenbacks") and made them legal tender (acceptable for payments of debts and taxes). After the war, the secretary of the treasury began to retire greenbacks because he and many others believed they destabilized money. Congress stopped him after he had called in about one-fourth of the greenbacks. It feared that the already rapid postwar deflation would get worse and would take the whole economy down with it. Thus greenbacks remained in circulation, and doubts about their value persisted. Was one greenback worth one gold dollar?

A related controversy involved the national banking system, which Congress created in 1864. The country now had a more stable banking system, but it could issue no more than $300 million in banknotes. That limitation and the tendency of the banks to cluster in major urban centers in the Northeast resulted in serious maldistributions. The southern and western states wanted and needed easier access to national banknotes and banking services. Moreover, the economy as a whole needed currency expansion in keeping with its rapid post–Civil War growth.

A financial panic in 1873 and the depression that followed reopened the greenback and banking issues. Producers, primarily farmers, demanded relief from deflation, which lowered prices for what they produced (and, at a slower rate, for what they bought) while increasing the costs of borrowing. Farmers borrowed heavily to buy or rent the land they needed and to carry themselves over the months between planting and selling their products. They wanted to increase the number of greenbacks and national banknotes. Opponents of these measures decried these steps as leading to an unstable currency that would adversely affect the economy. These defenders of "sound" or "honest" money pointed to the damage done the United States in the past by unstable currencies and attacked the so-called cheap-money measures as threats to lenders and investors and to America's critically important trade with foreign countries, especially Great Britain. Congress and the Grant administration passed compromise legislation, the Specie Resumption Act (1875), which put equal value on greenbacks and gold dollars and provided for an increase in the number of national banknotes. The new law ended uncertainties about the value of greenbacks. It did not, however, stimulate a significant expansion in national banknotes, because the reserve requirements of National Bank acts precluded more than minimal increases in notes. Thus the Resumption Act did not settle the monetary issues. They festered, then burst out from time to time when the economy faltered or when it became painfully obvious that the postwar deflationary trend was continuing.

Greenbackerism or antiresumption entered partisan politics in the 1870s. The Greenback party's presidential ticket drew a scant following in 1876. Two years later and under a new banner, the National Greenback-Labor party, Greenbacker candidates won fourteen seats in Congress, though none in the South. Greenbackers in northern Alabama, however, lent vigorous support to the successful congressional candidacy of William M. Lowe. Greenbackers showed considerable electoral strength in Texas and Arkansas in 1880, but that year marked the high tide of the Greenback-Labor party in the South.

Greenbackers' ideas outlasted their electoral success. Greenbacker leaders and ideologues espoused a subtle, sophisticated policy that belied the accusations of simpleminded inflationism their critics hurled at them. Greenbackers, who included politicians, farmers, manufacturers, theorists, and labor leaders, contended that the value of a nation's currency depended on the strength, real or perceived, of its economy. Hence Greenbackers attacked one of the cornerstones of the monetary theory and policy of their day: the belief that currency must be based on a metallic standard, preferably gold. The Coinage Act of 1873 drew special fire from the Greenbackers, as well as others. With this legislation, Congress left the bimetallic (gold and silver) standard and joined the international movement toward a monometallic (gold) standard. The move had a deflationary effect and soon became known among its critics as the "Crime of '73." Greenbackers argued that deflationary policies, such as the Resumption Act and the Coinage Act, limited economic growth and rewarded creditors while punishing producers and debtors. These ideas became elemental in American politics for years to come.

Reacting to the sentiments on which Greenbackerism fed and keenly aware of an unsettled economy, Congress tried its hand at compromise again, this time with respect to the monetary standard. The Bland-Allison Act (1878) required the secretary of the treasury to purchase no less than $2 million and no more than $4 million of silver per month and coin it as standard dollars. This mildly inflationary legislation may have appeased some inflationists, but it fell far short of the unlimited silver coinage they had sought. The Treasury Department further restrained the impact of the law by electing to purchase the least amount required.

The return of prosperity in 1879 eased pressures on Congress to act on monetary issues. The struggles over monetary policy, however, had portents for the future. Both major parties, the Republican and the Democratic, discovered that the "money question" was explosive. It caused sharp internal divisions in both parties and threatened the coalitional foundations of both. Therefore, both parties sought to avoid the money question, and both sought a more serviceable issue, which they found: the tariff. Monetary issues also stoked the latent fires of sectionalism—not North versus South but Northeast versus West and South. Monetary policy evoked intense feeling and abrasive rhetoric: "sound," "honest," or "cheap" money, "the moneyed interests," "good" and "evil," and so forth. People could march in two different monetary armies and feel righteous. The money question touched the most sensitive American nerves: a sense that there were stark inequalities in income and wealth and well-being in America; suspicions that some people prospered by conspiracy, not effort; and fears that equality of opportunity did not exist. The money issue was one of those fairly rare issues in American history which polarized Americans. During the latter part of the nineteenth century, the erratic fortunes of too many American farmers and the sometimes chaotic American economy kept divisive monetary issues alive. They percolated to the surface throughout the 1880s. Then, in the 1890s, monetary policy became *the* issue in American politics, thanks in large part to the Alliance movement.

THE ALLIANCE MOVEMENT: TEXAS ROOTS

The Alliance movement had uncertain origins and a complex family tree. The Alliance began in Texas prairie country in 1877 or in 1879, but its growth dates from the latter year. The founders, cotton farmers and small ranchers, initially developed their voluntary association as a way to deal with stray cattle, cattle thieves, "land sharks," and big ranchers, who preempted large areas of land by fencing. The Texas Farmers' Alliance (its official name) had 144 lodges or suballiances by 1881 and 500 by 1885, a testament to the Alliance's ability to respond to the needs of many people and to its organizing capacities. Not all of those needs were economic. Like the fraternal orders then found everywhere in the United States, the Alliance had a secret ritual, hand grips, passwords, and regalia. "Throughout its career," one scholar has noted, "the Alliance, particularly at the local level, was a cohesive social institution as well as agency for political and economic action." The Alliance was steeped in the morality and revivalism of nineteenth-century rural Protestantism. "We held an old-fashioned experience meeting," an Alliance member recalled. "We all owned up like men, told our respective shortcomings, and made good resolutions for the future. In that meeting I saw brethren embrace each other in loving embrace, and to this day, the effects of that meeting are plainly visible in Navarro County." Alliance lodges limited—"fenced," as Scottish Presbyterians say about communion—their membership to rural whites of all occupations, except lawyers, merchants, bankers, and their ilk. Townsmen were not welcome. Local notables, however, could prompt a more inclusive spirit. General (later Senator) John Brown Gordon was readily initiated into the Alliance when it expanded into Georgia. Save for the poorest, the membership of the Alliance included the entire spectrum of farmers, though probably most members were small landowners.

The Alliance employed paid lecturer-organizers extensively—$1 for each lodge organized, later $3.35. Local officers carried on the work of the suballiances after the lecturer-organizer moved on. The itinerant teachers created an informal school system in which hundreds of "students" heard and, presumably, digested Alliance teachings. Drawing on the 1870s, the Grange, and especially the Greenback movement, those teachings emphasized currency expansion or "soft money" and cooperatives. Cooperation was critical to the success of the Alliance. It founded a number of small cooperatives for buying and selling, and some cooperative cotton gins and compresses, flour mills, and grain elevators.

Antimonopoly sentiments and ideas permeated Alliance thought. The fear of monopoly or economic concentration was pervasive in the United States at the time. Large combinations in industry, banking, merchandising, and transportation presumably had the power to dictate prices to consumers and producers, to make vassals of labor, to manipulate politicians at will, and to destroy small enterprises. These "moneyed" behemoths could trample the economy, basic freedoms, and people. They were "parasites" living off the substance created by the "real producers."

Defining "producers" and arriving at interests they had in common proved to be very difficult for the Alliance and for its successors. The Alliance thought of industrial workers as "producers" and tried to develop ties with the Knights of Labor, the major labor organization in the United States in the 1880s. The Knights, who wanted one union for all workers and whose ranks grew very rapidly in the mid-1880s, had local units in Texas. When the Knights forced Jay Gould's Texas and Pacific Railroad to rescind a wage reduction in 1885, membership multiplied all over the country. Almost half of the nonfarm workers in Texas belonged to the union, and in some places suballiances and the Knights cooperated closely. Both were made up of "producers," and any railroad, but especially one of Jay Gould's, was an enemy they had in common. But did the interests of the Alliance members include support for longshoremen in Galveston, who, not incidentally, were black, or the Knights' boycotts of two Texas companies? More to the point, how would farmers react to the Knights' efforts to unionize farmworkers and make demands on their employers? Was a farm-labor coalition possible?

The issue remained unsettled into 1886, when the Knights and Gould clashed again. This time Gould won decisively. That defeat and the reactions against the Knights for allegedly precipitating the Haymarket riot in Chicago in June began the Knights' rapid decline. Many Alliance members, however, continued to be interested in some kind of coalition with organized labor. The Alliance had supported the Knights against Gould during the strikes in 1885 and

1886, even when the 1886 strike came close to being a pitched battle. Afterward, suballiances and local units of the Knights continued to work together in northern Texas, and 10,000 Alliancemen and Knights paraded in Dallas in August 1886.

Closely related to the debate over forming a coalition with organized labor was the debate about whether and how the Alliance ought to get involved in politics. The question of political involvement and the issue of a farm-labor coalition became so intense that they nearly split the Alliance permanently in 1886. The following year, the Alliance downplayed its divisions, plunged anew into cooperation, and expanded beyond the borders of Texas. Charles Macune led the way. A native midwesterner, Macune lived in California and Kansas, then in Texas, and taught himself pharmacy, medicine, and law, all of which he practiced at one time or another. He joined the Alliance in 1886, became editor of an Alliance newspaper, and quickly rose in the organization's ranks. As acting president and then president of the Texas Alliance, he got the Alliance to unite behind his plan for a state cooperative exchange. The Texas State Exchange, which was headquartered at Dallas and which Macune served as the elected business agent, was designed to by-pass the middlemen by having members sell their cotton directly to northeastern and European buyers and by buying farm equipment and supplies directly from the manufacturers. The exchange soon realized that many Alliancemen could not use the exchange because they had to mortgage their crops to country merchants in order to obtain supplies and provisions to start and go through a crop year until they could sell their products. So the exchange decided to make cash advances to Alliancemen provided they agreed to sell their cotton through the exchange. A year later, the exchange had to be liquidated. Macune and others blamed hostile bankers and middlemen, who undoubtedly were not pleased to see such a competitor. But probably more important was the exchange's lack of the capital reserves it needed to conduct such a large business and the inadequate backing of the promissory notes members signed when the exchange furnished them with supplies.

The creation of the exchange and the struggle to keep it going stimulated an extensive campaign in political education by the Alliance. Lecturer-organizers, Macune, other Alliance officials, Alliance newspapers, and newspapers sympathetic to the Alliance spread the gospel of cooperation, in Texas and then throughout the cotton belt and beyond. The failure of the Texas State Exchange was costly to the Alliance's members in Texas, and it never regained its earlier strength. The successful boycott conducted by cotton farmers against a combination of jute-bag manufacturers in 1888–1889 did, however, strengthen the Alliance. Cotton farmers forced manufacturers to cut prices on cloth the farmers used for bagging cotton. Cooperation and organization got a widespread, well-publicized demonstration of their potential effectiveness. By 1889 the Alliance had members in every state in the South on the border, and beyond. Its growing power and mounting farm discontent were forcing the issue of the Alliance's stance toward partisan politics. More and more Alliancemen were coming to the conclusion that the Alliance would have to get into politics if it was going to be successful with its program.

The Alliance enjoyed spectacular growth after 1886 and became a major force in American politics. Its greatest strength lay in the South and West. In 1887 the Texas Farmers' Alliance merged with the Louisiana Farmers' Union to form the National Farmers' Alliance and the Co-operative Union, the largest farm group in the United States. A year later it joined forces with the Agricultural Wheel to form the Farmers' and Laborers' Union of America, which then took in the North Carolina Farmers' Association. These merged groups were what is generally called the Southern Farmers' Alliance or Southern Alliance. The Agricultural Wheel had begun in Arkansas in 1882, absorbed the Brothers of Freedom, spread through much of Arkansas, and grown strong in Tennessee, Kentucky, Missouri, and especially Alabama. Leonidas L. Polk founded and led the North Carolina organization. An established farm leader, he was largely responsible for the creation of the North Carolina Department of Agriculture. He served as its first head, then left the department when he concluded that it was too reactionary, and in 1886 began a major farm periodical, *Progressive Farmer*.

Behind the rapid expansion of the Southern Alliance lay a strong sense of injustice and bitter feeling. Polk wrote in 1887:

> There is something radically wrong in our industrial system. There is a screw loose. The wheels have dropped out of balance. The railroads have never been so prosperous, and yet agriculture languishes. The banks have never done a better or more profitable business, and yet agriculture languishes. Manufacturing enterprises never made more money or were in a more flourishing condition, and yet agriculture languishes. Towns and cities flourish and "boom" and grow and "boom," and yet agriculture languishes.

In 1888 the Southern Alliance initiated efforts to unite several of the larger farm organizations into a confederation and to develop a working relationship with organized labor. The farm organizations included the National Farmers' Alliance (popularly known as the Northern Alliance), the Colored National Farmers' Alliance, and the Farmers' Mutual Benefit Association. Founded in Chicago in 1880 and financed largely by Milton George, editor of the *Western Rural*, the Northern Alliance had about 50,000 to 100,000 members in its loosely structured organization. The Colored Farmers' Alliance began in Texas in 1886. Though started by blacks as another of the many black self-help associations and officered largely by blacks, the Colored Alliance's most prominent public figure was Richard Manning Humphrey, a white Baptist minister and Confederate veteran. Though the claims of the Colored Alliance to a membership of 1 million were exaggerated, it did have an extensive following. The Farmers' Mutual Benefit Association had its base in Illinois, where it originated in the early 1880s; it had at least 150,000 members and concentrated its energies on marketing the grain of its members. It showed little interest in merging with other farm groups, but did agree to cooperate with them. The color barrier precluded a confederation between the Colored Alliance and the Southern Alliance.

Efforts toward a confederation centered therefore on the Southern Alliance and the Northern Alliance. To that end, they met separately in St. Louis in early 1889. The Southern Alliance drew delegations from all the southern and border states, as well as Kansas, Nebraska, and Indiana. Delegates from eight midwestern and western states and territories attended the meeting of the Northern Alliance. Negotiations between the organizations failed to produce a merger. The Alliances remained separate. Sectionalism and partisan politics contributed to the failure of the merger; so did the self-interest of the officers and members of the Alliances. Given the size of the two organizations, the Northern Alliance would have been swallowed up by the Southern, and the newly formed confederation would have been dominated by southerners and Democrats and would have been more militant than the Northern Alliance was. Possibly those prospects plus the loss of offices and titles proved too much for the leaders of the Northern Alliance.

The collapse of the unification attempt also reflected the conflicts of self-interest which often divided farmers by region and product. The heated politics of butter, oleomargarine, and lard, in particular, demonstrated these divisions. Dairy farmers, who were concentrated in the Northeast and Midwest, wanted federal protection for butter against oleomargarine ("bogus" butter), and midwestern hog farmers wanted the same thing for "pure" or pork lard against "blended" lards. Manufacturers used cottonseed oil, fast developing as an important element in the cotton industry, in both oleomargarine and blended lard. They also used cattle fat in blended lard. Not too surprisingly, cotton farmers and cattle growers fought vigorously against federal legislation designed to protect butter and pure lard. Farmers also differed over tariff policy. Though most opposed tariffs in general as adding to the costs of the manufactured goods they purchased, farmers modified their opposition to particular import duties on the basis of self-interest. Wheat farmers along the Canadian border, for example, favored high import duties on Canadian wheat.

Despite the failure of its negotiations with the Northern Alliance, the Southern Alliance did expand as a result of the St. Louis meeting. The Kansas Alliance and the South Dakota Alliance left the Northern Alliance, with which they had been affiliated, and joined the Southern. In 1890 the North Dakota Alliance did likewise. Thus the Southern Alliance took on a more national character. At its peak the Southern Alliance had organizations in thirty-two states and had 1.5 million members, three-quarters of whom were southerners. It was a mass movement. The expanding, increasingly militant Southern Alliance also opened its doors to industrial labor. It changed its constitution in order to allow mechanics to be members. Along with the Knights of Labor, which had become highly politicized even as its ranks dwindled, the Southern Alliance issued a list of "demands." The list strongly resembled the "platform" that the Northern Alliance issued at the same time in St. Louis. We may surmise, then, that it was not ideology that kept the Alliances apart. The differences in tone between "demands" and "platform," however, did reflect differences in militancy.

Refined, sharpened, and added to in at least one significant way, the documents drafted at St. Louis appeared as the Ocala Demands of the Southern Alliance (officially, the National Farmers' Alliance and Industrial Union) in December 1890. Delegates came from as far away as California, North Dakota, and New York to Ocala, Florida, where the list of demands was drafted. It represented the distillation of nearly twenty years of thinking and agitating for change. The Alliance demanded "the abolition of national banks," subtreasuries to lend "money direct to the people" at low interest rates "on non-perishable products" and on real estate, currency expansion "to not less than $50 per capita," free silver (put the United States on a bimetallic standard), "laws prohibiting alien ownership of land," the surrender of "all lands now held by railroads and other corporations in excess of such as is actually used and needed," lower tariffs, a graduated income tax, and "government control and supervision of the public means of communication and transportation, [or] government ownership of such." The Ocala meeting also called for severe limits on government spending in order to keep taxes down and for the direct election of United States senators in place of the then prevailing system of election by state legislatures. The Ocala Demands were a frontal assault on what many people believed were monopolies in land, credit, money, transportation, and communications.

The most novel of the demands was the subtreasury plan. It had first been introduced during the final hours of the meeting of the Southern Alliance in St. Louis. Charles Macune apparently was primarily responsible for the subtreasury scheme, which he may have derived in part from French and Russian precedents. Necessity also played a strong hand. Most of the Southern Alliance cooperatives had failed by 1889, and survivors faced grim prospects. The cooperatives could not raise enough capital to succeed; perhaps governments could. By 1889, moreover, the Southern Alliance had begun to give greater stress to currency expansion and an overhaul of the banking system.

The subtreasury appeared to meet these needs. According to the plan, the U.S. Department of the Treasury would open a branch (subtreasury) in every county in the nation which produced at least $500,000 worth of farm products. Every subtreasury would have facilities to store nonperishables such as cotton, wheat, sugar, corn, and tobacco. A farmer would be able to store products for up to one year and obtain a loan in subtreasury notes of up to 80 percent of the market value of the crop when it was stored. Costs to the farmer would be small: the subtreasury would charge a small fee for storage and handling and 1 percent interest on the loan, which could run up to twelve months.

The subtreasury plan had a multiple purpose. Farmers could end their dependence on local merchants, warehousers, and grain elevator operators, who often had local monopolies. Since they would have money from the subtreasuries, farmers would not have to sell their crops as soon as they harvested them; they could hold their crops in the hope of selling at better prices. Subtreasury notes would be legal tender and would displace national banknotes. Since subtreasury notes would be far more numerous than banknotes, the subtreasury plan also would substantially expand the amount of money in circulation. The subtreasury promised a way out of the "vast pawnshop" that entrapped so many farm families.

The subtreasury scheme was a new and certainly an ingenious proposal. Government had never remained aloof from the American economy; tariffs, subsidies to railroads, and tax revenues for education, to cite only a few examples, attested to that. But in 1890, despite such governmental activities, most Americans still believed that politics and economics occupied separate spheres, and they usually spurned government aid to the economy as "class legislation." The subtreasury elicited that criticism, and others, when it was proposed, and it probably never had much chance of passage in Washington.

To begin with, it was too innovative to gain quick acceptance. Governments (and people in general) tend to break new ground quickly only in extreme circumstances, in emergencies more serious even than the one posed by the American economy at the end of the nineteenth century. For instance, as its fortunes declined drastically after 1862, the government of the Confederate States became the first in North America to conscript troops and even built and operated war industries. The subtreasury also raised the specter of an unstable, expansive currency. Bankers and most middlemen opposed the subtreasury for obvious reasons. The subtreasury had more than a hint of class legislation about it since it favored farmers, but not all of them, and would adversely affect many others by raising food and fiber prices.

Many farmers were either hostile to the subtreasury or indifferent to it. The subtreasury appealed primarily to cotton and wheat farmers, who confronted especially hard times and whose products could be stored easily and for long periods of time. Corn, hog, dairy, vegetable, and fruit producers had little use for the subtreasury plan. Most farmed in the north-central and north Atlantic states and were considerably more prosperous than wheat or cotton farmers. Those states accounted for 70 percent of the farm wealth in the United States in 1890; the north-central states alone accounted for one-half of national farm wealth. Inflation, or currency expansion, might lessen the value of what farmers owned in those states. And if the government was going to lend them money, they were more interested in mortgages on land than in loans on crops. That explained why the Southern Alliance at the Ocala meeting added real estate to its demand for a subtreasury.

*T*HE ALLIANCE IN POLITICS

The issue of political activity also made itself felt during the Ocala meeting. Whether to be "in politics" was no longer the issue, as the Ocala Demands made clear. Now the question was how. They could lobby as a pressure group, work with and perhaps try to dominate the Democratic and Republican parties, or form a third party. The Ocala meeting indicated that the Alliance was leaning toward the last approach. It elected Leonidas L. Polk, who had third-party inclinations, to succeed Macune, who did not, to the presidency. Macune continued to function as editor of the *National Economist*, the official national newspaper of the Alliance; he used it to beat a steady drum for the subtreasury plan. A 1,000-member National Reform Press Association was also formed at Ocala.

But the Alliance wavered on its political tactics. The third-party strategy threatened to divide the organization permanently. The core of the Alliance, its southern white members, had a patriotic commitment to the Democratic party. Memories, habits, and a race phobia cemented the attachment. Moreover, some Democratic politicians had been receptive to the Alliance, and the Alliance became a force in several southern states by working with Democrats. The Republicans inadvertently reinforced that attachment. In 1890 the Republican House of Representatives passed the Lodge Election Bill, or the Force Bill, as it was called by its mostly southern opponents and as it has since been known. Proposed in 1889 by Henry Cabot Lodge, then a Massachusetts congressman, the bill provided for federal supervision of elections to ensure that blacks could vote freely in the southern states. Attacks of conscience and partisan politics prompted the Republican action. Violations of the political and civil rights of blacks were flagrant and routine in the South. Republicans also had a strong interest in expanding their voter base, because in national politics they confronted an equally powerful Democratic party.

For years the Republicans sought ways to increase their following in the South. Convinced that blacks offered their best hope and equally convinced that election frauds had prevented Republican successes in many places in the South, the Republicans turned to the Lodge Bill. Though it had little chance to pass in the Senate, the Lodge Bill set off alarms in the South and memories of resistance to Reconstruction. Recalling "that glorious era," the Atlanta *Constitution* opined that "what we did twenty years ago we can do again." Southern delegates to the Ocala meeting of the Alliance shouted their approval of a resolution protesting the bill. At the same time and at a separate meeting in Ocala, the Colored Alliance endorsed the Lodge Bill. Racial fears kept the Alliance close to the Democrats even as those same fears divided the Alliance movement along racial lines.

Election returns in 1890 gave the Alliance reason to hope that it could achieve its aims within Democratic ranks. In South Carolina, "Pitchfork Ben" Tillman used Alliance support to win the governorship as a Democrat while driving out his opponents in the Democratic party ("the aristocratic coterie") and establishing a personal political machine. James S. Hogg achieved a similar success in Texas with help from the Alliance, the Grange, and the Knights of Labor. Tennessee sent the president of the state Alliance to the governor's office, and more than a third of the state legislators had ties with the Alliance. In several states—North Carolina, Florida, Georgia, Alabama—the Alliance was a major force in legislative and congressional elections. An Alliance-supported candidate won the governorship of Georgia, and another nearly became governor of Alabama. The Alliance split in Arkansas, and a faction joined forces with the Union Labor party in a strong, though unsuccessful, third-party effort. In Virginia, Louisiana, and Kentucky, several congressmen pledged allegiance to the Alliance. Leonidas L. Polk celebrated the returns. "We are here to stay....The people of this country are desperately in earnest. They will no longer put up with this nonsense. Old Party fossils have lost their grip." An Allianceman sounded a triumphant theme: "Being Democrats and in the majority, we took possession of the Democratic Party."

What politicians meant when they took the pledge of allegiance to the Alliance, however, was not clear. The Alliance discovered that the Democrats whom they helped elect and who had expressed sympathy with the organization behaved more like Democrats than like Alliance enthusiasts. Tillman in South Carolina and Hogg in Texas embraced only part of the Alliance program; Hogg never accepted the subtreasury, and Tillman did so only to get elected. Hogg even tried unsuccessfully to destroy the Alliance. In Georgia, a supposedly Alliance-dominated legislature elected elderly General Gordon, one of the state's Bourbon triumvirate, to the U.S. Senate, failed to act on railroad regulation or any antitrust legislation, but did pass legislation to aid businesses.

THE MISSISSIPPI PLAN

Mississippi produced the most surprising and the most important outcome of the Alliance's involvement in politics in 1890. Exhorted by the Alliance, the state Grange, and others, the state legislature called a constitutional convention in order, according to James Z. George, U.S. senator and Mississippi's leading politician, "to devise such measures, consistent with the Constitution of the United States, as will enable us to maintain a home government, under the control of the white people of the state." The convention devised the "Mississippi Plan" as a legal mechanism to circumvent the Fourteenth and Fifteenth amendments and to preclude federal intervention in Mississippi elections, a possibility that the Force Bill suggested was hardly remote.

The Mississippi Plan was an important precursor to a Southwide movement to eliminate blacks and large numbers of poor whites from the political process. The new state constitution required voters to have resided in the state for at least two years and in their election districts for one, to have paid all their taxes for two years before registering to vote, and to register and pay a poll tax of $2, unless they qualified for one of the few exemptions. Voters had to "be able to understand" any part of the state constitution when it was read to them "or give a reasonable interpretation thereof." Drafters of the constitution had a general agreement that registrars would pass illiterate whites and fail blacks.

As soon became obvious, the constitutional interpretation or "understanding" clause did not, as had been promised, provide adequate insurance for the voting rights of poorer whites. The tax clause, especially the poll tax, effectively disfranchised many whites and most blacks in a state where the average income produced by a farm was about $400 a year. Given the transience of lower-income groups, the residency requirement tended to reinforce the class and race pattern of disfranchisement. The "understanding" clause invited fraud. Factions or machines in control of the electoral system could manipulate the clause for the desired effect, perhaps disfranchising some and enfranchising others, possibly blacks, in order to win elections.

After 1890, "the legal Negro voter, and consequently the Republican party," a student of Mississippi politics wrote, became "a negligible factor in state-wide elections." For instance, Republican vote totals in presidential elections plummeted from 43,000 in 1884 to 1,500 votes in 1892. Not until 1920 did a Republican presidential nominee again get as many as 6,000 votes. Of the 120,000 whites who could vote in 1890, only 68,000 registered in 1892. That year some 40,000 Mississippians voted for Grover Cleveland; in 1888, more than 85,000 had done so.

Disfranchisement, as these figures indicate, secured the dominance of white people in Mississippi politics and determined which whites would have predominance. Mississippi politics, to simplify somewhat, reflected the divisions between the delta counties (those near the Mississippi and its principal tributaries) and the rest of the state. The delta, with its enormously rich riverine soil, had large, highly productive, profitable landholdings or plantations, which were owned by whites and most of which were worked by black sharecroppers and day laborers. Blacks in the delta outnumbered whites by from 3 to as much as 15 to 1.

Northeastern Mississippi provided the delta planters with their strongest opposition. Whites in the northeast considerably outnumbered those in the delta, but they farmed inferior land and had much less income. The southeastern part of the state, the piney woods, afforded even fewer opportunities than were available in the northeast. The lumber boom did not reach the southeast until the mid-1890s, and even when the boom came, its primary beneficiaries were large lumber companies. What industry Mississippi had was located in the southern part of the state. Only after new sources of energy were available to make up for the lack of coal and the absence of water power did industry spread elsewhere in Mississippi. A strip of counties along the eastern edge of the delta had considerable agricultural wealth and provided a transitional area between the delta and the rest of the state. Large landholders and successful farmers in this strip and in areas scattered throughout the state were political allies of the delta planters, as were railroad leaders and prominent lawyers, merchants, bankers, and manufacturers. Most of the latter groups centered their activities in Jackson.

Black disfranchisement threatened to cost the delta dearly. Delta and other Bourbons or planters and their allies in the state had used black votes to maintain their strong position in Mississippi politics. The Bourbons employed intimidation, persuasion, and "fusion" to control black votes. "Fusion"—the division of local offices with blacks—was a tactic employed most frequently in the delta. Confronted by an increasingly restive agrarian movement in the state in the late 1880s, the Redeemers increasingly resorted to various fraudulent voting tactics. Such methods and the continuing insensitivity of the Redeemers to the needs of smaller farmers fueled demands by the Alliance and other radical agrarians for disfranchisement of blacks as a necessary first step to getting what the agrarians wanted from the legislature.

The Redeemer elements in the state constitutional convention, however, devised a means to shore up the power of the delta and other Redeemer elements. The new constitution shifted some representation away from the delta, but it still allowed these elements very disproportionate power. The result was gross overrepresentation of the delta. This disproportion was also carried over to methods used for electing governors, who were given wide powers, such as responsibility for the appointment of all judges in the state.

Ironically, as a result of the plunge of the Alliance and the Grange into politics, thousands of whites (as well as blacks) were deprived of their votes, and for some years anti-Alliance forces were strengthened. Mississippi Democrats also embraced free silver in the early 1890s. That position and the Mississippi Plan may have been enough to keep the Democrats firmly in power and to account for the failure of the Populist party in Mississippi in the 1890s.

Perhaps even more unsettling for the Alliance was what occurred in Washington. Congressional Democrats allowed a bill to create the subtreasury to die in committee. Congress did pass a mildly inflationary currency measure, the Sherman Silver Purchase Act, in 1890, as well as the Sherman Antitrust Act, a landmark antimonopoly statute. For many members of the Alliance, that was not enough. Then in 1891, when the now heavily Democratic House of Representatives could not pass the more inflationary Bland Silver Bill, many Alliancemen in the South became embittered and consequently more interested in what the Alliance had done in Kansas. There it had formed an independent party, the People's (Populist) party, in 1890, and had won sweeping victories at the polls.

THE POPULISTS

During 1891 the Populist party became a national party with supporters in every southern state, especially in Texas, Alabama, Georgia, North Carolina, and Florida. Delegates gathered for the party's national nominating convention in Omaha in July 1892. They met, according to a party statement, "in the midst of a nation brought to the verge of moral, political, and material ruin." The convention chose a slate and wrote a sweeping, highly specific platform, unlike the platitude-filled platforms that usually emerged from national political conventions.

The Populists called for election reforms that included the Australian (secret) ballot system; a graduated income tax; currency expansion and the replacement of national banknotes by government-issued notes; "free and unlimited

FAMILY REUNION, 1890s (Courtesy, Georgia Department of Archives and History)

coinage of silver and gold" at a ratio of 16 to 1; the subtreasury; government ownership of railroads, telephone, and telegraph; and an attack on land monopolies and landowning by aliens. Endeavoring mightily to build a farm-labor coalition, the Populists expressed the hope "that the union of the labor forces of the United States this day consummated shall be permanent and perpetual. . . . Wealth belongs to him who creates it. . . ." The platform urged greater protection against immigrant labor, which "crowds out our wage-earners," and expressed its sympathies with the Knights of Labor and with workers' efforts to organize and to get shorter hours. Though the Populists favored free and open elections and had a strong interest in them, since the Democrats had so effectively used their control of the election machinery in several southern states for partisan ends, the Populists opposed the Force Bill. Obviously, southern sentiments prevailed on this issue.

The Populists had some difficulty selecting their nominees for president and vice president. The strongest candidate from the South—which, of course, was an Alliance and Populist stronghold—had been lost when Leonidas L. Polk died suddenly in early 1892. The convention chose General James B. Weaver of Iowa as its presidential nominee. Weaver had served in the Union Army during the Civil War, but he had ties and friends in all sections of the country and was an experienced campaigner and politician. He left the Republican party in the 1870s and with Democratic support gained a seat in Congress in 1878 as a

MIDDLE-CLASS FARM HOME, 1890s (Courtesy, Georgia Department of Archives and History)

Greenbacker. In 1880 he ran for president on the Greenback ticket, campaigning throughout much of the country. In the 1880s he returned to Congress as a Greenback-Democrat. Then he joined the Populists. For vice president the Populists picked General James G. Field, a Confederate veteran from Virginia. A colonel during the Civil War, Field may have been "promoted" for his service as attorney general in Virginia or in the militia. Such "promotions" were not uncommon.

The Populists left Omaha in high spirits and with a sense of mission and an immense task. In addition to the usual problems faced by new political parties, the Populists faced the enormous barriers presented by sectionalism, race, and a militant opposition that knew few scruples. As new parties usually did, the Populists lacked a reservoir of good candidates with established reputations, especially at the state and local levels, and they did not have an experienced campaign organization, substantial sums of money for electioneering, or patronage to offer party workers. As assailers of the status quo, the Populists unsettled many voters, and their fiery rhetoric reinforced those feelings. Conversely, the Populists could draw upon the ideas, the emotions, and sometimes the organizations that the Alliance had produced. Certainly, many potential voters found the rebellious spirit of the People's party attractive. Many farmers in the South, however, were not in a rebellious mood because they were successful. Not all were on the verge of moral or material ruin.

The Populists also had to persuade people to break old party loyalties, loyalties complicated by sectionalism and especially by race. Party loyalty, as anal-

yses of American politics have shown repeatedly, is a powerful force. Party loyalty fell along ethnic and religious lines, strong factors everywhere in the
United States in the late nineteenth century. Protestants and Catholics in the
northern states, for instance, showed strong attachments to the Republicans
and the Democrats, respectively. In the southern version of ethnic politics,
Democrats drew a familiar and favorite equation: the Democratic party equaled
white supremacy and sectional patriotism. That equation was an enormous asset for the Democrats. Furthermore, they enjoyed the considerable advantages
of being the most entrenched party in the South and of having, in 1892, a likely
victor in the presidential race, Grover Cleveland. The Democrats also took over
some Populist issues. Governor Hogg of Texas, for example, succeeded in getting strong railroad regulatory legislation, while South Carolina's Tillman got
approval for an agricultural school, Clemson College (now Clemson University), and weakened the University of South Carolina, alleged to be an aristocratic Bourbon enclave.

Probably the greatest challenge faced by the Populists was to attract the
black voters they had to have if they were to succeed. "The negro vote will be
the balancing vote in Texas," a black delegate to the Texas state Populist convention declared. "If you are going to win, you will have to take the negro with
you." Just how far the Populists were willing or able to "take the negro" with
them was a matter of dispute in the 1890s and has been debated by historians
since.

In light of the sad history of black-white relations in the South especially,
but also in the country as a whole, it is tempting to see the Populists as bolder
innovators in race relations than they were. A desire to see the past as more
heroic than it was is entirely understandable, but it may lead one to see a past
that was not there.

The Populist approach to the blacks should be examined for motivation and
for what the Populists did and did not do. The Populists included blacks in their
meetings, usually on a segregated basis, and selected blacks for party offices,
but not for candidates for public office. John B. Rayner, a black, served as an
officer and very effective speaker for the Texas Populists. The Populists were
acting from self-interest. They assumed that they and the blacks, as the disinherited farmers of the South, had common interests. The Populists emphatically
rejected social equality or anything that approached it, but they had enough vision and sense to spurn blatant Negrophobia, something the Democrats did not
do. Tom Watson put the Populist appeal to blacks in cogent terms: "Once it
appear[s] plainly that it is to the interest of a colored man to vote with the white
man, ... he will do it."

The Populists dared to breach one of the most formidable barriers of the
South, the wall between blacks and poorer whites. Those breaches required
mental and sometimes physical courage. Moreover, unlike the Democrats, the
Populists did not exploit Negrophobia to advance their cause or advocate the
disfranchisement of blacks. Later, however, many disappointed, embittered

Populists, most notably Tom Watson, did look back on their defeats and hurl their pent-up fury at the blacks.

Blacks responded variously to Populist appeals. Not all saw an identity of interests with the Populists. Black political leaders had a stake in the Republican party—status and possibly a desired appointment. Most blacks had strong emotional ties to "the party of Lincoln," the party of emancipation. The small urban black middle class had good reason to fear the Populist program. Thousands of blacks were sharecroppers and farm day laborers, and their interests often differed from those of their white employers, who might be Populists. Blacks had bitter experiences with the Southern Alliance, the spiritual father of the People's party, which had kept the Colored Farmers' Alliance at arm's length. The Southern Alliance in Georgia, for instance, had supported laws that required segregation by race on railroad cars and had favored the revival of the whipping post for some crimes. In Mississippi, the Alliance had been in the forefront of the movement to disfranchise blacks.

In some instances the Democrats tried to speak to black concerns. In Georgia, Governor William J. Northen advocated more money for black schools and an end to lynching. But Northen also verbalized a stark, self-serving paternalism in which blacks were perpetual children consigned permanently to farm labor. Understandably blacks wondered with which whites they should ally themselves, whom they could trust. Given the alternatives, many impoverished blacks probably acted rationally when they sold their votes. Some blacks undoubtedly voluntarily voted for Democrats. Many more did so unvoluntarily.

The Populists also represented a challenge to the established order—to, among other things, the "right thinking" of the day on banking and currency, to men like Judge Emory Speer, and to those who built and promoted the Atlanta Exposition. "The wellspring of Populism," a sympathetic scholar has concluded, was its efforts

> to overcome a concentrating system of finance capitalism that was rooted in Eastern commercial banks and which radiated outward through trunk-line railroad networks to link in a number of common purposes much of America's consolidated corporate community. [The Populists'] aim was structural reform of the American economic system.

That aim alone would have triggered a furious response by the more established elements. Then add the challenge Populism presented to the Democratic party and to white supremacy, and the fiery rhetoric with which they issued it. In Georgia the Populists told voters as they got ready to vote:

> The hand of God is in our movement and will be until we triumph.
> We are slaves now. It used to be only the colored people.
> Fellow citizens, our homes and our liberties are at stake, and in the name of Almighty God let us pledge ourselves and not give up the fight until we win the victory.

The Augusta (Georgia) *Chronicle* replied:

Never has there been a time since the days of reconstruction, when it was so absolutely necessary for every southern man to do his duty at the ballot box to his God, his country and himself.

In the triumph of democratic doctrines and policies is the perpetuity of our government and the prosperity of our country.

The south and especially the tenth [congressional] district is threatened by anarchy and communism. The direful teaching of Thomas E. Watson, and the visionary promises of the demagogue have aroused the cupidity of the ignorant, and influenced the passions of intemperate men, who would sacrifice their country and their people to their own selfish desires.

These words accurately reflected the battlefield mentality that permeated the South during the 1892 election. General Weaver received a hostile reception when he campaigned in the South. Earlier, as a Greenbacker, he had not, but in 1892 Weaver constituted a much greater threat. Weaver was shouted down, rocked, and egged until he "was made a walking omelet by the Southern chivalry of Georgia." Mary E. Lease, Kansas Populist spokeswoman, remembered for advising farmers in her home state "to raise more hell and less corn," got similar treatment. The Populists were prepared to see women take a more active part in politics, but much of the South was not. The Greensboro (North Carolina) *Daily Record* felt that "the sight of a woman traveling around the country making political speeches . . . is simply disgusting," that "Southern manhood revolts at the idea of degrading womanhood to the level of politics."

The level of politics got very low in 1892 and probably unnecessarily so in the South. The Democrats won there easily. Weaver got one-third of his 1 million votes (out of 12 million cast in the nation) in the South, but none of his electoral votes. Only Alabama gave Weaver as much as a third of its votes (36.6 percent); Texas ranked second (23.6 percent).

A Populist-supported candidate did nearly win election as governor in Alabama. Reuben Kolb had developed a wide following among Alabama farmers, and he was probably the most popular politician in the state. Yet anti-Alliance Democrats controlled the nominating process and kept Kolb from getting the Democratic nomination in 1890 and 1892. After the second rebuff, Kolb and his followers formed a separate faction, the Jeffersonian-Democrats. They embraced much of the Populist program and joined forces with the Populists and the Republicans. The Republicans were attracted to the three-way alliance by, among other things, that portion of the Jeffersonian-Democrats' platform which declared, "We favor the protection of the colored race in their political rights."

The Democrats attacked that "nigger rights' section of the platform," but their hostility to it did not discourage them from using their control of the election machinery to marshal black votes to defeat independents in Alabama. Democrats favored black voting when they controlled that vote. The issue in Alabama was not whether or not blacks could vote; "the real question was *how* the Negro voted."

Kolb lost to the Democratic incumbent, Thomas G. Jones, in 1892 by 11,435 votes. Jones's strength lay in the black belt, where he had 30,217 more votes than Kolb and where most counties had more blacks than whites. It may have been the most fraudulent election in Alabama since Reconstruction. Desperate to stop Kolb, Jones's supporters threatened, intimidated, and bribed voters and stole ballot boxes. Such tactics were not exclusive to counties with black majorities, but the black belt provided the margin of victory for Jones. There, an Alabama wag noted, the planter, "by patience, perseverance and courage...has maintained his influence with the nigger and has neutralized nigger supremacy with nigger votes, which is the grandest political achievement of the century. He has knocked out the Republicans with the boomerang they hurled at him." The Democrat won with a formula that became an Alabama standard after the 1880s. The planters of the black belt combined forces with the Big Mules,* the commercial and industrial leaders of Birmingham and Mobile, to counter rural counties with white majorities.

Tom Watson met a similar fate in his congressional reelection campaign in Georgia. The former Democrat, now a Populist, ran into an urban version of Democratic election chicanery. Patrick Walsh, political boss of Augusta, led the way. Augusta reported twice as many votes in 1892 as there were legal voters in the city. Blacks reportedly were brought by wagonloads from South Carolina to vote for Watson's opponent. This was an old tradition in the area. In earlier years, whites from the Augusta area had crossed the Savannah River to help South Carolina Democrats defeat Republicans.

POLITICAL UPHEAVAL

The Democrats also won the presidential election in 1892, but that victory had the potential for disaster. Grover Cleveland, a militant gold-standard man, won. When the Democrats had renominated Cleveland, they had ignored the distressed farmers of the West and the South and gone for a winner, a former New York governor and former president who had failed to win reelection to the presidency in 1888 by a narrow margin. To the sure bloc of votes from the solid South, Cleveland added the votes of his home state and those of several other northern states and returned to the White House. Thus, ironically, even as the Populists were asserting themselves and many Democrats in the South were drawing close to the positions of the Alliance and the Populists, the presidency became a gold-standard stronghold occupied by a Democrat. Moreover, the new president took particular pride in assuming forthright positions and defending them at all costs. Cleveland had little taste or gift for the art of compromise.

Confronted by the depression of the 1890s, the worst economic crisis in American history until 1929, Cleveland did what was expected of a president

---

*The term was first coined in the 1930s. It has since come to be used retrospectively.

then—next to nothing. Cleveland expended his greatest efforts in defense of the gold standard, which he and many others thought was of critical importance to the economy. Cleveland waged a bitter, successful battle to repeal the Sherman Silver Purchase Act, and he moved with dispatch to preserve the government's gold reserves.

Cleveland's stand on the gold standard incensed the Populists and many Democrats in the South as well as in the West. They had embraced currency expansion and after 1892 had become committed to free silver as essential to the economic well-being of southern and western farmers and of the country as a whole. They saw these policies as fundamental to an effort to wrest power from the eastern "moneyed interests" so that a political and economic democracy might be restored. Cleveland talked about "the cankering rust of national dishonesty" and "national bad faith," and warned that "popular discontent and passion [were being] stimulated by the art of designing partisans to a pitch perilously near to class hatred or sectional anger." He saw a "line of battle [being] drawn between the forces of safe currency and those of silver monometallism." Ben Tillman declared that "when Judas betrayed Christ his heart was not blacker than this scoundrel, Cleveland, in deceiving" the Democratic party. Tillman promised to attack the "old bag of beef...with a pitchfork."

Like the last previous Jacksonian Democrat in the White House, Andrew Johnson, Cleveland refused to compromise. Ironically for a Jacksonian, Cleveland relied on Wall Street for advice, and he turned again to Wall Street—to J. P. Morgan and other bankers—to shore up the declining gold reserves of the government even as the Atlanta Exposition was opening. Thus as some people were celebrating the New South in Henry Grady's town with a blessing from the president, others saw no New South or did not like much of what they saw of it. They also believed that Cleveland's gold policies would lead to even harder times and greater disasters. In growing numbers they distanced themselves from the Cleveland Democrats by turning to Populism or to free silver within the Democratic party.

But Cleveland persisted and won, and in doing so contributed substantially to the near-destruction of the national Democratic party. The Republicans achieved something they had never been able to do: they became the majority party in the 1890s. Thereafter Republicans could largely ignore the South and still dominate national politics. That dominance lasted a generation, during which the solid South generally found itself excluded from national power.

The political turbulence occasioned by the depression of the 1890s gave the Populists their opportunity. Populism reached its electoral peak during the next major election year, 1894. It enjoyed greater success in the South than elsewhere in the nation and did best where Populists fused with Republicans or with dissident Democrats. In North Carolina the Populists joined ranks with the Republicans, who had strong support in the eastern part of the state, with its large black population, and in the largely white western part of the state. The Populists won control of the state senate and shared the state house of representatives with the Republicans. A Republican filled the unexpired term of the deceased senator Zebulon Vance, a Democrat who had been a fixture in North Carolina politics. The Populist Marion Butler won a six-year term to the United States Senate. Three Populists, two Republicans, and one Independent served North Carolina in the national house of representatives. The Populist-Republican fusion in North Carolina owed much of its success to the Populists' moderation. They softened their appeal to class interests and retreated from open efforts to build a black-white coalition.

Alabama Populists followed a similar course. They joined forces with Jeffersonian Democrats rather than with Republicans. There fusionists were awarded several congressional seats after they got disputed elections reversed by Congress. But Kolb lost the governorship again, probably for the same reasons he had lost in 1892. He and his followers staged their own "inaugural," but, faced by overwhelming police force, they dispersed after a brief informal ceremony. Kolb did attract more votes from the coal miners and ironworkers in and around Birmingham. Miners, 7,000 of whom went on strike in 1894, found Kolb particularly attractive. They thought he would be less inclined to use force and convict labor to break strikes than the Democrats, who had used such tactics against the miners' strike. Thus a farm-labor coalition existed in Alabama, if briefly. Industrial labor would play a significant role in Alabama politics thereafter. Tom Watson had an experience similar to Kolb's. He lost again in Georgia in his race for Congress, and again he may have been defrauded by unscrupulous Democrats.

In their search for electoral success, the Populists altered their positions on some issues, sometimes drastically. Populists in North Carolina and Alabama, for instance, dropped the Populist financial program and staked their entire economic appeal on free silver. Georgia Populists kept the faith on most economic issues, but like the Populists of North Carolina and Alabama, they muffled or completely altered their appeals to black voters. Only in Texas did the Populists refuse to endorse free silver as the key financial issue. There they adhered to class-interest politics. They kept the full Populist financial program, supported labor, and openly appealed to black voters.

Populist or fusion tickets got nearly 54 percent of the vote in North Carolina, 48 percent in Alabama, more than 36 percent in Texas, and, in 1895 and 1896 respectively, more than 25 percent in Mississippi and nearly 44 percent in Louisiana. Louisiana Populists joined antilottery Democrats to defeat an entrenched Democratic machine whose dubious assets included $10 million in profits per year from a state lottery that cost them only $40,000 for an exclusive franchise. Under Bourbon rule, public services in Louisiana sank to their nadir. Though Louisiana had more wealth than its neighbor Arkansas, it devoted less than one-half of the amount of tax money Arkansas did for public schools. As one historian noted sardonically, on the basis of literacy rates Louisiana "climbed from fifth to first place in ignorance between 1880 and 1890."

The 1894 election had other implications, most of which were not happy ones for the Populists. Outside the South, the Populists suffered setbacks where they had been a majority or a near majority—in Kansas, Colorado,

Idaho, the Dakotas, Nevada, and Wyoming. Much more important, the Republicans scored an enormous victory nationally in the congressional race. The 1894 election was a decisive factor in making the Republican party the dominant major party in the United States for more than three decades. The Republicans gained 117 seats in the House of Representatives and 5 seats in the Senate. They gained the upper hand for the 1896 presidential election while the Democrats counted casualties and fell into bitter divisions over whom to blame for their defeat and over policy, especially over gold versus silver. Eventually free silver triumphed among the Democrats. They nominated William Jennings Bryan for president in 1896. When the Republicans chose William McKinley as their nominee, the stage was set for one of the most dramatic and climactic elections in American history.

For the Populists, 1896 was also climactic. They faced hard choices. Fusion had been their most successful tactic, whether with the Democrats in Kansas or with the Republicans in North Carolina. But the national Republican party had rejected free silver and had adopted a moderate gold-standard plank in its platform. Moreover, the Republican party hardly suited the antielitism of the Populists, and the Republicans remained repugnant in most of the South, where Populist strength now was centered.

The Democrats had more appeal for the Populists. They had endorsed free silver and nominated Bryan, a populistic candidate—someone who could legitimately claim to be "a man of the people." Bryan's candidacy also demonstrated that the Democratic party had been sensitive to distressed farmers and had shifted politically in the direction of the Populists. Prominent southern Democrats became converts to free silver: Senator John Tyler Morgan of Alabama, James Z. George of Mississippi, and James K. Jones of Arkansas were Bourbons and major figures in the Senate. Secretary of the Interior Hoke Smith supported Bryan after he was nominated; Cleveland forced the Georgian to resign from the cabinet.

But fusion with the Democrats involved high risks and heavy costs. After all, southern Populists had fought bitter struggles with the Democrats; the Democrats had a populistic nominee for president, but in the South the party still had a distinctly Bourbon or standpat flavor. Moreover, the Democrats had chosen Arthur Sewall of Maine, who had made a fortune in shipping, for vice president. Middle-of-the-road Populists believed that fusion with either Republicans or Democrats meant extinction. Tom Watson warned: "The [Democratic] idea of fusion [is that] we play Jonah while they play the whale." Moreover, these Populists thought that in endorsing free silver and then trumpeting the issue so vigorously that the 1896 campaign was becoming a single-issue campaign, silver versus gold, the Democrats were following a simpleminded course. Middle-of-the-road Populists believed Populism had a far more thorough and better program for the country, that free silver in Democratic hands was a fatally adulterated Populism.

The Populists could have chosen to nominate a candidate of their own or endorsed none at all. But the first alternative would ensure Republican victory

TOM WATSON, POPULIST LEADER, AT 48 (Culver Pictures)

in the presidential race because the anti-Republican vote would be split. The second alternative would be unacceptable for a party that claimed to be a national party; it would signal that the Populists could not even select a presidential ticket. The Populists were sharply divided and ended up with an awkward, though understandable, compromise. They first nominated Watson for vice president, then Bryan for president. Bryan never formally accepted the nomination nor did he reject Sewall, the Democratic nominee for vice president, as the Populists asked him to do. Bryan did not have to do either. He had, in effect, captured the Populists without making a concession. Whether, if he won, he would have appointed some Populists to positions in his administration is uncertain. Many of the Populist leaders who favored fusion with the Democrats in 1896 certainly anticipated such rewards. Those hopes may explain part of their motivation for supporting Bryan.

Bryan lost the presidency in 1896, and the Populists lost ground everywhere except in North Carolina. They did well in Georgia, Alabama, and Texas and might have won in those states if the elections had been fair. In North Carolina, where the elections were generally free and open, the Populists won decisively, fusing with the Republicans and helping elect Daniel L. Russell, the only Republican governor in North Carolina between 1877 and 1973.

In 1898 the white Democrats in North Carolina mounted a scurrilous Negrophobic campaign and routed the Populists and Republicans. The rout reached its bloody finale at Wilmington, North Carolina, in late 1898, when local Democrats overthrew the black-majority city government and installed themselves. At least eleven blacks were killed and more were injured.

Elsewhere in the South after 1896, Populism faded quickly, though more quietly in Alabama and Georgia than in Texas, where it held its own a little longer. In Mississippi, Florida, and Louisiana it was virtually nonexistent. In South Carolina, Tillmanism, a weak variant of Populism, held sway. The Democrats in Arkansas, who had adopted free silver, easily bested their Republican opponents and absorbed remnants of the Populists. The strong one-party tradition of that state prevailed. In Tennessee the Populists never became more than a vocal but small faction amid the highly factionalized politics of the state. Democrats were, however, forced to call upon former governor Robert Love "Our Bob" Taylor. A skilled compromiser, Taylor pulled the Democratic factions together to defeat the Populists and a strong Republican challenge in 1896. It did not hurt that Bob Taylor was adept at the fiddle and storytelling. Republicans, however, remained as a force in Tennessee politics, a greater force there than in other southern states. Virginia Democrats used their tightly organized party structure and their control of the state electoral apparatus to contain the Populists, who enjoyed limited success in the 1890s and then withered. Most members of Virginia's strong Alliance balked at joining the People's party. Democrats used fears of blacks and Mahoneism effectively. They claimed William Mahone was covertly supporting the Populists. Nationally, the Populists faced an equally bleak future. Populist numbers in Congress shrank by 1900. The same year, the Populists followed Bryan again in the presidential race, and Bryan lost again. Four years later, they chose Tom Watson, who got only 114,501 popular votes and no electoral votes.*

THE POPULIST LEGACY

Though the Populists faded fast, the breadth of their following and the extent of their legacy suggested that they were not a momentary phenomenon. Some of their proposals later became law. The Federal Farm Loan Act and the Warehouse Act of 1916 derived their assumptions from the subtreasury plan. More important, the Populists increased public pressures for major shifts in public

---

*The Populists nominated a bizarre slate in 1900. For their presidential candidate a rump of the party selected Wharton Baker, an aged Philadelphia banker and monetary theorist who had joined the Populists in 1896. For vice president they chose Ignatius Donnelly of Minnesota, a none too stable veteran of many reform campaigns.

policy. Government ownership of the transportation and communications systems of the nation never received broad acceptance, but Congress increased its regulatory powers over both. In 1913 Congress created the Federal Reserve System. In the same year the ratification of the Sixteenth Amendment made federal income taxes constitutional, and four years later, as the United States entered World War I, Congress passed a graduated income tax as part of the War Revenue Act. The national government and various state and local governments enacted measures that implemented the direct democracy that the Populists often called for: the Australian ballot system, direct election of United States senators, primaries, initiative, referendum, and recall.

Monetary history also lent support to the position of the Populists. When gold discoveries in Alaska and South Africa markedly increased the supply of gold in the world and thus increased the amount of currency in circulation (inflation), the economy benefited. Moreover, the expanded supply of gold meant that when the United States passed the Gold Standard Act in 1898, the country could end the uncertainty about which monetary standard it would follow without contracting the currency (deflation).

The Populists obviously were not solely and perhaps not primarily responsible for the implementation of their ideas. Nor were all the ideas they espoused original. Even the Redeemers had called for a federal income tax and generally had supported railroad regulation. Still, they left a remarkable legacy. They developed and articulated a wide range of ideas and proposals for a society that was in disarray. Their creativity and boldness stood in stark contrast to the timidity and vacuity of both the Democrats and the Republicans. In challenging the color bar and in speaking for the dispossessed, they showed uncommon courage. A historian of Populism in Alabama concluded:

> To embrace Populism in the 1890s was an act of defiance. A man could not thereby increase his social prestige....No one voted Populist from habit for the People's Party was new. Men who voted Populist were frequently plagued by social ostracism, loss of financial credit, and sometimes physical intimidation. If the charges of white Democrats were true, Populists were guilty of treason to party, race, religion, and sacred Jeffersonian principles.

The strength of the Populists' legacy indicated the extent of their debt to the deep currents of postbellum reform thought and agitation, currents that had their sources in urban and industrial America as well as in rural America. That legacy also indicated that increasing numbers of Americans shared the sentiments if not the particular ideas the Populists espoused. More than anything else, the Populists were part of and shapers of a growing feeling that the government and the economy could not exist in separate spheres if the United States was to have any hope of living up to its expressed dreams and ideals. Thus, through the Alliance first and then the People's party, the South contributed in an elemental way to altering the course of the nation that only a generation earlier it had tried to sunder.

As an institution, the Populist party failed. In its earlier years, it enjoyed amazing success for a new party at the polls. But the Populists could not overcome the limitations imposed on all new political parties in the United States or the severe problems specific to their time and place. Racial animosities and fears and sectionalism took heavy tolls.

The Populist party, like the Alliance before it, created some of its own difficulties. Try as they might, the Populists could not keep from sounding like a single-interest movement. Too much of what they wanted appeared primarily to serve the interest of southern cotton growers and western wheat farmers. Other farmers spurned them or ignored them. So did industrial workers, for the most part. The Populists defined "producers" too narrowly, thus discounting the positive role of bankers, investors, merchants, and other "nonproducers" in aiding and sustaining economic growth and activity. In fact, the Populists became so caught up in their praises of agrarianism that they often appeared to be reactionaries in search of the lost world of Thomas Jefferson.

That they were not. Their proposals alone ought to silence the notion that Populism equaled agrarian antiquarianism. The Populists sensed the threat that concentration of economic and political power posed for American life. Yet the Populists never went so far as to break with their attachment to the concept of private property. They blamed "monopolies" for the problems of American agriculture and shied away from blaming a market-oriented economic system.

Within the South, the Populists took dead aim at the foundations of the Lost Cause and the New South. As one historian wrote,

> Southern Populism collided full tilt with the whole edifice of Southern Politics; with the romantic attachment to images of the past; with the separation of politics and economics; with the entombing one-party system, with the [white] folk unity forged by Reconstruction. The Populists talked the language of economics and self-interest. They spoke of class consciousness and class legislation, of combining farmers and laborers in one party, of using government to solve economic problems. Most alarming of all, they said that economic self-interest transcended race. They proposed to fit the Negro in somewhere in their great combination.

Moreover, the Populists did enjoy some success with working-class Americans in the south and elsewhere. The Knights of Labor enjoyed a resurgence after 1890, allied themselves with Eugene V. Debs's American Railway Union, and joined forces with the Populists. Some of these workers and their leaders subsequently became a part of the Socialist party, which showed surprising strength in Texas, Arkansas, Louisiana, and Oklahoma in the early twentieth century.

No wonder the Populists excited such hostility. Entrenched Democrats employed legal and illegal devices to stop the Populist party, then to eliminate it. Fraudulent elections and violence and threats of violence were common. The Democrats also had the advantage of being the established party and the white man's party. Moreover, many voters disagreed with Populist proposals or did not trust the Populists.

DISFRANCHISEMENT: JIM CROW AND SOUTHERN POLITICS

The Democrats discovered in the 1890s that their best weapon to ensure their dominance was the law. Seeking legal means to limit the franchise, they forged the law into an ornate iron gate that effectively barred the way to undesirable voters. Those means included poll taxes, complicated registration laws, such mystifying election procedures as multiple ballot boxes and vague secret ballots, literacy and property tests, and understanding clauses and grandfather clauses.* Most of these tortured statutes clearly discriminated against the poor and the less well educated. Most of these people were black, but many were white. Some efforts were made to lessen the impact on poorer whites, but not many. It is more than suggestive that of all the measures passed by the southern states to limit the franchise, only the poll tax was enacted in every state.

Only Mississippi, South Carolina, Louisiana, Alabama, and Virginia held constitutional conventions to constrict the franchise. Of those states, only Alabama submitted its revised constitution to the voters. Passage was secured by heavy majorities in the black belt. Either the result was fraudulent or Alabama blacks had taken the unusual step of voting to disfranchise themselves.

The disfranchisers overwhelmed white and black opponents, many of whom were Populists, in legislatures, in constitutional conventions, at the polls, and in the courts. In 1898, in *Williams* v. *Mississippi*, the United States Supreme Court upheld the constitutionality of the disfranchisement provisions of the Mississippi state constitution. The decision was the climactic moment for legal disfranchisement, which had begun modestly in the 1870s and early 1880s, accelerated and broadened dramatically after 1888, and reached its peak during the 1890s.

The decision of the Supreme Court meant that the federal government would not attempt to defend the political rights of blacks as it had done in the past. In making its decision, the Court fell back from the bolder constitutional innovations of the Reconstruction era and retreated to the more familiar ground where states had traditionally had the power to set eligibility rules for voters, even in federal elections. Disfranchisement had racial and class motives and im-

---

*"Understanding" clauses are discussed on p. 523. They were enacted in Mississippi, South Carolina, Georgia, and Virginia. North Carolina, Louisiana, and Oklahoma passed grandfather clauses, which exempted all men who could have voted before 1867 (before Republican governments came to power during Reconstruction) from property or literacy requirements. The exemptions sometimes applied to their descendants as well: the descendants of veterans could get exemptions in Alabama and Georgia under their "fighting grandfather" clauses.

These clauses provided only limited protection to poorer whites who could not meet other requirements for registering and voting, since the period of time during which these exemptions were available was limited. Only Mississippi put no time limit on its "understanding" clause. The small number of these clauses and the time limits imposed on them suggest that the men who designed them were concerned primarily to get the disfranchisement laws and constitutional changes past voters who might object to disfranchising low-income whites.

plications. In 1904 Mississippi Congressman Eaton J. Bowers explained that Mississippi had

> disfranchised not only the ignorant and vicious black, but the ignorant and vicious white as well, and the electorate in Mississippi is now confined to those, and to those alone, who are qualified by intelligence and character for the proper and patriotic exercise of this great franchise.

A disfranchisement leader in Louisiana assured

> the large class of the people of Louisiana who will be disfranchised under the proposed limitations of the suffrage [that] what we seek to do is undertaken in a spirit, not of hostility to any particular men or set of men, but in the belief that the State should see to the protection of the weaker classes; should guard them against the machinations of those who would use them only to further their own base ends; should see to it that they are not allowed to harm themselves. We owe it to the ignorant, we owe it to the weak, to protect them just as we would protect a little child.

Partisan aims were also served. Some Democrats wanted disfranchisement to protect the position of their party and to minimize competition. However, disentangling the motives of the disfranchisers in order to determine whether race, class, or partisanship played the biggest part is probably impossible. Most historians give primacy to race as a motive. Since blacks were poorer than whites and more likely to be Republicans, racial discrimination in registration and voting automatically involved class and partisan discrimination. But because many of the voting laws had a class bias—that is, they discriminated against people who were illiterate, did not have property, moved often, or could ill afford to pay the cumulative poll taxes—the voting laws adversely affected the political rights of the small white landowners who formed the base of the Populist party.

Disfranchisement had a major impact on southern politics. Declines of 50 percent in registration and voting were common. Blacks became nonentities as political participants. The Democrats became so entrenched that they had no effective political opposition except in some local elections and congressional races in eastern Tennessee, western North Carolina, and southwestern Virginia. For all practical purposes, the most important elections in the South were the Democratic primaries, and the Democrats limited their primaries to whites only. The South thus became a one-party region in which politicians did not have to appeal to the majority of the citizens.

The South reversed the long nineteenth-century trend of expanding the suffrage. Scholars see some comparable developments in the North, where politicians acted to limit the impact of the votes of the "new immigration" from eastern and southern Europe. Governments exist to solve problems that escape private solutions. Private efforts to create an electorate congenial to the southern Democrats had failed, and had repeatedly raised charges of fraud and threats of federal intervention in elections; so they turned to government to get that electorate for them. Coincidentally, as we shall see in Chapter 21, southern white governments erected an elaborate code of racial segregation governing virtually every facet of life in the South. Jim Crow, as the system of racial segregation was called, had been largely informal in the past. Now it was formalized.

THE FOUNDATION RESECURED

Disfranchisement probably ended any prospects the Populists might have had in the South. Then economic recovery eased anxieties and dampened ardor for reform. Farmers especially enjoyed better times. Coincidentally, Americans, north and south, joined in the war against Spain. Good times, "a splendid little war," new territorial acquisitions, and a heightened sense of the country's importance in the world caused memories of the depression and the political turmoil of the 1890s to fade. White supremacy at home and abroad seemed natural, indeed divinely ordained.

White supremacy was fixed in the South. So was the Democratic party, as was cotton, still. The Little Rock *Arkansas Gazette* declared in 1899: "Once more the South is getting up on its feet.... The wait has been a long one, but the hour of prosperity has come, and come to stay. Once more cotton is king."

Even if the Populists had gotten their subtreasury plan passed and had substantially changed the credit system, it is very doubtful that dependency on cotton would have been much altered or that the average southern farmer would have enjoyed sustained prosperity. Though much had changed in the South since 1865, as the Cotton States Exposition attested, most southerners were still overdependent on agriculture for their livelihood. The great majority of southerners no doubt correctly sensed that they had too few alternatives in the kingdom of cotton and that cotton was a miserly monarch. No doubt they resented those frequent homilies about diversified farming delivered by the likes of Judge Emory Speer. The judge told the inaugural audience at the exposition about a fruit and vegetable farm he had seen on a recent vacation trip to the Georgia mountains. He urged southern farmers to use such farms as models. Unfortunately, at the moment, that approach to farming was entirely inappropriate to and beyond the means of the vast number of southerners who toiled in the fields.

21

Divisions in Dixie

——————— ❖ ———————

T here were and (still are) many Souths. The two most obvious and most widely discussed are the black South and the white South. The distance between the two and the hostility between them became greater in the 1890s than it probably had ever been before and remained so for more than a generation. One man tried to bridge the gap.

THE ATLANTA COMPROMISE

In 1895 Booker T. Washington, who rose from slavery to become the founder and then president of Tuskegee Institute in Alabama, suggested terms for a truce or compromise between the black South and the white South in a speech he delivered at the Cotton States and International Exposition in Atlanta in September 1895. His remarks, which became known as "The Atlanta Compromise," fitted the occasion like a glove and mirrored the times and the place with arresting precision.

Washington spoke to a racially segregated, predominantly white audience, which initially gave him a cool reception. But when he finished, the audience cheered him wildly. Washington succeeded by saying what southern whites wanted to hear, by making blacks feel proud, and by praising northern whites "for the constant help that has come to our educational life,...especially from Northern philanthropists." He spoke in biblical terms while embracing the rampant materialism of the times and the place. Blacks were delighted to have one of their own recognized by southern whites. Such recognition was rare, and Washington did blacks proud by performing wonderfully. Initially few blacks dissented from his remarks; eventually many did.

Washington began his speech with an assertion that formed the foundation of his address: blacks and whites had mutual, entwined interests. "One-third of the population of the South is of the Negro race. No enterprise seeking the material, civil, or moral welfare of this section can disregard this element of our population and reach the highest success." He tacitly accepted the white version of the Reconstruction and post-Reconstruction eras and endorsed a grad-

ualist approach to black participation in southern politics. In the 1860s, "ignorant and inexperienced" former slaves had made the mistake of trying to start
"at the top instead of at the bottom...a seat in Congress or the state legislature
was more sought than real estate or industrial skill....It is at the bottom of life
we must begin." Washington decried efforts to encourage blacks to emigrate to
Africa and to encourage Europeans to swell the labor force in the New South.
He adroitly blended the "faithful Negro" theme, a southern white staple, with
allusions to labor conflicts in the immigrant-populated North. He could rely on
his audience to recall Haymarket, Homestead, and Pullman, three long-
remembered episodes of American industrial warfare that had occurred within
the past decade.

> As we have proved our loyalty to you in the past, in nursing your children, watch-
> ing by the sick-bed of your mothers and fathers, and often following them with tear-
> dimmed eyes to their graves, so in the future, in our humble way, we shall stand by
> you with devotion that no foreigner can approach, ready to lay down our lives, if
> need be, in defense of yours, interlacing our industrial, commercial, civil, and reli-
> gious life with yours in a way that shall make the interest of both races one.

Then, raising his hand high, Washington electrified the audience with a memorable gesture and reassuring words: "In all things that are purely social, we
can be separate as the fingers, yet one as the hand in all things essential to mutual progress." The "whole audience," a New York *World* reporter wrote, "was
on its feet in a delirium of applause."

Washington accepted or acquiesced in the divisions between the black

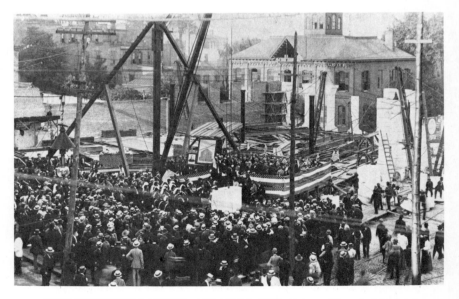

CORNERSTONE LAYING, ATLANTA, 1891 (Atlanta Historical Society)

South and the white South. He dismissed "the agitation of questions of social equality" as "the extremest folly.... Progress in the enjoyment of all the privileges that will come to us must be the result of severe and constant struggle rather than of artificial forcing." He implicitly suggested that the securing of political rights for blacks could wait until another, unspecified day. Washington did, however, make an oblique call for civil rights: he hoped that there would be "a determination to administer absolute justice...[and] a willing obedience among all classes to the mandates of the law."

Throughout, Washington based his remarks on the assumption that material progress had transformative powers, that it promised a better day (someday) for patient, hard-working blacks and for the entire South. He also assumed that blacks would play a subordinate role in this process, principally as a critically needed source of labor, especially on the farm. Such assumptions reflected the pervasiveness of materialism at the time and fitted neatly into white perceptions about the place of blacks in the nation.

*J*IM CROW

Many blacks then and more since criticized Washington as an "Uncle Tom," or a toady to southern whites. They had a point, but Washington's remarks reflected the realities of his day. The great majority of blacks lived in the South, where whites were dominant in every facet of life and were determined to remain so. The great majority of northern whites offered little support or encour-

BOOKER T. WASHINGTON STATUE (Tuskegee Institute, Alabama)

agement to blacks. Indeed, the attitudes of northern whites seemed to differ only slightly from those of southern whites. Blacks lacked the power and self-confidence at that time to put up more than token resistance.

In 1895 the Jim Crow system of de jure and de facto subordination of blacks in the South was beginning to reach its maturity. The Jim Crow system was a racial caste system. It was based on race in a starkly simple way. Anyone—from a pale-skinned mulatto to the very dark-skinned—who had Negroid physical characteristics was considered to be a Negro. Negroes were born into their caste and could not escape it by marriage or by personal achievement. They could never earn enough or achieve enough to escape their caste. Jim Crow was systematic. It involved the virtually total disfranchisement of blacks and sweeping racial segregation in social relations and, in many instances, in economic relations. The system grew out of white supremacy, or the idea that whites are inherently and culturally superior to "nonwhites." In the American South, blacks were the prime target of white supremacy, and there white supremacy involved more than prejudice and discrimination against people who had a particular ancestry and certain physical characteristics. In the South, white supremacy "suggest[ed] systematic and self-conscious efforts to make race or color a qualification for membership in the civil community." Jim Crow involved formal codes, restrictions written into law, and informal codes, unwritten but understood forms of behavior. The informal codes, for instance, required that blacks use only the back door at the home of a white and that blacks address a white by title and last name while whites almost always used the first name or nickname of a black. By law, blacks were segregated or excluded altogether from virtually all public places: public transportation, schools, housing, libraries, restrooms, drinking fountains, barber and beauty shops, the offices of physicians, dentists, and lawyers, hospitals, institutions for the incapacitated and dependent, and cemeteries. Perhaps eager to establish its identity as a southern state, Oklahoma required racially segregated telephone booths. Jim Crow, as we shall see, also involved blatant economic discrimination.

By 1895, when Washington spoke, most of the southern states had taken significant legal steps to restrict the civil and political rights of blacks. These measures, as we know, had been preceded by nonlegal measures. During Reconstruction, these measures first hampered and then undermined Republican state governments and Republican officeholders in the South and seemed to assure the Democrats of dominance. Legal disfranchisement measures began to appear after 1875, reached flood proportions in the 1890s, and continued to come until 1915. As blacks disappeared from the polls, they disappeared from public offices and from jury boxes. The last black congressman left office in 1901. There would not be another until 1928, and he was from Chicago.

Predictably, blacks did not receive equal protection of the law. Neither did their concerns command the attention of politicians and public officials. Blacks were three times as likely as whites to be incarcerated and received much harsher sentences for the same crime—a pattern that continued for many years. In South Carolina, 80 percent of the felons executed by the state from 1915 to

1962 were black. As we saw earlier, blacks were also overrepresented in the convict lease system and on chain gangs, the most brutal manifestations of the penal system. By 1910, however, most of the southern states abandoned the convict lease system after a series of newspaper exposés and legislative hearings revealed that the system was too grotesque even for the Jim Crow era. Embarrassment may have been a more powerful force for change than a stricken conscience.

Chain gangs remained, however. Local governments found them important sources of labor for services and projects. Penal systems and laws that resembled the infamous Black Codes were closely related to what southern whites thought were their needs for labor and to their concern to keep blacks "in their place." Vagrancy laws provided a useful means of obtaining labor when it appeared to be in short supply—short sometimes because employers conspired to create labor shortages by keeping wages low. In 1903 Alabama defined a vagrant as "any person wandering or strolling about in idleness, who is able to work, and has no property to support him; or any person leading an idle, immoral, profligate life, having no property to support him." The next year the Atlanta *Constitution* wryly notified the local police: "Cotton is ripening. See that the 'vags' get busy."

The number of blacks who were subjected to this form of involuntary servitude cannot be accurately calculated, nor can the number of those who worked in debt peonage (court-ordered hiring out to individuals to work off debts) or under surety contracts (court-ordered hiring out to individuals to work off fines and sentences). Debt peonage, which sometimes claimed white victims, was usually found in more remote areas, such as turpentining camps, where public attention was unlikely and where the work was harsh even without the brutalities that accompanied peonage. Peonage represented "the shadow of slavery," a shadow with real substance.

Southern white farmers and governments also continued their attempts to restrain the freedom of black farm laborers. To prevent blacks from leaving farms during the crop year, laws were passed making such departures criminal rather than civil offenses, and specifying fines both for the blacks who moved on and for the persons convicted of enticing them away. "Emigrant agents" who recruited black labor in the South faced stiff barriers. In 1891 the Carolinas passed laws that required such agents to buy a license in each county in which they operated, at $1,000 per county. Failure to do so could result in a fine of $5,000 and a sentence of two years. The "system of involuntary servitude was a unique blend of slavery and freedom which gave whites the option of limiting black movement while leaving Negroes otherwise free to come and go as they pleased"—and, it might be added, more responsible for their own survival than slaves had been. How successful these efforts to restrain the freedom of black farm laborers were is not clear. Very likely, the mobility of the laborers was constrained to a degree, but the size of black migrations from the South indicated that there were limits to the success of those constraints. The numbers of blacks

leaving the rural South became so large in the early twentieth century and remained so large for many years thereafter that the movement became known as
the "Great Migration."

Blacks were also the primary targets of extralegal "court systems" that operated in all the southern states. Between 1882 and 1951, vigilante mobs in the
United States "executed" or lynched—after a "trial" in which "evidence" was
given to and assessed by a "jury"—more than 4,900 people, more than four-
fifths of whom were blacks. Initially lynching had been a phenomenon primarily of the American frontier. After the mid-1880s, however, it shifted to the
South, where some 80 percent of lynchings were committed. The number of
recorded lynchings also increased dramatically. Nearly three-fourths of the
lynchings from 1882 to 1951 were committed in the quarter century after 1882.
The worst year was 1892, when perhaps 235 died, and the numbers did not fall
consistently below 100 until 1908.

Lynching was community-sanctioned murder. Crimes were alleged; trials
were summary; death, often accompanied by torture and mutilation, came by
hanging, shooting, burning, stabbing, dragging, and combinations thereof.
Lynchings often attracted large crowds, which frequently included women and
children. Lynchers were almost never arrested or convicted. Eventually national and community pressures brought the barbarous ritual to an end. In only
one-sixth of the lynchings in the South was rape of a white woman by a black
man even alleged, though this "crime against white womanhood" was the primary justification given for lynchings, and such lynchings were even publicly
defended by prominent public officials. Lynch victims were accused of everything from theft to arrogance toward whites to being "bad." Economic competition between blacks and low-income whites may have been the root cause in
most instances.

Thomas Pearce Bailey, a South Carolina–born psychologist and distinguished educator, summarized the racial credo of southern whites in 1914:

> 1. "Blood will tell." 2. The white race must dominate. 3. The Teutonic peoples stand
> for race purity. 4. The Negro is inferior and will remain so. 5. "This is a white man's
> country." 6. No social equality. 7. No political equality. 8. In matters of civil rights
> and legal adjustments give the white man, as opposed to the colored man, the ben-
> efit of the doubt; and under no circumstances interfere with the prestige of the white
> race. 9. In educational policy let the Negro have the crumbs that fall from the white
> man's table. 10. Let there be such industrial education of the Negro as will best fit
> him to serve the white man. 11. Only Southerners understand the Negro question.
> 12. Let the South settle the Negro question. 13. The status of peasantry is all the
> Negro may hope for, if the races are to live together in peace. 14. Let the lowest
> white man count for more than the highest Negro. 15. The above statements indi-
> cate the leadings of Providence.

Bailey, however, had a more moderate, even advanced view: "The real problem
is not the Negro, but the white man's attitude toward the Negro."

A LYNCHING (Library of Congress)

WHY JIM CROW?

Why Southern whites acted with such venom and so systematically is not clear. Nor can why they acted *when* they did be fully explained. But it may be helpful to examine four factors: the level of confidence and fear among southern whites, the strengths and weaknesses of outside pressures, the shifting role of the federal government, and the power of blacks.

After the Civil War, southern whites developed a reasonably acceptable (at least, to them) pattern of racial dominance in which sweeping segregation laws seemed unnecessary and were not sought. In the later 1880s, however, whites were saying more and more often that the pattern was not working. They talked about troublesome blacks, in particular about the coming of age of the first generation of blacks who had not been reared in slavery and thus had not been taught the proper roles and spheres of blacks and whites. By 1905, articles on "the Negro problem" or "Negro question" appeared in many publications. Most authors saw gloomy, often threatening prospects for race relations. Whites' perceptions of blacks had some factual basis, both narrowly and broadly conceived. The first generation of postslavery blacks was in fact reaching adulthood. More important, economic change and urbanization unsettled the racial modus vivendi of the postbellum South. Competition between blacks and whites as farm laborers, in services and industry, and sometimes in skilled trades rubbed against exposed nerves. Competition for housing and public services in urban areas became intense as southern towns and cities shared in the explosive growth of Gilded Age America. Towns and cities raised other volatile issues. Were the taboos and the understood rules of racial etiquette of the rural south known and applied in the urban South? Was it not necessary, indeed urgent, that they be codified or written into law, especially since blacks made up to 40 to 50 percent, sometimes more, of the population of cities and towns in the South?

The already fragile relationship between blacks and whites became much more tense when the economy collapsed in the 1890s. As we have seen, Democrats warred with one another, with the Populists, and with the Republicans in one of the most tumultuous decades in southern politics, and the political storm enveloped blacks. The dearth of jobs, the mounting debts and declining returns from farming, and the dwindling of money for the essentials of life fueled elemental fears. In turn, race relations suffered.

Fear also grew from less concrete sources than competition for jobs, housing, and public services. That fear had a phobic, irrational quality which had its sources in deep, tangled emotions. How else can the enormous anxiety of whites about the security of white women against sexual attacks by black men be explained? Or the firm belief of whites that efforts of blacks to secure their civil and political rights were an opening wedge for attempts to end social segregation and achieve some never-defined social equality? Or the fears of racial contamination that propelled white school officials to go so far as to keep school textbooks in racially segregated warehouses? Apparently thousands read *The Clansman* (1904), by the Reverend Thomas Dixon, Jr., despite its subtitle, *An Historical Romance of the Ku Klux Klan*. Part of its attraction was its lurid descriptions of blacks:

> He had the short, heavy-set neck of the lower order of animals. His skin was coal black, his lips so thick they curled both ways up and down with crooked bloodmarks across them. His nose was flat, and its enormous nostrils seemed in perpetual dilation. The sinister bead eyes, with brown splotches in their whites, were set wide apart and gleamed ape-like under his scant brows. His enormous cheekbones and jaws seemed to protrude beyond the ears and almost hide them.

D. W. Griffith made this novel into a highly successful film, *The Birth of a Nation* (1905), which was widely popular with white audiences.

Conversely, whites in the South were confident that white peoples were by birth and achievement superior to all other peoples. Whites virtually everywhere in the world at the time believed that. Southern whites were confident because they had long established their power and their will to dominate blacks. Southern whites were also confident by the 1890s because they faced little outside pressure of any kind, including interference from the federal government, to slow the course of Jim Crow. Finally, whites could be confident that blacks had little power to oppose them.

The federal government had retreated since the 1860s from intervention on the part of blacks in the South. Confronted after 1865 by the resurgence of the Democrats outside the South and by the return of the South to the Union, the Republicans had initially tried to establish beachheads south of the Mason-

Dixon line by enfranchising blacks and supporting those whites who had Union sentiments and presumably would join the Republican party. Reconstruction ended in defeat for this Republican strategy. So the Republicans had experimented with other approaches, also without much success. They had conciliated the white South with the Compromise of 1877, which made it explicit and widely known that southern whites had virtually a free hand in race relations in the South. In 1883 the Supreme Court struck down the Civil Rights Act of 1875, which on paper had outlawed racial discrimination in public accommodations. The Court ruled that though governments could not legally discriminate in public accommodations, individuals could. The Republicans had sought alliances with independent political movements, most notably with the Readjusters in Virginia in the 1870s and 1880s. In the 1890s, some Republicans in the South joined forces with the Southern Farmers' Alliance and then with the Populist party.

In 1890 Republicans in Congress tried to return to their basic strength in the South, blacks. In doing so, Republicans made their last major effort to use federal power on behalf of blacks. The Republican-controlled House of Representatives narrowly passed the Lodge Election Bill, which was designed to counter election frauds in the South by providing federal supervision of congressional elections when citizens petitioned to protest returns in those elections. Proponents of the measure claimed that fraudulent election returns were depriving the Republicans of electoral victories in the South. Opponents—primarily Democrats in all sections, but especially in the South—countered with visions of Reconstruction revived and federal government tyranny. Borrowing from the traditions of the American Revolution, they denounced the bill as the Force Bill. The name stuck, an ironic twist to the intent of the bill. The measure died in the Senate and with it Congress's last attempt for many years to assure blacks of their voting rights in the South.

Political developments in the 1890s reinforced this Republican retreat. The national debacle of the Democratic party in the 1890s helped the Republicans become the majority party in the country even though they received no electoral votes from the South and were seldom factors in any state election there. The Republicans dominated American politics from the mid-1890s until 1930 with no more than a shadow of a party in the South. The Republicans' newly achieved power allowed them for the first time in their history largely to ignore the South—and blacks. The functions of the Republicans in the South shrank to those of a "post office" party. Republican presidential hopefuls exchanged promises of political appointments (postmasterships and so forth) for southern Republican votes at national nominating conventions. No longer in need of southern votes to win national elections, Republicans acquiesced in white supremacy in the South. The Democrats were hardly likely candidates at that time to become champions of black rights.

The Supreme Court acknowledged the completeness of the retreat of the federal government as defender of the rights of blacks when it made several landmark decisions that gave judicial sanction to Jim Crow. In *Plessy* v. *Ferguson* (1896) the Court enunciated its famous "separate but equal" doctrine in ruling that a Louisiana law requiring racial segregation in public transportation was constitutional. Only Justice John M. Harlan, a Kentuckian from a family of former slaveholders, dissented. The Constitution, he contended, was color-blind. Two years later the Court ruled that Mississippi could require literacy tests and poll taxes for voter registration. Southern political leaders correctly perceived that the Fourteenth and Fifteenth amendments could be legally evaded, that Jim Crow was not an outlaw.

American blacks also suffered setbacks outside the South. Though black men generally retained the right to vote in the North, blacks faced mounting hostility there. State laws against racial discrimination remained largely unenforced. Segregation, in schools and elsewhere, was common. The never sub-stantial number of black officeholders in the North shrank. Support for the rights of blacks among organized labor declined. Though not always a consis-tent defender of black workers, the Knights of Labor treated them more fairly than virtually any other organization or institution in the United States at the time. But the American Federation of Labor (AFL), which in the 1880s displaced the Knights as the leading American labor union, tacitly accepted Jim Crow in the workplace. Two unions affiliated with the AFL, however, included many blacks among their ranks: the International Longshoremen's Association and the United Mine Workers. Moreover, scattered evidence suggests instances of racial cooperation in local trade unions. However, these were exceptions to the general pattern of growing hostility toward blacks, north and south.

Beyond the United States, pressures against Jim Crow were nonexistent. If anything, they reinforced Jim Crow. Ideologically and politically, white su-premacy was attaining new heights. History, achievements in the arts, eco-nomic development, and gains in technology were believed to give indisputable proof that whites were superior. A particular subspecies of white supremacy flourished: Anglo-Saxonism. Politically, whites had demonstrated their capacity to shape the world. Europeans and Americans carried their money, products, and culture throughout the world. In a remarkably short time Europeans ex-panded or established political control over much of Africa and Asia. The United States followed with new footholds in the Caribbean, Central America, and the Pacific. History and contemporary events seemed to justify and rein-force white supremacy. Thus white supremacy was not peculiar to the South, though the forms it took there and the intensity with which it was embraced were unusual even at that time.

Blacks did not retreat readily before these overwhelming odds. They con-tinued to assert their rights as citizens and human beings. Black men exercised their franchise in spite of mounting discouragements and barriers until the Jim Crow system eliminated virtually any possibility of voting. As they had done earlier, blacks protested segregation on public transportation and did so effec-tively as late as 1894 in Atlanta. Other boycotts of streetcars in southern cities, however, proved more indicative of the direction of southern race relations. Not one of a dozen such boycotts between 1896 and 1908 succeeded. Atlanta fell into step, too. Jim Crow prevailed on the streetcars there after 1906, the year of

a gruesome race riot in Atlanta. Blacks occasionally formed protest organizations, of which the Afro-American Council was the most important. Founded in
1890, the council stagnated by the middle of the 1890s and became extinct by
1908, testimony to black impotence against white power. Others sought a qui-
eter form of protest; they moved. Moving offered more safety and greater prospects for oneself and one's family. It was an old story that dated back to the
movements of free blacks within and out of the slave South, then to movements
of blacks during and after the Civil War. Cities and towns offered refuge and
hope—more safety from whites, greater personal freedom, better jobs, and
greater opportunities for education. Newer farm regions inside and outside the
South, as in Kansas in the 1870s, also beckoned.

Not until after 1910 did large numbers of blacks move outside the South.
Fifty years after the Civil War, 89 percent of American blacks lived in the South,
a decline of only 3 percent in a half century. Significant shifts occurred in that
half century, however. Migrations to Louisiana, Texas, Arkansas, and Oklahoma helped raise the black population in those states to nearly 2 million, almost one-fourth of the total number of blacks living in the South. At the same
time, 1.5 million blacks moved to urban areas in the South.

After the Civil War some blacks left the United States entirely. Most significant of the few emigrants were those who chose exile in Africa. Henry McNeal
Turner, a bishop in the African Methodist Episcopal church and a politician and
activist in Georgia, became the principal spokesman of back-to-Africa interests,
which had a brief but well-publicized life in the 1870s and periodically thereafter
until 1900. The meager response to Turner's appeals and to similar appeals by
others can, however, mislead us as to the importance of the back-to-Africa
movement. Turner preached black pride—pride in black skin, in the achievements of blacks, and in their African heritage. He and others who had similar
ideas thus presented a markedly distinctive message in a day of rampant Anglo-
Saxonism and European ethnocentrism.

The fact that Turner commanded an audience but made few converts to emigration had profound implications. Few blacks had a realistic alternative to living in the United States. Moreover, despite all that had happened to them,
blacks showed they were Americans with a deep attachment to America,
though they had an African heritage and a historical experience that was strikingly different from that of other groups in the United States. W. E. B. Du Bois,
the brilliant black scholar and activist, called this the "twoness" of being "an
American, a Negro; two souls, two thoughts, two unreconciled strivings." Du
Bois believed, as he said in 1901, that the

> history of the American Negro is the history of this strife . . . to merge his double self
> into a better and truer self. . . . He would not Africanize America, for America has too
> much to teach the world and Africa. He would not bleach his Negro soul in a flood
> of white Americanism, for he knows that Negro blood has a message for the world.
> He simply wishes to make it possible for a man to be a Negro and an American,
> without being cursed and spit upon by his fellows, without having the doors of Op-
> portunity closed roughly in his face.

Du Bois openly criticized Booker T. Washington, something blacks rarely did at the time because Washington was the most powerful black leader in the country. Washington, Du Bois argued publicly, put too much blame on blacks for their poverty and lack of education and too little blame on whites. Du Bois believed that in accepting whites' demands that blacks stay out of politics, Washington had conceded too much and did not realize that political participation was a prime means for blacks to register dissent and gain attention to their concerns. Finally, Du Bois attacked the basic philosophy of Tuskegee Institute, which stressed a vocational education that he thought was inadequate to prepare its students for life in the twentieth century.

Questions about the origins of Jim Crow have stimulated an extraordinarily rich debate among scholars and have left some very perceptive insights into the past of the American South. The debate has focused on several questions: Why was Jim Crow so systematic? What mode of race relations did it displace or augment? Why did Jim Crow emerge when it did? What were the alternatives to Jim Crow? Did Jim Crow represent a major break with the older modes of race relations in the South? The debate has extended beyond the boundaries of the United States as scholars have turned to comparisons between race relations in the American South and in South Africa. South Africa's system of rigid racial segregation, called *apartheid*, has close parallels to Jim Crow, yet the systems also have some striking differences.

Jim Crow displaced what has been called laissez faire segregation: a patchwork pattern of political segregation, some self-segregation, segregated parallel institutions, and understood behavior. Well before 1900, southerners were divided by race. Most blacks voted Republican, most whites voted Democratic. Blacks and whites segregated themselves in churches, in many businesses and professions, and in social relations. Schools were racially divided also. Thus parallel, racially segregated but similar structures evolved in the South. Blacks rode where they pleased on public transportation, sat where they pleased in theaters, ate in restaurants that they chose—in some places in the South but not in others. Whites employed random means to keep blacks "in their place"—

BLACK STUDENTS AT HAMPTON (Library of Congress)

lynchings and physical threats and abuse, discriminatory justice, intimidation. Paternalism and personal patronage softened the force of laissez faire racism, although both reinforced the notion and reality of white dominance.

Sometime, perhaps in the late 1880s, race relations took a noticeably negative turn. Jim Crow subsequently displaced laissez faire segregation. Clearly Jim Crow did not introduce racial segregation to the South, a fact underlined by the recent work of scholars. But Jim Crow did represent a sharp change in race relations because it was so thorough and sweeping and because it had the backing of the law, which was usually enforced. Jim Crow was put in place in the 1890s and the early twentieth century, not, as once was thought, when Reconstruction ended or when the North first showed it had little inclination to intervene on behalf of blacks. The economic and political turbulence of the 1890s stimulated Jim Crow enormously. Jim Crow then became entrenched and acquired the appearance of permanence, the appearance that it represented what had always been and what always would be.

Jim Crow examined reveals much more than that. Its creation was supported by the great majority of whites. That support came from upper- and middle-class whites, not just from poorer whites variously labeled "rednecks," "crackers," and "white trash." Southern white leaders found Jim Crow a useful means of building unity among whites and blurring class divisions among them. Jim Crow lay at the foundation of what has been called the "Herrenvolk democracy" of the South, a system of political democracy for whites only that ignored or obscured class divisions. Jim Crow brought order to race relations—a retrogressive, repressive order, but order. Once Jim Crow was in place, for instance, the number of lynchings declined. Elections became more orderly, though they were markedly less democratic, because so many adult males had been disfranchised. There were alternatives to Jim Crow; most were worse. Operative forces in the 1890s made a continuation of laissez faire segregation highly unlikely. Far more unlikely would have been developments comparable to those that occurred after World War II, when segregation and disfranchisement of blacks were ended. Massive, forced deportation of blacks did not occur, nor did forced removal to specially created reservations, nor did genocide. Could such horrors have taken place? Certainly they had occurred before, and they have occurred since in human history. Such happened to Indians in America.

Why did not even worse happen? Perhaps the ties, including deep emotional attachment, between southern blacks and whites played a part. Blacks in America assimilated white culture to a much greater extent than Africans in South Africa. The degree of assimilation was reflected in the range and depth of similarities between southern blacks and whites with respect to religion, family structure and roles, and commitment to materialism. After all, in an age of the self-made man, Booker T. Washington fitted hand in glove with the dominant white culture. Blacks and whites shared a common citizenship, though they received widely disproportionate shares of the fruits of that citizenship. Unlike white South Africans, for example, American whites could not treat blacks as aliens without certain rights, such as the right to remain in the United States. Moreover, blacks could (and did) move to states outside the South, where they hardly received warm receptions but did get to vote. The American tradition of adherence to the law, though often more honored in the breach than in the observance, must have had some influence here, as it has had throughout most of American history.

Probably the most important factor that precluded alternatives worse even than Jim Crow was the labor of blacks. As whites clearly understood, the economy of the South required large amounts of black labor. Agriculture, most of the extractive industries, some manufacturing, shipping, and services relied heavily on black workers. Moreover, competition between black and white labor tended to be blunted by chance or design. Unlike white workers in South Africa, those in the South were not faced by a mass of black workers whose numbers threatened to drive them from the labor market altogether. White South Africans were, and their government passed laws to exclude black Africans from most jobs. Southern states stopped short of wholesale legal exclusion.

Nor did employers in the South pay blacks far less than whites for the same work, as South African employers do. Demographic patterns had a part in that. Population patterns in the South softened black-white competition in farming: blacks predominated in those areas where plantation agriculture prevailed, while whites predominated in the piedmont and mountain areas. Blacks and whites who worked at the same or similar jobs in mining, iron and steel plants, shipping, and services usually worked in segregated units, but not always. Observers frequently commented on seeing blacks and whites work side by side in the South but never in the North. Booker T. Washington was not merely courting his audience at the Atlanta Exposition when he asserted that Negroes had greater economic opportunities in the South than in the North in the 1890s. He was stating a fact.

Economic competition between blacks and whites was eased in other ways, to the disadvantage of blacks. Certain positions were reserved for whites only, especially the more skilled, better-paying ones and supervisory positions. Over time, black artisans lost out to white artisans, except in bricklaying and stone masonry. Trade unions lent Jim Crow a hand by making racially discriminatory uses of their apprenticeship rules. When black businessmen competed with white businessmen, they had serious handicaps. Lack of capital, credit, and training ensured that black-owned businesses would be small and especially vulnerable to economic fluctuations. Moreover, most black businesses served a low-income clientele, since most had a black clientele. Black physicians, dentists, and other professionals faced similar difficulties.

Blacks were excluded from one highly important manufacturing industry, cotton textiles. This was a de facto practice, not a de jure practice; only South Carolina passed a Jim Crow law for industry, in 1915, and then only for textiles. Worker insistence, more than anything else, accounted for this action. At the time textiles had a unique labor force among industries: women, some of them quite young, made up approximately half of the labor force in the industry. Many families worked as units. White textile workers grasped at the opportunity to portray Jim Crow as a means to protect white womanhood. Attempts to deviate from strict segregation—even hints of such attempts—triggered strikes or threats of strikes and other protests.

This response discouraged textile company officials from hiring blacks, except in the most menial jobs, and thus from hiring those who might work for even lower wages. This did not, however, necessarily mean that the textile industry had to face inflated labor costs. (Wages and labor costs are not necessarily the same thing.) Had the industry attempted to force its white workers to work with blacks, it would have faced the heavy costs of strikes and of losing many or most of its more experienced workers. The industry probably would have encountered great difficulty recruiting other white workers and perhaps would have caused state and local governments to take negative action against the industry. Finally, the threat of black labor gave management a potent weapon for keeping its white workers in place, a weapon management did not hesitate to use. Jim Crow in textiles all but excluded blacks from the largest industrial employer in the South until the 1960s, and therefore excluded them from one of the principal means of modest self-advancement available to the less advantaged in the Southeast.

*T*HE BLACK WORLD

The American South had its own "twoness," a white world and a black world. Jim Crow reflected this "twoness," and exacerbated and perpetuated it. The existence of two worlds whose boundaries were marked by the physical charac-

WOMEN'S BIBLE CLASS, COTTON-MILL VILLAGE (South Carolina State Museum)

teristics—not necessarily the ancestry—of their inhabitants was not new in 1900, or even in 1860. But the depth and clarity of the divisions between the worlds were new.

Racial divisions became starkly simple. The "one drop" demarcation prevailed. Anyone with any African ancestry—"one drop of Negro blood"—was a Negro, though he or she might be fair-skinned and blue-eyed. Thus by the early twentieth century such terms as *mulatto* fell into disuse, and American Negroes came generally to be thought of and to think of themselves as one people, no matter how dark or light they were. Some Negroes, however, did elect to "pass"—that is, to become accepted as white if their physical appearance made it possible for them to do so. Nor did Negroes always ignore their own variations in pigmentation: lighter skin continued to be more desirable among many Negroes.

Poverty, or perhaps more accurately relative deprivation, gave shape and substance to the black world. Occupational structure and the evidences and opportunities for self-improvement made this very clear. Racial discrimination compounded by educational deficiencies and landlessness shaped the occupation structure among blacks in the South and limited their economic advancement. The occupation structure, in turn, molded the world of the blacks in the South in decisive ways. Like southern whites, most southern blacks earned their living from farming, but they were much more likely than whites to be tenants, sharecroppers, or farm laborers. Proportionately fewer blacks became professionals than whites, or merchants or clerks. The numbers of black dentists, teachers, clergy, and lawyers were very small—especially lawyers, who were excluded from courtrooms. Eight in ten black professionals were teachers or ministers. After 1865, the number of black artisans declined. The overwhelming majority of blacks worked at jobs that required physical labor. A much higher percentage of black women worked outside the home than did white women. Here, need—sometimes desperate need—played its part. As black women were more likely to be poor, more of them sought employment than white women, more continued to do so after marriage and childbirth, and more remained employed for most of their lives. Bias played a hand, too. White women scorned domestic labor—cooking, cleaning, and laundering for others—as suitable only for blacks. More than eight in ten female domestics in the South in 1920 were black. Despite its low per capita income, the South had considerably more servants per household than any other region in the United States. In 1920, for instance, Atlanta had 249 female domestics for every 1,000 families, whereas Boston had 82, New York 74, and Chicago 68. Even white textile workers in the South employed blacks as domestics.

Despite numerous barriers, blacks made significant economic and social gains after 1865. Between 1865 and 1915, the number of blacks in the United States doubled while birth rates and mortality rates declined markedly. This fact indicated that, despite their poverty, the conditions of blacks' lives had improved after slavery. During the same time period, literacy rates among blacks rose from approximately 5 percent to over 50 percent. Income per capita among

BLACK MOTHER AND SON, 1920s (South Caroliniana
Library)

blacks probably more than doubled between 1866 and 1900. That rate exceeded
the rate of increase for white incomes over the same years, but incomes of
blacks remained well below those of whites—approximately 35 percent of incomes of whites in the nation. Moreover, had there been no racial discrimination, incomes for black Americans would have been 10 percent higher. The
slave past, landlessness, and lower educational and skill levels, almost universal among blacks in 1865 and too persistent thereafter, probably account for
much of the difference in incomes (and the even greater difference in wealth)
between blacks and whites in the South. Evidence suggests that blacks got
about the same pay for comparable work, but blacks seldom got the better jobs.

Black gains after the Civil War came from several sources. No longer slaves,
blacks commanded higher wages and had greater control over their labor and
leisure. They used these advantages to improve their situations. They sought
education for themselves and their children. In fact, through taxes and private

giving and expenditures, blacks paid for a large part of the education they received, from elementary school through college. Blacks moved to areas that promised greater opportunities, and they worked and struggled. In 1910 the census reported that 71 percent of blacks over nine years of age in the United States had gainful employment, while 51 percent of whites did. Blacks created their own savings institutions, banks, realty companies, and insurance companies, which often grew out of various fraternal and religious bodies.

John Merrick, a Durham, North Carolina, barber-turned-entrepreneur, formed a group to take over a fraternal order and reorganize it into an insurance company. Eventually North Carolina Mutual would become the largest black business in the country. Alonzo Herndon, an Atlanta barber, founded the Atlanta Life Insurance Company in 1905; it became North Carolina Mutual's major competitor. Maggie Walker, the daughter of a former slave, founded the Penny Savings Bank in Richmond, her hometown. Under her presidency the bank prospered and later merged with other black banks to form the Consolidated Bank and Trust company. Walker also organized the Richmond Council of Negro Women. Its 1,400 members engaged in a variety of reform activities.

Negroes also joined in "buy black" campaigns in an effort to support black-owned businesses. Still, the great majority of black businesses remained very small—mom-and-pop grocery stores, pharmacies, and general merchandise stores. By 1910 some 218,000 blacks were part or full owners of nearly 15.7 million acres of southern farmland, worth more than $212 million. But there were six times as many white landowners, and their farms were valued at more than $3 billion and averaged twice as many acres as those owned by blacks. Moreover, such figures do not reflect differences in the values of farm buildings, livestock, and implements and machinery.

Maurice Evans, a South African who traveled extensively in the South and wrote about race relations there and in his native country, noted in *Black and White in the Southern States* (1915) that the "total advance of the negro people in material things since Emancipation has been indubitably very great." While Evans applauded this development, he saw it as potentially explosive. Evans saw black advances leading to competition with whites and then to conflicts and violent confrontation. Actually, that progression had already materialized. In the face of the competition in New South cities, the economic collapse of the 1890s, and the political turmoil of that decade, laissez faire segregation failed. A dramatic increase in random racial violence took many forms, of which lynching was the most brutal and notorious. Jim Crow restored order, at a very high cost to blacks and some costs to whites. The new rigid caste system stayed in place for more than a half century.

Blacks had to accept the system of American apartheid because they had no alternative. Behind the barriers of Jim Crow they created their own world, dependent on whites yet independent of them. "Even in the midst of the brutalities and injustices of the...postbellum race systems, black men and women were able to find the means to sustain a far greater degree of self-pride and group cohesion than the system they lived under ever intended for them to be able to do." But blacks could not remain in their own world all the time. Most had to deal with whites on a daily basis and be ever attuned to them. Richard Wright, the black novelist, recalled that as part of his growing up he had to learn "how to watch white people, their every move, their expressions, and what they said or left unsaid." But he found that "it was utterly impossible for me to calculate, to scheme, to act, to plot all the time. I would remember to dissemble for short periods, then I would forget and act straight and human again." Wright left the South as soon as he was able to because he feared for his life. Yet, even as blacks put on an Uncle Tom face for whites, they derided whites in a variety of ways, especially in songs and in jokes.

"Boy. What are you doin' in here? Don't you know this is a white church?
"Boss, I only got sent here to mop up the floor."
"Well, that's all right then. But don't let me catch you prayin'."

Industrial Workers in the New South

By 1900 the division between blacks and whites was only the most obvious division in the American South. As the new century began, more than 500,000 southerners earned their livings in manufacturing. Many of these people worked in small factories, but a majority worked in the larger factories that relied heavily on simple, repetitive, often hazardous and dirty labor, usually as machine tenders. In 1900 nearly 100,000 of these industrial workers were in textiles. Large numbers would be found in iron and steel, lumber, and tobacco manufacturing.

Most of the industrial workers of the South came from farms; few came from Europe. The move from farm to factory required major changes. Except for those who had been farm laborers, most of these former farmers had controlled their daily work routines, determining when to start and stop work, and what tasks would be done when. The factories required them to work according to a new concept of time, time measured in hours and minutes, and under close supervision at assigned tasks.

Industrial workers usually lived in racially and occupationally segregated communities or neighborhoods. Very often they lived in company housing, and almost always near the workplace. The former farmers thus entered a different world. During the initial stages of this transition, many apparently maintained strong rural ties and moved back and forth between farm and factory. Later, apparently, most of them gave up agriculture permanently. Those who made the transition sensed they were crossing a chasm between two worlds, that something was dying even as something was beginning.

Ben Robertson, who wrote about his memories of the South Carolina upcountry in *Red Hills and Cotton*, remembered seeing cotton mill workers at the store on Saturday afternoon. Looking at their pale faces, the result of working indoors all the time, he felt "that they had been captured, that they were imprisoned, that they had given up being free." Robertson also recalled the terrible dilemma a landless farmer confronted when he weighed his chances of success on the farm and in the factory.

Tom Rampey had rented thirty acres on shares from Robertson's family for twenty years. When a chance to work at a nearby cotton mill presented itself, Rampey anguished in indecision, then discussed his alternatives with the Robertsons.

> "I'm a landless man. As long as I stay with you, I have a house and I'll have something to eat, but what chance have I got to get ahead? What chance have I got ever to own any land of my own?...I could have money at the mill....I ought to be able to save enough in no time to buy a few acres of my own—it oughtn't to take me long to save enough for that....I want to improve my condition,...I want to educate my children. I want them to have things better than I have had them."
>
> A few days later the Rampeys piled their things into a two-horse wagon and drove off. They moved into a house on the side of a steep hill at Cateechee Mill....The whistle blew for them at half past four o'clock, and at six their work started. Six to six was their shift. It was a hard life for a family accustomed to the open, but Saturday was pay day—every Saturday. Sometimes on Sunday Mr. Tom would come back to see my Great-Aunt Narcissa at the Old House. He would eat dinner and my great-aunt would tell him he could move back if he cared to, and always this seemed to comfort him.
>
> Finally one Sunday at Praters Baptist Church the preacher announced that Brother Tom Rampey and family desired to remove their letters of membership from Praters to Cateechee Mill Baptist Church. When the preacher asked the congregation what was their wish in this matter, my Uncle Philip moved that the request be granted. One of the Boldings seconded the motion. Thus did the Rampeys cut their last tie. They bought a new coal stove with their cash money. They bought an icebox, a car, a radio. Mr. Tom's oldest boy eventually was graduated from college.

The Tom Rampeys were legion, products of the markedly uneven rewards farmers in the South received. The federal censuses recorded the tale. In 1910, for instance, the South had more than half the nation's farmers but produced less than 30 percent of the nation's farm products. Southern farmers earned about 55 percent of the national average farm income. The value of farm implements, machinery, and livestock in the South was about 60 percent of the national average. Southern farmers used two-thirds of the total fertilizers applied by American farmers, a reflection of the continuing dominance of soil-depleting cotton. These figures did not reveal the great disparities within the South. In 1910, plantations with five or more tenants occupied 5 million acres in Alabama, Georgia, and Mississippi, and a study of some 200 of those plantations found they had 50 or more tenants each and averaged more than 4,200 acres worth $114,000.

Rising land values after 1900 proved a mixed blessing. As values doubled in the ten years after 1900, many farmers gained but many more joined the ranks of tenants. The number of tenant farms in the South increased 25 percent, to more than 1.5 million. Two-thirds of the tenant farmers were black. Farm size continued to decline, usually an indication of low productivity and low profitability. Thus the pattern of smaller farms which had set in after 1860 persisted. According to John L. Coulter, an agricultural expert employed by the Census Bureau, average farm size shrank from 321 acres in 1860 to 84 in 1910.

Tenancy, of course, does not automatically mean poverty. Renting land can be profitable, sometimes very profitable, for renter and landlord alike. Farm renters may, for example, find it to their advantage to use the capital they might have tied up in land to purchase better equipment and machinery. Generally, however, farm tenants in the South in 1910 rented or worked on shares because they had no other choice, not because they were trying to invest their assets as wisely as possible. Nearly half of all farm tenants in the South moved each year, seeking to improve their fortunes. Coulter believed that tenancy resulted in the "poor agriculture, exhausted soils, poor roads, decaying bridges, and unpainted houses" he saw in much of the South.

Factories and cities promised better things. From 1880 to 1900, the capital invested in manufacturing in the South quadrupled and the value of manufactured products tripled, then increased by 268 percent and 197 percent respectively during the next decade. The number of workers in manufacturing grew from 627,169 in 1900 to 1.01 million in 1910, to 1.3 million in 1920. At the same time, the population of the urban South rose from 3 million to 5.3 million, a 56 percent increase—a rate of urban growth that considerably exceeded the national rate.

UNIONS AND UNIONIZATION IN THE NEW SOUTH

The growing numbers of industrial workers clearly indicated a changing South, a South more like the rest of the nation. So did the growth of unionization in the South and the increasing conflict between labor and management. The Knights of Labor enjoyed impressive, but brief, success in its efforts to organize southern workers. The American Federation of Labor (AFL), founded in 1886, eventually enjoyed greater success than the Knights. Committed to trade unionism and eschewing the broad reform goals that the Knights had enunciated, the AFL effectively organized printers, building tradesmen, railroaders, and the skilled workers among the longshoremen. A number of AFL affiliates, including the International Brotherhood of Boiler Makers and the International Association of Machinists, had their origins in the South. The AFL unions usually segregated blacks into separate units or excluded them altogether, as did the railroad brotherhoods and Eugene V. Debs's American Railway Union.

As elsewhere in the United States, industrial unionism enjoyed little success in the South before the 1930s, whereas trade and railroad unions were very active. These patterns of unionization mirrored patterns in the rest of the nation. Of course, union members were fewer in the South than in the North, and so were the efforts to unionize; both reflected the smaller amount of industrialization and urbanization in the South. Coal miners, especially in Alabama, made serious efforts to organize as early as the late 1880s. Unionization among textile workers grew significantly around 1900, then subsided. In 1894 coal miners in the Birmingham region initiated a major strike in which black and white miners joined in a pitched battle against employers. Here the use of convict labor as strikebreakers and as a means of keeping wages low was a major issue. The miners also got involved in the political upheaval of the 1890s in Alabama and threw their support to Reuben Kolb, the Jeffersonian opponent of the Bourbon Democrats. Kolb's defeat and the defeat of this strike left bitter feelings and a demoralized union. Yet four years later, Alabama miners cast their lot with the national United Mine Workers (UMW); by 1902, more than 60 percent of Alabama miners were unionized. Then a major strike devastated the UMW in Alabama in 1908 and left a legacy of acute racial hostility in the coal regions. The UMW enjoyed more success in the Southwest, and before World War I the union experienced a more general revival in the whole South. The militant actions of miners in Tennessee had a decisive role in the abolition of the convict lease system there in 1902.

Efforts to unionize cotton mill workers in the South resulted in some victories, but local unions seldom survived encounters with determined mill owners, and those few locals that survived had no discernible impact on the industry. The Knights, as we indicated earlier, had a large organization in Augusta; elsewhere in Georgia, textile workers had joined the Knights, as they had done in South Carolina, North Carolina, and Alabama.

In 1895 the National Union of Textile Workers (NUTW), an AFL affiliate, began major organizing efforts in the South. Augusta and Columbus, Georgia; Columbia, South Carolina; Alamance and Greensboro, North Carolina; and Danville, Virginia, were the focal points of these campaigns. Initially the AFL acted to prevent the Socialist Trade and Labor Alliance, led by Daniel De Leon, from getting a foothold in the textile South. But the growth of southern textiles also played a hand. Leaders of textile labor unions in the North feared competition, especially the competition of a nonunionized and cheaper labor force in the South. In 1899 the NUTW issued fifty-four charters to new locals in the South. Labor newspapers in the South—among the important by-products of union activity in the region—claimed that the 500-member NUTW local at Columbia, South Carolina, was "the largest textile [local] union in the world." By 1900 the NUTW had 5,000 dues-paying members, most in the South, and a southerner for president. The NUTW and the AFL lobbied unsuccessfully for child labor legislation in the southern states. They also proved to be vulnerable to the strong counterattacks waged by southern mill owners, who managed to scuttle textile unions in the South by the end of 1902.

As in the rest of the country, ethnic conflict marked and shaped labor relations in the South. In the industrial and mining regions of the Northeast and Midwest, for instance, there were sharp differences among native Europeans and native Americans, as there were on occasion in the Plains, the mountain states, and the Far West. In the West, confrontations between whites and Orientals were a major factor in successful efforts to limit Asian immigration severely or stop it entirely.

In the South, color had an immense impact on labor relations and occupations, whereas immigration, from either Europe or Asia, had almost no effect except in the coal and iron regions. Black and white workers formed alliances on several occasions in the 1880s and the 1890s. The Knights of Labor and the UMW demonstrated degrees of interracial solidarity that were unique for this era in the South or elsewhere, and indeed for many years to come in the South. Black and white Knights of Labor joined in the strikes against Jay Gould in 1885 and 1886. Black and white UMW members struck against coal operators in the Birmingham region in 1894. By 1902 the biracial union had the largest membership of any single union in the South. As subsequent events proved, however, the biracialism of the UMW was fragile.

Interracial cooperation among workers was not, however, limited to the Knights and the UMW. In 1892 a general strike called by an alliance of AFL unions in New Orleans involved 20,000 members of forty-two locals and virtually shut the city down for three days. It ended when the city's Board of Trade made concessions in regard to wages and hours but not in regard to union recognition or the closed shop (an agreement to hire only union members). The result conformed to the usual pattern of labor disputes of the era throughout the South and the nation. When employers made concessions—and they seldom did—they conceded points on narrow issues: wages, hours, working conditions. Employers almost never conceded on broader issues: recognition of a union as a collective bargaining agent or agreement to the closed shop.

Biracial solidarity among workers in the South also suffered setbacks. Racial divisions marred an 1894 strike in New Orleans. In 1908, Alabama coal miners divided along racial lines when they were confronted by mine owners and a state government determined to suppress their union even if they had to play to racial prejudice to do so. Jim Crow triumphed, erasing memories of interracial cooperation while erecting a segregationist tradition. The UMW declined sharply in Alabama, although the union did enjoy a revival in the state before World War I. The UMW, however, remained a strong force in Texas and Oklahoma, and retained its biracial character there. The Brotherhood of Timber Workers also adopted a biracial strategy during its brief lifetime in the Southwest, 1910–1913.

The racial exclusivism that marked almost all of organized labor after 1900 created an atmosphere conducive to strikebreaking by blacks. Organized labor rather quickly came to associate blacks with strikebreaking, though unionists usually ignored their own role in creating the situation. Excluded from almost all unions, often desperate for work, and eager to improve their earnings, blacks did not turn away from offers of the jobs of striking white workers. They took such jobs with increasing frequency after 1910, especially in the North, where real or alleged strikebreaking by blacks contributed to a series of violent racial confrontations around World War I.

Even when employers did not use blacks as strikebreakers, they still could and did threaten to do so. Ironically, employers also appealed to white racial solidarity. These appeals gave employers an advantage over their white employees similar to the advantage white elitist politicians and their class allies enjoyed over their poorer white constituents. Less advantaged whites derived benefits—often more emotional than economic—from Jim Crow. But employers and white elitist politicians gained even more from a racially divided work force and electorate.

New Divisions Among Protestants

The Protestant churches, a collective cornerstone of the South, also reflected the growth of divisions in Dixie. So numerous and pervasive were the Baptists and the Methodists in the postbellum South that after color, form of baptism was the most common distinction among southerners. In addition to racial and baptismal distinctions, social and economic distinctions found more overt expression among the denominations and among churches of the same denomination. "First Church," "Second Church," uptown church, mill church, country church reflected a social and economic geography that was familiar to most southerners.

New and striking divisions among Protestants developed in the 1880s and became very obvious in the early twentieth century. The Holiness movement attracted numerous adherents, as did Pentecostalism (from Pentecost, the day when, according to the New Testament, the spirit of God descended on the early Christians) and the Church of Christ. Each has grown as a force in the lives of southerners since then.

Initially the Holiness movement and Pentecostalism had their origins in Methodism. Convinced that their church had become "lukewarm," too worldly, too formal, emotionally dead, and too much a church of "birthright" members instead of a church of members by conversion and conviction, Methodists, north and south, joined "a Great Holiness Revival." Initially hailed as a blessing, the revival erupted into bitter battles between Methodists who believed the Holiness movement had become "disruptive and unseemly" and those who believed they were following God's will. Eventually new denominations evolved: the Church of the Nazarene, the Assemblies of God, and other Pentecostal groups. Each stressed spirituality or being "born again," a rigid or perfectionist moral code, and doctrinal purity. Each of these groups preferred its ministers to be divinely "called" to preach and unsullied by much formal education, and often expected them to derive most of their income from nonministerial employment. These groups differed among themselves, sometimes very sharply, over issues of belief and church organization. The Pentecostals emphasized the "gifts of God," or such charismatic phenomena as faith healing; an aversion to medical treatment and care; glossolalia, or "speaking in tongues"; and the imminent end of the world and the return of Christ.

The available evidence suggests that these new religious groups had their greatest appeal for the poorest among industrial workers and poorer farmers in the South and elsewhere. One student of American religion has noted:

Though sociological generalizations are risky, it is probably fair to say that the greater appeal [of these groups] . . . has been to the lower economic stratum, to those who, finding worldly goods denied them, have denied the world. At the same time they have affirmed a nobility of life which not only clearly distinguishes them from the world, but promises somehow to redeem elements of that world.

Ernest Troeltsch, a leading pioneer in the history of Christian social ethics, wrote some years ago:

The really creative, church-forming religious movements are the work of the lower strata. Here only can one find that union of unimpaired imagination, simplicity in emotional life, unreflective character of thought, spontaneity of energy and vehement force of need, out of which an unconditional faith in divine revelation, the naiveté of complete surrender, and the intransigence of certitude can rise.

Economic and social factors seem to have set the stage for these developments in southern Protestantism. As the New South became a reality, as the economy diversified, as cities and towns grew, and as disparities between the successful and the unsuccessful became more obvious, Protestant churches reflected these developments. The disinherited or neglected, finding too little for themselves in the conventional churches, went elsewhere to find preachers who spoke in understandable terms. They found churches where they felt welcome, and where they received assurances that they were purified, that they had greater virtue or the right relationship with God because they followed a stricter moral code, and that the inequities of this world would be suddenly and finally reversed. These new Protestant groups represented a blend of old religious ideas and sentiments with a particular set of social and economic factors. These groups reflected a recurring pattern in the history of Christianity, a pattern that earlier had produced the Anabaptists, Quakers, Methodists, and the Salvation Army, to name a few of the "churches of the disinherited."

The Churches of Christ had a history similar to that of the Pentecostals and the Holiness movement, but within a more traditional theological and biblical framework. Congregations within the Disciples of Christ denomination drew away from the Disciples over several issues, of which the use of instrumental music in worship was the most important stated issue. Unstated issues probably had greater weight: social and economic differences among the Disciples. This drawing away took explicit form by 1906. When the federal government took its religious census that year, the Churches of Christ asked to be enumerated separately from the Disciples. The new denomination has enjoyed phenomenal growth, eventually becoming the most dynamic of the large denominations in the South. It has had its greatest success in Tennessee, Kentucky, Arkansas, Texas, and Oklahoma. The Churches of God found their largest following in Kentucky, Tennessee, Alabama, Georgia, North Carolina, and Florida; the Church of the Nazarene in Oklahoma and Texas as well as Arkansas and Tennessee; and the Assemblies of God in Arkansas, Texas, and Oklahoma.

POLITICAL DEMAGOGUES

Electoral politics in the late nineteenth and early twentieth centuries reflected the serious divisions in the South, divisions that found political expression even after the end of the depression of the 1890s, the demise of the Populist party, and the reentrenchment of the Democratic party throughout the South. The most obvious political expression of group conflict was the profusion of political demagogues that the South produced in the early twentieth century. The demagogue was not a new phenomenon in the South—Ben Tillman had thrived in the 1890s in South Carolina, for instance—and the type continued to flourish in such latter-day versions as George Wallace of Alabama in the 1960s. Cole Blease succeeded Tillman in South Carolina in the early twentieth century. Mississippi produced first James K. Vardaman, then Theodore Bilbo; Georgia, Tom Watson; Tennessee, Fiddlin' Bob Taylor; Arkansas, Jeff Davis, who was variously described as "the Wild Ass of the Ozarks, the Tribune of Haybinders, a Karl Marx for Hillbillies."

Demagogue is too often a misleading political epithet or slur. Though these political leaders outraged many people with their vitriolic oratory and bizarre behavior, the epithet obscures their contributions to southern politics and what their existence and repeated successes at the polls meant. Their followings and their victories meant, among other things, that more conventional politics and politicians failed to meet the needs of many southerners. The demagogues were, as one historian has observed, "agrarian radicals [who] practiced a politics of catharsis and symbolic action." But their actions "probably inhibited radical change." They provided a voice, an emotional outlet, and symbols of success for the disinherited whites of the New South. Cotton mill workers felt so attached to Blease that they frequently wrote him to complain, especially about working conditions. Blease gave the mill hands a sense of importance, of having a political voice. In turn, cotton mill workers gave strong support to Blease at the polls.

Though some of the demagogues' contributions were concrete and noteworthy, it seemed at times that their major contribution was to the comic-opera aspects of southern politics. The demagogues flourished because the Dixie of the late nineteenth and the early twentieth centuries was deeply divided. The divisions were symptoms of the rapid social and economic change the South had experienced.

22

Southern Progressives

—————— ❖ ——————

M aterialism, as Booker T. Washington suggested in 1895, had dramatically altered the South since 1880, and southerners began to realize that they must bring some kind of order to their changed world. What kind of order? Who would be its agents? Those questions were addressed by the men and women of the Progressive Era.

Four southern progressives

James Kimble Vardaman, "the White Chief," served Mississippi as a legislator in the 1890s, then as governor (1904–1908) and United States senator (1913–1919). He was remembered more for his vitriolic racist demagoguery than for his political ideas and achievements. Typical of white politicians of his day, he used Negrophobia to appeal to voters. But he carried venomous racism further than most southern politicians.

Many of his contemporaries found his Negrophobic language and proposals more than they could abide even in that day. Vardaman wanted to repeal the Fifteenth Amendment, modify the Fourteenth, and stop spending even the small sums Mississippi spent for the education of "the black man" because "education only makes the Negro dissatisfied with his lowly position in society." When President Theodore Roosevelt entertained Booker T. Washington at lunch at the White House, the Mississippian favored the nation with his commentary:

> President Roosevelt takes this nigger bastard into his home, introduces him to his family and entertains him on terms of absolute social equality. He does more. He carries his daughter to another social function, where she and Washington ["the saddle-colored philosopher of Tuskeegee"] are to be among the special guest[s] of honor.

Was this not a presidential endorsement of the horror of horrors, interracial marriage?

Vardaman claimed he felt kindly toward blacks, that he wanted blacks to prosper in their place. To do so blacks had to stay out of politics and had to accept their subordinate social and economic position. As governor, Vardaman did suppress racial violence, and some of his legislative program aided blacks, though some of it certainly hurt them.

Vardaman's political power was rooted in his enormous popularity with the small white farmers of Mississippi. Vardaman provided a catharsis, a symbol, and something of a program for white farm families who had too little fertile land and received meager earnings despite their efforts, who saw other Mississippi farmers thrive (especially those in the delta), and who believed, not incorrectly, that prosperous farmers had an alliance with the railroads, banks, and the comfortable in the towns against the interests of people like themselves. At a time when two in three farmers and half of the white farmers were landless tenants and their ranks were swelling, Vardaman's appeal is not much of a mystery. Small farmers embraced a man who spurned the conventions of the established and successful and who spoke the language of the small farmers, literally and figuratively. Catching his spirit, they transformed the epithets *redneck* and *hillbilly* into badges of honor. They displayed these badges on posters and banners at political rallies, for instance, when they greeted Vardaman at Meridian as he stepped off a train in his familiar white suit and white boots, a black broad-brimmed hat atop his shoulder-length hair.

Vardaman's evolution as a politician was more conventional than his dress

JAMES K. VARDAMAN CAMPAIGNING (Courtesy of Mississippi Department of Archives and History)

or manner suggested. He early obtained a vehicle for himself and his views when he became owner and editor of the Greenwood *Enterprise*, a step aided by the substantial inheritance of the widow he married. He entered politics as a party regular and a partisan of the status quo in the 1890s—a Bourbon Democrat in Mississippi. His later break with the Bourbons can be attributed to personal ambition and a timely adjustment to changes in the politics of Mississippi. He sensed that he had little future among the regulars, since others had firm holds on higher rungs of the regular party ladder, and he became aware that the Bourbons had failed to respond adequately to the needs and fears of the majority of white voters in the state. Vardaman also took advantage of the opportunity presented by direct primaries, a new political device that made it easier to circumvent the power of the party establishment, which was based on control of party caucuses and conventions.

Vardaman broke with the Bourbons, then the old guard of Mississippi politics, and ran as a man of the people against the political establishment. Others did likewise at the time—for instance, Robert La Follette in Wisconsin, one of the patriarchs of the Progressive movement.

Vardaman adopted many positions that were conventional for a Progressive. He generally supported the concept of activist government, an attitude he showed even before he held public office. He was one of Greenwood's civic elite, who boosted the town and called for the expansion and improvement of public services. As governor he proposed measures to improve the judicial system; to obtain a more equitable tax system; to create a system for providing cheaper textbooks for schools; to secure better services for the mentally ill and incapacitated, the blind, the deaf and dumb, and those afflicted with tuberculosis; and to reform Mississippi's brutal, corrupt penal system. He moved to double appropriations for public education (for whites); to stiffen regulations and restraints on insurance companies, utilities, railroads, manufacturers, and large corporations; to create the office of agricultural commissioner; and to expand highway construction. He tried to obtain restrictions on child labor, state bank depositories for individuals and lower interest rates, and a state highway commission. Encouraged by Vardaman, the legislature passed Jim Crow laws for streetcars and a vagrancy law so harsh that it probably reduced many blacks to peonage. Employing his powers as governor, he led a campaign that effectively limited the spread of a yellow fever epidemic in 1905, a move that had no precedent in Mississippi. He used his office on perhaps nine occasions to halt lynchings, though he continued to uphold lynching "to defend the virtue" of white women. He directed a vigorous campaign against "whitecappers," groups who resembled the Ku Klux Klan and who used violence in southern Mississippi to force out black farm owners and tenants. Vardaman realized that whitecapping threatened the stability of the labor supply and discouraged businesses that wanted to operate in Mississippi. Even his opponents acknowledged that he was a good governor. In his autobiography, *Lanterns on the Levee*, William Alexander Percy, cousin of the novelist and essayist Walker Percy, described Vardaman as "a kindly, vain demagogue unable to think, and given to emotions he considered noble...a handsome, flamboyant figure of a man, immaculately overdressed,...[who] looked like a top-notch medicine man." Yet, Percy conceded, "he had made a good governor."

Later, as U.S. senator—an office he won after defeating Leroy Percy, father of William Alexander, in a bitter campaign—Vardaman followed his earlier course as a progressive Democrat. He also continued giving racist diatribes. For several years he toured much of the United States giving lectures, the most memorable of which was "The Impending Crisis!" The title of the lecture was an obvious imitation of Hinton R. Helper's antebellum alarm. The theme was vintage Vardaman: political equality for Negroes led to social equality and thence to interracial marriage; therefore, granting any political concessions to Negroes led inevitably to catastrophe. "Ambition in the negro is concreted in lust."

Edgar Gardner Murphy recoiled at the demagoguery of Vardaman and his kind. Murphy might have recoiled even more at the suggestion that he and the White Chief were fellow progressives. Born in Arkansas, educated at Sewanee (the University of the South) and at General Theological Seminary in New York, Murphy held several pastorates in the Episcopal church. He accepted a call to Montgomery, Alabama, in 1899, and there became involved in the Social Gospel movement. The Social Gospel, which evolved in response to the negative social ramifications of industrialization and urbanization—to brutalizing labor, growing disparities in income and wealth, and wretched urban conditions— emphasized the obligation of Christians to change social institutions and the social environment. Christianity, according to the Social Gospel, involved more than personal salvation, piety, and occasional gifts to the needy. The Social Gospel was on the cutting edge of a crucial shift in opinion about the human condition. Increasing numbers of people were coming to see environmental and social conditions as explanatory factors in the circumstances and behavior of human beings. People might have little education because they were poor, for example, not simply because they lacked motivation or ability.

Soon after he went to Montgomery, Murphy became aware of the plight of child laborers in the textile mills in Alabama. In an effort to restrict child labor, he founded the Alabama Child Labor Committee in 1900. Four years later he was the major figure in the founding of the national Child Labor Committee. By then he had resigned his pastorate and had become executive secretary of the Southern Education Board, which played an important role in the Southwide efforts to improve education in the early twentieth century.

Murphy also became involved in efforts to ameliorate the conditions of blacks in the South. He trod carefully here. He decried lynching but embraced Jim Crow. A thoroughgoing paternalist, Murphy rested his hopes for improving the conditions of blacks on the "better sort" of whites and on such means as industrial education. Predictably, Booker T. Washington and Tuskegee received lavish praise from Murphy. He feared that the racist demagoguery of the kind dispensed by Vardaman would enflame the white masses, and in his *Problems of the Present South* (1904) called upon the South "to do justice to the negro and to the more helpless elements of her industrial life." Whatever the biases he held in common with most of his generation, Murphy labored hard to implement his portion of the Social Gospel, an effort that may have been a factor in his early death.

Walter Hines Page joined Murphy in some of these efforts. Born in North Carolina in 1855, Page enjoyed a distinguished career as a journalist, editor, and publisher. While preparing for the Methodist ministry at Randolph-Macon College in Virginia, Page became a religious skeptic, a not unusual condition for educated Americans of his generation, who were heavily exposed to Darwinian thought and its ramifications. Page sought another calling. Two years of graduate study at Johns Hopkins University, then the most distinguished graduate institution in the United States, convinced him that scholarship was not his mission in life. Then he entered the newspaper business in North Carolina, and in 1886 left the South permanently to find greater opportunities in New York.

Page thus became a not uncommon southern figure, an expatriate who lectured the South on its deficiencies and proposed remedies. His lecterns eventually included at various times the *Atlantic Monthly*, the *Forum*, and *World's Work* and the publishing houses of Houghton Mifflin and Doubleday, Page. His early expatriate lectures in the form of weekly letters to the *State Chronicle* of Raleigh, North Carolina, reached a considerable audience and elicited mixed reactions. No doubt Page's argumentative style had something to do with those reactions. His "mummy" letter of February 1886 was long remembered. Upset by opposition in North Carolina to state-supported industrial education, a basic plank in the New South platform, Page wrote: "They don't want an Industrial School. That means a new idea, and a new idea is death to the supremacy of the mummies. Let 'em alone. The world must have some corner in it where men sleep and sleep and dream and dream and North Carolina is as good a spot for that as any." Opponents of innovation could simply ignore the reputation of North Carolina as "the laughingstock among the States," while "the most active and energetic men in North Carolina leave the state" and "bright and able men" drink themselves to death. "When every intellectual aspiration is discouraged, when all the avenues that lead to independent thought and to mental growth are closed... there is absolutely no chance for the ambitious men of ability, proportionate to their ability." The "mummy" letter, John Milton Cooper says, "was the most controversial and... influential piece of writing that he ever produced." That letter and "The Forgotten Man," his noted address on education to the first class graduated from North Carolina's school for teachers, made Page's reputation as a leader in educational reform in the South. Page became part of the efforts of a group of journalists, politicians, activists, educators, and other professionals who prodded North Carolina to transform itself. They scored major successes in the early twentieth century, especially during the administration of Governor Charles B. Aycock and particularly in education.

Page also worked to reconcile North and South, to explain each to the other. Page saw himself as "the Southerner as American." In so doing, he embodied one side in the long debate about how distinctive the South was and is from the rest of the nation. It is a debate about whether southerners are first southern or first American—a debate that lies at the heart of the historical experience of the South and southerners.

In 1911 Page also helped initiate the campaign to get Woodrow Wilson elected president. The campaign led eventually to the return of the Democrats to the White House and, for a time, the restoration of southern Democrats to the front ranks of national leadership. Page's reward was the American ambassadorship to Great Britain, a position he held until shortly before his death in 1918. The southern expatriate went far from Cary, North Carolina, to financial success, to the forefront of journalism and publishing in New York and Boston, to leadership in reform and in sectional reconciliation, to the Court of St. James's.

Kate Barnard did not go that far, but she went a long way in the border South. In 1907, voters in the new state of Oklahoma elected Barnard to be their first commissioner of charities and corrections, a position she held until 1915, when poor health forced her to retire from office. She came to the fore as Progressivism, southern style, became a shaping force in Oklahoma.

Barnard was an "eighty-niner." Like thousands of other Oklahomans, she had joined in the Oklahoma "run" of 1889, the first of a series of runs for homesteads on lands that the federal government had declared open for settlement. Like many other people, her father had migrated to Oklahoma in order to reverse his fortunes. Many succeeded, but John Barnard did not. He soon gave up his homestead and moved to Oklahoma City, one of the "cities" instantly created in 1889.

The instant city soon developed old familiar patterns and problems. A "strange thing happened which opened my eyes to a new view of life," Kate Barnard remembered.

> The well-to-do people gradually moved out from the district around our home and the poor began to take possession of their dwellings...out of these crowded pest-ridden "homes" came the strangest children I ever saw—peaked and poor and thin and sallow...little children who drifted around, hungry, cold, uncared for, unloved....I watched these children till my heart ached and I was compelled to cry out in their behalf.

A converted and deeply committed Catholic, Barnard felt prompted to act upon her Christian commitment. Barnard began a rapid transformation at thirty years of age, or twenty-six or -five or -three (somewhat uncharacteristically, Barnard followed the feminine convention of the day when asked her age). She started out in 1904 with private charities that practiced incidental relief—charities that took up occasional donations from the well-to-do and distributed them to the "deserving" poor. She quickly surmised that more than an occasional basket of food was required. She helped found the United Charities of Oklahoma City; then she turned to political and labor union activism. A local newspaper helped this transformation; the *Daily Oklahoman* paid Barnard's expenses for a nationwide tour to see how other cities dealt with the impoverished. Barnard met many of the leaders of the "social justice" faction of the Progressive movement. She soon came to share their belief that poverty was a social problem, not a personal problem or the result of personal failings. Working

KATE BARNARD (Western History Collections, University
of Oklahoma Library)

closely with organized labor and other groups, Barnard helped draft a constitution for Oklahoma which incorporated much of this thinking.

Seemingly determined to cover every eventuality, the Oklahoma constitutional convention drafted a document of more than 50,000 words, "easily the
world's longest constitution at the time." Reflecting the strong antimonopolistic
views that prevailed in much of the United States and certainly in the South in
1907, the constitution devoted nearly one-fifth of its coverage to efforts to restrain the powers of the "trusts." The constitution established several graduated taxes, including one on incomes and another on corporations; restrictions
on child labor; compulsory education; prohibition of contract labor and increased employer liability for occupational safety; an eight-hour day for miners
and public employees; home rule for urban areas with at least 2,000 people; and
a department of charities and corrections, whose elected commissioner could be
a man or a woman. It was the only statewide office that carried that stipulation,

which was intended to ensure that Kate Barnard would be its first occupant. Barnard received more votes than any other candidate in the state's first election—in which she could not vote because she was a woman.

The constitution also created a large number of elective offices, a reflection of the Populist legacy and the William Jennings Bryan tradition of Progressivism. The constitution clearly reflected the southern background of many of its drafters and the people who had elected them to the constitutional convention. The constitution did not give women the vote. Opponents of women's suffrage sounded the familiar objections, including the assertion that suffrage for women would open the way to suffrage for blacks. The constitution did attempt to render Oklahoma a dry state. In an article that had to be ratified separately, the constitution prohibited the sale of alcoholic beverages except for medicinal purposes. Voters approved the article by an overwhelming vote, and available evidence indicates that the new state began its career in cold sobriety. More certain is the fact that the state clung to prohibition long after many Oklahomans ceased abstaining. Will Rogers, the beloved humorist, once claimed that Oklahomans would vote for a dry state "as long as they could stagger to the polls and keep it that way."

The new constitution would have disfranchised blacks and racially segregated schools and public transportation if the delegates to the constitutional convention had had their way. President Theodore Roosevelt objected to their efforts to put Jim Crow in the Oklahoma constitution and threatened to prevent Oklahoma from becoming a state if they went ahead with their plans. The apprentice state demurred and waited until it gained admission to the Union and had more freedom to follow its inclinations. The first legislature of the new state moved promptly to disfranchise blacks and to adopt Jim Crow in schools, transportation, and public facilities, although only 5 percent of the populace was black. Black disfranchisement enjoyed only limited success, in part because of a 1915 ruling of the U.S. Supreme Court against the state's blatantly discriminatory grandfather clause. The efforts of the Democrats to prevent blacks from voting persisted, because they believed that blacks provided the margin of victory for Republicans in elections in parts of the state. As in Tennessee and another border state, Kentucky, the Republican party was strong enough to present a continuing challenge to the Democrats in Oklahoma. Jim Crow in schools, transportation, and public facilities did become fixed, giving Oklahoma a distinctly southern quality in its race relations. Other aspects of Oklahoma contributed to the "southernness" of the state: the longtime dominance of the Democrats in the state, the power and numbers of evangelical Protestants, especially the Southern Baptists, and a farm-based economy that was beleaguered by overdependence on cotton and high rates of tenancy. The last was worsened after World War I by soil depletion and the advent of the boll weevil.

At its inception, Oklahoma embraced most of the advanced ideas of Progressivism, southern style. Kate Barnard quickly discovered that the Sooner State could also beat a strategic retreat from some of the more advanced Progressive positions. Almost immediately the state fell back from its antimonopolistic position because it feared that business would be driven from the state. "Business Progressivism" gained sway, a Progressivism that reflected the concerns and interests of the commercial-civic elites of businessmen and professionals. Barnard and her allies, many from organized labor, immediately ran into strong opposition to implementing the restrictions on child labor which the state constitution called for. Only after Barnard led a strong lobbying effort in 1908 did the Oklahoma legislature pass, and the governor sign, a law to restrict child labor. It became a model for other states. Barnard also persuaded the state to adopt a series of penal reforms, including a juvenile court system, and to establish an institution for the "feebleminded." Impressed by her triumphs, Alexander McKelway of the National Child Labor Committee urged Woodrow Wilson to use her help in his 1912 presidential campaign because she was "the most consummate politician" in Oklahoma.

Exhausted and ill, Barnard did not run for reelection in 1914. She continued for some time to work with other "social justice" Progressives, but she was never again as active as she had been. By 1922 she had departed Oklahoma, a symbol of the decline of her brand of Progressivism and the advent of a "safer" brand.

PROGRESSIVISM, SOUTHERN STYLE

James K. Vardaman, Edgar Gardner Murphy, Walter Hines Page, and Kate Barnard make an unlikely quartet. Yet they illustrate the major characteristics, proclivities, assumptions, and achievements of southern Progressivism. All accepted the cardinal principle of Progressivism, the activist state. The diversity of this quartet also illustrates the diversity and diffuse nature of the Progressives and their movement, which have so often baffled historians and others. Progressivism in the South drew upon an antimonopolistic tradition that had its origins in the 1870s. That tradition received an enormous boost from Populism and the merger craze, which after 1895 produced business giants that were or seemed to be out of control. The power of the "trusts" caused apprehension throughout the South. As prices rose steeply after 1898, the power of U.S. Steel, of the Southern Railway and other major trunk lines, and even of the American Book Company, the "textbook trust" with which Vardaman warred, hardly was a phantom conjured up by politicians on the stump. Nor were local utilities and transportation companies that rendered indifferent or bad services at increasing costs to urbanites.

Progressivism in the South embraced antimonopolism at its height in 1907–1908. Jeff Davis fought a spectacular, if ineffectual, battle in Arkansas against outside companies. Governor Braxton Bragg Comer of Alabama warred with Milton H. Smith of the Louisville and Nashville Railroad until exhaustion forced a cease-fire. Texas passed the noted Robertson Act, which required out-of-state insurance companies to invest a percentage of their profits earned in Texas in the Lone Star State. Standard Oil lost its charter in Texas. In 1919 the state legislature gave the railroad commission power to regulate the oil industry. To the north, as we know, antimonopolism found a prominent place in Oklahoma's constitution. But antimonopolism soon subsided in the South, as elsewhere. The South needed capital too urgently to risk chasing it away.

Though Progressivism in the South retained some of its Populist aspects, it came to have a more middle-class, urban quality. Populist ideology left its mark in the institutionalizing of direct democracy: primary elections, secret ballots, an increase in the number of elective offices, the initiative, referendum, and recall. As we shall see, direct democracy had the ironic effect of increasing the power of interest groups at the expense of the power of political parties and the unorganized.

Progressivism dealt with a wide range of issues and left a substantial legacy. It left a much larger number of public agencies and public services, a much greater number of regulatory laws, and, inevitably, substantially higher taxes. Between 1903 and 1922, state revenues in the South increased 400 percent. (Nationally, they increased 300 percent.) The south Atlantic states led the way with a fivefold rise; North Carolina led all the states with a sixfold rise. Progressivism attempted to ameliorate some of the harsher consequences of industrialization and urbanization. Progressivism was prompted by humanitarian concerns, a direct and indirect result of the Social Gospel; it was driven by an urge to exercise social control over a society seemingly threatened by deep divisions, and by a "search for order" in an America that at the time was "a society of island communities." That society broke down under the twin forces of industrialization and urbanization. The United States could no longer rely primarily on local autonomy; Americans had to develop new approaches more appropriate to their needs. Turning from the personal, informal ways of the community, "Americans sought order through continuity and predictability," by creating new mechanisms and more centralized authority. Progressivism involved transformation, not revolution. Progressivism involved certain reforms of capitalism, not its rejection.

Southern Progressivism mirrored its locale. It accepted the basic structure of race relations in the South: white over black. Some observers contend that among the earliest reforms of the Progressives were disfranchisement of blacks and Jim Crow. From our perspective, such a contention appears to do violence to the concept of reform; but even greater evils might have been perpetrated in an era when racist orators appeared to know no limits and when the possibility of outright race war was not a fantasy of fanatics and the deranged. Moreover, turmoil during elections did seem to subside after the great majority of black men lost their voting rights. That loss significantly reduced the opportunities of white politicians to use the ballots of blacks for their own ends—to stay in power and protect their economic advantages and those of their allies. But blacks paid a high price for that change, and this was not the first or the last time whites in the South shifted the burden to the blacks. Moreover, as became very clear especially in the way public money was spent, without the vote blacks had even less opportunity to pressure public officials than they had had before.

Southern Progressivism was almost exclusively a Democratic affair. The Populist-Republican fusion in North Carolina set some precedents in the 1890s, especially in education, which progressive Democrats followed. Tennessee Republicans took advantage of a split among Democrats over prohibition and a murdered leader, Edward W. Carmack, to get two terms in the governor's office. Tennessee Republicans elected one other governor during the era. Kentucky Republicans elected several. Republicans won seats in state legislatures, but not majorities. They won some congressional elections—consistently in a few places—and they won some local and county offices. Otherwise, the Democrats dominated statewide elections in the South. Essentially, then, southern Progressives worked through the Democratic party. Progressivism was the product of bifactional politics, not partisan politics.

Southern Progressives expressed their regionalism in other ways. So intense and extensive was their interest in improving education (generally, for whites only) that the movement to upgrade schools and universities in the South became known as "the education crusade." Prohibition received early, strong support in the South. Abolition of the convict lease system, a Southwide institution with few imitations outside the region, became the most important of a series of penal reforms. Woman had an active role in Progressivism, sometimes as leaders, but they could not forget they were Southern Ladies. Indeed, feminine gentility could be a weapon in dextrous hands. But those dextrous women could guide only five southern states to ratify the Eighteenth Amendment, granting women the right to vote.

Progressives in the South paid particular attention to public health, child labor, and other issues of concern to working people. Tuberculosis, yellow fever, typhoid, smallpox, pellagra, hookworm, and malaria were the leading threats to life and health in the South in 1900. Within the United States by then, yellow fever, pellagra, and malaria were major diseases only in the South. Malaria killed few of its victims but contributed heavily to the chronic ill health of southerners. Tuberculosis took the most lives. Child labor, especially in the textile mills, became an explosive issue and a scandal.

Finally, Progressives remained loyal to the New South creed. Moreover, the New South creed fitted neatly with business Progressivism, which stressed orderly government and government services that facilitated the operations of private business.

THE ROOTS OF SOUTHERN PROGRESSIVISM

The roots of southern Progressivism were deep and extensive and intertwined with the basic elements of the American South as the nineteenth century gave way to the twentieth. Progressivism's growth and endurance throughout the South and its appeal to so many people suggest that it developed in response to widely perceived needs. Disarray was pervasive. The concrete achievements of the New South—the growth of industry, transportation systems, and urban areas—had brought blessings and unanticipated problems. The traditional response of passive government seemed woefully inadequate. The Progressives believed that the power of the state was required to meet the problems of society as they perceived and understood those problems. The Progressives also directed their attention to the needs of farmers and farming.

Progressivism did not develop in a vacuum of ideas, political, social, or economic. Though public funds were short, southern Democrats after 1880 had generally been willing to use the state to improve education, to provide some services to the needy, and to create new agencies, such as state boards of health. Most Democratic leaders had long been sensitive to the demands of farmers, who, after all, were the electoral majority. Lower tariffs, railroad regulation, currency inflation, and public services for farmers consistently found favor among most Democratic politicians. Obviously, the agrarian unrest of the late nineteenth century indicated that many farmers felt that what Democratic leaders offered was not enough. Those feelings should not, however, leave the erroneous impression of callous disregard for southern farmers.

Conservation, a major concern of the Progressives, also drew upon precedents from the late nineteenth century. The reputation of the Gilded Age for profit-driven exploitation of natural resources certainly was deserved. During the Gilded Age and the early twentieth century, extinctions or near-extinctions of major species occurred for the first time since the late Pleistocene epoch (a geological epoch that ended some 25,000 years ago). Victims included the whooping crane, cougar, timber wolf, red or Florida wolf, Carolina parakeet, and passenger pigeon. At the same time, whole forests fell to armies of loggers and to land-clearing farmers. Yet, drawing upon antebellum precedents, state legislatures passed laws to restrict fishing and hunting and to protect nongame animals, particularly birds. How effective these laws were is not clear. Changes in fashion may have done more to protect birds. Birds with spectacular plumage were safer after feathered hats became passé. Effective or not, these laws demonstrated that the Gilded Age South was not entirely indifferent to the environment.

Convinced that forests were also in danger of becoming things of the past, groups concerned about forest conservation proliferated dramatically in the 1890s. Their agitation led to the development of scientific forestry in the South. Support grew for the creation of federally owned forest preserves, support that helped secure federal legislation authorizing government land purchases in the Appalachians. Those purchases laid the foundation for what later became the Great Smoky Mountains National Park. Thus the Gilded Age South—including the Redeemers—left a more positive legacy for the Progressives than has often been realized.

Progressivism also owed something to Populism, though how much varied from state to state. Like Populism, Progressivism drew much of its motivation from a profound sense that the times were out of joint, especially in the 1890s. And, as we have seen, some Progressives had a strong Populist bent, which showed itself especially in the more rural-dominated states. In the case of Alabama, however, one historian concluded that Progressivism and Populism were parallel developments in the 1890s: "Progressivism, the alternative to Populism, was a substantially different reaction by a separate set of men to the same enemy Populism faced—the dominant industrial wing of the Democratic Party." Progressivism in the South eventually ran a course far different from that which

Populism envisioned. Developments in Alabama suggest rich insights into why their courses diverged so sharply. The Populists attempted to build a mass-based political movement. Their leaders were not among the state's elite, and they attempted to be spokesmen for the "dispossessed and powerless." The Populists focused their attention on modernizing agriculture and improving the position of farmers in the marketplace. They paid little attention to other sectors of the economy, though they were genuinely concerned about the plight of working people. The Alabama Progressives, ambitious businessmen, felt that "abolishing privilege was not enough." They believed that economic growth would increase equality of opportunity. Economic growth, they argued, depended on an increase in governmental services to stimulate development and help individuals to take advantage of greater opportunities.

The aspirations of the Progressives did not, of course, extend far toward the blacks. Nor did most Progressives display much concern for working people. Progressivism remained close to those "tenets shared by comfortable Americans everywhere."

EDUCATIONAL REFORM

A substantial number of comfortable southerners did feel distressed about the state of education in their region in 1900. The "great educational awakening" began with the painful awareness of the woeful state of schooling in the South; then came vigorous publicizing of alarming facts, conferences, lobbying, and the involvement of philanthropists from outside of the region. Remedies included substantial investments of money, large increases in public expenditures, expansion of public agencies, new laws, attempts to standardize, extensive use of experts, and the involvement of the universities of the region. Educational reform drew its breath from the urge of the "better elements" to uplift the lesser folk. It was a "mixture of paternalism and *noblesse oblige*." Educational reform reflected its local and state settings, and almost all the states of the South became heavily involved in it. Educational reform also stayed within the familiar confines of the New South, white supremacy, and male dominance.

Public education hardly existed outside of the larger cities, and few of the many private academies were a great improvement over the public schools.

> The public schools of the South at the opening of the century were for the most part miserably supported, poorly attended, wretchedly taught, and wholly inadequate for the education of the people. Far behind the rest of the country in nearly all respects, Southern education suffered from a greater lag than any other public institution in the region.

Perhaps 20 percent of whites and 50 percent of blacks were illiterate. In 1900 only two states in the South and border region—Texas and Oklahoma—spent as much as one-half the national average per pupil, $2.84. Alabama and North Carolina spent the least in the region, 50 cents. South Carolina followed at 67 cents; four others spent less than $1. These disparities represented years of fiscal tightfistedness, a legacy of the reaction to Reconstruction, the depression of the 1870s, and harsh realities that defied quick remedies and determined efforts. The ratio of children to adults in the South was nearly double that in the rest of the nation. Those adults also had less to spend on schooling. Taxable wealth per school-aged child was five times greater in Massachusetts, for instance, than in North Carolina. The costs of education in the South were compounded by other demographic factors: population was less dense in many southern states than in the northern states, and the South's racial segregation required dual school systems and faculties and staffs.

Fewer than half of the school-aged children attended school in the South. Few schools stayed open as long as four months a year. Teachers generally earned less than $30 a month. Yet more men taught in the South than elsewhere, a clear and unfortunate indication that in 1900 job opportunities in the South lagged behind those in the rest of the nation. Still, it is easy to overlook important shifts in attitudes toward public education before 1900. Southern states significantly increased funding for public education after the depression of the 1870s ended. Kentucky, for instance, increased taxes substantially in 1881 and 1882 to raise money for public education. So did Georgia. In 1888 Georgia created a state property tax to raise money for a state school fund. Three years later the state legislature created the Georgia Institute of Technology, and state support for higher education gradually increased. Most of the southern states tried to improve public education by making changes in education administration and by increasing opportunities for teacher training. In 1900, however, the South still lagged far behind the rest of the nation in quality and funding of public education.

EDUCATION REFORM (North Carolina Collection, University of North Carolina Library at Chapel Hill)

Having weathered the depression of the 1890s and the Populist challenge and buoyed by the easy victory in the Spanish-American War and the passing or defeat of an older generation of leaders, the South began an extensive, prolonged effort to overhaul public education. Initially a group of educators, journalists, and activists mounted a campaign of fact-finding, publicity, conferences, and lobbying. Northern philanthropists joined in, with substantial sums and quiet discretion.

Walter Hines Page played a strategic role in the early stages of the "educational awakening." He had long been interested in education reform. As editor of the *Forum* in the 1890s and later of *World's Work*, he had encouraged investigations into education. Page saw educational improvement as necessary if the New South were to be realized. In 1897 he delivered an address in Greensboro, North Carolina, which became a landmark. The "forgotten man," Page said, was the man who had not received an adequate education. Reflecting the Progressives' penchant for facts and figures, Page claimed that failure to support education had cost North Carolina dearly. The steady emigration of Tarheels had exacted a heavy toll in lost talent. Those left behind paid a heavy personal price and were a millstone around the neck of the state.

> In 1890, twenty-six percent of the white persons of the State were unable to read or write. One in four was wholly forgotten. But illiteracy was not the worst of it; the worst of it was that the stationary social condition indicated by generations of illiteracy had long been the general condition. The forgotten man was content to stay forgotten.

Page's speech was the public capstone of a concerted effort to elevate schooling in North Carolina. The extraordinarily bitter, violent politics of North Carolina in the 1890s had obscured the emergence of a widely shared determination to improve educational opportunities in the state. Led by the new president of the University of North Carolina, Edwin A. Alderman, and Charles D. McIver, president of the recently opened North Carolina State Normal and Industrial School for Women (now the University of North Carolina at Greensboro), the campaign first succeeded in obtaining a more secure tax base for public education. Charles B. Aycock, governor from 1900 to 1904, and James Y. Joyner, longtime state superintendent of education, assumed command of a crusade for education which marked a turning point in the history of North Carolina. Newspapers in the state aided the impressive efforts. Similar developments occurred elsewhere in the South.

Coincidentally, aid came from the outside. Led by Robert C. Ogden, a wealthy New York businessman and supporter of Hampton Institute in Virginia, the Conference for Education in the South began in 1898. Initially concerned about education for blacks, the conference soon shifted its primary emphasis to whites. The Southern Education Board (SEB) evolved out of the conference in 1901, and the SEB became the major vehicle for publicity and lobbying for the education crusade. Edgar Gardner Murphy became the executive director of the SEB, which supported campaigns for educational reform in every southern state and ran a bureau that collected and disseminated information.

Other northern philanthropists provided critically needed assistance, another example of the not always welcome hand of outside reformers. John D. Rockefeller, Sr., gave $53 million from 1902 to 1909 through one of his organizations, the General Education Board (GEB). Rockefeller expressed a "special interest in education in the South." The SEB and GEB worked together closely; in fact, several individuals served on the boards of directors of both agencies.

Aided by funds from the GEB, the SEB distributed a steady stream of bulletins, documents, and reports; encouraged state campaigns; and sent out agents during a series of campaigns that extended for more than a decade. No one could entirely escape the crusaders; they turned up to speak at public gatherings of all sorts, from church meetings to barbecues. They relied on concentrated verbal blitzes reminiscent of revival meetings. Where the spoken word did not reach, the written word did, in newspapers and magazines fortified by the latest release from the SEB.

The southern states increased their total expenditures for public schools nearly 300 percent, from $21.4 million in 1900 to $57.2 million in 1910, then nearly tripled that sum to $156.3 million in 1920. (The increase in North Carolina exceeded 1,200 percent for the same years, from $950,000 to more than $12 million.) Illiteracy rates declined sharply, more so for whites than for blacks, an indication of the severe racial discrimination in the distribution of educational expenditures. The proportion of school-aged children enrolled in school increased significantly, as did the length of the school year and salaries for teachers. The ratio of pupils to teachers declined somewhat. By 1920, every southern state had adopted a compulsory education law. Schools, especially in urban areas, offered greater varieties of courses. Certification and administrative procedures diminished the power of local politicians to use local schools for patronage. That development lessened political pressures on teachers and school administrators. As they became more professional, they tended also to be more bureaucratic and insulated from the pressures of their constituencies. But neither they nor the schools were insulated from Jim Crow or from the efforts of powerful people in the state to determine the goals of education. Businessmen, for instance, effectively pressed for schooling that was designed to produce "desirable" employees, though pupils often proved far less pliant than the champions of vocational education presumed. As late as 1940, every southern state spent far less on public education per pupil than other states spent, and not all of the disparities can be explained by income differentials among the states. It is possible, however, that the disparties between expenditures per pupil might have been much less if comparisons are limited only to white pupils.

In almost every measurable category, however, the South continued to lag behind the rest of the nation. Jim Crow, dependency on cotton, and demographic factors still outweighed the efforts and successes of the education crusade. No state in the South or the border region except Oklahoma equaled or exceeded the national average for length of school term or for expenditures per

SELECTED SCHOOL STATISTICS, 1900, 1920

	Average length of school term (in days)		Per pupil expenditures (per capita/total population)	
	1900	1920	1900	1920
United States	144.6	161.3	$2.84	$ 9.80
Alabama	78.3	123	.50	3.88
Arkansas	77.5	126	1.04	4.40
Florida	93	133	1.45	7.26
Georgia	112	145	.89	3.13
Kentucky	115.4	123	1.41	3.36
Louisiana	120	149	.82	6.32
Mississippi	105.1	140	.89	3.06
North Carolina	70.8	134	.50	4.75
Oklahoma	95.3	166	1.72	11.29
South Carolina	88.4	110	.67	3.94
Tennessee	96	133	.87	4.34
Texas	108.2	156	1.46	7.21
Virginia	119	147	1.07	5.62

pupil in 1920. All of the states in the region trailed behind the national averages in daily attendance and literacy.

Southern leaders pursued a deliberate policy of discriminating against Negroes in expenditures for education. From 1890 to 1930, for instance, Alabama increased the gap between educational expenditures for blacks and whites. The width of the gap varied from area to area within the state, but every area spent at least twice as much for whites' schooling as for blacks'. In 1930 Lowndes County appropriated $53,525 for 975 white children and $48,786 for 10,039 Negro children. Similar patterns prevailed in Virginia, the Carolinas, and Georgia. In North Carolina, "for every $1.00 expended on a Negro child of school age, $3.22 was expended on the education of a white child of school age" in 1915. That same year the state superintendent of education in South Carolina asked, "Is it too much to hope for a minimum of $25 per white child and $5 per negro child?" South Carolina actually spent less for both in 1915, but at an even more lopsided ratio, 12.37 to 1. Some, but not much, of this imbalance was offset by the work of private philanthropies, the GEB and the Slater, Jeanes, and Peabody funds. Some of these funds antedated the education crusade. At great sacrifice, blacks also supported Negro education financially as individuals and through religious groups. The disparities could have been even worse. Some southern leaders wanted to base appropriations for the education of blacks on the taxes blacks paid. Vardaman took the most extreme position here: he wanted to eliminate public expenditures for black schools altogether. In this case, however, moderates held off the extremists.

The philanthropies, especially the GEB, tried to channel blacks into industrial and vocational education. They had a willing ally in Booker T. Washington.

AVERAGE MONTHLY SALARIES OF TEACHERS, GEORGIA ELEMENTARY
SCHOOLS

	1901		1915	
White,	1st Grade	$36.90	White men	$60.25
White,	2nd Grade	28.11	White women	45.70
White,	3rd Grade	22.33		
Black,	1st Grade	25.60	Black men	30.14
Black,	2nd Grade	26.00	Black women	21.69
Black,	3rd Grade	16.30		

SOURCE: Louis R. Harlan, *Separate and Unequal: Public School Campaigns and Racism in the Southern Seaboard States 1901–1915*. New York: Atheneum, 1968, p. 245. Copyright © 1958 The University of North Carolina Press. Reprinted by permission.

Average Annual Salaries of Teachers in the Southern Seaboard, 1911–1913

State	Teachers		Salaries		Av. ann. salary	
	White	Black	White	Black	White	Black
Va.	8,576	2,441	$2,767,365	$ 421,381	$322.69	$172.63
N.C.	8,716	2,875	1,715,994	340,856	196.83	118.59
S.C.	4,363	2,760	1,454,098	305,084	333.28	110.54
Ga.	9,053	4,052	2,884,580	483,622	318.63	110.54
Sou. Seab.	30,708	12,128	8,822,037	1,550,943	287.29	127.88

SOURCE: Harlan, *Separate and Unequal*, p. 257.

Per Capita Expenditures for White and Negro in Southern Counties

County groups' % blacks in population	White teachers' salaries	Black teachers' salaries	Per capita white	Per capita black
Counties under 10%	$ 7,755,817	$ 325,579	$ 7.96	$7.23
Counties 10 to 25%	9,633,674	1,196,788	9.55	5.55
Counties 25 to 50%	12,572,666	2,265,945	11.11	3.19
Counties 50 to 75%	4,574,366	1,167,796	12.53	1.77
Counties 75% and over	888,759	359,800	22.22	1.78

SOURCE: Harlan, *Separate and Unequal*, p. 260.

Such an approach fitted the New South credo and the white view of the place of blacks. Yet, as W. E. B. Du Bois and others contended, much of what was called industrial education was training in crafts that were becoming obsolete. Du Bois pleaded, without much success, for a broad education for more able blacks (his "talented tenth") who would provide leadership for the race. Not many whites had an interest in developing such leaders.

Interest in better education reached beyond secondary education. Well it might, given the unhappy state of colleges and universities in the South in

1900. Few of them could meet the basic standards of the day for colleges—a four-year course in the liberal arts and sciences, a full-time faculty of at least six members, and a requirement that entering students have completed four years of high school. Most so-called colleges were no more than high schools. Funds for higher education were so limited that the annual income of Harvard University in 1901 exceeded the "total available income for the sixty-six colleges and universities of Virginia, North Carolina, South Carolina, Georgia, Alabama, Mississippi, and Arkansas." Several state universities received no state funds at all. Louisiana State University could receive no more than $10,000 from the state. The state constitution stipulated that sum, and it did not change until 1904, when the limit was raised to $15,000. Support for private education also lagged. In 1900 eighteen colleges and universities in the United States had endowments of $1.5 million or more. None was in the South. Only Tulane and Vanderbilt were among the thirty with endowments of at least $1 million. New York State had twice as much money for higher education as the entire South had.

The founding of the Southern Association of Colleges and Secondary Schools in 1895 signaled the determination of some southerners to improve this situation. Led by Chancellor James H. Kirkland of Vanderbilt University, the association set out to establish higher standards for scholarship, to codify differences between colleges and secondary schools, and to establish entrance requirements. Endowments increased to $12 million—a combination of gifts from the GEB and individuals. Some battles for academic freedom also were won. The efforts of sectarians to control higher education were blunted in some instances, and the effect of their attacks on institutions lessened. Vanderbilt established its independence from the Methodist College of Bishops. Trinity College (later Duke University) refused to dismiss Professor John Spencer Bassett after he called Booker T. Washington "the greatest man, save General Lee, born in the South in a hundred years" and not very subtly criticized white leaders who were "stirring up the fires of racial antipathy," a course he feared might lead "the country to an end which I dare not name." Bassett made his comments in the *South Atlantic Quarterly*, which he helped found in 1902. The quarterly, along with the *Sewanee Review* (founded in 1892), gave the South its first scholarly journals of real quality and continuing impact. Professor Andrew Shedd of Emory did not fare so well as Bassett. After he took mild exception to the racial orthodoxy of the South, Emory "accepted" his "resignation." Several years later, the college reinstated him.

Gains came slowly in academia. Eighteen years after its founding, the Southern Association counted only twenty-eight colleges and universities among its members, and but seven of them required four years of study for a baccalaureate degree. Despite improvements, serious deficiencies in financial support, facilities, library holdings, faculty, and student bodies remained. Even casual inspection revealed an abundance of institutions that were universities and colleges in name only. While some politicians led or at least encouraged the education crusade, others blundered. The worst incident occurred in the newest extension of the South, Oklahoma. There the governor summarily and without explanation dismissed a fifth of the faculty of the University of Oklahoma in 1908. The university's president also was dispatched, along with his Harvard doctorate, to be replaced by a man with no academic degree at all.

HEALTH REFORMS

Matters of the body as well as the mind were high on the Progressives' agenda. Indifference to water quality, garbage disposal, and sewerage services helped to explain why tuberculosis, yellow fever, malaria, diphtheria, smallpox, and typhoid topped the lists of causes of chronic illnesses and death. The quality of medical services and health care, low incomes, undrained lowlands, and a hot, humid climate made matters worse. Average longevity—accurate figures are not available—was probably no more than fifty years.

This picture was altered significantly in the next twenty or so years, in large part because of the discovery that many of these diseases had bacterial origins. State and local boards of public health were reorganized or established; they became enforcers of quarantines, dispensers of vaccines and antitoxins, and providers of laboratory services and information. Improved water, sewerage, and garbage services made urban living safer. These things had a measurable effect: by 1920, longevity averaged slightly more than fifty-five years. Much remained to be done, of course, before the chronic diseases were reduced to minimal threats to life and health. At the same time, extensive draining of lowlands, such as those in the lower Mississippi basin, and spraying for mosquitoes reduced the impact of malaria and yellow fever. Outbreaks of both during the great Mississippi flood of 1927 underscored the tenuousness of the victory over these two. Still, nothing like the 20,000 deaths from yellow fever which occurred in 1878 in the Mississippi basin happened again. Sustained economic growth in the South after 1940 resulted in raised incomes and better health. Thereafter, the threats of bacteria-based diseases in the South were reduced to a minimum.

Medicine in the South followed other national patterns. Encouraged by the American Medical Association, which had reorganized itself along more professional lines in 1885, local medical societies focused on efforts to improve the training of medical personnel and the care patients received. These efforts resulted in the closing of some medical schools and improvements in others and the licensing of medical personnel. Licensing required a determination of what a physician was, what training was satisfactory, and what codes of ethical and professional behavior physicians should establish. This process of identification, development of professional codes, and certification or accreditation also took place among other professionals, such as lawyers, teachers, and engineers. While improvement of services provided much of the stimulus for this process, so did self-interest. Professionals thus got the power to limit access to their services—to reduce competition. Women, save for teachers, found the gates to the professions narrow indeed, and among teachers men received markedly better pay than women. Blacks, of course, also had limited prospects in the professions. Physicians also found other ways to protect their self-interest. For instance, the American Medical Association and other physicians' organizations in Florida opposed cooperative medical insurance programs. Physicians preferred the fee-for-service system, which became a critical, formative factor in American medicine in the twentieth century.

Issues of public health could and did cast an embarrassing light on the South. Predictably, some southerners reacted defensively to the news that the South was a hotbed of hookworm and pellagra. They saw the nefarious hand of medical carpetbaggers, and their suspicion was heightened by the association of the Rockefellers with a campaign to eradicate hookworm. In 1902 Dr. Charles Wardell Stiles, a New York–born, German-trained zoologist, announced, according to the *New York Sun*, that he might have found the "germ of laziness." The "discoverer of the hookworm disease" had found a scientific explanation for an infection that afflicted perhaps 40 percent of southerners, most of them white. At first southerners greeted Stiles's work with laughter. True enough, a lot of poor whites and blacks were known for their laziness, but how could a worm have caused it?

Hookworm, an intestinal parasite, can cause its host to suffer anemia, to be pale and suffer indigestion, cause developmental problems in children, create a general sense of weakness or fatigue, and produce melancholia. Combined with the nutritionally poor diet that most low-income southerners had in 1900 (and for some years thereafter), hookworm could have a very damaging, even fatal impact on its host. Hidden in the intestines and not striking with the noticeable swiftness of yellow fever, say, hookworm long persisted as an undetected scourge.

Beginning with a million-dollar gift from John D. Rockefeller, Sr., the Rockefeller Commission for the Eradication of Hookworm Disease spread its efforts out over much of the South. The efforts involved a combination of science

BLACK MIDWIFE, C. 1935 (Courtesy Georgia Department of Archives and History)

and public education, administrative problems and innovations, evangelical fervor and public relations. The not always tactful Stiles was scorned as the Yankee "doctor of something else" (not medicine). Bishop Warren A. Candler of Georgia, brother to pharmacist-turned-entrepreneur Asa G. Chandler, founder of Coca-Cola, believed Rockefeller wanted to use the commission as a means to become a dominant force in southern education. Josephus Daniels, editor of the Raleigh *News and Observer*, a power among North Carolina Democrats and future secretary of the navy, wrote:

> Many of us in the South are getting tired of being exploited by advertisements that exaggerate conditions.... As to hookworm, this paper has accepted the statement of the widespread prevalence of that disease with many grains of allowance. Let us not canonize Standard Oil Rockefeller by putting laurels on his head because he seeks to buy the appreciation of the people whom he has been robbing for a quarter of a century.

Most southerners apparently felt otherwise about the commission. In fact, Walter Hines Page had helped connect Stiles with the people in charge of Rockefeller's philanthropies. Eradication of the disease involved delicate matters, most particularly the microscopic examination of samples of human feces and a campaign to persuade people without modern toilet facilities that they must construct, maintain, and use sanitary privies.

During its five-year life, more than a million people were examined and some 440,000 people were treated. Another 254,000 received treatment elsewhere—no doubt a direct result of the work of the commission. The commission found infestation rates as high as 50 percent in North Carolina, 60 percent in Georgia, and 67 percent in South Carolina. So prevalent was the disease among cotton mill hands and their families that it was often referred to as "cotton mill anemia."

The commission did not eradicate hookworm in the South but it came close to doing so. Certainly it improved the health of many southerners. It significantly reduced the incidence of hookworm and suggested a nonproscriptive explanation for the gaunt appearance and widely reported "laziness" of a large number of southerners who deserved better and who knew that the way they felt was not "all in their heads." Moreover, the Sanitary Commission aided in the evolution of the public health movement in America. Its most important legacy in the South may have been the encouragement it gave to the development of state and local public health agencies. Finally, the commission laid the base for the Rockefeller Foundation and may have facilitated the campaign of Dr. Joseph Goldberger against pellagra, a disease that in the United States was found only in the South.

Goldberger, a Jewish immigrant from Hungary, had been reared in New York, where he received his medical training. As an employee of the United States Public Health Service he began his landmark research on pellagra in 1914, about the time some southerners became intensely concerned about the disease. That concern had mounted in tandem with the number of reported cases of pellagra, a relatively unknown condition before 1900. Between 1907 and

1911, eight states in the South reported 15,870 cases, with a death rate of nearly 40 percent. And things seemed to be getting worse.

Victims (pellagrins) developed a distinctive butterfly-shaped facial rash that caused a burning sensation, digestive disorders, dizziness, and depression. Some cases were mild; others were severe, often fatal. Pellagrins were often stigmatized and sometimes were isolated, like lepers. The stigma also marked the South, which became known as "the land of hookworm and pellagra."

Dr. Goldberger soon came to suspect that pellagra was the result of poor diet, that it was an affliction of the poor. His research led him to connect the disease with the diet of cornmeal, fatback (cheap cuts of pork), and molasses that so many poor whites and blacks in the South regularly consumed. Several obstacles hindered his work. Nutrition was a relatively new area of medical research. Other physicians clung to their belief that the disease was caused by bacteria. When Goldberger tried to alert the public and leaders in the South about the disease and its causes, many people regarded his efforts as one more attempt to stigmatize their region. Goldberger's reports about pellagra were dismissed as "malicious propaganda." Florida worried that tourism would be adversely affected. Businessmen worried about the effects of the reports on business interests. Politicians talked about being made objects of scorn and charity. A number of state boards of health in the South denied that pellagra was a growing menace despite figures that indicated otherwise. Other public health officers in the region, however, concurred with Goldberger. Whatever its cause, pellagra was an urgent problem. Deaths from pellagra reached all-time highs in the South in the late 1920s, when some 200,000 cases were diagnosed.

The work on pellagra had struck the deep vein of southern defensiveness. That vein was the product of historical experience mixed with illusions and fears. The work on pellagra had laid the base for its eventual elimination as a major threat to the health of southerners. That victory came, however, a quarter century after Dr. Goldberger began his research and more than a decade after his death in 1929. Scientists found a direct relationship between the disease and deficiencies in the consumption of nicotinic acid (vitamin B-12), deficiencies that could readily be corrected by the consumption of more eggs, meat, and green vegetables. In time the image and reality of the South as the "land of hookworm and pellagra" ended.

CHILD LABOR REFORM

Trouble and embarrassment struck the South from another quarter, this time from within the region, at least initially. Interest in child labor reform in the South began before 1900. In 1901, however, it got a major boost. That year Edgar Gardner Murphy led a group that founded the Alabama Child Labor Committee. The committee's statewide activities sparked a nationwide effort to restrict the amount of work children of fifteen or under could do in manufacturing and some other areas of employment. Murphy acted after he became aware that child laborers in Alabama cotton mills worked as many as seventy-two hours a week—six twelve-hour days with Sundays off—in dusty, noisy, often hot mills for 30 cents a day.

Murphy soon realized that child labor was a national as well as a regional issue. Child textile workers were common throughout the South. Of the more than 83,000 mill workers in 1900 in the principal southern textile states (Alabama, Georgia, and the Carolinas), nearly 30 percent (about 25,000) were ten to fifteen years of age. Many were six to nine years old. Children were commonly employed in all parts of the country. New England mills employed almost 11,000 workers under sixteen (6.7 percent of their work force), and mills in the middle Atlantic states used more than 4,300 (12.4 percent of their work force). Glassmaking in West Virginia and coal mining in Pennsylvania and southern Appalachia, two industries that caught the attention of the National Child Labor Committee (NCLC) because of their especially harsh and dangerous working conditions, employed substantial numbers of children in several states. In 1900 and in 1910, more than 1.5 million children between the ages of ten and fifteen were gainfully employed in the United States, though their proportion of all the gainfully employed had declined and would continue to do so. Most of the attention and concern about child labor centered on the textile industry in the South, in part because of the size of the industry and the numbers of minors it employed. Southern textile manufacturers and their allies saw more sinister motives for the spotlight in which they found themselves, and they were not entirely wrong.

The NCLC and several state child labor committees mounted strong campaigns to reduce or eliminate child labor from textiles and other industries. The NCLC had strong southern roots. Murphy initiated its founding and attracted some of the most prominent "social justice" Progressives of the day to the committee. Alexander McKelway, a Presbyterian minister from North Carolina, directed NCLC activities in the South. Child labor reform ultimately involved major efforts at fact-finding and publicity. Lewis W. Hine left a valuable photographic record of child labor which helped establish his reputation as one of the giants of American photography. The federal government also contributed thorough studies of the employment and work lives of both children and women.

By 1920 these activities brought concrete results. Each of the major textile states in the South had passed legislation to restrict child labor. North Carolina, for example, limited minors and women to sixty hours a week, no more than eleven hours in any day. All of the states had compulsory school attendance laws, which varied in scope. Congress also had passed the Keating-Owen Act to restrict child labor, but the Supreme Court had declared it unconstitutional. Still, the NCLC could be pleased: child labor in southern textile mills had declined markedly. In 1919 the census reported that the proportions of mill workers under sixteen ranged from under 2 percent in Alabama to around 6 percent in the Carolinas.

The NCLC and its allies had overcome considerable opposition to get child labor laws passed. Restrictions on child labor involved complex issues and strong feelings. Child labor reform appeared to be a simple case of a struggle to protect the innocent and powerless from the greedy and powerful. Much more was involved, however, and it was not so morally unambiguous.

Child labor reform raised questions about the rights and powers of employers, of parents, and of children, and questions about where government ought to act or intrude. Should the state intervene on behalf of minors? If so, when and how? Child labor reform presented serious questions about law and its enforcement. If a parent swore that his or her child was of legal age or that the family was destitute and needed the labor of all in the family who could work, should public officials question such statements? The fact that many workers did not have birth certificates complicated matters. So did the obvious need of many families to increase their incomes if they were to survive.

Child labor reform aroused intense sectional feelings and defensiveness. Cotton manufacturers in the South claimed they needed the advantage of low wages if they were to compete against the more established mills of New England and the middle Atlantic states. They argued that the survival of the industry in the South was critically important because it was a large source of the jobs their region desperately needed. They saw the devious, self-serving hand of northern textile manufacturers and organized labor behind the effort to limit child labor. In fact, the American Federation of Labor did oppose child labor as a threat to adult workers and to unions. The AFL was the original source of Murphy's information on child labor in Alabama and continued to supply data to him. He persuaded the AFL to remain in the background because he feared charges of outside interference.

In addition to triggering sectional feelings and defensiveness, which were particularly strong in this case because New England was once again perceived to be the main villain, child labor reform called into question the widely boasted achievements of the New South. Moreover, the movement besmudged the most advertised icon of the New South, the textile industry. Southern textile manufacturers and their supporters predictably, and not implausibly, claimed they were the soldiers in a second Civil War. They also employed less emotional and more specific arguments. They claimed, for instance, that the reformers exaggerated the drudgery of minors' work in their industry. Moreover, they correctly asserted that many parents wanted their children to work in the industry because they needed the money, and they noted that traditionally children had worked (and still did work) in agriculture. The child labor issue thus revealed some of the unpleasant realities of the South's economy in the early twentieth century. Mill owners did exploit workers. They enjoyed high returns on their investment and should have been able to pay better wages. Still, even at the wages they did pay, the mills represented better opportunities than the farms the mill hands had left, where children also worked. For some years families survived and made modest economic and social gains by relying on the family wage system, or the pooling of family members' earnings in the mills. School was not a realistic alternative for many children, and probably was not a very desirable one. Education promised little to mill workers and their families in 1900. The education available to them was often woefully inadequate. And even if it had not been, they might very well have discounted it as not worth the costs. Given the jobs open to their children at that time, some mill families may have sensed that the costs of schooling were not worth bearing. Those costs sometimes included formal segregation in a separate school for "mill children" or informal segregation within a school. Over time mill workers did come to favor education for their children, but only after they were able to forgo the wages of young children and after they could see real economic and social benefits of education for their offspring. Such benefits became more obvious as the economy of the region continued to develop.

Mill workers had good reason to react coolly to child labor reformers. Child labor reform may have been essentially humanitarian, but it constituted a critical intrusion by outsiders in the lives of workers. Murphy defended such an intrusion on the grounds that the future of the children justified such action, for the sake of both the children and society in general. Murphy feared that the industry made mill hands "a fixed and semi-dependent class,—'once an operative, always an operative.'"

Child labor reformers carried a set of cultural assumptions to their crusade, and fears. A recent investigation concluded that child labor reform, at least in South Carolina, was rooted in cultural and political conflict. By 1900, as urbanization spread in South Carolina, an urban middle class emerged, composed primarily of business and professional families. These "town people" believed that "mill people" constituted a grave threat to their concept of a modern South Carolina, and, equally important, to white unity. The town people believed that mill people were isolated from modernization by their segregation in cotton mills and company-owned mill villages. Since approximately one-sixth of all whites in the state lived in those villages in 1905, the "mill problem"—a term and a notion conjured by the town people—was believed to be serious. What especially aroused the town people was the strong support mill hands gave to Cole Blease, a raucous demagogue who opposed modernization.

Alarmed at the growing division between the mill workers and the town people, the reformers (or Progressives) wanted to use the powers of government to attack what they believed was their basic cause: the cultural isolation of the mill villager from the town. The reformers realized that industrialization was creating a factory class that lived and worked in segregation by occupation. The supposedly anachronistic culture that workers brought with them from the country, reformers believed, reinforced that segregation. Disinclined to blame mill owners for creating the mill problem, the reformers courted the owners, praised them for the jobs they created and whatever other benefits they provided, and generally ignored the continuing opposition by most owners to the reformers' programs. Most of the reformers' criticism "was directed, instead, at the operatives, above all at the mill family; the attitudes and habits of mill parents, perpetuated through their children, were threats to the social order, to be combated by using state power to obtain at least partial control over the upbringing of the mill child."

Southern legislatures also gave attention to other areas of labor reform. By 1920 most southern states had created at least rudimentary workers' compensation plans. Several had laws calling for mine and factory inspections and for limits on the number of hours women could work in manufacturing jobs. Most also prohibited night work for women and minors.

It is not clear how much effect these various labor laws had on labor practices. The laws restricting child labor and requiring school attendance had many loopholes and were not systematically enforced. Compulsory school-attendance laws, where they were enforced, probably had greater impact than child labor laws. Economic and technological changes had even more impact than the laws. Mill owners found that their increasing reliance on adult male workers, partly as a result of technological changes, made child labor less and less advantageous. Moreover, minors were simply not as able and reliable as more mature workers. Thus mill owners became less convinced that child labor was an important asset in their battles with northern textile companies and with their competitors in the South. Mill owners came to agree that more educated workers would benefit the industry and the South. At the same time, the reliance of the southern textile industry on the family labor system declined. Around 1900, as dependence on child labor decreased sharply, a large number of women who previously had remained at home to keep house and tend to nearby vegetable gardens began to work in the mills. In a sense, they replaced their children, who now went to school. In doing so, these women took on a dual burden: they continued to run their homes, and they worked at physically exhausting jobs outside the home. In time, they, too, became objects of the reformers' concern.

Southern ladies

The image of southern women and the realities of their lives often differed, sometimes sharply, and not just among mill workers. This divergence existed before 1860 and became even greater afterward. The Civil War forced white women in the South to take on even greater responsibilities than they had assumed before the war. After the war, the deaths and severe disabilities of so many men, economic losses and disruptions, the ending of slavery, and then the evolution of a more industrial and urban South presented new burdens and new opportunities to women, white and black.

Immediately after the war, black men opposed fieldwork for black women. Apparently they felt that such work was not suitable for ladies. This was an opportunity for black men to assert their new freedom and control over their own lives and those of their wives and children, to act upon their notions about proper sex and family roles. Available evidence shows a sharp decline in the number of black women who worked in the fields. Whether or not that decline continued for a long time is not certain, but it is doubtful. The need to survive and the urge to get ahead very probably required black women in farm families to return to the fields eventually. White women among the thousands of poor families worked the land, too.

Economic realities prevailed over social assumptions. Poverty forced women out-of-doors or into new jobs in factories and cities and towns. Textiles provided the largest number of industrial jobs for white women. As late as 1890, one in two cotton mill operatives in the South (and New England as well) were women. During the next three decades, the proportion of female mill hands declined, more in the South than in New England (to 38.2 and 42.9 percent, respectively, in 1920), but the number of women working in southern cotton mills grew to almost 78,000. Black women were much more likely to be gainfully employed than white women, native- or foreign-born, and black women found most of their employment in domestic service, an area few white women entered. More than seven in ten black women who had nonagricultural employment were maids, cooks, or laundresses.

The Civil War and its aftermath created new opportunities for middle-class white women. Economic change subsequently reinforced these changes. Women became operators of farms and plantations and found greater outlets in writing and journalism. Like their male counterparts, most women writers found that they could attract more readers with sentimental stories and historical romances than with more realistic writing. Several women enjoyed success in newspaperwork. Eliza Poitevent Nicholson, who became the editor of the New Orleans *Picayune,* was the most notable of these journalists.

More and more white women found employment as office workers, clerks in stores, and teachers. Teaching began its shift from male dominance to female dominance (numerically, at least) after Reconstruction. Later, during the education crusade of the early twentieth century, this trend accelerated. Women found some openings in other professions, but not very many.

Middle- and upper-class women found their greatest outlets in the various reform and mission groups that became involved in a wide range of activities—temperance, child labor reform, day nurseries, foreign and domestic missions, penal reform, education reform, health care and public health, industrial relations, race relations, women's suffrage. Many of these groups had counterparts among black women. As early as the 1870s, women in the South found new outlets for self-expression and vehicles for their concerns in the women's missionary societies of their churches, especially among the Baptists and Methodists. The Women's Home Mission Society of the Methodist Church, South especially did not avoid controversial issues. Deeply concerned about family life, the society opposed child labor. Among other activities and concerns, the society also attempted to reduce racial tensions and eventually became involved in efforts to end lynching.

The Women's Christian Temperance Union (WCTU) blossomed in the 1880s. It crossed denominational and sectional lines, had a substantial membership, and used its influence and lobbying powers for temperance and other issues. The abuse of alcohol was not a laughing matter, given its negative impact on individuals and families. Activists in the WCTU went beyond temperance to work for penal reform, maternal education, prenatal care, and shorter working hours. By the 1890s, women in the South became involved in the club movement. Before 1910 every southern state had a state federation of such clubs, and by that year all had joined the General Federation of Women's Clubs. The clubs had by then given themselves over to a wide range of reform activities. "One social concern led to another, and the social concerns inevitably led to politics." Few women got involved in the ways Kate Barnard did, but many became expert at lobbying legislatures and other political bodies. As Patty Blackburn Semple noted, the woman's club of Louisville treated politics as taboo, "but gradually we found that our efforts in behalf of civic improvements and the correcting of outrageous abuses were handicapped at every turn by politics."

The experiences of women in missionary societies, the WCTU, and women's clubs laid the necessary foundation for the politicization of women and their struggle to gain the vote. These experiences provided a form of higher education for women at a time when their opportunities for college or university training were severely limited. These experiences also provided crucially important opportunities for women to learn to express their opinions, to strengthen their self-confidence and offset the psychological impact of the ideal of the submissive Southern Lady, and to learning how to organize and bring pressure. Still, the heritage of the submissive woman persisted during the battle to secure the vote.

Woman suffragists and their male allies encountered strong opposition and stirred deep emotions. Politicians worried about diminished power. Businessmen saw women as too disposed to support measures they opposed. Liquor interests saw a life-threatening link between women as voters and temperance. Some ministers criticized woman suffrage as against Scripture. Others saw socialism, foreign influences, and threats to domestic peace and marital harmony.

But most important was Negrophobia. Opponents pointed out that votes for women meant votes for black women. Supporters of woman suffrage employed Negrophobia in their own way: they pointed out that Jim Crow prevented black votes, male and female, from becoming a significant force in southern politics; thus, they argued, granting women the vote would have the happy effect of doubling the white electorate without greatly increasing the black vote. Some suffragists in the South, however, opposed amending the Constitution to grant women the vote. They preferred to have suffrage granted by each state, even if that procedure required many more years. Fearful of federal intervention, southerners, a northern suffragist remarked, "dreaded anything that called attention to the right of suffrage." Thus Laura Clay of Kentucky and Kate Gordon of Louisiana, two prominent suffragists, waged last-gasp battles against the ratification of the Nineteenth Amendment.

Most of the South resisted ratification, though the suffragists got a big boost from the surge of patriotic feelings during World War I and from the endorsement of the Nineteenth Amendment by President Woodrow Wilson, a southern-born Democrat. Texas broke southern ranks first, becoming the ninth state in the Union to approve the amendment. Arkansas, Kentucky, and Oklahoma followed later. Last came Tennessee. Its approval on August 18, 1920, gave the amendment the required three-fourths vote for adoption. Tennessee did not achieve this distinction gracefully. Liquor lobbyists plied the legislature so freely that, according to reports, at various times during the fight over ratification none of the members of the lower chamber was sober. Opponents in the state senate tried to prevent a quorum by fleeing to Alabama. Thus, on the eve of the 1920 elections, the object of this fright, the Southern Lady, continued her unfinished transition from pedestal to politics.

The South, even Southern Ladies, became a part of the Progressive Era before 1912. Activist government displaced passive government. Government agencies proliferated. State and local budgets swelled, as did taxes. Regulations of business increased—regulation of banking, insurance companies, railroads, and others. Limitations on the labor of children and women were imposed, workers' compensation systems were created, and compulsory school-attendance laws were passed. Professionals increased their role in the South, especially by making human services more professional—medicine, dentistry, public health, law, social work, and education. Professionals succeeded in imposing many of their standards on themselves and others. They formed national and regional organizations, such as the NCLC and the Southern Sociological Congress, in order to share ideas and data and to lobby for their goals.

Women found a larger place for themselves in public life and in employment than they had had before. Blacks enjoyed somewhat greater economic opportunities, but continued to find much of their private and public lives circumscribed by the suffocating Jim Crow. The Democratic party remained dominant, but political parties lost some of their impact to the growing power of other well-organized groups. Urban elites, as we shall see, held sway in the urban South.

Surging forward, then falling back, then surging again, prohibition eventually conquered the South and won its endorsement for the Eighteenth Amendment. Prohibition triumphed because, as one historian wrote, it "tied together most of the reform strands of the progressive era and offered a simple, moral solution to disturbing social ills." It afforded an opportunity to attack moral and political corruption. "It reaffirmed the evangelical ideals of southern Protestantism. It was both a coercive reform with strong racial and class overtones and an expression of social concern for those victimized by the South's new urbanization and industrialization." Enforcement of prohibition, however, proved to be far more difficult than passing legislation to mandate it.

Farmers, the largest group in the South, got some things from the Progressive Era, but not enough to protect them from the vicissitudes of the 1920s. That became painfully obvious only after the prosperity born of war came to an end for most southern farmers but continued for most townspeople, thus widening the distance between the farm and the town.

23

Restoration and Exile, 1912–1929

❖

W orld War I and the 1920s brought important changes to the South. But before war broke out, the South enjoyed a return to power in national politics such as it had not known since 1860. That return came in the wake of Woodrow Wilson's election to the presidency in 1912.

THE WILSON ADMINISTRATION

Three hundred thousand people looked on as Woodrow Wilson was sworn in as president of the United States on March 6, 1913. This crowd, the largest that had gathered for an inauguration up to that time, was an indication of the momentousness of Wilson's assumption of the presidency. Progressivism was at a high tide, the Democrats controlled both the White House and Congress for the first time since 1894, and Wilson was the first southern-born president since 1850.

It was purely coincidental that a former Confederate army officer, Chief Justice Edwin Douglass White, administered the oath to the new president, but the symbolism of the coincidence was not lost on the nation. The South, one observer wrote, "had come back to rule the Union." Carried away by the moment, another prematurely announced that "the return of the Democrats to power breaks down sectionalism."

The Wilson administration restored the South to a place in national politics which it had not enjoyed for more than half a century. From 1865 to 1912, no southerner or southern expatriate had been nominated for president or vice president by either major party. Few held cabinet or diplomatic posts. Only seven of thirty-one justices of the Supreme Court came from below the Mason-Dixon line. By contrast, southerners had occupied the White House for fifty of the seventy-two years from Washington to Lincoln, and they served for sixty of those years as chief justices of the nation's highest court. No wonder rebel yells and "Dixie" punctuated the inaugural festivities of 1913.

Wilson's road to the presidency ran through the South. Wilson thought of himself as rooted in the South, where he was born and reared. So were his most important initial supporters. Regional loyalties helped Wilson retain critically needed support during a difficult struggle to get his party's nomination. Then, aided by deep divisions among the Republicans during the 1912 presidential campaign, Wilson won a majority of electoral votes even though he won only 45 percent of the popular vote.

The Wilson presidency had a distinctly southern quality, as did the leadership of Congress, with which he worked closely. In general Wilson's legislative proposals had strong support in the South. Some had their origins in the South. But the Wilson administration represented more than the triumph of Dixie. The Democrats' successes in elections and in their efforts to secure their legislative program in Washington were indicative of national developments.

The Democrats showed that their sentiments lay with Progressivism. The forces of Populism, Bryanism, and Progressivism had transformed them into something quite different from the Cleveland Democrats who had held sway in the late nineteenth century. This new generation of Democrats generally chose to follow the course of activist government. The Democrats passed the first significantly lower tariff since 1857. The tariff legislation provided for a modest income tax, which opponents claimed was an attack on class and on the East by the South and West. The new banking system (the Federal Reserve System) which Congress created in 1913 answered some of the major complaints voiced by the South (and the West) in regard to the national banking acts. The old banking system, its critics said, was too centralized (in the Northeast), had too little government regulation, resulted in rigidities in the money supply, and failed to meet the credit needs of farmers. The Federal Reserve System, designed to answer these charges, was hailed by the South as a major victory. When the Democrats addressed the issue of monopoly, they chose what they believed was regulated competition (the Clayton Antitrust Act and the Federal Trade Commission Act).

Encouraged and sometimes led by southerners, Congress passed legislation to regulate the marketing and warehousing of cotton and created a federally sponsored farm land bank system, a system of extension education for farmers through county agents and land-grant colleges, and a program of federal aid for vocational education. The good roads movement, which enjoyed broad support in the South, reached a decisive milestone when the Federal Highways Act was passed.

The South also contributed to the dubious record of the Wilson administration on race relations. Wilson was not an extremist on race, but he permitted Jim Crow to flourish in official Washington. Numerous blacks lost positions in the civil service or were demoted. Racially segregated facilities became commonplace in public buildings. Such extremists as Ben Tillman of South Carolina and James K. Vardaman of Mississippi wanted even more than they got from the Wilson administration. But conscience, perhaps, and political expediency, certainly, stayed the hand of the president. Democrats were aware that blacks, some of whom supported Democrats, voted in significant numbers in such states as Illinois and New York as well as in the upper South and the border states. As the minority party, the Democrats needed every vote they could muster.

The president gave considerable ground to southern sentiments on race. He did not in other respects. With an eye to his reelection, Wilson endorsed labor legislation that received a cool or hostile reception from most southern leaders. In 1916 he lent his name to successful efforts to enact a federal child labor law (the Keating-Owen Act). Most of its opposition came from the southerners in Congress, especially those from the Southeast, where cotton mills were a major factor in the economy. A number of southern senators and congressmen did vote for the measure, however. Wilson also endorsed the Nineteenth Amendment, which gave women the right to vote—not a popular measure in the South, at least not among most men. Still, in the 1918 congressional election Republicans successfully attacked Wilson for allegedly being a captive of the South. They amassed a good deal of political capital with their claim that his wartime farm policy favored cotton more than other farm products, that sectional interests had won out over national interests during a national crisis. Such attacks helped the Republicans to regain control of the Senate and the House of Representatives and set the stage for a Republican victory in the 1920 presidential election.

During their brief return to national political power, however, southerners in Congress figured prominently in the remarkable legislative record of the Wilson administration, most of which was enacted without the stimulus of economic crisis or war. As their support indicated, southern leaders (and their constituents) embraced activist government. "Progressivism, an amalgam of agrarian radicalism, business regulation, good government, and urban social justice reforms, became in the end a movement for positive government [which found] general acceptance." But this mixture of disparate elements could not survive the centrifugal forces loosed by World War I.

A DISRUPTED SOCIETY: THE SOUTH DURING WORLD WAR I

In August 1914, World War I—or the Great War, as it was then called—enveloped Europe. The war soon made itself felt in the United States, first economically, then diplomatically, and finally militarily when Congress declared war on Germany in 1917. The war was a massive stimulant to the southern economy, and the resulting prosperity accelerated trends already set in motion before the conflict started. The town world continued to distance itself from the farm world. So many southerners joined the ongoing migration to towns and cities that the population patterns of the South of 1920 were markedly different from those of 1915. Many people, black and white, found life better at their destinations. These migrations also created and reflected social turmoil, which reverberated into the 1920s.

A powerful nationalism—100 percent Americanism—swept the nation. When the United States entered the war, local and state councils of defense directed the enormous wave of American nationalism which swept the South into voluntaristic efforts in support of the war effort. Unfortunately, and sometimes tragically, some of those energies spilled over into vigilantism, which was encouraged by the passage of espionage and sedition laws and by the policies and actions of public officials. For American radicals, the success of the Bolshevik revolution in Russia in 1917 made matters worse. Socialists became prime targets. Mounting antiradical sentiments among the public and repressive measures of government and private citizens combined with unprecedented farm prosperity to destroy the socialists, even in the Southwest, where they had had a strong following. The public also showed little tolerance for anyone they believed was lacking in patriotism, even the immensely popular Vardaman. The White Chief was hanged in effigy in Mississippi because of his opposition to the war; in 1918 he was soundly defeated in his attempt to be reelected to the U.S. Senate.

Vardaman's defeat removed one of the most outspoken, vitriolic Negrophobes from the national scene. The war, however, had little impact on Negrophobia in the South. Although the wartime surge of patriotism brought whites and blacks together in various efforts to support the war, Jim Crow remained intact. Racial animosities often worsened when the war stimulated social upheaval. As the ranks of the farm-to-town migrants swelled, competition for jobs, housing, and urban services grew. Blacks seemed to be rising out of their place.

The incidence of lynching, a bloody measure of the state of race relations, had been declining before the war, but that trend was reversed: the number of lynchings rose from sixty-seven in 1915 to eighty-three in 1919. No one, of course, counted the number of interracial confrontations between individuals or small groups. As returning black veterans discovered, not even the uniform of their country offered protection. Many whites were convinced that black servicemen had gotten "bad notions" from their experiences in the military and in Europe. Ten uniformed servicemen died at the hands of lynch mobs. And lynchings seemed to be getting even more grotesque: more black men were being burned alive.

Race riots erupted inside and outside the South. The first of a series of major racial conflicts broke out in East St. Louis, Illinois, and in Houston in 1917. Nineteen-nineteen was worse: Charleston, South Carolina; Longview, Texas; Washington, D.C.; Chicago; Knoxville; Omaha; and Elaine, Arkansas. In all, twenty-five urban race riots occurred in a period of six months in 1919. Perhaps two hundred were killed; at least two-thirds of the victims were blacks. James

Weldon Johnson, secretary of the National Association for the Advancement of Colored People (NAACP), called it the "red summer."

Two years later, Tulsa achieved the distinction of being the first American city to be attacked from the air. There a riot left thirty (many more, perhaps) dead and $1 million worth of property destroyed. Widespread looting and burning of black neighborhoods by whites caused most of the destruction. Some whites even used airplanes to strafe blacks and bomb them with dynamite. Tulsa blacks fought back, as blacks had done elsewhere during the race riots of the era. The poet Claude McKay spoke for blacks who risked their lives in defense of their dignity:

> If we must die, let it not be like hogs
> Hunted and penned in an inglorious spot,
> While round us bark the mad and hungry dogs,
> Making their mock at our accursed lot.

The fact that blacks had fought back, as the historian John Hope Franklin recalled of his boyhood, "had a great deal to do with eradicating the fear that a Negro boy growing up in Tulsa might have felt in the years following the riot."

Some southern blacks and whites reacted to these outbursts of racial violence by creating an interracial movement. Careful never to question or overtly

TULSA RACE RIOT, 1921 (Tulsa County Historical Society)

threaten Jim Crow, the Commission on Interracial Cooperation worked to resolve grievances, to relieve tensions and prevent violence, and to change attitudes through education and interracial contacts. The NAACP, which grew rapidly in those years, used a somewhat different approach: it cautiously began to challenge Jim Crow in the courts and lobbied on behalf of Negroes.

World War I prompted other efforts at social reform. Social work programs experienced a major revitalization. The war also served as a catalyst for the prohibition movement. The movement attracted a wide following; it reflected an urge for purity rooted in Protestantism and a belief in the power of the state to regulate morality. Prohibition had its less savory side: anti-Catholicism and hostility to immigrants from eastern and southern Europe. The Eighteenth Amendment, prohibiting "the manufacture, sale, or transportation of intoxicating liquors," was ratified in January 1919, only thirteen months after Congress proposed it. Amid these war-related activities, almost no one noticed "Colonel" William J. Simmons and his force of fourteen as they climbed to the top of Stone Mountain, outside of Atlanta, in late 1915. There they gathered before an altar covered by an American flag, ignited a large cross, and resurrected the Ku Klux Klan—according to Simmons, "The World's Greatest Secret, Social, Patriotic, Fraternal Beneficiary Order." The Klan had only a small following until after the war ended. Colonel Simmons discovered that lighting a fiery cross on Stone Mountain was easier than attracting members and their dues. Energies that might have found expression through the Klan found more official outlets during World War I.

Though race relations seemed unchanged, southern blacks actually experienced profound changes in their lives during World War I. Some of those changes had begun before the war started. Sometime around 1910, the migrations of blacks from farms to cities in the South and North grew so large that it came to be called the Great Migration. It reached the proportions of a flood during World War I. Blacks enjoyed unprecedented job opportunities. Faced with a smaller supply of labor, southern manufacturers, even textile manufacturers, employed increasing numbers of black workers. Northern industry also sought blacks as the war reduced the supply of unskilled European immigrants and coincidentally stimulated industrial expansion. Through labor recruiting and more often by word of mouth, newspapers, and magazines, blacks learned of opportunities in northern industries such as steel. Even at less than $2 a day for long, hard, and often dangerous work, jobs in steel mills looked better than work in cotton fields or occasional labor. While tighter labor markets provided a powerful pull on black (and white) migration, other factors provided strong pushes. First came the cotton crisis of 1914–1915, when World War I began; then came the boll weevil, which was eating its way eastward through cotton fields, and floods in the Deep South in 1915 and 1916. And there was the continuing hostility of southern whites.

Initially, whites welcomed the black exodus. But labor shortages soon caused some whites to reconsider and act to halt it. The fact that many of the migrants were skilled workers deepened these anxieties. Apparently convinced that southern blacks were not capable of making rational economic decisions and therefore must be being enticed away by outside labor agents, some communities tried to stop such activities. Montgomery prohibited labor recruiting altogether. Macon allowed recruiters to work if they had a license, which cost $25,000, and letters of commendation from local clergy, businessmen, and manufacturers. Others were more direct: they prevented blacks from boarding northbound trains. Some white leaders did work to persuade their communities to be less hostile toward blacks.

But the exodus did not stop or even slow. So many people were leaving that railroads ran special trains. For the first time ever, the center of the black populace in America stopped moving southwestward and shifted toward the northeast. Perhaps 800,000 to 900,000 blacks departed; most went to urban industrial centers in the North and Midwest. The exodus got the attention of numerous observers. One investigator asked blacks detraining in Washington, D.C., why they had come north. He listed their explanations:

> Economic exploitation...insecurity of life...high mortgage rates, and the lack of credit for Negro farmers. "Jim Crow"...crop failures due to boll weevil and floods. Lack of employment. Poor school facilities...attraction of the North...letters from relatives and friends...labor demand of the North. Unfair treatment of sharecroppers and tenants...labor agents...travel...new locations.

As blacks left the South, they carried their culture and religion with them. One consequence was the appearance of jazz as a major form of musical expression in the nation as a whole in the late 1920s.

GOOD TIMES: THE SOUTHERN ECONOMY AND WORLD WAR I

Like the social order, the economic order was shaken by World War I. Initially the war adversely affected the southern economy. The disruption in the sales of raw cotton, at a time when the cotton crop was the largest in history, plunged the South into a severe slump. Losses in 1914 totaled $500 million, about one-half of the value of the crop. Major cotton exchanges closed and did not reopen for three months. Cotton prices fell below 10 cents a pound, generally considered to be the break-even price. Even at 5 cents a pound cotton found no buyers. Cotton went unpicked. Landowners released renters from contracts. Cutoffs of provisions left renters and croppers without food or supplies. The Red Cross, the U.S. Department of Agriculture, and other organizations gave food or money to the destitute and to local communities for relief purposes. For years thereafter, cotton farmers spoke about 1914 in somber tones as "that year."

Then, less than a year after cotton prices plummeted, they rose to 11 cents, then to nearly 20, then to nearly 36. Cotton prices averaged 27 cents from 1917

SLOSS FURNACE, BIRMINGHAM, 1920s (Archives Department, Birmingham Public Library, Birmingham, Alabama)

to 1919, the best years ever, and well above increases in the cost of living. The latter year's crop sold for a record $2 billion. Negro tenants were reported to have "come to town with their pockets stuffed with paper money" to pay off debts and to buy. Landowners had to offer better-than-usual terms to prospective renters. "New houses, new barns, new roof paint, better roads, schoolhouses, churches, and better farm equipment" appeared in the countryside. Automobiles invaded the South. Prosperous landowners moved to new houses in town, complete with modern appliances and facilities, and commuted to their farm holdings in order to supervise renters and croppers.

The war-stimulated demand reached far beyond the cotton fields. Economic expansion stimulated such established industries as railroads, textiles, lumber, iron and steel, coal and oil, hydroelectric power, and tobacco manufacturing. The wartime boom spilled over into Appalachia, which hitherto had not been as affected by the forces of the New South as had other parts of the South. The economic surge that World War I had done so much to cause carried over into the 1920s in much of the South.

The military preparedness efforts of the federal government and then the nation's entry into the war altered the South and the lives of its inhabitants.

Some southerners experienced the war very directly and personally. From farms, towns, and cities, from Virginia to Florida to Texas, one million men entered the armed forces. Many went far greater distances than they had ever gone before, even if they only went to a military training camp. Most of the boot camps were located in the South, where year-round training was more practical than in much of the rest of the country. (Cynics might, of course, think that weather was a lesser factor in the camps' location than the power of southern Democrats in Washington.) Some southerners went much farther—to Europe, to battle—and many did not return.

American blacks who fought in Europe fought with French units, because the American army refused to use blacks in combat. The army's attitude mirrored that of the white public. Larger proportions of blacks than whites were taken by the draft. Racial prejudice undoubtedly played a large part in these decisions. Local white citizens became quite uneasy when black trainees were located at nearby installations. Southern black soldiers received a wary, even violent welcome when they returned home.

A full accounting of the impact of the federal budget, which in current dollars grew 2,600 percent between 1916 and 1919, is probably not possible. Every southern state had at least one military installation or defense industry. Naval bases and shipyards ran along the coast southward from Hampton Roads, Virginia, to Charleston, around the Florida peninsula, and along the Gulf Coast to New Orleans and Texas. The powder and chemical industries expanded. The most important of these firms were Du Pont in eastern Virginia, the nucleus of what developed as Tennessee Eastman at Kingsport, Tennessee, and a dam and a nitrate plant at Muscle Shoals, Alabama. The last, which was not completed when the war ended, became the initial step in the massive Tennessee Valley Authority. By the late 1920s, Allied Chemical and other firms had followed Du Pont into eastern Virginia and helped make Hopewell the center of a burgeoning chemical industry. They lifted chemicals to second place in value added among industries in Virginia. Rayon, the first fiber to be contrived by artificial means (though from natural plant products), held a comparable position in Tennessee.

Chemicals were in the vanguard of an industrial development that grew rapidly during the war and continued growing afterward. Petroleum and petrochemicals, hydroelectric power, pulpwood and paper, furniture, tobacco manufacturing, and aluminum joined the ranks. So did iron and steel, though without the same vigor as the others. Real estate agents followed in their wake, finding most urban areas attractive, even intoxicating. Southern Appalachia and Florida especially drew investors. The boom in Appalachia antedated the war and had sufficient strength to last into the early 1920s. Florida, by contrast, experienced its greatest growth in the early and middle 1920s; so great was this growth that it became famous as the "Florida land boom." The demand for lumber and then for bituminous or soft coal seemed to turn Appalachia upside down during the generation that stretched from around 1900 to 1930. But demand for these products would not be sufficient to create sustained economic development in Appalachia and make it the promised land its boosters predicted. The Florida bubble burst in 1926, but the bonanza of the 1920s left some solid foundations for future development in the state. Finally, textiles, the flagship of industry in the South, thrived during the war, but not thereafter, a circumstance that had considerable significance for the industry, its workers, and the Southeast.

The war rescued the oil industry from excess capacity, which had devastated prices. Wartime demand caused an acute shortage and escalating prices. New fields opened in Texas during the war, and in Louisiana, Oklahoma, and Arkansas after the war. The free-for-all atmosphere of new fields, wildcatters, instant towns, and even more instant fortunes (sometimes followed by instant bankruptcies) soon gave way to a more orderly world of substantial companies, then to the "majors"—the corporations that dominate the oil industry—and to oil refineries, networks of pipelines, and increasingly scientific and technical operations. In the 1920s, drilling for and piping natural gas, often to distant markets, became an important facet of the petroleum industry. Petrochemicals came later. Oil and gas fueled the rapid rise of Houston, Dallas, Fort Worth, Oklahoma City, and Tulsa as leading urban centers in the Southwest and lessened the dependence of each on cotton marketing as their principal source of income. Smaller towns that prospered with petroleum dotted the region: Ponca City and Bartlesville in Oklahoma; Wichita Falls, Amarillo, and Odessa in Texas; Lake Charles and Baton Rouge in Louisiana; and El Dorado and Smackover in Arkansas.

Electricity provided a growing portion of the energy used in the South. Using the power of dammed-up water (and readily accessible coal to generate steam power when it was needed), electric power companies grew rapidly along the rivers of the South. Generating capacity tripled in the South in the 1920s and by 1930 represented about 17 percent of the nation's capacity. Before the 1920s ended, large companies and outside investment characterized the electric power industry, and some companies had become household names—Alabama Power, Georgia Power, Gulf Power, Duke Power.

Southern forests continued to provide the raw materials for diverse industries. Lumber, turpentine, and rosins were well-established products. To them were added paper, pulpwood, furniture, and wood chemicals. High Point, North Carolina, became the center for furniture manufacturing in the South by 1922, and paper mills in the South produced half of the nation's paper by 1930. Rayon, made from cellulose, a wood by-product, introduced a new epoch in textiles. In North Carolina, Burlington Mills (now Burlington Industries) made a strong commitment to rayon and began its rise to the top of the world's textile industry.

Tobacco manufacturing expanded its strong base in North Carolina and Virginia. The war and changes in social habits which made cigarette smoking more acceptable provided enormous opportunities for an already substantial industry. Clever advertising and aggressive marketing were the weapons chosen by Reynolds Tobacco in 1913 to challenge the industry leader, the American To-

OIL BOOM, OKLAHOMA, 1920s (Archives and Manuscripts Division of the Oklahoma Historical Society)

bacco Company. Reynolds got the early lead in best-sellers with Camels. Liggett and Myers followed suit with Chesterfields. Then American, the largest of tobacco's Big Three, responded with Lucky Strikes. Cigarette consumption more than doubled during World War I. Thanks primarily to tobacco manufacturing, lumber and wood products, furniture making, and textiles, North Carolina became the most industrialized of the southern states by 1930. Georgia, also heavily industrialized, was the site of a growing beverage empire. As Americans doubled their consumption of carbonated drinks during the war, annual sales of Coca-Cola rose above $20 million; they exceeded $35 million before the end of the 1920s. Prohibition of alcoholic beverages may have helped stimulate these sales.

At the beginning of World War I, the Aluminum Company of America began large operations in Tennessee and North Carolina to manufacture aluminum and related products. The war gave some boost to the slow-growing iron and steel industry, centered in the Birmingham region. The faster growth continued after hostilities ceased. Southern steelmakers, most of whom were in Alabama, doubled their production of ingots by 1930, and the value added by steelworks and rolling mills had done likewise (from $15.6 to $34.7 million). A parallel development was taking place in the coal industry. The demand for coal, one of the most plentiful minerals in the South, soared. Lesser-known ores and minerals were also being exploited, as phosphates had been for years.

Many of those minerals came from southern Appalachia, which had only recently become a center of economic activity.

SOUTHERN APPALACHIA

Southern Appalachia runs north and east of northeastern Alabama, across northern Georgia and far northwestern South Carolina, through eastern Tennessee and western North Carolina, eastern Kentucky and western Virginia, and into southern West Virginia. (Though West Virginia is not generally considered a southern state, it has some southern characteristics, and some West Virginians, especially those in the lower part of the state, consider themselves to be southern.) Three mountain ranges compose southern Appalachia: the Blue Ridge, the Cumberland, and the Great Smoky. Not until 1870 did any railway line penetrate southern Appalachia. But before the century ended, the region had a rail network. The steel rails running to the rich natural resources of Appalachia carried a storm of change into the mountains.

Never static, southern Appalachia had been undergoing significant change before 1870. Despite its relative inaccessibility, it had felt the force of the Civil War, sometimes very directly. Then, after the war, this region of family farms, tiny communities, and small scattered towns began to feel the impact of a steady increase of population. Longer-established, better-off families took over more of the better plateau lands; others had to find land in more marginal areas. Sharp divisions based on wealth or the lack of it, however, did not exist yet.

SELLING OFF APPALACHIA (Courtesy of the Appalachian Photographic Archives, Alice Lloyd College)

Mountaineers raised most of their own food, did some hunting and gathering, and traded by barter or with cash, sometimes for manufactured goods from outside the region. They worshiped, visited, and married within a setting bounded by familiar ridges and waters. Few were black, as slaves had been rare in the mountains. Almost all were Scotch-Irish, Protestant, and overwhelmingly Baptist and Methodist.

Within a generation, a timber bonanza and then a coal bonanza shook the foundations of Appalachia. Coming by rail and then up along rivers, armies of lumberjacks cut into virgin forests. As the frenzy mounted, loggers cut over mountains. Companies, mostly from outside the region, bought up land in units of 10,000 acres. The holdings of the William M. Ritter Lumber Company, for instance, included nearly 200,000 acres in western North Carolina. There and in eastern Tennessee, the Champion Company owned 420,000 acres, from which it got the raw material for wood pulp to make into paper. Champion built a complex that required a whole new town: the mill at Canton, North Carolina, had more than 7,000 people on its payroll before World War I, and was the largest pulp and paper mill in the country by 1930.

It is probable that some 100,000 people worked in the southern Appalachian lumber industry during each of the boom years from 1890 to 1920. Lumber production in southern Appalachia peaked in 1909 at 8.5 million board feet (about 20 percent of the total production in the United States). Production declined thereafter despite greater reliance on heavy machinery in logging. By 1929, only 5.4 million board feet of lumber came from the region. As the number of timber workers fell by more than half, they had to look elsewhere for work. Some went to mining coal, bauxite, kaolin, and mica. Others turned to textiles, making up a small invasion force of mountaineers in the piedmont. Later, some textile companies reversed the process and set up plants in the mountains in order to take advantage of the low-wage labor force available there.

Coal began to be mined in southern Appalachia before 1890. Not until the late 1890s, however, did the industry show the rapid growth that was to characterize it until the mid-1920s. Bituminous coal from southern Appalachia had several advantages over its main competitor, the anthracite coal mined in the North. Most important, southern mountaineers worked for less than coal miners elsewhere in the United States, and the coal they mined was of better quality, more plentiful, and easier to extract. Costs to start mining were low, and small mines proliferated. Soon, however, profit margins narrowed, and large operators became dominant in the industry—and in the politics of the coal region.

A twentieth-century feudalism emerged. By-products of this development were legends and legendary figures, admixtures of fact and fiction and sordidness. John Calhoun Mayo taught school and moonlit as a land speculator. In less than a decade he acquired more than 500,000 acres of eastern Kentucky coal land. Mayo then combined forces with the Consolidated Coal Company, whose control extended over a million acres of southern Appalachia. Corporate giants entered the coal industry to assure themselves of steady supplies of the vital energy source: the J. P. Morgan interests, which included U.S. Steel and Southern Railway, International Harvester, Ford, and others.

Harlan County, Kentucky, began its legendary and often tragic career in coal in the early twentieth century. Rapid growth became runaway growth when wartime demand for coal soared. The population of Harlan also soared—from a prewar total of less than 11,000 to almost 65,000 in 1930. The populations of the neighboring coal counties, Pike and Perry, climbed rapidly, too: a twofold increase to more than 62,000 people in the first instance and a nearly fourfold increase to more than 42,000 in the second.

High earnings, especially in comparison with what could be earned from available alternatives, and plenty of work made coal mining very attractive to the mountaineers. The money also attracted European immigrants and southern blacks. Thousands became miners in spite of coal mining's well-deserved reputation as one the most dangerous jobs in the country.

Because of the isolation and newness of most coal mining operations, coal companies frequently owned their own housing and even towns for miners and their families. Some firms provided good housing, stores, and a variety of educational and social services. Others provided only the crudest housing and little else. Not a few employed the only police officers in and around their operations. Control of the local police or the sheriff often came directly from control over local politicians or alliances with them. The industry generally did little to make its mines safer places to work. Probably 300 to 500 coal miners died each year in southern Appalachia.

No company could make adequate provision for the sharp decline in coal consumption in the late 1920s as alternate sources of energy gained favor. Even before the decline began, coal companies had mechanized and laid off miners to cut costs in order to meet intensifying competition from oil, gas, and hydroelectric power. The severe drop in demand for coal reinforced these effects. Company payrolls, hourly wages, and welfare programs shrank after 1923. Every third miner had lost his job by 1930. Protests, work stoppages, strikes, and unionization could not reverse the trend. The coal boom in southern Appalachia was over.

The coal boom and the lumber bonanza left environmental and human disarray. Although many companies had bought land outright, many others had purchased only the rights to the minerals beneath the surface of the soil or only the right to log the land. Lumber companies left landowners with denuded land and acute environmental problems. Coal companies tore up the land to get to the seams of coal. Landowners usually received less than $3 an acre for their land and even less legal protection. The terms of the land deeds were so broadly written and so generally interpreted to favor the companies that landowners were often owners in name only. Those who resisted the sale of rights to their land or of the land itself frequently lost their land through fraud, a method made easier by the inadequacy of public records and the lack of precise titles.

By 1930, mountaineers found that many fewer of them had land of any use for farming, and most were wage-dependent in a region where the number of jobs was shrinking. They had become poor subjects in an economy dominated by absentee owners and by the owners' local political allies. Many of the people of southern Appalachia were reduced to squeezing a living from their depleted farms and forests or seeking jobs outside the region. Some turned prohibition laws to their advantage; they became moonshiners. Others found employment in the growing tourist industry in such towns as Asheville, North Carolina. Others went to work on the Biltmore estate, where George Washington Vanderbilt had constructed an elegant 250-room château and where Pisgah National Forest began. Pisgah became the site of some of the earliest efforts in scientific forestry and conservation in the United States. By 1930, some of the larger lumber and forest product companies had become involved in conservation and reforestation, sometimes in cooperation with U.S. Forestry Service. Appalachians often found the Forestry Service (and the Park Service) as economically and culturally imperious as others who came to the region. Like the lumber lords and coal barons, these agencies, and even self-described and often well-intentioned social and religious reformers, tarred Appalachia with the term *hillbilly*. A hillbilly was presumably backward, ignorant, lazy, and a quaint curiosity. The word underlined the social distance between Appalachia and the modernizing parts of the South, in particular the town world.

*T*HE TOWN WORLD

The economic changes that World War I did so much to stimulate slowed in southern Appalachia in the early 1920s, but not in the towns and cities of the interior South outside of Appalachia. New Orleans remained the largest city in the South in 1930, but Houston was closing in fast, as was Dallas. Louisville, Atlanta, and Birmingham remained near the top in size, though none expanded so rapidly as the Texas cities. Memphis, San Antonio, and Richmond followed. Then came Oklahoma City, a newcomer. Behind it came Fort Worth, Nashville, Tulsa, Jacksonville, and Norfolk. Numerous substantial towns would become important cities in another decade or so.

Patterns in this urban growth became discernible. The piedmont continued to prosper from Richmond to Atlanta and Birmingham, though it was not certain then that Atlanta would eclipse the other two and become the urban hub of the Southeast. Smaller urban developments, spawned primarily by the textile industry, continued their expansion. Among eastern coastal locales, Norfolk and Jacksonville prospered, Charleston and Savannah did not. Situated on a fine natural harbor, the Atlantic Ocean, and the Atlantic Intracoastal Waterway, Norfolk became a major port, primarily for such bulk cargo as coal, lumber, and pulpwood. World War I, as we have seen, brought a big boost to shipbuilding. Jacksonville, on the Atlantic and the St. John's River, grew as agriculture, manufacturing, and tourism developed in northern Florida. To the south, on the gulf coast, Tampa based its economy on phosphate mining, cigarmaking, proximity to Florida's expanding citrus and truck gardening, and developing industries in shipping and tourism. St. Petersburg, on the other side of Tampa Bay, relied much more heavily on tourism. On the Atlantic, Miami and Miami Beach grew out of sand, fertile imaginations, and the desire to be warm in the winter. Though development of the gulf coast and the interior was hardly as spectacular or well advertised as the Florida boom, urban growth increased steadily during the 1920s from New Orleans to Houston, up the Mississippi and some of its tributaries to Memphis, Shreveport, and Little Rock, and into the especially fast-growing oil regions of the Southwest. Nashville, Knoxville, and Chattanooga in Tennessee, Louisville, and Huntsville, Alabama, experienced steady growth in the upper central South and the Tennessee Valley.

In the 1920s the warm sun of southern Florida seemed to have addled the minds of the presumably sober. William Jennings Bryan became part of a public relations, sales, and land-speculation effort that resulted in a mushroom-like development of subdivisions. Some contained lavish homes that were reputed to be copies of Mediterranean styles but that one observer described as "the Bastard-Spanish-Moorish-Romanesque-Gothic-Renaissance-Bull-Market-Damn-the-Expense Style." Earlier, "snowbirds" had migrated south by rail and stayed at hotels and "tourist homes." Now they came by car, often using the new Dixie Highway, which ran from Michigan to Miami, and many bought homes. In 1926 disaster hit Florida. Fraud had a hand in it; so did gullibility and nature. Real estate salespeople sometimes made deceptive claims. More important, the land boom rested on an inadequate financial structure. The collapse left fortunes in ruins. Thousands of residents fled north. A hurricane struck six months after the financial bubble burst, destroying or damaging thousands of homes and leaving more than 400 people dead. Still, a foundation for future, bigger development had been laid—an expanded transportation and highway system and an extensive network of commercial buildings, residential developments, and new hotels. The 1920s was a benchmark in Florida's history. Thereafter, Florida would be less "southern" than it had been.

Cities in the South, like those elsewhere in the nation, offered more opportunities for social and economic mobility than rural areas, so they attracted growing numbers of newcomers. Those newcomers represented success and economic growth. They also presented problems: growing needs for water, sewerage, lighting, transportation, fire and police protection, some degree of regulation of social and economic activity, pollution control, street construction and repair, and traffic control. Most cities applied similar solutions to similar problems. Most cities were dominated by civic elites. They came from upper-income groups, and they sought to fashion urban politics and policy. These elites varied in makeup to some degree, a reflection of the differences among cities. Where industry was more important—say in Birmingham, Dallas, Greensboro, or Macon—manufacturers had greater influence than in New Orleans, where banking and commercial interests had the upper hand. The civic elites marched in the front ranks of the urban boosters, lineal descendants of the New South advocates, but with a crucial difference. The civic elites of the twentieth century were also Progressives—their New Southism had been shaped by the Social Gospel, the experience of the tumultuous 1890s, and the concern for order and professionalism so widely shared by the Progressives. Moreover, they had more power than the New South advocates to obtain the changes they sought.

The civic elites embraced vigorous growth and order at the same time, a course full of inherent contradictions. Many of the problems of urban order stemmed from the rapid growth that the elites generally hailed. Rapid urban expansion usually meant fast-growing populations (often with disproportionately large numbers of young male transients); housing shortages; inadequate services and facilities for education, fire and police protection, utilities, public transit, health, and the handicapped and the needy; and overtaxed systems of public streets.

The last problem was greatly compounded by automobiles, whose numbers grew geometrically during the 1920s. The horseless carriage brought with it a somber addition to the mortality statistics the government gathered and published: death by auto accident, a statistical category that grew at least as fast as the numbers of automobiles. Autos also contributed to air pollution, primarily by increasing the amount of dust in the air. (Most street were unpaved.) But it should be remembered that horses and horse-drawn vehicles were not free of serious problems; they, too, were involved in accidents, and the horses distributed pollutants of a particularly unsanitary kind. The dust and exhaust from the coal furnaces then widely used in industry, businesses, offices, and homes gave some cities a dark-brown cast and caused discomfort and serious health problems. The automobile did have a major multiplier effect on urban economies: sales agencies, service stations, parts stores, roadhouses, restaurants.

Civic elites applied similar solutions—with varying success—to the problems they perceived and felt required attention. They chose means that were compatible with business Progressivism, or what suited civic elites. The means they chose fitted urban boosterism and growth and stressed efficiency, bureaucracy, and government by the "better elements."

The urban leaders of the 1920s had precedents to draw on. Led by earlier civic elites, many cities and towns had changed their form of government from a large council with members elected by wards to a smaller council with members elected at large. This change further limited the political power of black voters, who had still exercised some power in local elections, and the power of others who were not part of the "better element" and might want policies that differed from those sought by civic elites. Those undesirable others included railroad workers, skilled tradesmen, and industrial workers. In 1912, for instance, Columbia, South Carolina, "reformed" its elections laws to minimize the political power of its substantial body of railroad workers, many of whom were unionized, and of textile mill workers.

Galveston, Texas, became a model for the kind of urban reform civic elites wanted in the early twentieth century and continued to seek in the 1920s. Faced by rising debts and declining public services, Galveston business leaders had called for changes in the city government to make it more efficient and more responsive to what they believed were community-wide needs. Their calls went largely unheeded until September 1900, when the worst hurricane in the history of Galveston struck, leaving more than 6,000 dead and destroying large portions of the city. The city quickly adopted a commission form of government to deal with the crisis. Five commissioners presided over clearly defined departments and attempted to run Galveston like a modern corporation.

Galveston's commission form of government was widely publicized and carefully watched, and frequently was credited with the city's quick recovery from the hurricane. Probably no change in government could have kept Galveston among the leading cities in Texas. Memories of the hurricane, a long history of severe storms, and the dredging of the Houston Ship Channel (1912–1914) speeded Galveston's displacement by Houston as Texas's premier port. Moreover, the enthusiasm of urban leaders for commission government cooled after they determined that it created too wide a gap between responsibilities for governing and responsibilities for public services. Civic leaders found the city manager (an appointed professional or expert urban manager) form of urban government more to their liking. By World War I, many civic leaders had become strong supporters of that approach to city governance.

Accordingly, cities and towns in the 1920s increased their reliance on experts and paid agencies, often in a conscious effort to copy the management approach of large corporations. Appointed city managers presumably brought expertise to city management and supposedly made decisions in an atmosphere free of political pressure. The urban South in the 1920s also raised taxes and spent increasing amounts of money to pave streets, lay sewer lines, provide better water and sanitation services and more fire and police protection, and increase the amount and quality of public education.

Expenditures tended to reflect the biases and concerns of civic elites. Few black neighborhoods had paved streets or city water and sewers. White schools received more money than black schools—in Birmingham in 1911, for instance, nearly seven times more. Marked disparities prevailed in teacher pay and training, length of school year, physical facilities, and course offerings. Some southern cities did, however, include a new item in their expenditures for public education: high schools for blacks. Urban leaders spurned the idea of public housing; they believed that housing should be a function of the private sector of the economy. Similarly, they believed that private charities, not public agencies, should provide any relief needed. Services and facilities available for blacks in the urban South were poor, where they existed at all. Less advantaged whites tended to receive not much more than blacks. Elites could and did occasionally divide among themselves over important issues, such as what kinds of taxes were desirable or what kinds of business activity should be regulated. The fact that cities and towns in the South had less wealth and less revenue to spend than those elsewhere in the United States obviously shaped expenditure patterns.

Cities seemed to raise serious moral issues: vice, the sale and use of alcoholic beverages, the content and form of public entertainment, and the appropriate way to keep the Sabbath. Civic elites generally eschewed the use of government to police morals. Other groups, especially the clergy, often led efforts to force city officials to act on these matters. Some places censored books, movies, magazines, and theaters and even outlawed dance halls. Almost all had laws against prostitution, vice, and gambling. Sunday closing laws were common.

However, these laws were not consistently and vigorously enforced. Limitations of manpower and money contributed to the disparity between the written law and its application. More important was public indifference and even hostility to such laws, feelings that were most forcefully expressed in attitudes toward prohibition. The urban South had opposed prohibition in the first place and continued to do so after it was made part of the Constitution and put into effect. Saloons, of which there had been hundreds in the South (Memphis alone had more than 500), closed. So did open sales of packaged beer, wine, and liquor. Covert and not very covert forms of saloons and sales of alcoholic beverages started up and flourished. Charleston, South Carolina, spurned such subterfuges and defiantly sold and served alcohol publicly. Memphis remained wayward, largely untouched by sporadic attempts to purify the river city. William Faulkner wrote of Memphis as a den of iniquity which lured the natives of the region with temptations of forbidden but highly accessible evils. Yet "bossism" and entrenched political machines were less prevalent in the cities in the South than elsewhere in the United States. The most notable of southern bosses was Edward H. "Boss" Crump, Jr., of Memphis. Crump developed an "easy" relationship with purveyors of booze and illicit activities. The Choctaw Club of New Orleans represented the political machine in its glory. By forming alliances throughout the state, the Choctaw Club wielded enormous power in Louisiana, as Crump did in Tennessee. At the same time, the South had many rural-oriented political machines. They were especially prevalent in the black-belt counties of the Deep South. The most famous, however, was in Virginia: the Byrd machine.

The urban South differed from the urban North in some important ways. Southern cities were smaller than northern cities, but after 1900 they grew three times faster. Southern cities and towns drew heavily on surrounding rural areas for much of their population growth. The urban South had fewer foreign-born residents, Catholics, and Jews and larger percentages of blacks. Whites in the urban South perceived blacks as a valuable but troublesome, even threatening presence. Blacks were believed to be valuable for the cheap labor the community required, but they were thought to be "irresponsible and unreliable" workers and inclined to antisocial behavior and crime.

"Most whites," a careful student of Birmingham has concluded,

> therefore favored frankly discriminatory law enforcement to render Negroes more available as a pool of cheap labor, to overcome their alleged unreliability as workers, and to curb their alleged criminal tendency....The police, sheriff's deputies, and courts usually automatically accepted the word of any white man against that of any black.

Blacks were the main targets of vagrancy laws, chain gangs, and convict leasing. Chain gang members and leased convicts, 80 to 90 percent of whom were
black, provided cheap labor for public works and private employers and occasionally served as strikebreakers. Their forced labor also reduced the costs of
chronically underfunded penal systems.

Fewer cities and towns in the South relied on manufacturing as their principal economic activity, and the population density was lower in the urban
South. Because urban areas developed later in the South than in the North,
they felt the impact of the car in a more formative way. Cities and towns were
more spread out and contained fewer high-rise buildings. Even southern ghettos differed from northern ones. Instead of tenements, urban copies of rural
farm shacks were thrown up along railroad tracks, on the flood plains of rivers,
and near factories. Blacks far outnumbered whites in southern slums. Labor
unions in the South, generally smaller than their northern counterparts, also
had lesser roles in urban politics.

Violence was much more common in the urban South than the urban
North, if statistics on murder are any indication. Southerners, white and black,
assaulted and murdered more often than northerners, white or black. The cities
with the five highest homicide rates in the nation were located below the
Mason-Dixon line—or, as a journalist wrote, "below the Smith and Wesson
Line." Memphis led the nation with a homicide rate of 89 per 100,000 people in
1916, when the national average for cities was 9.2 per 100,000. Atlanta stood
next (31), followed by New Orleans (25.6), Nashville (24.8), and Charleston
(23.1). Apparently the homicide rate had been rising in southern cities since the
first decade of the twentieth century, and the mayhem seems to have gotten
worse in the 1920s and 1930s.

BUSINESS PROGRESSIVISM AND STATE GOVERNMENT

Business Progressivism expanded from the small cities to the state capitals in
the 1920s. Stressing better education, good roads, and improved health services
while downplaying regulation of business, especially regulation of labor-
managment relations, southern state governments increased taxes and expenditures significantly. North Carolina led the way; in the process, the University
of North Carolina became the leading university of the South, displacing the
University of Virginia. The University of Texas and Duke University (formerly
Trinity College, now renamed for its principal benefactor) also gained national
reputations in the 1920s. The ranks of business Progressives among the gover-
nors of the South included Austin Peay in Tennessee, Thomas E. Kilby and
Bibb Graves in Alabama, Cameron Morrison and Angus M. McLean in North
Carolina, John E. Martineau in Arkansas, Huey Long in Louisiana, Harry Flood
Byrd in Virginia, Pat Neff and Dan Moody in Texas, and Lamartine G.
Hardaman in Georgia. The last three, however, were not able to achieve much.

Prohibition divided Texas Democrats, crippled the forces of Progressivism, and helped elect Miriam "Ma" Ferguson. She was the political stand-in for her husband, James E. Ferguson, who had been expelled from office in 1917 for corruption. In Georgia, Progressives at the state level faced a hostile legislature and the forces of the popular Eugene Talmadge. A gifted manipulator of rural sentiments and prejudices, Talmadge became a major force in Georgia politics. As governor in the 1930s and 1940s, he provided more emotional release for disadvantaged whites than concrete programs for them or for the state. Despite his "country" image and bright-red suspenders, Talmadge pursued a status quo politics that many businessmen found to their liking.

Louisiana's Huey Long (the "Kingfish") differed markedly from Georgia's Talmadge. A brilliant, enormously energetic lawyer from northern Louisiana, where Populism had once been strong, Long so effectively attacked corporations and entrenched power in his state that he was elected governor in 1928 when he was thirty-five years old. He had ready targets and ready tools. The latter included radio, a newly emerging means of mass communications, and a gift for riveting, outrageous oratory. His prime targets included lumber, sulfur, and oil and gas companies, which had formed alliances with large agricultural interests, sugar and cotton planters in particular. They worked closely with politicians who preferred the status quo. Established politicians remained established; taxes remained low; public services remained meager. Though Louisiana had very substantial natural resources (especially minerals), numerous prosperous farm operations, and the South's largest city and one of the nation's largest ports, the state had an appalling record of neglect of the needs of most of its citizens. For example, 40 percent of the native *white* males of twenty-five years of age had less than five years of schooling in *1940*; 15 percent had no schooling at all. In 1924, only 331 miles of the state's roads were paved.

As governor, Long boosted taxes on oil and other resources, a strategy that took advantage of Standard Oil's high visibility and unpopularity. Spurred by Long, the legislature went heavily into debt to pay for a greatly expanded list of public projects. A total of 3,754 miles of roads were paved by 1935. More than a hundred bridges were constructed—critical projects in a state laced with rivers, lakes, and bayous. Additions to public buildings included much-expanded facilities at Louisiana State University. Long got the legislature to provide free textbooks for all schoolchildren, public, private, and parochial. The last measure had broad appeal, not least among Louisiana's numerous Catholic voters.

In 1930 Long won election to the U.S. Senate, but chose to remain governor until 1932 to oversee his program and to secure a pliable successor in the statehouse. He created a statewide political machine that survived his death—by assassination in 1935—and divided the Louisiana Democratic party into bitter Long and anti-Long factions, the closest thing to two-party politics anywhere in the South until after World War II. Long increased taxes, state spending and indebtedness, corruption, and state programs, whose benefits reached many citizens. For all his anticorporate rhetoric, Long reached accommodations with business from which some businesses and the Kingfish personally benefited.

HUEY LONG AT A FOOTBALL GAME (Louisiana State Museum)

Like his fellow business Progressives, Long had a poor record on labor. He did little to improve workers' compensation. One popular myth about Louisiana politics had an element of truth: "Since Long, the people have the alternative of a venal administration with a dynamic program, or an honest, do-nothing administration belonging to the corporations."

Long kept a close watch and a heavy hand on state affairs even after he went to the Senate in 1932. There, the ever-energetic, hugely ambitious Louisianan launched a successful, though short-lived, effort to become a major figure in national politics. Unlike other southern demagogues, Long avoided religious bigotry and race-baiting, and he dealt with real issues—education, social services, regressive taxation, entrenched corporations, even the distribution of income and wealth.

Most business Progressives differed markedly from Long in their style and in the concerns they stressed, but they were not indifferent to the less fortunate. Every southern state but one had a public welfare agency by 1927, and Mississippi followed suit in 1934. Expenditures for public welfare increased dramatically. Obviously the Social Gospel was not dead, though it lost some of its force in the 1920s. Moreover, private philanthropic efforts were substantial. The Rosenwald Fund, the Milbank Memorial Fund, and especially the Rockefeller Foundation were the most notable. Between 1902 and 1947 the Rockefeller Foundation gave nearly $128 million to the southern states through its General Education Board and its International Health Board.

Despite steep increases in state revenues and expenditures in the 1920s, the southern states still lagged far behind the rest of the nation, taking in and spending only about one-half the national averages. Private giving could reduce these differentials only slightly. Serious, chronic deficiencies in health and education remained. Two measures of public health—the birth rate and the infant mortality rate—reflected the seriousness of these deficiencies. Southerners continued to have a higher birth rate than other Americans, and more of their infants died. In these categories the gaps between southern blacks and whites remained wide, and so did those between the rural and urban South.

By the 1920s the social and economic disparities within the town world became quite obvious. So did those between the town world and the farm world. Urbanites, especially the better off, illuminated their homes with electric lights, replaced their iceboxes with refrigerators, relied less and less on wood or coal for heating and cooking, and installed telephones. The prosperous had spacious homes with indoor plumbing on large, landscaped lots on tree-lined streets. Southern urbanites lived in more economically and racially segregated circumstances than ever before. The streetcar and automobile allowed people to live in racially and economically homogeneous neighborhoods at some distance from the places where they worked and traded.

Cities and towns reflected caste and class as never before. Whites might work closely with domestic (nearly always black) servants, of whom there was a large supply, and have no close dealings with any other blacks. The wives of the prosperous managed their homes, joined clubs and societies, and often worked to improve their city and state and to help the less fortunate. Their husbands wore sober-looking three-piece suits, ties, and starched shirts to work in offices or stores. In larger urban areas, their children usually attended schools with their social and economic peers, then played with their peers in neighborhood parks or, possibly, at local country clubs. In smaller urban areas, the bet-

CAUSEWAY NEAR MOBILE ON OPENING DAY (Erik Overbey Collection, University of South Alabama Archives)

ter off had to rely on well-known if less physically obvious means to define the boundaries of class and caste.

Clubs and churches also reflected the status of city dwellers. Catholics were not numerous and had little influence except in New Orleans, Mobile, and, surprisingly, Charleston and Savannah. Jews, who were strong in merchandising, were even fewer and were often excluded from clubs and some neighborhoods.

THE KU KLUX KLAN REBORN

Despite the predominance and power of white Anglo-Saxon Protestants in the cities and towns, the urban South in the 1920s developed a fortress mentality; southerners became almost hysterical about alien people and ideas. The social, economic, and political changes that came in the wake of World War I profoundly disturbed many Americans, north and south. That many of those changes were more apparent than real and that many were beneficial did little to soothe jangled nerves. Many southerners believed that foreigners and alien ideas constituted a grave threat to American values and even the very survival of the country. Aliens were vaguely defined to include immigrants, Catholics, Jews, blacks, communists, and socialists. Strange ideas were almost as vaguely defined: those that qualified included communism or bolshevism, socialism, modernist thought, evolution, science, and unconventional sexuality. Southerners were distressed by the recent tendency to be frank about sex and sexuality, the actual and apparent sexual freedom women seemed to have taken up during and after the war, and the demand of some women for changes in their roles both inside and outside their families.

Profound anxiety underlay the sudden growth of nativism, the Ku Klux Klan (KKK), and evangelical Protestantism. That anxiety was no less profound because some of its sources were more imagined than real. Few of the "new immigrants"—the great human tide that swept onto American shores from southern and eastern Europe between 1880 and 1920—settled in the South. In most places below the Mason-Dixon line the numbers of Catholics and Jews were insignificant. Even where they did congregate, their numbers did not compare with those in the urban North. Yet southern politicians increasingly became supporters of immigration restriction. Restrictionists finally won a major victory in 1917 and 1921 when Congress passed literacy requirements for immigrants and then severely reduced the number of immigrants the country would admit each year. Nativism in general and Anglo-Saxonism, its particular American variant, thrived in the South. Nativism was not, however, an altogether alien growth in the region. It found sustenance in the racism and war-stimulated patriotism of the region. Fear of domestic and foreign radicals soared during the war, especially with the success of the Bolsheviks in Russia.

The KKK benefited enormously from these circumstances and from rapid urbanization, among other factors. As southerners poured into the cities, they found uncertainties along with opportunities. Dependent on wages and salaries, often for the first time, and confronted by loss of individuality, often by unrealized expectations, and by a strange world, these people had very real needs that the Invisible Empire of the Ku Klux Klan seemed to serve.

In 1920 a catalyst emerged to spark the KKK's resurgence. Actually, two catalysts: Edward Young Clarke, a former newspaperman and salesman for fraternal organizations, and Elizabeth Tyler, a public relations expert and leader in the Republican party in Georgia. They owned and ran the Southern Publicity Association, a fund-raising agency whose accounts included the Theodore Roosevelt Memorial Fund, the Anti-Saloon League, and the Red Cross. They saw the commercial potential of the Klan and took it on as a client. Paid on the basis of the number of members they signed up, Clarke and Tyler organized a national network of recruiters, who also worked on commission. They enjoyed considerable success, but it was confined largely to the South until Congress lent an unwitting hand. Aroused by reports that the KKK was a secret, violent association, Congress held hearings. The result was helpful publicity. The head of the Klan, Colonel Simmons—colonel by courtesy of the Woodmen of the World, a fraternal order—was the star witness. Attired in Prince Albert coat, starched shirt, tie, and gold watch chain, he conveyed the image of respectability and 100 percent Americanism. Thereafter, Klan membership, which had been growing, soared to several million. So did profits—from initiation fees, dues, and sales of Klan regalia.

Approximately 40 percent of the Klan's membership at its peak in the early 1920s were southerners. Most of the members lived in urban areas. Some were prominent in their communities. Most were of the lower middle class. They represented a broad spectrum of occupations. Many were clergymen. Virtually every southern city or town that called itself a city had a vigorous local Klan. Of the larger cities, only New Orleans and Louisville did not. But even in the earliest days of its revival, the KKK faced opposition. Not all whites approved of the Klan or acquiesced in it. Such opposition, however, had little effect in the heyday of the reborn Klan.

The 1920s proved to offer an ideal environment for the growth of the Klan. The Klan offered much that southern (and many northern) whites seemed to need at the time: fraternity, idealism, secrecy, ritual and regalia, offices, a sense of self-importance, reform, and commitment to traditional moral values and sex roles. Only white Anglo-Saxon Protestant males could join. (Women were invited to join auxiliaries.) The Klan embraced evangelical Protestantism and biblical literalism. It espoused prohibition, attacked saloons, fought unions, favored immigration restriction, opposed the supposedly sweeping changes in sexual behavior and sex roles in the 1920s, and denounced political radicalism, prostitution, gambling, and the theory of evolution. Things foreign particularly incensed the Klan, as did deviations from isolationism: all non-WASPS, the League of Nations, and the World Court. The Klan thrived on anti-Catholicism, anti-Semitism, and antiradicalism, though the South had few Catholics, Jews, or radicals. Negrophobia played a secondary role, presumably because Jim Crow kept blacks so effectively "in their place." The Klan reserved its greatest alarm for the grave threats that they believed Catholics and the Pope represented for the United States. The "lure of the Klan," one scholar wrote, "was its anti-Catholicism and its promise...to bring Christian righteousness to society....The Klan, in short, appeared to be doing what the Church talked about."

Reformism, according to a careful study of the Klan in the Southwest, was more instrumental than nativism in the manifestations of the Invisible Empire in Texas, Arkansas, Louisiana, and Oklahoma. The Klan in the Southwest became vigilante reformers who wanted to restore private and public morality that they believed had recently fallen apart. In a way, the Klan was correct when it called itself "progressive," but it was a backward-looking, xenophobic, and dangerous variant of Progressivism.

To convey its message to the community, the Klan relied on intimidation and terrorism, although terrorism did not have the official sanction of the Klan's national leadership. The Klan conducted numerous masked demonstrations and parades, complete with fiery crosses, and it often resorted to violence. Klansmen flogged, branded, mutilated, beat, kidnapped, tarred, lynched, and otherwise murdered people they feared; for good measure they burned their houses.

Such atrocities contributed to the rapid fading of the Invisible Empire. More moderate members, including community leaders, abandoned an organization that attracted so many fanatics and sadists. Local and state governments turned against the KKK. The Klan was also damaged by internal dissension and power struggles, financial shenanigans, and the scandalous behavior of some of its officers. Finally, fear of the alien and the hysteria it triggered seemed to be subsiding by the mid-1920s.

By 1927, Klan membership in the South had plummeted from approximately 2 million in the early 1920s to somewhere around 50,000. At the same time, the Klan's political power virtually disappeared. It had elected or helped elect congressmen, U.S. senators in Oklahoma and Texas, and governors in Georgia and Louisiana, as well as in Colorado, Ohio, Oregon, and Maine. The Klan had dominated Indiana politics for a time, and it had been a critical force in the nomination of the Democratic candidate for president in 1924. Four years later, the Klan could not stop Alfred E. Smith, governor of New York—Irish Catholic, opponent of prohibition, and a product of Tammany Hall and ethnic politics—from being nominated by the Democrats. Nor was the Klan very important in Smith's loss to Herbert Hoover in the 1928 election. However, the Klan might have had more staying power in the South in the 1920s if blacks had not been so thoroughly and systematically subordinated.

THE BLACK WORLD

Although Jim Crow circumscribed the world of black southerners, they found avenues of self-assertion in the 1920s which contributed to and shaped critical changes in that world. The migration of so many of them had the most far-reaching impact. Since a substantial proportion of the black migrants took a wide variety of skills with them, the South found itself in greater need of skilled workers than ever. Individually and collectively, blacks continued to build and maintain a world apart from whites. Even faithful servants remained distant. The black world became institutionalized: black churches, stores, banks, parks, libraries, picture shows, theaters, hospitals, drugstores, insurance organizations, and professionals—lawyers, ministers, realtors, clergy, teachers. Residential segregation was reinforced and sometimes caused by zoning laws and the availability of public transportation for people who could not afford an automobile. In urban areas especially, a new black elite developed to serve a black clientele. Ironically, this elite had a vested interest in Jim Crow, which ensured a steady though not very prosperous flow of black customers and clients.

Generally, however, blacks had fewer chances for employment or careers and earned less after World War I ended. Blacks found fewer opportunities to work in services with a white clientele and in the building trades, where they had once been numerous. White-dominated labor unions acted to reduce job opportunities for blacks in railroading and most of the building trades. The International Longshoremen's Association, however, remained a stronghold for black workers, and in 1925 A. Philip Randolph started to organize railroad sleeping car porters, all of whom were black. Randolph later became a major figure in the civil rights movement. Blacks continued to make up much of the work force in the iron and steel industry in Alabama, but they seldom held the better-paying skilled jobs. Studies of wages in Virginia in the 1920s confirmed what some observers had suspected: even if blacks did the same work as whites, they usually received less pay.

One of the more obvious ways for blacks to assert themselves was to join the NAACP. Many of the black elite, who formed the backbone of the organization, supported its efforts even though the NAACP's attacks on Jim Crow threatened the self-interest of many of them. Membership in the NAACP multiplied during and after World War I. This growth reflected changing circumstances within and without the organization. Even before Booker T. Washington's death in 1915, his power had waned along with the appeal of his passive approach to change. The war accelerated these shifts. Led by southern black expatriates such as James Weldon Johnson and Walter White and galvanized by the aggressive, forcefully argued rhetoric of the brilliant W. E. B. Du Bois, editor of Crisis, the main organ of the NAACP, the organization grew from fewer than 20 chapters (one in the South) to 300. More than half of the chapters were located in the South, as were almost half of the 88,000 members of the association.

The NAACP persistently sought relief by legal action and lobbying. In 1915 the NAACP succeeded in getting Oklahoma's grandfather clause declared unconstitutional. Two years later it obtained a federal court ruling against laws requiring residential segregation in municipalities. Neither decision, however, had any practical effect. Oklahoma passed legislation to evade the court's decision, and municipalities simply ignored the courts and continued to pass laws requiring residential segregation. In the latter instance, laws were probably unnecessary, because community pressures and economic realities made residential segregation virtually inevitable.

Most blacks remained beyond the reach of the NAACP; it appealed almost exclusively to the well educated and highly articulate. Marcus Garvey's Universal Negro Improvement Association, which flourished for a time during the early 1920s, had mass appeal, but it had few overt followers in the South. The "New Negro" movement of the latter 1920s had more effect, particularly on the campuses of black colleges. There students and their allies succeeded in replacing white administrators with black administrators. Residential neighborhoods around these campuses came to be favored by black elites.

After the racial turmoil of the World War I era waned, southern whites seemed not to perceive blacks as a serious threat. Neither the restiveness of blacks nor the NAACP caused whites to question the security of white supremacy. Certainly, little occurred from day to day in the 1920s to shake that sense of dominance. In 1928 the foremost southern historian and one of the leading scholars of the time, Ulrich B. Phillips, pronounced what seem to be the final, definitive word on the relations of whites and blacks in the South: "the central theme of Southern history" was "a common resolve indomitably maintained" that the South "shall be and remain a white man's country."

THE WORLD OF THE FARM

Most southern farmers, black and white, lived a world away from the general prosperity of the towns in the 1920s. Gracie Turner, North Carolina sharecropper and mother of twelve, told an all too common story of farming in her childhood in the 1890s: the "most we cleared was $179 [a year]....Most years it was fifty and sixty dollars." Although southern farmers did better in the 1920s than they did when Gracie Turner was a child, they did not do much better. As in the 1890s, farms in the South were too small, too undercapitalized, and too dependent on a limited range of cash crops. Studies have indicated that farm income generally rises as farms get larger. Unfortunately, southern farms seemed to be headed in the opposite direction. The number of agricultural units with less than 50 acres under cultivation increased, while the number of those with more than a 100 acres declined. Farm values for land and buildings averaged some $4,300 in the South and some $11,000 in the North, and comparative figures for livestock and machinery and tools revealed even greater contrasts. Southern farmhouses were much less likely than those in the North to have electric lights, running water, and indoor plumbing, and were much more likely to be located along unimproved dirt roads. The gap between the North and South narrowed, however, with respect to automobile ownership. Large numbers of even the poorest southern farmers owned cars.

Cotton was still the principal cash crop of the South; it provided the only cash income for 50 percent of all southern farmers. Tobacco, rice, and sugar were the other major cash crops. The proportion of investment in or income derived from livestock and poultry was still very small. The value of beef cattle, dairy herds, and poultry declined in the 1920s. Southern farmers did grow a wider range of crops than they had raised in the late nineteenth century. Citrus fruits continued to be critical to Florida, where their cultivation expanded rapidly during the 1920s. At the same time, citrus growing was introduced to the lower Rio Grande Valley in Texas. The growing of other fruits, especially apples and peaches in the Southeast, expanded, as did truck farming and peanut and pecan growing in various parts of the South. Soybeans made their first appearance on southern farms during the 1920s. Southern farmers raised more of their own food and probably ate better than they had done before, but agricultural diversification did not add much to farm incomes.

Cotton still reigned, if in a miserly fashion. No challenger or alternative was readily available. World War I left the basic structure of southern agriculture intact. Incomes from cotton followed a roller-coaster pattern after World War I, and cotton-dependent farmers were unable to avoid being hapless riders. Sharp declines in the price of cotton (and of tobacco as well) in 1920 and 1921 and the boll weevil took a heavy toll on farm incomes and welfare and forced many independent farmers to become renters and sharecroppers. Then higher cotton prices returned in the mid-1920s, and the boll weevil was largely contained. In 1925, cotton production almost equaled the record set in 1914, yet prices remained good. The following year farmers grew 18 million bales of cotton on 47 million acres, both records. This time prices fell—from 18 cents a pound in 1925 to 10 cents in 1927. Earnings from cotton declined by $500 million. The Great Depression arrived in the cotton fields—and thus in most of the rural South— two years before the stock market crashed in 1929.

The devastation was worst in the older cotton-growing areas, especially in the southeastern and south-central states. There farmers had plowed up more land than ever and used larger and larger amounts of fertilizer to squeeze better yields from their never overly rich and ever more eroded soils. They had done so, for one thing, to compete with farmers who grew cotton in the rich soils of northeastern Arkansas and the Mississippi-Yazoo delta, both of which had recently been drained and cleared, and with cotton growers in Texas and Oklahoma. The boll weevil had a much lesser impact on the western cotton belt. More important, farmers there could mechanize and cut labor costs much more easily than farmers in the older cotton-growing areas. Finally, all cotton farmers faced increasing competition from foreign-grown cotton and from synthetic fibers. One clear indication of the difficulties of cotton farmers in the late 1920s and of southern agriculture in general was the sudden increase in the incidence of pellagra, a disease that fed upon poor diets.

The census of 1930 presented a generally somber picture of the farm world of the South at the end of the 1920s. Between 1920 and 1930, the ranks of farm owners shrank by some 350,000. The ranks of sharecroppers swelled; those of tenants declined slightly. Approximately 60 percent of southern farm operators worked someone else's land. Rates of tenancy increased for whites and decreased for blacks. More than 155,000 whites became sharecroppers in the 1920s, but blacks still accounted for a little more than half of the 770,000 croppers in the region. As these figures represent heads of households only, perhaps 4 million southerners were sharecroppers in 1930. Too many people in the South tried to make a living at an occupation that yielded them little beyond bare subsistence.

Yet, tragically, the economy of the South could not absorb the multitudes who were leaving the land. There were not enough nonfarm jobs for them. Some 1.3 million blacks left the South during the 1920s. At the same time, about 1.5 million whites left the older parts of the South. Many of them went to the Southwest, where the population grew by nearly 900,000 people during the decade as petroleum propelled rapid economic expansion. Even that impressive growth and the growth of much of the urban South could not, however, prevent the region from suffering a decline in personal incomes. It was the first such decline for the South since 1870. No other region in American history has ever suffered a decade-long decline in per capita income. Some of that decline was probably the result of a birth rate higher than the national average and a higher proportion of children and young people who produced little or no income.

Migrating seemed to be the only alternative for many people. Politics offered little hope. Congress did pass legislation to improve marketing and encourage farm cooperatives. Late in the 1920s Congress even passed the McNary-Haugen plan in an effort to raise farm prices by reducing surpluses of agricultural commodities through government purchases of those surpluses. The government was either to hold the purchased commodities off the domestic market until prices rose above fixed levels or to sell them abroad. However, President Calvin Coolidge vetoed the measure in 1927, and when Congress passed a revised version in 1928, he vetoed that, too. Still, it is doubtful that the legislation would have helped much; McNary-Haugen made no provision for limiting what farmers produced. Very likely farm production would have continued to exceed effective demand. Government-imposed crop restrictions offered greater hope, but they were a political impossibility in the 1920s. Instead, there were the usual calls for voluntary restrictions, and the usual failures of farmers to heed them.

Southern farmers had no organized, effective voice, and they lacked strong political allies. Nothing like the Alliance or the Populists emerged. The Farmers' Educational and Cooperative Union (Farmers' Union), the nonpolitical successor to the Populists, was moribund several years before World War I. It had no successor. The farm bloc in Congress, composed of some southern Democrats and some northern and western farm-state Republicans, fought continuing, sometimes successful battles with Republican administrations in Washington in the 1920s. Their efforts, however, were inadequate to meet the crisis thousands of farmers were experiencing. Even if farmers had been better organized, they would have had little chance to obtain legislation of the kind that might have aided the poorer farmers. The twenties were not the time for that—certainly not 1928.

THE END OF THE DECADE

In 1928 Republicans enjoyed their greatest political success in Dixie since Reconstruction. Noneconomic issues played a decisive part in that success. Alfred E. Smith, the Democratic nominee, carried too many liabilities for many southern whites. Not even the usual appeals to white supremacy could keep the South solidly Democratic. Seven southern states—Florida, Kentucky, North Carolina, Oklahoma, Tennessee, Texas, and Virginia—voted for Herbert Hoover, the Republican nominee. He ran well in traditionally Republican areas in the South and in the more prosperous urban areas that earlier had shown Republican leanings.

The Republicans continued to dominate the politics of the nation. The Wilson administrations and the Democratic Congress seemed now to be only an interlude, albeit a creative one, in a Republican era. Claims of a Democratic restoration or a South "come back to rule the nation" had been rendered hollow by subsequent events. Despite its electoral behavior in 1928, the South remained committed to the Democrats and white supremacy. Thus the South was politically isolated, part of a Democratic minority. The South's isolation had economic and cultural dimensions as well. Economically beleaguered despite the gains of the previous half century and still considered a cultural backwater despite evidence to the contrary, the South was the exile region of the nation.

Coincidentally, the distance between the farm world, including southern Appalachia, and the town world grew. It could be seen in the presence or absence of electric lights, running water, and paved streets, in diets, and in human expectations. Much of the urban South, especially the Southwest, enjoyed prosperity in the 1920s. There the events of World War I had altered the structure of the economy. Buoyed by the confidence generated by the material progress they perceived, the business Progressives—small-scale copies of Herbert Hoover—embraced the "New Era" of the twenties and confidently looked to even better days.

Then the Great Depression struck. Suddenly the distance between the farm and the town shrank. In the wake of the worst economic collapse in American history, a major revolution in southern agriculture was launched, the Democrats became dominant in the nation's politics, the political isolation of the South ended, and white supremacy came under its severest challenge since the 1890s.

24

Religion and Culture in the New South

------- ❖ -------

The South was long perceived by observers within and without the region as the "benighted South," a cultural and social backwater. The Scopes, or "monkey," trial, which occurred in 1925, underscored that reputation and helped make the South, once again, the object of scorn and condescension. Ironically, even as the trial was being held, revolutionary changes in the thought and literature of the South were taking place. The trial hastened those changes.

THE SCOPES TRIAL

The origins of the Scopes trial were innocent and not wholly peculiar to the South. John Washington Butler did not set out in 1925 to become a catalyst for one of the most famous trials in American history. Butler devoted most of his adult life to tilling the 120 acres of a farm in Macon County, Tennessee, which had been in his family for four generations. However, he was hardly a "simple farmer," whatever that is. He had shown considerable skill at baseball when he was young, and he passed on his fondness for music—and probably his talent for it—to his sons, who formed a band. In time he went into politics. A very active, committed Christian, John Butler worried about threats to the faithful and to people who might become faithful if they could be protected from the lure of false doctrine. In particular, he worried that Darwin's theory of evolution would undermine religious faith.

As a member of the Tennessee state legislature in 1925, he called for legislation to forbid the teaching of evolution in any public school in the state. He drafted an

Act prohibiting the teaching of the Evolution Theory in all the Universities, Normals [teachers' colleges] and all other public schools of Tennessee . . . [whereby] it shall be unlawful...to teach any theory that denies the story of the Divine Creation of man as taught in the Bible, and to teach instead that man has descended from a lower order of animals.

The Butler Act did not have wide support in the state. Substantial numbers of clergy and laity gave the measure strong vocal support, but they were not even a large minority. Opponents—including most but not all of the academics in the state as well as many of the state's cultural, business, and political leaders—either were indifferent to the measure or feared the power of its supporters. Legislators were not inclined to risk a vote that might be construed as a vote against God.

Similar fears gnawed at Governor Austin Peay. A Progressive and one of Tennessee's best governors, Peay had managed a state debt crisis in the early 1920s, then persuaded the state to spend more money to improve highways, hospitals, and public schools and universities. The governor hesitated, then signed the bill. "This bill," he explained, "is a distinct protest against an irreligious tendency to exalt so-called science, and deny the Bible in some schools and quarters—a tendency fundamentally wrong and fatally mischievous in its effects on our children, our institutions and our country."

Americans in the 1920s, as the governor indicated, worried a great deal about their country and their institutions, about what they believed was a general decline in morals and values, and about what was happening to their children. John Butler was no hillbilly, and he was not alone in his unease. Still, not much was made initially of the Butler Act. Governor Peay said that he did not think the act would ever be enforced because schoolbooks in Tennessee contained nothing "with which this bill will interfere in the slightest manner." The governor's prediction might have proved correct if it had not been for the American Civil Liberties Union (ACLU).

Founded during World War I to protect the rights of pacifists, the ACLU expanded its concerns to civil and individual rights in general after the war. Having decided to test the constitutionality of the growing number of antievolution laws and policies being passed or implemented by state and local authorities in the 1920s, the ACLU published nationwide offers to pay the defense costs of anyone who wanted to challenge an antievolution law in the hope of getting such laws and policies declared unconstitutional. At that point John Thomas Scopes, a teacher in Tennessee, stepped forward, somewhat reluctantly. The twenty-four-year-old Scopes, a recent graduate of the University of Kentucky, taught science and coached football at a high school in Dayton, Tennessee. He did not particularly want to be arrested or to be the center of attention. Moreover, he thought that evolution and the biblical account of creation could easily be reconciled, and he knew that, contrary to what the governor said, Tennessee high school science teachers used a state-approved textbook that included a discussion of evolutionary theory.

Dayton was the small but prosperous seat of Rhea County, in the lowlands of southern Appalachia. Dayton had some 2,000 residents, several paved streets, municipally owned plants for electricity and water, and the range of Protestant churches usually found in a southern community, though about half of the people in the town and the county were unchurched. It had a Progressive Club founded and run by community leaders with rising expectations for themselves and their community, perhaps 400 black residents who were thoroughly segregated, and no local Ku Klux Klan. Obviously Dayton was not an isolated, reactionary backwater. It had not, however, continued the growth it enjoyed in the late nineteenth century. It was increasingly overshadowed by Chattanooga, a city of more than 100,000 with a strong diverse economy, only forty miles or an hour and a half away.

Rhea County had a diverse economy, but it needed more diversity and greater growth. About half of its residents farmed, most of them on holdings of fewer than 100 acres. Half of the county's work force found employment outside agriculture, in construction or mining or in the sawmills, cotton mills, or knitting mills. Several hundred of them worked in the coal and iron mines operated by the Cumberland Coal Company under George Rappelyea, a thirty-one-year-old college-trained engineer from New York.

Rappelyea's position, background, and age were hardly likely to endear him to Rhea County natives. Still, he took an active part in the life of the town and served as superintendent of the Sunday school at the Methodist church. But he had an impolitic habit of expressing his opinions on such emotional topics as patriotism (he claimed to be a descendant of an American colonist who arrived in the New World in 1623) and evolution at two of Dayton's more important meeting places, the barbershop and Robinson's drugstore. The owner of the barbershop once bit Rappelyea during a dispute over evolution: the barber thought the engineer had called his family monkeys. Despite his less than winning ways, Rappelyea succeeded in convincing first local leaders and then Scopes that they ought to challenge the Butler Act.

Rappelyea persuaded the proprietor of Robinson's, who chaired the local school board, and the superintendent of the county schools that since Chattanooga's leaders had announced that they would drop their intended challenge to the Butler Act, Dayton ought to fill the void. No doubt the urge to put Dayton on the map made the leaders more receptive to Rappelyea's arguments. If so, they succeeded beyond their wildest expectations. Dayton became synonymous with the Scopes trial or the "monkey trial." John Scopes got part of his wish, too. Though the trial bore his name, he was shunted from center stage by more dramatic figures: H. L. Mencken, acid-tongued columnist, author, and literary critic with the *Baltimore Sun*; Clarence Darrow, the most famous trial attorney of his day; and William Jennings Bryan, former congressman, presidential candidate, and secretary of state.

Mencken saw the trial as a chance to display the South in all its backwardness and thus to defeat the opponents of freedom of thought and modern culture. Mencken's reporting of the trial, which he attended, and about Dayton and Tennessee reflected these motives and was, in some instances, distorted by this bias. He could, for example, have shown greater understanding of the serious religious and moral concerns of the antievolutionists. Mencken's reports went to much of the nation through the *Sun* and the wire services. Indeed, the trial and the town were besieged by the media. Other newspapers and magazines sent journalists, newsreel cameras whirred, radio announcers stood by their microphones to report the latest flash, and some members of the press even chartered an airplane to fly over Dayton, presumably to gain some perspective on the town.

Darrow happily volunteered to defend Scopes without charge. Long known as a defender of underdogs and dissidents and a profound religious skeptic, he found in the Scopes trial an unusual opportunity to defend personal and religious liberty and freedom of scientific inquiry. Like Mencken, he relished a chance to disturb the peace of the conventional world, and he shared Mencken's dislike of Bryan, though he had agreed with Bryan on many issues during Bryan's heyday as the foremost spokesman in American politics for the common people.

Bryan in the 1920s had assumed the role of major spokesman for biblical literalism, the belief that every word in the Bible was the literal word of God. Biblical literalists believed, for example, that what the Bible said about creation was what actually occurred: God made the world in six days, made Adam out of dust, and made Eve out of Adam's rib. Evolution and biblical literalism could not coexist. Bryan, predictably, became a major opponent of the theory of evolution. He genuinely believed, as did many others, that the teaching of evolutionary theory would undermine religious faith and consequently American society, which, as he saw it, was based on Christian faith, morals, and values. The nation—"man's last best hope"—was at risk. Bryan saw the Scopes trial as a duel to the death between religion and the theory of evolution. When the World's Christian Fundamentals Association asked Bryan to join the prosecution, he quickly agreed, and the prosecution welcomed him.

Bryan and Darrow occupied the center stage of the trial, sometimes sharing it with Judge John T. Raulston, over whose bench hung a banner that said, "Read Your Bible." The judge helped create and sustain an atmosphere that was more appropriate for a carnival than for a fair judicial hearing. Darrow correctly anticipated that even-handed justice was not to be dispensed. But he hoped that he could get the court to allow the case to be argued on broad constitutional grounds—freedom of speech and of religion. He wanted to air the need for unhindered scientific inquiry and to tackle the question whether there was a conflict between science and Christianity. But Judge Raulston narrowed the issue to whether the state of Tennessee had the authority to pass the Butler Act and whether or not Scopes had broken that law. Once the judge ruled that indeed the state had that authority under the police powers guaranteed the states by the Constitution, the outcome of the trial was not in doubt, because Scopes readily admitted he had broken the law. The guilty verdict was anticlimactic when it came. Bryan and Darrow both had their moments during the trial, however.

Bryan told the court that the law was not the beginning of a broad attack on the freedom of speech and thought. Rather, the law reflected the concern of parents to protect their children's religious faith and welfare from such grave threats as evolutionism. Moreover, what children were taught should be determined by their parents and the majority of the community through local school boards, Bryan declared, not by school administrators, teachers, or outsiders with advanced academic degrees. Darrow decried the banning of evolution from the classroom as the first step toward the banning of books and newspapers, the setting of one religious group against another, and attempts to force one set of religious views on the holders of other views.

When Darrow managed to lure Bryan to the witness stand, the Great Commoner was more thoroughly routed than he could admit. Darrow led Bryan through a series of questions and answers that revealed how little he knew about biblical scholarship and history and how much he deviated from the biblical literalism he was supposed to accept and represent. But the best moments of the trial came from neither Darrow nor Bryan but from David Dudley Malone. "The truth," Malone said in his opening statement for the defense, "does not need the force of Government."

The trial attracted large crowds, food vendors, curio salesmen, and religious cranks. One man wore a sign proclaiming he was the world's leading authority on the Bible. Banners and exhibits urged all to read their Bible or be damned. Others had already given up, at least on Dayton. One woman was convinced that Dayton had "the mark of the beast." She took her children and fled to the surrounding mountains. "The thing is genuinely fabulous," Mencken exulted. "I have...enough material stored up to last me the rest of my life." By imposing "Baptist and Methodist barbarism," Mencken charged, the southern clergy had created a cultural vacuum and a fear of ideas. He referred to the people of Rhea County as "yokels," "morons," "hillbillies," and "peasants." He watched a nighttime Pentecostal revival outside Dayton and described the highly emo-

SPA BEACH IN ST. PETERSBURG, FLORIDA (St. Petersburg Times)

tional service in unflattering detail and with little understanding of its meaning. Of course, many Daytonians also scorned such revivals of Pentecostals or "Holy Rollers." This scorn reflected a basic division in the South of the 1920s, the gap (sometimes a chasm) between the town and the farm.

Mencken left the trial early. He had seen enough, he said, and he knew what the verdict would be. Scopes was found guilty and fined $100. The *Baltimore Sun* posted bond, and Scopes was free to go. He left Dayton and teaching, went to graduate school, and became a geologist for petroleum companies. The Tennessee Supreme Court saved the state's face when it reversed the verdict on a technicality. The court, however, upheld the constitutionality of the Butler Act. It was not repealed until 1967. George Rappelyea left for New Orleans. No doubt some of his former neighbors thought he had gone to Sodom. Rappelyea said he felt isolated in Dayton, a feeling that may have been reinforced by local law officials. After the trial started, they ticketed him three times in six days for speeding.

Save for Bryan, the other principals continued their lives as before. Judge Raulston, however, did not survive the next election; Rhea County voters retired him. Bryan died five days after the trial ended. His death was probably due to the diabetes from which he suffered, its effects exacerbated by the humid heat of July and the exertions of the trial. The trial itself so darkened the image of antievolutionism that it lost what momentum it had had before the "monkey trial" and declined rapidly.

The trial powerfully reinforced the image of the benighted South. Revelations of the South's deficiencies poured forth through the media: reactionary fundamentalism, antievolutionism, prohibition, lynchings, chain gangs, debt peonage, forced labor in lumber and turpentine camps, the Ku Klux Klan, convict leasing, shootings, hookworm, pellagra, venereal diseases, dietary deficiencies, poor whites, degenerate white politicians, systematic repression of impoverished blacks, labor strife, repressive mill villages, poor schools, inferior colleges and universities, a void in intellectual life and activity, and a general reactionary attitude that numbed the mind. So negative was the image of the South, one distant observer recalled, that people just knew that the South could produce "nothing but fundamentalism and intolerance." Though the image of the benighted South was distorted and tended to obscure the genuinely positive accomplishments of the region, it contained a great deal of truth. And if the South was benighted, the religious heritage it had brought with it into the twentieth century had helped substantially to make it so.

THE RELIGIOUS HERITAGE OF THE TWENTIETH-CENTURY SOUTH

Possibly because of its preoccupation with the Lost Cause, the South was slow to feel the impact of the intellectual and scientific ideas that challenged established religious beliefs in the North after 1860. The theory of evolution, biblical criticism, and historical theology, to cite only three of the most important areas of intellectual and scientific investigation, presented revolutionary threats. Evolutionary theory appeared to reduce the biblical account of human origins to a perceptive, perhaps inspiring fable. Biblical criticism—the study of the Bible as literature and as a historical document—also seemed to raise serious doubts about the authority of the Bible, or at least about some of its passages and episodes. Historical theology suggested that basic Christian doctrines and beliefs, such as the second coming of Christ, were produced or shaped by particular historical settings. Eventually members of the clergy and the laity were forced to respond to evolutionary theory, biblical criticism, and historical theology, either by rejecting them altogether, by accommodating to them, or by abandoning Christian doctrine.

In the South, the most powerful and vocal response was rejection. Biblical literalism, in particular, became a very widely held position and a pervasive force. Literalists adhered to the letter of Scripture and frequently ignored the historical setting or context of Bible passages. Scripture interpreted as written, literalists maintained, provided the ultimate authority for true religion and moral values.

Biblical literalists are not the same thing as fundamentalists, though the two are commonly confused. Products of a long, complicated, and often highly disputatious process that involved Christians in every region of the country, the fundamentalists got their name from the publication of their basic beliefs in a series titled *The Fundamentals: A Testimony of the Truth* (1910–1913). Fundamentalists believe that true Christians accept certain basic beliefs: the virgin birth of Christ; his physical resurrection; the atonement (reparation) of Christ, who was sinless, for the sins of human beings by his acceptance of the crucifixion; the inerrancy of the Bible in every detail; and the imminent physical second coming of Christ. Most biblical literalists do not accept and stress all of these doctrinal positions of the fundamentalists, though they usually accept most of them. Finally, biblical literalism was considerably more influential than fundamentalism in the South of the 1920s. Fundamentalism has enjoyed much greater influence in the region since 1950. Clearly, both biblical literalists and fundamentalists reject the theory of evolution as well as most of biblical criticism and historical theology.

This rejection dates from the late nineteenth century. At that time southern Protestantism generally took an anti-intellectual and antiscientific posture. The Baptist and Methodist majority simply ignored or were largely unaware of the intellectual and scientific revolution going on around them. They concentrated their energies on evangelism, public piety, and internal disputes, all with considerable success. The ranks of the Baptists and the Methodists continued to expand despite internal divisions. The Baptists did so well that they became the leading denomination in the South in the early twentieth century. Baptists and Methodists alike became increasingly militant about public piety, or proper public behavior with respect to gambling and cardplaying, alcoholic beverages and tobacco, dancing and theatergoing. Self-interest caused modifications in the code of public piety, however. Carolinians, for instance, had a forgiving attitude toward the production and consumption of tobacco. Baptists divided sharply among themselves, especially over the Landmark issue. The Landmark Baptists claimed that they were the only true Baptists—and indeed the only true Christians—because they were directly descended from the original Christian church, the church of the New Testament. Eventually these particular divisions subsided. Obviously, they did not hinder the growth of the denomination and may have actually helped, as various Baptist groups competed to attract followers.

Not all southern Protestants maintained an anti-intellectual and anti-scientific stance in the late nineteenth century. The Presbyterians, better educated in general and more inclined to stress theology, were also more aware of the intellectual and scientific revolution of their times. The Presbyterians' theological orthodoxy, however, insulated them from the challenges of evolutionary theory, biblical criticism, and historical theology. Robert Lewis Dabney led the defenders of orthodoxy in religion as well as with respect to the Lost Cause. Having an "apparently inexhaustible reservoir of rancor," a Dabney biographer noted, he fought the "Yankee" (northern) Presbyterian church first from Union Seminary in Richmond, where he was professor of theology, then from Austin, where he was professor of moral philosophy at the University of Texas and where he helped found a Presbyterian seminary. Dabney figured prominently in one of the few instances in which evolutionary theory made a conspicuous

BAPTISMAL AND SUNDAY SCHOOL SCENE, MILL VILLAGE (South Carolina State Museum)

entry into the citadels of southern Presbyterianism before 1900. James Woodrow, uncle of Woodrow Wilson and professor at the Presbyterian seminary in Columbia, South Carolina, indicated a willingness in 1884 to accept the theory of evolution. Dabney assumed a leading role in the efforts to dismiss Woodrow, which led to his ouster in 1888. Thus Presbyterians in the South adopted a conservative position on evolution similar to that taken by Presbyterians in the North.

On the whole, Episcopalians in the South devoted more of their energies to disputes over forms of worship and to ensuring that their seminaries enjoyed intellectual freedom than they devoted to doctrine. Few Episcopalians knew about William Porcher Du Bose. Soon after returning from service in the Civil War, Du Bose joined the faculty at the University of the South at Sewanee, Tennessee, and dedicated the rest of his life to rebuilding it and its seminary and to teaching and writing about theology. Noted for his pastoral concern and his brilliance, Du Bose was one of America's most gifted theologians.

Like the Episcopalians, the Lutherans and the Catholics had little to do with the theological issues that preoccupied most of the other denominations in the South. Since the South attracted few immigrants after 1860, Lutherans and Catholics in the South, unlike those elsewhere in the country, did not face serious internal divisions occasioned by the arrival of large numbers of new immigrants in their churches. Southern Lutherans, in contrast to the Baptists, Methodists, and Presbyterians, tended to stress unity with other American Lutherans. Catholics in the South were preoccupied primarily by support of the "Americanists," those who said the Catholic church in America had to assimilate with the dominant society and could do so without sacrificing its basic principles. Edward Fitzgerald, the bishop of Little Rock, was one of only two bishops who voted against the doctrine of papal infallibility at the First Vatican Council in 1870. Almost all of the few Quakers in the postbellum South lived in North Carolina. In the late nineteenth century, Quakers lost much of their distinctiveness as they began to model themselves on their evangelical Protestant neighbors. This adaptation may have saved the southern Quakers from extinction, but the sense of something lost tempered their pleasure at seeing their numbers increase. Some Quakers wondered if they had compromised too much.

Similar concerns troubled white evangelical Protestants in the late nineteenth century. Those concerns, which never involved questions about the morality of Jim Crow, led to major disruptions among the South's largest Protestant denominations, a major religious revival, and a surge of growth among Christian sects. Those disruptions left changes that still shape the religious landscape of the South. Most of these disruptions were related to the growing social and economic divisions that came in the wake of urbanization and industrialization. Churches and their congregations, the styles of their worship and practices, and their beliefs reflected the social and economic positions of the believers. Religious dissidents decried the "lukewarm" religion of "birthright" Christians, or those who had been born into their faith rather than converted to

it. In order to appeal to the "plain people," some evangelists and their supporters called for more informal and emotional worship, simpler creeds, and ministers with less formal training and presumably more spirituality.

The Holiness movement and Pentecostalism, which reshaped much of religion in the South after the mid-1880s, were the primary products of the religious discontent and revivalism of the late nineteenth century. By the time of
the Scopes trial, the Holiness movement and Pentecostalism had so thoroughly
penetrated southern Appalachia that the region cannot have been so culturally
isolated as it is often thought to have been. When the Holiness movement and
Pentecostalism entered southern Appalachia, they became part of the most religiously diverse portion of the South. Baptists especially had long abounded
there in numbers and in kinds, though few were Southern Baptist and very few
were black. Southern Appalachia had few blacks of any kind. The small Protestant religious bodies in southern Appalachia stressed demonstrative worship
and practice. When preachers were moved by the spirit, their highly charged
sermons often seemed unintelligible, at least to the uninitiated. Speaking in
tongues was common. Foot washing was not uncommon. A very few practiced
snake handling as a demonstration of the power of faith. Music was central to
the experience: gospel songs, not hymns, sung to a wide variety of instruments,
but not organs. No wonder Mencken and many others found the religion of
southern Appalachia strange, even outrageous, and too often missed the spiritual yearning that permeated it.

Most of these sects, which were hardly limited to southern Appalachia, had
broadly democratic qualities. Governing structures were weak or nonexistent.
Participation in decisions was wide. Some groups had women preachers. Some
welcomed blacks as members of their congregations. Almost all stressed public
piety and the need for continuing spiritual experiences. Most saw little connection between religion and political issues. They did not accept the Social Gospel. They did, however, stress concern and care for one another. In doing so,
they met very real needs, especially in light of the straitened economic circumstances that prevailed in most of southern Appalachia. Not a few of their adherents believed that the Kingdom of God was at hand and that one must be
prepared for its coming. Thus they stressed evangelism and revivalism. Unfortunately, many of these sects were xenophobic and fanatic, inclined to see "the
mark of the beast" on places such as Dayton.

Evangelicalism and revivalism were part of the religious heritage of the
twentieth-century South. As the South became more urban and less rural and
agricultural, however, camp meetings declined in number and importance. In
their place came "protracted meetings," series of revival services usually held in
local churches and usually held at night to accommodate urban and industrial
populations. The Methodist Sam Jones became the leading urban revivalist of
the late nineteenth-century South after his conversion and the ending of his dependence on the bottle. Billy Sunday more or less followed in Jones's footsteps.
The former baseball player made a number of forays into the South, though he
carried on most of his work as an evangelist elsewhere. J. Frank Norris, Baptist

evangelist, attracted so many worshipers to his church in Fort Worth that by the early 1930s it was the largest Baptist church in the world, with 8,000 members. Norris attacked evolution in his characteristically controversial way. In the 1920s he managed to rid Texas of at least six professors whom he accused of finding Darwin's theory reasonable. How many others Norris intimidated is uncertain. He may have had a hand, directly or indirectly, in persuading Governor Miriam Ferguson to censor biology textbooks. As head of Texas's state textbook commission, the governor imposed a policy of approving only texts that made no mention of evolution.

The religious heritage of the South was expressed also in the growth of educational institutions in the late nineteenth century and especially in the early twentieth century. Major denominations built or expanded colleges, universities, and seminaries. The seminaries reflected the growth of professionalism among the clergy. Being moved by the spirit was still of critical importance, but ministers were also expected to be educated. The number of Bible colleges and institutes expanded to give advanced training to people who felt called to church work and were not ready for or could not afford regular college, university, or seminary training. Bible colleges and institutes also promised to be safe havens for people who thought that secular academic institutions were unsafe for the faithful.

MARDI GRAS, MOBILE, ALABAMA, 1920s (Erik Overbey Collection, University of South Alabama Archives)

CULTURE IN THE POSTBELLUM SOUTH

If cultural heritages are measured by the quality and quantity of creative literature, music, and art produced by a society, the South inherited less culture than religion from the late nineteenth century. If the definition of cultural heritage is broadened to include folk arts, then the South's cultural heritage is much more substantial. This is particularly the case with respect to music and, to a lesser extent, such literary forms as folk stories and tall tales. But few people paid attention to the cultures of southern Appalachia, poorer whites in general, and southern blacks. Those who did attend to them often caricatured them, and those caricatures unfortunately received wide circulation and were accepted as realistic representations.

Lack of money and concentrations of population contributed to the small number and low quality of museums, galleries, concert halls, orchestras, theaters, and dance and theatrical companies in the South. Other deficiencies, however, had perhaps a greater negative impact on cultural institutions. The South lacked a strong tradition of support for cultural activities, colleges and universities of high quality, or a good system of public education. Moreover, the cultural institutions that had existed before the Civil War often suffered grievously from wartime casualties and destruction and from loss of morale. During the war, book publishers, newspapers, magazines, and literary journals became impoverished or collapsed altogether. Few recovered after the war. The novelist William Gilmore Simms lost his home and his library of 11,000 volumes. "I could wish," he told a friend, "to have some books sent me....I have had nothing to read for 4 years." During the war and for some years afterward the arts had to be neglected while more immediate needs were served. Finally, the Civil War and Reconstruction constricted artistic imagination in the South, placing it in service first to the Lost Cause, then to the romanticized Old South. At least both, especially the magnolia-scented Old South, had the virtue of being highly marketable.

Writing was probably the strongest cultural enterprise in the South in the half century or so after the Civil War. Yet, while the body of literature from the South of the late nineteenth century was notable, it was not remarkable. Sidney Lanier earned an honored place among poets, though the Georgian's poor health and his need to make a living limited his output. When local-color literature became a nationwide literary movement in the 1880s, southern authors were well received. Their acceptance reflected the growing reconciliation between South and North: in the immediate postbellum years, southern writers had not been welcomed by northern readers. Local-color writers tried to take selective verbal photographs. They stressed things that were peculiar to particular American regions: physical settings and the speech, dress, mannerisms, and thought patterns of the people of America's various regions. Antebellum plantation blacks, Louisiana Creoles, white mountaineers, and poor whites or "crackers," "rednecks," and "hillbillies" became staples of this literary genre. Of the local-colorists of the South, the most important were George Washington

Cable, Thomas Nelson Page, Joel Chandler Harris, Mary Noailles Murfree, Kate Chopin, and, above all, Mark Twain.

Cable's *Old Creole Days* (1879), about life among Louisiana's French-speaking people, was widely acclaimed as the best treatment of Creole life ever published. Vocal critics in Louisiana complained that Cable demeaned the Creoles by the indelicacy of his descriptions. When the New Orleans native and former Confederate officer continued to publish stories and novels about Creoles and Louisiana and dared to mention such matters as miscegenation, his Louisiana readers angrily joined in attacks against him. Deeply attached to the South but unable to ignore its worst features, Cable called for more equitable treatment of blacks in *The Silent South* (1885). Thereafter, made to feel thoroughly unwelcome by southerners who believed he had betrayed them, Cable left to spend the rest of his long writing career in New England.

Grace King was one of the New Orleans readers who believed that Cable had slandered the South in general and Creoles in particular. She set out to correct him. In her earliest work, "Monsieur Motte," a story she later expanded into a book, King told a complex tale whose primary focus was the roles played by black and white women. King made a career of writing. She read and was influenced by French realists, maintained close ties with leading literary circles in the North, and engaged in research in this country and in Europe. She produced short stories, novels, and serious works of southern history. Scholars have recently called attention to *Tales of a Time and Place* (1892) and *Balcony Stories* (1893), collections of her short stories, and several of her histories, including *Creole Families of New Orleans* (1921).

Thomas Nelson Page, unlike Cable, did not offend, at least not most of the readers of his day. Nor, unlike King, did he tell complex stories. Page's significance lay primarily in his fictional treatment of the Lost Cause. His novels enjoyed great popularity and gave the Lost Cause wide circulation both inside and outside the South. In such books as *In Ole Virginia* (1887) and *The Burial of the Guns* (1894), Page presented an overly romanticized version of antebellum plantation life. He established a formula that was and continues to be extraordinarily attractive to readers: idyllic plantations where chivalry reigned in a world of gentlemen planters, demure charming ladies, and happy faithful slaves. His plantation world only remotely resembled the real plantation world of the antebellum South. Still, readers north and south liked Page, no matter what the critics said, and fictional descendants of Page's historical romances continue to attract droves of readers. More than a generation of southern children learned about the Lost Cause from Page's *Two Little Confederates* (1888) and *Among the Camps* (1891).

More creative and lasting than the work of Thomas Nelson Page were *Uncle Remus: His Songs and Sayings* (1880) and *Nights with Uncle Remus* (1883). These ingenious tales, more than the simple stories for children they appeared to be, were the creations of Joel Chandler Harris, a Georgian who was born and reared in slim circumstances and worked his way up in journalism from printer's apprentice to columnist. Harris had a wonderful sense of the sights, sounds, and thoughts of middle Georgia towns and plantations. As the aged Uncle Remus told stories to a white child in a heavy dialect, he wondered out loud about the mysteries of life and reflected on what he had seen and experienced in his long years. Harris mixed humor, shrewd insight, and animal tales to create literature of memorable quality. The stories of the triumphs of the rabbit (Brer Rabbit) over the fox (Brer Fox) drew upon an African folk tradition carried to America by the slaves. Harris probably was unaware of this African element in his stories, but he was quite well aware that his animal fables reflected the view of southern blacks that the weak but clever could win out over the strong.

Mary Noailles Murfree (also known by one of her pseudonyms, Charles Egbert Craddock) drew heavily on her eastern Tennessee background and summer vacations in Tennessee's Cumberland Mountains to write a series of stories and mountain romances. *In the Tennessee Mountains* (1884) was so successful that her subsequent works had an instant market, and eventually she was able to drop her male pseudonyms. Unfortunately, like Page, she created stereotypes that lasted despite their distortions. She did not understand the folk culture of the mountains, the complexity of the life there, or the speech patterns of the region. She viewed the mountains from an outsider's perspective. Her mountaineers were simple, quaint folk caught in a physical environment that controlled their lives, and their dialect owed more to her imagination than to her ear.

Kate Chopin, "one of the acknowledged belles of St. Louis," is remembered best for her portrayal of Louisiana Creole life in *Bayou Folk* (1894) and *A Night in Acadie* (1897) and for *The Awakening* (1899). The last is a story about a married woman who leaves her businessman husband and two children and later has an affair. An especially well-crafted and beautifully written novel, *The Awakening* touched sensitive nerves, scandalized Chopin's contemporaries, and ended her writing career. Neither readers nor publishers welcomed Chopin's feminist themes or her probing of the realities of the Victorian patriarchal family and the supposed bliss of orderly domesticity. Chopin's writing reflected a deep sense of dissatisfaction that was all but inevitable among educated women confined to the role of Southern Lady in a time of social and intellectual ferment. Only recently has Kate Chopin received the acclaim she deserves.

Despite the role assigned them, a number of southern women had successful careers as writers. Most avoided the risks that Chopin took. Their careers attested to their talents and their hard work and to the lack of occupational alternatives available to educated gifted women. Most of these women, like comparable men writers, left little writing of enduring quality. Mary Johnston enjoyed the greatest commercial success. *To Have and to Hold* (1900), a historical romance about early Jamestown, Virginia, became a record-breaking best-seller and was twice made into a movie.

Charles Chesnutt, the first important black fiction writer in America, wanted, like Kate Chopin, to use local-color writing to send a message that no one wanted to hear. His unpopular purpose was to attack the notion of the blissful life on the antebellum plantation and to assert the humanity and rights of blacks. The North Carolina native used black narrators to tell stories that were intended to show that masters sought to make as much money as possible at the expense of their slaves, who lived lives of drudgery and fear. But most readers did not discover Chesnutt's intent because they were so charmed by the dialect stories in his most widely known work, *The Conjure Woman* (1899). His later work expressed his aims more bluntly and not so creatively, and his earlier success in attracting readers was not repeated. Critics took aim at his awkward plotting and melodramatic writing, but similar flaws did not prevent the Reverend Thomas Dixon's crudely white-supremacist novels (*The Leopard's Spots* [1902] and *The Clansman* [1905]) from being very successful. Sutton Elbert Griggs, a black minister in Texas, challenged Dixon in *The Hindered Hand* (1902), one of several novels that added a black perspective to southern fiction. Unfortunately, Griggs's artistic skill was no better than Dixon's and he had far fewer readers.

Mark Twain grew up in Hannibal, Missouri, a town on the Mississippi, and first achieved literary fame in the 1860s as a local-colorist and humorist of the West. But his greatest work was based on the South. In *Life on the Mississippi* (published serially as "Old Times on the Mississippi" in 1875 and as a book in 1883) Twain wrote a loosely constructed memoir based on his experiences as a river pilot. Then he pushed local-color writing to previously untried depths in *Adventures of Huckleberry Finn* (1884), a classic of American literature which is regarded as Twain's greatest book. In *Huckleberry Finn* he set idyllic scenes peopled by simple innocents, detailed daily events with delicious humor, and then lured unsuspecting readers into dark, almost nightmarish scenes to explore lost innocence, violence, slavery, religion and the religious, government, and socioeconomic class.

On the whole, however, southern writers of the late nineteenth century adopted largely uncritical attitudes toward their region and its people. Moreover, southern writings of the period seldom indicate that their authors knew about recent trends in literature, though realism and naturalism were major literary movements well before the end of the century. Some of them, however, gave indications of change. The *Sewanee Review* and the *South Atlantic Quarterly* were vehicles for critical analyses of southern writing and more generally of the region and its condition. The *Review* was quartered at the University of the South in Sewanee, the *Quarterly* at Trinity College (Duke University after 1924), indications of the role some universities in the South would play as critics of the region.

Still, a stronger uncritical mentality persisted in the turn-of-the-century South. Wilbur Cash later described it as the "savage ideal," which he traced to attitudes that developed in the slave South and persisted thereafter. In *The Mind of the South* (1941) Cash described that ideal as one

whereunder dissent and variety are completely suppressed and men become, in all their attitudes, professions, and actions, virtual replicas of one another. Tolerance, in sum, was pretty well extinguished all along the line, and conformity made a nearly universal law. Criticism, analysis, detachment, all those activities and attitudes so necessary to the healthy development of any civilization, every one of them took on the aspect of high and aggravated treason.

Southern writers stepped gingerly into the twentieth century, generally avoiding frontal assaults on their culture of the type that had been going on in the North for some years. Ellen Glasgow led the way, usually with muffled words. Glasgow witnessed the disorder and division of the New South from her upper-middle-class neighborhood in Richmond and then wrote about the disarray she saw as part of her attempt to create "a well-rounded social record of Virginia," though she wrote as much about her own personality and her own inner disarray as that of the world around her. Glasgow's work was one of the early forays into realism in southern literature. Eventually realism would become one of the hallmarks of southern literature and an elemental force in what is called the southern literary renaissance. The best of her books include *Barren Ground* (1925), a novel about the meager rewards of small farms and the heavy toll they exacted from the people who worked them, and *They Stooped to Folly: A Comedy of Morals* (1929), a novel about the morals and manners of the upwardly mobile in New South Richmond. *The Sheltered Life* (1932) is a masterly novel about the determination of tidewater Virginians to preserve their self-image and their innocence while they steadfastly ignore realities.

James Branch Cabell, Glasgow's neighbor and friend, produced a large and varied body of writing. They and other writers in Richmond at the time gave the city a very active and productive literary group from the end of World War I to the late 1920s and a national reputation as a literary center. During Cabell's early years, gossip swirled around him. For that his mother was largely responsible. She divorced her husband. Proper ladies did not do things like that, or smoke cigarettes and drink cocktails, as she did. After her lover, a cousin, was murdered, rumors spread that Cabell had done the deed. Marriage at thirty-four apparently calmed his life. Though he had been an active writer before, thereafter he became much more industrious. He had the good fortune to have one of his books (*Jurgen* [1919]) declared indecent in 1920 by the New York Society for the Suppression of Vice. He and his publisher won in court while benefiting from the publicity. However, he never attracted the wide following that Glasgow did.

Cabell's writing confused and bewildered many people who attempted to read it. He mixed realism, romanticism, and naturalism in a highly complex style. At the heart of his work lay paradox or contradiction. Human beings need ideals and dreams, yet they mislead the dreamers because they are unattainable. He loved legend and myth and used both in his major work, the eighteen-volume *Biography of Manuel* (1927–1930), which pulled together some of his earlier works and expanded upon them in a work that ranged over seven centuries, from an imaginary medieval land to contemporary Richmond. Late in his life he appeased some people in his native city and state by paying his respects to General Robert E. Lee and Virginia in *Let Me Lie* (1951). Even then, he could not resist a pun. Cabell received enough critical acclaim, including that of Mencken, to have a national reputation. Scholars, however, have generally neglected him; the complexity of Cabell's work may have deterred them.

THE WAR WITHIN

In 1917, when Mencken launched his famous attack on the South as the "Sahara of the Bozart" (beaux arts), the best work of Glasgow and Cabell had not yet appeared, and no other southern authors of the stature they would achieve were being published. Southern culture seemed locked in pious contemplation of the Old South and in thrall to the uncritical mentality of the New South. Mencken offered his own explanation for the South's cultural torpor. The South, he said, had fallen into cultural darkness after the Civil War because semiliterate Baptist and Methodist clergymen had achieved dominance in southern religion, culture, and politics. Mencken pictured the South as an "awe-inspiring blank" where "a poet is now almost as rare as an oboe-player, a drypoint etcher or a metaphysician." Of "critics, . . . composers, painters, sculptors, architects, . . . there is not even a bad one between the Potomac mud-flats and the Gulf. Nor an historian . . . sociologist . . . philosopher . . . theologian . . . [or] scientist." Though Mencken's charges were exaggerated, they were largely valid.

Mencken's "Sahara of the Bozart" essay helped initiate a war within elite cultural circles in the South in the 1920s. When the smoke cleared around 1930, the Old South was no longer an object of unquestioning worship in intellectual and academic circles. Nor were the New South assurances of orderly progress toward a better life under the leadership of captains of industry accepted with only minor reservations. The war within helped produce the southern literary renaissance and southern regionalism, whose impact extended from the arts to economics and politics.

Mecken fired his barrage from the periphery of the South, Baltimore. Other critics shot from closer range. Gerald W. Johnson of the Greensboro (N.C.) *Daily News* produced a steady stream of clear, pointed editorials flavored by a "keen and relentless self-criticism" that Johnson believed the South desperately needed. In succeeding years, other journalists followed Johnson's lead. William Henry Skaggs, former mayor of Talladega and leader of Alabama's Populists, published *The Southern Oligarchy: An Appeal in Behalf of the Silent Masses of Our Country Against the Despotic Rule of the Few* (1924). Skaggs let his fury get the best of him; it alienated readers who might have profited from his perceptive analysis and rich collection of data. That same year the historian Frank Tannenbaum, who was not a native of the region, explored the Klan, cotton mill workers and mill villages, and race relations in *Darker Phases of the South*.

Such attacks inspired others to race to the defense, a posture in which southerners all too often found themselves. Most defenders failed miserably. They hurled mud at Mencken in particular. He sneered his replies. Virginius Dabney of the Richmond *Times-Dispatch* offered a partially successful argument for the persistence of southern liberalism from Thomas Jefferson on in his *Liberalism in the South*. Reacting strongly to the Scopes trial, Edwin Mims, a Vanderbilt professor, attempted in *The Advancing South* to show that

southerners who favored freedom of thought, self-criticism, and forward thinking were gaining ground on their opponents.

Dabney and Mims claimed too much, but they had a point. As should have
been obvious even to casual observers, the South hardly had an exclusive hold
on xenophobia in the United States during World War I and the years that followed. Nor was the South blindly attempting to restore the Old South. Whatever its limitations, the business Progressivism that was predominant in the
1920s was not reactionary, though it was overly materialistic. And the reformist
Progressives remained active, though they were less vocal and less effective
than they had been.

Stung by the surge of interracial violence during and immediately after
World War I, small groups of southern whites and blacks took the small but
bold step of forming the Commission on Interracial Cooperation in 1919. The
commission contributed to efforts that eventually led to profound changes in
southern race relations. The clergy, Mencken's favorite target, provided much
of the leadership of the commission. Clergy also figured prominently in efforts
to limit antievolutionism and then to force it to retreat in every southern state.

The Young Men's Christian Association (YMCA) and the Young Women's
Christian Association (YWCA) continued to pursue programs to study and relieve social problems. Women took particularly active parts in reform efforts in
the 1920s. Drawing upon experience and confidence gained from their work in
missionary societies, the Women's Christian Temperance Union, women's

KLAN PARADE, MONTGOMERY, ALABAMA, 1921 (Collection of the Alabama
State Department of Archives and History)

clubs, the YWCA, and the suffragist movement, women took on a wide range of issues: maternal and infant health, child care and child labor, working women, industrial relations, race relations and the conditions of blacks, and political reforms, especially the abolition of poll taxes. The YWCA directed particular attention to industrial relations. In addition to a program of legislation, the YWCA ran programs to educate college women about industrial labor and held conferences for women factory workers. Some of the women affiliated with the Southern School for Women Workers in Industry later became labor union activists, while others became recognized authorities on industrial relations. In 1930 churchwomen from the rural and small-town South, led by Jessie Daniel Ames, founded the Association of Southern Women for the Prevention of Lynching. The most lasting achievement of women reformers in the 1920s may have been the part they played in the effort to persuade business and political leaders as well as the public that government had a continuing responsibility for public welfare.

But defenders of the South in the 1920s could win only skirmishes. Arts in the South, like much else in the elite culture of the region, remained tied to the dead past. And the New South had a host of grave social, economic, and political deficiencies. Elite culture in the South remained trapped in Victorianism as late as the 1920s, long after the rest of the country had embraced "modernism." Not even Ellen Glasgow could bring herself fully, as she said, to "encounter reality." She remained a Victorian, though one in transition.

Victorianism assumed that the world was divided into separate compartments, the "civilized" and the "savage." Victorians believed that an educated, cultured upper class or cultural aristocracy presided over this bipolar world. The upper class was responsible for controlling the "savage" elements or "lower orders," whose ranks included the poor, factory workers, landless farmers, transients, the fallen, and similar sorts. The cultured "betters" could handle their formidable task because, Victorians assumed, the civilized were rational. Reason was the guiding force in the Victorian world. The civilized, at least civilized men, were presumed to be rational and able to control themselves and the world around them. Southern Victorianism had its peculiar regional twist. Slaveholding planters were still believed to have been a gentlemanly aristocracy who had held slaves, poor whites, and money-hungry Yankees in check until the defeat of the South in the Civil War. After the war, large landholders and New South industrializers and urbanizers assumed the role of the defeated slaveholding aristocracy and set the South on a progressive course.

Modernism assaulted the rock on which Victorianism was built. Drawing upon the insights of Darwinian biology and Freudian psychology, modernism rejected the idea that there was a sharp dichotomy between the civilized and the savage and the assumption that anyone was altogether rational. Thus the slave owner and the slave, the factory owner and factory worker shared a common humanity. Other major intellectual developments in the nineteenth century, such as Marxian social analysis and cultural anthropology, shaped and fueled the modernist inclination to analyze and to challenge basic institutions and practices.

Modernism sank deep roots in the South almost a generation after it had taken hold elsewhere in American culture. Once the South discovered it, it dealt mortal blows to piety toward the Old South and unquestioning praise for the New South. Nowhere was this changed state of affairs clearer than in the southern literary renaissance.

THE SOUTHERN LITERARY RENAISSANCE

Beginning in the 1920s, the quality, range, and quantity of southern literature soared; for the next forty years, the South dominated the American literary scene. The southern literary renaissance was so extensive that it is impossible here to do more than sketch its basic outlines and major figures. The most important writers of this renaissance were John Crowe Ransom, Allen Tate, Robert Penn Warren, Donald Davidson, Andrew Lytle, Caroline Gordon, Thomas Wolfe, William Faulkner, Cleanth Brooks, Katherine Anne Porter, Carson McCullers, Eudora Welty, Flannery O'Connor, and Tennessee Williams.

Ransom, Tate, Davidson, and Warren were part of a group called the Fugitives—from *The Fugitive*, a literary magazine they helped to start in 1922. Natives of Kentucky and Tennessee, they clustered in and around the English department of Vanderbilt University in Nashville, a city that could accurately boast of being a leader in higher education. The Fugitives became a very influential group in American literary history. They wanted to break new ground in literature and, at least initially, to dissociate themselves from their region in general and from its literary conventions. They found the worship of the Old South and the hymns to the New South equally repellent. In their poetry and their literary criticism, they stressed complexities in form, content, and language which appeared to be opaque and even completely meaningless to casual readers. They succeeded wonderfully in their efforts to break new ground in literature. Eventually some of the Fugitives changed course and embraced their region, but not with blind or stultifying affection.

In 1930 Ransom, Tate, and Warren, along with other southern authors and academics, wrote *I'll Take My Stand: The South and the Agrarian Tradition*. Prompted in part by their reaction to the Scopes trial, they called for a reassertion of past values to offset the materialism of the New South and the rationalism and skepticism of Mencken and Darrow. Those values, they contended, included religion and faith, but they rejected the rigid religious stand taken by most evangelical Protestants. Convinced that industrialization and urbanization undermined human values and personal dignity, the Agrarians, as they came to be known, called for a return to the land. Theirs was a perceptive if shortsighted view of the South of their day—and a lament. As most of the people who worked the soil of the South—something the Agrarians had not done—knew, the future of the great majority of southerners did not lie in the land. But *I'll Take My Stand* was a striking document and triggered wide debate about the nature and future of the region. Thus the Agrarians helped to reinforce and expand the growing self-awareness and self-examination that were powerful forces in the South after the mid-1920s. They served as catalysts, as Mencken and the Scopes trial had done.

Andrew Lytle, one of the contributors to *I'll Take My Stand*, became a major novelist whose best work was about the central role of the family in the South. *The Long Night* (1936) is set in the antebellum South and revolves around the powerful force of family loyalty and blood revenge. Lytle's best novel, *The Velvet Horn* (1957), traces the destruction a family brings upon itself when, during Reconstruction, it withdraws into obsessive isolation. Lytle's memoir/chronicle, *A Wake for the Living* (1975), has received high praise. Caroline Gordon, whose husband was Allen Tate, was an Agrarian, though she was not a contributor to *I'll Take My Stand*. Gordon used memories from her family and her region for material for several novels. *Penhally* (1931) is the story of an antebellum Kentucky dynasty that disintegrates when it loses its sense of mutual dependence and its own destructive character flaws gain dominance. *None Shall Look Back* (1937) has been praised as possibly the best southern novel about the Civil War experience ever written.

Some writers outside Agrarian circles also became part of the growing self-examination of the region as part of their own maturation. Thomas Wolfe was one of those. Wolfe's reputation rests essentially on *Look Homeward, Angel*, a highly autobiographical novel about a young man's coming of age in Altamont, North Carolina (the thinly disguised Asheville, Wolfe's home). Wolfe described Asheville, the surrounding mountains, and the people in rich, evocative detail that did not sharply differentiate fact from fiction. Many people in Asheville, but not his family, resented the book, though it received wide critical and popular acclaim and made Wolfe famous. That resentment was understandable, given the often unflattering portrayals in the novel. But too many readers missed a crucial point: though the book's protagonist was eager to get away from his hometown, he was anxious to take it with him, anxious not to lose his roots. Like the Agrarians, Wolfe could not or would not tear himself away from his southern past. Seven years after his masterpiece was published and Wolfe had become an international literary celebrity, Asheville welcomed him home with open arms. But death at thirty-seven ended a promising career.

The same year that *Look Homeward, Angel* appeared, 1929, William Faulkner published *Sartoris*, the first of his Yoknapatawpha County novels, which were only a part, though a substantial part, of the writing he published between 1922 and 1962. Faulkner's fictional county and its inhabitants bore a strong resemblance to the rural counties and peoples, past and present, of Faulkner's home state, Mississippi. The county had old plantations in various states of repair, some still occupied by old families. Other families had left their plantations and moved to town to run stores, banks, and various businesses. Older families found themselves displaced by ambitious, driven seekers of money and power who had once lived on the scruffier marginal lands of the county. Poorer whites farmed much of the county, some as landowners, most as renters. Below them were the white trash, who drifted about the county without visible means of support and only occasionally surfaced to be condescendingly noticed and dismissed. Blacks helped shape the life and texture of the county as farmers, farmworkers, domestics, and occasional laborers. They, Faulkner suggested, had a clearer understanding of the people and the life of Yoknapatawpha County than did most whites.

But Faulkner's Yoknapatawpha novels ranged far beyond history and social commentary. His writing has been called "southern Gothic" because it explores in depth the horrors of life: cancerous ambition, violence, self-destruction, mental incapacity, insanity, stunted lives, and poisonous race relations. He often used a convoluted, highly repetitive style. Faulkner was one of the most perceptive observers of the South and a literary genius. In 1950 he was awarded the Nobel Prize for literature. Throughout he made extensive use of the region to which he was deeply attached, even while he exposed the dark, even demonic aspects of its people and its life.

Cleanth Brooks established himself as one of the foremost figures in modern

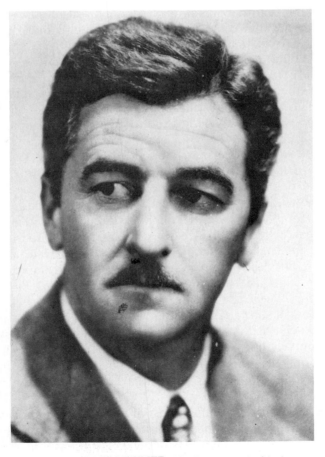

WILLIAM FAULKNER (The Bettmann Archive)

literary criticism. His critical analysis of Faulkner is considered to be the best analysis of Faulkner ever done. Legions of college and high school students have been influenced by his textbooks about understanding and analyzing poetry, fiction, and drama. Porter, a Texan, used materials drawn from the South and Southwest, a biting sardonic wit, and an extraordinarily economical style to create some of the finest short stories in American fiction. Carson McCullers also found material for her work close by—from places like Columbus, Georgia, where she grew up, and especially from personal relationships. The latter had a gothic quality like much of her writing. McCullers is best remembered for *The Heart Is a Lonely Hunter* (1940) and *The Member of the Wedding* (1946), which was adapted into a highly successful play and movie. Eudora Welty's exquisitely balanced, evocative novels and short stories have attracted a wide audience and much critical acclaim. *Delta Wedding,* set in her native Mississippi, is a subtle blend of memory, the sense of tradition, and divergent perspectives as a family prepares for a wedding on its plantation in 1923. Flannery O'Connor used rural middle Georgia as Welty used Mississippi for the settings and characters of her stories and novels. In *A Good Man Is Hard to Find* (1955) and *Everything That Rises Must Converge* (1965), collections of her stories, and in her novels, *Wise Blood* (1952) and *The Violent Bear It Away* (1960), O'Connor powerfully combined literary realism and a religious perspective that was consistently orthodox but expressed in unconventional terms. Tennessee Williams, born in Mississippi and reared in St. Louis, was one of the best playwrights America has produced. *The Glass Menagerie* (1944) and *A Streetcar Named Desire* (1947) are the best of a very substantial body of work.

Mencken's Sahara had blossomed. The blossoming was obvious as early as the late 1920s, and Mencken happily acknowledged the literary outburst, whose dimensions and duration neither he nor anyone else could have anticipated. Southern writers had deliberately and decisively broken with the Victorian genteel tradition and embraced modernism. In doing so, they cast a withering, introspective eye on the South without the sneers and caricatures of Mencken. They held that it was possible to examine one's region honestly and critically without being a traitor to one's homeland. Generally, that was a novel idea in the South in the 1920s, and not always a welcome one. Moreover, they helped set the stage for the conscious regional self-examination and determination to change the South which became major forces in the late 1920s and for years thereafter.

The critical attitudes of the 1920s carried over to blacks. The blacks in Faulkner's work were not the shuffling, aged, deferential, but wise denizens of happy slave times. Nor were those in the writing of Du Bose Heyward, Julia Peterkin, and Jean Toomer. Heyward caught the vibrancy and resilience of lower-class black life in Charleston, South Carolina, in *Porgy* (1925) and in Charleston and New York City in *Mamba's Daughters* (1929). Ira and George Gershwin used *Porgy* as the base for their opera *Porgy and Bess* (1929), a classic of American musical theater. Peterkin's work paralleled Heyward's. She tried to convey a faithful, moving picture of black life from what she knew from living on a plantation in the South Carolina low country. The heroine of Peterkin's

Scarlet Sister Mary (1928) is interesting, combative, sensuous, and no simple heart-of-gold mammy. Her story won a Pulitzer prize for Peterkin.

Jean Toomer inspired his fellow black writers to explore their roots more fully and to express their feelings more candidly and less self-consciously. He is best remembered for *Cane* (1923), a collection of poems, vignettes, and stories. A native of Washington, D.C., Toomer was the grandson of P. B. S. Pinchback, who served as acting governor of Louisiana during Reconstruction. Visits to rural Georgia, where his family lived, gave Toomer much of the material and many of the ideas for *Cane*. Toomer's work fitted with the New Negro movement and Harlem renaissance of the 1920s, which was centered in New York but reverberated throughout the South. One aspect of the Harlem renaissance which attracted a wide audience among blacks and whites was its music: jazz and blues. These African-American creations are two of most significant original and influential musical traditions ever created by Americans.

SOUTHERN REGIONALISM IN THE 1920S AND 1930S

The Scopes trial had heightened the image of the benighted South, an isolated, stagnant cultural backwater. Whatever else one might have concluded about the South five years later, culturally it was alive. One aspect of that vitality was southern regionalism, or a deep commitment to regional self-examination and reform. Numerous southern writers and journalists, scholars, intellectuals, and activists became heavily involved in southern regionalism after the early 1920s. Never before had criticisms from within the South been so thorough and so sweeping. Southern regionalists defended their analyses as a necessary prelude to the change that the South needed to seek.

Southern regionalism found institutional support in the 1920s and 1930s in several universities, especially the University of North Carolina, which was then moving quickly to become a leading American university. Howard Washington Odum stood at the center of that development. He established or helped to establish the Department of Sociology, first of its kind in the South, the Institute for Research in the Social Sciences, the *Journal of Social Forces*, and the University of North Carolina Press, all of which became major forces in the South's self-examination.

The University of North Carolina Press published a steady stream of critical assessments of the South, some of which remain crucial to an understanding of the region. These works include, to name only a few, Rupert B. Vance's *Human Factors in Cotton Culture: A Study of the Social Geography of the American South* (1929) and *Human Geography of the South* (1932), Odum's *Southern Regions of the United States* (1936), Harriet L. Herring's *Welfare Work in Mill Villages* (1929), Arthur Franklin Raper's *Tragedy of Lynching* (1933) and *Preface to Peasantry* (1936), and *The Collapse of Cotton Tenancy* (1936) by Charles S. Johnson, Edwin Embree, and Will Alexander. Presiding over these and numerous other studies was the director of the University of North Carolina Press, William Terry

Couch, who was only twenty-four when he took the job. Under him the press became the single most important means of bringing the work of the South's social critics before the public. During the interwar decades, the press became a major cultural force, a singular achievement for a university press. Couch also edited two valuable works: *Culture in the South* (1935), a model collection of essays on numerous facets of life and culture in the region, and *These Are Our Lives* (1939), a collection of oral histories of ordinary southerners and a pioneer among oral histories. The latter book grew out of Couch's strongly negative reaction to Erskine Caldwell's two best-selling novels, *Tobacco Road* (1932) and *God's Little Acre* (1933). Couch perceptively criticized their overdrawn picture of poor whites and the assumption that Caldwell's characters were typical southern whites. But Caldwell, a Georgian, was closer to the mark in his portrayal of the South's poorest whites than Couch acknowledged.

Caldwell later worked with the photographer Margert Bourke-White to produce a famous photo-documentary on southern tenant farmers: *You Have Seen Their Faces* (1937). Widely praised now, though little noted at the time, was the Tennessean James Agee's study of white tenant farmers in Alabama, *Let Us Now Praise Famous Men* (1941), which included photographs by Walker Evans. Evans's work soon came to be recognized as classic, but the ironically titled book was a commercial failure, largely because of Agee's convoluted, introspective prose. In the 1960s, however, it was reissued to critical acclaim.

Other writers shared Erskine Caldwell's interest in southern industrial workers. The famous textile strike of 1929 in Gastonia particularly stimulated several "proletarian novelists," as they were called, to write novels with a social message about industrial workers. Unfortunately, the message usually overshadowed the plots and characters. They and numerous other writers who were part of the southern literary renaissance attacked southern racism. Their attacks were usually oblique, but not Lillian Smith's. In *Strange Fruit* (1944) Smith struck at southern racism's most sensitive nerve, interracial love. In this novel and by other means she took a forthright stance against Jim Crow. She was a rare person for her day: a native white southerner who openly and explicitly challenged the racial caste system of the South.

The most widely read and noted product of the self-examination encouraged by southern regionalism was Wilbur Cash's *Mind of the South*. More about the temperament and character of the South than about its mind, the book combined history, insight, and dazzling prose to argue that southerners, in the Old and New South, were inclined to rampant hedonism and Puritan guilt and disinclined to reflection and abstract thought. The South was

> proud, brave, honorable by its lights, courteous, personally generous, loyal, swift to act, often too swift, [and was characterized by] violence, intolerance, aversion and suspicion toward new ideas, an incapacity for analysis, . . . exaggerated individualism and a too narrow concept of social responsibility, attachment to fictions and false values, above all too great an attachment to racial values and a tendency to justify cruelty and injustice in the name of those values.

Cash's book enraged many readers, but it became a primer for southerners who were determined to shake the ghosts of the past and build a modern South. For a generation after its publication, it also had a unique influence on students of southern history.

The book came too late, however, to influence people who believed the depression of the 1930s and the New Deal of President Franklin Roosevelt offered unusual opportunities to realize urgently needed changes in the South. Some of them were actively involved in the Roosevelt administration, in Congress, and elsewhere in shaping economic policy for the South. Their efforts and thinking were reflected in a major document of the 1930s, *Report of the Economic Conditions of the South*, which opened with the memorable statement: "The South [is]...the Nation's No. 1 economic problem." A number of these southern New Deal liberals formed an organization, the Southern Conference for Human Welfare (SCHW), in 1938 to work to transform the South. It attracted important political leaders, labor union activists, journalists, and academicians. "For the first time in the history of the region...the lonely Southern liberals met in great numbers—actually more than twelve hundred." Confronted by strong opposition and deeply troubled by internal divisions between liberals and radicals, the SCHW did more talking than acting. Its most important work was its campaign to abolish the poll tax. That campaign contributed to growing dissatisfaction with the tax, a major barrier to voting by low-income whites as well as blacks. Increasingly subject in the 1940s to charges that it was under communist influence and faced with declining interest, the SCHW disbanded in 1948.

The SCHW was also beset by allegations that it favored racial equality. Actually, it stepped lightly whenever it approached Jim Crow, though it did have a biracial membership, then a virtually unheard-of violation of racial etiquette. Few southern white liberals questioned Jim Crow. Instead, they supported efforts to rid the South of its worst racial excesses and to make "separate but equal" a reality—an advanced position at the time. Arthur Raper took exception to this approach. He described southern race relations in terms that accurately reflected its pathology and strongly implied that "separate but equal" did not and could not work. Raper assisted in a major study of race relations and the condition of American blacks which was published as *An American Dilemma: The Negro Problem and Modern Democracy*. Published in 1944, it is the single most important book ever written about American race relations, a source and stimulus for the civil rights revolution in the post–World War II South.

Blacks, of course, had long been critics of the South. The most important during the interwar decades was probably W. E. B. Du Bois. Certainly he was the most vocal. Returning to Atlanta University in 1934 after his long tenure as editor of *Crisis*, the journal of the National Association for the Advancement of Colored People, Du Bois resumed his career as scholar and teacher while remaining a vigorous critic of American race relations, of white supremacy and black subordination and submissiveness. In 1935 he published *Black Reconstruction in America*, an important revisionist interpretation of Reconstruction. Richard Wright, however, reached a wider audience. A survivor of poverty and blatant racial discrimination, Wright followed a migratory pattern not unlike that of other Mississippi blacks. He drifted to Memphis, got a series of jobs there when he was fifteen, and saved enough to move on to Chicago. He read whenever and whatever he could, caught on with the Federal Writers' Project, a New Deal program, and published his *Uncle Tom's Children* in 1938. Two years later came *Native Son*, his best work and the one that established his reputation as a major writer. Though it was set in Chicago, *Native Son* drew heavily on Wright's experiences in the South. In 1945 he used those experiences much more explicitly in *Black Boy: A Record of Childhood and Youth*, a blunt revelation of black life in the South. It suggested something that by the end of World War II would become increasingly obvious: blacks were no longer willing to submit to Jim Crow, and open challenges to the system were likely to increase.

GONE WITH THE WIND

The critical analyses of the southern literary renaissance and southern regionalism disturbed and often angered many southerners. Stark Young and Margaret Mitchell, for instance, reacted with memorable novels set in the plantation South. Young, one of the authors of *I'll Take My Stand*, used Mississippi legends and his family's history to reassert the values of the agrarian South in a very popular novel, *So Red the Rose* (1934). Similar motives prompted Mitchell, a former newspaper reporter and housewife. *Gone with the Wind*, published in 1936, enjoyed instant enormous success. Determined to show a South blissfully free of the grotesqueries described by Faulkner and Caldwell, Mitchell set her novel in the South of sumptuous antebellum cotton plantations, the Civil War, and Reconstruction. It combined historical fact and myth, powerful characters, and a compelling story of the South from antebellum splendor to crushing defeat to determined efforts to recover. The public, south and north, snapped up copies of *Gone with the Wind*. Within six months of its publication, a million copies were sold. Its sales now exceed 21 million. The cultural elite may have accepted modernism and cast aside the plantation myth, but not the mass public.

Gone with the Wind won a Pulitzer prize and was turned into the most successful movie ever produced and probably the most widely seen movie ever made. The novel and the movie, which had a lavish premiere in Atlanta in 1939, obviously struck a responsive note in a nation eager to recover from the Great Depression, its worst domestic crisis since the Civil War. That crisis did not end until the early 1940s, more than two years after World War II had begun. With the end of the Depression, the sense of the South as benighted faded. The loss of that sense was not, however, a product of economic change alone. It was also a product of conscious regional self-examination, determination to engage in major self-reform, and the southern literary renaissance, which had poured out its riches over more than two decades and would continue to do so for twenty more years.

The Changing South: People and Cotton

―――――― ❖ ――――――

Populaton changes in the South mirror the profound changes that have occurred in the region since the Civil War, especially since 1880. Initially, and for some years thereafter, the westward drift of the population of the South continued. Since 1900 the economic growth in the oil and gas states, in Florida, along the Piedmont, in the Chesapeake Bay region, and in the resurgent urban centers of the Middle South, such as Nashville and Memphis, have reshaped the southern landscape into an area that is highly urban and sometimes metropolitan. As the map for 1930–1990 indicates, the South has been much more prosperous in the last half century than it was in the half century prior to 1930.

That prosperity often did not include blacks who over the years left the region in hopes of better opportunities and greater safety and personal dignity elsewhere. Black out-migration and white in-migration since 1955 largely account for the South having proportionately fewer blacks today than at any time since the seventeenth century.

The prevalence of cotton in 1930 and its disappearance or decline to secondary importance in the rural South by 1959 also graphically reflect the transformation of the South since the Great Depression. Cotton is hardly the whole story of the South, or even of southern agriculture, but cotton is one telling barometer we have of the history of the South.

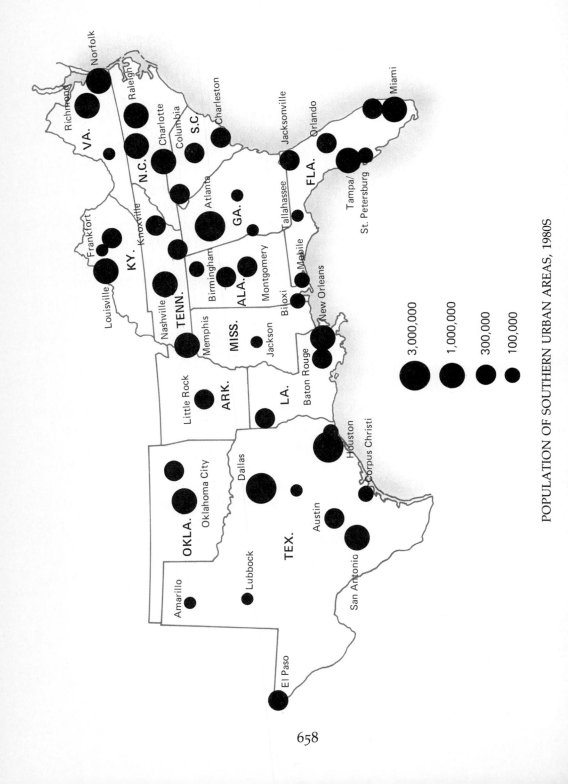

POPULATION OF SOUTHERN URBAN AREAS, 1980S

3,000,000

1,000,000

300,000

100,000

Norfolk

Richmond

Raleigh

VA.

Charlotte

Columbia

Charleston

S.C.

N.C.

Jacksonville

Orlando

FLA.

Miami

Frankfort

Atlanta

GA.

Tallahassee

Tampa/
St. Petersburg

Knoxville

KY.

Louisville

Nashville

TENN.

Birmingham

Montgomery

ALA.

Mobile

Biloxi

New Orleans

Memphis

MISS.

Jackson

Little Rock

ARK.

LA.

Baton Rouge

Oklahoma City

OKLA.

Dallas

Houston

Corpus Christi

Austin

TEX.

Lubbock

San Antonio

Amarillo

El Paso

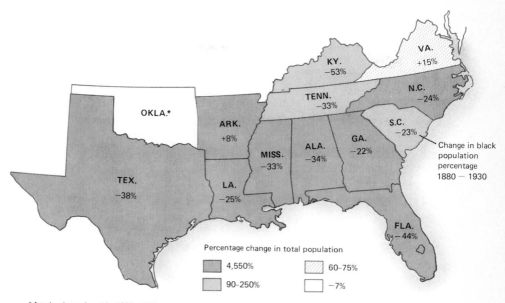

POPULATION CHANGES, 1880–1930

Percentage change in total population

- 4,550%
- 90–250%
- 60–75%
- −7%

*Attained statehood in 1907; 1930 population was 2.4 million.

Change in black population percentage 1880 – 1930

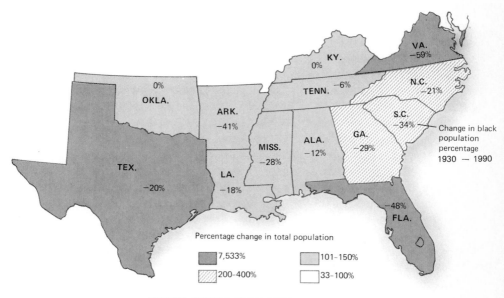

POPULATION CHANGES, 1930–1990

Percentage change in total population

- 7,533%
- 200–400%
- 101–150%
- 33–100%

Change in black population percentage 1930 – 1990

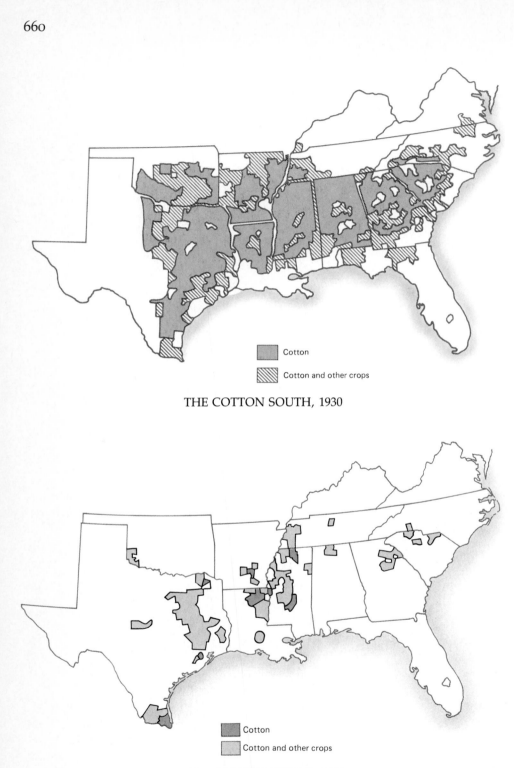

Cotton

Cotton and other crops

THE COTTON SOUTH, 1930

Cotton

Cotton and other crops

THE COTTON SOUTH, 1959

25

The Emergence of the Modern South, 1930–1945

❖

*I*n 1937, Brian and Mary Sue Smith left Portland, Texas, a town of perhaps 500 near Corpus Christi, after they lost their home and business during the Depression. They moved to Blanco County, fifty miles west of Austin, in the hill country of Texas. Though it had thin soil and slight rainfall, it "was the only place where land was cheap enough so we could buy a farm." The Smiths probably shook hands that year with the twenty-eight-year-old Lyndon Baines Johnson, who was running for Congress in a special election. A man of great ambition and enormous energy, Johnson "pressed the flesh" with virtually every voter in Blanco County and with a majority of the other voters in the ten-county, 140-mile-wide Tenth Congressional District.

A lot more was involved here, however, than shaking hands and vote-getting. The Depression, which began in 1929, struck with such ferocity that it drove thousands back to the land. So many went back that the 1930s became the first decade in American history in which more people migrated to the countryside than to the cities. So desperate were people in the South that they fled to the land despite a 60 percent decline in farm incomes from 1929 to 1932.

Lyndon Johnson was desperate, too. Propelled by his ambition and his personal inclinations and circumstances, he left the hill country to pursue political power and personal fortune. Johnson went to Washington, D.C.—not to Austin, where his father had once been a prominent state legislator—in 1931. He had a job in Washington—in politics, which he loved, and away from the limited opportunities the hill country offered.

Johnson served as a secretary to a congressman (1931–1935), New Deal administrator (1935–1937), congressman (1937–1949), United States senator (1949–1960), vice president (1961–1963), and president (1963–1968). In 1964 he became only the second southerner to be elected president since 1848. Woodrow Wilson was the first, and Wilson initially achieved political prominence outside the South, when he was elected governor of New Jersey.

Lyndon Johnson's political career and that of the modern South became intertwined; his career mirrored the evolution and transformation of the American South after the 1930s.

In 1937, however, Johnson concerned himself with present, not future, prospects. He told voters in the hill country what the New Deal had done for them and what it would do for them. The government, for instance, could help farmers obtain electricity, without which modern living and farming were impossible. That message must have struck a responsive note: in 1930 less than 5 percent of the farms in the South had electricity, compared with more than 14 percent nationally, 45 percent in New England, 33 percent in the middle Atlantic states, 22 percent in the Midwest, and 57 percent in the Pacific states. Fewer than 2 in 100 farms in Mississippi and fewer than 3 in 100 in Alabama, Arkansas, and Louisiana had electricity. Mary Sue Smith remembered that "moving from Portland into the Hill Country was like moving from the twentieth century back into the Middle Ages."

Russell Baker, author and noted columnist with the *New York Times*, recalled from his childhood in the settlement of Morrisonville in northern Virginia that

> my mother and grandmother kept house very much as women did before the Civil War. Their lives were hard, endless, dirty labor. They had no electricity, gas, plumbing, or central heating. No refrigerator, no radio, no telephone, no automatic laundry, no vacuum cleaner. Lacking indoor toilets, they had to empty, scour, and fumigate each morning the noisome slop jars which sat in bedrooms during the night.
>
> For baths, laundry, and dishwashing, they hauled buckets of water from a spring at the foot of a hill. To heat it, they chopped kindling to fire their wood stoves. They boiled laundry in tubs, scrubbed it on washboards until knuckles were raw, and wrung it out by hand. Ironing was a business of lifting heavy metal weights heated on the stove top.
>
> They scrubbed floors on hands and knees, thrashed rugs with carpet beaters, killed and plucked their own chickens, baked bread and pastries, grew and canned their own vegetables, patched the family's clothing on treadle-operated sewing machines, deloused the chicken coops, preserved fruits, picked potato bugs and tomato worms to protect their garden crop, darned stockings, made jelly and relishes, rose before men to start the stove for breakfast and pack lunch pails, polished the chimneys of kerosene lamps, and even found time to tend the geraniums, hollyhocks, nasturtiums, dahlias, and peonies that grew around every house. By the end of a summer day a Morrisonville woman had toiled like a serf.

It should come as no surprise that the great majority of southerners eagerly embraced Franklin Roosevelt and the New Deal. Lyndon Johnson benefited from that embrace. Most people who went to the polls in 1937 had fresh, bitter memories of economic disaster and a federal government controlled by Republicans which in their eyes had done little to help a nation in distress. Cloaking himself in the mantle of Franklin Roosevelt and the New Deal, Johnson carried the Tenth District to become one of the youngest members of Congress and a member of the powerful Texas congressional delegation.

THE DEPRESSION AND THE SOUTH

The Great Depression was the worst economic crisis in American history. From 1929 to 1932, per capita incomes fell by 44 percent in the southern states; elsewhere in the United States they fell by 46 percent. Still, southerners made less than half of what Americans outside the South made. Since unemployment statistics for regions are inadequate for this time, it is impossible to determine whether jobs were harder to find in the South than elsewhere in the country. In the nation as a whole, unemployment rose from around 3 percent in 1929 to about 25 percent in 1932, and, except for one year, it remained above 15 percent until 1940. Industrial production in the South declined by half. Ten thousand miles of rail lines were in the hands of receivers. By 1931 the Southern Railway owed the federal government $15 million for loans. Bankruptcy even threatened governments. Louisiana, South Carolina, and Arkansas defaulted on their debts. Most southern state and local governments survived only by making drastic cuts in their spending; by paying their employees in scrip, which could be used to pay property taxes but nothing else; and by searching for new sources of revenue. The last effort led to general sales taxes, which became staples in the revenue policies of the South and which fell most heavily on the people least able to pay.

BIRMINGHAM STEEL MILLS, 1936 (Library of Congress)

The state government of Tennessee had a brush with bankruptcy when the Nashville firm of Caldwell and Company, a large investment brokerage, collapsed. The fall of the "Morgan of the South" took $6.5 million from the state treasury and triggered a panic that swept away more than a hundred banks in seven states. In the five years after the Depression began, more than a third of the banks in the South failed altogether or disappeared in forced mergers, and 60 percent of the bank assets of the region (some $2.5 billion) were lost. Southern banking lost more heavily than banking elsewhere because the economy of the South was more vulnerable and its banks were more dependent on larger banks outside of the region.

Numbers, however, cannot convey the human toll the Great Depression exacted. There is no way to calculate the costs of permanently impaired health, early death, shattered families, lost hopes, or the investments of lifetimes in farms, businesses, and homes that had been lost. The town world and the farm world were drawn together for a time by common adversity. According to the federal government, Birmingham was "probably the hardest hit city in the nation." An Alabama congressman stated in 1932 that of the 108,000 wage and salary earners in his district, which included the "Magic City" of the South, only 8,000 "have their normal incomes. At least 25,000 are altogether without work. Some of them have not had a stroke of work for more than 12 months." He reported that many farm owners could no longer furnish their tenants and croppers and were letting them go to provide for themselves wherever and however they could. "Any thought that there has been no starvation...is the rankest nonsense."

Relief workers estimated that of San Antonio's 280,000 residents, 88,000 were on relief. Of Houston's 380,000 residents, some 60,000 were on relief. It would have had more, but Houston officials, as one said, were "turning away as many Negroes as we can. We've got to, because of the mental attitude of the whites. We've been threatened with riots here." Mexican-Americans probably received similar treatment from relief agencies in the South.

Economic distress, however, was not new to large numbers of southern farmers. They had struggled through hard times before, especially in the 1920s. "Well, we didn't know the difference in a depression," a Mississippi tenant farmer recalled, "except...what we would hear. It just increased the fear a little bit of maybe not being able to get any food at all. We was just living on the bare necessities anyhow." Many southerners had a far easier time. Ben Robertson remembered that "when the depression...hit us, we retrenched...we stayed at home and we did without. We lived on fried chicken and beef and turnip greens and sweet potatoes and string beans and cornbread and sweet milk...and we waited for the hard time to pass." As in the rest of the country, many people did not stay home. Large numbers of them became nomads. John Steinbeck's novel *The Grapes of Wrath* made some of the nomads famous: the 150,000 "Okies" (and "Arkies") who fled westward along U.S. highway 66 from the Mississippi Valley through Arkansas, Oklahoma, and northern Texas and finally on to California.

Others turned to direct action. In January 1931 some fifty farmers climbed on a truck owned by H. C. Coney, a white tenant farmer, and rode into England, Arkansas, to ask for food for their families. If politeness failed, they intended to take the food. When the Red Cross quickly rushed in relief, the "riot" ended. Several other Arkansas communities had similar experiences. Arkansas was particularly distressed because it was most adversely affected by the Southwide drought of 1930–1931. The severe drought was one of the worst in American history. In 1932 the Sharecroppers' Union, an organization of black farmers in Alabama, charged dues of a few cents. It "would back you up and fight your battles with you." That appealed to Ned Cobb. "Ever since I been in God's world, I've never had no rights, no voice in nothin that the white man didn't want me to have—even been cut out of education, book learnin, been deprived of that." Cobb joined the organization. Later, without the help of the union—it was very weak and soon collapsed—he stood up to the sheriff's deputies who were confiscating the livestock of indebted farmers. Cobb survived the shootout that ensued—others did not—and spent the next twelve years in prison.

Labor unrest also became overt. Textile workers had engaged in work stoppages earlier, in the aftermath of World War I and toward the end of the 1920s when management moved aggressively to increase productivity. Efforts at increasing output per worker-hour usually took the forms of speedups and stretchouts: management forced workers to work much faster and reduced the number of workers without reducing the amount of work required or increasing

MIGRANT FAMILY IN THE OZARKS, 1930s (Library of Congress)

pay. Mill hands worked in unventilated rooms where the air was saturated by mechanical humidifiers while managers stood nearby and timed their work with stopwatches. "I had seen women, one of them my own daughter," one textile worker recalled, "going all day long in that unbearable heat with their clothes stuck to their bodies like they had been dipped in a pool of water." Such conditions triggered a series of walkouts in the late 1920s. The most celebrated of these strikes took place at Gastonia, North Carolina, in 1929. It attracted national attention, inspired a substantial body of literature, resulted in several deaths, and ended in emotional trials, miscarriages of justice, and the complete defeat of the union.

The American Federation of Labor (AFL) sought to take advantage of the unrest among southern textile workers by mounting an organizing campaign in 1930. Less than a year later, the AFL claimed more than a hundred new locals, including twenty-five in textiles, which were organized under the United Textile Workers of America (UTW). But the organizing campaign sustained a crippling defeat at Danville, Virginia, when the UTW lost a four-month strike against the Dan River and Riverside cotton mills, where 4,000 workers walked out in September 1930. Neither the AFL nor the UTW had the human or financial resources to sustain that large a strike for more than a few weeks. The AFL also continued to demonstrate that it lacked the boldness such campaigns required and the commitment to organize industrial workers. The intransigence of the company and racial divisions also contributed to the defeat of the UTW at Danville. As a concession to white workers, the union excluded the few black workers at Dan River and Riverside. Blacks countered by crossing the picket lines.

Encouraged by local communists, cigar workers in Tampa marched to protest their plight. The action evoked a swift reaction. Local police and volunteers from the American Legion dispersed the march. When workers struck to protest this action, the cigar companies beat them handily, and resumed their operations on a nonunion basis. Predictably, labor strife lasted longer and was more violent among the coal miners. More than 10,000 miners in Harlan County became involved. So did the sheriff's department, mine guards, and the National Guard. Seemingly everyone had a gun, and most used them. The "Battle of Evarts" left four dead. The United Mine Workers retreated from what they believed was a sure defeat for unionization. A communist-controlled union, the National Mine Workers Union, tried to fill the vacuum and was routed, in part by the miners themselves. Harlan became a subject of intense study and publicity as it joined Gastonia as a hallmark in the history of industrial relations in the South.

Most southerners, however, avoided activism. Most of those who could vote expressed themselves through the ballot box. Once again the South gave its electoral votes to the Democratic presidential nominee in 1932. This time, however, there was a very significant difference. The solid South in 1932 found itself on the side of a large majority.

In THE DEMOCRATIC MAJORITY

The Great Depression transformed the political fortunes of the South. Economic disaster became political disaster for the Republicans. The Democratic party became the dominant party, a position it had not had since the 1850s. Southern Democrats consequently rose to unaccustomed power and prominence. They enjoyed important positions in the administrations of Franklin Roosevelt. Those administrations, however, which lasted from 1933 to 1945, never had the strong southern flavor those of Woodrow Wilson had had. With the exception of Senator James F. Byrnes of South Carolina, southern Democrats were not part of the inner circle at the White House. Vice President John Nance Garner's experience was typical. A Texas congressman who became Speaker of the House, he lent southern balance to the Democratic ticket in 1932 and again in 1936, but he was not a close adviser of Roosevelt. Nor were the three cabinet members from the South.

The real power of the southern Democrats lay in Congress, where seniority allowed them to chair most of the committees and to serve as floor leaders in the Senate and the House. Using this congressional power base, the southern Democrats helped create and shape the New Deal. Some southern Democrats in Congress, however, opposed the New Deal from its earliest days, generally for doing too much, for spending too much. Meanwhile Huey Long, the most vocal southern critic of the New Deal, attacked it for not doing enough.

Initially, however, the president enjoyed almost undivided support from his party. For most Democrats (as for most Republicans), party loyalty was a powerful, persistent force. Extensive experience as a political minority reinforced party cohesion among the Democrats. So did the profound sense of economic and political crisis triggered by the Depression. Finally, Roosevelt had personal charisma and he employed it skillfully.

The Depression went on and on, and a sense of crisis could not be sustained indefinitely. Disenchantment with New Deal programs and proposals set in when full economic recovery was not forthcoming, though the worst of the depression had passed and the disenchantment deepened when times grew tougher in 1937–1938. Disagreements developed along sectional, rural and urban, and ideological lines. Convinced that low wages were a major asset for attracting the industrial investment the South so urgently wanted, southern leaders worked to obstruct efforts to close sectional wage differentials. As politicians from a predominantly rural region they supported measures that favored rural areas over more urbanized areas. They vigorously supported the landmark farm legislation of the New Deal designed to relieve agricultural distress, but they were often indifferent to or hostile toward relief of unemployed city dwellers. Fears of expanded federal powers and concerns about balanced budgets and rising governmental expenditures drove a number of southern leaders in Congress away from the New Deal. Southern Democrats accounted for about half of the party's anti–New Deal votes in the House of Representatives from 1933 to 1939 and almost one-third of such votes in the Senate. Other southerners in Congress remained vigorous New Dealers, sometimes outdistancing the president in pushing the New Deal leftward. Southern Democrats remained united, however, on race. White supremacy still stood as the cornerstone of the Democrats in Dixie, and the cornerstone seemed firmly in place in 1932, when Franklin Roosevelt was first elected.

Roosevelt's New Deal profoundly affected the lives of most Americans. The New Deal assumption that the federal government was responsible for the economic well-being of the country became a given in American politics and economics. For the first time the federal government gave direct relief to the unemployed and the needy, expanded its efforts to regulate and stabilize banking and finance, encouraged organized labor and collective bargaining, protected and stimulated private homeownership with government-supported loans, and created the social security system, which "brought government into the lives of people as nothing since the draft and the income tax."

THE NEW DEAL AND SOUTHERN AGRICULTURE

Two facets of the New Deal had particular impact on the South: its agricultural policies and its labor policies. The New Deal passed and implemented the most sweeping government farm program in American history. New Deal policies—reinforced by market forces—set the stage for an agricultural revolution in the South. By the end of the 1930s, the basis for more diverse, modern farming had been laid. The dawning of a new era in southern agriculture became evident in the fate of cotton. In a reversal of a history spanning more than two hundred years, cotton acreage began a long-term decline.

Southern cotton farmers had struggled after World War I. Supply exceeded demand, and the situation was made worse by synthetic fibers and domestic and foreign competition in cotton growing. American manufacturers in the 1920s produced 120 million pounds of rayon annually. They tripled that output during the next decade. Farmers in California and Arizona became important cotton producers before 1930. Led by China, India, Brazil, and Egypt, foreign countries captured a growing share of the world's cotton supply, a development that reduced exports and prices for southern cotton farmers. Then the Depression sent shock waves into the already weakened foundations of the cotton kingdom.

For several years, however, the foundation remained secure—at least to the naked eye. During the long, hot summers from 1930 to 1935, the kingdom must have seemed permanent to the nearly 8 million southerners who were dependent on cotton. The wife of a white sharecropper told one of the dozens of writers (and scholars, journalists, and photographers) who examined and publicized the plight of the small farmer in the South during the 1930s: "We seem to move around in circles like the mule that pulls the syrup mill. We are never still, but we never get anywhere. For twenty-three long years we have begun each year with nothing and when we settled here in November we had the same." Three-fourths of all the farmers who produced less than $1,000 annually lived in the South. Fifty-five percent of southern farmers (60 percent of cotton farmers) were tenants, with little or no hope of ever owning their own land. It has been estimated that the ten principal cotton states of the South had 1.8 million tenant families, of whom 1.1 million were white. Tenants lived in virtual peonage in the cotton belt, in a "miserable panorama of unpainted shacks, rain-gullied fields, straggling fences, rattle-trap Fords, dirt poverty, disease, drudgery, and monotony that stretche[d] for a thousand miles." This harsh panorama did not end at the borders of the cotton kingdom; it ran on to the tobacco belt of the Southeast, to farms in the cut-over pine and hardwood forests along the coastal plains, into Appalachia and the Ozarks, and to the dry, plowed-up grasslands of the western reaches of the South.

Yet as early as 1935 New Deal farm programs had initiated a process to reshape this panorama and all of the agriculture of the South. Then, enormously stimulated by World War II and postwar economic developments, the process resulted in the transformation of southern agriculture. In 1935 about 45 in 100 southerners farmed; in 1970 about 5 in 100 did. Farm output and methods underwent a similar transformation. By 1970 the average farm in the South was much larger, was heavily mechanized, was cultivated by scientific methods, and was more likely to grow grains, livestock and poultry, fruits and vegetables, hays, soybeans, and trees for lumber, furniture, pulp, and paper than cotton.

The cornerstone of the New Deal's farm policy was the belief that raising farm incomes to parity (making them equal to or on a par with *real* farm incomes from 1909 to 1914 for most commodities, and from 1919 to 1929 for tobacco) should be the primary concern of the agricultural policy of the federal government. All other concerns were secondary. To raise farm incomes, the New Deal stressed a decrease in farm output and modernization of agricultural methods. The strategy was to encourage larger farms, mechanization and scientific farming, crop specialization, and production for cash. Other strategies might have been attempted; for instance, committing the necessary human and financial resources to develop smaller-scale, more self-sufficient farms, with less dependence on a cash crop. Whether this strategy would have worked will never be known. Political—and perhaps economic—realities precluded more than modest attempts at implementing such a strategy. The Resettlement Administration, later the Farm Security Administration, tried to rehabilitate small farmers. Neither agency had the financial or human resources to do much, and neither could match the power of the governmental and business interests that favored a big-farm strategy for agricultural recovery and reform.

To raise farm incomes by decreasing farm output and modernizing agriculture, the New Deal adopted an interventionist, sometimes contradictory policy that had mixed results and high human and financial costs. The haves gained more than the have-nots from government farm policies in the 1930s, as they have continued to do. Though this was not the intended result, economic and political circumstances were more influential than intent in shaping the policy. Whether any farm program that could have been implemented would have significantly aided the majority of poor farmers, or even large numbers of them, is doubtful at best. Moreover, the better-off farmers had considerable advantages. They worked closely with and through the Department of Agriculture, local county farm agents, schools of agriculture in state universities, and such well-organized groups as the American Farm Bureau Federation. Probably the most influential person in the Agricultural Adjustment Administration was Oscar Johnson, a Mississippian who was the largest planter in the nation. The have-nots lacked personal resources and had few organizations or spokesmen to defend their interests.

The government assumed unprecedented powers to reduce farm output. In the past, farmers of most commodities had great difficulty in altering their output in response to demand. Chronic surpluses and low farm incomes resulted. Given the large number of farmers and the dearth of their options, there was little likelihood that these surpluses would end without government intervention or a complete collapse of agriculture and the further spread of human misery. Voluntary reduction programs had been repeatedly urged. Some had been attempted, but few had succeeded.

Now the New Deal forced or induced farmers to reduce output in return for government benefits. Benefits (implemented under the Agricultural Adjustment acts, the Bankhead Cotton Control Act, the Tobacco Control Act, and the Soil Conservation and Domestic Allotment Act) were based on reductions in the number of cultivated acres and in the production of the commodities covered by these programs (among them cotton, rice, wheat, hogs, dairy products, tobacco, sugar, peanuts, and cattle). Thus the larger the farm, the more benefits received. The hundreds of thousands of smaller farmers in the South got little. Nearly half of the farmers in the South got less than $40 in benefit payments from the government in 1938, hardly enough to improve their standard of living. Such improvements were possible only if a farmer could take at least thirty to sixty acres out of production. Differences in benefits obtained could be startling. The British-owned Delta and Pine Land Company, in the Mississippi delta, got $114,480 for its 1933 crop reductions. The government could not have avoided such imbalances in benefits, however, given the program it adopted and its need for support from the bigger farmers in order to pass and implement that program.

New Deal farm credit programs drastically reduced the cost of money to farmers, provided, of course, that they were considered good risks. Not since the Civil War had southern farmers had such ready access to credit. Easier credit and benefit payments for crop and land reductions allowed farmers to make basic changes. Many did. They changed the kind and the quantities of the crops they grew; they took less fertile soils out of cultivation; and they relied less on sharecroppers, for whom they had year-round responsibilities, and more on day laborers. Farmers increased their investments in machinery, a major step toward capital-intensive agriculture and away from the labor-intensive agriculture that had long been characteristic of most of the South.

Southern farmers harvested 11 million fewer acres in 1939 than they had in 1929. More significantly, they decreased their harvested cotton acreage by 22 million acres (about 50 percent) and their cotton production by 277,700 bales (20 percent). They grew more corn, soybeans, peanuts, hay, wheat, and truck crops. Tobacco production remained virtually constant. Apparently tobacco was impervious to economic downturns, and it was bolstered by a special, particularly generous parity price (based on the higher 1920–1929 prices, as opposed to the more usual standard of 1910–1914).

The size of the farm population remained almost constant during the 1930s, or so it seemed. Actually, it grew by 500,000 from 1930 to 1935, then declined by a like number during the next five years. More significantly, the ranks of tenants and sharecroppers shrank by nearly 300,000 between 1930 and 1940. Many of the former tenants became day laborers on farms or, worse, could find only seasonal work, such as picking cotton.

New Deal farm programs had a large if unintentional hand in this process. The government encouraged landlords to sign agreements to divide and distribute benefit payments between themselves and their tenants, in the same way they had divided crops in the past. A sharecropper working on "halves," for instance, should have received half of the benefit payment. Instead, many landlords kept the cash and reduced a tenant's debt by a like amount, or used the tenant's share of the benefits to pay bills the tenant owed to local merchants. Fraud sometimes compounded wrong. Landlords sometimes reduced their own land under cultivation but not that of their tenants, then claimed all of the benefit payments for themselves. Whatever happened, tenants had little or no recourse. Direct government payments to tenants would have required a more elaborate bureaucracy than even the New Deal farm programs developed and would have required the government to interpose itself between landowner and tenant. Landowners stood rigidly opposed to that policy because it would have threatened what one scholar has called "the traditional condition of sharecropper dependence," a condition that was often reinforced by the racial caste system. The general shift to more capital-intensive agriculture probably had an equally adverse effect on tenants and sharecroppers as well as on many small farm owners.

Reforestation and soil conservation programs permanently altered southern forests and lands. The New Deal reforested much of the South and launched the most comprehensive soil conservation effort ever to be undertaken there. The region had nearly two-thirds of the 150 million eroded acres in the United States. Severe erosion or loss of topsoil blighted every southern state. Virginia, for example, had lost the topsoil from 1.5 million acres; Alabama, from 4 million; Georgia, from 5 million; and Arkansas and Tennessee, from 3 million each. The Dust Bowl of 1934–1935, which came on the heels of the drought of 1930–1931, was the worst drought disaster in American history. Dust storms hit Oklahoma, Texas, and Arkansas especially hard and darkened skies as far as the Atlantic and gulf coasts. Convinced that soil erosion was a major problem, Congress passed new soil conservation and reforestation legislation in 1935. During the next decade, the "plans [of the Soil Conservation Service] for land use, crop rotation, grasses, woodlands, contour plowing, terracing, strip cropping, ponds, drainage, and the planting of legumes like soybeans, kudzu, and lespedeza" were applied to 26.7 million acres in the South. That massive effort contributed significantly to the diversification of agriculture and the expansion of forest products in the South but not to the primary goal of New Deal farm policy, the reduction of output. Farmers removed their poorest land from cultivation while they cultivated their better lands more intensively. Yields per acre increased, and total farm output remained high.

New Deal relief programs, most of which took the form of work relief, provided some help for the landless and the small farm owners and also aided nonfarmers in both the urban and the rural South. But the relief programs did not do nearly enough to alleviate the desperate circumstances poorer people experienced in the 1930s. The Federal Emergency Administration (FERA) and the Public Works Administration, created by the Federal Emergency Relief Act in 1933, and other federal agencies provided relief to millions. In October 1933 more than 4 million people in the South were on relief, over 90 percent of which came from the federal government. By 1940, when most of the relief programs had ended, the combined expenditures of FERA, the Works Progress Administration (or WPA, which was later called the Works Projects Administration), and the Civil Works Administration reached nearly $2 billion in the South. Ei-

SOIL EROSION SCENE, ALABAMA, 1937 (Library of Congress)

ther inability or unwillingness kept the southern states from obtaining more federal funds to meet federal matching requirements. Whatever the reasons, the southern states received less for relief from the federal government than other states did, though the South had the greater need.

Millions found employment under these and other government programs, including the Civilian Conservation Corps (CCC), the Tennessee Valley Authority (TVA), and the National Youth Administration. Some people found work as teachers in financially devastated schools, in public health, in research, in surveying historical records, in libraries and archives, in writing state guidebooks and oral histories, and in drama, art, and music. Others found work building public housing, dams, schools, courthouses, playgrounds, privies, highways, and bridges, including the first bridge connecting the Florida keys.

New Deal relief programs had ambiguous results. Those programs established crucial precedents and laid the basis for a transformation of social work in the United States, but the programs did little to alter the established order of the South. President Roosevelt asked for and Congress appropriated the funds for the largest relief measures in American history. The funds were dispensed as grants—not as loans, as under the Hoover administration—to state and local governments for distribution as direct relief to needy "unemployables" and as work relief for needy "employables," who were put to work on government projects. Those grants often required that federal funds be matched by state and local funds and that the administration of relief meet certain federal standards. This pattern continued and became fixed with the passage of the Social Security Act of 1935. In addition to its most important program, benefits for the elderly and for dependent survivors of deceased workers covered by the program, the Social Security Act included aid to dependent children and the blind and provisions for public health, maternal, and child-welfare services.

Even Virginia, then in the grasp of the tightfisted political oligarchy headed by Senator Harry F. Byrd, retreated from its commitment to "a negative policy on public services." A keen student of southern politics noted later that Byrd's Virginia, when faced with "an apparent demand...will grudgingly yield a bit here and there." As a result of the Depression and the New Deal, public assistance for the needy and pension benefits for the elderly became a fixed part of American public policy. The welfare agencies that they spawned at every level of government also became permanent.

New Deal relief efforts established crucial precedents, but they did little to alter the basic attitude "that many, if not most, of the destitute are undeserving," and those efforts contoured themselves to fit the farm season and Jim Crow. Programs for the needy too infrequently included rehabilitation. Finally, direct-relief and work-relief programs revealed the fault lines in the economy and the politics of the South.

Expenditures for relief programs followed the farm seasons: they rose during the winter months and fell in the spring. New Deal agencies often cut their work-relief rolls when the demand for farm labor increased, particularly at harvesttime. Agencies did differ with landlords over who should bear respon-

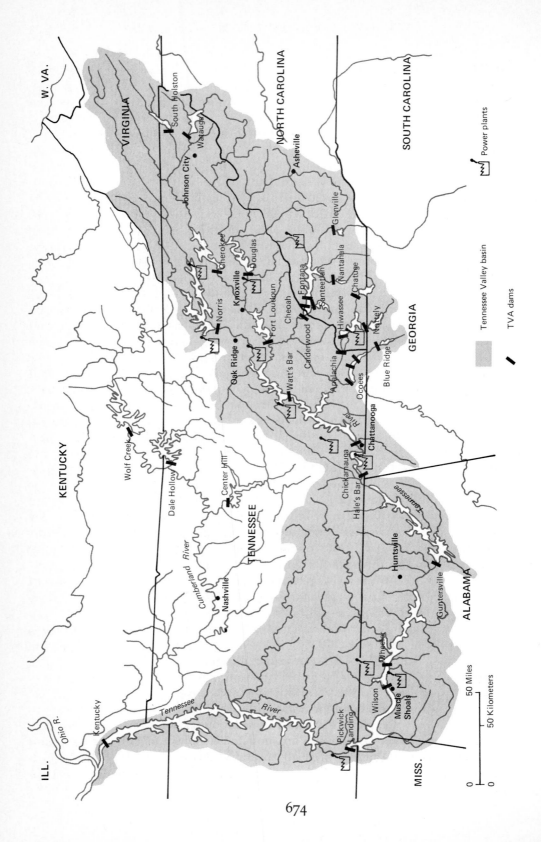

THE TENNESSEE VALLEY AUTHORITY

Tennessee Valley basin

TVA dams

Power plants

W. VA.

VIRGINIA

NORTH CAROLINA

SOUTH CAROLINA

KENTUCKY

TENNESSEE

GEORGIA

ALABAMA

MISS.

ILL.

Ohio R.

South Holston

Watauga

Johnson City

Asheville

Cherokee

Douglas

Fontana

Glenville

Nantahala

Chatuge

Norris

Knoxville

Fort Loudoun

Cheoah

Santeetlah

Hiwassee

Calderwood

Appalachia

Nottely

Oak Ridge

Watt's Bar

Ocoees

Blue Ridge

Wolf Creek

Chickamauga

Chattanooga

Hale's Bar

Dale Hollow

Center Hill

Cumberland River

Nashville

Tennessee

Huntsville

Guntersville

Wheeler

Kentucky

Tennessee River

Pickwick Landing

Wilson

Muscle Shoals

50 Miles

50 Kilometers

0

0

674

sibility for tenants. Initially, many landlords got the agencies to assume that burden; later, the agencies shifted the burden back to the landlords. When they wanted to hire workers at low wages, landlords attacked relief programs as a threat to the farmer, though the agencies often paid less than prevailing wages in local communities. One landlord told a North Carolina welfare worker, "I don't like this welfare business. I can't do a thing with my niggers. They aren't beholden to me any more. They know you won't let them perish."

New Deal agencies seldom came into conflict with Jim Crow. Blacks had more trouble than whites getting direct or work relief, and they received less from the same programs. Blacks, who were much more likely than whites to be unemployed, received less than half of the relief funds, though they outnumbered whites on relief rolls 3 to 1. The CCC had racially segregated camps, disproportionately low enrollments of blacks, and no black supervisors. Later, under considerable pressure, the CCC altered its policies with respect to the last two matters. Public housing financed by federal money was segregated, but half of the total housing constructed in the South was for blacks. The Federal Housing Administration perpetuated and widened racial segregation in private housing, reinforcing the growing trend toward residential segregation. The TVA also followed the racial caste system. Some New Deal agencies did require certain percentages of blacks to be hired on federal construction projects. In doing so, they set precedents for racial hiring quotas for subsequent government programs.

Some New Deal programs discriminated unintentionally against blacks. When the industrial codes written under the National Recovery Administration (NRA), which was created by the National Industrial Recovery Act in 1933, raised manufacturing wages, thousands of blacks lost industrial jobs to whites. Already victimized by rising unemployment in domestic services and in agriculture, their principal sources for employment, blacks expressed their bitterness with the NRA by labeling it the "Negro Removal Administration." New Deal farm programs also victimized blacks. Disproportionately represented among sharecroppers and tenants, blacks suffered disproportionately from the crop-limitation efforts of the New Deal.

The New Deal did little to rehabilitate the rural poor, who paid high personal prices for the federal farm programs. Neither the Farm Security Administration (FSA) nor its predecessor, the Resettlement Administration, had enough money or staff to go beyond meager first steps toward resettlement communities, land use planning, and the transformation of more able tenants into landowning family farmers. The FSA, for example, made rehabilitation loans to only 15,000 farmers at a time when the number of tenant farmers in the southern states numbered nearly 2 million.

Despite the most sweeping government farm program in American history, much of southern agriculture in 1940 was still characterized by small cultivation units, too little diversification, low earnings, and poor living standards. On the average, farmers harvested fewer than thirty-five acres, and fewer than 10 percent had either a tractor or a truck. They had diversified their output modestly but had hardly increased their livestock holdings. Earnings remained low. Per capita *gross* annual earnings from 1924 to 1937 averaged $162 for farm people in Arkansas, Louisiana, Tennessee, Mississippi, Alabama, Georgia, and North and South Carolina. Earnings averaged $381 in the rest of the country. Living standards among farmers also had changed little by 1940. Too many families lived in poor housing without running water or any modern conveniences. A farm with a telephone or a radio was as uncommon as a farm with electricity or access to an adequate school or even a paved road.

Yet few families left the farm. They had little choice. So in 1940 southerners were still more dependent on farming than other Americans. More than twice as many people in the South (39 percent) farmed for a living as in the remainder of the United States (15 percent). Only a massive demand for labor could alter that situation—the kind of demand that would be generated by a major war.

Still, farming in the South had not remained static during the 1930s. Farmers grew more hay, corn, oats, and peanuts. Soybeans had become an important crop. Most significant, the amount of cotton produced declined by one-half—a landmark in the history of the region. Major steps toward reforestation and better soil management had been taken. Other less dramatic but important changes had occurred. Like diversification, mechanization had increased somewhat, as had electricification, under the auspices of another New Deal agency, the Rural Electrification Administration (REA). About one-fifth of the farms in the region had electricity, an increase of 400 percent. The REA and the TVA accounted for most of this growth and laid the foundation for much greater expansion of rural electrification during and especially after World War II.

The Tenth Congressional District in Texas got electricity sooner than most. Thanks in large part to the explosive energies of Congressman Lyndon Johnson, electric power lines reached into distant corners of the district by 1940. Johnson had delivered on the promises he made Brian and Mary Sue Smith in 1937. He expected to be remembered at the polls, and he was; he easily won reelection to Congress in 1940.

*T*HE NEW DEAL AND SOUTHERN INDUSTRY

Like agriculture, industry did not remain static during the 1930s. And again the New Deal—assisted by market forces—played a formative role. Industry recovered slowly but more rapidly in the South than in the rest of the nation because of the predominance of nondurable consumer goods in southern manufacturing. By the end of the 1930s, industrial output in the region had returned to the highs of 1929, and total wages had climbed to within 10 percent of the 1929 level.

Industry also became more diversified during the Depression decade. Chemicals and paper led the way. The chemical industry developed or expanded major facilities in Louisiana, especially at Baton Rouge, along the gulf coast of Texas, at Hopewell, Virginia, and elsewhere. Innovations in chemical processing enlarged the range of paper products that could be made from the trees in southern forests, even from scrub pines and the waste from lumbering. Paper manufacturers invested $200 million in the South in the 1930s, locating plants in coastal areas that had long been economic backwaters.

Market forces, of course, had much to do with these and other changes that took place in the industrial South in the 1930s. So did the New Deal, directly and indirectly. Government spending poured enormous sums of money into a money-scarce economy. The Reconstruction Finance Corporation (RFC), for instance, lent funds to insolvent banks and financial institutions, insurance companies, and railroads. It also provided capital for government-owned corporations. Chaired by Texas millionaire Jesse Jones, a farm boy whose fortunes soared with Houston's, the RFC dispensed more than $10 billion to the nation in the 1930s. Jones saw that the South got its share, perhaps more. Government-assisted hydroelectric power development and rural electrification expanded energy sources for industrial growth. Federally funded public works, especially highway construction, enhanced opportunities for economic development.

But the New Deal may have had its greatest impact on the industrial South by its labor policy. The New Deal raised wages, set maximum hours, and encouraged unionization and collective bargaining. The New Deal initiated these policies as early as 1933, when the National Industrial Recovery Act was passed. That law sanctioned business self-regulation in order to stabilize production and employment and to help the economy recover.

Protected from antitrust litigation by the new law, industry groups, such as cotton textile manufacturers, devised industry-wide codes that limited production in order to bring output more in line with demand, set prices, established maximum hours and minimum wages, and abolished child labor. Section 7(a) of the act guaranteed the right of workers "to organize and bargain collectively through representation of their own choosing." The nation's cotton textile manufacturers became the first to adopt such a code, acting speedily in the hope of restoring solvency to the industry. The seriousness of the industry's plight was indicated by the concessions southern manufacturers made on wages and hours. They accepted large reductions in regional differences in wages and a shorter workweek, advantages they had long valued. They agreed to a minimum wage of $12 for a forty-hour week. Elsewhere it was $13. They also accepted a two-shift operation limit (a total of 80 hours). But southern mill managers, as they demonstrated subsequently, made no concessions to unionization and collective bargaining.

The NRA code had an immediate and in some ways a lasting impact on cotton textile manufacturing in the South. Business improved markedly after the code was in place. So did workers' earnings—those of workers who kept their jobs. Confronted by higher labor costs, companies countered by laying off workers and increasing the productivity of those they kept. The stretchout and the speedup reappeared or became more obvious. But these measures proved inadequate. After the initial surge, sales fell and inventories mounted. In December 1933 the NRA implemented a thirty-hour, two-shift workweek. The new limits remained in force for several months and reduced workers' earnings by a fourth. Manufacturers talked of reimposing the shorter week and cutting wages sometime in 1934. Workers responded by unionizing. By mid-1934 the United Textile Workers of America (UTW), an affiliate of the AFL, had more than 250,000 members, most of them in the South. Propelled by mounting frustration and anger over pay and working conditions, local union members initiated a general textile strike in Alabama and then persuaded the UTW to call a national strike for September.

The largest industrial strike in American history followed. During the months the strike lasted, perhaps 400,000 workers walked out from Alabama to Maine. Half the cotton mills in the South were shut down at one time or another. In some locales, every mill was closed. Workers divided among themselves; some of the divisions led to violence and bitter memories. At least seven strikers died in the South, two in New England. In general, government officials adopted promanagement positions. None went so far as Governor Eugene Talmadge of Georgia, who called out the state militia to arrest strikers and put them behind barbed wire at Fort McPherson in Atlanta. Reacting to Talmadge's "concentration camps" and other instances of harsh treatment of strikers, a prominent North Carolina Democrat expressed his concern for workers who were "forced in some mills to work long hours for compensation below proper sustenance....It makes me sick to see soldiers beat them down, even when they make demands greater than the industry can stand in days of weak demand for their goods."

In 1934 cotton manufacturers could do little to meet demands to increase hours and wages, and their swollen inventories allowed them to wait out strikers. Workers were very vulnerable, as was the UTW. Workers had few resources, financial or otherwise, to wage a protracted struggle. Most lived in company housing; they could be—and often were—evicted for strike or union activities. The UTW also lacked the funds and staff to carry on a long strike, particularly one of such unprecedented proportions.

The strike, which had begun with great enthusiasm, faltered in its second week, staggered in its third, and fell apart within a month. The union might have been more successful if it could have delayed the strike until economic conditions improved. But, as one union leader noted, the "strike was the result of an emotional wave that could not have been stopped by God himself." For years thereafter, textile union officials and organizers heard about the Great Strike. "The big argument all over the South was, 'Lord, we don't want to get into that Union and have happen to us what they did to our mothers and fathers in 1934.' "

Such memories probably contributed to labor's limited success in organizing southern textile workers in the late 1930s, during World War II, and in the decades thereafter. That limited success contrasted with labor's triumphs elsewhere. From 1935 to 1945, organized labor enjoyed its greatest growth in American history. Membership among nonfarm workers rose from 3.6 million to 14.3

(38.5 percent of nonfarm workers). The South shared in that growth, though by the 1960s the proportion of southern workers who were organized was half the rate in the remainder of the nation, and the proportions of unionized workers in the South varied widely by industry.

Clearly, many workers in the south joined labor unions; clearly, most textile workers did not. The largest, most important manufacturing industry in the South was still largely nonunion. That left organized labor with a critical weakness in a major region in the United States. That weakness had broad implications for the economy and the political life of the South.

What is not so clear is why unions failed so dismally in the textile South. Several factors may account for this failure. Nineteen-thirty-four left bitter memories and damaged the credibility of unions and unionism among southern textile workers. Probably the most important factor was the nature of the textile industry—highly competitive, labor-intensive. Such an industry was bound to be especially hostile to organized labor. Unable to pass along increased labor costs to its customers, the besieged industry fought unionism by fair means and foul—and usually with success, even during the boom days of unionization.

The large pool of unskilled and semiskilled labor in the South gave management a great advantage. It could readily replace strikers and union activists. Moreover, the agricultural crisis of the 1930s and New Deal farm policies expanded that pool of labor. Other New Deal programs reduced the numbers of the unemployed, but not so quickly as their numbers were growing. Other factors may have contributed to the overall failure to unionize textiles in the South. Analysts have pointed to the dependence that life in mill villages supposedly

PERCENTAGE OF UNIONIZED WORKERS IN THE SOUTH, 1962, BY INDUSTRY

Industry	Percent
Primary metal	95
Petroleum and coal products	88
Transportation equipment	86
Rubber products	81
Paper and allied products	79
Electrical machinery and equipment	73
Tobacco products	72
Stone, clay, and glass products	65
Chemicals and allied products	62
Printing and publishing	61
Fabricated meta	54
Apparel	30
Furniture and fixtures	28
Lumber and wood products	27
Textile mill products	14

SOURCE: F. Ray Marshall, *Labor in the South* (Cambridge, Mass.: Harvard University Press, 1967), p. 317. Reprinted by permission of Harvard University Press.

created in workers, the otherworldly quality of much of the religious life of the workers, the cultural tradition of individualism and deference, the promanagement policies of government officials, the perceptions of union officials as outsiders, and the quality of textile union leadership in the 1930s.

The Great Strike may have left more than bitter memories and a dismal legacy for unionism. By reacting so strongly to cuts in their earnings in 1933 and 1934, textile workers may have helped ensure that the minimum wage and maximum hours established by the NRA became permanent standards, even after the U.S. Supreme Court declared that the NRA was unconstitutional. Most businesspeople welcomed the end of the NRA and its codes.

Southern employers had a special grievance against the NRA: it narrowed regional differences in wages. They assumed that smaller differences in wages, which remained even after the NRA had been abolished, weakened their competitive position in relation to New England textile firms. But the New England industry, burdened by lax management, old plants and machinery, and somewhat higher labor costs, continued its decline and virtually collapsed during the 1930s. Some of the larger of the New England companies moved south. In the decade after the Depression began, textile employment in New England declined to about 80,000 workers, a loss of some 40,000 jobs. Textile employment in the South grew by a comparable amount, to a total of more than 300,000 jobs. That growth was, of course, too small to accommodate the thousands of southerners who needed an alternative to farming. At the same time, bankruptcies and mergers significantly reduced the number of textile companies operating in the South. Still, the industry remained one of the most competitive in the country. It also faced what it believed was a grave challenge from a new source, Japan. Southern textile leaders acted as if they had sighted a typhoon. In alarm they turned to Washington and persuaded the government to restrict imports of Japanese textiles. They overreacted. Japanese textile manufacturers lacked the capacity to export much to the United States in the 1930s. We should note, however, that even the modest amount of textiles imported into this country exceeded exports of American textiles.

Southern employers had an even greater grievance with another legacy of the NRA. In 1935 Congress revived the collective bargaining portion of the NRA by passing the National Labor Relations (Wagner) Act. The Wagner Act probably had the effect of raising wages because it gave unions a powerful legal and psychological tool for getting and staying organized. The relationship between unionization and wages is often disputed. Numerous studies show clearly that organized and unorganized employees in the same industry have similar earnings. Therefore, some observers conclude that unionization has no impact on wages. But it is impossible to determine what the unorganized workers would earn if there were no pressure from unions. After World War II, for instance, the textile industry often increased wages and benefits for its workers as a preventive measure against unionization. Studies do show clearly that unions have often prevented cuts in their members' wages and thus have helped create a floor for wages.

New Deal assaults on low wages went beyond the NRA and the Wagner Act. The Fair Labor Standards Act (FLSA), passed by Congress in 1938, set maximum hours and minimum wages and forbade child labor. Again certain standards were put in place and established important precedents, though many workers did not initially enjoy the protection of the new law. Domestic workers and farm laborers were excluded, and some regional wage differentials were tolerated. To a large extent, these provisions represented concessions made to southern Democrats, without whose support the act could not have been passed. New Deal work-relief programs, especially the WPA, eventually adopted a policy similar to the minimum wage. For instance, the WPA initially based the wages it paid its workers on the wage rates that prevailed in the local area. By 1938 the WPA shifted from this "prevailing wage" policy to one that reduced regional wage differentials considerably.

CRACKS IN THE SOLID SOUTH

The legislative battle over the FLSA revealed the growing dissatisfaction of many southern Democrats with the New Deal, with Roosevelt, and with the national Democratic party. Southern Democrats had given Roosevelt and the New Deal, including the Wagner Act, strong support until 1936. The South had benefited considerably from the New Deal. Seemingly content, southern Democrats joined in the campaign to reelect the president and, coincidentally, accepted a major change in the nominating procedure for Democratic presidential candidates. During their 1936 national nominating convention, the Democrats repealed the requirement that their presidential nominee had to receive a two-thirds vote of the convention, a provision that had substantially enhanced the power of factions or sections, such as the South, in the nominating process. The rule had also resulted in deadlocked conventions. In 1924 the Democrats had sweltered through 103 ballots before they could choose a presidential candidate.

Party harmony at the Democratic convention lapsed at least once, however, for a few revealing minutes. South Carolina Senator Ellison D. "Cotton Ed" Smith walked out when a black minister stood to give an invocation. Later, during his campaign to be reelected to the Senate in 1938, Smith told and retold a carefully rehearsed version of the event. "[When a] slew-footed, blue-gummed, kinky-headed Senegambian...started praying,...I started walking, and as I...walked...it seemed to me that old John Calhoun leaned down from his mansion in the sky and whispered...you did right, Ed."

Smith's walkout showed how quickly southern Democrats could react to any challenge to their preconceptions. His actions also reflected a growing restiveness among southern Democrats who perceived their party becoming "northernized," urban, non-Protestant, and prolabor. Important southern Democrats began reluctantly to conclude that Roosevelt and the New Deal were converting the national Democratic party into the party of northern liberalism. Their restiveness intensified markedly in late 1936, after Roosevelt had been reelected, when a number of unions affiliated with the Congress of Industrial Organizations (CIO) adopted the militant tactic of the sit-down strike. Instead of walking out when a strike was announced, workers stopped working and stayed where they were, blocking any effort to turn their machines over to strikebreakers. With food and other supplies brought by supporters and hauled up through the windows, they could stay there for weeks. The president remained aloof while others worried that the sit-ins constituted a massive assault on the sanctity of private property and the beginnings of a revolution. Prominent southern Democrats broke with President Roosevelt because of his failure to oppose the sit-down strikes.

That break widened in 1937, when the president attempted to overhaul the U.S. Supreme Court with his "Court-packing" plan. Fearful that the elderly conservatives on the Supreme Court were going to undo the New Deal, Roosevelt tried to alter the makeup of the Court by increasing the number of justices, or "packing" the Court. Southern opponents of the scheme had several motives. Most were inclined to the concepts of states' rights and limited government. They saw the Supreme Court, largely secure from the winds of political change and shifts in public opinion, as a bulwark for such things as Jim Crow. Finally, they used their opposition to the Court plan as an indirect means of expressing their growing reservations about particular New Deal programs and about Franklin Roosevelt. Those reservations grew and were more openly expressed as the country fell into the severe recession of 1937–1938, a slump that demonstrated that the "magic" of the New Deal recovery was ephemeral at best.

Most southern leaders liked the New Deal farm programs. New Deal relief programs and attacks on low wages, however, got a much more mixed reception. Southern political leaders knew that the human needs that relief programs addressed were real and that many workers' wages were far too low, but these New Deal programs created a dilemma for them. Recipients of relief, if they could and did vote, remembered the politician who supported relief measures. So did the beneficiaries of higher wages and shorter hours. But so did employers, who had very different interests and whose ranks included thousands of farmers.

New Deal policies also threatened the basic strategy the South used to industrialize and diversify its economy. The South had historically relied on a strategy of cheap labor, as measured in wages, for economic growth and development. Relief programs and laws establishing a minimum wage and maximum hours endangered this approach by raising the floor for wages, if only modestly in some instances, and by reducing labor's dependency on employers. Cotton Ed Smith attacked the FLSA as an attempt to raise wages in South Carolina to equal those of New England despite the lower living costs in South Carolina. "Why...don't some of these people call in God and tell Him that He must stop this thing of making one section more advantageous than another."

Southern leaders successfully defended some of their regional advantage in cheap labor. New Deal legislation and policy generally favored the regional wage differential, though sometimes they narrowed it. Self-interest, of course, figured prominently in this battle. The South's low wages obviously benefited employers, some of whom were major forces in politics. Conversely, those wages harmed northern employers and organized workers, most of whom were outside the South.

But more than narrow self-interest was involved. Needing desperately to diversify its economy much more than it had already done, the South had little alternative in the 1930s to an emphasis on low wages, its greatest advantage as a region in its struggle for economic development. Southern leaders reacted hostilely to any real or imagined threat to this advantage. They included damn yankees in their indictments of labor unions. Northern competitors, so the argument went, encouraged attempts to organize southern workers in the hope of raising wages and thus undermining the South's most important competitive advantage. Predictably, the FLSA received strong support from labor unions and northern political and business leaders. It was, one observer declared, "a sectional bill disguised as a humanitarian reform."

Sectionalism reared its head in other economic matters. None got greater publicity than freight rates. Those rates, which were regulated by the Interstate Commerce Commission (ICC), favored the shipment of semiprocessed raw materials out of the South and the flow of manufactured goods into the region. Convinced that the South was being victimized by a domestic version of mercantilism designed to keep the southern economy in a subordinate or "colonial" position, southern leaders mounted a concerted attack to alter the rates. The actual economic impact of differential freight rates is hard to determine. Apparently they had some effect, but not as much as southern leaders claimed. Still the issue served a number of uses. It provided a means for venting sectional feelings and a way to put some of the blame for economic conditions in the South on others while deflecting attention from the serious internal economic weaknesses of the region. The struggle over freight rates also touched very deep emotions in the South, particularly its defensiveness vis-à-vis the rest of the nation and its sense that it was unfairly treated. Those emotions found expression in the parallel and widely held notion that the South was an economic colony of the North. Though the "colonial economy" concept had serious analytical deficiencies, it had a powerful appeal. After a five-year effort led by southern governors, the ICC altered the freight rate structure in 1939. The Southern Governors' Conference evolved from this struggle, a lasting product of the freight rate battles.

New Deal relief measures also stirred sectional feelings. These sentiments became more pronounced after 1936 as more southern Democrats began openly to criticize federal relief programs. Convinced, despite the serious recession of 1937–1938, that the worst of the Depression was over, they saw less need for such programs as the WPA than for a tax cut for business to stimulate economic activity. They worried about creating a welfare state and an expanded federal bureaucracy and about adding to the federal deficit. Southern Democrats believed, correctly, that more federal relief money went to the cities than to rural areas, and that the money was more likely to go to the North than to the South.

Southern Democrats charged favoritism by the federal government but ignored offsetting factors. The South got more money from the federal government for agricultural programs than the North did, and because its incomes were lower, the South paid less in federal taxes. Race, as usual, also figured in the controversy over federal relief. Southern Democrats believed, again correctly, that federal relief efforts attracted black voters to the national Democratic party. They especially feared that northern Democrats would become too dependent on black voters. Conversely, southern Democrats thought that federal welfare measures would make blacks less dependent on whites for labor, and therefore would cause wages to rise in the South and hurt southern employers, particularly farmers.

Not all southern Democrats broke with the New Deal after 1936. The great majority of southerners who liked the New Deal were devoted to Franklin Roosevelt, the president they believed cared about them. Both Lister Hill of Alabama and Claude Pepper of Florida, for instance, strongly supported the New Deal, and both won Senate seats in 1938, Pepper for his second term. Alben Barkley of Kentucky, another New Deal loyalist, also won reelection with an assist from President Roosevelt. The president had less success with his highly publicized efforts to defeat two opponents in the Senate. Walter F. George of Georgia and Cotton Ed Smith had signed the "Conservative Manifesto," a document drafted and released in July 1938 by conservatives in the Senate. Of the ten signers, five were southern Democrats. The other three were Harry F. Byrd and Carter Glass of Virginia and Josiah W. Bailey of North Carolina. The manifesto called for tax reductions to encourage investment, a balanced budget, an end to sit-down strikes as a violation of private property and the right of workers to work, support of private enterprise, and "the vigorous maintenance of States' rights, home rule and local self-government."

Senators George and Smith won handily despite the president's campaign efforts against them. They were particularly effective at portraying the president as an intruder in the affairs of their states. Smith summoned up memories of federal intervention during Reconstruction. He claimed he was acting in the spirit of Wade Hampton and Robert E. Lee, and he repeatedly recited the story of his triumphant march out of the national Democratic convention in defense of white supremacy. After Smith won, a university professor wrote a colleague in South Carolina that he knew his friend was "rejoicing that States' rights, white supremacy, Bourbonism, low wages, long hours, and the right to ignorance, prejudice and superstition are no longer in jeopardy in S.C."

Although Roosevelt had not been completely routed in his efforts to align the Democratic party more closely with the New Deal, the defeats in Georgia and South Carolina were well publicized and were interpreted as indicating that southern Democrats who opposed the New Deal could be neither changed nor defeated. Thereafter, powerful southern Democrats appeared to work so closely with Republicans that a bipartisan coalition was thought to be a major force in American politics.

JIM CROW: AN UNCERTAIN FUTURE

The racial caste system faced growing though oblique challenges in the 1930s. Attacks came from several quarters, the most threatening from within the Democratic party, from blacks, and, to a lesser degree, from southern whites. Those challenges became serious enough by 1940 to make the future of Jim Crow somewhat uncertain for the first time in the twentieth century.

That the Democratic party became a threat to Jim Crow was ironic. Since the Civil War the South had relied on that party to defend its peculiar system of race relations. The solid South's defenses faltered during the 1930s as black voters shifted their allegiance to the Democrats. This development was very important because the Great Migration had shifted large numbers of blacks to cities outside the South, and there they voted. In 1936 probably more than 70 percent of the blacks who went to the polls supported Franklin Roosevelt. They did so despite the very mixed blessings bestowed on them by the New Deal and despite Roosevelt's inconsistent support of their interests. Still, mixed blessings, inconsistencies, and all, the federal government did more for American blacks under Roosevelt than it had done since the Emancipation Proclamation and Reconstruction.

Convinced that the Republicans had ignored them for years and grateful to Roosevelt and the New Deal, blacks left the party of Abraham Lincoln in droves. They quickly made their presence felt in the Democratic party. In 1934 Chicago sent the first black Democrat to Congress, and black voters provided the margin for Democratic victories in Pennsylvania and Louisville, both Republican strongholds. The number of black faces at Democratic conventions increased, including some from Kentucky and West Virginia in 1936.

Roosevelt, who had not shown particular concern for blacks when he was governor of New York, had altered course as president. He had a "black cabinet"—blacks who held high-ranking (but noncabinet) positions in his administration. This group included Mary McLeod Bethune, founder and president of Bethune-Cookman College; the economist Robert C. Weaver, who in 1966 became the first black to hold an official cabinet post when Lyndon Johnson appointed him secretary of housing; and the political scientist Ralph Bunche, who won the Nobel Peace Prize in 1950 for his efforts as a United Nations mediator in the Middle East.

Roosevelt also appointed southern whites who by the standards of the day were liberals on racial issues. The most prominent were Will Alexander and Aubrey Williams. Formerly a Methodist minister with roots in Missouri and Tennessee, Alexander helped found the Commission on Interracial Cooperation and directed it for a long time. He worked under Roosevelt in the Resettlement Administration and then in the Farm Security Administration. Williams, an Alabamian, was a social worker who held positions with the WPA and the National Youth Administration. Alexander and Williams became two of the most forceful and persistent defenders of the rights and interests of blacks and the poor in general.

Williams worked closely at times with Eleanor Roosevelt. The president's wife publicly and repeatedly defended the rights of blacks and decried racial discrimination. In doing so, she attracted severe criticism from southern whites and the lasting devotion of blacks. The president shared her concerns, but he had to be more cautious, as he had to work closely with powerful southern Democrats in Congress. Thus he refused to give federal antilynching bills his full endorsement because southern Democrats vigorously opposed such measures. Still, he did nothing to restrain his wife's activities on behalf of civil rights.

The president was caught in a dilemma that entrapped many American politicians. If they defended the rights of blacks, they risked offending whites, especially *but not only* in the South. If they failed to defend the rights of blacks, they risked offending blacks and losing their votes. Black votes in the South had been critically important to the Republicans after the Civil War. Black votes in the North became critically important to the Democrats when blacks switched to the party of Franklin Roosevelt. The number of black voters outside the South soared in the 1930s. Without blacks' shift in allegiance and their increasing eagerness to register and vote, the solid South would have remained secure for many more years, perhaps indefinitely.

Southern blacks also had a hand in shaking the foundations of the solid South during the 1930s—some by leaving, some by staying and becoming more active in politics. Perhaps 400,000 blacks left the South during the decade. Many became voters. At the same time, blacks who remained in the South became more active politically, especially in urban areas. Even modest increases in registering and voting had some impact, particularly in such border states as Kentucky, West Virginia, and Missouri. Black candidates won local offices in North Carolina in 1936, one in Raleigh and one in Durham. Public services for blacks improved in Miami and Tampa. Here and there, police and fire departments added blacks to their forces. Still, the scope of this new black political activism in the South was very limited. In 1940 only about 250,000 of the more than 4 million people in the old Confederate states who voted in the presidential election were black.

Still, whites worried. An official in Macon, Georgia, feared that "the ignorant class of white people we have got in Georgia" might form a political coalition with blacks. Happily, they were "violent nigger haters" who would probably be repelled by such an alliance. An official in Greenville, South Carolina, revealed that his county had been having "a lot of trouble about niggers registering." The "churches and preachers and the school and all kinds of organizations," a Charleston voter registrar explained, "are after them about their rights." A Montgomery registrar explained her reluctance to register blacks this way: "All niggers—educated and uneducated—have one idea back in their mind—that they want equality....It is necessary to keep the Negro from voting, for voting would lead to social equality." Yet Montgomery leaders tolerated "token registration" by "the upper ranks of Negro society," since the white primary preserved white supremacy in politics. The Democratic party was, according to party officials, "a private party, like a social club...it is for white people."

The increases in political activism by blacks reflected some important changes among southern blacks—most of all, a lessening of their dependence on whites and their growth in self-confidence. The third generation of blacks who had never been slaves was coming of age. For the first time in their history, less than half of the blacks in the South lived and worked on farms. Most had family members and friends who lived outside the South and were doing better. While black families in the South earned one-third to one-half what white families did, a tiny upper class of blacks had established itself, as had a slightly larger middle class, which included a growing number of professionals. Blacks had created and now sustained vigorous institutions—schools, churches, and fraternal orders. They had achieved much against terrible odds, and they wanted more.

So in the late 1930s the NAACP focused its attention on educational inequalities, one of the strongest of the deliberately constructed barriers against the efforts of blacks to improve themselves. The barriers they assaulted were high. In 1935–1936, the expenditures of ten southern states averaged $13.09 per black student and $37.87 per white student. (Nationally, expenditures per student averaged $67.88 in 1936.) Black teachers earned about 40 percent of what white teachers earned. High schools for blacks were still rare. No public institution in the South offered graduate or professional training for blacks.

Thanks in large part to the work of the NAACP, the gap between the salaries of black and white teachers was narrowed. Otherwise, the gap between expenditures for black and white education remained. The NAACP also succeeded in breaching Jim Crow in higher education, and at the same reopened the issue of the constitutionality of "separate but equal" for the first time since 1896. The courts ordered law schools at the University of Maryland (1936) and the University of Missouri (1938) to admit black applicants because both states had provided law schools for whites but not for blacks and thus were in violation of the equal protection clause of the Fourteenth Amendment to the Constitution ("No State shall make or enforce any law which shall abridge the privileges or immunities of the citizens of the United States...; nor deny to any person within its jurisdiction the equal protection of the laws"). In the Missouri case (*Missouri ex. rel. Gaines* v. *Canada*), the Supreme Court suggested for the first time that the "separate but equal" doctrine might not be secure. Although the Court found nothing legally wrong with the doctrine, it did imply that the courts ought to consider whether "separate but equal" was obtainable. If not, one could infer that "separate but equal" failed the equal protection clause and thus was unconstitutional.

Indeed, before the *Gaines* case the Court had shown a growing inclination, as one legal expert wrote, to use the due process clause for "protecting black men from oppressive and unequal treatment by whites." Beginning in 1925, the justices had ruled that defendants had a right to a trial free from an atmosphere of hysteria and intimidation. Then, in rulings involving the notorious Scottsboro rape case (1931), the court decided that due process in capital cases required that defendants have competent counsel and that the juries in such cases could not be selected by a process that systematically excluded blacks.

Another, more subtle indication that the foundation on which Jim Crow rested was becoming increasingly shaky can be seen in the behavior of southern whites. Subtle changes in attitudes were becoming apparent. Many southern whites, while accepting Jim Crow, rejected its more brutish versions and openly sought to do away with them. The numbers and the outspokenness of such people increased significantly during the 1930s. Just as important, they shifted their positions on Jim Crow. Some of them had their initiation in racial liberalism in the home mission societies of their churches, in the YMCA or YWCA, or in the Commission on Interracial Cooperation. In none of the interracial contacts or educational programs on race relations they sponsored did these organizations challenge racial segregation—probably the only reasonable course, given the times in which they operated. Still, the antilynching campaign organized by the Interracial Commission seems to have had a real impact. Encouraged by Will Alexander, then head of the commission, Jessie Daniel Ames launched the Association of Southern Women for the Prevention of Lynching (ASWPL) in 1930. The ASWPL's campaign undermined the principal justification for lynching: the defense of southern womanhood. Its members, 43,000 strong, succeeded in getting more public officials and leaders to take an open stand against lynching. At least one study indicates that those efforts had an impact. Happily, for whatever reasons, the incidence of lynchings in the South declined from 21 in 1930 to 5 in 1940 and remained very low thereafter.

The Southern Conference for Human Welfare (SCHW, 1938–1948) edged closer to an open break with Jim Crow. Composed of southern New Dealers and New Deal sympathizers, the SCHW drew politicians, journalists, academics, union leaders and activists, and reformers of various stripes, black and white. The SCHW's most concrete action was a vigorous but unsuccessful assault on the poll tax. That attack alarmed most southern politicians. According to Virginia Durr, the Birmingham native who led the antipoll tax campaign,

> Southern congressmen were just terrified of the race issue. They immediately translated the fight against the poll tax into the race issue. The Negro had no rights, couldn't vote, had no power whatever. The unions were coming South and some of them were integrated. White Southerners thought that getting rid of the poll tax would give all these people the right to vote—the unions and the Negroes and all these new labor people. The world would turn over. Cheap labor was the great selling point of the South. Every Southern state, every chamber of commerce, and every corporation thought the way to make the South prosperous was cheap labor.

When a delegation of white women tried to get a senator from the deep South to support repeal of the poll tax, Durr recalled that he exploded in anger: "I know what you women want—black men laying on you!"

Organized labor did represent a challenge to Jim Crow, though hardly a consistent challenge. Most of the unions affiliated with the AFL practiced Jim Crow, excluding blacks altogether or keeping them in the most menial positions. To protect the jobs of white members, the railroad brotherhoods had become virtually lily-white. Most of the black porters who worked the dining cars and sleeping cars on the railroads belonged to an AFL affiliate, the Brotherhood of Pullman Car Porters. The CIO, which was founded in 1937, welcomed black members and had some black officers—a factor in its rapid growth in some industries. Local CIO unions, however, frequently ignored the national union's biracial policy: racial discrimination and exclusion were not unusual in CIO locals in the South. Communist-led unions had long had a policy of desegregation, but as their following was small, that policy had little effect on blacks.

If the challenges to Jim Crow made its future less certain in 1940, they did no more than that. No one could have foreseen the enormous impact World War II would have on the racial caste system of the South, or on almost every aspect of southern life.

WORLD WAR II

World War II brought more rapid and greater change to the South than it had experienced since the Civil War. In 1945 the economy of the South differed significantly from that of 1940, Jim Crow was threatened, and the cracks in the solid South had become increasingly difficult to plaster over. Cotton, segregation, and one-party politics (Democratic, in this instance), the three pillars of the post-Reconstruction South, were in grave danger.

The war led the federal government to spend unprecedented sums in the region. It invested more than $7 billion on military bases and industrial plants in the South. Industry received another billion from private sources. Of the income payments in the region, which increased by 250 percent during the war, the federal government provided one-fourth. Thus the war, with its massive deficit spending, did what the New Deal could not do: it brought jobs, money, and renewed hope. Many southerners enjoyed prosperity for the first time in twenty years.

The South received a disproportionate share of military bases. Weather, readily available open spaces, and the power of southern congressional delegations probably accounted for that. After the war, many of those bases were expanded and made permanent. The prevalence of military personnel and retirees in the South since 1945 can be traced directly to World War II.

Still, the South received less than its share of government investment in war plants. Southern congressmen and senators charged regional discrimination, but it was historical circumstances rather than sectionalism that accounted for this disparity. Investment in war plants tended to go to places where industry was already strong. Production of military vehicles, for instance, was concentrated in the industrial Midwest, where automobile and truck production was

JOBS, WORLD WAR II (Library of Congress)

well established. Still, the number of production workers in the South more than doubled, to almost 3 million.

Ordnance plants were closed after the war ended, as few of them could be converted to other uses; but one ordnance operation became a permanent fixture. Built to process uranium for atomic bombs, Oak Ridge, a spin-off of TVA located near Knoxville, Tennessee, required 110,000 workers during its construction and 82,000 during its peak production period in 1945. Extractive industries received much heavier investments than did electrical machinery or vehicle manufacturing or steel and iron milling. Important, lasting investments were made in petrochemicals and other chemicals, oil pipelines, aluminum and tin milling, and shipyards and shipbuilding. Developments in shipbuilding were particularly noticeable, especially at Newport News and Norfolk, Charleston, Tampa, Mobile, Pascagoula, New Orleans, and Houston. These developments along the coast indicated a significant change in the geography of industrial and urban growth in the South. The coastal regions thus regained some of the ground they had lost to the interior after 1865. Similar though smaller developments occurred in aircraft manufacturing. Areas along the gulf coast received a disproportionate share of the new industrial capacity, with Texas leading the way by a wide margin, followed by Louisiana and Alabama.

Many of these gains remained in place after World War II. The industrial capacity of the region was estimated to have grown 40 percent; from 1939 to

1929 STRIKE OF MILL WORKERS, GASTONIA, NORTH CAROLINA (AP/Wide World Photos)

1947, value added from the industry of the region soared from $3 billion to $10.7 billion. The ranks of production workers had grown by almost 50 percent during the same period, from 1.3 million to 2 million. Personal income in the South rose almost two and a half times in five years, from $13.6 billion to $32.1 billion. Per capita income increased from about 59 percent of the national average to 69 percent, the biggest gain the South had ever made. After the war personal income would continue to rise faster in the South than in the rest of the nation.

Some of the changes in the southern economy reflected deliberate policy choices by the federal government. The government continued its assault on low wages in the South by the way it implemented the Fair Labor Standards Act and through the National War Labor Board, a wartime agency. Washington's encouragement of unionization contributed to the substantial growth of organized labor in the South. Federal support may have made possible the organization of oil and chemical workers in the South during World War II. The Roosevelt administration selected the southwestern gulf coast for the site of most of the production facilities of an important new industry, synthetic rubber, and the federal government financed the construction of those facilities. The growth of metal fabrication plants in the Southwest was also a result of conscious government policy, as was the development of aircraft manufacturing and shipbuilding in the South during the war. The Southwest—Texas, Louisiana, Oklahoma, and Arkansas—led all the regions of the United States in the growth of manufacturing during World War II.

At the same time, the Tennessee Valley Authority made a major change in course. Initially it had concentrated on generating electric power, controlling floods, improving river navigation, and producing fertilizer. These activities reflected the TVA's policy of moderate improvement of the economy and life of the region it served, rather than basic changes that might result in new industries and more and better-paying jobs. In 1942, however, the TVA began to seek new manufacturing industries for its region.

Tragically, little attention was given to the major victims of the federal government's assault on low wages: the people who for one reason or another were not qualified to hold jobs that paid better. They lost their jobs. As long as the war lasted, their plight was eased somewhat by opportunities to serve in the military and by a shortage of farm labor. After the war, they found themselves isolated from the new prosperity, from jobs, from any meaningful place in American society, South or North.

Willingly and unwillingly, perhaps one-fourth of the people in the South moved inside or outside the region. More than 4 million southerners served in the armed forces; more than 3 million left the rural South, a decline of more than 20 percent; 2 million blacks left the South altogether. At the same time, more than 6 million nonsoutherners invaded the region, most to serve in the military, some in civilian capacities. Unlike the invaders of the 1860s, they were friendly though not uncritical forces. Enemy prisoners of war joined the inmigration. Some 277,000 of the 372,000 captured Germans imprisoned in the United States were held in the South. German POWs praised the physical beauty of the South and reported the region to be generally prosperous. Nazis though they might be, however, they joined with American nonsoutherners in condemning the mistreatment of blacks. Conscripted as farm laborers, often as cotton pickers, many of the captured Germans developed a keen appreciation for the hard work blacks did.

Civilians migrated to take advantage of the extraordinary employment opportunities the war created. They left agriculture, though farm wages doubled and even tripled during the war. Perhaps 4 million women were gainfully employed in the South in 1940; perhaps 5 million held jobs in 1945, and more of them were married, middle-aged, and mothers. Black women fled domestic service. Their flight may have prompted one of the more exotic rumors of the war. Despite the absence of any firm evidence, stories of "Eleanor [Roosevelt] Clubs" blossomed in profusion. These organizations of black domestics supposedly intended to place "a white woman in every kitchen." A jocular Tennessean observed that though white women in the South might not feel themselves personally threatened by Hitler, they "certainly recognized what a crisis the loss of a cook is."

Job seekers and military bases and industrial plants triggered unprecedented urban growth. Mobile's population nearly doubled. Public services fal-

WOMEN WELDERS, WORLD WAR II (Erik Overbey Collection, University of South Alabama Archives)

tered badly. Some schools operated in double shifts, and still classrooms were overcrowded. Waterless faucets were not uncommon, nor were queues outside movie theaters and diners. Virtually any enclosed space could be rented for housing. Crime, delinquency, and prostitution increased. Conditions in Norfolk became so bad that journalists nominated it for the title of "Our Worst War Town." Finally, after Congress investigated, the citizens of Norfolk made concerted efforts to deal with the problems.

People who stayed on the farm enjoyed good times, better than farmers in the South had enjoyed in a generation. Net farm income in the region tripled between 1940 and 1944, but the per capita net income of farmers in the South was still considerably less than of other American farmers, $454 compared with $530. The number of mules decreased; the number of trucks, tractors, and automobiles increased. More farms had running water, telephones, and electricity. Electricity, which had reached fewer than one farm in five in the South in 1940, reached almost one in three in 1945. The Rural Electrification Administration and the Tennessee Valley Authority had much to do with that growth. The number of tenants and sharecroppers declined significantly and the number of farm owners expanded somewhat.

These changes reflected a crucial development in southern agriculture: the steady flow of large amounts of capital into farming and the marked decline in the availability of farm labor. That circumstance created an unusual need and an unusual opportunity. Southern farmers had to turn to less labor-intensive, more capital-intensive agriculture. More than ever before, they could afford to diversify and mechanize their operations. Peanut and soybean production doubled. The output of rice and sugar cane increased. Dairy farming, however, grew only modestly. Cattle and pig raising, as well as truck and fruit farming, grew faster, but not as much as had been predicted. Tobacco farmers, though they continued their largely unmechanized methods, had never had better times; the demand for tobacco, especially for cigarettes, soared, and so did prices.

Most farmers in the South still relied heavily on cotton, and that reliance persisted through World War II. About half of all farm income in the South came from cotton, which remained the principal cash crop of almost half of the farmers in the region. During the war King Cotton rewarded them more generously than he had for a long time as cotton prices more than doubled. In response to wartime demand, American manufacturers absorbed almost all the cotton American farmers grew. Some southerners must have thought that the cotton South was returning to its best days.

But there were clear indications that cotton prosperity was going to be a wartime phenomenon for most growers and that the nature of cotton farming was continuing to undergo fundamental changes that had long-term implications. Carry-overs—the unsold cotton carried over from one crop year to be sold in the next—provided a telling clue. Despite strong demand for cotton, the carry-overs of cotton remained virtually unchanged from 1939 to 1945. Domestic demand was likely to decline after the war (as in fact it did). Renewed access to foreign markets would only partially offset this decline. Cotton growers also faced growing competition from foreign producers, primarily those in Brazil, China, and India, and from synthetic fibers, primarily rayon, but also nylon, a recently developed product. Total national output rose to as much as 10 million bales a year, but the amount of cotton acreage declined by more than 20 percent, from 22.8 million acres in 1939 to 17.6 in 1945. Yield per acre had risen significantly. A major factor in that increase was the continuation of cotton's westward march into heavily mechanized, irrigated lands in Texas, Arizona, and California. Moreover, even after 1943, when the government removed its restrictions on the number of acres that could be planted in cotton, total cotton acreage did not increase because of labor shortages and the availability of more profitable alternatives.

These developments, which had strong roots in the Depression and the New Deal, clearly indicated that Dixie was not necessarily the land of cotton. Another crucial development was graphically demonstrated by the International Harvester Company in the fall of 1944. While 2,500 people looked on at the Hopson Brothers Plantation outside Clarksdale, Mississippi, mechanical pickers harvested 1,000 pounds of cotton each an hour, about the amount that required fifty to sixty adult males to pick in the same time. Thus the threat of massive displacement confronted thousands of tenants, sharecroppers, and farmworkers. The prospect was particularly grim for blacks, because they were disproportionately represented in these groups. Mechanical cotton pickers were not so rapidly adopted in the postwar years as many people had anticipated, however. High purchasing and operating costs delayed adoption of the pickers.

Jim Crow faced more immediate threats during World War II. The most serious was a change in the attitudes of blacks. Howard Odum observed, "It was as if some universal message had come through to the great mass of negroes, urging them to dream new dreams and to protest against the old order." "By the way, Captain," a black sharecropper remarked to his employer soon after the attack on Pearl Harbor, "I hear the Japs done declared war on you white folks." Between 1940 and 1946 the NAACP grew from a membership of 50,556 in 355 branches to nearly 450,000 in 1,073 branches: the NAACP had a grass-roots following for the first time in its history. Here and there blacks challenged segregation in public facilities. In 1944, at the invitation of the University of North Carolina Press, a group of black leaders produced a collection of essays, *What the Negro Wants*. Although the group represented a wide range of opinion, from conservative to radical, they agreed unanimously that blacks wanted political and civil rights, equal educational and job opportunities, and equal access to public facilities—now. Their impatience was widely shared. A traveler in the South reported that blacks expressed "a sense of not belonging, and protest, sometimes not loud but deeply felt." Blacks developed their own version of the widely popular *V*-for-victory sign—double *V*, for victory abroad and at home.

Their wartime experiences demonstrated that this rendering of the signal was all too appropriate. Perhaps 300,000 black men and women from the South

JIM CROW MOVIE (Library of Congress)

served in the armed forces, which were thoroughly segregated by race. Initially the Marine Corps and the Army Air Corps (predecessor to the Air Force) excluded blacks altogether. The U.S. Navy restricted blacks to menial capacities. The U.S. Army allowed blacks to serve in a wider range of activities but restricted the majority to menial positions. Proportionately fewer blacks became officers, and they were limited to all-black units whose superior officers were white. The Air Corps did eventually create a separate black unit of pilots, who trained at Tuskegee Institute and then served in combat in Europe.

Military bases maintained racially separate and usually unequal facilities. Separate and unequal treatment off the bases was, of course, routine in the South and not rare elsewhere. Black and white military personnel fought each other—on a few occasions with live ammunition. Blacks reported that white officers and military police were often blatantly discriminatory and verbally and physically abusive. They complained even more about the civilian police they encountered off their bases. There were assaults and killings, some of which were never solved.

William H. Hastie, dean of the law school at Howard University and civilian aide to Secretary of War Henry L. Stimson, observed that "only the sensational cases of shootings, killings and rioting...attract public attention. But day by day the Negro soldier faces abuse and humiliation." The army, he contended in a letter to Secretary Stimson, had no comprehensive plan for dealing with this pervasive situation. The army investigated and reported, transferred individuals and occasionally court-martialed them, and sometimes shifted regiments to other stations. "The Army itself is busy with booklets, lectures and various devices of indoctrination, teaching our soldiers how to treat the peoples of India, the South Sea Islanders, the Arabs, everyone but their fellow American soldiers."

Blacks continued to receive separate and unequal treatment in civilian employment. Congress, marching steadily rightward, gutted federal relief programs faster than blacks could find jobs in a racially biased job market. Not until 1942 did that market grow enough to make even menial positions readily available for blacks, and only after 1943 were more skilled positions opened to blacks. In addition to carrying the burden of lower rates in literacy and skills, largely imposed by long years of racial discrimination, blacks had to overcome the discriminatory attitudes and practices of white employers and employees. A 1941 survey of defense contractors in Georgia revealed that 95 percent of their jobs were for whites only. The region's largest industry, textiles, maintained its policy of a virtually all-white work force. Pressed by the federal government and a growing shortage of suitable white workers, shipbuilders in Mobile opened skilled and semiskilled positions to blacks in 1944. Their predominantly white work force started a riot that ended only when military forces intervened. A compromise was subsequently struck. Several shipyards began working all-black and all-white crews. That arrangement gave blacks an opportunity to advance to better jobs. Trade unions usually maintained their Jim Crow traditions, but industrial unions continued to deviate somewhat from those traditions.

Railroad brotherhoods in the South resisted all efforts at desegregation, despite considerable pressure from the federal government.

Even after job opportunities for blacks had improved, most blacks were still employed to do the heaviest, least desirable work. The legendary shipbuilder Andrew Jackson Higgins was a rarity. The New Orleans industrialist provided equal pay and work to blacks and whites, and even worked cooperatively with unions. By the end of the war, black employment in manufacturing had grown so much that the number of black industrial workers equaled the pre-Depression number. Those gains, however, had a soft underpinning. Among the last hired, blacks were usually the first fired during postwar reconversion.

In fact, blacks seldom found effective allies in the federal government during the war. After a threatened mass march by blacks on Washington on the eve of the United States entry into World War II seemed likely to materialize, President Roosevelt issued an executive order requiring nondiscrimination clauses in defense contracts and forbidding discrimination by defense contractors. To enforce these provisions the president established the Fair Employment Practices Commission (FEPC), which walked softly and seldom carried even a small stick. It applied persuasion but would not touch its most formidable weapon, recommendations that defense contracts be canceled. The FEPC took no initiative in specific cases; it responded if someone complained, but people who complained risked retaliation. The president made some use of his patronage powers in an attempt to appease his black critics; for instance, he appointed Judge Hastie to the War Department to be a spokesman for blacks.

In 1944, however, the Supreme Court dealt white supremacy a major defeat. The Court ruled in *Smith* v. *Allwright* that the Texas white primary law violated the Fifteenth Amendment and was therefore unconstitutional. The upper South acquiesced in the decision, and the number of blacks in the upper South who registered to vote increased substantially in the ensuing decade. The impact of increased black voter registration was limited because blacks made up a small proportion of the registered voters in the upper South.

The lower South, where blacks made up a large proportion of the population, held its ground firmly on Jim Crow at the ballot box. Governor Olin Johnston of South Carolina even called the state legislature into special session to make the state Democratic party a private club, which could then set its own membership rules. The courts soon declared the new laws unconstitutional. Thereafter, South Carolina, like other southern states, used literacy tests and understanding clauses as its primary means of keeping blacks from exercising their rights as citizens. Southern whites seemed as determined to sustain white supremacy in 1940 or 1945 as they were in 1900. But a knowledgeable South Carolinian thought otherwise. "The Southerner's attitude," wrote John A. Rice in 1942, "is incredibly more humane than it was in the South I knew as a child."

Southern Democrats in Congress, however, resisted change. During World War II they helped to dismantle some New Deal programs and blocked the expansion of others by making effective use of their strength in Congress. They had numbers (a strong, often united minority), seniority-based control of many congressional committees, the power of the filibuster in the Senate, and something approaching an informal alliance with congressional Republicans. So armed, the southern Democrats were able to defend most of the programs that southern farm owners wanted while virtually destroying the already enfeebled Farm Security Administration, whose programs were intended to aid landless farmers. It was replaced by the Farmers Home Corporation, which had reduced programs for tenant purchases of farms. The other liberal New Deal agencies— the WPA, the NYA, the CCC—were abolished.

When northern Democrats attempted to create a massive public housing program, southern Democrats emasculated the measure. In comparison with their northern colleagues, they had few urban constituents who would benefit from the program. Southern Democrats persisted in their strong opposition to organized labor; they pushed for legislation to forbid unions to make contributions to political campaigns or to strike during wartime. Southern state legislatures adopted a wide array of antiunion laws; the most popular were so-called right-to-work laws, which outlawed collective bargaining agreements that required employees to join the union. And of course southern Democrats held firmly to Jim Crow. They successfully killed federal anti-poll-tax legislation. Fearing that blacks might find a back door to voting booths in the South, they eviscerated national legislation designed to allow soldiers to cast absentee ballots easily.

Southern Democrats also held firmly, though with growing doubt and discomfort, to the party of their fathers. Although their disagreements with President Roosevelt's domestic policies were sharp and very public, southern Democrats gave strong support to the president's foreign policy. That support was particularly important during the months of crisis between the start of World War II and the United States' entry into the war, and again when the president was working to establish the United Nations and to ensure American participation in that organization. They also supported the reelection of the president in 1944, as they had done in 1940, after some hesitation on both occasions. In 1944 they put pressure on Roosevelt to replace Vice President Henry A. Wallace, a New Deal liberal. In Wallace's place the president chose Senator Harry S. Truman of Missouri, a border state with strong southern characteristics. The old balance of power between North and South in the Democratic party seemed to have been revived. That balance seemed even more secure when Truman succeeded Roosevelt. On April 12, 1945, as Roosevelt was sitting for a portrait in his cottage at Warm Springs, Georgia, he suddenly slumped over. Within minutes the man who so earnestly wanted to see a modern South was dead.

Five months later, on September 2, 1945, Japan surrendered. World War II was over, and a different world order was emerging. So was a different South, a modern South, where the three pillars of the prewar South were endangered or had started to crumble: Jim Crow, the solid South, and economic dependence on agriculture in general and cotton in particular. The Great Depression, the New Deal, and World War II had struck the region with elemental force. White southerners, at least those in seats of power, were shaken. A young newspaper reporter privately noted a year before the war ended that the South was "unhappy, restless, confused, embittered, torn by pressures steadily mounting. As far as the eye can see there is discontent and bitterness, faint intimations of a coming storm like a rising wind moving through tall grass."

Several months later, a South Carolina soldier sent an unintended warning that some of the storm clouds gathering over the South were generated within the region. He had tried to vote as an absentee but found he could not do so because his state legislature refused to allow voters from his state to use ballots distributed through the armed forces. Legislators feared that blacks might use this means to obtain ballots.

Stung by the experience, the soldier wrote a letter of protest to his hometown newspaper. He declared that he was an "ardent Southerner" who was "always ready" to defend his state and the South. "But I can no longer hide the fact that actually I am ashamed of my state." He was distressed because, among other things, he had seen many southerners do poorly on examinations in the military because of their educational deficiencies. For that situation the South had itself to blame.

> Yet often South Carolina leads the South in wailing about the injustices brought on us, such as high freight rates, or Elanor's medling [sic]. It's time we cleaned our own house, maybe if we did this, the yankees would quit trying to do it for us....It seems to me that the average South Carolinian is so afraid that the negro will get ahead that he is willing to sacrifice his own rights just to make sure the negro won't have any. Are our fine Southerners afraid that if they meet the negro on equal terms, that they will be beaten?

The obsession of white southerners with maintaining their superior status and with keeping blacks in their place would drive away the outside business investment that the South wanted. "We can expect no prosperity as other states have it until we wise up to ourselves."

The soldier's letter at least suggested that Negrophobia, for some two hundred years the cornerstone of southern politics and society, rested on uncertain ground. The letter also suggested that the veterans of World War II were returning with different attitudes or more open minds. If so, then World War II had shaken Wilbur Cash's "savage ideal" and had helped prepare white southerners for the sweeping changes that transformed much of their world in the quarter century that followed the end of the war.

26

The End of Jim Crow

The Civil Rights Revolution

——————— ❖ ———————

Rosa Parks had worked all that Thursday in 1955 at her job as a seamstress in a Montgomery, Alabama, department store. Her feet hurt as she got on the 5:30 bus, which, like all Montgomery buses, was required by law to segregate black and white passengers. The first ten rows of seats on the buses were reserved for whites. Blacks sat behind those seats, or they stood. Blacks could not take empty seats in the other section if their own was filled, but whites could do so. If a white person did sit in the back, that row instantly became a white row and all the blacks seated in it had to move. Further, blacks had to pay their fares at the front door and then go out and enter again by the back door. The white bus drivers were often condescending, rude, and even abusive to black passengers. They sometimes drove off before blacks could board at the rear after paying their fares. Parks herself had once been physically thrown off a bus by a driver when she refused after paying her fare to disembark and reboard at the rear. Her clear recollections of that episode were stirred when she got on the bus that Thursday. The driver was the same one who had put her off the bus seven years before.

This bus quickly became crowded. When the white section was filled, a white man moved toward the row where Parks was seated. The driver ordered blacks in that row to give up their seats. Someone remembered that he used a familiar phrase: "Niggers, get back." Others moved, but Parks did not. Long an advocate of self-assertion in defense of one's rights, Parks had had enough. She was, as she said later, more than just physically tired. She was tired from "the accumulation of many years of oppression, of humiliation, of deprivation, and of just the attempt of those in power to make me feel less than a person—that is what it was designed to do." Too many times she had watched black parents instruct their children to stand on buses with empty seats, teaching them the lesson that they themselves had learned from Jim Crow—that they were of an inferior order of beings. Asked if she intended to move, she simply said, "No." The driver left the bus and called the police. They came, arrested Parks, and took her to jail.

Rosa Parks had never before been arrested. A high school graduate who had attended Alabama State, she was a pillar of her church, was active in the Women's Political Council (WPC) of Montgomery, had served as secretary for the local NAACP chapter, and was working actively with the youth council of the local NAACP. The chapter president, E. D. Nixon, soon learned of her arrest and acted promptly to secure her release, with the assistance of a white lawyer, Clifford Durr. Then Nixon began to work with Parks to build a case to test the constitutionality of the law that required racial segregation on public transit in Montgomery, hoping the case might become a focal point for a protest movement.

The WPC also immediately grasped the larger significance of Parks's case. Frequent complaints about the bus system had usually been received politely by city officials, but had gone unheeded. Searching for a new, more effective strategy, the WPC developed the idea of a bus boycott. When Jo Ann Gibson Robinson, president of the WPC, learned of Parks's arrest, she recruited a colleague from the Alabama State faculty and two students. By Friday morning they had mimeographed 52,500 leaflets calling for a one-day boycott of the bus system on Monday, December 5, to protest the Parks case. They and others from the WPC distributed the leaflets to black Montgomery. Meanwhile, individuals and groups worked over the weekend to arrange for car pools and reduced-fare taxi services to get the boycotters to work and home again.

Then the anxious waiting began.

Robinson later recalled, "The suspense was almost unbearable, for no one was positively sure that taxi drivers would keep their promises, that private car owners would give absolute strangers a ride, that Negro bus riders would stay off the bus. And then there was the cold and the threat of rain."

The boycott proved to be amazingly effective. Black ridership on city buses dropped almost to zero. Monday night 5,000 to 6,000 people gathered at a church to celebrate and shouted their approval of a proposal to extend the boycott until they received better treatment on city buses. They chose the Reverend Dr. Martin Luther King, Jr., to lead them. Day after day Montgomery blacks endured the monetary and personal costs of relying on taxis, privately owned cars, and car pools. Some risked their jobs. Many gave nickels, dimes, and quarters to car pool drivers. A group of college students stayed out of school to drive boycotters. When King told a weary elderly woman that she ought to give up walking and go back to the buses, she refused. "Oh, no. I'm gonna walk till it's over." "But aren't your feet tired?" "Yes...but my soul is rested."

Probably no one realized that the boycott would drag on for thirteen difficult, sometimes violent, months. No one could have anticipated that the Montgomery bus boycott would become a national and international event, and that King would become the leading figure in a movement that was to transform the post–World War II South.

Rosa Parks's quiet rebellion was not an isolated event. Blacks, sometimes supported by a few whites, had been protesting Jim Crow individually and collectively since World War II. Circumstances more than personalities put Montgomery on the world stage. Montgomery showed how deep and widespread

LUNCH-COUNTER SIT-IN IN JACKSON, MISSISSIPPI, 1963 (AP/Wide World Photos)

was the anger of blacks about Jim Crow, how tired they were of being kept "in their place." The Montgomery boycott, like the civil rights movement to which it contributed, was a grass-roots movement.

JIM CROW AND THE TRUMAN ADMINISTRATION

The Montgomery boycott, of course, occurred within a larger context. World War II had eroded the ideas and attitudes that were vital underpinnings for the South's peculiar system of race relations. The gap between the claims and the practices of American democracy had become painfully obvious to most white Americans, even to some in the South, and utterly unacceptable to blacks. Racism—the assumption that one or another race is inherently superior—was losing its respectability. Physical and social scientists had destroyed its claims. Hitler had made it odious.

America's newly assumed role of world leader and Cold War competition made Jim Crow an unacceptable international liability. Communists kept up a steady stream of criticism of the treatment blacks received in the United States. As the world leader of democracy and a prime mover in the United Nations, the

United States could not afford to ignore its commitment to equality. Jim Crow and that commitment could not coexist. Their coexistence became even more untenable as European colonies in Africa and Asia asserted and obtained their independence after 1945, and Third World nationalism became a force in international politics. Cold War considerations figured prominently in President Harry S. Truman's conclusion that the federal government had to take steps to oppose segregation and racial discrimination.

So did domestic political considerations. Here American blacks assumed the initiative more forcefully and effectively than they ever had done before. Stronger economically and especially politically than at any other time in their three-hundred-year American experience, blacks after World War II could now make themselves heard. They could force American political leaders to become less evasive about racial discrimination and perhaps even to move against it.

A generation after the waves of black migration from the rural South had begun, the numbers of black voters in the North and border states made them a force to be reckoned with. For instance, the Truman administration concluded that it could not win the 1948 presidential election without attracting strong black support outside the South, even at the risk of infuriating the white South. Moreover, the president was said to have been stunned by NAACP reports of increased racial violence and lynchings and a new wave of Negrophobic literature.

However mixed his motives were, Truman was the first president since Lincoln to act forthrightly on behalf of black Americans. Truman created the Civil Rights Committee in 1947. Its fifteen members included corporate, labor, and academic leaders, as well as two prominent blacks. Its final report, *To Secure These Rights*, became a landmark in civil rights history. The committee called for "the elimination of segregation based on race, color, creed, or national origin from American life." It urged passage of federal antilynching and anti-poll-tax legislation; an end to segregation and discrimination in the armed forces, in interstate transportation, and in public services; and nondiscrimination in elections, education, and housing. To enforce these policies, the committee called for a fair employment practices act and asked that federal agencies charged with protecting civil rights be enlarged and strengthened and that Congress make its grants-in-aid to state and local governments dependent on nondiscrimination. State governments, the committee declared, ought to adopt similar policies and ought to outlaw discrimination in public accommodations.

The report had little immediate effect. President Truman endorsed most of the report in early 1948 in an address to Congress. Southern Democrats, who had more than enough power to stall civil rights legislation in Congress, reacted with such hostility that the president retreated on civil rights for a while. No consensus for implementing any but the most modest proposals of the commission existed in 1948 or for some years thereafter. Not until the mid-1960s did the necessary consensus develop, and then only after the civil rights movement had forced the issue.

None of the seventeen states that had Jim Crow laws and policies altered course. Mounting disagreements among Democrats over major issues portended a political civil war. Of these issues, civil rights was the most explosive. Truman, who in 1948 was battling to get his party's nomination for the presidency, wavered as his party divided into warring factions. Truman finally acted decisively in late July. By then the Democratic National Convention had endorsed most of the recommendations in *To Secure These Rights* and had nominated Truman for reelection after a number of southern Democrats had bolted the party. The president used his executive authority to order the gradual elimination of racial segregation and discrimination in the armed forces and in federal employment. Thus began the slow but steady decline of Jim Crow in the American armed forces. Racially mixed units of American forces fought in the Korean war (1950–1953).

The coalition that had made the Democrats the dominant national party since 1930 splintered. Some left-wing Democrats departed to support Henry A. Wallace, the former vice president, who ran as the nominee of the hastily formed Progressive party. Much more important, then and thereafter, were the Dixiecrats. When the Democratic party adopted a strongly worded civil rights plank in its 1948 platform, the Mississippi delegation and half of the Alabama delegates walked out of the national convention. By prearrangement, they and other southerners met in Birmingham three days later to create the States' Rights party. The States' Rights Democrats—or the Dixiecrats, as they were popularly known—nominated Governor J. Strom Thurmond of South Carolina for president and Governor Fielding Wright of Mississippi for vice president. A speaker at the Birmingham meeting caught the spirit of the occasion when he denounced President Truman and his civil rights program as "threats to make Southerners into a mongrel, inferior race by forced intermingling with Negroes." Thurmond declared in his acceptance speech: "There is [sic] not enough troops in the Army to force the Southern people to break down segregation and admit the Negro race into our theaters, into our swimming pools, into our homes, and into our churches."

The Dixiecrats believed that the national Democratic party had betrayed the South, the region that had been most loyal to the party. Traditionally, the Democratic party's greatest asset in the South had been its ability to keep blacks in their place and to prevent the federal government from intervening to alter that arrangement. That ability was clearly in jeopardy in 1948. The Republicans, however, were not an acceptable alternative for most southern whites in 1948. Traditional aversion to the Republican party and the strong civil rights stand that the national Republicans adopted in 1948 kept most southern Democrats from joining forces with the Republicans. Memories of the Depression and the New Deal may also have deterred some southern Democrats from switching parties.

The Thurmond-Wright slate carried four states—South Carolina, Alabama, Mississippi, and Louisiana—in all of which they ran under the official Democratic party label. The Dixiecrats did very well for a new third party, though they failed to achieve their goal of capturing enough electoral votes to force the election into the House of Representatives, where they might have been strong enough to engineer the election of a president more congenial to them. Loyalty to the traditional party of the region and the reluctance of most Democratic regulars to take the risk of deserting Truman counted heavily against the Dixiecrats.

However, Negrophobia or hostility toward any attempt to change Jim Crow significantly would in time dramatically change politics in the solid South. Nineteen forty-four was the last time the Democrats captured all the electoral votes of the South. Joined with other forces—opposition to the economic policies of the national Democratic party and conservatives' reactions to the liberal policies of Democrats of the urban North—Negrophobia and defenses of Jim Crow dramatically transformed politics in the South and consequently those in the nation.

More immediately, the Democrats maintained an uneasy peace nationally. President Truman could do little with the well-entrenched southern Democrats in Congress, and he tried little beyond ordering the military to desegregate. More energy was spent—with some success—in making compromises across sectional lines within the Democratic party in preparation for future elections. Thus neither the Congress nor the Truman administration did much to lend substance to the report of Truman's Civil Rights Committee or to the civil rights plank of the 1948 Democratic party platform. But the Supreme Court did. In 1950 the Court dealt racially segregated public education a major blow in a case that challenged the exclusion of blacks from a publicly supported law school.

THE SUPREME COURT AND "SEPARATE BUT EQUAL"

When Heman Sweatt, a World War II veteran, applied for admission to the law school at the University of Texas in February 1946, the state had 7,701 white lawyers and 23 black lawyers, and no publicly supported law school for blacks. The university rejected Sweatt's application because he was black. Sweatt sued, asserting that his rejection violated the "separate but equal" doctrine. The state responded by establishing a separate law school for blacks. Sweatt's NAACP attorneys argued and a number of leading figures in legal education testified that the new school could not compare with that at the University of Texas. This approach reflected the NAACP's legal strategy of forcing the "separate but equal" doctrine by insisting on *real* equality. Some supporters, including Truman's attorney general, Tom C. Clark, a Texan, went much further. They filed *amicus curiae* (friend of the court) briefs challenging the constitutionality of the cornerstone of Jim Crow, *Plessy* v. *Ferguson*, the "separate but equal" decision of 1896. That decision, they said, violated the Fourteenth Amendment of the Constitution, and therefore the Court was obliged to declare the doctrine unconstitutional. Texas and eleven other states that filed *amicus* briefs countered with a defense of racial segregation as constitutional and with the assertion that the right of the states to abide by the traditions and preferences of their citizens in educational and racial matters was well established in law and in practice.

The Supreme Court ruled that the University of Texas had to admit Sweatt to its law school, but it did not declare "separate but equal" unconstitutional. It found the newly established law school for blacks to be unequal to that of the University of Texas because the latter had more faculty, students, course offerings, and opportunities to specialize, as well as a law review. "What is more important, the University of Texas Law School possesses to a far greater degree those qualities which are incapable of objective measurement but which make for greatness in a law school...to name but a few,...reputation of the faculty, experience of the administration, position and influence of the alumni, standing in the community, traditions and prestige." The new black law school could not possibly meet the "separate but equal" standard. "It is," the Court concluded "difficult to believe that one who had a free choice between these law schools would consider the question close."

At the same time, the Supreme Court struck two more blows against Jim Crow. On grounds similar to those in the *Sweatt* decision, the Court ordered the University of Oklahoma to cease segregating George W. McLaurin, a black graduate student. Earlier the university had lost its legal battle to exclude McLaurin altogether. Then it attempted to segregate him within the university. When he attended a class, or studied in the library, he sat in an anteroom or alcove by himself. If he wished to eat in the cafeteria, he could do so only before or after whites ate there. The Court declared that since the restrictions imposed on McLaurin denied him an opportunity to study and learn equal to that accorded to white students, those restrictions violated the "separate but equal" constitutional standard. The Court also ruled that the Southern Railway violated the Constitution when it denied equal treatment to black passengers on its dining cars by restricting them to specific tables that were marked by signs and set apart by screens and barriers.

The *Atlanta Constitution* trumpeted that the *Sweatt* decision meant that "'Separate but Equal' Still Stands." It stood, but on a very insecure foundation. How could the South meet the criteria set forth by the Court for law schools, medical schools, dental schools, engineering schools, graduate schools—all publicly supported educational institutions? The railway decision reinforced the Court's growing determination to refuse to sanction racial segregation on trains and buses that crossed state lines.

In the decade after the *Sweatt* decision, desegregation of higher education in the South increased substantially. The numbers grew from 200 blacks in twenty-one graduate and professional schools in 1950 to perhaps 2,000 in regular sessions and several thousand in summer sessions in 1954. By 1960, 131 previously segregated public institutions of higher education, 14 of which had been all-black, had been desegregated. Most of them were graduate and professional schools. Perhaps 200 private colleges and universities had desegregated voluntarily. The Deep South, predictably, held out the longest, although Louisiana State University had lowered its racial barrier under a court order in

1950 and had more than 150 black students by 1953. Georgia admitted its first black student in 1960, but higher education in South Carolina, Alabama, and Mississippi remained completely segregated. The last two states would become stages for major civil rights confrontations in the 1960s.

Although racial barriers in interstate and intrastate public transportation had eroded, largely because of pressures from the federal government, those barriers held firm in most of the Deep South. Jim Crow remained intact in public education, but many people anticipated that this would be the next and most explosive battleground in desegregation. Public school desegregation would become the most divisive domestic political issue in the twentieth-century United States.

The mood of the South after the Court's decisions expressed itself tellingly in two senatorial elections in 1950, then in the presidential election of 1952. Perceived as soft on segregation (and too close to organized labor), Florida's Senator Claude Pepper lost his reelection bid in a campaign loaded with racial overtones. Frank Graham's defeat in North Carolina had an even greater shock effect. Graham had presided over the rise of the University of North Carolina to the front ranks in education in the South. Buttressed by his reputation as a great educator and his personal popularity, Graham carried a large lead from the first primary election in May into the runoff. Then came the Court's 1950 decisions on racial segregation. Graham's opponents quickly linked a vote for Graham with "your children sitting in Negro schools." Negrophobia spread like a prairie fire in North Carolina, from low-income and working-class whites who feared school desegregation and job competition from blacks to middle- and upper-income whites who wanted all-white schools. Labeled a "nigger lover," Graham watched his substantial lead disappear within days, and he lost his bid to return to the Senate.

The Democrats also suffered major defeats in the South in the 1952 presidential election. Four southern states—Virginia, Tennessee, Florida, and Texas—voted for Dwight D. Eisenhower, the successful Republican presidential candidate, as support for the president increased in the South to nearly 50 percent from about 35 percent four years earlier. Eisenhower's greatest strength came from traditionally Republican mountain areas and from urban areas where the economic policies of the national Democrats were very unpopular. Counties with large black majorities and acute sensitivity to any changes along the color line also favored the Republican nominee.

More direct efforts to keep Jim Crow in place in public education were made in the early 1950s. Attempts to make "separate but equal" a fact, not a theory, increased markedly. Steps toward equalization had already been taken in teacher pay and in the provision of school buses and high schools for blacks. Large gaps remained, however. South Carolina, for example, tacitly acknowledged these gaps when it instituted a 3 percent sales tax in 1951 to fund a $75 million bond program designed to improve black schools. By 1952 the southern states spent 70 percent as much on education for blacks as for whites, up from 43 percent in 1940.

However, "separate but equal" was running a losing race. It was explicitly challenged in several court cases in 1952. Then in December of that year the

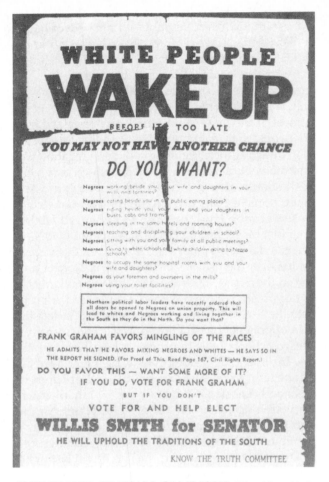

ANTI-FRANK GRAHAM CAMPAIGN (The New York
Public Library)

Supreme Court heard arguments on several desegregation cases that collectively came to be known as *Brown* v. *Board of Education of Topeka*. After hearing
arguments, then rearguments a year later, then extensively deliberating the
cases, the Court unanimously declared on May 17, 1954, that "separate but
equal" was unconstitutional, reversing *Plessy* v. *Ferguson*. "We conclude that in
the field of public education that doctrine of 'separate but equal' has no place.
Separate but equal facilities are inherently unequal." Justice Hugo Black, an Alabamian who was one of the first of the justices to conclude that *Plessy* was constitutionally indefensible, reportedly warned his colleagues when they were deciding on *Brown* that if they overturned *Plessy*, "it would mean the end of
Southern liberalism for the time being. The Bilbos and the Talmadges would
come even more to the fore.... The guys who talked nigger would be in charge,

there would be riots, the Army might have to be called out." Still, Black "was determined to overrule it on principle." Justice Black's warnings ultimately proved correct. Almost everywhere in the South, *Brown* met strong resistance— blunt, overt opposition or deliberate evasion.

*B*ROWN: *MASSIVE RESISTANCE, CALCULATED EVASION*

Overt opposition to school desegregation found expression in a variety of ways, including the revival of the Ku Klux Klan. In its third life, the Klan focused its anger on blacks and on school desegregation. Also born in the wake of *Brown* were white-collar or country-club segregationist groups. Peopled by local and regional elites, the Association of Citizens' Councils and such allies as the Virginia Defenders of State Sovereignty and Individual Liberties, the North Carolina Patriots, and the Georgia States' Rights Council formed a loose confederation, the Citizens' Councils of America (popularly known as the White Citizens' Councils). Numbering 250,000 members at their peak, the White Citizens' Councils had their greatest influence in the Deep South states of Louisiana, South Carolina, Mississippi, and Alabama. The councils exerted more influence than the Klan and generally opposed the violence associated with the KKK. In Mississippi and Alabama the councils functioned as unelected governments for a time. Elsewhere they aggravated community anxieties and encouraged reprisals. Encouraged by local councils, businessmen in several South Carolina communities used economic pressures to silence the NAACP and other dissenters. After the names of the black signers of petitions calling for school desegregation were published in local newspapers, signers lost their jobs, were evicted, could not get insurance policies renewed or receive credit, and had difficulties with their home mortgages. Soon the number of petitioners shrank. Some blacks retaliated by taking their business to other communities. Those actions and growing national pressure forced the councils to temper their use of economic boycotts. White Citizens' Councils and other groups also founded and ran racially segregated schools, or "seg academies," designed to preserve racial separation in education.

The forces of official opposition to *Brown* came from the Deep South and Virginia. Senator Harry F. Byrd of Virginia issued a call for "massive resistance," which became their rallying cry. Choosing a strategy of confrontation, they spurned the Supreme Court's invitation to present plans or suggestions for implementing *Brown*, and they attempted to barricade their schools against desegregation. Their bluntest tactic was their apparent willingness to abandon the public schools. In some instances, these states forbade the spending of public funds on integrated schools, repealed compulsory school attendance laws and provisions for public schools in state constitutions, and authorized the sale or lease of public school property and public aid to students attending private schools. To muffle dissent, steps were taken to weaken teachers' tenure.

The rest of the South adopted a less confrontational but no more conciliatory strategy on school desegregation. Such states as Tennessee, Texas, and Arkansas resisted passively and effectively, though in each some schools were desegregated in areas where blacks made up small minorities. State leaders in
North Carolina, led by Governor Luther Hodges, employed a school segregation strategy that permitted them to outflank both extreme segregationists who
wanted to close the schools and integrationists. The North Carolina legislature
passed laws permitting school districts to choose to desegregate or not. If they
chose not to do so, they could then decide to close their schools. The state provided for financial aid for students to attend private schools if public schools in
their districts were closed. North Carolina officials also initiated pupil assignment laws designed to minimize integration and encouraged blacks "voluntarily" to attend racially segregated schools. Thus the Tarheel State maintained its
moderate image while effectively keeping Jim Crow in public education for a
decade after *Brown*.

Such events as the Montgomery bus boycott added to the anxieties of those
whites who were trying to preserve the racial caste system. Southern blacks had
boycotted public transit systems earlier in the 1950s. In fact, some of the lessons
blacks learned during a brief, unsuccessful bus boycott in Baton Rouge in 1953
were applied in Montgomery. Nor was the Montgomery demonstration the
only one at the time. Tallahassee blacks conducted an even more effective boycott. But the charisma of Martin Luther King, Jr., drew the public spotlight to
Montgomery.

The Montgomery campaign also introduced a critical new element in the
challenge to Jim Crow: the televised mass demonstration, which became a cat-
alytic force in the early 1960s. Montgomery, as well as Baton Rouge and Tallahassee, revealed the extent of black discontent with segregation. Whites tried to
claim that such protests were the result of "outside agitators," a few local mal-
contents who misled ordinary blacks, and even communists. The substantial
size of the boycotts and their spontaneity belied these claims.

The Montgomery boycott received support from some local whites, and not
just from those who considered their maids indispensable. White moderates
walked or tiptoed an uncomfortable, often risky, even dangerous line between
blacks and whites. Some lost customers; others received threats of business
losses. A socially prominent architect in Montgomery whose racial moderation
became known left after his clientele vanished. Virginia Durr's husband's law
practice virtually evaporated. The Sunday school class Clifford Durr taught did
evaporate. At one time a prominent attorney before he became a high-ranking
official in the New Deal and then commissioner of the Federal Communications
Commission, Durr struggled the rest of his life to make a living. Families were
ostracized, sometimes threatened. At least two local churches—one Presbyterian, one Episcopal—hired police to bar blacks from services. When the Episcopal pastor objected, he was forced to leave. A white Lutheran clergyman shared
a distinction with King and King's closest ally, Ralph Abernathy: each survived
a bombing of his home.

The intransigence of the white leaders in Montgomery worsened the boycott. Initially the blacks in Montgomery had not sought an integrated bus system. They had asked for a more flexible version of segregated seating, such as the one already in place in Mobile and other southern cities; for the hiring of black drivers for routes that were heavily traveled by blacks; and for more courteous treatment by all drivers. White political leaders refused, although the bus company was willing to be more conciliatory. Black leaders then changed their demands: now they would settle for nothing less than a completely desegregated bus system. The final settlement came in November 1956, when the Supreme Court confirmed a lower court's decision, issued by Alabama federal judges Frank M. Johnson, Jr., and Richard T. Rives, that the Montgomery ordinance requiring racial segregation in public transit was unconstitutional. The Court based its decision on the Fourteenth Amendment and the precedent of *Brown*, thus widening the effect of *Brown* beyond public education.

The city of Montgomery exercised its last legal option and asked the Court to reconsider its decision. The Court refused. The decision became effective December 20. Early the next morning, Rosa Parks, E. D. Nixon, King, Abernathy, and Glen Smiley, a white, Texas-born civil rights activist, boarded a Montgomery bus at the front door and quietly took seats near the front. Photographers and cameramen recorded the event; it became a landmark in the demise of Jim Crow. Bitterness lingered, however. A major break in the racial caste system had occurred, but strong resistance remained. In the late 1950s Montgomery officials closed parks and a zoo to avoid integrating them and removed the seats from the public library after it was desegregated.

The situation in Montgomery did not, however, indicate what would happen if state or local officials chose to ignore or disobey a court order to desegregate. Would the federal government intervene to enforce the order? And if so, how? Events in 1956 were not reassuring for the champions of desegregation. In February 1956 Autherine Lucy won her three-year battle for admission to the University of Alabama. During Lucy's three-day academic career at Tuscaloosa, mobs rioted in protest. To quell the riots, state police expelled Lucy. The university's board of trustees made her expulsion permanent after she charged that the university administration had conspired with the mobs. "The lesson was clear," one analyst said. "Federal court orders could be forcibly nullified— provided that sufficient elements of the white power structure countenanced or encouraged it."

When another important element of the white power structure bluntly challenged *Brown* and the Supreme Court in March 1956, President Eisenhower said nothing. Nineteen of the 22 senators and 101 of the 128 congressmen from the former Confederate states signed the "Declaration of Constitutional Principles," or what was called the Southern Manifesto. It denounced *Brown* as a "clear abuse of judicial power," a threat to the rights of states and parents, and destructive of "the amicable relations between the Negro and white races." Tennessee's senators, Albert Gore and Estes Kefauver, refused to sign. By arrangement, the sponsors of the manifesto did not ask Lyndon Johnson of

Texas, the majority leader in the Senate, to sign. None of the nonsigners in the Senate or the House came from the Deep South. Political considerations very probably prompted the manifesto and Eisenhower's silence: 1956 was an election year.

The failure of President Eisenhower to intervene on behalf of a flagrantly violated federal court order raised serious doubts about the civil rights policy of his administration. Eisenhower's position on civil rights was ambiguous. He had grave reservations about the *Brown* decision, he never publicly put the authority of his office or his person behind the decision by endorsing it, but he enforced *Brown* where he felt he had clear authority. On his orders, public schools and federal facilities in Washington, D.C., were quickly desegregated. He also pushed desegregation and nondiscrimination in the armed forces and in federal employment. Eisenhower's policy on civil rights was shaped by his conservative view of presidential and federal powers, his belief that intervention would make race relations worse rather than better, and very probably a lack of sensitivity in regard to the never-ending insults suffered by blacks. The failing was, of course, shared by the vast majority of American whites, north and south. Eisenhower also thought he could rely on quiet persuasion to get southern white leaders to make concessions. He obviously underestimated their intransigence.

Six months after the manifesto appeared, state officials in Texas explicitly refused to obey a federal court order to admit blacks to two all-white schools. Earlier, desegregation of public schools had gone smoothly in southwest Texas. Eastern Texas was another story. Part of the Old South with large black minorities, eastern Texas was a hostile setting for desegregation. Governor Allan Shivers revived the widely discredited pre–Civil War interposition doctrine— the concept that the federal government is not the sole judge of its powers and that the states may insert or interpose themselves between the federal government and individuals in the states. He used this doctrine along with the Texas Rangers to stop school desegregation in eastern Texas.

Growing hostility to *Brown* also led to not very subtle attempts to disfranchise blacks or to slow the significant increase in black voter registration that had been occurring since the white primary had been declared unconstitutional in 1944. Citizens' Council members advised some registered black voters to disfranchise themselves "voluntarily." By 1955 fifteen Mississippi counties had no black voters at all. Louisiana passed legislation in 1954 which allowed local officials to review the qualifications of registered voters and remove from voting rolls those deemed to be unqualified. Guided by a pamphlet, *Voter Qualification Laws in Louisiana—The Key to the Segregation Struggle*, registrars removed the names of more than 10,000 blacks from voter rolls.

In response to these and other developments, the Eisenhower administration and Congress passed the first federal civil rights legislation since 1875. The Civil Rights Act of 1957 provided for the creation of the Civil Rights Commission to investigate denial of voting rights and of equal protection of the laws, elevated the Civil Rights Section of the Justice Department to a division, and gave the Justice Department authority to intervene in voting rights cases. The legislation passed only after a compromise with southern congressional leaders diluted the measure. Majority Leader Lyndon Johnson's support was necessary for the bill's passage. Whatever prompted Johnson in this instance and in cleverly arranging to avoid signing the Southern Manifesto, he was keenly aware that no southern Democrat could cling adamantly to Jim Crow and ever be elected president. Other southerners in Congress from outside the Deep South—from Texas, Tennessee, Florida, Kentucky, and Oklahoma—also supported the civil rights act. Missouri, West Virginia, and Maryland, states with strong segregationist traditions, also supplied votes for the new legislation.

PUBLIC SCHOOL DESEGREGATION: LITTLE ROCK AND NEW ORLEANS

The most serious and highly publicized challenges to *Brown* in the 1950s did not, ironically, come from the Deep South. A number of school boards outside the Deep South adopted gradual, often token desegregation plans. Under these plans, very small numbers of black applicants were admitted to previously all-white schools, usually high schools. The school board of Little Rock, Arkansas, had such a plan. After opponents of the Little Rock plan lost their legal battle to stop it, school officials prepared to admit nine black students to Central High in September 1957.

Governor Orval Faubus, who was not known as an extreme segregationist, suddenly intervened to prevent desegregation. Claiming he was acting to prevent violence and was justified in doing so by the doctrine of interposition, Faubus dispatched the Arkansas National Guard to maintain order at Central High by preventing blacks from enrolling. Overnight Little Rock became a national news item. Court battles, negotiations, and protests went on for several weeks before they reached a climax. Faced with a federal injunction, Faubus withdrew the National Guard. A near riot and several days of disturbances followed. On September 24 President Eisenhower reluctantly federalized the Arkansas National Guard and sent units of the 101st Airborne Division to Little Rock to maintain order in and around Central High and to ensure the enforcement of the court order to desegregate the school. For the first time since Reconstruction, the federal government had used its military force on behalf of blacks. Also for the first time, Eisenhower had put the force of his office behind *Brown*.

The paratroopers remained for two months. Elements of the National Guard stayed for the rest of the year. Black students lived through an awkward, difficult, and sometimes intimidating school year. In June, Ernest Green became Central's first black graduate. Twenty years later, Green, a lawyer, served as an undersecretary in the Labor Department for President Jimmy Carter.

But in September 1958, Little Rock closed all four of its high schools, black and white, and they stayed closed for that academic year. Authorized by recently passed state laws, Little Rock voted 19,470 to 7,561 to close the schools

rather than integrate them. Clearly, most whites were expressing a deep commitment to segregation. They pointed to what they believed was the hypocrisy
of northern whites, noting that blacks were often treated poorly outside the
South and that many northern school systems were racially segregated. Whites
resented the use of military force. Class complicated matters. Upper-income
whites had less to lose than other whites. Most of the high school students from
the more affluent homes attended newly opened Hall High, which was to remain all-white.

Sensitive to themselves as victims and insensitive to the victimization of
blacks and their own role in that victimization, most whites in Little Rock
fought to preserve Jim Crow in public education. Governor Faubus demonstrated the handsome political benefits that could accrue to militant opponents
of *Brown*. He won reelection by a wide margin in 1958 and was reelected every two years thereafter until 1966, when he chose not to run again. State
legislators joined Faubus's "massive resistance" campaign and in 1958
passed laws that allowed school officials to close public schools rather than
desegregate them.

The Supreme Court ruled against the Arkansas school-closing legislation in
September 1958, holding that the rights of black students "can neither be nullified openly and directly by state legislators or state executive officials nor nullified indirectly by them by evasive schemes for segregation." Still, public high
schools in Little Rock stood empty during the 1958–1959 school year.

In August 1959 the high schools reopened. Four black students enrolled at
Central High and Hall High. The action of federal courts and the forces for compromise had weakened the resolve to maintain segregation at all costs. Conscience and necessity had worked their way. The first factor is harder to document than the second. Fears about the adequacy of private education and about
the children whose families who could not pay its costs outweighed fears of desegregated schools. As Little Rock's image as a progressive New South city
shattered and, more to the point, as companies abruptly lost interest in locating
facilities there, Little Rock's business leaders became more supportive of school
desegregation. They also began quietly working with local black leaders to desegregate public facilities. A student of the Little Rock crisis saw "more than
simply a desire for economic gain.... The emphasis on 'image' also reflected a
desire to join, at last, the American mainstream."

Virginia also initially closed schools rather than desegregate them. Governor J. Lindsay Almond took the initiative; school systems under court orders to
desegregate were closed by the governor in 1958. But the closings came to an
end when the Virginia supreme court ruled that the state's school closing law
was unconstitutional. The national media may well have influenced the situation. *Time* and the *New York Times* ran articles on "the lost class of '59." Edward
R. Murrow and *CBS Reports* gave the issue extensive prime-time coverage. Only
in Prince Edward County did schools stay closed to avoid desegregation. There
the schools remained locked for five years, and white students received grants
from county funds for their private school expenses.

In 1960 New Orleans provided the next major battleground when public schools there became the first in the Deep South to be required to integrate. Eight years after a suit to desegregate New Orleans public schools had been filed, U.S. District Court Judge J. Skelly Wright ordered the schools to drop their racial barriers. Turmoil followed as four black students enrolled in two all-white elementary schools in November 1960. A prominent Louisiana politician, Leander Perez, warned 5,000 protesters: "Don't wait for your daughter to be raped by these Congolese. Don't wait until the burr-heads are forced into your schools. Do something about it now." All the white students were quickly withdrawn from one of the schools. A small number stayed at the other. For weeks they and their parents were confronted daily by mobs that abused them verbally and physically. Local authorities provided no protection. Economic pressures were also applied. One nonboycotting white lost his job and could not find another. The parent of a black student was also fired. His employer explained that he regretted firing him but had done so to placate customers who threatened to trade elsewhere if the employee was not dismissed. First white, then black teenagers rampaged through the streets. Called into special session by Governor Jimmie Davis, the state legislature resuscitated interposition to pass school-closing legislation and other measures designed to block desegregation.

Before the struggle reached a climax in early 1961, Judge Wright had issued injunctions or restraining orders against the governor, the legislature, the attorney general, the state superintendent of education, the National Guard, and the state police. Never had a judge gone so far to enforce a court order or to defend the supremacy of the federal government. Ninety percent of the people in New Orleans recognized the name of "that integration judge." Old friends avoided him and stopped speaking. He received numerous threats on his life. Federal marshals protected the judge at all times. The legislature gave a standing ovation to a coffin containing Wright's blackened effigy. But Wright persisted, and the forces of moderation and federal law finally prevailed.

Mob rule might have been avoided in New Orleans, which was not a typical Deep South city. Its ethnically diverse population gave the city a cosmopolitan character. Some public facilities had been quietly integrated before the crisis over the schools. Substantial numbers of blacks voted, and the move in the 1950s to disfranchise black voters in Louisiana largely by-passed New Orleans. However, race relations in the city were volatile. Serious racial violence had occurred there, and there were organized extremists among the segregationists in New Orleans.

Local and state leaders made matters worse, even when their intentions were not altogether obstructive. The school board acquiesced in desegregation only after a long legal battle. Then it made no effort to plan for desegregation until late in the day. The board chose to begin by desegregating two schools in lower-income neighborhoods, both of which had been long neglected by city officials. These neighborhoods felt they were being doubly victimized. And by desegregating only two schools, the board allowed extremists to concentrate their forces.

BLACK FIRST-GRADER, NEW ORLEANS (AP/Wide World Photos)

Mayor de Lesseps S. Morrison, a Democrat who aspired to higher office, carefully avoided offending the segregationists. He provided little public leadership during the turmoil and failed to order the police to disperse the mobs and restore order at the schools. Business leaders were divided or indifferent and caught in crosscurrents. As the televised "Battle of New Orleans" raged, the critically important tourist trade declined sharply. But moderates faced threats of economic retaliation and social ostracism. New Orleans' leaders had apparently learned little from events in Little Rock and Virginia. They failed to assert the kind of leadership that leaders in Atlanta and other southern cities demonstrated when their schools were desegregated. Politicians in Louisiana did learn from Faubus and others that resistance to school desegregation won favor with the majority of voters. At the state level, Louisiana had the best record of desegregation in higher education in the South. Yet the governor and the state legislature reacted with massive resistance to public school desegregation, going, as Governor Jimmie Davis said melodramatically, to the "last step before secession." Some church leaders in New Orleans publicly advocated desegregation and open schools. Other church leaders did the reverse. Most remained silent. Few of the laity heeded the admonitions of those clerics who advocated integration. The pronouncements of the local Catholic archbishop, for example, had little discernible effect.

Massive resistance failed in New Orleans, and, unlike Little Rock, New Orleans desegregated its schools without federalized National Guard troops or the intervention of the United States Army. The Eisenhower administration made early and extensive use of federal marshals, something it had not done in Little Rock. The administration also sided with desegregationists in the courtroom. These actions suggested that the federal government was becoming more inclined to act in support of desegregation and in defense of the rights of black citizens. That inclination was also indicated by the passage of the Civil Rights Act of 1960. Though it was weak, the law did authorize federal judges to appoint referees to register qualified blacks who had been denied registration.

Desegregation of public schools provoked massive resistance or calculated evasion because it bluntly probed the most sensitive nerves of southern whites. Daily close contact among people of both sexes and races stirred the deepest phobias, and the contact was not necessarily limited to school hours. A prominent South Carolina journalist wrote in 1960:

> The white Southerner's concern over race relations is in substantial measure a concern over sex relations.... Back of this preoccupation is a complex of reasons, both rational and irrational, which makes it impossible to raise the prospect of integration without raising the specter of interracial marriage, or of interracial sexual relations. Perhaps more than any other single factor, this apprehension has solidified white resistance to integration.

Integration of public schools also raised less personal but still powerful concerns. Education has long been closely linked with economic and social mobility. If integration threatened the quality of education, as many whites believed, then integration might jeopardize social and economic mobility. That was hardly a minor matter under any circumstances, and for southern whites who had only recently joined the American middle class it was a vital concern.

Southern whites genuinely believed that blacks were inferior. So did most other American whites. More than 300 years of discrimination and acculturation reinforced that view. Class complicated whites' assessment of blacks. Collectively blacks were poorer than whites, had poorer schooling and health, lower skills, less opportunity to enter the middle class. Almost entirely blocked from avenues to the middle class by barriers erected by whites, blacks had much less incentive to pay the costs associated with schooling.

Schools and homeownership could easily become intertwined. Decisions to buy a home were often shaped by perceptions of the public schools in the area. The reputation of local schools, merited or not, could have a positive or negative effect on the largest single financial asset a family had. People often think of the school in their area as "theirs," a possession that, like their home, is regarded with affection, boasted of, and defended against real and imagined threats. Similar attachments dampened the enthusiasm of many blacks for school desegregation. Their schools were their cultural strongholds. School officials reinforced such attachments by making significant improvements in public education for blacks in the 1950s. Desegregation held out the promise of a better education but involved the possible loss of one's school and of oneself in a white-dominated school. More concretely, black teachers and school administrators could be and were displaced or discharged when schools were integrated. Thus, whereas Montgomery blacks had been united in their bus boycott, that unity evaporated when King and others pressed for desegregation of public schools.

Realizing the highly divisive implications of *Brown* and the great variety of conditions and circumstances prevailing in public school systems, the Supreme Court gave the lower courts wide discretion in deciding how and when schools should be desegregated. In its second *Brown* decision (1955), known as *Brown II*, the court stipulated only that desegregation should take place "with all deliberate speed." The federal judges primarily responsible for implementing *Brown* were district court judges in the South, most of whom were natives of their areas and were either openly hostile to *Brown* or quietly opposed to it. Most school boards and officials in the South had similar backgrounds and attitudes. Implementation also depended on the initiation of suits by desegregationists, primarily blacks, which involved personal risks and considerable expense that often strained the limited resources of the NAACP and its supporters. The result was prolonged delays.

School boards and school officials became accomplished at evading school desegregation. Officials made artful uses of pupil-assignment laws and "freedom of choice" desegregation plans to preserve segregation, either entirely or very substantially. After 1965, "freedom of choice" became the favored means for evasion. School systems announced that their schools were open to all races and that students and their parents were free to choose the schools they wished to attend. Judge John J. Parker of the U.S. Circuit Court of Appeals had provided the legal defense for pupil-assignment laws and "freedom of choice" plans. In *Briggs* v. *Elliott* (1955), Parker had declared:

> Nothing in the Constitution or in the [*Brown*] decision of the Supreme Court takes away from the people the freedom to choose the schools they attend. The Constitution, in other words, does not require integration. It merely forbids discrimination. It does not forbid such discrimination as occurs as a result of voluntary action. It merely forbids the use of governmental power to enforce segregation.

Not surprisingly, few blacks got assigned or chose to go to all-white or predominantly white schools. No whites got assigned or chose to go to black schools.

Blacks could be discouraged subtly or not so subtly from requesting transfers. As one prominent Mississippi journalist wrote, "Most Negroes work for white people in the South—and almost everywhere else. In a majority of instances a white employer need only mention to his Negro employee that he is certain that both agree that school segregation is the wisest course for all concerned." Harry and Liza Briggs learned about such things. *Briggs* v. *Elliott* evolved in part from their efforts to get their children admitted to the better, all-white public schools of Clarendon County in the South Carolina low country. A navy veteran and father of five, Briggs lost his job in a local service station and his credit at the bank. Liza Briggs was fired from her job as a maid in a nearby motel.

Tokenism in school desegregation proved more effective and less risky and disruptive than massive resistance. Dramatic conflicts such as those in Little Rock and New Orleans were rare. Ten years after *Brown*, nearly 98 percent of blacks attending public school went to all-black schools. Almost all black students who attended previously all-white public schools lived in urban areas in the upper South, in the Southwest, or in the border states. Jim Crow prevailed in public education a decade after the Supreme Court had declared "separate but equal" unconstitutional.

In the face of tokenism in school desegregation and the intransigence of whites, blacks became more assertive and innovative in pursuit of their rights. They forced the federal government to take unprecedented steps. In doing so, they had an improbable ally: the Fifth Circuit Court of Appeals, then sitting in New Orleans. The court became a major force in establishing precedent-setting legal doctrines that helped implement the *Brown* v. *Board of Education* decision in the classroom, in politics, and in the jury room. The court, which was dominated by Judges Elbert P. Tuttle, John Minor Wisdom, John R. Brown, and Richard Taylor Rives, devised the legal basis for forcing schools to take steps to end segregation speedily, for overcoming past discrimination through affirmative action, for making reapportionment more equitable, and for making it more likely that defendants would be tried before a jury of their peers. The impact of the court extended from jury boxes to schools to local governments, state legislatures, and congressional districts. In sum, the Fifth Circuit functioned like "an institutional equivalent of the civil rights movement."

THE CIVIL RIGHTS MOVEMENT

For several years after the *Brown* decision, assaults on Jim Crow focused on public schools, and most of those assaults occurred in courtrooms. However, significant challenges to segregation were also made through politics and organized protests. The latter evolved into the mass civil rights movement.

The voting power of Negroes had become important at several levels. By 1948 black voters had established their importance in close presidential elections, as well as in some congressional elections outside the South. By 1960 strong black support of John F. Kennedy in such key states as Illinois and Michigan played a significant role in his narrow defeat of Richard Nixon. Congressional candidates in some nonsouthern states actively sought black voters. Thus civil rights legislation and attacks on Jim Crow often had Republican and Democratic support. Within the South itself, more than 25 percent of voting-age blacks had registered by 1960, and strong black support for Kennedy provided his narrow margin of victory in South Carolina. Proportions ran considerably higher in the upper South (except in Virginia) than in the lower South. Blacks sometimes had enough votes to have a limited voice in local elections, and white leaders became more responsive to black constituents. More money was spent on black schools; recreational facilities for blacks were improved; cities hired a few blacks for their police forces; public transit systems were desegregated; occasionally Jim Crow signs over water fountains and on restroom doors disappeared. Still, more than a decade after the publication of *To Secure These Rights* by the Truman administration, Jim Crow remained largely intact.

King and others, primarily black clergymen, had organized the Southern Christian Leadership Conference (SCLC) in 1958 to build on the gains made during the Montgomery boycott and to expand their civil rights efforts in other parts of the South and to other issues. A regional organization committed to desegregation and nondiscrimination, the SCLC struggled to find a feasible program and adequate financing. SCLC leaders expended most of their energies in the important but slow and difficult task of voter education and registration. The NAACP continued to confine most of its fight against segregation to the courtroom and to lobbying. The Congress of Racial Equality (CORE) was a direct-action group and lobby that had a small membership and was based in the North. The forces for desegregation appeared to be inadequate to the task. Jim Crow remained entrenched and apparently would remain so unless a more effective strategy could be devised.

Ezell Blair, Jr., Franklin McCain, Joseph McNeil, and David Richmond talked a lot about segregation during the fall of 1959. Then in February 1960 the four seventeen-year-old freshmen at all-black North Carolina A&T College in Greensboro decided to do something on their own. After arranging for the local newspapers to be informed, they went to a store in downtown Greensboro, made several purchases, and then went to the lunch counter and asked to be served. The store refused; it was following the customary policy of serving whites only at its lunch counter. The students remained seated. A policeman watched them closely. Two older white women praised their actions. Several others criticized them, including one older black woman. When the store closed, they got up and went back to their campus. Word spread. Twenty or so A&T students joined them the next day. A few white students from the University of North Carolina Women's College (now the coeducational University of North Carolina at Greensboro) joined in several days later. The sit-ins spread to other downtown stores, then to shopping centers. Crowds of white teenagers gathered to heckle. The demonstrators did not respond, even to physical abuse. By the following Saturday, hundreds of students were being confronted by gangs of white youths. After the stores were closed in an effort to dampen the explosive situation, a mass meeting of A&T students voted to halt demonstrations. It was the first of a series of demonstrations and racial confrontations that disrupted Greensboro for more than three years.

SITTING IN, GREENSBORO, NORTH CAROLINA (Bruce Roberts/Photo Researchers)

The Greensboro sit-ins came as a shock, at least to whites. North Carolina had a reputation as a progressive state, moderate on race relations. Greensboro was believed to be in the forefront of progress and moderation. It had removed some vestiges of Jim Crow in the early 1950s, and a black won a seat on the city council in 1951. Greensboro had been the first city in the South to announce it would comply with *Brown*, and in 1957 six black students enrolled in two previously all-white schools. Their numbers did not increase, however, and they met persistent harassment at school. Like other school systems in North Carolina, Greensboro's used recently passed school legislation to stifle desegregation while seeming to comply with *Brown*. Black parents who wanted their children to attend desegregated schools had to make their way through a bureaucratic maze, meet a complex set of criteria, and stand firm in an intimidating atmosphere—sometimes more. When two families succeeded in getting their children transferred to a previously all-white school, the school board then transferred all the white students, faculty, and staff out of the school.

Such measures stifled public school desegregation in North Carolina: the rate of integration in the state progressed to 0.026 percent by 1961. A Little Rock school official told a colleague in North Carolina: "You North Carolinians have devised one of the cleverest techniques of perpetuating segregation that we have seen." Yet the state maintained its moderate image by not openly engaging in the massive resistance practiced by its neighbors, Virginia and South

Carolina. Under Luther Hodges, widely praised as a moderate, North Carolina did pass legislation to allow local districts to close schools rather than desegregate. But none ever used that option.

Just as blacks found few places in Greensboro's white schools, they found few good places for employment or careers, though the city had a significant number of educated blacks. The tokenism of school desegregation, limited job and career opportunities, and other continuing evidences of racial prejudice and discrimination gave Greensboro's blacks a very different image of the city than most whites had. The contradictions between image and reality helped set the stage for the sit-ins.

When the Greensboro Four decided to take some action, they could not have anticipated that they would be giving impetus to a mass movement that would hasten the collapse of the South's racial caste system and have implications far beyond the South. A week after the first Greensboro demonstration, sit-ins started occurring elsewhere in North Carolina, then elsewhere in the South. By mid-April they were taking place in some sixty cities. Thousands of people were involved, mostly black college students. Small numbers of whites, usually students, joined in, as did faculty members at black colleges and a few local black leaders who were not academics. Protesters from twelve southern states met in Raleigh over Easter and formed the Student Nonviolent Coordinating Committee (SNCC, or "Snick"), which became a major force in the civil rights movement.

During the next five years, demonstrations and protests on behalf of the rights of blacks became familiar occurrences as blacks and their allies found that direct action was both necessary and effective. The sit-ins took place mostly in 1960 and 1961, then sporadically thereafter. Thirty-six hundred people were arrested in the first twelve months. Amazingly, there were few reported instances of violent confrontations between groups of blacks and whites. The protesters refused to be provoked. From the start, the sit-ins were "a movement of nonviolence...a Christian movement." John Lewis, a founder and chairman of SNCC who was elected to Congress in 1986 from an Atlanta district, said that nonviolence "became a way of life. You would put on your church-going clothes, Sunday clothes, and we took books and papers and did our homework at the lunch counter, just quiet and trying to be as dignified as possible."

Such conduct required discipline and courage. During a sit-in in Nashville, the manager of a hamburger stand locked demonstrators in and fumigated them, "the same thing that you use to fumigate for insects—the man just turned on this machine, and this huge foam covered the whole place....He refused to let us out. We stayed in there, and finally the Nashville Fire Department came down, and they broke the window of the place." On another day in Nashville, hecklers cursed and spat on protestors as they sat stoically at a lunch counter, extinguished cigarettes on them, struck them, and jerked them off the stools. An elderly white woman intervened when a man threatened a young woman with battery acid. Another white bystander, perhaps a college student, forcibly disarmed another man who threatened to attack a demonstrator with a knife. Ann Moody was part of a group of black and white men and women protestors who in 1963 were dragged off stools in a store in Jackson, Mississippi, kicked, and carried or dragged out to the street. They returned immediately and sat quietly for three hours as they were taunted, smeared with food, and sprayed with paint. Police arrested hundreds of demonstrators—an estimated 3,600 in the first year alone—but few of their attackers. Sit-ins and their variant forms—pray-ins, stand-ins, sleep-ins, jail-ins, consumer boycotts—did not achieve dramatic results before 1964. Piecemeal desegregation over several years was the norm.

But despite the modest initial results, the sit-ins contributed significantly to the development of the direct-action strategy of the civil rights movement. Young people, especially college students, joined the movement en masse, supplying it with an army of volunteers willing to take serious risks and disinclined to compromise. They refined the tactics of nonviolent confrontation, learning how to alert the news media to dramatic events to come, causing businesses and communities to suffer economic losses and raising the specter of greater losses, distressing the image-conscious urban South, going to jail and refusing to leave, and remaining nonviolent despite provocations and assaults. They had taken the high ground in a moral crusade in a region (and a nation) deeply commited to religious values. The sit-ins escalated the process of forcing the white South to stifle or ignore its segregation-at-any-costs minority and retreat, however reluctantly, from Jim Crow. The sit-ins and SNCC also forced older black leaders to act more vigorously. Finally and crucially, pressures on the federal government to engage Jim Crow more directly and powerfully increased as the civil rights movement became more youthful and militant.

THE KENNEDY ADMINISTRATION AND CIVIL RIGHTS

The Kennedy administration faced mounting pressure from civil rights activists early in its inaugural year. Its first civil rights crisis passed quickly in January 1961. Georgia officials resisted a court order to integrate the University of Georgia by withholding funds from the university. But state officials suddenly reversed field and decided to desegregate the university rather than risk a showdown with the federal government and possibly more turmoil on the campus.

The next civil rights crisis was much more serious. In May, activists from CORE, joined by some from SNCC, started the "freedom rides," a move that put enormous pressure on President Kennedy and his advisors to act more decisively on behalf of civil rights. CORE freedom riders challenged racial segregation on interstate buses and in bus terminals. (The Supreme Court had ruled these forms of segregation unconstitutional in 1946 and 1960, respectively, but throughout the South both rulings were ignored.) Two busloads of black and white riders who had been trained in nonviolent tactics left Washington in early May for the South. The well-publicized journey proceeded uneventfully through Virginia and North Carolina. After some trouble in South Carolina, then none in Georgia, the buses entered Alabama. A mob near Anniston stopped one of the buses by shooting its tires out, then set it on fire. According to most accounts, the occupants were at first prevented from fleeing the burning bus. When finally they got out, they were beaten. Doctors and nurses at the local hospital refused to treat the injured. A caravan of armed blacks rescued the freedom riders after a white mob gathered at the hospital and it became apparent that law enforcement officials would not protect the demonstrators.

When the other bus reached the terminal in Birmingham, a planned assault began: white men beat the defenseless, unresisting freedom riders with baseball bats and chains for nearly fifteen minutes before the first police arrived on the scene. The next day CORE leaders agreed to a cooling-off period arranged by U.S. Attorney General Robert Kennedy in the hope of calming matters and per- haps achieving some compromise. Though the SNCC activists were convinced that Alabama leaders could not or would not make acceptable concessions, they refused to stop the ride.

John Lewis and new volunteers from Nashville resumed the ride. James Farmer, executive director of CORE, reluctantly rejoined the ride, but Martin Luther King, Jr., declined an invitation to join, something SNCC activists long remembered. Heavily protected by state authorities on the road from Birming- ham, they arrived at a suspiciously quiet bus station in Montgomery. Several hundred men "with ax handles, chains and everything else" soon appeared and attacked the riders. John Lewis later recalled lying on the ground while "the Attorney General of Alabama [was] serving this injunction... saying that it was unlawful for interracial groups to travel." Also badly hurt was John Siegenthaler, administrative assistant to Robert Kennedy, who had been sent to Alabama as an observer.

SEPARATE WAITING ROOM (Library of Congress)

Two days later, another mob of angry whites gathered outside a black church in downtown Montgomery where a large gathering had assembled to support the freedom riders. Rampaging whites forced church doors open and charged in. Marshals, who had been dispatched by the Kennedy administration, pushed the attackers out and kept them precariously at bay. The possibility that the mob would burn the church while it was occupied by several hundred people was very real. Inside, King, the featured speaker of the evening, worked to calm the audience between urgent telephone conversations in which he explained the nature and gravity of the situation to Robert Kennedy. The state of Alabama finally took the decisive action Washington had been pleading for. Governor John Patterson declared martial law and sent 800 National Guard troops to the scene. They may have prevented the rioters from overwhelming the marshals and destroying the church and its occupants. By this time the story of the freedom ride was being featured prominently in the national and international news.

The rides soon began again, this time with heavy protection from the Alabama National Guard and, after crossing the state line, by the Mississippi National Guard. At Jackson, however, the freedom riders were arrested—for their own protection, claimed Governor Ross Barnett. After they refused to pay their fines, they served forty-day sentences in various Mississippi jails, including notorious Parchman Prison, where their stay was made as miserable as possible. Eventually some 300 riders served sentences. The freedom rides cost CORE more than $300,000 and nearly bankrupted the organization. Initially CORE had planned to use Gandhian tactics ("Fill up the jails, as Gandhi did in India, fill them up to bursting if we had to.") in order to make segregation so expensive that southern leaders would conclude "that they no longer could afford it." That tactic did not succeed immediately, but the freedom rides achieved a great deal, perhaps as CORE had planned. Farmer wrote later that his organization had set out

> with the specific intention of creating a crisis. We were counting on the bigots in the South to do our work for us. We figured that the government would have to respond if we created a situation that was headline news all over the world, and affected the nation's image abroad. An international crisis, that was our strategy.

The Kennedy administration did respond, eventually, finding it could not ignore the crisis created by the intrepid band of bus riders. A week after the arrests in Jackson, Attorney General Robert Kennedy announced that he had asked the Interstate Commerce Commission to ban segregation in interstate travel, and the commission complied with the request that fall. Many communities defied the new regulation. The Kennedy administration also intervened in the crisis as a mediator, then as an advocate. Robert Kennedy pressed state and local officials to furnish protection for the riders and persuaded very reluctant bus companies to provide buses and drivers. The administration sent federal marshals and threatened to use even more force. Its sympathies clearly lay with the civil rights movement.

Still, President Kennedy temporized on civil rights. Narrowly elected, the president lacked a clear mandate to take a strong stand on politically divisive issues. Nor was there a clear national consensus on civil rights in the very early 1960s. Kennedy also had to be concerned about the southern Democrats, whose power in Congress could undermine his legislative program. The administration devoted less attention to domestic policy than to foreign policy. Black votes and an election-eve endorsement by Martin Luther King, Sr., had been crucial to Kennedy's election, but the president did not meet personally with King, Jr., until nine months after his inauguration.

The Kennedy administration did give blacks greater recognition in its appointments than its predecessor had done, and it privately urged southern political and business leaders to abandon segregation and racial discrimination. On the other hand, during its first eighteen months the administration acquiesced in the appointment of some archsegregationists to the lower federal courts in the South and ignored the advice of Vice President Lyndon Johnson about how to work with Congress to secure the passage of new civil rights legislation. The federal government did go to court and later used force to ensure the admission of James Meredith, a black army veteran and native of Mississippi, to the University of Mississippi. Tragically, two people were killed and many were injured in a riot that broke out as the university's first black student enrolled. Eight months later, the Kennedy administration symbolically stood toe to toe with Governor George Wallace as the University of Alabama desegregated. The Kennedys also gave strong support to efforts to register black voters in the South. That these registration efforts could be made without highly publicized crises and politically awkward moments undoubtedly had appeal to the White House.

But civil rights leaders wanted greater and faster results than could be secured either in the courts or at the ballot box. To fight a long string of cases through the courts is a time-consuming, expensive process that is subject to a variety of limitations. For example, there was no federal law banning racial segregation in public accommodations and public facilities. Relief through the ballot box did not appear to be very promising, either. Few southern whites were willing to end segregation, and blacks lacked the necessary electoral power to defeat Jim Crow on their own. As late as 1962, less than 30 percent of voting-age blacks in the South were on the voting rolls. Poverty and defeatism contributed to low registration, as did fear, intimidation, evasion, violence, and state and local laws aimed at systematically limiting political participation by blacks. Of the means used to discourage blacks politically, economic intimidation and the poll tax were important, but "character," literacy, and "understanding" (of state constitutions) tests had the greatest impact. Gains in black voter registration were slow even though the Justice Department under Kennedy greatly increased its activities on voting rights cases. The Kennedy administration began to realize that its original strategy of working behind the scenes and stressing voter registration efforts by southern blacks was not very effective, that southern whites and their leaders remained largely intransigent or willing to make only minor concessions to blacks. Implicitly acknowledging the weaknesses of the Civil Rights acts of 1957 and 1960 and sensing the urgency of the civil rights issue, President Kennedy sent Congress his first major message on voting rights in February 1963 and two months later a proposal for new voting rights legislation. But by then militant civil rights leaders had conceived of and started a plan to force the federal government and the white South to do more.

BIRMINGHAM AND THE MARCH ON WASHINGTON

In early April, King and the SCLC implemented "Project C" (for Confrontation) in Birmingham. King hoped to force concessions from what had been called "the most segregated city in America" and to pressure the federal government into a more vigorous role on behalf of civil rights. The SCLC had chosen Birmingham deliberately. Its public safety commissioner, Eugene "Bull" Connor, seemed ideal for the sort of confrontation they had in mind. Connor was an intemperate, aggressive racist spoiling for a fight, and this was a fight he might welcome as an opportunity to further the political ambitions he apparently had. Earlier, at Albany, Georgia, the SCLC had learned that no confrontation was possible if law enforcement officials kept their tempers and avoided using excessive force. The civil rights demonstrations that King had helped lead in Albany had stalled as Chief Laurie Pritchett refused to be drawn into a dramatic confrontation. It was a critical defeat for King. The SCLC could not afford another Albany.

The SCLC launched an economic boycott against stores in downtown Birmingham in early April. They wanted the stores to desegregate their facilities (dressing rooms, restrooms, drinking fountains, lunch counters, and restaurants) and hire on a nondiscriminatory basis. The SCLC also asked the city to offer blacks equal employment opportunities in municipal jobs and to form a broad-based committee charged with extending desegregation beyond these first stages. Project C did not take hold, however, not even after King went to jail. While there he wrote his "Letter from Birmingham Jail" to local white clergymen in response to their criticisms of him and the SCLC. In what became one of the principal documents of the civil rights movement, King explained that other methods, including attempts at negotiation, had failed to dent segregation in Birmingham. He analyzed and justified the civil disobedience philosophy and tactics of the civil rights movement. He declared that blacks had waited long enough—"waited for more than 340 years for our constitutional and God given rights." And he criticized the white clergy for failing to lead efforts to end racial segregation.

> If I have said anything in this letter that is an overstatement of truth and is indicative of an unreasonable impatience, I beg you to forgive me. If I have said anything in this letter that is an understatement of the truth and is indicative of my having a

patience that allows me to settle for anything less than brotherhood, I beg God to forgive me.

Soon freed from jail, King returned to a movement that seemed to be stalemated. He desperately sought some way to give it needed life and force the confrontation he believed the movement had to have. Finally, with grave reservations, King asked schoolchildren to march. Several thousand joined in. After several days of demonstrations, Connor rounded up 4,000 blacks, some of them children, in a city park and attacked them with high-pressure water hoses. Connor had also used clubs and police dogs on demonstrators. Blacks who had been bystanders entered the fray and fought police. A full-blown, bloody riot throughout Birmingham was a real possibility. News media gave the story extensive coverage. Millions read about it and watched on television as Birmingham policemen and firemen assaulted children and adults. A fortuitous development increased this exposure greatly: the networks had only recently inaugurated their half-hour national news programs. Andrew Young, an SCLC leader and later mayor of Atlanta, later explained:

> We were consciously using the mass media to try to get across to the nation what our message was. The movement was really about getting publicity for injustice. ...The injustice was there under the surface and as long as it stayed below the surface, nobody was concerned about it. You had to bring it out into the open.

On May 10, black and white leaders, aided by officials of the Kennedy administration, announced a settlement that provided for desegregation of public facilities and lunch counters and for improvements in job opportunities for blacks. A biracial committee was created to deal with employment practices. The settlement broke the segregationist logjam in Birmingham, and the city started on a steady though uneven course toward desegregation. In Birmingham's wake there were demonstrations in perhaps 200 other southern cities and towns, many of which ended with agreements like the one reached in Birmingham. One scholar of civil rights declared, "More racial change came in these few months than occurred in three-quarters of a century."

It was not altogether a victory for King's aggressive nonviolent direct-action strategy. Violent encounters between blacks who were not associated with King and the Birmingham police and the Alabama Highway Patrol prompted Birmingham's less rigid segregationist leaders to compromise before matters got even worse. Rioting broke out after the bombing of the home of A. D. King, a brother of the SCLC leader, and when King's motel room, which happened to be empty at the time, was also bombed, the rioting threatened to spread. President Kennedy federalized the Alabama National Guard to remove it from the control of Governor Wallace and stationed army troops near Birmingham. A month later the federal government defeated Wallace's attempt to keep the University of Alabama segregated. At Wallace's inauguration in January 1963 he had shouted, "Segregation now—segregation tomorrow—segregation forever!" and he had vowed to "stand in the schoolhouse door" to prevent the entry of black students. Now federal officials stepped past the governor to escort two black students to classes at Tuscaloosa. That night President Kennedy announced that he would soon send Congress new civil rights legislation. He became the first American president to give resounding support to civil rights for blacks.

> We preach freedom around the world, and we mean it. And we cherish our freedom here at home. But are we to say to the world—and much more importantly to each other—that this is the land of the free, except for the Negroes; that we have no second-class citizens, except Negroes; that we have no class or caste system, no ghettos, no master race, except with respect to Negroes....
>
> We face, therefore, a moral crisis as a country and a people. It cannot be met by repressive police action. It cannot be left to increased demonstrations in the streets. It cannot be quieted by token moves or talk. It is a time to act in the Congress, in your state and local legislative body, and, above all, in all of our daily lives.

Only a few hours after the president spoke, a sniper shot Medgar Evers, field secretary of the NAACP in Mississippi, in the back as he got out of his car. Ripped open by the blast from a high-powered hunting rifle, Evers died in his front yard in Jackson as his wife and children tried to comfort him. His accused killer was never convicted.

Evers was one of at least forty men, women, and children who between 1954 and 1970 lost their lives during the civil rights struggle. Many more people were victims of serious, often severe, beatings and intimidation. Probably some seventy churches, homes, and businesses were destroyed by bombings and fire. The figure for the dead does not include the number of those who died as the result of racial confrontations and riots. Still, as violent as the struggle over civil rights was at times, confrontations between labor and management in the United States have been even bloodier.

The civil rights movement kept pressing throughout the summer and fall of 1963. Demonstrations in support of the movement were held all over the country. They reached a climax on August 28, when more than 200,000 marchers, about one-fourth of them white, marched in Washington. It was the largest demonstration ever held in the United States. Movie stars appeared; so did many politicians and union leaders. Celebrities of the music world entertained as the throng gathered in front of the Lincoln Memorial. The audience joined in the singing. The theme song of the civil rights movement, "We Shall Overcome," rolled across the center of the nation's capital. Speeches went on into the afternoon. The crowd began to drift as the afternoon faded. Many people did not wait to hear King's memorable speech with its haunting repetitions of "I have a dream." Hazel Mangel Rivers, wife of a truck driver and mother of eight, twice jailed for demonstrating in Birmingham, her home, declared, "If I ever had any doubts before, they're gone now." She had paid $8, about a tenth of her husband's weekly pay, for a bus ticket to ride to Washington, the farthest north she had ever been. "When I get back there now I am going to do whatever needs to be done."

MARCH ON WASHINGTON (UPI/Bettmann Newsphotos)

Opinion polls indicated that most Americans believed that civil rights had become the nation's greatest domestic issue. President Kennedy's proposed civil rights legislation remained tied up in Congress, however, the result of a filibuster in the Senate led by James Eastland of Mississippi and Strom Thurmond of South Carolina. The emotional groundswell that followed the tragic assassination of President Kennedy and the force and legislative skills of his successor, Lyndon Johnson, finally broke through the Senate.

Eight months after John Kennedy's death, Congress passed the Civil Rights Act of 1964, the most comprehensive and powerful law in support of racial equality ever enacted in the United States. It required that states apply the same "standards, practices, and procedures" to all persons who sought to register and vote and that literacy tests for voters must be administered on a nondiscriminatory basis. Racial segregation in public accommodations and public facilities was banned, the Civil Rights Commission was made permanent and given more power, the Equal Employment Opportunities Commission was established, and discrimination in employment because of "race, color, religion, sex, or national origin" was forbidden. The law forbade discrimination in any program that had federal assistance. Failure to comply with this provision could result in the withdrawal of funds. The Department of Health, Education, and Welfare (HEW) was authorized to help school districts desegregate.

Less than a decade after Rosa Parks refused to give up her seat, the federal government had created the most powerful weapon for civil rights since the passage of the Fourteenth Amendment. The civil rights movement had played an indispensable role in these events. One of its principal and certainly best-known leaders, Martin Luther King, Jr., had been transformed from a local pastor into a national and international figure. He received the Nobel Peace Prize in December 1964. Southern blacks and their allies had undermined Jim Crow, one of the cornerstones of southern society since Reconstruction.

THE VOTING RIGHTS ACT

The Voting Rights Act of 1965 was designed to ensure that blacks could register and vote. By the mid-1960s, black voter registration had grown significantly in most of the South, but not in the black belt—not in places such as Dallas County, Alabama. There only 156 of the more than 15,000 voting-age blacks were registered. Using the authority granted it by the Civil Rights acts of 1957 and 1960, the Justice Department took the county to court in 1961, charging discrimination against blacks who attempted to register. The county delayed, evaded, and then allowed 71 more blacks (of 114 who had applied) to register. A federal district court judge in Alabama decided that the county was no longer discriminating against black registrants and ruled against the Justice Department. When SNCC started a voter registration drive in Dallas in 1963, the sheriff intimidated and harassed the organizers and the black citizens who applied to register. Would-be registrants also faced economic reprisals. Attempts to desegregate public facilities drew equally hostile responses in Dallas County. Though litigation was pursued more forcefully in Dallas County than anywhere else in the South, the number of black voters in the county failed to rise above 335.

In January 1965 King and SCLC opened a campaign to register black voters in the county. Working with SNCC, SCLC launched a series of demonstrations in Selma, the county seat. On Sunday afternoon, March 7, Alabama highway patrol troopers stopped a column of 600 people who had announced their intention to march to Montgomery to protest. The officer in charge ordered the column to disperse within two minutes. The column remained in place. Perhaps a minute passed. The officer ordered the troopers to charge; they rushed forward with clubs, tear gas, and electric cattle prods. A posse numbering over a hundred, many on horseback, joined in. Blacks fled in terror. Officers of the law pursued the demonstrators into their neighborhoods, even into their homes, repeatedly clubbing and stunning with the cattle prods those they could catch. Clusters of white spectators applauded and cheered. The Selma police intervened and finally persuaded the troopers and the posse to desist. Chief of Police Wilson Baker, with the full support of the mayor, had tried to contain Sheriff Jim Clark and the highway patrol. He feared that their tendency to resort to brutality when they dealt with black demonstrators would make Selma infamous. His fears were realized. Selma became a grim landmark in the history of the civil rights movement as millions watched the assault on television.

SELMA MARCH, 1965 (Bruce Davidson/Magnum Photos)

"Bloody Sunday" triggered a flurry of activity. President Johnson immediately gave first place to the new voting rights legislation his administration had
been working on since the first of the year. On March 15 he addressed a joint
session of Congress and made an urgent plea for his legislation. In his Texas
drawl the president told Congress: "We have waited one hundred years and
more and the time for waiting is gone. We *shall* overcome." Five days later, protected by a federal court order and the federalized Alabama National Guard, the
Selma-to-Montgomery march resumed. It ended four days later at the state capital with 25,000 in attendance and millions watching on television.

In August the president signed the Voting Rights Act. Its provisions gave
the attorney general the power to appoint federal examiners who would supervise voter registration in those states and voting districts that had literacy or
other qualifying tests and where less than 50 percent of the residents of voting
age were registered or had voted in 1964. This portion of the law was applied in
parts or all of seven states—Virginia, the Carolinas, Georgia, Alabama, Mississippi, and Louisiana. The act provided for stiff penalties for interference with
voting rights, abolished literacy requirements, forbade the creation of new voter
qualifications unless they had been cleared by the Justice Department or by a
federal court in the District of Columbia, and directed the Justice Department to
test the constitutionality of poll taxes in state and local elections. (The Twenty-
fourth Amendment to the Constitution [1964] abolished poll taxes in federal
elections.) Four states—Texas, Alabama, Mississippi, and Virginia—still had

poll taxes for state and local elections. In 1966, in a case involving Virginia, the Supreme Court declared poll taxes in state elections unconstitutional.

Congress subsequently voted to extend the life of the Voting Rights Act and widened its coverage. In 1970 Congress altered the law to include cities and counties outside the South where literacy tests had been required, and lowered the voting age to eighteen. A year later the ratification of the Twenty-sixth Amendment made the new voting age permanent and ensured its application to state and local elections. In 1975 Congress amended the act to protect the voting rights of American Indians, native Alaskans, Asian-Americans, Americans of Spanish heritage, and illiterates. In 1982 Congress again strengthened and extended the Voting Rights Act. Shielded and encouraged by the federal government, black voter registration grew rapidly in the South. In 1964 an estimated 43 percent of voting-age blacks in the old Confederacy were registered. In 1968, 62 percent were registered. After that the proportion fluctuated, reaching 66 percent in 1984.

*D*ISILLUSIONMENT

Less than a week after the Voting Rights Act became law, the country was shaken by a serious urban riot. More than ten days of rioting and looting left 34 dead, more than 1,000 injured, and $40 million in property damage in the Watts area of Los Angeles. Similar explosions took place in more than 100 cities in the next three years. Most of the riots occurred outside the South and often began innocently enough, perhaps when a white police officer stopped a black driver for speeding. The eruptions grew from deep cores of black resentment. Unemployment, for example: 30 percent of the employable residents of Watts had no jobs; or housing: residents lived crowded together in dilapidated housing because discrimination bottled up even financially able blacks in "their areas." Expectations had soared in the wake of the civil rights movement, but the realities of the lives of most blacks had not changed much, if at all. Opportunities for political participation had improved dramatically. So had educational opportunities. But job opportunities had not, at least not much. "Colored only" and "white only" signs were gone or were going. But lack of money kept many doors closed to the great majority of blacks. For blacks, the restrictions of caste had been greatly reduced, but for the majority, not the restrictions of class. Frustration turned to rage when blacks failed to find a starting place in the circular route to the American dream: income—educational opportunity—educational achievement—upward mobility—income.

By 1968 the national consensus that had supported the assault on Jim Crow vanished, its disappearance hastened by the riots. But support for that assault never included a willingness to undertake a sustained, deliberate effort to close the gap in income between blacks and whites. Moreover, other points of strong resistance remained in the South. Whites accepted little more than tokenism in public school desegregation and not even tokenism in desegregation of private housing. Residential segregation remained intact. So did racially separate social worlds. In race relations, the South now closely resembled the rest of the nation.

The civil rights movement declined after 1965. Its white support waned. King split with Lyndon Johnson and attacked the United States' commitment to the war in Vietnam. The movement's never entirely harmonious factions split into warring camps. Different styles and aims, egos, generational divisions, and tactical disputes fueled the split. The movement's leaders disputed among themselves about black separatism versus racial integration, about how to attack the seemingly intractable problems of poverty, about whether to risk a break with Lyndon Johnson and openly oppose the war in Vietnam.

SNCC in particular reflected the growing sense of futility among civil rights leaders and many blacks. SNCC embraced black power, stridently demanding black control of the civil rights movement, openly challenging the intentions and abilities of older black leaders, and declaring that no "honky" (white) was to be trusted. Bitter experiences had shaped SNCC's attitudes. SNCC workers had attacked Jim Crow in its darkest, most resistant regions. Physically threatened, beaten, shot at, fire-bombed, even murdered, SNCC activists knew how deeply entrenched southern white hatred and resistance were. They saw blacks who attempted to register to vote lose their jobs, access to credit, and household utilities. SNCC volunteers, most of them middle-class college students, witnessed and experienced poverty and deplorable living and working conditions. The illiteracy and wretched education they found among rural blacks shocked them. A SNCC worker recalled a family with eleven children: "Seven of the children are school age, and not one...is in school because they have no money, no food, no clothes." Their house had "no paper or nothing on the walls and you can look at the ground through the floor and if you were not careful you will step in one of those holes and break your leg or ankle."

At the same time, SNCC lost all faith in the nation's white leaders. White liberals, particularly politicians such as John and Robert Kennedy and Lyndon Johnson, appeared all too ready to compromise the interests of blacks and naive about the seriousness of their problems. Johnson infuriated SNCC and its allies in 1964 when he compromised at the Democratic National Convention with the regular Mississippi Democratic party, which was blatantly racist and often viciously discriminatory, and did not fully support the Mississippi Freedom Democratic party, which was biracial and had a grass-roots following among Mississippi blacks. Federal law enforcement officials seemed indifferent and even hostile. SNCC frequently reported that agents of the Federal Bureau of Investigation stood by and took notes as blacks were beaten or crudely discriminated against. Perhaps SNCC should have had a greater appreciation for the legal limits under which federal officials worked. But when SNCC activists and others were being openly threatened and assaulted by whites who had the approval and even the active support of state and local law officers, they had an understandable tendency to forget that assault is a violation of state law but not of federal law.

With its call for radical change or perhaps revolution, black power had obvious appeal to many blacks (and some young whites, few of whom hailed from the South). Many young blacks in particular had concluded that the plight of blacks was hopeless short of revolutionary change. Black power also provided a way to express outrage, to strike out at "honkies," to intimidate *them* for a change. Stokely Carmichael, who became president of SNCC in 1966, urged blacks in Mississippi to reject the reform strategy of King:

> The only way we are going to stop them from whuppin' us is to take over. We've been saying freedom for six years and we ain't got nothin'.... The time for running has come to an end.... Black Power. It's time we stand up and take over; move on over, whitey, or we'll move on over you.

Black-power rhetoric was heady stuff. It had understandable appeal. It was also reckless, divisive, and rather silly. Black power was reckless because it suggested a racial civil war whose principal victims would have been blacks. Black power was divisive: it divided blacks among themselves and divided blacks and whites. Black power was silly when it talked of revolution: the means for revolution or radical change in the political and economic system of the United States did not exist.

Black power did contribute significantly to the self-image of blacks. Blacks took greater pride in their history and culture and resisted the idea that the price for desegregation and the end of racial discrimination was their becoming "white." But, ironically, this determination to preserve "blackness" and black institutions, such as black colleges and universities, strongly resembled the determination of white segregationists to preserve "whiteness" and white institutions.

The black power movement was short-lived but important. More than anything else, it demonstrated the enormous difficulties the United States faced in trying to create an equitable society. Those difficulties preoccupied and often depressed Martin Luther King during the last three years of his life. Then an assassin's bullet stilled the clearest and most eloquent voice of the civil rights movement. King's death marked a climax in that movement and badly damaged the hopes the movement had stirred.

Extraordinarily high hopes had been required to sustain the civil rights movement in the face of continual verbal and physical abuse, even death. Those high hopes created unrealistic expectations of what could be achieved. Bitterly disappointed blacks, particularly young blacks, focused on what the movement had not done. Conversely, whites focused on what had been done. Almost everywhere in the South, and in a remarkably few years, Jim Crow was dead or dying. Whites added President Johnson's antipoverty program to the things they believed had been done for blacks, though whites also benefited from the "War on Poverty." Moreover, Johnson's program was a limited war with a modest budget and short life. Such considerations, however, had little effect on the perceptions of whites.

Moreover, whites in the South after 1964 perceived a new and grave threat to their public schools. By various means, schools in the South had remained overwhelmingly segregated in spite of *Brown*. But that situation was changing. The percentage of black students enrolled in previously all-white schools increased to 7.5 in 1965, then to 12.5 in 1966. Pressures from the Johnson administration accounted for most of these increases. Acting with the authority of the 1964 Civil Rights Act, the Department of Health, Education, and Welfare (HEW) developed guidelines for school desegregation and then pushed their implementation. Also in 1966, the federal courts made a landmark ruling that greatly accelerated the desegregation of public schools.

THE END OF "FREEDOM OF CHOICE"

Declaring that "the clock has ticked the last tick on tokenism and delay in the name of 'deliberate speed,' " Circuit Court of Appeals Judge John Minor Wisdom fashioned a decision that was the most important judicial ruling on school integration since *Brown* v. *Board of Education* and *Briggs* v. *Elliott*. In *United States* v. *Jefferson County Board of Education* (1966), Wisdom, a native of Louisiana and a Republican appointed by President Eisenhower, set forth three principles. First, public school systems that had practiced de jure (by law) racial segregation had to do more than adopt nondiscriminatory policies. They had an affirmative duty to desegregate. Second, in doing so, they had to devise desegregation plans that followed HEW guidelines. Wisdom issued detailed instructions on such things as pupil assignments; the hiring, firing, and assignment of faculty and staff; and school bus systems. "Eradicating the vestiges of the dual system" was Wisdom's intention. School systems were free to choose from a variety of means to achieve this aim, but "the only school desegregation plan that meets constitutional standards is one that works." The third principle in *Jefferson* was compensatory justice: the remedies that schools instituted must constitute "the organized undoing of the effects of past segregation."

The Supreme Court accepted the *Jefferson* decision and expanded on it. Thus, after more than a decade as a passive agent in school desegregation, the Supreme Court ended "freedom of choice" as an option in school desegregation plans because it had left segregated schools largely in place. For instance, the board of education in the small rural county of New Kent, Virginia, kept its two schools completely segregated until 1965, when it adopted "freedom of choice" desegregation in order to continue to receive federal funds. No whites chose the black school; 115 blacks chose the white school. Eight-five percent of the black students remained in the black school. This arrangement also required the county to bus students of both races across the county to attend the school of their choice. In a 1968 ruling the Court said the public schools in the South had the "affirmative duty to take whatever steps necessary to convert to a unitary system in which racial discrimination would be eliminated root and branch." These two decisions also had the effect of transferring the initiative for desegregation from blacks to white school boards.

The impact of the Johnson administration's support of school desegregation and these two court decisions appears to have been immediate. The Civil Rights Commission reported that nearly a third of the black public school students in the South were attending schools with whites in 1968. "Deliberate speed" was dead. Its demise brought joy in some quarters in the South, outrage in others.

The 1968 presidential election accurately reflected the mood of the country that year: division and turmoil. It was an election in which the South would play a decisive role, one that reflected the profound changes that had occurred in southern politics. Of the many things that contributed to the turmoil in 1968, probably the most important were a war in Vietnam that seemed endless, a troubled economy, racial conflict, and a "cultural revolution" that shocked more than it transformed. The Democratic party fell into disarray. Less than four years after his overwhelming victory in November 1964, President Johnson announced that he would not seek reelection in 1968. After an acrimonious campaign, during which Senator Robert F. Kennedy was assassinated, and a chaotic national convention, the Democrats nominated Vice President Hubert H. Humphrey for president.

Humphrey lost by a narrow margin in popular votes (43.4 percent to 42.7) but by a wide margin (301 to 191) in the electoral college. Richard Nixon's victories in Virginia, the Carolinas, Florida, Kentucky, Tennessee, and Oklahoma figured heavily in his election. For the first time since 1876, electoral votes from the South had been critically important in electing a Republican president. Humphrey became the first Democratic presidential candidate in the twentieth century to win only one state in the South; he carried only Lyndon Johnson's home state of Texas.

Large numbers of white voters in the South rejected Humphrey but were not ready to vote for a Republican. Instead, they supported George Wallace, the Democratic governor of Alabama, who ran on the ticket of the American Independent party—the party for "the little man," the party that promised to "get the Federal Government out of the local schools." Like Thurmond in 1948, Wallace fell far short of his goal of denying either Nixon or Humphrey a majority of electoral votes and thus throwing the election into the House of Representatives, where the South might obtain concessions that Wallace hoped to dictate. "White backlash," hostility toward blacks and their demands, had drawn much of its energy from anger over school desegregation and had had much to do with the outcome of the election.

To heighten the turmoil of those difficult times, Martin Luther King, Jr., was assassinated in April 1968, while helping black garbage collectors in Memphis with their efforts to get better pay and working conditions. The murder of the nation's leading prophet of nonviolence triggered a wave of rioting, burning, and looting throughout the country. Thousands mourned King's death, which had occurred only a dozen years after the then young Baptist minister reluctantly agreed to lead the Montgomery bus boycott.

Remarkable changes had taken place in the dozen years since Montgomery. Racial segregation in public facilities was dead. Barriers against registration and voting by blacks had been largely torn down, and the number of black office-holders was increasing. Blacks had greater access to schooling and jobs than ever before. After more than a decade of delay, evasion, and massive resistance, *Brown* v. *Board of Education* was being implemented in the South. Black faces multiplied in classrooms, on athletic teams, among police and firefighters, behind counters in stores, at desks in government agencies, at front doors rather than back doors. A new etiquette for race relations evolved along with a greater sensitivity toward blacks. Politicians learned to solicit black votes. Sheriffs, police, and local courts treated blacks more evenhandedly.

Whites played critical if somewhat secondary roles in these remarkable changes. With rare exceptions, whites in the South—and elsewhere—had taken little initiative in the early stages of the assault on Jim Crow. Most whites accepted or acquiesced in desegregation and did so more quickly and quietly than most people believed was possible. Demographics and economic change helped. The ratio of blacks to whites had declined in every southern state since 1900. In none were blacks a majority in 1960; in that year one in four people living in the South was black. Consequently, whites felt less threatened. Whites also enjoyed the greater security that post-1940 prosperity had brought with it. Still, few observers would have concurred with what Leslie Dunbar, the executive director of the Southern Regional Council, a pioneering biracial organization, predicted in 1961. Dunbar said that whites would fight desegregation because they felt duty-bound to defend their culture and their past, but they would accept desegregation rather quickly.

> Once the fight is decisively lost (the verdict has to be decisive), once the Negro has secured the right to vote, has gained admittance to a public library, has fought his way into a desegregated public school, has been permitted to sup at a lunch counter, the typical white Southerner will shrug his shoulders, resume his stride, and go on. He has, after all, shared a land with his black neighbors for a long while; he can manage well enough even if patterns change. There is now one less fight which history requires of him. He has done his ancestoral duty. He...can relax a bit more.

These remarkably perceptive comments suggest a more thorough transformation in race relations in the South than in fact has come about. As we shall see, patterns of racial separation persist, most noticeably in social relations, but they are still very obvious also in public schools and in housing; and the persistence of separation has had major consequences, most obviously in the politics of the South—and of the nation. The pattern of race relations in the South has changed from conscious subordination of blacks to a less conscious but hardly accidental pattern of avoidance. Perhaps that was all that one realistically could have expected in a quarter of a century, but that was all that was achieved.

27

The Modern South

--- ❖ ---

O ne hundred years after the disputed Hayes-Tilden presidential election of 1876 and the end of Reconstruction, Americans chose James Earl "Jimmy" Carter, Jr., of Plains, Georgia, to be the thirty-ninth president of the United States, the first resident of the Deep South to be elected president in almost 130 years. Carter's electoral victory indicated that much had changed in the intervening decades.

Indeed, the South of 1976 bore only faint resemblance to the South of 1876. The overwhelmingly impoverished agrarian world of the 1870s had given way to a prosperous modern South of metropolitan complexes and cities, of diverse manufacturing and growing service industries, of agribusiness, retirement centers, and tourism. The 1870s elite of planters and their business and professional allies had been displaced by a more cosmopolitan elite whose base lay in the region's urban centers, in banking, insurance, law, manufacturing, services, and education.

Just as economic life in the South had been transformed, so had political life. Blacks had regained the vote and the access to public office that they had enjoyed in the 1870s, and this time their hold on both seemed more secure. The southern Democrats had moved from the politics of white supremacy to desegregation, even integration. By 1976 southern Democrats had forged an alliance of blacks and whites to meet the challenge of a revived Republican party in the South. The solid or one-party Democratic South was becoming a relic.

Another relic was Jim Crow. The rigid caste system of earlier days had collapsed, though more vestiges of it remained than many people cared to acknowledge. Even the humid heat of the long southern summers had been blunted, if not banished, by air conditioning. Standing in the air conditioned comfort of hotel rooms in Atlanta or Dallas, visiting corporate executives from Chicago or New York could gaze out over a landscape of skyscrapers, freeways, and interstate highways, franchise stores and eating places, suburban developments and shopping centers spilling over the horizon. Understandably, they might conclude that the South they saw was just like the rest of the United States, that the South was no longer clearly differentiated from the rest of the nation.

Striking distinctions remained, however, even if they were not so easily perceived as the economic backwardness, the one-party politics, and the racial caste system that once clearly delineated an older South. The South still had a disproportionate share of the nation's poor, undereducated, and unskilled. The South remained more Protestant—more Baptist, more Methodist—than the rest of the country, and less ethnically diverse, though it had the highest proportion of blacks. Southerners continued to talk with soft drawls, to attach more importance to manners, to live at what appeared to be a slower pace, and to murder and assault one another more often than their fellow Americans. Southerners still maintained a peculiar attachment to their region, though usually they were aware of its deficiencies.

The South and southerners still had a distinctive identity a hundred years after Reconstruction, but that identity had lost some of its edge, had become murkier than at any time since the mid-eighteenth century. Historians and similar sorts had once been able to identify the South and southerners easily. By 1977, as Jimmy Carter prepared to enter the White House, that identification was no longer so straightforward. The task has become even more difficult in the intervening years. That difficulty may help explain why journalists seemed quickly to get a clear focus on who Jimmy Carter was and what Plains was, only to have the images blur and leave them puzzled.

JIMMY CARTER AND PLAINS, GEORGIA

Plains has a deceptively simple appearance that suggests an older South that has not changed. Yet it also suggests a very new South. A look at Plains does not take very long. It has a diameter of a mile, and some 680 people, more than half of whom are black, live there. (Shortly after President Carter took office, the population in Plains declined by 2 percent, from 683 to 672 people, presumably a result of Carter's move to Washington.) Settled in the 1830s, Plains was incorporated in the 1890s when the railroad recentered the geography and economy of the town and the surrounding area. The arrival of a trunk line (which became part of the Seaboard Airline) pulled the center of Plains to the new railway station, shortened the village's biblically inspired name, Plains of Dura, and accelerated the development of cash-crop farming. Cotton growing increased steadily around the turn of the century; so did sharecropping. Of the 2,878 farm operators in Sumter County (where Plains is located) in 1910, 2,286 were tenants or croppers, and more than 2,000 of them were black. Of the 592 farm owners in 1910, 138 were black.

Thus Sumter County resembled many rural counties in the Deep South in the early twentieth century. That was still the case in the 1970s. Sumter County in the 1970s reflected the impact of the dramatic changes that had occurred in southern agriculture in the twentieth century. Population growth had stopped or even declined in many rural areas. When Jimmy Carter announced his candidacy for the presidency in 1974, the entire population of Sumter County was

27,797, or 1,200 fewer people than had lived there in 1910. Sumter had only 404 farm operators, 360 of whom owned part or all of their farms. About one in four earned more money off the farm than on the farm. Black farm tenants had become virtually extinct; only 3 of the 44 farm tenants in the county were black. Thirty-three blacks owned part or all of the land they cultivated. Most of the blacks who still worked in agriculture were day laborers. Some 25 percent of the county lived below the poverty level. Livestock, poultry, dairy farming, and peanut growing overshadowed cotton.

Like many rural counties in the South, Sumter had resisted the civil rights revolution. In the 1960s the county was reputed to be especially hostile to the movement. Some local whites took pride in the fact that in 1961 Martin Luther King, Jr., spent time in the county jail in Americus, where he had endured being called "boy" and had to sweep the floors. Two years later, officials arrested four civil rights workers in Americus and charged them with insurrection, a capital offense. A federal judge eventually intervened to stop their prosecution. In 1965 a federal judge enjoined county officials from enforcing segregation. Two years later the U.S. Fifth Circuit Court of Appeals set aside county election results because of what the court called "gross, spectacular, completely indefensible state-imposed, state-enforced racial discrimination." As late as 1976 blacks complained that local whites were perpetuating racial discrimination in politics by backing Uncle Toms (blacks who were overly susceptible to white pressure and not sufficiently attuned to the interests of blacks) for local office and by arranging voting districts to dilute the power of black voters. At the same time, there were reports of marked improvements in race relations in the Americus high school and significantly increased enrollments of white students in the black-majority school. The high school football team, which had won two state championships, received considerable credit for these changes.

The Carter farm and peanut-processing facilities were major employers of black men in the area. Blacks attended the desegregated white schools, voted, and held public office. Not much else had been desegregated, however, including the local churches. Whites generally lived north of the railroad line, blacks generally south. Whites lived in homes with plumbing; blacks lived in poorer houses, two-thirds of which had no plumbing. Almost all the homes, however, had electricity. Plains was a direct beneficiary of the Rural Electrification Administration.

The Carter family was the most prosperous in Plains. The Carter homestead was one of the first to be connected to the power lines under the REA. His father, "the Prince of Plains," had been so successful in merchandising and agribusiness that he was able to send all of his children to college. Jimmy was the best student of the four, and the first member of the Carter family to get a college degree. Following a year of study at a nearby community college, which Carter's father had strongly supported, and at Georgia Institute of Technology, the future president went to the U.S. Naval Academy. After his graduation in 1947 and further study in nuclear engineering, Carter began what he intended to be a lifelong career in the navy. Like many young, ambitious southerners of the World War II era, he had chosen to leave the land, get an education, and pursue a career outside the rural South. Like many southerners before him, he initially sought success in the military.

He changed course in 1953. When his father died, Carter resigned his navy commission, returned to Plains, and took charge of the family business, which had declined during his father's last years. Jimmy Carter revived the business, concentrating his efforts on peanut processing and peanut seeds. The successful agribusinessman also got involved in community affairs and then in politics. He served on local and regional economic development commissions in Georgia, then was elected to the state senate for the first of two terms in 1961.

Five years later Carter was one of three Democrats to run for governor, his first statewide race, and lost in the primary to Lester Maddox, who got more votes than any other candidate but fell short of a majority. The Democratic-controlled Georgia legislature elected Maddox governor. Maddox, an Atlanta restaurateur and political novice, had achieved notoriety by threatening to apply an ax handle to the heads of demonstrators who attempted to desegregate his restaurant. Furious reactions to recently passed federal civil rights legislation, federal court decisions on civil rights, and moves to accelerate desegregation of public accommodations and schools provided the impetus for his unexpected victory. Maddox's victory tarnished the moderate image of Atlanta, the city "too busy to hate."

Carter, who had run as a racial moderate, returned to Plains a disillusioned man. He had not anticipated the depth of the anger that desegregation would arouse in Georgia whites. He had deviated from the segregationist mentality of most Georgia whites before he entered politics. In the 1950s he openly broke from his father's paternalist-segregationist position to adopt a desegregationist stance similar to that of Lillian Carter, his mother. Carter refused to join the White Citizens' Council in 1955, a move that hurt his business for a while and could have destroyed it. In 1964 he tried unsuccessfully to persuade the Plains Baptist Church to accept black members.

After his return to Plains in 1966, Carter had a profound religious experience. Bolstered by the experience of being "born again" and his considerable ambition and energy, Carter ran for governor again in 1970. Running as an antiestablishment candidate against Carl Sanders, a popular former governor and Atlanta attorney, Carter won the Democratic primary decisively. Then he easily beat his Republican opponent in the general election. Carter's coalition included, ironically perhaps, the "little people" whose political heroes had been Maddox and George Wallace, the populistic governor of Alabama and several times presidential candidate who had built a large following by his dramatic show of resistance to desegregation.

At his inauguration as governor, Carter took a stance that few earlier white leaders in the South would have assumed, certainly not Maddox or Wallace. He told the inaugural audience: "I say to you quite frankly that the time for racial discrimination is over....No poor, rural, weak, or black person should ever have to bear the burden of being deprived of the opportunity of an education, a job, or simple justice." Carter subsequently ordered a portrait of Martin

Luther King, Jr., to be displayed in the state capitol and appointed a number of blacks to state agencies and boards.

Personal conviction and political necessity influenced these actions. After the civil rights revolution and the rebirth of southern Republicanism in the 1960s, southern Democrats had to ally themselves with blacks. In other respects, too, Governor Carter showed himself to be a reflection of the modern South. He worked very hard to reorganize the state government in the hope of making it more efficient and less costly, and he spent much of his time and energy on efforts to attract new industries and businesses to Georgia in order to continue to diversify the state's economy and to create greater job opportunities for Georgians.

Carter, who could not succeed himself as governor, announced his presidential candidacy in 1974. In 1976 this relatively unknown political figure won the presidential election. Carter's southern roots influenced the outcome powerfully. Save for Virginia and Oklahoma, he carried the entire South and all the border states. It was a better performance in the formerly solid South than could be claimed by any Democrat since Franklin Roosevelt in 1944. Unlike Roosevelt's electoral victories in the South, however, Carter's victory depended heavily on southern blacks. Without them Carter would not have won any southern state.

Carter's sudden rise to political prominence in the nation and his electoral success triggered enormous interest in him and in the world from which he emerged. That interest was reinforced and shaped by the nation's recurring urge to understand the South and southerners. Carter did not make it easy to satisfy that urge. At various times, partly because of the way he projected him-

CARTER AND BLACK LEADERS (Jimmy Carter Library)

self, Carter was perceived both as a modern man and as a rural rustic. He symbolized the modern South—desegregated, upwardly mobile, more cosmopolitan in its politics, a champion of agribusiness, well educated, adroit in public imagery. But he was also perceived as a simple peanut farmer and small-town Southern Baptist from a rural fantasyland where few people wore shoes, neighbors were neighborly, and traditional values and ways persisted—except for Jim Crow, which had wondrously vanished one warm summer morning.

Carter's kin also attracted the curious and often left them puzzled. His wife, Rosalynn, appeared to be a timid Southern Lady, until she spoke; then she was impressive. Perceptive listeners sensed that she had brains, energy, and ambition in ample measure. "Miss Lil," the mother and former Peace Corps worker, rocked on her front porch and entertained with stories that seemed to obscure as much as they revealed. Carter's only and younger brother smoked packs of unfiltered cigarettes, drank beer by the sixpack, and spun tales for reporters at the filling station he owned and operated. They thought they had found that perennial archetype of the South, the good ole boy. Few suspected that he was fully capable of running the Carter family enterprise, as he did after Jimmy Carter left for the White House.

The president's older sister, Gloria Carter Spann, a born-again Christian, lived in modest circumstances with her husband in Americus and sped about the countryside on a motorcycle to conduct an informal ministry. Ruth Carter Stapleton, the younger sister, resided in North Carolina, in a comfortable, post–World War II suburb with her husband, a dentist, and their children. She traveled frequently as a Christian evangelist and faith healer. She counseled Jimmy Carter when he had his born-again experience. Carter's beliefs were hardly as simple as some people thought. He read and digested the complexities of modern Christian theology and social ethics. His religious faith and thinking and the man himself defied stereotyping and simplistic labeling, but the stereotyping and labeling went on.

Carter's religious commitment and the way he expressed that commitment reflected his southern roots. So did his sense of place and attachment to agriculture, his extended family and ties to the military, and his determination that the South must modernize, relying heavily on science and industry to do so. He combined the traditions of evangelical Protestantism, agrarianism, Populism, and Whiggery, all southern traditions. The resulting combination may have been too complicated for easy public consumption. Certainly the public found Carter a puzzle it could not solve and eventually did not care to solve. The elusiveness of Carter may symbolize the South at the end of the twentieth century.

THE RISE OF THE SOUTHERN REPUBLICANS

Some things about the South were clear in the last decades of the twentieth century. The Republican party had become a major force in the region. The Republican revival, which began shortly after World War II, received its initial stimulus from divisions among Democrats. Traditionally the Democratic party's greatest asset in the South had been its ability to keep blacks in their place and to prevent the federal government from intervening to alter that arrangement. By the 1940s, southern Democrats faced serious threats to their power to do either of these things. Faced by the renomination of Harry Truman and the national Democratic party's endorsement of a strong civil rights plank in its platform, many voters fled. Traditional aversion to the Republican party and the strong civil rights stand that the Republicans had adopted in 1948 kept most angry southern Democrats from joining the Republicans. Those southern Democrats who broke with the national Democrats either retreated to the sidelines to wait out the election or became Dixiecrats.

Republican presidential fortunes improved dramatically in 1952. Except for Herbert Hoover in 1928, no Republican presidential nominee had done well in the South since Reconstruction. Dwight D. Eisenhower captured Virginia, Florida, Tennessee, Texas, and Oklahoma in 1952. To these states Eisenhower added Louisiana during his successful reelection campaign in 1956. The Democrats recaptured Texas and Louisiana when John F. Kennedy defeated Richard Nixon in 1960. The victories in those states were probably largely the result of Kennedy's choice of Lyndon Johnson of Texas, then Senate majority leader, as his vice presidential running mate. Johnson provided an urgently needed cohesive force for a divided Democratic party and strong regional appeal for southern voters. Johnson had been a cohesive force for the Democrats before. During the late 1950s he had stood midway between northern Democrats who wanted to abolish Jim Crow quickly and southern Democrats who adamantly opposed almost every facet of desegregation. A moderate on race, a politician who aspired to national office, and a master of political strategy, he realized that the Democratic party could not survive if it ignored the aspirations of blacks and tried to keep Jim Crow. Johnson, like a small but growing number of southern whites, seems to have believed that Jim Crow was immoral and was unworthy of a great nation, especially one that claimed to be a democracy and world leader.

Conversely, Johnson knew that an all-out government assault on Jim Crow would drive the great majority of southern Democrats out of the party, perhaps into the Republican party. Thus he adopted a convoluted course of action. He carefully and quietly avoided signing the Southern Manifesto in 1956. He orchestrated passage of the Civil Rights acts of 1957 and 1960. As weapons against Jim Crow, both measures had serious deficiencies, especially in their provisions for enforcement. Johnson was strongly criticized for that lack. Critics said he had so diluted the new laws to get them passed that they were civil rights laws in name only. Others, however, noted that Johnson's actions made passage of the laws possible, that they were the first of their kind since Reconstruction and thus constituted important precedents for stronger civil rights legislation in the future, and that the new laws were intended to be warning signals to the South.

Republican successes in the South from 1952 to 1960 reflected the economic and demographic changes the region had been undergoing, especially since

1940. In the surge of post-1940 prosperity, the ranks of the urban middle class swelled. Professionals, managers, businesspeople, and corporate officials, most of whom were college educated, found the national Republican party more compatible with their views than the national Democratic party, which they perceived as too liberal, too inclined to support labor unions, and too disinclined to foster private business. Republicans had shown strength in the urban South before, as long ago as 1920. In the 1950s and thereafter, that strength was broader and more durable, in part because of precedent-setting court decisions on reapportionment.

Some of the Republican-leaning inhabitants of the new suburbs, with centrally air conditioned and heated homes, expansive green lawns, second cars, private kindergartens, and dancing and music lessons for often reluctant offspring, were only a generation from farms, mines, and factories. Probably more came from second- and third-generation city families. Migrating "Yankees" added to the numbers of these two groups. As early as 1950, native whites born outside the South made up 30 percent of the white population of Florida. (No other southern state had as many as 15 percent until 1970.) Northern white migrants tended to concentrate in urban areas outside the Deep South, particularly in southern Florida, in northern Virginia, along the Chesapeake Bay, at Richmond, and in Dallas, Fort Worth, Houston, and San Antonio. Many of these newcomers had Republican ties or, like many of the other prosperous southern city dwellers, had only weak ties to the Democrats. Traditionally Republican areas—eastern Tennessee, western North Carolina and Virginia, portions of northern Alabama and northern Georgia, northeastern Oklahoma, northwestern Arkansas, the "German" counties in Texas—continued to vote Republican. That loyalty and the votes of the urban middle class accounted for the success of the Republican presidential candidates in the South in the late 1950s and early 1960s. Those successes ended in 1964—temporarily, as it turned out.

THE COLLAPSE OF THE SOLID SOUTH

Nineteen sixty-four marked a decisive turning point in the demise of the solid South, as it did also in the collapse of Jim Crow. In the decade or so after 1964, Democratic strength in the South declined precipitously while Republican fortunes soared. "The breadth of the Democratic collapse is staggering," two political scientists commented. "It would be difficult to find comparable instances in American political history of such a rapid and comprehensive desertion of an established majority party by an entire region."

Ironically, during the 1964 election the Democrats looked very strong in the region. Lyndon Johnson won the presidency in his own right in a landslide victory over Barry Goldwater, the Republican nominee. Johnson thus became only the second successful presidential candidate from one of the former Confederate states since Zachary Taylor. Johnson swept the border states and the upper

South, areas where Republicans had been showing growing strength since World War II. The Democrats also made very strong showings in most of the congressional, state, and local elections in the South in 1964.

Many southerners, however, did not rejoice in Johnson's victory. Repelled by Johnson's embrace of civil rights, part of an evolving pattern of close ties between the national Democratic party and blacks, white voters in the Deep South flocked to the Republican candidate. Louisiana, Mississippi, Alabama, Georgia, and South Carolina joined Arizona, Goldwater's home state, as the only states that gave their electoral votes to the Republican senator. Goldwater's opposition to the *Brown* decision and to the Civil Rights Act of 1964 had great appeal in the South. He received 54 percent of the vote in Georgia, 59 percent in South Carolina, almost 69.5 percent in Alabama, and 87 percent in Mississippi to become the first Republican candidate to win those states since Reconstruction. Alabama also elected five Republicans to the House of Representatives, Georgia and Mississippi one each.

President Johnson's electoral triumph benefited as much from the personality of Senator Barry Goldwater of Arizona as from his own appeal. A militant conservative, Goldwater alarmed moderates and liberals alike. They feared he would lead the United States into a wider, costlier war in Vietnam, risk nuclear confrontation with the Soviet Union, and undermine domestic programs many citizens thought were critically important. The senator had an unusual talent for triggering alarms. While campaigning in Florida, he convinced many elderly voters that he wanted to abandon social security; in Tennessee, he suggested that he wanted to sell the Tennessee Valley Authority to private investors.

But Goldwater attracted strong support in the Deep South, where race was the paramount issue. Convinced that the Republicans could not "get the Negro vote as a bloc" in 1964 and 1968, he had told a Republican audience in 1961 that they "ought to go hunting where the ducks are." Goldwater declared that school desegregation was "the responsibility of the states" and that he did not want his party to "assume it is the role of the federal government to enforce integration in the schools." The Arizona senator had opposed the *Brown* decision as an invasion of the rights of states and an overly broad interpretation of the constitutional powers of the Supreme Court. For similar reasons, Goldwater voted against the Civil Rights Act of 1964.

Conversely, the Democratic party under Kennedy and then Johnson had increasingly allied itself with the civil rights movement. That process had accelerated in 1963 as a result of the prolonged civil rights conflict in Birmingham, the march on Washington, and the nation's grief in the wake of the assassination of President Kennedy. Johnson now had the votes to push the Civil Rights Act through Congress, and he did so. The Texas Democrat had moved to embrace the civil rights movement and to ensure that blacks would be part of the winning political coalition he was constructing.

Segregationists eagerly joined the Goldwater forces and helped him win the Republican presidential nomination. They liked more than his stance on civil rights. His strongly conservative positions—for states' rights, against communism, for reduced government spending on social programs and an increase in spending for the military—paralleled theirs. Most climbed on the Goldwater bandwagon so eagerly that they missed a subtle point. The senator had long believed that segregation was wrong. He differed with President Johnson, King, and others over means, not ends; over *how* segregation should be attacked, not over *whether* it should be attacked. Critics noted that Goldwater's chosen means—the states—were unlikely to dismantle Jim Crow, that his position on civil rights put him effectively, if unintentionally, in the segregationists' camp.

THE REPUBLICAN PARTY SECURES ITS PLACE IN DIXIE

The size of the Democratic victory in 1964 obscured most of the critical political changes that were occurring within the Republican party in the South. The nature of that party changed significantly. Before 1964 the Republican party in the South had been evolving by fits and starts from a party whose primary concern was the distribution of federal patronage to one that could beat the Democrats. That goal required a more vigorous organization, slates of viable candidates, and infusions of talent and money. Goldwater's candidacy stimulated this process, especially in the Deep South. Young, ambitious men and women embraced the Republican party as the party of the future. They could rise more rapidly there than in the Democratic party. They saw the Democratic party as entrenched, self-satisfied, and resistant to change, new ideas, and new people. Breaking away from the Democrats was a way to break from one's parents. Not a few of the young Goldwaterites were converted Democrats. Senator Strom Thurmond, the most successful politician in South Carolina's electoral history, also switched parties in 1964, bringing with him an important cadre of South Carolina political activists.

Most of the Goldwaterites were ideological conservatives. Almost all of them opposed rapid desegregation; some were outright segregationists. One observer described the Goldwater or "New Guard" Republicans in Tennessee as "prepared to exploit the older norms of white supremacy, laissez-faire, anti-unionism, and businessman Bourbonism." They were "politically inexperienced, but ideological and impatient with the supineness of the Old Guard," ready to employ "the hard sell, the grass roots drive, and the systematic organization which generated success in the business world" in pursuit of their political aims. The New Guard took over much of the Republican party structure and was ready to outorganize and outwork the Democrats, who were ill prepared for vigorous partisan battles after so many years of one-party politics.

Circumstances provided a strong stimulus for the growth of the Republican party in the South. Nineteen-sixty-four was a year of widespread unrest in reaction to the war in Vietnam, an outspoken counterculture, and racial conflict.

Unrest grew in the South as the pace of public school desegregation quickened after 1964. Only two years after enjoying their greatest victories in the South since 1948, Democrats suffered defeats throughout the region in 1966. That year the Republicans in the South added a total of seven seats in the House of Representatives (though they lost two of their Alabama seats), elected a senator in Tennessee, reelected Thurmond as a Republican in South Carolina, elected governors in Florida and Arkansas, nearly won the governorship in Georgia, and almost doubled their seats in the state legislatures in the region. Voters thus swelled the ranks of the southern Republicans at the time that New Guard Republicans were taking over the leadership of the party.

As the New Guard pushed the Republican party to the right, it became whiter. Republican moderates and black Republicans found themselves shoved to the periphery or out of the party altogether. Ironically, moderates had been important in earlier Republican successes in the South. They had been prominent in the Eisenhower and Nixon campaigns, and they had been rewarded. Republican moderates appointed to the bench by President Eisenhower— Judges Elbert P. Tuttle, John R. Brown, and John Minor Wisdom—and Judge Richard T. Rives, a Democrat appointed by President Harry Truman, led the Fifth Circuit Court of Appeals when that court became the foremost judicial force in the dismantling of Jim Crow. This judicial circuit, which then covered Texas, Louisiana, Mississippi, Alabama, Georgia, and Florida, made a series of landmark decisions in civil rights in the 1950s and 1960s.

Judge Frank M. Johnson, Jr., another Republican whom Eisenhower appointed, was also part of the judicial vanguard whose decisions undermined segregation and laid the foundation for sweeping political change in the South. Sitting on a special three-judge panel, Johnson and Rives formed the 2-to-1 majority that in 1956 declared unconstitutional the Montgomery ordinance requiring racial segregation on public transportation. They concluded that the ordinance violated the principle established by the Supreme Court in *Brown* v. *Board of Education* that "separate but equal" violated the Fourteenth Amendment. Judge Johnson later was involved in several dramatic confrontations with Governor George Wallace of Alabama over desegregation and civil rights demonstrations. Not all of Eisenhower's judicial appointees in the South were moderates, much less forces for desegregation. Judge Benjamin F. Cameron of the Fifth Circuit, an unbending segregationist, did his best to preserve Jim Crow, even if he had to ignore Supreme Court rulings to do so.

The Goldwaterites also carried the Republican party into the previously overwhelmingly Democratic black belt. John Grenier, an Alabama Republican who became a national party leader, later contended that the 1964 election gave the South a major voice in the national party. In the wake of Republican victories in the South and the growing weaknesses of the Republicans in the northeastern states, traditionally an area of Republican power, Grenier said, the South and the West had become the dominant regions in the national Republican party. These developments help explain the nominations of two Californians, Richard Nixon in 1968 and 1972 and Ronald Reagan in 1980 and 1984.

Certainly Republican presidential candidates have done well in the South since 1964. In 1968 Nixon carried Virginia, Tennessee, Oklahoma, and Florida, as Eisenhower had done, and added North Carolina and South Carolina. However, he lost Texas to Humphrey, the Democratic nominee, and Louisiana, Mississippi, Alabama, and Georgia to George Wallace, who ran as a third-party candidate on the American Independent party ticket. When President Nixon ran for reelection in 1972 he swept the South, something a Republican had never done before.

In both elections Nixon used a more subtle version of Goldwater's appeal to southern white voters. Nixon's "southern strategy" combined strong conservative positions on defense and on economic and social issues with obvious but not blunt appeals to the racial sentiments of whites. Nixon called for less government intervention in support of desegregation, and he said that the South ought to be given more time to adjust to the dramatic advances of desegregation from 1963 to 1968. Privately, Nixon was less subtle and more specific. To ensure his nomination in 1968, Nixon obtained the support of Senator Strom Thurmond by promising the South Carolinian that his administration would downplay school desegregation, appoint a southerner to the Supreme Court, and support a strong national defense.

When Nixon campaigned, he particularly criticized busing as a means of implementing school desegregation. He—and others—continued these attacks though they knew it was often impossible to desegregate schools without busing some students, and that busing had in fact long been used to maintain segregated schools. He and his political advisers correctly sensed that the majority of both whites and blacks opposed busing. Hostility to school busing for segregation stemmed from a complex array of ideas, feelings, fears, and sometimes misinformation. Moreover, this strong negative attitude created a large dilemma. Could school desegregation, which most people after 1970 said they favored or accepted, be achieved without busing, which most people said they opposed?

Busing aroused strong feelings because it undermined the concept of the neighborhood school, it had a strong impact on millions of families, it could be very expensive, and it raised issues of economic and social class. Busing raised all kinds of concerns, many of which were reasonable and some of which were not. Among those concerns were the safety of children, the expense of busing, and its effect on the education of children and the schedules of families, especially at a time when most adults were employed outside the home. Busing also seemed to be one more instance of the transfer of power over a basic institution to faceless judges and bureaucrats, who appeared to be moving students (and sometimes teachers) like pawns to meet racial quotas and seemed to order changes in desegregation plans every year.

Opponents of school busing claimed that it would only cause resegregation of public schools because whites, who had more money than blacks, would put their children in private schools or move from urban districts to suburban districts. Many whites did in fact turn to private schools or move. But white flight was motivated by more than a desire to avoid integrated schools or busing.

Suburbs provided newer, often more pleasant, and frequently less costly housing than was available in many older urban areas. The flight to the suburbs reinforced the decline of central cities in the South as residential areas. Conversely, the decline of central cities reinforced the migration to the periphery.

Opponents of busing usually ignored facts that conflicted with their position. Busing, as we have noted, had long been used to keep schools racially
segregated, and long-distance busing was not uncommon. Some desegregation
plans actually involved less travel for students and lower busing costs than the
transportation programs some schools had in place before desegregation. Supporters of busing to facilitate desegregation rightly suspected that the real opposition was not to busing per se but to school desegregation by any means.

The busing issue created a dilemma for the national Democratic party. In
the 1960s the Democrats became the political leaders of the attack on Jim Crow
and consequently led the political assault on segregated public education. In
1966 the courts ordered that school districts that had once been legally segregated by race must assume the initiative to desegregate and must have racially
unitary school systems. To obey these judicial orders, school districts frequently
had to bus large numbers of pupils considerable distances because of residential
segregation. Residential segregation tended to be most pronounced in the large
cities, where the majority of voters now lived. This set of circumstances led voters to associate the Democratic party with a highly unpopular policy. Southern
Democrats tried to dissociate themselves from the party's position by decrying
school busing.

Thus circumstances gave the Republicans a great political opportunity, particularly in the 1968 presidential election. Nixon quickly seized the opportunity,
frequently denouncing busing and simultaneously appealing to racial moderates and strong segregationists. The results at the polls in 1968 indicated that
the southern strategy worked.

Once in office, President Nixon openly joined efforts to slow school desegregation. Moreover, southerners were appointed to high and very visible positions in the administration. Opposition in the Senate and the president's own
ineptitude initially prevented him from putting a southerner on the Supreme
Court. After two rejections, however, in 1971 the Senate confirmed Lewis F.
Powell, Jr., of Virginia, Nixon's third nominee, for a seat on the Supreme
Court. In 1972 Nixon's southern strategy helped him to capture the votes of
people who had supported George Wallace in 1968 and to carry the entire South
in a landslide victory. Republican successes in the South created a power base
that had implications for national politics.

Only once in the five presidential elections since 1964 have the Democrats
done well in the South. (And only once have they won a presidential election.)
Jimmy Carter carried eleven of thirteen southern states in 1976—all but Virginia
and Oklahoma. The Democratic victory was short-lived. Carter had the misfor-
tune to assume the presidency at an extraordinarily difficult time, when the
United States was stumbling from one economic crisis to another and appeared
to be impotent in international affairs. Four years later those problems re-

mained, and Carter, one of the more intelligent presidents to serve this country, appeared to be confused and indecisive. The Iranian hostage crisis in particular emphasized the perceptions of America's—or at least of Carter's—weaknesses. Carter's inability to secure the release of Americans being held hostage by Islamic militants in Teheran seemed to be clear evidence that he lacked political skills. Public opinion polls showed that the "man from Plains" was one of the most unpopular presidents in this century. To virtually no one's surprise, he failed to win reelection.

When Carter lost to Ronald Reagan in 1980, he lost everywhere in the South except Georgia, his home state. President Reagan captured every southern state when he was reelected in 1984, as did George Bush during his successful 1988 presidential campaign. Carter's unpopularity abetted the emergence of a new "solid South," Republican style, at least in presidential politics. A striking indication of the new reality was the strength of President Bush's support in the South. He buried his opponent, Michael Dukakis, in Dixie by a margin of 58 percent of the vote to 42 percent, by far the largest margin of victory in any region. Elsewhere Bush won by about 52 percent to 48 percent.

But the Republicans have had less success at other levels. Southern Democrats still outnumber southern Republicans in the U.S. Senate and House of Representatives. Both senators from Virginia in 1984 were Republicans, however, and so were the majority of its representatives. In 1988 Charles S. Robb, son-in-law of Lyndon Johnson and former Democratic governor of Virginia, defeated one of Virginia's Republican senators. Most of the governors' mansions in the region remained in Democratic hands. Republican strength in the South should increase, however, because economic and demographic factors favor the Republican party. The number of southern white voters, who are more likely to vote Republican, has grown faster since 1960 than has the number of black voters, who are more likely to vote Democratic. One indication of the growing strength of the Republicans in the South was that Republicans steadily increased their overall numbers in state and local offices. Obviously a two-party South had emerged. In its politics the South had come to resemble the rest of the nation. The solid South had gone with Jim Crow.

THE TRANSFORMATION OF THE SOUTHERN DEMOCRATS

Just as the political terrain of the South has been transformed since World War II, so has the Democratic party in the South. The Democrats had to learn that not all white voters—other than eccentrics and mountaineers—were Democrats, that their power base in the black belt had been eroded, and that attracting and winning black voters were essential to survival. Initially the great majority of Democratic leaders sought to maintain their party's birthright as the party of white supremacy. White flight to the Republican party, the civil rights movement, and the weight of the courts and the federal government forced first a retreat, then the development of a new strategy. Some Democrats, such as Carter, welcomed the change. Most Democratic leaders changed because they had no choice; they either changed or lost.

Southern Democrats learned in the 1960s that many races could not be won without black votes. They learned they had to build political coalitions with black leaders and voters and support black candidates for office. In less than a decade after the Southern Manifesto appeared, the party of white supremacy became biracial. The transition was not easy. There was open conflict, suspicion, and misunderstanding. White Democrats often found themselves caught between the need to satisfy the demands of blacks and anxieties about white flight. President Johnson and then Senator Hubert H. Humphrey, a long-time civil rights advocate, infuriated blacks when they refused to support the efforts of the predominantly black Freedom Democratic party of Mississippi to be seated as the state's official delegation at the Democratic National Convention in 1964. Fearing white backlash in Mississippi, Johnson and Humphrey refused to exclude the delegates of the regular Democratic party in Mississippi, though they were avowed segregationists and openly disloyal to the national party ticket.

Converts to biracial politics, however, eventually outnumbered unreconcilable segregationists. Herman Talmadge was one of the more conspicuous converts. He had inherited the strong personal support of his father, Eugene, and had nurtured that support with racist rhetoric in successful gubernatorial and senatorial campaigns. A Supreme Court decision ruling unconstitutional the system by which Georgia managed to give greater weight to rural (white) votes than to votes in urban areas (where more blacks were registered to vote) and the Voting Rights Act of 1965 persuaded Herman Talmadge that he had to take a different tack. Senator Talmadge addressed a luncheon meeting of Atlanta's black leaders in 1966 and declared that "all candidates are going to solicit the votes of all Georgia citizens." Asked why he had not appeared before them five or six years earlier, Talmadge responded: "Five or six years ago, you didn't invite me."

Democrats who openly favored racial moderation did very well in gubernatorial elections in 1970. The newly elected Democratic governors of Florida (Reubin Askew), Arkansas (Dale Bumpers), Georgia (Jimmy Carter), and South Carolina (John C. West) called for an end to segregation and racial discrimination. Republicans could, of course, also endorse racial moderation, as Linwood Holton of Virginia did. A "mountain Republican" from Virginia, the state that once had led the "massive resistance" campaign against public school desegregation, and the first member of his party to be elected governor in Virginia in the twentieth century, Holton told his inaugural audience:

> Here in Virginia we must see that no citizen of the Commonwealth is excluded from full participation in both the blessings and responsibilities of our society because of his race. . . . As Virginia has been a model for so much else in America in the past, let

us now endeavor to make today's Virginia a model in race relations. Let us, as Lincoln said, insist upon an open society "with malice toward none; charity for all."

Commentators hailed these governors as New South political leaders. Obviously the New South had retained its plasticity and its pleasing quality.

The limited involvement of southern blacks in politics changed dramatically after 1965. Black voter registration in the eleven former Confederate states increased from 1.5 million in 1960 to 2.7 in 1966, 3.4 in 1970, and 4.3 in 1980, and the percentage of the electorate that was black increased from 11 to 17 percent. There were some 2,600 black elected officials in these states in 1980. Tuskegee, for instance, elected its first black mayor, Johnny Ford, in 1972. Other first-time black mayors—Birmingham's Richard Arrington, Atlanta's Maynard Jackson, Charlotte's Harvey Gantt, Richmond's Henry Marsh—were more conspicuous because they served much larger cities. Andrew Young, who had been one of King's closest advisers and a former Carter administration official, succeeded Jackson in 1982. John Lewis, former SNCC leader and militant civil rights activist, won a seat in Congress in 1986 when he defeated another prominent black civil rights figure, Julian Bond.

The growth of southern blacks' political power was impressive and unprecedented. But blacks were still a minority, albeit a franchised minority. Even with gains in black voter registration, 83 percent of the electorate in the former Confederate states were white. Moreover, the number of white voters in the South has grown faster since the 1960s than the number of black voters. Blacks have had their greatest political successes either when whites divided more or less evenly by party or candidate and blacks remained united or when blacks had majorities or near majorities. They are not a majority in any state. In only three states—South Carolina, Mississippi, and Louisiana—did blacks make up as much as 25 percent of the registered voters in 1984.

Other blunt realities have compounded the frustrations of the franchised minority. Most whites have refused to vote for black candidates. Consequently, blacks have difficulty winning elections in which they must attract more than a small number of white voters. Statewide races have proved to be especially difficult for black candidates. Only one black office seeker has won statewide elections in the South since Reconstruction: Virginia elected L. Douglas Wilder lieutenant governor in 1986, and in 1989 he was elected governor by a slim margin over an antiabortion Republican. The Democratic party must attract black voters to survive but cannot appear to be a black party and do well. Conversely, the Republican party does not need to attract black voters to survive or even to do well. If the Republicans concede the votes of blacks to the Democrats, however, they will be in danger in any election in which Democrats attract a substantial portion of white voters. That is what happened when Carter swept most of the South in 1976. Southern Republicans have therefore dropped their once rather blatant racist appeals, though often only for more subtle versions. They have attempted to attract black voters with some success, especially middle-class blacks. Racial polarization along party lines, however, may be so strong a force that neither party can prevent it. In 1984 a political scientist in South Carolina was invited by a local businessman to switch to the Republican party: "Why don't you leave the niggers behind and come and join us?" Understandably, fears persist that the South's recently acquired two-party politics may become one party for blacks and one party for whites, a disquieting reminder of the past.

The 1980 and 1984 presidential elections reinforced those fears. Reagan got 61 percent of the white vote in 1980 and 70 percent in 1984. Eighty-nine percent of the black voters in 1980 supported Carter; 90 percent supported Walter Mondale, the Democratic nominee in 1984. Similar voting patterns appeared in the 1988 presidential election. But again, racial voting does not fully explain the success the Republican party has enjoyed in the South since World War II. Ronald Reagan's enormous personal popularity accounted for some of this success in the 1980s. More broadly, Republicans have benefited greatly from the rise of a new urban middle class in the South and the economic distance the region has

JESSE JACKSON (UPI/Bettmann Newsphotos)

come since the desperate days of the Great Depression. As much as anything else, the economic transformation of the region since World War II has transformed the politics of the South. Accompanying these economic developments has been the shift of political power in the South from the rural areas to the cities and suburbs, from the farm world to the town world and now to the metropolitan world.

The political power of the rural South fell rapidly in the 1960s. This decline had its beginnings earlier, largely in the massive migrations from rural to urban areas and the growth of the economic and political power of the cities. The courts hastened the political decline. In the process they broke new constitutional ground, setting new standards for representation in state legislatures, for state and local elections, and for the boundaries of political units.

The pivotal case for the courts involved political boundaries in Tuskegee, Alabama. Tuskegee typified the politics of the black belt. Blacks outnumbered whites about 4 to 1 (4,360 to 1,340), but whites controlled the politics of the town because very few blacks could vote. Intimidation, sometimes not very subtly applied, and paternalism kept blacks in their places. Tuskegee had what many whites in the South thought were "good race relations."

Tuskegee was not, however, a typical black belt town. It was the site of Booker T. Washington's Tuskegee Institute and a large Veterans Administration hospital that served black veterans exclusively. Tuskegee therefore had an unusually high proportion of well-educated blacks. Almost all voting-age whites were already registered, and preventing blacks from registering was becoming increasingly difficult. To block access to the ballot box and to public office, white officials administered literacy and understanding tests. Officials found an unusually large number of people with masters' and doctoral degrees who became stupid or illiterate when they entered the voting registrar's office, and they often complicated matters by applying arcane procedural rules arbitrarily and by making the time and place of voter registration as inconvenient as possible. As elsewhere in the South, these devices had proved to be the most effective barriers to enfranchisement of blacks in the years since the end of the white primary.

When these barriers became increasingly difficult to maintain, Tuskegee whites asked the Alabama legislature for help. It obliged in 1957 by passing Alabama Act Number 140, creating new boundaries for the town. The legislature's new creation had twenty-eight sides, resembled "a stylized sea horse," and was artfully designed to include all of the residences of the Tuskegee whites and to exclude almost all of the residences of the Tuskegee blacks. The blacks countered by turning to the courts. Asserting that the new boundaries were an attempt to disfranchise them, the plaintiffs argued that the redistricting was unconstitutional. The lower courts reluctantly refused to rule for the plaintiffs since the courts had traditionally held that setting political boundaries was a political issue and therefore not a matter to be reviewed or settled in the courts. "Courts," Supreme Court Justice Felix Frankfurter had declared in 1946, "ought not to enter this political thicket."

In 1960, however, the Supreme Court broke tradition and entered the "political thicket" in the case of *Gomillion* v. *Lightfoot*. It ruled that Alabama Act Number 140 was unconstitutional because it violated the equal protection clause of the Fourteenth Amendment and the Fifteenth Amendment, which states that no citizen's rights shall be "denied or abridged...on account of race, color, or previous condition of servitude." The Court also noted that the history of the Fifteenth Amendment indicated conclusively that the authors of the amendment had intended it to be a means to secure "the freedom of the slave race...from the oppression of those who had formerly exercised unlimited dominion over him."

In *Gomillion* the Court established new, crucial linkages between political representation and individual voting rights. It then strengthened those links in several important rulings in the 1960s. In *Baker* v. *Carr* (1962), a case that involved the failure of Tennessee to reapportion its legislature every ten years, as the state's constitution required, the Court declared that the federal courts had the authority and duty to consider the constitutionality of the apportionment of state legislatures. A year later, in *Gray* v. *Sanders*, the Court declared Georgia's county-unit system of apportioning votes in state primaries unconstitutional. Under that system, candidates had to obtain a majority of county units to win primaries. County units were assigned according to a formula that discriminated heavily against urban areas. The least populous 40 percent of the state's population had almost 60 percent of the county units. Fulton County (Atlanta) had 556,376 people in 1960 and six units, while small counties such as Chattahoochee (13,011) and Echols (1,876) had two units each. One vote in Chattahoochee had the same impact as fourteen in Fulton; one vote in Echols equaled ninety-nine in Fulton. The county-unit system also diluted the political impact of blacks in Georgia. Many rural counties had black majorities or large black minorities, but few blacks could vote there, whereas many urban blacks were registered voters.

Georgia's peculiar political institution permitted what V. O. Key, Jr., the noted political scientist, called the "rule of the rustics." Leaders of Georgia's rural white minority dominated the legislature and state offices and indulged themselves in what had long been a favorite Georgia pastime, attacking cities in general and Atlanta in particular. Eugene Talmadge had once been among the principal beneficiaries of this pastime. Affecting the image of a small farmer, the "Wild Man from Sugar Creek" mounted stumps, stands, steps, and backs of wagons all over Georgia, snapped his red galluses, and railed, especially against blacks. During a twenty-year period that ended in 1946, Talmadge ran in every state primary and was elected commissioner of agriculture three times and governor four times.

When it voided Georgia's county-unit system as a violation of the equal protection clause of the Fourteenth Amendment, the Court erected a new standard for apportionment and for redistricting political units—"one person, one vote," known more commonly as "one man, one vote." This decision, in conjunction with other factors, especially the civil rights movement and the Voting Rights

Act of 1965, altered the basic structure of southern politics. Eugene Talmadge's boy Herman joined other southern Democrats in shifting to biracial politics. The Republican party also found *Gray* v. *Sanders* useful in attacking apportionment measures written by Democratic legislatures. Thus blacks and southern Republicans have benefited the most from "one person, one vote." The principle has been applied widely outside the South, and Chicanos in the Southwest have taken particular advantage of it.

THE SUNBELT

Like politics in the South after 1945, economic life has undergone a remarkable transformation. But like politics, the economy of the South also has unfortunate vestiges of the past. Personal income in the southern states grew more than 400 percent in real terms between 1945 and 1980. Still, the post–World War II generation of southerners has had considerably more income than any previous generation of southerners ever had. Moreover, the gap in personal income between the South and the rest of the country narrowed after World War II. Per capita income increased from about one-half the national average in 1945 to two-thirds in 1960 to nearly nine-tenths in 1980, a ranking the South has not enjoyed since the firing started at Fort Sumter. The region that had been called the "Nation's No. 1" economic problem emerged almost magically as part of America's Sunbelt, that belt of warmth, newness, and prosperity stretching from the Chesapeake through the South, then westward to Arizona and California. Regional pride and self-confidence soared as thousands of southerners entered the middle class for the first time.

But distressing vestiges of the past lingered. While some southern states—Florida, Virginia, Texas, Oklahoma—were near or above the national average in per capita income in 1982, most were not. But more recently, personal incomes in Texas, Oklahoma, and Louisiana have declined sharply because of a recession in the petroleum industry, which is so important to those states. The gap between personal incomes in the South and those in the rest of the nation has remained about the same since the 1970s. Six of the ten poorest states in America in 1982 were located in the South. Lower living costs reduced these differences but only to a degree, and lower living costs also meant that less was being spent for such services as health care and education. The South had 40 percent of America's poor though it had only 25 percent of its people. While impoverished whites outnumbered impoverished blacks in the region (8.3 million to 5.5 million), the proportion of blacks in that category far exceeded that of whites (49 percent to 12 percent).

There were other familiar disturbing patterns. Urban and particularly suburban areas were generally more prosperous than rural areas. Most of southern Appalachia had remained a distressed region. Personal incomes among its predominantly white populace were only 80 percent of the national average. Ratios in the Appalachian regions of Kentucky fell to as low as 63 percent, in Virginia to 71 percent. Industrial workers still earned less and received less legal protection against unhealthful or dangerous working conditions than their counterparts elsewhere. The South still led the nation in infant and maternal deaths and trailed it in longevity of its inhabitants. Despite considerable advances, educational statistics still revealed serious deficiencies. Fewer people in the South had graduated from high school, and the South still spent less on education. The persistence of poverty and low incomes may help explain an aspect of voting behavior in the South. The percentage of voting-age people who have voted in presidential races has been declining since 1968, from 52 percent to 44 percent. (Outside the South, there were comparable developments: from 64 percent in 1968 to 51 percent in 1988.) Voter turnout has consistently been lower in the South, as low as 38 percent in South Carolina. Of course, turnout for nonpresidential elections is even lower than for presidential elections.

Wide differences in postwar economic change caused some observers to suggest a new geographical arrangement for the South: the outer South (the Chesapeake area, Florida, Texas, and Oklahoma); the middle South (the Carolinas, Georgia, and Louisiana); and the inner South (Arkansas, Mississippi, Alabama, Tennessee, and Kentucky). Marked postwar differences in economic growth rates, types of economic activity, occupational diversity, and urbanization justify this new economic geography. The outer South has experienced the greatest change. Military and defense spending during World War II had a particularly strong impact on the outer South, and during the Cold War the

MIAMI BEACH (Florida Department of Commerce, Division of Tourism)

military-defense industry became a permanent fixture there. Among the benefits it brought were the expanded port facilities that were in place when the national economy became much more internationalized. A reciprocating chain reaction ensued: more international trade led to more international banking, trading, and services activities, which led to more economic growth in areas around ports. Since the 1950s, more than 40 percent of the people on military payrolls resided in the South or close to its borders, most of them in the outer South. About 135,000 civilian employees of the Defense Department lived in the Chesapeake Bay region in 1980; 78,000 of them resided in metropolitan Washington and 40,000 in Norfolk–Newport News.

The outer South has been able to take particular advantage of the postwar economic trends: the expansion of financial, communications, and transportation services, the internationalization of trade, the shift away from manufacturing as the United States entered the postindustrial era, the boom in tourism and retirement, and the development and expansion of services that rely on sophisticated technology and communications. The value of the export-import trade reached $74 billion in the gulf ports of Texas and Louisiana in 1982, and $27 billion in the Chesapeake ports. Such a large trade has had a substantial ripple effect, encouraging the growth of insurance companies, banks, law firms, and highly educated and skilled work forces. Northern Virginia, northern Florida, Houston, and Dallas–Fort Worth have led the region in high-tech development,

EGLIN AIR FORCE BASE

well ahead of other important centers of this area of activity such as Atlanta; Huntsville, Alabama; Oak Ridge, Tennessee; and Raleigh–Durham–Chapel Hill (the Research Triangle), North Carolina.

Oil and gas provided much of the economic growth and diversification in Texas and Oklahoma. Both, especially Texas, have petrochemical complexes, and recently both have found that boom-and-bust cycles still plague the oil and gas industry. Nor, as Louisiana has shown, do large reserves of oil and gas or a large petrochemical industry necessarily elevate a state's economy to the upper ranks of the region.

Much of the gap between the outer South and the middle South can be explained by the latter's greater dependence on manufacturing. Textile production has been and continues to be the leading industry in the middle South, though its preeminence is rapidly declining. More than 216,000 jobs in textiles—a 30 percent reduction—were lost between the mid-1970s and 1987. Similar declines, though smaller in absolute terms, occurred in tobacco, furniture, and wood products manufacturing. While manufacturing has become more diverse in the middle South, neither total manufacturing employment nor the real wages of industrial workers have increased. The Middle South has less urban and metropolitan development than the outer South, despite the striking growth of Charlotte, Greensboro, Raleigh–Durham–Chapel Hill, Columbia, Charleston, Myrtle Beach, Baton Rouge, and, most of all, Atlanta.

The inner South lags well behind its neighbors. Arkansas and Mississippi have been the least industrialized, least economically diversified of the southern states. Major industries in the inner South—aluminum, coal, and iron and steel—have suffered severe reverses. The new industries that have developed, such as the new manufacturing plants built by foreign and domestic automobile manufacturers, have not offset losses in older industries; nor have the activities at such high-tech centers as Huntsville and Oak Ridge. Only two cities in the inner South have been among the leaders in metropolitan growth in the South—Memphis and Nashville. Tennessee has generally had more economic success than its neighbors and may not belong in the inner South. In the 1980s Tennessee's population growth was modest, like that in the rest of the inner South, but Tennessee has considerably outpaced its neighbors in degree of urbanization, the growth and output of its manufacturing, and the success of its farmers.

Some of Tennessee's economic success may be attributed to the Tennessee Valley Authority, the largest effort at regional development in American history. But elsewhere in the inner South, not even the TVA has managed to overcome the problems that slowed economic growth. In fact, critics claimed that the rates the TVA charged nearly equaled those of private utilities; that it had overbuilt its generating capacity, especially its nuclear power plants; and that its heavy use of coal made it a major polluter in the region. Hope for economic expansion in some of the inner South rested in part on the Tennessee-Tombigbee Waterway, a $2 billion project completed in 1985 and designed to provide a cheaper means of transporting heavy cargo from the southern Appalachian states to Mobile and the gulf coast by a canal system linking the Tennessee River to the Tombigbee River.

The Tennessee-Tombigbee Waterway is only one of the more recent examples of the adeptness with which southern leaders have pursued federal funds for their region. The ability of Congressman L. Mendel Rivers of South Carolina and Congressman Carl Vinson and Senator Richard Russell of Georgia to attract Defense Department dollars made them legendary figures. Where military spending has involved complex scientific and engineering work, it has tended to create new facilities and groups of scientists and engineers and to expand existing ones. The location of the army's Redstone arsenal at Huntsville, Alabama, for example, revived Huntsville and led to the creation of the University of Alabama at Huntsville. The National Aeronautics and Space Administration has had a similar impact along the gulf coast, especially in Houston, where it is headquartered. In the last instance, the hand of Lyndon Johnson was very evident.

Before World War II the South did not seek federal funding as readily as other regions did. That situation changed after the war, especially after 1950. Southern leaders in politics and business adopted much more Whiggish attitudes: they, like the pre–Civil War Whigs, advocated certain kinds of government spending as a means of achieving economic growth. The modern Whigs found money in state and local treasuries to provide matching funds for interstate highways, airports, stadiums, and similar facilities that promised to stimulate the southern economy in ways they approved of. The advent of post–World War II Whigs to positions of power also indicated the decline of older leaders with ties to the black belt counties, county courthouses, local banks, and older manufacturing industries.

The expansion of airports and highways has had a profound effect on the geography of the South. Postwar highway construction, to which the Interstate Highway Act (1955) gave a massive stimulus, reinforced these developments, especially as trucks displaced railroads as the primary means for transporting freight. The horizontal growth pattern of the urban South has continued, geometrically in such cities as Houston and Atlanta. Urban experts have noted that Atlanta may be the model for American cities of the future: metropolises with multiple centers or nuclei. In other instances, transportation systems have reinforced the dispersed pattern of manufacturing facilities in the South. Tourism and the retirement industry have been enormously stimulated by post–World War II developments in the transportation systems in the southern states, as well as in air conditioning. Chilled air also made some manufacturing and medical processes possible for the first time in the hot, humid South.

Fiscal and budgetary policies in the South also reflected Whiggish attitudes. Before World War II the South had higher corporate taxes than the rest of the nation; after the war, lower. On the other hand, most southern states have relied heavily on sales taxes, which weigh disportionately on low-income groups. Moreover, state and local spending for social services is still generally lower in the South than elsewhere in the nation, though recently the pattern of expenditures for higher education has changed as leaders have concluded that quality in higher education and economic growth are closely connected.

"COTTON FIELDS NO MORE"

Whatever the relative economic position of the various parts of the South, one thing is clear: agriculture has undergone revolutionary change since 1940. When World War II began, more than 40 percent of southerners (15.6 million) farmed. Forty years later, only 3 to 4 percent (1.6 million) did. The number of farms had declined from 2.9 million to 949,000. The average size of farms, the value of farmland and buildings, and the value of their output had increased, often dramatically. Recent figures indicated that the decline in the number of farms in the South has continued, and at a faster rate than in the rest of the nation.

Clearly the volume of output per farm had soared. Comparable changes can be seen in the kinds of outputs produced. Beef cattle, poultry, soybeans, tobacco, and dairy products had become the leading farm products. Production of vegetables, fruits, and nuts had also increased, aided by improved transport and refrigeration. Some farmers, especially in the Southeast, added significantly to their incomes by selling off timber. However, nonfarmers, particularly large wood and paper products manufacturers, became the principal owners of timberlands in the South. Private corporations owned 133 million acres of southern forests, which by 1977 produced pulpwood for two-thirds of the paper manufactured in the United States and a fourth of the nation's yearly output of lumber. In no state was cotton the leading cash crop, though it ranked second in Texas and Mississippi. The land of cotton had come to look more like the land of soybeans, grass, cattle, and pine trees.

These radical changes resulted from the conjunction of numerous factors: mechanization; electrification; fertilizers; improved seeds; better control of

AVERAGE NUMBER OF HARVESTED ACRES AND AVERAGE VALUE OF LAND, BUILDINGS, AND FARM PRODUCTS PER FARM IN THREE SOUTHERN STATES, 1940, 1978, AND 1987

	Acres			Land and buildings			Farm products		
	1940	1978	1987	1940	1978	1987	1939[a]	1978	1987
Florida	27.0	93.1	98.8	$5,211	$351,646	$543,830	$1,494	$69,148	$119,033
Alabama	30.7	83.9	78.2	1,764	128,260	168,161	349	27,398	44,053
Virginia	22.0	54.7	64.4	3,860	163,918	232,374	713	22,933	35,464

[a] Reported in 1940.

SOURCE: Gilbert C. Fite, *Cotton Fields No More: Southern Agriculture, 1865–1980* (Lexington, Ky., 1984); U.S. Bureau of the Census, *1987 Census of Agriculture* (Washington, D.C., 1987), Vol. I, Pt. 1, p. 1; Pt. 9, p. 1; Pt. 46, p. 1.

pests, diseases, and weeds; better breeding stock; development of good pasture; removal of poor soils from production; the work of agricultural schools and extension services; greater attention to careful management; and more accessible credit, capital, and markets. Profits from current production (a large part of them generated by World War II), loans and payments from federal agencies and programs, and loans from commercial banks provided most of the capital and credit. People who were considered good credit risks got loans readily, but not marginal farmers, and they were legion. The process favored bigger farm owners over small farm owners, tenants, and sharecroppers. The most successful were agribusinessmen. Regardless of the nature or size of their operations, most farmers became dependent on high-volume production, credit, and chemicals. The use of chemicals entailed unanticipated costs, which have been and often still are ignored. For instance, only after a long battle was the toxic chemical DDT banned in 1978. As a result of the post-1940 agricultural revolution in the South, a whole way of life disappeared in a generation: most family farms and almost all the tenants, sharecroppers, mules, and cotton gins. Networks of human relations—burdened though they were by racism, debt, and perennial disappointment—collapsed. So did many wood-shack homes. Church pews emptied till the churches were abandoned. So did country schools and stores.

The agricultural revolution blessed many farmers and even more nonfarmers. Nonfarmers benefited from more, better, and cheaper farm products. Those farmers who were able to make the transition to modern, large-scale agriculture improved their incomes, sometimes dramatically. Some became wealthy. Their children, like Jimmy Carter, went to college, often the first members of their families to do so. They regularly shopped in places where they had seldom gone before, such as Columbus and Atlanta. Their involvement in community affairs went beyond their immediate locales. They joined civic clubs in nearby towns. Many worked with recently formed county and regional development boards and agencies to diversify declining rural economies and to offset the staggering loss of jobs created by the agricultural revolution in the South.

That revolution exacted a very high price in human terms, primarily from people who could not or did not make the transition to modern farming and who found inadequate employment opportunities even in the rapidly growing economy of the post-1940 South. In "one of the greatest movements of people in history to occur within a single generation," nearly 14 million southerners left the farms between 1940 and 1980, most of them for cities in the South and the North. In the 1950s and 1960s so many people climbed aboard northbound trains in the Carolinas clutching sacks of home-fried chicken for the journey that the trains came to be known as the Chicken-Bone Special. Thousands of these rural exiles failed to find enough nonagricultural employment to raise them above the poverty level. Minimal skills and meager schooling limited many of them, especially those who were black—a disproportionate part of the South's displaced farm population.

Blacks also faced overt racial barriers in the job market until at least the mid-1960s. (Covert racial barriers have remained, though they appear to be coming down slowly.) Even where blacks found traditional nonfarm work, they were limited by lack of skills and inferior schooling. Racial preferences often precluded their rise to skilled or supervisory positions. Before the mid-1960s, white workers frequently joined with management to perpetuate racial discrimination. Strong worker sentiment in the textile industry, which was still largely nonunion, kept the work force of that industry virtually all-white. There was, in fact, a good deal of evidence of a tacit agreement between white workers and management in textiles: if the workers kept unions out, management would keep blacks out. Only after labor shortages and pressures from the federal government forced management's hand did racial barriers begin to drop in the textile industry. In less than a decade the most racially segregated labor force in the South became one of the most desegregated.

During the post-1940 economic boom the number of nonagricultural jobs in the South more than tripled, from nearly 7.8 million in 1940 to 25.9 million in 1980; manufacturing employment almost doubled, from 1.9 million to 3.4 million. But the displaced farmers had to compete with more skilled and better-educated people. Most of their competitors came from southern towns and cities, though many of them were northerners who migrated southward after World War II. Modern air conditioning encouraged this migration by easing the ordeal of Dixie's hot, humid summers. By the 1960s the South had passed a major demographic landmark: for the first time in a century, in-migration exceeded out-migration, though not among blacks. Then in the 1970s, for the first time since Emancipation, more blacks moved into the South than moved out.

The post-1950s decline in America's heavy industries, traditionally the first step up the social and economic ladder for impoverished farmers, compounded the difficulties of rural exiles and their children, especially young males. Industrial decay came first in the North, then spread to the South in the 1970s. Industrial wages in the South remained low. Only in Louisiana, Kentucky, and Oklahoma were the average hourly earnings of industrial workers higher than the $7.27 national average in 1980. In the most industrialized states of the South—Virginia, the Carolinas, and Georgia—hourly earnings of industrial workers averaged less than $6. The South's most industrial state, North Carolina, had the lowest industrial wages in the country. Its heavily industrialized neighbor, South Carolina, was a close second. The predominance of textiles probably explains that. The textile industry has traditionally paid low wages because it uses relatively unskilled workers, many of them women. The labor intensity of the highly competitive textile industry has kept wages low. The weakness of labor unions in the Carolinas also contributes to the low wages in manufacturing.

Workers in the South still tend to be less unionized than other American workers. Less than 10 percent of textile workers were unionized in the 1980s, despite numerous attempts to organize them. The largest of those efforts took place shortly after World War II. Operation Dixie, whose primary target was textiles, lasted from 1946 to 1950, cost at least $5 million, and ended in almost complete failure.

The textile industry proved to be as subtle and resourceful as it was resistant. The industry relied less on blunt intimidation than on public relations and on timely pay raises and improvements in benefits. The industry also received encouragement from local and state governments, which saw labor unions as threats to their efforts to attract industrial investors. Moreover, most southern states had "right-to-work" laws, stipulating that workers could not be forced to join a union in order to get or retain a job. Whether or not right-to-work laws actually deterred unionization is a matter of dispute, though both labor and management believed that they did. As late as the 1970s southern Democrats played major roles in defeating federal legislation that they believed favored organized labor. Labor leaders were convinced that President Carter had failed to act decisively to get the Labor Reform Bill of 1978—a name its opponents disputed, of course—passed by Congress. The bill was designed to make unionization easier by making the procedures stipulated by the National Labor Relations (or Wagner) Act simpler and more quickly implemented.

In the face of massive, swift agricultural change and inadequate opportunities off the farm, thousands of displaced farmers had few options. Most were landless or became landless when farm costs increased rapidly after 1940. Black farm owners became virtually extinct. Some black and white farmers who managed to keep their small holdings farmed part-time and did odd jobs, often in seasonal farmwork. Over time, however, migrant labor took over much of the seasonal work. Factory jobs, where they could be found in rural areas, tended to be low-skill, low-pay, and unpredictable. Welfare provided minimal benefits and unwelcome dependency. Welfare policy and practices encouraged out-migration. Southern states had fewer resources to spend on welfare and proportionately more people who needed welfare than most other states. All the same, southern states were tightfisted in regard to the needy. In 1987, welfare payments to individuals in the United States averaged $120.15 a month; in Alabama they averaged $38.99, in Georgia $78.04, and in Florida $79.08.

The civil rights revolution hastened the displacement of black farmers. As the traditional mode of white dominance and black subservience came under assault, personal relations between blacks and whites became more distant and white paternalism seemed to evaporate. A black farmer in Alabama remarked in 1967 that "them white folks got a lot more interested in machinery after the civil rights bill was passed." Government had little interest in the economic welfare of the displaced farmers. The plight of these people did not trigger federal or state programs or financial assistance that even remotely approximated their need.

Many rural counties in the South, especially in the black belt, Appalachia, and parts of the Ozarks, more closely resembled Third World countries than the Sunbelt. In such places as Greene County, Alabama, perhaps half of the residents got government assistance in 1979. The civil rights revolution had made life better politically for the county's black majority but not economically. In an effort to improve things, the black-dominated county approved the opening of a dog track. It increased county revenues by nearly $2 million a year, but it did not create many jobs.

THE METROPOLITAN SOUTH

When farmers displaced by the South's agricultural revolution left their farms, many did not move far. So many black and white Mississippians moved to Memphis after World War II that it was called the "largest city in Mississippi." The migrants from the farms joined others from small towns in and outside the South to make southern cities among the fastest growing in America after 1940.

The urban South offered jobs. It also offered attractive services, recreational and cultural opportunities, and desirable educational systems. Riding the wave of the post–World War II economic boom, the urban South worked feverishly to secure or expand the hallmarks of modernization: large airports, freeways, shopping malls, skyscrapers, major banks and other financial institutions, corporate headquarters, convention centers, museums, orchestras, restaurants and theaters, ballet and opera companies, sophisticated medical complexes, colleges and universities, and professional sports teams. The urban South also offered the possibility of living in an urban world that was leisurely, friendly, and mannerly, or claimed to be. Whatever the precise fit between possibility and actu-

POPULATION OF SOUTHERN METROPOLITAN AREAS, 1940–1980 (IN THOUSANDS)

	1940*	1960	1970	1980
Dallas/Fort Worth	473	1,738	2,378	2,975
Houston	385	1,430	1,999	2,905
Atlanta	302	1,169	1,596	2,030
Miami	172	935	1,268	1,626
Tampa–St. Petersburg	169	772	1,106	1,614
New Orleans	495	907	1,046	1,187
San Antonio	254	736	888	1,072
Memphis	293	727	834	913
Louisville	319	754	807	906
Oklahoma City	204	512	719	861
Nashville	167	597	699	851
Birmingham	268	747	767	847
Jacksonville	173	530	622	738
Richmond	193	462	548	632

*Urban only.

SOURCE: U.S. Department of Commerce, *Statistical Abstract of the United States* (Washington, D.C., 1942, 1962, 1982).

ality, southern cities have acted as magnets, as their growth since World War II clearly indicates.

Improvements in the quality and range of education offered in the South reflect the economic growth of the region and the large role urban areas played in it. The changes since the 1930s are striking. Then the American Council on Education concluded that only seven universities in the entire South had departments that were qualified to offer doctoral degrees, and that the South had only 42 of the 661 such departments in the nation. Only 2 of the 230 departments believed to have attained "eminence" were in the South. Collectively, primary and secondary schools in the South still were below national standards in 1980. But the gap had closed substantially. Moreover, many of these schools —public and private—met or exceeded national standards. The same could be said of postsecondary schools. Community colleges, technical colleges, and branch campuses of state universities had proliferated. Some professional schools had achieved national and even international distinction: the Texas Medical Center in Houston, the medical school at the University of Alabama in Birmingham, the Medical College Division of Virginia Commonwealth University, the law and medical schools at the University of Virginia, at Duke, Vanderbilt, and Emory, and the schools of engineering and architecture at Rice University. Among private universities, several had achieved high national ranking: Rice, Duke, Vanderbilt, Emory, Wake Forest, and Tulane. Three public universities had achieved similar status: the University of North Carolina, the University of Virginia, and the University of Texas. The University of Florida had almost joined that company by 1980. Colleges of distinction in the region include William and Mary, Washington and Lee, Richmond, Davidson, Wofford, Sewanee, Birmingham Southern, Milsaps, Rhodes, and Trinity. Every southern state had accredited graduate and professional programs in a wide range of fields.

The civil rights revolution contributed to the enhanced status of the universities and colleges of the South. Racial segregation had created a negative academic climate; in particular, it raised serious questions about academic freedom. Among the positive effects of desegregation are improved chances of attracting faculty and students from outside the region and a more open atmosphere on campuses. Yet desegregation has had a negative effect on traditionally all-black colleges and universities, as many black students have chosen to enroll in formerly all-white schools. Many black faculty have taken a similar route.

Though obviously education in the South had improved markedly since World War II, serious concerns remained in 1980. Almost two-thirds of Americans who were twenty-five years of age or older had completed high school; but in only one southern state, Florida, was the proportion that high. The majority of southern states had fewer that six in ten high school graduates among that age group. Illiteracy also remained disproportionately high in the South. Southern states, despite great exertions, still spent considerably less for each school-age resident than most states outside the South. These facts disturbed government and business leaders, as they had come to perceive a direct connection between continued economic growth on the one hand and educational achievement and the status of educational institutions on the other. State development boards, which had become sophisticated agencies for economic development, found that potential investors tended more than ever to shy away from places where schools were below their standards. It was no accident that a number of southern states made strong commitments in the 1980s to improve education. One of the striking developments of the postwar South is the amount of thought and energy poured into efforts to create jobs. Surely Henry Grady would have delighted in the sophistication of state and local efforts at economic development and the willingness of political leaders to pursue potential investors across the globe.

By 1980, however, and in some cases earlier, southerners discovered that the rapid economic and urban growth it had experienced had some major negative aspects. Not least was the fading of the more relaxed way of life that had long characterized the region. Most of the costs were more tangible: pollution, crime, personal violence, urban sprawl, traffic jams, commuting, overtaxed public services, blighted neighborhoods. White suburbs proliferated around older urban cores where the less advantaged were trapped with little hope of leaving. These people were more likely to be black than white, more likely to be older, less educated, and less skilled.

To be sure, variations could be found in almost every southern city, sometimes reflecting a history or economic characteristics peculiar to itself. Miami had a large, prosperous Cuban community. Houston and San Antonio had large Chicano communities, portions of which had become middle class. Almost every southern city had "gentrified" neighborhoods, inner-city areas that had been reclaimed and refurbished by upper-middle-class professionals, and

STREET SCENE (The Charlotte Observer)

most southern cities had considerable black populations, more than cities elsewhere could claim. Among blacks there was a growing middle class, some of
whom lived in racially desegregated neighborhoods. Still, southern cities were
more racially segregated in 1980 than ever before. School desegregation had
had a large part in that development as whites had taken flight to suburbs, to
all-white or nearly all-white school districts. As a result of that flight and the
growth of enrollments in private schools, many public schools were becoming
resegregated. Public schools in Little Rock, scene of the South's first major clash
over public school desegregation, found themselves nearly as racially segregated as they had been in 1957. Similar trends could be seen outside the urban
South. In many places no resegregation had occurred because the schools had
never been desegregated to any significant degree. Race, however, was not the
only reason that parents were turning away from public schools. Concerns
about quality of education, moral values, and religious beliefs prompted many
parents to send their children to private schools, though they were costly. Unfortunately, these schools were all-white or virtually all-white. These trends in
education clearly suggested that Jim Crow was not entirely dead and that some
seemingly intractable class differences between whites and blacks tended to
persist.

As early as the 1970s, as the South entered its most expansive decade since
the Civil War, observers had wondered if the urban South would repeat the
mistakes of the urban North. Southern cities, one observer believed, had several advantages: they were smaller and generally younger, had less heavy industry, and had fewer areas that had decayed or had been abandoned. But two
national trends threatened to erase these advantages: most of the jobs and most
of the whites were in the suburbs, and the majority of blacks and the poor were
concentrated in inner-city ghettos. Little that occurred in southern cities in the
1970s indicated that the path they had followed differed in any significant respect from the course taken by northern cities. Indeed, in the 1970s the differences between the South and the rest of the nation became so blurred that more
than a few observers wondered if the South had lost its distinctiveness.

28

No Eden in Dixie

--------- ❖ ---------

Since the earliest days of European settlement in North America, the historian Charles Roland remarked in 1970, people have been predicting that the American South "was just about to become the garden spot of the universe." Expectations, however, have repeatedly exceeded performance. "The South...has been, and remains today, a land becoming and not a land become—a garden spot that beckons only to recede like a mirage when approached. It is America's will-o'-the-wisp Eden."

As early as 1588, Thomas Hariot assured readers of *A Brief and True Report of the New Found Land of Virginia* that "the ayre there is so temperate and holsome, the soyle so fertile,...in short time...they may raise...those sortes of commodities which shall both enrich them selves, as also others that shall deale with them." Hariot's brief career as a colonist apparently did not dampen his spirits. The English mathematician, scientist, and preacher had been one of the 108 men who founded the first English colony in the New World. As we know, the colony lasted ten months. Disease, food shortages, and hostile Indians largely accounted for the short life of one of England's early attempts to create a great overseas empire.

Generations of boosters of the South have followed in Hariot's footsteps. Hopes—as well as judgments about the wholesomeness of the climate of the South, the fertility of its soil, and the extent of its natural resources—have repeatedly exceeded realities. In 1811 Thomas Jefferson foresaw an agrarian utopia in which the federal debt would be retired and modest taxes would generate enough revenue to pay for "canals, roads, schools, etc." The "farmer will see his government supported, his children educated, and the face of his country made a paradise."

Less than a decade after Jefferson retired from politics, new political voices endorsed the economic nationalism of Jefferson's fiercest enemy, Alexander Hamilton. Henry Clay of Kentucky and John C. Calhoun of South Carolina called for a strong federal government, supported by the revenues produced by a high tariff, which would lead the way toward a strong, diverse American economy based on agriculture, commerce, and manufacturing. The result of this policy, Calhoun declared, would help American farmers, who made up the majority of the population of the United States and especially of the South. "The farmer," he predicted, "will find a ready market for his surplus produce; and what is almost of equal consequence, a certain and cheap supply of all his wants. His prosperity will diffuse itself to every class in the community."

The South, however, did not subscribe to Hamiltonian economic nationalism. It sought its fortunes instead in cotton, slavery, and free trade. Calhoun soon reversed his course. He rejected economic nationalism and the policy of a strong federal government, embraced states' rights, and spent much of the remainder of his political life trying to devise some means to protect the interests of the South within the Union.

The economic success of the antebellum South, particularly the prosperity of the 1850s, seemed to justify the course the South had taken. In 1857 Senator James H. Hammond, a successor to Calhoun, declared, "Cotton is king." Confident of its economic strength, the South seceded three years later. It suffered massive military defeat, in part because of the gap between expectations generated by the cotton kingdom and its realities.

Boosterism, however, survived disunion and war. Even during the Civil War, at least early in the conflict, hope for southern self-sufficiency thrived. Another vision of southern prosperity was widely held in the North. According to that vision, slavery was the snake that had kept the South from being a garden of Eden. Once the snake was destroyed, "schools and churches will be multiplied under Northern inspiration and example, ... industry, production, and intelligence will follow our arms, and when our forces withdraw instead of leaving a desolate country behind them, they will point to it as a blossoming and regenerated Eden." Similar smug thoughts provided much of the motivation and some of the policies of Radical Reconstruction.

After Reconstruction, the prophets of the New South called continually for southerners to make an Eden with their own hands. Of those prophets, Henry Grady of the *Atlanta Constitution* was the most prescient. Again and again Grady pleaded for economic diversification in the South, where

> is centered all that can please or prosper humankind. A perfect climate above a fertile soil, yields to the husbandman every product of the temperate zone.... There, are mountains stored with exhaustless treasures; forests, vast and primeval, and rivers that, tumbling or loitering, run wanton to the sea.

Few dissented from the pursuit of Eden in Dixie. Some religious folk had grave reservations about attempts to construct man-made Edens, but the religious dissidents were a small minority. The cultural elite provided a number of dissenters: Mark Twain, Ellen Glasgow, the Agrarians, Thomas Wolfe, and William Faulkner, to name only some of the most obvious. Stronger, more persistent voices in the 1920s and 1930s decried the gap between the realities of the New South and even a pale version of Eden. Their dissent found its most powerful vehicle in *Economic Conditions of the South*. Written by the National Emergency Council, which President Franklin Roosevelt created, and published in

1938 as the nation was still mired in the worst economic crisis in American history, the report declared: "The Nation's No. 1 economic problem is the South." Like so many people before them, the council members believed that the South could do much better because it had good soils, a temperate climate, great quantities of water, and rich resources. "The paradox of the South is that while it is blessed by Nature with immense wealth, its people as a whole are the poorest in the country."

Soon after the report appeared, the South began three decades of economic growth unequaled in its history. By the early 1970s, the South was celebrating its place in the Sunbelt. By almost any conceivable measure, the South was far better off than it had been at the beginning of World War II. In 1940 southerners earned about half what other Americans earned, and the great majority of them made their living in dirty, physically arduous, and frequently hazardous work on farms and in factories, forests, and mines. Tuberculosis, hookworm, pellagra, and malnutrition were not uncommon in 1940. By 1970 each of these serious health problems had been very substantially reduced or nearly erased, and personal income had increased by more than 400 percent in *real* terms. Great improvements had also been made in housing, education, and leisure. By 1980, for the first time, the majority of white southerners had middle-class occupations. They indeed had much to celebrate.

The Sunbelt looked so much like the rest of postwar America that it provoked a nagging question: Had the South disappeared? The question had a bittersweet flavor. No one, for instance, lamented the end of the poverty of the 1930s or the disappearance of hookworm. Some whites mourned the passing of Jim Crow, but most did not. Large numbers of southerners, white as well as black, rejoiced at the ending of the racial caste system. But urban and industrial pollution unsettled many people. The appearance of air conditioning pleased nearly everyone, but not the disappearance of front porches and front-porch culture. People went inside and watched television, which projected a homogenized national culture.

The boundaries of the South are no longer so clearly delineated. Yet certain distinguishing features remain, among them regional speech patterns and food habits, a concern for manners, and strong interest in tradition. The South has exported some of its tastes in food. Kentucky Fried Chicken has enjoyed considerable success outside of Dixie. So, more recently, has Cajun cooking. Southern speech patterns have received a more mixed reception. Southerners who are concerned that they might sound "slow" or "dumb" are offered courses designed to erase their accents. Conversely, southern girls are urged by "everybody north of Baltimore": "Whatever you do, *don't* lose that lovely southern accent of yours."

Life may still take a slower pace in the South than in the rest of country, but in many parts of the region, the easy pace has become a thing of the past. The population of the South remains blacker but less ethnically diverse than the rest of the United States. However, the growing Chicano population of the Southwest is rapidly altering the ethnic composition of such states as Texas. That change is also increasing the size and importance of the Catholic population in parts of the South. Similar developments have occurred in southern Florida.

Evangelical Protestantism still permeates the South, however, and since the 1950s fundamentalism and Pentecostalism, the hard and soft sides of evangelical Protestantism, have been especially vigorous. Southerners also tend more than nonsoutherners to believe in God, to accept the Bible as literally true, and to belong to religious bodies and attend religious services. The religious hegemony of the Southern Baptists remains; since 1945 the numbers of Baptists in the South have steadily increased, and their conservatism strongly influences public and religious life in the South. Southern Baptists still resist the ordination of women and exclude them from boards of deacons, the ruling bodies of local churches. Disagreements over the role of women in the church and especially over biblical literalism have produced grave divisions among Southern Baptists.

The South has produced the leading Protestant evangelists of post–World War II America—Billy Graham, Oral Roberts, Jimmy Swaggert, Jerry Falwell, and Pat Robertson—and much of their following. Making especially effective use of radio and television, the "televangelists" have presented old-time religion in contemporary terms to large numbers of people looking for assurance in a rapidly changing world, a world that seems beyond the power of individuals to understand or to alter in significant ways. The God of the evangelists is personal and accessible. Their message is personal, intense, immediate, and based on the Bible as the infallible, unambiguous authority. Graham has enjoyed the greatest and longest success of these evangelists. He has preached to more than 50 million people all over the world and has reached audiences through his books, newspaper columns, interviews, and films. Perhaps ironically, he has been more effective outside the South than in it.

The influence of the televangelists has not been limited to religion. Following the example of the ministers who were active in the civil rights movement, some televangelists have become deeply involved in politics. They and their supporters have devoted themselves particularly to anticommunism, the restoration of prayer in public schools, and opposition to abortion, feminism, homosexuality, and pornography. Staunch defenders of the values they consider traditional, they favor censorship of school and library books, the teaching of "creation science" as an alternative to evolution, and Christian schools as alternatives to public schools. Since the great majority of the Christian schools operated by the televangelists were founded after the public schools began to be desegregated, and since most of those schools have few black students, critics have denounced them as thinly disguised attempts to perpetuate racial segregation. Generally, however, that is an unfair criticism. In fact, several televangelists counseled moderation in interracial relations before that position was generally accepted among whites in the South.

Falwell and Robertson have been especially active in politics. Falwell became a particularly vocal, vigorous supporter of the candidacy and presidency of Ronald Reagan. Robertson actively campaigned for the American presidency in 1988. In doing so, he was following a course taken by Jesse Jackson, a black

BILLY GRAHAM (AP/ Wide World Photos)

minister and civil rights leader. Television, the diverse directions taken by conservative Christian revivalists, and the unsettling effect of the rapid changes and disruptions that have marked American society since 1960 have greatly increased the impact of the southern-rooted evangelical revival. It has had much greater effect than the fundamentalist revival of the early decades of the century. Thus Protestant evangelicalism has joined southern literature, jazz, blues, rock and roll, and country music as a major means by which the South has shaped the nation's life and culture.

Defenders of the Protestant evangelists praise them for their efforts to bring people to God and to create a stable moral society. Critics say that the evangelists present an overly narrow, simplistic theology and espouse a religion that supports the status quo rather than one that provides a means to change it. Modern televangelists extol the patriarchal family as divinely ordained even as increasing numbers of women work outside the home in order to meet their families' basic needs or to enable them to enjoy the material benefits of the modern South.

Just as evangelical Protestantism has persisted in the modern South, so has physical violence. Southerners murder each other—usually a friend or family member—much more frequently than non-Southerners do. On occasion religion and violence have mixed in bizarre ways. In the 1950s a son reportedly shot and killed his father on the steps of a church in eastern North Carolina during a dispute over a Bible passage. Fortunately, such mixings of faith and violence have been rare, but southerners do own more guns than non-southerners do. Southern men are more likely to hunt and to attach significance to hunting, an activity which is heavy with masculine overtones. Southerners more readily endorse corporal punishment from spanking to execution; the South also leads the nation in the percentage of people incarcerated in jails and prisons. Attacks on property and assaults associated with theft, however, have been more common outside the South, as have suicides.

For all its changes, the South remains committed to religion and physical force in every facet of life—in individual relationships, sports and leisure, and public policy issues ranging from the discipline of children and criminals to foreign affairs. Asked in 1989 to explain why high school football games in Douglas County, Georgia, began with public prayer, a county attorney said that the prayer was intended "to add a solemn and dignified tone to the proceedings." The conjunction of prayer and football may express the continuing conflict in the southern mentality between piety and social control on the one hand and violence and unrestrained individualism on the other. Some observers have seen in this conflict a sort of battle of the sexes, a struggle between control, presumably a feminine attribute, and unfettered physicality, presumably a masculine characteristic. For longer than anyone can remember the Southern Lady has been expected to save the raucous South from itself.

Whether or not football games have been microcosms of the southern mentality, they have been one of the prime products of southern high schools, colleges, and universities. Even as colleges and universities have sought to appease alumni with winning teams, they have won national recognition by improving themselves academically. More attuned to national and professional standards than they once were, the South's institutions of higher education have become strongholds of national and international culture. Few have remained academic outposts of regional culture, though the conduct of their students has often run counter to this trend. While these schools' broadened perspectives and gains in quality have generally been welcome, many southerners mourn a lessening of concern about local and regional problems, particularly in the universities.

Southern writers have continued to produce a large body of fine work. Mississippi's Eudora Welty has written steadily for some fifty years, and her works have been widely read and have received high praise from critics. Though less well known, Peter Taylor (*The Collected Stories of Peter Taylor* [1969]) has for forty years explored the conflict between the values of the southern small town and those of the big city. Ralph Ellison and William Styron have created novels of lasting value. Ellison's *Invisible Man* (1952) is a classic novel

A COLLEGE FOOTBALL GAME (The University of Texas at Austin, Eugene C. Barker, Texas History Center)

that combines complex forms and perspectives with African-American folk devices that have a jazzlike quality. He takes his nameless black hero from the Jim Crow South to a still largely racially segregated, anonymous, bureaucratic New York City. Styron went in the opposite direction, from New York to the South, in his widely praised *Lie Down in Darkness* (1951), a somber tale about individuals caught between the two sets of traditional southern values.

Robert Penn Warren has produced novels, essays, short stories, meditations, and poetry of lasting quality. *All the King's Men* (1946), based loosely on the life of Huey Long of Louisiana, is a powerful novel about politics and power. Some of Warren's most recent poetry appeared in *Rumor Verified* (1981). Randall Jarrell and James Dickey are two major southern poets. Less and less of the work of major southern writers is clearly identifiable with the South. Anne Tyler's *Dinner at the Homesick Restaurant* (1982), a novel of disintegrating traditions and collapsing family structures, is set in her native Baltimore, but the story could have taken place almost anywhere. Though he used Tennessee as the setting for his *Orchard Keeper* (1969) and *Child of God* (1974), Cormac McCarthy is not regional in his graphic explorations of human depravity. Walker Percy used a thoroughly modern, almost pastless South to follow modern men who are searching for meaning and purpose: *The Moviegoer* (1960), *Love in the Ruins* (1971), and *Second Coming* (1980).

Percy's South may be the South of the 1990s—a region that is hardly distinguishable from the rest of the country. Perhaps the author-journalist John Egerton was right when he wrote in 1973 that "for good or ill, the South is just about over as a separate and distinct place." That assessment, however, appears to require that too much of the life and culture of the South be dismissed as peripheral and of little meaning. Moreover, it underestimates the stubborn determination of southerners to remain "southern" in the face of strong countervailing forces. That stubbornness takes many forms, some dubious, such as waving the Confederate flag, and some interminable, such as symposia on the New South. That stubbornness also reflects the deep attachment of southern whites and blacks to their region.

Finally, more than a few vestiges of unhappier times cast shadows over the Sunbelt South and raise haunting memories of a past that is not altogether gone. Of those vestiges, the most troubling is the persistence of racial division, inadequacies in education and health, and poverty. Black and white southerners have long had much in common historically and culturally. They also share a profound sense that the South is their place, and often have close, deep personal relationships with one another. Moreover, much of the South is more racially desegregated than the rest of America. But blacks and whites remain deeply divided about many matters and by their very different economic standings. Economic differences tend to reinforce racial divisions. In 1979, 45 percent of black families and 19 percent of white families in the South had annual incomes of less than $10,000; 77 percent of black families and 51 percent of white families, less than $20,000.

Attitudes and perceptions, as the accompanying graphs indicate, vary substantially between the races. Some people had predicted that once Jim Crow had declined and politicians could no longer use blatant racist appeals to attract white voters while ignoring important economic issues, black and working-class white voters would form an alliance based on economic interests. The graphs suggest, however, that such an alliance is unlikely to materialize. Also, though public schools in the South are generally more desegregated than those outside the South, thousands of black and white students attend schools where there are few or no members of the other race. Resegregation has become widespread enough to occasion considerable comment.

Moreover, politicians have discovered that subtle and not so subtle racist appeals are effective with both blacks and whites. In 1980 Ronald Reagan launched his presidential campaign in Neshoba County, Mississippi. A small rural county in a state with only a handful of electoral votes seemed like a curious place to begin a presidential campaign. Probably not too many voters remembered Neshoba as a site of intense civil rights activity in the 1960s or as the place where three civil rights workers were beaten and murdered by a party of lynchers, whose ranks included officials of local law enforcement. Reagan did not mention James Chaney, Andrew Goodman, or Michael Schwerner, the civil rights movement, or the remarkable changes in race relations in Mississippi since the 1960s. Instead, he announced that he "believed[d] in states' rights" and would work as president to "restore to states and local governments the powers that properly belong to them." Some observers saw this avowal of states' rights as an attempt to reach Mississippi's and the South's white electorate through code words loaded with racial overtones. At the same time, much

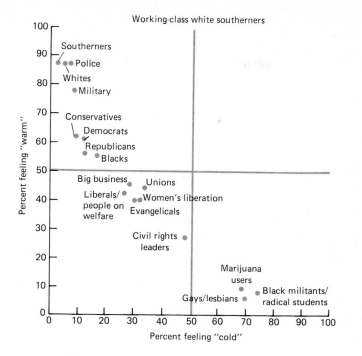

Working-class white southerners

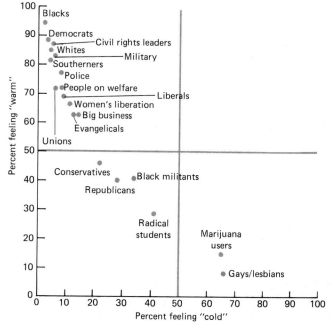

Black southerners

BLACK/WHITE REACTIONS TO POLITICAL SYMBOLS

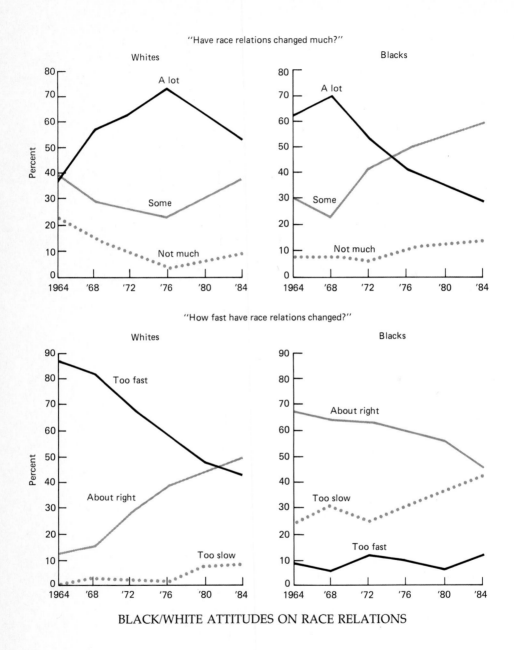

BLACK/WHITE ATTITUDES ON RACE RELATIONS

of Jesse Jackson's success—and lack of success—can be attributed to the fact that he is black.

Low incomes could become a major political issue in the 1990s. Southerners, black and white, still earn less than their fellow Americans. In 1985, in only one state in the South, Virginia, was per capita income above the national average.

Florida and Texas nearly equaled the national average. Several states—Mississippi, Alabama, Arkansas, Kentucky, Tennessee, and South Carolina—fell well below. As might be expected, education lagged behind as well. Every state in the South falls below the national average in years of completed schooling. These deficiencies have persisted despite the very substantial efforts made to improve education since World War II, and they are deeply disturbing as the South enters the postindustrial era. Though much of the South gets a high rating as "an ideal place to live" and for a "good business climate," it still draws sharp criticism for its "climate for workers." Workers in the South earn less than most other American workers, even when the lower cost of living is taken into account, and have fewer benefits and less protection. One hundred and three years after Henry Grady charmed a banquet audience in New York City with his talk of the New South, the wages of industrial workers in the South average less than $8 an hour, the lowest in the nation.

Even after nearly fifty years of unequaled economic growth and improvements in the standard of living, the South is still "a land becoming and not a land become...America's will-o'-the-wisp Eden."

BIBLIOGRAPHICAL ESSAY

—————— ❖ ——————

No full bibliography of southern history exists. For the period between 1820 and 1860, however, Fletcher M. Green and J. Isaac Copeland, *The Old South* (Arlington Heights, Ill., 1980), is fairly comprehensive, though the scholarship it incorporates obviously stops short some years ago. In this essay we make no claim for inclusiveness; at least another volume of equal length would be required to discuss thoroughly the vast body of writing on southern history. Our goal here is to provide a guide to the major literature on the history of the South.

For any student of the South several basic reference works provide indispensable assistance. David C. Roller and Robert W. Twyman, eds., *The Encyclopedia of Southern History* (Baton Rouge, La., 1979), in its almost 1,400 pages treats briefly an incredible number and variety of topics. Charles R. Wilson and William Ferris, eds., *Encyclopedia of Southern History* (Chapel Hill, N.C., 1989), reflects an extraordinarily broad definition of culture, with entries ranging from Architecture to Wrestling. For scholarly assessments of the historical literature both Arthur S. Link and Rembert W. Patrick, eds., *Writing Southern History: Essays in Historiography in Honor of Fletcher M. Green* (Baton Rouge, La., 1967), and John B. Boles and Evelyn Thomas Nolen, eds., *Interpreting Southern History: Historiographical Essays in Honor of Sanford W. Higginbotham* (Baton Rouge, La., 1987), are essential. For superb coverage of southern literary history from the colonial era forward, consult the older Jay B. Hubbell, *The South in American Literature, 1607–1900* (Durham, N.C., 1954), and the more modern Louis D. Rubin, Jr. et al., eds., *The History of Southern Literature* (Baton Rouge, La., 1985). *Historical Statistics of the United States: Colonial Times to 1970*, 2 vols. (Washington, D.C., 1975), and Donald B. Dodd and Wynelle S. Dodd, comps., *Historical Statistics of the South, 1790–1970* (University, Ala., 1973), provide ready access to statistical data taken overwhelmingly from United States censuses. At least one of these titles is relevant to every subject discussed in this book.

The best general study of the early colonial South is still Wesley Frank Craven, *The Southern Colonies in the Seventeenth Century, 1607–1689* (Baton Rouge, La., 1949). No comparable book is yet available for the eighteenth century. T. H. Breen, ed., *Shaping Southern Society: The Colonial Experience* (New York, 1976), brings together notable articles on the colonial South. Excellent introductions to the individual colonies can be found in a modern series covering all of the original colonies. The volumes dealing with the South include Warren W. Billings et al., *Colonial Virginia: A History* (White Plains, N.Y., 1986); Kenneth Coleman, *Colonial Georgia: A History* (New York, 1976); Aubrey C. Land, *Colonial Maryland: A History* (Millwood, N.Y., 1981); Hugh T. Lefler and William S. Powell, *Colonial North Carolina: A History* (New York, 1973); and Robert M. Weir, *Colonial South Carolina: A History* (Millwood, N.Y., 1983).

Studies on specific subjects abound. On the Indians see Charles M. Hudson's massive *Southeastern Indians* (Knoxville, Tenn., 1976); James H. Merrell, *The Indians' New World: Catawbas and Their Neighbors from European Contact through the Era of Removal* (Chapel Hill, N.C., 1989); and J. Leitch Wright, Jr., *The Only Land They Knew: The Tragic Story of the American Indians in the Old South* (New York, 1981), which concentrates heavily on the colonial period and also makes controversial claims for Indian populations. In three books that cover all the colonies, not just the southern ones, James Axtell has argued for the centrality of the interaction between the Europeans and the natives: *The European and the Indian: Essays in the Ethnohistory of Colonial North America* (New York, 1981), *The Invasion Within: The Contest of Cultures in Colonial North America* (New York, 1985), and *After Columbus: Essays in the Ethnohistory of Colonial North America* (New York, 1988). Samuel Eliot Morison, *The European Discovery of America: The Northern Voyages, A.D. 500–1600* (New York, 1971), is wonderful on Spanish and French exploration as well as on English efforts before 1600. On the first serious English attempt at colonization see also David B. Quinn, *Set Fair for Roanoke: Voyages and Colonies, 1584–1606* (Chapel Hill, N.C., 1985). Alden T. Vaughan, in his *American Genesis: Captain John Smith and the Founding of Virginia* (Boston, 1975), discusses the key figure in early Jamestown. Still useful is Verner W. Crane, *The Southern Frontier, 1670–1732* (Ann Arbor, Mich., 1929), which deals with a significant subject. John J. McCusker and Russell R. Menard, *The Economy of British North America, 1607–1789* (Chapel Hill, N.C., 1985), is the best treatment of the colonial economy. On economic matters in specific colonies see Paul G. E. Clemens, *The Atlantic Economy and Colonial Maryland's Eastern Shore: From Tobacco to Grain* (Ithaca, N.Y., 1980); Converse D. Clowse, *Economic Beginnings in Colonial South Carolina, 1670–1730* (Columbia, S.C., 1971); Peter A. Coclanis, *The Shadow of a Dream: Economic Life and Death in the South Carolina Low Country, 1670–1920* (New York, 1989); John C. Rainbolt, *From Prescription to Persuasion: Manipulation of Eighteenth [Seventeenth] Century Virginia Economy* (Port Washington, N.Y., 1974). Julia C. Spruill, *Women's Life and Work in the Southern Colonies* (Chapel Hill, N.C., 1938), is still the only general account, though many of the titles discussed below address the role and place of women in southern society.

Social, cultural, and intellectual life have drawn considerable recent attention. On intellectual matters a good beginning is Richard Beale Davis's encyclopedic *Intellectual Life in the Colonial South, 1585–1763*, 3 vols. (Knoxville, Tenn., 1978). Sumptuously illustrated, Jessie Poesch, *The Art of the Old South: Painting, Sculpture, Architecture, and the Products of Craftsmen* (New York, 1983), covers an important area. Although, as the following paragraphs show, much recent and innovative work has been done on the social history of the southern colonies, Carl Bridenbaugh, *Myths and Realities: Societies of the Colonial South* (Baton Rouge, La., 1952), is still the only general study.

Studies that focus on specific colonies or people have great value. Edmund S. Morgan, *American Slavery, American Freedom: The Ordeal of Colonial Virginia* (New York, 1975), at the same time the best study of seventeenth-century Virginia and a brilliant investigation of the origins of slavery, and Rhys Isaac, *The Transformation of Virginia, 1740–1790* (Chapel Hill, N.C., 1982), which uses the perspective and methodology of cultural anthropology, are probably the most notable of these books. Others that merit attention include Richard R. Beeman, *The Evolution of the Southern Backcountry: A Case Study of Lunenberg County, Virginia, 1746–1832* (Philadelphia, 1984); T. H. Breen, *Tobacco Culture: The Mentality of the Great Tidewater Planters on the Eve of Revolution* (Princeton, N.J., 1985); Wesley Frank Craven, *White, Red, and Black: The Seventeenth-Century Virginian* (Charlottesville, Va., 1971); Harold E. Davis, *The Fledgling Province: Social and Cultural Life in Colonial Georgia, 1733–1776* (Chapel Hill, N.C., 1976); Richard B. Davis, *Literature and Society in Early Virginia, 1608–1840* (Baton Rouge, La., 1973); Wesley M. Gewehr, *The Great Awakening in Virginia, 1740–1790* (Durham, N.C., 1930); Harvey H. Jackson and Phinizy Spalding, eds., *Forty Years of Diversity: Essays on Colonial Georgia* (Athens, Ga., 1984); Aubrey C. Land, *The Dulanys of Maryland: A Biographical Study of Daniel Dulany the Elder (1685–1753) and Daniel Dulany the Younger (1722–1797)* (Baltimore, 1984); Kenneth A. Lockridge, *The Diary and Life of William Byrd II of Virginia, 1674–1744* (Chapel Hill, N.C., 1987); Gloria Main, *Tobacco Colony: Life in Early Maryland, 1650–1720* (Princeton, N.J., 1983); George C. Rogers, Jr., *Charleston in the Age of the Pinckneys* (Norman, Okla., 1969); Darrett B. Rutman and Anita H. Rutman, *A Place in Time: Middlesex County, Virginia, 1650–1750* (New York, 1984); Thad W. Tate and David L. Ammerman, eds., *The Chesapeake in the Seventeenth Century: Essays on Anglo-American Society* (Chapel Hill, N.C., 1979); Stephen S. Webb, *1676: The End of American Independence* (New York, 1984), which has considerable material on seventeenth-century Virginia as part of a full, though controversial, treatment of Bacon's Rebellion; and Louis B. Wright, *The First Gentlemen of Virginia: Intellectual Qualities of the Early Colonial Ruling Class* (San Marino, Cal., 1940).

The first three volumes of Douglas Southall Freeman's mammoth *George Washington: A Biography* (completed by J. A. Carroll and Mary W. Ashworth, 7 vols.; New York, 1948–1957) contains an enormous amount of material on social, economic, and political matters in eighteenth-century Virginia.

Studies of slavery deal with the social and cultural life of whites as well as blacks. Three of them have special significance: David Brion Davis, *The Problem of Slavery in the Age of Revolution, 1770–1823* (Ithaca, N.Y., 1975), a probing analysis of the question of slavery in the midst of revolution for liberty; Winthrop Jordan, *White over Black: American Attitudes toward the Negro, 1550–1812* (Chapel Hill, N.C., 1968), an impressive study of racial perceptions; and Morgan, *American Slavery, American Freedom.* Other worthy and informative books include Ira Berlin and Ronald Hoffman, eds., *Slavery and Freedom in the Age of the American Revolution* (Charlottesville, Va., 1983), a valuable collection of essays; Allan Kulikoff, *Tobacco and Slaves: The Development of Southern Cultures in the Chesapeake* (Chapel Hill, N.C., 1986); Daniel C. Littlefield, *Rice and Slaves: Ethnicity and the Slave Trade in Colonial South Carolina* (Baton Rouge, La., 1981); Duncan J. MacLeod, *Slavery, Race, and the American Revolution* (Cambridge, Eng., 1974); Gerald W. Mullin, *Flight and Rebellion: Slave Resistance in Eighteenth-Century Virginia* (New York, 1972); Mechal Sobel, *The World They Made Together: Black and White Values in Eighteenth-Century Virginia* (Princeton, N.J., 1987), which stresses the impact of each race and culture on the other; Betty Wood, *Slavery in Colonial Georgia, 1730–1775* (Athens, Ga., 1984); and Peter Wood, *Black Majority: Negroes in Colonial South Carolina from 1670 through the Stono Rebellion* (New York, 1974), which emphasizes the contribution of the slaves to the colony's economic success.

On African slavery consult Paul E. Lovejoy, *Transformation in Slavery: A History of Slavery in Africa* (New York, 1983), and Suzanne Miers and Igor Kopytoff, eds., *Slavery in Africa: Historical and Anthropological Perspectives* (Madison, Wis., 1977). Philip D. Curtin's *Atlantic Slave Trade: A Census* (Madison, Wis., 1969) revolutionized the quantitative dimension of the slave trade while James A. Rawley, *The Trans-Atlantic Slave Trade* (New York, 1981), contains a full, descriptive account of that trade.

Political subjects are treated in numerous books. In *Liberty and Slavery: Southern Politics to 1860* (New York, 1983), William J. Cooper, Jr., presents an interpretive analysis. Jack P. Greene, *The Quest for Power: The Lower Houses of Assembly in the Southern Royal Colonies, 1689–1776* (Chapel Hill, N.C., 1963), provides superb treatment of a major theme. See also Richard M. Brown, *The South Carolina Regulators* (Cambridge, Mass., 1963); Kenneth Coleman, *The American Revolution in Georgia, 1763–1789* (Athens, Ga., 1958); A. Roger Ekirch, *"Poor Carolina": Politics and Society in Colonial North Carolina, 1729–1776* (Chapel Hill, N.C., 1981); Ronald Hoffman, *A Spirit of Dissension: Economics, Politics, and the Revolution in Maryland* (Baltimore, 1973); Eugene Sirmans, *Colonial South Carolina: A Political History* (Chapel Hill, N.C., 1966); and Charles S. Sydnor, *American Revolutionaries in the Making: Political Practices in Washington's Virginia* (New York, 1965), a sparkling account of political culture in one state.

For the Revolutionary era one must always recognize that the southern colonies acted in conjunction with the northern colonies. Thus major works on the period contain much of value on the southern experience. Bernard Bailyn, *The Ideological Origins of the American Revolution* (Cambridge, Mass., 1967) and *The Origins of American Politics* (New York, 1968), and Gordon S. Wood, *The Creation of the American Republic, 1776–1789* (Chapel Hill, N.C., 1969), discuss fundamental questions of ideology and politics. Edmund S. and Helen M. Morgan, *The Stamp Act Crisis: Prologue to Revolution* (Chapel Hill, N.C., 1953), is the standard account. Edmund S. Morgan's *Inventing the People: The Rise of Popular Sovereignty in England and America* (New York, 1988) illuminates the origins of what became a basic principle of the Revolution; in addition see his engaging and enlightening *Meaning of Independence: John Adams, George Washington, and Thomas Jefferson* (Charlottesville, Va., 1976). Also helpful are Robert A. Becker, *Revolution, Reform, and the Politics of American Taxation, 1763–1783* (Baton Rouge, La., 1980); Richard Beeman et al., eds., *Beyond Confederation: Origins of the Constitution and American National Identity* (Chapel Hill, N.C., 1987), a first-rate collection of essays; H. James Henderson, *Party Politics in the Continental Congress* (New York, 1974); Alice H. Jones, *Wealth of a Nation to Be: The American Colonies on the Eve of the Revolution* (New York, 1980), an investigation of wealth in Revolutionary America; Forrest McDonald, *Novus Ordo Seclorum: The Intellectual Origins of the Constitution* (Lawrence, Kans., 1985); Pauline S. Maier, *The Old Revolutionaries: Political Lives in the Age of Samuel Adams* (New York, 1980); Jackson T. Main, *The Social Structure of Revolutionary America* (Princeton, N.J., 1965); Peter Onuf, *Statehood and Union: A History of the Northwest Ordinance* (Bloomington, Ind., 1987); J. G. A. Pocock, *The Machiavellian Moment: Florentine Political Thought and the Atlantic Republican Tradition* (Princeton, N.J., 1975); Jack N. Rakove, *The Beginnings of National Politics: An Interpretive History of the Continental Congress* (New York, 1979); and Garry Wills, *Inventing America: Jefferson's Declaration of Independence* (New York, 1978). There is no good study of southern loyalists or Tories, but Paul H. Smith, *Loyalists and Redcoats: A Study in British Revolutionary Policy* (Chapel Hill, N.C., 1964), discusses the importance the British placed on them. Staughton Lynd, *Class Conflict, Slavery, and the United States Constitution: Ten Essays* (Indianapolis, 1968), and Donald Robinson, *Slavery in the Structure of American Politics, 1765–1820* (New York, 1979), make massive, often exaggerated claims for the centrality of slavery. They find it in every crevice of national affairs.

On the South specifically see John R. Alden, *The South in the American Revolution, 1763–1789* (Baton Rouge, La., 1957) and *The First South* (Baton Rouge, La., 1961), which addresses the intriguing questions of the beginnings of southern distinctiveness. Jeffrey

J. Crow and Larry E. Tise, eds., *The Southern Experience in the American Revolution* (Chapel Hill, N.C., 1978), contains helpful articles on diverse topics. James R. Morrill, *The Practice and Politics of Fiat Finance: North Carolina in the Confederation, 1783–1789* (Chapel Hill, N.C., 1969), and Charles G. Singer, *South Carolina in the Confederation* (Philadelphia, 1941), analyze events in two states during the Confederation period.

On the military conflict in the South, Don Higginbotham, *The War of American Independence: Military Attitudes, Policies, and Practice, 1763–1789* (New York, 1971); Charles Royster, *A Revolutionary People at War: The Continental Army and American Character, 1775–1783* (Chapel Hill, N.C., 1979); John Shy, *A People Numerous and Armed: Reflections on the Military Struggle for American Independence* (New York, 1976); and Christopher Ward, *The War of the Revolution*, 2 vols. (New York, 1952), supply a full background and a rich context. On key actions see John S. Pancake, *This Destructive War: The British Campaign in the Carolinas, 1780–1782* (University, Ala., 1985); M. F. Treacy, *Prelude to Yorktown: The Southern Campaigns of Nathanael Greene* (Chapel Hill, N.C., 1963); and Russell F. Weigley, *The Partisan War: The South Carolina Campaign of 1780–1782* (Columbia, S.C., 1970). Volume 5 of Freeman's *George Washington* is thorough on Yorktown.

Primary documents, including the letters, diaries, speeches, and travel accounts of contemporaries, have no match for imparting the flavor of a particular time. Especially notable published collections for the colonial and Revolutionary South include James C. Ballagh, ed., *The Letters of Richard Henry Lee*, 2 vols. (New York, 1912–1914); Philip L. Barbour, ed., *The Complete Works of Captain John Smith, 1580–1631*, 3 vols. (Chapel Hill, N.C., 1986); Warren M. Billings, ed., *The Old Dominion in the Seventeenth Century: A Documentary History of Virginia, 1606–1689* (Chapel Hill, N.C., 1975); Julian P. Boyd et al., eds., *The Papers of Thomas Jefferson*, 22 vols. to date (Princeton, N.J., 1950–); Edmund C. Burnett, ed., *Letters of Members of the Continental Congress*, 8 vols. (Washington, D.C., 1921–1936); Thomas D. Clark, ed., *Travels in the Old South: A Bibliography*, 3 vols. (Norman, Okla., 1956–1959), a superior guide to travel accounts; Elizabeth Donnan, ed., *Documents Illustrative of the Slave Trade to America*, 4 vols. (Washington, D.C., 1930–1935); Jonathan Elliot, ed., *The Debates in the Several State Conventions on the Adoption of the Constitution...*, 5 vols. (Philadelphia, 1907); Hunter D. Farish, ed., *Journal and Letters of Philip Vickers Fithian, 1773–1774: A Plantation Tutor of the Old Dominion* (Williamsburg, Va., 1943); John C. Fitzpatrick, ed., *The Writings of George Washington from the Original Manuscript Sources, 1745–1799*, 37 vols. (Washington, D.C., 1931–1944); Worthington Ford et al., eds., *Journal of the Continental Congress, 1774–1789*, 34 vols. (Washington, D.C., 1904–1937); Jack P. Greene, ed., *The Diary of Colonel Landon Carter of Sabine Hall, 1752–1778*, 2 vols. (Charlottesville, Va., 1965); Philip M. Hamer et al., eds., *The Papers of Henry Laurens*, 11 vols. to date (Columbia, S.C., 1968–); Don Higginbotham, ed., *The Papers of James Iredell*, 2 vols. (Raleigh, N.C., 1976); Richard J. Hooker, ed., *The Carolina Backcountry on the Eve of the Revolution: The Journal and Other Writings of Charles Woodmason, Anglican Itinerant* (Chapel Hill, N.C., 1953); William T. Hutchinson et al., eds., *The Papers of James Madison*, 15 vols. to date (Chicago and Charlottesville, Va., 1962–); Merrill Jensen et al., eds., *The Documentary History of the Ratification of the Constitution*, 8 vols. to date (Madison, Wis., 1976–), superior to Elliot's edition but not yet complete; Aubrey C. Land, ed., *Bases of Plantation Society* (New York, 1969); Elsie Pinckney and Marvin R. Zahnisner, eds., *The Letterbook of Eliza Lucas Pinckney, 1739–1762* (Chapel Hill, N.C., 1972); Robert A. Rutland, ed., *The Papers of George Mason, 1725–1792*, 3 vols. (Chapel Hill, N.C., 1970); Paul H. Smith et al., eds., *Letters of Delegates to Congress, 1774–89*, 16 vols. to date (Washington, D.C., 1976–), superior to Burnett's edition but not yet complete; Charles C. Tansill, ed., *Documents Illustrative of the Formation of the Union of the American States* (Washington, D.C., 1927), a convenient source for numerous documents related to the Constitutional Convention; Marion Tinling, ed., *The Correspondence of the Three William Byrds of Westover, Virginia, 1684–1776,* 2 vols. (Charlottesville, Va., 1977); Richard Walsh, ed., *The Writings of Christopher Gadsden, 1746–1805* (Columbia, S.C., 1966); Maude H. Woodfin and Marion Tinling, eds., *Another Secret Diary of William Byrd of Westover, 1696–1726* (Richmond, Va., 1942); Louis B. Wright, ed., *The Prose Works of William Byrd of Westover: Narratives of a Colonial Virginian* (Cambridge, Mass., 1966); and Wright and Marion Tinling, eds., *The Secret Diary of William Byrd of Westover, 1709–1712* (Richmond, Va., 1941).

No single book covers in detail southern affairs from the 1780s to the 1840s. Cooper, *Liberty and Slavery,* offers an interpretive analysis of politics in the period. Thomas P. Abernethy, *The South in the New Nation, 1789–1819* (Baton Rouge, La., 1961), goes over the chronological ground of thirty crucial years, albeit in uneven fashion. Strong on geographical expansion and Indian relations, it slights ideology and politics and contains practically nothing on slavery. Charles S. Syndor, *The Development of Southern Sectionalism, 1819–1848* (Baton Rouge, La., 1948), is best on the 1820s and weakest on the 1840s. Robert F. Durden's argument in *The Self-Inflicted Wound: Southern Politics in the Nineteenth Century* (Lexington, Ky., 1985), that the South moved in the 1820s from liberal and optimistic to conservative and defensive, overlooks the fundamental commitment made to slavery during the Revolution. Durden's interpretation follows that of William E. Dodd in two old but obviously influential books: *Statesmen of the Old South, or From Radicalism to Conservative Revolt* (New York, 1911) and *The Cotton Kingdom* (New Haven, Conn., 1920). Henry Adams's classic *History of the United States during the Administrations of Jefferson and Madison,* 9 vols. (New York, 1889–1891), still has enormous value, and because of their intimate involvement in the nation, southerners occupy a major place in his story. Merrill Peterson's *Great Triumvirate: Webster, Clay, Calhoun* (New York, 1987) uses the lives of these three individuals as avenues to approach American history between the War of 1812 and 1850; here, as in Adams, southerners and the South play leading roles. James S. Young, *The Washington Community, 1800–1828* (New York, 1966), makes an intriguing argument on how the capital city's rude character and living arrangements affected politics.

On the party that dominated the South in the early national period, Noble E. Cunningham has two basic volumes, *The Jeffersonian Republicans: The Formation of Party Organization, 1789–1801* (Chapel Hill, N.C., 1957) and *The Jeffersonian Republicans in Power: Party Operations, 1801–1809* (Chapel Hill, N.C., 1963). Three especially valuable studies emphasizing ideology are Joyce Appleby, *Capitalism and a New Social Order: The Republican Vision of the 1790s* (New York, 1984); Lance Banning, *The Jeffersonian Persuasion: Evolution of a Party Ideology* (Ithaca, N.Y., 1978); and Drew R. McCoy, *The Elusive Republic: Political Economy in Jeffersonian America* (Chapel Hill, N.C., 1980). In his *Last of the Fathers: James Madison and the Republican Legacy* (New York, 1989) McCoy brilliantly analyzes Madison's thought while he probes the meaning of the constitutional Union. For detailed treatment of the southern Republicans who refused to follow party shifts, see Norman K. Risjord, *The Old Republicans: Southern Conservatism in the Age of Jefferson* (New York, 1965), and Robert E. Shalhope, *John Taylor of Caroline: Pastoral Republican* (Columbia, S.C., 1980). Concentrating on Randolph's character, Robert Dawidoff's *Education of John Randolph* (New York, 1979) also discusses the Virginia statesman's views of his world. Alexander DeConde, *This Affair of Louisiana* (New York, 1976), illuminates a primary event of the Jefferson years.

For the history of southern Federalists three books are required reading: George C. Rogers, Jr., *Evolution of a Federalist: William Loughton Smith of Charleston, 1758–1812* (Columbia, S.C., 1962), absolutely first-rate; Lisle A. Rose, *Prologue to Democracy: The Feder-*

alists in the South, 1789–1800 (Lexington, Ky., 1968); and James H. Broussard, *The Southern Federalists, 1800–1816* (Baton Rouge, La., 1978). Also see Joseph W. Cox, *Champion of Southern Federalism: Robert Goodloe Harper of South Carolina* (Port Washington, N.Y., 1972). Although it has little on the South, Linda Kerber, *Federalists in Dissent: Imagery and Ideology in Jeffersonian America* (Ithaca, N.Y., 1970) is revealing on why the Federalists had so much trouble in the South. Also the South did not share equally in the party's renewed vigor sparked by younger Federalists claimed by David H. Fischer, *The Revolution of American Conservatism: The Federalist Party in the Era of Jeffersonian Democracy* (New York, 1965).

Monographs on activities in individual states during this time are Richard R. Beeman, *The Old Dominion and the New Nation, 1788–1801* (Lexington, Ky., 1972); Joan Wells Coward, *Kentucky in the New Republic: The Process of Constitution Making* (Lexington, Ky., 1972); Delbert H. Gilpatrick, *Jeffersonian Democracy in North Carolina, 1789–1816* (New York, 1931); Norman K. Risjord, *Chesapeake Politics, 1781–1800* (New York, 1978), the best of these books; and John H. Wolfe, *Jeffersonian Democracy in South Carolina* (Chapel Hill, N.C., 1940).

On the dynamic relationship between slavery and politics, Davis, *Slavery in the Age of Revolution*, and Jordan, *White over Black*, remain pertinent. See also Robert McColley, *Slavery and Jeffersonian Virginia* (Urbana, Ill., 1973), and John C. Miller, *The Wolf by the Ears: Thomas Jefferson and Slavery* (New York, 1977).

For this era in southern history biographies of major actors are especially useful. Volumes 6 and 7 of Freeman's *George Washington* detail the course of the first national hero; for solid, and considerably briefer, treatment see John R. Alden, *George Washington: A Biography* (Baton Rouge, La., 1984). Dumas Malone's monumental *Jefferson and His Time*, 6 vols. (Boston, 1948–1981); Merrill Peterson's excellent *Thomas Jefferson and the New Nation: A Biography* (New York, 1970); and Noble E. Cunningham's thoughtful *In Pursuit of Reason: The Life of Thomas Jefferson* (Baton Rouge, La., 1987) contain a wealth of information on ideology and politics in general as well as on Jefferson, the first dominant force in southern politics. The next, Andrew Jackson, has received thorough, sympathetic biographical treatment in Robert V. Remini's massive *Andrew Jackson*, 3 vols. (New York, 1977–1984); James C. Curtis's insightful and much briefer *Andrew Jackson and the Search for Vindication* (Boston, 1976) looks at Jackson from a different vantage point. John C. Calhoun's influential and tortured career has been documented in Charles M. Wiltse's *John C. Calhoun*, 3 vols. (Indianapolis, 1944–1951), and in John Niven's careful and suggestive *John C. Calhoun and the Price of Union: A Biography* (Baton Rouge, La., 1988). Charles G. Sellers, Jr., *James K. Polk*, 2 vols. to date (Princeton, N.J., 1957–) details the rise to the White House of a Democratic loyalist and contains a mass of material on Tennessee. Superb coverage of the War of 1812 can be found in J. C. A. Stagg's substantial *Mr. Madison's War: Politics, Diplomacy, and Warfare in the Early American Republic, 1783–1830* (Princeton, N.J., 1983), which concentrates on the war. On the southern front, specifically the Indian campaigns and the contest for New Orleans, the first volume of Remini's *Andrew Jackson* tells the story in detail. Also see Frank L. Owsley, Jr., *Struggle for the Gulf Borderlands: The Creek War and the Battle of New Orleans, 1812–1815* (Gainesville, Fla., 1981).

Historians have not avidly pursued the important issues reflected in the disintegration of the Jeffersonian Republican party. This theme does, however, form a part of George Dangerfield's lively *Era of Good Feelings* (New York, 1952), which does not slight southern developments. No good monographs analyze the South and such central topics as the tariff, internal improvements, the second Bank of the United States, the Panic of 1819, and the critical election of 1824, though Albert R. Newsome, *The Presidential Election of 1824 in North Carolina* (Chapel Hill, N.C., 1939), looks at one state. The Missouri crisis receives thorough treatment in Glover Moore, *The Missouri Controversy, 1819–1821* (Lexington, Ky., 1953). Missouri is also the initial crisis discussed by Don E. Fehrenbacher, *The South and Three Sectional Crises* (Baton Rouge, La., 1980). Fletcher M. Green, *Constitutional Development in the South Atlantic States, 1776–1860* (Chapel Hill, N.C., 1930), first called attention to the democratization of southern politics.

Jacksonianism has occupied the talents of a legion of historians. The most complete study of the party in the South is William J. Cooper, Jr., *The South and the Politics of Slavery, 1828–1856* (Baton Rouge, La., 1978). Other books that have particular pertinence for students of southern history include Richard P. McCormick, *The Second American Party System: Party Formation in the Jacksonian Era* (Chapel Hill, N.C., 1966); Marvin Meyers, *The Jacksonian Persuasion: Politics and Belief* (Stanford, Calif., 1960); Robert V. Remini, *The Legacy of Andrew Jackson: Essays on Democracy, Indian Removal, and Slavery* (Baton Rouge, La., 1988); Arthur M. Schlesinger, Jr., *The Age of Jackson* (Boston, 1945); and John William Ward, *Andrew Jackson: Symbol for an Age* (New York, 1955). On the key issues of the Jackson presidency see Richard E. Ellis, *The Union at Risk: Jacksonian Democracy, States' Rights, and the Nullification Crisis* (New York, 1987); William W. Freehling, *Prelude to Civil War: The Nullification Controversy in South Carolina, 1816–1836* (New York, 1966); William G. McLoughlin, *Cherokee Renascence in the New Republic* (Princeton, N.J., 1986); Merrill D. Peterson, *Olive Branch and Sword: The Compromise of 1833* (Baton Rouge, La., 1982); Robert V. Remini, *Andrew Jackson and the Bank War* (New York, 1967); and Ronald N. Satz, *American Indian Policy in the Jacksonian Era* (Lincoln, Neb., 1975).

For the growth of the Whig opposition and the resulting Whig party, see the Cooper and McCormick volumes cited above along with Thomas Brown, *Politics and Statesmanship: Essays on the American Whig Party* (New York, 1985); George R. Poage, *Henry Clay and the Whig Party* (Chapel Hill, N.C., 1936); and Arthur C. Cole's older *Whig Party in the South* (Washington, D.C., 1913). In his *Political Culture of the American Whigs* (Chicago, 1979), Daniel W. Howe underestimates the special characteristics of southern Whiggery. Two statistical analyses of congressional voting emphasize the existence of party loyalty: Thomas B. Alexander, *Sectional Stress and Party Strength: A Computer Analysis of Roll-Call Voting Patterns in the United States House of Representatives, 1836–1860* (Nashville, Tenn., 1967), and Joel H. Silbey, *The Shrine of Party: Congressional Voting Behavior, 1841–1852* (Pittsburgh, 1967).

A number of substantial state and local studies illuminate both the Democratic-Whig competition and the southern political world between the 1820s and 1860. Without question the best of them are J. Mills Thornton III, *Politics and Power in a Slave Society: Alabama, 1800–1860* (Baton Rouge, La., 1978), and Lacy K. Ford, Jr., *Origins of Southern Radicalism: The South Carolina Upcountry, 1800–1860* (New York, 1988). Other worthy titles include William H. Adams, *The Whig Party of Louisiana* (Lafayette, La., 1973); Charles H. Ambler, *Sectionalism in Virginia from 1776 to 1861* (Chicago, 1910); Paul H. Bergeron, *Antebellum Politics in Tennessee* (Lexington, Ky., 1982); Herbert J. Doherty, Jr., *The Whigs of Florida, 1845–1854* (Gainesville, Fla., 1959); William S. Hoffman, *Andrew Jackson and North Carolina Politics* (Chapel Hill, N.C., 1958); Marc W. Kruman, *Parties and Politics in North Carolina, 1836–1865* (Baton Rouge, La., 1983); John V. Mering, *The Whig Party in Missouri* (Columbia, Mo., 1967); Edwin A. Miles, *Jacksonian Democracy in Mississippi* (Chapel Hill, N.C., 1960); Horace Montgomery, *Cracker Parties* (Baton Rouge, La., 1950); Paul Murray, *The Whig Party in Georgia, 1825–1853* (Chapel Hill, N.C., 1948); Ulrich B. Phillips, *Georgia and State Rights* (Washington, D.C., 1902); Arthur W. Thompson, *Jacksonian Democracy on the Florida Frontier* (Gainesville, Fla., 1961); and Harry L. Watson, *Jacksonian Politics and Community Conflict: The Emergence of the Second Party System in Cumberland County, North Carolina* (Baton Rouge, La., 1981), absolutely first-rate. A clear, modern vantage point for Virginia politics is Craig M. Simpson's *A Good Southerner: The Life of Henry A. Wise of Virginia* (Chapel Hill, N.C., 1985). On the structure of politics see also two books by Ralph A. Wooster, *Politicians, Planters, and Plain Folks: Courthouse and Statehouse in the Upper South, 1850–1860* (Knoxville, Tenn., 1975) and *The People in Power: Courthouse and Statehouse in the Lower South, 1850–1860* (Knoxville, Tenn., 1969).

Published primary materials especially relevant for this period include *Annals of Congress* (1789–1824), *Register of Debates in Congress* (1825–1837), *Congressional Globe* (1833–1861), for congressional debates; John S. Bassett, ed., *Correspondence of Andrew Jackson*, 7 vols. (Washington, D.C., 1926–1935); Chauncey S. Boucher and Robert P. Brooks, eds., *Correspondence Addressed to John C. Calhoun, 1837–1849* (Washington, D.C., 1930); Boyd et al., eds., *Papers of Jefferson*; Clark, ed., *Travels in the Old South*, the guide to travel accounts; Noble E. Cunningham, ed., *Circular Letters of Congressmen to Their Constituents, 1789–1829*, 3 vols. (Chapel Hill, N.C., 1978); Fitzpatrick, ed., *Writings of Washington*; Paul L. Ford, ed., *The Writings of Thomas Jefferson*, 10 vols. (New York, 1892–1899); William W. Freehling, ed., *The Nullification Era: A Documentary Record* (New York, 1967); Hutchinson et al., eds., *Papers of Madison*; James F. Hopkins et al., eds., *The Papers of Henry Clay*, 9 vols. to date (Lexington, Ky., 1959–); J. Franklin Jameson, ed., *Correspondence of John C. Calhoun* (Washington, D.C., 1900); Robert L. Meriwether et al., eds., *The Papers of John C. Calhoun*, 16 vols. to date (Columbia, S.C., 1959–); Milo M. Quaife, ed., *The Diary of James K. Polk: During His Presidency, 1845–1849*, 4 vols. (Chicago, 1910); Herbert Weaver et al., eds., *The Papers of James K. Polk*, 7 vols. to date (Nashville, Tenn., 1969–).

Lewis C. Gray published the standard history of antebellum southern agriculture more than fifty-five years ago. Full on cultivation, processing, and marketing, *History of Agriculture in the Southern United States*, 2 vols. (Washington, D.C., 1933), remains a remarkable achievement and an invaluable aid. Complementing Gray, Sam B. Hilliard, *Atlas of Antebellum Southern Agriculture* (Baton Rouge, La., 1984) provides marvelous cartographic treatment of the subject. Other noteworthy volumes include Sam B. Hilliard, *Hog Meat and Hoecake: Food Supply in the Old South, 1840–1860* (Carbondale, Ill., 1972), which focuses on both the food supply and internal trade patterns; Harold D. Woodman, *King Cotton and His Retainers: Financing and Marketing the Cotton Crop of the South, 1800–1925* (Lexington, Ky., 1968), which details marketing processes; and Gavin Wright, *The Political Economy of the Cotton South: Households, Markets, and Wealth in the Nineteenth Century* (New York, 1978), the best analysis of the cotton economy in the prewar South.

Other basic crops have also had their historians: Henry C. Dethloff, *A History of the American Rice Industry, 1685–1985* (College Station, Tex., 1988); James F. Hopkins, *A History of the Hemp Industry in Kentucky* (Lexington, Ky., 1957); Joseph C. Robert, *The Tobacco Kingdom: Plantation, Market, and Factory in Virginia and North Carolina, 1800–1860* (Durham, N.C., 1938); and J. Carlyle Sitterson, *Sugar Country: The Cane Sugar Industry in the South, 1753–1950* (Lexington, Ky., 1953).

For agricultural developments in specific states see in addition James C. Bonner, *A History of Georgia Agriculture, 1732–1860* (Athens, Ga., 1964); Cornelius O. Cathey, *Agricultural Developments in North Carolina* (Chapel Hill, N.C., 1956); Coclanis, *Shadow of a Dream*; Richard G. Lowe and Randolph B. Campbell, *Planters and Plain Folk: Agriculture in Antebellum Texas* (Dallas, 1987); John H. Moore, *The Emergence of the Cotton Kingdom in the Old Southwest: Mississippi, 1770–1860* (Baton Rouge, La., 1988); Alfred G. Smith, Jr., *Economic Readjustment of an Old Cotton State: South Carolina, 1820–1860* (Columbia, S.C., 1958).

No subject in southern history has attracted more attention or drawn a more talented group of scholars than slavery. The initial classic, Ulrich B. Phillips, *American Negro Slavery* (New York, 1918), explored virgin territory but was marred by the racial outlook of the author and his time. Replacing Phillips, Kenneth M. Stampp, *The Peculiar Institution: Slavery in the Ante-Bellum South* (New York, 1956), combined massive archival research with a modern view of race. In an early emphasis on the human beings who were slaves, Melville J. Herskovits argued for the significance of their African cultural background in *The Myth of the Negro Past* (New York, 1941). For our time Stanley Elkins, *Slavery: A Problem in American Institutional and Intellectual Life* (Chicago, 1959), has probably had more influence than any other single book. This slim volume directed attention to the slaves and their behavior rather than to the institution. That perspective, along with the civil rights movement, shifted the chief approach of slavery scholarship to an effort to understand slaves in their bondage.

To date the major result of this inquiry has been Eugene D. Genovese, *Roll, Jordan, Roll: The World the Slaves Made* (New York, 1974), an impressively researched study that places the slaves in the forefront as it probes their world. Two other books also deserve special mention: Herbert G. Gutman, *The Black Family in Slavery and Freedom, 1750–1925* (New York, 1976), which focuses on the family as critical in slave life, and Lawrence W. Levine, *Black Culture and Black Consciousness: Afro-American Folk Thought from Slavery to Freedom* (New York, 1977), which illuminates the cultural world of the slaves.

Studies that cast light on other important areas of slavery include Frederic Bancroft, *Slave Trading in the Old South* (New York, 1931), still the only monograph on this critical topic; John W. Blassingame, *The Slave Community: Plantation Life in the Antebellum South* (New York, 1979), and George P. Rawick, *From Sundown to Sunup: The Making of the Black Community* (Westport, Conn., 1972), which emphasize the positive characteristics of the slave community; Paul D. Escott, *Slavery Remembered: A Record of Twentieth-Century Slave Narratives* (Chapel Hill, N.C., 1979); Jacqueline Jones, *Labor of Love, Labor of Sorrow: Black Women, Work, and the Family from Slavery to the Present* (New York, 1985); Leslie H. Owens, *This Species of Property: Slave Life and Culture in the Old South* (New York, 1976); Albert J. Raboteau, *Slave Religion: The "Invisible" Institution in the South* (New York, 1978); Todd L. Savitt, *Medicine and Slavery: The Diseases and Health Care of Blacks in Antebellum Virginia* (Urbana, Ill., 1978), a model for further investigation of this crucial topic; Robert S. Starobin, *Industrial Slavery in the Old South* (New York, 1970), a pathbreaking book, and Ronald L. Lewis, *Coal, Iron, and Slaves: Industrial Slavery in Maryland and Virginia, 1715–1865* (Westport, Conn., 1979); William L. Van Deburg, *The Slave Driver: Black Agricultural Labor Supervisors in the Antebellum South* (Westport, Conn., 1979); Richard C. Wade, *Slavery in the Cities: The South, 1820–1860* (New York, 1964), a valuable study, though it exaggerates the incompatibility between cities and slavery; Thomas L. Webber, *Deep Like the River: Education in the Slave Community* (New York, 1978); and Deborah G. White, *Ar'nt I a Woman? Female Slaves in the Plantation South* (New York, 1985).

During the past decade a number of books have clarified the legal dimensions of slavery. Paul Finkelman has been in the forefront of this effort: *An Imperfect Union: Slavery, Federalism, and Comity* (Chapel Hill, N.C., 1981), which concentrates on slavery's meaning for the federal system; *Slavery in the Courtroom: An Annotated Bibliography of American Cases* (Washington, D.C., 1988); and *The Law of Freedom and Bondage: A Casebook* (New York, 1986). In *The American Law of Slavery, 1810–1860: Considerations of Humanity and Interest* (Princeton, N.J., 1981) Mark V. Tushnet maintains that slavery forced the creation of a distinctive southern legal system. Two studies focus on developments in the states: Michael S. Hindus, *Prison and Plantation: Crime, Justice, and Authority in Massachusetts and South Carolina, 1767–1868* (Chapel Hill, N.C., 1980), and Philip J. Schwarz, *Twice*

Condemned: Slaves and the Criminal Laws of Virginia, 1705–1865 (Baton Rouge, La., 1988). Also see the notable collection of articles in Kermit L. Hall, ed., *The Law of American Slavery: Major Interpretations* (New York, 1987).

Eugene D. Genovese, *From Rebellion to Revolution: Afro-American Slave Revolts in the Making of the Modern World* (Baton Rouge, La., 1979), places the southern story in a hemispheric context, albeit within a Marxist framework. Herbert Aptheker, *American Negro Slave Revolts* (New York, 1963) covers all the major revolts, though it greatly overestimates the number of organized attacks on the system. For discussions of the major revolts (except the one in Louisiana in 1811, which has not been thoroughly studied) see Wood, *Black Majority*, on the Stono Rebellion; Mullin, *Flight and Rebellion*, on Gabriel Prosser's conspiracy; Freehling, *Prelude to Civil War*, and John Lofton, *Denmark Vesey's Revolt: The Slave Plot That Lit a Fuse to Fort Sumter* (Kent, O., 1983), on the Vesey conspiracy; and Stephen B. Oates, *The Fires of Jubilee: Nat Turner's Fierce Rebellion* (New York, 1975), on the most famous revolt.

Published to wide acclaim as the culmination of quantitative research on slavery, Robert W. Fogel and Stanley L. Engerman, *Time on the Cross*, 2 vols. (Boston, 1974), soon came under withering attack for methodological flaws. For a sweeping critique consult Paul A. David et al., *Reckoning with Slavery: A Critical Study in the Quantitative History of American Negro Slavery* (New York, 1976). Fogel and Engerman, however, did push a point made by earlier scholars, that slavery was economically vibrant and generally profitable. Eugene D. Genovese, by contrast, in *The Political Economy of Slavery: Studies in the Economy and Society of the Slave South* (New York, 1965), argued for the backwardness and lack of profitability in the system.

A number of state and local studies have value. Those written before the revolution in the historiography of slavery focus on the institution, not on the slaves. They include J. Winston Coleman, *Slavery Times in Kentucky* (Chapel Hill, N.C., 1940); Chase C. Mooney, *Slavery in Tennessee* (Bloomington, Ind., 1957); James B. Sellers, *Slavery in Alabama* (University, Ala., 1950); Charles S. Sydnor, *Slavery in Mississippi* (New York, 1933); Joe Gray Taylor, *Negro Slavery in Louisiana* (Baton Rouge, La., 1963); and Orville W. Taylor, *Negro Slavery in Arkansas* (Durham, N.C., 1958). More modern studies include Randolph B. Campbell, *An Empire for Slavery: The Peculiar Institution in Texas, 1821–1865* (Baton Rouge, La., 1989); Barbara J. Fields, *Slavery and Freedom on the Middle Ground: Maryland during the Nineteenth Century* (New Haven, Conn., 1985); Charles Joyner, *Down by the Riverside: A South Carolina Slave Community* (Urbana, Ill., 1984); Julia F. Smith, *Slavery and Plantation Growth in Antebellum Florida, 1821–1860* (Gainesville, Fla., 1973) and *Slavery and Rice Culture in Low Country Georgia, 1750–1860* (Knoxville, Tenn., 1985). For a solid distillation of recent scholarship see John B. Boles, *Black Southerners, 1619–1869* (Lexington, Ky., 1983). For brief introductions to a wide variety of subjects, Randall M. Miller and John Davis Smith, eds., *Dictionary of Afro-American Slavery* (New York, 1988), is helpful.

Investigations of planters and plantation management help immensely to understand the slave plantation. Drew G. Faust's brilliant *James Henry Hammond and the Old South: A Design for Mastery* (Baton Rouge, La., 1982) explores with insight and imagination the activities of a large planter and slave owner. See also Malcom Bell, Jr., *Major Butler's Legacy: Five Generations of a Slaveholding Family* (Athens, Ga., 1987); Avery O. Craven, *Rachel of Old Louisiana* (Baton Rouge, La., 1975); Weymouth T. Jordan, *Hugh Davis and His Alabama Plantation* (University, Ala., 1948); and Theodore Rosengarten, *Tombee: Portrait of a Cotton Planter* (New York, 1986). John S. Otto, *Cannon's Point Plantation, 1794–1860: Living Conditions and Status Patterns in the Old South* (Orlando, Fla., 1984), presents the results of an extensive archaeological investigation. William K. Scarborough, *The Overseer: Plantation Management in the Old South* (Baton Rouge, La., 1966), discusses that crucial position. Ulrich B. Phillips, *Life and Labor in the Old South* (Boston, 1929), is still worthwhile on the texture of rural life.

Comparative studies provide a broader perspective for comprehending slavery in the American South. The first comparison was with other slave societies in the New World. Pertinent titles include Carl M. Degler, *Neither Black nor White: Slavery and Race Relations in Brazil and the United States* (New York, 1971); Laura Foner and Eugene D. Genovese, eds., *Slavery in the New World: A Reader in Comparative History* (Englewood Cliffs, N.J., 1969); and Herbert S. Klein, *Slavery in the Americas: A Comparative Study of Virginia and Cuba* (Chicago, 1967). More recently other unfree systems have also been analyzed; two especially notable books are Peter Kolchin, *Unfree Labor: American Slavery and Russian Serfdom* (Cambridge, Mass., 1987), with its different angle on slavery in the South, and Orlando Patterson, *Slavery and Social Death: A Comparative Study* (Cambridge, Mass., 1982), an ambitious attempt to devise an all-inclusive theory of slavery.

On free blacks, Ira Berlin, *Slaves without Masters: The Free Negro in the Antebellum South* (New York, 1974), is an excellent general treatment. Two meritorious books on unusual individuals illuminate the complex, precarious world of the free black: Michael P. Johnson and James L. Roark, *Black Masters: A Free Family of Color in the Old South* (New York, 1984), and Gary B. Mills, *The Forgotten People: Cane River's Creoles of Color* (Baton Rouge, La., 1977). Also see Letitia W. Brown, *Free Negroes in the District of Columbia, 1790–1846* (New York, 1972); Edwin A. Davis and William R. Hogan, *The Barber of Natchez* (Baton Rouge, La., 1954); John Hope Franklin, *The Free Negro in North Carolina, 1790–1860* (Chapel Hill, N.C., 1943); Luther P. Jackson, *Free Negro Labor and Property Holding in Virginia, 1830–1860* (New York, 1942); Dickson J. Preston, *Young Frederick Douglass: The Maryland Years* (Baltimore, 1980); Herbert E. Sterkx, *The Free Negro in Antebellum Louisiana* (Rutherford, N.J., 1972); and Marina Wikramanayake, *A World in Shadow: The Free Black in Antebellum South Carolina* (Columbia, S.C., 1973).

Lewis P. Simpson in three books, *Mind and the American Civil War: A Meditation on Lost Causes* (Baton Rouge, La., 1989), *The Brazen Face of History: Studies in the Literary Consciousness in America* (Baton Rouge, La., 1980), and *The Dispossessed Garden: Pastoral and History in Southern Literature* (Athens, Ga., 1975) places the intellectual history of the antebellum South in the context of American and Western European development. Drew G. Faust, *A Sacred Circle: The Dilemma of the Intellectual in the Old South, 1840–1860* (Baltimore, 1977), took southern intellectuals and their endeavors seriously while showing that they did also. Michael O'Brien and David Moltke-Hansen, eds., *Intellectual Life in Antebellum Charleston* (Knoxville, Tenn., 1986), illustrates the variety and the complexity in one of the region's chief centers of intellectual activity. Louis D. Rubin, Jr., *The Edge of the Swamp: A Study in Literature and Society of the Old South* (Baton Rouge, La., 1989), emphasizes the impact of slavery on southern writers. On the leading literary figure also consult Mary Ann Wimsatt, *The Major Fiction of William Gilmore Simms: Cultural Traditions and Literary Form* (Baton Rouge, La., 1989). Three studies focus on the Virginia debate around 1830 over the nature and future of the state and the place of slavery in it: Dickson D. Bruce, Jr., *The Rhetoric of Conservatism: The Virginia Convention of 1829–30 and the Conservative Tradition in the South* (San Marino, Calif., 1982); Alison Goodyear Freehling, *Drift toward Dissolution: The Virginia Slavery Debate of 1831–1832* (Baton Rouge, La., 1982); John C. Robert, *The Road from Monticello: A Study of the Virginia Slavery Debate of 1832* (Durham, N.C., 1941). In *The Freedom-of-Thought Struggle in the Old South* (New York, 1964), Clement Eaton stressed the closing of the southern mind on the subject of slavery. Two other books by Eaton, *The Growth of Southern Civilization, 1790–1860* (New York, 1961) and *The Mind of the Old South* (Baton Rouge, La., 1967), provide general descriptions of a diversity of topics. Other meritorious works on various subjects include Robert J. Brugger, *Beverly Tucker: Heart over Head in the Old South* (Baltimore, 1978); Jesse T. Carpenter, *The South as a Conscious Minority, 1789–1861: A Study in Political Thought* (New York, 1930); James X. Corgan, ed., *The Geological Sciences in the Antebellum South* (University, Ala., 1982); Richard Beale Davis, *Intellectual Life in Jefferson's Virginia, 1790–1830* (Chapel Hill, N.C., 1964); Neal C. Gillispie, *The Collapse of Orthodoxy: The Intellectual Ordeal of George Frederick Holmes* (Charlottesville, Va., 1972); C. Hugh Holman, *The Roots of Southern Writing: Essays on the Literature of the American South* (Athens, Ga., 1972); Ronald L. Numbers and Todd L. Savitt, eds., *Science and Medicine in the Old South* (Baton Rouge, La., 1989); Michael O'Brien, *A Character of Hugh Legaré* (Knoxville, Tenn., 1985), and O'Brien, ed., *All Clever Men Who Make Their Way: Critical Discourse in the Old South* (Fayetteville, Ark., 1982); J. V. Ridgely, *Nineteenth-Century Southern Literature* (Lexington, Ky., 1980) and *John Pendleton Kennedy* (New York, 1966); Lester D. Stephens, *Joseph LeConte: Gentle Prophet of Evolution* (Baton Rouge, La., 1982); John D. Wade, *Augustus Baldwin Longstreet: A Study in the Development of Culture in the South* (New York, 1924); and Jon L. Wakelyn, *The Politics of a Literary Man: William Gilmore Simms* (Westport, Conn., 1973). Waldo W. Braden, ed., *Oratory in the Old South, 1828–1860* (Baton Rouge, La., 1970), provides an introduction to what many southerners considered an art.

On the proslavery argument specifically five books command attention: George M. Fredrickson, *The Black Image in the White Mind: The Debate on Afro-American Character and Destiny, 1817–1914* (New York, 1971); Eugene D. Genovese, *The World the Slaveholders Made: Two Essays in Interpretation* (New York, 1969), which has an important discussion of George Fitzhugh; Reginald Horsman, *Josiah Nott of Mobile: Southerner, Physician, and Racial Theorist* (Baton Rouge, La., 1987); William S. Jenkins, *Pro-Slavery Thought in the Old South* (Chapel Hill, N.C., 1935), the first and still the only general survey; and Larry E. Tise, *Proslavery: A History of the Defense of Slavery in America, 1701–1840* (Athens, Ga., 1987), a not entirely successful effort to redefine the conventional chronological framework and to place the proslavery stance at the center of the conservative tradition.

On religion four titles are essential: John B. Boles, *The Great Revival, 1787–1805* (Lexington, Ky., 1972); James O. Farmer, Jr., *The Metaphysical Confederacy: James Henley Thornwell and the Synthesis of Southern Values* (Macon, Ga., 1986); Anne C. Loveland, *Southern Evangelicals and the Social Order, 1820–1860* (Baton Rouge, La., 1980); and Donald G. Mathews, *Religion in the Old South* (Chicago, 1977). Additional items meriting attention are David Bailey, *Shadow on the Church: Southwestern Evangelical Religion and the Issue of Slavery, 1783–1860* (Ithaca, N.Y., 1985); John B. Boles, *Religion in Antebellum Kentucky* (Lexington, Ky., 1976); Samuel S. Hill, Jr., *The South and the North in American Religion* (Athens, Ga., 1980); E. Brooks Holifield, *The Gentlemen Theologians: American Theology in Southern Culture, 1795–1860* (Durham, N.C., 1978); John W. Kuykendall, *Southern Enterprise: The Work of National Evangelical Societies in the Antebellum South* (Westport, Conn., 1982); and Donald G. Mathews, *Slavery and Methodism: A Chapter in American Morality, 1780–1845* (Princeton, N.J., 1965). The two strongest denominational histories are David E. Harrell, Jr., *Quest for a Christian America: The Disciples of Christ and American Society to 1866* (Nashville, Tenn., 1966), and Ernest T. Thompson, *Presbyterians in the South, 1607–1861* (Richmond, Va., 1963). See also three books by Walter B. Posey: *The Development of Methodism in the Old Southwest, 1783–1824* (Tuscaloosa, Ala., 1933), *The Presbyterian Church in the Old Southwest, 1778–1838* (Richmond, Va., 1952), and *The Baptist Church in the Lower Mis-*

sissippi Valley, 1776–1845 (Lexington, Ky., 1957); and Leonard Dinnerstein and Mary D. Palsson, eds., *Jews in the South* (Baton Rouge, La., 1973).

The history of education, both precollegiate and collegiate, in the antebellum South has not yet received the attention it deserves. Eaton, *Growth of Southern Civilization*, probably has the best survey, though a thin one. As of now the story must be pieced together from various books on religion and intellectual life; many of the titles cited on pages 793–794 touch on education. For the precollege level there are really no substantive monographs. The best studies of institutions of higher learning are Thomas G. Dyer, *The University of Georgia: A Bicentennial History* (Athens, Ga., 1985), and Daniel W. Hollis, *South Carolina College* (Columbia, S.C., 1951). Of the older and dated treatments, Kemp P. Battle, *History of the University of North Carolina*, 2 vols. (Raleigh, N.C., 1907, 1912), and Philip A. Bruce, *History of the University of Virginia*, 5 vols. (New York, 1920–1922), stand out. E. Merton Coulter wrote a delightful account of student life at the University of Georgia in his *College Life in the Old South* (Athens, Ga., 1951). See also Nora C. Chaffin, *Trinity College, 1830–1892: The Beginnings of Duke University* (Durham, N.C., 1950), and Albea Godbold, *The Church College in the Old South* (Durham, N.C., 1944).

Numerous superb publications of primary materials contribute to an understanding of slavery, slave owners, and southerners who thought about slavery. The best and most helpful among them include John S. Bassett, ed., *The Southern Plantation Overseer as Revealed in His Letters* (Northampton, Mass., 1925); John Blassingame, ed., *Slave Testimony: Two Centuries of Letters, Speeches, Interviews, and Autobiographies* (Baton Rouge, La., 1977); Carol Bleser, ed., *Secret and Sacred: The Diaries of James Henry Hammond, a Southern Slaveholder* (New York, 1988); James O. Breeden, ed., *Advice among Masters: The Ideal in Slave Management in the Old South* (Westport, Conn., 1980); Helen T. Catterall, ed., *Judicial Cases Concerning American Slavery and the Negro*, 5 vols. (Washington, D.C., 1926–1937); Edwin A. Davis, ed., *Plantation Life in the Florida Parishes of Louisiana, 1836–1846, as Reflected in the Diary of Bennett H. Barrow* (New York, 1943); J. H. Easterby, ed., *The South Carolina Rice Plantation as Revealed in the Papers of Robert F. W. Allston* (Chicago, 1945); Drew G. Faust, ed., *The Ideology of Slavery: Proslavery Thought in the Antebellum South, 1830–1860* (Baton Rouge, La., 1981), the best modern compilation; William R. Hogan and Edwin A. Davis, eds., *William Johnson's Natchez: The Ante-Bellum Diary of a Free Negro* (Baton Rouge, La., 1951); Michael P. Johnson and James L. Roark, eds., *No Chariot Let Down: Charleston's Free People of Color on the Eve of the Civil War* (Chapel Hill, N.C., 1984); Frances Anne Kemble, *Journal of a Residence on a Georgian Plantation in 1838–1839*, ed. John A. Scott (Athens, Ga., 1984), an account by the English wife of a sea island planter; Michael Meyer, ed., *Frederick Douglass: The Narrative and Selected Writings* (New York, 1984), an excellent collection including the autobiography and other writings of the famous former slave who became an abolitionist; Robert M. Myers, ed., *The Children of Pride: A True Story of Georgia and the Civil War* (New Haven, Conn., 1972), the correspondence of a slave-owning family; Solomon Northup, *Twelve Years a Slave*, eds. Sue Eakin and Joseph Logsdon (Baton Rouge, La., 1968), a fascinating autobiography of a slave; Charles L. Perdue et al., eds., *Weevils in the Wheat: Interviews with Virginia Ex-Slaves* (Charlottesville, Va., 1976); Mary C. Simms Oliphant et al., eds., *The Letters of William Gilmore Simms*, 6 vols. (Columbia, S.C., 1952–1982); Frederick Law Olmsted, *The Cotton Kingdom: A Traveller's Observations on Cotton and Slavery in the American Slave States*, ed. Arthur M. Schlesinger, Sr. (New York, 1984), an excellent edition of the writings of the man who wrote the most thorough accounts of travel in the slave states; George P. Rawick, ed., *The American Slave: A Composite Autobiography*, 41 vols. (Westport, Conn., 1972–1979), the fullest documentary record of the slave experience based on interviews conducted in the

796 BIBLIOGRAPHICAL ESSAY

twentieth century with former slaves; Willie Lee Rose, ed., *A Documentary History of Slavery in North America* (New York, 1976); Robert S. Starobin, ed., *Blacks in Bondage: Letters of American Slaves* (New York, 1974), and Starobin, ed., *Denmark Vesey: The Slave Conspiracy of 1822* (Englewood Cliffs, N.J., 1970), a collection of documents; Henry I. Traigle, *The Southampton Slave Revolt of 1831: A Compilation of Source Material Including the Full Text of the "Confessions" of Nat Turner* (Amherst, Mass., 1971), also a collection of documents.

The ideology and social dynamics of the antebellum South remain lively topics of debate among historians. In several extremely influential works Eugene D. Genovese has depicted the antebellum South as a premodern culture dominated by slaveholding planters who had a strong antipathy to both capitalism and democracy. See three of his books already cited, *Political Economy; Roll, Jordan, Roll*; and *World the Slaveholders Made*. Cooper, *Politics of Slavery* and *Liberty and Slavery*, Thornton, *Politics and Power*, and Ford, *Origins of Southern Radicalism*, present a different view of the southern political world, though they certainly do not agree on all issues. Thornton and Ford also have superb discussions of the white social world, and both conclude that unity prevailed over disunity. James Oakes, *The Ruling Race: A History of American Slaveholders* (New York, 1982), places the planters fully in the capitalist world and disagrees fundamentally with Genovese on their world view. See also Randolph B. Campbell and Richard G. Lowe, *Wealth and Power in Antebellum Texas* (College Station, Tex., 1977); Bruce Collins, *White Society in the Antebellum South* (New York, 1985); Paul D. Escott, *Power and Privilege in North Carolina, 1850–1900* (Chapel Hill, N.C., 1985); Kenneth S. Greenberg, *Masters and Statesmen: The Political Culture of American Slavery* (Baltimore, 1985); John C. Inscoe, *Mountain Masters, Slavery, and the Sectional Crisis in Western North Carolina* (Knoxville, Tenn., 1989); and Raimondo Luraghi, *The Rise and Fall of the Plantation South* (New York, 1978), a Marxist interpretation considerably less powerful and subtle than Genovese's.

On the yeomen, an older study that should not be forgotten is Frank L. Owsley, *Plain Folk in the Old South* (Baton Rouge, La., 1949). Also see Everett Dick, *The Dixie Frontier: A Social History of the Southern Frontier from the First Transmontane Beginnings to the Civil War* (New York, 1948), and Grady McWhiney's controversial *Cracker Culture: Celtic Ways in the Old South* (Tuscaloosa, Ala., 1988), as well as Edward Magdol and Jon L. Wakelyn, eds., *The Southern Common People: Studies in Nineteenth-Century Social History* (Westport, Conn., 1980), a collection of informative articles. In his first-rate *Plain Folk and Gentry in a Slave Society: White Liberty and Black Slavery in Augusta's Hinterlands* (Middletown, Conn., 1985), J. William Harris found unity dominant. No student of the antebellum South should overlook two books by contemporary southerners: Hinton R. Helper, *The Impending Crisis of the South: How to Meet It*, ed. George M. Fredrickson (Cambridge, Mass., 1968), condemns the regime, while Daniel R. Hundley, *Social Relations in Our Southern States*, ed. William J. Cooper, Jr. (Baton Rouge, La., 1979), presents it in a positive fashion. Poesch's *Art of the Old South* contributes to an understanding of the architectural environment.

Important books that probe critical dimensions of southern society include W. J. Cash's unique and remarkable *Mind of the South* (New York, 1941); Fred Hobson's intriguing *Tell about the South: The Southern Rage to Explain* (Baton Rouge, La., 1983); John M. McCardell's suggestive *Idea of a Southern Nation: Southern Nationalists and Southern Nationalism, 1830–1860* (New York, 1979); William R. Taylor's imaginative *Cavalier and Yankee: The Old South and American National Character* (New York, 1961); and Bertram Wyatt-Brown's provocative *Southern Honor: Ethics and Behavior in the Old South* (New York, 1982).

Many other books contribute to an understanding of southern society. The most worthy of them include Dickson D. Bruce, Jr., *Violence and Culture in the Antebellum South* (Austin, Tex., 1979); John Hope Franklin, *A Southern Odyssey: Travelers in the Antebellum*

North (Baton Rouge, La., 1976), a study of southern travelers reacting to the North, and *The Militant South, 1800–1861* (Cambridge, Mass., 1956); Guion G. Johnson, *Antebellum North Carolina: A Social History* (Chapel Hill, N.C., 1937); Rollin G. Osterweis, *Romanticism and Nationalism in the Old South* (New Haven, Conn., 1949); Rosser H. Taylor, *Antebellum South Carolina: A Social and Cultural History* (Chapel Hill, N.C., 1942); and Jack K. Williams, *Dueling in the Old South: Vignettes of Social History* (College Station, Tex., 1980).

Women have not until recently begun to receive the scholarly attention they deserve. The starting point for consideration of women is Anne F. Scott, *The Southern Lady: From Pedestal to Politics, 1830–1930* (Chicago, 1970), the first modern treatment. Since then a number of historians have mined the substantial archival materials on women in the antebellum South. Catherine Clinton, *The Plantation Mistress: Woman's World in the Old South* (New York, 1982), concentrates entirely on the mistresses of large plantations along the seaboard. A first-rate local study that points the way to further fruitful work is Suzanne Lebsock, *The Free Women of Petersburg: Status and Culture in a Southern Town, 1784–1860* (New York, 1984). Wyatt-Brown's *Southern Honor* discusses insightfully the place and role of women in antebellum southern society. Elizabeth Fox-Genovese, *Within the Plantation Household: Black and White Women of the Old South* (Chapel Hill, N.C., 1988), with a strong theoretical dimension, and George C. Rable, *Civil Wars: Women in the Crisis of Southern Nationalism* (Urbana, Ill., 1989), provide superb in-depth coverage. Five other books that emphasize the family are Orville Vernon Burton, *In My Father's House Are Many Mansions: Family and Community in Edgefield, South Carolina* (Chapel Hill, N.C., 1985); Jane T. Censer, *North Carolina Planters and Their Children, 1800–1860* (Baton Rouge, La., 1984); Robert C. Kenser, *Kinship and Neighborhood in a Southern Community: Orange County, North Carolina, 1849–1881* (Knoxville, Tenn., 1987); Jan Lewis, *The Pursuit of Happiness: Family and Values in Jefferson's Virginia* (New York, 1983); and Steven M. Stowe, *Intimacy and Power in the Old South: Ritual in the Lives of the Planters* (Baltimore, 1987).

On the southern economy Gavin Wright's *Political Economy of the Cotton South* is helpful. Although much work remains to be done, several important books investigate the industrial sector of that economy and analyze public policy. See Fred Bateman and Thomas Weiss, *A Deplorable Scarcity: The Failure of Industrialization in the Slave Economy* (Chapel Hill, N.C., 1981), and Laurence Shore, *Southern Capitalists: The Ideological Leadership of an Elite, 1832–1885* (Chapel Hill, N.C., 1986). In his *Banking in the American South from the Age of Jackson to Reconstruction* (Baton Rouge, La., 1987), Larry Schweikart argues that southern banks assisted economic development and growth. Worthy state studies include George D. Green, *Finance and Economic Development in the Old South: Louisiana Banking, 1804–1861* (Stanford, Calif., 1972); Milton S. Heath, *Constructive Liberalism: The Role of the State in Economic Development in Georgia to 1860* (Cambridge, Mass., 1954); Smith, *Economic Readjustment of an Old Cotton State*; and Peter Wallenstein, *From Slave South to New South: Public Policy in Nineteenth-Century Georgia* (Chapel Hill, N.C., 1987). For individual industries and industrialists consult James P. Baughman, *Charles Morgan and the Development of Southern Transportation* (Nashville, Tenn., 1968); Charles B. Dew, *Ironmaker to the Confederacy: Joseph R. Anderson and the Tredegar Iron Works* (New Haven, Conn., 1966); Ernest M. Lander, Jr., *The Textile Industry in Antebellum South Carolina* (Baton Rouge, La., 1969); Randall M. Miller, *The Cotton Mill Movement in Antebellum Alabama* (New York, 1978); Broadus Mitchell, *William Gregg: Factory Master of the Old South* (Chapel Hill, N.C., 1928); John H. Moore, *Andrew Brown and Cypress Lumbering in the Old Southwest* (Baton Rouge, La., 1967); and Merl E. Reed, *New Orleans and the Railroads: The Struggle for Commercial Empire* (Baton Rouge, La., 1966).

Four useful titles on cities are Blaine A. Brownell and David R. Goldfield, eds., *The City in Southern History: The Growth of Urban Civilization in the South* (Port Washington,

N.Y., 1977), a collection of helpful articles; David R. Goldfield, *Urban Growth in the Age of Sectionalism: Virginia, 1847–1861* (Baton Rouge, La., 1977) and *Cotton Fields and Skyscrapers: Southern City and Region, 1607–1980*, rev. ed. (Baltimore, 1989); and Lawrence H. Larsen, *The Rise of the Urban South* (Lexington, Ky., 1985). For specific locations consult Harriet E. Amos, *Cotton City: Urban Development in Antebellum Mobile* (University, Ala., 1985); D. Clayton James, *Antebellum Natchez* (Baton Rouge, La., 1968); James M. Russell, *Atlanta, 1847–1890: City Building in the Old South and the New* (Baton Rouge, La., 1988); and Kenneth W. Wheeler, *To Wear A City's Crown: The Beginnings of Urban Growth in Texas, 1836–1865* (Cambridge, Mass., 1966).

The sectional conflict between 1845 and 1861 has stimulated a number of major studies in which southern developments occupy a prominent place. Consult Allan Nevins's magnificent *Ordeal of the Union*, 2 vols. (New York, 1947) and *The Emergence of Lincoln*, 2 vols. (New York, 1950); Roy F. Nichols's impressive *Disruption of American Democracy* (New York, 1948); and David M. Potter's superlative *Impending Crisis, 1848–1861*, completed by Don E. Fehrenbacker (New York, 1976). Michael F. Holt takes a bold and imaginative look at the final antebellum decade in *The Political Crisis of the 1850s* (New York, 1978). A straightforward, now dated account focusing on southern opinion, especially newspaper opinion, is Avery O. Craven, *The Growth of Southern Nationalism, 1848–1861* (Baton Rouge, La., 1953). Recent brief surveys are Roger L. Ransom, *Conflict and Compromise: The Political Economy of Slavery, Emancipation, and the Civil War* (New York, 1989), with emphasis on economics broadly viewed, and Richard W. Sewell, *A House Divided: Sectionalism and Civil War, 1848–1865* (Baltimore, 1988).

Best on the Mexican War is K. Jack Bauer, *The Mexican War, 1846–1848* (New York, 1974). Robert W. Johannsen, *To the Halls of Montezuma: The Mexican War in the American Imagination* (New York, 1985) analyzes the American, including southern, reaction to Mexico. In a tidy little book, *Reluctant Imperialists: Calhoun, the South Carolinians, and the Mexican War* (Baton Rouge, La., 1980), Ernest M. Lander, Jr., discovered a dearth of enthusiasm for war in the state supposedly the most hot-blooded.

The great question of slavery and the territories has been a central theme. Cooper, *Politics of Slavery*, provides a thorough treatment that relates ideological foundations to political manifestations. In addition to the books already cited on the 1845–1861 period, see also Genovese, *Political Economy of Slavery*; Fehrenbacker, *The South and Three Crises*; Holman Hamilton, *The Crisis and Compromise of 1850* (Lexington, Ky., 1964); Frederick Merk, *Slavery and the Annexation of Texas* (New York, 1972); Chaplain Morrison, *Democratic Politics and Sectionalism: The Wilmot Proviso Controversy* (Chapel Hill, N.C., 1967); Oakes, *Ruling Race*; Gerald W. Wolff, *The Kansas-Nebraska Bill: Party, Section, and the Coming of the Civil War* (New York, 1977). Fehrenbacker has a superb discussion of the legal and constitutional issues in *The Dred Scott Case: Its Significance in American Law and Politics* (New York, 1978). On the most important northern Democrat of the 1850s, a man most southerners regarded as a turncoat by 1860, see Robert W. Johannsen's excellent *Stephen A. Douglas* (New York, 1973). On key events during the crisis of 1850 consult John Barnwell, *Love of Order: South Carolina's First Secession Crisis* (Chapel Hill, N.C., 1982), and Thelma N. Jennings, *The Nashville Convention: Southern Movement for Unity, 1848–1851* (Memphis, Tenn., 1980).

On events in individual states consult the state studies cited above on pages 789–790. W. Darrel Overdyke, *The Know-Nothing Party in the South* (Baton Rouge, La., 1950), though dated, is the only general study of that phenomenon. Local studies are not plentiful, but see Jean H. Baker, *Ambivalent Americans: The Know-Nothing Party in Maryland* (Baltimore, 1975), and Leon C. Soulé, *The Know-Nothing Party in New Orleans* (Baton Rouge, La., 1961).

Several studies emphasize the minority of southerners who were determined to expand the South's boundaries in a southerly direction and those few who agitated for a renewal of the international slave trade: Charles A. Brown, *Agents of Manifest Destiny: The Lives and Times of the Filibusters* (Chapel Hill, N.C., 1980); Robert E. May, *John A. Quitman: Old South Crusader* (Baton Rouge, La., 1985) and *The Southern Dream of a Caribbean Empire, 1854–1861* (Baton Rouge, La., 1973); and Ronald T. Takaki, *A Pro-Slavery Crusade: The Agitation to Reopen the African Slave Trade* (New York, 1971).

Secession remains a most vexing question. Although scholars have been scrutinizing secession for many years, no general treatment has yet replaced Dwight L. Dumond's still useful *The Secession Movement, 1860–1861* (New York, 1931), but see William L. Barney, *The Road to Secession: A New Perspective on the Old South* (New York, 1972). Ralph A. Wooster, *The Secession Conventions of the South* (Princeton, N.J., 1962), charts convention membership. The two most recent overviews present conflicting interpretations: Cooper, *Liberty and Slavery*, and Holt, *The Political Crisis*. An important recent book on the upper South is Daniel W. Crofts, *Reluctant Confederates: Upper South Unionists in the Secession Crisis* (Chapel Hill, N.C., 1989). The best of the state studies are Thornton, *Politics and Power*, which also has the fullest discussion of the fire-eaters, and Ford, *Origins of Southern Radicalism*. On the fire-eaters also consult Robert May, *John A. Quitman*, and Laura White, *Robert Barnwell Rhett: Father of Secession* (New York, 1931). Other worthy monographs are Jean H. Baker, *The Politics of Continuity: Maryland Political Parties from 1858 to 1870* (Baltimore, 1973); William L. Barney, *The Secessionist Impulse: Alabama and Mississippi in 1860* (Princeton, N.J., 1974); Walter L. Buenger, *Secession and the Union in Texas* (Austin, Tex., 1984); Steven Channing, *Crisis of Fear: Secession in South Carolina* (New York, 1970); William J. Evitts, *A Matter of Allegiances: Maryland, 1850–1861* (Baltimore, 1974); Michael P. Johnson, *Toward a Patriarchal Republic: The Secession of Georgia* (Baton Rouge, La., 1977); Marc Kruman, *Parties and Politics in North Carolina*; Harold S. Schultz, *Nationalism and Sectionalism in South Carolina, 1852–1860: A Study of the Movement for Southern Independence* (Durham, N.C., 1950); Joseph C. Sitterson, *The Secession Movement in North Carolina* (Chapel Hill, N.C., 1939); and James M. Woods, *Rebellion and Realignment: Arkansas's Road to Secession* (Fayetteville, Ark., 1987).

For understanding the party that most of the white South perceived as the great enemy, these volumes are essential: Eric Foner, *Free Soil, Free Labor, Free Men: The Ideology of the Republican Party before the Civil War* (New York, 1970), on ideology; William E. Gienapp, *The Origins of the Republican Party, 1852–1856* (New York, 1987), on party formation; David M. Potter, *Lincoln and His Party in the Secession Crisis* (New Haven, Conn., 1962); and Kenneth M. Stampp, *And the War Came: The North and Secession Crisis, 1860–1861* (Baton Rouge, La., 1950) on the secession crisis.

Books on the Civil War and the Confederacy are legion. Allan Nevin's *War for the Union*, 4 vols. (New York, 1959–1971), is history in the grand manner. For a superb but much briefer account see James M. McPherson, *Battle Cry of Freedom: The Civil War Era* (New York, 1988), which concentrates on the war years. On the Confederacy two general studies provide good starting points: E. Merton Coulter's detailed *Confederate States of America, 1861–1865* (Baton Rouge, La., 1950) and Emory M. Thomas's more historiographically current and interpretive *Confederate Nation, 1861–1865* (New York, 1979). Shelby Foote's magnificent *The Civil War: A Narrative*, 3 vols. (New York, 1958–1974), is a beautifully written narrative with a broad sweep. Drew Gilpin Faust, *The Creation of Confederate Nationalism: Ideology and Identity in the Civil War South* (Baton Rouge, La., 1988), is an intelligent inquiry into a difficult subject.

The political history of the Confederacy has generally been poorly served by historians. Exceptions are Thomas B. Alexander and Richard E. Beringer's meticulous *Anat-*

omy of the Confederate Congress: A Study of the Influence of Member Characteristics on Legisla-tive Voting Behavior, 1861–1865 (Nashville, Tenn., 1972); Paul D. Escott's suggestive *After Secession: Jefferson Davis and the Failure of Confederate Nationalism* (Baton Rouge, La., 1978); and Thomas E. Schott's superb *Alexander H. Stephens of Georgia: A Biography* (Baton Rouge, La., 1988). Other books that merit consultation are Albert B. Moore, *Conscription and Conflict in the Confederacy* (New York, 1924); Frank L. Owsley, *State Rights in the Con-federacy* (Chicago, 1925); Rembert W. Patrick, *Jefferson Davis and His Cabinet* (Baton Rouge, La., 1944); May S. Ringold, *The Role of the State Legislatures in the Confederacy* (Athens, Ga., 1966); William M. Robinson, Jr., *Justice in Grey: A History of the Judicial System of the Con-federate States of America* (Cambridge, Mass., 1941); and Richard C. Todd, *Confederate Fi-nance* (Athens, Ga., 1954).

On Confederate diplomacy the standard work is Frank L. Owsley, *King Cotton Di-plomacy: Foreign Relations of the Confederate States of America* (Chicago, 1959); see also D. P. Crook, *Diplomacy during the American Civil War* (New York, 1975). John C. Schwab's *Con-federate States of America, 1861–1865: A Financial and Industrial History of the South during the Civil War* (New York, 1901) has not been replaced.

On the civilian front Charles W. Ramsdell, *Behind the Lines in the Southern Confederacy* (Baton Rouge, La., 1944), is still valuable. Other worthy titles are James W. Silver, *Con-federate Morale and Church Propaganda* (Tuscaloosa, Ala., 1957); Gardiner H. Shattuck, Jr., *A Shield and Hiding Place: The Religious Life of Civil War Armies* (Macon, Ga., 1987); and Bell I. Wiley, *The Road to Appomattox* (New York, 1968). For the story of women, Rable, *Civil Wars*, is best; also see Mary Elizabeth Massey, *Bonnet Brigades* (New York, 1966), and Bell I. Wiley, *Confederate Women* (Westport, Conn., 1975). Books on individual states usually address economic, political, and social as well as military topics. They include John G. Barrett, *The Civil War in North Carolina* (Chapel Hill, N.C., 1963); John K. Bettersworth, *Confederate Mississippi: The People and Policies of a Cotton State in Wartime* (Baton Rouge, La., 1943); T. Conn Bryan, *Confederate Georgia* (Athens, Ga., 1953); Charles E. Cauthen, *South Carolina Goes to War, 1861–1865* (Chapel Hill, N.C., 1950); John E. Johns, *Florida during the Civil War* (Gainesville, Fla., 1963); and John D. Winters, *The Civil War in Lou-isiana* (Baton Rouge, La., 1963).

Several interesting books discuss the questions the war raised for masters and slaves. Bell I. Wiley, *Southern Negroes, 1861–1865* (New Haven, Conn., 1938), was for many years the standard account and still has great value. Robert F. Durden, *The Gray and the Black: The Confederate Debate on Emancipation* (Baton Rouge, La., 1972), focuses on the emancipation issue. Leon F. Litwack, *Been in the Storm So Long: The Aftermath of Sla-very* (New York, 1979), tells the story of the slaves' response to freedom, while James L. Roark, *Masters without Slaves: Southern Planters in the Civil War and Reconstruction* (New York, 1977), delineates the slave owners' response to the reaction of their slaves. For the story in three locations see Clarence L. Mohr, *On the Threshold of Freedom: Masters and Slaves in Civil War Georgia* (Athens, Ga., 1986); Janet S. Hermann, *The Pursuit of a Dream* (New York, 1981); and Willie Lee Rose's masterful *Rehearsal for Reconstruction: The Port Royal Experiment* (Indianapolis, 1964).

On the military history of the Confederacy the books have no end. Here we will point only to those that deal with major topics. Douglas Southall Freeman's *R. E. Lee: A Biography*, 4 vols. (New York, 1934–1935), remains unmatched on the greatest warrior of the Confederacy. Also on the war in the east, Freeman's superlative history of the Army of Northern Virginia, *Lee's Lieutenants: A Study in Command*, 3 vols. (New York, 1942–1944), is the best overall. On the western war Thomas L. Connelly has two excellent vol-umes on the Army of Tennessee: *Army of the Heartland: The Army of Tennessee, 1861–1862* (Baton Rouge, La., 1967) and *Autumn of Glory: The Army of Tennessee, 1862–1865* (Baton

Rouge, La., 1971). For the often forgotten Trans-Mississippi theater consult Albert Castel, *General Sterling Price and the Civil War in the West* (Baton Rouge, La., 1968), and Robert L. Kerby, *Kirby-Smith's Confederacy: The Trans-Mississippi South, 1863–1865* (New York, 1972). Richard M. McMurry, *Two Great Rebel Armies: An Essay in Confederate Military History* (Chapel Hill, N.C., 1989), compares the two most significant Confederate field armies. On Confederate command and strategy see Thomas L. Connelly and Archer Jones, *The Politics of Command: Factions and Ideas in Confederate Strategy* (Baton Rouge, La., 1973); Archer Jones, *Confederate Strategy from Shiloh to Vicksburg* (Baton Rouge, La., 1961); Frank Vandiver, *Rebel Brass: The Confederate Command System* (Baton Rouge, La., 1956). Bell I. Wiley's classic *Life of Johnny Reb: The Common Soldier of the Confederacy* (Indianapolis, 1943) tells the story of the private soldier. For the revolution in weaponry and the reality of combat see Gerald F. Linderman, *Embattled Courage: The Experience of Combat in the American Civil War* (New York, 1987); Grady McWhiney and Perry D. Jamieson, *Attack and Die: Civil War Military Tactics and the Southern Heritage* (University, Ala., 1982); and Reid Mitchell, *Civil War Soldiers* (New York, 1988). Virgil C. Jones has written the fullest account of the naval war, *The Civil War at Sea*, 3 vols. (New York, 1960–1962). On the epochal *Monitor-Virginia* battle see William C. Davis, *Duel between the First Ironclads* (New York, 1975). The most recent attempt to explain the defeat of the Confederacy, Richard E. Beringer et al., *Why the South Lost the Civil War* (Athens, Ga., 1986), is not convincing.

Published primary materials are extraordinarily rich for the late antebellum and Confederate years. The chief works include John Q. Anderson, ed., *Brokenburn: The Journal of Kate Stone, 1861–1868* (Baton Rouge, La., 1972); Ira Berlin et al., eds., *Freedom: A Documentary History of Emancipation, 1861–1867* ...(New York, 1982); *Congressional Globe*, for congressional debates; Lynda L. Crist et al., eds., *The Papers of Jefferson Davis*, 6 vols. to date (Baton Rouge, La., 1971–); E. Merton Coulter, *Travels in the Confederate States: A Bibliography* (Norman, Okla., 1948), the guide to travel accounts; Clifford Dowdey, ed., *The Wartime Papers of R. E. Lee* (Boston, 1961); Dwight L. Dumond, ed., *Southern Editorials on Secession* (New York, 1931); Le Roy P. Graf et al., *The Papers of Andrew Johnson*, 7 vols. to date (Knoxville, Tenn., 1967–); Robert U. Johnson and Clarence C. Buel, eds., *Battles and Leaders of the Civil War*, 4 vols. (New York, 1888), the finest compilation of accounts by participants; J. B. Jones, *A Rebel War Clerk's Diary at the Confederate States Capital*, 2 vols. (Philadelphia, 1866); *Journal of the Congress of the Confederate States of America, 1861–1865*, 7 vols. (Washington, D.C., 1904–1905), contains only a record of legislative activities, no speeches; Albert D. Kirwan, ed., *The Confederacy* (Cleveland, O., 1959), a convenient collection of documents on diverse subjects; John F. Marszalek, ed., *The Diary of Miss Emma Holmes, 1861–1866* (Baton Rouge, La., 1979); Robert Myers, ed., *The Children of Pride: Official Records of the Union and Confederate Navies in the War of the Rebellion*, 30 vols. (Washington, D.C., 1894–1922), the basic published documentary record of the naval war; Oliphant et al., eds., *Letters of Simms*; Ulrich B. Phillips, ed., *Correspondence of Robert Toombs, Alexander Stephens, and Howell Cobb* (Washington, D.C., 1913); James D. Richardson, ed., *A Compilation of the Messages and Papers of the Confederacy, Including the Diplomatic Correspondence, 1861–1865*, 2 vols. (Nashville, Tenn., 1906); Dunbar Rowland, ed., *Jefferson Davis, Constitutionalist: His Letters, Papers, and Speeches*, 10 vols. (Jackson, Miss., 1923); William K. Scarborough, ed., *The Diary of Edmund Ruffin*, 3 vols. (Baton Rouge, La., 1972–1989); *War of the Rebellion: A Compilation of the Official Records of the Union and Confederate Armies*, 128 vols. (Washington, D.C., 1880–1901), the basic published documentary record of the land war; C. Vann Woodward, ed., *Mary Chesnut's Civil War* (New Haven, Conn., 1981), and Woodward and Elisabeth Muhlenfeld, eds., *The Private Mary Chesnut: The Unpublished Civil War Diaries* (New York, 1984).

So many books have been written about the South since 1865 that those discussed here must necessarily be only a selection. Three volumes of the ten-volume *History of the South* (Baton Rouge, 1947–), edited by Wendell Holmes Stephenson and E. Merton Coulter, are extremely useful to any serious student of the American South since 1865. E. Merton Coulter, *The South during Reconstruction, 1865–1877* (1951), contains a wealth of information, but Coulter was too sympathetic toward southern whites and too hostile toward Republicans and what they were attempting to do. His treatment of blacks reflects the racial assumptions common among most whites in the South (and a great many in the North) in his day. C. Vann Woodward's *Origins of the New South, 1877–1913* (1951), a landmark in the interpretation of southern history, represented a major shift in tone and interpretation. Spurning the racism and sectionalism that mars Coulter's book, Woodward concludes that southern political and economic leaders after 1865 did more than the Old South, the Civil War, or Reconstruction to create the New South. George B. Tindall's *Emergence of the New South, 1913–1945* (1967) is even more comprehensive than either the Coulter or the Woodward volume. It is a massive but clear synthesis of critical decades in the twentieth-century South. All three volumes contain very useful essays on sources. Charles P. Roland's *Improbable Era: The South since World War II* (Lexington, Ky., 1972) and David R. Goldfield's *Promised Land: The South since 1945* (Arlington Heights, Ill., 1987) are good syntheses of the South since World War II.

Of symposia on the South there seems to be no end. Of particular merit are William T. Couch, ed., *Culture in the South* (Chapel Hill, N.C., 1935), and John C. McKinney and Edgar T. Thompson, eds., *The South in Continuity and Change* (Durham, N.C., 1965). Several sources provide lists of recently published articles and books and recently completed dissertations. See *Writings in American History*, a publication of the American Historical Association; *America: History and Life* and *Southern Exposure*. The *Journal of Southern History* and the *Journal of American History* periodically publish lists of recent publications and dissertations. Thomas D. Clark, ed., *Travels in the New South* (Norman, Okla., 1962), is very useful for finding firsthand accounts of the South since 1865. Three important sources contain materials from southern blacks during Reconstruction (despite their titles): George Rawick, ed., *The American Slave*; Ira Berlin et al., eds., *Freedom: A Documentary History of Emancipation*; and B. A. Botkin, ed., *Lay My Burden Down: A Folk History of Slavery* (Athens, Ga., 1989).

Historical Statistics and Donald Dodd and Wynette Dodd, eds., *Historical Statistics of the South* are invaluable. Updated statistics are available in *Statistical Abstract of the United States*, an annual publication of the U.S. Department of Commerce. Other federal government publications, including the *Congressional Globe* and the *Congressional Record*, as well as records of congressional hearings, are extremely useful.

Reconstruction has proved to be one of the most difficult of terrains for historians to traverse. At one time most historians accepted the interpretation of William Dunning, who held that the white South knew it had been defeated, was willing to deal fairly with the former slaves, and wanted to rejoin the Union. But Radical Republicans spurned reconciliation, imposed Republican governments on the southern states, and enforced black suffrage with bayonets. Motivated by unreasoning hate, partisanship, and greed, the Republicans created "Black Republican" governments that were singularly corrupt and peopled by "unscrupulous 'carpetbaggers' from the North, unprincipled southern white 'scalawags,' and ignorant freedmen." After a prolonged period of corruption and misrule, southern whites "redeemed" the South by overthrowing the Republican governments and restoring "home rule," or government by themselves. Good government,

Dunning assumed, could not include blacks, who supposedly lacked the capacity to govern or to participate in governing.

The clearest, most concise refutation of Dunning is Kenneth M. Stampp's *Era of Reconstruction, 1865–1877* (New York, 1965). Most recent general histories of the period reflect Stampp's influence. James M. McPherson's *Ordeal by Fire: The Civil War and Reconstruction* (New York, 1982) contains a brief but carefully balanced retelling of the Reconstruction story. Eric Foner's *Reconstruction: America's Unfinished Revolution, 1863–1877* (New York, 1988), part of the New American Nation series, is a comprehensive account based on copious research.

Particularly useful for overviews of the period between the collapse of the Confederacy and the beginning of Reconstruction are Dan T. Carter, *When the War Was Over: The Failure of Self-Reconstruction in the South, 1865–1867* (Baton Rouge, La., 1985), and Michael Perman, *Reunion without Compromise: The South and Reconstruction, 1865–1868* (Cambridge, Eng., 1973). In *The Road to Redemption: Southern Politics, 1869–1879* (Chapel Hill, N.C., 1984), Perman traces political developments across the South from the start of Reconstruction to "redemption" and its impact on the configuration of politics in the New South.

A number of Reconstruction studies focus on individual states or regions, and some of them cover more than Reconstruction. These works include Stephen V. Ash, *Middle Tennessee Society Transformed, 1860–1870* (Baton Rouge, La., 1987); Horace Mann Bond, *Negro Education in Alabama: A Study in Cotton and Steel* (Washington, D.C., 1939); Alan Conway, *The Reconstruction of Georgia* (Minneapolis, 1966); W. McKee Evans, *Ballots and Fence Rails: Reconstruction on the Lower Cape Fear* (Chapel Hill, N.C., 1967); Barbara Fields, *Slavery and Freedom on the Middle Ground;* William C. Harris, *Presidential Reconstruction in Mississippi* (Baton Rouge, La., 1967) and *The Day of the Carpetbagger: Republican Reconstruction in Mississippi* (Baton Rouge, La., 1979); Jack P. Maddex, Jr., *The Virginia Conservatives* (Chapel Hill, N.C., 1970); Carl H. Moneyhon, *Republicanism in Reconstruction Texas* (Austin, Tex., 1980); William E. Parrish, *Missouri under Radical Rule, 1865–1870* (Columbia, Mo., 1965), Jerrell H. Shofner, *Nor Is It Over Yet: Florida in the Era of Reconstruction, 1863–1877* (Gainesville, Fla., 1974); Roger W. Shugg, *Origins of Class Struggle in Louisiana* (Baton Rouge, La., 1959); Joe G. Taylor, *Louisiana Reconstructed, 1863–1877* (Baton Rouge, La., 1974); George H. Thompson, *Arkansas and Reconstruction* (Port Washington, N.Y., 1976); and Ted Tunnell, *Crucible of Reconstruction: War, Radicalism, and Race in Louisiana, 1862–1877* (Baton Rouge, La., 1984).

Several topical studies about Reconstruction are important and useful: Martin Abbott, *The Freedmen's Bureau in South Carolina, 1865–1872* (Chapel Hill, N.C., 1967); George R. Bentley, *A History of the Freedmen's Bureau* (Philadelphia, 1955); Carol R. Bleser, *The Promised Land: The History of the South Carolina Land Commission, 1869–1890* (Columbia, S.C., 1969); Richard N. Current, *Those Terrible Carpetbaggers: A Reinterpretation* (New York, 1988); Edmund L. Drago, *Black Politicians and Reconstruction in Georgia* (Baton Rouge, La., 1982); Thomas Holt, *Black over White: Negro Political Leadership in South Carolina during Reconstruction* (Urbana, Ill., 1977); Peyton McCrary, *Abraham Lincoln and Race: The Louisiana Experiment* (Princeton, N.J., 1978); George R. Rable, *But There Was No Peace: The Role of Violence in the Politics of Reconstruction* (Athens, Ga., 1984); James E. Sefton, *The United States Army and Reconstruction, 1865–1877* (Baton Rouge, La., 1967); Mark W. Summers, *Railroads, Reconstruction, and the Gospel of Prosperity: Aid under the Radical Republicans, 1865–1877* (Princeton, N.J., 1984); Allen W. Trelease, *White Terror: The Ku Klux Klan Conspiracy and Southern Reconstruction* (New York, 1974); Peter Wallenstein, *From Slave*

South to New South; and Sarah W. Wiggins, *The Scalawag in Alabama Politics, 1865–1881* (University, Ala., 1977).

After the Civil War, southerners had to rebuild their economy and develop a new system of race relations and a labor system without slavery. The historians who have studied this difficult, highly complex process have produced a rich literature. Willie Lee Rose's landmark study *Rehearsal for Reconstruction* is still valuable. James Roark, *Masters without Slaves* discusses the adjustment of slave masters to the loss of their slaves and the rapid decline of their economic and social status. Works on related topics include Louis Gerteis's *From Contraband to Freedman: Federal Policy toward Southern Blacks, 1861–1865* (Westport, Conn., 1973); C. Peter Ripley, *Slaves and Freedmen in Civil War Louisiana* (Baton Rouge, La., 1976); and Theodore Bratner Wilson, *The Black Codes of the South* (University, Ala., 1966).

A number of books stress the adjustment of former slaves to emancipation and help us to see that the South was a mutual creation of blacks and whites: Orville Burton, *In My Father's House Are Many Mansions;* Ronald L. F. Davis, *Good and Faithful Labor: From Slavery to Sharecropping in the Natchez District, 1860–1890* (Westport, Conn., 1982); Janet Hermann, *The Pursuit of a Dream;* Peter Kolchin, *First Freedom: The Responses of Alabama's Blacks to Emancipation and Reconstruction* (Westport, Conn., 1972); Leon Litwack, *Been in the Storm So Long;* Lawrence Powell, *New Masters: Northern Planters during the Civil War and Reconstruction* (New Haven, Conn., 1980); Michael Wayne, *The Reshaping of Plantation Society: The Natchez District, 1860–1880* (Baton Rouge, La., 1983); and Joel Williamson, *After Slavery: The Negro in South Carolina during Reconstruction, 1861–1877* (New York, 1965). Also see John Boles, *Black Southerners,* for a good synthesis of recent scholarship.

Race relations in the post–Civil War South have long attracted the attention of historians. No one doubts that Jim Crow was firmly entrenched by around 1900, but historians disagree as to why and when Jim Crow was imposed. A good way to follow this discussion is C. Vann Woodward's *Strange Career of Jim Crow,* 4th rev. ed. (New York, 1974). Major contributions to an understanding of Jim Crow include John Cell, *The Highest Stage of White Supremacy: The Origins of Segregation in South Africa and the American South* (New York, 1982); George Frederickson, *The Black Image in the White Mind and White Supremacy: A Comparative Study in American and South African History* (New York, 1981); J. Morgan Kousser, *The Shaping of Southern Politics: Suffrage Restrictions and the Establishment of the One-Party South, 1880–1910* (New Haven, Conn., 1974); and Joel Williamson, *The Crucible of Race: Black-White Relations in the American South since Emancipation* (New York, 1984). John Hope Franklin, *From Slavery to Freedom: A History of Negro Americans,* 6th ed. (New York, 1988); August Meier and Elliott M. Rudwick, *From Plantation to Ghetto: An Interpretive History of American Negroes* (New York, 1966); and Jacquelyn Jones, *Labor of Love, Labor of Sorrow* should also be consulted. So should Eric Anderson, *Race and Politics in North Carolina, 1872–1901* (Baton Rouge, La., 1981); Joseph H. Cartwright, *The Triumph of Jim Crow: Tennessee Race Relations in the 1880s* (Knoxville, Tenn., 1976); H. Leon Prather, *We Have Taken a City: The Wilmington Massacre and Coup of 1898* (Rutherford, N.J., 1984); George B. Tindall, *South Carolina Negroes, 1877–1900* (Columbia, S.C., 1952); Vernon Lane Wharton, *The Negro in Mississippi, 1865–1890* (Chapel Hill, N.C., 1947); and Charels E. Wynes, *Race Relations in Virginia, 1870–1902* (Charlottesville, Va., 1961), as well as the fine two-volume biography of Booker T. Washington by Louis R. Harlan, *Booker T. Washington: The Making of a Black Leader* (New York, 1972) and *Booker T. Washington: The Wizard of Tuskegee* (New York, 1983).

The postbellum systems of labor relations and race relations were shaped by the economic and political alternatives available. The general histories of the South cited above are very helpful for understanding the economy, as are general histories of the United States and of the American economy. Two essays are particularly helpful: William N. Parker, "The South in the National Economy, 1865–1970," *Southern Economic Journal* 46 (1983): 7–27; and Harold D. Woodman, "Sequel to Slavery: The New History Views the Postbellum South," *Journal of Southern History* 43 (1977): 523–554.

Gavin Wright's *Political Economy of the Cotton South* and *Old South, New South: Revolutions in the Southern Economy since the Civil War* (New York, 1986) are essential, as are Gilbert C. Fite, *Cotton Fields No More: Southern Agriculture, 1865–1980* (Lexington, Ky., 1984), and Harold D. Woodman, *King Cotton and His Retainers*. Related important books include Robert L. Brandfon, *Cotton Kingdom of the New South: A History of the Yazoo Mississippi Delta from Reconstruction to the Twentieth Century* (Cambridge, Mass., 1967); Thomas D. Clark, *Pills, Petticoats, and Plows: The Southern Country Store* (New York, 1944); Stephen DeCanio, *Agriculture in the Postbellum South* (Cambridge, Mass., 1974); Robert Higgs, *Competition and Coercion: Blacks in the American Economy, 1865–1914* (Chicago, 1980); Jay R. Mandle, *The Roots of Black Poverty: The Southern Plantation Economy after the Civil War* (Durham, N.C., 1975); Daniel A. Novak, *The Wheel of Servitude: Black Forced Labor after Slavery* (Lexington, Ky., 1978); and Roger Ransom and Richard Sutch, *One Kind of Freedom: The Economic Consequences of Emancipation* (Cambridge, Eng., 1977).

Historians have debated whether the New South was very different from the Old South and whether the planter elite maintained political and economic power after the Civil War. Woodward contended in *Origins of the New South* that the Redeemers were "new men" who rejected agrarianism in favor of economic diversification. That view has been challenged or modified by a number of historians. James Tice Moore, "Redeemers Reconsidered: Change and Continuity in the Democratic South, 1870–1900," *Journal of Southern History* 44 (1978): 357–378, and Numan V. Bartley, "Another New South?" *Georgia Historical Quarterly* 65 (1981): 119–137, are good introductions to the debate. Dwight B. Billings, Jr., *Planters and the Making of a "New South": Class, Politics, and Development in North Carolina, 1865–1900* (Chapel Hill, N.C., 1979), and Jonathan Wiener, *Social Origins of the New South: Alabama, 1860–1880* (Baton Rouge, La., 1978), sharply challenge the "new men" thesis. Others modify it; they include William J. Cooper, Jr., *The Conservative Regime: South Carolina, 1877–1890* (Baltimore, 1968); Paul D. Escott, *Many Excellent People: Power and Privilege in North Carolina* (Chapel Hill, N.C., 1985); Jack Maddex, *Virginia Conservatives*; and James Russell, *Atlanta, 1847–1890*. Woodward's argument receives strong support from David L. Carlton, *Mill and Town in South Carolina, 1880–1920* (Baton Rouge, La., 1982), and Michael Wayne, *The Reshaping of Plantation Society: The Natchez District, 1860–1880* (Baton Rouge, La., 1983). The rhetoric and ideas of the New South boosters are explored in Paul M. Gaston, *The New South Creed: A Study in Southern Mythmaking* (New York, 1970).

By the end of Reconstruction, the solid or Democratic South was well established, though it had not yet reduced the Republicans or political independents to impotence. The place to begin reading about politics in the South after 1865 is V. O. Key, *Southern Politics in State and Nation* (New York, 1949). As Key and others have shown, the solid South had deep divisions throughout its history. Perhaps the most striking divisions occurred in the late nineteenth century, when disaffected farmers and their allies fueled an agrarian revolt that threatened the solid South for more than a decade. Theodore Saloutos, *Farmer Movements in the South, 1865–1933* (Berkeley and Los Angeles, 1960), provides a broad overview of that revolt. Other very useful studies include Steven

Hahn, *The Roots of Southern Populism: Yeoman Farmers and the Transformation of the Georgia Upcountry, 1850–1890* (New York, 1983); William Ivy Hair, *Bourbonism and Agrarian Protest: Louisiana Politics, 1877–1900* (Baton Rouge, La., 1969); Roger L. Hart, *Redeemers, Bourbons, and Populists: Tennessee, 1870–1896* (Baton Rouge, La., 1975); Albert D. Kirwan, *Revolt of the Rednecks: Mississippi Politics, 1876–1925* (Lexington, Ky., 1951); Allen W. Moger, *Virginia: Bourbonism to Byrd, 1870–1925* (Charlottesville, Va., 1968); William Warren Rogers, *One-Gallused Rebellion: Agrarianism in Alabama, 1865–1896* (Baton Rouge, La., 1970); and Edward C. Williamson, *Florida Politics in the Gilded Age, 1877–1893* (Gainesville, Fla., 1976).

John D. Hicks, *The Populist Revolt: A History of the Farmers' Alliance and the People's Party* (Minneapolis, 1931), is still the best place to get an overview of the Populists. Hicks has been challenged, most vigorously and successfully by Lawrence Goodwyn, *Democratic Promise: The Populist Movement in America* (New York, 1976). One need not accept Goodwyn's assertion that the Populists sought sweeping changes to be persuaded by his argument that southern Populism deserved more attention for its innovative thinking. Other good studies of southern Populism include Robert F. Durden, *The Climax of Populism: The Election of 1896* (Lexington, Ky., 1965); Gerald H. Gaither, *Blacks and the Populist Revolt: Ballots and Bigotry in the "New South"* (University, Ala., 1977); Sheldon Hackney, *Populism to Progressivism in Alabama* (Princeton, N.J., 1969); Robert C. McMath, Jr., *Populist Vanguard: A History of the Southern Farmers' Alliance* (Chapel Hill, N.C., 1975); Bruce Palmer, *"Man over Money": The Southern Populist Critique of American Capitalism* (Chapel Hill, N.C., 1980); Michael Schwartz, *Radical Protest and Social Structure: The Southern Farmers' Alliance and Cotton Tenancy, 1880–1890* (New York, 1976); and Barton C. Shaw, *The Wool-Hat Boys: Georgia's Populist Party* (Baton Rouge, La., 1984).

Some of the works listed above are also useful, directly or for background, in regard to the period from the Progressive Era through the 1920s. Dewey Grantham, *Southern Progressivism: The Reconciliation of Progress and Tradition* (Knoxville, Tenn., 1983), is a good overview. For general background, consult Arthur S. Link, *Woodrow Wilson and the Progressive Era* (New York, 1954). The diversity of the politics of Progressivism is reflected in some fine state studies: Danny Goble, *Progressive Oklahoma: The Making of a New Kind of State* (Norman, Okla., 1980); Lewis L. Gould, *Progressives and Prohibitionists: Texas Democrats in the Wilson Era* (Austin, Tex., 1973); David D. Lee, *Tennessee in Turmoil: Politics in the Volunteer State, 1920–1932* (Memphis, Tenn., 1979); Franklin D. Mitchell, *Embattled Democracy: Missouri Democratic Politics, 1919–1932* (Columbia, Mo., 1968); and Raymond H. Pulley, *Old Virginia Restored: An Interpretation of the Progressive Impulse, 1870–1930* (Charlottesville, Va., 1968), are particularly helpful.

Other aspects of Progressivism, such as city governance, women's rights, education, health, and labor reform, are dealt with below. Hugh C. Bailey, *Liberalism in the New South: Southern Social Reformers and the Progressive Movement* (Coral Gables, Fla., 1968), and Bruce Clayton, *The Savage Ideal: Intolerance and Intellectual Leadership in the South, 1980–1914* (Baltimore, 1972), are valuable guides to the narrowness of the Progressives' mentality. For a better understanding of the political climate of those years, consult Charles C. Alexander, *The Ku Klux Klan in the Southwest* (Lexington, Ky., 1965); David M. Chalmers, *Hooded Americanism: The First Century of the Ku Klux Klan, 1865–1965* (Garden City, N.Y., 1965); Willard B. Gatewood, Jr., *Preachers, Pedagogues, and Politicians: The Evolution Controversy in North Carolina, 1920–1927* (Chapel Hill, N.C., 1966); and Kenneth T. Jackson, *The Ku Klux Klan in the City, 1915–1930* (New York, 1967). On southern Republicans during this era, see Paul D. Casdorph, *Republicans, Negroes, and Progressives in the*

South, 1912–1916 (University, Ala., 1981); Gordon B. McKinney, *Southern Mountain Republicans, 1865–1900: Politics and the Appalachian Community* (Chapel Hill, N.C., 1978); and Olive Hall Shadgett, *The Republican Party in Georgia: From Reconstruction through 1900* (Athens, Ga., 1964). On the socialists in the South, see Garin Burbank, *When Farmers Voted Red: The Gospel of Socialism in the Oklahoma Countryside, 1910–1924* (Norman, Okla., 1980), and James R. Green, *Grass-Roots Socialism: Radical Movements in the Southwest, 1895–1943* (Baton Rouge, La., 1978).

Finally, biographies are always useful. See Raymond Arsenault, *Wild Ass of the Ozarks: Jeff Davis and the Social Bases of Southern Politics* (Philadelphia, 1984); Monroe Lee Billington, *Thomas P. Gore: The Blind Senator from Oklahoma* (Lawrence, Kans., 1967); Nelson M. Blake, *William Mahone of Virginia, Soldier and Political Insurgent* (Richmond, Va., 1935); Keith L. Bryant, Jr., *Alfalfa Bill Murray* (Norman, Okla., 1968); John Milton Cooper, *Walter Hines Page: The Southerner as American, 1855–1918* (Chapel Hill, N.C., 1977); Robert C. Cotner, *James Stephen Hogg: A Biography* (Austin, Tex., 1959); Wayne Flynt, *Cracker Messiah: Governor Sidney J. Catts of Florida* (Baton Rouge, La., 1977); Dewey W. Grantham, Jr., *Hoke Smith and the Politics of the New South* (Baton Rouge, La., 1958); William F. Holmes, *The White Chief: James Kimble Vardaman* (Baton Rouge, La., 1970); Jack Temple Kirby, *Westmoreland Davis: Virginia Planter-Politician, 1859–1942* (Charlottesville, Va., 1968); William D. Miller, *Mr. Crump of Memphis* (Baton Rouge, La., 1964); Stuart Noblin, *Leonidas La Fayette Polk: Agrarian Crusader* (Chapel Hill, N.C., 1949); Oliver H. Orr, Jr., *Charles Brantley Aycock* (Chapel Hill, N.C., 1961); Samuel Proctor, *Napoleon Bonaparte Broward: Florida's Fighting Democrat* (Gainesville, Fla., 1950); Daniel M. Robison, *Bob Taylor and the Agrarian Revolt in Tennessee* (Chapel Hill, N.C., 1935); Francis B. Simkins, *Pitchfork Ben Tillman, South Carolinian* (Baton Rouge, La., 1944); T. Harry Williams, *Huey Long* (New York, 1969); and C. Vann Woodward, *Tom Watson: Agrarian Rebel* (New York, 1938).

For an overview of the New Deal, see William E. Leuchtenburg, *Franklin D. Roosevelt and the New Deal* (New York, 1963). Frank Freidel, *F.D.R. and the South* (Baton Rouge, La., 1965), provides useful background. Economic and social conditions in the South on the eve of and during the Depression are discussed in a variety of sources. See especially Howard W. Odum, *Southern Regions of the United States* (Chapel Hill, N.C., 1936), a gold mine of statistical data; Twelve Southerners, *I'll Take My Stand* (New York, 1930); and Rupert B. Vance, *Human Factors in Cotton Culture* (Chapel Hill, N.C., 1929) and *Human Geography of the South* (Chapel Hill, N.C., 1932). Two anthologies of oral histories of ordinary southerners provide unique perspectives: William T. Couch, ed., *These Are Our Lives* (Chapel Hill, N.C., 1939), and Tom E. Terrill and Jerrold Hirsch, eds., *Such as Us: Southern Voices of the Thirties* (Chapel Hill, N.C., 1978). Also see James Agee and Walker Evans, *Let Us Now Praise Famous Men* (New York, 1941); Pete Daniel, *The Shadow of Slavery: Peonage in the South, 1901–1969* (Urbana, Ill., 1972); J. Wayne Flynt, *Dixie's Forgotten People: The South's Poor Whites* (Bloomington, Ind., 1979); Margaret Jarman Hagood, *Mothers of the South: Portraiture of the White Tenant Farm Woman* (Chapel Hill, N.C., 1939); H. L. Mitchell, *Mean Things Happening in This Land: The Life and Times of H. L. Mitchell* (Montclair, N.J., 1979); Arthur Raper, *Preface to Peasantry: A Tale of Two Black Belt Counties* (Chapel Hill, N.C., 1936); Raymond Wolters, *Negroes and the Great Depression: The Problem of Economic Recovery* (Westport, Conn., 1970); and Donald E. Worster, *Dust Bowl: The Southern Plains in the 1930s* (New York, 1979).

For a summary of the agricultural programs of the New Deal, see Theodore Saloutos, *The American Farmer and the New Deal* (Ames, Ia., 1982). Important works on specific programs include Anthony J. Badger, *Prosperity: The New Deal, Tobacco, and North Carolina* (Chapel Hill, N.C., 1980); D. Clayton Brown, *Electricity for Rural America: The Fight for the REA* (Westport, Conn., 1980); Wilmon Henry Droze, *High Dams and Slack Waters: TVA Builds a River* (Baton Rouge, La., 1965); Preston J. Hubbard, *Origins of the TVA: The Muscle Shoals Controversy, 1920–1932* (Nashville, Tenn., 1961); Thomas K. McGraw; *TVA and the Power Fight, 1933–1939* (Philadelphia, 1971); and Michael J. McDonald and John Muldowny, *TVA and the Dispossessed: The Resettlement of Population in the Norris Dam Area* (Knoxville, Tenn., 1982). Thomas D. Clark, *The Greening of the South: The Recovery of Land and Forest* (Lexington, Ky., 1984), has a good deal of material on the New Deal's conservation and reforestation efforts. For the story of the New Deal's failure with respect to poorer farmers, see David Eugene Conrad, *The Forgotten Farmers: The Story of Sharecroppers in the New Deal* (Urbana, Ill., 1965); Donald H. Grubbs, *Cry from the Cotton: The Southern Tenant Farmers' Union and the New Deal* (Chapel Hill, N.C., 1971); and Paul E. Mertz, *New Deal Policy and Southern Rural Poverty* (Baton Rouge, La., 1978). Two books include perceptive discussions of the impact of the New Deal agricultural programs on the South: Pete Daniel, *Breaking the Land: The Transformation of Cotton, Tobacco, and Rice Cultures since 1880* (Urbana, Ill., 1985), and Jack Temple Kirby, *Rural Worlds Lost: The American South, 1920–1960* (Baton Rouge, La., 1986).

James T. Patterson, *Congressional Conservatism and the New Deal: The Growth of the Conservative Coalition in Congress, 1933–1939* (Lexington, Ky., 1967), is important. Also see his *New Deal and the States: Federalism in Transition* (Princeton, N.J., 1969) and John Braeman, Robert H. Bremner, and David Brody, eds., *The New Deal: The State and Local Levels* (Columbus, O., 1975). Several books discuss the New Deal in the various states. Among them are Ronald L. Heineman, *Depression and New Deal in Virginia: The Enduring Dominion* (Charlottesville, Va., 1983), and John Dean Minton, *The New Deal in Tennessee, 1932–1938* (New York, 1979).

Again, biographies can be very useful. See Robert A. Caro, *The Years of Lyndon Johnson: The Path to Power* (New York, 1982); Ronnie Dugger, *The Politician: The Life and Times of Lyndon Johnson: The Drive for Power, from the Frontier to the Master of the Senate* (New York, 1982); Charles W. Eagles, *Jonathan Daniels and Race Relations: The Evolution of a Southern Liberal* (Knoxville, Tenn., 1982); Virginia Van der Veer Hamilton, *Hugo Black: The Alabama Years* (Baton Rouge, La., 1972); John Robert Moore, *Senator Josiah William Bailey of North Carolina: A Political Biography* (Durham, N.C., 1968); Lionel V. Patenaude, *Texans, Politics, and the New Deal* (New York, 1983); and Martha H. Swain, *Pat Harrison: The New Deal Years* (Jackson, Miss., 1978).

Efforts by southern liberals and radicals to change the South can be followed in Anthony P. Dunbar, *Against the Grain: Southern Radicals and Prophets, 1929–1959* (Charlottesville, Va., 1981); Wilma Dykeman and James Stokely, *Seeds of Southern Change: The Life of Will Alexander* (Chicago, 1962); Richard B. Henderson, *Maury Maverick: A Political Biography* (Austin, Tex., 1970); Rackham Holt, *Mary McLeod Bethune: A Biography* (New York, 1940); Thomas A. Krueger, *And Promises to Keep: The Southern Conference for Human Welfare, 1938–1948* (Nashville, Tenn., 1967); and John A. Salmond, *A Southern Rebel: The Life and Times of Aubrey Willis Williams, 1890–1965* (Chapel Hill, N.C., 1983).

Efforts to update V. O. Key's famed *Southern Politics* have produced several useful books, including Jack Bass and Walter De Vries, *The Transformation of Southern Politics: Social Change and Economic Consequence since 1945* (New York, 1976); William Havard, ed., *The Changing Politics of the South* (Baton Rouge, La., 1972); and Alexander P. Lamis, *The Two-Party South* (Baton Rouge, La., 1984). Earl Black and Merle Black, *Politics and Society in the South* (Cambridge, Mass., 1987), is the best study of southern politics to appear since Key's book.

Other valuable studies are Numan V. Bartley, *The Rise of Massive Resistance: Race and Politics in the South during the 1950s* (Baton Rouge, La., 1984) and *The Creation of Modern Georgia* (Athens, Ga., 1983); Earl Black, *Southern Governors and Civil Rights* (Cambridge, Mass., 1976); Bernard Cosman and Robert J. Huckshorn, *Republican Politics: The 1964 Campaign and Its Aftermath for the Party* (New York, 1968); Chandler Davidson, *Biracial Politics: Conflict and Coalition in the Biracial South* (Baton Rouge, La., 1972); Steven F. Lawson, *In Pursuit of Power: Southern Blacks and Electoral Politics, 1965–1982* (New York, 1985); Neil R. McMillen, *The Citizens' Council: Resistance to the Second Reconstruction* (Urbana, Ill., 1971); Louis M. Seagull, *Southern Republicanism* (Cambridge, Mass., 1975); and George B. Tindall, *The Disruption of the Solid South* (New York, 1972).

Several biographies and studies give insights into some of the important political leaders of the post–World War II South: Charles L. Fontenay, *Estes Keafauver: A Biography* (Knoxville, Tenn., 1980); Marshall Frady, *Wallace* (New York, 1968); Joseph Bruce Gorman, *Keafauver: A Political Biography* (New York, 1971); and J. Harvie Wilkinson III, *Harry Byrd and the Changing Face of Virginia Politics, 1945–1966* (Charlottesville, Va., 1968). On Jimmy Carter, see his *Keeping the Faith: Memoirs of a President* (New York, 1982) as well as Gary M. Fink, *Prelude to the Presidency: The Political Career of and Legislative Leadership Style of Governor Jimmy Carter* (Westport, Conn., 1980); Erwin C. Hargrove, *Jimmy Carter as President: Leadership and the Politics of the Public Good* (Baton Rouge, La., 1988); Charles O. Jones, *The Trustee Presidency: Jimmy Carter and the United States Congress* (Baton Rouge, La., 1988).

Southerners, especially southern leaders, did not restrict themselves to domestic politics alone, as the following works make clear: Alfred O. Hero, Jr., *The Southerner and World Affairs* (Baton Rouge, La., 1965); Charles O. Lerche, Jr., *The Uncertain South: Its Changing Patterns of Politics in Foreign Policy* (Chicago, 1964); and Tennant S. McWilliams, *The New South Faces the World: Foreign Affairs and the Southern Sense of Self, 1877–1950* (Baton Rouge, La., 1988).

Gunnar Myrdal's massive two-volume *American Dilemma: The Negro Problem and Modern Democracy*, 2 vols. (New York, 1944), is still the most important book on race relations available. David W. Southern has a fine discussion of the book and its impact: *Gunnar Myrdal and Black-White Relations: The Use and Abuse of "An American Dilemma"* (Baton Rouge, La., 1987). General histories of black Americans, like those by John Hope Franklin and August Meier and Elliot Rudwick, ought to be consulted. Two important studies of recent years are Herbert Gutman, *The Black Family in Slavery and Freedom* , and Lawrence Levine, *Black Culture and Black Consciousness.* Among the several studies of blacks in various states, see John Dittmer, *Black Georgia in the Progressive Era, 1900–1920* (Urbana, Ill., 1977); Lester C. Lamon, *Black Tennesseans, 1900–1930* (Knoxville, Tenn., 1977); Neil R. McMillen, *Dark Journey: Black Mississippians in the Age of Jim Crow* (Urbana, Ill., 1989); and I. A. Newby, *Black Carolinians: A History of Blacks in South Carolina from 1895 to 1968* (Columbia, S.C., 1973). Two published autobiographical works on blacks are particularly good: Theodore Rosengartern, *All God's Dangers: The Life of Nate Shaw [Cole]* (New York, 1974), and *He Included Me: The Autobiography of Sarah Rice*, transcribed and edited by Louise Westling (Athens, Ga., 1989).

There is no general history of the massive migration of blacks from the South. Daniel M. Johnson and Rex B. Campbell, *Black Migration in America: A Social Demographic History* (Durham, N.C., 1981) is too brief. Two books deal with the 1870s migration of blacks to

Kansas: Nell Irvin Painter, *The Exodusters: Black Migration to Kansas after Reconstruction* (New York, 1976), and Robert G. Athearn, *In Search of Canaan: Black Migration to Kansas, 1879–80* (Lawrence, Kans., 1978). Migration to Africa attracted the interest of some blacks. This is the subject of Edwin S. Redkey's *Exodus: Black Nationalism and Back-to-Africa Movements, 1890–1910* (New Haven, Conn., 1969). That interest was stirred again during World War I and especially during the 1920s by Marcus Garvey, who led the first mass black protest movement in America: E. David Cronon, *Black Moses: The Story of Marcus Garvey and the Universal Negro Improvement Association* (Madison, Wis., 1955).

Studies of race relations have generally tended to focus on particularly critical moments, such as the surge of Jim Crow legislation in the late nineteenth century, the wave of race riots after World War I, and the civil rights revolution. Arthur I. Waskow's *From Race Riot to Sit-in, 1919 and the 1960's: A Study in the Connections between Conflict and Violence* (Garden City, N.Y., 1966) is a good general introduction. For a study of a specific riot, see Scott Ellsworth, *Death in a Promised Land: The Tulsa Race Riot of 1921* (Baton Rouge, La., 1982). Arthur F. Raper's *Tragedy of Lynching* (Chapel Hill, N.C., 1933) is still the best work on that terrible practice. W. E. B. Du Bois, *The Souls of Black Folk* (Chicago, 1903) is a classic, beautifully written and full of insights. Du Bois's autobiographical writings also contain many treasures.

Rich insights about race relations in the 1930s can be found in intensive studies done during that decade: Allison Davis, Burleigh B. Gardner, and Mary B. Gardner, *Deep South: A Social Anthropological Study of Caste and Class* (Chicago, 1941); John Dollard, *Caste and Class in a Southern Town* (New York, 1937); and Hortense Powdermaker, *After Freedom: A Cultural Study in the Deep South* (New York, 1958). Dan T. Carter's study of the notorious Scottsboro trial, *Scottsboro: A Tragedy of the American South*, rev. ed. (Baton Rouge, La., 1979), and James R. McGovern's discussion of a 1934 lynching, *Anatomy of a Lynching: The Killing of Claude Neal* (Baton Rouge, La., 1982), are full of insights. The best introduction to what blacks found in the American military during World War II and the Korean War is Richard M. Dalfiume, *Desegregation of the U.S. Armed Forces: Fighting on Two Fronts, 1939–1953* (Columbia, Mo., 1969).

No general survey of the civil rights revolution is available, but see Genna Rae McNeil, *Groundwork: Charles Hamilton Houston and the Struggle for Civil Rights* (Philadelphia, 1983); Aldon D. Morris, *The Origins of the Civil Rights Movement: Black Communities Organizing for Change* (New York, 1984); Harvard Sitkoff, *The Struggle for Black Equality, 1954–1980* (New York, 1981); and Mark V. Tushnet, *The NAACP's Legal Strategy against Segregated Education, 1925–1950* (Chapel Hill, N.C., 1987). Richard Kluger, *Simple Justice: The History of "Brown v. Board of Education" and Black America's Struggle for Equality*, (New York, 1976), is valuable and compelling. The role of the courts, especially the federal courts, is discussed in Jack Bass, *Unlikely Heroes: The Dramatic Story of the Southern Judges of the Fifth Circuit Court Who Translated the Supreme Court's "Brown" Decision into a Revolution for Equality* (New York, 1981); Tinsley E. Yarbrough, *Judge Frank Johnson and Human Rights in Alabama* (University, Ala., 1983); J. Harvie Wilkinson III, *From "Brown" to "Bakke": The Supreme Court and School Integration, 1954–1978* (New York, 1979); and Raymond Wolters, *The Burden of "Brown": Thirty Years of School Desegregation* (Knoxville, Tenn., 1984). Bass and Yarbrough laud the judges. Wilkinson has reservations about the expansion of judicial authority in the school cases. Wolters is generally critical of the role of the courts in school desegregation.

Several books deal with the divergent ways southern liberals dealt with Jim Crow in the 1930s and 1940s. The most general of these works is Morton Sosna, *The Silent South: Southern Liberals and the Race Issue* (New York, 1977). Also see the books by Dunbar, Eagles, and Salmond cited above, as well as John M. Glen's recent study of Highlander School: *Highlander: No Ordinary School, 1932–1962* (Lexington, Ky., 1988). Lillian Smith was one of the few southern whites who bluntly attacked Jim Crow: *Killers of the Dream* (New York, 1949). In the 1960s, James McBride Dabbs made an eloquent, ethically based attack on race relations in his native region: *Who Speaks for the South?* (New York, 1964), while a fellow South Carolinian, William D. Workman, argued in *The Case for the South* (New York, 1960) against federal intervention in racial matters. The South should be left alone to deal with its own racial problems, Workman argued, but he was vague as to when and how the South ought to act.

David J. Garrow and Taylor Branch have written extensive, rich studies of Martin Luther King, Jr., and the civil rights movement: Garrow, *Bearing the Cross: Martin Luther King, Jr., and the Southern Christian Leadership Conference* (New York, 1986); and Branch, *Parting the Waters: America in the King Years, 1954–1963* (New York, 1988). Howell Raines, *My Soul Is Rested: Movement Days in the Deep South Remembered* (New York, 1983), conveys the emotion behind the movement and provides facts and insights that help us to realize the diversity of both the movement and its leadership and the great risks many people took when they challenged Jim Crow. For the Student Nonviolent Coordinating Committee, see Clayborne Carson, *In Struggle: SNCC and the Black Awakening of the 1960s* (Cambridge, Mass., 1981). Of personal reminiscences of the civil rights movements, two of the best are Mary King, *Freedom Song: A Personal Story of the 1960s Civil Rights Movement* (New York, 1987), and Anne Moody, *Coming of Age in Mississippi* (New York, 1969).

The following are very useful for understanding particular events or groups: Catherine A. Barnes, *Journey from Jim Crow: The Desegregation of Southern Transit* (New York, 1983); William H. Chafe, *Civilities and Civil Rights: Greensboro, North Carolina, and the Black Struggle for Freedom* (New York, 1981); David J. Garrow, *Protest at Selma: Martin Luther King, Jr., and the Voting Rights Act of 1965* (New Haven, Conn., 1978); Robert J. Norell, *Reaping the Whirlwind: The Civil Rights Movement in Tuskegee* (New York, 1985); Jo Ann Gibson Robinson, *The Montgomery Bus Boycott and the Women Who Started It: The Memoirs of Jo Ann Gibson*, ed. with a foreword by David J. Garrow (Knoxville, 1987); Charles V. Hamilton, *The Bench and the Ballot: Southern Federal Judges and Black Voters* (New York, 1973); and J. Mills Thornton, "Challenge and Response in the Montgomery Bus Boycott of 1955–1956," *Alabama Review* 33 (1980): 163–235. The last study is extremely valuable. Elizabeth Jacoway and David R. Colburn, eds., *Southern Businessmen and Desegregation* (Baton Rouge, La., 1982), recounts the role businessmen played in encouraging acceptance of desegregation and their motives for doing so. Michael V. Namorato, ed., *Have We Overcome? Race Relations since "Brown"* (Jackson, Miss., 1979) is a reassessment of the civil rights movement. For an argument that economic and institutional factors are more important than racial factors in determining the place and future of American blacks, see William Julius Wilson, *The Declining Significance of Race: Blacks and Changing American Institutions* (Chicago, 1978) and *The Truly Disadvantaged: The Inner City, the Under Class, and Public Policy* (Chicago, 1987).

Women in the South are a comparatively new area of historical study. The best place to start is Jacquelyn Dowd Hall and Anne Frior Scott, "Women in the South," in John Boles and Evelyn Nolen, *Interpreting Southern History*. Several works of a general nature are important, especially Anne Scott's *Southern Lady*. Several other important works give some attention to the South: David M. Katzman, *Seven Days a Week: Women and Domestic Service in Industrializing America* (New York, 1978); Alice Kessler-Harris, *Out to Work: A History of Wage-Earning Women in the United States* (New York, 1982); and Barbara Mayer Wertheimer, *We Were There: The Story of Working Women in America* (New York, 1977).

Jacqueline Dowd Hall's *Revolt against Chivalry: Jessie Daniel Ames and the Women's Campaign against Lynching* (New York, 1979) is a major contribution that focuses on women, feminism, religion, and social reform.

Women in the New South assumed leading roles in the churches, social reform, and, of course, the drive to secure the vote for women. Eleanor Flexner, *Century of Struggle: The Woman's Rights Movement in the United States* (New York, 1979), provides a useful general introduction. A. Elizabeth Taylor wrote extensively about the campaign for women's suffrage in articles and in *The Woman Suffrage Movement in Tennessee* (New York, 1957). Paul E. Fuller, *Laura Clay and the Women's Rights Movement* (Lexington, Ky., 1975), is about one of the South's leading suffragists.

The importance of women in religious groups and religiously based reform efforts is stressed in Jean E. Friedman, *The Enclosed Garden: Women and Community in the Evangelical South, 1830–1900* (Chapel Hill, N.C., 1985), and John Patrick McDowell, *The Social Gospel in the South: The Woman's Home Mission Movement in the Methodist Episcopal Church* (Baton Rouge, La., 1982).

Also see Daisy Bates, *The Long Shadow of Little Rock: A Memoir* (New York, 1962); Septima Poinsette Clark, *Echo in My Soul* (New York, 1962); Couch, *These Are Our Lives*; *Outside the Magic Circle: The Autobiography of Virginia Foster Durr*, ed. Hollinger F. Barnard (University, Ala., 1985); Sara Evans, *Personal Politics: The Roots of Women's Liberation in the Civil Rights Movement and the New Left* (New York, 1979); Hagood, *Mothers of the South*; Jacquelyn C. Hall et al., *Like a Family: The Making of a South Carolina Mill World* (Chapel Hill, N.C., 1987); Gerda Lerner, ed., *Black Women in White America: A Documentary History* (New York, 1972); Anne C. Loveland, *Lillian Smith: A Southerner Confronting the South: A Biography* (Baton Rouge, La., 1986); Katharine Du Pré Lumpkin, *The Making of a Southerner* (New York, 1947); Lucy Mason Randolph, *To Win These Rights: A Personal Story of the CIO in the South* (New York, 1952); Pauli Murray, *Proud Shoes: The Story of an American Family* (New York, 1956); Lillian Smith, *Killers of the Dream*; Tom Terrill and Jerrold Hirsch, *Such as Us*; and Ida B. Wells, *Crusade for Justice: The Autobiography of Ida B. Wells*, ed. Alfreda M. Duster (Chicago, 1970). More impressionistic but useful and sometimes amusing are Shirley Abbott, *Womenfolks: Growing Up Down South* (New Haven, Conn., 1983); Rosemary Daniell, *Fatal Flowers: On Sin, Sex, and Suicide in the Deep South* (New York, 1980); and Florence King, *Southern Ladies and Gentlemen* (New York, 1975). Southern women novelists also provide important perceptions and perspectives. See Barbara Christian, *Black Women Novelists: The Development of a Tradition, 1892–1976* (Westport, Conn., 1976); Anne Goodwyn Jones, *Tomorrow Is Another Day: The Woman Writer in the South, 1859–1936* (Baton Rouge, La., 1981); and, of course, the works of the novelists these books discuss.

Women have long been a critical part of the southern work force, both at home and away from home. Thus labor history is often also women's history. Women have also been leaders in efforts to improve working conditions and the lives of working people's families. In addition to the works cited above and some that are cited in the section on labor, useful material may be found in Dolores E. Janiewski's *Sisterhood Denied: Race, Gender, and Class in a New South Community* (Philadelphia, 1985); Kathy Kahn, *Hillbilly Women* (Garden City, N.Y., 1981); and Cathy L. McHugh, *Mill Family: The Labor System in the Southern Cotton Textile Industry, 1880–1950* (New York, 1986). Mary Frederickson's study, *A Place to Speak Our Minds: The Southern School for Women Workers, 1927–1950* (Bloomington, Ind., 1990), casts new light on the relationship among middle-class women activists, women workers, and organized labor.

The amount of scholarly work on the history of labor in the South is not extensive, but it is growing. Even less is available about the history of industry, and that body of work is hardly growing. The best overview available is James C. Cobb, *Industrialization and Southern Society, 1877–1984* (Lexington, Ky., 1984), but it is spotty—a reflection, in part, of the state of the literature. Cobb's *Selling of the South: The Southern Crusade for Industrial Development, 1936–1980* (Baton Rouge, La., 1982) is a lucid account of the region's pursuit of investors. Victor S. Clark, *The History of Manufactures in the United States*, 3 vols. (New York, 1929), is still useful, as are Harriet L. Herring, *Southern Industry and Regional Development* (Chapel Hill, N.C., 1940), and Broadus Mitchell and George S. Mitchell, *The Industrial Revolution in the South* (Baltimore, 1930).

Several books are very valuable as starting points on the economy of the South as a whole. They include the work of Gavin Wright cited above; Melvin L. Greenhut and W. Tate Whitman, eds., *Essays in Southern Economic Development* (Chapel Hill, N.C., 1964); and Calvin B. Hoover and B. U. Ratchford, *Economic Resources and Policies of the South* (New York, 1951). Government publications are very important sources for statistics and for analytical studies. Also see the publications of the National Bureau of Economic Research.

The growth of the southern economy has been examined extensively. Among the most helpful works is Bernard L. Weinstein and Robert E. Firestine, *Regional Growth and Decline in the United States: The Rise of the Sunbelt and the Decline of the Northeast* (New York, 1978). Also helpful are the publications of the Southern Growth Policies Board, especially its overview of the economy of the South: *The Future of the South* (Research Triangle Park, N.C., 1981). The Southern Regional Council, whose activities include the publishing of studies of the contemporary South, continues to remind us of the shady spots in the Sunbelt. On the way southerners interact with the physical environment they say they love, see Albert E. Cowdrey, *This Land, This South* (Lexington, Ky., 1983). Nelson M. Blake, *Land into Water—Water into Land: A History of Water Management in Florida* (Tallahassee, Fla., 1980), is a sobering analysis of one specific environmental case.

Individual industries have received varying degrees of attention from scholars over the years. Two of the more glamorous industries, railroads and oil, have fared best. John Stover, *Railroads of the South, 1865–1900: A Study in Finance and Control* (Chapel Hill, N.C., 1955), is a good general introduction. The best history of an individual railroad company is Maury Klein, *The Richmond Terminal: A Study of Businessmen and Business Strategy* (Charlottesville, Va., 1970). Another fine recent study of railroads in the South is James P. Baughman, *Charles Morgan and the Development of Southern Transportation* . Among the several good books on the oil industry are Carl Coke Rister, *Oil! Titan of the Southwest* (Norman, Okla., 1949); John S. Spratt, *The Road to Spindletop: Economic Change in Texas, 1875–1901* (Dallas, 1955); and Harold F. Williamson et al., *The American Petroleum Industry*, 2 vols. (Evanston, Ill., 1957–1963). Arthur M. Johnson has written the basic study of pipelines, a vital aspect of the petroleum industry: *The Development of American Petroleum Pipelines: A Study in Private Enterprise and Public Policy, 1826–1906* (Ithaca, N.Y., 1956) and *Petroleum Pipelines and Public Policy, 1906–1959* (Cambridge, Mass., 1967).

Unfortunately, neither the coal nor the iron industry has attracted as much scholarly attention as the oil industry. Ethel M. Armes, *The Story of Coal and Iron in Alabama* (Salem, N.H., 1910) is useful in spite of its boosterism. Material can also be gleaned from H. H. Chapman et al., *The Iron and Steel Industries of the South* (University, Ala., 1955). On the decline of the coal industry after its years of expansion, see McAlister Coleman, *Men and Coal* (New York, 1943), and Malcolm H. Ross, *Machine Age in the Hills* (New York, 1933).

The economic and social plight of Appalachia, partially the result of the decline of the coal industry, has received considerable attention. Harry Caudill has written extensively and passionately about that region. For instance, see his *Night Comes to the Cumberlands: A Biography of a Depressed Area* (Boston, 1963). Ronald D. Eller's fine historical study, *Miners, Millhands, and Mountaineers: Industrialization of the Appalachian South, 1880–1930* (Knoxville, Tenn., 1982), surveys economic development and exploitation in southern Appalachia. Eller also effectively undermines the notion that the people of Appalachia lived in naive simplicity in wooded mountains cut off from the rest of the nation. Other books on coal mining and life and politics in the Appalachian South include David Allen Corbin, *Life, Work, and Rebellion in the Coal Fields: The Southern West Virginia Miners, 1880–1922* (Urbana, Ill., 1981); John Gaventa, *Power and Powerlessness: Quiescence and Rebellion in an Appalachian Valley* (New York, 1980); and John W. Hevener, *Which Side Are You On? The Harlan County Miners, 1931–39* (Urbana, Ill., 1978). The black minority in Appalachia has begun to receive scholarly attention: Ronald L. Lewis, *Black Coal Miners in America: Race, Class, and Community Conflict, 1780–1980* (Lexington, Ky., 1989), and William Turner and Edward Cabell, eds., *Blacks in Appalachia* (Urbana, Ill., 1989). Durwood Dunn, *Cade's Cove: The Life and Death of a Southern Appalachian Community, 1818–1937* (Knoxville, Tenn., 1988), is a recent study of a once-successful farm area that was taken over by the National Park Service and tourists.

Several works on textiles are helpful. Broadus Mitchell's *Rise of the Cotton Mills of the South* (Baltimore, 1921) is valuable, though it lionizes the first generation of New South mill builders. Similar reservations apply to Holland Thompson, *From the Cotton Field to the Cotton Mill: A Study of the Industrial Transition in North Carolina* (New York, 1906). Melvin T. Copeland, *The Cotton Manufacturing Industry of the United States* (Cambridge, Mass., 1912), is also useful. Jack Blicksilver, *Cotton Manufacturing in the Southeast: An Historical Analysis* (Atlanta, 1959), brings the story up to more recent times but is brief. David Carlton's *Mill and Town* is a perceptive analysis of the early years of the textile industry and the reaction that followed the emergence of a large working class in the industrializing South. Louis Galambos's fine study, *Competition and Cooperation: The Emergence of a National Trade Association* (Baltimore, 1966), traces industry efforts from the 1890s to the 1930s to strike a balance between competition and cooperation. The best single company history is Robert S. Smith, *Mill on the Dan: A History of Dan River Mills, 1882–1950* (Durham, N.C., 1960).

Nannie May Tilley's excellent *Bright-Tobacco Industry, 1860–1929* (Chapel Hill, N.C., 1948) covers every aspect of bright-leaf tobacco, its history, cultivation, and final processing into consumer products. For a similar fine study of sugar, see Carlyle Sitterson, *Sugar Country*. Tilley also wrote a fine company history: *The R. J. Reynolds Tobacco Company* (Chapel Hill, N.C., 1985). Other than company- or industry-sponsored histories, little is to be found on such highly significant industries as banking, utilities, trucking, chemicals, and lumbering and forest products. Still, sponsored histories should not be completely ignored; some of them contain useful information.

Robert F. Durden's *Dukes of Durham* (Durham, N.C., 1975) is a good study of one of the most powerful business families in the South. Two useful books on merchandising are Hugh G. Baker, *Rich's of Atlanta: The Story of a Store since 1867* (Atlanta, 1953), and LeGette Blythe, *William Henry Belk: Merchant of the South* (Chapel Hill, N.C., 1950). Unfortunately, we have no solid history of either Coca-Cola or Pepsi Cola, two bubbling giants of the South.

General histories of the American worker and organized labor provide valuable direct and indirect data and perspectives on labor in the South. See, for instance, Ronald L. Filipelli, *Labor in the United States* (New York, 1984). David Brody's *Workers in Industrial America: Essays on the Twentieth-Century Struggle* (New York, 1980) provides useful insights. Christopher L. Tomlins, *The State and the Unions: Labor Relations, Law, and the Organized Labor Movement in America, 1880–1960* (New York, 1985), is a fine study of an important topic. F. Ray Marshall's *Labor in the South* (Cambridge, Mass., 1967) is a general study of organized labor in the South. Merl E. Reed, Leslie S. Hough, and Gary M. Fink, eds., *Southern Workers and Their Unions, 1880–1975* (Westport, Conn., 1981) is a collection of useful papers. For a careful assessment of the importance of unions in contemporary America and a useful corrective to the unions-no-longer-serve-a-useful-purpose theme, see Richard D. Freeman and James L. Medoff, *What Do You Unions Do?* (New York, 1984).

Leon Fink, *Workingmen's Democracy: The Knights of Labor and American Politics* (Urbana, Ill., 1983); Melton Alonzo McLaurin, *Paternalism and Protest: Southern Cotton Mill Workers and Organized Labor, 1875–1905* (Westport, Conn., 1971); and McLaurin, *The Knights of Labor in the South* (Westport, Conn., 1978), deal with organized labor and worker protest in the South in the late nineteenth century. For a study of racial cooperation and conflict among workers in an important industrial state, see Robert D. Ward and William W. Rogers, *Labor Revolt in Alabama: The Great Strike of 1894* (Austin, Tex., 1965). Ruth A. Allen also wrote about labor in Texas during these years: *Great Southwest Strike* (Austin, Tex., 1942) as well as *Chapters in the History of Organized Labor in Texas* (Austin, Tex., 1941) and *East Texas Lumber Workers, 1870–1950* (Austin, Tex., 1961).

Child labor was at one time common in the South. On that topic consult Elizabeth H. Davidson, *Child Labor Legislation in the South in the Southern Textile States* (Chapel Hill, N.C., 1931); Walter I. Trattner, *Crusade for the Children: A History of the National Child Labor Committee and Child Labor Reform in America* (Austin, Tex., 1970); and Stephen B. Wood, *Constitutional Politics in the Progressive Era* (Austin, Tex., 1968). David Carlton's *Mill and Town* discusses workers' resistance to child labor legislation.

Perhaps because of their numbers, textile workers have received more attention than other workers in the South. Herbert J. Lahne, *The Cotton Mill Worker* (New York, 1944), is a valuable introduction. Jacquelyn Hall et al., *Like a Family*, and Allen Tullos, *Habits of Industry: White Culture and the Transformation of the Carolina Piedmont* (Chapel Hill, N.C., 1989), discuss the world the early textile workers came from and the world they helped to create. Also see the fine recent study of I. A. Newby, *Plain Folk in the New South: Social Change and Cultural Persistence, 1880–1915* (Baton Rouge, La., 1989). Cathy McHugh's *Mill Family* is a study of labor policy during the early years of the industry. Background to the labor strife that marked the industry in the 1920s and 1930s may be found in Irving Bernstein, *The Lean Years: A History of the American Worker, 1920–1933* (Boston, 1960); and George S. Mitchell, *Textile Unionism and the South* (Chapel Hill, N.C., 1931).

On the labor-management turmoil of the 1930s and on the labor policy of the New Deal, see Irving Bernstein, *Turbulent Years: A History of the American Worker, 1933–1941* (Boston, 1970) and *The Caring Society: The New Deal, the Worker, and the Great Depression: A History of the American Worker, 1933–1941* (Boston, 1985); James A. Hodges, *New Deal Labor Policy and the Southern Cotton Textile Industry, 1933–1941* (Knoxville, Tenn., 1985); and Liston Pope, *Millhands and Preachers: A Study of Gastonia* (New Haven, Conn., 1942). For a good firsthand account by a participant in the famous Gastonia strike of 1929, see Thomas Tippett, *When Southern Labor Stirs* (New York, 1931). The general textile strike of 1934 has not been fully treated by historians, but Jacquelyn Hall et al., *Like a Family*, and Hodges,

New Deal Labor Policy, are the best available studies. On the change and decline of a major working-class institution in the South, read Harriet L. Herring, *Passing of the Mill Village: Revolution in a Southern Institution* (Chapel Hill, N.C., 1940). Barbara Griffith has written about Operation Dixie, organized labor's unsuccessful attempt to expand its base in the South: *The Crisis of American Labor: "Operation Dixie" and the Defeat of the CIO* (Philadelphia, 1988). Mimi Conway's *Rise Gonna Rise: A Portrait of Southern Textile Workers* (New York, 1979) is an interesting though journalistic account of the struggle to organize the J. P. Stevens mill at Roanoke Rapids, North Carolina, site of one battle in the long war between Stevens and organized labor.

Among the valuable books on black labor are Philip S. Foner and Ronald L. Lewis, eds., *Black Workers: A Documentary History from Colonial Times to the Present* (Philadelphia, 1989), and Julius Jacobson, ed., *The Negro and the American Labor Movement* (Garden City, N.Y., 1968). For earlier years, see Gerald David Jaynes, *Branches without Roots: Genesis of the Black Working Class in the American South, 1862–1882* (New York, 1986), and Peter J. Rachleff, *Black Labor in the South: Richmond, Virginia, 1865–1890* (Philadelphia, 1984). William Hamilton Harris, *Keeping the Faith: A. Philip Randolph, Milton P. Webster, and the Brotherhood of Sleeping Car Porters, 1925–1937*, deals with the first black union admitted to the AFL and the men who created it. Randolph was the most important black labor leader in America and a major force in the civil rights movement. Nell Irvin Painter, *The Narrative of Hosea Hudson: His Life as a Negro Communist in the South* (Cambridge, Mass., 1979), is the story of a very different kind of black activist.

Information on workers and organized labor in the South can also be found in studies that are not specifically about the South: Melvyn Dubofsky, *We Shall Be All: A History of the Industrial Workers of the World* (Chicago, 1969); Walter Galenson, *The CIO Challenge to the AFL: A History of the American Labor Movement, 1935–1941* (Cambridge, Mass., 1960); Daniel Nelson, *American Rubber Workers and Organized Labor, 1900–1941* (Princeton, N.J., 1988), and Robert H. Zieger, *Rebuilding the Pulp and Paper Workers' Union, 1933–1941* (Knoxville, Tenn., 1984).

Urban history has been relatively neglected by historians of the South, and a good part of the scanty material available is to be found only in articles. *The City in Southern History*, a collection of historiographical essays edited by Blaine Brownell and David Goldfield, is useful but dated. Goldfield has since published an overview of southern urban history in which he stresses the close ties between the South as a region and the character of its cities: his *Cotton Fields and Skyscrapers* contains a good bibliographical essay.

Older histories of southern cities—for instance, William D. Miller, *Memphis during the Progressive Era, 1900–1917* (Memphis, Tenn., 1957), and Joy L. Jackson, *New Orleans in the Gilded Age: Politics and Urban Progress, 1880–1896* (Baton Rouge, La., 1969)—are more descriptive than analytical, but they provide useful information. Much more analytical and suggestive are Carl V. Harris, *Political Power in Birmingham, 1871–1921* (Knoxville, Tenn., 1977), and Eugene J. Watts, *Social Bases of City Politics: Atlanta, 1865–1903* (Westport, Conn., 1978). Atlanta has received more serious scholarly attention than most other southern cities. The best biography of a southern mayor is probably Harold H. Martin, *William Henry Hartsfield: Mayor of Atlanta* (Athens, Ga., 1978). J. Michael Russell's study of early Atlanta, cited earlier, is very good. Howard L. Preston has examined Atlanta at a later time, when it was reshaped by the horseless carriage: *Automobile Age Atlanta: The Making of a Southern Metropolis, 1900–1935* (Athens, Ga., 1979). Scholars have also examined Nashville carefully. For instance, there are Don H. Doyle's studies of Nashville since 1880: *Nashville in the New South, 1880–1930* (Knoxville, Tenn., 1985) and

Nashville since the 1920s (Knoxville, Tenn., 1985). The impact of World War II on the urban South is well known, but one unusual instance of that impact is the subject of Charles W. Johnson and Charles O. Jackson: *City Behind a Fence: Oak Ridge, Tennessee, 1942–1946* (Knoxville, Tenn., 1981).

Several historians have written fine monographs about particular aspects of southern urbanization. They include John W. Blassingame, *Black New Orleans, 1860–1880* (Chicago, 1973); Robert W. Ingalls, *Urban Vigilantes in the New South: Tampa, 1882–1936* (Knoxville, Tenn., 1988); and Howard Rabinowitz's *Race Relations in the Urban South*, cited earlier. Two very useful anthologies are Roger W. Lotchin, *The Martial Metropolis: U.S. Cities in War and Peace* (New York, 1984), and David C. Perry and Alfred J. Watkins, eds., *The Rise of the Sunbelt Cities* (Beverly Hills, Calif., 1977). Some readers may dispute Carl Abbott's definition of the Sunbelt, but many will find his *New Urban America: Growth and Politics in Sunbelt Cities of the South* (Chapel Hill, N.C., 1981) informative and insightful.

There is no history of culture or religion in the South per se. The two most perceptive interpretations of the mind-set and values of the South are Wilbur Cash's *Mind of the South* and Vann Woodward's *Burden of Southern History* (Baton Rouge, La., 1960). Both are efforts to penetrate the paradoxes in the culture and religion of the South: extreme individualism coexisting with suffocating social conformity; egalitarianism with social stratification; paternalism with a ferocious sense of independence; sectional loyalism with fierce, unquestioning national patriotism; a one-party political tradition that disguised intense, ongoing political conflict and division; and deep religious and moral commitments with a blatantly discriminatory, dehumanizing racial caste system that was one of the cornerstones of southern life and politics.

Cash saw a continuing mind-set that survived the Civil War and persisted to his day. Cash contended that southerners did not think, they felt. They were romantics rather than realists, individualists who abhorred restraints, especially institutional restraints. Ironically, the masses were easily seduced by flamboyant rhetoric. They espoused personal independence, then loyally followed the lead of the political and economic elite of the region. The dominant white majority was obsessed by the large black minority. The region's pervasive evangelical Protestantism and the anguished coexistence of righteousness and guilt contorted the soul of the South.

Woodward took a different tack. The burden of history, he said, had shaped the South. Its experiences had made it different from the rest of the country: guilt for slavery and then Jim Crow; military defeat, occupation, and political reconstruction; and long-term poverty, relative to the rest of the country and the Western world. This burden has lost a good deal of its persuasive power in the last decade or so, but this is still a very perceptive approach to southern history.

Some historians have argued that the modern South has shaken off the burden of its past so completely that it is no longer distinctive as a region. That is one theme of John Egerton's thoughtful book *The Americanization of Dixie: The Southernization of America* (New York, 1974). As the title suggests, Egerton also sees the South "southernizing" the rest of the nation. Though a native of Dixie, Egerton does not think this process altogether good. The best answer to the contention that Dixie is dead is John Shelton Reed, *The Enduring South: Subcultural Persistence in Mass Society* (Lexington, Mass., 1972). When he carefully analyzed Gallup polls, Reed found that the South had retained a great deal of its regional distinctiveness. Reed has followed this work with *One South: An Ethnic Approach to Regional Culture* (Baton Rouge, La., 1982) and *Southerners: The Social Psychology of Sectionalism* (Chapel Hill, N.C., 1983). Carl Degler in *Place over Time: The Continuity of*

Southern Distinctiveness (Baton Rouge, La., 1977) and George B. Tindall in *The Ethnic Southerners* (Baton Rouge, La., 1976) also argue for southern distinctiveness, as do Fifteen Southerners in *Why the South Will Survive*, ed. Clyde N. Wilson (Athens, Ga., 1981). But should readers become so involved in the issue of southern regional identity that they perceive a second secession, they ought to remember that southerners are Americans. On that subject a good reminder is Charles B. Sellers, Jr., ed., *The Southerner as American* (Chapel Hill, N.C., 1960).

Writers of the South have and still are creating treasures that serious students of southern culture must read and ponder. For guidance, consult Louis Rubin, et al., eds., *The History of Southern Literature*, which covers a very broad spectrum of materials and times. To understand fundamental changes in the literature of the South and in the assumptions of the elite culture of the region, Daniel Joseph Singal's *War Within: From Victorian to Modernist Thought in the South, 1919–1945* (Chapel Hill, N.C., 1982) is essential. Also see Michael O'Brien, *The Idea of the American South, 1920–1941* (Baltimore, 1979), and Richard H. King, *A Southern Renaissance: The Cultural Awakening of the American South, 1930–1955* (New York, 1980).

Evangelical Protestantism has permeated and shaped the South. For a general, thorough history of religion in America, see Sydney E. Ahlstrom, *A Religious History of the American People* (New Haven, Conn., 1972). Other very useful works of a general nature are Edwin S. Gaustad, *Historical Atlas of Religion in America*, rev. ed. (New York, 1976), and Samuel S. Hill, Jr., ed., *Encyclopedia of Religion in the South* (Macon, Ga., 1984). Two collections of essays are important: Charles R. Wilson, ed., *Religion in the South* (Jackson, Miss., 1985), and David Edwin Harrell, Jr., ed., *Varieties of Southern Evangelicalism* (Macon, Ga., 1981). Also see Samuel S. Hill, Jr., ed., *Religion and the Solid South* (Nashville, Tenn., 1972) and Hill, *The South and the North in American Religion*.

There are a number of studies of various denominations, black and white, Protestant and Catholic, by region, subregion, and state. Most are institutional in focus. Three histories that give special consideration to the social, economic, and political contexts within which particular denominations functioned demonstrate this shift in focus: David Harrell, *Quest for a Christian America* and *The Social Sources of Division in the Disciples of Christ, 1865–1900* (Atlanta, 1973); and Clarence E. Walker, *A Rock in a Weary Land: The African Methodist Episcopal Church during the Civil War and Reconstruction* (Baton Rouge, La., 1982).

Christian sects have been important in the history of the South, especially for the dispossessed, black and white. They have begun to receive the careful, sensitive attention they deserve. Consult the works of a general nature cited above as well as such books as David Harrell's *All Things Are Possible: The Healing and Charismatic Revivals in Modern America* (Bloomington, Ind., 1975); W. J. Hollenweger, *The Pentecostals: The Charismatic Movement in the Churches* (Peabody, Mass., 1972); and Vinson Synan, *The Holiness-Pentecostal Movement in the United States* (Grand Rapids, Mich., 1971).

Jews, a small but important group of southerners, have been seriously studied by a number of people. Two useful collections of essays are good starting points: Leonard Dinnerstein and Mary Palsson, eds., *Jews in the South*, and Nathan M. Kaganoff and Melvin I. Urofsky, eds., *"Turn to the South": Essays on Southern History* (Charlottesville, Va., 1979). Eli Evans, *The Provincials: A Personal History of Jews in the South* (New York, 1973), is valuable but unapologetically impressionistic. Other groups that have been or are somewhat outside the southern ethnic and religious mainstreams have received little or no attention. Those groups include some that have had or are beginning to have a significant impact on the South: Irish-Americans, Quakers or Friends, Greek-Americans, Lebanese-Americans, and especially Cuban-Americans and Mexican-Americans.

German-Americans, however, have been studied rather extensively, as in Terry G. Jordan, *German Seed in Texas Soil: Immigrant Farmers in Nineteenth-Century Texas* (Austin, Tex., 1966), and Klaus Wust, *The Virginia Germans* (Charlottesville, Va., 1969). The early Italian, Cuban, and Spanish immigrants to Florida are the subjects of a serious historical work: Garry Ross Mormino and George E. Pozzetta, *The Immigrant World of Ybor City: Italians and Their Latin Neighbors in Tampa, 1885–1985* (Urbana, Ill., 1985). Finally, there is a fine study of Chinese-Americans in Mississippi, modern-day manifestations of an attempt to import Chinese laborers to be farmworkers: James W. Loewen, *The Mississippi Chinese: Between Black and White* (Cambridge, Mass., 1971). It is also a somber reminder that racial and ethnic discrimination is more persistent than some of us like to believe.

Charles R. Wilson, *Baptized in Blood: The Religion of the Lost Cause, 1865–1920* (Athens, Ga., 1980), is a perceptive analysis of the Lost Cause as the civil religion of the postbellum South. Another fine study of the Lost Cause is Gaines Foster, *Ghosts of the Confederacy: Defeat, the Lost Cause and the Emergence of the New South, 1865 to 1913* (New York, 1987). A provocative analysis of the patron saint of the Lost Cause is Thomas L. Connelly, *Marble Man: Robert E. Lee and His Image in American Society* (New York, 1977).

Critics and interpreters of religion in the South have at times been too ready to find fault with it and to find its adherents insensitive or indifferent to social causes and reforms. We are now more aware that that was not the case with respect to such issues as prohibition and sabbath laws. At the same time, the charges are on target with respect to such highly sensitive issues as Jim Crow and the civil rights revolution, workers' rights and working conditions, women's rights, and poverty. Such blind spots have often been present among the faithful outside the South. Moreover, some sects are quiescent because they have rejected this world and have focused on the next.

There are exceptions, of course, to all of these observations. Many black religious people joined in the civil rights movement; the black church and clergy were the prime catalysts of the biggest social revolution in American history since emancipation. Many of the South's outspoken and active dissidents have been motivated by their faith. Finally, one ought to remember that generalizations are necessary but they often distort and often are very unfair. A book to ponder is James McBride Dabb's memoir: *Haunted by God* (Richmond, Va., 1972).

Education within the South must, of course, be placed within its national context first. Consult, for instance, R. Freeman Butts and Lawrence A. Cremin, *History of Education* (1953), for primary and secondary education, and Frederick Rudolph, *The American College and University: A History* (New York, 1962). Laurence R. Veysey, *The Emergence of the American University* (Chicago, 1965), is a very perceptive study of the governance of the American colleges and universities. Much more needs to be done on the impact of desegregation, recent demographic shifts, conservative religion, increasing professionalism, and the federal government on education at all levels. For a study of the pernicious effects of Jim Crow on the education of blacks, see Louis R. Harlan, *Separate and Unequal: Public School Campaigns and Racism in the Southern Seaboard States, 1901–1915* (Chapel Hill, N.C., 1965). Lower-income whites also received unequal treatment in the public schools. In his *Mill and Town*, David Carlton convincingly demonstrates that students in mill schools received less financial support than whites in other schools. J. Morgan Kousser arrived at similar conclusions in "Progressivism—For Middle-Class Whites Only: North Carolina Education, 1880–1910," *Journal of Southern History* 46 (May 1980): 169–194. The most recent historical and scholarly study of education in the South is William A. Link, *A Hard Country and a Lonely Place: Schooling, Society, and Reform in Rural Virginia, 1870–1920* (Chapel Hill, N.C., 1986).

There are numerous biographies of educators and histories of educational institutions and of the educational efforts of religious bodies. Older institutional histories include Daniel W. Hollis, *University of South Carolina*, 2 vols. (Columbia, S.C., 1951–1956), and Louis Round Wilson, *The University of North Carolina, 1900–1930: The Making of a Modern University* (Chapel Hill, N.C., 1957). Two fine studies are Paul K. Conkin, *Gone with the Ivy: A Biography of Vanderbilt University* (Knoxville, Tenn., 1985), and Robert McMath et al., *Engineering the New South: Georgia Tech, 1885–1985* (Athens, Ga., 1985).

Most of life, of course, went on outside the halls of ivy. Too much of it went on in courtrooms, jails, and prisons. The most thoughtful recent examination of crime in the South is Edward L. Ayers, *Vengeance and Justice: Crime and Punishment in the Nineteenth-Century South* (New York, 1984). Though criticized for its statistical methodology, Sheldon Hackney's article on violence in the South is still essential for studying that grievous aspect of Dixie: "Southern Violence," *American Historical Review* 74 (1969): 906–925. Mark Carlton wrote a history of Louisiana's penal system: *Politics and Punishment: The History of the Louisiana State Penal System* (Baton Rouge, La., 1971).

Health and medicine have attracted the interest of too few historians. But the efforts of some historians have resulted in some very good work: Edward H. Beardsley, *A History of Neglect: Health Care for Blacks and Mill Workers in the Twentieth-Century South* (Knoxville, Tenn., 1987); Elizabeth Etheridge, *The Butterfly Caste: A Social History of Pellagra in the South* (Westport, Conn., 1972); John Ettling, *The Germ of Laziness: Rockefeller Philanthropy and Public Health in the New South* (Cambridge, Mass., 1981); James H. Jones, *Bad Blood: The Tuskegee Syphilis Experiment* (New York, 1981); and Kenneth Kiple and Virginia Himmelsteib King, *Another Dimension to the Black Diaspora: Diet, Disease, and Racism* (Cambridge, Eng., 1981).

Southerners, like other Americans, love sports. For general background, Benjamin G. Rader, *American Sports: From the Age of Folk Games to the Age of Spectators* (Englewood Cliffs, N.J., 1983), is useful. So is Allen Guttmann, *A Whole New Ball Game: An Interpretation of American Sports* (Chapel Hill, N.C., 1988); its bibliographical essay is virtually one of a kind. Most of the action in Jules Tygiel's *Baseball's Great Experiment* (New York, 1983) occurred outside the South, but the story of racial desegregation of baseball has significance for the modern South.

The music of the South, one of its greatest contributions to American and world culture and to general enjoyment, ought to receive more attention by historians. The following are useful: William Ferris, *Blues from the Delta* (New York, 1979); Sheldon Harris, *Blues Who's Who: A Biographical Dictionary of Blues Singers* (New Rochelle, N.Y., 1979); Paul Kingsbury and Alan Axelrod, eds., *Country: The Music and the Musicians* (New York, 1988); Bill C. Malone, *Southern Music, American Music* (Lexington, Ky., 1979); and Martin Williams, *Jazz Heritage* (New York, 1985). Fortunately or unfortunately, moviemakers have paid the South a lot of attention. Two assessments of the results are Edward D. C. Campbell, *The Celluloid South: Hollywood and the Southern Myth* (Knoxville, Tenn., 1981), and Jack Temple Kirby, *Media-Made Dixie: The South in the American Imagination* (Baton Rouge, La., 1978).

Index